Marketing
Concepts and Strategies

Lyndon Simkin
University of Warwick

William M. Pride
Texas A & M University

O. C. Ferrell
Colorado State University

HOUGHTON MIFFLIN   Boston   New York

Sponsoring Editor: *Morten Fuglevand*
Senior Associate Editor: *Susan M. Kahn*
Senior Project Editor: *Nancy Blodget*
Project Editor: *Liz Napolitano*
Editorial Assistant: *Elisabeth Kehrer*
Senior Production/Design Coordinator: *Jill Haber*
Senior Manufacturing Coordinator: *Marie Barnes*
International Sales and Marketing Director: *Chris Hall*
International Marketing Manager: *Suzanne Morgan*

Cover design: *Diana Coe/ko Design Studio*
Cover illustration: *Minko T. Dimov, MinkoImages*

Printed in the U.S.A.

ISBN: 0-395-96244-7

123456789-DOW-04 03 02 01 00

Brief Contents

Contents

Note: Each chapter contains a Summary, a list of Important Terms, Discussion and Review Questions, and Recommended Readings.

Preface

Marketing affects everyone: we are all consumers. Most businesses depend on marketing to provide an understanding of the marketplace, to ensure their products and services satisfy the needs of customers and that they are competing effectively. There is little doubt that marketing is an important facet of today's society and commerce. In the majority of business schools and colleges in the UK, Eire, Benelux and Scandinavia, *Marketing: Concepts and Strategies* is used to introduce students to the nature and scope of marketing. The first edition of *Marketing: Concepts and Strategies* appeared in 1991. Since then, this text has become the leader in its market. Whether for undergraduates seeking a comprehensive introduction to marketing, MBAs requiring a grounding in marketing analysis or marketing management, or students in colleges wishing to pass degrees and diplomas, *Marketing: Concepts and Strategies* is used by lecturers and teaching staff to provide an accessible, topical and enlightening insight into the world of marketing. *Marketing: Concepts and Strategies* is also recommended by the Chartered Institute of Marketing and the Marketing Institute of Ireland. This edition has been totally revised to reflect the current core themes of marketing in terms of academic content but also—given the authors' wide ranging experiences outside the lecture theatre—from a practitioner's perspective.

The Authors

Sally Dibb and Lyndon Simkin have been at the leading UK university management centre, Warwick Business School, since the mid-1980s, teaching undergraduates, MBAs—full-time, part-time and distance learning—and executives the basics of marketing, advanced strategic marketing, buyer behaviour, marketing communications and marketing research. Sally and Lyndon's research focuses on services marketing, market segmentation, marketing planning, retail modelling, marketing communications and teaching methods, in which areas they have published extensively in the academic journals in the UK and USA. In addition to being joint authors of *Marketing: Concepts and Strategies,* they produced the innovative *The Marketing Casebook: Cases and Concepts* (Routledge) in 1994, mixing real-world cases with overviews of theory, and in 1996 *The Market Segmentation Workbook* and *The Marketing Planning Workbook* (both International Thomson Business Press), aimed at assisting marketing practitioners to reassess their target markets and understand the complexities of marketing planning. These workbooks were based on their consultancy experiences with organisations as diverse as Andersen Consulting, DRA (MoD), Forte, ICI, JCB, Jet, McDonald's, PowerGen, Standard Chartered, Tesco and Zeneca.

Bill Pride and O.C. Ferrell first teamed up to produce *Marketing* for Houghton Mifflin in 1977. Since then the American sister of *Marketing: Concepts and Strategies,* now in its eleventh edition, has been used by over one million students and become one of the principal marketing texts in the USA. O.C. is Professor of Marketing in the College of Business at Colorado State University. Prior to his arrival at Colorado State he was Distinguished Professor of Marketing and Business Ethics at the University of Memphis, where he had also been Dean. He is past president of the Academic Council for the prestigious American Marketing Association (AMA). He chaired committees that developed the AMA Code of Ethics and the AMA Code of Ethics for Marketing on the Internet. O.C. is the author of many texts, including *Marketing Strategy* (Dryden), *Business Ethics: Ethical Decision Making and Cases* (Houghton Mifflin) and *Business: A Changing World* (Irwin/McGraw-Hill). Bill Pride is Professor of Marketing at Texas A&M University where he specialises in marketing communications, strategic marketing planning and business marketing education. As with O.C., Bill has published a large number of journal papers and is widely recognised in the marketing field. Bill is also co-author of *Business* (Houghton Mifflin).

Changes for the Fourth Edition

Marketing is a quickly evolving discipline in a rapidly changing world. Businesses once deterred by acts of violence in Northern Ireland have sought to establish operations in a newly emerging marketplace. Such "external" forces affecting the attractiveness of markets are not unusual to marketers, and they do not result only from the violence in the former Yugoslavia or the Gulf. Only a decade ago, the Berlin Wall stood as a very real barrier facing trade between western and eastern Europe: today, the markets in the former eastern bloc are a major opportunity for many businesses. A few years ago, German households sorting their rubbish into separate containers depending on the recyclability of their trash seemed quirky to many observers. Now, with the "greening" consumer, most businesses must be environmentally aware. The Internet is no longer the preserve only of computer buffs, with increasing numbers of households using the *net* to purchase goods. Ethics and social responsibility were once discussed in lecture theatres but rarely in Board rooms: now they are increasingly integral to companies' marketing strategies. In such a fast moving world, it is essential to keep abreast of developments. This is particularly true in marketing. After all, in most businesses, it is the responsibility of the marketers to make their colleagues aware of trends in the marketplace, the actions of competitors and perpetually changing customer requirements.

For the authors, writing the fourth edition was also prone to external environmental forces. The arrival of baby Mae led to prudent time management, insights into a whole new world of marketing examples and even the use of time to revise the services chapter while awaiting the surgeon's knife. We apologise if there are too many baby product examples cited in this edition!

The fourth edition of *Marketing: Concepts and Strategies* strives to explain the nature of marketing and the importance of understanding the complexities of the marketplace. In so doing, the intention as ever is for the text to be easy to read, informative, interesting and topical. To this end, there has been a restructuring of the twenty-four chapters. Each Part has improved scene-setting and *postscripts* to explain the inter-relationships of the many concepts and strategies introduced. The Parts follow a logical structure which follows the premise that for effective marketing there must first be analysis of the marketplace, then the recommendation of a marketing strategy, and finally the production of marketing programmes with control processes which facilitate implementation of the desired strategy.

In addition, every chapter has been up-dated in terms of the current research and thinking in the area, the latest statistics and industry figures where relevant, and to reflect the views of leading academics and practitioners who have kindly reviewed the chapters, provided thought-provoking quotes and suggested the key readings in their area of expertise as additional references. Many of these experts have kindly provided their thoughts regarding the future of marketing *per se* in the new millennium.

The principal aim of *Marketing: Concepts and Strategies* has always been to provide a book which students find easy to use and which reflects accurately the current thinking in the world of marketing. There have been extensive changes to the fourth edition, but they are to reflect students' needs, suggestions by peers and the current developments in marketing as identified by practitioners, the journals and at conferences. In summary, the improvements for the fourth edition include:

- Extensive coverage of currently in-vogue topics:
    Relationship marketing and developing on-going customer interaction
    Internal marketing and organisational management
    Green marketing and social awareness
    Direct marketing in channel selection and the promotional mix
    The role of the Internet in marketing research, promotional strategy, direct marketing channels and marketing in general
- Greater explanation of marketing strategy:
    Corporate strategy and mission enactment
    Marketing opportunity analysis
    Strategic focus and options
    Target marketing
    Competitive forces and positions
- Significant attention to implementation issues:
    Marketing mix programmes
    Internal marketing
    Controls and managerial processes
    Performance measures and benchmarking
    Cultural and organisational operational barriers
- Appendices aimed to offer applied help to students, examining how to:
    Tackle case studies
    Write reports
    Make presentations
    Revise and prepare for examinations
    Handle job interviews, and
    Produce CVs
- More balanced coverage of the issues relating to marketing in consumer services and business-to-business markets

- More extensive cross-referencing between chapters and Parts
- The inclusion of the insights of leading marketing "gurus", their reviews, recommended further readings and quotes
- New chapter opening vignettes, Marketing Insights illustrating current developments, and end of chapter cases for discussion
- Up-dated industry/market statistics, figures and examples for the EU and leading brands
- Ancillaries for tutors including Powerpoint visual aids, testbank software, video material, case answers and a web site
- Web site support for users of *Marketing: Concepts and Strategies*:
  Powerpoint visual aids
  Student testbank
  Web links with case companies, brands and topics
  Extra cases
  Suggested examination formats and questions
  Q&A topics and solutions
  Financial analyses in marketing
  Full glossary of key terms
  Topical insights and evolving concepts

As ever, *Marketing: Concepts and Strategies* is supported by comprehensive indexing, a full glossary of key terms appearing in the margins of the relevant chapters, questions for discussion and full listing of the key terms and jargon detailed chapter by chapter.

The views of student users and fellow academics have guided changes for this fourth edition. These modifications have been made to improve *Marketing: Concepts and Strategies,* up-rate its usability and to reflect how the discipline of marketing is evolving. Current adopters of *Marketing: Concepts and Strategies* should find little difficulty in incorporating the new look in their teaching. New readers should find that *Marketing: Concepts and Strategies* is even more accessible and topical.

Running Order of *Marketing: Concepts and Strategies,* Fourth Edition

Part I: Marketing Defined—An introduction to the nature and scope of marketing, the composition of the marketing environment and the importance of global marketing.

Part II: Understanding and Targeting Markets—Consumer and business-to-business buying behaviour, marketing research and the principal task in developing a marketing strategy: target market selection.

Part III: Product, Branding, Packaging and Service Decisions—The first ingredients of the marketing mix, product and people decisions.

Part IV: Place (Distribution and Channel) Decisions—The nature of marketing channels in the marketing mix and the key participating players.

Part V: Promotion Decisions—The use of advertising, publicity and public relations, sponsorship, personal selling, sales promotion, direct mail, the Internet and direct marketing in marketing communications.

Part VI: Pricing Decisions—The concepts of price and value, setting price and determining pricing policies.

Part VII: Manipulating the Marketing Mix—Adapting the marketing mix for business-to-business, services and global markets.

Part VIII: Marketing Management—Strategic marketing and competitive strategy; marketing planning and sales forecasting; implementing strategies, internal marketing and measuring performance; ethics and social responsibility in modern marketing.

End Piece: Marketing in the New Millennium—The Thoughts of Leading Exponents.

Appendix A: Case Study Analysis—How to tackle case study learning plus five strategic marketing cases.

Appendix B: Revision Tips

Appendix C: Careers in Marketing

Acknowledgments

This text would not have happened without the support and encouragement of American authors Bill Pride and O.C. Ferrell, plus the comments and enthusiasm from fellow marketing lecturers at Warwick and, above all, from our students past and present. Specific thanks must go to:

Colin Egan, *Leicester De Montfort University*
Peter Jackson, *Adsearch, Richmond-Upon-Thames*
Hans Kasper, *University of Limburg*
John Wringe, *Lansdown Conquest (WPP), London*

And also to Pat Ibbotson and Miriam Catterall, both of *University of Ulster,* for their assistance with the initiation of the web support package.

We are also indebted to those who generously contributed chapter opening quotes and recommended readings in their areas of expertise:

Michael Baker, *University of Strathclyde*
Dave Birks, *University of Bath*
Martin Christopher, *Cranfield University School of Management*
Peter De Pelsmacker, *University of Antwerp*
Peter Doyle, *Warwick Business School*
Colin Egan, *Leicester De Montfort University*
John Fernie, *University of Abertay at Dundee*
O.C. Ferrell, *Colorado State University*
Gordon Foxall, *University of Keele*
David Ford, *University of Bath*
Norman Hart, *CIM/Hart Inc*
Susan Hart, *University of Strathclyde*
Hans Kasper, *Rijksuniversiteit Limburg, Maastricht*
Constantine Katsikeas, *Cardiff Business School*
Peter Leeflang, *Rijksuniversiteit Groningen*
Malcolm McDonald, *Cranfield University School of Management*
Peter McGoldrick, *Manchester Business School*
Elaine O'Brien, *University of Strathclyde*
Nigel Piercy, *Cardiff Business School*
David Shipley, *Trinity College, University of Dublin*
Antonis Simintiras, *The Open University*

Michael Thomas, *University of Strathclyde*
Eric Waarts, *Erasmus University, Rotterdam*
Robin Wensley, *Warwick Business School*

A number of individuals have made many helpful comments and recommendations in their reviews of this and previous editions. We appreciate the inestimable help of these reviewers:

Stewart Arnold, *University of Hull*
David Arnott, *Warwick Business School*
Marylyn Carrigan, *The University of Birmingham*
Derrick Chong, *Royal Holloway University of London*
David Crick, *University of Leicester*
Leslie de Chernatony, *The Open University*
Aidan Daly, *University of Galway*
Deane Ford, *American University of Cairo*
Andrea Frame, *University of Central England*
Audrey Gilmore, *University of Ulster at Jordanstown*
Robert Grafton Small, *University of St. Andrews*
Al Halborg, *Coventry University*
Phil Harris, *Manchester Metropolitan University*
Benson Honig, *University of St. Andrews*
Andrew Inglis, *London Guildhall University*
Irish Marketing Institute
Colin Jenkins, *Nene College*
David Marshall, *University of Edinburgh*
Danielle McCartan-Quinn, *University of Ulster*
Sally McKechnie, *The University of Nottingham*
Vincent W. Mitchell, *UMIST*
Sandra Mohabir-Collins, *University of Paisley*
Elaine O'Brien, *University of Strathclyde*
Daragh O'Reilly, *University of Bradford*
David Pickton, *Leicester De Montfort University*
Veronica Premchand, *Maastricht University*
Susan Scoffield, *Manchester Metropolitan University*
Viv Shaw, *Otago University*
Antonis Simintiras, *The Open University*
Peter Stoney, *The University of Liverpool*
Richard I. Taylor, *Swansea Business School*
Ann M. Torres, *National University of Ireland, Galway*
Dominic Wilson, *UMIST*

Sally Dibb
Lyndon Simkin
William M. Pride
O.C. Ferrell

I Marketing Defined

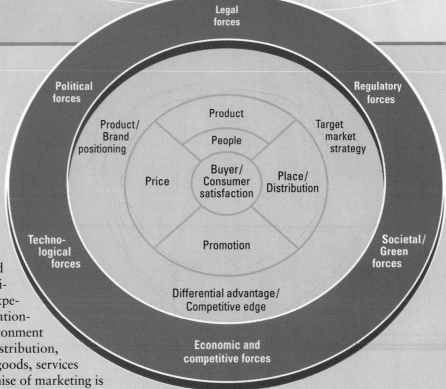

Marketing consists of individual and organisational activities that facilitate and expedite satisfying exchange relationships in a dynamic environment through the creation, distribution, promotion and pricing of goods, services and ideas. The simple premise of marketing is that to be successful, any organisation must understand its customers' requirements and satisfy them in a manner that gives the organisation an edge over its competitors. This involves offering the "right" mix of product, people, service, pricing, promotion and distribution channel. Marketing also depends on constant up-dating of ideas. Customers are often surprisingly fickle and modify their needs and wants, rivals alter their strategies and forces in the marketplace regularly change.

Part I of *Marketing: Concepts and Strategies* introduces the concept of marketing and explores its nature and scope.

Chapter 1, "An Overview of the Marketing Concept", defines marketing; establishes its importance to business organisations and to consumers; and outlines the major components of marketing

strategy—notably marketing opportunity analysis, target market selection and the development of marketing mix programmes that implement the marketing strategy. The chapter also establishes the ethos of *Marketing: Concepts and Strategies*, describes the structure of the text and presents an overview of the continuing development of the text over the past decade. Important concepts presented in Chapter 1 are deliberately repeated throughout the text. It is important for the reader to understand and accept them before progressing to the following chapters.

Chapter 2, "The Marketing Environment", examines the many forces at work in a market over which consumers and businesses have little or no control but which tangibly affect the nature of the products and services marketed. These forces of what is termed "the macro marketing environment" include economic, political, legal, regulatory, societal and technological impacts. Competitive forces—"the micro marketing environment"— often have a more specific impact on separate businesses. The chapter also examines the concept of environmental scanning, the process many businesses use to address the marketing environment.

Chapter 3, "Marketing in International Markets", acknowledges that today many businesses operate across national borders and modify their marketing practices accordingly. The chapter defines the nature of marketing internationally, establishes why the concept is so important and explains the need for international marketing intelligence. The discussion then focuses on how forces of the marketing environment differ between territories and how regional trade alliances create the need to treat non-domestic markets differently. The chapter concludes with an examination of alternative market entry strategies for companies wishing to become involved in international marketing activities.

By the conclusion of Part I of *Marketing: Concepts and Strategies,* readers should understand what is meant by the term *marketing* and be able to grasp its nature and scope. The essential themes in Part I are developed further as the text continues.

1 An Overview of the Marketing Concept

"Marketing is concerned with the establishment and maintenance of mutually satisfying exchange relationships."

Michael Baker, University of Strathclyde

O B J E C T I V E S

- To understand the definition of marketing
- To understand the importance of marketing
- To gain insight into the basic elements of the marketing concept and its implementation
- To understand the major components of a marketing strategy and the marketing mix
- To gain a sense of general strategic marketing issues, such as market opportunity analysis, target market selection and marketing mix development
- To grasp the ethos and structure of this text

Little Chef is Britain's largest roadside restaurant brand. There are now over 400 Little Chefs located across the British Isles, so you need never to feel hungry when you are travelling around the country as you will never be far away from one of our restaurants!

Perhaps with such an extensive number of locations it is not surprising that every year Little Chef customers plough their way through 17 million rashers of bacon, 26 million sausages, 17 million eggs and 12 million cups of tea! Much has changed in the life span of Little Chef, now owned by Granada. The first was an 11-seater snack bar in Reading and opened in 1958. While the buildings now are breakthrough in design, being pre-assembled in a factory and erected rapidly on site; the interiors air-conditioned, brightly decorated and complete with free newspapers, a top-up shop to help travellers on their way and provide telecommunications points; and the menus constantly up-dated to reflect the changing eating patterns of customers, the core values remain unaltered more than three decades since the first branch opened.

The Little Chef proposition is simple: delicious, simple food, freshly prepared to order. Although the newest and busiest branches now may seat over one hundred customers, there is still table service and fresh food cooked to order. Famous for its traditional English breakfasts, the menus also offer a varied mix of grills, salads, desserts and vegetarian meals. Children receive special menus, activity packs and a warm welcome. Babies, too, are well catered for with high chairs and free baby food. The shops provide hassled parents, lost tourists or bemused business commuters with a welcome range of books, CDs, confectionery, drinks, toys and maps. The constantly evolving menu has recently been supplemented with a *Flaming Good Idea,* as Little Chef has teamed up with Burger King. In over 40 "combi" restaurants, the Little Chef sit-down dining experience is complemented by a Burger King take-away counter for travellers desiring an on-the-move "pit stop".

The *Flaming Good Idea* is not the only way in which Little Chef has evolved over the years. Forte Hotels operated the budget-priced motorway lodge hotel chain, Travelodge. New owner Granada merged these with its own lodges to create an extensive trunk road and city chain of over 170 budget hotels. Although the hotel rooms are well equipped—spacious en suite rooms, free satellite TV, tea and coffee making equipment, Hypnos beds, free morning newspaper, fax/phone facilities and ample parking—the hotels contain no bars or restaurants. This is where Little Chef has come to support its sister Granada operation, Travelodge. Each Travelodge hotel is adjacent to a Burger King, Rock Island Diner, Harry Ramsden's fish restaurant, La Brioche Doree, or in around 120 instances, to a Little Chef, which provides bar and restaurant facilities for travellers and hotel guests. This dual site proposition has enabled Granada to rapidly develop a major hotel chain, now extending into Eire and parts of the EU. It reflects the continued evolution of the highly successful Little Chef brand: success built on decades of modifying its proposition to reflect market trends, customers' needs and competitors' activities, with a well positioned and effectively communicated branding.

Families eat for less at Little Chef.

Feeding your family on the move needn't be an uphill struggle. Simply bring this voucher to any Little Chef and get 20% off your bill. With Kid's Fun Meals including a free toy and free Heinz baby food, it's no wonder we've been voted Best Roadside Restaurant in the Tommy's Campaign Parent Friendly Awards.

STOP **LITTLE CHEF** ↑

STOP AT LITTLE CHEF. START AFRESH.

20% Discount Terms & Conditions. This voucher entitles you to a 20% discount off your bill at any Little Chef. Discount is only available for party sizes of 2 or more. Voucher valid for one transaction only. Not to be used in conjunction with any other voucher based offer. No cash alternative. Offer is only valid with this voucher. Photocopied or defaced vouchers will not be accepted. Not valid at Little Chef Express Outlets. Voucher valid until 3.1.2000.

SOURCES: Granada plc, 1999; "On the Move", Little Chef, Summerhouse Publishing Ltd., "Update Little Chef", Little Chef; **www.little-chef.co.uk,** 1999. *Advertisement:* Courtesy of Little Chef.

T his first chapter of *Marketing: Concepts and Strategies* provides an overview of the concepts and decisions covered in this text. This chapter first develops a definition of marketing and explains each element of the definition. It next focuses on some of the reasons people should study marketing and on why marketing is important. The text then introduces the marketing concept and examines several issues associated with successful implementation. The chapter goes on to define and discuss the major tasks associated with marketing strategy: market opportunity analysis, target market selection, marketing mix development and the management of marketing activities. It concludes by discussing the organisation and running order of this text. Like all the chapters in *Marketing: Concepts and Strategies*, this one contains detailed illustrative examples in the Marketing Insight boxes, presents cases for discussion at its conclusion, lists all the key terms presented in the chapter and provides discussion and review questions to emphasise the key themes. In addition, as the principal definitions are introduced in the text, they are repeated in the margins for ease of understanding.

Marketing Defined

Asking members of the public to define marketing is an illuminating experience. They will respond with a variety of descriptions, including "advertising", "selling", "hype", "conning people", "targeting", "packaging". In reality, marketing encompasses many more activities than most people realise and depends on a wealth of formal concepts, processes and models not implied by the soundbites just listed. Since it is practised and studied for many different reasons, marketing has been, and continues to be, defined in many different ways, whether for academic, research or applied business purposes. This chapter begins with an examination of what is meant by the term **marketing**.

Marketing Individual and organisational activities that facilitate and expedite satisfying exchange relationships in a dynamic environment through the creation, distribution, promotion and pricing of goods, services and ideas

> Marketing consists of individual and organisational activities that facilitate and expedite satisfying exchange relationships in a dynamic environment through the creation, distribution, promotion and pricing of goods, services and ideas.
>
> *Dibb, Simkin, Pride and Ferrell*

The basic rationale of marketing is that to succeed, a business requires satisfied and happy customers who return to the business to provide additional custom. In exchange for something of value, typically payment or a donation, the customers receive a product or service that satisfies their needs. Such a product has an acceptable level of quality, reliability, customer service and support, is available at places convenient for the customer at the "right" price and is promoted effectively by means of a clear message that is readily comprehended by the customers in question. For example, in return for quenching thirst at affordable prices with a reliable product that is widely available in easy to use containers, Coca-Cola receives a great deal of money from customers. Unfortunately for companies and their marketers, customers' requirements change as their needs alter, marketing messages infiltrate their thinking, friends and colleagues discuss purchases and competing products are pushed by rival businesses. In the dynamic world of marketing, an effective solution to satisfying customer needs does not have longevity. High specification turntables no longer satisfy the majority of music lovers' needs: compact disc players, therefore, have taken over the dominant share of Sony's range. Marketers must constantly assess their customers' requirements and be prepared to modify their marketing activity accordingly. An assessment of marketing opportunities is an ever evolving process requiring regular revision and up-dating.

> Marketing is the management process responsible for identifying, anticipating and satisfying customer requirements profitably.
>
> *Chartered Institute of Marketing*

Understanding customers and anticipating their requirements is a core theme of effective marketing.[1] So, too, is understanding general market trends and developments that may affect both customers' views and the activities of businesses operating in a particular market. These factors may include social trends, technological enhancements, economic patterns and changes in the legal and regulatory arena, as well as political influences. These forces are often termed "the marketing environment". Compared with five years ago, for example, look at how many companies now produce products in "environmentally friendly" packaging in line with the social trend of the "greening consumer". A business does not have a marketplace to itself. There are direct competitors, new entrant rivals, substitute products with alternative solutions to a customer's specific need.

Construction equipment giant JCB markets trench digging equipment to utilities and local authorities. The growth of subterranean tunnelling robotic "moles" for pipe laying, requiring no trench digging, is a substitute for the traditional JCB backhoe loader and a major competitive threat. The competitive context is of fundamental importance to marketers of any good or service. So, too, are the internal resource base and the strengths and weaknesses within the business that will determine which market opportunities are in fact viable for the business to pursue. Marketing, therefore, depends on the successful analysis of customers, the marketing environment, competition and internal capabilities.

> The aim of marketing is to make selling superfluous. The aim is to know and to understand the customer so well that the product or service fits him/her and sells itself!
>
> *US management guru Peter Drucker*

With an understanding of these aspects of the marketplace, a business must then develop a marketing strategy. Even the mighty global organisations such as GM/Vauxhall or ICI choose not to offer a product for every type of consumer or customer need. Instead, they attempt to identify groups of customers where each separate group, or *market segment,* has "similar" needs. Each group of customers may then be offered a specifically tailored product or service proposition and a *marketing mix* programme. The Ford Maverick off-roader appeals to a separate group of customers than does the Ford Focus town car, and it is marketed totally differently. In developing unique marketing programmes for individual market segments—groups of customers—a business must prioritise which particular groups of customers it has the ability to serve and which will provide satisfactory returns. Resources will not permit all segments in a market to be targeted. In deciding on which segments to target, a business must be clear about the message—or *positioning*—it intends to offer to each group of customers. The business should endeavour to serve those customers it targets in a manner that gives it an edge over its competitors. Knowing how to group customers sensibly into homogeneous market segments, determining which to ultimately target, selecting a suitable positioning platform and seeking superiority over rivals are the core elements of marketing strategy.

> The marketing concept holds that the key to achieving organisational goals lies in determining the needs and wants of target markets and delivering the desired satisfaction more efficiently and effectively than the competition.
>
> *US marketer Philip Kotler*

Once a company has devised a marketing strategy, its attention must switch to marketing mix programmes.[2] As consumers of food brands, audio products or banking services, all readers of this text will have experienced the marketing mix programmes of major companies such as Cadbury's, Sony or Lloyds TSB. These are the tactical actions of marketing departments, which are designed to implement the desired marketing strategy. The product or offer must be clearly defined in line with target customer needs, service levels and guarantees must be determined, pricing and payment issues decided, channels of distribution established to make the product or service available and promotional strategies devised and executed to communicate with the targeted customers. These tactical aspects of marketing—the marketing mix—must be supported with carefully managed control programmes in a business to ensure their effective execution and the monitoring of their effectiveness.

It is important to remember the following simple sequential process: analysis, strategy, programmes for implementation (A-S-P). Marketers must understand their markets—customers, competitors, trends—and their own capabilities before developing marketing mix tactical programmes. A marketing strategy must be determined which reflects the analyses before the marketing mix programmes required to action the recommended strategy are specified. Analysis first, then strategy, with finally programmes—A-S-P. The focus must be on providing customer satisfaction, but in a manner that leads to the business's successful performance. For example, by addressing customers' needs and adopting a marketing culture incorporating clear controls, JCB has recently enjoyed the most successful financial returns in the company's history.

The intention of this introductory marketing text is to explore these facets of marketing comprehensively and thus provide a sound conceptual basis with which to understand the nature and activities of marketing. There are many definitions of marketing, since it is not a pure science. However, certain core ingredients of the various definitions collectively indicate the basic priorities of marketing:

- satisfying customers
- identifying/maximising marketing opportunities
- targeting the "right" customers
- facilitating exchange relationships
- staying ahead in dynamic environments
- endeavouring to beat or pre-empt competitors
- utilising resources/assets effectively
- increasing market share
- enhancing profitability

These aims form the objectives for many marketing directors and marketing departments. They are featured throughout this text, which adopts the following definition: *marketing consists of individual and organisational activities that facilitate and expedite satisfying exchange relationships in a dynamic environment through the creation, distribution, promotion and pricing of goods, services and ideas.* A definition of marketing must acknowledge that marketing relates to more than just tangible goods, that marketing activities occur in a dynamic environment and that such activities are performed by individuals as well as organisations.[3] The ultimate goal is to satisfy targeted customers, seeking their loyalty and consumption. This should be achieved in a manner which is differentiated in the view of customers vis-à-vis competitors' marketing mixes, which provides a company with a competitive edge over rivals and which is regularly up-dated to reflect market forces and developments.

The Definition Explored

Marketing Consists of Activities
The marketing of products or services effectively requires many activities. Some are performed by producers; some are accomplished by intermediaries, who purchase products from producers or from other intermediaries and re-sell them; and some are even performed by purchasers. Marketing does not include all human and organisational activities, but only those aimed at facilitating and expediting exchanges. Table 1.1 lists several major categories and examples of marketing activities, as ultimately encountered by the consumer, who remains at the "sharp

Marketing Mix Variables

Product	Develop and test market new products; modify existing products; eliminate products that do not satisfy customers' desires; formulate brand names and branding policies; create product guarantees and establish procedures for fulfilling guarantees; plan packages, including materials, sizes, shapes, colours and designs
Place/Distribution	Analyse various types of distribution channels; design appropriate distribution channels; select appropriate channel members and partners; design an effective programme for dealer relations; establish distribution centres; formulate and implement procedures for efficient product handling; set up inventory controls; analyse transportation methods; minimise total distribution costs; analyse possible locations for plants and wholesale or retail outlets
Promotion	Set promotional objectives; determine major types of promotion to be used; select and schedule advertising media; develop advertising messages; measure the effectiveness of advertisements; recruit and train salespeople; formulate payment programmes for sales personnel; establish sales territories; plan and implement sales promotion efforts such as free samples, coupons, displays, competitions, sales contests and co-operative advertising programmes; prepare and disseminate publicity releases; evaluate sponsorships; provide direct mail; and establish web sites or Internet facilities
Price	Analyse competitors' prices; formulate pricing policies; determine method or methods used to set prices; set prices; determine discounts for various types of buyer; establish conditions and terms of sales; determine credit and payment terms; understand the consumers' notion of value
People	Manipulate the marketing mix and establish service levels, guarantees, warranties, expertise, sales support, after sales back-up, customer handling requirements, personnel skills training and motivation (people as marketers); make products and services available (people as intermediaries); provide market for products (people as consumers)

Table 1.1   Possible decisions and activities associated with marketing mix variables

end" of such tactical decisions. Note that this list is not all-inclusive. Each activity could be subdivided into more specific activities.

Marketing Is Performed by Individuals and Organisations   All organisations perform marketing activities to facilitate exchanges. Businesses as well as not-for-profit and public sector organisations such as colleges and universities, charitable organisations, community theatres and hospitals perform marketing activities. For example, colleges and universities and their students engage in exchanges. To receive instruction, knowledge, entertainment, a degree, the use of facilities and sometimes room and board, students give up time, money and perhaps services in the form of labour; they may also give up opportunities to do other things! Many organisations engage in marketing activities. Various police forces have surveyed their communities in order to prioritise services and re-assure the general public that people's concerns will be addressed. Politicians now conduct analyses before determining strategies; they think of target markets rather than just the electorate. Even the sole owner of and worker in a small corner shop decides which products will sell, arranges deliveries to the shop, prices and displays products, advertises and serves customers.

Marketing Facilitates Satisfying Exchange Relationships

Exchange The provision or transfer of goods, services and ideas in return for something of value

For an **exchange** to take place, four conditions must exist. (1) Two or more individuals, groups or organisations must participate. (2) Each party must possess something of value that the other party desires. (3) Each party must be willing to give up its "something of value" to receive the "something of value" held by the other party. The objective of a marketing exchange is to receive something that is desired more than is given up to get it: that is, a reward in excess of costs. (4) The parties to the exchange must be able to communicate with each other to make their "something of value" available.[4]

Figure 1.1 illustrates the process of exchange. The arrows indicate that the parties communicate and that each has something of value available to exchange. Note, though, that an exchange will not necessarily take place just because these four conditions exist. Nevertheless, even if there is no exchange, marketing activities still have occurred. The "somethings of value" held by the two parties are most often products and/or financial resources, such as money or credit. When an exchange occurs, products are traded for other products or for financial resources.

Customer satisfaction A state that results when an exchange meets the needs and expectations of the buyer

An exchange should be *satisfying* to both the buyer and the seller. In fact, in a study of marketing managers, 32 per cent indicated that creating **customer satisfaction** was the most important concept in a definition of marketing.[5] Marketing activities, then, should be oriented towards creating and maintaining satisfying exchange relationships. To maintain an exchange relationship, the buyer must be satisfied with the goods, service or idea obtained in the exchange; the seller must be satisfied with the financial reward or something else of value received in the exchange.

Maintaining a positive relationship with buyers is an important goal for a seller, regardless of whether the seller is marketing cereal, financial services or a construction plant. Through buyer-seller interaction, the buyer develops expectations about the seller's future behaviour. To fulfil these expectations, the seller must deliver on promises made. Over time, a healthy buyer-seller relationship results in interdependencies between the two parties. The buyer depends on the

Figure 1.1 Exchange between buyer and seller

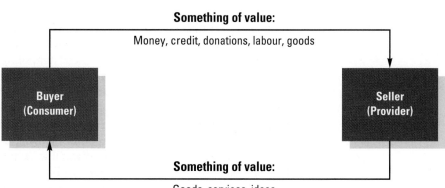

Something of value:

Money, credit, donations, labour, goods

Buyer (Consumer)

Seller (Provider)

Something of value:

Goods, services, ideas

seller to furnish information, parts and service; to be available; and to provide satisfying products in the future.

Marketing Occurs in a Dynamic Environment

Marketing environment External changing forces within the trading environment: laws, regulations, political activities, societal pressures, economic conditions and technological advances

The **marketing environment** consists of many external changing forces within the trading environment: laws, regulations, political activities, societal pressures, changing economic conditions and technological advances. Each of these dynamic forces has an impact on how effectively marketing activities can facilitate and expedite exchanges. For example, the development and acceptance of the Internet in home PCs has given businesses another vehicle through which to promote their products. Another example is the impact EU regulations have had on reducing distribution headaches within much of Europe, along with recent strides towards economic monetary union and the launch of the euro.

Marketing Involves Products, Distribution, Promotion, Pricing and People

Marketing means more than simply advertising or selling a product; it involves developing and managing a product that will satisfy certain needs. It focuses on making the product available at the right place, at the right time, at a price that is acceptable to customers and with the right people and service support. It also requires transmitting the kind of promotional information that will help customers determine whether the product will in fact be able to satisfy their needs.

Marketing Focuses on Goods, Services and Ideas

Product A good, service or idea

Good A physical entity that can be touched

Service The application of human and mechanical efforts to people or objects in order to provide intangible benefits to customers

Idea A concept, philosophy, image or issue

The word *product* has been used a number of times in this chapter. For purposes of discussion in this text, a **product** is viewed as being a good, a service or an idea. A **good** is a physical entity that can be touched. A Ford Focus, a Sony compact disc player, Kellogg's Cornflakes, a bar of Lux soap and a kitten in a pet shop are examples of goods. A **service** is the application of human and mechanical efforts to people or objects in order to provide intangible benefits to customers. Services such as air travel, dry cleaning, hairdressing, banking, medical care and child care are just as real as goods, but an individual cannot actually touch them. Marketing is utilised for services but requires certain enhancements in order to be effective (see Part VII). **Ideas** include concepts, philosophies, images and issues. For instance, a marriage counsellor gives couples ideas and advice to help improve their relationships. Other marketers of ideas include political parties, churches, schools and marketing lecturers.

The Importance of Marketing

Marketing Activities Are Used in Many Organisations

The commercial importance of marketing and its relevance as a topic worth studying are apparent from the definition of marketing just presented. This section discusses several less obvious reasons why marketing should be studied.

In Europe and the United States between 25 and 33 per cent of all civilian workers perform marketing activities. The marketing field offers a variety of interesting and challenging career opportunities, such as personal selling, advertising, packaging, transport, storage, marketing research, product development, wholesaling, retailing, strategic planning and consultancy. In addition, many individuals who work for not-for-profit organisations—such as charities or health—engage in marketing activities. Marketing skills are used to promote political, cultural, church, civic and charitable activities. The advertisement in Figure 1.2 encourages support of the British Heart Foundation, a non-profit organisation. Whether a person earns a living through marketing activities or

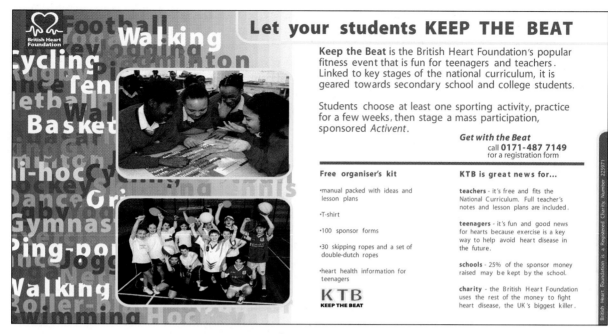

Figure 1.2 Promotion of a non-profit organisation. The British Heart Foundation uses marketing to communicate its message. SOURCE: Courtesy of the British Heart Foundation.

performs them without compensation in non-business settings, marketing knowledge and skills are valuable assets. For both commercial and non-profit organisations there are needs to satisfy, exchanges to expedite, changing circumstances to monitor and decisions to make.

Marketing Activities Are Important to Businesses and the Economy

A business organisation must sell products to survive and to grow. Directly or indirectly, marketing activities help sell an organisation's products. By doing so, they generate financial resources that can be used to develop innovative products. New products allow a company to better satisfy customers' changing needs, which in turn enables the company to generate more profits. Charities and other not-for-profit organisations use marketing to generate revenues and funds, as described in Marketing Insight 1.1.

Europe's highly complex economy depends heavily on marketing activities. They help produce the profits that are essential not only to the survival of individual businesses but also to the health and ultimate survival of the economy as a whole. Profits are essential to economic growth because without them businesses find it difficult, if not impossible, to buy more raw materials, recruit more employees, attract more capital and create the additional products that in turn lead to more profits.

Marketing Knowledge Enhances Consumer Awareness

Besides contributing to a country's economic well-being, marketing activities permeate everyone's lives. In fact, they help to improve the quality of life. Studying marketing activities enables the costs, benefits and flaws of marketing to be evaluated. The need for improvement and ways to accomplish changes can be determined. For example, an unsatisfactory experience with a guarantee may lead consumers to demand that laws be enforced more strictly to make sellers fulfil their promises. Similarly, there may be the desire for more information about a product—or more accurate information—before purchase. Understanding marketing leads to the evaluation of the corrective measures (such as laws, regulations and industry guidelines) that may be required to stop unfair, misleading or unethical marketing practices. The results of the survey presented in Table 1.2 indicate that there is a considerable lack of knowledge about marketing activities, as reflected by the sizeable proportion of respondents who agree with the myths in the table.

Marketing Costs Consume a Sizeable Portion of Buyers' Incomes   The study of marketing emphasises that many marketing activities are necessary to provide people with satisfying goods and services. Obviously, these marketing activities cost money. A family with a monthly income of £1,000, of which £300 goes towards taxes and savings, spends about £700 on goods and services. Of this amount, typically £350 goes towards marketing activities. Clearly, if marketing expenses consume that much income, it is necessary to know how this money is used.

Business Performance   Marketing puts an emphasis on satisfying customers. Marketing analyses should lead a business to develop a marketing strategy that takes account of market trends, aims to satisfy customers, is aware of competitive activity and targets the right customers with a clear positioning message. In so doing, a business should benefit from customer loyalty and advantages over its rivals, while making the most efficient use of resources to effectively address the specific requirements of those markets it chooses to target. Hence, marketing should provide both a financial benefit and a greater sense of well-being for the organisation.

The Marketing Concept

Some organisations have tried to be successful by buying land, building a factory, equipping it with people and machines, and then making a product that they believe consumers need. However, these organisations frequently fail to attract

Myths	Strongly Agree	Somewhat Agree	Neither Agree nor Disagree	Somewhat Disagree	Strongly Disagree
Marketing is selling	14%	34%	26%	18%	8%
Marketers persuade	21%	25%	20%	11%	23%
Dealers' profits significantly increase prices consumers pay	21%	32%	12%	8%	27%
Marketing depends on advertising	17%	44%	12%	9%	18%
Strategic planning has nothing to do with marketing	19%	19%	21%	17%	24%

SOURCES: Student surveys.

Table 1.2   Popular marketing myths

Charities Turn to Marketing: Promoting the Children's Society

FMCGs (fast moving consumer goods) used to be the domain of marketing managers. The need to identify customers' needs and satisfy them no longer applies only to the likes of Heinz and Kellogg's. Irrespective of their products or markets, some of the most successful organisations in the world are experts in marketing, be they American Express, British Airways, JCB, Nestlé or Unilever. It is no longer just the manufacturers of baked beans or cornflakes that worry about keeping their customers happy, staying abreast of market trends and endeavouring to be ahead of their rivals. The service sector, especially banking and financial services, leisure and tourism, has in recent years been a major employer of marketing graduates. There are few areas of commercial activity in which the concepts and strategies of marketing are not employed. One area that is currently adopting the ethos of marketing and engaging in the practices once left only to the FMCG companies is the charity sector.

The increasing use of marketing by charities is both a response to the strategies of other businesses seeking alliances and an ever important foundation for the charities' own fund raising initiatives. Some businesses perceive that by allying with "good causes", not only will these causes benefit but so too will the businesses, as their own customers see them in a better light. For example, Midland Bank (HSBC) has invested over £1 million in bolstering its position as a community bank, signing support deals with Shelter, Age Concern and the National Deaf Children's Society. Charity involvement at business events is growing too. Companies organising conferences are benefiting from having charities on board, making presentations or exhibiting in the foyer. The event's patrons gain a "feel good" factor, while the charity benefits from much needed exposure and goodwill.

The charities themselves are increasingly exploiting marketing. By identifying why members of the public or businesses donate to good causes and targeting those who do so regularly, Oxfam's marketers help the charity maximise use of scarce publicity and promotional resources to generate the maximum income for the charity. The Children's Society has recently embarked on a major advertising campaign. While cynics will say it is a waste of £500,000, the charity on the other hand knows that many potential donors have been deterred by uncertainty over who benefits from its fund raising: the 360,000 children with a disability, the 43,000 runaways, the 160,000 homeless families or the two million children living with asthma.

The campaign aims to explain to the public that there are significant issues that need tackling and many thousands of youngsters who require financial or material support. The Children's Society aims to work with disadvantaged children and young people, regardless of race, culture or creed to (a) help them grow as valued members of the community, (b) listen to them and help them make their own decisions, and (c) help change the conditions that stand in their way. Having determined that these issues were not being raised in the media or being adequately linked to the charity's own fund raising, the Children's Society confidently expects not only to cover the costs of the campaign by increasing the level of donations being received but also to awaken people's desire to improve conditions for the children and families it supports. Target marketing is increasing donations and the awareness of this charity's message. Shrewd promotion is providing a stimulus for interest in the charity's activities and for growing support. As in most charities, marketing today plays a significant role.

Sources: Andy Fry, "When justice is child's play", *Marketing*, 4 July 1996, p. 31; Pat Anderson, "Cause and effect", *Marketing Week*, 21 October 1994, pp. 66–67; Harriot Lane Fox, "Good cause better effect", *Marketing*, 11 January 1996, pp. 25–27; "Midland ties in with charity trio", *Marketing*, 11 January 1996, p. 8; the Children's Society, London, 1999; Oxfam, Oxford, 1999.

buyers with what they have to offer because they defined their business as "making a product" rather than as "helping potential customers satisfy their needs and wants". Such organisations have failed to implement the marketing concept. It is not enough to be "product-led", no matter how good the product. An organisation must be in tune with consumer requirements.

According to the **marketing concept,** an organisation should try to provide products that satisfy customers' needs through a co-ordinated set of activities that also allows the organisation to achieve its goals. Customer satisfaction is the major aim of the marketing concept. First, an organisation must find out what will satisfy customers. With this information, it then attempts to create satisfying products. But the process does not end there. The organisation must continue to alter, adapt and develop products to keep pace with customers' changing desires and preferences. The marketing concept stresses the importance of customers and emphasises that marketing activities begin and end with them.[6]

In attempting to satisfy customers, businesses must consider not only short run, immediate needs but also broad, long term desires. Trying to satisfy customers' current needs by sacrificing their long term desires will only create future dissatisfaction. For instance, people want efficient, low cost energy to power their homes and cars, yet they react adversely to energy producers who pollute the air and water, kill wildlife or cause disease or birth defects. To meet these short and long run needs and desires, a company must co-ordinate all its activities. Production, finance, accounting, personnel and marketing departments must work together.

The marketing concept is not a second definition of marketing. It is a way of thinking—a management philosophy guiding an organisation's overall activities. This philosophy affects all the efforts of the organisation, not just marketing activities. However, the marketing concept is by no means a philanthropic philosophy aimed at helping customers at the expense of the organisation. A company that adopts the marketing concept must not only satisfy its customers' objectives but also achieve its own goals, or it will not stay in business long. The overall goals of a business might be directed towards increasing profits, market share, sales or a combination of all three. The marketing concept stresses that an organisation can best achieve its goals by providing customer satisfaction. Thus, implementing the marketing concept should benefit the organisation as well as its customers.

Evolution of the Marketing Concept

The marketing concept may seem an obvious and sensible approach to running a business. However, business people have not always believed that the best way to make sales and profits is to satisfy customers. A famous example is the marketing philosophy for cars widely attributed to Henry Ford in the early 1900s: "The customers can have any colour car they want as long as it is black." The philosophy of the marketing concept emerged in the third major era in the history of business, preceded by the **production era** and the **sales era.** Surprisingly, it took nearly forty years after the **marketing era** began before many businesses started to adopt the marketing concept. The more advanced marketing-led companies have now entered the **relationship marketing era.**

The Production Era During the second half of the nineteenth century, the Industrial Revolution was in full swing in Europe and the United States. Electricity, railways, the division of labour, the assembly line and mass production made it possible to manufacture products more efficiently. With new technology and new ways of using labour, products poured into the marketplace, where consumer demand for manufactured goods was strong. This production orientation continued into the early part of the last century, encouraged by the scientific management movement that championed rigidly structured jobs and pay based on output.

Part I   Marketing Defined

The Sales Era In the 1920s, the strong consumer demand for products subsided. Businesses realised that products, which by this time could be made quite efficiently, would have to be "sold" to consumers. From the mid-1920s to the early 1950s, businesses viewed sales as the major means of increasing profits. As a result, this period came to have a sales orientation. Business people believed that the most important marketing activities were personal selling and advertising.

The Marketing Era By the early 1950s, some business people began to recognise that efficient production and extensive promotion of products did not guarantee that customers would buy them. Businesses found that they had to first determine what customers wanted and then produce it, rather than simply making products first and then trying to change customers' needs to correspond to what was being produced. As organisations realised the importance of knowing customers' needs, businesses entered into the marketing era—the era of customer orientation.[7]

The Relationship Marketing Era By the 1990s, many organisations had grasped the basics of the marketing concept and had created marketing functions. However, their view of marketing was transaction based. The priority for marketing was to identify customer needs, determine priority target markets and achieve sales via marketing mix tactical programmes. The focus was on the individual transaction or exchange. Long term success and market share gains depend on such transactions but also on maintaining a customer's loyalty and on repeatedly gaining sales from existing customers. This requires ongoing, committed, re-assuring and tailored relationship-building marketing programmes. As this era of relationship orientation has developed, it has been suggested that it is not only relationships with customers which are important. Suppliers, agents, distributors, recruiters, referral bodies (such as independent financial advisers recommending financial services companies' products), influencers (such as government departments, national bank or the EU), all should be "marketed to" in order to ensure their support, understanding and resources. The internal workforce must be motivated and provided with a clear understanding of a company's target market strategy, marketing mix activities and, indeed, of the corporate strategy and planned direction. Hence, the current era is moving away from transaction based marketing towards relationship marketing.[8] Marketing Insight 1.2 describes one industry making this move.

Implementing the Marketing Concept

A philosophy may sound reasonable and look good on paper, but that does not mean it can be put into practice easily. The marketing concept is a case in point. To implement it, an organisation must focus on some general conditions and recognise several problems. Because of these conditions and problems, the marketing concept has yet to be fully accepted by some businesses.

Because the marketing concept affects all types of business activities, not just marketing activities, the top management of an organisation must adopt it wholeheartedly. High level executives must incorporate the marketing concept into their philosophies of business management so completely that it becomes the basis for all the goals and decisions that they set for their companies. They must also convince other members of the organisation to accept the changes in policies and operations that flow from their acceptance of the marketing concept. Costs and budgetary controls are important, products and manufacturing essential, and personnel management necessary; but all are to no avail if the organisation's products or services are not desired by the targeted customers.

As the first step, management must establish an information system that enables it to discover customers' real needs and to use the information to create satisfying products. Because such a system is usually expensive, management must be willing to commit money and time for development and maintenance. Without an adequate information system, an organisation cannot be customer oriented.

Management's second major task is to restructure the organisation. If a company is to satisfy customers' objectives as well as its own, it must co-ordinate all its activities. To achieve this, the internal operations and the overall objectives of one or more departments may need restructuring. If the head of the marketing unit is not a member of the organisation's top level management, he or she should be. Some departments may have to be abolished and new ones created. Implementing the marketing concept demands the support not only of top management but also of managers and staff at all levels within the organisation.

Even when the basic conditions of establishing an information system and reorganising the company are met, the business's new marketing approach may not work perfectly. (1) There is a limit to a company's ability to satisfy customers' needs for a particular product. In a mass production economy, most business organisations cannot tailor products to fit the exact needs of each customer. (2) Although a company may attempt to learn what customers want, it may be unable to do so, and when the organisation does correctly identify customers' needs, it often has a difficult time developing a product that satisfies those needs. Many companies spend considerable time and money to research customers' needs and yet still create some products that do not sell well. (3) By striving to satisfy one particular segment of society, a company sometimes dissatisfies other segments. Certainly, government and non-business organisations also experience this problem. (4) A business organisation may have difficulty maintaining employee morale during any restructuring needed to co-ordinate the activities of various departments. Management must clearly explain the reasons for the various changes and communicate its own enthusiasm for the marketing concept. Adoption of the marketing philosophy takes time, resources, endurance and commitment.

Marketing Strategy

Marketing strategy One that encompasses the selection and analysis of a target market and the creation and maintenance of an appropriate marketing mix that will satisfy those people in the target market

Marketing mix The tactical "toolkit" of product, place/distribution, promotion, price and people that an organisation can control in order to facilitate satisfying exchange

To achieve the broad goal of expediting desirable exchanges, an organisation's marketing managers are responsible for developing and managing marketing strategies. Specifically, a **marketing strategy** encompasses selecting and analysing a target market (the group of people whom the organisation wants to reach) and creating and maintaining an appropriate **marketing mix** (the tactical "toolkit" of product, place/distribution, promotion, price and people) that will satisfy those customers in the target market. A marketing strategy articulates a plan for the best use of the organisation's resources and tactics to meet its objectives.

When marketing managers attempt to develop and manage marketing activities, they must deal with three broad sets of variables: (a) those relating to the marketing mix, (b) those inherent in the accompanying target market strategy, and (c) those that make up the marketing environment. The marketing mix decision variables—product, place/distribution, promotion, price and people—and the target market strategy variables are factors over which an organisation has control. As Figure 1.3 shows, these variables are constructed around the buyer or

Banks Enter the Relationship Marketing Era

Retail banks were not known for their customer-friendly orientation. Security fears, the seriousness of dealing with people's financial matters and the austere architecture of many branches did not lend themselves to the creation of a relaxing, informal trading environment. In the late 1980s, the first efforts were made to "move with the times" and throughout the 1990s there were significant developments. Longer, more flexible opening hours, customer service personnel, desks and easy chairs rather than formal counters and security grills, open-plan layouts and glass fronted, well lit buildings—all brought the retail banking environment more in line with other high street shops and consumers' increasing expectation of improved service.

As the 1990s drew to a close, there was to be a further move towards focusing on the customer rather than operational issues. Many of the major retail banking operations such as ABN Amro, HSBC and Lloyds TSB turned to relationship marketing as a means to enhance customer service, motivate branch personnel and strive to maintain customer loyalty. IT systems were re-designed with a focus on capturing data which were customer-specific rather than product-specific. Customers were profiled in order to better understand their evolving financial requirements. This enabled the leading high street banks to tailor product offers, mailings and customer service calls to individual customer accounts.

HSBC (Midland) identified a series of lifestage events which trigger different patterns of expenditure, savings and financial planning. For example, leaving school for university, purchasing a house, having children, retirement—each involves not only a radical change in financial circumstances, but also the need to save, borrow, plan longer term and take out various insurance or savings policies. Many first-time parents suddenly become aware that until the arrival of their baby, they had not really planned for long term financial security or taken out precautionary insurance policies to cover for untimely death. In addition to monitoring these major lifestage events, the tracking of customers' use of debit cards reveals their lifestyle spending patterns and types of consumption. Favourite restaurants, frequently used petrol forecourts, entertainment venues, propensity for overseas holidays or certain retail outlets are only a few of the numerous trackable profile-building characteristics that can be monitored. Many of the banks, while safeguarding consumers' rights to confidentiality and security of financial information, have endeavoured to use this enhanced insight into individual customers in order to target specific services and products at individual customers.

This one-to-one approach is perhaps the ultimate in honing a product proposition to reflect customer needs, perceptions and expectations. It has to be carefully controlled to ensure some standardisation of product offer, bank branding and equity in the eyes of consumers, and to guarantee cost effective returns for these relationship-building banks. It has also been necessary to re-focus employees to think one-to-one, to become less operationally oriented and to emphasise the provision of customer service. A clear target market strategy and an understanding of which consumers should be primary targets for marketing activity are still important objectives. Products and services must be developed with more than an individual customer in mind in order to gain adequate scale economies. The aim, though, for most retail banks in the new millennium is to better match available products, services and promotional messages to individual customers so that the products and marketing communications genuinely reflect a customer's needs, interests and expectations. In this way, a bank's products and marketing campaigns are less likely to be ignored and customers, it is expected, will be more satisfied with their bank.

SOURCES: Sally Dibb and Maureen Meadows, "The application of a relationship marketing perspective in retail banking", working paper, Warwick Business School, 1999; Maureen Meadows and Sally Dibb, "Assessing the implementation of market segmentation in retail financial services", *International Journal of Service Industry Management*, 9 (3), 1998, pp. 266–285; Midland Bank, 1999.

consumer. The marketing environment variables are political, legal, regulatory, societal/green, technological, and economic and competitive forces. These factors are subject to less control by an organisation, but they affect buyers' needs as well as marketing managers' decisions regarding marketing mix variables.

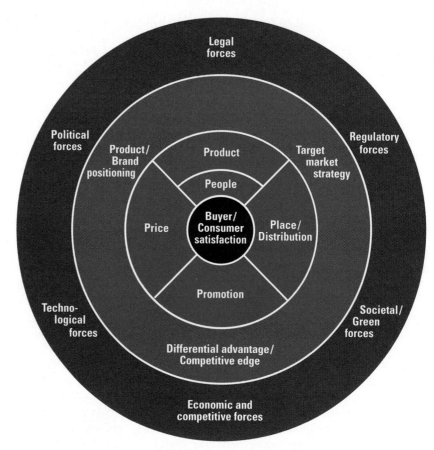

The circular diagram shows concentric rings. From the center outward:

Buyer/Consumer satisfaction (center)

The marketing mix ring contains: **Product**, **People**, **Price**, **Place/Distribution**, **Promotion**

Marketing strategy ring contains: **Product/Brand positioning**, **Target market strategy**, **Differential advantage/Competitive edge**

The marketing environment (outer ring) contains: **Legal forces**, **Regulatory forces**, **Societal/Green forces**, **Economic and competitive forces**, **Technological forces**, **Political forces**

Legend:
- ■ Consumer satisfaction
- ■ The marketing mix
- ■ Marketing strategy
- ■ The marketing environment

Figure 1.3 The marketing environment, marketing strategy, the marketing mix and customer satisfaction. Consumers and businesses are affected by the forces of the marketing environment. Businesses must determine a marketing strategy, implemented through the ingredients of the marketing mix, which aims to satisfy targeted customers.

To develop and manage marketing strategies, marketers must focus on several marketing tasks: marketing opportunity analysis (the marketing analyses), target market selection (determination of the marketing strategy), marketing mix development and effective marketing management (the programmes that facilitate and control implementation of the marketing strategy). Figure 1.4 lists these tasks, along with the chapters of this book in which they are discussed.

Marketing Strategy: Marketing Opportunity Analysis

Marketing opportunity One that exists when circumstances allow an organisation to take action towards reaching a particular group of customers

A **marketing opportunity** exists when circumstances allow an organisation to take action towards reaching a particular group of customers. An opportunity provides a favourable chance or opening for a company to generate sales from identifiable markets. For example, during a heat wave, marketers of electric fans have a marketing opportunity—an opportunity to reach customers who need electric fans.

Marketers should be capable of recognising and analysing marketing opportunities. An organisation's long term survival depends on developing products that satisfy its customers. Few organisations can assume that products popular today will interest buyers ten years from now. A marketing organisation can choose among several alternatives for continued product development through which it

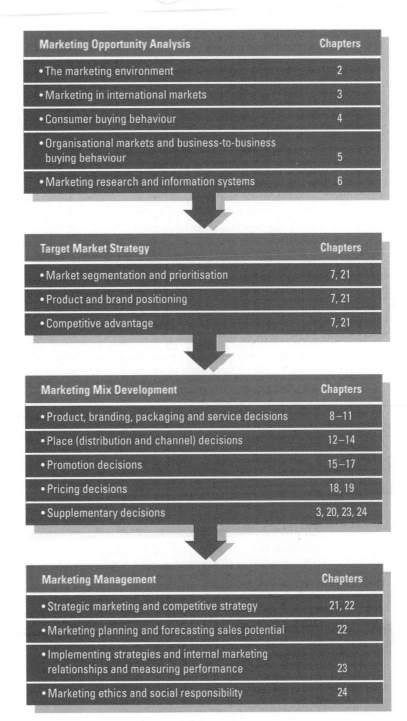

Marketing Opportunity Analysis	Chapters
• The marketing environment	2
• Marketing in international markets	3
• Consumer buying behaviour	4
• Organisational markets and business-to-business buying behaviour	5
• Marketing research and information systems	6

Target Market Strategy	Chapters
• Market segmentation and prioritisation	7, 21
• Product and brand positioning	7, 21
• Competitive advantage	7, 21

Marketing Mix Development	Chapters
• Product, branding, packaging and service decisions	8–11
• Place (distribution and channel) decisions	12–14
• Promotion decisions	15–17
• Pricing decisions	18, 19
• Supplementary decisions	3, 20, 23, 24

Marketing Management	Chapters
• Strategic marketing and competitive strategy	21, 22
• Marketing planning and forecasting sales potential	22
• Implementing strategies and internal marketing relationships and measuring performance	23
• Marketing ethics and social responsibility	24

Figure 1.4 Marketing tasks: analysis, strategy and programmes for implementation and control

can achieve its objectives and satisfy buyers. It can modify existing products (for example, by removing preservatives from jams and sauces to address increasing health consciousness among customers), introduce new products (such as Windows 98, pay-as-you-talk mobile phone packages or Hitachi digital TVs) and delete some that customers no longer want (such as disc cameras or turn-tables). A company may also try to market its products to a greater number of customers, persuade current customers to use more of a product or perhaps expand marketing activities into additional countries. Diversification into new product offerings through internal efforts or through acquisitions of other organisations may be viable options for a company. For example, BSN Groupe, a French consumer goods marketer of pasta, bakery goods and other products, bought RJR Nabisco's European consumer goods division, gaining the rights to market a number of highly successful Nabisco products in Europe, and Grand Metropolitan's purchase of Pillsbury led to the European appearance of Häagen-Dazs premium adult ice creams. An organisation's ability to pursue any of these alternatives successfully depends on its internal characteristics and the forces within the marketing environment.

Internal Organisational Factors

The primary factors inside an organisation that should be considered when analysing marketing opportunities are organisational objectives, financial resources, managerial skills, organisational strengths and weaknesses, and cost structures. Most organisations have overall organisational objectives. Some marketing opportunities may be consistent with these objectives; others are not, and to pursue them is hazardous. Frequently, the pursuit of such opportunities ends in failure or forces the company to alter its long term objectives.

Obviously, a business's financial resources constrain the type of marketing opportunities it can pursue. Typically, an organisation does not develop projects that can bring economic catastrophe. In some situations, however, a company must invest in a high risk opportunity, because the costs of not pursuing the project are so high. Thus, despite an economic recession and reduced house and road building, construction equipment manufacturer JCB continued to launch new ranges and enter new markets. It developed and launched its Compact Division, emphasising mini escavators, at a cost of millions, to respond to changing market requirements.

The skills and experience of management also limit the types of opportunities that an organisation can pursue. A company must be particularly cautious when exploring the possibility of entering unfamiliar markets with new products. If it lacks appropriate managerial skills and experience, the business can sometimes acquire them by recruiting additional managerial personnel.

Like people, most organisations have strengths and weaknesses. Because of the types of operations in which a company is engaged, it normally has employees with specialised skills and technological information. Such characteristics are a strength when launching marketing strategies that require them. However, they may be a weakness if the company tries to compete in new, unrelated product areas.

An organisation's cost structure may be an advantage if the company pursues certain marketing opportunities and a disadvantage if it pursues others. Such factors as geographic location, employee skills, access to raw materials and type of equipment and facilities all can affect the cost structure.

Marketing Environment Forces

The marketing environment, which consists of political, legal, regulatory, societal/green, technological, and economic and competitive forces, surrounds the buyer (consumer) and the marketing mix (see Figure 1.3). Each major environmental force is explored in considerable depth in Chapter 2. Marketers know that they cannot predict changes in the marketing environment with certainty. Even so, over the years marketers have become more systematic in taking these forces into account when planning their competitive actions.[9]

Marketing environment forces affect a marketer's ability to facilitate and expedite exchanges in three general ways. (1) They influence customers by affecting their lifestyles, standards of living, preferences and needs for products. Because a marketing manager tries to develop and adjust the marketing mix to satisfy consumers, the effects of environmental forces on customers also have an indirect impact on the marketing mix components. (2) Marketing environment forces help determine whether and how a marketing manager can perform certain marketing activities. (3) The environmental forces may affect a marketing manager's decisions and actions by influencing buyers' reactions to the company's marketing mix.

Although forces in the marketing environment are sometimes viewed as "uncontrollables", a marketing manager may be able to influence one or more of them. However, marketing environment forces fluctuate quickly and dramatically, which is one reason marketing is so interesting and challenging. Because these forces are highly interrelated, a change in one may cause others to change. For example, from Freons in fridges to additives in foods, most consumers have become increasingly aware of health and environmental issues. Manufacturers have altered product specifications and production methods. Legislators and regulatory bodies have also responded to expert and consumer opinions with new regulations and informal agreements, forcing companies to re-think their manufacturing and marketing policies.

Even though changes in the marketing environment produce uncertainty for marketers and at times impede marketing efforts, they can also create opportunities. After the 1989 oil spills, for example, more companies began developing and marketing products designed to contain or dissipate spilled oil. The BSE beef crisis gave producers of other meats significant opportunities. Environmental concerns have encouraged car manufacturers to develop emission-free engines. Thus a marketer must be aware of changes in environmental forces not only to adjust to and influence them but also to capitalise on the opportunities they provide.

Marketing Strategy: Target Market Selection

Target market A group of people for whom a company creates and maintains a marketing mix that specifically fits the needs and preferences of that group

A **target market** is a group of people for whom a company creates and maintains a marketing mix that specifically fits the needs and preferences of that group.[10] When choosing a target market, marketing managers try to evaluate possible markets to see how entering them would affect the company's sales, costs and profits. Marketers also attempt to determine whether the organisation has the resources to produce a marketing mix that meets the needs of a particular target market and whether satisfying those needs is consistent with the company's overall objectives. The size and number of competitors already marketing products in possible target markets are also of concern.

Marketing managers may define a target market as a vast number of people or as a relatively small group. For example, Ford produces cars suitable for much of the population (although specific models are quite narrowly targeted, such as the family runaround Focus or the executive Mondeo). Porsche focuses its marketing effort on a small proportion of the population, believing that it can compete more effectively by concentrating on an affluent target market. Although a business may concentrate its efforts on one target market through a single marketing mix, businesses often focus on several target markets by developing and employing multiple marketing mixes. Reebok, for example, markets different types of shoes to meet the specific needs of joggers, walkers, aerobics enthusiasts and other groups.

Target market selection is crucial to generating productive marketing efforts. At times, products and organisations fail because marketers do not identify the appropriate customer groups at which to aim their efforts. Organisations that try to be all things to all people typically end up not satisfying the needs of any customer group very well. It is important for an organisation's management to designate which customer groups the company is trying to serve and to have adequate information about these customers. The identification and analysis of a target market provide a foundation on which a marketing mix can be developed.

Marketing Strategy: Marketing Mix Development

As mentioned, the marketing mix consists of four major components: product, place/distribution, promotion and price. Increasingly, people are becoming the fifth component. These components are called marketing mix decision variables because a marketing manager decides which type of each component to use and in what amounts. A primary goal of a marketing manager is to create and maintain a marketing mix that satisfies consumers' needs for a general product type. Notice in Figure 1.3 that the marketing mix is built around the buyer (as is stressed by the marketing concept). Bear in mind, too, that the forces of the marketing environment affect the marketing mix variables in many ways.

Marketing mix variables often are viewed as controllable variables because they can be changed. However, there are limits to how much these variables can be altered. For example, because of economic conditions or government regulations, a manager may not be free to adjust prices daily. Changes in sizes, colours, shapes and designs of most tangible goods are expensive; therefore, such product features cannot be altered very often. In addition, promotional campaigns and the methods used to distribute products ordinarily cannot be changed overnight. People, too, require training and motivating, and cannot be recruited or sacked overnight.

Marketing managers must develop a marketing mix that precisely matches the needs of the people in the target market. Before they can do so, they have to collect in-depth, up-to-date information about those needs. The information might include data about the age, income, ethnic origin, sex and educational level of people in the target market; their preferences for product features; their attitudes towards competitors' products; and the frequency and intensity with which they use the product. Armed with these kinds of data, marketing managers are better able to develop a product, service package, distribution system, promotion programme and price that satisfy the people in the target market.

This section looks more closely at the decisions and activities related to each marketing mix variable (product, place/distribution, promotion, price and people—the "5Ps"). Table 1.1 on page 8 contains a list of the decisions and activities associated with each marketing mix variable.

Product variable The aspect of the marketing mix that deals with researching consumers' product wants and designing a product with the desired characteristics

The Product Variable A product can be a good, a service or an idea. The **product variable** is the aspect of the marketing mix that deals with researching consumers' product wants and designing a product with the desired characteristics. It also involves the creation or alteration of packages and brand names and may include decisions about guarantees and repair services. The actual manufacturing of products is not a marketing activity.

Product variable decisions and related activities are important because they directly involve creating products and services that satisfy consumers' needs and wants. To maintain a satisfying set of products that will help an organisation achieve its goals, a marketer must be able to develop new products, modify existing ones and eliminate those that no longer satisfy buyers or yield acceptable profits. For example, after realising that competitors were capturing large shares of the low calorie market, Heinz introduced new product items under its Weight Watchers name.

The Place/Distribution Variable   To satisfy consumers, products must be available at the right time and in a convenient location. In dealing with the **place/distribution variable,** a marketing manager seeks to make products available in the quantities desired to as many customers as possible and to keep the total inventory, transport and storage costs as low as possible. A marketing manager may become involved in selecting and motivating intermediaries (wholesalers, retailers and dealers), establishing and maintaining inventory control procedures, and developing and managing transport and storage systems.

The Promotion Variable   The **promotion variable** relates to communication activities used to inform one or more groups of people about an organisation and its products. Promotion can be aimed at increasing public awareness of an organisation and of new or existing products. In addition, promotion can serve to educate consumers about product features or to urge people to take a particular stance on a political or social issue. It may also be used to keep interest strong in an established product that has been available for decades. The advertisement in Figure 1.5 is an example.

The Price Variable   The **price variable** relates to activities associated with establishing pricing policies and determining product prices. Price is a critical component of the marketing mix because consumers are concerned about the value obtained in an exchange. Price often is used as a competitive tool; in fact, extremely intense price competition sometimes leads to price wars. For example, airlines like United, British Airways and Virgin Atlantic Airways are engaged in ruthless price cutting in the battle for transatlantic routes. Price can also help to establish a product's image. For instance, if Chanel tried to sell Chanel No. 5 in a two litre bottle for £3, consumers probably would not buy it because the low price would destroy the prestigious image of Chanel's de luxe brand.

The People Variable   *Product, place/distribution, promotion* and *price* are the principal elements of the marketing mix—the "4Ps". Marketers of services include *people* as a core element. Whether part of the product element or a separate element of the marketing mix, there is no doubt that people are important. As marketers they manipulate the rest of the marketing mix. As intermediaries in the marketing channel they help make products and services available to the marketplace. As consumers or buyers they create the need for the field of marketing. In the marketing mix, the **people variable** reflects the level of customer service, advice, sales support and aftermarket back-up required, involving recruitment policies, training, retention and motivation of key personnel. For many products and most services, personnel interface directly with the intended purchaser and are often perceived by such consumers as being part and parcel of the product offering.

Place/distribution variable   The aspect of the marketing mix that deals with making products available in the quantities desired to as many customers as possible and keeping the total inventory, transport and storage costs as low as possible

Promotion variable   The aspect of the marketing mix that relates to activities used to inform one or more groups of people about an organisation and its products

Price variable   The aspect of the marketing mix that relates to activities associated with establishing pricing policies and determining product prices

People variable   The aspect of the marketing mix that reflects the level of customer service, advice, sales support and aftermarket back-up required, involving recruitment policies, training, retention and motivation of key personnel

Figure 1.5 Promoting an established brand. Champagne house Moët & Chandon uses its heritage in its advertising to reinforce its brand appeal. SOURCE: Courtesy of Olivia Beasley.

Developing and maintaining an effective marketing mix is a major requirement for a strong marketing strategy. Thus, as indicated in Figure 1.4, a large portion of this text (Chapters 8 through 20) focuses on the concepts, decisions and activities associated with the components of the marketing mix. It is the marketing mix that readers, as consumers, will most frequently have experienced. It is important to remember, however, that analysis must precede the development of a marketing strategy which in turn must be formulated before the marketing mix is determined for a product or a service.

Marketing Strategy: Marketing Management

Marketing management A process of planning, organising, implementing and controlling marketing activities to facilitate and expedite exchanges effectively and efficiently

Marketing management is a process of planning, organising, implementing and controlling marketing activities to facilitate and expedite exchanges effectively and efficiently. Effectiveness and efficiency are important dimensions of this definition. *Effectiveness* is the degree to which an exchange helps achieve an organisation's objectives. *Efficiency* is the minimisation of resources an organisation must spend to achieve a specific level of desired exchanges. Thus the overall goal of marketing management is to facilitate highly desirable exchanges and to minimise as much as possible the costs of doing so.

Marketing planning is a systematic process of assessing opportunities and resources, determining marketing objectives, developing a marketing strategy and developing plans for implementation and control. Planning determines when and how marketing activities will be performed and who is to perform them. It forces marketing managers to think ahead, to establish objectives and to consider future marketing activities. Effective marketing planning also reduces or eliminates daily crises.

Organising marketing activities refers to developing the internal structure of the marketing unit. The structure is the key to directing marketing activities. The marketing unit can be organised by function, product, region, type of customer or a combination of all four.

Proper implementation of marketing plans hinges on co-ordination of marketing activities, motivation of marketing personnel and effective communication within the unit. Marketing managers must motivate marketing personnel, co-ordinate their activities and integrate their activities both with those in other areas of the company and with the marketing efforts of personnel in external organisations, such as advertising agencies and marketing research businesses. An organisation's communication system must allow the marketing manager to stay in contact with high level management, with managers of other functional areas within the company and with personnel involved in marketing activities both inside and outside the organisation.

The marketing control process consists of establishing performance standards, evaluating actual performance by comparing it with established standards and reducing the difference between desired and actual performance. An effective control process has four requirements. (1) It should ensure a rate of information flow that allows the marketing manager to quickly detect differences between actual and planned levels of performance. (2) It must accurately monitor different kinds of activities and be flexible enough to accommodate changes. (3) It must be economical so that its costs are low relative to the costs that would arise if there were no controls. (4) Finally, it should be designed so that both managers and subordinates can understand it. To maintain effective marketing control, an organisation needs to develop a comprehensive control process that evaluates marketing operations at regular intervals. Chapters 22 and 23 examine the planning, organising, implementing and controlling of marketing activities in greater detail.

The Organisation of This Book

The structure of this book adheres to the principle that it is important to analyse marketing opportunities, then develop strategies and finally construct programmes that implement the desired marketing strategy—the A-S-P process. Marketing analyses develop a thorough understanding of the marketplace—particularly customers, competitors and market trends. This knowledge of the marketplace provides a sound basis on which to devise marketing strategies. These should identify attractive target market segments, with a clear positioning and awareness of the competitive situation. Finally, to implement the recommended target market strategy, marketing programmes must be designed with marketing mix combinations and control processes to ensure effective implementation. This analysis-strategy-programmes process is fundamental to sound marketing practice and is the sentiment behind Figure 1.4.

The first two parts of *Marketing: Concepts and Strategies,* therefore, address marketing opportunity analysis and target market selection:

- Part I: Marketing Defined
- Part II: Understanding and Targeting Markets

The next five parts examine in detail the core ingredients of the marketing mix. These are the tactical marketing activities at the heart of marketing programmes that take a product or service to the targeted consumers:

- Part III: Product, Branding, Packaging and Service Decisions
- Part IV: Place/Distribution and Channel Decisions
- Part V: Promotion Decisions
- Part VI: Pricing Decisions
- Part VII: Manipulating the Marketing Mix

Finally, the implementation issues of effective marketing management are discussed in the last part of the book. This set of chapters returns to the core issues of marketing strategy and additionally discusses marketing planning, implementing strategies and the important consideration of ethical and social responsibility concerns in marketing:

- Part VIII: Marketing Management

Marketing: Concepts and Strategies also includes:

- an indexed margin/glossary of key terms
- full subject and name indexing
- a section of extended cases to enhance readers' understanding of key topics, supported with extensive guidance on how to tackle cases
- an appendix providing a summary of career choices and opportunities in marketing
- an appendix presenting revision hints and tips for readers about to take marketing examinations
- detailed illustrative examples in every chapter
- up-to-date statistics for the marketing industry
- support material on its own web site

S U M M A R Y

Marketing consists of individual and organisational activities that facilitate and expedite satisfying exchange relationships in a dynamic environment through the creation, distribution, promotion and pricing of goods, services and ideas. An *exchange* is the provision or transfer of goods, services and ideas in return for something of value. Four conditions must exist for an exchange to occur: (1) two or more individuals, groups or organisations must participate; (2) each party must have something of value desired by the other; (3) each party must be willing to give up what it has in order to receive the value held by the other; and (4) the parties to the exchange must be able to communicate with each other to make their "somethings of value" available. In an exchange, products are traded either for other products or for financial resources, such as cash or credit. *Products* can be goods, services or ideas. Through the exchange, the recipient (the customer) and the provider (the business) must be *satisfied*.

It is important to study marketing because it permeates society. Marketing activities are performed in both business and non-business organisations. Moreover, marketing activities help business organisations generate profits and income, the life-blood of an economy. The study of marketing enhances consumer awareness. Marketing costs absorb about half of what the consumer spends. Marketing practised well improves business performance.

The *marketing concept* is a management philosophy that prompts a business organisation to try to satisfy customers' needs through a co-ordinated set of activities that also allows the organisation to achieve its goals. Customer satisfaction is the major objective of the marketing concept. The philosophy of the marketing concept emerged during the 1950s, as the *marketing era* succeeded the *production* and the *sales eras*. As the 1990s progressed into the *relationship marketing era*, transaction based marketing was replaced by relationship marketing. To make the marketing concept work, top management must accept it as an overall management philosophy. Implementing the marketing concept requires an efficient information system and sometimes the restructuring of the organisation.

Marketing strategy involves selecting and analysing a target market (the group of people whom the organisation wants to reach) and creating and maintaining an appropriate *marketing mix* (product, place/distribution, promotion, price and people) to satisfy this market. Marketing strategy requires that managers focus on four tasks to achieve set objectives: (1) marketing opportunity analysis, (2) target market selection, (3) marketing mix development and (4) marketing management.

Marketers should be able to recognise and analyse *marketing opportunities,* which are circumstances that allow an organisation to take action towards reaching a particular group of customers. Marketing opportunity analysis involves reviewing both internal factors (organisational objectives, financial resources, managerial skills, organisational strengths, organisational weaknesses and cost structures) and external ones in the *marketing environment* (the political, legal, regulatory, societal/green, technological, and economic and competitive forces).

A *target market* is a group of people for whom a company creates and maintains a marketing mix that specifically fits the needs and preferences of that group. It is important for an organisation's management to designate which customer groups the company is trying to serve and to have some information about these customers. The identification and analysis of a target market provide a foundation on which a marketing mix can be developed.

The five principal variables that make up the marketing mix are product, place/distribution, promotion, price and people—"the 5Ps". The *product variable* is the aspect of the marketing mix that deals with researching consumers' wants and designing a product with the desired characteristics. A marketing manager tries to make products available in the quantities desired to as many customers as possible and to keep the total inventory, transport and storage costs as low as possible—the *place/distribution variable*. The *promotion variable* relates to activities used to inform one or more groups of people about an organisation and its products. The *price variable* refers to establishing pricing policies and determining product prices. The *people variable* controls the marketing mix; facilitates the product's distribution, sale and service; and—as consumers or buyers—gives marketing its rationale. Marketing exists to encourage consumer satisfaction.

Marketing management is a process of planning, organising, implementing and controlling marketing activities to facilitate and expedite exchanges effectively and efficiently. Marketing planning is a systematic process of assessing opportunities and resources, determining marketing objectives, developing a marketing strategy and developing plans for implementation and control. Organising marketing activities refers to developing the internal structure of the marketing unit. Properly implementing marketing plans depends on co-ordinating marketing activities, motivating marketing personnel and effectively communicating within the unit. The marketing control process consists of establishing performance standards, evaluating actual performance by comparing it with established standards and reducing the difference between desired and actual performance.

Important Terms

Marketing	Marketing concept	Target market
Exchange	Production era	Product variable
Customer satisfaction	Sales era	Place/distribution variable
Marketing environment	Marketing era	Promotion variable
Product	Relationship marketing era	Price variable
Good	Marketing strategy	People variable
Service	Marketing mix	Marketing management
Idea	Marketing opportunity	

Discussion and Review Questions

1. What is marketing? How did you define marketing before you read this chapter?
2. Why should someone study marketing?
3. Discuss the basic elements of the marketing concept. Which businesses use this concept? Have these businesses adopted the marketing concept? Explain.
4. Identify several business organisations that obviously have not adopted the marketing concept. What characteristics of these organisations indicate non-acceptance of the marketing concept?
5. Describe the major components of a marketing strategy. How are these major components related?
6. Identify the tasks involved in developing a marketing strategy.
7. What are the primary issues that marketing managers consider when conducting a market opportunity analysis?
8. What are the variables in the marketing environment? How much control does a marketing manager have over environmental variables?
9. Why is the selection of a target market such an important issue?
10. Why are the elements of the marketing mix known as variables? What are these variables?
11. What type of management activities are involved in the marketing management process?
12. Why is it important to adhere to the principle of analyses first, then marketing strategy development, followed ultimately by programmes for implementing the recommended strategy?

Recommended Readings

M. Baker, "The nature and scope of marketing", in the *Companion Encyclopaedia of Marketing*, M. Baker, ed. (London: International Thomson Business Press, 2000).

M. Baker, "What is marketing?" in *The Marketing Book*, M. Baker, ed. (Oxford: Butterworth-Heinemann, 1999).

J. Lynch, "What is marketing?" in *Effective Industrial Marketing*, N. Hart, ed. (London: Kogan Page, 1994).

T. Levitt, "Marketing myopia", *Harvard Business Review*, 1960, vol. 38, no. 4, pp. 45–56.

● C A S E S

1.1 *Sweden's IKEA Marches On*

When Swedish home furnishings retailer IKEA opened its first store in the UK, a retail shed near the M6 at Warrington, curious shoppers found queues jamming nearby roads, parking spaces at a premium and retailing analysts by the score. With just one store, IKEA had the UK furniture industry on its toes: large retail groups and manufacturers alike feared large market share losses. With its acquisition of the UK's Habitat, IKEA has conquered yet another territory. Such an impact is not confined to the UK market.

IKEA has grown from one store in 1958 to 140 stores in 28 countries, 22,000 employees and sales of over £3.5 billion. Close to 80 per cent of sales are from within Europe, but recent expansion in North America, South East Asia and Australasia is now increasing *rest of the world* sales—despite some initial franchising difficulties in certain territories. IKEA's distinctive catalogue is produced in-house and now printed in 14 languages. IKEA is perhaps one of the world's most successful retailers with a brand name that is known, recognised and discussed; a retail concept that stands for value, style and quality; everything for the home under one roof, with easy parking, children's play areas and cafés—"a day out"! As the company succinctly states in its advertising:

> IKEA: the furnishings store from Sweden
> More for your money
> IKEA is more than just furnishing ideas. It's a
> day out for all the family.

Most of the time, beautifully designed home furnishings are created for a small part of the population—the few who can afford them. From the beginning, IKEA has taken a different path. We have decided to side with the many.

That means responding to the home furnishing needs of people throughout the world. People with many different needs, tastes, dreams, aspirations . . . and wallets. People who want to improve their home and create a better everyday life.

For IKEA, helping create a better everyday life means offering a wide range of home furnishings in IKEA stores. Home furnishings that combine good design, good function and good quality with prices so low that as many people as possible can afford them.

IKEA's huge volumes, cheap out-of-town sites and dedication to keeping costs low through self-assembly packs mean that unlike many competitors, the company coped with the recession of the early 1990s. Low prices have been the key to IKEA's success, but price alone cannot create an internationally long term marketing success story. Products are up-dated consistently to match consumers' expectations and lifestyles. In-store service and staff training are integral to the IKEA shopping experience. Sites are chosen to maximise catchment areas, to make access easy for shoppers and to bring the brand name to the attention of the whole community. Logistics give IKEA an edge, with carefully managed ordering and delivery reducing both stock-holdings and stock-outs. Promotion emphasises the "style without expense" philosophy and the IKEA name. The result has been a country by country revolution as staid furniture markets have been rejuvenated with the entry of IKEA. Shoppers intending to buy just a sofa return home with a sofa, a chair, some lamps and a general excitement about a new store where they can buy home furnishings at unbelievable prices.

The latest strategic developments for IKEA include entering eastern European markets, developing a new IKEA format and expanding its mail order/electronic ordering. Eastern Europe has been the recent target for expansion, with IKEA stores opening in Poland, the Czech Republic and Hungary. The company is also sourcing furniture from eastern European manufacturers, which now supply 15 per cent of its range. The standard "big box" IKEA concept has been brought to a smaller stage with the New York opening in Manhattan of the first IKEA *Marketing Outpost,* a 720 square metre (7,500 square foot) "boutique", significantly smaller than the normal 19,000 square metre (200,000 square foot) IKEA superstore. Even more unusual is the decision to offer only a selected, themed, reduced range at any moment in time. For example, *IKEA Cook* showcases the company's kitchen-related merchandise. Every eight to 12 weeks the store closes completely, to re-open with a new look, different merchandise, signage, lighting and staff uniforms. If successful, the *Marketing Outpost* concept will be rolled out into other cities and countries. IKEA is also recognising the growing use of the Internet and is developing sales tools to utilise this new technology.

IKEA has its ideals and operating philosophies: standards matter. IKEA has a forceful, well directed marketing strategy actioned through two tightly developed marketing mixes: one for the core superstores, and another for the new *Marketing Outpost* operation. The result is a successful, expanding company, satisfied target customers and unhappy competitors.

SOURCES: Helen Jones, "IKEA's global strategy is a winning formula", *Marketing Week*, 15 March 1996, p. 22; Jennifer Pellet, "IKEA takes Manhattan!", *Discount Merchandiser,* October 1995, pp. 22–23; "IKEA", *Retail Business,* March 1995, pp. 78–81; Jonathan Pell, "IKEA successfully penetrates east European consumer markets", *Central European,* June 1994, pp. 13–14; *IKEA Facts,* 1990 and 1992; B. Solomon, "A Swedish company corners the business: worldwide", *Management Review,* 80 (4), 1991, pp. 10–13; IKEA HQ, 1998.

Questions for Discussion

1. Explain why IKEA is successful.
2. To whom does the *Marketing Outpost* concept appeal? Why has IKEA developed this novel format?
3. In what ways does IKEA deploy the marketing concept?

1.2 Marketing: Concepts and Strategies *Responds to Market Feedback*

Marketing seeks to satisfy customers, fend off competitors, create a competitive and differentiated product and branding proposition, stay abreast of market trends and to seek adequate financial returns. None of this can occur without an understanding of the marketplace and a suitable phase of marketing analysis. When companies introduce new products or when they modify existing ones, most do so having analysed their market: trends, competitors' propositions and, above all, their targeted customers' needs and expectations. Many of the products which fail (see Chapter 6) do so because they have not been well researched or carefully thought through. The launch of Ford's Focus, the 1998 replacement for the company's best selling and long established Escort range, followed several years of such research. Initially this analysis concentrated on the prototype design and concept testing, but latterly moved on to the determination of model specifications in the range, pricing and the selection of a suitable brand name and identity. Finally, the analysis moved to the launch message, brand positioning and promotional campaign required to introduce the Focus first to dealerships and the motoring press, and then to the car buying public. The four or five years' research and analysis typical in the launch of a new car are perhaps extreme in terms of time, detailed planning and resource allocation for marketing analysis, but the capital costs, marketing spends and longevity of the car product necessitate such shrewd planning. Nevertheless, such a process of analysis and thinking, even if over a much shorter time period and with much smaller budgets, is central to the introduction of most products—even for a textbook such as *Marketing: Concepts and Strategies.*

Marketing: Concepts and Strategies was conceived in the late 1980s and launched in 1991. Now in its fourth edition, there have been many changes in content, format, structure and design.

Irrespective that barely a word remains *in situ* from the first edition to this, a brief glance at Table 1.3 will reveal some immediately clear changes in content. In the 1980s marketing concentrated on the "4Ps" of the marketing mix: product, place/distribution, promotion and pricing—the tactical ingredients manipulated by marketers as they produce sales and marketing programmes. Throughout the 1990s, the thrust in mainstream marketing grew to be (a) building and maintaining relationships with customers, while (b) ensuring that the marketing process deployed was a rigorous one incorporating astute marketing analysis, clear and objective strategic decision-making, with the outputs leading into the marketing mix deployment, supported by internal operating controls and mechanisms to ensure implementation of the desired target market strategy and associated tactical marketing mix programmes. The structure, running order and content of this edition of *Marketing: Concepts and Strategies* very tightly reflect these changes.

Marketing: Concepts and Strategies was the first leading textbook to devote a chapter to the important consideration of practising marketing ethically and with social consideration, concepts that are now top of the agenda for many blue chip international businesses. The importance of services in the economy and to users of this text led to the inclusion of the people ingredient of the marketing mix, plus greater attention to branding and services in Part III. Most businesses now include sponsorship, direct mail and the Internet as part of their promotional mixes, so the traditional view of the promotional mix had to be up-graded: advertising, PR, personal selling and sales promotion no longer sufficed. Marketing grew up in the consumer goods corporations of the United States. Textbooks tended to reflect this, with "asides" devoted to industrial, services and international markets and marketing. These areas are now mainstream

First Edition, 1991	Fourth Edition, 2001
I: An Analysis of Marketing Opportunities	**I:** Marketing Defined
1. An Overview of Strategic Marketing	1. An Overview of the Marketing Concept
2. The Marketing Environment	2. The Marketing Environment
3. Segmenting Markets, Targeting, Positioning and Evaluation	3. Marketing in International Markets
4. Consumer Buying Behaviour	**II:** Understanding and Targeting Markets
5. Organisational Markets and Buying Behaviour	4. Consumer Buying Behaviour
6. Marketing Research and Information Systems	5. Organisational Markets and Business-to-Business Buying Behaviour
II: Product Decisions	6. Marketing Research and Information Systems
7. Product Concepts	7. Segmenting Markets, Targeting and Positioning
8. Developing and Managing Products	**III:** Product, Branding, Packaging and Service Decisions
III: Distribution Decisions	8. Product Decisions
9. Marketing Channels	9. Branding and Packaging
10. Wholesaling	10. Developing and Managing Products
11. Retailing	11. The Marketing of Services
12. Physical Distribution	**IV:** Place/Distribution and Channel Decisions
IV: Promotion Decisions	12. Marketing Channels
13. Promotion: An Overview	13. Wholesalers, Distributors and Physical Distribution
14. Advertising and Publicity	14. Retailing
15. Personal Selling and Sales Promotion	**V:** Promotion Decisions
V: Pricing Decisions	15. Promotion: An Overview
16. Pricing Concepts	16. Advertising, Publicity and Sponsorship
17. Setting Prices	17. Personal Selling, Sales Promotion and Direct Mail, the Internet and Direct Marketing
VI: Marketing Management	**VI:** Pricing Decisions
18. Strategic Market Planning	18. Pricing Concepts
19. Implementing Strategies and Measuring Performance	19. Setting Prices
20. Marketing Ethics and Social Responsibility	**VII:** Manipulating the Marketing Mix
VII: Selected Applications	20. Modifying the Marketing Mix for Various Markets
21. Industrial Marketing	**VIII:** Marketing Management
22. Services Marketing	21. Marketing Strategy
23. International Marketing	22. Marketing Planning and Forecasting Sales Potential
	23. Implementing Strategies, Internal Marketing Relationships and Measuring Performance
	24. Marketing Ethics and Social Responsibility

Table 1.3 *Marketing: Concepts and Strategies* reflects changing emphases in marketing over the past decade

employers of marketers and fully fledged users of the marketing toolkit. Indeed, many of the latest developments utilised by the consumer goods businesses originated from services marketing! To reflect this change in orientation and the growing importance of marketing in business-to-business and services organisations, *Marketing: Concepts and Strategies* has evolved throughout its four editions with modified running order, content and chapter headings. The cases, examples and statistics used throughout the text also reflect this balanced coverage of the marketing domain: business-to-business, services, international *and* consumer goods markets. As the content of journal papers, conference presentations and lectures evolves, so too must the format and content of this book. Relationship marketing, technology in marketing, e-commerce, green marketing, direct marketing and internal marketing are just some of the themes receiving greater attention in this edition.

So much for the content. This book has two sets of users: course tutors and you, the reader. The third edition introduced the Part Openers, Part Postscripts and the end-of-part "road map" showing progress through the text and the relationship of the various Parts. This proved to be very popular with student users as the summaries and road mapping offered greater clarity and guidance. Student feedback indicates the "how to do" appendices are well appreciated. The chapters have always been well referenced and sourced, but had not suggested specific additional chapter-by-chapter readings for students (and lecturers) wishing to find out more. The result was each chapter's recommended further readings, suggested by leading gurus in the relevant field (e.g. Peter Doyle on branding, Peter McGoldrick on retail marketing or Nigel Piercy on implementation). Many of these gurus also reviewed the chapters, suggesting improvements and topical material up-dates. For this edition, the purposely designed web site has provided greater opportunity to provide back-up material, up-to-date readings and links with the web sites of many

of the organisations detailed in the chapter cases. The first edition of *Marketing: Concepts and Strategies* was supported with acetates, a *Tutor's Manual,* a videotape and a floppy disk testbank of questions. These all still exist, but are now housed on the web site alongside more than a dozen tutor and student ancillary tools. These reflect the current teaching requirements of tutors and students, plus the growing importance of the Internet in education.

Much has changed, while the core values of *Marketing: Concepts and Strategies* which made such an immediate impact back in 1991 remain. The changes to content, style, running order, ancillaries on the web are not ad hoc, poorly planned whims. They result from a constant programme of market evaluation: (a) feedback from tutors and students, (b) suggestions from colleagues, (c) an appraisal of current marketing developments and evolving teaching methods, (d) the content and modifications of competitors' products. More than anything, the changes respond directly to "customer" observations and changing needs. It takes over twelve months to revise each edition of *Marketing: Concepts and Strategies*. The aim in revising an already effective product is to respond to marketing analyses and develop a more successful product—just as when Ford plans a new model launch.

SOURCES: Sally Dibb and Lyndon Simkin, Warwick Business School, January 2000.

Questions for Discussion

1. Why must marketing analyses play a part in the development and launch of a product?
2. Which are the key audiences to research in developing a textbook such as *Marketing: Concepts and Strategies*? How might their needs differ?
3. How would you research the needs, expectations and product perceptions of these target markets? Defend your choices.

2 The Marketing Environment

"All businesses operate within an environment, which directly or indirectly affects the way in which they function, just as we as consumers live within a cultural and social environment which to a greater or lesser degree determines the way in which we behave as individuals."

Elaine O'Brien, University of Strathclyde

OBJECTIVES

- To understand the concept of the marketing environment and the importance of environmental scanning and analysis
- To explore the broad forces of the macro marketing environment:

  Identifying the types of political forces relevant to marketers

  Understanding how laws and their interpretation influence marketing practices

  Determining how government regulations and self-regulatory agencies affect marketing

  Identifying societal issues that marketers must deal with as they make decisions

  Exploring the effects of new technology on society and on marketing activities

  Understanding how economic and competitive factors affect organisations' ability to compete and customers' willingness and ability to buy products

- To examine the company-specific micro marketing environment forces:

  The business

  Suppliers

  Marketing intermediaries

  Buyers

  Competitors

  Publics

- To understand the role of the marketing environment in marketing opportunity analysis and the importance of strategic windows

In 1947 the launching of the Marshall Plan presented a blueprint for the economic reconstruction of a Europe devastated by the Second World War. This led in 1948 to the creation of the Organisation for European Economic Co-operation (OEEC), the precursor of today's Economic Union. In March 1957 the Treaty of Rome was signed to establish the European Economic Community (EEC). By 1973, with the arrival of Denmark, Ireland and the UK, the EEC had grown to nine member states. Greece joined in 1981 and Portugal and Spain in 1986 to create the "Euro 12". The momentous signing of the Maastricht Treaty in 1992 established the European Union (EU) and by 1 January 1993 the European single market was at last a reality. The single market is defined by the EU as *"an economic area within which persons, goods, services and capital have unrestricted freedom of movement, which entails not only the elimination of customs barriers, but also of technical, tax and legislative obstacles"*. Many more countries now wish to join the EU, notably former eastern bloc communist states, but until they offer an open economy capable of standing up to competition from western Europe and democratic institutions attentive to human rights, the EU will block further moves by these states to join.

The single market has a significant impact on the populations of member and non-member trading states, as well as on marketers representing their companies. With the removal of so many bureaucratic barriers on 1 January 1993, professionally qualified personnel could seek employment without retraining in other member states; companies could tender for government contracts throughout the EU; imports and exports became subject to far fewer restrictions, less red tape, reduced customs controls

and much freer movement within and between EU states. Immigration and travel have become much quicker and simpler than before. Health and safety working regulations have been harmonised, as have air travel regulations and even standards for mobile phone networks and VAT collection.

The EU has many critics, not least due to its Common Agricultural Policy (CAP), which takes more than half of the entire EU budget, is a significant drain on the resources of the richer member states and currently is being renegotiated. There are moans about the often top-heavy bureaucracy of European government in Brussels; and the inevitable formalisation of so many working practices when so many countries' rules and regulations are combined to form a single, cohesive approach. However, there are few marketers who would claim that in the years since the harmonisation of Europe in 1993, doing business across Europe has not been simplified, opening up significant marketing opportunities for many businesses and presenting new competitive threats. The EU continues to present new challenges and a reason to re-think marketing strategies. There is little doubt that the EU is an external factor in the marketing environment of most businesses and consumers that cannot be ignored.

SOURCES: EU policy documents, 1990–1999; *Europe in Figures*, Eurostat, Luxembourg, 1995; *Europe on the Move, From Single Market to European Union, Internal Market*: all EU, Brussels, publications. *Photo*: Tony Freeman/Photo Edit.

The EU has a tremendous impact on the decisions and activities of marketers. Using examples to illustrate this theme, this chapter explores the external forces which impact on an organisation's trading and ability to satisfy its customers. These forces are termed the marketing environment and fall into two categories. The very broad forces are the macro marketing environment—the political, legal, regulatory, societal, technological, and economic and competitive forces that impact on all businesses operating in a market and on their ability to carry out their affairs. After defining the marketing environment and considering why it is critical to scan and analyse it, each of these macro forces is discussed. Authors have increasingly distinguished these broad forces from an additional set of company-specific forces termed the micro marketing environment forces. This chapter discusses both macro and micro forces, commencing with the broader macro issues. The chapter concludes with an examination of how an understanding of these marketing environment forces assists a company in identifying strategic windows and maximising marketing opportunities.

Examining and Responding to the Marketing Environment

Marketing environment The external forces that directly or indirectly influence an organisation's acquisition of inputs and generation of outputs, comprising six categories of forces: political, legal, regulatory, societal/green, technological, and economic and competitive

The **marketing environment** consists of external forces that directly or indirectly influence an organisation's acquisition of inputs and generation of outputs. Inputs might include personnel, financial resources, raw materials and information. Outputs could be information (such as advertisements), packages, goods, services or ideas. As indicated in Chapter 1 and as shown in Figure 1.3 on page 18, the broad marketing environment consists of six categories of forces: political, legal, regulatory, societal/green, technological, and economic and competitive. Although there are numerous environmental factors, most fall into one of these six categories. These are termed the *macro forces* of the marketing environment as they affect all organisations operating in a particular market. The *micro forces* are more situation- and company-specific, including the business's internal environment, suppliers, marketing intermediaries, buyers, competitors and the company's publics.

Whether they fluctuate rapidly or slowly, environmental forces are always dynamic. Changes in the marketing environment can create uncertainty, threats and opportunities for marketers. Although the future is not very predictable, marketers can estimate what will happen, although some fail to do so, thus negatively affecting the performance of their businesses. Astute marketers continually modify their marketing strategies in response to the dynamic environment. Marketing managers who fail to recognise changes in environmental forces leave their companies unprepared to capitalise on marketing opportunities or to cope with threats created by changes in the environment.

Organisations that cannot deal with an unfavourable environment are at risk of going under.[1] For example, during the OPEC-led recession of the mid-1970s many manufacturers cut back on their workforces, causing unemployment rates of over 40 per cent in many suburbs. Many local retailers and small shopkeepers, restaurants, take-aways and garages had anticipated neither the extent of the unemployment nor its effect on their businesses. Dozens of small, local businesses closed down. The 1990 Persian Gulf Crisis caused huge increases in the price of petrol. The car buying public became even more concerned about fuel consumption, with a resultant decline in the sales of high horsepower sports cars and executive saloons. The Gulf Crisis also hit business travel and tourism, affecting the fortunes of many airlines and hotel operators. Civil war in what was once Yugoslavia has had tragic implications for the peoples of that region and an economic impact on the tour operators who specialised in holidays to the Yugoslavian coastline. The BSE beef crisis affected farmers, meat producers and supermarkets. Genetically modified foods caused a more recent storm with implications for food manufacturers and supermarkets. Thus monitoring the environment is crucial to an organisation's survival and to the long term achievement of its goals.

Environmental Scanning and Analysis

Environmental scanning The process of collecting information about the forces in the marketing environment

Environmental analysis The process of assessing and interpreting the information gathered through environmental scanning

To monitor changes in the marketing environment effectively, marketers must engage in environmental scanning and analysis. **Environmental scanning** is the process of collecting information about the forces in the marketing environment. Scanning involves observation; keeping "an ear to the ground"; perusal of secondary sources, such as business, trade, government and general interest publications; and marketing research. However, managers must be careful not to gather so much information that sheer volume makes analysis impossible. **Environmental analysis** is the process of assessing and interpreting the information gathered through environmental scanning. A manager evaluates the information for accuracy, tries to resolve inconsistencies in the data and, if warranted, assigns significance to the findings. Through analysis, a marketing manager seeks to describe current environmental changes and to predict future changes. By evaluating these changes, the manager should be able to determine possible threats and opportunities linked to environmental fluctuations. Understanding the current state of the marketing environment and recognising the threats and opportunities arising from changes within it help marketing managers assess the performance of current marketing efforts and develop marketing strategies for the future.

JCB, the construction equipment producer, allocates to individual managers the task of monitoring aspects of the macro marketing environment: political, legal, regulatory, societal—particularly the green movement—technological, economic and competitive. A small committee meets to prepare short papers and presentations to interested colleagues. When the laws relating to roadworks were amended, making contractors responsible for the safety of their sites and the long term quality of the re-laid road surface, JCB recognised that many of its customers would have to alter their working practices as a result. So the company produced guides to assist these contractors in responding to the new legislation. In so doing, JCB was able to enhance its image and at the same time promote its products.

Responding to Environmental Forces

In responding to environmental forces, marketing managers can take two general approaches: to accept environmental forces as uncontrollable or to confront and mould them. If environmental forces are viewed as uncontrollable, the organisation remains passive and reactive towards the environment. Instead of trying to influence forces in the environment, its marketing managers tend to adjust current marketing strategies to environmental changes. They approach marketing opportunities discovered through environmental scanning and analysis with caution. On the other hand, marketing managers who believe that environmental forces can be shaped adopt a proactive approach. For example, if a market is blocked by traditional environmental constraints, marketing managers may apply economic, psychological, political and promotional skills to gain access to it or operate within it. Once they identify what blocks a marketing opportunity, marketers can assess the power of the various parties involved and develop strategies to try to overcome environmental forces.[2] As described in Marketing Insight 2.1, supermarket retailer Iceland has taken a proactive approach to genetically modified foods.

In trying to influence environmental forces, marketers may seek to create new marketing opportunities or to extract greater benefits relative to costs from existing marketing opportunities. For instance, a company losing sales to competitors with lower priced products may strive to develop technology that would make its production processes more efficient; greater efficiency would allow it to lower the

Food Retailers Tackle the Regulators

From seemingly nowhere in early 1999 there emerged a new food scare: genetically modified (GM) foods. Leading agrochemicals businesses such as Monsanto and Zeneca had produced strains of soya, tomatoes, even tobacco, genetically modified to exaggerate their proliferation and ability to ward off disease and pests. Coming after consumers' fears about farming methods' interference with meat production, notably BSE in beef cattle, a further instance of natural farming techniques being artificially aided caused great concern. A NOP research poll revealed that despite government assurances, over half of the general public were concerned about eating genetically modified food. Eighty-eight per cent were aware of GM foods while 60 per cent worried about eating them. Only 34 per cent checked the labelling on food products, but many others stated there was little point owing to the lack of clear labelling.

The reaction from the major supermarket groups was swift. They promised to seek assurances from suppliers about the content of GM ingredients in products delivered to them. Once clarified by the suppliers, the supermarkets intended to provide better labelling. Ultimately, though, the onus was on the consumer to make the choice. Consumer groups believe that packaging information was initially inadequate to permit such considered choices. While seeking to improve labelling, the supermarkets' responses were varied:

Iceland: "We are unsure of the long term effects of GM foods."

Somerfield: "Until the EU addresses the issue there is not a lot we can do."

Sainsbury's: "We are looking hard to find alternatives but have to look at the long term."

Tesco: "Customer calls peak every time there is media interest."

Asda: "The food has been passed as safe by the government . . . we are taking a responsible approach."

Although these comments reflect a diverse set of views, the implication was that "the powers that be" had deemed GM food safe to consume, so until they altered their stance, it was to be stocked by the retailers. Politicians joined the debate with many MPs calling for a moratorium on the sale of GM foods pending further safety testing. While Prime Minister Tony Blair stated he was happy to eat GM foods, the government did promise additional research funding. The difficulty for the supermarkets was that government had passed the GM products as safe for consumption, despite growing consumer fears.

Tesco and Safeway had already clearly labelled GM modified lines. Their rivals followed suit. Sainsbury's set up a dedicated hotline to help address consumers' queries and fears. A third of all customer enquiries to Sainsbury's related to the GM food issue. Iceland immediately reacted by banning GM ingredients from its own label brands, but still stocked manufacturer brands containing GM ingredients, notably soya based lines. The remaining supermarkets in conjunction with the British Retail Consortium put pressure on the government to make the decisions about GM foods. Somerfield had lobbied the US government since 1997 and in 1999 switched to pressurising the British government and EU regulators. This proactive pressure on regulators was an acknowledgement by retailers of the role of macro marketing environment forces.

Sources: "Sainsbury's sets up helpline to quash fears over GM foods", *Marketing Week*, 18 February 1999, p. 9; Alexandra Jardine, "GM scare strains retailers", *Marketing*, 18 February 1999, p. 7; "Public resist GM food", *Marketing*, 25 February 1999, p. 4; Julia Hinde, "GM circus comes to town", *The Times Higher*, 12 March 1999, pp. 20, 60.

prices of its own products. Political action is another way of affecting environmental forces. UK retailers, for example, successfully lobbied government to permit longer Sunday trading and legal opening of retail outlets all day. A proactive approach can be constructive and bring desired results. However, managers must recognise that there are limits on how much an environmental force can be shaped and that these limits vary across environmental forces. Although an organisation may be able to influence the enactment of laws through lobbying, it is unlikely that a single organisation can significantly increase the national birth rate or move the economy from recession to prosperity!

Generalisations are not possible. It cannot be stated that either of these approaches to environmental response is better than the other. For some organisations, the passive, reactive approach is more appropriate, but for other companies, the aggressive approach leads to better performance. The selection of a particular approach depends on an organisation's managerial philosophies, objectives, financial resources, customers and human skills, and on the specific composition of the set of environmental forces within which the organisation operates.

The rest of this chapter explores in detail the macro and micro marketing environment forces, and then examines the link between an understanding of these issues and marketing opportunity analysis.

Political Forces

The political, legal and regulatory forces of the marketing environment are closely interrelated. Legislation is enacted, legal decisions are interpreted by the courts and regulatory agencies are created and operated, for the most part, by people elected or appointed to political offices or by civil servants. Legislation and regulations (or the lack of them) reflect the current political outlook. Consequently, the political force of the marketing environment has the potential to influence marketing decisions and strategies.

Marketers need to maintain good relations with elected political officials for several reasons. When political officials are well disposed towards particular companies or industries, they are less likely to create or enforce laws and regulations unfavourable to these companies. For example, political officials who believe that oil companies are making honest efforts to control pollution are unlikely to create and enforce highly restrictive pollution control laws. In addition, governments are big buyers, and political officials can influence how much a government agency purchases and from whom. Finally, political officials can play key roles in helping organisations secure foreign markets.

Many marketers view political forces as beyond their control; they simply try to adjust to conditions that arise from those forces. Some businesses, however, seek to influence political events by helping to elect to political office individuals who regard them positively. Much of this help is in the form of contributions to political parties. A sizeable contribution to a campaign fund may carry with it an implicit understanding that the party, if elected, will perform political favours for the contributing company. There are, though, strict laws governing donations and lobbying in most countries and increasingly ethical considerations for donor marketers (see Chapter 24).

Legal Forces

A number of laws influence marketing decisions and activities. This discussion focuses on procompetitive and consumer protection laws and their interpretation.

Procompetitive Legislation

Procompetitive legislation is enacted to preserve competition and to end various practices deemed unacceptable by society, for example, monopolies and mergers.

Procompetitive legislation Laws enacted to preserve competition and to end various practices deemed unacceptable by society

Office of Fair Trading UK government office set up to oversee trading practices of organisations and individuals in the UK

Competition Commission An independent body in the UK that investigates monopolies to determine whether they operate against the public interest

In the UK the President of the Board of Trade and the Director General of the **Office of Fair Trading** can refer monopolies for investigation by the **Competition Commission,** an independent body whose members are drawn from a variety of backgrounds, including lawyers, economists, industrialists and trade unionists. The legislation defines a monopoly as a situation in which at least a quarter of a particular kind of good or service is supplied by a single person or a group of connected companies, or by two or more people acting in a way that prevents, restricts or distorts competition. Local monopolies can also be referred to the Commission. If the Commission finds that a monopoly operates against the public interest, the President of the Board of Trade has power to take action to remedy or prevent the harm that the Commission considers may exist. Alternatively, the Director General of the Office of Fair Trading may be asked to negotiate undertakings to remedy the adverse effects identified by the Commission. The government believes that the market is a better judge than itself of the advantages and disadvantages of mergers, so most take-overs and proposed mergers are allowed to be decided by the companies' shareholders. However, when too much power would be placed in the hands of one organisation, company or person, the government will insist on a Monopolies and Mergers Commission appraisal. If the Commission believes it is against the public interest for a take-over or merger to proceed, then it will prohibit any agreement between the companies or organisations involved. For example, national generator PowerGen was prevented from taking over regional electricity company Midlands Electricity. The EU has a commissioner responsible for competition. In recent years, the commissioner has ruled on anti-competitive practices in many industries, from airlines to financial services, forcing companies to alter their trading practices and encouraging competition from a broader base of organisations.

Under the Financial Services Act of 1986, the Director General of the Office of Fair Trading is required to consider the implications for competition of rules, regulations, guidance and other arrangements and practices of the regulatory bodies, investment exchanges and clearing houses. The Director General must report to the President of the Board of Trade whenever a significant or potentially significant effect on competition has been identified. This legislation is for the protection of investors, and the Secretary of State may refuse or revoke recognition of the organisation or require it to make alterations to its activities. Under anti-competitive practices legislation, the Director General of the Office of Fair Trading can investigate any business practice, whether in the public or private sector, that may restrict, distort or prevent competition in the production, supply or acquisition of goods or services. The Secretary of State has power to take remedial action. With the introduction of the Restrictive Trade Practices Act in 1976, if two or more people who are party to the supply of goods or services accept some limitation on their freedom to make their own decisions about matters such as prices or conditions of sale, the Office of Fair Trading must be notified and such an agreement must be registered. Once an agreement has been registered, the Director General is under a general duty to refer it to the Restrictive Practices Court, and the court must declare the restrictions in it contrary to the public interest unless the parties can satisfy the court that the public interest is not an issue. The vast majority of agreements never reach the court because parties elect to give up the restrictions rather than go through such a procedure.

Within the European Union, the objective of the competition policy is to ensure that there is free and fair competition in trade among member states and that the government trade barriers which the Treaty of Rome seeks to dismantle are not replaced by private barriers that fragment the Common Market. The EU has powers to investigate and terminate alleged infringements and to impose fines. The Treaty of Rome prohibits agreements or concertive practices that may affect trade among member states and aims to prevent restriction or distortion of competition within the Common Market.[3] Most countries have similar procompetitive legislation. For example, in the United States the Sherman Anti-Trust Act prevents monopolistic situations; the Clayton Antitrust Act specifically prohibits price discrimination; and the Federal Trade Commission Act broadly prohibits unfair methods of competition and empowers the Federal Trade Commission to work with the Department of Justice to enforce the provisions of the Clayton Antitrust Act. The Wheeler-Lea Act essentially makes unfair and deceptive acts or practices unlawful, regardless of whether they incur competition. The Robinson-Patman Act deals with discriminatory price differentials.[4]

Consumer Protection Legislation

The second category of regulatory laws, consumer protection legislation, is not a recent development. However, consumer protection laws mushroomed in the mid-1960s and early 1970s. A number of them deal with consumer safety, while others relate to the sale of various hazardous products such as flammable fabrics and toys that might injure children. In the UK, the Fair Trading Act (1973) provides a machinery—headed by the Director General of the Office of Fair Trading—for continuous review of consumer affairs, for actions dealing with trading practices that unfairly affect consumers' interests, for action against persistent offenders under existing law and for the negotiation of self-regulatory codes of practice to raise trading standards. Consumers' interests with regard to the purity of food, the description and performance of goods and services, and pricing information are safeguarded by the Food Act (1984), the Medicines Act (1968), the Misrepresentations Act (1967), the Trade Descriptions Act (1968), the Prices Act (1974), the Unfair Contract Terms Act (1977), the Sale of Goods Act (1979) and the Supply of Goods and Services Act (1982). The marking and accuracy of quantities are regulated by the Weights and Measures Act (1985). The Consumer Credit Act (1974) provides comprehensive protection for consumers who enter into credit or hire transactions. The Consumer Protection Act (1987) implements a harmonised European Union code of civil law covering product liability, creates a general criminal offence of supplying unsafe consumer goods, makes it an offence to give any misleading price indication and consolidates the powers provided under safety related acts. The Financial Services Act (1986) offers greater protection to investors by establishing a new regulatory framework for the industry. Currently legislation is pending concerning the production, supply and use of food.

In addition, consumer advice and information are provided to the general public at the local level by the Citizens' Advice Bureaux and the Trading Standards or Consumer Protection departments of local authorities, and in some areas by specialist consumer advice centres. The independent, non-statutory National Consumer Council, which receives government finance, ensures that consumers' views are made known to those in government and industry. Nationalised industries have consumer councils whose members investigate questions of concern to the consumer, and many trade associations in industry and commerce have established codes of practice. In addition, several private organisations work to further consumer interests, the largest of which is the **Consumers' Association,** funded by the subscriptions of its membership of over one million people. The association

Consumers' Association A private organisation, funded by members' subscriptions, that works to further consumer interests

Part I   Marketing Defined

conducts an extensive programme of comparative testing of goods and investigation of services; its views and test reports are published in its monthly magazine *Which?* and other publications.

Interpreting Laws

Laws certainly have the potential to influence marketing activities, but the actual effects of the laws are determined by how marketers and the courts interpret them. Laws seem to be quite specific because they contain many complex clauses and sub-clauses. In reality, however, many laws and regulations are stated in vague terms that force marketers to rely on legal advice rather than their own understanding and common sense. Because of this vagueness, some organisations attempt to gauge the limits of certain laws by operating in a legally questionable way to see how far they can go with certain practices before being prosecuted. Other marketers, however, interpret regulations and statutes very conservatively and strictly to avoid violating a vague law. Although court rulings directly affect businesses accused of specific violations, they also have a broader, less direct impact on other businesses. When marketers try to interpret laws in relation to specific marketing practices, they often analyse recent court decisions, both to understand better what the law is intended to do and to gain a clearer sense of how the courts are likely to interpret it in the future.

Regulatory Forces

Interpretation alone does not determine the effectiveness of laws and regulations; the level of enforcement by regulatory agencies is also significant. Some regulatory agencies are created and administered by government units; others are sponsored by non-governmental sources.

Government

In the UK, the Ministry of Agriculture, Fisheries and Food develops and controls policies for agriculture, horticulture, fisheries and food; it also has responsibilities for environmental and rural issues and food policies. The Department of Employment controls the Employment Service, employment policy and legislation; training policy and legislation; health and safety at work; industrial relations; wages councils; equal opportunities; small firms and tourism; statistics on labour and industrial matters for the UK; the Careers Service; and international representation on employment matters and educational policy. The Department of the Environment controls policies for planning and regional development, local government, new towns, housing, construction, inner city matters, environmental protection, water, the countryside, sports and recreation, conservation, historic buildings and ancient monuments. The Export Credit Guarantee Department is responsible for the provision of insurance for exporters against the risk of not being paid for goods and services, access to bank finance for exports and insurance cover for new investment overseas.

The Central Statistical Office prepares and interprets statistics needed for central economic and social policies and management; it co-ordinates the statistical work of other departments. The Department for Trade and Industry/Board of Trade controls industrial and commercial policy, promotion of enterprise and competition in the UK and abroad, and investor and consumer protection. Specific responsibilities include industrial innovation policy; regional industrial policy; business development, management development and business/education links; international trade policy; commercial relations and export promotions;

competition policy; company law; insolvency; consumer protection and safety; radio regulations; and intellectual property. The Department of Transport is responsible for land, sea and air transport; rail network regulation; domestic and international civil aviation; international transport agreements; shipping and ports industries; navigation issues, HM Coastguard and marine pollution; motorways and trunk roads; road safety; and overseeing local authority transport. JCB's advertising of its compact equipment range shows how the company responded to changing regulations in general, and the Streetworks Act in particular (Figure 2.1). These examples of British government departments are not unusual. Similar administrative bodies exist in most countries. Increasingly in the EU, political, legal and regulatory forces are being harmonised to reflect common standards and enforcement.

Local Authorities The functions of UK local authorities are far reaching; some are primary duties, whereas others are purely discretionary. Broadly speaking, functions are divided between county and district councils on the basis that the county council is responsible for matters requiring planning and administration over wide areas or requiring the support of substantial resources, whereas district councils on the

Figure 2.1 Responding to regulatory changes. JCB's compact equipment range advertising responds to changing regulations and the Streetworks Act. SOURCE: John Braley, JCB Sales Ltd. Agency: CB Brookes Advertising Ltd.

whole administer functions of a more local significance. English county councils are generally responsible for strategic planning, transport planning, highways, traffic regulations, local education, consumer protection, refuse disposal, police, the fire service, libraries and personal social services. District councils are responsible for environmental health, housing decisions, most planning applications and refuse collection. They may also provide some museums, art galleries and parks. At both county and district council level, arrangements depend on local agreements.

Most countries in Europe have a similar structure: resource-hungry issues with wide ranging social and political consequences are controlled centrally. Planning and service provision within the community are viewed as being better controlled at the local level by the actual communities that will experience the advantages or problems resulting from such decision-making. The European Union aims to establish commonly accepted parameters for planning, service provision and regulation, and a framework to assist in inter- and intra-country disputes.

Non-governmental Regulatory Forces   In the absence of governmental regulatory forces and in an attempt to prevent government intervention, some businesses try to regulate themselves. For example, many newspapers have voluntarily banned advertisements for telephone chat services used for undesirable activities, even though such services are technically not illegal. Trade associations in a number of industries have developed self-regulatory programmes. Even though these programmes are not a direct outcome of laws, many were established to stop or stall the development of laws and governmental regulatory groups that would regulate the associations' marketing practices. Sometimes trade associations establish codes of ethics by which their members must abide or risk censure by other members, or even exclusion from the programme. For example, many cigarette manufacturers have agreed, through a code of ethics, not to advertise their products to children and teenagers. The ITC Code of Advertising Standards and Practice aims to keep broadcast advertising "legal, decent, honest and truthful".[5]

Self-regulatory programmes have several advantages over governmental laws and regulatory agencies. They are usually less expensive to establish and implement, and their guidelines are generally more realistic and operational. In addition, effective industry self-regulatory programmes reduce the need to expand government bureaucracy. However, these programmes also have several limitations. When a trade association creates a set of industry guidelines for its members, non-member organisations do not have to abide by them. In addition, many self-regulatory programmes lack the tools or the authority to enforce guidelines. Finally, guidelines in self-regulatory programmes are often less strict than those established by government agencies.

Deregulation   Governments can drastically alter the environment for companies. In the UK the privatisation of the public utilities created new terms and conditions for their suppliers and sub-contractors. The state's sales of Jaguar and Rover in the car industry and of British Airways created commercially lean companies that suddenly had new impetus to become major competitors in their industries. Deregulation in the European Union has created opportunities across borders and also new threats. Car manufacturers were previously able to restrict certain models to specific countries. They placed rigorous controls on their dealers, forbidding them to retail cars produced by rival manufacturers in the same showroom or on the same site. Many of these controls have since been swept aside.

Societal/Green Forces

Societal/green forces Individuals and groups and the issues engaging them that pressure marketers to provide high living standards and enjoyable lifestyles through socially responsible decisions and activities

Societal/green forces comprise the structure and dynamics of individuals and groups and the issues that engage them. Society becomes concerned about marketers' activities when those activities have questionable or negative consequences. For example, in recent times, well publicised incidents of unethical behaviour by marketers and others have perturbed and even angered consumers. Chapter 24 takes a detailed look at marketing ethics and social responsibility. When marketers do a good job of satisfying society, praise or positive evaluation rarely follows. Society expects marketers to provide a high standard of living and to protect the general quality of life. This section examines some of society's expectations, the means used to express those expectations, and the problems and opportunities that marketers experience as they try to deal with society's often contradictory wishes.

Living Standards and Quality of Life

Most people want more than just the bare necessities; they want to achieve the highest standard of living possible. For example, there is a desire for homes that offer not only protection from the elements but also comfort and a satisfactory lifestyle. People want many varieties of safe and readily available food that is also easily prepared. Clothing protects bodies, but many consumers want a variety of clothing for adornment and to project a certain image to others. Consumers want vehicles that provide rapid, safe and efficient travel. They want communications systems that give information from around the globe—a desire apparent in the popularity of products such as organisers, mobile phones, facsimile machines and the 24 hour news coverage provided by cable and satellite television networks and by the Internet. In addition, there is a demand for sophisticated medical services that prolong life expectancy and improve physical appearance. Education is expected to help consumers acquire and enjoy a higher standard of living.

Society's high material standard of living often is not enough. Many desire a high degree of quality in their lives. People do not want to spend all their waking hours working: they seek leisure time for hobbies, voluntary work, recreation and relaxation. The quality of life is enhanced by leisure time, clean air and water, unlittered beaches, conservation of wildlife and natural resources, and security from radiation and poisonous substances. A number of companies are expressing concerns about the quality of life. Consumers too are expressing concern over "green" issues such as pollution, waste disposable and the so-called greenhouse effect. Society's concerns have created both threats and opportunities for marketers. For example, one of society's biggest environmental problems is lack of space for refuse disposal, especially of plastic materials such as disposable nappies and Styrofoam packaging, which are not biodegradable. In the United States, several cities have passed laws banning the use of all plastic packaging in stores and restaurants, and governments around the world are considering similar legislation. This trend has created problems for McDonald's and other fast food restaurants, which have now developed packaging alternatives. Other companies, however, see such environmental problems as opportunities. Procter & Gamble, for example, markets cleaners in bottles made of recycled plastic.[6] Environmentally responsible, or green, marketing is increasingly extensive. For example, the German companies Audi, Volkswagen and BMW are manufacturing "cleaner" cars that do not pollute the atmosphere as much as traditional ones. BP has launched a "green" diesel fuel with hardly any noxious emissions.

Italian chemical companies are investing billions to reduce toxic wastes from their plants, and British industry is investing equally large sums to scrub acid emissions from power stations and to treat sewage more effectively.[7]

Green movement The trend arising from society's concern about pollution, waste disposal, manufacturing processes and the greenhouse effect

The **green movement** is concerned about these environmental issues. Several years ago few consumers were concerned about the well-being of their natural environment—their planet. Resources were not seen as scarce, pollution was poorly acknowledged and people had a short term, perhaps selfish, perspective. Now there is a growing awareness that is affecting everyone: consumers, manufacturers and legislators. Supermarket shelves are rapidly filling with packaging that can be recycled or re-used and products for which manufacturing processes have altered. Children are now taught in the classroom to "re-educate" their parents to take a more responsible view of the earth's environment. The changes are not just in the supermarkets and schools, as highlighted by BMW in Marketing Insight 2.2. The rising importance and role of the green aspect of the societal forces must not be underestimated. Changes in the forces of the marketing environment require careful monitoring and often demand a clear and effective response. Since marketing activities are a vital part of the total business structure, marketers have a responsibility to help provide what members of society want and to minimise what they do not want.

Consumer Movement Forces

Consumer movement A diverse collection of independent individuals, groups and organisations seeking to protect the rights of consumers

The **consumer movement** is a diverse collection of independent individuals, groups and organisations seeking to protect the rights of consumers. The main issues pursued by the consumer movement fall into three categories: environmental protection, product performance and safety, and information disclosure. The movement's major forces are individual consumer advocates, consumer organisations and other interest groups, consumer education and consumer laws.

Consumer advocates, such as David Tench, take it upon themselves to protect the rights of consumers. They band together into consumer organisations, either voluntarily or under government sponsorship. Some organisations, such as the Consumers' Association, operate nationally, whereas others are active at local levels. They inform and organise other consumers, raise issues, help businesses develop consumer oriented programmes and pressure legislators to enact consumer protection laws. Some consumer advocates and organisations encourage consumers to boycott products and businesses to which they have objections.

Educating consumers to make wiser purchasing decisions is perhaps one of the farthest reaching aspects of the consumer movement. Increasingly, consumer education is becoming a part of school curricula and adult education courses. These courses cover many topics: for instance, what major factors should be considered when buying specific products, such as insurance, housing, cars, appliances and furniture, clothes and food. The courses also cover the provisions of certain consumer protection laws and provide the sources of information that can help individuals become knowledgeable consumers. Figure 2.2 is an example of the EU educating consumers and manufacturers regarding new labelling protection systems.

Technological Forces

The word *technology* brings to mind creations of progress such as computers, superconductors, lasers and heart transplants. Even though such items are

Figure 2.2 Consumer Protection. The EU is protecting consumers through new labelling protection systems.
SOURCE: Courtesy of European Protection Systems.

Technology The knowledge of how to accomplish tasks and goals

out-growths of technology, none of them *is* technology. **Technology** has been defined as the knowledge of how to accomplish tasks and goals.[8] Often this knowledge comes from scientific research. The effects of technology are broad in scope and today exert a tremendous influence on everyone's lives. Technology grows out of research performed by businesses, universities and not-for-profit organisations. Much of this research is paid for by governments, which support investigations in a variety of areas, including health, defence, agriculture, energy and pollution. Because much centrally funded research requires the use of specialised machinery, personnel and facilities, a sizeable proportion of this research is conducted by large business organisations or research institutions that already possess the necessary specialised equipment and people.

The rapid technological growth of recent decades is expected to continue in the new millennium. Areas that hold great technological promise include digital electronics, artificial intelligence, superconductors, materials research and biotechnology. Current research is investigating new forms of memory chips and

Part I   Marketing Defined

Social Awareness: BMW Recycling the Consumer

The European Recovery and Recycling Association (ERRA) is indicative of the growing concern for the environment and consumer awareness of this social issue. With members including Cadbury Schweppes, Coca-Cola, Heineken, Nestlé, L'Oréal, Petrofina and Tetra Pak, the Brussels based ERRA has developed a recycling scheme that could lead to the regular collection of discarded packaging—containers and bottles from housing estates, factories, schools, offices and shops—and their sorting and re-use. The scheme in many countries is far from becoming reality, requiring the significant commitment of government, local authorities and, of course, consumers. However, ERRA exists, supported by an extensive array of manufacturers and environmental pressure groups. The public's interest in the environment and in safeguarding the planet and its resources for generations to come has led companies to pay real attention to the green lobby.

BMW, the German de luxe car maker, has been stressing the "recyclability" of its vehicles in its television and press advertising for its 3 Series range. These cars are produced using more environmentally friendly production processes, with a greater proportion of components suitable for reworking. BMW's commitment to the future, however, goes further. In Landshut, Germany, it has a recycling factory. Two workers can strip all the re-usable parts from a 1970s car in under 45 minutes, including the careful draining of all fluids, at a cost of about £90.

Landshut's role is as a huge scrap merchant, but one that adheres to the strictest code of ethical working practices and the latest understanding of how to dispose of "dead" vehicles with the least harm to the environment. BMW executives support the notion of a European wide initiative, requiring an authorised recycler to issue a disposal certificate for every car at the end of its life. Until such a certificate is issued, the last registered owner would continue to be liable to pay road taxes. This initiative would eventually require legislation and the support of governments. Meanwhile, several leading car manufacturers have joined forces, adopting standardised colour coding for all re-usable parts.

The investment for BMW is significant, but anticipating eventual EU legislation to enforce recycling, the German manufacturer believes it is thinking strategically and is working towards maintaining its position as a major producer of vehicles. BMW has 30 partner recycling plants worldwide, with its first UK site in Sussex. By 1995, the company had an international network, with more than 5 sites in the UK. Simultaneously, BMW is striving to make more of its cars reclaimable; 40 per cent of the current 3 Series can be stripped down and re-used.

It is not only companies such as BMW which have responded to increasing social awareness of environmental and green issues. Bottle banks, which exist in most towns at multiple locations, have been joined by collection containers for waste paper, tin cans and even discarded clothes. Charity Oxfam has provided clothing collection banks in many car parks nationwide. Local councils collect householders' waste paper separately from their refuse for recycling. School children are taught to care for their environment and encourage their parents to use bottle banks and waste paper collections. Societal pressure has created a new way of thinking which marketers must reflect.

SOURCES: "The can and bottle story: environment", Coca-Cola & Schweppes Beverages Ltd, 1993; "Helping to solve the waste management puzzle", ERRA, Brussels, 1991; John Eisenhammer, "Where cars will go when they die", *The Independent on Sunday*, 21 February 1993, pp. 24–25; "Helping the earth begins at home", Central Office of Information, Department of the Environment, HMSO, 1992; BMW 3 Series promotional material, 1995; Warwickshire County Council, 1999; Oxfam, Kenilworth, 1999.

computers that will think for themselves or be more responsive to their specific users' characteristics. Because these and other technological developments will clearly have an impact on buyers' and marketers' decisions, it is important to discuss here the effects of technology on society and marketers and to consider several factors that influence the adoption and use of technology.

The Impact of Technology

Marketers must be aware of new developments in technology and their possible effects because technology does affect marketing activities in many different ways. Consumers' technological knowledge influences their desires for goods and services. To provide marketing mixes that satisfy consumers, marketers must be aware of these influences. The various ways in which technology affects marketing activities fall into two broad categories. It affects consumers and society in general, and it influences what, how, when and where products are marketed.

Effects of Technology on Society Technology determines how consumers as members of society satisfy their physiological needs. In various ways and to varying degrees, eating and drinking habits, sleeping patterns, sexual activities and health care are all influenced both by existing technology and by changes in technology. Technological developments have improved standards of living, thus creating more leisure time; they have also enhanced information, entertainment and education. Nevertheless, technology can detract from the quality of life through undesirable side effects, such as unemployment, polluted air and water, and other health hazards. Some people believe that further applications of technology can soften or eliminate these undesirable side effects. Others argue, however, that the best way to improve the quality of our lives is to decrease the use of technology.

Effects of Technology on Marketing Technology also affects the types of products that marketers can offer. The introduction and general acceptance of cassette tapes and compact discs drove most manufacturers of vinyl long playing (LP) albums out of business or forced them to invest in new technology. Yet this technology provided new marketing opportunities for recording artists and producers, record companies, retailers and those in related industries. The following items are only a few of the many thousands of existing products that were not available to consumers 20 years ago: PC digital cameras, cellular telephones, ultra-light lap-top computers, high resolution televisions and hand-held video cameras.

Computer technology helps make warehouse storage and keeping track of stored products more efficient and, therefore, less expensive. Often these savings can be passed on to consumers in the form of lower prices. Because of technological changes in communications, marketers can now reach large masses of people through a variety of media more efficiently. The development and widespread use of facsimile machines and services, for example, allow marketers to send their advertisements or sales specifications directly to selected groups of customers who want their products. In recent years the Internet has permeated the lives of many, bringing a world of information into the home and allowing consumers to shop for products on-line. Technological advances in transport enable consumers to travel farther and more often to shop at a larger number of stores. Changes in transport have also affected producers' ability to get products to retailers and wholesalers. The ability of present day manufacturers of relatively lightweight products to reach any of their dealers within 24 hours (via overnight express delivery services, such as TNT and Federal Express) would astound their counterparts of 50 years ago.

Adoption and Use of Technology

Technology assessment A procedure by which managers try to foresee the effects of new products and processes on their company's operation, on other business organisations and on society in general

Through a procedure known as **technology assessment,** some managers try to foresee the effects of new products and processes on their company's operation, on other business organisations and on society in general. With the information gained through a technology assessment, management tries to estimate whether the benefits of using a specific kind of technology outweigh the costs to the business and to society at large. The degree to which a business is technologically based will also influence how its management responds to technology. Companies whose products and product changes grow out of recent technology strive to gather and use technological information. Although available technology could radically improve their products (or other parts of the marketing mix), some companies may put off applying this technology as long as their competitors do not try to use it. The extent to which a business can protect inventions stemming from research also influences its use of technology. The extent to which a product is secure from imitation depends on how easily others can copy it without violating its patent. If new products and processes cannot be protected through patents, a company is less likely to market them and make the benefits of its research available to competitors. How a company uses (or does not use) technology is important for its long run survival. A business that makes the wrong decisions may well lose out to the competition. Poor decisions may also affect its profits by requiring expensive corrective actions. Poor decisions about technological forces may even drive a company out of business.

Economic and Competitive Forces

Economic and competitive forces
Factors in the marketing environment—including the effects of general economic conditions, buying power, willingness to spend, spending patterns, types of competitive structure, competitive tools and competitive behaviour—that influence both marketers' and consumers' decisions and activities

The **economic and competitive forces** in the marketing environment influence both marketers' and customers' decisions and activities. This section first examines the effects of general economic conditions, also focusing on buying power, willingness to spend and spending patterns. Then the discussion moves to the broad competitive forces, including types of competitive structure, competitive tools and some methods for monitoring competitive behaviour. The strategic importance of competition is discussed in Chapters 7 and 21.

General Economic Conditions

Business cycle Fluctuations in the economy that follow the general pattern of prosperity, recession, depression and recovery

Prosperity A period during which unemployment is low and total income is relatively high

Recession A period during which unemployment rises and total buying power declines

The overall state of the economy fluctuates in all countries. Table 2.1 presents some economic measures of performance for Europe. These changes in general economic conditions affect (and are affected by) the forces of supply and demand, buying power, willingness to spend, consumer expenditure levels and the intensity of competitive behaviour. Therefore, current economic conditions and changes in the economy have a broad impact on the success of organisations' marketing strategies. Fluctuations in the economy follow a general pattern often referred to as the **business cycle**. In the traditional view, the business cycle consists of four stages: prosperity, recession, depression and recovery. During **prosperity**, unemployment is low and total income is relatively high. Assuming a low inflation rate, this combination causes buying power to be high. To the extent that the economic outlook remains prosperous, consumers generally are willing to buy. In the prosperity stage, marketers often expand their marketing mixes (product, place/distribution, promotion, price and people) to take advantage of the increased buying power. They sometimes capture a larger market share by intensifying distribution and promotion efforts.

Unemployment rises during a **recession,** so total buying power declines. The pessimism that accompanies a recession often stifles both consumer and business spending. As buying power decreases, many consumers become more price- and value-conscious; they look for products that are basic and functional. For instance, people ordinarily reduce their consumption of more expensive convenience foods and strive to save money by growing and preparing more of their own food. Individuals buy fewer durable goods and more repair and do-it-yourself products. During a recession, some companies make the mistake of drastically reducing their marketing efforts and thus damage their ability to survive.

Table 2.1 Main economic indicators for eastern and western European countries

Country	Gross National Product (GNP)—Current Prices (national currency)	Gross National Product per Capita (national currency)	Gross Domestic Product (GDP) (national currency)	Retail Sales Value Index (100)	Retail Price Index (100)	Industrial Production Index (100)	Unemployment %	Interest Rate %	Trade Balance	Hourly Manufacturing Wages Index (100)	Industrial Share Price Index (100)
Austria	2,514 Sch bn	311.5 Sch 000s	2,517 Sch bn	117	121	115	7.1	2.50	−6.1 US$ bn	137	76
Belgium	8,805 BFr bn	866.6 BFr 000s	8,673 BFr bn	119	117.1	106	13.3	2.75			177
Bulgaria			17,103 Leva bn		118,050	74.7	10.5		0.24 US$ bn		
Czech Republic			1,649.5 Kc bn		254.8	80.7	4.4	13.0			75.6
Denmark	1,109.5 DKr bn	210.1 DKr 000s	1,120.9 DKr bn	123	115	123	7.8	3.50			195
Estonia			65.1 Kr bn		493.8				−1,124 US$ bn		
Finland	485.6 FMk bn	95.4 FMk 000s	622.1 FMk bn	103	114	131	14.5	4.00	10.08 US$ bn	131	233
France	8,147 FFr bn	139.8 FFr 000s	8,130 FFr bn	111.5	115.2	103.8	12.5	3.24	US$ bn		152
Germany	3,446 DMk bn	42.2 DMk 000s	3,646 DMk bn	103	122.9	104	11.5	2.5			158
Greece	33,096 Dra bn	3,145 Dra 000s	33,026 Dra bn	190.4	218.4	99.8	10.0	14.5	−15.6 US$ bn	204	146
Hungary			6,845 Ft bn		453.0	102.3	10.5				
Ireland	41.92 Irf bn	11,644 Irf	48.2 Irf bn	145	116.8	197.1	10.2	6.75		126	214

(continued)

Table 2.1 Main economic indicators for eastern and western European countries *(cont.)*

Country	Gross National Product (GNP)—Current Prices (national currency)	Gross National Product per Capita (national currency)	Gross Domestic Product (GDP) (national currency)	Retail Sales Value Index (100)	Retail Price Index (100)	Industrial Production Index (100)	Unemployment %	Interest Rate %	Trade Balance	Hourly Manufacturing Wages Index (100)	Industrial Share Price Index (100)
Italy	1,930 Llt tri	33.6 Llt mn	1,951 Llt tri	122	136.0	107.7	12.3	5.5		135	131
Latvia			3,211 Lat mn		14,367				−610 Lat mn		
Lithuania			38,201 Litas mn		48,471				−7,136 Litas mn		
Luxembourg	549.0 LFr bn	1,339.0 LFr 000s	573.7 LFr bn	120	118.0	107.5		3.46	−82.80 LFr bn	114.9	248.1
The Netherlands	710.3 HFl bn	45.5 HFl 000s	703.4 HFl bn	120	119.2	113	5.5	5.0			302
Norway	1,075.1 NKr bn	243.8 NKr 000s	1,084.8 NKr bn	140	116.8	139	4.1	5.5	12.72 US$ bn	129	258
Poland			444.09 Zl bn		827.1		11.5	22.0	223.38 Zl bn		
Portugal	12,476 Esc bn	1,264 Esc 000s	17,905 Esc bn		149.1	103.3		5.31	−10.4 US$ bn		200
Romania			249,750 Lei bn		33,588	73.5	7.4				
Russia			2,602 Rb bn		626,797	97.0	9.3				
Slovenia			2,552.7 Tl bn		1,402.1	81.8	13.8	10.0			
Spain	72.7 Pta tri	1.85 Pta mn	77.8 Pta tri	108.4	135.8	109.1	20.8	4.75	−18.5 US$ bn		215
Sweden	1,400 SKr bn	160.6 SKr 000s	1,739 SKr bn	109	126	129	8.0	2.5	19.28 US$ bn	138.9	263

(continued)

Table 2.1 Main economic indicators for eastern and western European countries (*cont.*)

Country	Gross National Product (GNP)—Current Prices (national currency)	Gross National Product per Capita (national currency)	Gross Domestic Product (GDP) (national currency)	Retail Sales Value Index (100)	Retail Price Index (100)	Industrial Production Index (100)	Unemployment %	Interest Rate %	Trade Balance	Hourly Manufacturing Wages Index (100)	Industrial Share Price Index (100)
Switzerland	377.6 SFr bn	53.6 SFr 000s	370.1 SFr bn	104.6	118.4	108	5.2	1.0	0.24 US$ bn	116.2	308
Turkey	1,270.6 LTk tri	21,095 LTk 000s	13,345 LTk tri		6,093	140.6	6.4	50.0	−22.32 US$ bn		
Ukraine			8,450 Krb tri		489,075		0.6				
United Kingdom	798.8 £ bn	13,536 £	786.6 £ bn	116.2	124.9	109.4	5.7	6.6			189

1997 data throughout where available.
Local currencies unless stated otherwise.
Tri = trillion; bn = billion; 000s = thousands.

SOURCES: IFL, EU, IFS, OECD, CCET, World Bank, National Accounts, CIA, European Bank for Reconstruction and Development, Eurostat, EIU World Outlook, NTC Publications.

Obviously, marketers should consider some revision of their marketing activities during a recessionary period. Because consumers are more concerned about the functional value of products, a company must focus its marketing research on determining what product functions buyers want and then make sure that these functions become part of its products. Promotional efforts should emphasise value and utility.

A **depression** is a period in which unemployment is extremely high, wages are very low, total disposable income is at a minimum and consumers lack confidence in the economy. Governments have used both monetary and fiscal policies to off-set the effects of recession and depression. Monetary policies are employed to control the money supply, which in turn affects spending, saving and investment by both individuals and businesses. Through the establishment of fiscal policies, the government is able to influence the amount of savings and expenditures by adjusting the tax structure and by changing the levels of government spending. Some economic experts believe that the effective use of monetary and fiscal policies can completely eliminate depressions from the business cycle.

Recovery is the stage of the business cycle in which the economy moves from depression or recession to prosperity. During this period, the high unemployment rate begins to decline, total disposable income increases and the economic gloom that lessened consumers' willingness to buy subsides. Both the ability and the willingness to buy rise. Marketers face some problems during recovery—for example, the difficulty of ascertaining how quickly prosperity will return and of forecasting the level of prosperity that will be attained. During this stage, marketers should maintain as much flexibility in their marketing strategies as possible to be able to make the needed adjustments as the economy moves from recession to prosperity. Fluctuations in economic conditions have a significant impact on marketers' activities and fortunes.

Consumer Demand and Spending Behaviour

Marketers must understand the factors that determine whether, what, where and when people buy. Chapters 4 and 7 look at behavioural factors underlying these choices, but here the focus is on the economic components: buying power, willingness to purchase and spending patterns.

Buying Power   The strength of a person's **buying power** depends on the size of the resources that enable the individual to purchase and on the state of the economy. The resources that make up buying power are goods, services and financial holdings. Fluctuations of the business cycle affect buying power because they influence price levels and interest rates. For example, during inflationary periods, when prices are rising, buying power decreases because more pounds or ECUs are required to buy products. Table 2.2 indicates some trends in UK consumers' expenditure. The major financial sources of buying power are income, credit and wealth. From an individual's viewpoint, **income** is the amount of money received through wages, rents, investments, pensions and subsidy payments for a given period, such as a month or a year. Normally, this money is allocated among taxes, spending for goods and services, and savings. However, because of the differences in people's educational levels, abilities, occupations and wealth, income is not equally distributed in any country.

Marketers are most interested in the amount of money that is left after payment of taxes. After-tax income is called **disposable income** and is used for spending or saving. Because disposable income is a ready source of buying power, the

---

Depression   A period during which unemployment is extremely high, wages are very low, total disposable income is at a minimum and consumers lack confidence in the economy

Recovery   The stage of the business cycle in which the economy moves from depression or recession to prosperity

Buying power   Resources such as goods, services and financial holdings that can be traded in an exchange situation

Income   The amount of money received through wages, rents, investments, pensions and subsidy payments for a given period

Disposable income   After-tax income, which is used for spending or saving

Table 2.2 UK consumer expenditure. SOURCE: *Marketing Pocket Book, 1999.* Reprinted by permission of NTC Publications, Ltd.

Growth Rates[1]	Percentage change		
	1997/1987	1997/1992	1997/1996
Housing	28.5	17.1	3.6
Domestic fuel/power	−11.7	−9.4	−10.6
Food (in-home)	..	3.4	−1.3
Alcohol	9.6	9.5	1.2
Tobacco	8.5	12.2	5.2
Clothing/footwear	6.4	16.9	3.6
Personal gds./servs.	30.9	16.5	6.8
Household goods	19.0	18.0	7.0
Domestic services	29.3	18.7	1.5
Motoring	27.6	25.8	7.1
Fares/travel costs	23.5	19.0	7.0
Leisure goods	29.0	21.2	4.7
Leisure services	59.9	25.3	5.6
Financial services	47.6	23.8	5.7
Other	36.0	9.9	2.3
Total	**23.4**	**16.1**	**3.6**

[1]Deflated by the Retail Prices Index (1997 = 100).

Household expenditure, 1997   £ per Year

Category	£ per Year
Housing	3,246
Leisure services	2,804
Motoring	2,360
Food (home)	2,188
Household goods	1,336
Clothing, etc.	1,207
Alcohol	1,202
Leisure goods	1,031
Financial	914
Personal	831
Domestic services	750
Fares/travel	732
Fuel/power	609
Tobacco	529
Other	1,072

total amount available in a nation is important to marketers. Several factors affect the size of total disposable income. One, of course, is the total amount of income. Total national income is affected by wage levels, rate of unemployment, interest rates and dividend rates. These factors in turn affect the size of disposable income. Because disposable income is the income left after taxes are paid, the number of taxes and their amount directly affect the size of total disposable income. When taxes rise, disposable income declines; when taxes fall, disposable income increases. Disposable income that is available for spending and saving after an individual has purchased the basic necessities of food, clothing and

Discretionary income Disposable income that is available for spending and saving after an individual has purchased the basic necessities of food, clothing and shelter

shelter is called **discretionary income.** People use discretionary income to purchase entertainment, holidays, cars, education, pets and pet supplies, furniture, appliances and so on. Changes in total discretionary income affect the sales of these products—especially cars, furniture, large appliances and other costly durable goods. The marketers of such products must monitor factors likely to alter their target customers' discretionary income.

Credit enables people to spend future income now or in the near future. However, credit increases current buying power at the expense of future buying power. Several factors determine whether consumers use or forgo credit. First, credit must be available to them. Interest rates, too, affect consumers' decisions to use credit, especially for expensive purchases such as homes, appliances and cars. When credit charges are high, consumers are more likely to delay buying expensive items. Use of credit is also affected by credit terms, such as the size of the down payment and the amount and number of monthly payments. Many marketers offer "interest-free credit" or low interest rates as part of the marketing proposition for their products.

Wealth The accumulation of past income, natural resources and financial resources

A person can have a high income and very little wealth. It is also possible, but not likely, for a person to have great wealth but not much income. **Wealth** is the accumulation of past income, natural resources and financial resources. It may exist in many forms, including cash, securities, savings accounts, jewellery, antiques and property. Like income, wealth is unevenly distributed. The significance of wealth to marketers is that as people become wealthier they gain buying power in three ways: they can use their wealth to make current purchases, to generate income and to acquire large amounts of credit. Buying power information is available from government sources, trade associations and research agencies. One of the most current and comprehensive sources of buying power data is the Central Statistical Office's *National Income and Expenditure Survey.* The EU's *Eurostat* provides similar data. Income, wealth and credit equip consumers to purchase goods and services. Marketing managers should be aware of current levels and expected changes in buying power in their own markets because buying power directly affects the types and quantities of goods and services that consumers purchase, as explained later in the discussion of spending patterns. Just because consumers have buying power, however, does not necessarily mean that they will buy. Consumers must also be willing to use their buying power. Marketers must encourage them to do so.

Willingness to spend A disposition towards using buying power, influenced by the ability to buy, expected satisfaction from a product and numerous psychological and social forces

Consumers' Willingness to Spend People's **willingness to spend** is, to some degree, related to their ability to buy. That is, people are sometimes more willing to buy if they have the buying power. However, a number of other elements also influence willingness to spend. Some elements affect specific products; others influence spending in general. A product's absolute price and its price relative to the price of substitute products influence almost everyone. The amount of satisfaction currently received or expected in the future from a product already owned may also influence consumers' desire to buy other products. Satisfaction depends not only on the quality of the functional performance of the currently owned product, but also on numerous psychological and social forces.

Factors that affect consumers' general willingness to spend are expectations about future employment, income levels, prices, family size and general economic conditions. If people are unsure whether or how long they will be employed, willingness to buy ordinarily declines. Willingness to spend may increase if people are reasonably certain of higher incomes in the future. Expectations of rising prices in the near future may also increase willingness to spend in the present. For a given level of buying power, the larger the family, the greater the willingness to buy. One of the reasons for this relationship is that as the size of a family increases, a larger amount of money must be spent to provide the basic necessities of life to sustain the family members. Finally, perceptions of future economic conditions influence willingness to buy. For example, rising short term interest rates cool consumers' willingness to spend.

Consumer Spending Patterns Marketers must be aware of the factors that influence consumers' ability and willingness to spend, but they should also analyse how consumers actually spend their disposable incomes. Marketers obtain this information by studying consumer spending patterns. **Consumer spending patterns** indicate the relative proportions of annual family expenditures or the actual amount of money spent on certain kinds of goods and services. Families are usually categorised by one of several characteristics, including family income, age of the household head, geographic area and family life cycle. There are two types of spending patterns: comprehensive and product-specific.

The percentages of family income allotted to annual expenditures for general classes of goods and services constitute **comprehensive spending patterns.** Comprehensive spending patterns or the data to develop them are available in government publications and in reports produced by the major marketing research companies and by trade associations. **Product-specific spending patterns** indicate the annual monetary amounts families spend for specific products within a general product class. Information sources used to construct product-specific spending patterns include government publications, trade publications and consumer surveys. A marketer uses spending patterns to analyse general trends in the ways that families spend their incomes for various kinds of products. Analyses of spending patterns yield information that a marketer can use to gain perspective and background for decision-making. However, spending patterns reflect only general trends and thus should not be used as the sole basis for making specific decisions.

Assessment of Competitive Forces

Few organisations, if any, operate free of competition. Broadly speaking, all companies compete with each other for consumers' money. From a more practical viewpoint, however, a business generally defines **competition** as those organisations marketing products that are similar to, or can be substituted for, its own products in the same geographic area. For example, a local Tesco or Aldi supermarket manager views all grocery stores in a town as competitors, but almost never thinks of other types of local or out-of-town stores (DIY or electrical, for example) as competitors. This section considers the types of competitive structure and the importance of monitoring competitors.

Types of Competitive Structure The number of businesses that control the supply of a product may affect the strength of competition. When only one or a few companies control supply, competitive factors will exert a different sort of influence on marketing activities than when there are many competitors. Table 2.3 presents four general types of competitive structure: monopoly, oligopoly, monopolistic competition and perfect competition.

A **monopoly** exists when a company turns out a product that has no close substitutes. Because the organisation has no competitors, it completely controls the supply of the product and, as a single seller, can erect barriers to potential competitors. In reality, the monopolies that survive today are some utilities, such as

Consumer spending patterns
Information indicating the relative proportions of annual family expenditures or the actual amount of money spent on certain kinds of goods and services

Comprehensive spending patterns
The percentages of family income allotted to annual expenditures for general classes of goods and services

Product-specific spending patterns
The annual monetary amounts families spend for specific products within a general product class

Competition Those companies marketing products that are similar to, or can be substituted for, a given business's products in the same geographic area

Monopoly A market structure that exists when a company turns out a product that has no close substitutes

Type of Structure	Number of Competitors	Ease of Entry into Market	Product	Knowledge of Market	Examples
Monopoly	One	Many barriers	Almost no substitutes	Perfect	Non-privatised railways, many government departments
Oligopoly	Few	Some barriers	Homogeneous or differentiated (real or perceived differences)	Imperfect	Airlines, petroleum retailers, some utility providers
Monopolistic competition	Many	Few barriers	Product differentiation with many substitutes	More knowledge than oligopoly; less than monopoly	Jeans, fast food, audio-visual
Perfect competition	Unlimited	No barriers	Homogeneous products	Perfect	The London commodity markets, vegetable farms

Table 2.3　Selected characteristics of competitive structures

telephone, electricity and some railways (in many countries), and cable companies, which are heavily regulated. These monopolies are tolerated because of the tremendous financial resources needed to develop and operate them; few organisations can obtain the resources to mount any competition against a local electricity producer, for example. An **oligopoly** exists when a few sellers control the supply of a large proportion of a product. In this case, each seller must consider the reactions of other sellers to changes in marketing activities. Products facing oligopolistic competition may be homogeneous, such as aluminium, or differentiated, such as cigarettes and cars. Usually, barriers of some sort make it difficult to enter the market and compete with oligopolies. For example, because of the enormous financial outlay required, few companies or individuals could afford to enter the oil refining or steel producing industries. Moreover, some industries demand special technical or marketing skills that block the entry of many potential competitors.

Monopolistic competition exists when a business with many potential competitors attempts to develop a differential marketing strategy to establish its own market share. For example, Levi's has established a differential advantage for its blue jeans through a well known trademark, design, advertising and a quality image. Although many competing brands of blue jeans are available, this company has carved out its market share through use of a differential marketing strategy. **Perfect competition**, if it existed at all, would entail a large number of sellers, not one of which could significantly influence price or supply. Products would be homogeneous, and there would be full knowledge of the market and easy entry into it. The closest thing to an example of perfect competition would

Oligopoly　A market structure that exists when a few sellers control the supply of a large proportion of a product

Monopolistic competition　A market structure that exists when a business with many potential competitors attempts to develop a differential marketing strategy to establish its own market share

Perfect competition　A market structure that entails a large number of sellers, not one of which could significantly influence price or supply

be an unregulated agricultural market. Few, if any, marketers operate in a structure of perfect competition. Perfect competition is an ideal at one end of the continuum, with monopoly at the other end. Most marketers function in a competitive environment that falls somewhere between these two extremes.

Competitive Tools   Another set of factors that influences the level of competition is the number and types of competitive tools used by competitors. To survive, a business uses one or several available competitive tools to deal with competitive economic forces. Once a company has analysed its particular competitive environment and decided which factors in that environment it can or must adapt to or influence, it can choose among the variables that it can control to strengthen its competitive position in the overall marketplace. Probably the competitive tool that most organisations grasp is price. Bic, for example, markets disposable pens and lighters that are similar to competing products but less expensive. However, there is one major problem with using price as a competitive tool: competitors will often match or beat the price. This threat is one of the primary reasons for employing non–price competitive tools that are based on the differentiation of market segments, product offering, service, promotion, distribution or enterprise.[9] By focusing on a specific market segment, a marketer sometimes gains a competitive advantage. For instance, Saab cars and Porsche sports coupes are narrowly targeted at specific groups of consumers. Most manufacturers try to gain a competitive edge by incorporating product features that make their brands distinctive to some extent. Companies use distinguishing promotional methods to compete, such as advertising and personal selling. Competing producers sometimes use different distribution channels to prevail over one another. Retailers may compete by placing their outlets in locations that are convenient for a large number of shoppers. Dealers and distributors offer wide ranges, advice and service.

Monitoring Competition   Marketers in an organisation need to be aware of the actions of major competitors. They should monitor what competitors are currently doing and assess the changes occurring in the competitive environment. **Competitor monitoring** allows businesses to determine what specific strategies competitors are following and how those strategies affect their own. It can also guide marketers as they try to develop competitive advantages and can aid them in adjusting current marketing strategies, as well as in planning new ones. Information may come from direct observation or from sources such as salespeople, customers, trade publications, syndicated marketing research services, distributors and marketing studies. An organisation needs information about competitors that will allow its marketing managers to assess the performance of its own marketing efforts. Comparing their company's performance with that of competitors helps marketing managers recognise strengths and weaknesses in their own marketing strategies. Data about market shares, product movement, sales volume and expenditure levels can be useful. However, accurate information on these matters is often difficult to obtain.

Competition exists in most markets and situations. Even charities compete with one another and with manufacturers for consumers' attention and financial commitment. Marketing places an emphasis on meeting consumers' needs and offering satisfaction. To be successful, however, competing organisations need to identify unique marketing mixes; otherwise all rival products and services will merely replicate each other. The search for a competitive edge—achieved through a differential advantage in a market over competitors—is central to effective

Competitor monitoring   The process by which a company studies the actions of its major competitors in order to determine what specific strategies they are following and how those strategies affect its own; also used by marketers as they try to develop competitive advantages, adjust current marketing strategies and plan new ones

Part I   Marketing Defined

marketing strategy. As well as monitoring direct compe[...] be aware of new entrants coming into a market with com[...] of the danger of substitute products or services being [...] understanding of competition is also addressed in Ch[...] *Marketing: Concepts and Strategies.*

Figure 2.3 The f[...] the marketin[...] ment: m[...]

The Micro Marketing Environment

Macro marketing environment
The broader forces affecting all organisations in a market—political, legal, regulatory, societal/green, technological, economic and competitive

Micro marketing environment The more company-specific forces reflecting the nature of the business, its suppliers, marketing intermediaries, buyers, all types of competitors—direct, substitute and new entrant—and its publics

Many authors, notably Michael Porter,[10] have made a distinction between the very broad forces of the **macro marketing environment** discussed up to now in this chapter—political, legal, regulatory, societal/green, technological, economic and competitive—and a set of more company-specific forces often termed the **micro marketing environment** forces. The distinction, put simply, is that the broad macro forces have an impact on every organisation operating in a particular market, from manufacturers to distributors to customers, and such an impact is universally felt by such organisations. The micro forces, on the other hand, often have an organisation-specific impact subject to the characteristics and status of the individual business.

Although categorisations vary among authors, the core aspects of the micro marketing environment worthy of note include the business, suppliers, marketing intermediaries, buyers, competitors and publics. See Figure 2.3.

The Business It is necessary when creating and implementing marketing strategies and marketing mix programmes to consider the reaction, attitudes and abilities of the *internal* environment: top management, finance, research and development, purchasing, manufacturing, sales and marketing, logistics. The marketing function's recommendations must be consistent with senior management's corporate goals, be conveyed to other functions within the business and reflect colleagues' views, input, concerns and abilities to implement the desired marketing plan. Marketers must be aware of these organisational factors, monitor them and modify their actions accordingly to ensure internal take-up of their ideas and plans.

Suppliers Most organisations source raw materials, components or supplies from third parties. Without the understanding and co-operation of these other organisations, a business would fail to deliver a quality product or service which satisfies its customers' needs. Marketers must be aware of aspects of supply which might affect the way in which their business functions in satisfying its customers. These forces could include supplier innovations; deals with rivals; supply shortages, delays or quality concerns; strikes or recruitment difficulties; legal actions or warranty disputes; supply costs and price trends; new entrants into the supply chain; or anything prone to altering the business's receipt of its required supplies.

Marketing Intermediaries Some businesses sell directly to their targeted customers. Most, though, utilise the skills, network and resources of intermediaries to make their products available to the end-user customer. Intermediaries are discussed later in *Marketing: Concepts and Strategies* (see Part IV) and include resellers—such as retailers, wholesalers, agents, brokers, dealers—plus physical distribution companies responsible for logistical needs, providers of marketing

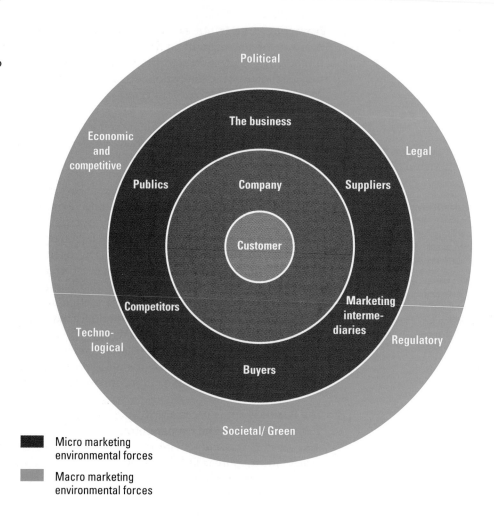

Political

The business

Economic
and
competitive

Legal

Publics

Company

Suppliers

Customer

Competitors

Marketing
interme-
diaries

Techno-
logical

Regulatory

Buyers

Societal/ Green

▮ Micro marketing
environmental forces

▮ Macro marketing
environmental forces

services such as advertising agencies or packaging design consultancies, and financial facilitators of credit lines and export guarantees. Without the smooth co-operation of such intermediaries, a business is unlikely to be able to deliver its products as required by its customers. For example, the collapse of a credit company or bank such as BCCI severely reduces the ability of a client business to fund its activities. A striking workforce in a business's preferred road haulage company will lead to the urgent need to negotiate alternative logistical support with a new haulier, requiring time and perhaps legal intervention given existing contractual arrangements. An advertising agent's new account win might be that of a direct rival to an existing client. The existing client business might sensibly choose to find a different advertising agency, but this move will have a penalty in terms of management time and perhaps the timely execution of a planned advertising campaign. In each of these examples, shrewd awareness of developments by a business's marketers would have reduced the likelihood of any impediment to its own activities and ability to serve its own customers. Failure to pick up on any of these events would have resulted in a loss of business as the marketers and colleagues in other business functions sought alternative lines of credit, haulage agreements or advertising expertise.

Buyers Customers are central to the marketing concept. They are often fickle and have ever changing requirements, needs and perceptions which marketers must understand, anticipate and satisfy. As Chapters 4 and 5 describe, consumers and businesses' customers must be analysed, and the marketing mix developed by a set of marketers must be designed to satisfy these customers' requirements. Each individual business will have a unique set of resources, skills, marketing mix programmes and products to offer its customers. Therefore, as customers' needs evolve, separate businesses will find that their required response is different. As the consumer has come to demand more customer service from supermarket retailers, Tesco and Sainsbury have been better placed to upgrade their service-oriented propositions than say Somerfield or Iceland. This micro environmental force has had a variable impact on these retailers' strategies.

Competitors Marketers must strive to satisfy their target customers but in a manner which differentiates their product, brand and overall proposition from competing companies' marketing mixes. In order to achieve this, marketers require an in-depth understanding of their competitive arena (see Chapter 21). There are two important considerations in this analysis. First, competition stems not only from like-for-like or direct rivals. There are substitute solutions to monitor and new entrants to anticipate. For example, construction equipment manufacturer JCB competes with a plethora of similar businesses such as Caterpillar or Case. Iseki manufactures none of the same equipment, but it produces a micro-bore tunnelling "mole" which lays pipes without the need to dig trenches, thus rendering the need for a JCB backhoe loader digger redundant. Such substitute competition can seriously erode a business's market position if not observed and combated. New entrant car producer Daewoo has made significant sales inroads in the European small and medium car market. Certain car manufacturing rivals had anticipated Daewoo's arrival with pre-emptive product launches and marketing campaigns. Other rivals had no contingency plans and saw their market share seriously eroded. The second consideration is the business's own position: resources, market standing, capabilities, strengths and any differential advantage—competitive edge—held over rivals. These characteristics are different for each business so the impact of any competitive activity will vary between businesses. Marketers must be aware of direct, substitute and new entrant competitor activity but also should gauge the likely impact of competition on their own business in the context of a sound understanding of their capabilities and standing.

Publics The micro marketing environment also includes any group—public—which does or could impact on a business's ability to satisfy its target customers and achieve its corporate objectives.[11] These include financial bodies such as banks, investment houses, financial analysts or shareholders; newspaper, magazine, radio, television, or Internet media which carry features about a business, its products and activities; government bodies which may intervene over operating or consumer issues; consumer and pressure groups; neighbourhood publics such as residents adjacent to a large manufacturing plant; the general public whose view of a business must be assessed and taken into account when developing marketing mix programmes; and internal publics such as the workforce. Most businesses are increasingly recognising the importance of communicating effectively with these sets of people. The notion of relationship marketing outlined in Chapter 1 is designed to emphasise the need to address more publics than solely customers through marketing programmes and communications. (See also

Chapter 23.) In order to effectively achieve this, however, it is necessary for a business to understand these micro marketing environment forces.

The Marketing Environment and Strategic Opportunities

Strategic windows   Major developments or opportunities triggered by changes in the marketing environment

When changes occur in the marketing environment they can trigger major developments. If large enough, such changes are called **strategic windows** or paradigm shifts.[12] If market leaders have failed to spot the underlying development or evolutionary change, rivals may have an opportunity to gain an advantage over established companies and brands by "stepping through the open window". The established company must strive to "close the window" with its own proposition speedily enough to pre-empt competitors' inroads. Failure to monitor the marketing environment and take appropriate action invariably results in a business being unable to react quickly enough to the change to keep out competitors. Marketing strategists believe there are six broad causes of strategic windows opening[13]:

New Technology   Duracell over took market leader EverReady because Duracell took advantage of new lithium technology before EverReady modified its product range. Direct Line gained leadership in the car insurance market because it turned to direct selling via telephone call centres before any of the major insurance companies recognised this evolving use of technology.

New Markets   Security services and logistics company Securicor was quick to spot the likely take-off of the mobile phone market, taking the majority share in leading network provider Cellnet. This awareness of new markets enabled Securicor to firmly establish itself as a multi-faceted communications business.

New Distribution Channels   Telecommunications provider Vodafone was quick to recognise that some customers were reluctant to venture into the specialist mobile phone shops, feeling they would be confused by the salesperson's fast patter. Vodafone created point-of-sale displays with self-service selection for mainstream retailers such as Woolworth's or Halford's. This self-selection appealed to a segment of the market and this innovative channel of distribution—cutting out mobile phone shops and specialists—helped to expand Vodafone's market share.

Market Re-definition   NCR—National Cash Registers—used to dominate the market for providing electronic cash tills in retailers' stores. As retailers discovered the convenience of stock management through barcodes and EPoS systems, they turned to more sophisticated systems. Retail management's desire to monitor and record detailed sales data altered the buyer's requirement of in-store technology. ICL and Nixdorf were quick to spot this change and build on their computer industry resources to develop all-in retail systems which incorporated the cash till with much more. This re-definition of the market eroded NCR's once dominant position while giving rivals a marketing opportunity.

New Legislation and Regulation   Laws, regulations and international agreements create strategic windows. The "open skies" policy of the EU has created route opportunities for smaller airlines once precluded from hubs by state protected national airlines. Privatisation of the rail network enabled Stagecoach and Virgin to diversify their businesses into rail services.

Financial and Political Shocks Sudden changes in currency prices, interest rates, trade agreements, inflation, unemployment levels, protectionist policies or political leadership can have major impact on business. A new government might decide to privatise state owned assets or more tightly regulate an industry's activities. A trade war between states will impact on businesses operating in such markets.

Often managers only notice sales dips months after a marketing environment force has created a problem. In the meantime, this has created a window for competitors to enter. While there are many psychological factors which can hinder managerial activity, such as a preference for retrenchment and an aversion to change,[14] a common problem is simply the failure to formally and routinely monitor the forces of the marketing environment through environmental scanning—the process of collecting and analysing information about the forces of the marketing environment. A business must determine which aspects of the marketing environment—macro and micro—to monitor and how. Strategists believe a regular and routinised system enables identification of strongly signalled issues that senior management or a marketing function can then prioritise for more detailed investigation. Clearly, given the vast array of issues examined in this chapter, it is not feasible or desirable for a set of managers to address every conceivably pertinent facet of the trading environment.

Companies opt for different solutions.[15] Some require line managers to undertake environmental scanning in addition to their other responsibilities. Occasionally, a strategic planner undertakes such monitoring, although this head office position is often too divorced from the business's operations to identify the crucial core forces to investigate. A few large companies have created a bespoke marketing environment unit of cross-functional managers responsible for researching, analysing, disseminating and recommending. This ensures scanning occurs but is costly and again can be too removed from a company's operations. More frequently, marketing planning identifies core trends and evolving forces to monitor.[16] Marketing planning is practised in most medium and large companies, and part of the cross-functional, multi-hierarchical team's remit is to annually report on marketing environment forces likely to have implications for the business (see Chapter 22). Some companies have no more than a box in the centre of an open-plan office in which any manager can deposit marketing environment information stemming from press comments, customer feedback, dealer observations, trade show intelligence, analysts' reports, or any other inputs. This material is then regularly sifted, summarised and circulated, with individual issues being followed up as determined by managerial judgement. Other businesses have formalised this approach using e-mail and Intranet newsletters to personnel and sites within the organisation, often globally, with interactive dialogue aiding the understanding of the environmental forces noted.

No matter how it is orchestrated, it is essential that the marketing environment be thoroughly and regularly monitored[17]. This must translate into managerial recommendations when necessary, with target market strategies and marketing mix programmes reflecting the issues identified. An understanding of the marketing environment—macro and micro forces—is essential for a rigorous and meaningful assessment of marketing opportunities. Without such an analysis, any recommended marketing strategy is unlikely to take account of unfolding strategic windows. Competitors may be offered the chance to make inroads and the business may fail to benefit from potential marketing opportunities.

The *marketing environment* consists of external forces that directly or indirectly influence an organisation's acquisition of inputs (personnel, financial resources, raw materials, information) and generation of outputs (information, packages, goods, services, ideas). Generally the forces of the marketing environment are divided into two categories: macro and micro. The macro marketing environment comprises political, legal and regulatory forces; societal forces, including green concerns for the earth's natural environment; and technological forces. Along with economic forces and trends, these macro, broader aspects of the marketing environment have an impact on manufacturers and their customers. The forces of the micro marketing environment are more company-specific and include the business's internal environment, suppliers, marketing intermediaries, buyers, competitors and publics.

To monitor changes in these forces, marketers should practise environmental scanning and analysis. *Environmental scanning* is the process of collecting information about the forces in the marketing environment; *environmental analysis* is the process of assessing and interpreting the information obtained in scanning. This information helps marketing managers predict opportunities and threats associated with environmental fluctuation. Marketing management may assume either a passive, reactive approach or an active, aggressive approach in responding to these environmental fluctuations. The choice depends on an organisation's structure and needs and on the composition of the environmental forces that affect it.

The political, legal and regulatory forces of the marketing environment are closely interrelated. The current political outlook is reflected in legislation and regulations or the lack of them. The political environment may determine what laws and regulations affecting specific marketers are enacted and how much the government purchases and from which suppliers; it can also be important in helping organisations secure foreign markets.

Legislation affecting marketing activities can be divided into *procompetitive legislation*—laws designed to preserve competition and to end various practices deemed unacceptable by society—and consumer protection laws. In the UK the Restrictive Trade Practices Act and the Competition Act sought to prevent monopolies and activities that limit competition; legislation such as the Financial Services Act, the Sale of Goods Act and the Consumer Credit Act was directed towards more specific practices. Consumer protection laws generally relate to product safety and information disclosure. The actual effects of legislation are determined by how marketers and the courts interpret the laws.

Regulatory agencies influence most marketing activities. For example, in the UK the *Competition Commission* and the *Office of Fair Trading* usually have the power to enforce specific laws and some discretion in establishing operating rules and drawing up regulations to guide certain types of industry practices. Self-regulation by industry represents another regulatory force; marketers view this type of regulation more favourably than government action, because they have more opportunity to take part in creating the guidelines. Self-regulation may be less expensive than government regulation, and its guidelines are often more realistic. However, such regulation generally cannot assure compliance as effectively as government agencies.

Societal/green forces refer to the structure and dynamics of individuals and groups and the issues that concern them. Many members of society want a high standard of living and a high quality of life, and they expect business to help them achieve these goals. Of growing concern is the well-being of the earth, its resources, climate and peoples. The *green movement* is increasing general awareness of the natural environment and is altering product design, manufacture, packaging and use. The *consumer movement* is a diverse collection of independent individuals, groups and organisations that attempt to protect the rights of consumers. The major issues taken up by the consumer movement fall into three categories: environmental protection, product performance and safety, and information disclosure. Consumer rights organisations inform and organise other consumers, raise issues, help businesses develop consumer oriented programmes, and pressure legislators to enact consumer protection laws. Some are quite formally organised, such as the *Consumers' Association*.

Technology is the knowledge of how to accomplish tasks and goals. Product development, packaging, promotion, prices and distribution systems are all influenced directly by technology. Several factors determine how much and in what way a particular business will make use of technology; these factors include the company's ability to use technology, consumers' ability and willingness to buy technologically improved products, the business's perception of the long run effects of applying technology, the extent to which the company is technologically based, the degree to which technology is used as a competitive tool and the extent to which the business can protect technological applications through patents. Many businesses conduct a *technology assessment*.

The *economic forces* that can strongly influence marketing decisions and activities are general economic conditions, buying power, willingness to spend, spending patterns and *competitive forces*. The overall state of the economy fluctuates in a general pattern known as the *business cycle*. The stages of the business cycle are *prosperity, recession, depression* and *recovery*.

Consumers' goods, services and financial holdings make up their *buying power*—that is, their ability to purchase. The financial sources of buying power are *income*, credit and wealth. After-tax income used for spending or saving is called *disposable income*. Disposable income left after an individual has purchased the basic necessities of food, clothing and shelter is called *discretionary income*. It is important to identify levels of *wealth*. Two measures of buying power are effective buying income (which includes salaries, wages, dividends, interest, profits and rents, less taxes) and the buying power index (a weighted index consisting of population, effective buying income and retail sales data). The factors that affect consumers' *willingness to spend* are product price, the level of satisfaction obtained from currently used products, and expectations about future employment, family size, income, prices and general economic conditions. *Consumer spending patterns* indicate the relative proportions of annual family expenditures or the actual amount of money spent on certain kinds of goods and services. *Comprehensive spending patterns* specify the percentages of family income allotted to annual expenditures for general classes of goods and services. *Product-specific spending patterns* indicate the annual amounts families spend for specific products within a general product class.

Competition is a fundamental concern for all marketers. Although all businesses compete for consumers' spending, a company's direct competitors are usually the businesses in its geographic area marketing products that resemble its own or can be substituted for them. The number of businesses that control the supply of a product may affect the strength of competition. There are four general types of competitive structure: *monopoly, oligopoly, monopolistic competition* and *perfect competition*. Marketers use *competitor monitoring* to determine what competitors are currently doing and to assess the changes occurring in the competitive environment.

Increasingly marketers make a distinction between the broader trading *macro marketing environment* forces—political, legal, regulatory, societal/green, technological, economic and competitive—and the more company-specific forces of the *micro marketing environment*. Micro forces include the business in question, its suppliers, marketing intermediaries, buyers, business-specific competition—direct, substitute and new entrant rivals—and the various publics of an organisation: financial bodies, media, government, consumer and pressure groups, neighbours, the general public and the internal workforce.

Changes in the marketing environment often create *strategic windows* which, if they are not quickly identified, can enable rivals to steal an edge. There are six key causes for the creation of strategic windows, all aspects of the macro or micro marketing environment: new technology, new markets, new distribution channels, market re-definition, new legislation and regulation, plus financial and political shocks. Often managers fail to notice sales dips until months after the impact of an aspect of the marketing environment. This may be because they are averse to change and prefer retrenchment, but often it stems from a lack of environmental scanning. Strategists believe a regular and routinised assessment of the marketing environment is essential prior to the formulation of any target market strategies or marketing mix programmes. Companies adopt different solutions to monitoring the marketing environment: line managers, strategic planners, bespoke units or as an integral part of the annual marketing planning process. It is essential that the marketing environment—macro and micro forces—is continually monitored in order to maximise marketing opportunities and fend off competitors' actions.

Important Terms

Marketing environment
Environmental scanning
Environmental analysis
Procompetitive legislation
Office of Fair Trading
Competition Commission
Consumers' Association
Societal/green forces
Green movement
Consumer movement
Technology
Technology assessment
Economic and competitive forces

Business cycle
Prosperity
Recession
Depression
Recovery
Buying power
Income
Disposable income
Discretionary income
Wealth
Willingness to spend
Consumer spending patterns
Comprehensive spending patterns

Product-specific spending
  patterns
Competition
Monopoly
Oligopoly
Monopolistic competition
Perfect competition
Competitor monitoring
Macro marketing environment
Micro marketing environment
Strategic windows

Discussion and Review Questions

1. Why are environmental scanning and analysis so important?
2. How are political forces related to legal and regulatory forces?
3. Describe marketers' attempts to influence political forces.
4. What types of procompetitive legislation directly affect marketing practices?
5. What is the major objective of most procompetitive laws? Do the laws generally accomplish this objective? Why or why not?
6. What types of problems do marketers experience as they interpret legislation?
7. What are the goals of the Competition Commission? How does the Commission affect marketing activities?
8. Name several non-governmental regulatory forces. Do you believe that self-regulation is more or less effective than governmental regulatory agencies? Why?
9. How is the so-called green movement altering the shape of business?
10. Describe the consumer movement. Analyse some active consumer forces in your area.
11. What does the term *technology* mean to you?
12. How does technology affect you as a member of society? Do the benefits of technology outweigh its costs and dangers?
13. Discuss the impact of technology on marketing activities.
14. What factors determine whether a business organisation adopts and uses technology?
15. In what ways can each of the business cycle stages affect consumers' reactions to marketing strategies?
16. What is the current business cycle stage? How is this stage affecting businesses in your area?
17. Define income, disposable income and discretionary income. How does each type of income affect consumer buying power?
18. How is consumer buying power affected by wealth and consumer credit?
19. How is buying power measured? Why should it be evaluated?

20. What factors influence a consumer's willingness to spend?
21. What are the principal types of competition?
22. What differentiates the forces of the micro marketing environment from those of the macro marketing environment?
23. Why must marketers monitor changes in supplier and marketing intermediary practices?
24. Marketers should not track only direct, like-for-like competitors. Why not? What other types of competitors are there?
25. Why should marketers be aware of their company's publics?
26. How does an assessment of marketing environment forces assist in marketing opportunity analysis?
27. What are the main causes for the opening of strategic windows?
28. How can a business instigate environmental scanning?

Recommended Readings

A. Palmer and B. Hartley, *The Business and Marketing Environment* (Maidenhead: McGraw-Hill, 1996).

P. Drucker, *Management in Turbulent Times* (London: Butterworth-Heinemann/Pan, 1993).

M. E. Porter, "How competitive forces shape strategy", *Harvard Business Review,* March–April 1979, pp. 137–145.

K. Peattie, *Environmental Marketing Management* (London: Pitman, 1995).

P. S. H. Leeflang and W. F. van Raaij, "The changing consumer in the European Union: a meta-analysis", *International Journal of Research in Marketing,* 1995, vol. 12, no. 5, pp. 373–387.

● C A S E S

2.1 The Race against Regulation

Throughout the 1980s and 1990s, the anti-smoking lobby had grown in stature. Governments responded by banning TV tobacco advertising and most employers created no-smoking areas in offices, canteens and on the shop floor. Some even prohibit smoking totally. Restaurants and bars are encouraged by the government to provide no-smoking areas and air purification equipment, public transport is largely a no-smoking zone and British Airways bans in-flight smoking. Despite these measures, the tobacco industry is huge with the majority of youths smoking, particularly teenage girls. Most forecourt shops, CTN newsagents, supermarkets and convenience stores stock the leading brands of cigarettes.

For the manufacturers there is the need to promote their brands against rivals' products. Once popular T.V.B advertising has been prohibited. Advertising in any form has been ruled against by EU legislators. An alternative was sports sponsorship: football competitions, tennis tournaments, horse racing all received lucrative sponsorship from the major cigarette producers. Nothing was more high profile, though, than the tobacco industry's multi-faceted sponsorship of F1 grand prix motor racing. The famous black cars carrying the John Player Special design led the way in the 1970s, followed by many years of success on the track for the Marlborough sponsored McLaren team. Winfield supported once dominant Williams. Half of Jordan's sponsorship of £38m comes from Gallaher's Benson & Hedges. Although sponsorship comes from many other industries, including car manufacturers, clothing producers and management consultants, the tobacco industry has for thirty years provided the bulk of the sport's income, excluding television rights. The world audience tuning in to live coverage of F1 races is the primary reason for the huge amounts of sponsorship poured into this sport. Gallaher openly states that F1 is seen as a major advertising opportunity with the Benson & Hedges brand on TV, in the press, in magazines and all over the media, aggressively putting the brand in front of a worldwide audience.

At the start of the 1999 season, the newest team to join the F1 roadshow, British American Racing, revealed its two cars, which were very different in appearance to each other. Jacques Villeneuve's car was red and white, matching Lucky Strike cigarette's—a leading brand in Latin America—pack design, while Ricardo Zonta's car promoted Far East cigarette brand 555. British American Racing, owned by British American Tobacco (BAT), was clearly promoting the tobacco industry and the Lucky Strike and 555 brands specifically. Some onlookers felt the cars resembled cigarette packets with wheels! There then followed a dispute with the sports ruling body FIA, which argued that a team's cars must be virtually identical. Here was a case of a sponsor truly attempting to maximise the brand exposure gained from its financial outlay. Not all teams are quite so extreme in the tobacco links. Japanese brand Mild 7 supports the Benetton team, but the Italian clothing giant's own colours dominate its cars.

For BAT, direct ownership of its own team has stemmed from the impending ban of tobacco sponsorship of F1 motor racing. There are few prominent places for tobacco advertising and promotion. F1 is one. The EU and the British government are banning tobacco sponsorship in an attempt to reduce teenage smoking and the health risks in general associated with this market. BAT hopes that by owning a team and naming its cars and racing team after its products, it might circumvent some of the impending regulation changes. The advertisements will come off the cars in 2006 and it remains to be seen whether direct ownership by BAT of the team will provide any protection against a total loss of media exposure for its cigarette brands.

The European ban will go into effect in 2006 but the F1 "circus" visits Australia, Japan, North America and a growing number of non-EU countries. China, South Korea, Malaysia, Indonesia and South Africa have shown interest in staging F1 races, as the industry seeks to attract the huge sums of sponsorship required to keep a leading team going: between £30m and £60m annually. Most Asian companies are much more relaxed about smoking than the EU. The economic collapse of these so-called Tiger economies has put a question mark over these new entrants' ability to stage such events. China's scheduled 1999 race was cancelled after it failed to meet financial commitments. While the F1 managers hoped to work around the EU's ban on tobacco advertising and sponsorship by seeking new territories, this unexpected collapse of the Pacific Rim economy placed any hope of attracting new venues in doubt. As a result, it seems likely that the FIA may well have to comply with the EU's desire for a worldwide ban on F1 tobacco sponsorship.

Action on Smoking & Health (ASH) believes there may well be a watered down compromise. F1 is a multi-billion pound industry which brings significant income and employment to EU countries, notably France, Italy and Britain. There are many vested interests opposed to any external forces likely to minimise its success and future growth. However, the government's stance and EU regulations are quite specific. The opportunity of turning to the Pacific Rim Tiger economies has fallen foul of that region's economic troubles. There is perhaps no better example of an industry and of marketers having to grapple with the changing forces of the marketing environment than the F1 motor racing business.

SOURCES: Richenda Wilson, "Race against time", *Marketing Week*, 21 January 1999, pp. 51–53; Roger Baird, "Winning formula", *Marketing Week*, 4 March 1999, pp. 37–38; Richard Foster, "Why sponsors need to negotiate the rule book", *Marketing Week*, 25 February 1999, p. 16.

Questions for Discussion

1. What are the marketing environment forces at play in the F1 market?
2. What strategies have been adopted by the tobacco companies as they strive to maintain a high profile for their brands?
3. What other external forces might in future affect this industry?

2.2 Ericsson Sights Global Markets

Sweden has many internationally known organisations, many of which are leaders in their respective fields: Saab Scania in aerospace and vehicles; Volvo in cars and trucks; Electrolux in domestic appliances and electrical goods; IKEA in home furnishings; Tetra Pak in packaging and Ericsson in electronics and telecommunications. These companies all succeed by having a global focus and the ability to exploit technological niches. In the early 1980s, Ericsson anticipated that mechanical switching in telecommunications would be replaced by the faster and more efficient electronic switching, with the total transformation of telephone exchanges worldwide. By taking the decision to accept this trend and become one of the instigators of such change, Ericsson created an enviable lead in the marketplace and achieved significant market share increases.

It is perhaps not too surprising, therefore, that in the rapidly growing cellular (mobile) phone market, the world leader should be Sweden's Ericsson. Globally, 9 million new subscribers to mobile telephones are currently being added every three months, making it the fastest growing sector within the rapidly growing telecommunications industry. It is estimated that 40 per cent of all mobile phones in the world are connected to cellular networks delivered by Sweden's Ericsson. In Sweden, which has the highest penetration of mobile phones—40 per cent of the population, compared with 25 per cent in the UK—there are no signs of saturation, and penetration of an incredible 90 per cent is expected.

While Ericsson has succeeded in this marketplace largely because of insightful business planning and product development, the external marketing environment acted in favour of this Swedish multinational. There are various technologies at work in the rival cellular networks. A regional initiative by the Swedish, Norwegian and Finnish authorities established the Nordic Mobile Telephone (NMT) standard. It is a fact of most industries that an organisation's view of the world and of global customer needs is heavily influenced and biased by what is happening in a business's domestic marketplace. In this instance, the NMT standard for Scandinavia was more homogeneous than that applied in other parts of the world. While this forced Ericsson and Nokia to invest in new and

more expensive technologies initially, the result was a product capability and knowledge genuinely superior to that being developed elsewhere in the world. It is not surprising, therefore, that network operators throughout Europe turned to Ericsson to provide infrastructure and networks. By contrast, the US has significant regulatory inconsistencies and barriers, as a result of which domestic US manufacturers produce equipment not deemed desirable worldwide. Indeed, through a joint venture with GE, the large American electronics conglomerate, Ericsson has successfully entered the US market and has beaten Motorola in its own home market. As a result, Ericsson now has 80 per cent of the joint venture with GE and is the fastest expanding player in the North American telecommunications market.

In a world market dominated by global players, Ericsson has been able to compete successfully with rivals such as AT&T, Northern Telecom, Alcatel and Siemens. The company's current focus is on providing technical services that can genuinely be company-specific. Ericsson has recognised that in the high tech world of telecommunications, each company's needs as a customer of Ericsson will be unique. A second important requirement is to facilitate integration with other businesses. While such an awareness of market trends and customer needs has figured prominently in Ericsson's success, so has the company's ability to maximise opportunities offered by the broader marketing environment. The NMT standard in Scandinavia gave Ericsson, perhaps by default, a viable standard on which to build. In North America, Ericsson used its joint venture with GE to penetrate the market, but its global knowledge and size allowed it to overcome many of the regulatory and political barriers impeding the growth of domestic US manufacturers. In the telecommunications market, however, the ground rules are continually changing, and regulatory bodies are particularly prone to protect domestic markets and specific consumers.

SOURCES: R. Olins, "Mobile phone war hots up", *Sunday Times*, 19 November 1995; T. Jackson, "New kids on the telephony block", *Financial Times*, 15 May 1995; T. Grey and C. Price, "Orange aims to float in March", *Financial Times*, 12 January 1996; Andrew Pickford, Combitech Traffic Systems; "A visit to telecom's magic kingdom", *America's Network*, 15 March 1995, pp. 52–54; Matthew Lynn, "Calling for partners", *Management Today*, July 1992, pp. 80–81.

Questions for Discussion

1. Why is it important for Ericsson to monitor the marketing environment?

2. To compete in Europe with companies like Ericsson, what must Motorola or Sony find out about the marketing environment in these target markets?

3. What are likely to be the most significant aspects of the marketing environment for Ericsson as it continues its attack on world markets?

3 Marketing in International Markets

"An international perspective on marketing management is critical in the contemporary era of global competition."

Colin Egan, Leicester De Montfort University

O B J E C T I V E S

- To define international marketing and understand the nature of international involvement
- To understand the importance of international marketing intelligence
- To recognise the impact of environmental forces on international marketing efforts
- To become aware of regional trade alliances and markets
- To look at alternative market entry strategies for becoming involved in international marketing activities

Six months after PepsiCo Food International (PFI), Frito-Lay's overseas snack division, introduced Cheetos in China, the brand was so popular that the company could barely keep up with demand. How did PFI convince so many Chinese—who eat almost no snack foods—to indulge in the crunchy, salty morsels? Before marketing its product, PFI conducted extensive research and development, testing 100 brand names and 600 flavours. In China, as in all of its global markets, Frito-Lay's key to success is understanding each market and adapting products to local tastes. This strategy has made the company the world's largest snack food enterprise outside of the United States, owning 35 per cent of the global snack market, and offering products in 34 countries from the Netherlands to Korea to Brazil.

The strategy has been shaped by bitter experience. When the company introduced Cheetos to the United Kingdom without doing consumer research, the product failed. In Spain, adults loved PFI's "Matutano" snacks, which they bought in grocery stores and restaurants. Children, however, could not get Matutanos in the outdoor kiosks where they typically buy snacks and could not afford to buy them elsewhere. To increase acceptance among children, the company packaged the snacks in single-serving bags, expanded distribution to smaller outlets and increased outdoor advertising.

Mistakes taught Frito-Lay's marketers to become experts in distinctive local tastes and behaviours.

Today, the company makes essential changes in seasonings, textures, product positioning and promotion based on brand managers' information about global markets and consumer snacking habits.

Frito-Lay now knows that British snackers favour salted potato crisps, Germans prefer paprika flavouring and Koreans like cuttlefish peanut snacks. The company gave the British a thinner, lighter textured Dorito, more like the potato crisps they love. A £5.5 million ad campaign and sampling that reached 7 million consumers boosted British sales of Doritos to over £60 million in the first year. In China, the company took the cheese out of Cheetos because dairy products are not a staple in Chinese diets. Instead, Chinese snackers can munch on popcorn flavoured Savory American Creams or teriyaki tasting Zesty Japanese Steak. The company supported the product launch with an aggressive marketing campaign comprising television ads, massive product sampling and consumer promotions featuring spokescartoon Chester Cheetah, or Qi Duo Bao as he is known in China. Six months after Chinese Cheetos rolled onto the market, stores were selling out.

Building on global successes like these, the snack food giant plans to introduce Cheetos, Doritos and other snacks in eastern Europe, India and the Middle East.

SOURCES: Karen Benezra, "Fritos 'round the world", *Brandweek*, 27 March 1995, pp. 32, 35; Lara Mills, "Hostess reformulates with famous faces", *Marketing Magazine*, 6 March 1995, p. 4; and Anita Sharp, "Pepsico's net jumped 16% in 4th quarter", *Wall Street Journal*, 8 February 1995, p. A4. *Advertisement*: Courtesy of Pepsi Co. Food International.

International marketing generally refers to marketing activities performed across national boundaries.[1] Companies such as PepsiCo, which operate globally, must manage all aspects of their operations with considerable care. In many cases, serving foreign target markets requires significant adjustments to marketing strategies. In this example Frito-Lay, the snack division of PepsiCo, has needed to modify certain aspects of its snack brands to cater for local differences in tastes and buying behaviour.

This chapter looks closely at the unique features of international marketing. It begins by examining companies' level of commitment to and degree of involvement in international marketing and then considers the importance of international marketing intelligence when a company is moving beyond its domestic market. Next the chapter focuses on the need to understand various environmental forces in international markets and discusses several regional trade alliances and markets. A review of the latest developments in the European Union is an important feature of this section. The concluding section describes alternative market entry strategies for becoming involved in international marketing.

Involvement in International Marketing

Before international marketing could achieve its current importance, enterprises with the necessary resources had to develop an interest in expanding their businesses beyond national boundaries. Once interested, marketers engage in international marketing activities at several levels of involvement. Regardless of the level of involvement, however, they must decide on the degree to which it is possible to standardise their marketing strategies for different markets.

Levels of International Involvement

Domestic marketing Marketing activities directed exclusively in a business's home market

Export marketing Marketing activities through which a business takes advantage of opportunities outside its home market but continues production in the home country

International marketing Marketing activities in which a business reduces reliance on intermediaries and establishes direct involvement in the countries in which trade takes place

Multinational marketing Adaptation of some of a company's marketing activities to appeal to local culture and differences in taste

Multinational companies Companies that behave in their foreign markets as if they were local companies

Global marketing A total commitment to international marketing, in which a company applies its assets, experience and products to develop and maintain marketing strategies on a global scale

The level of involvement in international marketing covers a wide spectrum, as shown in Figure 3.1. A business that undertakes marketing activities exclusively in its home market is involved in **domestic marketing.** Such organisations may have deliberately chosen to restrict their business to domestic customers or may simply not have considered the possibility of international marketing. **Export marketing** takes place when a business takes advantage of opportunities outside its home market. In some cases exporting activity begins almost by accident. For example, the products of a small medical supplies manufacturer might occasionally be purchased by hospitals or clinics in nearby countries; its products might also be purchased by other countries through an export agent. Whatever the reasons behind the initial export activity, production in the home country will be used to supply these new markets; for most businesses the domestic market will remain the key area of business. Companies that go beyond simple exporting become involved in **international marketing,** reducing their reliance on intermediaries and establishing direct links in the countries in which trade takes place. At this stage a foreign subsidiary may be set up, and products may be sourced away from the domestic market.

Multinational marketing takes marketing for non-domestic markets one step further by adapting some of the company's marketing activities, such as marketing communications, to appeal to local culture and differences in tastes. **Multinational companies** are those that behave in their foreign markets as if they were local companies. Full scale **global marketing** requires total commitment to international marketing and involves applying the organisation's assets, experience and products to develop and maintain marketing strategies on a global scale. Marketing Insight 3.1 explains the global marketing approach of ABB Asea Brown Boveri.

Understanding Global Marketing

Global marketing is the most extreme case of international involvement, representing the full integration of international marketing into strategic planning.[2] The underlying principle is to identify products or services for which similarities across many markets allow a single global strategy to be pursued. This approach is attractive to managers because one marketing strategy can be used across a number of markets; a business can spread the costs of its research and development, technology and distribution, taking advantage of economies of scale in the process.

Despite the fact that global marketing strives for a single over-arching global strategy,[3] it is a mistake to assume that local differences can be ignored. During the 1980s marketers sought to globalise the marketing mix as much as possible by employing standardised products, promotion campaigns, prices and distribution channels for all markets. The potential economic and competitive pay-offs for such an approach were certainly great. More recently marketers have realised that, while it may be feasible to standardise a company's offerings in different

Domestic marketing	Export marketing	International marketing	Multinational marketing	Global marketing
Home market involvement only.	This is an attempt to create sales without significant changes in the company's products and overall operations. An active effort to find foreign markets for existing products is most typical.	Greater commitment to international markets. International marketing activities are seen as part of overall planning. Direct investment in non-domestic markets is likely and products may also be sourced away from the home market.	Further steps are taken to adapt to local tastes. Modifications may be made to aspects of the marketing mix to make them more appealing to local markets.	Total commitment to international marketing which involves applying the organisation's assets, experience and products to develop and maintain marketing strategies on a global scale. Although a single global marketing strategy is required, some adaptation to local needs is still needed.

Domestic orientation ←――――――――――――――――――――――――→ **Global orientation**

Figure 3.1 Levels of involvement in international marketing

markets, a degree of adaptation to local differences is also required. While brand name, product characteristics, packaging and labelling may be relatively straightforward to standardise, media allocation, retail outlets and price may be more difficult. For example, a supplier of animal feeds may decide to send promotional material about a new product range to farmers and producers in a variety of different markets. Although the business may have decided upon a suitable platform for the promotion, help may be needed from each country's marketing team to devise an appropriate mailing list.

Some companies have moved from customising or standardising products for a particular region of the world to offering globally standardised products that are advanced, functional, reliable and low in price.[4] Reebok, for example, provides a standardised product worldwide. Examples of globalised products are electrical equipment, videos, films, soft drinks, rock music, cosmetics and toothpaste. Sony televisions, Levi jeans and UK confectionery brands seem to make annual gains in the world market. Even McDonald's restaurants seem to be widely accepted in markets throughout the world. Yet even here there is some adaptation to local tastes, with small variations in menus in certain countries. For example, in Portugal there is more emphasis on ice creams than in the UK. Some products that are regarded by many as globally standard, such as Coca-Cola (see Figure 3.2), are in fact adapted for certain markets.

Debate about the feasibility of globalised marketing strategies has continued for nearly 40 years. Questions about standardised advertising have been a primary concern. The debate about customisation versus globalisation will doubtless

The Logic of Global Business: An Interview with ABB's Percy Barnevik

Percy Barnevik, president and CEO of ABB Asea Brown Boveri, is a corporate pioneer. He is moving more aggressively than any CEO in Europe, perhaps in the world, to build the new model of competitive enterprise—an organisation that combines global scale and world-class technology with deep roots in local markets. He is working to give substance to the endlessly invoked corporate mantra, "Think global, act local".

Headquartered in Zurich, ABB is a young company forged through the merger of two venerable European companies. Asea, created in 1890, has been a flagship of Swedish industry for a century. Brown Boveri, which took shape in 1891, holds a comparable industrial status in Switzerland. In August 1987, Barnevik altered the course of both companies when he announced that Asea, where he was managing director, would merge with Brown Boveri to create a potent new force in the European market for electrical systems and equipment.

The creation of ABB became a metaphor for the changing economic map of Europe. Barnevik initiated a wrenching process of consolidation and rationalisation—lay offs, plant closings, product exchanges between countries—that observers agreed will one day come to European industries from steel to telecommunications to cars. And soon more than a metaphor, Barnevik's bold moves triggered a wholesale restructuring of the Continent's electrical power industry.

In this interview, Percy Barnevik, 49, offers a detailed guide to the theory and practice of building a "multidomestic" enterprise.

The interview was conducted at ABB's Zurich headquarters by *Harvard Business Review* associate editor William Taylor.

HBR: *Companies everywhere are trying to become global, and everyone agrees that ABB is more global than most companies. What does that mean?*

Percy Barnevik: ABB is a company with no geographic centre, no national axe to grind. We are a federation of national companies with a global coordination centre. Are we a Swiss company? Our headquarters is in Zurich, but only 100 professionals work at headquarters and we will not increase that number. Are we a Swedish company? I'm the CEO, and I was born and educated in Sweden. But our headquarters is not in Sweden, and only two of the eight members of our board of directors are Swedes. Perhaps we are an American company. We report our financial results in US dollars, and English is ABB's official language. We conduct all high level meetings in English.

My point is that ABB is none of those things—and all of those things. We are not homeless. We are a company with many homes.

HBR: *Are all businesses becoming global?*

No, and this is a big source of misunderstanding. We are in the process of building this federation of national companies, a multidomestic organisation, as I prefer to call it. That does not mean all of our businesses are global. We do a very good business in electrical installation and service in many countries. That business is superlocal. The geographic scope of our installation business in, say, Stuttgart does not extend beyond a ten-mile radius of downtown Stuttgart.

We also have businesses that are superglobal. There are not more than 15 combined-cycle power plants or more than three or four high voltage DC stations sold in any one year around the world. Our competitors fight for nearly every contract—they battle us on technology, price, financing—and national borders are virtually meaningless. Every project requires our best people and best technology from around the world.

The vast majority of our businesses—and of most businesses—fall somewhere between the superlocal and the superglobal. These are the businesses in which building a multidomestic organisation offers powerful advantages. You want to be able to optimise a business globally—to specialise in the production of components, to drive economies of scale as far as you can, to rotate managers and technologists around the world to share expertise and solve problems. But you also want to have deep local roots everywhere you operate—building products in the countries where you sell them, recruiting the best local talent from the universities, working with the local government to increase exports. If you build such an organisation, you create a business advantage that's damn difficult to copy.

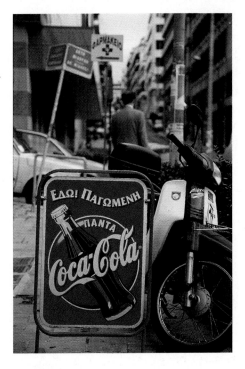

Figure 3.2 Example of globalisation. Although Coca-Cola is available globally, in some markets the flavour and packaging are adapted to local tastes. SOURCE: Jeff Greenberg/Photo Edit.

continue, although neither is implemented in its pure form.[5] In the end, the feasibility of globalisation is determined by the degree of similarity among the various environmental and market conditions. For some products—such as training shoes—a global marketing strategy, including advertising, seems to work well, while for other products—such as beer—strategies must make considerable concessions to accommodate local, regional and national differences.[6] Some marketers now believe that some of the best global opportunities are presented by "global market segments".

International Marketing Intelligence

Despite the ongoing debate over globalisation, most businesses perceive international markets as differing in some ways from domestic markets. Analyses of international markets and possible marketing efforts can be based on many dimensions. Table 3.1 lists the types of information that international marketers need. (Chapter 6 contains a detailed discussion of marketing research and data collection.)[7]

Gathering secondary data (see Table 3.2) should be the first step in analysing a foreign market. Sources of information include government publications, financial services firms, international organisations such as the United Nations, foreign governments and international trade organisations. UK companies seeking to market their products in Russia, for example, can obtain information about Russian markets and regulations from the Department of Trade and Industry (DTI), the Russian Chamber of Commerce and Industry, the Russian trade organisation Amtorg and numerous other organisations. Marketers must, however, be vigilant in assuring the reliability, validity and comparability of data, as information from some sources may be misleading.

Preliminary Screening	Analysis of Industry Market Potential	Analysis of Company Sales Potential
Demographic/Physical Environment	**Market Access**	**Sales Volume Forecasting**
Population size, growth, density Urban and rural distribution Climate and weather variations Shipping distance Product significant demographics Physical distribution and communications network Natural resources	Limitations on trade: tariff levels, quotas Documentation and import regulations Local standards, practices, other non-tariff barriers Patents and trademarks Preferential treaties Legal considerations: investment, taxation, repatriation, employment, code of laws	Size and concentration of customer segments Projected consumption statistics Competitive pressures Expectations of local distributors/agents
Political Environment		**Landed Cost**
System of government Political stability and continuity Ideological orientation Government in business Government in communications Attitudes towards foreign business (trade restrictions, tariffs, non-tariff barriers, bi-lateral trade agreements) National economic and developmental priorities	**Product Potential** Customer needs and desires Local production, imports, consumption Exposure to and acceptance of product Availability of linking products Industry-specific key indicators of demand Attitudes towards products of foreign origin Competitive offerings Availability of intermediaries	Costing method for exports Domestic distribution costs International freight insurance Cost of product modification **Cost of Internal Distribution** Tariffs and duties Value added tax Local packaging and assembly Margins/commission allowed for the trade Local distribution and inventory costs Promotional expenditures
Economic Environment	Regional and local transport facilities Availability of manpower Conditions for local manufacture	**Other Determinants of Profitability**
Overall level of development Economic growth: GNP, industrial sector Role of foreign trade in economy Currency, inflation rate, availability, controls, stability of exchange rate Balance of payments Per capita income and distribution Disposable income and expenditure patterns		Going price levels Competitive strengths and weaknesses Credit practices Current and projected exchange rates
Social/Cultural Environment		
Literacy rate, educational level Existence of middle class Similarities and differences in relation to home market Language and other cultural considerations		

SOURCE: Adapted from S. Tamer Cavusgil, "Guidelines for export market research", *Business Horizons*, November–December 1985, pp. 30–31. Used by permission.

Table 3.1 Information needed for international marketing analyses

Type of Information	Sources	Other Sources
Foreign market information	Foreign economic trends Overseas business reports International economic indicators Foreign governments (e.g. US Department of Commerce) DTI EU (Eurostat, etc.)	*Financial Times* surveys *Business International* Dun & Bradstreet International Chase World Information Corp. *International Trade Reporter* Accounting and stock market firms Foreign trade organisations Economist Intelligence Unit
Export marketing research	Country market sectoral surveys Global market surveys International marketing research	Marketing research firms Advertising agencies Publishing companies Trade associations
International statistics	Export statistics profile Customer service statistics	Predicasts Foreign brokerage houses United Nations International Monetary Fund OECD, EU, GATT
Overseas representatives	Customised export mailing list World trader data reports Agent/distributor service	Banks International chambers of commerce Consulting firms Direct telephone contact
Sales leads	Trade opportunities programme Strategic and industrial product sales group Major export projects programme Export information reference room	Banks International chambers of commerce Consulting firms Development agencies
Reference data on foreign markets	World trader data reports	Banks International chambers of commerce Consulting firms Development agencies Corporate information databases

SOURCES: S. Tamer Cavusgil, "Guidelines for export market research", *Business Horizons*, November–December 1985, p. 32; and Leonard M. Fuld, "How to gather foreign intelligence without leaving home", *Market News*, 4 January 1988, pp. 24, 47.

Table 3.2 Sources of secondary information for international marketing

In some circumstances marketers may need primary data to understand consumers' buying behaviour in the country under investigation. (Buying behaviour is discussed in detail in Chapters 4 and 5.) Marketers may have to adjust their techniques of collecting primary data for foreign markets. Attitudes towards privacy, unwillingness to be interviewed, language differences and low literacy rates can be serious research obstacles. In a bi-cultural country such as Canada, a uniform national questionnaire cannot be used because of the cultural and language differences. In China, restrictions on free speech mean that many businesses are reluctant to respond to questionnaires.

Primary research should uncover significant cultural characteristics before a product is launched so that the marketing strategy is appropriate for the target market. It may be necessary to investigate basic patterns of social behaviour, values and attitudes to plan a final marketing strategy. Overall, the cost of obtaining such information may be higher than the cost of domestic research; the reasons include the large number of foreign markets to be investigated, the distance between the marketer and the foreign market, unfamiliar cultural and marketing practices, language differences and the scarcity or unreliability of published statistics.[8]

After analysing secondary and primary data, marketers should plan a marketing strategy. A full assessment of the market situation will enable decisions to be made about whether to withdraw from the foreign market, to continue to expand operations or to consider additional foreign markets.

Environmental Forces in International Markets

A detailed analysis of the environment is essential for any business considering entry into a foreign market. If a marketing strategy is to be effective across national borders, the complexities of all the environments involved must be understood. This section examines how the cultural, social, economic, political and legal, and technological forces of the marketing environment in different countries vary.

Cultural Forces
Culture can be defined as the concepts, values and tangible items (such as tools, buildings and foods) that make up a particular society. Culture is passed on from one generation to another and is a kind of blueprint for acceptable behaviour in a particular society. When products are introduced into one nation from another, acceptance is far more likely if there are similarities between the two cultures.

The connotations associated with body motions, greetings, colours, numbers, and shapes, sizes and symbols vary considerably across cultures. For example, as shown in Table 3.3, the use of colour has different connotations in different cultures. In many parts of Europe black has negative overtones, whereas in the Middle East it has positive connotations. Marketing Insight 3.2 presents further examples of colour differences across cultures. Yet even here it is important to watch for more subtle cultural differences. For example, Table 3.3 treats the whole of Europe as if it were one nation, although in practice it is very difficult to generalise for the region as a whole. This is important because multinational marketers know that cultural differences have implications for product development, personal selling, advertising, packaging and pricing. For example, the illustration of feet is regarded as despicable in Thailand. An international marketer must also know a country's customs regarding male-female social interaction. In Italy it is unacceptable for a salesman to call on a woman if her husband is not at home.

A Cross-Cultural Comparison of Colour and International Branding

In a recent paper, Anthony Grimes and Isobel Doole explored the relationship between colour and international branding. Their cross-cultural comparison, which focused on consumers in the UK and Taiwan, used a series of semi-structured focus groups to examine perceptions of colour and international branding. The findings of their research appear to suggest that associations of colour are surprisingly similar across national boundaries and apparently support the notion that standardisation of brand colours across international markets may be possible. However, the research also highlights that colour is only one aspect of the make-up of an international brand and, as such, may have a relatively small role to play in developing brand image. This is clearly demonstrated by the fact that while perceptions of colour across cultures may fluctuate relatively little, impressions of international brands may vary widely.

Colour association in the UK and Taiwan

Colour	UK Associations	Taiwan Associations
Green	Inexpensive, reliable, light and good-tasting Old, quiet, traditional, trustworthy and safe Life, calm, tenderness, health and happiness Environment, natural, pure and fresh Ireland, and Italy to some extent	Inexpensive, reliable, light and good-tasting Quiet, calm, male and old Safe, trustworthy, unadventurous and stable Environment, life, tender, pure, fresh, natural Ireland, and to some extent UK
Red	Expensive, premium, high quality and good-tasting Young, warm, fun, loud, playful and happy Dangerous, adventurous, luxurious and exciting Life, love, passion, power and aggression China, and the US to some extent	High quality, expensive and good-tasting Warm, female, loud, playful and adventurous Love, passion, danger and aggression Life, excitement and happiness US, and to some extent Italy
Blue	Heavy, reliable, high quality and expensive Male, mature, quiet, subdued, calm and thoughtful Serious, trustworthy, dependable, dignified and sad US and UK to a limited extent	Heavy, reliable, high quality and expensive Male, old, quiet, serious Calm, dignified, trustworthy Sadness, depression and to some extent power
Black	Expensive, high quality, high tech and premium products Old, heavy and reliable objects Male, old, quiet and serious Mysterious, luxurious, sophisticated and dangerous Death, dignity, power and aggression	High quality, high tech, premium and expensive Old, male, quiet and heavy Mysterious, sophisticated and serious Death, sadness, depression, power, fear and aggression Strongly associated with China
Yellow	High quality, expensive, reliable, light and good-tasting Pert, fresh and playful Luxury, sophistication and to some extent safety Life, happiness, tenderness and warmth	New, expensive, light and good-tasting Young, warm, loud, playful and adventurous Life, love, happiness and power Strongly associated with China
Purple	Expensive, luxurious and good-tasting Warm, and to some extent female Sophisticated and mysterious Death, dignity, passion and power France, and to some extent Japan	High quality, premium and expensive Warm, female, old and quiet Love, passion, luxury, sophisticated and mystery Serious, sadness, dignity, power and aggression France, and to some extent Japan

Perceptions of key brands in the UK and Taiwan

Brand	UK	Taiwan
Pepsi	Male, muscular, young, sexy and energetic Wild, fun and sporty Associated with beach settings Not very healthy—sugar and caffeine Challenger to Coca-Cola and the status quo	Male, muscular, young, energetic, sporty and attractive Fun, sexy, loud, wild and a little crazy Associated with the beach, the sun and the Spice Girls Good tasting and refreshing Intensely competitive with regard to Coca-Cola
Marlboro	Original brand is masculine, American and red Cool, sexy, wild, adventurous and strong Rough but with a lot of style Associated with cowboys, the desert and music Unhealthy and anti-social—cancer, smoke and smells Marlboro Lights are less damaging and more popular Associated with pubs, music, youth and the colour gold	Masculine, American and red Cool, strong, young, adventurous and exciting Powerful and stylish Associated with cowboys, the desert and music
Kodak	Masculine, mature, intelligent, creative and well-respected Warm, friendly and colourful High quality, high technology and very professional Associated with happy times, sunshine, happiness, fun, colourfulness and the colour yellow Safe, reliable, trustworthy, affordable and popular	Masculine, intelligent, innovative and creative High quality, expensive and professional Modern, colourful and hugely popular Associated with high technology
Cadbury's	Feminine, smooth, silky, sexy and sultry Beautiful, luxurious, stylish and expensive High in quality, reliability and class Associated with velvet, satin and silk Old, friendly, aristocratic and eccentric Very young, sweet and cute	Masculine, old, friendly, warm, loving but poor brand Feminine, young, sweet, sensual and cute Overall: low quality, cheap, no class and largely unpopular A sticky, sickly, lazy brand, predominantly for children
BP	Masculine, big, old, greedy, rich, powerful and British Grey, faceless, boring, uncaring, mysterious, even sinister and arrogant to some extent Associated with intelligence, power, wealth, technology, heavy production and pollution	Masculine, rich, powerful, distinguished and serious High in class and style, intelligent and authoritative—a leader
Guinness	Masculine, modern, young, cool, streetwise, sociable, attractive, quiet, secretive and mysterious Old, traditional, simple and genuine Associated with goodness, honesty and hard work Overall: smooth, creamy, bitter, heavy and good quality	Male, powerful, intelligent, attractive and mysterious Calm, quiet and distant on the surface, but crazy inside Independent, unique, stylish and dangerous

TABLE AND TEXT SOURCE: Reprinted with Permission from the *Journal of Marketing Management*, Vol. 15, No. 6, pp. 449–462. Copyright © Westburn Publishers Ltd., 1995.

Country/Region	Body Motions	Greetings	Colours	Numbers	Shapes, Sizes, Symbols
Japan	Pointing to one's own chest with a forefinger indicates one wants a bath. A forefinger to the nose indicates "me".	Bowing is the traditional form of greeting.	Positive colours are in muted shades. Combinations of black, dark grey, and white have negative overtones.	Positive numbers are 1, 3, 5, 8. Negative numbers are 4, 9.	Pine, bamboo or plum patterns are positive. Cultural shapes such as Buddha shaped jars should be avoided.
India	Kissing is considered offensive and is not usually seen on television, in films or in public places.	The palms of the hands touch and the head is nodded for greeting. It is considered rude to touch or shake hands with a woman.	Positive colours are bold such as green, red, yellow or orange. Negative colours are black and white if they appear in relation to weddings.	To create brand awareness, numbers are often used as a brand name.	Animals such as parrots, elephants, tigers or cheetahs are often used as brand names or on packaging. Sexually explicit symbols are avoided.
Europe	When counting on one's fingers, the number 1 is often indicated by thumb, 2 by thumb and forefinger.	It is acceptable to send flowers in thanks for a dinner invitation, but not roses (for sweethearts) or chrysanthemums (for funerals).	Generally, white and blue are considered positive. Black often has negative overtones.	The numbers 3 or 7 are usually positive; 13 is a negative number.	Circles are symbols of perfection. Hearts are considered favourably at Christmas time.
Latin America	General arm gestures are used for emphasis.	The traditional greeting is a hearty embrace and slap on the back.	Popular colours are generally bright or bold yellow, red, blue or green.	Generally, 7 is a positive number. Negative numbers are 13, 14.	Respect religious symbols. Avoid national symbols such as flag colours.
Middle East	The raised eyebrow facial expression indicates "yes".	The word "no" must be mentioned three times before it is accepted.	Positive colours are brown, black, dark blues and reds. Pink, violets and yellows are not favoured.	Positive numbers are 3, 5, 7, 9; 13, 15 are negative.	Round or square shapes are acceptable. Symbols of six-pointed star, raised thumb or Koranic sayings are avoided.

Sources: James C. Simmons, "A matter of interpretation", *American Way*, April 1983, pp. 106–111; "Adapting export packaging to cultural differences", *Business America*, 3 December 1979, pp. 3–7.

Table 3.3 Sampling of cultural variations

It is also important for marketers to tune into changes in culture. For example, in Japan, the government has expressed concern about its citizens' emphasis on work and has declared that people should start enjoying life. With an official reduction of the working week to forty hours, many new leisure industry opportunities are being created. In one year alone, two hundred companies applied for permits to develop new theme parks. Meanwhile, to help people deal with these new leisure opportunities, the National Recreation Association is offering a one year course on how to enjoy life.[9]

Product adoption and use are also influenced by consumers' perceptions of other countries.[10] When consumers are generally unfamiliar with products from another country, their perceptions of the country itself affect their attitude towards and adoption of the products. If a country has a reputation for producing quality products, marketers will want to make the country of origin well known. For example, a generally positive image of western computer technology has fueled sales of Compaq and IBM personal computers and Microsoft software in Japan.[11]

Culture may also affect marketing negotiations and decision-making behaviour of marketers, industrial buyers and other executives. Research has shown that when marketers use a problem solving approach—that is, gain information about a particular client's needs and tailor products or services to meet those needs—it leads to increased customer satisfaction in marketing negotiations in France, Germany, the United Kingdom and the United States. Furthermore, the role and status of the seller are particularly important in both the UK and France.[12] However, the attractiveness of the salesperson and his or her similarity to the customer increase the levels of satisfaction only for Americans.

Social Forces   Marketing activities are primarily social in purpose; therefore, they are structured by the institutions of family, religion, education, health and recreation (see Figure 3.3). For example, in the UK, where listening to music on hi-fi systems is a common form of relaxation, Japanese products have a large target market. In all countries, these social institutions can be identified. By finding major deviations in institutions among countries, marketers can gain insights into the adaptation of a marketing strategy. Although American football is a popular sport in the United States and a major opportunity for many television advertisers, soccer is the most popular television sport in Europe. Yet football hooliganism caused major advertisers in the United Kingdom to have second thoughts about supporting such events with vast sums spent on advertising.[13] The role of children in the family and a society's overall view of children also influence marketing activities. For example, in the Netherlands, children are banned from appearing in advertisements for sweets, and confectionery manufacturers are required to place a little toothbrush symbol at the end of each confectionery advertisement.[14]

Economic Forces   Economic differences dictate many of the adjustments that must be made in marketing abroad. The most prominent adjustments are caused by differences is standards of living, availability of credit, discretionary buying power, income distribution, national resources and conditions that affect transport. Exchange rate fluctuations and differences in interest rates can also have a major impact. Recently, the strength of the UK's currency and high interest rates have made it difficult for businesses to make money exporting their goods and services.

Gross domestic product (GDP) The total value of all goods and services produced by a country's income

Gross domestic product (GDP) is the total value of all goods and services produced by a country's income. A comparison of GDP for Europe, the US and Japan shows that the United States has the largest gross domestic product in the world. By dividing this figure by the size of the population, an understanding of

So small, it will change your perspective.

Forget those big mobile phones of the past. The Ericsson GF788 is
so small it hides in your hand. Forget poor sound quality, here is a phone that
lets you sound like you. Forget about having to keep your calls short,
with this phone you can talk for hours. The Ericsson GF788 is easy to use,
even though it is packed with features. And it comes in four discreet colours.
It will change the way you look at mobile phones.

Figure 3.3 The societal aspects of international marketing. Widespread acceptance of relaxing to music enables Philips to produce a range of advertisements with relevance in many markets. SOURCE: Courtesy Ericsson Mobile Communications/HCYR.

the standard of living can be achieved. In this way it is possible to gain insight into the level of discretionary income or buying power of individual consumers. Knowledge about aggregate GDP, credit and the distribution of income provides general insights into market potential.

Opportunities for international marketers are certainly not limited to countries with the highest incomes. Indeed, as recent events in the Asia Pacific region have shown, high income is no guarantee of an attractive market. Some countries are progressing faster than they were even a few years ago; and these countries—especially in eastern Europe, Latin America, Africa and the Middle East—have great market potential for specific products. However, marketers must first understand the political and legal environment before they can convert buying power into actual demand for specific products.

Political and Legal Forces

A country's political system, national laws, regulatory bodies, national pressure groups and courts all have great impact on global marketing. A government's policies towards public and private enterprise, consumers and foreign companies influence marketing across national boundaries. The types of measures a government can take to govern cross-border trade include the use of tariffs, quotas and non-tariff barriers. For example, the Japanese have established many barriers to imports into their country. Even though they are reducing the tariffs on certain items, many non-tariff barriers still make it difficult for other companies to export their products to Japan.[15] **Tariffs** are taxes that affect the movement of goods across economic or political boundaries and can affect imports, exports or goods in transit.[16] These taxes provide government with revenue and can give domestic companies an important advantage. For example, import tariffs in the form of import duties effectively increase the price of imported products, giving local companies an automatic advantage. **Quotas** involve physical restrictions on the amount of goods that can be imported into a particular country or region. The imposition of quotas is not always in the best interest of consumers, as choice is limited and allocations tend to be used up on imports of goods carrying the greatest profit margin. **Non-tariff barriers** are much more difficult to define; they include a wide range of rules, regulations and taxes that have an impact upon trade. As shown in Table 3.4, these barriers can include anything from port and border taxes to trademark and health and safety regulations. For example, just a few years ago, companies exporting electronic equipment to Japan had to wait for the Japanese government to inspect each item. A government's attitude towards co-operation with importers has a direct impact on the economic feasibility of their exporting to that country. As barriers to trade decline, opportunities are presented. Attempts to bring trade barriers down and improve the flow of goods between countries have come to the forefront in recent decades. The rules and frameworks for world trade are partly determined by the General Agreement on Tariffs and Trade (GATT). From a marketing standpoint, principles such as those defended by GATT increase competition.

Differences in political and government ethical standards are enormous. The use of pay-offs and bribes is deeply entrenched in many governments, while in others such involvement is prohibited. European companies that do not engage in such practices may have a hard time competing with foreign businesses that do. Some businesses that refuse to make pay-offs are forced to hire local consultants, public relations firms or advertising agencies—resulting in indirect pay-offs. The ultimate decision about whether to give small tips or gifts where they are customary must be based on a company's code of ethics.

Technological Forces

Much of the marketing technology used in Europe and other industrialised regions of the world may be inappropriate for developing countries. For example, promoting products via the Internet will be difficult in countries where computer ownership is low. Nonetheless, many countries—particularly China, South Korea, Mexico and the countries of the former Soviet Union—want to engage in international trade, often through partnerships with American, European and Japanese businesses, so that they can gain valuable industrial and

Tariffs Taxes that affect the movement of goods across economic or political boundaries and can also affect imports, exports or goods in transit

Quotas Physical restrictions on the amount of goods that can be imported into a particular country or region

Non-tariff barriers A wide range of rules, regulations and taxes that have an impact upon trade

Formal Trade Restrictions

A. Non-Tariff Import Restrictions (Price Related Measures)

Surcharges at border
Port and statistical taxes
Non-discriminatory excise taxes and registration charges
Discriminatory excise taxes, government insurance requirements
Non-discriminatory turnover taxes
Discriminatory turnover taxes
Import deposit
Variable levies
Consular fees
Stamp taxes
Various special taxes and surcharges

B. Quantitative Restrictions and Similar Specific Trade Limitations (Quantity Related Measures)

Licensing regulations
Ceilings and quotas
Embargoes
Export restrictions and prohibitions
Foreign exchange and other monetary or financial controls
Government price setting and surveillance
Purchase and performance requirements
Restrictive business conditions
Discriminatory bi-lateral arrangements
Discriminatory regulations regarding countries of origin
International cartels
Orderly marketing agreements
Various related regulations

C. Discriminatory Freight Rates (Flag Protectionism)

Administrative Trade Restrictions

D. State Participation in Trade

Subsidies and other government support
Government trade, government monopolies, and granting of concessions or licences
Laws and ordinances discouraging imports
Problems relating to general government policy
Government procurement
Tax relief, granting of credit and guarantees
Boycott

E. Technical Norms, Standards, and Consumer Protection Regulations

Health and safety regulations
Pharmaceutical control regulations
Product design regulations
Industrial standards
Size and weight regulations
Packing and labelling regulations
Package marking regulations
Regulations pertaining to use
Regulations for the protection of intellectual property
Trademark regulations

F. Customs Processing and Other Administrative Regulations

Anti-dumping policy
Customs calculation bases
Formalities required by consular officials
Certification regulations
Administrative obstacles
Merchandise classification
Regulations regarding sample shipment, return shipments and re-exports
Countervailing duties and taxes
Appeal law
Emergency law

SOURCE: Beatrice Bondy, *Protectionism: Challenge of the Eighties* (Zurich: Union Bank of Switzerland Economic Research Department, 1983), p. 19. Reprinted by permission.

Table 3.4   Non-tariff trade barriers

agricultural technology. However, there may be export restrictions which limit trade in certain goods. For example, the export of defence equipment is tightly controlled by many European governments.

Regional Trade Alliances and Markets

While some businesses are beginning to view the world as one huge marketplace, opportunities for companies are affected by a range of regional trade alliances. This section examines several regional trade alliances and changing markets, including the European Union, the Pacific Rim markets, changing conditions in central and eastern Europe, and the North American Free Trade Agreement.

European Union

European Union (EU) One of three major market groups in western Europe, the EU has 15 members: Austria, Belgium, Denmark, Finland, France, Germany, Greece, Ireland, Italy, Luxembourg, the Netherlands, Portugal, Spain, Sweden and the UK

Maastricht Treaty The treaty, signed in 1992, that established the European Union

The **European Union** (EU) is one of three major market groups in western Europe.[17] Formed by the Treaty of European Union, the EU has its origins in the European Common Market, set up in 1958, which later became known as the European Community (EC). Following the signing of the **Maastricht Treaty** in 1992 and the creation of the single European market in 1993, the group became known as the European Union. Today the EU has 15 members: Austria, Belgium, Denmark, Finland, France, Germany, Greece, Ireland, Italy, Luxembourg, the Netherlands, Portugal, Spain, Sweden, United Kingdom. The objectives of the Union are set out in the following extract from Article B of the Treaty on European Union.[18]

—to promote economic and social progress which is balanced and sustainable, in particular through the creation of an area without internal frontiers, through the strengthening of economic and social cohesion and through the establishment of economic and monetary union, ultimately including a single currency in accordance with the provisions of this Treaty;

—to assert its identity on the international scene, in particular through the implementation of a common foreign and security policy including the eventual framing of a common defence policy, which might in time lead to a common defence;

—to strengthen the protection of the rights and interests of the nationals of its Member States through the introduction of a citizenship of the Union;

—to develop close co-operation on justice and home affairs.

On 1 January 1999 the European Union moved closer to economic and monetary union with the launch of the euro, the unit of European currency.[19] Eleven of the 15 European Union members became committed to the new currency. Only Sweden, Denmark and Britain postponed participation in the single currency, while Greece failed to meet the economic criteria. Although the issue of euro notes and coins will be delayed until 2002, many businesses will now need to set prices in euros, and customers will be able to pay in the currency using cheques or credit cards.

To coincide with the euro launch, the European Commission proposed fixed conversion rates between the euro and the currencies of the participating countries. The rates are:

1 euro	=	40.3399	Belgian francs
	=	1.95583	German marks
	=	166.386	Spanish pesetas
	=	6.55957	French francs
	=	0.787564	Irish punts
	=	1936.27	Italian lire
	=	40.3399	Luxembourg francs

1 euro	=	2.20371	Dutch guilders
	=	13.7603	Austrian schillings
	=	200.482	Portuguese escudas
	=	5.94573	Finnish markka

The price of British sterling will continue to fluctuate against the euro, but is currently around 70 British pence.[20]

European Free Trade Association (EFTA) Set up in 1960 to encourage free trade between member countries

The **European Free Trade Association (EFTA)** was set up in 1960 with the intention of encouraging free trade between member countries. In 1994, Austria, Finland and Sweden, formerly members of EFTA, joined the EU, bringing the number of member states to 15 (see Figure 3.4 for EU and EFTA membership as at the end of 1996). EFTA has been successful in meeting its objectives to eliminate customs duties and other restrictions on the trade of industrial products between members. However, in the period preceding the completion of the single European market, the need to

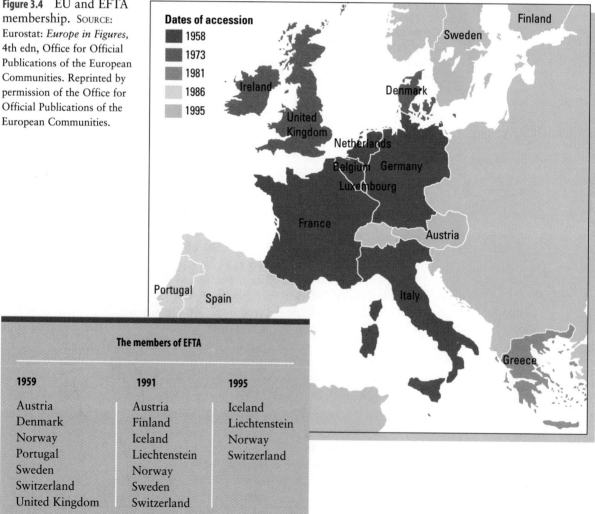

Figure 3.4   EU and EFTA membership. SOURCE: Eurostat: *Europe in Figures,* 4th edn, Office for Official Publications of the European Communities. Reprinted by permission of the Office for Official Publications of the European Communities.

Dates of accession
- 1958
- 1973
- 1981
- 1986
- 1995

The members of EFTA

1959	1991	1995
Austria	Austria	Iceland
Denmark	Finland	Liechtenstein
Norway	Iceland	Norway
Portugal	Liechtenstein	Switzerland
Sweden	Norway	
Switzerland	Sweden	
United Kingdom	Switzerland	

European Economic Area (EEA) An agreement, beginning in 1993, that encourages free trade between EFTA and the EU

re-organise the EFTA arrangement became apparent. Negotiations for a **European Economic Area (EEA)** were completed in 1993 and the EEA came into force on 1 January 1993. In addition to the then 12 EU countries, the agreement also covered EFTA members (except Switzerland, which decided not to join, and Liechtenstein, which joined two years later). Since the initial agreement was signed, EFTA members Austria, Finland and Sweden have anyway joined the EU. The EEA agreement, which covers 377 million consumers, extends the earlier arrangement on free trade in industrial products to allow EFTA countries free movement of goods, services, people and capital within the EU.

Although the 15 nations of the EU essentially function as one large market and consumers in the EU are likely to become more homogeneous in their needs and wants, marketers know that cultural and social differences among the 15 member nations may require modifications in the marketing mix for consumers in each nation. Some researchers believe that eventually it will be possible to segment the European Union into six markets on the basis of cultural, geographic, demographic and economic variables. For example, the United Kingdom and Ireland would form one market, while Greece and southern Italy would form another.[21] Differences in taste and preferences among these markets are significant for international marketers. For example, the British consume far more instant coffee than their other European neighbours. Consumers in Spain eat far more poultry products than Germans do.[22] In some geographic regions, preferences even vary within the same country. Thus international marketing intelligence efforts remain very important in determining European consumers' needs and in developing marketing mixes that will satisfy those needs. It is also clear that EU organisations will have to face up to considerable changes in the way they operate, and for some, such as pharmaceutical companies, the prospects include harmonisation of prices and formulations and likely job losses.

Pacific Rim Nations

Countries in the Pacific Rim represent an enormous part of the world market with 60 per cent of the world's population living there. Although the region is characterised by considerable diversity, in general companies of the Pacific Rim nations—Japan, China, South Korea, Taiwan, Singapore, Hong Kong, the Philippines, Malaysia, Indonesia, Australia and Indochina—have become increasingly competitive and sophisticated in their marketing efforts in the last three decades. Throughout the early to mid-1990s the performances of Japan and the four so-called Tiger economies of the region—South Korea, Singapore, Taiwan and Hong Kong—were particularly impressive.[23] The Japanese in particular made considerable inroads into the world consumer markets for cars, motorcycles, watches, cameras and audio-visual equipment. Products made by Sony, Sanyo, Toyota, Honda, Canon, Suzuki and others are sold all over the world and have set quality standards by which other products are often judged. Through direct investment in Europe, the Japanese built strong distribution and developed a keen understanding of the market. However, Japan's marketing muscle attracted criticism in certain quarters, fuelled partly by fears that Japanese products might swamp the market. These concerns are compounded by Japan's reluctance to accept imports from other countries.[24] In practice, the sale of Japan's products in Europe is limited by the existence of quotas, but many of these quotas are nearing their end.

South Korea also became very successful in world markets with familiar brands such as Samsung, Daewoo and Hyundai. Korean companies even took market share away from Japanese companies in the world markets for video cassette recorders, colour televisions and computers, despite the fact that the Korean market for these products is limited. In Canada, the Hyundai Excel overtook Japan's Honda in just 18 months.[25] Towards the end of the 1990s many Far Eastern markets were substantially affected by economic recession. Currency markets in Japan, South Korea and Hong Kong were strongly hit, affecting the economic strength of the Pacific Rim region. It remains to be seen what lasting impact this period of recession will have.

Less visible Pacific Rim regions, such as Singapore, Taiwan and Hong Kong, are major manufacturing and financial centres. Singapore also has large world markets for pharmaceutical and rubber goods. Hong Kong continues to face an uncertain future following its move in 1997 from British control to control by the People's Republic of China. Taiwan may have the most promising future of all the Pacific Rim nations. It has a strong local economy and has lowered many import barriers, sending imports up. Taiwan has privatised state run banks and is also opening its markets to foreign businesses. Some analysts believe that it may replace Hong Kong as a regional financial power centre.[26]

Much attention is now being given to the four Pacific Rim nations that have reached the point of massive industrial growth. Thailand, Malaysia, Indonesia and China all offer considerable marketing potential.[27] For example, the People's Republic of China has great market potential and opportunities for joint venture projects. Analysts are keeping a close watch on how these countries are affected by economic uncertainty in the region. In the case of China, an important consideration is the risk associated with doing business there. Political and economic instability have the potential to spoil the chances of businesses seeking a stake in this growing market.[28]

In general, attempts to form groups promoting trade and other links between Pacific Rim countries have not been particularly successful. Perhaps the best known is the **Association of South East Asian Nations (ASEAN),** formed in 1967, which aims to build trade and other links between its six members: Brunei, Indonesia, Malaysia, the Philippines, Singapore and Thailand. With 340 million consumers in the group and a combined GNP of some £300 billion, in practice the progress towards the trading links that the organisation sought has been hampered by the inability of member states to agree on key issues.[29] At the moment it seems that the future of ASEAN is in the balance, with an economic treaty being discussed that aims to set up a free trade area by the year 2008.[30] More recently, the **Asia Pacific Economic Co-operative (APEC)** has been set up to include the six ASEAN members, the United States, Australia, Canada, New Zealand, Japan, China, South Korea, Hong Kong and Taiwan.[31] Currently APEC is little more than a weakly joined group of countries aiming to promote trade, and what the future holds is unclear.

Central and Eastern Europe (CEE)

Central and Eastern Europe (CEE) encompasses the Commonwealth of Independent States (formerly the Soviet Union), the Balkan states, the Czech and Slovak Republics, Hungary and Poland. The decline of communism in central and eastern Europe, the fall of the Berlin Wall in 1989 and the break up of the former Soviet Union in 1990 resulted in a host of new marketing opportunities in the region.

Following a policy of *perestroika*, encompassing considerable political and economic change, the CEE countries are replacing the Communist Party's centrally planned economies with marketing-oriented democratic institutions. This process of market reforms, designed to lead to greater imports and exports, has not been without difficulty. The challenge for many of the eastern European countries has been to move forward from the inefficiencies of state

Association of South East Asian Nations (ASEAN) Formed in 1967 with the intention of building trade and other links among its six members: Brunei, Indonesia, Malaysia, the Philippines, Singapore and Thailand

Asia Pacific Economic Co-operative (APEC) Aims to promote trade between its members: the six ASEAN members plus the United States, Australia, Canada, New Zealand, Japan, China, South Korea, Hong Kong and Taiwan

Central and Eastern Europe (CEE) Encompasses the Commonwealth of Independent States (formerly the Soviet Union), the Balkan states, the Czech and Slovak Republics, Hungary and Poland

owned industry and to develop the marketing expertise, business culture, infrastructures and legal frameworks required to trade with capitalist countries.[32] If the CEE countries wish to compete effectively with nations from other parts of the world, these changes are essential. For example, the poorly developed distribution infrastructure in many parts of central and eastern Europe currently restricts the outlets where western products can be sold and limits the opportunities domestic companies can pursue.[33] However, the move towards market change has resulted in considerable social upheaval and, in some cases, unrest in countries going through it. For example, in Russia, annual inflation rates of up to 900 per cent have dampened the people's enthusiasm for reform.

The **Commonwealth of Independent States (CIS)** emerged in 1996 as a loosely connected group of former Soviet Union states. The member states of the CIS include Azerbaijan, Armenia, Belarus, Estonia, Georgia, Kazakhstan, Kyrgyzstan, Latvia, Lithuania, Moldova, Russia, Tajikistan, Turkmenistan, Ukraine and Uzbekistan. Reviewing key economic data for the CIS and comparing it with EU countries provides a stark reminder of the difficult position in which many eastern European nations find themselves. The highest GNP per capita figure for the CIS, £1,940, is found in Belarus, while the lowest for the region, £320, is in Tajikistan. These figures compare with an EU high of £23,507 in Luxembourg and a low of £4,787 in Greece.[34]

Although after it was set up there were potential opportunities for the CIS to trade as a market group, in practice this idea has been severely restricted by the lack of co-operation between member states and, in particular, by the continuing economic and political problems in Russia.[35] The importance of Russia—the largest market, with 150 million consumers—cannot be overlooked in the region's development.[36] For western companies, the potential is considerable. Hewlett-Packard enjoyed a four fold increase in sales in 1993 alone, and others—such as Coca-Cola and McDonald's—have also taken advantage of the new opportunities.

The reformers of the CEE economies want to reduce trade restrictions on imports and offer incentives to encourage exports to and investment in their countries.[37] One such move involved seven UK companies, which formed a consortium to look at opportunities in the personal care and food and drink areas of the Russian market. So far, the initiative has led to a number of developments, including joint venture agreements between Tambrands and the Ukrainian ministry of public health to sell tampons to a market of 70 million women and between Allied Lyons and the Russian ministry of trade to market 8 million gallons of ice cream a year under the Baskin-Robbins label.[38] Because of these economic and political reforms, productivity in central and eastern Europe is expected to increase as workers are given more incentives and control. There is also speculation that some of the eastern European nations will ultimately join the European Union, allowing freer trade across all European borders.[39] In free elections, East Germany voted in 1990 to re-unify with West Germany. Although there have been initial teething problems and some social unrest, the unification of Germany is also having a great impact on the European Union and world economy. Exactly how the changing face of the CEE in general will affect world trade remains to be seen. However, because of the swift and uncontrolled nature of the changes taking place in eastern Europe and the former Soviet Union, businesses considering marketing their products in these countries must carefully monitor events and proceed cautiously.

North American Free Trade Agreement (NAFTA) Implemented in 1994 and designed to eliminate all tariffs on goods produced and traded between Canada, Mexico and the United States, providing for a totally free trade area by 2009

The **North American Free Trade Agreement (NAFTA)**, implemented on 1 January 1994, created a market of about 374.2 million people. This market consists of Canada, the United States and Mexico and has an estimated annual output of $7 trillion. NAFTA is built on the Canadian Free Trade Agreement (FTA), signed by the United States and Canada in 1989, and on the substantial trade and investment reforms undertaken by Mexico since the mid-1980s. Initiated by the Mexican government, formal negotiations on NAFTA began in June 1991 between the governments of Canada, Mexico and the United States. In August 1992 trade representatives from the three countries announced the successful conclusion of the NAFTA negotiations. The support of NAFTA by President Bill Clinton, past US presidents Ronald Reagan and Jimmy Carter, and Nobel Prize winning economists provided support in the United States for ratifying NAFTA in November 1993. Mexico's involvement in NAFTA provides important links between the United States and other Latin American countries. Chile is expected to become the fourth member of NAFTA, although politics may delay its entry.[40]

NAFTA will eventually eliminate all tariffs on goods produced and traded between Canada, Mexico and the United States to provide for a totally free trade area by 2009. In addition, the agreement liberalises US investment in Mexico and Canada, provides for intellectual property rights (of interest to producers of high tech goods and entertainment), expands trade in services by requiring equal treatment of US firms in both countries and simplifies country of origin rules, hindering Japan's use of Mexico as a staging ground for further penetration into US markets. Most competitive products immediately have qualified for tariff-free treatment: aerospace equipment, semiconductors, telecommunications and electronics, medical equipment, car parts, machine tools and paper.

Though tariffs on imports to the United States will be eliminated, duties on the more sensitive products, such as household glassware, footwear, and some fruits and vegetables, will be phased out over a 15 year period. For other US products, US export tariffs will be phased out over a 10 year period. NAFTA also contains special rules that allow re-instatement of certain tariffs or other measures to protect US farmers and workers in the case of injury from a sudden surge of imports from Mexico or Canada.

Additional supplemental agreements have also been negotiated concerning labour and the environment. The supplemental agreement on the environment provides measures for enforcing federal and international environmental laws. NAFTA is the first trade agreement in history to contain specific provisions for protecting the environment.

Alternative Market Entry Strategies

The level of commitment to international marketing is a major variable in deciding what kind of involvement is appropriate. A company's market entry options range from occasional exporting to expanding overall operations (production and marketing) into other countries. This section examines exporting, licensing, franchising, joint ventures, trading companies, foreign direct investment and other approaches to international involvement.[41]

Exporting

Exporting is the lowest and most flexible level of commitment to international marketing. A business may find an exporting intermediary that can perform most marketing functions associated with selling to other countries. This approach entails minimum effort and cost. Modifications in packaging, labelling, style or colour may be the major expenses in adapting a product. There is limited risk in using export agents and merchants because there is no direct investment in the foreign country.

Export agents bring together buyers and sellers from different countries; they collect a commission for arranging sales. Export houses and export merchants purchase products from different companies and then sell them to foreign countries. They specialise in understanding customers' needs in foreign countries.

Foreign buyers from companies and governments provide a direct method of exporting and eliminate the need for an intermediary. Foreign buyers encourage international exchange by contacting domestic businesses about their needs and the opportunities available in exporting. Domestic companies that want to export with a minimum of effort and investment seek out foreign importers and buyers.

Licensing

When potential markets are found across national boundaries—and when production, technical assistance or marketing know-how is required—**licensing** is an alternative to direct investment. The licensee (the owner of the foreign operation) pays commissions or royalties on sales or supplies used in manufacturing. An initial fee may be charged when the licensing agreement is signed. Exchanges of management techniques or technical assistance are primary reasons for licensing agreements. Yoplait yoghurt is a French yoghurt that is licensed for production in the United States; the Yoplait brand tries to maintain a French image.

Licensing is an attractive alternative to direct investment when the political stability of a foreign country is in doubt or when resources are unavailable for direct investment. This approach is especially advantageous for small manufacturers wanting to launch a well known brand internationally. For example, Pierre Cardin has issued 500 licences and Yves St Laurent 200 to make their products.[42] Löwenbrau has used licensing agreements to increase sales worldwide without committing capital to build breweries.

Franchising

Another alternative to direct investment in non-domestic markets is **franchising.** This form of licensing, which grants the right to use certain intellectual property rights, such as trade names, brand names, designs, patents and copyrights, is becoming increasingly popular in Europe.[43] Under this arrangement the franchiser grants a licence to the franchisee, who pays to be allowed to carry out business under the name owned by the franchiser. The franchiser retains control over the manner in which the business is conducted and assists the franchisee in running the business. The franchisee retains ownership of his or her own business, which remains separate from that of the franchiser.[44]

Franchising has recently experienced a period of rapid growth. Companies such as Benetton, Burger King, Holiday Inn and IKEA are particularly well known for their commitment to growing global business in this way. There are various reasons why the popularity of franchising has increased so rapidly.[45] First, the general world decline in manufacturing and shift to service industries has increased the relevance of franchising. This is significant, because franchising is a very common internationalisation process for service organisations. Second, franchising has been relatively free of restrictions from legislation, especially in the EU. Third, an increase in self-employment has provided a pool of individuals willing to become involved in franchising, and this activity has generally been supported by the major clearing banks.

Joint Ventures

Joint venture A partnership between a domestic company and a foreign company or government

In international marketing, a **joint venture** is a partnership between a domestic company and a foreign company or government. Joint ventures are especially popular in industries that call for large investments, such as natural resources extraction or car manufacturing. Control of the joint venture can be split equally or can be retained by one party. Joint ventures are often a political necessity because of nationalism and governmental restrictions on foreign ownership. They also provide legitimacy in the eyes of the host country's people. Local partners have first hand knowledge of the economic and socio-political environment, access to distribution networks, or privileged access to local resources (raw material, labour management, contacts and so on). Moreover, entrepreneurs in many less developed countries actively seek associations with an overseas partner as a ready means of implementing their own corporate strategy.[46]

Joint ventures are assuming greater global importance because of cost advantages and the number of inexperienced businesses entering foreign markets. They may be the result of a trade-off between a company's desire for completely unambiguous control of an enterprise and its quest for additional resources. They may occur when internal development or acquisition is not feasible or unavailable or when the risks and constraints leave no other alternative. As project sizes increase in the face of global competition and businesses attempt to spread the huge costs of technological innovation, there is increased impetus to form joint ventures.[47] Several European truck makers used mergers and joint ventures with other European companies to consolidate their power after the unification of the EU in 1992 and the deregulation of the European haulage industry in 1993. Volvo and Renault developed such a partnership.[48] Of course, joint ventures are also possible between partners from different continents. LDV, a European truck manufacturer, has recently joined forces with Korean company Daewoo.

Joint ventures are sometimes criticised as being inherently unstable,[49] or because they might result in a take-over attempt. For businesses trying to build longer term joint ventures, there is also the danger that the relationship stifles flexibility. Of course, for many companies that become involved in joint ventures this may be their only feasible mode of entry at the time and may anyway be regarded purely as a transitional arrangement.[50] For example, European construction companies bidding for business in Saudi Arabia have found that joint ventures with Arab construction companies gain local support among the handful of people who make the contracting decisions.

Strategic alliances Partnerships formed to create a competitive advantage on a worldwide basis

Strategic alliances, the newest form of international business structure, are partnerships formed to create a competitive advantage on a worldwide basis. They are very similar to joint ventures. Strategic alliances have been defined as "co-operation between two or more industrial corporations, belonging to different countries, whereby each partner seeks to add to its competencies by combining its resources with those of its partner".[51] The number of strategic alliances is growing at an estimated rate of about 20 per cent per year.[52] In fact, in some industries, such as cars and high technology, strategic alliances are becoming the predominant means of competing. International competition is so fierce and the costs of competing globally so high that few businesses have the required individual resources, and it makes sense to collaborate with other companies.[53]

The partners forming international strategic alliances share common goals yet often retain their distinct identities, each bringing a distinctive competence to the union. What distinguishes international strategic alliances from other business structures is that member companies in the alliance may have been traditional rivals competing for market share in the same product class.[54] Table 3.5 shows some examples of strategic alliances.[55]

Trading Companies

Trading company A company that provides a link between buyers and sellers in different countries

A **trading company** provides a link between buyers and sellers in different countries. As its name implies, a trading company is not involved in manufacturing or owning assets related to manufacturing. It buys in one country at the lowest price consistent with quality and sells to buyers in another country. An important function of trading companies is taking title to products and undertaking all the activities necessary to move the products from the domestic country to a foreign country. For example, large grain trading companies control a major portion of the world's trade in basic food commodities. These trading companies sell agricultural commodities that are homogeneous and can be stored and moved rapidly in response to market conditions.

Table 3.5 Examples of international strategic alliances

Partners	Products
General Motors; Toyota	Cars
CompuServe; Microsoft	Internet
Recticel SA; Foamex	Autoparts
British Airways; American Airlines	Airlines
Lufthansa; Scandinavian Airlines Systems (SAS)	Airlines
Alfa Romeo; Nissan; Fiat	Cars
AT&T; Olivetti	Office equipment; computers
Amdahl; Fujitsu	Computers
ICL; Fujitsu	Computers
AT&T; Philips	Telecommunications equipment
Honeywell; L.M. Ericsson	PBX system
General Motors; Fanuc	Robotics
AEG Telefunken; JVC; Thorn-EMI; Thomson	Video recorders
General Electric; Matsushita	Electrical appliances
Corning Glass; Siemens	Optical cables
Hercules; Montedison	Polypropylene resin
United Technologies; Rolls Royce	Aircraft engines

SOURCES: Adapted from S. Young, J. Hamill, C. Wheeler and R. Davies, *International Market Entry and Development*, 1st edn (London: Harvester Wheatsheaf, 1989), p. 273; *Information World Review*, 116, July/August 1996, p. 9; *Chemical Marketing Reporter*, 26, 24 June 1996, p. 31; *Economist*, 1 June 1996, p. 68; *Aviation Week*, 144, 22 January 1996, p. 21.

Trading companies reduce risk for companies interested in getting involved in international marketing, assisting producers with information about products that meet quality and price expectations in domestic or international markets. Additional services a trading company may provide include consulting, marketing research, advertising, insurance, research and development, legal assistance, warehousing and foreign exchange.

Foreign Direct Investment

Foreign direct investment (FDI)
A long term commitment to marketing in a foreign nation through direct ownership of a foreign subsidiary or division

Once a company makes a long term commitment to foreign marketing, direct ownership of a foreign subsidiary or division is a possibility. **Foreign direct investment (FDI)** involves making a long term commitment to marketing in a foreign nation through direct ownership of a foreign subsidiary or division. The expenses of developing a separate foreign distribution system, in particular, can be tremendous. For example, as French hypermarket chain Carrefour has discovered, the opening of retail stores in neighbouring countries can require a large financial investment in facilities, research and management.

Multinational enterprise
A company with operations or subsidiaries in many countries

The term **multinational enterprise** refers to companies that have operations or subsidiaries located in many countries. Often the parent company is based in one country and cultivates production, management and marketing activities in other countries. The company's subsidiaries may be quite autonomous in order to respond to the needs of individual international markets. Companies such as ICI, Unilever and General Motors are multinational companies with worldwide operations. Table 3.6 lists the top 20 European companies, ranked by market

Table 3.6 Top 20 European companies, ranked by market capitalisation

Rank					
1997	1996	Company	Country	Market Capital $m	Turnover $m
1	1	Royal Dutch/Shell	Neth./UK	191,002.3	131,557.9
2	..	Novartis	Switzerland	104,467.6	24,639.9
3	5	HSBC Holdings	UK	91,339.4	..
4	3	British Petroleum	UK	85,905.0	71,695.8
5	2	Roche Holding	Switzerland	85,852.8	10,857.5
6	4	Glaxo Wellcome	UK	79,715.9	13,369.1
7	14	Lloyds TSB Group	UK	72,094.9	..
8	8	Unilever plc/NV	Neth./UK	57,484.2	53,729.8
9	10	Allianz Holding	Germany	56,013.3	..
10	7	Nestlé	Switzerland	54,315.6	41,135.7
11	13	SmithKline Beecham	UK	53,304.1	12,702.4
12	..	Deutsche Telekom	Germany	52,515.4	35,300.5
13	9	ENI	Italy	49,876.9	49,934.0
14	21	Ericsson LM	Sweden	46,174.0	16,156.9
15	16	Daimler-Benz	Germany	42,709.9	59,513.7
16	12	BT	UK	42,017.5	23,938.1
17	26	Barclays	UK	40,636.1	..
18	15	Siemens	Germany	37,357.7	52,708.8
19	22	ING Group	Netherlands	37,345.8	..
20	23	Deutsche Bank	Germany	36,991.1	..

SOURCE: Reprinted by permission of *Financial Times European 500*. Copyright © 1998.

capitalisation. Most of these companies are active in different countries and across several continents.

A wholly owned foreign subsidiary may be allowed to operate independently of the parent company so that its management can have more freedom to adjust to the local environment. Co-operative arrangements are developed to assist in marketing efforts, production and management. A wholly owned foreign subsidiary may export products to the home country. Some car manufacturers, such as Ford and General Motors, for example, import cars built by their foreign subsidiaries. A foreign subsidiary offers important tax, tariff and other operating advantages. The greatest advantages of direct foreign investment are greater strategy control and enhanced market capacity. To maximise these, a subsidiary may operate under foreign management, so that a genuinely local identity can be developed. A company's success in achieving these advantages will tend to depend on whether the business has a competitive advantage allowing it to recover the costs of its investment.

● S U M M A R Y

Marketing activities performed across national boundaries are usually significantly different from domestic marketing activities. International marketers must have a profound awareness of the foreign environment. The marketing strategy is ordinarily adjusted to meet the needs and desires of markets across national boundaries.

The level of involvement in international marketing covers a wide spectrum from *domestic marketing* to *export marketing, international marketing, multinational marketing* and *global marketing*. Although all companies involved in international marketing must make some modifications to their marketing effort, full scale global marketing requires total commitment to international marketing and involves applying the company's assets, experience and products to develop and maintain marketing strategies on a global scale. *Multinational companies* are those that operate in overseas markets as if they were local companies.

Marketers must rely on international marketing intelligence to understand the complexities of the international marketing environment before they can formulate a marketing mix. Therefore, they collect and analyse secondary data and primary data about international markets.

Environmental aspects of special importance include cultural, social, economic, political and legal, and technological forces. Cultural aspects of the environment that are most important to international marketers include customs, concepts, values, attitudes, morals and knowledge. Marketing activities are primarily social in purpose; therefore, they are structured by the institutions of family, religion, education, health and recreation. The most prominent economic forces that affect international marketing are those that can be measured by income and resources. *Gross domestic product (GDP)* is the total value of all goods and services produced by a country's income. Credit, buying power and income distribution are aggregate measures of market potential. Political and legal forces include the political system, national laws, regulatory bodies, national pressure groups and courts.

Measures that governments can take to govern cross-border trade include the use of tariffs, quotas and non-tariff barriers. *Tariffs* are taxes that affect the movement of goods across economic or political boundaries. *Quotas* involve physical restrictions on the amount of goods that can be imported. *Nontariff barriers* include a wide range of rules, regulations and taxes that have an impact upon trade. The foreign policies of all nations involved in trade determine how marketing can be conducted. The level of technology helps define economic development within a nation and indicates the existence of methods to facilitate marketing.

Various regional trade alliances and specific markets are creating both difficulties and opportunities for organisations. In Europe there are three major market groups. The *European Free Trade Association (EFTA)* was set up in 1960 to promote trade between members. The creation of the single European market in 1993 following the signing of the *Maastricht Treaty* in 1992 led to the formation of the *European Union (EU)*. The *European Economic Area (EEA)*, which was completed in 1993, attempts to encourage free trade between EU and EFTA members. The best known trading group in the Pacific Rim is the *Association of South East Asian Nations (ASEAN)*, which was formed in 1967. More recently, the *Asia Pacific Economic Co-operative (APEC)* has been set up to promote trade in the region. The group includes the US, Australia, Canada, New Zealand, Japan, China, South Korea, Hong Kong, Taiwan and ASEAN members. Trade in the Asia Pacific region has recently been substantially affected by economic recession. *Central and Eastern Europe (CEE)* encompasses the *Commonwealth of Independent States (CIS)*, the Balkan states, the Czech and Slovak Republics, Hungary and Poland. The *North American Free Trade Agreement (NAFTA)*, set up in 1994, aims to eliminate all tariffs on goods produced and traded between Canada, Mexico and the US and to provide for a totally free trade area by 2009.

There are several ways of becoming involved in international marketing. *Exporting* is the easiest and most flexible method. *Licensing* is an alternative to direct investment; it may be necessitated by political and economic conditions. *Franchising* is a form of licensing granting the right to use certain intellectual property rights such as trade names, brand names, designs, patents and copyrights. *Joint ventures* and *strategic alliances* are often appropriate when outside resources are needed, when there are governmental restrictions on foreign ownership or when changes in global markets encourage competitive consolidation. *Trading companies* are experts at buying products in the domestic market and selling to foreign markets, thereby taking most of the risk in international involvement. *Foreign Direct Investment (FDI)* in divisions or subsidiaries is the strongest commitment to international marketing and involves the greatest risk. When a company has operations or subsidiaries located in many countries, it is termed a *multinational enterprise.*

Important Terms

Domestic marketing
Export marketing
International marketing
Multinational marketing
Multinational companies
Global marketing
Gross domestic product (GDP)
Tariffs
Quotas
Non-tariff barriers
European Union (EU)
Maastricht Treaty

European Free Trade Association (EFTA)
European Economic Area (EEA)
Association of South East Asian Nations (ASEAN)
Asia Pacific Economic Co-operative (APEC)
Central and Eastern Europe (CEE)
Commonwealth of Independent States (CIS)

North American Free Trade Agreement (NAFTA)
Exporting
Licensing
Franchising
Joint venture
Strategic alliances
Trading company
Foreign direct investment (FDI)
Multinational enterprise

Discussion and Review Questions

1. How does international marketing differ from domestic marketing?
2. What must marketers consider before deciding whether to become involved in international marketing?
3. Are the largest industrial companies in Europe committed to international marketing? Why or why not?
4. Why do you think so much of this chapter is devoted to an analysis of the international marketing environment?
5. A manufacturer recently exported peanut butter with a green label to a nation in the Far East. The product failed because it was associated with jungle sickness. How could this mistake have been avoided?

6. How do religious systems influence marketing activities in foreign countries?
7. Recent recession in the Asia Pacific region has affected trade opportunities for many European businesses. How could such businesses minimise the impact of such problems?
8. If you were asked to provide a small tip (or bribe) to have a document approved in a foreign nation where this practice was customary, what would you do?
9. What should marketers consider as they decide whether to license or to enter into a joint venture in a foreign nation?
10. Discuss the impact of strategic alliances on marketing strategies.

Recommended Readings

F. Bradley, *International Marketing Strategy*, 3rd ed. (Hemel Hempstead: Prentice-Hall, 1998).

C. Egan and P. McKiernan, *Inside Fortress Europe: Strategies for the Single Market* (Wokingham: Addison-Wesley, 1994).

J-P. Jeannet and H. D. Hennessey, *Global Marketing Strategies*, 4th edn (Boston: Houghton Mifflin, 1998).

S. Paliwoda and J. K. Ryans, Jr., eds, *International Marketing Reader* (London: International Thomson Business Press, 1996).

J. A. Quelch and C. A. Bartlett, eds, *Global Marketing Management* (London: Longman, 1998).

● C A S E S

3.1 Porsche AG: The International Tradition Continues

German high performance car maker Porsche AG was founded in 1930 by Dr Ferdinand Porsche as a research and development company. It accepted contracts from individuals and companies for new cars, aeroplanes and ships based on customer design. In 1948 Dr Ferry Porsche—Ferdinand Porsche's son—established a company that would itself design, as well as produce, sports cars under the Porsche name. Despite intermittent tough economic periods, the company persevered and prospered. By 1973, Porsche AG had built and sold some 200,000 cars, gaining worldwide recognition as the maker of the finest sports cars in the world. As the company promised the customer, to drive a Porsche was to experience "driving in its purest form".

The popularity of Porsche cars stems from their reputation for outstanding performance. Not only are the vehicles produced in painstakingly detailed fashion, but Porsche also takes maintenance and repair very seriously. Company mechanics receive five days of instruction annually at the Porsche Marketing Centre in Ludwigsburg, a higher level of training than that provided by any other car manu-facturer in the world. Until 1984, Porsche mechanics in the United States also flew to Germany for this training. Now, however, they receive instruction at company training centres established in the United States.

Despite Porsche's impeccable reputation for excellence, the company has not been immune from trying times. For example, its sales suffered when it had to raise prices on cars sold in the United States because of fluctuating exchange rates and a new tax on luxury cars priced at over $30,000. These developments, a weak US dollar, and increased US- and Japanese-based competition in the American high performance sports car market brought down sales in its largest market from 30,000 in 1986 to about 3,700 in 1993. Since US sales traditionally account for about 60 per cent of the company's total global sales, such a drastic drop was particularly troublesome to its overall global operations. For example, Porsche sold only 23,000 cars worldwide in 1992, as compared with 50,000 in 1986. Consequently, the company made a loss of nearly £30 million in 1992, its first annual deficit in over 20 years, and even larger losses in 1993 as a result of what many industry observers considered the company's over-dependence on the American market.

In an effort to combat its mounting problems, Porsche laid off more than 20 per cent of its US based work force, lowered production output, cut manufacturing costs, reduced its prices, pulled out of the lower end of the American luxury car market and made public plans to enter promising new international markets such as Spain and Japan. In 1993 the company announced two additional moves designed to revive worldwide sales. Early in the year, Ferry Porsche, then 83 years old, asked to be relieved of his position as the company's chairman of the board. The appointment of Helmut Sihler as his replacement marked the first time in the organisation's 63 year history that someone from outside the controlling family was named to head the company. The move was applauded by many shareholders, who had attributed the company's financial troubles to the Porsche family's unwillingness to relinquish operational control. Besides this transition in leadership, the German company announced both the continuation of substantial cost cutting programmes and new developments on the product front. Specifically, Porsche AG disclosed plans to unveil five new versions of the company's three lines of sports cars. Porsche spent £13 million to launch a newly redesigned 1995 911 Carrera. Launched at the Frankfurt motor show in September 1995, the 911 Targa and Carrera 4S arrived in the UK two months later with price tags starting from £64,250 and £74,795 respectively. The company also announced plans for production of a two-seat sports car similar to its highly acclaimed Boxster show car, which was launched in 1995.

SOURCES: Martha T. Moore, "Porsche smooths 'jerky' image", *USA Today*, 11 February 1994, p. 2B; "Business briefs", *Wall Street Journal*, 6 May 1993, p. B4; "Business briefs", *Wall Street Journal*, 9 March 1993, p. B4; Jerry Flint, "Porsche turns", *Forbes*, 1 February 1993, p. 104; "Porsche AG names Helmut Sihler to head Board of Supervisors", *Wall Street Journal*, 26 January 1993, p. B6; James R. Henley, "Porsche puts on brakes", *USA Today*, 29 January 1992, p. 2B; Karen Miller and Terrence Roth, "Porsche, a favorite in times of plenty, struggles to survive in a more frugal era", *Wall Street Journal*, 27 January 1992, pp. B1–B2; Thomas L. Bryant, "Miscellaneous ramblings", *Road and Track*, December 1991, p. 53; Jim Henry, "Luxury car tax may speed sales", *Advertising Age*, 10 December 1990, p. 17; David Vivian, "Heavenly bodies", *Marque*, 2, 1995, pp. 6–7.

Questions for Discussion

1. Evaluate international marketing opportunities for Porsche AG. What are the company's strengths and weaknesses?
2. What obstacles must Porsche overcome to succeed in selling its cars in the United States?
3. What is the role of diversification in the Porsche AG corporate strategy?

3.2 Carrefour's International Strategy

Carrefour has been in the business of managing hypermarkets for more than 35 years. The original business idea was generated in the early 1960s, when Marcel Fournier and Denis and Jacques Defforey visited a retailing conference in the United States. The hypermarket concept which they developed is based on choice, low prices, self-service and free car parking, allowing consumers to do all of their shopping under one roof. The first outlets were opened in the Paris suburbs, followed in 1966 by Europe's largest self-service hypermarket outside Lyon.

The main features of the Carrefour concept are:

- Large, spacious stores with wide aisles and free car parks
- Store size of around 10,000 square metres, serving three million shoppers each year
- Flexibility in product and service offerings to reflect local tastes
- Food representing about 45 per cent of sales, gross margins of about 18 per cent
- Narrow profit margins and high volume purchases, allowing discount prices to be offered on a daily basis
- A choice of branded, private and generic labels, usually arranged on the shelves vertically in this order

An early foray into international expansion, with new stores in Belgium, Italy, Switzerland and the United Kingdom, was not particularly successful and the group quickly abandoned this activity to concentrate on its home operations. However, in the mid-1970s a period of organic growth began, with new openings in France, Spain and Brazil. This

The World of Carrefour

Country	Type of Store	First Opening	Stores
France		1963	
Carrefour	Hypermarkets		116
Carrefour Optique	Eyewear shops		38
Picard Surgelés	Frozen food		321
Erteco	Discount stores		367
Comptoirs Modernes*	Supermarkets		386
Metro France*	Cash and carry		61
Office Depot France*	Office supplies		2
Cora	Hyper- and supermarkets		56
Spain		1973	
Pryca	Hypermarkets		56
Comptoirs Modernes*	Supermarkets		80
Italy		1993	
Carrefour	Hypermarkets		6
Portugal		Acquisition 1991	
Carrefour	Hypermarkets		4
Turkey		1993	
Carrefour	Hypermarkets		2
Poland		1997	
Carrefour	Hypermarkets		1
Brazil		1975	
Carrefour	Hypermarkets		57
Argentina		1982	
Carrefour	Hypermarkets		19
Mexico		1994	
Carrefour	Hypermarkets		17
Taiwan		1989	
Carrefour	Hypermarkets		18
Carrefour Optique	Eyewear shop		1
China		1995	
Carrefour	Hypermarkets		8
Hong Kong		1996	
Carrefour	Hypermarkets		2
South Korea		1996	
Carrefour	Hypermarkets		4
Thailand		1996	
Carrefour	Hypermarkets		7
Malaysia		1994	
Carrefour	Hypermarkets		4

SOURCE: Carrefour's 1998 *Annual Report* and corporate home page (www.carrefour.fr)
*Participation: Comptoirs Modernes (23%), Metro France (20%) and Office Depot France (50%).

continued until the early 1980s, with Carrefour opening its first Argentinian and Taiwanese outlets. During this same time period, Carrefour France concentrated on developing new retail concepts and formats which might be adopted in overseas markets. Once such initiative was the change of name in Spain from Carrefour to Pryca.

At the beginning of the 1990s, Carrefour decided to concentrate on growth by acquisition, buying the French chains Montlaur and Euromarche. But Carrefour was not confining its growth to the hypermarket sector. By acquiring Picard Sugelés, a French frozen food business, Carrefour was signalling its expansion into other retail sectors. The company's 1998 *Annual Report* provides details of hypermarkets, supermarkets, eyewear, frozen food, discounter, cash and carry and office supply stores in 15 different countries.

Carrefour's commitment to an international strategy was initially encouraged by problems in developing its domestic business. These difficulties were caused partly by government regulations designed to protect small retailers. For example, tight controls were imposed on the opening of new stores and, in some cases, on the increase of selling space in existing outlets. For Carrefour, this restricted new domestic opportunities to those which could be gleaned through the acquisition of existing businesses. Once these opportunities had been exploited, the only other growth option for Carrefour was to expand overseas.

The international success which the business has enjoyed can be attributed to a number of factors. First, the business has been a fast mover in many of the countries in which it has expanded. By carefully choosing the right time to enter new countries, Carrefour has been able to make the most of appropriate retail conditions. Second, Carrefour has consistently applied its proven and well developed hypermarket concept. In many cases, by maintaining the same basic operational and marketing characteristics, the business has been able to simply transplant its operation to a new market. However, Carrefour has also shown the flexibility to make appropriate modifications to local taste where required. Finally, the business has a deep-seated commitment to its international expansion strategy. In the words of company Chairman Daniel Bernard:

. . . internationalisation is a difficult learning curve which is expensive at the outset. After setting up the basics, it becomes necessary to be patient enough to fine-tune the concept and to await profitability, which may be quite distant. Internationalisation represents long-term investment.

In recent years attempts to improve profit margins have focused on supply chain management. In 1993, Carrefour teamed up with food suppliers to develop "controlled supply chains", making use of the latest developments in EDI and ECR. The aim was to offer consumers healthy, good quality products at margins which are attractive to the business and its suppliers. Using new technology allowed Carrefour to achieve this by providing suppliers with information on store product sales, allowing for better stock level control.

The Carrefour commitment to expansion means that the business has often been prepared to forgo short term profits in the interests of longer term competitive advantage. However, as retail globalisation continues, Carrefour will have to continue reacting with speed and flexibility if it is to maintain its position. In particular, as the growing use of the Internet and home shopping begin to alter buying behaviour, the business must address whether or not the hypermarket concept will be able to adapt to changing consumer needs and profiles.

SOURCES: M. Rocha, "The globalisation of supermarkets: a case study approach", MBA project, Warwick Business School, 1998; Carrefour, *Annual Report,* Paris, 1997; Carrefour, *Annual Report,* Paris, 1998; P. Damour, "Carrefour keeps its customers loyal", *International Journal of Retail and Distribution Management,* 23(2), 1995; R. Redman, "Carrefour details its international expansion plans", *Supermarket News,* 7 October 1996, pp. 41, 46; D. Merrerfield, "Carrefour: exporting formats risky", *Supermarket News,* 7 June 1993, pp. 23, 43; D. Merrerfield and M. Tosh, "Carrefour's crossroad", *Supermarket News,* 6 June 1992, pp. 1, 42; K. Morris, "Carrefour: hyper-extension", *Financial World,* 26 May 1992, pp. 11, 161; J. Veenker, "European food retail: industry report", *Meespierson,* 14 May 1997; J.L. Johnson, "Carrefour revisited", *Discount Merchandiser,* August 1990.

Questions for Discussion

1. In what ways has Carrefour expanded its businesses internationally?
2. What new international opportunities might be open to Carrefour?
3. In what way have local needs altered Carrefour's store format?

Effective marketing hinges on satisfying customers and establishing relationships. There are many forces at work, however, which affect how organisations endeavour to achieve these goals. Part I of *Marketing: Concepts and Strategies* has explored the nature and scope of the concept of marketing, continuing to describe the forces of the macro and micro marketing environment and the essential requirements for marketing in global markets.

The focus of *Marketing: Concepts and Strategies* now turns to the customer. As outlined in Figure 1.4, the customer must be at the centre of the marketing process. Businesses must target specific groups of customers, understand their needs and endeavour through their marketing activities to satisfy these needs. It is essential, though, to recognise that a business does not deal with its customers in a vacuum: there are many marketing environment forces at work, affecting the behaviour of customers and those organisations attempting to market to them. For businesses operating across national borders, involved with marketing in global markets, the impact of these forces and the trading decisions required are even more complex. These are the issues that have been examined in Part I.

Before progressing, readers should be confident that they are now able to do the following:

Define and explain the marketing concept

• What is marketing? • Why is marketing important? • How has marketing evolved? • What are the core stages of marketing strategy? • What is the marketing mix?

Outline the forces at work in the marketing environment

• What is environmental scanning? • Why are the forces of the marketing environment important considerations for marketers? • What are the macro and micro marketing environment forces?

Describe the additional complexities facing marketers engaged in international markets

• What is the nature of international marketing? • Why is marketing intelligence so important? • Why are the forces of the marketing environment integral to international marketing? • Why are regional trade alliances important considerations? • What market entry strategies can businesses use to become involved in international marketing activities?

Marketing Opportunity Analysis	Chapters
• The marketing environment	2
• Marketing in international markets	3
• Consumer buying behaviour	4
• Organisational markets and business-to-business buying behaviour	5
• Marketing research and information systems	6

Target Market Strategy	Chapters
• Market segmentation and prioritisation	7, 21
• Product and brand positioning	7, 21
• Competitive advantage	7, 21

Marketing Mix Development	Chapters
• Product, branding, packaging and service decisions	8–11
• Place (distribution and channel) decisions	12–14
• Promotion decisions	15–17
• Pricing decisions	18, 19
• Supplementary decisions	3, 20, 23, 24

Marketing Management	Chapters
• Strategic marketing and competitive strategy	21, 22
• Marketing planning and forecasting sales potential	22
• Implementing strategies and internal marketing relationships and measuring performance	23
• Marketing ethics and social responsibility	24

II Understanding and Targeting Markets

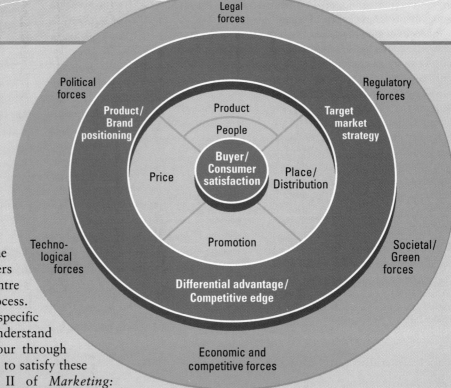

Legal forces

Political forces

Regulatory forces

Product/Brand positioning

Target market strategy

Product

People

Price

Buyer/Consumer satisfaction

Place/Distribution

Promotion

Technological forces

Societal/Green forces

Differential advantage/Competitive edge

Economic and competitive forces

A s outlined in the figure, customers must be at the centre of the marketing process. Businesses must target specific groups of customers, understand their needs and endeavour through their marketing activities to satisfy these customer needs. Part II of *Marketing: Concepts and Strategies* commences with a thorough examination of the nature of consumer buying behaviour and buying processes and continues to examine the nature of buying in business-to-business organisational markets. There are times when managers' existing knowledge of their customers is sufficient for marketing decision-making, or when they are content to trust their intuition. On many occasions, however, marketers may not feel confident with the level of marketing intelligence available and will instigate marketing research in order to fill any gaps in their understanding of customers, competitors or market trends. The nature, uses and types of marketing research are introduced in Part II of *Marketing: Concepts and Strategies*. Having developed an understanding of a marketplace and particularly

the customers within, marketers must then develop a marketing strategy. This should identify which customers they wish to target, what positioning they intend to use and which approach will provide an advantage over competitors. Part II concludes, therefore, with an examination of marketing strategy and, specifically, with target market strategy selection.

Part II of *Marketing: Concepts and Strategies* examines buying behaviour for consumers and organisations, the nature of marketing research and the issues concerned with target market strategy selection.

Chapter 4, "Consumer Buying Behaviour", describes the different types of consumer buying behaviour, the stages of consumer buying decision-making and the different categories of buying decisions. The chapter examines how personal, psychological and social factors influence the consumer buying decision process. Finally, it explains why marketers must understand consumer buying behaviour and use their understanding to determine marketing strategy.

Chapter 5, "Organisational Markets and Business-to-Business Buying Behaviour", familiarises readers with the various types of organisational markets, identifies the major characteristics of business-to-business buyers and transactions, outlines the attributes of business-to-business demand and presents the concept of the buying centre. The chapter emphasises the notion of relationship marketing and exchanges between industrial buyers and sellers. The focus then shifts to the stages of the business-to-business buying process and the factors that influence it. The chapter concludes by examining how to select and analyse business-to-business target markets.

Chapter 6, "Marketing Research and Information Systems", explains the importance of research and information systems in marketing decision-making, distinguishes between research and intuition in solving marketing problems, and outlines the five basic steps for conducting formal marketing research. The fundamental methods of gathering data for marketing research are examined. The chapter then introduces the wide variety of marketing research tools and explains their relative pros and cons.

Chapter 7, "Segmenting Markets, Targeting and Positioning", explains the core aspect of developing a marketing strategy: the process of target market strategy selection. The chapter commences by defining the concept of a market and outlining the various types of markets. The focus then shifts to how businesses segment markets, how they make targeting decisions and prioritise target markets, and how they determine a brand or product positioning strategy for each segment selected as a target market. The chapter also highlights how important it is for an organisation to attempt to develop an edge over its competitors in the market(s) it has chosen to target.

By the conclusion of Part II of *Marketing: Concepts and Strategies,* readers should understand buying behaviour in consumer and business-to-business markets, the nature and use of marketing research, and the fundamentals of target market strategy selection.

4 Consumer Buying Behaviour

OBJECTIVES

- To understand the different types of consumer buying behaviour
- To recognise the stages of the consumer buying decision process and understand how this process relates to different types of buying decisions
- To explore how personal factors may affect the consumer buying decision process
- To learn about the psychological factors that may affect the consumer buying decision process
- To examine the social factors that influence the consumer buying decision process
- To understand why it is important for marketers to attempt to understand consumer buying behaviour and the role of this behaviour in marketing strategy

"Anticipating consumer behaviour is not an option for marketing managers: it is their job description."

Gordon Foxall, University of Keele

For many couples, having a baby is a major life event. The arrival of a new family member will usually have major repercussions on how they organise their lives, buying behaviour and day-to-day expenditure. For many couples, including those who enjoyed a comparatively high level of disposable income prior to the new arrival, the need to take maternity leave also reduces spending power. Later on, the purchase of child care may continue to affect their available disposable income. Overall, the family will need to allocate its income in new ways, buying a host of new products and services which previously may not have been relevant.

The arrival of a new baby generally signals a major learning exercise. Couples must collect information and learn about a variety of novel products from pushchairs, car seats and prams, to nappies, baby formula and sterilising units. Such new parents are not alone in their search for inspiration. A range of specif-ically targeted magazines and retail outlets are geared to help. Publications such as *Practical Parenting, Mother & Baby*, and *Pregnancy Plus* are just a few of those which provide a diverse mix of guidance on everything from antenatal care provision and baby care, to education options, new product ideas and buying guides. For example, a recent edition of one such magazine included consumer tests for sterilisers, activity centres and toy storage.

The baby and child retailer Mothercare is another source of help and assistance, with the following clearly stated commitment to parents and their babies.

Nothing is more important to us than you and your baby. From the moment you know you are pregnant to the day you hold your precious little one in your arms for the first time, we're there for you. And even when that tiny bundle has grown into a miniature tornado, full of fun and chattering nineteen to the dozen, we'll still be here for you both to call on.

For all of us here at Mothercare, helping you provide the very best care for your little ones is a way of life. We've watched proudly as Mothercare babies grow up and come to us with babies of their own, and we are totally committed to continuing our tradition of service to the nation's little ones and their parents.

Offering a full range of maternity clothing, baby wear, bedding, safety items, cosmetics and baby equipment such as cots, prams, car seats and pushchairs, the company has recently launched a *Personal Shopper Service*. Providing advice from fully trained sales advisers, help with a comprehensive range of products, and expertise and knowledge on product features and benefits, this service is specifically aimed at couples seeking guidance on the purchasing decisions associated with their change in family status. For couples wishing to spread the cost of their purchases, a Nursery Plan and Mothercare account card are also on offer, while those without the time to visit the store are catered for with home shopping facilities.

SOURCES: *Mothercare Newborn to Toddler Catalogue,* 1998; *Practical Parenting,* October 1998; *Practical Parenting,* November 1998; *Practical Parenting,* December 1998; *Mother & Baby,* December 1998; *Mother & Baby,* Special Edition 1999; *Pregnancy Plus,* November/December 1998. *Advertisement*: Courtesy of Mothercare.

Free wellies with kids' coats & jackets at mothercare*

Buy any kids' coat or jacket & get a free pair of wellies.

Buying behaviour The decision process and actions of people involved in buying and using products

Consumer buying behaviour The buying behaviour of ultimate consumers—those who purchase products for personal or household use

Throughout their lives consumers purchase numerous products of all kinds. However, for many couples the arrival of a baby signals a period of learning about and purchasing a wide variety of new products. The importance of the occasion is reflected in the time and care that is dedicated to these purchases. It is not surprising that retailers often make considerable efforts to determine their customers' needs and gain a better understanding of their buying behaviour.

The decision process and actions of people involved in buying and using products are termed their **buying behaviour.**[1] **Consumer buying behaviour** is the buying behaviour of ultimate consumers—those who purchase products for personal or household use. Consumer buying behaviour is not concerned with the purchase of items for business use.

There are important reasons for marketers to analyse consumer buying behaviour. The success of a company's marketing strategy will depend on how buyers react to it. As indicated in Chapter 1, the marketing concept stresses that the marketing mix which companies develop must be designed with customer needs in mind. To find out what satisfies customers, marketers must examine the main influences on what, where, when and how consumers buy. By understanding these factors better, marketers are better able to predict how consumers will respond to marketing strategies. Ultimately, this information helps companies compete more effectively in the marketplace and leads to more satisfied customers.

Although marketers try to understand and influence consumer buying behaviour, they cannot control it. Some critics credit them with the ability to manipulate buyers, but marketers have neither the power nor the knowledge to do so. Their knowledge of behaviour comes from what psychologists, social psychologists and sociologists know about human behaviour in general. Even if marketers wanted to manipulate buyers, the lack of laws and principles in the behavioural sciences would prevent them from doing so.

This chapter begins by examining the types of decision-making in which consumers engage. It then analyses the major stages of the consumer buying decision process and the personal, psychological and social factors that influence it. The chapter concludes by assessing the importance of understanding consumer buying behaviour.

Types of Consumer Buying Behaviour

Different consumers have a varied and wide range of needs and wants. The acquisition of products and services helps these consumers to satisfy their current and future needs. To achieve this objective, consumers make many purchasing decisions. For example, people make many decisions daily regarding food, clothing, shelter, medical care, education, recreation or transport. As they make these decisions, they engage in different decision-making behaviour. The amount of time and effort, both mental and physical, that buyers expend in decision-making varies considerably from situation to situation—and from consumer to consumer. Consumer decisions can thus be classified into one of three broad categories: routine response behaviour, limited decision-making and extensive decision-making.[2]

Routine response behaviour
Behaviour that occurs when buying frequently purchased, low cost, low risk items that need little search and decision effort

A consumer practises **routine response behaviour** when buying frequently purchased, low cost, low risk items that need very little search and decision effort. When buying such items, a consumer may prefer a particular brand, but he or she is familiar with several brands in the product class and views more than one as being acceptable. The products a consumer buys through routine response behaviour are purchased almost automatically. For most buyers, the time and effort involved in selecting a bag of sugar or a bar of soap is comparatively minimal. If the supermarket has run out of the required brand, the buyers will probably select an alternative brand instead.

Limited decision-making Behaviour that occurs when buying products purchased only occasionally, for which a moderate amount of information gathering and deliberation is needed

Buyers engage in **limited decision-making** when they buy products occasionally and when they need to obtain information about an unfamiliar brand in a familiar product category. This type of decision-making requires a moderate amount of time for information gathering and deliberation. For example, if Sega launches a new computer game aimed at teenagers, buyers may seek additional information about the new product, perhaps by asking a friend who has tested the game or seen it reviewed. Similarly, if a well known brand appears in a new form, the consumer will take extra time.

Extensive decision-making
Behaviour that occurs when a purchase involves unfamiliar, expensive, high risk or infrequently bought products for which the buyer spends much time seeking information and comparing brands before deciding on the purchase

The most complex decision-making behaviour, **extensive decision-making**, comes into play when a purchase involves unfamiliar, expensive, high risk or infrequently bought products—for instance, cars, homes, holidays or personal pensions. The buyer uses many criteria to evaluate alternative brands or choices and spends much time seeking information and comparing alternative brands before deciding on the purchase.

Impulse buying Behaviour that involves no conscious planning but results from a powerful, persistent urge to buy something immediately

By contrast, **impulse buying** involves no conscious planning but a powerful, persistent urge to buy something immediately. For some individuals, impulse buying may be the dominant buying behaviour. Impulse buying, however, often provokes emotional conflicts. For example, a teenager may purchase a new pair of fashionable boots, but later regrets the expense because the boots are uncomfortable to wear. Marketers often capitalise on the tendency towards impulse buying—for example, by placing magazines and confectionery next to supermarket checkout counters.

The purchase of a particular product does not always elicit the same type of decision-making behaviour.[3] In some instances, buyers engage in extensive decision-making the first time they purchase a certain kind of product but find that limited decision-making suffices when they buy the product again. If a routinely purchased, formerly satisfying brand no longer pleases, a consumer may use either limited or extensive decision processes to switch to a new brand. For example, if the video tapes a family usually buys are becoming damaged too easily, a better quality brand may be sought through limited or extensive decision-making.

The Consumer Buying Decision Process

Consumer buying decision process
A five stage process that includes problem recognition, information search, evaluation of alternatives, purchase and post-purchase evaluation

As explained earlier, a major part of buying behaviour is the decision process used in making purchases. The **consumer buying decision process**, shown in Figure 4.1, includes five stages: (1) problem recognition, (2) information search, (3) evaluation of alternatives, (4) purchase and (5) post-purchase evaluation. Although it is important to conduct a detailed review of these stages, a number of general observations are also pertinent. First, the actual act of purchasing is only one stage in the process; the process is begun several stages before the actual purchase. Second, not all decision processes lead to a purchase, even though the

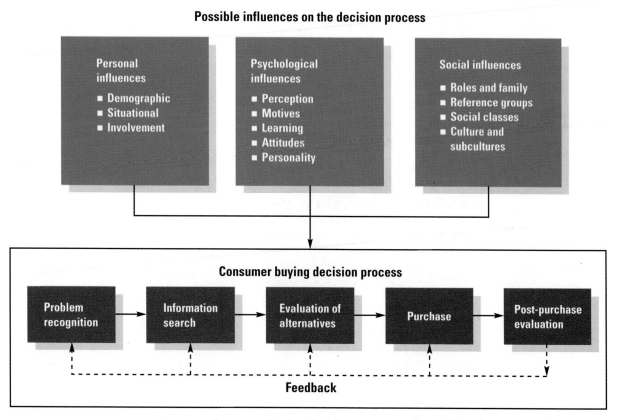

Figure 4.1   Consumer buying decision process and possible influences on the process

process implies that it does. A consumer may stop the process at any time. It is also possible that a different sequence of stages will be followed, with buyers revisiting certain stages. Finally, consumer decisions do not always include all five stages. People engaged in extensive decision-making usually go through all stages of this decision process, whereas those engaged in limited decision-making and routine response behaviour may omit certain parts.

Problem Recognition   Problem recognition occurs when a buyer becomes aware that there is a difference between a desired state and an actual condition. For example, consider a sales manager who needs to keep a record of appointments. When, at the end of the year, her old diary is finished, she recognises that a difference exists between the desired state—a current diary—and the actual condition—an out-of-date one. She therefore makes the decision to buy a new diary.

Sometimes a person has a problem or need but is unaware of it. As shown in Figure 4.2, some consumers might be concerned about their weight but might not be aware that Hellmann's has introduced a low calorie mayonnaise. Marketers use sales personnel, advertising, sales promotion and packaging to help trigger

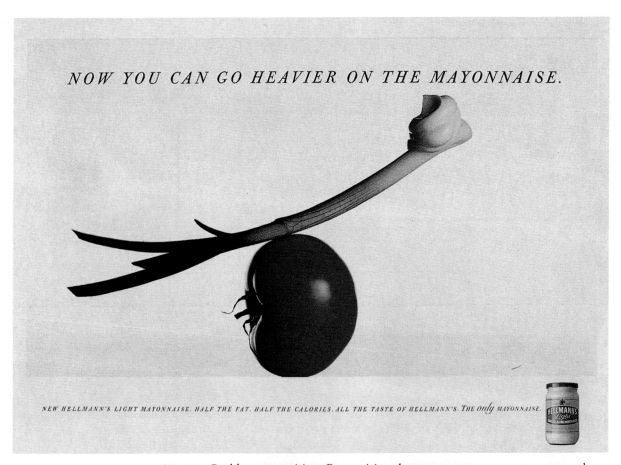

Figure 4.2 Problem recognition. Recognising that many consumers are concerned about their weight, Hellmann's has introduced a low calorie mayonnaise.
SOURCE: Hellmann's is a registered trademark of CPC International.

recognition of such needs or problems. For example, travel agents may advertise package holidays immediately after the Christmas and New Year holidays. People who see the advertisements may realise that now is a good time to plan their summer holidays. The speed of consumer problem recognition can be either slow or rapid, depending on the individual concerned and the way in which need recognition was triggered.

Information Search

After recognising the problem or need, the buyer (if continuing the decision process) searches for information about products that will help resolve the problem or satisfy the need. For example, the people mentioned above, after recognising the need to plan their holiday, may search for information about different tour operators, travel options and possible locations. Information is acquired over time from the consumer's surroundings and ever more frequently on the Internet. The impact which the information has will depend on how the consumer interprets it.

There are two aspects to information search. In the **internal search,** buyers search their memory for information about products that might solve the problem. If they cannot retrieve enough information from their memory for a decision, they seek additional information in an **external search.** The external search may involve communicating with friends and colleagues, comparing available brands and prices, or reviewing television or press advertisements, and public sources including the World Wide Web. An individual's personal contacts—friends, relatives, associates—are often viewed as credible sources of information because the consumer trusts and respects them. A consumer study has shown that word-of-mouth communication has a stronger impact on consumer judgements of products than do printed communications, unless the buyer has a well defined prior impression or unless printed information about a product is extremely negative.[4] Using information sources which have been generated by marketers, such as salespeople, advertising, package labelling, in-store demonstrations and displays, typically does not require much effort on the consumer's part. Buyers can also obtain information from public sources—for instance, government reports, news stories, the World Wide Web, consumer publications and reports from product testing organisations. Many companies use public relations to try to capitalise on these sources because consumers often perceive them as factual and unbiased. The external search is also characterised by the extensiveness, manner and order in which brands, stores, attributes and sources are considered. For example, a schoolboy choosing a new pair of training shoes may look at or try on several brands at a number of sports shops before reaching a final decision.

Consumer groups are increasingly demanding access to greater quantities of relevant product information. However, research indicates that buyers make poorer choices if overloaded with large amounts of information.[5] Improving the quality of information and stressing features important to buyers in the decision process may help buyers make better purchase decisions.

How consumers use and process the information obtained in their search depends on features of the information itself, namely, availability, quantity, quality, repetition and format. If all the necessary information for a decision is available in the store, consumers may have no need to conduct an internal information search and the decision process may be easier.[6] It is important to recognise that adequate information may not always be available. Sometimes consumers must make do with whatever data are on hand at the time of purchase. For example, a motorist replacing a broken windscreen following a road accident may not have

Internal search One in which the buyer searches his or her memory for information about products

External search One that focuses on information not available from the consumer's memory

enough time to review all relevant sources of information because the car is needed again urgently.

Repetition, a technique well known to advertisers, increases consumer learning of information. When seeing or hearing an advertising message for the first time, the recipient may not grasp all its important details but learns more details as the message is repeated. Nevertheless, even when commercials are initially effective, repetition eventually causes the phenomenon of "wear-out": consumers pay less attention to the commercial and respond to it less favourably than they did at first.[7] Consumers are more likely to be receptive to repetition when making a low involvement purchase. **Involvement** refers to the level of interest, emotion and activity which the consumer is prepared to expend on a particular purchase. For example, a consumer who buys a pack of audio tapes may have very low interest in the product itself but may elect to buy the particular brand because it is being offered at a discounted price.

The format in which information is transmitted to the buyer may also determine its use. Information can be presented verbally, numerically or visually. For many consumer tasks, pictures are remembered better than words, and the combination of pictures and words further enhances learning.[8] Consequently, marketers pay great attention to the visual components of their advertising materials.

A successful information search yields a group of brands that a buyer views as possible alternatives. This group of products is sometimes called the buyer's **evoked set.** For example, an evoked set of compact disc players might be those manufactured by Sony, Aiwa, JVC and Philips.

Evaluation of Alternatives

When evaluating the products in the evoked set, a buyer establishes criteria for comparing the products. These criteria are the characteristics or features that the buyer wants (or does not want). For example, one buyer may favour a compact disc player with remote control, whereas another may have no preference as to the size of the machine but be unwilling to pay a premium for the remote control. The buyer also assigns a certain **salience,** or level of importance, to each criterion; some features and characteristics carry more weight than others. The salience of criteria varies from buyer to buyer. For example, when choosing a newspaper one buyer may consider the political stance of the editorial to be crucial, while another might place more importance on the quality and coverage of sports. Using the criteria, a buyer rates and eventually ranks the brands in the evoked set. Obviously this involves comparing the brands with each other as well as with the salient criteria. If the evaluation stage does not yield a brand that the buyer is willing to purchase, a further information search may be necessary. Marketing Insight 4.1 considers how the criteria used by car buyers are changing.

Marketers can influence consumers' evaluation by *framing* the alternatives— that is, by the manner in which the alternative and its attributes are described. Framing can make a characteristic seem more important to a consumer and can facilitate its recall from memory. For example, by emphasising the lycra in women's hosiery, manufacturers can encourage the consumer to consider this particular aspect significant. Framing affects the decision processes of inexperienced buyers more than those of experienced ones.[9] If the evaluation of alternatives yields one or more brands that the consumer is willing to buy, the consumer is ready to move on to the next stage of the decision process—the purchase.

Purchase

The purchase stage, when the consumer chooses which product or brand to buy, is mainly the outcome of the consumer's evaluation of alternatives, but other fac-

Involvement The level of interest, emotion and activity which the consumer is prepared to expend on a particular purchase.

Evoked set The group of products that a buyer views as possible alternatives after conducting an information search

Salience The level of importance a buyer assigns to each criterion for comparing products

Car Buyers Shun Speed and Sex

The annual national motor shows such as those staged in Paris, Frankfurt or at Birmingham's NEC feature bright lights, shiny paintwork, glamorous models, loud music and the latest in visual floorshows. For decades, car launches have focused on performance, sex appeal and sporty imagery. Results from the latest survey by the AA (Automobile Association) of 9,400 of its members reveal that car advertisements featuring speed and sex appeal now fail to seduce motorists in most markets. The average driver is more concerned with safety and reliability. Complex dashboards with trendy gadgets fall well behind features such as fuel economy and good brakes. Speed performance came only 27th in a list of 40 factors influencing car buyers. No longer included in this year's top 10 most desired attributes were high tech features, high speed and sex appeal.

According to the AA, "Mr and Mrs Ordinary Motorist are more turned on by mechanical reliability, good all-round vision, reassuring brakes and ease of getting in and out of the car . . . Theft and safety are fundamental concerns." Most drivers want comfortable cars suitable for school runs and long journeys, with hard wearing interiors, reasonable fuel economy and—befitting the latest promotional campaigns by Ford, Vauxhall or VW—safety and security. While some manufacturers have helped create this switch, government anti-theft campaigns have also instilled the changing attitudes of today's motorist. Ford recently ran a series of high profile television and press advertisements emphasising safety features such as anti-lock brakes, side impact protection mouldings, crumple zones and air bags—plus security features such as deadlocks, alarms, immobilisers and tracking systems. This focus on safety and security is taken right through Ford's communications package: advertising, press releases, dealer videos for showrooms, brochure features and salesforce training. With the usual concern for reliability, the top 10 features from the AA's survey confirm the switch away from performance and sex appeal to safety and security as key requirements for car buyers.

Top 10 Features
1 Reliability
2 Vision
3 Accident avoidance
4 Fuel economy
5 Security against thieves
6 Air pollution control
7 Ease of getting in and out
8 Supportive, adjustable driver's seat
9 Injury prevention
10 Roadholding ability

While companies such as Ford help determine the views of the car buying public, such consumer opinions are also influenced by media coverage, personal experience, the comments of family and friends, and the actions of regulatory bodies and consumer watchdogs, as well as by the marketing campaigns for other products and services. Safety and security are emotive issues that through a variety of sources have come to dominate customer needs in many segments of the car market. As the AA survey implies, far fewer motorists today are concerned with *911* acceleration or *XR3i* image appeal. There are still groups of car buyers who desire such performance and sex appeal, and manufacturers do cater for them with separate models or revved up model derivatives. The mainstream car buying segments, though, changed significantly in their wants and worries as the 1990s came to a close.

Sources: "Speed and sex appeal low down on list for drivers", *Evening Telegraph*, 18 June 1995; The AA PR Office, Hampshire, 1995/1996; *What Car?* magazine.

tors have an impact, too. The closeness of alternative stores and product availability can both influence which brand is purchased. For example, if the brand the buyer ranked highest is not available in the local supermarket, an alternative may be selected.

During this stage, the buyer also picks the seller from whom the product will be purchased and finalises the terms of the sale. Other issues such as price, delivery, guarantees, service agreements, installation and credit arrangements are discussed and settled. Finally, the purchase takes place, although in some cases the consumer terminates the buying decision process before reaching that point.

Post-purchase Evaluation After the purchase has taken place, the buyer begins evaluating the product to check whether its actual performance meets expected levels. Many of the criteria used in evaluating alternatives are applied again during the post-purchase evaluation. This stage will determine whether the consumer is satisfied or dissatisfied. Either outcome strongly influences consumers' motivation and information processing. Consumers' satisfaction or dissatisfaction determines whether they make a complaint, communicate with other possible buyers or purchase the product again.[10] A recent study shows that UK consumers are more likely to complain about products than in the past. Figure 4.3 illustrates the type of action which consumers are prepared to take. Some marketing experts believe that this rise in consumer assertiveness is a positive move which illustrates industry's willingness to respond to feedback about products and services.[11] The impact of the post-purchase evaluation is illustrated by the feedback loop in Figure 4.1.

Cognitive dissonance Doubts that occur as the buyer questions whether he or she made the right decision in purchasing the product

Shortly after the purchase of an expensive product, the post-purchase evaluation may result in **cognitive dissonance**—doubts that occur because the buyer questions whether the right decision was made in purchasing the product. For example, after buying a new personal computer, an accountant may feel anxious about whether the brand will be reliable or if the warranty is adequate. A buyer who experiences cognitive dissonance may attempt to return the product or may seek positive information about it to justify the choice. For example, motoring journalists often note with amusement that car shows and exhibitions are frequented by consumers who have just recently purchased a new car.

As shown in Figure 4.1, three major categories of influences are believed to affect the consumer buying decision process: personal, psychological and social factors. These are the factors that determine which particular newspaper, choco-

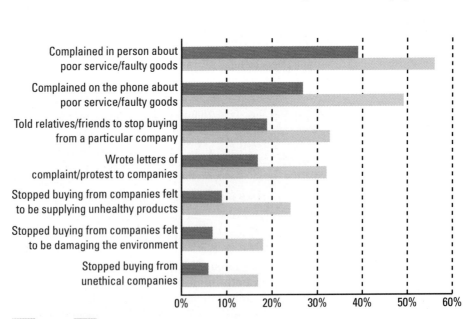

Figure 4.3 The nature of customer complaints. SOURCE: Neill Denny, "Why complaining is our new hobby", from *Marketing Magazine,* 26 November 1998, p. 16. Reprinted with permission.

late bar, washing powder, camera, holiday, car or house a certain consumer will buy. Understanding these aspects helps marketers gain valuable insights into their customer base and can help ensure that a more suitable marketing mix is developed. The remainder of this chapter focuses on these factors. Although each major factor is discussed separately, it is important to realise that it is a combination of their effects which influences the consumer buying decision process.

Personal Factors Influencing the Buying Decision Process

Personal influencing factors
Factors unique to a particular individual

Personal factors are unique to a particular person. Many different personal factors can influence purchasing decisions. In this section three types are considered: demographic factors, situational factors and level of involvement.

Demographic Factors

Demographic factors Individual characteristics such as age, sex, race, ethnic origin, income, family life cycle and occupation

Demographic factors are individual characteristics such as age, sex, race, ethnic origin, income, family life cycle and occupation. (These and other characteristics are discussed in Chapter 7 as possible variables for segmentation purposes.) Demographic factors have a bearing on who is involved in family decision-making. For example, it was estimated that by the late 1990s the UK would have the largest market for children's toys and clothes in the EU and the highest proportion of children in the population.

Children aged 6 to 17 are known to have more influence in the buying decision process for breakfast cereals, ice cream, soft drinks, holidays and even the family car than ever before.[12] This influence is increasingly reflected in the way such products are designed and marketed. For example, holiday brochures now contain pictures and information designed to appeal to children and teenagers. Demographic factors may also partially govern behaviour during a specific stage of the decision process. During the information stage, for example, a young person may consult a greater number of information sources than an older, more experienced adult. Marketing Insight 4.2 shows how mobile telephone companies are developing products specifically designed to appeal to younger consumers.

Demographic factors also affect the extent and way in which products in a specific product category are used. While consumers aged 18 to 30 may purchase furniture, appliances and other household basics as they establish their own households, those aged 45 to 54 spend more money on luxury and leisure products after their children have left home.[13] Brand preferences, store choice and timing of purchases are other areas on which demographic factors have some impact. Consider, for example, how differences in occupation result in variations in product needs. A car mechanic and a nanny may earn similar incomes, yet spend their earnings entirely differently. While both require work clothes to carry out their jobs, the mechanic will buy heavy duty boots and overalls, while the nanny opts for a smart, more formal uniform. Their choice of vehicle will also be quite different. While the mechanic selects a basic, but robust, van, the nanny buys a small four door hatchback with room for her charges and a pushchair. Thus occupation clearly affects consumer buying behaviour.

Situational Factors

Situational factors External circumstances or conditions that exist when a consumer is making a purchase decision

Situational factors are the external circumstances or conditions that exist when a consumer is making a purchase decision. These factors can influence the buyer at any stage of the consumer buying decision process and may cause the individual to shorten, lengthen or terminate the process. For example, a college lecturer who usually communicates with overseas colleagues by e-mail may be forced to use the fax machine when her computer breaks down. Alternatively, a young couple planning their wedding may postpone their plans following the death of a close relative.

The effects of situational factors can be felt throughout the buying decision process in a variety of ways. Uncertainty about employment may sway a consumer against making a purchase. On the other hand, a conviction that the supply of a particular product is sharply limited may impel a person to buy it. For example, consumers have purchased and hoarded petrol, food products and even toilet tissue when these products were believed to be in short supply. These and other situational factors can change rapidly; their influence on purchase decisions is generally as sudden as it is short lived.

The amount of time a consumer has available to make a decision is a situational factor that strongly influences buying decisions. If there is little time for selecting and purchasing a product, a person may quickly decide to buy a readily available brand. The amount of available time also affects the way consumers process the information contained in advertisements[14] and the length of the stages within the decision process. For example, if a family is planning to buy a new television set, its members may gather and consider a wide range of information from a variety of sources. They may read consumer magazines, consider mail order catalogues, talk to friends and salespersons, look at a number of advertisements and spend a good deal of time doing comparative shopping in a number of stores and on the Internet. However, if the family's 10 year old television set suddenly breaks down and cannot be repaired, the extent of the information search, the number of alternatives considered and the amount of comparative shopping may be much more restricted. Indeed, given the time factor, if these family members were reasonably satisfied with the performance of the old set and service arrangements, they may buy an up-to-date model of the same brand.

Levels of Involvement

Level of involvement The level of interest, emotional commitment and time spent searching for a product in a particular situation

Many aspects of consumer buying decisions are affected by the individual's **level of involvement.** This term refers to the level of interest, emotional commitment and time spent searching for a product in a particular situation. A buyer's level of involvement determines why he or she is motivated to seek information about certain products and brands but virtually ignores others. The extensiveness of the buying decision process varies greatly with the consumer's level of involvement. The sequence of the steps in this process may also be altered. Low involvement buyers may form an attitude towards a product—perhaps as a result of an advertising campaign—and evaluate its features after purchasing it rather than before.[15] Conversely, high involvement buyers spend much time and effort researching their purchase beforehand. For example, the purchase of a car, such as the Honda shown in Figure 4.4, is a high involvement decision.

The level of consumer involvement experienced is linked to a number of factors. Consumers tend to be more involved in the purchase of high priced goods and products that are visible to others, such as clothing, jewellery or cars. As levels of perceived risk increase, involvement levels are likely to rise. Furthermore, individuals may experience enduring involvement with a product class. *Enduring involvement* is an ongoing interest in a product class because of personal relevance. For example, people often have enduring involvement with products associated with their leisure activities. These individuals engage in ongoing search and information gathering processes for these products over extensive periods of time, irrespective of whether or not a purchase is imminent. Golf enthusiasts often read about the sport

Cellnet Targets "U"

A battle is afoot for a stake in the pre-paid mobile phone market. These flexible pay-as-you-go packages, which allow users to enjoy the benefits of mobile phone ownership without the binding commitment of a contract, have injected new life into the market. In just 12 months, 1.5 million new UK subscribers have bought into pre-paid packages. It seems that the growth is just beginning, with research indicating room for considerable increases in the pre-pay market. With UK penetration figures of just 20 per cent, considerably behind the 30–40 per cent norms seen in the rest of Europe, it is not hard to see why. Early indications suggest that young adults are particularly interested in this flexible proposition. For the first time, mobile phone ownership is within the grasp of the under 18s, who previously had been barred by contractual requirements. Now, more than ever, mobile phone ownership is seen as young and trendy and open to more consumers. Even parents are considering mobile phone ownership as an option for their children. On the back of the upsurge in interest, a new study published by Continental Research suggests that penetration of mobile phones in the UK could double within five years.

Growth in UK Subscribers Network
(Number of subscribers)

	12/96	12/97	9/98
Cellnet GSM	883,000	2,060,000	2,856,000
Cellnet Analogue	1,797,000	930,000	530,000
Total Cellnet	2,680,000	2,990,000	3,386,000
Vodafone GSM	1,220,000	2,335,000	3,092,000
Vodafone Analogue	1,580,000	805,000	857,000
Total Vodafone	2,800,000	3,140,000	3,949,000
Orange	785,000	1,120,000	1,650,000
One 2 One	545,000	1,014,000	1,485,000
Total UK	6,810,000	8,264,000	10,470,000

SOURCE: Continental Research

First to launch its UK pre-pay service was One 2 One, which was closely followed by Orange and Vodafone offerings. Now Cellnet has also entered the fray, initially going to market with its Easylife pre-pay service. More recently the company has emphasised its presence with the £3.5m launch of its new "U" service, which targets 16 to 24 year olds. This is an important time for the company, which has seen its market share fall from about 39 per cent at the end of 1996 to 32 per cent by September 1998. Cellnet is clear about the focus of "U" upon the youth market, launching the service with a series of television advertisements which portray difficult dilemmas for individuals to resolve. The emphasis of the programme is on freedom from interference, culminating in the statement "It's your call". According to board account director Will Harris, "The aim was to create a brand that appeals directly and exclusively to the young." Marketing director Kent Thexton adds, "The flexibility of no subscription, no bills, no contract and no credit check clearly appeals to this age group." A print, radio, poster and cinema advertising campaign are supporting the programme of TV advertisements.

SOURCES: Robert McLuhan, "Cellnet plays freedom card", *Marketing*, 26 November 1998, p. 23; "Cellnet to try out second youth brand", *Marketing Week*, 22 October 1998, p. 9; Martin Croft, "Factfile: upwardly mobile market", *Marketing Week*, 22 October 1998, pp. 40–41.

HONDA

Produced by Haymarket Motoring Group Special Projects for Honda (UK) Ltd, 4 Power Road, Chiswick, London W4 5YT
Photography Julian Mackie **Assistant** Jono Teighe **Design** Dave Alexander

First man, then machine

Figure 4.4 Reaching consumers who have a high level of involvement. Choosing a car is a high involvement purchase decision, as leading car manufacturer Honda knows. SOURCE: Courtesy of Honda UK.

and may avidly follow televised tournaments. They may visit championship golf courses and browse mail order catalogues to see the latest golf related products.

Situational involvement is experienced by buyers as a result of the particular circumstance or environment in which they find themselves. This type of involvement, sometimes also called pre-purchase involvement, is temporary because the conditions that triggered the high degree of involvement may change.[16] If a man is searching for an engagement ring for his prospective fiancée, for example, he will probably experience a high level of involvement in the purchase decision. His information search and evaluation of alternatives may be extensive. However, once the selection has been made, he may no longer see an engagement ring as being personally relevant.

Many purchase decisions do not generate great involvement on the consumer's part. When the involvement level is low, as with routine response purchases, then buying is almost automatic, and the information search and evaluation of alternatives are extremely limited. The purchase of floor cleaner, for example, represents a low involvement purchase decision for many consumers; the product is chosen out of habit and with minimal effort.

Psychological factors Factors that influence consumer behaviour, including perception, motives, learning, attitudes and personality

Psychological factors operating within individuals partly determine people's general behaviour and thus influence their behaviour as consumers. The primary psychological influences on consumer behaviour are (1) perception, (2) motives, (3) learning, (4) attitudes and (5) personality. Even though these psychological factors operate internally, it will become apparent later in this chapter that they are highly affected by social forces external to the individual.

Perception

Perception The process of selecting, organising and interpreting information inputs to produce meaning

Information inputs The sensations received through sight, taste, hearing, smell and touch

Are the horsemen in Figure 4.5 riding to the left or to the right? It could be either way depending on how you perceive the riders. People's perception of the same thing varies. Similarly, the same individual at different times may perceive the same item in a number of ways. **Perception** is the process of selecting, organising and interpreting information inputs to produce meaning. **Information inputs** are the sensations received through sight, taste, hearing, smell and touch. Each time we see an advertisement, go on-line, visit shops or use a product, we receive information inputs.

As the definition indicates, perception consists of three steps. The first step of the perceptual process is the selection of information. Although individuals receive numerous pieces of information simultaneously, only a few of them reach awareness. Certain inputs are selected while others are ignored. This **selective exposure** occurs because consumers cannot be conscious of all inputs at the same time, and involves people selecting inputs that are to be exposed to their awareness. A student word-processing a report may be unaware that the light is on, that the computer is making a humming sound, that there is background noise in the room or that other students are working at the same table. Even though these inputs are being received, the student will ignore them until they are mentioned.

Selective exposure
The selection of inputs that people expose to their awareness

An input is more likely to reach awareness if it relates to an anticipated event. If a violent storm has damaged the roof of a couple's house, they are much more

Figure 4.5 Perception. Are the horsemen riding to the left or to the right? SOURCE: © 1988 M.C. Escher c/o Cordon Art-Baarn-Holland.

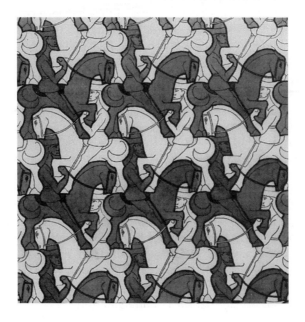

likely to notice a local newspaper advertisement promoting a building and repairs service. An input is more likely to reach awareness if the information helps satisfy current needs. Thus, hungry people are more likely to notice a TGI Friday's sign than are those who are not. Finally, an input is more likely to reach awareness if its intensity changes significantly. When a store manager reduces a price slightly, consumers may not notice because the change is not significant, but if the manager cuts the price in half, they are much more likely to recognise the reduction.

The selective nature of perception leads to two other conditions: selective distortion and selective retention. **Selective distortion** is the changing or twisting of currently received information. This sometimes occurs when a person receives information that is inconsistent with personal feelings or beliefs. For example, an individual who reads some favourable publicity about a company he or she dislikes is likely to distort the information to make it more consistent with personally held views. The publicity may therefore have much more impact on another consumer who views the same brand more positively. In the **selective retention** phenomenon, a person remembers information inputs that support personal feelings and beliefs and forgets inputs that do not. After hearing a sales presentation and leaving the shop, a customer may forget many of the selling points if they contradict pre-existing beliefs.

Selective distortion The changing or twisting of currently received information

Selective retention The process of remembering information inputs that support personal feelings and beliefs and of forgetting those that do not

The information inputs that do reach awareness are not received in an organised form. For them to produce meaning, an individual must enter the second step of the perceptual process—organising and integrating the new information with that already stored in the memory. Although this step is usually carried out quickly, it may take longer when the individual is considering an unfamiliar product area.

Interpretation—the third step in the perceptual process—is the assignment of meaning to what has been organised. A person bases interpretation on what is familiar, on knowledge already stored in memory. For this reason, a company that changes a package design or logo faces a major problem. Since people look for the product in the old, familiar package, they may not recognise it in the new one. Unless a package or logo change is accompanied by a promotional programme that makes people aware of the change, a company may lose sales. Even in cases in which such a programme is conducted, positive reaction from the consumer cannot be guaranteed. For example, when British Airways changed its corporate identity and redesigned its aeroplane tail fins to reflect themes from around the world, consumer reaction to the reduction in the company's overt Britishness was mixed. Companies often try to get around this difficulty by making only small changes to their logo or brand identity.

Although marketers cannot control people's perceptions, they often try to influence them. This may be difficult to achieve for a number of reasons. First, a consumer's perceptual process may prevent the information from being received. Second, a buyer may receive the information but perceive it differently from the way that was intended. For example, when a toothpaste producer advertises that "35 per cent of the people who use this toothpaste have less decay", a customer could infer that 65 per cent of the people who use the product have more tooth decay. Third, buyers who perceive information inputs to be inconsistent with their personally held beliefs are likely to forget the information quickly. In some cases the problem of interpreting information is made more complex by the large number of information inputs that consumers encounter each day.[17] For example, a student travelling by bus to college may pass more than 30 different advertising hoardings, but actually notice only one or two.

In addition to perceptions of packages, products, brands and organisations, individuals also have self-perceptions. That perception is called the person's **self-concept** or self-image. It seems likely that a person's self-concept affects purchase decisions and consumption behaviour. The results of some studies suggest that buyers purchase products that reflect and enhance their self-concepts. For instance, one individual might buy a Rolex watch to project an up-market image, while another might buy a Swatch to enhance acceptability among that person's peer group.

Self-concept   A person's perception of himself or herself; self-image

Motives

A **motive** is an internal, energy giving force that directs a person's activities towards satisfying a need or achieving a goal. Motivation is the set of mechanisms for controlling movement towards goals.[18] A buyer's actions at any time are affected by a set of motives rather than by just one. Each buyer's motives are unique and, at a single point in time, some motives in the set have priority, but the priorities of motives vary from one occasion to another. For example, a person's motives for taking a shower are particularly strong after a trip to the gym. Motivation also affects the direction and intensity of behaviour. Individuals must choose which goals to pursue at a particular time.

Motive   An internal, energy giving force that directs a person's activities towards satisfying a need or achieving a goal

Motives influencing where a person purchases products on a regular basis are called **patronage motives.** A buyer may use a particular shop because of such patronage motives as price, service, location, honesty, product variety or friendliness of salespeople. To capitalise on patronage motives, a marketer should try to determine why regular customers patronise a store and then emphasise these characteristics in the store's marketing mix (see Figure 4.6).

Patronage motives   Those motives that influence where a person purchases products on a regular basis

Although motivation research can be used to analyse the major motives that influence consumers to buy or not buy products, this is not always straightforward. Motives that are subconscious are especially hard to judge, because people are by definition unaware of them and marketers cannot elicit them through direct questioning. Most motivation research relies on interviews or projective techniques.

When researchers study motives through interviews, they may use individual in-depth interviews, focus groups or a combination of the two. In an **in-depth interview,** the researcher tries to get the subject to talk freely about anything at all in order to create an informal atmosphere. Although there is some variation in approach, usually the researcher asks general, non-directed questions and then probes the subject's answers by asking for clarification. An in-depth interview may last for several hours. In a **focus group,** the moderator—through leadership that is not highly structured—tries to generate discussion about one or several topics in a group of six to 12 people. Through what is said in the discussion, the moderator attempts to discover people's motives relating to some issue such as the use of a product. The researcher usually cannot probe as far in a focus group as in an in-depth interview, and some products may not be suitable for such group discussion. To determine the subconscious motives reflected in the interviews, motivation researchers must exhibit a range of qualities: they must be perceived as non-threatening by members of the group, must be able to adopt a demeanour appropriate for the characteristics of the individuals in the group and must be extremely well trained in clinical psychology. The use of sound and video recordings can simplify the process of analysis. Moderators' skill in uncovering

In-depth interview   The collection of data from an individual by an interview

Focus group   A semi-structured discussion involving six to 12 people, led by a moderator

Figure 4.6   Identifying consumer motives.   SOURCE: Courtesy of Alliance & Leicester Pic.

subconscious motives from what is said in an interview determines the effectiveness of their research. Both in-depth and focus group techniques can yield a variety of information. For example, they might help marketers discover why customers continue to buy high cholesterol red meats despite the fact that most say they are working towards reducing their intake of high fat foods.

Projective techniques Tests in which subjects are asked to perform specific tasks for particular reasons, while actually being evaluated for other purposes

Projective techniques are tests in which subjects are asked to perform specific tasks for particular reasons, while actually being evaluated for other purposes. Such tests are based on the assumption that subjects will unconsciously "project" their motives as they perform the required tasks. Researchers trained in projective techniques can analyse the materials a subject produces and make predictions about the subject's subconscious motives. Some common types of projective techniques are word association tests, sentence completion tests and bubble drawings. These are illustrated in Figure 4.7. Such tests can be useful to marketers in a number of ways, such as helping to make advertising more effective.[19]

Motivation research techniques can be reasonably effective but are far from perfect. Marketers who want to research people's motives should obtain the services of professional psychologists skilled in the methods of motivation research.[20]

Figure 4.7 Common types of projective techniques

Word association tests

Subjects are asked to say what words come into their minds when a particular topic/product is mentioned.

Fresh foods are . . .	Frozen foods are . . .
Natural	Processed
Fresh	Quick
Healthy	Simple
Expensive	Convenient
Good for you	Preservatives
Real	Manufactured

Sentence completion tests

Subjects are asked to complete the sentences.

"People who use re-cycled toilet tissue . . ."
"People who look for the ingredients on packets before they buy them are . . ."
"People who buy Swatch watches . . ."

Bubble drawings

Subjects are asked to say what the man is thinking.

CAR SHOWROOM

I just love the one with flowers on it!

Learning

Learning Changes in a person's behaviour caused by information and experience

Learning refers to changes in a person's behaviour caused by information and experience. The consequences of behaviour strongly influence the learning process. Behaviour that results in satisfying consequences tends to be repeated. For example, if consumers purchase a facial moisturising cream which they believe improves their skin tone and makes them look younger, they are more likely to buy the same brand next time. In fact, they may continue to purchase the brand until they are no longer satisfied with it. If the consumers suffer from a sudden and prolonged attack of spots, they may switch their allegiance to an alternative brand.

The ability of buyers to process information when making purchasing decisions varies. For example, when purchasing a computer, a well educated potential buyer who has experience with computers may be able to read, comprehend and synthesise the considerable quantities of information found in the technical brochures for various competing brands. On the other hand, another buyer with more limited abilities may be incapable of performing this task and will have to rely on information obtained from advertisements or from a sales representative of a particular brand.

A critical aspect of an individual's ability to process information is knowledge. **Knowledge** has two components: familiarity with the product and expertise—the ability to apply the product.[21] The duration and intensity of the buying decision process depends on the buyer's familiarity with or prior experience in purchasing and using the product. For example, in Figure 4.8, SOLA builds consumer awareness by informing potential purchasers about the benefits of its varifocal lenses. The individual's knowledge influences his or her search for, re-call and use of information.[22]

When making purchase decisions, inexperienced buyers may use different types of information from more experienced shoppers who are familiar with the product and purchase situation. Inexperienced buyers use price as an indicator of quality more frequently than buyers who have some knowledge of a particular product category.[23] Thus two potential buyers of a pedigreed dog may use quite different types of information in making their purchase decision. The more experienced buyer, wishing to take the animal to dog shows, may seek detailed information about the dog's pedigree; the less experienced buyer, looking for a loyal family pet, may judge the animal by how approachable and friendly it is.

Consumers who lack expertise are more likely to seek the advice of others when making a purchase. More experienced buyers have greater confidence; they also have more knowledge about the product or service and can tell which features are reliable indicators of product quality. For example, consider two families choosing a long haul holiday. Members of one family are unused to overseas travel, are unsure of the suitability of locations offered in travel brochures and do not understand how to investigate flight options or medical and insurance requirements. Members of the other family have taken holidays abroad regularly in many countries. Although on this occasion they intend to visit a country that is new to them, they are sufficiently conversant with this type of travel to make their purchase without assistance and with confidence.

Marketers sometimes help customers to learn about their products and to gain experience with them. Free samples encourage trial and reduce purchase risk. In-store demonstrations help consumers acquire knowledge of product uses. DIY retailer B & Q recently ran a series of extended television advertisements offering detailed guidance on home improvements and decorating. Each advertisement featured step-by-step instructions towards the completion of a particular project. This helps consumers to learn and can create a more favourable attitude towards the company's products. Consumers also learn when they experience products indirectly, by way of information from salespeople, friends and relatives.

Although marketers seek to influence what a consumer learns, their attempts are seldom fully successful. Marketers encounter problems in attracting and holding consumers' attention, providing consumers with the kinds of information

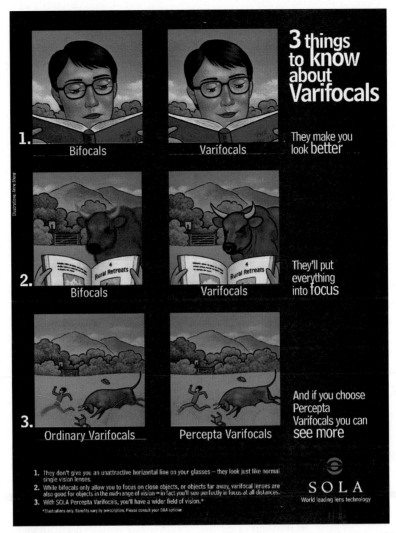

Figure 4.8 Building consumer awareness. SOLA promotes awareness of its varifocal lenses. SOURCE: Courtesy of SOLA.

that are important for making purchase decisions, and convincing them to try the product. These attempts are most likely to be successful when carefully designed to appeal to the target market.

Attitudes

Attitude An individual's enduring evaluation, feelings and behavioural tendencies towards an object or activity

An **attitude** refers to an individual's enduring evaluation, feelings and behavioural tendencies towards an object or activity. The objects or activities towards which we have attitudes may be tangible or intangible, living or non-living. Some attitudes relate to things that have a major impact on our lives, while others are less important. For example, we have attitudes towards relationships, culture and politics, just as we do towards rock music, skiing and pizza.

An individual learns attitudes through experience and interaction with other people. Just as attitudes are learned, they can also be changed. Nevertheless, an individual's attitudes remain generally stable and do not change from moment to moment. Likewise, at any one time, some attitudes will be stronger than others.

For example, members of a family which has recently suffered a house burglary may develop attitudes towards rising crime which are particularly clearly defined. An attitude consists of three major components: cognitive, affective and behavioural. The cognitive component is a person's knowledge and information about the object or idea, whereas the affective component comprises feelings and emotions towards the object or idea. The behavioural component is composed of the action tendencies one exhibits towards the object or idea. Changes in one of these components may or may not alter the other components. Thus consumers may become more knowledgeable about a specific brand without changing the affective or behavioural components of their attitude towards that brand.

Consumer attitudes towards a company and its products greatly influence the success or failure of the company's marketing strategy. When consumers have strong negative attitudes towards one or more aspects of a business's marketing practices, they may not only stop using the business's product but also urge their relatives and friends to do likewise. For example, following the execution of human rights activists in Nigeria, some motorists chose to boycott Shell petrol because of allegations about Shell's activities in Nigeria.

Since attitudes can play such an important part in determining consumer behaviour, marketers should measure consumer attitudes towards prices, package designs, brand names, advertisements, salespeople, repair services, store locations, features of existing or proposed products, and social responsibility activities. Several methods can help marketers gauge these attitudes. One of the simplest ways is to question people directly. A marketing research agency carrying out attitude research for Rayban, for example, might question consumers about their opinions on the latest trends in eye wear. Sometimes marketers evaluate attitudes through attitude scales. An **attitude scale** usually consists of a series of adjectives, phrases or sentences about an object. Subjects are asked to indicate the intensity of their feelings towards the object by reacting to the adjectives, phrases or sentences in a certain way. For example, a researcher measuring attitudes towards "green" products might ask respondents to state the degree to which they agree or disagree with a number of statements, such as "Recycling paper packaging is good for the environment".

If marketers identify particularly negative attitudes towards an aspect of a marketing mix, they may try to change consumer attitudes to make them more favourable. This task is generally long, expensive and difficult and may require extensive promotional efforts. For example, in the UK, Post Office Counters has been advertising to draw customers' attention to the fact that local post offices offer a wide range of services. This publicity is attempting to alter customers' perceptions away from the traditional view that the Post Office exists purely for mailing letters and parcels.

Attitude scale   A series of adjectives, phrases or sentences about an object used by a subject to indicate his or her feelings towards the object

Personality

Personality   All the internal traits and behaviours that make a person unique

Personality includes all the internal traits and behaviours that make a person unique. Each person's unique personality is both inherited and the result of personal experiences. Personalities are typically described as having one or more characteristics, such as compulsiveness, ambitiousness, gregariousness, dogmatism, authoritarianism, introversion, extroversion, aggressiveness and competitiveness. Marketing researchers have for many years attempted to find relationships among such characteristics and buying behaviour, but the results of many studies have been inconclusive. Some researchers see the apparently weak association between personality and buying behaviour as due to unreliable measures rather than because no such relationship exists.[24] A number of marketers are convinced that a consumer's personality does influence the types and brands of products purchased. For example, the type of clothing or cars that people buy, as well as the way their hair is styled and the leisure activities they engage in, may reflect one or more personality characteristics.

At times, marketers aim advertising campaigns at general types of personalities. In doing so, they use positively valued personality characteristics, such as gregariousness, independence or competitiveness. Products promoted in this way include drinks, cars, cigarettes, clothing and computer games. For example, television advertising promoting the launch of new product Tony's Freezer Cocktails aims to appeal to young, outgoing consumers.

Social Factors Influencing the Buying Decision Process

Social factors The forces other people exert on buying behaviour

The forces that other people exert on buying behaviour are called **social factors.** As shown in Figure 4.1, they can be grouped into four major areas: (1) roles and family, (2) reference groups, (3) social classes and (4) culture and sub-cultures.

Roles and Family

Role A set of actions and activities that a person in a particular position is supposed to perform, based on the expectations of both the individual and surrounding people

All of us occupy positions within groups, organisations and institutions. Associated with each position is a **role**—a set of actions and activities that a person in a particular position is supposed to perform, based on the expectations of both the individual and surrounding people. Because people occupy numerous positions, they also have many roles. For example, one man may perform the roles of father, husband, grandfather, son, machine tool operator, part time youth club organiser and member of the local rambling association. Thus there are several sets of expectations placed on each person's behaviour.

An individual's roles influence both general behaviour and buying behaviour. The demands of a person's many roles may be inconsistent and confusing. To illustrate, assume that a man is thinking about buying a boat. While he wants a boat for fishing, his children want one suitable for water skiing. His wife wants him to delay the boat purchase until next year. A colleague at work insists that he should buy a particular brand, known for high performance. Thus an individual's buying behaviour may be partially affected by the input and opinions of family and friends.

Family roles relate directly to purchase decisions. The male head of household is likely to be involved heavily in the purchase of products such as household insurance and alcohol. Although female roles have changed, women still make buying decisions related to many household items, including healthcare products, washing products, household cleaners and food. Husbands and wives participate jointly in the purchase of a variety of products, especially durable goods. Some students aged 16 to 24 may be rebellious; their brand loyalty can be quite changeable. Marketers frequently promote their products during school and college holidays to catch this hard to reach group at a time when they are more receptive to a promotional message.[25] Others in this age group may seek their parents' advice about products with which they are not personally familiar. For example, many college students bank with the same bank as their parents. Children are making many purchase decisions and influencing numerous household purchase decisions that traditionally were made only by husbands and wives. Some buying decisions are made by the whole family. For example, parents and children will usually all be involved in choosing a family holiday, although different family members may play different roles in the process. When two or more individuals participate in a purchase, their roles may dictate that each is responsible for performing certain tasks: initiating the idea, gathering information, deciding whether to buy the product or selecting the specific brand. The particular tasks performed depend on the types of products being considered.

Marketers need to be aware of how roles affect buying behaviour. To develop a marketing mix that meets precisely the needs of the target market, marketers must know not only who does the actual buying but also what other roles influence the purchase.

Reference Groups

Reference group A group with which an individual identifies so much that he or she takes on many of the values, attitudes or behaviour of group members

A group is referred to as a **reference group** when an individual identifies with it so much that he or she takes on many of the values, attitudes or behaviour of group members. Most people have several reference groups, such as families, friends, work colleagues, and social, religious and professional organisations.

A group can be a negative reference group for an individual. Someone may have been a part of a specific group at one time but later have rejected its values and members, even taking specific action to avoid a particular group.[26] However, in this discussion reference groups mean those that the individual involved views positively.

A reference group may serve as a point of comparison and a source of information for an individual. A customer's behaviour may change to be more in line with the actions and beliefs of group members. For example, an elderly lady might stop visiting a particular hairdresser on the advice of a close friend. An individual may seek information from a reference group about the best brand to buy or about other purchase factors, such as where to buy a certain product. The degree to which a reference group will affect a purchase decision depends on an individual's susceptibility to its influence and the strength of his or her involvement with the group. Young people are often especially susceptible to this kind of influence. In general, the more conspicuous a product, the more likely the brand decision will be influenced by reference groups.

A marketer sometimes tries to use reference group influence in advertisements by suggesting that people in a specific group buy a product and are highly satisfied with it. In this type of appeal, the advertiser hopes that many people will accept the suggested group as a reference group and buy (or react more favourably to) the product as a result. Whether this kind of advertising succeeds depends on three factors: (1) how effectively the advertisement communicates the message, (2) the type of product, and (3) the individual's susceptibility to reference group influence.

Opinion leader The member of a reference group who provides information about a specific sphere of interest to reference group participants seeking information

In most reference groups, one or more members stand out as opinion leaders. An **opinion leader** provides information about a specific sphere of interest to reference group participants who seek such information. Opinion leaders are viewed by other group members as being well informed about a particular area and easily accessible. Often because such individuals know that they are opinion leaders, they feel a responsibility to remain informed about the sphere of interest and thus seek out advertisements, manufacturers' brochures, salespeople, web sites and other sources of information.

Social Classes

Social class An open group of individuals who have similar social rank

Within all societies, people rank others into higher or lower positions of respect. This ranking results in social classes. A **social class** is an open group of individuals who have similar social rank. A class is referred to as "open" because people can move into and out of it. The criteria for grouping people into classes vary from one society to another. In the UK, as in other western countries, many factors are taken into account, including occupation, education, income, wealth, race, ethnic group and possessions. In the former Soviet Union, wealth and income are less important in determining social class than education and occupation: although Russian doctors and scientists do not make a great deal of money, they are highly valued in Russian society. A person who is ranking someone does not necessarily apply all of a society's criteria. The number and importance of the factors chosen depend on the characteristics of the individual being ranked and the values of the person who is doing the ranking. For example, one individual may particularly respect status within a church or religious sect, while another may regard it as having little relevance.

To some degree, people within social classes develop and assume common patterns of behaviour. They may have similar attitudes, values, language patterns and possessions. Social class influences many aspects of people's lives. For example, it affects whom they marry, their likelihood of having children and the children's chances of surviving infancy. It influences childhood training, choice of religion, selection of occupation and the way in which people spend their time. Because social class has a bearing on so many aspects of a person's life, it also affects buying decisions. For example, up-market fashion labels Chanel and Versace are popular among upper class Europeans because they believe these brands symbolise their status, income and aspirations.

Social class affects the type, quality and quantity of products that a person buys and uses. Social class also affects an individual's shopping patterns and the types of stores patronised. Advertisements are sometimes based on an appeal to a specific social class. See Table 4.1 for an analysis of the categories of social class which have been used in the UK for many years. In a recent development, it is possible that a new social classification system will replace the old ABC1 approach. A sociology professor was asked to create a new classification system for use by the UK's Office for National Statistics. This system was unveiled in December 1998 and is subsequently undergoing a review by a panel of experts.[27]

The new system, like the old ABC1 approach, is based on occupation, but aims to reflect more closely consumers' purchasing power on the basis of their position in the labour market. Table 4.2 illustrates the proposed system, the success of which will depend partly on the willingness of marketers and marketing research companies to embrace a move away from the familiar territory of ABC1.

Culture and Sub-cultures

Culture All the things around us that are made by human beings: tangible items, such as food, furniture, buildings, clothing and tools; and intangible concepts, such as education, the legal system, healthcare and religion; plus values and behaviours

Culture consists of everything in our surroundings that is made by human beings. It includes tangible items, such as food, furniture, buildings, clothing and tools, and intangible concepts, such as education, the legal system, healthcare and religion. Culture also includes the values and wide range of behaviours that are acceptable within a specific society. The concepts, values and behaviours that make up a culture are learned and passed on from one generation to the next.

Culture influences buying behaviour, determining what people wear and eat, how they socialise, where they live and travel. Certainly, society's interest in the healthiness of food has affected companies' approaches to developing and promoting their products. Culture also influences how consumers buy and use products and the satisfaction gained from them. In many western cultures, shortage of time is a growing problem because of the increasing number of women who work and the current emphasis placed on physical and mental self-development. Many people do time saving shopping and buy convenience and labour saving products to cope with this problem.[28]

Because culture, to some degree, determines how products are purchased and used, it in turn affects the development, promotion, distribution and pricing of products. Food marketers, for example, have had to make a multitude of changes

Approximate Social Grade	Social Status	Head of Household's Occupation	Percentage of Families
A	Upper middle class	Higher managerial, administrative or professional	3
B	Middle class	Intermediate managerial, administrative or professional	10
C1	Lower middle class	Supervisory or clerical and junior managerial, administrative or professional	24
C2	Skilled working class	Skilled manual workers	30
D	Manual workers	Semi- and unskilled manual workers	25
E	Those at lowest levels of subsistence	State pensioners or widows (no other earner), casual or lowest grade workers	8

A—Upper middle class: The head of the household is a successful business or professional person, senior civil servant, or has considerable private means. A young person in some of these occupations who has not fully established himself/herself may still be found in Grade B, though he/she should eventually reach grade A. In country or suburban areas, A-grade householders usually live in large detached houses or in expensive flats. In towns, they may live in expensive flats or town houses in the better parts of town.

B—Middle class: In general, the heads of B-grade households will be quite senior people but not at the very top of their profession or business. They are quite well off, but their style of life is generally respectable rather than rich or luxurious. Non-earners will be living on private pensions or on fairly modest private means.

C1—Lower middle class: In general it is made up of the families of small tradespeople and non-manual workers who carry out less important administrative, supervisory and clerical jobs, i.e. what are sometimes called "white collar" workers.

C2—Skilled working class: Consists in the main of skilled manual workers and their families: the serving of an apprenticeship may be a guide to membership of this class.

D—Semi-skilled and unskilled manual workers: Consists entirely of manual workers, generally semi-skilled or unskilled.

E—Those at lowest levels of subsistence: Consists of old age pensioners, widows and their families, casual workers and those who, through sickness or unemployment, are dependent on social security schemes, or have very small private means.

SOURCE: From Peter M. Chisnall, *Marketing: A Behavioural Analysis,* Third Edition, (Berkshire, England: McGraw-Hill Publishing Co., Ltd., 1995), pp. 144–145. Reprinted by permission.

Table 4.1 Socio-economic classification (JICNARS)

in their marketing efforts. Thirty years ago most families ate at least two meals a day together, and the mother devoted four to six hours a day to preparing those meals. Now more than 60 per cent of women aged 25 to 54 are employed outside the home, and average family incomes have risen considerably. These shifts, along with lack of time, have resulted in dramatic increases in per capita consumption of shelf-stable foods like Pot Rice and Pot Noodles, frozen meals and take-away foods.[29] As a result of increasing demands from those wishing to "eat on the move", petrol stations now stock a variety of prepared sandwiches and snacks.

Table 4.2 Towards a new ABC1?

> ### Towards a new ABC1?
>
> In his newly revised Social Class System, Professor Rose proposes that consumers be divided into 17 narrow classifications by occupation, taking into consideration employment relationships between managers and the managed. These 17 classifications can be grouped into eight broad categories.
>
> 1 Professionals (currently ABC1s): doctors, vets, teachers, lawyers, librarians and social workers, plus business executives and successful entrepreneurs.
>
> 2 Junior managers in smaller organisations (currently C1s): journalists, police sergeants and constables, plus hospital nurses, research executives and market researchers.
>
> 3 Intermediate occupations (currently C2s): clerical workers, secretaries, those formerly classified as skilled manual, plus dental nurses, telephone engineers and computer technicians.
>
> 4 Small employers with fewer than 25 employees; the self-employed.
>
> 5 Supervisors of those in semi-routine and routine occupations, i.e. working class supervisors.
>
> 6 Semi-routine occupations (currently Ds): sales assistants, supermarket cashiers, all drivers and assembly line or factory workers.
>
> 7 Routine occupations: domestics, couriers, porters, refuse collectors and all labourers.
>
> 8 Never worked or long term unemployed.
>
> SOURCE: Reproduced with the permission of the copyright owner, Haymarket Business Publications, Ltd.

When marketers sell products overseas, they often see the tremendous impact that culture has on the purchase and use of products. International marketers find that people in other regions of the world have different attitudes, values and needs, which in turn call for different methods of doing business. Some international marketers fail because they do not or cannot adjust to cultural differences. As Case 4.2 illustrates, manufacturers of white goods must adjust the design and marketing of their products to take account of cultural differences. The effect of culture on international marketing programmes was discussed in greater detail in Chapter 3.

Sub-cultures Sub-divisions of culture according to geographic regions or human characteristics, such as age or ethnic background

A culture can be divided into **sub-cultures** according to geographic regions or human characteristics, such as age or ethnic background. In any country, there are a number of different sub-cultures. Within these, there are even greater similarities in people's attitudes, values and actions than within the broader culture, resulting in stronger preferences for specific types of clothing, furniture or leisure activity. For example, the wearing of kilts tends to be confined to Scotland rather than England or Wales. Marketers must recognise that even though their operations are confined to one country, state or city, sub-cultural differences may dictate considerable variations in what products people buy and how they make their purchases. To deal effectively with these differences, marketers may have to alter their product, promotion, distribution systems, price or people to satisfy members of particular sub-cultures.

Understanding Consumer Behaviour

Marketers try to understand consumer buying behaviour so that they can offer consumers greater satisfaction. For example, consumer concerns about factory farming methods have encouraged supermarkets to stock more free-range products. An appreciation of how and why individuals buy products and services helps marketers design more appealing marketing programmes.[30] At the same time, consumer expectations of products and services are rising. To keep consumers satisfied, now more than ever marketers must focus on the marketing concept and on being consumer oriented. In particular, they must be equipped with a clear understanding of the process and motivations of consumer buying.

The fact that it may be difficult to precisely analyse consumer behaviour does not detract from the importance of doing so. Even though research on consumer buying behaviour has not supplied all the knowledge that marketers need, progress has been made during the last 20 years and is likely to continue in the future. Not only will refinements in research methods yield more information about consumer behaviour, but the pressures of an increasingly competitive business environment will also make obtaining such information much more urgent for marketers.

● S U M M A R Y

Buying behaviour refers to the decision processes and actions of people involved in buying and using products. *Consumer buying behaviour* refers to the buying behaviour of ultimate consumers—those who purchase products for personal or household use, not for business purposes. Analysing consumer buying behaviour is important to marketers; if they are able to determine what satisfies customers, they can implement the marketing concept and better predict how consumers will respond to different marketing programmes.

Consumer decisions can be classified into three categories: routine response behaviour, limited decision-making and extensive decision-making. A consumer uses *routine response behaviour* when buying frequently purchased, low cost, low risk items that require very little search and decision effort. *Limited decision-making* is used for products purchased occasionally or when a buyer needs to acquire information about an unfamiliar brand in a familiar product category. *Extensive decision-making* is used when purchasing an unfamiliar, expensive, high risk or infrequently bought product. *Impulse buying* is an unplanned buying behaviour involving a powerful, persistent urge to buy something immediately. The purchase of a certain product does not always elicit the same type of decision-making behaviour. Individuals differ in their response to purchase situations. Even the same individual may make a different decision in other circumstances.

The *consumer buying decision process* includes five stages: problem recognition, information search, evaluation of alternatives, purchase and post-purchase evaluation. Decision processes do not always culminate in a purchase, and not all consumer decisions include all five stages. Problem recognition occurs when a buyer becomes aware that there is a difference between a desired state and an actual condition. After recognising the problem or need, the buyer searches for information about products that will help resolve the problem or satisfy the need. In the *internal search,* buyers search their memory for information about products that might solve the problem. If they are unable to retrieve from memory sufficient information to make a decision, they seek additional information through an *external search. Involvement* refers to the level of interest, emotion and activity which the consumer is prepared to expend on a particular purchase. A successful information search will yield a group of brands, called an *evoked set,* that a buyer views as possible alternatives. To evaluate the products in the evoked set, a buyer establishes certain criteria and assigns each a certain *salience*—or level of importance—by which to compare, rate and rank the different products. Marketers can influence consumers' evaluation by framing the alternatives.

In the purchase stage, the consumer selects the product or brand on the basis of results from the evaluation stage and on other factors. The buyer also chooses the seller from whom he or she will buy the product. After the purchase, the buyer evaluates the product to determine if its actual performance meets expected levels. Shortly after the purchase of an expensive product, for example, the post-purchase evaluation may provoke *cognitive dissonance*—dissatisfaction brought on by the consumer's doubts as to whether he or she should have bought the product in the first place. The results of the post-purchase evaluation will affect future buying behaviour.

Three major categories of influences are believed to affect the consumer buying decision process: personal, psychological and social factors. A *personal factor* is one that is unique to a particular person. Personal factors include demographic factors, situational factors and level of involvement. *Demographic factors* are individual characteristics such as age, sex, race, ethnic origin, income, family life cycle and occupation. *Situational factors* are the external circumstances or conditions that exist when a consumer is making a purchase decision, such as the time available. An individual's *level of involvement*—the level of interest, emotional commitment and time spent searching for a product in a particular situation—also affects the buying deci-

sion process. Enduring involvement is an ongoing interest in a product class because of personal relevance. Situational involvement is a temporary interest resulting from the particular circumstance or environment in which buyers find themselves.

Psychological factors partly determine people's general behaviour and thus influence their behaviour as consumers. The primary psychological influences on consumer behaviour are perception, motives, learning, attitudes and personality. *Perception* is the process of selecting, organising and interpreting *information inputs* (the sensations received through sight, taste, hearing, smell and touch) to produce meaning. The first step in the perceptual process is the selection of information. *Selective exposure* is the phenomenon of people selecting the inputs that are to be exposed to their awareness; *selective distortion* is the changing or twisting of currently received information. When a person remembers information inputs that support personal feelings and beliefs and forgets inputs that do not, the phenomenon is called *selective retention.* The second step of the perceptual process requires organising and integrating the new information with that already stored in memory. Interpretation—the third step in the perceptual process—is the assignment of meaning to what has been organised. In addition to perceptions of packages, products, brands and organisations, individuals also have a *self-concept,* or self-image.

A *motive* is an internal, energy giving force directing a person's activities towards satisfying a need or achieving a goal. *Patronage motives* influence where a person purchases products on a regular basis. To analyse the major motives that influence consumers to buy or not buy products, marketers conduct motivation research, using *in-depth interviews, focus groups* or *projective techniques.* Common types of projective techniques include word association tests, bubble drawings and sentence completion tests.

Learning refers to changes in a person's behaviour caused by information and experience. *Knowledge* has two components: familiarity with the product and expertise—the ability to apply the product.

Attitude refers to an individual's enduring evaluation, feelings and behavioural tendencies towards an object or activity. Consumer attitudes towards a company and its products greatly influence the success or failure of the company's marketing strategy. Marketers measure consumers' attitudes towards an object through *attitude scales*.

Personality comprises all the internal traits and behaviours that make a person unique. Though the results of many studies have been inconclusive, some marketers believe that personality does influence the types and brands of products purchased.

The forces that other people exert on buying behaviour are called *social factors*. Social factors include the influence of roles and family, reference groups, social classes, and culture and sub-cultures. All of us occupy positions within groups, organisations and institutions, and each position has a *role*—a set of actions and activities that a person in a particular position is supposed to perform, based on the expectations of both the individual and surrounding persons. A group is a *reference group* when an individual identifies with the group so much that he or she takes on many of the values, attitudes or behaviours of group members. In most reference groups, one or more members stand out as *opinion leaders*. A *social class* is an open group of individuals who have similar social rank. *Culture* is everything in our surroundings that is made by human beings. A culture can be divided into *sub-cultures* on the basis of geographic regions or human characteristics, such as age or ethnic background.

Marketers try to understand consumer buying behaviour so that they can offer consumers greater satisfaction. Refinements in research methods will yield more information about consumer behaviour, and the pressure of rising consumer expectations combined with an increasingly competitive business environment will spur marketers to seek a fuller understanding of consumer decision processes.

Important Terms

Buying behaviour	Personal factors	Focus group
Consumer buying behaviour	Demographic factors	Projective techniques
Routine response behaviour	Situational factors	Learning
Limited decision-making	Level of involvement	Knowledge
Extensive decision-making	Psychological factors	Attitude
Impulse buying	Perception	Attitude scale
Consumer buying decision process	Information inputs	Personality
Internal search	Selective exposure	Social factors
External search	Selective distortion	Role
Involvement	Selective retention	Reference group
Evoked set	Self-concept	Opinion leader
Salience	Motive	Social class
Cognitive dissonance	Patronage motives	Culture
	In-depth interview	Sub-cultures

Discussion and Review Questions

1. Name the types of buying behaviour consumers use. List some products that you have bought using each type of behaviour. Have you ever bought a product on impulse? In what circumstances?
2. What are the five stages in the consumer buying decision process? Are all these stages used in all consumer purchase decisions?
3. What are the personal factors that affect the consumer buying decision process? How do they affect the process?
4. How does a consumer's level of involvement affect his or her purchase behaviour?
5. What is the function of time in a consumer's buying decision process?

6. What is selective exposure and what effect does it have on consumer buying?
7. How do marketers attempt to shape consumers' learning?
8. Why are marketers concerned about consumer attitudes?
9. Describe reference groups. How do they influence buying behaviour? Name some of your own reference groups.
10. In what ways does social class affect a person's purchase decisions?
11. What is culture? How does it affect a person's buying behaviour?
12. Describe the sub-cultures to which you belong. Identify buying behaviour that is unique to your sub-culture.
13. What is the impact of post-purchase evaluation on future buying decisions?
14. If consumers are dissatisfied with a particular purchase, what actions are open to them? What can marketers do to respond to these actions?

Recommended Readings

H. Assael, *Consumer Behaviour and Marketing Action* (Cincinnati: South-Western, 1998).

J. F. Engel, R. D. Blackwell and P. W. Miniard, *Consumer Behaviour* (Fort Worth: Dryden, 1997).

G. R. Foxall, *Consumers in Context* (London and New York: Routledge, 1996).

G. R. Foxall, *Consumer Psychology for Marketing* (London and New York: International Thomson Business Press, 1997).

J. O'Shaughnessy, *Explaining Buyer Behaviour* (New York: Oxford University Press, 1992).

 C A S E S

4.1 IKEA: Stylish Furnishings at Affordable Prices

Swedish company IKEA is a mass market producer of cheap and stylish home furnishings that appear to transcend national boundaries. The company was founded in 1943 by Ingvar Kamprad, a small town handyman from southern Sweden, who devised the company name by combining his initials with the first initials of his farm (Elmtaryd) and the parish (Agunnaryd) where he was raised. Today, IKEA's business mission is clear. In the words of the company's founder, "We shall offer a wide range of furnishing items of good design and function, at prices so low that the majority of people can afford to buy them."

Since expanding internationally in 1973, IKEA's incremental growth approach to spreading into overseas markets has continued. Today the company is the world's largest retailer. Now located in more than 25 countries, with over 120 outlets, the company almost tripled its turnover worldwide between 1984 and 1990. Offering affordable and varied furniture is central to IKEA's strategy. The company maintains its cost advantages by doing what it does best and concentrates on its core business and on the adoption of a long term strategy.

IKEA's ability to maintain its success across so many markets is impressive. Some studies suggest that one possible reason for this success is that when prices are very competitive, cultural barriers become smaller and it becomes easier to reach a larger percentage of the total furniture buying population. To maintain its low cost base, the company needs to shift volume, which it does by selling broadly the same range of stylish, flat packed Swedish products in all of its stores worldwide.

Price is not the only reason for IKEA's success. In the design of its stores and products, IKEA has done much to appeal to consumers' underlying reasons for buying. The company understands that shopping is a purposeful activity: people buy in order to make their lives richer. In IKEA's case, the challenge has been to make the apparent essence of a Swedish lifestyle—beautiful homes and high quality living—

available at affordable prices. IKEA has also used the opportunity to innovate where it can. For example, the retailer recently opened its first New York outlet, a 7,400 square foot scaled down version of its usual 200,000 square foot stores. The "boutique-style" outlet is essentially a marketing vehicle for the company. Known as the Marketing Outpost, the shop aims to concentrate on only one product at a time. Every eight to 12 weeks IKEA will close the store for a complete refit and transformation.

Consumer interest in IKEA has revived the flagging fortunes of furniture retailers. In areas where new IKEA stores have opened, the company's lively approach has led to an increase in the time spent shopping for home related products. Research also suggests that the proportion of their income that consumers are prepared to spend on these products is increasing. IKEA therefore believes it is competing with purchases of new cars and holidays—anything that claims the disposable income in the consumers' pocket—not just with other furniture retailers.

Although the company does not deliberately use demographic and psychographic variables to segment its customer base, IKEA products seem to appeal particularly to people in their twenties and thirties. In order to expand the product line further into other life cycle stages, the company is trying to grow with its customers by adopting a policy of offering products that cater for families with teenage children and those whose children have left home.

While IKEA recognises that consumers shop to improve their lives, the company also acknowledges their practical needs. People are much more likely to visit retail outlets that are conveniently located and where the shopping experience is fun. IKEA meets these important needs by locating its stores close to motorways and major trunk roads and by offering extensive parking, child care, toilet and restaurant facilities. A full range of furnishings is presented in real room settings that combine expensive, high risk purchases such as living room suites and carpets with cheaper, lower involvement items such as pictures, ornaments and lampshades.

SOURCES: Jennifer Pellet, "IKEA takes Manhattan!", *Discount Merchandiser,* October 1995; "IKEA", *Retail Business—Retail Trade Reviews,* 33, March 1995; Peter Wingard, "A study of six Swedish firms' approach to marketing", Warwick Business School MBA Programme, 1991; S. Redmond, "Home truths", *Marketing,* 7 April 1988; J. Bamford and A. Dunlap Smith, "Why competitors shop for ideas at IKEA", *Business Week,* 9 October 1989; P. Corwin, "The Vikings are back—with furniture", *Discount Merchandiser,* 27 (4), April 1987; B. Saporito, "IKEA's got 'em lining up", *Fortune,* 123 (5), 11 March 1991; J. Reynolds, "IKEA: a competitive company with style", *Retail and Distribution Management,* 16 (3), 1988; "Report on the UK Furniture Market", *Key Note,* 1989.

Questions for Discussion

1. How do families go about purchasing a new item of furniture? Who influences and who is involved in the buying decision process?
2. What factors influence the way in which a newly married couple buy furniture?
3. How important is price to IKEA because of its position as a retailer of home furnishings?

4.2 European White Goods Manufacturers Tune in to Customer Expectations

European manufacturers of white goods—washing machines, dishwashers, fridges and freezers—need to cater for many cultural and regional variations across the markets they serve. In the UK, consumer preference for front loading washing machines results in a product quite different from the top loading French equivalent. But not all variations are caused by differing consumer preferences. The warm, sunny climate in Italy also has an effect on product features. Here, much slower spin speeds are required by the clothes washing public than in Germany, where the climate is much colder and wetter. With the increasing use of electric tumble dryers, it is not clear for how long this difference will be significant.

Meanwhile, also in Germany, the powerful environmental movement is having an impact on the products offered to the consumer. For example, Freon gas in fridges and freezers has already been outlawed, and a move towards washing machines that use less water seems inevitable.

In 1995 Electrolux, Whirlpool Europe BV (WEBV) and Bosch-Siemens, three of Europe's top appliance manufacturers, signalled their intention to increase their pursuit of global expansion. The biggest player, Electrolux, with about 22 per cent market share (by retail value), aims to use one global brand and three pan-European brands to segment its geographic market. Second placed Bosch-Siemens, with 14 per cent market share, sees future globalisation opportunities in markets in eastern Europe, China, South America and the US. Meanwhile WEBV, which serves its share of the European appliance market through 20 sales companies in 20 countries, aims to use the findings of extensive marketing research to identify and gear its marketing to the distinct needs of different segments. With a clearly stated intention to become the world's largest appliance manufacturer, Whirlpool will need to keep catering for regional differences in customer requirements.

Local and cultural differences have an important impact on the marketing programmes companies develop. WEBV has adopted an unusual approach in its attempts to implement its marketing and advertising effort in Europe. In 1989 WEBV launched the first pan-European advertising campaign in this industry. This approach has been developed in the company's current *Fantastic World* campaign, which is unusual in its product-specific focus. Most manufacturers communicate at a local level, because they believe this helps to overcome differences in the way advertising messages are interpreted. Some also argue that traditional, American-style advertising is unpopular in certain European markets.

Although there has been much discussion about possible convergence of product offerings in European markets, it is not yet clear how much regional differences can or will be ignored. For key industry players the challenge is to establish the values, opinions, attitudes, behaviour and expectations of consumers in order to identify similarities and differences between them.

Armed with a better understanding of the needs of key customer groups across Europe, manufacturers should be better able to match consumer requirements and make comparisons across national boundaries. Although the potential of merged marketing programmes is still unknown, opportunities exist to rationalise the way customers are grouped, thus reducing marketing costs.

SOURCES: Hoover's web company profiles, 1999; "Whirlpool in Europe," Whirlpool Corporation web site, 1998; Peter Wingard, "A study of six Swedish firms' approach to marketing", Warwick Business School MBA Programme, 1991; T. A. Stewart, "A heartland industry takes on the world", *Fortune*, 121 (6), 12 March 1990, pp. 110–112; J. Kapstein, "The fast spinning machine that blew a gasket", *Business Week*, 10 September 1990, pp. 50–52; C. Harris, "Women of Europe put Whirlpool in a spin", *Financial Times*, 30 October 1990; "Marketing: phase 2", *Appliance Manufacturer*, 43 (2), February 1995; "Big plans for Europe's big three", *Appliance Manufacturer*, 43 (4), April 1995; James Stevens, "Electrolux marketshare leader by units in Europe", *Appliance Manufacturer*, 42 (7), July 1994.

Questions for Discussion

1. What role do cultural and regional variations play in the purchase of white goods?
2. How might manufacturers of white goods cater for the regional variations that they encounter? Should the manufacturers try to ignore these variations?
3. What are the likely advantages and disadvantages of adopting a pan-European advertising campaign in this situation? Would you expect Whirlpool's strategy to be successful in the long term?

5 Organisational Markets and Business-to-Business Buying Behaviour

O B J E C T I V E S

- To become familiar with the various types of organisational markets

- To identify the major characteristics of business-to-business buyers and transactions

- To understand several attributes of business-to-business demand

- To become familiar with the major components of a buying centre

- To understand relationship marketing and exchanges between industrial buyers and sellers

- To understand the stages of the business-to-business buying decision process and the factors that affect this process

- To learn how to select and analyse business-to-business target markets

"Business marketing is not simply about making sales. It's the task of establishing, developing and managing a portfolio of customer relationships."

David Ford, University of Bath

Courtaulds Textiles is a large international producer of fabrics to garment makers and ready-made garments to retailers including Marks & Spencer, Bhs and Tesco. With production facilities across the globe, the company has significant design and manufacturing interests in the UK and France. The business is divided into two units: fabrics and garments. The fabric marketers are constantly innovating in terms of fabrics, designs and seaming techniques. The latest products are fabrics which when warm release smells such as citrus odours—very useful in sports and swimwear, but also in promotional ploys. Only a few of the fabric brands are known to consumers: Calais produced Desseilles lace is world-renowned. On the whole, however, the various fabric brands are familiar only to Courtaulds' immediate customers, the garment makers and retailer merchandisers. Most consumers wear Courtaulds' textiles without identifying the textile manufacturer. Instead they see the retailer

or garment maker's branding. For the garment producing side of Courtaulds Textiles, it is a very different story. Most of the clothing produced is retailer own-label branded goods, purchased by consumers as St Michael (M&S), Bhs or Tesco own label branded merchandise. In addition, Courtaulds' garment brands include many which are promoted directly to the consumer under the very familiar lingerie and clothing names of Well (France), Aristoc, Berlei, Gossard, Georges Rech, Zorbit and Christy towels.

Although Berlie or Gossard underwear is advertised in consumer magazines and Aristoc lingerie appears on billboards, the vast majority of the marketing activity is pitched at companies retailing or manufacturing clothing: business-to-business marketing. For Courtaulds Textiles' businesses supplying the large retail chains, retail merchandisers expect them to provide all the packaging, design, labelling, photography, but to the retailers' own briefs. Courtaulds must do much more than simply produce a satisfactory product for a customer such as Marks & Spencer (M&S). Subsidiary Meridian, for example, pays for photography, packaging, hangers, ticketing and displays for Bhs and Tesco. The retailers only have to find space for the display stand and manage inventory levels.

For garments, each season between 25 and 35 new products are offered by Courtaulds Textiles per each single one which is included in the ranges sold in M&S or Bhs. There is a lead time of three seasons to enable the design, selection, manufacturing and promotion of the new ranges. First there are fabric searches, then design searches. The garment makers and separately the retailer merchandisers travel the world on "shopping trips" for ideas—fabrics, seaming methods and designs. Retailers give some guidelines to their garment makers. Then the garment makers produce prototypes in the right colours and fabrics in order to pitch their wares to M&S or Bhs. There is a round of selection meetings which turns down most prototypes and makes the final choice. A supplier is almost assured that if the garment maker supplied three items in this season's M&S range, it will receive three slots in next season's range. The difficulty is in seeking the fourth item, particularly as the overall range will not grow: any additional item will be at the expense of a competitor garment maker. To win an additional inclusion requires innovation in design, method, fabric or price—a new look by itself will not suffice. The fact is that before a new line in lingerie, nightwear or clothing is even stocked in a retailer's stores, let alone before a member of the public has made any purchase, the fabric and made-up garment have both been marketed to Courtaulds Textiles' customers: the retailers. While most of us are consumers and are on the receiving end of retailers' and manufacturers' marketing campaigns, many marketers work instead to entice other companies to purchase their companies' products and services.

SOURCES: Well; Courtaulds Textiles; Desseilles Textiles, France and the UK, 1999. *Photo*: Courtesy of Courtalds Textiles.

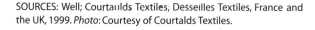

Organisational (or **industrial**) **market** Individuals or groups that purchase a specific type of product for re-sale, for use in making other products or for use in daily operations

The large international fabric and garment producer Courtaulds Textiles supplies a diverse mix of organisational markets. An **organisational** (or **industrial**) **market** is defined as consisting of individuals or groups that purchase a specific type of product for re-sale, for use in making other products or for use in daily operations. To maintain its international standing as a fabric and garment manufacturer supplying many large clothing makers and retailers, Courtaulds has had to adapt to the needs of its diverse business-to-business customer base. This has involved building an understanding of the characteristics of the companies that buy its products and an appreciation of their buying behaviour.

This chapter looks more closely at organisational markets and business-to-business buying decision processes.[1] In addition, it considers how such markets can be analysed and industrial targets identified. The first section discusses the various kinds of organisational markets and the types of buyers that make up these markets. The next section explores several dimensions of industrial buying, such as the characteristics of the transactions, the attributes and concerns of the buyers, the methods of buying and the distinctive features of the demand for products sold to business-to-business purchasers. The chapter then examines business-to-business buying decisions by considering how they are arrived at and who makes the purchases. The final section examines the selection and analysis of business-to-business target markets.

Types of Organisational Markets

There are four kinds of organisational, or industrial, markets: producers, resellers, governments and institutions (see also Chapter 7). The following section describes the characteristics of the customers that make up these markets. Table 5.1 shows the employment patterns in these markets across Europe.

Producer Markets

Producer markets Buyers of raw materials and semi-finished and finished items used to produce other products or in their own operations

Individuals and business organisations that purchase products for the purpose of making a profit by using them to produce other products or by using them in their own operations are classified as **producer markets.** Producer markets include buyers of raw materials and semi-finished and finished items used to produce other products. For example, a manufacturer buys raw materials and component parts to use directly in the production of its products. Grocers and supermarkets are producer markets for numerous support products, such as paper and plastic bags, displays, scanners and floor care products. Hotels are producer markets for food, cleaning equipment, laundry services and furniture. Figure 5.1 illustrates some products targeted at hotels. Producer markets cover a broad array of industries, ranging from agriculture, forestry, fisheries and mining to construction, transport, communications and public utilities.

Manufacturers tend to be geographically concentrated. This concentration occurs in Europe too, with heavy industry centred on the Ruhr Valley in Germany and on the Midlands and North West in the UK. Sometimes an industrial marketer may be able to serve customers more efficiently as a result. Within certain areas, production in just a few industries may account for a sizeable proportion of total industrial output.

Reseller Markets

Reseller markets Intermediaries, such as wholesalers and retailers, who buy finished goods and re-sell them to make a profit

Reseller markets consist of intermediaries, such as wholesalers and retailers, who buy finished goods and re-sell them to make a profit. (These intermediaries are discussed in Chapters 13 and 14.) Other than making minor alterations, resellers do not change the physical characteristics of the products they handle. With the exception of items that producers sell directly to consumers, all products sold to consumer markets are first sold to reseller markets.

Wholesalers Intermediaries who purchase products for re-sale to retailers, other wholesalers and producers, governments and institutions

Wholesalers purchase products for re-sale to retailers, other wholesalers and producers, governments and institutions. Although some highly technical products are sold directly to end users, many products are sold through wholesalers, who in turn sell products to other companies in the distribution system. Thus wholesalers are very important in helping to get a producer's product to customers. Wholesalers often carry many products, perhaps as many as 250,000 items. From the reseller's point of view, having access to such an array of products from a single source makes it much simpler to buy a variety of items. When inventories are vast, the re-ordering of products is normally automated and the wholesaler's initial purchase decisions are made by professional buyers and buying committees.

Sector	Austria	Belgium	Denmark	Finland	France	Germany	Greece	Ireland	Italy	Netherlands	Norway	Portugal	Spain	Sweden	Switzerland
Agriculture, forestry	7.1	2.9	5.2	8.6	5.1	3.0	21.3	10.5	7.5	4.0	5.3	11.3	10.1	3.4	5.6
Mining, quarrying	0.4	0.3	0.1	0.2	0.3	0.3	0.5	0.4	0.5	0.1	1.2	0.5	0.5	0.2	0.1
Manufacturing	26.0	20.7	19.8	19.5	19.6	29.1	15.6	16.3	22.9	17.8	14.9	23.8	20.3	18.3	23.6
Electricity, gas, water	1.1	0.8	0.6	1.1	0.9	1.2	1.1	0.9	1.1	0.7	1.1	0.7	0.7	0.8	0.6
Construction	8.1	7.1	5.8	6.2	6.8	6.5	7.0	5.2	8.5	6.0	5.8	8.1	9.2	5.6	8.9
Wholesale, retail, restaurants, hotels	18.8	17.9	15.8	14.8	16.9	17.1	21.3	18.0	21.7	17.3	17.1	19.4	21.0	14.5	20.3
Transport, storage and communications	6.6	6.9	7.2	7.8	6.4	5.8	6.7	5.1	5.7	6.3	8.1	4.7	5.9	6.9	6.3
Finance, insurance and business services	7.4	9.9	10.1	8.9	10.4	9.0	5.9	17.8	7.6	10.8	7.9	6.9	6.5	9.6	11.0
Community, social and personal services	23.9	33.0	34.6	32.8	33.5	28.0	20.6	4.8	24.5	34.7	38.5	24.6	25.7	40.5	23.6
Not defined	0.6	0.5	0.7	0.2	—	—	—	—	—	2.3	0.1	—	—	0.1	—

SOURCE: From *European Marketing Pocket Book 1996*, p. 14. Reprinted by permission of NTC Publications, Ltd.

Table 5.1 Percentage of the workforce employed in different sectors across Europe, 1993

Figure 5.1 Focus on re-seller markets. Cafe and restaurant operators must purchase a wide variety of products in order to satisfy their customers, the final consumers. SOURCE: Courtesy of Pritchitt Foods.

Retailers Intermediaries that purchase products and re-sell them to final consumers

Retailers purchase products and re-sell them to final consumers. Some retailers carry a large number of items. Chemists, for example, may stock up to 12,000 items, and some supermarkets may handle in excess of 20,000 different products. In small, family owned retail stores, the owner frequently makes purchasing decisions. Large department stores have one or more employees in each department who are responsible for buying products for that department. As for chain stores, a buyer or buying committee in the central office frequently decides whether a product will be made available for selection by store managers. For many products, however, local store managers make the actual buying decisions for a particular store.

When making purchase decisions, resellers consider several factors. They evaluate the level of demand for a product to determine in what quantity and at what prices it can be re-sold. They assess the amount of space required to handle a product relative to its potential profit. Sometimes resellers will put a product on trial for a fixed period, allowing them to judge customers' reactions and to make better informed decisions about shelf space and positions as a result. Retailers, for example, sometimes evaluate products on the basis of sales per square metre of selling area. Since customers often depend on a reseller to have a product when they need it, a reseller typically evaluates a supplier's ability to provide adequate quantities when and where wanted. Resellers also take into account the ease of

	1981	1986	1991	1992	1993	1994
			Percentages			
Social security	27	31	32	33	34	34
Health	11	12	14	14	13	14
Education	12	12	13	13	12	13
Defence	11	12	10	10	9	8
Public order and safety	4	4	6	5	5	5
General public services	4	4	5	5	4	4
Housing and community amenities	6	5	4	4	4	4
Transport and communication	4	2	3	3	2	2
Recreational and cultural affairs	1	2	2	2	2	2
Agriculture, forestry and fishing	1	1	1	1	2	1
Other expenditure	19	16	11	11	12	13
All expenditure (= 100%) (£ billion in real terms[1])	224.6	241.0	250.9	268.1	278.3	285.7

[1]Adjusted to 1994 prices using the GDP market prices deflator.

SOURCE: Central Statistical Office, *Social Trends: 1996 Edition*. © Crown Copyright 1995. Reproduced by permission of the Office for National Statistics.

Table 5.2 UK central government expenditure: by function

placing orders and the availability of technical assistance and training programmes from the producer. More broadly, when resellers consider buying a product not previously carried, they try to determine whether the product competes with or complements products the company is currently handling. These types of concerns distinguish reseller markets from other markets. Sometimes resellers will start stocking a new line of products in response to specific requests from customers. Marketers dealing with reseller markets must recognise these needs and be able to serve them.

Government Markets

Government markets Departments that buy goods and services to support their internal operations and to provide the public with education, water, energy, national defence, road systems and healthcare

National and local governments make up **government markets.** They spend billions of pounds annually for a variety of goods and services to support their internal operations and to provide the public with education, water, energy, national defence, road systems and healthcare. Table 5.2 shows UK central government expenditure on goods and services from 1981 to 1994. In Europe, the amount spent by local governments varies from country to country depending on the level and cost of services provided. As a result of the European single market, the services provided by different governments may eventually become standardised.

The types and quantities of products bought by government markets reflect social demands on various government agencies. As the public's needs for government services change, so do the government markets' demands for products. Because government agencies spend public funds to buy the products they need to provide services, they are accountable to the public. This accountability is responsible for their relatively complex set of buying procedures. Some businesses, unwilling to deal with so much red tape, do not even try to sell to government buyers, while others have learned to deal efficiently with government procedures. For certain companies, such as British Aerospace, and for certain products, such as defence related items, the government may be one of only a few customers.

Governments usually make their purchases through bids or negotiated contracts. To make a sale under the bid system, a company must apply and receive approval to be placed on a list of qualified bidders. When a government unit wants to buy, it sends out a detailed description of the products to these qualified bidders. Businesses that wish to sell such products then submit bids. The government unit is usually required to accept the lowest bid. When buying non-standard or highly complex products, a government unit often uses a negotiated contract. Under this procedure, the government unit selects only a few companies, negotiates specifications and terms, and eventually awards the contract to one of the negotiating companies. Most large defence contracts held by such companies as British Aerospace, GEC and Raytheon are reached through negotiated contracts.

Although government markets have complicated requirements, they can also be very lucrative. When government departments or healthcare providers modernise obsolete computer systems, for example, successful bidders can make many millions of pounds during the life of a contract, which may last for five years or more. Some companies have established separate departments to facilitate marketing to government units, while others specialise entirely in this area.

Institutional Markets

Institutional markets Organisations with charitable, educational, community or other non-business goals

Organisations with charitable, educational, community or other non-business goals constitute **institutional markets.** Members of institutional markets include libraries, museums, universities, charitable organisations and some churches and hospitals. Institutions purchase millions of pounds' worth of products annually to provide goods, services and ideas to club members, congregations, students and others. For example, a library must buy new books for its readers; pay rent, fuel and water bills; fund the staffing and cleaning of its buildings; and pay to produce publicity material about its services. Because such institutions often have different goals and fewer resources than other types of organisations, marketers may use special marketing activities to serve these markets.

Dimensions of Business-to-Business Buying

Having clarified the different types of organisational customers, the next step is to consider the dimensions of business-to-business buying. After first examining several characteristics of business-to-business transactions, this section then discusses various attributes of business-to-business buyers and some of their primary concerns when making purchase decisions. Next it looks at methods of business-to-business buying and the major types of purchases organisations make. The section concludes with a discussion of how the demand for industrial products differs from the demand for consumer products.

Characteristics of Business-to-Business Transactions

Although the marketing concept is equally applicable to organisational and consumer markets, there are several fundamental differences between the transactions that occur in each. Business-to-business buyers tend to order in much larger quantities than do individual consumers. Suppliers must often sell their products in large quantities to make profits; consequently, they prefer not to sell to customers who place small orders.

Generally, business-to-business purchases are negotiated less frequently than consumer sales. Some purchases involve expensive items, such as machinery or office equipment, that are used for a number of years. Other products, such as raw materials and component items, are used continuously in production and may have to be supplied frequently. However, the contract regarding the terms of sale of these items is likely to be a long term agreement, requiring periodic negotiations.

Negotiations in business-to-business sales may take much longer than those for consumer sales. Purchasing decisions are often made by a committee; orders are frequently large, expensive and complex; and products may be custom built. There is a good chance that several people or departments in the purchasing organisation will be involved. One department might express a need for a product; a second department might develop its specifications; a third might stipulate the maximum amount to be spent; and a fourth might actually place the order. This approach allows individuals with relevant expertise to be incorporated into the process when required.

One practice unique to business-to-business sales is **reciprocity,** an arrangement in which two organisations agree to buy from each other. In some countries, reciprocal agreements that threaten competition are illegal and action may be taken to stop anti-competitive reciprocal practices. Nonetheless, a certain amount of reciprocal dealing occurs among small businesses and, to a lesser extent, among larger companies as well. Such companies often find that developing long term relationships of this kind can be an effective competitive tool.[2] Reciprocity can create a problem because coercive measures may be used to enforce it or because reciprocity influences purchasing agents to deal only with certain suppliers.[3]

Attributes of Business-to-Business Buyers

Business-to-business buyers are usually thought of as being different from consumer buyers in their purchasing behaviour because they are better informed about the products they purchase. To make purchasing decisions that fulfil an organisation's needs, business-to-business buyers demand detailed information about a product's functional features and technical specifications.

Business-to-business buyers, however, also have personal goals that may influence their buying behaviour. Most buyers seek the psychological satisfaction that comes with promotion and financial rewards. In general, agents are most likely to achieve these personal goals when they consistently exhibit rational buying behaviour and perform their jobs in ways that help their companies achieve their organisational objectives. Suppose, though, that an organisational buyer develops a close friendship with a certain supplier. If the buyer values the friendship more than organisational promotion or financial rewards, he or she may behave irrationally from the company's point of view. Dealing exclusively with that supplier regardless of better prices, quality or service from competitors may indicate an unhealthy or unethical alliance between the buyer and seller. Companies have different ways of dealing with such problems. Some require more than one person to be involved in buying products, while others periodically review their use of suppliers.

Primary Concerns of Business-to-Business Buyers

When they make purchasing decisions, business-to-business customers take into account a variety of factors. Among their chief considerations are quality, delivery, service and price.[4] For example, in Figure 5.2 quality is stressed by the construction engineers. Product range and innovation may also be significant considerations.

Figure 5.2 Primary concerns of business-to-business buyers. In this instance, the construction engineers who built the bridge depended on the quality of the concrete supplied. SOURCE: Courtesy of Beton.

Most business-to-business customers try to achieve and maintain a specific level of quality in the products they offer to their target markets. To accomplish this goal, they often buy their products on the basis of a set of expressed characteristics, commonly called *specifications*. These allow a business-to-business buyer to evaluate the quality of the products being considered according to particular features and thus to determine whether or not they meet the organisation's needs.

Meeting specifications is extremely important to business-to-business customers. If a product fails to meet specifications and malfunctions for the ultimate consumer, that product's supplier may be dropped and an alternative sought. On the other hand, a business-to-business buyer is usually cautious about buying products that exceed specifications, because such products often cost more and thus increase production costs. Suppliers therefore need to design their products carefully to come as close as possible to their customers' specifications without incurring any unnecessary extras.

Business-to-business buyers also value service. The services offered by suppliers directly and indirectly influence their customers' costs, sales and profits. When tangible goods are the same or quite similar—as with most raw materials—they may have the same specifications and be sold at the same price in the same kind of containers. Under such conditions, the mix of services a business-to-business marketer provides to its customers represents its greatest opportunity to gain a competitive advantage.

Among the most commonly expected services are market information, inventory maintenance, on-time delivery, warranty back-up, repair services and credit facilities. Specific services vary in importance, however, and the mix of services companies need is also affected by environmental conditions.

Business-to-business buyers in general are likely to need technical product information, data regarding demand, information about general economic conditions or supply and delivery information. For example, when technology is changing rapidly, forcing companies to change their production machinery, the demand for consultancy support services and warranty assurances will be especially high. It is critical for suppliers to maintain an adequate inventory in order to keep products accessible when a business-to-business buyer needs them and to reduce the buyer's inventory requirements and costs. Reliable, on-time delivery by suppliers also enables business-to-business customers to carry less inventory. Purchasers of machinery are especially concerned about adequate warranties. They are also keen to obtain repair services and replacement parts quickly, because equipment that cannot be used is costly.

Suppliers can also give extra value to business-to-business buyers by offering credit. Credit helps to improve a business-to-business customer's cash flow, reduces the peaks and troughs of capital requirements and thus lowers the company's cost of capital. Although no single supplier can provide every possible service to its customers, a marketing oriented supplier will try to create a service mix that satisfies the target market.

Service quality has become a critical issue because customer expectations of service have broadened. Marketers also need to strive for uniformity of service, simplicity, truthfulness and accuracy; to develop customer service objectives; and to monitor or audit their customer service programmes. Companies can monitor the quality of their service by formally surveying customers or calling on them informally to ask questions about the service they have received. Marketers with a strong customer service programme reap a reward: their customers keep coming back long after the first sale.[5] With customer expectations increasing, it is becoming more difficult for companies to achieve a differential advantage in these areas, and companies must take care to ensure that complaints are properly handled.[6] This reduces the likelihood that dissatisfied customers will give negative feedback to others in the marketplace.[7] Marketing Insight 5.1 explains one company's efforts to stay in touch with customer expectations.

Price matters greatly to a business-to-business customer because it influences operating costs and costs of goods sold, and these costs affect the customer's selling price and profit margin. When purchasing major equipment, an industrial buyer views the price as the amount of investment necessary to obtain a certain level of return or savings. Such a purchaser is likely to compare the price of a machine with the value of the benefits that the machine will yield. Caterpillar lost market share to foreign competitors because its prices were too high. A business-to-business buyer does not compare alternative products by price alone, though; other factors, such as product quality and supplier services, are also major elements in the purchase decision. For example, one study found that in the buying decision process for mainframe computer software operating systems, intangible attributes, such as the seller's credibility and understanding of the buyer's needs, were very important in the buyer's decision process.[8]

Methods of Business-to-Business Buying

Although no two business-to-business buyers go about their jobs in the same way, most use one or more of the following purchase methods: *description, inspection, sampling* and *negotiation*. When products being purchased are commonly standardised according to certain characteristics (such as size, shape, weight and colour) and graded using such standards, a business-to-business buyer may be able to purchase simply by describing or specifying quantity, grade and other attributes. Agricultural produce often falls into this category. In some cases a buyer may specify a particular brand or its equivalent when describing the desired product. Purchases on the basis of description are especially common between a buyer and seller who have established an ongoing relationship built on trust.

Certain products, such as large industrial machinery, used vehicles and buildings, have unique characteristics and are likely to vary in condition. For example, a transport depot may need its parking area to be re-surfaced. Consequently, buyers and sellers of such products must base their purchase decisions on inspection.

In buying based on sampling, a sample of the product is taken from the lot and evaluated. It is assumed that the characteristics of this sample represent the entire lot. This method is appropriate when the product is homogeneous—for instance, grain—and examination of the entire lot is not physically or economically feasible.

Some industrial purchasing relies on negotiated contracts. In certain instances, a business-to-business buyer describes exactly what is needed and then asks sellers to submit bids. The buyer may take the most attractive bids and negotiate with those suppliers. In other cases, the buyer may not be able to identify specifically what is to be purchased but can provide only a general description—as might be the case for a special piece of custom made equipment. A buyer and seller might negotiate a contract that specifies a base price and contains provisions for the payment of additional costs and fees. These contracts are most likely to be used for one-off projects, such as buildings and capital equipment. For example, the prices that Orbital Sciences Corporation charges its customers for launching and placing satellites in orbit are determined through negotiated contracts.

Types of Business-to-Business Purchases

New task purchase   An organisation's initial purchase of an item to be used to perform a new job or to solve a new problem

Modified re-buy purchase   A new task purchase that is changed when it is re-ordered or the requirements associated with a straight re-buy purchase are modified

Straight re-buy purchase   A routine re-purchase of the same products under approximately the same terms of sale

Most business-to-business purchases are one of three types: new task purchase, modified re-buy purchase or straight re-buy purchase. The type of purchase affects the number of individuals involved and the length of the buying process. In a **new task purchase,** an organisation makes an initial purchase of an item to be used to perform a new job or to solve a new problem. This may take a long time because it may require the development of product specifications, supplier specifications and procedures for future purchases. To make the initial purchase, the business-to-business buyer usually needs a good deal of information. A new task purchase is important to the supplier because it may lead to the sale of large quantities of the product over a period of years.

In a **modified re-buy purchase,** a new task purchase is changed the second or third time it is ordered, or the requirements associated with a straight re-buy purchase are modified. For example, an organisation might seek faster delivery, lower prices or a different quality of product specifications. When modified re-buying occurs, regular suppliers may become more competitive to keep the account. Competing suppliers may have the opportunity to obtain the business.

A **straight re-buy purchase** occurs when a buyer re-purchases the same products routinely under approximately the same terms of sale. For example, when re-ordering photocopying paper, a buyer requires little additional information

Asea Brown Boveri Group: Combining Global Orientation and Local Flexibility

Swiss-Swedish international electrical engineering group Asea Brown Boveri Group (ABB) provides electrical systems and equipment worldwide to customers in the electrical power generation, transmission, industrial, environmental control and mass transit markets. Formed in 1987 from a merger between Asea from Sweden and Brown Boveri from Switzerland, the company's position as world leader in many of its key markets led to a restructuring of the global power industry.

At the centre of ABB's success is its ability to globalise engineering and production, while maintaining a local presence in the countries in which it operates. ABB does this by operating a matrix structure to its business. One dimension of the matrix consists of ABB's global network, where product strategy and sales development are the responsibility of business area managers around the world. Around 500 of ABB's managers are global managers, experts on maintaining the company's advantages globally. The second dimension consists of traditionally run national companies that are well established in their home markets. The role of the country managers is to ensure that responsiveness is maintained at the local level.

The company already has about 25,000 employees in a wide range of locations, and it is not afraid to enter markets other companies may not regard as particularly politically or economically stable. For example, ABB now has a presence in the Czech Republic, Estonia, Hungary, Kazakhstan, Latvia, Poland, Romania, Russia and the Ukraine. All in all, the company now controls 58 companies in 16 eastern European countries. Such investment has been at a price, with profits falling during the late 1990s. However, the company believes that investment in eastern Europe is an appropriate long term strategy.

To keep its diverse customer base satisfied, ABB has implemented its own mix of total quality management, just-in-time management and time based management philosophies. The initiative aims to put the customer first and to offer higher standards of quality, delivery and customer support. Staff rotation and teamwork are encouraged, and sales and marketing, product development and production departments work together in functional units.

With interests in so many national markets, ABB is susceptible to a variety of important changes in environmental conditions. Most significant, the European power equipment industry is becoming increasingly oligopolistic as a result of mergers and acquisitions. Concern for the environment is also affecting ABB's market. As it moved forward into the late 1990s, the company sought to capitalise on its experience in environmentally friendly technology by making products for use in "green" applications. For example, the company became involved in a joint project with Volvo and the Royal Institute of Technology in Stockholm to create an environmental concept car. The Volvo ECC, as it is called, uses a gas turbine for highway driving and a rechargeable battery for electrically powered city driving. This project fits in with the company's relationship-building philosophy, which helps it stay in touch with market needs by understanding and responding to changes in the environment in which it operates.

SOURCES: Paul Hofheinz, "Yes, you can win in eastern Europe", *Fortune,* 16 May 1994, pp. 110–112; John McClenahen, "Percy Barnevik . . . and the ABBs of competition", *Industry Week,* 6 June 1994, pp. 20–24; "A local touch in global sales", *Business Europe,* 1 May 1995; Michael Maccoby, "Human engineering leads to operating principles for global management", *Research-Technology Management,* 38 (5), September/October 1995; Michael Valenti, "Hybrid car promises high performance and low emissions", *Mechanical Engineering,* 116 (7), July 1994, pp. 46–49; Peter Wingard, "A study of six Swedish firms' approach to marketing", Warwick Business School MBA Programme, 1991; "Asea Brown Boveri: power play", *The Economist,* 28 May 1988; W. Taylor, "The logic of global business: an interview with ABB's Percy Barnevik", *Harvard Business Review,* March–April 1991.

and can usually place the order relatively quickly, often using familiar suppliers that have provided satisfactory service and products in the past. These suppliers try to set up automatic re-ordering systems to make re-ordering easy and convenient for business-to-business buyers and may even monitor the organisation's inventory to indicate to the buyer what needs to be ordered.

Demand for Industrial Products

Products sold to business-to-business customers are called industrial products and, consequently, the demand for these products is called industrial demand. Unlike consumer demand, industrial demand is (1) derived, (2) inelastic, (3) joint and (4) more fluctuating.

Derived Demand As business-to-business customers, especially producers, buy products to be used directly or indirectly in the production of goods and services to satisfy consumers' needs, the demand for industrial products arises from the demand for consumer products; it is therefore called **derived demand.** In fact, all industrial demand can in some way be traced to consumer demand. This occurs at a number of levels, with industrial sellers being affected in various ways. For instance, consumers today are more concerned with good health and nutrition than ever before and as a result are purchasing food products containing less cholesterol, saturated fat, sugar and salt. When some consumers stopped buying high cholesterol cooking fats and margarine, the demand for equipment used in manufacturing these products also dropped. Thus factors influencing consumer buying of various food products have ultimately affected food processors, equipment manufacturers, suppliers of raw materials and even fast food restaurants, which have had to switch to lower cholesterol oils for frying. Changes in derived demand result from a chain reaction. When consumer demand for a product changes, a wave is set in motion that affects demand for all of the items involved in the production of that consumer product.

Inelastic Demand The demand for many industrial products at the industry level is **inelastic demand,** that is, a price increase or decrease will not significantly alter demand for the item. (The concept of price elasticity of demand is discussed further in Chapter 19.) Because many industrial products contain a number of parts, price increases that affect only one or two parts of the product may yield only a slightly higher per unit production cost. Of course, when a sizeable price increase for a component represents a large proportion of the total product's cost, demand may become more elastic, because the component price increase will cause the price at the consumer level to rise sharply. For example, if manufacturers of aircraft engines substantially increase the price of these engines, forcing Boeing in turn to raise the prices of its aircraft, the demand for aircraft may become more elastic as airlines re-consider whether they can afford them. An increase in the price of windscreens, however, is unlikely to affect greatly the price of the aircraft or the demand for them.

   The characteristic of inelasticity applies only to industry demand for the industrial product, not to the demand curve faced by an individual company. For example, suppose that a car component company increases the price of rubber seals sold to car manufacturers, while its competitors retain their lower prices. The car component company would probably experience reduced unit sales because most of its customers would switch to the lower priced brands. A specific organisation is vulnerable to elastic demand, even though industry demand for a particular product is inelastic.

Joint Demand The demand for certain industrial products, especially raw materials and components, is subject to joint demand. **Joint demand** occurs when two or more items are used in combination to produce a product. For example, a company that manufactures cork noticeboards for schools and colleges needs

---

Derived demand Demand for industrial products which arises from the demand for consumer products

Inelastic demand Demand which is not significantly affected by a price increase or decrease

Joint demand Demand that occurs when two or more products are used in combination to produce a product

supplies of cork and wood to produce the item; these two products are demanded jointly. A shortage of cork will cause a drop in the production of wooden surrounds for noticeboards.

Marketers selling many jointly demanded items must realise that when a customer begins purchasing one of the jointly demanded items, a good opportunity exists for selling related products. Similarly, when customers purchase a number of jointly demanded products, the producer must take care to avoid shortages of any one of them, because such shortages jeopardise sales of all the jointly demanded products. The susceptibility of producers to the shortage of a particular item is clearly illustrated when industrial action at companies producing microchips results in a halt in production at manufacturers of computers and other white goods.

Fluctuating Demand   Because the demand for industrial products fluctuates according to consumer demand, when particular consumer products are in high demand, their producers buy large quantities of raw materials and components to ensure that they can meet long run production requirements. Such producers may also expand their production capacity, which entails the acquisition of new equipment and machinery, more workers, a greater need for industrial services, and more raw materials and component parts.

Conversely, a decline in the demand for certain consumer goods significantly reduces the demand for industrial products used to produce those goods. When consumer demand is low, industrial customers cut their purchases of raw materials and components and stop buying equipment and machinery, even for replacement purposes. This trend is especially pronounced during periods of recession.

A marketer of industrial products may notice changes in demand when its customers change their inventory policies, perhaps because of expectations about future demand. For example, if several dishwasher manufacturers who buy timers from one producer increase their inventory of timers from a two week to a one month supply, the timer producer will experience a significant immediate increase in demand.

Sometimes price changes can lead to surprising temporary changes in demand. A price increase for an industrial item may initially cause business-to-business customers to buy more of the item because they expect the price to rise further. Similarly, demand for an industrial product may be significantly lower following a price cut as buyers wait for further price reductions. Such behaviour is often observed in companies purchasing information technology. Fluctuations in demand can be significant in industries in which price changes occur frequently.

Business-to-Business Buying Decisions

Business-to-business (or industrial) buying behaviour   The purchase behaviour of producers, resellers, government units and institutions

Business-to-business (or **industrial**) **buying behaviour** refers to the purchase behaviour of producers, resellers, government units and institutions. Although several of the same factors that affect consumer buying behaviour (discussed in Chapter 4) also influence business-to-business buying behaviour, a number of factors are unique to the latter. This section first analyses the buying centre to learn who participates in making business-to-business purchase decisions and then focuses on the stages of the buying decision process and the factors that affect it.

The Buying Centre

Most business-to-business purchase decisions are made by more than one person. The group of people within an organisation who are involved in making business-to-business purchase decisions are usually referred to as the **buying centre**. These individuals include users, influencers, buyers, deciders and gatekeepers, although one person may perform several of these roles.[9] Participants in the buying process share the goals and risks associated with their decisions.

Users are those in the business who actually use the product being acquired. They frequently initiate the purchase process and/or generate the specifications for the purchase. After the purchase, they also evaluate the product's performance relative to the specifications. Although users do not ordinarily have sufficient power to make the final decision to buy, it is important that their views be considered. A user who is unhappy with a piece of equipment may not work efficiently. Influencers are often technical personnel, such as engineers, who help develop the specifications and evaluate alternative products. Technical personnel are especially important influencers when the products being considered involve new, advanced technology. For example, a chemicals manufacturer seeking to install new processing equipment may take advice from a wide range of technical experts.

Buyers are responsible for selecting suppliers and actually negotiating the terms of purchase. They may also become involved in developing specifications. Buyers are sometimes called purchasing agents or purchasing managers. Their choices of suppliers and products, especially for new task purchases, are heavily influenced by individuals occupying other roles in the buying centre. For straight re-buy purchases, the buyer plays a major role in the selection of suppliers and in negotiations with them. Deciders actually choose the products and suppliers. Although buyers may be the deciders, it is not unusual for different people to occupy these roles. For routinely purchased items, buyers are commonly the deciders. However, a buyer may not be authorised to make purchases that exceed a certain monetary value, in which case higher level management personnel are the deciders. Gatekeepers, such as secretaries and technical personnel, control the flow of information to and among others in the buying centre. The flow of information from supplier sales representatives to users and influencers is often controlled by buyers or other personnel in the purchasing department. Unfortunately, relations between members of the buying centre at times can become strained.

The size and characteristics of an organisation's buying centre are affected by the number of its employees and its market position, the volume and types of products being purchased and the company's overall managerial philosophy regarding exactly who should be involved in purchase decisions. A marketer attempting to sell to a business-to-business customer needs to know who is in the buying centre, the types of decisions each individual makes and which individuals are the most influential in the decision process. Then the marketer will be in a position to contact those in the buying centre who have the most influence.

Relationship Marketing and Managing Exchange Relationships

The relationship that exists between a supplying organisation and its customers is an important aspect of the buying process that deserves special consideration. In fact, marketing experts have recently become much more interested in marketing relationships in general.[10] The term **relationship marketing** has been used to express this particular development. Instead of being concerned about individual transactions between suppliers and buyers, the relationship marketing approach emphasises the importance of the whole relationship between the parties. Relationship marketing can therefore be regarded as all of the activities an organisation uses to build, maintain and develop customer relations.[11]

Put simply, relationship marketing is concerned with getting and keeping customers by ensuring that an appropriate combination of marketing, customer service and quality is provided.[12] Underlying the relationship marketing concept is the idea that the relationship between a supplying organisation and its buyers is essentially similar to the relationship between two individuals. For example, bitumen company Nynas, featured in Case 5.1, has achieved market leadership through building ongoing relationships with a diversity of customers 24 hours a day, 365 days a year. Such relationships are conducted over a period of time through a series of meetings, which allow each party to get to know the other, to share information, to adapt to each other and generally to build trust and co-operation.[13]

As explained in Chapter 1, the concept of relationship marketing is changing the way in which marketers are looking at marketing. However, it is also particularly pertinent to this chapter's discussion of the exchange relationships that develop between buyers and sellers.[14] When a company buys a product or service from another company, both organisations become involved in an exchange process. During the transaction, both buyer and seller will exchange items of value in return for something else. For example, when a software company provides a printer with a desktop publishing package, it will provide the buyer with a package of benefits that include the software disks, detailed users' guide, warranty details, a variety of payment options and the opportunity to attend a training course. In exchange the buyer will agree to pay the price negotiated with the manufacturer. Figure 5.3 shows the range of factors that can be exchanged during the purchase process.

It is often in the interests of both parties to develop long term relationships. If buying and selling companies are used to dealing with each other, they are more likely to be able to adapt to each other's needs and to reach an agreement quickly and easily. Long term relationships are often attractive to both companies because they reduce the level of risk (financial and practical) associated with the purchase. The trend towards long term relationships has resulted in the development of what is called **relationship management**.[15] This process encourages a match between the seller's competitive advantage and the buyer's requirements over the life cycle of the item being purchased.

Relationship management The process of encouraging a match between the seller's competitive advantage and the buyer's requirements over an item's life cycle

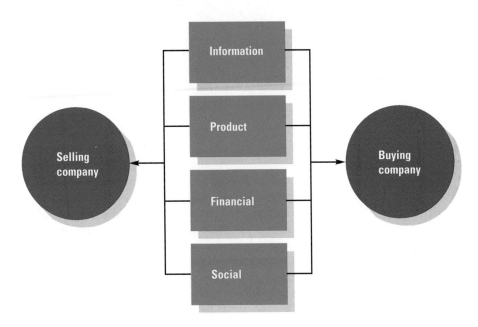

Figure 5.3 The exchange process in business-to-business buying

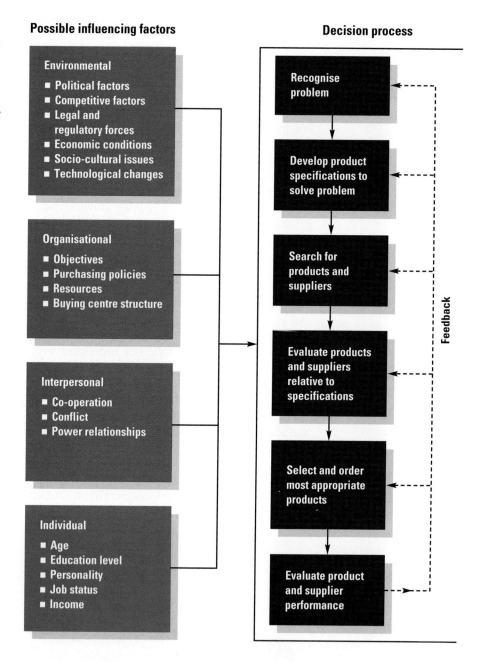

Figure 5.4 Business-to-business buying decision process and factors that may influence it.
SOURCE: Adapted from Frederick E. Webster, Jr, and Yoram Wind, *Organisational Buying Behaviour* (Englewood Cliffs, N.J.: Prentice-Hall, 1972), pp. 33–37. Adapted by permission.

Possible influencing factors

Environmental
- Political factors
- Competitive factors
- Legal and regulatory forces
- Economic conditions
- Socio-cultural issues
- Technological changes

Organisational
- Objectives
- Purchasing policies
- Resources
- Buying centre structure

Interpersonal
- Co-operation
- Conflict
- Power relationships

Individual
- Age
- Education level
- Personality
- Job status
- Income

Decision process

Recognise problem

Develop product specifications to solve problem

Search for products and suppliers

Evaluate products and suppliers relative to specifications

Select and order most appropriate products

Evaluate product and supplier performance

Feedback

Stages of the Business-to-Business Buying Decision Process

Like consumers, businesses follow a buying decision process. This process is summarised on the right hand side of Figure 5.4. In the first stage, one or more individuals recognise that a problem or need exists. Problem recognition may arise under a variety of circumstances, either from inside or outside the company. For example, a machine might reach the end of its working life and need to be replaced, or changes in fire regulations might dictate the need for a new approach to manufacturing. Individuals in the buying centre, such as users, influencers or buyers, may be involved in problem recognition, but it may be stimulated by external sources, such as sales representatives or customers.

The second stage of the process—development of product specifications—requires those involved to assess the problem or need and to determine what is

The *Academy* Expands to Meet New Customer Needs

A common experience for most managers is the in-company training programme or the workshop seminar. While many large companies have their own purposely designed conference suites and training centres, many opt to utilise the growing selection of facilities operated by the major hotel chains. Posthouse and Crest Hotels were established by Forte in the 1970s as business travel expanded and companies required comfortable, city or trunk road hotel accommodation for salespeople and executives. As the training and conference market expanded, these hotels built meeting rooms, seminar rooms equipped with audio-visual aids, plus larger exhibition and conference halls. For Forte, the conference market has emerged as a major target market and one in which the company is investing large sums so as to cater for this burgeoning business opportunity. The bespoke conference operation has even been given its own brand identity, marketing budget and specialised sales staff. The *Academy* is ear-marked for nationwide expansion. At over £1.2 million per location, this marks a serious attempt by Forte to establish a significant presence in the conference market.

The *Academy* caters for meetings and conferences, offering rooms and a full range of services including fax, word processing and photocopying. The suites are purpose built and can accommodate small groups right up to 300 people in the main halls. A full time meetings and conference organiser is on duty to help companies plan their corporate events. However, a major feature in each *Academy* is a state-of-the-art multi-media facility which uses computerised projection techniques from behind, instead of the once staple overhead projector. So impressive are the facilities that one new *Academy* location had advanced bookings of over £3 million for its first year of operations.

It is not only hotels which have seen the significant growth in conferences, training events and trade shows as a priority target market. Most universities now supplement their income with conferences held during vacation time. Warwick University has been so successful at targeting this market that it built, at over £5 million, three bespoke all-year-round conference centres. These each house four-star standard residential accommodation, fully equipped seminar and meeting suites, leisure facilities and business centres. A growing proportion of the market is being catered for by specialist conference centres. The Sundial Group, for example, has a network of rural country houses, modernised to incorporate seminar rooms, lecture theatres, syndicate suites, full residential and recreational facilities. As innovators in this sector almost forty years ago, the Sundial Group has expanded to support growing client demand. Sundial only operates conference centres and is "dedicated to providing the perfect environment for learning and creative thinking . . . offering a relaxing yet stimulating atmosphere which fosters learning, discussion and innovative thinking". In order to offer such specialist services, operators such as Forte's *Academy*, Warwick University's Scarman House or the Sundial Group must invest in well run and up-to-date facilities. These must be effectively marketed not to consumers but to businesses organising corporate events such as training sessions, sales meetings, product launches or "away day" strategic planning workshops. Many client companies, such as Barclays, Courtaulds or Safeway, have specialist managers who are responsible for organising corporate events and booking suitable venues. The marketers of the *Academy* or Sundial seek to develop marketing strategies and campaigns which will entice these managers to become their customers.

SOURCES: Bill Pollock, The *Academy*, Forte; Stewart Smith, "Academy opens for hire", *The Evening Telegraph*, 8 December 1998, p. 12; Tim Chudley, Sundial Conference and Training Group, Northampton; Scarman House, University of Warwick.

---

necessary to resolve or satisfy it. During this stage, users and influencers, such as technical personnel and engineers, often provide information and advice for developing product specifications. By assessing and describing needs, the organisation should be able to establish product specifications.

Searching for possible products to solve the problem and then locating suitable suppliers is the third stage in the decision process. Search activities may involve surfing the Internet, looking in company files and trade directories, contacting suppliers for information, visiting trade shows, soliciting proposals from known suppliers, and examining catalogues and trade publications. Marketing Insight 5.2 illustrates

Figure 5.5 Does the product meet specifications? These advertisements from New Holland and Massey Ferguson illustrate the features of the product proposition.
SOURCE: *left:* Courtesy of New Holland. *right:* Courtesy of Massey Ferguson.

how one hotel operator has responded to the demand for conference and training facilities, focusing on the business's efforts to entice prospective clients using its bespoke operation with its own-brand identity and marketing budget. Suppliers may be viewed as unacceptable because they are too small to supply the quantities needed, or because they do not have the necessary information technology systems to keep appropriate delivery records. In some instances the product may not be available from any existing supplier and the buyer must then find an innovative company, such as 3M, that can design and build the product.

If all goes well, the search stage will result in a list of several alternative products and suppliers. The fourth stage is evaluating the products on the list to determine which options (if any) meet the product specifications developed in the second stage. The advertisements in Figure 5.5 stress the particular product, service and supplier attributes that may help customers evaluate whether a particular offering meets their requirements. At this point, too, various suppliers are evaluated according to multiple criteria, such as price, service and ability to deliver.

The results of the deliberations and assessments in the fourth stage are used during the fifth stage to select the most appropriate product and supplier. In some cases the buyer may decide on several suppliers. In others only one supplier is

Sole sourcing A buying process that involves the selection of only one supplier

selected—a situation known as **sole sourcing**. Sole sourcing has traditionally been discouraged except when a product is available from only one company. In recent times sole sourcing has become more popular, partly because such an arrangement means better communications between buyer and supplier, stability and higher profits for the supplier, and often lower prices for the buyer. However, most organisations still prefer to purchase goods and services from several suppliers to reduce the possibility of disruption caused by strikes, shortages or bankruptcy. The actual product is ordered in this fifth stage and specific details regarding terms, credit arrangements, delivery dates and methods, and technical assistance are worked out.

During the sixth stage, the product's performance is evaluated by comparing it with specifications. Sometimes, even though the product meets the specifications, its performance does not adequately solve the problem or satisfy the need recognised in the first stage. In that case, the product specifications must be adjusted. The supplier's performance is also evaluated during this stage, and if it is found wanting, the buyer seeks corrective action from the supplier or searches for a new supplier. Buyers are increasingly concerned with obtaining high quality service from suppliers and may formally set performance targets for them. The results of such performance evaluations become feedback for the other stages and influence future purchase decisions.

This business-to-business buying decision process is used in its entirety primarily for new task purchases. Several of the stages, but not necessarily all, are used for modified re-buying and straight re-buying, and fewer individuals are likely to be involved in these decisions.

Influences on Business-to-Business Buying

Environmental factors Uncontrollable forces such as politics, competitive and economic factors, legal and regulatory issues, technological changes and socio-cultural issues

Figure 5.4 also lists the four major categories of factors that influence business-to-business buying decisions: environmental, organisational, interpersonal and individual.

Chapter 2 explained that **environmental factors** are uncontrollable forces such as politics, laws, regulations and regulatory agencies, activities of interest groups, changes in the economy, competitors' actions and technological changes. These forces generate a considerable amount of uncertainty for an organisation, which can make individuals in the buying centre apprehensive about certain types of purchases. Changes in one or more environmental forces can create new purchasing opportunities. For example, changes in competition and technology can make buying decisions difficult in the case of products like computers, a field in which competition is increasingly affected by new co-operative strategies between companies. Compaq Computers, for instance, grew into a billion dollar company by competing only against IBM and developing co-operative relationships with all other potential competitors.[16]

Organisational factors Include the buyer's objectives, purchasing policies and resources, as well as the size and composition of its buying centre

Organisational factors influencing the buying decision process include the buyer's objectives, purchasing policies and resources, as well as the size and composition of its buying centre. An organisation may have certain buying policies to which buying centre participants must conform. For instance, a company's policies may require long term contracts, perhaps longer than most sellers desire. The nature of an organisation's financial resources may require special credit arrangements. Any of these conditions could affect purchase decision processes.

Interpersonal factors The relationships among the people in the buying centre

Interpersonal factors are the relationships among the people in the buying centre, where the use of power and the level of conflict significantly influence organisational buying decisions. Certain persons in the buying centre may be better communicators than others and thus more persuasive. Often these interpersonal dynamics are hidden, making them difficult for marketers to appraise.

Individual factors The personal characteristics of individuals in the buying centre, such as age, education, personality, position in the organisation and income level

Individual factors are the personal characteristics of individuals in the buying centre, such as age, education, personality, position in the organisation and income level. For example, a 60 year old manager who left school at 16 and has been with the organisation ever since may affect the decisions of the buying centre differently than a 30 year old with a two year employment history who left university with a business studies degree and an MBA. How influential these factors will be depends on the buying situation, the type of product being purchased and whether the purchase is new task, modified re-buy or straight re-buy. The negotiating styles of individuals will undoubtedly vary within an organisation and from one organisation to another. To be effective, a marketer needs to know customers well enough to be aware of these individual factors and the effects they may have on purchase decisions.

Selection and Analysis of Business-to-Business Markets

Marketing research is becoming more important in industrial business-to-business markets. Most of the marketing research techniques discussed in Chapter 6 can be applied to **industrial marketing.** This section focuses on important and unique approaches to selecting and analysing industrial markets.

Industrial marketing Activities directed towards facilitating and expediting exchanges between Industrial markets and industrial producers

Industrial marketers have easy access to a considerable amount of information about potential customers, for much of this information appears in government and industry publications. However, comparable data about ultimate consumers are not available. Even though marketers may use different procedures to isolate and analyse target markets, most follow a similar pattern: (1) determining who potential customers are and how many there are, (2) locating where they are and (3) estimating their purchase potential.[17]

Identifying Potential Customers

Much information about industrial customers is based on the **Standard Industrial Classification (SIC) system,** which provides information on different industries and products and was developed to classify selected economic characteristics of industrial, commercial, financial and service organisations. In the UK this system is administered by the Central Statistical Office. Table 5.3 shows how the SIC system can be used to categorise products. The most recent SIC manual contains 10 broad divisions, each denoted by a single digit from 0 to 9. These are sub-divided

Standard Industrial Classification (SIC) system A system that provides information on different industries and products, and classifies economic characteristics of industrial, commercial, financial and service organisations

Table 5.3 The Standard Industrial Classification (SIC) system for categorising industrial customers

0	Agriculture, forestry and fishing
1	Energy and water supply industries
2	Extraction of minerals and ores other than fuels; manufacture of metals, mineral products and chemicals
3	Metal goods, engineering and vehicles
4	Other manufacturing industries
5	Construction
6	Distribution, hotels and catering; repairs
7	Transport and communication
8	Banking, finance, insurance, business services and leasing
9	Other services

Table 5.4 Types of government information available about industrial markets (based on SIC categories)

Value of industry shipments
Number of establishments
Number of employees
Exports as a percentage of shipments
Imports as a percentage of apparent consumption
Compound annual average rate of growth
Major producing areas

into classes (each denoted by the addition of a second digit), the classes are divided into groups (three digits) and the groups into activity headings (four more digits). There are 10 divisions, 60 classes, 222 groups and 334 activity headings. For example, Division 4 (see Table 5.3), "Other manufacturing industries", has 8 classes, 50 groups and 91 activity headings. The numbering system follows that of NACE (Nomenclature Générale des Activités Économiques dans les Communautés Européennes) as far as possible.[18] To categorise manufacturers in more detail, the *Census of Distribution* further sub-divides manufacturers.

Data are available for each SIC category through various government publications and departments. Table 5.4 shows the types of information that can be obtained from government sources. Some data are available by town, county and metropolitan area. Business-to-business market data also appear in such non-government sources as Dun & Bradstreet's *Market Identifiers*.

The SIC system is a ready-made tool that allows business-to-business marketers to divide industrial organisations into market segments based mainly on the type of product manufactured or handled. Although the SIC system is a vehicle for segmentation, it must be used in conjunction with other types of data to enable a specific business-to-business marketer to determine exactly which customers it can reach and how many of them can be targeted.

Input-output analysis works well in conjunction with the SIC system. This type of analysis is based on the assumption that the output or sales of one industry are the input or purchases of other industries. For example, component manufacturers provide products that form an input for manufacturers of white goods such as washing machines, dishwashers and fridges. **Input-output data** tell what types of industries purchase the products of a particular industry.

Input-output data Information on what types of industries purchase the products of a particular industry

After discovering which industries purchase the major portion of an industry's output, the next step is to find the SIC numbers for those industries. Because businesses are grouped differently in the input-output tables and the SIC system, ascertaining SIC numbers can be difficult. However, the Central Statistical Office does provide some limited conversion tables with the input-output data. These tables can assist business marketers in assigning SIC numbers to the industry categories used in the input-output analysis. Having determined the SIC numbers of the industries that buy the company's output, a business-to-business marketer is in a position to ascertain the number of establishments that are potential buyers nationally, by town and by county. Government publications report the number of establishments within SIC classifications, along with other types of data, such as those shown in Table 5.4.

Once industrial marketers have achieved this level of information, they can identify and locate potential customers using the Internet or business-to-business

Figure 5.6 Locating business-to-business customers. This advertisement for the Dutch Automobile Association targeted travel agencies. Source: Courtesy ANWB Royal Dutch Touring Club.

directories, such as *Kompass* and *Kelly's*. These sources contain such information about a company as its name, SIC number, address, phone number and annual sales, allowing organisations to develop lists of potential customers by area.

A second approach, which is more expedient but also more expensive, is to use one of the many marketing research agencies. For example, Market Locations is able to provide lists of organisations which fall into particular SIC groups. Information can include name, location, sales volume, number of employees, type of products handled and names of chief executives. Industrial marketers can then decide which companies on the list to pursue. This will usually involve an assessment of attractiveness and purchase potential (see Figure 5.6).

In industrial marketing, situation-specific variables may be more relevant in segmenting markets than general customer characteristics. Industrial customers concentrate on benefits sought; therefore, understanding the end use of the product is more important than the psychology of decisions or socio-economic characteristics. Segmenting by benefits rather than by customer characteristics can provide insight into the structure of the market and opportunities for new customers.[19]

To estimate the purchase potential of business-to-business customers or groups of customers, a marketer must find a relationship between the size of potential customers' purchases and a variable available in SIC data, such as the number of employees. For example, a fabric manufacturer might attempt to determine the average number of metres of different materials purchased by a specific type of potential clothing manufacturer relative to the number of people employed. If the marketer has no previous experience in this market segment, it will probably be necessary to survey a random sample of potential customers to establish a relationship between purchase sizes and numbers of people employed. Once this relationship has been established, it can be applied to potential customer segments to estimate their purchases. After deriving these estimates, the marketer selects the customers to be included in the target market.

SUMMARY

Organisational (or *industrial, business-to-business*) *markets* consist of individuals or groups that purchase a specific kind of product for re-sale, for direct use in producing other products, or for use in day-to-day operations. *Producer markets* include those individuals and business organisations that purchase products for the purpose of making a profit by using them either to produce other products or in their own operations. Intermediaries, such as *wholesalers* and *retailers*, who buy finished products and re-sell them for the purpose of making a profit are classified as *reseller markets*. *Government markets* consist of national and local governments, which spend billions of pounds annually for goods and services to support their internal operations and provide citizens with needed services. Organisations that seek to achieve charitable, educational, community or other non-business goals constitute *institutional markets*.

Business-to-business transactions differ from consumer transactions in several ways. The transactions tend to be larger, and negotiations occur less frequently, though they are often lengthy. Business-to-business transactions sometimes involve more than one person or one department in the purchasing organisation. They may also involve *reciprocity*, an arrangement in which two organisations agree to buy from each other, although some countries have strict rules governing such agreements. Business-to-business customers are usually viewed as more rational and more likely to seek information about a product's features and technical specifications than are ultimate consumers.

When purchasing products, business-to-business customers must be particularly concerned about quality, delivery, service and price. Quality is important because it directly affects the quality of the organisational buyer's ultimate product. To achieve an exact standard, organisations often buy their products on the basis of a set of expressed characteristics, called specifications. Reliable and quick delivery is crucial to many organisations whose production lines must be fed with a continuous supply of component parts and raw materials. Because services can have a direct influence on a company's costs, sales and profits, such matters as market information, on-time delivery and availability of parts can be crucial to a business-to-business buyer. Although a business-to-business customer does not decide which products to purchase solely by their price, cost is of prime concern because it directly influences a company's profitability.

Business-to-business buyers use several purchasing methods, including description, inspection, sampling and negotiation. Most business-to-business purchases are new task, modified re-buy or straight re-buy. In a *new task purchase*, an organisation makes an initial purchase of an item to be used to perform a new job or to solve a new problem. In a *modified re-buy purchase,* a new task purchase is changed the second or third time it is ordered, or the requirements associated with a straight re-buy purchase are modified. A *straight re-buy purchase* occurs when a buyer re-purchases the same products routinely under approximately the same terms of sale.

Industrial demand differs from consumer demand along several dimensions. *Derived demand* is the demand for industrial products which arises from the demand for consumer products. At the industry level, *inelastic demand* is a demand that is not significantly affected by a price increase or decrease. If the price of an industrial item changes, demand for the product will not change proportionally. Some industrial products are subject to *joint demand,* which occurs when two or more items are used in combination to make a product. Finally, because industrial demand ultimately derives from consumer demand, the demand for industrial products can fluctuate widely.

Business-to-business (or *industrial*) *buying behaviour* refers to the purchase behaviour of producers, resellers, government units and institutions. Business-to-business purchase decisions are made through a *buying centre*—the group of people who are involved in making organisational purchase decisions. Users are those in the organisation who actually use the product. Influencers help develop the specifications and evaluate alternative products for possible use. Buyers are responsible for selecting the suppliers and negotiating the terms of the purchases. Deciders choose the products and suppliers. Gatekeepers control the flow of information to and among persons who occupy the other roles in the buying centre.

When a company buys a product or service from another company, both organisations enter into a process during which items of value are exchanged in return for something else. This exchange process may lead to a long term relationship between buyer and seller. *Relationship marketing* is the term used to explain the special attention being given to this area and is defined as the activities an organisation uses to build, maintain and develop customer relations. The trend toward long term relationships has resulted in *relationship management.*

The stages of the business-to-business buying decision process are problem recognition, development of product specifications to solve the problem, search for products and suppliers, evaluation of products relative to specifications, selection and ordering of the most appropriate product and evaluation of the product's and the supplier's performance. The evaluation of product and suppliers will directly affect future purchasing decisions. *Sole sourcing,* the process of selecting only one supplier, is becoming more popular.

Four categories of factors influence business-to-business buying decisions: environmental, organisational, interpersonal and individual. *Environmental factors* include politics, laws and regulations, economic conditions, competitive forces and technological changes. *Organisational factors* include the buyer's objectives, purchasing policies and resources, as well as the size and composition of its buying centre. *Interpersonal factors* refer to the relationships among the people in the buying centre. *Individual factors* refer to the personal characteristics of individuals in the buying centre, such as age, education, personality, position in the organisation and income.

Industrial marketing is a set of activities directed at facilitating and expediting exchanges involving industrial products and customers in industrial markets.

Industrial marketers have a considerable amount of information available to them for use in planning their marketing strategies. Much of this information is based on the *Standard Industrial Classification (SIC) system,* which classifies businesses into major industry divisions, classes, groups and activities. The SIC system provides business marketers with information needed to identify market segments. It can best be used for this purpose in conjunction with other information, such as *input-output data.* After identifying target industries, the marketer can locate potential customers by using the Internet or industrial directories or by employing a marketing research agency. The marketer must then estimate the potential purchases of business-to-business customers by finding a relationship between a potential customer's purchases and a variable available in published sources.

Important Terms

Organisational (or industrial, business-to-business) market
Producer markets
Reseller markets
Wholesalers
Retailers
Government markets
Institutional markets
Reciprocity
New task purchase

Modified re-buy purchase
Straight re-buy purchase
Derived demand
Inelastic demand
Joint demand
Business-to-business (or industrial) buying behaviour
Buying centre
Relationship marketing

Relationship management
Sole sourcing
Environmental factors
Organisational factors
Interpersonal factors
Individual factors
Industrial marketing
Standard Industrial Classification (SIC) system
Input-output data

Discussion and Review Questions

1. Identify, describe and give examples of four major types of organisational markets.
2. Why are business-to-business buyers generally considered more rational in regard to their purchasing behaviour than ultimate consumers?
3. What are the primary concerns of business-to-business buyers?
4. List several characteristics that differentiate business-to-business transactions from consumer ones.
5. What are the commonly used methods of business-to-business buying?
6. Why do buyers involved in a straight re-buy purchase require less information than those making a new task purchase?
7. How does industrial demand differ from consumer demand?
8. What are the major components of a buying centre?
9. What elements may be exchanged by a buyer and seller when a purchase transaction takes place?
10. Why has relationship management attracted so much interest in business-to-business markets?
11. Identify the stages of the business-to-business buying decision process. How is this decision process used when making straight re-buys?
12. What impact does the evaluation of a particular purchase have on future buying decisions?
13. How do environmental, organisational, interpersonal and individual factors affect organisational purchases?
14. What function does the SIC system help industrial marketers perform?
15. List some sources that an industrial marketer can use to determine the names and addresses of potential customers.

Recommended Readings

D. Ford, *Understanding Business Markets* (London: Academic Press, 1997).
M. D. Hutt and T. W. Speh, *Business Marketing Management: A Strategic View of Industrial and Organisational Markets* (Fort Worth: Dryden Press, 1998).

T. L. Powers, *Modern Business Marketing* (St. Paul, Minn.: West, 1991).
F. E. Webster, *Industrial Marketing Strategy* (New York: John Wiley, 1995).

5.1 In the Black and Leading

For most people, oil is evident as fuel for cars, heating and the generation of electricity or as the basis for the plastics industry. What about the black surfaces of pavements, roads, driveways, car parks and school playgrounds? Bitumen is an oil based product most of us take for granted but which is a major part of the revenue for companies such as Shell, BP, Esso, Total, Colas or Lanfina. The leading bitumen player in the UK, Scandinavia and much of western Europe is Stockholm based Nynas. In the UK, this relatively small player in the petro-chemicals industry has overall market leadership in the bitumen market and is renowned for its innovative product development with polymer formulations.

Bitumen is one of the most ubiquitous materials made by industry, underfoot almost everywhere as a core ingredient of the macadams and asphalts in roads and pavements. There are numerous specialist applications too, such as the backing to carpet tiles, roofing felts, sealants for mighty dams and waterproofing for bridge decks. Inevitably this results in a diverse customer base for an organisation such as Nynas. In a market with competitors as large as Esso or Shell, Nynas's leadership has not occurred by accident. Nynas has established its enviable position by astutely utilising the resources required to develop innovative products, customer service schemes and flexible delivery capabilities in order to ensure customer satisfaction. At the heart of its business strategy is a desire to innovate, listen to customers and develop services which genuinely enable customers to be properly served.

Nynas believes it has several important edges over its rivals:

> Customer dialogue—as a major producer with significant R&D technical support, Nynas's laboratories can determine a product formulation for most bitumen based applications. Whether the customer is a local authority requiring a cost effective thin surfacing for a housing estate's ageing pavements, a contractor such as Tarmac requiring 24 hour supply of high quality, state-of-the-art bitumen for the construction of a new motorway, or a builder buying polymer enhanced mastic asphalts to act as a waterproofing membrane for regency

mews properties, Nynas can develop a quality bitumen based product.

> Consistent quality and innovative product development—refineries in Belgium, Sweden and the UK, supported with a network of terminals and research laboratories across Europe, enable Nynas to continually improve its products and their performance. Customers do not want to frequently re-surface major roads or busy shopping centre pavements. Specialist applications such as waterproofing dams or houses are time consuming, costly and inconvenient remedial activities which clients do not want to repeat in a hurry. Nynas has access to high grade Venezuelan bitumen, not readily available to its major competitors, which gives it added flexibility in producing high quality bitumen grades for specific applications. Whether it is for a routine commodity bulk job such as a school playground surface or an unusual requirement for waterproofing a royal building, Nynas has developed a reputation as being a leading supplier.

> Logistical support—users of bitumen often require deliveries at very short notice, in specific quantities and to guaranteed quality levels. These deliveries may be anywhere at any time. A contractor repairing a busy commuter route out of daylight hours needs on-time delivery of ready-to-use bitumen products. Repairs to a remote bridge still require guaranteed on-time delivery. Nynas's depots operate around the clock despatching computer monitored deliveries by tanker to clients as and when the customer has specified. Twenty-four hours, 365 days a year, Nynas prides itself on its high levels of responsiveness and reliability of delivery.

The composition of customers is varied. A major new road building scheme will involve formal tendering and guarantees with penalties against inferior product or missed deliveries. The buying process of such customers will be highly formal, involving numerous managers and functions as diverse as purchasing, technical support, construction, finance and logistical support. On both sides—customer and Nynas—cross-functional teams of scientists, engineers, managers and the field force will spend many months agreeing on the product requirement, contractual obligations, delivery requirements and application techniques. For other customers, the purchase is perhaps more of a routine re-buy with only limited interaction and discussion between Nynas and the customer. On other occasions, the Nynas helpline may receive a midnight telephone call from a highways agency surveyor who has just discovered cracks in a major road's surface and requires immediate assistance in both identifying the cause of the problem and rectifying the situation before commuters awaken the next morning.

For a rather bland looking substance such as bitumen, the market is diverse and challenging. Nynas has established its successful position in the European market for bitumen based products by practising the best principles of marketing. The company strives to understand its customers' needs and to offer reliable products supported with effective customer service, round the clock. Product innovation is at the forefront of the company's strategy and, coupled with constantly improving ways of offering peace of mind to customers, offers an edge over rivals. Shrewd marketing analysis constantly monitors product changes, customers' expectations, competitors' activities and those aspects of the marketing environment—notably technological and regulatory forces—which will impact on the business's fortunes. Resources are allocated to match this thorough assessment of market opportunities and marketing requirements.

SOURCES: Siobhan McKelvey and Willie Hunter, Nynas UK; *Network* magazine, 1997–1999; "Your guide to bitumen specialists", Nynas; the Nynas *Annual Review*, 1996–1999.

Questions for Discussion

1. Who are Nynas's customers?
2. What types of organisational markets (as classified in this chapter) purchase the products Nynas makes?
3. Would most purchases of Nynas's products be new task, modified re-buy or straight re-buy?
4. What product and service features does Nynas offer its customers?

5.2 Selling a White Powder: No Easy Matter

A white powder little known by most consumers appears as a core ingredient in all paints, inks and most plastics: TiO_2 or titanium dioxide, produced from ilmenite and synthetic rutile. With plants focused primarily in North America, Europe, Australia and southern Africa, the market was dominated by the UK's ICI—through its operating subsidiary Tioxide—and the US's DuPont. In the Americas, DuPont has the edge, whereas in Europe Tioxide is the dominant player. Smaller companies such as Kemira, Kerr McGee, Kronos and SCM also have slices of the market. For this commodity product used in the production process for so many materials, continuity of supply and purity of the pigment are important considerations. Customers for Tioxide or Kerr McGee are quite diverse, ranging from international masterbatch companies requiring long production runs (perhaps producing packaging or film products) to PVC and linoleum flooring manufacturers, marine engineers producing boat mouldings, the paint giants ICI Dulux and Crown, and the manufacturers of road marking paints!

The task facing Tioxide or DuPont varies according to which type of customer the company is dealing with. An international packaging company may well have a buying centre comprising a senior purchasing officer, a technical manager, a laboratory technician for technical approval, a production manager whose job depends on having the right supplies and a senior financial controller to sign off on any orders. Not all will be involved throughout the buying process, but DuPont or Tioxide must be aware of their views and attempt to influence and comfort them as required. Such packaging companies will be very large and understand their own markets well, with the result that they will have very specific and well defined product requirements from suppliers such as DuPont or Kronos.

The key customer needs in such a market may include product consistency over time and throughout production runs, guarantee of supply and long term supplier relationships with reputable companies. The buying process will be much more complicated than for any consumer purchase. It will usually commence when the need for TiO_2 is noted and suppliers are contacted. Samples will be tested by the packaging company's own laboratory technical experts. If the samples are deemed fit, the production department will be asked for its approval. In some circumstances the packaging company's key customers will be asked to approve the quality, purity and appearance of the final products. At this point in the buying process, there will be a group meeting in the packaging company involving commercial and technical personnel to agree on order quantities, delivery requirements and payment terms. After a period of negotiation, DuPont, Kerr McGee or Tioxide may be lucky enough to be awarded a contract, after which the whole process will re-commence. During the course of such deliberations in the buying process, numerous market factors will influence those involved—opinions voiced at trade association meetings, customer specifications, sales agents, equipment manufacturers, technical seminars, EU legislation and even the sales efforts of the TiO_2 suppliers.

By contrast, if Kerr McGee or SCM wishes to sell to a flooring manufacturer, the process is relatively simple. The buying centre may consist only of a purchasing manager. The main influencing factors will usually relate to trends in the construction industry—which can be monitored easily—and to anti-PVC moves because of "green" concerns. Such manufacturers will require reliability of supply, but any of the major players can meet that need. A competitive price and solid relationship with locally based sales personnel will continue to be dominant customer needs. Given that the product is a raw ingredient chemical, the buying process will still involve technical laboratory approval, production trial and senior level negotiation. With a much smaller buying centre, though, the process may be managed with more ease.

SOURCES: DuPont and Tioxide sales literature, 1996; Peter Fairly, "Tioxide grows materials group", *Chemical Week*, 5 July 1995, p. 18; Brent Shearer, "TiO_2 producers mull new plants", *Chemical Marketing Reporter*, 9 January 1995, p. 3; Marjorie Coeyman, "DuPont, Tioxide plan capacity hike", *Chemical Week*, 19 October 1994, p. 14; Ian Young, "Kronos deal prompts Tioxide exit from minerals company", *Chemical Week*, 2 March 1994, p. 18.

Questions for Discussion

1. In industrial markets, why does the buying process often seem more complicated than in consumer goods markets? Explain your views.
2. Why is it so important to understand the factors that influence decision-makers in industrial buying?
3. How should DuPont or Tioxide attempt to monitor the buying behaviour of its core customers? Describe with examples.

6 Marketing Research and Information Systems

> *"The researcher's challenge is not just generating data, but in creating a vision from that data."*
>
> Dave Birks, University of Bath

OBJECTIVES

- To understand the importance of and relationship between research and information systems in marketing decision-making
- To distinguish between research and intuition in solving marketing problems
- To learn the five basic steps of the marketing research process
- To understand the fundamental methods of gathering data for marketing research
- To gain a sense of the relative advantages and disadvantages of marketing research tools

All too frequently businesses turn to marketing research in order to diagnose the reasons for failing or failed products. Unfortunately, this can even be for products only recently and expensively launched. Marketing research has an invaluable role to play in focusing the attention of those responsible for creating, branding and launching new products and services. Research house Market Profiles, for example, conducted research for electric heater manufacturer Dimplex, which had invested in developing a dual fuel fire with gas for heat and electricity for powering the accompanying visual flame effect. A realistic looking model was produced and placed in British Gas Energy Centres in order to determine consumer reaction. While aesthetically pleasing, consumers gave the likely retail price the thumbs down, with the result that Dimplex was able to avoid a costly mistake. The product went no further and certainly the findings justified the expense of the marketing research.

Market Profiles also made realistic looking models when undertaking marketing research for brown goods manufacturer Panasonic. In the 1960s and 1970s most television sets were cased in wood or wood-effect finishes such as teak, rosewood or mahogany. During the 1980s most TVs, videos and hi-fi systems were produced in black plastic finishes. One proposal on the table at Panasonic was to produce a new range of TVs in wood or wood-effect cases. The researchers sought consumers' views of the wood-look dummy TVs: consumers in the UK were not impressed, but timber-loving Scandinavians and Germans were much more enthusiastic.

Norwegian plastics company Pivco developed an environmentally friendly electric car, the CityBee. With an electric engine rather than the more conventional petrol or diesel engines familiar to car buyers, it was important to test out the proposition before embarking on full scale production. Equally revolutionary was the body work, which was made from scratch-free, dent resistant, cheap to produce plastic. Pivco was keen to ascertain how consumers would react to such an unusual car concept. Prototype models were shipped to the UK and California, where marketing researchers ran discussion groups around the innovative CityBee car. The results were highly encouraging, but also identified aspects requiring further design input prior to any full scale product launch.

In each of these cases, the companies could have adopted the "product first" mentality which predominated in the production and sales eras prior to the marketing era of the 1950s and 1960s. The product came first, then target markets were identified and the product sold aggressively in order to gain rapid sales growth to cover the design, tooling and production costs. Had Dimplex, Panasonic or Pivco followed such a course of action, products would have entered full scale production and been launched with resource-eating promotional campaigns, only to fail to fully address target market customer needs and expectations. The marketing research undertaken during the product development stage by these companies enabled them to make more informed decisions, opting to either pull back from entering into production or to further modify their products prior to any market entry.

SOURCES: Richenda Wilson, "Test for success", *Marketing Week*, 15 October 1998, pp. 77–79; Chris Paxton, Market Profiles, 1998; Dimplex, 1998; Pivco, Oslo, 1998. *Cartoon:* Courtesy of *Marketing Week*.

To implement the marketing concept, marketers require information about the characteristics, needs and wants of their target markets. Given the intense competition in today's marketplace, it is unwise to develop a product and then look for a market where it can be profitably sold. The Sinclair C5 electric car is a prime example of product first, market second; it failed to satisfy customers' needs. Marketing research and information systems that provide practical, unbiased information help organisations avoid assumptions and misunderstandings that could result in poor marketing performance, as detailed in the chapter's opener.

This chapter focuses on the ways of gathering information needed to make marketing decisions, first distinguishing between managing information within an organisation (a marketing information system) and conducting marketing research. The discussion next addresses the role of marketing research in decision-making and problem solving, compares it with intuition and examines the individual steps of the marketing research process. The chapter also takes a close look at experimentation and various methods of collecting data. The final section considers the importance of marketing research and marketing information systems.

Defining Marketing Research and Marketing Information Systems

As the preceding chapters have made clear, marketers must understand customers, competitors, market trends and aspects of the marketing environment. To do this, they require information and marketing intelligence.[1] These may be

Marketing research The process of gathering, interpreting and reporting information to help marketers solve specific marketing problems or take advantage of marketing opportunities

judged inadequate to tackle a specific decision or marketing task, in which case it is probable that marketing research would provide the additional insights required. **Marketing research** is the systematic design, collection, interpretation and reporting of information to help marketers solve specific marketing problems or take advantage of marketing opportunities. It is a process for gathering information not currently available to decision-makers. Marketing research is conducted on a special project basis, and research methods are adapted both to the problems being studied and to changes in the environment. The marketing research industry is huge, highly competitive and increasingly dominated by international research agencies. Figure 6.1 reveals the scope of the marketing research industry.

The Market Research Society defines research as follows:

> the collection and analysis of data from a sample of individuals or organisations relating to their characteristics, behaviour, attitudes, opinions or possessions. It includes all forms of marketing and social research such as consumer and industrial surveys, psychological investigations, observational and panel studies.[2]

There are broadly two types of marketing research: quantitative and qualitative.[3] In **quantitative research,** techniques and sample sizes lead to the collection of data that can be statistically analysed and whose results can be expressed numerically. These data tend to come from large surveys, sales data or market forecasts. **Qualitative research** deals with information that is too difficult or expensive to quantify: subjective opinions and value judgements that are not amenable to statistical analysis and quantification,[4] typically unearthed during depth interviews or discussion groups.

Quantitative research Research aimed at producing data that can be statistically analysed and whose results can be expressed numerically

Qualitative research Research that deals with information too difficult or expensive to quantify, such as subjective opinions and value judgements, typically unearthed during interviews or discussion groups

Marketing information system (MIS) The framework for the day-to-day management and structuring of information gathered from sources both inside and outside an organisation

A **marketing information system (MIS)** is the framework for the day-to-day management and structuring of information gathered regularly from sources both inside and outside an organisation. As such, an MIS provides a continuous flow of information about prices, advertising expenditure, sales, competition and distribution expenses.[5] When information systems are strategically created and then institutionalised throughout an organisation, their value is enhanced.[6] Figure 6.2 illustrates the chief components of an MIS.

The inputs into a marketing information system include the information sources inside and outside the organisation assumed to be useful for future

Figure 6.1 European marketing research markets, 1990. The total is approximately 2,474 million ECUs. SOURCE: ESOMAR, the European Society for Opinion and Marketing Research, J. J. Viottastraat 29, 10/1 JP Amsterdam, The Netherlands. Tel 31-20-664-2141; FAX: 31-20-664-2922.

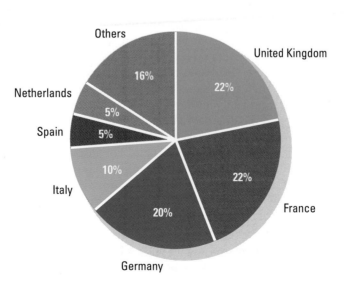

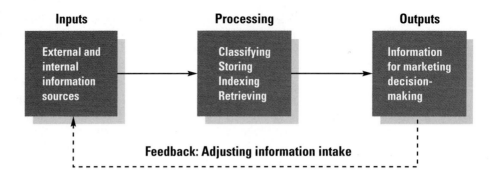

Figure 6.2 An organisation's marketing information system

Inputs	Processing	Outputs
External and internal information sources	Classifying Storing Indexing Retrieving	Information for marketing decision-making

Feedback: Adjusting information intake

decision-making. Processing information involves classifying it and developing categories for meaningful storage and retrieval. Marketing decision-makers then determine which information—the output—is useful for making marketing decisions. Finally, feedback enables those who are responsible for gathering internal and external data to adjust the information inputs systematically.[7]

Regular reports of sales by product or market categories, data on inventory levels and records of salespeople's activities are all examples of information that is useful in making marketing decisions. In the MIS, the means of gathering data receive less attention than do the procedures for expediting the flow of information. The main focus of the marketing information system is on data storage and retrieval, as well as on computer capabilities and management's information requirements. RJR Nabisco, for example, handles hundreds of thousands of consumer contacts each year, usually enquiries about product usage, nutrition and ingredients. This consumer feedback is computerised and made available on demand throughout the company's operating divisions.

The main difference between marketing research and a marketing information system is that the former is an information gathering process for specific situations, whereas the latter provides continuous data input for an organisation. Non-recurring decisions that deal, for example, with the dynamics of the marketing environment often call for a data search structured according to the problem and decision. Marketing research is usually characterised by in-depth analyses of major problems or issues. Often the information needed is available only from sources outside an organisation's formal channels of information. For instance, an organisation may want to know something about its competitors or to gain an unbiased understanding of its own customers. Such information needs may require an independent investigation by a marketing research company.

Data brought into the organisation through marketing research become part of its **marketing databank,** a file of data collected through both the MIS and marketing research projects. The marketing databank allows researchers to retrieve information that is useful for addressing problems quite different from those that prompted the original data collection. Often a research study developed for one purpose proves valuable for developing a research method of indicating problems in researching a particular topic. For instance, data obtained from a study by Ford on the buying behaviour of purchasers of its models may be used in planning future models. Consequently, marketers should classify and store in the databank all data from marketing research and the MIS to facilitate their use in future marketing decisions.

Databanks vary widely from one organisation to another. In a small organisation, the databank may simply be a large notebook, but many organisations

Marketing databank A file of data collected through both the MIS and marketing research projects

employ a computer storage and retrieval system to handle the large volume of data. Figure 6.3 illustrates how marketing decision-makers combine research findings with data from an MIS to develop a databank. Although many organisations do not use the term *databank,* they still have some system for storing information. Smaller organisations may not use the terms *MIS* and *marketing research,* but they normally do perform these marketing activities. All organisations have some **marketing intelligence**, although often it is found to be inadequate for specific problem solving, leading to ad hoc commissioning of marketing research. Marketing intelligence is the composite of all data and ideas available within an organisation, for example, a company or a marketing department that assists in decision-making.

After a marketing information system—of whatever size and complexity—has been established, information should be related to marketing planning.[8] The following section discusses how marketers use marketing information, intuition and judgement in making decisions. Marketing Insight 6.1 illustrates the importance of marketing research to marketing decision-makers. It is not always necessary in marketing decision-making to undertake marketing research, but it is necessary to have relevant marketing intelligence and accessible marketing information.

Marketing intelligence The composite of all data and ideas available within an organisation that assists in decision-making

Information Needs and Decision-Making

The real value of marketing research and marketing information systems is measured by improvements in a marketer's ability to make decisions. Marketers

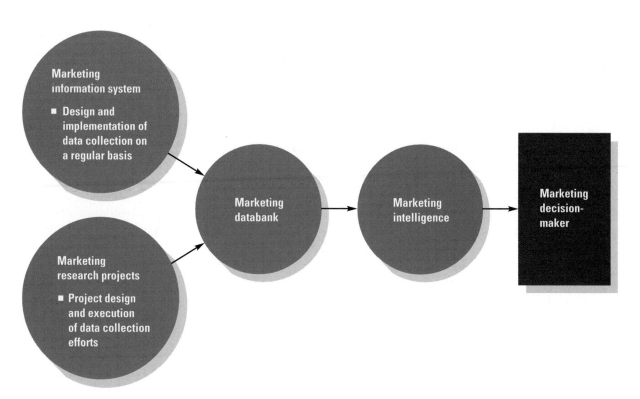

Figure 6.3   Combining marketing research and the marketing information system

should treat information in the same manner as other resources utilised by the company, and they must weigh the costs of obtaining information against the benefits derived. Information is worthwhile if it results in marketing mixes that better satisfy the needs of the company's target markets, leads to increased sales and profits, or helps the company achieve some other goal.

Marketing research and marketing information systems provide the organisation with customer feedback, without which a marketer cannot understand the dynamics of the marketplace. As managers recognise its benefits, they assign marketing research a much larger role in decision-making. For example, Japanese managers, who put much more faith in information they get directly from wholesalers and retailers, are beginning to grasp the importance of consumer surveys and scientific methods of marketing research as they seek ways to diversify their companies.[9]

The increase in marketing research activities represents a transition from intuitive to scientific problem solving. In relying on **intuition,** marketing managers base decisions on personal knowledge and past experience. However, in **scientific decision-making,** managers take an orderly and logical approach to gathering information. They seek facts on a systematic basis, and they apply methods other than trial and error or generalisation from experience.

Despite the obvious value of formal research, marketing decisions are often made without it. Certainly, minor, low risk problems that must be dealt with at once can and should be handled on the basis of personal judgement and common sense. If good decisions can be made with the help of currently available information, costly formal research may be superfluous. However, as the financial, social or ethical risks increase or the possible courses of action multiply, full scale research as a prerequisite for marketing decision-making becomes both desirable and rewarding.

The suggestion here is not that intuition has no value in marketing decision-making. Successful decisions blend both research and intuition. Statistics, mathematics and logic are powerful tools in problem solving, and the information they provide can reduce the uncertainty of predictions based on limited experience. But these tools do not necessarily bring out the right answers. Consider an extreme example. A marketing research study conducted for Xerox Corporation in the late 1950s indicated a very limited market for an automatic photocopier. Xerox management judged that the researchers had drawn the wrong conclusions from the study, and they decided to launch the product anyway. That product, the Xerox 914 copier, was an instant success. An immediate backlog of orders developed, and the rest is history. Although the Xerox example is certainly an extreme one, by and large a proper blend of research and intuition offers the best formula for a correct decision. Table 6.1 distinguishes between the roles of research and intuition in decision-making.

The Marketing Research Process

To maintain the control needed for obtaining accurate information, marketers approach marketing research in logical steps. The difference between good and bad research depends on the quality of the input, which includes effective control over the entire marketing research process. Figure 6.4 illustrates the five basic steps of the marketing research process: (1) defining and locating problems, (2) developing hypotheses, (3) collecting data with which to test and modify the

Why Products Fail: A Marketing Research Gap

The importance of marketing research and information systems is perhaps best understood by looking at product failures. Eight out of ten new products eventually fail. Strong marketing research can help companies reduce the likelihood of product failures.

At the end of 1998, radio based telephone service provider Ionica announced redundancies, a curtailment of network development and refinancing moves. The innovative telecommunications company had targeted domestic telephone users with a radio based system avoiding use of BT landlines. There was insufficient up-take to warrant the hefty network development and promotional costs. Better marketing research may have identified a more viable target market segment.

The National Lottery teamed up with football pools operator Vernons to launch a lottery based football game called EasyPlay. The rules proved too complex for most punters, who failed to purchase tickets in adequate quantities. Throughout the 1990s, the alcoholic beverages companies sought to re-position their recently launched slightly alcoholic fizzy drinks, such as Hooper's Hooch. Lemonade with a hint of alcohol had been targeted at young adults. Instead, teenagers saw the opportunity to illegally consume alcohol. The drinks businesses were harangued by MPs, consumer groups and parents. A predictable response, perhaps, but not one anticipated by the likes of Bass.

In 1996, Britain's newest Sunday newspaper, *The Planet on Sunday,* closed after one issue. Sales were only 110,000, far fewer than the hoped for 250,000 copies. The ethos of "green" environmental issues, so important to the publisher, was not apparently a core concern to the majority of Sunday newspaper readers. This relatively unresearched product failed.

When the film *Crocodile Dundee* was popular in the 1980s, so too was anything Australian. In jumped Australia's Foster's Lager beer. Foster's promotion revolved around its Australian heritage. But when the Australian fever ended, Foster's lost more than 40 per cent of its sales. In a highly competitive market, Foster's failed to convey a clear image to consumers beyond its Australian origins, and the product never found a market niche of its own. Targeting a saturated market requires marketing research to determine niches that may have an interest in the product.

In the late 1980s, four new colognes for men and women were introduced. There was nothing too unusual about the colognes except their brand name: Bic. Upon introducing the product, Bic sank £13/£14 million into its marketing campaign, but disappointing sales contributed to a 22 per cent drop in company profits. Advertising for the colognes focused more on the novel shape of the package—similar to a cigarette lighter—and less on the fragrance. Consumers were confused by the packaging and reluctant to purchase a cologne that they could not test before purchasing. More extensive marketing research could have revealed that the Bic brand name had been over extended. What makes for a great pen, lighter or razor doesn't necessarily create a great cologne.

These examples highlight the importance of marketing research, test marketing and establishing marketing information systems both within and outside of the company. Without critical research, products may fail, resulting in substantial losses. Marketing research can identify successful product formulae—and pre-empt disastrous launches or marketing programmes.

Sources: *Private Eye,* June 1996; "Lighters and smokers' requisites", *Retail Business,* May 1995, pp. 118–137; Robert Lever, "Bic writes on the alchemy of success in a pen", *Europe,* February 1995, pp. 19–20; Ros Snowdon, "Courage's £5m backs Foster's", *Marketing,* 26 January 1995, p. 2; Jennifer Comiteau, "A Foster's four pack", *Adweek,* 16 January 1995, p. 6; *Financial Times,* ad nauseam, 1998; all national press, 1998; BBC Teletext, *Ceefax,* November 1998.

hypotheses, (4) analysing and interpreting research findings, and (5) reporting research findings. These five steps should be viewed as an overall approach to conducting research rather than a rigid set of rules to be followed in each project. In planning research projects, marketers must think about each of the steps and how they can best be adjusted for each particular problem.

Table 6.1 Distinctions between research and intuition in marketing decision-making

	Research	Intuition
Nature	Formal planning, predicting based on scientific approach	Preference based on personal feelings or 'gut instinct'
Methods	Logic, systematic methods, statistical inference	Experience and demonstration
Contributions	General hypotheses for making predictions, classifying relevant variables, carrying out systematic description and classification	Minor problems solved quickly through consideration of experience, practical consequences
Situation	High risk decision-making involving high costs, investment, strategic change or long term effects	Low risk problem solving and decision-making

Step 1: Defining and Locating Problems

Problem definition The process of uncovering the nature and boundaries of a negative, or positive, situation or question

Problem definition, the first step towards finding a solution or launching a research study, focuses on uncovering the nature and boundaries of a negative, or positive, situation or question. The first sign of a problem is usually a departure from some normal function, such as conflicts between or failures in attaining objectives. If a company's objective is a 12 per cent return on investment and the current return is 6 per cent, this discrepancy should be a warning flag. It is a symptom that something inside or outside the organisation has blocked the attainment of the desired goal or that the goal is unrealistic. Decreasing sales, increasing expenses or decreasing profits also signal problems. Conversely, when an organisation experiences a dramatic rise in sales, or some other positive event, it may conduct marketing research to discover the reasons and maximise the

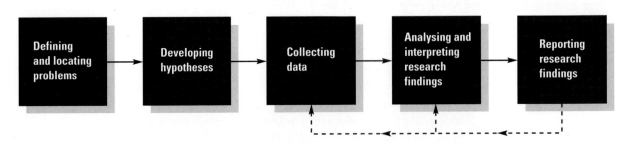

Figure 6.4 The five steps of the marketing research process

Part II   Understanding and Targeting Markets

opportunities stemming from them. In Figure 6.5 BMRB promotes its ability to isolate and identify problems.

To pin down the specific causes of the problem through research, marketers must define the problem and its scope in a way that requires probing beneath the superficial symptoms. The interaction between the marketing manager and the marketing researcher should yield a clear definition of the problem. Depending on their abilities, the manager and the researcher can apply various methods to shape this definition. Traditionally, problem formulation has been viewed as a subjective, creative process. Today, however, more objective and systematic approaches are utilised. For example, the **Delphi method** for problem definition consists of a series of interviews with a panel of experts. With repeated interviews, the range of responses converges towards a "correct" definition of the problem.[10] This method introduces structure as well as objectivity into the process of problem definition. Researchers and decision-makers should remain in the problem definition stage until they have determined precisely what they want from the research and how they will use it.

The research objective specifies what information is needed to solve the problem. Deciding how to refine a broad, indefinite problem into a clearly defined and

Delphi method   A method for problem definition that consists of a series of interviews with a panel of experts

Figure 6.5   Defining and locating problems. BMRB promotes its ability to target the most appropriate consumer types and their locations for profitable marketing investment.   SOURCE: Courtesy of BMRB International.

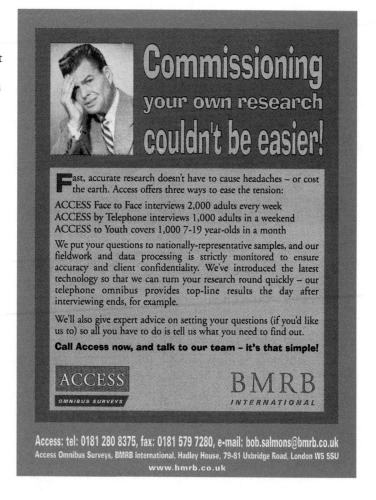

researchable statement is a prerequisite for the next step in planning the research: developing the type of hypothesis that best fits the problem.

Step 2: Developing Hypotheses

Hypothesis An informed guess or assumption about a certain problem or set of circumstances

The objective statement of a marketing research project should include hypotheses drawn from both previous research and expected research findings. A **hypothesis** is an informed guess or assumption about a certain problem or set of circumstances. It is based on all the insight and knowledge available about the problem from previous research studies and other sources. As information is gathered, a researcher can test the hypothesis. For example, a food manufacturer such as H. J. Heinz might propose the hypothesis that children today have more influence than those of previous generations on their families' buying decisions in regard to ketchup and other grocery products. A marketing researcher would then gather data, perhaps through surveys of children and their parents, and draw conclusions as to whether or not the hypothesis was correct. Sometimes several hypotheses are developed during the actual study; the hypotheses that are accepted or rejected become the study's chief conclusions.

Step 3: Collecting Data

Exploratory studies Deliberately flexible data gathering used to discover the general nature of a problem and the factors that relate to it

The kind of hypothesis being tested determines which approach will be used for gathering general data: exploratory, descriptive or causal. When marketers need more information about a problem or want to make a tentative hypothesis more specific, they may conduct **exploratory studies.** Exploratory studies discover the general nature of a problem and the factors that relate to it. The design is deliberately flexible.[11] For instance, they may review the information in the company's databank or examine publicly available data. Questioning knowledgeable people inside and outside the organisation may also yield new insights into the problem. An advantage of the exploratory approach is that it permits marketers to conduct mini-studies with a very restricted database. It also allows hypotheses to be developed further.

Descriptive studies Data collection that focuses on providing an accurate description of the variables in a situation

If marketers need to understand the characteristics of certain phenomena to solve a particular problem, **descriptive studies** can aid them. Descriptive studies focus on providing an accurate description of the variables in a situation. Such studies may range from general surveys of consumers' education, occupation or age to specifics on how many consumers purchased Ice Cream Mars last month or how many adults between the ages of 18 and 30 eat some form of high fibre cereal at least three times a week. Some descriptive studies require statistical analysis and predictive tools. For example, a researcher trying to find out how many people will vote for a certain political candidate may have to survey registered voters to predict the results. Descriptive studies generally demand much prior knowledge and assume that the problem is clearly defined. The marketers' major task is to choose adequate methods of collecting and measuring data.

Causal studies Data collection that assumes that a particular variable X causes a variable Y

Hypotheses about causal relationships call for a more complex approach than a descriptive study. In **causal studies,** it is assumed that a particular variable X causes a variable Y. Marketers must plan the research so that the data collected prove or disprove that X causes Y. To do so, marketers must try to hold constant all variables except X and Y. For example, to find out whether new carpeting, curtains and ceiling fans increase the leasing rate in a block of flats, marketers need to keep all variables constant except the new furnishings and the leasing rate. Table 6.2 compares the features of these types of research studies.

Marketing researchers have two types of data at their disposal. **Primary data** are observed and recorded or collected directly from respondents. This type of data must be gathered by observing phenomena or surveying respondents. **Secondary data** are compiled inside or outside the organisation for some purpose other than the current investigation. Secondary data include general reports supplied to an enterprise by various data services. Such reports might concern market share, retail inventory levels and consumer buying behaviour. Figure 6.6 illustrates how primary and secondary sources differ. Commonly, secondary data are already available in private or public reports or have been collected and stored by the organisation itself. Because secondary data are already available— "second hand"—to save time and money they should be examined prior to the collection of any primary data. Clearly, primary data collection is bespoke and therefore both time consuming and costly. For relatively straightforward problems, secondary data may prove adequate. More complex or risky situations may require specific primary data collection. Figure 6.7 illustrates Millward Brown International's data collection services. The next sections discuss the methods of gathering both secondary and primary data.

Secondary Data Collection

Marketers often begin the marketing research process by gathering secondary data. They may use available reports and other information from both internal and external sources to study a marketing problem.

Internal sources of secondary data can contribute tremendously to research. An organisation's marketing databank may contain information about past marketing activities, such as sales records and research reports, that can be used to test hypotheses and pinpoint problems. An organisation's accounting records are also an excellent source of data but, strangely enough, are often overlooked. The large volume of data that an accounting department collects does not automatically flow to the marketing area. As a result, detailed information about costs, sales, customer accounts or profits by product category may not be part of the MIS.

Primary data Information gathered by observing phenomena or surveying respondents

Secondary data Information compiled inside or outside the organisation for some purpose other than the current investigation

Table 6.2 Comparison of data gathering approaches

Project Component	Exploratory Studies	Descriptive or Causal Studies
Purpose	Provide general insights	Confirm insights Verify hypotheses
Data sources	Ill-defined	Well defined
Collection form	Open-ended	Structured
Sample	Small	Large
Collection procedure	Flexible	Rigid
Data analysis	Informal	Formal
Recommendations	Tentative	Conclusive

SOURCE: A. Parasuraman, *Marketing Research*, p. 122, © 1986. Reprinted by permission.

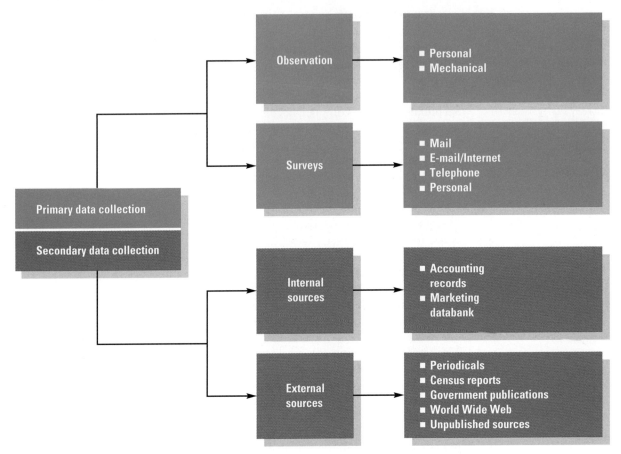

Figure 6.6 Approaches to collecting data

This situation occurs particularly in organisations that do not store marketing information on a systematic basis.

Secondary data can also be gleaned from periodicals, census reports, government publications, the world wide web and unpublished sources. Periodicals such as *Investors' Chronicle, Marketing, Campaign, Marketing Week, Wall Street Journal* and *Fortune* print general information that is helpful for defining problems and developing hypotheses. *Business Monitor* contains sales data for major industries. Mintel publishes sector reports. *The Marketing Pocket Books* are an excellent source of consumer, market, media and product information for national and international marketing. Table 6.3 summarises the major external sources of secondary data, excluding syndicated services.

Syndicated data services periodically collect general information, which they sell to clients. BARB, for example, supplies television stations and media buyers with estimates of the number of viewers at specific times. SAMI furnishes monthly information that describes market shares for specific types of manufacturers. Nielsen AGB provides data about products primarily sold through retailers. This information includes total sales in a product category, sales of clients' own brands and sales of important competing brands. In the US, the Market Research Corporation of America (MRCA) collects data through a national

Syndicated data services
Organisations that collect general information and sell it to clients

panel of consumers to provide information about purchases. The data on brands maintained by the MRCA are classified by age, race, sex, education, occupation and family size. Similar samples exist in most countries.

Another type of secondary data, which is available for a fee, is demographic analysis. Companies, such as CACI or Experian (formerly CCN), that specialise in demographic databanks have special knowledge and sophisticated computer systems to work with the very complex census databanks. These are explored further in Chapter 7. As a result, they are able to respond to specialised requests. Such information may be valuable in tracking demographic changes that have implications for consumer behaviour and the targeting of products.[12]

Primary Data Collection

The collection of primary data is a more lengthy and complex process than the collection of secondary data and is typically more costly, involving experimentation, sampling, survey methods, questionnaire construction and observation methods. The acquisition of primary data often requires an experimental approach to determine which variable or variables caused an event to occur.

Experimentation Data collection that involves maintaining certain variables constant so that the effects of the experimental variables can be measured

Experimentation Experimentation involves keeping certain variables constant so that the effects of the experimental variables can be measured. For instance, when Apple tests a change in its AppleWorks word processing computer program, all sales and marketing variables should be held constant except the change

Trade Journals	Virtually every industry or type of business has a trade journal. These journals give a feel for the industry—its size, degree of competition, range of companies involved and problems. To find trade journals in the field of interest, check *The Source Book*, a reference book that lists periodicals by subject.
Trade Associations	Almost every industry, product category and profession has its own association. Depending on the strength of each group, they often conduct research, publish journals, conduct training sessions and hold conferences. A telephone call or a letter to the association may yield information not available in published sources.
International Sources	Periodical indices, such as *Anbar*, are particularly useful for overseas product or company information. More general sources include the *United Nations Statistical Yearbook* and the *International Labour Organisation's Yearbook of Labour Statistics*.
Commercial Sources	Market survey/report organisations produce many sector reports and analyses of companies or brands, for example, *Verdict, Mintel, Kompass, The Times 1000, Key British Enterprises*.
Governments	Governments, through their various departments and agencies, collect, analyse and publish statistics on practically everything. Government documents also have their own set of indices. A useful index for government generated information in the UK is the government's weekly *British Business*.
Books in Print (BIP)	*BIP* is a several volume reference book found in most libraries. All books issued by publishers and currently in print are listed by subject, title and author.
Periodical Indices	Library reference sections contain indices on virtually every discipline. *ABI Inform (Pro-Quest)*, for example, indexes each article in all major periodicals.
Computerised Literature Retrieval Databases	Literature retrieval databases are periodical indices stored on computer disks. Books and dissertations are also included. Key words (such as the name of a subject) are used to search a database and generate references. Examples include *Textline, Harvest,* and *Pro-Quest*.
WWW pages	Many companies have established "home pages" on the Internet's World Wide Web for disseminating information on their products and activities.

Table 6.3   Guide to external sources of secondary data

Marketing experimentation   A set of rules and procedures by which data gathering is organised to expedite analysis and interpretation

Independent variable   A variable not influenced by or dependent on other variables in experiments

Dependent variable   A variable that is contingent on, or restricted to, one value or a set of values assumed by the independent variable

in the program. **Marketing experimentation** is a set of rules and procedures by which data gathering is organised to expedite analysis and interpretation.

In experimentation, an **independent variable** (a variable not influenced by or dependent on other variables) is manipulated and the resulting changes measured in a **dependent variable** (a variable contingent on, or restricted to, one value or a set of values assumed by the independent variable). Figure 6.8 illustrates the relationship between these variables. For example, when Houghton Mifflin Company introduces a new edition of its *American Heritage Dictionary,* it may want to estimate the number of dictionaries that could be sold at various levels of advertising expenditure and prices. The dependent variable would be sales, the independent variables would be advertising expenditures and price. Researchers

Figure 6.8 Relationship between independent and dependent variables

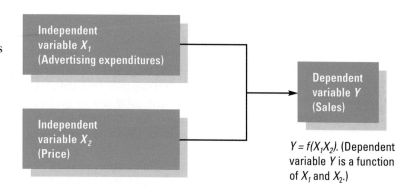

Independent variable X_1 (Advertising expenditures)

Independent variable X_2 (Price)

Dependent variable Y (Sales)

$Y = f(X_1 X_2)$. (Dependent variable Y is a function of X_1 and X_2.)

would design the experiment to control other independent variables that might influence sales, such as distribution and variations of the product.

In designing experiments, marketing researchers must ensure that their research techniques are both reliable and valid. A research technique has **reliability** if it produces almost identical results in successive repeated trials. But a reliable technique is not necessarily valid. To have **validity**, the method must measure what it is supposed to measure, not something else. A valid research method provides data that can be used to test the hypothesis being investigated. For example, experiments on cold fusion by scientists at various institutions have been held to lack both reliability and validity because the results were not repeated in successive trials and the scientists were not sure whether their experiments were measuring energy produced as a result of fusion or some other process.

In the United States, one marketing research company, Information Resources Inc., has brought a new dimension to experimental research by combining cable television, supermarket scanners and computers. The company has placed its BehaviorScan microcomputers on televisions in thousands of households in major cities. The company can thus track every advertisement its panelists watch and every purchase they make in a supermarket or chemist's. The information provided by Information Resources helps marketers assess the effectiveness of their advertising by determining whether a viewer saw a particular advertisement and whether the advertisement led the viewer to buy the product.[13] Case 6.1 discusses how the use of technology in marketing research assists with experimentation and marketing decision-making.

Experiments may be conducted in the laboratory or in the field; each research setting has advantages and disadvantages. In **laboratory settings,** participants or respondents are invited to a central location to react or respond to experimental stimuli. In such an isolated setting it is possible to control independent variables that might influence the outcome of an experiment. The features of laboratory settings might include a taste kitchen, video equipment, slide projectors, tape recorders, Internet hook-ups, one-way mirrors, central telephone banks and interview rooms. In an experiment to determine the influence of price (independent variable) on sales of a new canned soup (dependent variable), respondents would be invited to a laboratory—a room with table, chairs and sample soups—before the soup was available in stores. The soup would be placed on a table with competitors' soups. Analysts would then question respondents about their reactions to the soup at various prices.

One problem with a laboratory setting is its isolation from the real world. It is simply not possible to duplicate all the conditions that affect choices in the

Reliability The quality of producing almost identical results in successive repeated trials

Validity A condition that exists when an instrument measures what it is supposed to measure

Laboratory settings Central locations at which participants or respondents are invited to react or respond to experimental stimuli

marketplace. On the other hand, by controlling variables that cannot be controlled in the real world, laboratory experiments can focus on variables that marketers think may be significant for the success of a marketing strategy. Test market laboratories are being used more frequently today.[14]

The experimental approach can also be used in **field settings.** A field setting is a "real world" environment. A taste test of Stork SB margarine conducted in a supermarket is one example of an experiment in a field setting. Field settings give the marketer an opportunity to obtain a more direct test of marketing decisions than do laboratory settings.

There are, however, several limitations to field experiments. Field experiments can be influenced or biased by unexpected events, such as the weather or major economic news. Carry-over effects of field experiments are impossible to avoid. What respondents have been asked to do in one time period will influence what they do in the next. For example, evaluations of competing advertisements may influence attempts to obtain objective evaluations of a company's proposed advertising. The fact that they have viewed previous advertising influences respondents' evaluation of future advertising. There is often an unfortunate experimental "effect". In **home placements** (when a product is used in the home in a real setting) or **diary tests** (when households log their weekly purchases and consumption patterns), people become too involved with the product—artificially so. They might sniff items they would not normally sniff, or ask for their children's opinions about a food item when normally they would just give their children the meal and expect them to eat it.[15] Respondents may not co-operate properly because they do not understand their role in the experiment. Finally, only a small number of variables can be controlled in field experiments. It is impossible, for example, to control competitors' advertising or their attempts to influence the outcome of the experiment. Tactics that competitors can use to thwart field efforts include couponing, reducing prices temporarily and increasing advertising frequency.

Experimentation is used in marketing research to improve hypothesis testing. However, whether experiments are conducted in the laboratory or in the field, many assumptions must be made to limit the number of factors and isolate causes. Marketing decision-makers must recognise that assumptions may diminish the reliability of the research findings. For example, viewing proposed advertisements on a video cassette recorder in a laboratory is different from watching the advertisements on television at home.

The gathering of primary data through experimentation may involve the use of sampling, survey methods, observation or some combination of these techniques.

Sampling   By systematically choosing a limited number of units, or **sample,** to represent the characteristics of a total population, marketers can project the reactions of a total market or market segment. The objective of **sampling** in marketing research, therefore, is to select representative units from a total population. Sampling procedures are used in studying the likelihood of events based on assumptions about the future.

Since the time and the resources available for research are limited, it would be almost impossible to investigate all the members of a population. A **population,** or "universe", comprises all elements, units or individuals that are of interest to researchers for a specific study. For example, if a Gallup poll is designed to predict the results of an election, all the registered voters in the country would constitute the population. A representative national sample of several thousand

---

Field settings   "Real world" environments in which experiments take place

Home placements   Experiments in which a product is used in a home setting

Diary tests   Experiments in which households log their weekly purchases and consumption patterns

Sample   A limited number of units chosen to represent the characteristics of a total population

Sampling   The selection of representative units from a total population

Population   All elements, units or individuals that are of interest to researchers for a specific study

registered voters would be selected in the Gallup poll to project the probable voting outcome. The projection would be based on the assumption that no major political events would occur before the election. Sampling techniques allow marketers to predict buying behaviour fairly accurately on the basis of the responses from a representative portion of the population of interest. Sampling methods include random sampling, stratified sampling, area sampling and quota sampling.

When marketers employ **random sampling,** all the units in a population have an equal chance of appearing in the sample. Random sampling is basic probability sampling. The various events that can occur have an equal or known chance of taking place. For example, a specific playing card in a pack has a 1/52 probability of being drawn at any one time. Similarly, if every student at a university or college has a unique identification number and these numbers are mixed up in a large basket, each student's number would have a known probability of being selected. Sample units are ordinarily chosen by selecting from a table of random numbers statistically generated so that each digit from zero to nine will have an equal probability of occurring in each position in the sequence. The sequentially numbered elements of a population are sampled randomly by selecting the units whose numbers appear in the table of random numbers.

In **stratified sampling,** the population of interest is divided into groups according to a common characteristic or attribute, and a probability sampling is then conducted within each group. Employing a stratified sample may reduce some of the error that could occur as a result of using a simple random sample. By ensuring that each major group or segment of the population receives its proportionate share of sample units, investigators avoid including too many or too few sample units from each stratum. Usually, samples are stratified when researchers believe that there may be variations among different types of respondents. For example, many political opinion surveys are stratified by sex, race and age.

Area sampling involves two stages: (1) selecting a probability sample of geographic areas, such as streets, census tracts or census enumeration districts, and (2) selecting units or individuals within the selected geographic areas for the sample. This approach is a variation of stratified sampling, with the geographic areas serving as the segments, or primary units, used in sampling. To select the units or individuals within the geographic areas, researchers may choose every nth house or unit, or they may adopt random selection procedures to pick out a given number of units or individuals from a total listing within the selected geographic areas. Area sampling may be used when a complete list of the population is not available.

Quota sampling differs from other forms of sampling in that it is judgemental; that is, the final choice of respondents is left to the interviewers. A study of consumers who wear glasses, for example, may be conducted by interviewing any person who wears glasses. In quota sampling, there are some controls—usually limited to two or three variables such as age, sex and education—over the selection of respondents. The controls attempt to ensure that representative categories of respondents are interviewed. In the marketing research industry, quota sampling is by far the most commonly employed form of sampling.

Quota samples are unique because they are not probability samples; not everyone has an equal chance of being selected. Therefore, sampling error cannot be measured statistically. Quota samples are used most often in exploratory studies, in which hypotheses are being developed. Often a small quota sample will not be projected to the total population, although the findings may provide valuable insights into a problem. Quota samples are useful when people with some unusual characteristics are found and questioned about the topic of interest. They are also useful

Random sampling A sampling method in which all the units in a population have an equal chance of appearing in the sample

Stratified sampling A sampling method in which the population of interest is divided according to a common characteristic or attribute and a probability sampling is then conducted within each group

Area sampling A sampling method that involves selecting a probability sample of geographic areas and selecting units or individuals within the selected areas for the sample

Quota sampling A sampling method in which the final choice of respondents is left to the interviewers, who base their choices on two or three variables (such as age, sex and education)

in focusing on a specific core target market segment. A probability sample used to study people allergic to cats would be highly inefficient. Readers who have been stopped in the street by a researcher with a clipboard and a few questions may well have been subject to quota sampling because they fitted, for example, an age or apparent social class "stereotype" deemed appropriate for the specific study.

Survey methods Interviews by mail or telephone and personal interviews

Survey Methods Survey methods include interviews by mail, e-mail, or telephone and personal interviews. Selection of a survey method depends on the nature of the problem, the data needed to test the hypothesis and the resources, such as funding and personnel, that are available to the researcher. Table 6.4

	Mail Surveys	Telephone Surveys	Personal Interview Surveys
Economy	Potentially the lowest cost per interview if there is an adequate return rate; increased postage rates are raising costs	Avoids interviewers' travel expenses; less expensive than in-home interviews; most common survey method	In-home interviewing is the most expensive interviewing method; shopping mall and focus group interviewing may lower costs
Flexibility	Inflexible; questionnaire must be short, easy for respondents to complete; no probing questions; may take more time to implement than other survey methods	Flexible because interviewers can ask some probing questions, encourage respondents to answer questions; rapport may be gained, but observations are impossible	Most flexible method; respondents can react to visual materials, help fill out questionnaire; because observation is possible, demographic data are more accurate; in-depth probes are possible
Interviewer Bias	Interviewer bias eliminated; questionnaires can be returned anonymously (although often they are coded)	Some anonymity; may be hard to develop trust among respondents	Refusal may be decreased by interviewers' rapport-building efforts; interviewers' personal attributes may bias respondents
Sampling and Respondents' Co-operation	Obtaining a complete mailing list is difficult; non-response is a major disadvantage—33 per cent response rates are common in consumer surveys; 1–2 per cent rates in business-to-business surveys	Sample must be limited to respondents with telephones and listed numbers; engaged signals, no answers and non-response—including refusals—are problems; samples must cope with out-at-work non-responses	Not-at-homes are more difficult to deal with; focus groups, shopping mall interviewing may overcome these problems

SOURCE: Adapted from Milton M. Pressley, "Try these tips to get 50% to 70% response rate from mail surveys of commercial populations", *Marketing News*, 21 January 1983, p. 16. Reprinted by permission of the American Marketing Association.

Table 6.4 Comparison of the three basic survey methods

Part II   Understanding and Targeting Markets

summarises and compares the advantages of the various methods. Researchers must know exactly what type of information is needed to test the hypothesis and what type of information can be obtained through interviewing. Table 6.5 summarises marketing research issues and techniques in the UK, and Table 6.6 gives a break down of the total European marketing research markets.

Gathering information through surveys is becoming more difficult because respondent rates are declining. There is also an indication that people with higher incomes and education are the most likely to respond. Problems include difficulty in recruiting qualified interviewers and respondents' reluctance to take part in surveys because of over-long questionnaires, dull topics and time pressures.[16] Moreover, fear of crime makes respondents unwilling to trust interviewers. The use of "sugging"—sales techniques disguised as market surveys—has also contributed to decreased respondent co-operation: respondents wrongly suspect that the marketing researcher will switch over to a "hard sell" for a specific brand.

a. Expenditure on Market Research

AMSO Members' Source of Income by Clients' Business, 1996

	£m	%		£m	%
Food/soft drinks	61.3	+12	Household products	16.4	−2
Media	39.6	+9	Alcoholic drinks	16.2	−2
Public services and utilities	35.0	+9	Travel and tourism	14.2	+1
Financial services	31.5	+10	Advertising agencies	10.1	+4
Pharmaceuticals	30.3	+9	Oil	5.8	+50
Health and beauty	29.4	+12	H'hold durables/hardware	5.1	−3
Vehicles	27.5	+6	Tobacco	2.7	−2
Business and industrial	25.9	+17	Other direct clients	41.3	+7
Retailers	25.9	+40	Other AMSO cos. (mainly	7.4	
Govt., public bodies	20.8	+13	subcontracted fieldwork)		

Nature of AMSO Members' Fieldwork (Percentage of total), 1996

Personal interview	43.1	Group discussion	9.9
Telephone interview	18.3	Self-completion/postal	8.0
Hall test	11.1	Depth interviews	4.0
Continuous Research		Street interviews	2.6
Audits and panels	70	Mystery shopping	2.2
Advertising/Brand			
Tracking	48		
Customer Satisfaction	36		
Media	22		
Others	11		

Note: The AMSO accounts for more than two-thirds of all marketing research conducted in the UK.

SOURCES: From *Marketing Pocket Book 1999.* Reprinted by permission of NTC Publications, Ltd.

(Continues)

Table 6.5   The nature of the UK marketing research industry

b. AMSO's "League Table"

Overall Ranking by Turnover	1996 turnover £000s	Change % 1995–1996	Domestic ranking	International ranking
1. Taylor Nelson AGB Plc	68,441	+8.2	1	3
2. NOP Research Group Ltd	54,838	+10.4	2	4
3. Research International Ltd	50,264	+17.0	4	1
4. Millward Brown International Plc	44,700	+10.1	3	2
5. BMRB International Ltd	25,277	+18.5	5	13
6. RSL—Research Services Ltd	24,762	+16.4	6	5
7. MORI (Market & Opinion Research Int'l)	16,511	+16.0	7	19
8. The Research Business Group	13,769	−8.3	10	6
9. The MBL Group Plc	13,286	+16.1	9	9
10. IRI Infoscan Ltd*	11,066	+16.6	8	—
11. Martin Hamblin Group	10,602	+32.1	13	8
12. Harris Research Centre	10,510	+6.2	12	10
13. Simon Godfrey Associates (SGA)	7,017	+26.5	25	11
14. Gordon Simmons Research Group	6,905	+7.4	14	17
15. Infratest Burke Group Ltd	6,417	+1.6	17	15
16. PAS (Public Attitude Surveys Ltd)	6,088	+0.8	11	—
17. ISIS Research Group*	5,934	+32.5	37	7
18. BEM Ltd	5,396	+7.5	15	29
19. Pegram Walters Group	5,310	+1.0	20	16
20. FDS International Ltd	4,961	−14.8	16	27
21 = The Added Value Company	4,853	+15.2	28	14
21 = The Gallup Organisation Ltd	4,853	+9.7	19	21
23. Business & Market Research Ltd	4,474	+19.6	18	26
24. Hall & Partners*	4,321	+20.6	24	18
25. Marketing Sciences Ltd	3,825	+30.1	23	22
26. Audits and Surveys Europe	3,754	+26.1	38	12
27. Market Research Solutions Ltd	3,101	+4.2	26	28
28. Research & Auditing Services/INRA UK	3,077	+7.6	21	32
29. Continental Research	3,068	no change	31	23
30. Hauck Research Services Ltd*	3,015	+20.8	30	25
31. ESA Market Research Ltd	3,009	+37.0	22	33
32. Surveyplan (Market Research)	2,617	+18.9	27	—
33. Numbers	2,307	+8.5	29	—
34. GfK Great Britain Ltd	2,143	+2.6	35	20
35. DVL Smith Ltd*	1,753	+5.2	33	30
36. IRB International Ltd	1,636	−7.2	32	31
37. Scantel Ltd	1,594	+13.4	36	24
38. Marketing Direction Ltd	953	+12.1	34	—
Total Turnover of AMSO Members	446,407	+11.6		

*New members of AMSO. All turnover changes from 1995 include the previous year's data for these five companies to ensure compatibility.

SOURCES: From *Marketing Pocket Book 1999*. Reprinted by permission of NTC Publications, Ltd.

Table 6.5 The nature of the UK marketing research industry *(cont.)*

Table 6.6 European marketing research markets—aggregation of individual total market sizes, 1997

	Turnover (mill. EURO)	%
United Kingdom	1,192	25
Germany	1,035	22
France	749	16
Italy	340	7
Spain	237	5
Netherlands	196	4
Sweden	182	4
Switzerland	113	2
Belgium	94	2
Austria	79	2
Turkey	70	2
Norway	58	1
Denmark	55	1
Finland	48	1
Russia	44	1
Portugal	40	1
Poland	40	1
Greece	37	1
Ireland	28	1
Czech Republic	20	—
Hungary[1]	15	—
Croatia	5	—
Slovenia	4	—
FR Yugoslavia[1]	3	—
Bulgaria	2	—
Luxembourg	2	—
Total Europe	4,688	100

[1]No up-dated data provided; 1996 market size figure retained.

SOURCE: Copyright © ESOMAR® 2000. Permission for using this material has been granted by ESOMAR®, Amsterdam, The Netherlands (www. esomar.ni).

Mail surveys Questionnaires sent by mail or e-mail to respondents, who are encouraged to complete and return them

In **mail surveys,** questionnaires are sent by mail or e-mail to respondents, who are encouraged to complete and return them. Mail surveys are used most often when the individuals chosen for questioning are spread over a wide area and funds for the survey are limited. A mail survey is the least expensive survey method as long as the response rate is high enough to produce reliable results. The main disadvantages of mail surveys are the possibility of a low response rate or of misleading results, if respondents are significantly different from the population being sampled.

Researchers can boost response rates in mail surveys by offering respondents some incentive to return the questionnaire. Incentives and follow-ups have consistently been found to increase response rates. On the other hand, promises of anonymity, special appeals for co-operation and questionnaire length have no apparent impact on the response rate. Other techniques for increasing the response rate, such as advance notification, personalisation of survey materials, type of postage, corporate or university sponsorship, or foot-in-the-door techniques, have had mixed results, varying according to the population surveyed.[17] Although such techniques may help increase the response rates, they can introduce sample composition bias, or non-response bias, which results when those responding to a survey differ in some important respect from those not responding to the survey. In other words, response-enhancing techniques may alienate some people in the sample and appeal to others, making the results non-representative of the population of interest. Businesses devote relatively little funding to mail surveys.

Premiums or incentives encouraging respondents to return questionnaires have been effective in developing panels of respondents who are regularly interviewed by mail. **Mail panels** of consumers selected to represent a market or market segment are especially useful for evaluating new products, providing general information about consumers and providing records of consumers' purchases. Many companies use consumer mail panels; others use **consumer purchase diaries.** These surveys are similar to mail panels, but consumers keep track of purchases only. Consumer mail panels and consumer purchase diaries are much more widely used than mail surveys, but they do have shortcomings. Research indicates that the people who take the time to fill out a consumer purchase diary have a higher income and are better educated than the general population. If researchers include less well educated consumers in the panel, they must risk poorer response rates.[18]

In **telephone surveys,** respondents' answers to a questionnaire are recorded by interviewers on the phone. A telephone survey has some advantages over a mail survey. The rate of response is higher because it takes less effort to answer the telephone and talk than to fill out a questionnaire and return it. If there are enough interviewers, telephone surveys can be conducted very quickly. Thus they can be used by political candidates or organisations seeking an immediate reaction to an event. In addition, this survey technique permits interviewers to gain a rapport with respondents and ask some probing questions. According to a survey by the Council of American Survey Research Organizations (CASRO), telephone interviewing is the preferred survey method in more than 40 per cent of the projects conducted by commercial survey research firms.[19] Nearly all businesses engaged in marketing research at some time employ telephone interviewing.

Telephone interviews do have drawbacks. They are limited to oral communication; visual aids or observation cannot be included. Interpreters of results must make adjustments for subjects who are not at home or who do not have telephones. Surveys that specify quotas of respondents hit problems of non-response: secretaries "gatekeep" calls at businesses, thereby preventing researchers from talking to their targets; adult members of households who work outside the home are difficult to contact—and calls in the evening will not be welcome as people want to relax after work.

Telephone surveys, like mail and personal interview surveys, are sometimes used to develop panels of respondents who can be interviewed repeatedly to measure changes in attitudes or behaviour. Reliance on such panels is increasing.

Computer assisted telephone interviewing integrates questionnaire, data collection and tabulations, and provides data to aid decision-makers in the shortest time possible. In computer assisted telephone interviewing, the paper questionnaire is replaced by a computer monitor or video screen. Responses are entered on a terminal keyboard, or the interviewer can use a light pen (a pen shaped torch) to record a response on a light sensitive screen. On the most advanced devices, the interviewer merely points to the appropriate response on a touch sensitive screen with his or her finger. Open-ended responses can be typed on the keyboard or recorded with paper and pencil.

Mail panels Groups of consumers selected to represent a market or market segment who agree to be regularly interviewed by mail

Consumer purchase diaries A marketing research tool in which consumers record their purchases

Telephone surveys Surveys in which respondents' answers to a questionnaire are recorded by interviewers on the phone

Computer assisted telephone interviewing A survey method that integrates questionnaire, data collection and tabulations, and provides data to aid decisions-makers in the shortest time possible

Computer assisted telephone interviewing saves time and facilitates monitoring the progress of interviews. Entry functions are largely eliminated; the computer determines which question to display on the screen, skipping irrelevant questions. Because data are available as soon as they are entered into the system, cumbersome hand computations are avoided and interim results can be quickly retrieved. With some systems, a lap-top computer may be taken to off-site locations for use in data analysis. Some researchers say that computer assisted telephone interviewing—including hardware, software and operation costs—is less expensive than conventional paper and pencil methods.[20]

Personal interview survey Face-to-face situation in which the researcher meets the consumer and questions him or her about a specific topic

Marketing researchers have traditionally favoured the **personal interview survey,** chiefly because of its flexibility. A personal interview is a face-to-face situation in which the researcher meets the consumer and questions him or her about a specific topic.[21] Various audio-visual aids—pictures, products, diagrams or prerecorded advertising copy—can be incorporated into a personal interview. Rapport gained through direct interaction usually permits more in-depth interviewing, including probes, follow-up questions or psychological tests. In addition, because personal interviews can be longer, they can yield more information. Finally, respondents can be selected more carefully, and reasons for non-response can be explored. A **depth interview** is a lengthy, one-to-one structured interview examining a consumer's views about a product in detail.

Depth interview A lengthy, one-to-one structured interview, examining in detail a consumer's views about a product

The nature of personal interviews has changed. In the past, most personal interviews, which were based on random sampling or pre-arranged appointments, were conducted in the respondent's home. Today, most personal interviews are conducted in shopping centres or malls or on pavements. **Shopping mall/pavement intercept interviews** involve interviewing a percentage of people who pass by certain "intercept" points in a shopping centre or pavement. Shopping mall/pavement intercept interviewing is a popular survey technique, after telephone surveys and focus group interviewing.

Shopping mall/pavement intercept interviews Personal interviewing of a percentage of individuals who pass by certain "intercept" points in a shopping centre or pavement

Like any face-to-face interviewing method, shopping mall/pavement intercept interviewing has many advantages. The interviewer is in a position to recognise and react to respondents' non-verbal indications of confusion. Respondents can be shown product prototypes, video tapes of advertisements and the like, and reactions can be sought. The environment lets the researcher deal with complex situations. For example, in taste tests, researchers know that all the respondents are reacting to the same product, which can be prepared and monitored from the mall test kitchen or some other facility. In addition, lower cost, greater control and the ability to conduct tests requiring bulky equipment make shopping mall/pavement intercept interviews popular.

Research indicates that given a comparable sample of respondents, shopping mall/pavement intercept interviewing is a suitable substitute for telephone interviewing.[22] In addition, there seem to be no significant differences in the completeness of consumer responses between telephone interviewing and shopping mall/pavement intercept interviewing. In fact, for questions dealing with socially desirable behaviour, shopping mall/pavement intercept respondents appear to be more honest about their past behaviour.[23]

On-site computer interviewing A survey method that requires respondents to complete a self-administered questionnaire displayed on a computer monitor

In **on-site computer interviewing,** a variation of the shopping mall/pavement intercept interview, respondents complete a self-administered questionnaire displayed on a computer monitor. For example, MAX (Machine Answered eXamination), a microcomputer based software package developed by POPULUS, conducts such interviews in shopping malls. After a brief lesson on how to operate MAX, respondents can proceed through the survey at their own pace. According to its developers, MAX provides not only faster and more accurate information but also

Figure 6.9 Primary data collection. Viewing facilities are often used for experiments or for conducting focus group interviews. SOURCE: Courtesy of West Midland Viewing Facility.

Focus group interview A survey method that aims to observe group interaction when members are exposed to an idea or concept

Quali-depth interviews 25 to 30 minute intercept interviews that incorporate some of the in-depth advantages of focus group interviews with the speed and flexibility of shopping mall/pavement intercept interviews

consistency, for each respondent is asked questions in the same way. MAX is flexible because it can ask different sets of relevant questions depending on the respondents' previous answers. In addition, respondents' answers are entered directly into a computer and do not need to be coded and keyed in before being analysed; nor is there any chance of information being incorrectly encoded. Its developers assert that "MAX is the interviewer we would all like to be. MAX is patient, nonjudgmental, remembering all that he is taught, and he keeps track of every answer."[24]

The object of a **focus group interview** is to observe group interaction when members are exposed to an idea or concept. Focus groups frequently are held in viewing facilities as illustrated in Figure 6.9. Often these interviews are conducted informally, without a structured questionnaire. Consumer attitudes, behaviour, lifestyles, needs and desires can be explored in a flexible and creative manner through focus group interviews. Most companies use focus group interviewing. Questions are open-ended and stimulate consumers to answer in their own words. Researchers can ask probing questions to clarify something they do not fully understand or something unexpected and interesting that may help to explain consumer behaviour. When Cadbury's used information obtained from focus groups to change its advertising and test product concepts, the new advertisements and product launches pushed up sales.[25] Case 6.2 describes the future of this marketing research technique. Focus group interviews commence with a general discussion, typically among eight consumers of the same sex, led by a moderator. This marketing researcher narrows the conversation during the session, homing in on a specific brand, product or advertisement—hence the term "focus" group.

Quali-depth interviews are 25 to 30 minute intercept interviews that incorporate some of the in-depth advantages of focus group interviews with the speed and flexibility of shopping mall/pavement intercept interviews. Typically, intercepted consumers are taken to a nearby hall or café and asked more probing and searching questions than is possible in a 3 to 4 minute shopping mall/pavement intercept interview. They can also be shown a greater variety of stimulus material. This is a useful approach for sensitive issues that people might not wish to discuss in a group—gambling and drugs, for example.

Another research technique is the **in-home** (door-to-door) **interview.** Because it may be desirable to eliminate group influence, the in-home interview offers a clear advantage when thoroughness of self-disclosure is important. In an in-depth interview of 45 to 90 minutes, respondents can be probed to reveal their real motivations, feelings, behaviours and aspirations. In-depth interviews permit the discovery of emotional "hot buttons" that provide psychological insights.[26]

In-home interview   45 to 90 minute interview in which the researcher visits the respondent in his or her home

Questionnaire Construction   A carefully constructed questionnaire is essential to the success of any survey. A **questionnaire** is a base document for research purposes that provides the questions and the structure for an interview or self-completion and has provision for respondents' answers.[27] Questions must be designed to elicit information that meets the study's data requirements. These questions must be clear, easy to understand and directed towards a specific objective. Researchers need to define the objective before trying to develop a questionnaire because the objective determines the substance of the questions and the amount of detail. A common mistake in constructing questionnaires is to ask questions that interest the researchers but do not yield information useful in deciding whether to accept or reject a hypothesis. Finally, the most important rule in composing questions is to maintain impartiality.

Questionnaire   Base document for research purposes, providing the questions and structure for an interview or self-completion and providing space for respondents' answers

The questions are usually of four kinds: (1) open-ended, (2) dichotomous, (3) multiple choice, and (4) Likert scale.

1. OPEN-ENDED QUESTION
   What is your general opinion of the American Express Optima Card?
   _____
   _____
   _____

2. DICHOTOMOUS QUESTION
   Do you presently have a retailer loyalty card?
   Yes _____ Card? _____
   No _____

3. MULTIPLE CHOICE QUESTION
   What age group are you in?
   Under 20   _____
   20–29   _____
   30–39   _____
   40–49   _____
   50–59   _____
   60 and over _____

4. LIKERT SCALE QUESTION
   To what extent do you expect up-coming government legislation to help your exports?
   Not at   A great
   all |__|__|__|__|__| deal
            1   2   3   4   5

The design of questionnaires is extremely important because it will affect the validity and usefulness of the results. It is therefore useful to test questionnaires on a few respondents before conducting the full survey. The questions must relate to the research objectives. The layout of the questionnaire must not be off-putting to respondents or to the researchers conducting the work. These days, carefully laid out questionnaires can be read (scanned) and analysed by computers. Open-ended questions can be the most revealing, but are time consuming—and therefore off-putting—for respondents, as well as difficult to analyse across respondents. Dichotomous questions are straightforward but not very revealing; and often the answer is not a full yes or no. Multiple choice questions are popular, but care must be exercised in the choice of categories. Likert scale questions are very popular and can enable batches or strings of questions to be listed together in a space-saving style which can be time-saving for the respondent. They have the added benefits of permitting respondents to express degrees of a positive or negative response—rather than give an absolute yes or no—or the option of a "neutral" ("3") answer. Most questionnaires include a mix of question styles.

It is good practice when developing a questionnaire to ensure that throughout, from page to page, the "negative" response option (i.e. "no" or "not at all"—1) always appears on the same side (e.g. the left), while the "positive" response option (i.e. "yes" or "a great deal"—5) should always appear on the other side (e.g. the right). If these are mixed, the respondent may not notice, thus rendering responses unreliable. Researchers must be very careful in wording questions that a respondent might consider too personal or that might require him or her to admit to activities that other people are likely to condemn. Questions of this type (e.g. income or educational attainment questions) should be worded in such a way as to make them less offensive, and are often placed towards the end of the questionnaire.

For testing special markets, where individuals (for instance, executives, scientists and engineers) are likely to own or have access to a personal computer, questionnaires may be programmed on a computer disk and the disk delivered through the mail. This technique may cost less than a telephone interview and eliminate bias by simplifying flow patterns in answering questions. Respondents see less clutter on the screen than on a printed questionnaire; the novelty of the approach may also spark their interest and compel their attention. The Internet is now being used for this purpose.[28]

Observation Methods When using **observation methods**, researchers record respondents' overt behaviour, taking note of physical conditions and events. Direct contact with respondents is avoided; instead, their actions are examined and noted systematically. For example, researchers might use observation methods to answer the question, "How long does the average McDonald's restaurant customer have to wait in line before being served?"

Observation may also be combined with interviews. For example, during personal interviews, the condition of a respondent's home or other possessions may be observed and recorded, and demographic information such as ethnic origin, approximate age and sex can be confirmed by direct observation. Observation is not confined to consumers; shops and service establishments can be observed, too, through "mystery shopper" research—as detailed in Marketing Insight 6.2.

Data gathered through observation can sometimes be biased if the respondent is aware of the observation process. An observer can be placed in a natural market environment, such as a grocery store, without biasing or influencing shoppers' actions. However, if the presence of a human observer is likely to bias the outcome or if human sensory abilities are inadequate, mechanical means may be used to record behaviour. **Mechanical observation devices** include cameras, recorders, counting machines and other equipment that records physiological changes in individuals. For instance, a special camera can be used to record the

"Mystery Shopper" Research Programmes: Pros and Cons

Retailers and providers of services depend increasingly not only on the products they sell or deliver but also on the ability, attitude and quality of their personnel and the internal environment of their branch outlets. The regional directors and head office managers who check such standards all too often enter through the staff door at the rear of the branch, focusing primarily on operations and not on customer concerns. The branch's customers enter from the front, having first seen the exterior of the branch. They deal with all levels of personnel, not just the manager or manageress to whom the visiting director talks. These customers are not wrapped up in the company's products and operations; they seek help and advice. They expect courtesy and professionalism.

Customers buy a company's products; quite often the company's management never does, instead requesting items direct from storage at staff discount rates without ever visiting shops or showrooms. Car manufacturers give their senior management vehicles and offer all employees highly attractive deals. The result is that few senior managers ever visit a showroom or dealer—even their servicing is taken care of—so they never see the "sharp end", their dealers, as customers do.

Rover Cars instigated a programme of "mystery shopper" surveys. This programme involved visits by bogus potential car buyers to dealers to rate the up-keep and appearance of showrooms, technical knowledge and attitude of personnel, quality of displays, negotiating criteria and adherence to company policies. Dealers did not know who the bogus buyers were, nor when they were to visit. Service reception staff were similarly targeted. A favourite ploy by the researchers was to book a car service by telephone and then phone again to cancel, judging the receptionist's response to the lost business. As a result of these frequent, always anonymous, visits, Rover was able to improve the standards of its dealers, the attitude of its personnel and ultimately the quality of its service and customer satisfaction.

This form of marketing research, "mystery shopper", is one of the fastest growing areas in the industry. The largest company in the UK, BEM, has 3,000 mystery shoppers on its books, many working part time; and its annual sales exceed £5 million; £3.5 million from mystery

shopper surveys. BEM's employees are trained to evaluate how customers are greeted, how the store looks and whether shop assistants understand the products on sale. They are expected to blend in inconspicuously while assessing branches; they are not loud customers visibly asking awkward questions. For many businesses, mystery shopper researchers are evaluating standards and service quality and supplying management with measures of performance and benchmarks against which improvements can be made.

The European Society for Opinion and Marketing Research—ESOMAR—is attempting to clamp down on the use of mystery shopper research, arguing that it is laudable for organisations to wish to improve the appearance of their facilities and the capabilities of their personnel, but not by tricking employees into handling awkward customers in an off-hand or aggressive manner. ESOMAR is concerned that the staff member does not have the up-front opportunity to withdraw from the interview—something respondents can do in other forms of research surveys—and that the process of dealing with the mystery shopper takes up valuable staff time which may place pressure on the member of staff when dealing with the next customer. Another concern is that in most forms of ethical marketing research, the respondent is guaranteed anonymity, but if mystery shopper research is deployed to check up on staff or to develop "league tables" of branch performance, it is difficult for the research findings not to identify the personnel in question. ESOMAR's recommendations are that mystery shopper research must not waste informants' time and should permit anonymity, or that staff should be told beforehand of the impending research and the ultimate uses for the findings. A study intended to form a supervisory procedure for checking individuals' performance is not permitted under ESOMAR's code: the purpose of any mystery shopper research should be solely to boost consumer demand.

SOURCES: *Marketing Guides: Market Research*, 13 June 1996; Customer Concern and BEM promotional literature; Rover Cars; Peter Jackson, Adsearch, 1999; ESOMAR, Amsterdam, 1998.

eye movements of respondents looking at an advertisement and to detect the sequence of reading and the parts of the advertisement that receive greatest attention. Electronic scanners in supermarkets are mechanical observation devices that offer an exciting opportunity for marketing research. Scanner technology can provide accurate data on sales and consumers' purchase patterns, and marketing researchers may buy such data from the supermarket (see Case 6.1).

Observation is straightforward and avoids a central problem of survey methods: motivating respondents to state their true feelings or opinions. However, observation tends to be descriptive. When it is the only method of data collection, it may not provide insights into causal relationships. Another drawback is that analyses based on observation are subject to the biases of the observer or the limitations of the mechanical device.

Step 4: Analysing and Interpreting Research Findings

After collecting data to test their hypotheses, marketers analyse and interpret the research findings. Interpretation is easier if marketers carefully plan their data analysis methods early in the research process. They should also allow for continual evaluation of the data during the entire collection period. They can then gain valuable insight into areas that ought to be probed during the formal interpretation. It is important to give consideration to data analysis techniques prior to the collection of data. Many students discover after a survey has been completed, for example, how different wording or ordering of questions, as well as of categories, could have reduced the complexity of the analysis. It also helps when interpreting findings to keep in mind the target audience for the results—the report or presentation—so that the level of analysis and interpretation of the findings can be geared to their understanding.

The first step in drawing conclusions from most research is displaying the data in table format. If marketers intend to apply the results to individual categories of the things or people being studied, cross-tabulation may be quite useful, especially in tabulating joint occurrences. For example, a cross-tabulation of data using the two variables gender and purchase rates of car tyres would show differences in how men and women purchase car tyres. Various statistical procedures exist that facilitate simultaneous analysis and examine the interactions of many variables.[29]

Statistical interpretation An analysis of data that focuses on what is typical or what deviates from the average

After the data are tabulated, they must be analysed. **Statistical interpretation** focuses on what is typical or what deviates from the average. It indicates how widely responses vary and how they are distributed in relation to the variable being measured. This interpretation is another facet of marketing research that relies on marketers' judgement or intuition. Moreover, when they interpret statistics, marketers must take into account estimates of expected error or deviation from the true values of the population. The analysis of data may lead researchers to accept or reject the hypothesis being studied.[30]

Data require careful interpretation by the marketer. If the results of a study are valid, the decision-maker should take action; however, if it is discovered that a question has been incorrectly worded, the results should be ignored. For example, if a study by an electricity company reveals that 50 per cent of its customers believe that meter-readers are "friendly", is that finding good, bad or indifferent? Two important benchmarks help interpret the result: how the 50 per cent figure compares with that for competitors and how it compares with a previous time period. The point is that managers must understand the research results and relate the results to a context that permits effective decision-making.[31]

Step 5: Reporting Research Findings

The final step in the marketing research process is reporting the research findings. Before preparing the report, the marketer must take a clear, objective look at the findings to see how well the gathered facts answer the research question or support or negate the hypotheses posed in the beginning. In most cases, it is extremely doubtful that the study can provide everything needed to answer the research question. Thus in the report the researcher must point out the deficiencies and the reasons for them, perhaps suggesting areas that require further investigation.

The report presenting the results is usually a formal, written one. Researchers must allow time for the writing task when they plan and schedule the project. Since the report is a means of communicating with the decision-makers who will use the research findings, researchers need to determine beforehand how much detail and supporting data to include. They should keep in mind that corporate executives prefer reports that are short, clear and simply expressed. Often researchers will give their summary and recommendations first, especially if decision-makers do not have time to study how the results were obtained. Such summary findings tend to be presented via an audio-visual presentation. A technical report allows its users to analyse data and interpret recommendations because it describes the research methods and procedures and the most important data gathered. Thus researchers must recognise the needs and expectations of the report user and adapt to them.

When marketing decision-makers have a firm grasp of research methods and procedures, they are better able to integrate reported findings and personal experience. If marketers can spot limitations in research from reading the report, their personal experience assumes additional importance in the decision-making process. Marketers who cannot understand basic statistical assumptions and data gathering procedures may misuse research findings. Consequently, report writers should be aware of the backgrounds and research abilities of those who will rely on the report in making decisions. Clear explanations presented in plain language make it easier for decision-makers to apply the findings and less likely that a report will be misused or ignored. Talking to potential research users before writing a report can help researchers supply information that will indeed improve decision-making.

The Importance of Ethical Marketing Research

Marketing research and systematic information gathering increase the chances of successful marketing. Many companies, and even entire industries, have failed because of a lack of marketing research. The conventional wisdom about the evaluation and use of marketing research by marketing managers suggests that in future managers will rely on marketing research to reduce uncertainty and to make better informed decisions than they could without such information.[32]

Clearly, marketing research and information systems are vital to marketing decision-making. Because of this, it is essential that ethical standards be established and followed. Attempts to stamp out shoddy practices and establish generally accepted procedures for conducting research are important developments in marketing research. Other issues of great concern relate to researchers' honesty, manipulation of research techniques, data manipulation, invasion of privacy and failure to disclose the purpose or sponsorship of a study in some situations. Too often respondents are unfairly manipulated and research clients are not told about flaws in data.

One common practice that hurts the image of marketing research is "sugging" ("selling under the guise of marketing research"). More recently, direct marketers have disguised their selling mailings with questionnaires, adding to respondents' confusion and dislike of honest marketing research.[33] A leading marketing research association, ESOMAR, is encouraging research companies and marketing research organisations worldwide to adopt codes and policies prohibiting this practice.[34] In the UK, the Market Research Society lays down strict guidelines.

Because so many parties are involved in the marketing research process, developing shared ethical concern is difficult. The relationships among respondents who co-operate and share information, interviewing companies, marketing research agencies that manage projects, and organisations that use the data are interdependent and complex. Ethical conflict typically occurs because the parties involved in the marketing research process have different objectives. For example, the organisation that uses data tends to be results oriented, and success is often based on performance rather than a set of standards. On the other hand, a data gathering sub-contractor is evaluated on the ability to follow a specific set of standards or rules. The relationships among all participants in marketing research must be understood so that decision-making becomes ethical. Without clear understanding and agreement, including mutual adoption of standards, ethical conflict will lead to mistrust and questionable research results.[35]

Marketing research is essential in planning and developing marketing strategies. Information about target markets provides vital input in planning the marketing mix and controlling marketing activities. It is no secret that companies can use information technology as a key to gaining an advantage over the competition.[36] In short, the marketing concept—the marketing philosophy of customer orientation—can be implemented better when adequate information about customers, competition and trends is available.

● S U M M A R Y

To implement the marketing concept, marketers need information about the characteristics, needs and wants of their target markets. Marketing research and information systems that furnish practical, unbiased information help businesses avoid the assumptions and misunderstandings that could lead to poor marketing performance.

Marketing research is the systematic design, collection, interpretation and reporting of information to help marketers solve specific marketing problems or take advantage of marketing opportunities. Marketing research is conducted on a special project basis, with the research methods adapted to the problems being studied and to changes in the environment. *Quantitative research* leads to findings that can be quantified and statistically analysed. *Qualitative research* examines subjective opinions and value judgements.

The *marketing information system (MIS)* is a framework for the day-to-day managing and structuring of information regularly gathered from sources both inside and outside an organisation. The inputs into a marketing information system include the information sources inside and outside the organisation considered useful for future decision-making. Processing information involves classifying it and developing categories for meaningful storage and retrieval. Marketing decision-makers then determine which information—the output—is useful for making marketing decisions. Feedback enables those who are responsible for gathering internal and external data to adjust the information inputs systematically. Data brought into the organisation through marketing research become part of its *marketing databank*, a file of data collected through both the MIS and marketing research projects. Any information—an idea or piece of research—that assists in decision-making is *marketing intelligence.*

The increase in marketing research activities represents a transition from intuitive to scientific problem solving. Intuitive decisions are made on the basis of personal knowledge and past experience. *Scientific decision-making* is an orderly, logical and systematic approach to gathering information. Minor, non-recurring low risk problems can be handled successfully by *intuition.* As the number of risk and alternative solutions increases, the use of research becomes more desirable and rewarding.

The five basic steps of planning marketing research are (1) defining and locating problems, (2) developing hypotheses, (3) collecting data in order to test and further develop hypotheses, (4) analysing and interpreting research findings, and (5) reporting research findings.

Problem definition—the first step towards finding a solution or launching a research study—means uncovering the nature and boundaries of a negative, or positive, situation or question. The *Delphi method* for problem definition consists of interviews with experts. A problem must be clearly defined for marketers to develop a *hypothesis*—an informed guess or assumption about a certain problem or set of circumstances—which is the second step in the research process.

To test the accuracy of hypotheses, researchers collect data—the third step in the research process. Researchers may use *exploratory, descriptive* or *causal studies. Secondary data* are compiled inside or outside the organisation for some purpose other than the current investigation. Secondary data may be collected from an organisation's databank and other internal sources; from periodicals, census

reports, government publications, the World Wide Web and unpublished sources; and from *syndicated data services,* which collect general information and sell it to clients. Secondary data "pre-exists" and should be examined prior to the collection of any primary data.

Primary data are observed and recorded or collected directly from respondents for the specific marketing research task being instigated. *Experimentation* involves maintaining as constants those factors that are related to or may affect the variables under investigation, so that the effects of the experimental variables can be measured. *Marketing experimentation* is a set of rules and procedures according to which the task of data gathering is organised to expedite analysis and interpretation. In experimentation, an *independent variable* is manipulated and the resulting changes are measured in a *dependent variable.* Research techniques are *reliable* if they produce almost identical results in successive repeated trials; they have *validity* if they measure what they are supposed to measure and not something else. Experiments may take place in *laboratory settings,* which provide maximum control over influential factors, or in *field settings,* which are preferred when marketers want experimentation to take place in "real world" environments, such as with *home placements* and *diary tests.*

Other aspects of collecting primary data include sampling, surveys and observation. *Sampling* involves selecting a limited number of representative units, or *sample,* from a total *population.* In *random sampling,* all the units in a population have an equal chance of appearing in the sample. In *stratified sampling,* the population of interest is divided into groups according to a common characteristic or attribute, and then a probability sampling is conducted within each group. *Area sampling* involves selecting a probability sample of geographic areas such as streets, census tracts or census enumeration districts, and selecting units or individuals within the selected geographic areas for the sample. *Quota sampling* differs from other forms of sampling in that it is judgemental.

Survey methods include *mail surveys* and *mail panels, e-mail* and *Internet surveys, consumer purchase diaries, telephone surveys, computer assisted* telephone interviewing and personal interview surveys, such as depth interviews, shopping mall/pavement intercept interviews, on-site computer interviewing, focus group interviews, quali-depth interviews, and in-home interviews. Questionnaires are instruments used to obtain information from respondents and to record observations; they should be unbiased and objective. Observation methods involve researchers recording respondents' overt behaviour and taking note of physical conditions and events. Observation may be facilitated by mechanical observation devices.

To apply research findings to decision-making, marketers must tabulate, analyse and interpret their findings properly. Statistical interpretation is analy-sis of data that focuses on what is typical or what deviates from the average. After interpreting their research findings, researchers must prepare a report of the findings that the decision-makers can use and understand.

Marketing research and systematic information gathering increase the probability of successful marketing. Because marketing research is essential to the planning and development of marketing strategies, attempts to eliminate unethical marketing research practices and establish generally accepted procedures for conducting research are important goals. However, because so many parties are involved in the marketing research process, shared ethical concern is difficult to achieve.

Important Terms

Marketing research
Quantitative research
Qualitative research
Marketing information system (MIS)
Marketing databank
Marketing intelligence
Intuition
Scientific decision-making
Problem definition
Delphi method
Hypothesis
Exploratory studies
Descriptive studies
Causal studies
Primary data
Secondary data
Syndicated data services

Experimentation
Marketing experimentation
Independent variable
Dependent variable
Reliability
Validity
Laboratory settings
Field settings
Home placements
Diary tests
Sample
Sampling
Population
Random sampling
Stratified sampling
Area sampling
Quota sampling
Survey methods

Mail surveys
Mail panels
Consumer purchase diaries
Telephone surveys
Computer assisted telephone interviewing
Personal interview survey
Depth interview
Shopping mall/pavement intercept interviews
On-site computer interviewing
Focus group interview
Quali-depth interviews
In-home interview
Questionnaire
Observation methods
Mechanical observation devices
Statistical interpretation

Discussion and Review Questions

1. What is the MIS of a small organisation likely to include? Do all organisations have a marketing databank?
2. What is the difference between marketing research and marketing information systems? In what ways do marketing research and the MIS overlap?
3. What are the differences between quantitative and qualitative marketing research?

4. How do the benefits of decisions guided by marketing research compare with those of intuitive decision-making? How do marketing decision-makers know when it will be worthwhile to conduct research?
5. Give specific examples of situations in which intuitive decision-making would probably be more appropriate than marketing research.

6. What is the difference between defining a research problem and developing a hypothesis?
7. What are the differences between exploratory, descriptive and causal studies in marketing research?
8. What are the major limitations of using secondary data to solve marketing problems?
9. List some of the problems of conducting a laboratory experiment on respondents' reactions to the taste of different brands of beer. How would these problems differ from those of a field study of beer taste preferences?
10. In what situation would it be best to use random sampling? Quota sampling? Stratified or area sampling?
11. *Non-response* is the inability or refusal of some respondents to co-operate in a survey. What are some ways to decrease non-response in personal door-to-door surveys?
12. Suggest some ways to encourage respondents to co-operate in mail surveys.
13. If a survey of all homes with listed telephone numbers is conducted, what sampling design should be used?
14. What are the benefits of the focus group technique?
15. Give some examples of marketing problems that could be solved through information gained from observation.
16. Why is questionnaire design important? Why should questionnaires be tested?
17. What is "sugging"? Why is it damaging to the marketing research industry?

Recommended Readings

R. P. Bagozzi, ed., *Principles of Marketing Research* (Oxford: Blackwell, 1994).

R. Birn, *The Effective Use of Market Research* (London: Kogan Page, 1999).

P. M. Chisnall, *Marketing Research* (Maidenhead: McGraw-Hill, 1997).

E. F. McQuarrie, *The Market Research Toolbox: A Concise Guide for Beginners* (London: Sage, 1996).

D. S. Tull and D. I. Hawkins, *Marketing Research* (New York: Macmillan, 1990).

● C A S E S

6.1 Technology Comes to Marketing Research

AGB's *Superpanel*, launched in 1990, took the supermarket barcode wands one step further. No longer was scanning only for the benefit of retailers' stock control. Some 8,500 households—28,000 individual consumers—were provided with barcode swipe wands in their kitchens. Weekly shopping purchases were swiped, first by the checkout assistants and a second time in the consumer's home. The collected data were automatically downloaded by telephone hook to AGB's central computer. The resulting analyses enabled AGB to relate consumer purchases by retailer and manufacturer brands to demographics and lifestyles. The sales of one brand could be examined by type of household, stockist retailers, competitive purchases and brand switching, pricing policies and promotional activity. Technology allowed this data collection to take place on a weekly—even daily—basis.

According to AGB, 12 million marketing research interviews now take place each year in the UK. Around 70 per cent are pen and paper or clipboard exercises—small scale, ad hoc surveys. Five hundred interviews in a survey do not always warrant the use of software and lap-top computers by interviewers. Close to 70 per cent of all sales in the United States are barcoded, and Europe is follow-ing suit. Even most cars sold now have a barcode! Anticipating significant growth in electronic point-of-sale and in-home data capture, AGB invested over £12 million in three years to create Superpanel.

In the US, the barcode technology is being developed by leading food manufacturers to target specific consumers. Companies such as Quaker Oats, Kraft General Foods and Procter & Gamble are developing in-house databases that should soon include the names and addresses of 25 per cent of their end-user customers—the shoppers in the supermarkets. The names and data in this "relationship marketing" are collected from scanners at supermarket checkouts and from individually coded money back coupons mailed directly to millions of households. Once the personalised coupon has been redeemed, the consumer's code is instantly recorded in the scanner's database and purchases can be monitored.

Quaker Oats was a pioneer of this approach. It sent 10 coupons apiece to 18 million shoppers, each coupon inscribed with a separate family code and packaged with "involvement devices" such as competition entries and tie-ins with television programmes. Despite the high costs—double those for standard mailings—and the lengthy lead time before a database could be compiled from the feedback, other manufacturers quickly emulated Quaker Oats's initiative. Many US shoppers now carry "customer convenience cards", which reward—usually with price discounts—their compliance and brand loyalty.

Barcode scanning—in stores, at home and for manufacturers—is creating the biggest advance in data capture since the marketing research industry discovered telephone interviewing. The use of scanners, web home pages, telecommunications and software has increased sample sizes and the amount and accuracy of the information collected, and it has reduced the time lags between data collection, analysis and interpretation of results.

SOURCES: Larry Black, "Homing in on the American household", *The Independent on Sunday*, 10 March 1991, p. IB21; Bill Blyth at AGB; Phil Dourado, "Clipboard makes way for barcode", *The Independent on Sunday*, 13 January 1991, p. IB21; AGB promotional video; Suzanne Bidlake, "Tesco plans smart loyalty breakthrough", *Marketing*, 14 January 1993, p. 3.; AMSO, 1998.

Questions for Discussion

1. How does *Superpanel* work? How has technology enabled "live" tracking of consumer purchases?
2. Why would a marketing manager wish to profile the shopping basket composition of different households?
3. How would the resulting information lead to more prudent marketing mix development decisions?

6.2 Focus Group Interviewing: In-Depth Views from Group Discussions

Focus group interviews, which are generally informal group discussions about marketing ideas or concepts conducted by a marketer or marketing research firm, are used by most major organisations in developing marketing or business plans. In the 1980s, focus group interviewing became one of the most widely practised types of marketing research, expanding from the packaged goods industry into financial services and industrial applications.

However, the function of focus group interviewing is expected to change. Traditionally, companies have relied on focus group interviews to define the input going into quantitative studies, but the new trend is to conduct focus group interviews after tabulating research results, to provide insight into why the results were achieved. The trend is also towards higher costs (the average today is £1,400 for 90 minutes and £1,900 for an extended, video recorded group lasting two and a half hours).

Other changes pertain to moderator guides and their reports. The moderator guides will be expected to involve clients in the development process. Their reports will concentrate on providing conclusions that interpret the findings and on making recommendations for action by the client. The reports will also contain fewer actual quotations from individual focus group participants. The post-focus group debriefing techniques are also being altered. The shift is towards disciplined debriefing that asks participants their reactions to the group session. Such debriefing can provide the link between concept development and application and can serve as a rough check on validity and reliability.

Another new development in focus group interviewing is the use of electronics to offer three-way capabilities. Computerised decision-making software can supplement research findings and consolidate opinions from three different audiences. For example, in healthcare research in a hospital setting, the three audiences would be former patients, medics and employees. The advantages of using electronics include easier scheduling of participating groups and more interaction among the three audiences.

A major UK service retailer was faced with declining sales and two new competitors. In order to re-establish itself as the dominant force in its market, it decided to undertake some in-depth qualitative marketing research using focus groups. The retailer's new competitors were opening stores at the rate of six per month, and the company realised it had to act quickly to defend its position. However, it had conducted no consumer research for many years and was uncertain why its customers preferred its stores, how competitors were perceived and what types of people constituted its customer profile. Before modifying its marketing mix and launching an advertising campaign to combat its new competitors, the company had to gain a better understanding of its target market. For approximately £14,000 (1989), using a specialist consumer qualitative agency, in just three weeks the company had a good "feel" for its standing in its core trading area, as perceived by customers. The table shows that the information resulted from a fairly "standard" programme of focus groups.

Each group had eight consumers, four of whom were shoppers in the retailer's stores, four of whom shopped in competitors' stores. Each group lasted three hours, and a free merchandise voucher and buffet meal were provided for participants. The same moderator ran all eight groups to maintain consistency. Each session was tape recorded, the tapes being transcribed later into a report and presentation to the retailer's board of directors. Two sessions were video recorded, and several were secretly viewed by the company's marketing executives.

SOURCES: Lynne Cunningham, "Electronic focus groups offer 3-way capability", *Marketing News,* 8 January 1990, pp. 22, 39; Thomas L. Greenbaum, "Focus group spurt predicted for the '90s", *Marketing News,* 8 January 1990, pp. 21, 22; Nino DeNicola, "Debriefing sessions: the missing link in focus groups", *Marketing News,* 8 January 1990, pp. 20, 22; Peter Jackson, Adsearch, Richmond.

Questions for Discussion

1. What are the strengths and benefits of focus group marketing research?
2. This retailer chose to commission a programme of focus groups. Given the aims of the company's research, what other research tools might the company have used? Explain your selection.

Group Composition	Social Class*	Location
1. Male 25–39, white collar commuters†	A, B	Eastcheap
2. Male 40–55, white collar commuters	A, B	Hitchin
3. Female 25–44, executives/PAs	A, B, C1	Bristol
4. Female 25–44, semi-skilled	C2	Working
5. Female 35–40 "housewives"†	A, B	Leamington
6. Female 25–34, "housewives"	C1, C2	Sheffield
7. Male 18–29, young earners†	C1, C2	Ealing
8. Female 18–29, young earners	C1, C2	Telford

*For socio-economic classification, see Table 4.1, p. 130.
†Held in branches after hours

7 Segmenting Markets, Targeting and Positioning

OBJECTIVES

- To understand the definition of a market
- To recognise different types of markets
- To learn how companies segment markets
- To understand targeting decisions
- To discover how marketers prioritise target markets
- To learn about strategies for positioning
- To understand the importance of developing an edge over competitors

"The essence of successful segmentation lies not in fragmentation but in building an excellent understanding of the marketplace."

Sally Dibb, Warwick Business School

The UK government's 1998 Green Paper *Transport: The Way Ahead* indicated a projected growth in traffic of up to 80 per cent by the year 2025. With increasing use of vehicles and journey length, there are congestion and environmental problems. A combination of rising levels of carbon dioxide, nitrogen dioxide and sulphur dioxide have already caused acid rain, global warming problems and an increase in respiratory disease. A variety of UK and EU legislation has drawn attention to the environmental difficulties associated with road usage trends. The European Commission's Auto Oil Package has focused attention on air quality standards, demanding considerable reductions in vehicle emissions. The expectation is that the future will bring increasingly stringent national and EU legislation.

It is possible that European moves to reduce vehicle emissions will follow a similar pattern to that seen in California. There, strict environmental legislation requires that by 2003, 10 per cent of all new vehicles (some 800,000) must be zero emission. Not surprisingly, car manufacturers have invested heavily in developing a range of alternative fuel technologies in their drive towards more environmentally friendly vehicles. Currently, only battery-powered electric vehicles (EVs) are able to achieve zero emissions.

Other fuels under investigation include alcohol, compressed natural gas, hydrogen, liquefied petroleum gas, coal derived liquid fuels and fuels derived from biological materials such as soya beans. Chrysler, Ford, General Motors, Honda, Nissan and Toyota are just some of the manufacturers which have actively developed EVs for the California market.

In Europe too, the move towards more environmentally friendly vehicles continues apace. PSA Peugeot/Citroën has been a major player in the *Coventry Electric Vehicle Project*. This £400,000 joint initiative with the Energy Saving Trust involved five fleet operators—Coventry City Council, East Midlands Electricity, Peugeot, PowerGen and the Royal Mail—testing electric-powered Peugeot 106 cars and vans. The aim was to increase awareness of EVs. Peugeot's involvement in electric vehicle development is long established. Following early developments of technology in 1968, the company became the first European car manufacturer to offer EVs to its customers. Now the company is looking to establish the electric 106 through its dealer network. This fits with PSA Peugeot/Citroën's long term strategy to introduce electric versions of the Peugeot 106 and the Citroën Saxa throughout Europe.

Despite the ecological benefits of these innovative vehicles, many consumers remain unconvinced.

Images of slow electric milk floats and the Sinclair C5 electric trike are commonly associated with EVs. It is true that EVs require frequent recharging and do not have high top speeds. Nevertheless, many consumers desire more environmentally friendly vehicles. EVs are very quiet on the roads and, with no clutch or gears, relatively straightforward to drive. They are highly manoeuvrable and easy to park. EV batteries are currently expensive but running costs are remarkably low. The tasks facing the car manufacturers are to identify which types of consumers are likely to purchase an EV and to determine the product features and image necessary to stimulate sufficient demand to make such models commercially viable. The target market segments need to be defined and clear positioning strategies designed to appeal to these targeted consumers.

SOURCES: C.D. Haywood, "An analysis of the market potential for electric vehicles in the United Kingdom", MBA dissertation, University of Warwick, 1997; J. M. Dunne, "Status of emissions legislation", Vehicles Standards and Engineering Department of Transport, London; "Nissan switches to electricity", *Coventry Evening Telegraph,* 7 January 1997, p. 48; P. Foster, "Air pollution exceeds limits every five days", *The Times,* 26 September 1997, p. 4; "Positively all my own work", *Auto Express,* 3 January 1997; "Selling fuel cells: electric cars", *Economist,* 25 May 1996; "Survey on living with the car: a partly electric future", *Economist,* 22 June 1996; **http://www.aqmd.gov/monthly/white.html** (The case for electric vehicles); **http://www.ford.com/electricvehicle/qvm.html** (Ford's electric vehicle site); **http://www.bsi.ch/vel/velen01.htm** (The light electric vehicle project, Mendrisio, Switzerland). *Advertisement:* Courtesy of Honda.

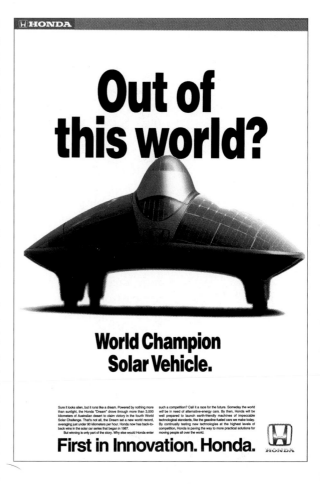

This case shows the importance of focusing on the process of market segmentation, from the identification of different consumer needs right through to the identification and implementation of suitable marketing programmes for these individuals. Companies like Peugeot realise that not all consumers want the same things. To satisfy these different needs it is necessary for companies to single out groups of customers and aim some or all of their marketing activities at these groups. The key is then to develop and maintain a marketing mix that both satisfies the particular requirements of customers in these groups and is positioned in such a way as to be meaningful to them.

This chapter considers the nature of markets, first defining the term and describing the different types. It then reviews the concepts of segmentation, targeting and positioning by considering the variables used to segment markets. Next, it considers the strategies often used to select and prioritise target markets and approaches to product positioning. Finally, it reviews the importance of developing an edge over competitors. The process of market segmentation and the aspects of marketing strategy detailed in this chapter are pivotal to effective marketing. Indeed, many marketers believe these facets of marketing to be the most important decisions made by marketers.[1]

What Are Markets?

The word *market* has a number of meanings. It used to refer primarily to the place where goods were bought and sold. It can also refer to a large geographic area. In some cases the word refers to the relationship between the demand and supply of a specific product. For instance, "What is the state of the market for oil?" Sometimes, "market" is used to mean the act of selling something. The dictionary defines *market* as an occasion on which goods are publicly exposed for sale, a place in which goods are exposed for sale, or to offer for sale. In marketing terms, a market is defined in terms of customers, their need for a product and ability to purchase or consume.

Market An aggregate of people who, as individuals or as organisations, have a need for certain products and the ability, willingness and authority to purchase such products.

For the purposes of this text, a **market** is an aggregate of people who, as individuals or as organisations, have needs for products in a product class and who have the ability, willingness and authority to purchase such products. In general use, the term *market* sometimes refers to the total population—or mass market—that buys products. However, the definition used here is more specific; it refers to individuals seeking products in a specific product category. For example, students are part of the market for text books, as well as being markets for calculators, pens and pencils, paper, food, music and other products. Obviously, there are many different markets in any economy. In this section, the requirements for markets are considered in conjunction with these different types.

Requirements for a Market

For a group of people to be a market, the members of the group must meet the following four requirements:

1. They must need or want a particular product or service.
2. They must have the ability to purchase the product or service. Ability to purchase is related to buying power, which consists of resources such as money, goods and services that can be traded in an exchange situation.
3. They must be willing to use their buying power.
4. They must have the authority to buy the specific products or services.

Individuals can have the desire, the buying power and the willingness to purchase certain products but may not be authorised to do so. For example, secondary school students may want, have the money for and be willing to buy alcoholic beverages; but a brewer does not consider them a market because until they are 18 years old, they are prohibited by law from buying alcohol. An aggregate of people that lacks any one of the four requirements thus does not constitute a market.

Types of Markets

Markets can be divided into two categories: consumer markets and business-to-business markets. These categories are based on the characteristics of the individuals and groups that make up a specific market and the purposes for which they buy products. A **consumer market** consists of purchasers and/or individuals in their households who personally consume or benefit from the purchased products and who do not buy products primarily to make a profit. Each of us belongs to numerous consumer markets for such products as housing, food, clothing, vehicles, personal services, appliances, furniture and recreational equipment. Consumer markets are discussed in more detail in Chapter 4.

Consumer market Purchasers or individuals in their households who personally consume or benefit from the purchased products and do not buy products primarily to make a profit

Business-to-business market Individuals or groups that purchase a specific kind of product to re-sell, use directly in producing other products or use in general daily operations

A **business-to-business market** (also referred to as an *organisational* or *industrial market*) consists of individuals or groups that purchase a specific kind of product for one of three purposes: re-sale, direct use in producing other products or use in general daily operations. The four categories of organisational (or industrial) markets—producer, reseller, government and institutional—are discussed in Chapter 5.

Selecting Target Markets

Chapter 1 defined a marketing strategy as having four components: (1) the analysis of marketing opportunities, (2) the selection of the organisation's target market, (3) the creation and maintenance of a marketing mix that satisfies that market's needs for a specific product, and (4) marketing management to plan, organise, implement and control marketing activities. Because products are classified according to use, the same product may be classified as both a consumer product and an industrial product, widening the potential market. Irrespective of the general types of markets on which a company focuses, marketers must select the company's target markets. The next section examines two general approaches to identifying target markets: the total market approach and market segmentation.

Total Market Approach or Market Segmentation?

Undifferentiated or **total market approach**   An approach that assumes that all customers have similar needs and wants and can be served with a single marketing mix

Sometimes marketers define the total market for a particular product or service as their target market. Companies that develop a single marketing mix aimed at all potential customers in a market are said to be adopting an **undifferentiated** or **total market approach.** The assumption is that all customers in the market have similar needs and wants and can, therefore, be satisfied with a single marketing mix—a standard product or service, similar price levels and personnel, one method of distribution and a promotional mix aimed at everyone.

Increasingly, marketers in both consumer and business-to-business markets are accepting that because of the varying characteristics, needs, wants and interests of customers, there are few markets where a single product or service is satisfactory for all. The extensive array of goods on supermarket shelves reflects basic differences in customers' requirements. The trend, it seems, is away from a mass marketing approach, and even markets that were traditionally undifferentiated are changing, with an ever increasing number of products on offer. For instance, the market for food seasoning used to be dominated by salt. Now, low sodium substitutes are being offered as alternatives for the increasingly health-conscious consumer.

The mass or total marketing approach is appropriate only under two conditions. The first, which is increasingly rare, is when there is little variation in the needs of customers for a specific product. The second condition is that the organisation must develop and sustain one marketing mix that satisfies everyone. If the number of customers is large, the commitment in terms of company resources and managerial expertise can be considerable.

When an undifferentiated approach is inappropriate or impractical, marketers use market segmentation to try to increase customer satisfaction. This technique involves identifying groups of customers in markets who share similar buying needs and characteristics. By identifying and understanding such groups, marketers are better able to develop product or service benefits that are appropriate for them (see Figure 7.1). They do this by designing products and brands to appeal to particular target segments and to be supported by an appropriate promotional campaign, relevant customer service, and suitable pricing and place/distribution strategies. For example, clothing sold through Top Shop or New Look is manufactured for youthful female consumers. This is reflected in both the product styling and the promotional campaign.

Figure 7.1 Market
segmentation approach

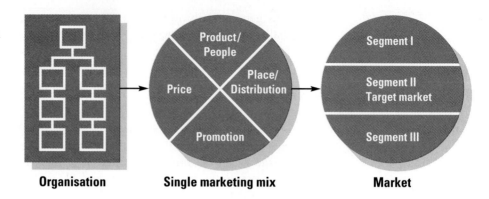

Organisation   **Single marketing mix**   **Market**

Applying Market Segmentation

Heterogeneous markets Markets in
which all customers have different
requirements

Markets in which all customers have different requirements are termed **heterogeneous markets.** For example, the market for wrist watches is quite diverse.
Swatch designs relatively low priced watches for the fashion-conscious customer.
Rotary markets much more conservative and expensive designs for an older customer group.

In completely heterogeneous markets the only way to satisfy everyone is by
offering tailor made or bespoke products. This situation is more prevalent in
business-to-business markets, where, for example, plant machinery is designed
for a specific task and situation. However, while it may not be feasible to offer
every customer a tailor made product, it is often possible to aggregate customers into groups with similar product needs and wants. **Market segmentation**
is the process by which customers in markets with some heterogeneity can be
grouped into smaller, more similar or homogeneous segments. In so doing, a
balance is sought between obtaining reasonably substantial groups and ensuring sufficient similarity to allow individuals to be offered a standard marketing
mix. Market segmentation is the identification of target customer groups in
which customers are aggregated into groups with similar requirements and buying characteristics.

Market segmentation The process
of grouping customers in markets with
some heterogeneity into smaller, more
similar or homogeneous segments. The
identification of target customer groups
in which customers are aggregated into
groups with similar requirements and
buying characteristics

Having identified market segments, marketers must decide which, if any, they
intend to enter. A marketing programme covering all elements of the marketing
mix can then be designed to suit the particular requirements of those segments
targeted. Ford-owned Jaguar Cars had a portfolio of products aimed at the luxury and executive segments of the car market. With a starting price of around
£35,000, Jaguar recognised it was not targeting the young professionals buying
BMW 3/5 Series. Jaguar therefore launched the S Type at the 1998 NEC Motor
Show, sized, specified and priced to appeal to a new target market segment for
Jaguar—young professionals.

Companies have turned to market segmentation with good reason. Whitbread,
Diner's Club and Bird's Eye Walls have all demonstrated that success can follow
the effective implementation of market segmentation strategies. For example, the
variety of offerings in the market for frozen, ready-to-eat meals illustrates the
spread of customer needs: healthy options, quick snacks, gourmet selections.

Careful segmentation and the customer understanding underlying it can make
it easier for companies to identify and exploit different market opportunities. For

example, segmentation can help minor players in the market achieve a foothold in a particular niche, perhaps by identifying an opportunity not directly exploited by market leaders. In general, segmentation helps companies pursue four types of product and market opportunities (see Ansoff's box in Figure 21.12 on page 681):

1. *Market penetration* involves increasing the percentage of sales in present markets by taking sales from the competition. For example, Coca-Cola and PepsiCo engage in advertising programmes that compete for each other's market share.
2. *Product development* offers new or improved products to existing markets by expanding the range of products on offer. For example, the washing powder market has undergone much change over recent years with the introduction of new micro-powders and products aimed specifically at washing coloured clothing or very smelly items.
3. *Market development* develops existing products in new markets by finding new applications and/or customer groups. Evian, one of the major players in the market for mineral water, now offers its product in a mist spray. The Evian Brumisateur atomiser (see Figure 7.2) is being marketed as a new concept in skin moisturisers.
4. *Diversification* involves moving into different markets by offering new products. For example, Bic followed its success in the ballpoint pen market by moving into disposable razors and perfumes. Construction equipment manufacturers CAT and JCB have launched rugged clothing and footwear ranges.

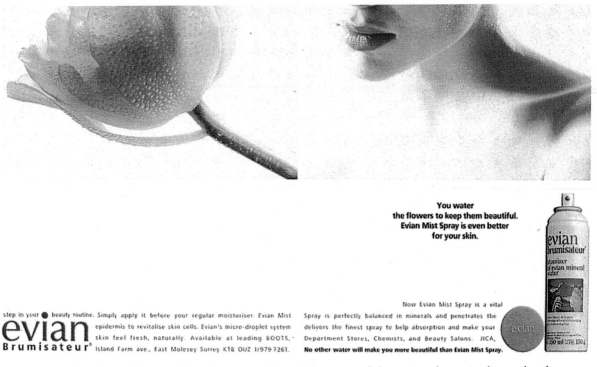

Figure 7.2 Developing existing products in new markets. Evian, one of the major players in the market for mineral water, now offers its product as a mist spray for skin care. SOURCE: Courtesy of PBWA Advertising, Inc. for Laboratoire d'Hygiene Dermatologique d'Evian.

The Advantages of Market Segmentation

Segmentation is seen to offer businesses a number of advantages that make it easier to develop and capitalise on opportunities such as those described above. These advantages can be considered at the customer level, in relation to the competition or in terms of the effectiveness of resource allocation and strategic planning.[2]

Customer Analysis

Segmenting markets allows a better understanding of customers' needs, wants and other characteristics to be achieved. The sharper focus that segmentation offers allows the personal, situational and behavioural factors that characterise customers in a particular segment to be considered. In short, questions about how, why and what customers buy can be addressed. By being closely in touch with segments, marketers can respond quickly to even slight changes in what target customers want.

Competitor Analysis

Most markets are characterised by intense competition. Within this environment, companies need to understand the nature of the competition they face. Who are the main competitors? At which segments are they targeting their products? Answering these questions allows marketers to make decisions about the most appropriate segments to target and the kind of competitive advantage to seek. Companies that do not understand how the market is divided up risk competing head-on against larger organisations with superior resources.

Effective Resource Allocation

All companies have limited resources. To target the whole of the market is usually unrealistic. The effectiveness of personnel and material resources can be greatly improved when they are more narrowly focused on a particular segment of customers. With limited resources, Saab and Porsche target only a few market segments compared with Ford or GM. Segmentation enables Saab and Porsche to identify homogeneous groups of customers at whom the Saab 9^5 or Porsche 911 models can be targeted. This maximises these companies' use of resources and marketing mix activities.

Strategic Marketing Planning

Companies operating in a number of segments are unlikely to follow the same strategic plans in them all. Dividing markets up allows marketers to develop plans that give special consideration to the particular needs and requirements of customers in different segments. The time scale covered by the strategic plan can also be structured accordingly, because some segments change more rapidly than others. The market for recorded music is a typical example. While tastes in classical music remain fairly steady, tastes in pop music change very rapidly. Companies like EMI or Sony clearly need to consider this factor when developing corporate plans.

The benefits of segmentation are illustrated in the following example. Despite recent problems, IBM is still regarded as something of a legend in the computer industry. During the 1960s, the company recognised that there was a need for certain industry standards. IBM argued that when customers' needs changed, it would not be feasible for customers to dispose of existing equipment and expertise and begin all over again. They had to be able to upgrade to equipment that spoke similar languages and had similar physiology. Through this insight, IBM became that standard. The company was able to offer a complete package of service, training, consultancy, maintenance and software support. It built its corporate image to the point that, according to an often quoted industry joke, "no-one ever got fired for buying IBM". For IBM's competitors this powerful competitive advantage presented a dilemma. How could they compete successfully against such odds? Curiously, for some companies the best solution was not to compete directly at all, but instead to specialise and focus on certain segments or niches in the market. For example, NCR concentrated on the retailing and banking markets, Apple on the education and graphic artist markets.

Segmenting, Targeting and Positioning

There are three stages to carrying out market segmentation: segmentation, targeting and positioning. Figure 7.3 gives an overview of these stages.

Segmenting the Market There are many ways in which customers can be grouped and markets segmented. In different markets, the variables that are appropriate change. The key is to understand which are the most suitable for distinguishing between different product requirements. Understanding as much as possible about the customers in the segments is also important, as marketers who "know" their targets are more likely to design an appropriate marketing mix for them. For example, car company Daewoo used extensive customer research as the basis for its entry into the UK car market. The research revealed an inherent consumer dislike of car showrooms and the high pressure selling techniques associated with them. Daewoo used its understanding to develop a new kind of distribution outlet, staffed by non-commissioned advisors. The impact of Daewoo's marketing approach is now being seen in the way other car manufacturers are gearing up their selling effort.

Figure 7.3 Basic elements of segmentation

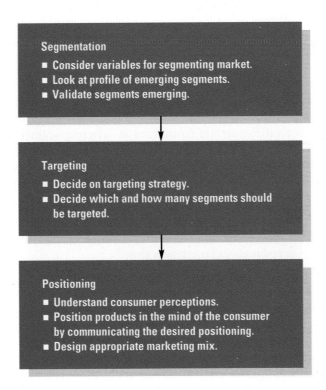

Segmentation
- Consider variables for segmenting market.
- Look at profile of emerging segments.
- Validate segments emerging.

Targeting
- Decide on targeting strategy.
- Decide which and how many segments should be targeted.

Positioning
- Understand consumer perceptions.
- Position products in the mind of the consumer by communicating the desired positioning.
- Design appropriate marketing mix.

| **Targeting Strategy** | Once segments have been identified, decisions about which and how many customer groups to target can be made. There are several options: |

- Concentrate on a single segment with one product and marketing programme.
- Offer one product and marketing programme to a number of segments.
- Target a different product and marketing programme at each of a number of segments.

These options are explored in more detail later in this chapter. The choices companies make must take resource implications into consideration. The actions of NCR and Apple or Saab and Porsche described above illustrate that careful focusing of resources is essential.

| **Positioning the Product** | Companies must decide precisely how and where within the targeted segments to aim a product or products, brand or brands. The needs and wants of targeted customers must be translated into a tangible mix of product/service, personnel, price, promotion and place/distribution. The consumers' view of the product and where it is positioned relative to the competition is particularly critical. After all, the paying public does not always perceive a product or brand in the way the manufacturer would like. For example, to the dismay of those who developed it, the Sinclair C5 electric trike was perceived as an object of ridicule. |

Targeting and positioning issues will be examined in more detail, but first the act of segmentation requires exploration.

Choosing Segmentation Variables

Segmentation variables or **bases** The dimensions or characteristics of individuals, groups or businesses that are used for dividing a total market into segments

Segmentation variables or **bases** are the dimensions or characteristics of individuals, groups or businesses that are used for dividing a total market into segments. There is rarely a single or best way to segment a market. Companies must choose from an array of different options.[3] In consumer markets, background characteristics like age, sex and occupation—which are relatively easy to obtain and measure through observation and questioning—are very widely used. In business-to-business markets, customer size, location and product use are often the focus.

Several factors are considered in selecting segmentation variables. The variables chosen should relate to customers' needs for, uses of or behaviour towards the product or service. Indeed, there is no "magic" associated with segmentation. Clifford and Cavanagh succinctly put the technique into perspective:

> High growth companies succeed by identifying and meeting the needs of certain kinds of customer, not all customers, for special kinds of products and service, not all products or all services. Business academics call this market segmentation. Entrepreneurs call it common sense.[4]

Stereo hi-fi equipment marketers might segment the stereo market on the basis of income and age—but not on the basis of religion, because one person's music equipment needs do not differ much from those of people of other religions. Furthermore, if individuals or businesses in a total market are to be classified accurately, the segmentation variable must be measurable. For example, segmenting a market on the basis of intelligence or moral standards would be quite difficult because these attributes are hard to measure accurately.

Variables for Segmenting Consumer Markets

Companies developing their strategy for segmentation can choose one or several variables or bases from a wide range of choices. Table 7.1 comprehensively illustrates the options available for the marketer of consumer goods. These divide into variables like demographics and socio-economics that relate to basic customer characteristics and product related behavioural factors, such as purchase and usage behaviour. It is rare for marketers to apply only one of these base variables: Generally a combination is selected.

Basic Customer Characteristics

Because of the ease with which information concerning basic customer characteristics can be obtained and measured, the use of these variables is widespread.

Demographics

Age
Sex
Family
Race
Religion
The family life cycle concept is an imaginative way of combining demographic variables (see Table 7.3).

Socio-Economics

Income
Occupation
Education
Social class
Different income groups have different aspirations in terms of cars, housing, education, etc.

Geographic Location

Country
Region
Type of urban area (conurbation/village)
Type of housing (affluent suburbs/inner city)

Personality, Motives and Lifestyle

Holiday companies often use lifestyle to segment the market. Club Med, for example, concentrates on young singles while other tour operators cater especially for senior citizens or young families. "Couch potatoes" and participating sports buffs have very different lifestyles, personalities and motives for purchasing and consuming products or services: satellite TV versus health club membership.

Product Related Behavioural Characteristics

Purchase Behaviour

Customers for frozen ready meals may be highly brand loyal to Heinz or Bird's Eye or may shop purely on the basis of price.

Purchase Occasion

A motorist making an emergency purchase of a replacement tyre while on a trip far from home is less likely to haggle about price than the customer who has a chance to shop around.

Benefits Sought

When customers buy washing powder or fabric conditioner, they seek different benefits. For some, cleaning power and softness are essential, whereas for others a product's environmental friendliness is the key. Ecover products try to cater for this latter group.

Consumption Behaviour and User Status

Examining consumption patterns can indicate where companies should be concentrating their efforts. Light or non-users are often neglected. The important question to ask is why consumption in these groups is low. Can it be stimulated or is the product currently offered simply inappropriate?

Attitude towards Product

Different customers have different perceptions of and preferences for products offered. Concern about environmental issues has altered many consumers' perceptions of household cleaning products and has resulted in a host of so-called environmentally friendly products.

Table 7.1 Variables for segmenting consumer markets

wonderful sights late summer light through trees brad pitt in jeans (only) a small white tooth

Halfway through his first year, a baby's teeth start to put in an appearance. It's one of the first real signs that your bundle of gurgles is starting to become just like you. The small, soft pieces in Farley's Junior Choice and Heinz 7 month meals may not be steak and chips, but they are an important move on from pureed food. And a wonderful sight for a hungry baby.

Farley's & Heinz
FOR EVERY LITTLE STEP

Figure 7.4 Demographic variables. Heinz baby food is promoted to new parents.
SOURCE: Courtesy of Heinz.

Basic Customer Characteristics

Demographic Variables The ease with which demographic variables can be measured has largely contributed to their widespread usage in segmenting markets. The characteristics most often used include age, sex, family, race and religion. Because these factors can be closely related to customers' product needs and purchasing behaviour, understanding them often helps target their efforts more effectively. For example, as shown in Figure 7.4, Heinz targets new parents with its baby foods. Manufacturers of ready-to-eat breakfast cereals, such as Kellogg's and Nabisco, offer their products in packages of different sizes to satisfy the needs of consumers ranging from singles to large families.

Financial institutions such as banks and building societies attempt to interest children in their products by offering free gifts such as book vouchers. Meanwhile, retired customers are targeted with products designed for a leisure oriented lifestyle. The emphasis is on tailoring the service package to suit the particular needs.

Population statistics help marketers to understand and keep track of changing age profiles (see Table 7.2). With the population of western Europe increasing at a rate of 0.6 per cent a year, there will have been a 7 per cent fall in the 0 to 19 year old age band between 1990 and 2000. Over the same period, however, the number of 20 to 59 year olds will have remained steady, with the number of people over 60 increasing by 9 per cent. This will inevitably affect new opportunities for marketers, who must increasingly cater for an ageing population. Given the relative affluence of this particular group, a wide range of companies (for example, the leisure and service industries) reaped the benefits of this increase by the end of the century.

		Austria	Belgium	Denmark	France	Germany	Ireland	Italy	Netherlands	Norway	Spain	Sweden	Switzerland	United Kingdom
Total population, 1996	millions	8.06	10.16	5.26	58.38	81.91	3.63	57.38	15.52	4.38	39.26	8.84	7.07	58.78
Population change at annual rates														
1986/96	%	0.6	0.3	0.2	0.5	0.5	0.1	0.1	0.6	0.5	0.2	0.6	0.8	0.3
1995/96	%	0.1	0.2	0.6	0.4	0.3	1.1	0.3	0.4	0.5	0.1	0.1	0.4	0.3
Population by sex and age, 1996														
Male	%	48.5	48.9	48.7	48.7	48.7	49.6	48.5	49.5	49.4	48.9	49.4	48.8	49.0
Female	%	51.5	51.1	50.6	51.3	51.3	50.4	51.5	50.5	50.6	51.1	50.6	51.2	51.0
Under 15	%	17.5	17.9	17.5	19.4	16.2	24.0	14.9	18.4	19.5	16.4	18.8	17.7	19.4
15–64	%	67.3	66.1	71.2	65.3	68.3	64.5	68.3	68.3	64.6	68.1	63.7	67.5	64.9
65 and over	%	15.2	16.0	11.3	15.3	15.5	11.5	16.8	13.3	15.9	15.5	17.5	14.8	15.7
Births, 1996	per 000's	11.0	11.1	12.9	12.6	9.3	13.9	9.2	12.2	13.8	9.0	10.8	11.7	12.2
Marriages, 1995	per 000's	5.3	5.1	6.6	4.4	5.3	4.3	4.9	5.3	5.0	5.0	3.8	5.8	5.5
Inhabitants per sq. km, 1997	no.	96.1	332.9	122.1	108.0	230.0	53.0	191.0	379.0	14.0	77.6	20.0	172.0	244.0
Number of households, 1995[1]	millions	3.1	4.1	2.5	23.1	36.4	1.1	20.4	6.4	1.8	12.1	3.8	2.9	24.5
Persons per household, 1995	no.	2.6	2.5	2.1	2.5	2.2	3.2	2.8	2.4	2.5	3.2	2.3	2.5	2.4
Commonly used unemployment rate 1997														
Proportion of labour force	%	4.4	9.2	5.5	12.4	10.0	10.1	12.1	5.2	4.1	20.8	9.9	3.9	7.0
Civilian employment by main sectors, 1996[2]														
Agriculture	%	7.2	2.6	4.3	5.1	3.3	10.7	7.0	3.9	5.2	8.7	2.9	4.5	2.0
Industry	%	33.2	27.7	27.0	27.7	37.5	27.2	32.1	22.2	23.4	29.7	26.1	27.8	27.4
Services	%	59.6	69.7	69.0	67.2	59.1	62.3	60.9	73.3	71.5	61.6	71.0	67.7	71.0

Notes:
1. Data for Denmark, Norway and Sweden refer to 1993.
2. Austrian data refer to 1994, Belgium and France data refer to 1993 and Norwegian data refer to 1995.

SOURCE: *The Marketing Pocket Book 1999*, pp. 160–161. Reprinted by permission of NTC Publications, Ltd.

Table 7.2 Demographic profile of western Europe

In some markets, including clothes, cosmetics, alcoholic drinks, books, magazines and even cigarettes, gender has long been a key demographic variable. In other markets, its use is more recent. European Union statistics show that while women and girls represent 51.4 per cent of the population, men and boys account for 48.6 per cent. The confectionery market is one that traditionally did not segment on the basis of sex. Chocolate manufacturers, including Cadbury's, tried to change this by developing assortments aimed primarily at men. In general, despite the care taken in each product's design, packaging and promotion, they were not successful.

The way in which marketers treat ethnicity varies in different parts of the world. For instance, in the US, where one quarter of the population is made up of ethnic minorities, ethnicity is widely used as a means of segmenting markets for goods and services of all kinds. The US Hispanic population illustrates the importance of ethnicity as a segmentation variable. Comprising people of Mexican, Cuban, Puerto Rican, and Central and South American heritage, this ethnic group is growing five times faster than the general population. Consequently, it is being targeted by more and more companies—including AT&T, Campbell Soup Co., Nabisco and Procter & Gamble. However, targeting Hispanic customers is not an easy task. For example, although marketers have long believed that Hispanic consumers are exceptionally brand loyal and prefer Spanish language broadcast media, recent research has failed to support this notion. Not only do advertisers disagree about the merits of Spanish language media, they also question whether it is appropriate to advertise to Mexicans, Puerto Ricans and Cubans using a common Spanish language.[5] In other areas the proportion of ethnic minorities is much lower than in the US, affecting the level of marketing attention they receive. In the UK, where only 5 per cent of the population come from an ethnic minority, marketers are much more reluctant to develop bespoke marketing programmes for particular groups. As explained in Case 7.1, they fear that such action may lead to accusations of ethnic stereotyping and racism.

Product and service needs also vary according to marital status and by number and age of children. Figure 7.5 illustrates patterns of expenditure on a full range

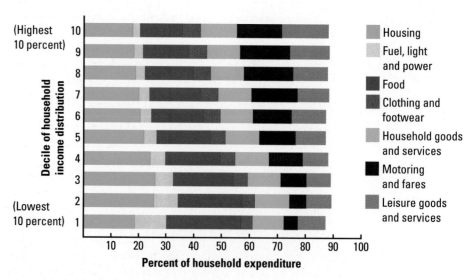

Figure 7.5 Pattern of expenditure by decile groups of gross income (1991). SOURCE: *Family Expenditure Survey*, Office for National Statistics, ©Crown Copyright 1991.

Note: Percentages are expenditure on commodity or service group as a percentage of total household expenditure.

Table 7.3 Wells and Gubar life cycle stages

Bachelor stage (young single people not living with parents)
Newly married couples without children
Full nest I (youngest child under 6)
Full nest II (youngest child 6 or over)
Full nest III (older married couple with dependent children)
Empty nest I (no children living at home, family head working)
Empty nest II (family head retired)
Solitary survivor (working)
Solitary survivor (retired)

SOURCE: Copyright © ESOMAR® 2000. Permission for using this material has been granted by ESOMAR®, Amsterdam, The Netherlands (www.esomar.ni).

of products for different household incomes. These factors are collectively taken into consideration by the *family life cycle* concept. Some of the more obvious markets in which the impact of different life cycles is seen are tourism, housing and financial services. The family life cycle has been broken down in several different ways. Table 7.3 illustrates a fairly comprehensive scheme that is sometimes used.

The scheme is based on the assumption that individuals at different life cycle stages have varying product needs. Marketers can respond to this by targeting such groups with marketing mixes designed to capitalise on the differences. For example, parents whose children have grown up and left home tend to have more disposable income than those with young children and tend to spend more on the home, holidays and new cars. Banks and financial institutions in particular are getting better at gearing their marketing efforts to life cycle changes. Critics of the life cycle concept point out that it can be difficult to decide to which categories families belong. Some households, such as single parent families and older married couples who never had children, do not appear to fit in at all.

Obviously, this discussion of demographic variables is not exhaustive. However, the variables described above probably represent the most widely used demographics. Other examples of the use of demographics include segmenting the cosmetic and hair care markets on the basis of race and directing certain types of foods and clothing towards people of specific religious sects.

Socio-Economic Variables This group of variables includes income, occupation, education and social class. Some marketing academics and practitioners include certain of these variables under the demographics label.

Income can be a very useful way of dividing markets because it strongly influences people's product needs (see Figure 7.5). It affects their ability to buy (discussed in Chapter 2) and their aspirations for a certain style of living. Obvious products in this category include housing, furniture, clothing, cars, food, certain kinds of sporting goods and leisure activities.

The occupations of the members of the household are known to have an impact on the types of products and services that are purchased. The type of housing individuals and families own or rent is strongly linked to this variable. It is obvious, for example, that sales of products for refurbishment and decoration, such as paints, fabrics and wallpapers, will occur predominantly among those professions that have owner-occupier status. Occupation is also known to affect the types of sporting and leisure activities people prefer. For example, professionals may be active with walking, swimming, cycling and jogging, but not so involved with darts or soccer. Intermediate managers enjoy walking, swimming and keep fit/yoga. Unskilled manual workers are not particularly active in sports and physical activities.[6]

Other socio-economic variables that may be used to segment markets include education level and social class.

Geographic Variables   The needs of consumers in different geographic locations may be affected by their local climate, terrain, natural resources and population density. Markets may be divided into regions because one or more geographic variables may cause customers' needs to differ from one region to another. A company that sells products throughout the European Union will, for example, need to take the different languages spoken into account when labelling its goods.

City size can be an important segmentation variable. For example, one franchised restaurant organisation will not locate in cities of less than 100,000 people because experience shows that a smaller population base could make the operation unprofitable. The same company may add a second, or even a third, restaurant once the city reaches a certain size. Other businesses, however, seek out opportunities in smaller towns. The major petroleum retailers, such as Esso and Shell, have traffic density thresholds, below which they perceive a local market as unviable. It is, therefore, quite common—particularly in villages and small towns in rural areas—for petroleum retailing to be dominated by independent garage owners and the smaller petroleum companies.

Market density The number of potential customers within a unit of land area

Market density refers to the number of potential customers within a unit of land area, such as a square kilometre. Although market density is generally related to population density, the correlation is not exact. For example, in two different geographic markets of approximately equal size and population, the market density for office supplies might be much higher in the first than in the second if the first contains a significantly greater proportion of business customers. Market density may be a useful segmentation variable because low density markets often require different sales, advertising and distribution activities from high density markets.

In Europe, climate can be used as a geographic segmentation variable. Companies entering new markets in Europe increasingly need to consider the impact of climate on their customer base. For example, washing machines sold in Italy do not require such fast spin speeds as those sold in Germany because the Italian climate is much sunnier. Other markets affected by climate include air conditioning and heating equipment, clothing, gardening equipment, recreational products and building materials.

Locality: ACORN   ACORN (A Classification of Residential Neighbourhoods) develops geographic location as a segmentation base one stage further. Information taken from census data allows people to be grouped according to a number of factors, including geography, socio-economics and culture. In total, 40 different variables are considered, among them household size, number of cars, type of occupation, and family size and characteristics.

The underlying concept is that customers living in different residential neighbourhoods have different profiles in respect of these variables. Their product

Categories	% Pop.	Groups	% Pop.
A Thriving	19.8	1 Wealthy achievers, suburban areas	15.2
		2 Affluent greys, rural communities	2.3
		3 Prosperous pensioners, retirement areas	2.3
B Expanding	11.5	4 Affluent executives, family areas	3.7
		5 Well off workers, family areas	7.8
C Rising	7.6	6 Affluent urbanites, town and city areas	2.2
		7 Prosperous professionals, metropolitan areas	2.1
		8 Better off executives, inner city areas	3.3
D Settling	22.3	9 Comfortable middle agers, mature home owning areas	13.5
		10 Skilled workers, home owning areas	8.8
E Aspiring	13.7	11 New home owners, mature communities	9.7
		12 White collar workers, better off multi-ethnic areas	4.0
F Striving	22.6	13 Older people, less prosperous areas	3.6
		14 Council estate residents, better off homes	11.5
		15 Council estate residents, high unemployment	2.7
		16 Council estate residents, greatest hardship	2.7
		17 People in multi-ethnic, low income areas	2.1
Unclassified	2.4		2.4

SOURCE: Copyright © CACI Limited, 2000. Reprinted by permission.
ACORN is a registered trademark of CACI Limited.

Table 7.4 The ACORN consumer targeting classification

needs in terms of styling and features therefore also vary. Consumers can be classified under ACORN on the basis of the postcode of their home address and then allocated to one of the groups in Table 7.4.

These categories further sub-divide to give a total of 17 groups and 54 neighbourhood types (see Figure 7.6). For example, the Aspiring (E) category splits into two groups:

- new home owners, mature communities.
- white collar workers, better off multi-ethnic areas.

These in turn further sub-divide into six ACORN types.

Personality, Motives and Lifestyle Variables such as personality characteristics, motives and lifestyle are sometimes used to segment markets. The variables can be used by themselves to segment a market or in combination with other variables, such as demographics or socio-economic statistics.

Personality characteristics are useful when a product is similar to many competing products and when consumers' needs are not significantly affected by other segmentation variables. However, attempting to segment a market according to personality characteristics has caused problems. Although marketing practitioners have long believed that consumer choice and product use should vary

Figure 7.6 ACORN Category C, Group 6, Type 17.
CACI's ACORN classification, based on demographic data from the census, is used extensively by marketers and planners in the UK for profiling purchasing and lifestyle behaviour. ACORN classifies people into 6 categories, which are subdivided into 17 groups and 54 neighborhood types. This illustration is for ACORN category C, Group 6, Type 17: Flats and Mortgages, Singles and Young Working Couples. This type is found in affluent areas in London, the Home Counties and central Scotland. SOURCE: CACI and ACORN are the trademarks and/or servicemarks of CACI Limited.

with personality and lifestyle, marketing research has shown only weak relationships. However, the weakness of such relationships may be due to the difficulty of accurately measuring personality traits, because most existing personality tests were developed for clinical use, not for segmentation purposes. As the reliability of more recent measurement instruments increases, a greater association between personality and consumer behaviour has been demonstrated.[7] For example, it has been shown that personality sometimes influences the clothes, make-up and hair styles individuals adopt.

When a market is segmented according to a motive, it is divided on the basis of consumers' reasons for making a purchase. Product durability, value for money, concern for the environment, convenience and status are all motives affecting the types of product purchased and the choice of stores in which they are bought. For example, one consumer might be motivated to purchase recycled kitchen paper out of concern for the environment. Another might travel to a large supermarket in order to buy the most absorbent, high quality brand of kitchen towels.

Lifestyle segmentation groups individuals according to how they live and spend their time, the importance of items in their surroundings (their homes or their jobs, for example), their beliefs about themselves and broad issues, and some socio-economic characteristics, such as income and education.[8] Lifestyle analysis provides a broad view of buyers because it encompasses numerous characteristics related to people's activities, interests and opinions (see Table 7.5). It can be thought of as going beyond a simple understanding of personality. Marketing Insight 7.1 reveals how CACI has developed a lifestyle database to assist marketers.

Psychographics is the main technique used to measure lifestyle. However, its use continues to be limited because psychographic variables are more difficult to measure accurately than are other types of segmentation variables. In addi-

Table 7.5 Characteristics related to activities, interests and opinions

Activities	Interests	Opinions
Work	Family	Themselves
Hobbies	Home	Social issues
Social events	Job	Politics
Holidays	Community	Business
Entertainment	Recreation	Economics
Club membership	Fashion	Education
Community	Food	Products
Shopping	Media	Future
Sports	Achievements	Culture

SOURCE: Reprinted, adapted from Joseph Plummer, "The concept and application of life style segmentation", *Journal of Marketing*, January 1974, p. 34. Reprinted by permission of the American Marketing Association.

tion, the relationships between psychographic variables and consumers' needs are sometimes obscure and unproven, and the segments that result from psychographic segmentation may not be reachable.[9] For example, a marketer may determine that highly compulsive individuals want a certain type of clothing. However, no specific stores or particular media—such as television or radio programmes, newspapers or magazines—appeal precisely to this group and this group alone. Psychographic variables can sometimes offer a useful way of better understanding segments that have been defined using other base variables.

Product Related Behavioural Characteristics

Marketers can also segment markets on the basis of an aspect of consumers' behaviour towards the product. This might relate to the way the particular product is used or purchased, or perhaps to the benefits consumers require from it.

Purchase behaviour can be a useful way of distinguishing between groups of customers, giving marketers insight into the most appropriate marketing mix. For example, brand loyal customers may require a different kind of treatment from those who switch between brands. On-pack sales promotions are often geared towards building loyalty in brand switchers.

The occasion on which customers buy a particular product may impact upon product choice because in different sets of circumstances different product selection criteria may be applied. For instance, a customer who replaces a car tyre in an emergency will probably be less concerned about price than one who is routinely maintaining his or her car.

Benefit segmentation The division of a market according to the benefits consumers want from the product

Benefit segmentation is the division of a market according to the benefits consumers want from the product.[10] Although most types of market segmentation are based on the assumption that there is a relationship between the variable and customers' needs, benefit segmentation is different in that the benefits the customers seek *are* their product needs. By determining the benefits desired, marketers may be able to divide people into groups seeking certain sets of benefits.

The effectiveness of benefit segmentation depends on several conditions. First, the benefits people seek must be identifiable. Second, using these benefits, marketers must be able to divide people into recognisable segments. Finally, one or more of the resulting segments must be accessible to the companies' marketing efforts.

Home Search Turns to Lifestyle Targeting

Lifestyles uk is CACI's lifestyle database which is designed to enable clients to target over 44 million consumers by around 300 different lifestyle characteristics. These range from charity concerns, consumption patterns, financial matters, health, holidays, to household characteristics and personal information, to newspaper readership, motoring and even pet ownership. A company can select any combination of these variables in order to identify interested consumers. These could be consumers with similar lifestyle traits to existing customers, or they could be consumers exhibiting a different lifestyle to enable the company to expand or diversify its customer base.

The *Lifestyles uk* standard selections include:

Charity concerns	Cancer · Children · Disabled · Disaster relief · Elderly · Environment · Homeless · Human rights · Medical · Mental health · Pets · Religious · Third world · Wildlife
Charity donors	Less than £25 · £25–£49 · £50–£99 · £100–£200 · over £200 · By post · Committed givers · Single gift donors
Finance	Never pay credit card in full · Rarely pay credit card in full · Usually pay credit card in full · Always pay credit card in full · Charge card consider · Charge card have · Credit card consider · Credit card have · Debit card consider · Debit card have · Type of card – affinity · Type of card – gold/platinum · Life Insurance consider · Life insurance have · Loan for consolidation · Loan for spending · Need personal loan – possibly · Need personal loan – yes · Shop for loan – bank branch · Shop for loan – direct mail · Shop for loan - newspaper · Shop for loan – radio/television · Employer's pension · Own funded pension · State pension · Personal pension · Personal pension consider · Consider a will · Have a will · Funeral plan consider · Funeral plan have · Current account consider · Current account have · Deposit account have · Regular savings consider · Regular savings have · Child savings consider · Child savings have · PEP consider · PEP have · TESSA consider · TESSA have · Savings/Investments – Growth Bonds · Savings/Investments – Guaranteed Income Bonds · Stocks and shares consider · Stocks and shares have · Unit trust consider · Unit trust have · Lump sum investment under £5,000 · Lump sum investment £5,001 to £10,000 · Lump sum investment over £10,001 · Mortgage consider · Mortgage have · Possibly change account · Dissatisfied with bank · Telephone bank consider · Telephone bank have
General	Family income £0–£9,999 · Family income £10,000–£19,999 · Family income £20,000–£29,999 · Family income £30,000–£49,999 · Family Income £50,000–£79,999 · Family Income £80,000+ · Length of residence 0–2 years · Length of residence 3–5 years · Length of residence 6–10 years · Length of residence 11+ years · Number of cars 0 · Number of cars 1 · Number of cars 2+ · Number of children 0 · Number of children 1–2 · Number of children 3+ · Children aged 0–4 · Children aged 5–10 · Children aged 11–15 · Children aged 16+ · Pets–cat · Pets – dog
General personal	Change buildings insurance · Change car insurance · Change contents insurance · Change health insurance · Insurance legal consider · Insurance redundancy consider · Work from home · Accident compensation possibly · Accident/temp disability insurance consider · Critical illness insurance consider · Consider private medical insurance · Long term care insurance consider · Permanent disability insurance consider · Have company med insurance · Have private med insurance · Contact lenses · Spectacles · Health aids / alternative · Health aids / health foods
Holidays	Activity / lakes & mountains · Boating (all types) · Camping / Caravan · Car across channel · Coach tour · Cottage / villa / gltc etc. · Cruise · Package · skiing holidays · Theme parks all · Weekend break · Africa · Asia / Australia / NZ · Caribbean · Europe / Med · UK + Ireland · USA/Canada · Travel insurance direct · Travel insurance indirect · Business flights frequent · Business flights occasional · Cost up to £500 · Cost £501 to £1,000 · Cost £1,001 to £1,500 · Cost £1,501 to £2,000 · Cost £2,001 plus.
Home/Domestic	Double glazing have · Double glazing in 6/12 mths · Home owned · Home council owned · Home rented private · Home type bungalow · Home type detached · Home type flat/maisonette · Home type semi-detached · Home type terraced · Home Value 0–60k · Home Value 60–100k · Home Value 100–200k · Home Value 200k · When home built – pre 1920 · When home built – 1920 to 1945 · When home built – 1946 to 1954 · When home built – 1955 to 1979 · When home built – 1980 and later · Council tax A/B · Council tax C/D · Council tax E/F · Council tax G/H · International calls never · International calls occasionally · International calls regularly · International calls frequently · Cable phone have · Cable TV have · Internet service consider · Internet service have · Satellite TV have · Security system have · Building insurance not tied · Building insurance tied · Consider mobile phone · Have mobile phone · Have dishwasher · Have e-mail at home · Have e-mail at school · Have e-mail at work · Have Microwave · Have camcorder · Central Heating Fuel Bottled Gas · Central Heating Fuel Coal · Central Heating Fuel Electricity · Central Heating Fuel Mains Gas · Central Heating Fuel Oil · Central Heating Fuel Other Types · Elec Supply Cost Dissat./V.Dissat · Elec. Supply Cost Neither · Elec Supply Cost V. Sat./Sat. · Elec. Supply Customer Dissat./V.Dissat. · Elec. Supply Customer Neither · Elec. Supply Customer V. Sat./Sat. · Elec. Supply Environment Dissat./V.Dissat. · Elec. Supply Environment Neither · Elec. Supply Environment V. Sat./Sat. · Elec. Supply General Dissat/V. Dissat. · Elec. Supply General Neither · Elec. Supply General V. Sat./Sat. · Change

Product usage is another method marketers sometimes use to segment their customers. Individuals can be divided into users and non-users of a particular product. Users can then be classified further as heavy, moderate or light. To satisfy a specific user group, marketers sometimes create a distinctive product, set special prices or initiate special promotion and distribution activities. Thus airlines such as British Airways or KLM offer frequent flier programmes to reward their regular customers with free trips and discounts for car hire and hotel accommodation. Light users or non-users of products often receive little attention from companies. There is a tendency sometimes to dismiss these groups when developing a marketing programme. For example, research in the holiday industry

	Utilities Suppliers Electricity • Change Utilities Suppliers Mains Gas • Change Utilities Suppliers Telephone • Change Utilities Suppliers Water • Electricity Quarterly bill Under £75 • Electricity Quarterly bill £75 to £99 • Electricity Quarterly bill £100 to £150 • Electricity Quarterly bill £150 Plus • Gas Quarterly Bill Under £75 • Gas Quarterly Bill £75 to £99 • Gas Quarterly Bill £100 to £150 • Gas Quarterly Bill £150 plus • Telephone Quarterly Bill Under £75 • Telephone Quarterly Bill £75 to £99 • Telephone Quarterly Bill £100 to £150 • Telephone Quarterly Bill £150 plus • Water Quarterly Bill Under £75 • Water Quarterly Bill £75 to £99 • Water Quarterly Bill £100 to £150 • Water Quarterly Bill £150 Plus • Pay bills by direct debit • Save utility bills – electricity • Save utility bills – gas • Save utility bills – telephone • Mercury phone have • Phone charge card • Appliance insurance consider
Interests	Angling • Boating • Bicycles & cycling • Bingo • Book club consider • Book club member • Cinema • Cookery • Current affairs • DIY • Fashion/Clothes • Football pools • Gardening • Listening to music • Lottery • Magazines subscribe • Men's Interests • Mother & baby • Motoring • Pub • Romantic fiction • Skiing/Snowboarding • Television 0–2 hours • Television 3–4 hours • Television 5+ hours • Theatre/arts • Watching videos • Wine • Women's interests
Leisure	Computer consider • Computer have • Computer games • Music: classical • Music: folk/country • Music: jazz • Music: pop etc. • Music: easy listening/vocal • National Trust member
Sports	Football • Golf • Rugby • Watery
Motoring	Annual mileage under 2,500 • Annual mileage 2,501 to 5,000 • Annual mileage 5,001 to 12,000 • Annual mileage 12,001 plus • Car insurance cost up to £299 • Car insurance cost £300 to £499 • Car insurance cost £500 and over • Car type 4 x 4 • Car type estate • Car type MPV • Car type saloon • Company car • Company car / own choice • Private car • Bought car new • Bought car used • Next car new • Next car used • Replace car within 3 months • Replace car within 6 months • Finance private car – cash • Finance private car – hire purchase • Finance private car – personal lease • Finance private car – personal loan • Next car price under £5,000 • Next car price £5,000 to £9,999 • Next car price £10,000 to £14,999 • Next car price £15,000 to £19,999 • Next car price £20,000 to £24,999 • Next car price £25,000 and over • Motor assistance • No claims – none • No claims – 1 year • No claims – 2 years • No claims – 3 years • No claims – 4 years and over • Insurance arrange own • Insurance direct • Insurance through broker
Newspapers	Daily Express • Daily Mail • Daily Mirror/Record • Daily Telegraph • FT • Guardian • Independent • Star • Sun • Times • Sunday Express • Mail on Sunday • Sunday Mirror • Sunday Telegraph • Observer • Independent on Sunday • The People • News of the World • Sunday Times
Shopping	Up-market catalogues Down-market catalogues • Mail order music • Mail order books • Mail order fashion • Mail order garden products • Mail order hampers • Mail order videos • Mail order film processing • Mail order buyer • Herbal tea • Low calorie hot chocolate • Washing powders • Lager 1– 4 pints/bottles p/wk • Lager 5-8 pints/bottles p/wk • Lager 9-12 pints/bottles p/wk • lager 14-24 pints/bottles p/wk • Lager 25+ pints/bottles p/wk • Spirits 1 to 2 bottles per year • Spirits – 3 to 4 bottles per year • Spirits – 5 or more bottles per year • Wine 0–1 per week • Wine 2-3 per week • Wine 4-7 per week • Wine 7+ per week • Own brand (use with caution!) • Supermarket spend under £20 p/wk • Supermarket spend £20 to £40 p/wk • Supermarket spend £41 to £60 p/wk • Supermarket spend £61 to £80 p/wk • Supermarket spend £81 to £100 p/wk • Supermarket spend over £100 p/wk • Cosmetics – heavy user • Cosmetics – medium user • Cosmetics – light user • Washing/styling hair <15 mins per day • Washing/styling hair 15 to 30 mins per day • Washing/styling hair 30+ mins per day.

SOURCE: Copyright © CACI Limited, 2000. Reprinted by permission.

Home Service specialises in insurance products co-branded with electricity and water companies. Currently recruiting around ten thousand new members every week via direct mail and leaflet drops through letterboxes, Home Service has utilised CACI's *Lifestyles uk* database to profile existing customers of each of its core products. With these profiles, the full database of 44 million consumers has been screened to identify those non-users who match the desired customer lifestyle characteristics. These consumers are then mailed with details of Home Service's insurance product. In this way, Home Service has utilised a mix of demographic, socio-economic, geographic, consumption and lifestyle data to tightly define the target market for each of its products and to help search CACI's database for prospective customers fitting the target segment profile criteria.

SOURCES: CACI web site, 1998; *Lifestyles uk*, CACI, 1997; *Marketing Systems Today*, 13 (1), 1998, p. 11; Home Service Ltd, 1998.

tends to focus on feedback from current customers, often forgetting to question why non-users failed to buy.

How customers apply the product may also determine segmentation. To satisfy customers who use a product in a certain way, some feature—say, packaging, size, texture or colour—may have to be designed with special care to make the product easier to use, more convenient or more environmentally friendly. For instance, Lever Brothers and Procter & Gamble are focusing more and more on the development of re-fill packs of detergents and other household products, to cater for increasing consumer concerns about the environment.

The varying attitude of customers towards products constitutes another set of variables that can be used to segment markets. Clothing retailers like River Island and Benetton are particularly conscious of this. While one customer seeks outfits that are practical and comfortable, another is concerned with achieving a highly fashionable image.

As this brief discussion shows, consumer markets can be divided according to numerous characteristics. Ultimately, the choices marketers make will depend on a host of market and company factors.

Variables for Segmenting Business-to-Business Markets

Like consumer markets, business-to-business (industrial or organisational) markets are often segmented, but the marketer's aim is to satisfy the needs of organisations for products. Marketers may segment business-to-business markets according to geographic location, type of organisation, company age and size, product type and product use. Marketing Insight 7.2 shows how construction equipment company JCB segments its market.

There are various reasons why businesses may find it difficult to segment their markets.[11] The particular characteristics of the market or the distribution structure in place may restrict the types of segment bases that can be used. For example, many European car manufacturers are dependent upon the fleet car market. This market tends to be structured on the basis of car engine and vehicle size, with companies providing their more senior managers with more powerful, larger and expensive vehicles. It is likely that customers would resist a move away from this accepted structure by the car manufacturers, who are therefore not in a position to use possibly contradictory segmentation approaches. Various segmentation approaches have been developed to try to make it easier for companies to deal with these kinds of constraints.[12]

Whatever the approach adopted, just as in consumer markets, some segment bases are easier to measure and apply than others.[13] For example, it is much more straightforward to segment on the basis of company size, which is a measurable and visible characteristic, than on the basis of buying centre structure (see Chapter 5), which may be much more difficult to appraise. Table 7.6 provides an overview of the variables for segmenting business-to-business markets and illustrates the relative ease with which they can be measured. Variables at the base of the table are easier to measure and more objective than those at the top.

Company Demographics Variables relating to the type of business or industry, geographic location, company age and size are probably the most widely used segmentation variables in business-to-business markets.

A company sometimes segments a market by the types of businesses within that market, perhaps on the basis of industry area or SIC code (see Chapter 5 and Table 5.3). Different types of organisations often require different product features, distribution systems, price structures and selling strategies. Given these variables, a company may either concentrate on a single segment with one marketing mix (concentration strategy) or focus on several groups with multiple mixes (multi-segment strategy). A paint manufacturer could segment customers into several groups, such as paint wholesalers, do-it-yourself retail outlets, vehicle manufacturers, decorators and housing developers.

The demand for some consumer products can vary considerably by geographic area because of differences in climate, terrain, customer preferences or similar factors. Demand for business-to-business products also varies according to geographic location. For example, the producers of certain types of timber divide their markets geographically because their customers' needs vary regionally. Geographic

Digging for Industrial Segments: The JCB Experience

Construction and agricultural equipment manufacturers produce a diversity of machines designed to cut and dig, carry and load, tunnel and excavate, climb on tracks up severe slopes or travel on public highways at speeds of up to 45 miles per hour. Some are designed to carry many tonnes of earth or rubble, others only small loads in often confined spaces.

The product ranges of most manufacturers have expanded gradually. Some companies have diversified and added new product groups, while others concentrate on developing improved models in existing product groups. Sales and marketing activities are often geared towards the different product groups, with teams of managers handling one set of products across national borders and customer groups. Distribution can be set up in a similar way: JCB customers may have to deal with several salespeople—even different dealers—when sourcing machines from different product groups.

The customers are almost as varied as the product technology. Their needs are also diverse: the contractor, who wants a few telescopic handlers and backhoe loaders; the farmer, who uses harvesters, tractors, combines and telehandlers, but who perhaps purchases only tractors and telescopic handlers; the plant hirer, whose staple products are backhoe loaders, skid-steer loaders, mini-excavators and telescopic handlers, which are rented out to contractors and individual users; the large house building and quarrying companies, which have purchasing officers and large fleets. In general, the industry groups customers by product technology, industrial sector and country. These divisions have arisen historically for practical reasons and do not necessarily relate to different customer needs.

Although much of the company's success is built on the backhoe yellow digger, JCB has a wide range of other construction products. In early 1993, the company launched its new skid-steer range, positioning it as the safest and most environmentally friendly in the industry. At the same time JCB realised that the needs of buyers of skid steers and other small equipment, such as the mini-excavator and smaller backhoe loaders, could be better served by a single selling and marketing effort, instead of

The Customers	The Products
Agriculture	All-terrain trucks
Civil engineering	Articulated dump trucks
Contractors	Asphalt finishers
Defence departments	Attachments
Earthmoving	Backhoe loaders
House building	Combines
Industrial services	Crawler dozers
Landscaping	Crawler excavators
Local authorities	Crawler loaders
Manufacturing services	Fork lifts
Mining and quarrying	Harvesters
Plant hire	Mini-excavators
Public utilities	Motor graders
Tool hire	Motor scrapers
Waste disposal	Rigid dump trucks
	Rough terrain lift trucks
	Skid-steer loaders
	Spreaders
	Telescopic handlers
	Tractors
	Wheeled excavators
	Wheeled loaders

different sales teams and promotional campaigns for each product type. With this in mind, the company has recently launched its Compact Division to handle the sales and service of these smaller machines.

The Compact Division cuts across traditional industry sectorisation of customers and selling, recognising that users of smaller equipment, irrespective of their business sector or country of origin, share common needs and expectations. These customers require a sales, service and distribution operation geared specifically to their needs. JCB's use of targeting and market segmentation through its Compact Division has given the company a significant advantage in its market.

SOURCES: Tony McBurnie and David Clutterbuck, *Give Your Company the Marketing Edge* (London: Penguin Books, 1988); "The JCB experience", JCB, 1992; JCB company reports; Matthew Lynn, "Digging for victory", *Business,* October 1990, pp. 112–115.

segmentation may be especially appropriate for reaching industries that are concentrated in certain locations, for example, textiles in West Yorkshire, cutlery in Sheffield, brewing in Burton and lace in Nottingham, or information technology

Table 7.6 Variables for segmenting business-to-business markets

Personal Characteristics of Buyers

Just as in consumer markets, the demographics, personality and lifestyle of those individuals in the buying centre impact upon purchasing decisions, practices, attitudes towards risk and loyalty to suppliers.

Situational Factors

The urgency of purchase, size of order or product application can play an important role in the choices that are made.

Purchasing Approach

Buying centre structure (centralised/decentralised), buying policies (sealed bidding, service contracts, leasing), nature of existing relationships (focus on new or existing customers), balance of power among decision-makers and buying criteria (quality, delivery, service, price, product range, innovation) may shape an organisation's purchase decisions.

Operating Variables

The technologies applied by an organisation, the manner in which products are used or customer capabilities can fundamentally affect purchase choice.

Demographics

Company age, location, industry (SIC code) and size are likely to alter product requirements.

(IT) along the M4 corridor in England. Examples of such concentration in Europe include heavy industry around Lille or in the Ruhr Valley and banking in Zurich.

A business's size may affect its purchasing procedures and the types and quantities of products it wants. To reach a segment of a particular size, marketers may have to adjust one or more marketing mix components. For example, customers who buy in extremely large quantities are sometimes offered discounts.

Operating Variables Customer requirements can be affected in a range of ways by different operating variables such as the technology applied by the buying organisation or the product types used. Certain products, especially raw materials such as steel, petrol, plastics and timber, are used in numerous ways. Sometimes the technology used by a company will play an important role. How a company uses products affects the types and amounts it purchases, as well as the method of making the purchase.[14] For example, computers are used for engineering purposes, basic scientific research, business operations such as word processing and bookkeeping, plus Internet access and games in the home. A computer manufacturer may segment the computer market by types of use because organisations' needs for computer hardware and software depend on the purpose for which the products are purchased.

Purchasing Approach Although it may be difficult for a company to appraise the buying approach of its customers, this is nonetheless sometimes an appropriate way for business-to-business markets to be segmented. The characteristics of the buying centre, including its structure (where the balance of buying power lies), and the nature of any buying policies can all affect the product requirements of customers.

For example, suppliers of building materials must organise their sales efforts to satisfy a wide array of customer types who organise their buying activities in vastly different ways. While dealing with large buyers such as Wimpey or Tarmac will require an understanding of a relatively complex buying structure, small local builders may be perfectly satisfied with a much simpler supply arrangement.

Situational Factors Sometimes it is appropriate to segment a business-to-business market on the basis of situational factors such as the urgency or size of the order. How urgently the order is required may have an impact on the importance a customer attaches to particular product features. For example, if a robot on a car production line has broken down, bringing the entire production process to a standstill, the price of replacement parts to fix it may be less important than their availability. However, if the same part is being replaced as part of a routine service, price may be the most important factor. The size and frequency of different orders can be effective segmentation variables because they have ramifications concerning the way the customer relationship is handled. For example, a university that regularly orders vast amounts of stationery would expect a different level of service than a small business that only infrequently buys small quantities of paper and envelopes.

Personal Characteristics Although individuals involved in business-to-business buying may not have as much control over the products and services selected as when they are making purchases for personal or family use, their individual characteristics still play a role in the preferences they demonstrate. For this reason it is sometimes appropriate to segment business-to-business markets on the basis of the characteristics of individuals within the buying centre. For example, the demographics, personality and lifestyle of managers tasked with buying a selection of new office furniture will influence the preferred designs. If power in the buying centre rests with one senior manager who strongly dislikes modern designs, this will influence the final selection of products.

Single Variable or Multivariable Segmentation

Selecting the appropriate variable for market segmentation is an important marketing management decision, because the variable is the primary factor in defining the target market.[15] So far, segmentation by one variable has been discussed. In fact, more than one variable can be used, and marketers must decide on the number of variables to include.

Single variable segmentation, which is the simplest to perform, is achieved by using only one variable, for example, country. However, the sales of one product in different countries will differ and the numbers of relevant consumers in each country will vary. A single characteristic gives marketers only moderate precision in designing a marketing mix to satisfy individuals in a specific segment.

To achieve **multivariable segmentation,** more than one characteristic is used to divide a total market (see Figure 7.7). Notice in the figure that the market is segmented by three variables: annual income, population density and volume usage. The people in the highlighted segment earn more than £40,000, are urban dwellers and are heavy users. Multivariable segmentation provides more information about the individuals in each segment than does single variable segmentation. This additional information may allow a company to develop a marketing mix that will satisfy customers in a given segment more precisely.

The major disadvantage of multivariable segmentation is that the larger the number of variables used, the greater the number of resulting segments likely to be identified. This proliferation reduces the sales potential of many of the segments. Another disadvantage is that it may be more complicated to resource and

Single variable segmentation
Segmentation achieved by using only one variable, the simplest type of segmentation to perform

Multivariable segmentation
Segmentation using more than one characteristic to divide a total market

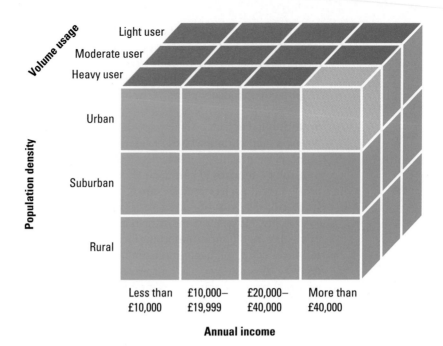

Figure 7.7 Multivariable segmentation

manage the proliferation of segments that result. While the use of additional variables can help create and maintain a more exact and satisfying marketing mix, when deciding on single variable or multivariable segmentation, a marketing manager must consider whether additional variables will actually help improve the company's marketing mix. If using a second or third variable does not provide information that ensures greater precision, there is little reason to spend more money to gain information about the extra variables. Where many variables are deployed, it may be prudent to utilise multivariate statistical techniques—such as cluster analysis[16]—to assist in the grouping of customers into market segments.

Segmentation Analysis Stages

Segmentation analysis invariably involves several stages[17]:

Objectives—Marketers must know the purpose of the exercise and have clear objectives.

Data—The information required for the analysis and decision-making must be specified and collected. This often involves a mix of qualitative and quantitative research. The qualitative phase develops a robust view of consumer attitudes, motives, behaviour and perceptions—often based around one-to-one interviews or focus group discussions (see Chapter 6). The quantitative research involves larger samples and statistical analysis of questionnaire responses to identify segments more reliably.

Analysis—There are various statistical packages such as SPSS containing the required routines. Factor analysis, conjoint analysis and particularly cluster analysis are some of the more commonly used techniques for analysing the collected data.[18] Multidimensional scaling (MDS) is widely used in product positioning studies. However, these are complex techniques and should not be applied by marketing personnel unfamiliar with the required statistical rigour. These techniques will all provide an "answer", but if not handled competently and sensibly, the proposed solutions will not be valid.[19]

Interpretation—The various statistical techniques all provide options in terms of proposed solutions. Marketers must interpret the suggested schemes to ensure any adopted segmentation scheme is statistically valid (complies with the relevant statistical significance tests) and managerially or intuitively valid, and that it presents market segments which are effective. Ultimately, the analysis should be sufficiently rigorous as to comply with the acknowledged statistical validity tests. However, any recommendation likely to be implemented must also be sensible in the view of managers.[20]

Recommendation—The final proposed solution must be packaged first for the internal audience of senior and line managers expected to approve the segments and then actioned for the external audience of distributors and customers. A clear positioning strategy is integral to this recommendation.

Segmentation Effectiveness

Whatever base variables are used, haphazard implementation can lead to ineffective market segmentation, missed opportunities and inappropriate investment. To avoid such difficulties marketers should take note of the following criteria. The first is that there must be real differences in the needs of consumers for the product or service. There is no value in segmenting a homogeneous market. Equally, dissimilar consumers in terms of their needs and purchasing behaviour must not be grouped together in the same market segment. In addition, the segments revealed must be:

- *measurable*—easy to identify and measure. Some basis must be found for effectively separating individuals into groups or segments with relatively homogeneous product or service needs.
- *substantial*—large enough to be sufficiently profitable to justify developing and maintaining a specific marketing mix.
- *accessible*—easy to reach with the marketing mix developed. For example, the promotional effort should target the relevant consumers.
- *stable*—the question of segment stability over time is not often addressed. If companies are to make strategic decisions on the basis of revealed segments, they need to be reasonably certain that those segments will be around long enough for action to be taken.
- *useful*—the selected segments must be meaningful to the managers tasked with operationalising them and be likely to enable the company to better satisfy its target market.

Using market segmentation also requires a good deal of common sense. It is often difficult for companies to implement totally new segmentation schemes because they would be at odds with the existing marketing structures and ways of doing things. In such cases companies sometimes choose to make minor changes to what is already in place.

Profiling Market Segments

Whatever the variable, or combination of variables, used to group customers, a more comprehensive understanding of the characteristics of individuals is likely to be required. For example, a company that segments the market for shoes on the basis of age, focusing on customers in their late teens, would do well to understand as much as possible about its particular target group in other respects. What reference groups influence them? Where do they live? Where and when do they shop? What social background are they from? What motivates them? The more comprehensive the image developed, the better the opportunity to develop an effective marketing mix with maximum appeal.

Profiling *The task of building up a fuller picture of the target segments*

Descriptors *Variables used to profile or build a fuller picture of target segments*

Profiling is the task of building up a fuller picture of target segments, and the variables being used in the description are termed **descriptors.** The types of descriptors available to marketers are broadly the same as the variables used to segment markets in the first place, that is, demographics, socio-economics and so on. This is sometimes a cause of confusion for students who struggle to remember whether they are dealing with base or descriptor variables. It helps to note that while base variables should discriminate between customer needs, descriptors are simply used to enrich the picture, to help summarise what else can be gleaned about the customers in a particular segment. This gives added inspiration to the creative team developing the product and promotional material and helps to fine-tune decisions on price and distribution. Overall, profiling segments in this way ensures that the impact of the marketing mix on the customer is maximised. If segments are not properly profiled, it is unlikely sales personnel, advertising agency staff or senior managers will fully comprehend the proposed segmentation scheme. Therefore its effective implementation may be jeopardised.

Targeting Strategies

Targeting *The decision about which market segment(s) a business decides to prioritise for its sales and marketing efforts*

Targeting is the decision about which market segment(s) a business decides to prioritise for its sales and marketing efforts. Decisions about targeting centre on two major segmentation strategies: the concentration strategy and the multisegment strategy. Whether a company chooses to adopt one or the other, the decision should be based on a clear understanding of company capabilities and resources, the nature of the competition and the characteristics of the product markets in question.

Concentration Strategy

Concentration strategy *A process by which a business directs its marketing effort towards a single market segment through one marketing mix*

When a business directs its marketing efforts towards a single market segment by creating and maintaining one marketing mix, it is employing a **concentration strategy.** The fashion house Chanel, for example, targets the exclusive fashion segment, directing its marketing effort towards high income customers who want to own the most chic apparel. The chief advantage of the concentration strategy is that it allows a company to specialise. The company can analyse the characteristics and needs of a distinct customer group and then focus all its energies on satisfying that group's needs. A company may be able to generate a large sales volume by reaching a single segment. In some cases, concentrating on a single segment permits a company with limited resources to compete with much larger organisations, which may have overlooked some smaller segments.

Concentrating on one segment also means that a company puts "all its eggs in one basket"—clearly a disadvantage. If a company's sales depend on a single segment and the segment's demand for the product declines, the company's financial strength declines as well. When the North American sports coupé market declined in the late 1980s, Porsche found itself in severe trouble as it had no exposure to other parts of the car market. Moreover, when a company penetrates one segment and becomes well entrenched, its popularity may keep it from moving into other segments. For example, it is hard to imagine that Rolex would start producing low cost watches, or that Swatch might compete at the high end of the luxury watch segment.

Figure 7.8   Multisegment
strategy

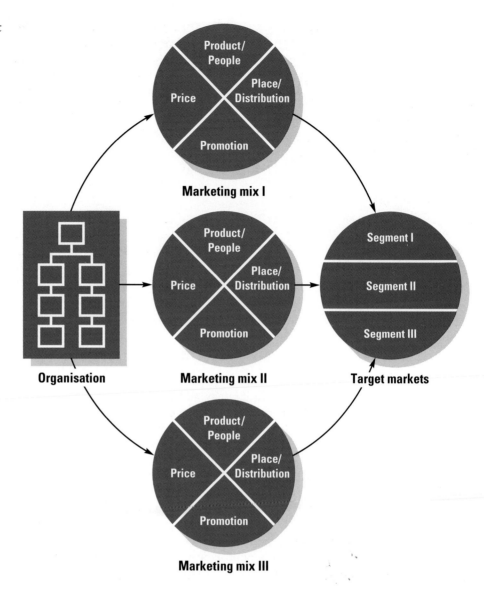

Marketing mix I

Organisation   **Marketing mix II**   **Target markets**

Marketing mix III

Multisegment Strategy

Multisegment strategy   A strategy
by which a business directs its marketing
efforts towards two or more market segments by developing a marketing mix
for each

With a **multisegment strategy** (see Figure 7.8), a business directs its marketing
efforts at two or more market segments by developing a marketing mix for each
selected segment. Sometimes this is a natural progression from the successful
application of a concentration strategy in one market segment. For example,
Jockey underwear has traditionally been aimed at one segment: men. However,
the company has expanded its efforts and now markets underwear for women
and children as well. The marketing mixes used for a multisegment strategy may
vary as to product/service differences, place/distribution methods, promotion
methods and prices. The majority of users of Gatwick Airport near London are
packged holiday travellers. A significant minority, however, are business users as
targeted in Figure 7.9.

A business can usually increase its sales in the aggregate market through a multisegment strategy because the organisation's mixes are being aimed at more people. For example, a company with excess production capacity may find a

Figure 7.9 Targeting strategy. Gatwick Airport targets its business users.
SOURCE: Courtesy of Gatwick Airport.

multisegment strategy advantageous because the sale of products to additional segments may absorb this excess capacity. On the other hand, a multisegment strategy often demands a greater number of production processes, materials and people; thus production costs may be higher than with a concentration strategy. Keep in mind also that a company using a multisegment strategy ordinarily experiences higher marketing costs. Because a multisegment strategy usually requires more research and several different promotion plans and place/distribution methods, the costs of planning, organising, implementing and controlling marketing activities increase.

Irrespective of whether or not a company chooses to adopt a concentration strategy or a multisegment strategy, when faced with the decision about whether or not to enter a new segment, it must consider a number of issues (see Figure 7.10). These issues include (1) the nature of the needs and wants of end users; (2) the size, structure and future potential of the segment; (3) the availability of company resources; (4) the intensity of the competition; (5) the size of the company's existing market share; and (6) the possibility of any production/marketing scale economies.

Figure 7.10 sums up the core factors affecting the choice of target market strategy. A company may recognise that a fit between its products or capabilities and target customer needs is stronger and more "marketable" in one market segment than in another, deeming the former to be more attractive. There are occasions when corporate strategy decisions to expand into new areas, markets, or territories may mean the converse, as when a company purposively targets markets where currently product and marketing proposition have a poor fit with customer needs, with the intention of rectifying such shortcomings. Certain markets' size or value makes them attractive, as does a company's existing or potential sizeable market share. There may be economies of scale available in targeting a particular market segment alongside related ones, so that certain aspects—but not all—of the production, sales and marketing activity may be shared. (Please

Figure 7.10 Factors
affecting choice of
target market strategy.
SOURCE: Data from D.
Cravens, *Strategic Marketing*
(Homewood, Ill.: Irwin,
1982).

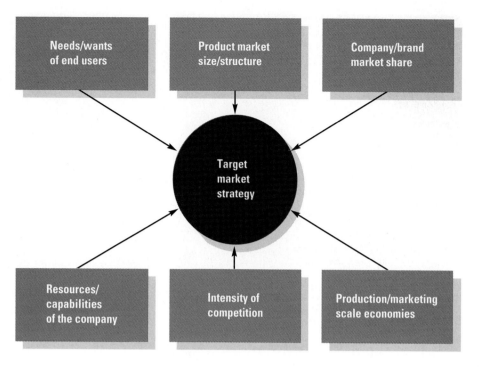

note: if truly homogeneous market segments have been identified, then each segment will require certain unique aspects of sales and marketing activity. If two segments really can be treated identically in terms of tactical marketing mix programmes, then they are probably one segment.) Highly intensive and well established competition may to some companies be something of a "turn off", whereas others may take such competitor activity to be indicative of extensive market growth and business opportunity. Finally, a company even the size of Ford or GM does not have the time, people or financial resources to develop a marketing mix for every single segment in the vehicle market. Available resources play a significant role in management's target market decisions.

There are many factors considered by companies determining which markets to target and which target market strategy to deploy. Figure 7.10 is nevertheless a useful summary of the core factors. Marketing planning (see Chapter 22) guru Malcolm McDonald suggests[21] a variety of issues to consider when determining which and how many target market segments to prioritise. These include market, competition, financial and economic, technological, socio-political and regulatory factors—the forces of the marketing environment (see Chapter 2) and core market trends:

- *Market factors*—size (money, units or both); growth rate per annum; diversity of the market; sensitivity to price, service features and external factors; cyclicality; seasonality; bargaining power of upstream and downstream suppliers.
- *Competition*—types of competitors; degree of concentration; changes in type and mix; entries and exits; changes in market shares; substitution by new technology; degrees and types of integration.
- *Financial and economic*—contribution margins; leveraging factors such as economies of scale and experience; barriers to entry or exit; capacity utilisation.
- *Technology*—maturity and volatility; complexity; differentiation; patents and copyrights; manufacturing process technology required.

Companies' Market Attractiveness Criteria

First Tier:

- Profitability

Second Tier:

- Market growth
- Market size
- Likely customer satisfaction
- Sales volume

Third Tier:

- Likelihood of a sustainable differential advantage over rivals
- Ease of access for the business
- Opportunities in the industry
- Product differentiation
- Competitive rivalry

- Market share
- Relative strength/key functions
- Customers' price sensitivity
- Customer image of company

Fourth Tier:

- Technological factors
- Fit with business strategy
- Stability of market
- Environmental factors
- Threat of substitutes
- Barriers to entry
- Negotiating power of buyers
- Ease of profiling customers
- Supplier power

SOURCE: Reprinted with permission from S. Dibb and L. Simkin, "Marketing planning: still barriers to overcome", European Marketing Academy Conference Proceedings, Warwick Business School, University of Warwick, UK.

Table 7.7   Market attractiveness factors adopted by UK companies

- *Socio-political and regulatory*—social attitudes and trends; influence with pressure groups, government and regulatory bodies; laws, government and EU regulations; human factors such as unionisation and community acceptance.

A recent survey[22] of marketing practices in the largest UK companies revealed an interesting set of variables utilised in determining target market attractiveness (see Table 7.7). This study revealed the extent to which UK businesses are overly restricted by *The City*'s short-termism and the emphasis placed by financial journalists and pundits on performance only in terms of profitability in the most recent few months. US, German and South East Asian financial markets tend not to be quite so short-termist in thinking.[23] Outside the UK, businesses worry about market share *and* profitability, not just for today and tomorrow, but for a few years to come! A market may well be targeted because of its future potential, not just because of current sales. It is reassuring to see customer satisfaction, sustainable differential/competitive advantage and likely product differentiation well up the list of factors considered in the UK, as Chapter 1 explained the importance in marketing of satisfying customers, outpacing competitors and developing differentiation. It is not so good to see the marketing environment and issues relating to non-direct competitor activity so low down the list. Businesses really should adopt a balanced list of criteria, mixing short term and longer term issues and internal and external factors—market characteristics, financial considerations and trends.

Positioning

Figure 7.3 illustrated the link between market segmentation, targeting and positioning. Having identified the segments in a market and decided on which segment (or segments) to target, a company must position its product, service or idea. According to Wind,

> a product's positioning is the place a product occupies in a given market, as perceived by the relevant group of customers; that group of customers is known as the target segment of the market.[24]

Harrison states that the positioning of a product is

> the sum of those attributes normally ascribed to it by the consumers—its standing, its quality, the type of people who use it, its strengths, its weaknesses, any other unusual or memorable characteristics it may possess, its price and the value it represents.[25]

Positioning The process of creating an image for a product in the minds of target customers

Positioning starts with a product—a piece of merchandise, a service, a company, an institution or even a person. **Positioning** is not what is done to the product—it is what is created in the minds of the target customers; the product is positioned in the minds of these customers and is given an image.[26] There may be a few cosmetic changes to the product—to its name, price, packaging, styling or channel of distribution—but these are to facilitate the successful promotion of the image desired by the target customers. The product must be perceived by the selected target customers to have a distinct image and position vis-à-vis its competitors. Product differentiation is widely viewed as the key to successful marketing; the product must stand out and have a clearly defined positioning.

Determining a Position

Positioning is based on customers' perceptions and is therefore only partly within the control of marketers. Positionings are described by variables and within parameters that are important to the customers and are essentially selected by them. Price may be the key in grocery shopping, service level in selecting a bank, quality and reliability in buying computer hardware, value for money in choosing which theme park to visit. In-depth marketing research (often focus group discussions) is required if customer motivations and expectations in a particular market are to be fully understood. Management's intuition is not always sufficient. For example, research revealed that consumers often have to decide between replacement living room or dining room furniture and a family packaged holiday abroad. Managers at most leading furniture retailers perceived other furniture retailers to be their competitors, when in reality they were additionally competing for consumer's disposable income against other diverse product areas. In the budget-conscious sector of the furniture buying market, retailers believed only price to be important. In-depth research proved that value for money, a concept that includes product quality and durability in addition to price, was perceived to be the main purchase consideration.

Consumers generally assign positionings to a company or a product that is the market leader—and probably has the highest profile—and the limited number of competitors they can recollect are oriented to this market leader. For example, in the market for tomato ketchup, perceptions of brands are oriented towards market leader Heinz. Occasionally the brand consumers regard as the market leader may not be the genuine market leader in terms of market share, but simply the one most visible at that time, possibly because of heavy promotional exposure. Customers respond to the attributes of a product and to its promotional imagery, but the product's positioning as perceived by its target customers is affected by the reputation and image of the company,

Figure 7.11 Positioning map of hypothetical consumer preferences. SOURCE: From D. Knee and D. Walters, *Strategy in Retailing* (Herts, England: Philip Allan, 1985), p. 27. Reproduced by permission of Philip Allan, a division of Prentice-Hall International.

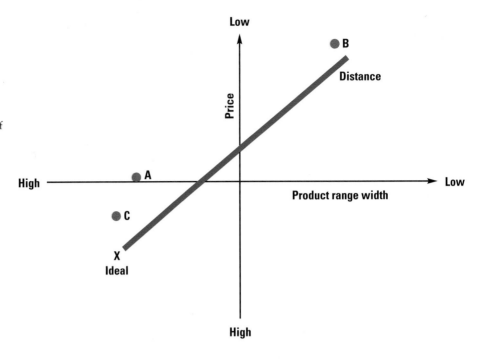

Perceptual mapping A tool used by marketers and marketing researchers to visually depict consumer perceptions and prioritising of brands and their perceived attributes

coupled with its other products, and by the activities of its competitors. For example, bad publicity, such as that experienced by British Airways following allegations of dirty tricks against Virgin Atlantic, can negatively affect a brand's positioning.

In-depth marketing research leads to an understanding of how consumers perceive different brands and companies, which marketing variables they believe to be most important and by what magnitude. **Perceptual mapping** is a tool commonly adopted by marketers and marketing researchers to visually depict such consumer perceptions and prioritising of brands and their perceived attributes. Figure 7.11 illustrates a hypothetical example in which consumers thought product range width and price were the key characteristics of the market. A cross marks the ideal position, with high product range width and above average price (typical of high quality shopping goods such as cameras or hi-fi systems). Brands (or companies) *A* and *C* are perceived as being relatively close to the ideal—their pricing policy does not fully match the image required—but brand (or company) *B* is viewed as being too cheap, with inadequate product range width. Figure 7.12 illustrates how consumers of children's wear in the UK realised that the positioning of Adams had shifted to reflect improvements in the quality of its merchandise, stores and personnel. Adams had successfully re-positioned its brand to move away from being perceived as a budget oriented retailer.

Steps in Determining a Positioning Plan

Although customers' perceptions play an important role in product positioning, the role of marketers is also crucial. There should be no mystique associated with positioning a product. Common sense and a step-by-step approach are essential in establishing a clear positioning for a product:

1. Define the segments in a particular market.
2. Decide which segment (or segments) to target.
3. Understand what the target consumers expect and believe to be the most important considerations when deciding on the purchase.

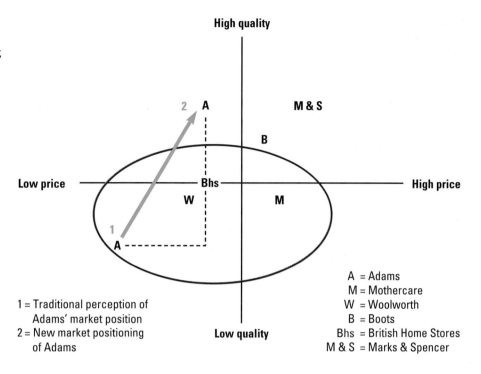

Figure 7.12 UK children's wear: positioning of major retailers, featuring the re-positioning of Adams

High quality

2 A

M & S

B

Low price ——————— Bhs ——————— High price

W   M

1

A

Low quality

1 = Traditional perception of
    Adams' market position
2 = New market positioning
    of Adams

A = Adams
M = Mothercare
W = Woolworth
B = Boots
Bhs = British Home Stores
M & S = Marks & Spencer

4. Develop a product (or products) that caters specifically for these needs and expectations.
5. Evaluate the positioning and images, as perceived by the target customers, of competing products in the selected market segment (or segments).
6. Select an image that sets the product (or products) apart from the competing products, thus ensuring that the chosen image matches the aspirations of the target customers. (The selected positioning and imagery must be credible: consumers would not believe Lada or Skoda if they promoted their cars in the same manner as Porsche or Lotus.)
7. Inform target consumers about the product. Although this is primarily a promotional task, it is also vital that the product is made readily available at the right price, through the development of the full marketing mix.

There are various options when determining a positioning. (1) The approach most plausible in terms of the consumer and the most defensible against competitors' marketing ploys is to identify product attributes or features which are superior, desirable and matched by few or no rivals. This is at the heart of the positioning deployed by Bang & Olufsen, BMW or Bosch. (2) The next best option is to identify key benefits encountered as a result of consumption, as illustrated by Anadin's painkiller advertising or Andrew's Salts saving the day from *that* hangover! If a product has no such distinctions or is lagging behind major rivals, there are other approaches, such as (3) emphasising specific usage occasions (Campbell's soups as a cooking ingredient), (4) depicting user groups (the Pepsi Generation), (5) deliberately adopting a head-to-head positioning against a rival ("Avis is No. 2, but we try harder" ran for over two decades), or if all else fails, (6) dissociating from direct rivals in order to develop a clear image and differentiation (Dr Pepper and 7 Up both try to persuade the marketplace they are fizzy and refreshing drinks, but not colas).

The final stage in developing a positioning in many instances is the determination of a suitable **positioning statement,** a plausible, memorable image-enhancing written summation of a product's or brand's desired stature. This should strike a chord with the targeted consumers; reflect the nature of the product, its branding and attributes; plus demonstrate to targeted consumers the business's understanding of customer needs—similar to a strapline in advertising. Everest double glazing's positioning statement is decades old, yet instantly recognisable: "Fit the best, fit Everest." "The ultimate driving machine" can only be BMW; "Because I'm worth it" is L'Oréal; "We try harder" is still used by car rental firm Avis; and, "You can't get better than a Kwik-Fit fitter" is tyre fitting company Kwik-Fit's proposition. Ultimately, a product or brand positioning must be memorable, plausible and relevant to the target market's perceptions. The intention is to develop a distinctive image for the product or service and, through a well honed positioning statement, to establish a platform for its effective communication.

Positioning statement A plausible, memorable image-enhancing written summation of a product's or brand's desired stature

Competitive Edge

Decisions about which marketing strategy to follow and which segments a business should target cannot possibly be made without considering the competitive arena (see Chapter 2).[27] Competitors' strengths and their ability to satisfy customers' needs may well influence the selection of target market priorities, particularly if a company feels certain that its competitors are much better equipped to match customer requirements in a particular market segment.[28] A business must identify what is referred to as a **basis for competing,** which hinges on identifying a differential advantage and making the most of any strengths held over rivals. A **differential advantage** is something that is highly desired by the target market's customers, which a business or its product has, that is not currently matched by rival companies or products. Without a differential advantage, success in the marketplace in the longer term is unlikely,[29] and a business will be highly vulnerable to competitors' moves. Companies with a differential advantage should gear their marketing programmes around it so as to emphasise its existence to targeted customers through sales and marketing activities. It must be remembered that while companies strive for such a competitive edge, they are not always successful in achieving their goal. Specific product attributes are easy to substantiate if they genuinely provide an advantage over rivals, but aspects of the service product often assist in developing an edge over competitors (see Chapter 8). For example, Toyota stresses in its press advertising the capabilities and friendliness of its dealers; Chanel, the eminence of its brands and fragrances; the AA, its coverage and ability to help; 3M, its innovative creativity; DHL, its speed and reliability; Duracell, the longevity of its cells; BA Club Europe, the added service, comfort and convenience; and JCB, the value and reliability inherent in its brand. Where a differential advantage exists, a business's brand positioning and promotion must utilise and emphasise the attribute in question.

Basis for competing A differential advantage and any strengths held over competitors

Differential advantage An attribute of a product or a business that is not currently matched by rival companies or products and is highly desired by the target market's customers

Steps in Determining a Differential Advantage

There is a straightforward sequence of steps a particular business's marketers follow when attempting to identify a differential advantage.[30]

1. Identify the market's segments.
2. Establish what product and service attributes are desired and demanded by each segment.

3. Decide which of these attributes the business in question offers.
4. Determine which attributes the business's competitors offer.
5. Consider what the marketplace perceives the competitors' genuine strengths to be.
6. Identify whether any gaps exist between customer expectations of the product/ service on offer and perceptions of the competitors' offers.
7. Consider whether any gaps identified in step 6 are matched by the business and its own offerings. If the business is able to match one or more of these gaps, the potential exists for a differential advantage to be developed.
8. Question whether any of these potential advantages for the business can be emphasised through sales and marketing programmes.
9. Consider the sustainability of these advantages for the business. How easily and quickly can competitors catch up? Is it possible for the business to defend these advantages?
10. If there are no current advantages for the business, given the gaps identified between competitors' offerings and customer expectations, consider which areas offer potential for developing a future differential advantage.
11. In order to maximise any existing or potential differential advantages, detail the changes the business must make to its research and development, engineering, sales and marketing activities.

It is important to remember that companies frequently examine their relative strengths and weaknesses in relation to their rivals (see Chapter 22). A strength is not the same as a differential advantage. For example, many rivals may also have strong brand awareness or high profitability. A differential advantage is something that targeted customers want and value and that only one supplier is able to provide. It is also important to avoid stressing aspects of the product or marketing mix as though they are differential advantages when they are, in effect, "givens" in a marketing programme. Indeed, customers take these aspects for granted. Most competitors in a market will in any case include these features, for example, guaranteed delivery or product quality, in their marketing programmes. Without such attributes—the "givens"—a customer may not even consider a particular company's products or services to be of interest. The basic requirements of customers and a business's numerous strengths may be important aspects of a company's basis for competing, but they do not constitute a differential advantage, which is the ultimate and most desirable basis for competing. Strategic issues of competition are addressed more extensively in Chapter 21.

Evaluating Markets and Forecasting Sales

Whatever segmentation choices businesses make, measuring the sales potential of the chosen target market or markets is crucial. Moreover, a marketing manager must determine the portion or share of the selected market that the company can capture relative to its objectives, resources and managerial skills, as well as to those of its competitors. Developing and maintaining a marketing mix consume a considerable amount of a company's resources. Thus the target market or markets selected must have enough sales potential to justify the costs of developing and maintaining one or more marketing mixes.

The potential for sales can be measured along several dimensions, including product, geographic area, time and level of competition.[31] With respect to product, potential sales can be estimated for a specific product item (for example, Diet Coke) or an entire product line (for example, Coca-Cola, Coca-Cola Classic, Diet Coke, Diet Caffeine-Free Coke, and Cherry Coca-Cola are one product line). A manager must also determine the geographic area to be included in the estimate. In relation to time, sales potential estimates can be short range (one year or less), medium range (one to five years), or long range (longer than five years). The competitive level specifies whether sales are being estimated for a single company or for an entire industry. Thus marketers measure sales potential both for the entire market and for their own companies and then develop a sales forecast. A detailed discussion of market potential, sales potential and sales forecasting is given in Chapter 22.

● S U M M A R Y

A *market* is an aggregate of people who, as individuals or as organisations, have needs for products in a product class and who have the ability, willingness and authority to purchase such products. A *consumer market* consists of purchasers and/or individuals in their households who intend to consume or benefit from the purchased products and who do not buy products for the main purpose of making a profit. A *business-to-business* (also known as an organisational or industrial) *market* consists of people and groups who purchase a specific kind of product for re-sale, direct use in producing other products or use in day-to-day operations. Profit is not always necessarily a motive. Because products are classified according to use, the same product may be classified as both a consumer product and an industrial product.

Marketers use two general approaches to identify their target markets: the total market and the market segmentation approaches. A company using an *undifferentiated* or *total market approach* designs a single marketing mix and directs it at an entire market for a particular product. The total market approach can be effective when a large proportion of individuals in the total market have similar needs for the product and the organisation can develop and maintain a single marketing mix to satisfy those needs.

Markets made up of individuals with diverse needs are called *heterogeneous markets*. The *market segmentation* approach divides the total market into smaller groups of customers who have similar product needs and buying characteristics. A market segment is a group of individuals, groups or organisations sharing one or more similar characteristics that cause them to have relatively similar product needs. *Segmentation variables* or *bases* are the dimensions or characteristics of individuals, groups or businesses that are used for dividing a total market into segments. The segmentation variable should be related to customers' needs for, uses of or behaviour towards the product. Segmentation variables for consumer markets can be grouped into two broad categories that relate either to customer characteristics—demographics (age, sex, family, race, religion), socio-economics (income, occupation, education, social class), geography (country, region, urban area, housing), personality, motives and lifestyle—or to product related behaviour—purchase behaviour and occasion, benefits sought (*benefit segmentation*), consumption behaviour and user status, and attitude towards product. *Market density* refers to the number of potential customers within a unit of land area. Segmentation variables for business-to-business markets include demographic factors, operating variables, purchasing approach, situational factors and the personal characteristics of buyers. Besides selecting the appropriate segmentation variable, a marketer must also decide how many variables to use. *Single variable segmentation* involves only one variable, but in *multivariable segmentation,* more than one characteristic is used to divide a total market. The latter is often more meaningful.

Certain conditions must exist for market segmentation to be effective. First, consumers' needs for the product should be heterogeneous. Second, the segments of the market should be measurable so that the segments can be compared with respect to estimated sales potential, costs and profits. Third, at least one segment must be substantial enough to have the profit potential to justify developing and maintaining a special marketing mix for that segment. Fourth, the company must be able to access the chosen segment with a particular marketing mix. Fifth, the segment should be reasonably stable over time. Sixth, the resulting segmentation scheme must be managerially useful. Customers with dissimilar needs and buying behaviour must not be grouped together in the same market segment.

Profiling segments using *descriptor* variables can help the marketer build up a fuller picture and design a marketing mix (or mixes) that more precisely matches the needs of people in a selected market segment (or segments). *Targeting* is the task of prioritising which market segment(s) to address. There are two major types of targeting strategy. In the *concentration strategy,* a business directs its marketing efforts towards a single market segment through one marketing mix. In the *multisegment strategy,* a business develops different marketing mixes for two or more market segments. The decisions about which segment or segments to enter are linked to considerations about company resources, expertise and the nature of customers and competitors.

Having decided which segment or segments to target, the marketer must position the product in order to create a clearly defined image in the minds of its target consumers. The product's *positioning* must be perceived by its consumers to be different from the positionings of competing prod-

ucts. *Perceptual maps* assist marketers in graphically depicting the relative positionings of the products in a particular market. Although a product's attributes and styling, along with its pricing, service levels and channel of distribution, contribute to how consumers perceive the product, a marketer uses mainly promotion to establish a product's positioning. The final stage in developing a positioning is the *positioning statement,* a plausible and memorable written summation of a product's or brand's desired stature.

To trade successfully, a business must endeavour to satisfy its target customers in a manner that gives it a competitive edge over its rival businesses. Companies therefore create a basis for competing as part of their marketing strategy. A *basis for competing* hinges on identifying a differential advantage and making the most of any edge over competitors. A *differential advantage* is something that is highly desired by the target market's customers, which a business or its product has, that is not currently matched by rival companies or products. It is important to remember that a differential advantage is not merely an edge over competitors, as several other rivals could actually share a certain business strength. Aspects taken for granted by customers as basic entry points in a market's product and marketing offerings, the "givens", must also not be designated as a business's differential advantage. The basis for competing and particularly any identified differential advantage must be emphasised in the selected marketing mix programmes deployed. Whichever segments marketers target, irrespective of the positioning adopted, they must be able to measure the sales potential of the target market or markets.

Important Terms

Market
Consumer market
Business-to-business market
Undifferentiated or total
  market approach
Heterogeneous markets
Market segmentation
Segmentation variables
  or bases

Market density
Benefit segmentation
Single variable segmentation
Multivariable segmentation
Profiling
Descriptors
Targeting
Concentration strategy
Multisegment strategy

Positioning
Perceptual mapping
Positioning statement
Basis for competing
Differential advantage

Discussion and Review Questions

1. What is a market? What are the requirements for a market?
2. In the area where you live, is there a group of people with unsatisfied product needs who represent a market? Could this market be reached by a business organisation? Why or why not?
3. Identify and describe the two major types of market. Give examples of each.
4. What is the total market approach? Under what conditions is it most useful? Describe a current situation in which a company is using a total market approach. Is the business successful? Why or why not?
5. What is the market segmentation approach? Describe the basic conditions required for effective segmentation. Identify several companies that use the segmentation approach.
6. List the differences between concentration and multisegment strategies. Describe the advantages and disadvantages of each strategy.
7. Identify and describe four major categories of base variables that can be used to segment consumer markets. Give examples of product markets that are segmented by variables in each category.
8. What dimensions are used to segment business-to-business markets?
9. How do marketers decide whether to use single variable or multivariable segmentation? Give examples of product markets that are divided through multivariable segmentation.
10. Choose a product and discuss how it could best be positioned in the market. Determine a suitable positioning statement.
11. Explain what is meant by the term *differential advantage*.
12. Describe the steps a business should take to create a differential advantage.
13. Why is it important to establish a basis for competing? Consider a leading supermarket chain or a car manufacturer: what is its basis for competing?

Recommended Readings

S. Dibb, "Developing a decision tool for identifying operational and attractive segments", *Journal of Strategic Marketing,* vol. 3, 1995, pp. 189–203.

S. Dibb and L. Simkin, "Implementation problems in industrial market segmentation", *Industrial Marketing Management,* vol. 23, 1994, pp. 55–63.

S. Dibb and L. Simkin, "Prioritising target markets", *Marketing Intelligence & Planning,* vol. 16, no. 7, 1998, pp. 407–417.

S. Dibb and L. Simkin, *The Market Segmentation Workbook: Target Marketing for Marketing Managers* (London: International Thomson Business Publishing, 1996).

G. Hooley and J. Saunders, *Competitive Positioning: The Key to Marketing Strategy* (London: Prentice-Hall, 1993).

M. McDonald and I. Dunbar, *Market Segmentation* (London: Macmillan Press, 1995).

● C A S E S

7.1 *Ethnic Marketing or Racial Stereotyping?*

While their US counterparts are using a host of marketing tools and techniques specifically to target ethnic groups, many UK companies are still uncomfortable with the whole idea of ethnic marketing. At a time when the UK ethnic community is expected to double in the next three decades, the unwillingness of many businesses to capitalise on the new opportunities that are arising seems surprising. In practice, this reluctance stems from concerns that doing so may provoke accusations of racism or of emphasising racial division. The outcome is that ethnic marketing in the UK tends to focus on ensuring that ethnic groups are not excluded, rather than being specifically targeted.

With new Office of National Statistics figures suggesting that the purchasing power of ethnic groups is on the increase, it seems inevitable that the situation will soon change. For example, there are now almost half a million Pakistani consumers in the UK, over half of whom hold managerial or professional positions. Since more than 60 per cent of these UK Pakistanis are under age 25, the potential for future growth in this group is also large. These characteristics are vital, as it seems likely that the success of ethnic marketing will be driven by the economic affluence of the groups being targeted. For a host of religious, cultural or language reasons, some groups may be too fragmented or small to attract specifically designed products and marketing programmes. For example, the 800,000 strong Indian community, the UK's largest ethnic group, is broken down into subgroups speaking five or more different languages, making targeting a complex affair.

The US, where more than 25 per cent of the population come from ethnic minorities, is not necessarily an appropriate point of comparison. The sheer size of the ethnic groups in the US simply cannot be ignored, and large companies such as Coca-Cola, Nabisco, Procter & Gamble and Sears are all developing specifically targeted marketing programmes for different ethnic minorities. In the UK, only around 5 per cent of the population come from ethnic minorities, a much lower proportion. These ethnic groups also tend to be more integrated into the population as a whole than in the US, so racial divisions are less clearly defined.

As companies in the UK continue to grapple with the strategic issue of ethnic marketing, attempts to include minorities at the tactical marketing level are increasing. For example, advertisers are making greater use of black and Asian actors in their promotions than previously. Yet members of these ethnic minorities are still rarely used in certain types of advertisements, such as those for cars, perfume, jewellery and financial services. The result is that accusations of tokenism and of reinforcement of racial stereotypes still abound. For example, in 1996 a Vauxhall Astra television advertisement featuring hundreds of babies attracted criticism because almost all of them were white. In spite of this, a spokesperson for the Commission for Racial Equality believes that the advertising business has at least progressed in recent years. The challenge now, it seems, is for companies to move away from the passive, sometimes minimalist inclusion of ethnic minorities and actively seek the opportunities that this important part of the population represents.

In North America, a recent conference presented the notion that, in effect, over half of the population is made up of ethnic minorities, encouraging companies as diverse as Coors and Microsoft to recognise the importance of marketing specifically to ethnic groups within their target markets. Most businesses do not perceive ethnic groups to be additional target markets—many black, white or yellow skinned people share similar lifestyles, income profiles and aspirations—but acknowledge that cultural and ethnic backgrounds may require them to modify their marketing mix programmes as they respond to the needs and buying behaviour of their target market. Although in the EU, ethnic proportions are much less than in the US, the buying power of ethnic minorities is still highly significant. As in the EU, the UK has still to witness the bespoke ethnic and racial marketing programmes that have developed in the US during the past few years. There are indications that marketers are acknowledging the need to be more flexible in their marketing styles in order to properly reflect the ethnic mix of their current and potential customer base.

SOURCES: Veronica Lyons, "Just a stereotype?", *Marketing Week,* 21 June 1996, pp. 40–41; Alicia Clegg, "Colour blind", *Marketing Week,* 21 June 1996, pp. 38–40; Peter Jackson, Adsearch, Richmond-upon-Thames, 2000; Jennifer Porter Grove, "Ethnic marketing may become the norm", *Bank Marketing,* 30 (9), 1998, pp. 12–14.

Questions for Discussion

1. "Ethnic marketing may become the norm" is a phrase being cited in North America. To what extent is such an assertion relevant in the EU?
2. Are certain brands or products more likely to be marketed along these more flexible lines? If so, which and why?
3. For a product as ubiquitous as Coca-Cola, does the notion of ethnic or racial marketing present any benefits or potential? Why or why not?

7.2 No Longer Just the Mini-Van or an Espace: The MPV Market Comes of Age

The famous VW Camper mini-van with its removable bench seats, sink unit and versatility was throughout the 1960s and 1970s the only real alternative to the large estate car for many large families. Then came Renault's Espace: more car-like than van-like, with space for seven passengers and some luggage at levels of speed and comfort almost equivalent to those of a car. Certainly not cheap—the latest models are priced between £18,000 and £28,000—the Espace quickly established a reputation for reliability, comfort, utility and a dash of French flair in what is now classed as the multipurpose vehicle (MPV) or "people carrier" market.

As the 1980s drew to a close, yet another category of vehicles in the car market took off and expanded: the 4x4 off-roader. Led initially by the genuine working vehicles built by Land Rover, more often than not mud-coated and prone to a harsh existence, Land Rover identified a market segment requiring 4x4 versatility combined with the comfort of the executive car. The resulting Range Rover and then the Discovery were trend setters in the growing 4x4 market, just as the Renault Espace had led the way in the MPV market.

In the 4x4 market, Land Rover's success was noted by the major Japanese players with the arrival of the Shogun, Land Cruiser and Trooper. Now the 4x4 market has been further segmented: the Toyota Rav4 and Suzuki Vitara cater for the cheaper, "fun" leisure users; the Ford Maverick, GM Frontera and Land Rover Freelander aim at the middle family market; and the Mitsubishi Shogun and Range Rover target company executives and country gentry. Few of these versatile off-roaders, increasingly bought as "fashion statements" by their image-conscious owners, ever see a muddy embankment or field. Despite a record year in terms of sales, Land Rover no longer has the 4x4 market to itself. The latest development has been the entry of the South Korean manufacturers into this seemingly crowded market. The SSang Yong Musso (Daewoo) is big, brash and glitzy; it has the off-road performance of the Range Rover and the design flair of Ken Greenley, the man behind Aston Martin's supercar, the Virage. German giant Mercedes has confidence in the new South Korean player: it owns 5 per cent of the company, provides the engines and permits the use of its logo and brand in the Musso's advertising. New entrants into this top-end 4x4 market, Mercedes and BMW aim to compete with the Range Rover and Jeep Cherokee. Even the creator of the breed, Land Rover, has brought out a new model to compete in the "fun" sector—the Freelander.

A similar competitive pattern is evident in the MPV market. For well over a decade, the Espace was not really challenged by any major manufacturer outside North America. Honda launched the Shuttle and Daihatsu the Hijet in 1993; the VW Sharan, Fiat Ulysee, Peugeot 806, Citroën Synergie and Chrysler Voyager appeared in 1994 and 1995. Ford formed the AutoEuropa joint venture with VW to produce the Ford Galaxy and VW Sharan. Even mighty Mercedes entered the European MPV market, aiming for a slice of the 300,000 vehicles sold annually with its Viano (V-class). In the middle of 1995, the Espace still had 50 per cent of the market, followed by Toyota, Nissan and Mitsubishi. However, despite a decade's lead over its rivals, significant brand awareness and re-styling, the Ford Galaxy is now out-selling Renault's ageing Espace. The Ford-VW plant in Portugal, which has the capacity to produce 180,000 Sharan/Galaxy models a year, is clearly intended to dominate the marketplace for MPVs. Ford's high spending promotional campaigns, pan-European branding, extensive dealer network and long standing customer base perhaps give cause for surprise only that the company waited until late 1995 to enter this rapidly growing market sector.

Perhaps the most significant development, though, is the re-emergence of America's Chrysler in European markets, not seen since the late 1970s. In the mid-1990s, the US giant re-launched the famous Jeep 4x4 range in Europe. In 1996 the top selling MPV Chrysler Voyager arrived, "the Espace of the US market". To universal press and critical acclaim, the "people eating" Voyager looks set to revolutionise the people carrier market so long dominated by Renault's Espace. With the Ford-VW joint venture and MPV launches by Mercedes (the V-class) and Vauxhall/GM (US-made Sintra), the market is becoming crowded. The entry of these manufacturers is, however, an indication of the importance they place on this market.

The 4x4 off-road market was created during the aftermath of the Second World War as Land Rovers and Jeeps were converted for commercial use and farming applications. Land Rover built on its expertise in the consumer oriented 1970s to create the larger Range Rover. Originally also a work horse, the Range Rover was re-positioned at the executive and country estate markets. Now there are 4x4 off-road product offerings from most major manufacturers, catering for executives, farmers, outdoor enthusiasts and families at all price points and specifications. There are initial signs that a similar evolution of models and targeting is about to be evident in the MPV market. Few manufacturers do not have an MPV on offer, and success will depend increasingly on more carefully honed target market strategies and marketing programmes. Rival manufacturers are having to further segment the people carrier market and are working even harder to create brand and product identities that differentiate their MPVs.

SOURCES: *The New Portugal Magazine,* February 1995, p. 6; *The Renault Magazine,* 131, Winter/Spring 1995, pp. 11–14; K. Done, "Espace—the final frontier", *Financial Times,* 12 April 1995; I. Morton, "Car makers scramble into people carriers", *Evening Standard,* 9 June 1995; Stewart Smith, "Far East flash of the Musso", *Evening Telegraph,* December 1995; *What Car?,* January 1996; Land Rover Ltd, 1998; *What Car?,* October 1998.

Questions for Discussion

1. What market and consumer trends have led to the growth of the MPV market?
2. In the 4x4 market, separate segments have emerged. Is this likely to happen in the MPV market? If so, why?
3. How might a new MPV be positioned in the existing marketplace?

Academics and practitioners define marketing as involving the understanding and satisfying of customers. It is not possible to accomplish these requirements without a sound understanding of buying behaviour, the processes involved and the associated influencing factors. Accordingly, Part II of *Marketing: Concepts and Strategies* has presented a comprehensive examination of the nature of consumer buying behaviour and then business-to-business buying behaviour.

Over time, marketers develop knowledge of their markets. Many marketing decisions are based on this experience and on the intuition of the managers concerned. Frequently, though, marketers recognise that they do not fully understand their customers, competitors or aspects of the marketing environment forces. In such instances they conduct marketing research. The nature and use of marketing research have also been discussed in Part II, along with an examination of the principal element of marketing strategy: target market selection.

Before progressing, readers should be confident that they are now able to:

Describe consumer buying behaviour

• What are the types and stages of consumer buying decision-making and the associated influencing personal, psychological and social factors? • Why should marketers understand consumer buying behaviour?

Describe business-to-business buying behaviour

• What are the types of organisational markets and the characteristics of business-to-business buyers and transactions, business-to-business demand and the buying centre? • Why are relationships so important? • What are the stages of the buying process? • How can business-to-business markets be selected and analysed?

Outline the core aspects of marketing research and information systems

• What is the importance of research and information systems in marketing? • What distinguishes intuition from marketing research? • What are the five steps of the marketing research process? • What are the basic tools for conducting marketing research?

Explain the process of target market selection

• Why is target market selection so important? • What types of markets are there? • How do marketers determine market segments? • How do companies choose which market segments to target? • What is the role of positioning in the target market process? • Why should companies strive for a differential advantage over competitors?

Marketing Opportunity Analysis	Chapters
• The marketing environment	2
• Marketing in international markets	3
• Consumer buying behaviour	4
• Organisational markets and business-to-business buying behaviour	5
• Marketing research and information systems	6

Target Market Strategy	Chapters
• Market segmentation and prioritisation	7, 21
• Product and brand positioning	7, 21
• Competitive advantage	7, 21

Marketing Mix Development	Chapters
• Product, branding, packaging and service decisions	8–11
• Place (distribution and channel) decisions	12–14
• Promotion decisions	15–17
• Pricing decisions	18, 19
• Supplementary decisions	3, 20, 23, 24

Marketing Management	Chapters
• Strategic marketing and competitive strategy	21, 22
• Marketing planning and forecasting sales potential	22
• Implementing strategies and internal marketing relationships and measuring performance	23
• Marketing ethics and social responsibility	24

III Product, Branding, Packaging and Service Decisions

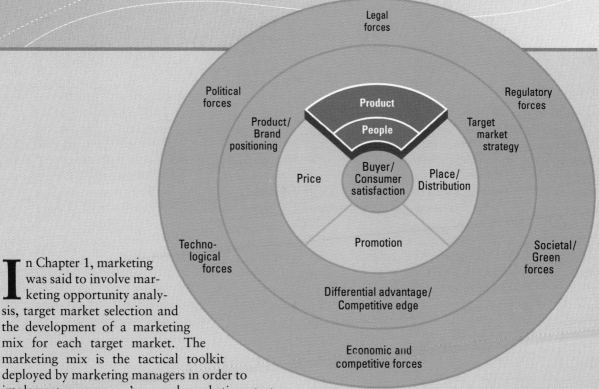

In Chapter 1, marketing was said to involve marketing opportunity analysis, target market selection and the development of a marketing mix for each target market. The marketing mix is the tactical toolkit deployed by marketing managers in order to implement a company's agreed marketing strategy. The marketing mix centres on the "5Ps" of product, people, place/distribution, promotion and pricing decisions. The marketing mix must endeavour to match the identified needs of target customers in order to satisfy these customers' requirements. It must also communicate the desired brand or product positioning and emphasise any differential advantage held by a business and its products over its rivals.

Part III of *Marketing: Concepts and Strategies* examines the product and people ingredients of the marketing mix, along with the integral issues of branding, packaging and customer service.

Chapter 8, "Product Decisions", introduces the concepts of how marketers define and classify products; examines the differences between product item, product line and product mix; and explores the product life cycle. The chapter then discusses organisational structures available to manage products, and concludes by examining the importance of the levels of a product in determining a competitive edge over rivals' products.

Chapter 9, "Branding and Packaging", recognises the fundamental importance of brands and brand equity in marketing and looks at different types of brands, their benefits, selection, naming, protection and licensing. The chapter goes on to discuss the functions of packaging, design considerations and the role of packaging in marketing strategy. Finally, it explores the functions of labelling and the associated legal issues.

Chapter 10, "Developing and Managing Products", outlines the organisational alternatives for managing products, explains how a business develops a product idea into a commercial product and analyses the role of product development in the marketing mix. The chapter includes a discussion of how products should be managed during the various stages of a product's life cycle. In conclusion, it discusses how existing products can be modified and how product deletion can sometimes benefit a marketing mix.

Chapter 11, "The Marketing of Services", explores how services differ from tangible goods and explores the implications for marketers. The chapter begins by explaining the nature and characteristics of services, classifying services and the development of marketing strategies for services. It goes on to discuss the significant problems encountered in developing a differential advantage for a service and also addresses the crucial concept of service quality. The chapter then explores the concept of marketing in non-business situations, the development of marketing strategies in non-business organisations and methods for controlling non-business marketing activities.

By the conclusion of Part III of *Marketing: Concepts and Strategies,* readers should understand the core product decisions that must be made in determining a marketing mix, including branding, packaging, people and service issues.

8 Product Decisions

OBJECTIVES

- To learn how marketers define products
- To define product levels
- To understand how to classify products
- To become familiar with the concepts of product item, product line and product mix and understand how they are connected
- To understand the concept of product life cycle
- To understand the types of organisational structures used to manage products
- To grasp the importance of the levels of a product in determining a competitive edge

"Developing great new products is not just about great ideas. It's about transforming them into products and services that customers want, that competitors have difficulty in copying and that exploit the strengths of the company."

Susan Hart, University of Strathclyde

Ambrosia, Apple, Bouquet, Coffee, Cola, Eau de Cologne, Fiji, Forest, Lavender, Lemon, Lime, Orange, Peppermint, Pineapple, Pizza, Rose, Strawberry, Tropical Paradise, Vanilla, Wild Flowers, Floral Bouquet, Jasmine and Banana.

So, what is the connection between these exotic sounding names? Foods? Paint colours? Brand names? No, the connection is they are all odours! Courtaulds Textiles has developed an innovative range of Fragrance Fabrics. The "micro-encapsulated" scent is adhered to the fabric via an acrylic polymer and applied in solution to the fabric during its final production process, the stenter run. When the fabric is rubbed, the scent "capsules" are broken, releasing the fragrance. Staggeringly, after over thirty washes at 40°C, the fragrance is still evident.

The Japanese producers of the micro-capsules have carried out extensive skin sensitivity tests at the Japanese Laboratory for Cutaneous (Skin) Health. Courtaulds Jersey Underwear Ltd has found ways of adhering the fragrance to 150g cotton single jersey and to 150g cotton/Lycra fabrics. The following are the core fragrances in demand:

Lemon—A refreshing scent characteristic for its up-lifting properties, associated with cleansing and ability to revive the skin.

Orange—A slightly sweet scent known for calming qualities.

Rose—The "queen" of essential oils, associated with beauty, femininity and purity, and a relaxed state of mind.

Vanilla—Commonly linked with taste, a distinctive smell which is obtained from the pods of a beautiful tropical orchid.

Lavender—A beautiful scent with endearing qualities, peaceful sleep and balancing properties. Widely used in perfumery and with an oil base to ease away muscular aches and pains.

Apple and Strawberry—Fresh and fruity fragrances that are the essence of a sunny summer.

Forest and Wild Flowers—Mirroring the scents of woodland, two fragrances that combine tranquillity and freshness.

247

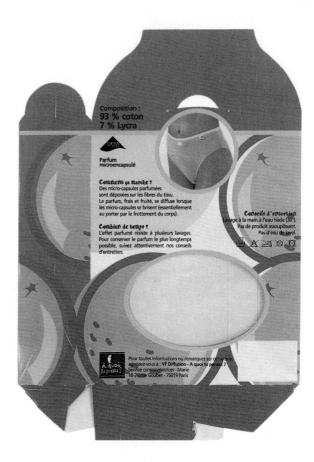

So why the excitement? Well, in fabric development innovations tend to be based around texture and durability—for example, the stretchy Lycra phenomenon. New product development rarely has been so innovative in this market, and for Courtaulds Textiles the result has been a competitive edge over rivals. The main target market is presently for sportswear: clothing which with this new technology emits a pleasant odour when the wearer becomes hot and sweaty on the squash court or in the gym. It is not only overly hot sports enthusiasts for whom this new product technology has appeal. The technology also exists for intelligent fabrics which can detect, for example, when a women is menstrual, releasing lavender or soothing rose fragrances.

It would seem that in the next few years, many clothing applications will be found to combine with the micro-encapsulated scents. The task for the fabric manufacturers' marketers will be to promote these attributes to the garment makers, whose marketers will need to entice retailers to stock these new lines and consumers to trial these fragrant products.

SOURCES: *Fragrance Fabrics* and *Essential Oils and Their "Well Being" Qualities*, Courtaulds Jersey Underwear; Courtaulds Textiles, Nottingham. *Advertisements:* Courtesy of Courtaulds Textiles.

The product is an important variable in the marketing mix. Products such as the Fragrance Fabrics devised by Courtaulds, are among a company's most crucial and visible contacts with buyers. If a company's products do not meet its customers' desires and needs, the company will have to adjust its offering in order to survive. Developing a successful product requires knowledge of fundamental marketing and product concepts. Courtaulds' range of Fragrance Fabrics will need to appeal both to the garment makers and to consumers if it is to achieve long term success.

This chapter's first section introduces and defines the concepts that help clarify what a product is and looks at how buyers view products. The next section examines the concepts of product mix and product line as an introduction to product planning. The chapter then explores the stages of the product life cycle. Each life cycle stage generally requires a specific marketing strategy, operates within a certain competitive environment and has its own sales and profit pattern. The final section discusses the elements that make up a product.

What Is a Product?

Product Everything, both favourable and unfavourable, tangible and intangible, received in an exchange of an idea, service or good

Good A tangible physical entity

Service The application of human and mechanical efforts to people or objects in order to provide intangible benefits to customers

Ideas Concepts, philosophies, images or issues that provide the psychological stimulus to solve problems or adjust to the environment

A **product** is everything, both favourable and unfavourable, that is received in an exchange. It is a complexity of tangible and intangible attributes, including functional, social and psychological utilities or benefits.[1] A product can be an idea, a service, a good or any combination of these three. This definition also covers supporting services that go with goods, such as installation, guarantees, product information and promises of repair or maintenance. A **good** is a tangible physical entity, such as a bar of Lux facial soap or a Rod Stewart CD. A **service,** by contrast, is intangible; it is the result of the application of human and mechanical efforts to people or objects. Examples of services include music tuition, holiday insurance and dental treatment. (Chapter 11 provides a detailed discussion of services marketing.) **Ideas** are concepts, philosophies, images or issues. They provide the psychological stimulus to solve problems or adjust to the environment. For example, Oxfam provides famine relief and attempts to improve the long term prospects of people in hunger stricken countries.

When buyers purchase a product, they are really buying the benefits and satisfaction they think the product will provide. A designer label sweatshirt, for example, is purchased for status and fashion, not just for warmth. Services, in particular, are bought on the basis of promises of satisfaction. Promises, with the images and appearances of symbols, help consumers make judgements about tangible and intangible products.[2] Often, symbols and cues are used to make intangible products more tangible or real to the consumer. MasterCard, for example, uses globes to symbolise the company's financial power and worldwide coverage.

Classifying Products

Consumer products Items purchased to satisfy personal or family needs

Industrial or **business-to-business products** Items bought for use in a company's operations or to make other products

Products fall into one of two general categories. Products purchased to satisfy personal and family needs are **consumer products.** Those bought for use in a company's operations or to make other products are **industrial** or **business-to-business products.** The same item can be both a consumer product and an industrial product. For example, when consumers purchase light bulbs for their homes, light bulbs are classified as consumer products. However, when a large company purchases light bulbs to provide lighting in a factory or office, the light bulbs are considered industrial products because they are used in the daily operations of the company. Thus the buyer's intent—or the ultimate use of the product—determines whether an item is classified as a consumer or an industrial product. It is common for more people to be involved in buying an industrial product than in a consumer purchase. Chapters 4 and 5 explain the differences in buying and decision-making for consumer and business-to-business products.

The main reason why it is important to know about product classifications is that different classes of products are aimed at particular target markets and classification affects distribution, promotion and pricing decisions. Furthermore, the types of marketing activities and efforts needed—in short, the entire marketing mix—differ according to how a product is classified. This section examines the characteristics of consumer and industrial products and explores the marketing activities associated with some of them.

Consumer Products The most widely accepted approach to classifying consumer products relies on the common characteristics of consumer buying behaviour. It divides products into four categories: convenience, shopping, speciality and unsought products. However, not all buyers behave in the same way when purchasing a specific type of product. Thus a single product can fit into more than one category. To minimise this problem, marketers think in terms of how buyers *generally* behave when purchasing a specific item. In addition, they recognise that the "correct" classification can be determined only by considering a particular company's intended target market.

Convenience Products Relatively inexpensive, frequently purchased and rapidly consumed items on which buyers exert only minimal purchasing effort are called **convenience products.** They range from bread, soft drinks and chewing gum to petrol and newspapers. The buyer spends little time planning the purchase or comparing available brands or sellers. Even a buyer who prefers a specific brand will readily choose a substitute if the preferred brand is not conveniently available.

Convenience products Inexpensive, frequently purchased and rapidly consumed items that demand only minimal purchasing effort

Classifying a product as a convenience product has several implications for a company's marketing strategy. A convenience product is normally marketed through many retail outlets. Because sellers experience high inventory turnover, per unit gross margins can be relatively low. Producers of convenience products such as Persil washing powder and Kellogg's Bran Flakes expect little promotional effort at the retail level and thus must provide it themselves in the form of advertising, sales promotion and how the item is packaged. The package in particular may have to sell the product, because many convenience items are available only on a self-service basis at the retail level. The use of on-pack sales promotion is one way to maximise the impact of the package.

Shopping Products Items that are more carefully chosen than convenience products are called **shopping products.** Buyers are willing to expend considerable effort in planning and purchasing these items. They allocate time for comparing stores and brands with respect to prices, credit, product features, qualities, services and perhaps guarantees. Appliances, furniture, bicycles, stereos, jewellery and cameras (as shown in Figure 8.1) are examples of shopping products. These products are not frequently purchased and are expected to last a fairly long time. Even though shopping products are more expensive than convenience products, few buyers of shopping products are particularly brand loyal. If they were, they would be unwilling to shop and compare among brands.

Shopping products Items chosen more carefully than convenience products; consumers will expend considerable effort in planning and purchasing these items

Marketers seeking to market a shopping product effectively must consider that shopping products require fewer retail outlets than convenience products. Because they are purchased less frequently, inventory (stock) turnover is lower and middlemen expect to receive higher gross margins. Although large sums of

Als je serieus genomen wilt worden, heb je soms meer nodig dan een leuke babbel. Een Sony Handycam Traveller dus.
Superkleine en verdichlichte Video 8 camera's, die ideaal zijn voor op reis. En daarmee leg je alles haarscherp vast.
Om te beginnen is er de TR45 (f 1.999,-). De kleinste en lichtste (700 gram) ter wereld. Uitgerust met een krachtige

zoomlens (6x), digitale Superimpose en een sluitertijd tot 1/4000 seconde, zodat niets hem meer te snel af is.
Ben je nog veeleisender, dan kies je voor de TR50. (f 2.295,-) Die heeft ook nog eens een handige Auto Lock Cover, een Fader, LCD-display en liefst 8x zoom.
Wie helemaal het onderste uit de kan wil, neemt de TR75

(f 2.599,-). Dan geniet je tevens van Hifi-stereo en een superieure beeldkwaliteit (470.000 beeldpunten).
Wat ze allemaal hebben, is 't gemak van Video 8: perfect geluid, drie uur op één bandje en direct afspelen op je tv.
En zelfs 't afrekenen word je makkelijk gemaakt met The Sony Card. Dus loop snel eens binnen bij de Sony-

dealer. Dan kun je de sterke verhalen voortaan aan anderen overlaten. UITEINDELIJK WIL JE TOCH EEN SONY

ZONDER EEN SONY TRAVELLER BLIJFT 'T EEN STERK VERHAAL.

Figure 8.1 Shopping products. Sony cameras, as well as most other brands of camera, are shopping products. SOURCE: Courtesy of Sony Europa.

money may be required to advertise shopping products, an even larger proportion of resources is likely to be used for personal selling. Indeed, the quality of the service may be a factor in the consumer's choice of outlet. Thus a family which purchases a new computer game system might expect sales personnel in their chosen retail outlet to explain fully the advantages and features of competing brands. In many cases, the producer and the middlemen also expect some co-operation from one another with respect to providing parts and repair services and performing promotional activities.

Speciality Products Products that possess one or more unique characteristics and for which a significant group of buyers is willing to expend considerable effort to obtain are called **speciality products**. Buyers carefully plan the purchase of a speciality product; they know exactly what they want and will not accept a substitute. An example of a speciality product is a painting by L. S. Lowry or a Cartier watch. When searching for speciality products, buyers do not compare alternatives; they are concerned primarily with finding an outlet that has a pre-selected product available.

The marketing of a speciality product is very distinctive. The exclusivity of the product is accentuated by the fact that speciality products are often distributed through a limited number of retail outlets. Some companies go to considerable lengths to control this aspect of their distribution. Like shopping goods, speciality

Speciality products Items that possess one or more unique characteristics; consumers of speciality products plan their purchases and will expend considerable effort to obtain them

products are purchased infrequently, causing lower inventory turnover and thus requiring relatively high gross margins.

Unsought Products   Products that are purchased when a sudden problem arises or when aggressive selling is used to obtain a sale that otherwise would not take place are called **unsought products.** In general, the consumer does not think of buying these products regularly. Emergency plumbing services and headstones are examples of unsought products. Life insurance and encyclopaedias, in contrast, are examples of products that need aggressive personal selling.

Industrial or Business-to-Business Products

Industrial products are usually purchased on the basis of a business's goals and objectives. Generally, the functional aspects of the product are more important than the psychological rewards sometimes associated with consumer products. Industrial products can be classified into seven categories according to their characteristics and intended uses: raw materials, major equipment, accessory equipment, component parts, process materials, consumable supplies and industrial services.[3]

Raw Materials   The basic materials that become part of physical products are **raw materials.** They include minerals, chemicals, agricultural products and materials from forests and oceans. They are usually bought and sold in relatively large quantities according to grades and specifications.

Major Equipment   Large tools and machines used for production purposes, such as cranes and spray painting machinery, are types of **major equipment.** Major equipment is often expensive, may be used in a production process for a considerable length of time and is often custom made to perform specific functions. For example GEC Large Machines manufactures purpose built large gears and turbines. Other items are standardised and perform similar tasks for many types of companies. Because major equipment is so expensive, purchase decisions are often long and complicated and may be made by high level management. Marketers of major equipment frequently must provide a variety of services, including installation, training, repair and maintenance assistance, and may even help in financing the purchase. This may lead to long term relationships being developed between suppliers of major equipment and their customers.

Accessory Equipment   Equipment that does not become a part of the final physical product but is used in production or office activities is referred to as **accessory equipment.** Examples of accessory equipment include typewriters, fractional horsepower motors, telephones and tools. Compared with major equipment, accessory items are usually much cheaper, are purchased routinely with less negotiation and are treated as expenditure items rather than capital items because they are not expected to last as long. More outlets are required for distributing accessory equipment than for major equipment, but sellers do not have to provide the multitude of services expected of major equipment marketers.

Component Parts   Parts that become a part of the physical product and are either finished items ready for assembly or products that need little processing before assembly are called **component parts.** Although they become part of a larger product, component parts can often be easily identified and distinguished. Tyres, spark plugs, gears, lighting units, screws and wires are all component parts of a delivery van. Buyers purchase such items according to their own specifications or industry standards. They expect the parts to be of specified quality and delivered on time so that production is not slowed or stopped. Producers that are primarily assemblers, such as most lawn mower or car manufacturers, depend heavily on the suppliers of component parts.

Process Materials   Materials that are used directly in the production of other products are called **process materials.** Unlike component parts, however, process materials are not readily identifiable. For example, Reichhold Chemicals markets a treated fibre product: a phenolicresin, sheet moulding compound used in the production of flight deck instrument panels and aircraft cabin interiors. Although the material is not identifiable in the finished aircraft, it retards burning, smoke and formation of toxic gas when subjected to fire or high temperatures.

Consumable Supplies   Supplies that facilitate production and operations but do not become part of the finished product are referred to as **consumable supplies.** Paper, pencils, oils, cleaning agents and paints are in this category. Because such supplies are standardised items used in a variety of situations, they are purchased by many different types of businesses. Consumable supplies are commonly sold through numerous outlets and are purchased routinely. To ensure that supplies are available when needed, buyers often deal with more than one seller. Consumable supplies can be divided into three sub-categories—maintenance, repair and operating (or overhaul) supplies and are sometimes called **MRO items.**

Industrial Services   Industrial **business-to-business services** are the intangible products that many businesses use in their operations. They include financial, legal, marketing research, computer programming and operation, caretaking and printing services for business. Some companies decide to provide their own services internally, while others obtain them outside the organisation. This decision depends largely on the costs associated with each alternative and the frequency with which the services are needed.

The Three Levels of Product

The product may appear obvious—a carton of fresh orange juice or a Mercedes van—but generally the purchaser is buying much more than some juice or a vehicle. To be motivated to make the purchase, there must be a perceived or real core benefit or service to be gained from the product. This level of product, termed the **core product,** is illustrated in Figure 8.2. The **actual product** is a composite of several factors: the features and capabilities offered, quality and durability, design and product styling, packaging and, often of great importance, the brand name.

In order to make the purchase, the consumer will often require the assistance of sales personnel; there may be delivery and payment credit requirements and, for bulky or very technical products, advice regarding installation. The level of warranty back-up and after sales support, particularly for innovative, highly technical or high value goods, will be of concern to most consumers. Increasingly, the overall level of customer service constitutes part of the purchase criteria, and in many markets it is deemed integral to the product on offer. These "support" issues form what is termed the **augmented product** (see Figure 8.2).

When a £25,000 BMW 5 Series executive car is purchased, the vehicle's performance specification and design may have encouraged the sale. Speed of delivery and credit payment terms may have been essential to the conclusion of the

Process materials   Materials used directly in the production of other products, but not readily identifiable

Consumable supplies   Supplies that facilitate production and operations but do not become part of the finished product

MRO items   Consumable supplies in the sub-categories of maintenance, repair and operating (or overhaul) supplies

Industrial services   The intangible products that many businesses use in their operations, including financial, legal, marketing research, computer programming and operation, caretaking and printing services

Core product   The level of a product that provides the perceived or real core benefit or service

Actual product   A composite of the features and capabilities offered in a product, quality and durability, design and product styling, packaging and brand name

Augmented product   Support aspects of a product, including customer service, warranty, delivery and credit, personnel, installation and after sales support

Figure 8.2 The three levels of product: core, actual and augmented

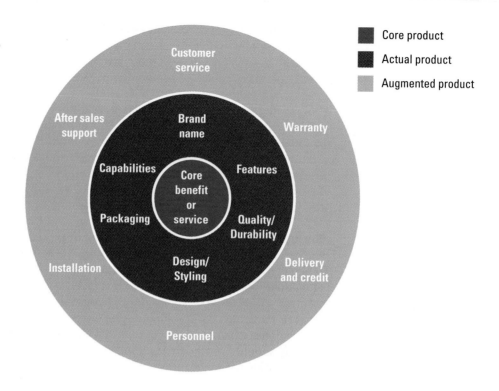

Legend:
- Core product
- Actual product
- Augmented product

Diagram labels:

Customer service

After sales support — Warranty

Brand name

Capabilities — Features

Core benefit or service

Packaging — Quality/Durability

Installation — Delivery and credit

Design/Styling

Personnel

deal. The brand's image, particularly in the case of a car costing £25,000, will also have influenced the sale. Once behind the wheel of the BMW, its new owner will expect reliability and efficient, friendly, convenient service in the course of maintenance being required. The purchase might have been lost at the outset had the salesperson mishandled the initial enquiry. Repeat servicing business and the subsequent sale of another new car would equally be ruled out if the owner encountered incompetent, unhelpful service engineers. The core benefit may have been a car to facilitate journeys to work, transport for the family or the acquisition of a recognised status symbol. Customer satisfaction will depend on the product's actual performance and also on service aspects of the augmented product. This example is not unusual. For most consumer or industrial products and services, the consumer is aware of—and influenced by—the three levels of the product: core, actual and augmented.

Many marketers now recognise the importance which personnel play in product exchanges. People are responsible for the design, production, marketing and sale of products and services. In the distribution channel they help to make products available to the marketplace. As consumers, people make decisions and ultimately adopt products for use and consumption. It is not surprising therefore that companies now pay more attention to the skills, attitudes and motivations of personnel involved in the marketing channel, recognising the key role played by their personnel, particularly when interacting with consumers. As explained in Chapter 11, this role is especially significant for services, but as discussed in Chapter 1, personnel also constitutes an essential ingredient of the marketing mix for consumer and industrial goods.

Product Line and Product Mix

Product item   A specific version of a product that can be designated as a distinct offering among a business's products

Product line   A group of closely related product items that are considered a unit because of marketing, technical or end use considerations

Product mix   The composite group of products that a company makes available to customers

Marketers must understand the relationships between all their business's products if they are to co-ordinate their marketing. The following concepts help describe the relationships between an organisation's products. A **product item** is a specific version of a product that can be designated as a distinct offering among a business's products, for example, Procter & Gamble's Pantene shampoo. A **product line** includes a group of closely related product items that are considered a unit because of marketing, technical or end use considerations. All the shampoos manufactured by Procter & Gamble constitute one of its product lines. Figure 8.3 illustrates the product line for Neutradol. Marketing Insight 8.1 explains how manufacturers of nicotine replacement products are expanding their product line to allow them to capitalise on the opportunities which this market provides. To come up with the optimum product line, marketers must understand buyers' goals. Specific items in a product line reflect the desires of different target markets or the different needs of consumers.

A **product mix** is the composite, or total, group of products that a company makes available to customers. For example, all the personal care products, laundry detergent products and other products that Procter & Gamble manufactures

Figure 8.3   Product line. This selection of products makes up part of Neutradol's product line.   SOURCE: Courtesy of Neutradol Inc.

Depth (of product mix) The number of different products offered in each product line

Width (of product mix) The number of product lines a company offers

constitute its product mix. The **depth** of a product mix is measured by the number of different products offered in each product line. The **width** of a product mix is measured by the number of product lines a company offers. Figure 8.4 shows the width of the product mix and the depth of each product line for selected Procter & Gamble products in the US. Procter & Gamble is known for using distinctive technology, branding, packaging and consumer advertising to promote individual items in its detergent product line. Tide, Bold, and Era—all Procter & Gamble detergents—share similar distribution channels and manufacturing facilities. Yet due to variations in product formula and attributes, each is promoted as distinct, adding depth to the product line.

Product Life Cycles

Product life cycle The four major stages for products: introduction, growth, maturity and decline

Just as biological cycles progress through growth and decline, so do **product life cycles.** A new product is introduced into the marketplace; it grows; it matures; and when it loses appeal and sales decline, it is terminated.[4] As explained in Chapter 10, different marketing strategies are appropriate at different stages in the product life cycle. Thus packaging, branding and labelling techniques can be used to help create or modify products which have reached different points in their life.

As Figure 8.5 shows, a product life cycle has four major stages: (1) introduction, (2) growth, (3) maturity and (4) decline. As a product moves through its cycle, the strategies relating to competition, promotion, place/distribution, pricing and market information must be periodically evaluated and possibly changed. Astute marketing managers use the life cycle concept to make sure that the introduction, alteration and termination of a product are timed and executed properly. By understanding the typical life cycle pattern, marketers are better able to maintain profitable products and drop unprofitable ones. Marketing Insight 8.2 shows how Gillette has successfully marketed an array of products around the world by ensuring a continual stream of new product introductions.

Laundry detergents	Toothpastes	Bar soaps	Deodorants	Shampoos	Tissue/Towel
Oxydol 1914	Gleem 1952	Ivory 1879	Old Spice 1948	Head & Shoulders 1961	Charmin 1928
Ivory Snow 1930	Crest 1955	Camay 1926	Secret 1956	Pantene Pro 1965	Puffs 1960
Dreft 1933		Zest 1952	Sure 1972	Vidal Sassoon 1974	Bounty 1965
Tide 1946		Safeguard 1963		Pert Plus 1979	Royale 1996
Cheer 1950		Oil of Olay 1993		Ivory 1983	
Bold 1965					
Gain 1966					
Era 1972					

Product line depth

Product mix width

Figure 8.4 The concepts of width of product mix and depth of product line applied to selected Procter & Gamble products. SOURCE: Information provided and reprinted by permission of The Procter & Gamble Company, Public Affairs Division, 1 Procter & Gamble Plaza, Cincinnati, OH 45202-3315.

Quitting the Habit: Developing Nicotine Replacement Products

Novartis, the company behind Nicotinell nicotine replacement gum and patches, is planning the launch of food products designed to help smokers quit the habit. Many consumers are already familiar with the Nicotinell brand. As smoking becomes increasingly socially unacceptable, the company now believes that there are a variety of new product development opportunities for its brand. Novartis is currently launching a nicotine replacement lozenge which when sucked provides a continual, low level boost of nicotine. Other initiatives include the possible development of nicotine-enhanced food and a detoxification programme for ex-smokers.

It is not difficult to understand the attractions of the nicotine replacement therapy market (NRT) and to appreciate why Novartis is seeking to extend its product offerings. As millions seek to leave their smoking habit behind, estimates suggest that between 1992 and 1998 the value of the UK NRT market increased from £22 million to £40 million. Indications also show that one in 20 of those attempting to "kick the habit" will use some form of nicotine replacement therapy. Not surprisingly, Novartis is not alone in seeking to develop its product range. Since NRT products were first launched in the UK a decade ago, three companies have dominated the market: Novartis, with its Nicotinell patch and gum; Pharmacia & Upjohn (P&U), with its Nicorette gum, inhalator and patches; and Boots, with its own label patches and gum. Recent launches include the Boots' inhalator and competing brand Nicorette's launch of its micro-tab, a kind of nicotine pill which when placed under the tongue, takes half an hour to dissolve.

Perhaps the most aggressive challenge to the market has come from pharmaceutical giant SmithKline Beecham (SKB), which recently spent £12 million on the UK launch of NiQuitin CQ (CQ stands for "committed quitters"). SKB claims this as the largest ever over the counter launch in the UK. Clearly the company expects that the brand, already the best seller in the US, will claim a large slice of the UK market. Company representatives suggest that this will be achieved by the unique "personalised literature pack" included with the NiQuitin CQ product. This pack includes a questionnaire for smokers to fill in, detailing the circumstances in which they are most vulnerable to lighting up. Advice is then offered which is tailored to match the answers provided in the questionnaire. According to Elaine MacFarlane, SKB's director of consumer healthcare communications, this represents a unique approach in the NRT market. She explains, "When these products first launched, they were positioned as a magic bullet—'take this and you won't want to smoke'. Now with all the noise from the political, health and economic perspectives, you know it doesn't make sense to smoke any more, and we felt the time was right for a more mature consideration of people's motivation."

In such a volatile market, future trends are difficult to predict. When NRT products were first launched in the UK in 1993, they were met with considerable consumer excitement. However, following an initial growth in sales, consumer confidence in the capabilities of the products declined. Today, as the products become available for the first time in supermarkets and to accompany the government's White Paper "Smoking Kills", the key players are looking for innovative ways to ensure that their products play a major role in the continued fight against smoking. New product development is likely to be just part of the solution with manufacturers also seeking a fresh and more realistic promotional stance. For Novartis, with the new slogan, *Helps you set yourself free from smoking*, this involves re-positioning the brand to stress its role in harm reduction. With smokers over 35 years old as the key target, and the biggest increase in new smokers among those in their early teens and twenties, the market potential is considerable. Time will tell whether Novartis and the other players can meet the challenge.

SOURCES: Neil Denny, "Smokers may be offered nicotine food to help quit", *Marketing*, 28 January 1999, p. 1; Sue Beenstock, "Queuing up to quit", *Marketing*, 28 January 1999, p. 1.

Introduction

Introduction stage A product's first appearance in the marketplace, before any sales or profits have been made

The introduction stage of the life cycle begins at a product's first appearance in the marketplace, when sales are zero and profits are negative. Profits are below zero because a new product incurs development costs, initial revenues are low and at the same time a company must generally incur large expenses for

Figure 8.5 The four stages of the product life cycle

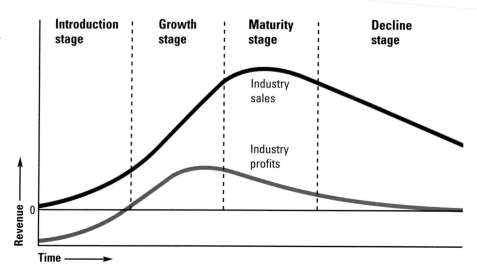

| Introduction stage | Growth stage | Maturity stage | Decline stage |

Industry sales

Industry profits

0

Revenue

Time

promotion and distribution. As time passes, sales should move upwards from zero and profits should build up from the negative position (see Figure 8.5).[5]

Because of cost, very few product introducitons represent major inventions. Developing and introducing a new product can mean an outlay of many millions of pounds. The failure rate for new products is quite high, ranging from 60 to 90 per cent depending on the industry and on how product failure is defined. For example, in the food and drinks industry, 80 per cent of all new products fail.[6] More typically, product introductions involve a new deodorant, a new type of hair dryer or a new restaurant concept rather than a major product innovation.

Potential buyers must be made aware of the new product's features, uses and advantages. Two difficulties may arise at this point. Only a few sellers may have the resources, technological knowledge and marketing know-how to launch the product successfully; and the initial product price may have to be high in order to recoup expensive marketing research or development costs. Given these difficulties, it is not surprising that many products never get beyond the introduction stage; indeed many are never launched commercially at all.

Growth

Growth stage The stage at which a product's sales rise rapidly and profits reach a peak, before levelling off into maturity

During the **growth stage**, sales rise rapidly and profits reach a peak and then start to decline (see Figure 8.5). The growth stage is critical to a product's survival because competitive reactions to its success during this period will affect the product's life expectancy. For example, Mars successfully launched Ice Cream Mars, the first ice cream version of an established confectionery product. Today the product competes with more than a dozen other brands. Already some of the competing brands have failed and others will follow. Profits decline late in the growth stage as more competitors enter the market, driving prices down and creating the need for heavy promotional expenses. At this point a typical marketing strategy encourages strong brand loyalty, perhaps using sales promotion, and competes with aggressive emulators of the product. During the growth stage, a company tries to strengthen its market share and develop a competitive position by emphasising the product's benefits.

Aggressive promotional pricing, including price cuts, is typical during the growth stage. The Internet industry is currently in the growth stage, and com-

Gillette's Products: A Global Success Story

Gillette markets an extraordinary array of products in over 200 countries. Although in some parts of the world the name *Gillette* has become synonymous with the words *razor blades,* this organisation markets much more than sharpened steel. In addition to razors and blades, Gillette's product offerings include Parker and Paper Mate pens, Liquid Paper, Oral-B toothbrushes, Braun small appliances and toiletries such as Right Guard deodorant. Although it does sell razors in Russia and blades in Bulgaria, the company also sells toothbrushes in Turkey and pens in Panama. In each of its divisions and in all of its international markets, Gillette's strategy is the same—aggressively roll out new products.

For over a hundred years, ever since King C. Gillette came up with the idea for disposable razor blades in 1895, the Gillette Company has been a world-class product innovator. While other organisations die out, asserts Gillette's president, his company thrives by continuously rejuvenating and re-inventing its products. In its personal care products division, Gillette originated clear gel deodorant and strengthened its brand image among women by introducing women's shave gel. In its shaving division, Gillette will not launch a product unless there is another new one already under development.

In addition to new product introductions, expansion into international markets is fuelling Gillette's phenomenal growth in sales and profits. Today, almost 70 per cent of the company's sales come from outside the United States. Gillette's strategy for global expansion is to enter into joint ventures with local organisations. Penetrating the Russian and eastern European markets, however, was not easy. Politics and currencies were unstable, borders were still evolving, and communication systems were unreliable at best. Gillette forged ahead, however, recognising that if it waited for stability, its competitors would have a head start.

In a joint venture with a Russian government group, Gillette invested about £35 million to construct a factory that produces blades and razors. Responding to modest Russian incomes, Gillette altered its product mix to feature lower end razors and more affordable packages containing fewer blades. To reach Russian shoppers, Gillette sells its brands in free-standing marketplace kiosks. By acquiring 80 per cent of a Polish razor blade company, Gillette was recently able to expand its operations to Poland. Several new joint ventures are on the drawing boards, and experts agree that Gillette's brand name recognition and distribution expertise virtually guarantee success in other foreign markets, as long as it keeps the new products coming.

SOURCES: Clive Chajet, "Breaking down image barriers", *Executive Speeches,* February/March 1995, pp. 32–35; Pam Weisz, "The razor's edge", *Brandweek,* 24 April 1995, pp. 26–28, 30, 32; Gary Hoover, Alta Campbell, and Patrick J. Spain, *Hoover's Handbook of American Business 1995* (Austin, Texas: Reference Press, Inc., 1995), pp. 560–561; "The process view: how marketing needs to change", *Planning Review,* March/April 1995, p. 11; John Wyatt, "Biggest U.S. companies promise you a profitable year", *Fortune,* 15 May 1995, pp. 65–66; Avraham Shama, "Entry strategies of U.S. firms to the newly independent states, Baltic states, and eastern European Countries", *California Management Review,* Spring 1995, pp. 90–109; Alex Pham, "Seventh annual Globe 100", *Boston Globe,* 23 May 1995, p. 36; and Tom Nutile, "Gillette's product development a key", *Boston Herald,* 13 March 1995, p. 23.

petitors are entering the market. Companies like Microsoft must battle hard to maintain their existing positions in this competitive arena.

Maturity

Maturity stage The stage during which a product's sales curve peaks and starts to decline, and profits continue to decline

During the **maturity stage,** the sales curve peaks and starts to decline, and profits continue to decline (see Figure 8.5). This stage is characterised by severe competition, with many brands in the market. Competitors emphasise improvements and differences in their versions of the product. Inevitably, during the maturity stage some weaker competitors are squeezed out or switch their attention to other products. For example, some brands of compact disc players are perishing now that the product is in the maturity stage.

During the maturity phase, the producers who remain in the market must make fresh promotional and distribution efforts. These efforts must focus on dealers as much as on consumers to ensure that brand visibility is maintained at the point of sale. Advertising and dealer oriented promotions are typical during this stage of the product life cycle. The promoters must also take into account the fact that, as the product reaches maturity, buyers' knowledge of it attains a high level. Consumers of the product are no longer inexperienced generalists but rather experienced specialists.

Decline

Decline stage The last stage of a product's life cycle, during which sales fall rapidly

During the **decline stage**, sales fall rapidly (see Figure 8.5). New technology or a new social trend may cause product sales to take a sharp turn downwards. When this happens, the marketer considers pruning items from the product line to eliminate those not earning a profit. At this time, too, the marketer may cut promotion efforts, eliminate marginal distributors and, finally, plan to phase out the product.

Because most businesses have a product mix consisting of multiple products, a company's destiny is rarely tied to one product. A composite of life cycle patterns is formed when various products in the mix are at different stages in the cycle. As one product is declining, other products are in the introduction, growth or maturity stage. Marketers must deal with the dual problems of prolonging the life of existing products and introducing new products to meet organisational sales goals. For example, Kodak has prolonged the product life cycle of its 110mm cameras by adding built-in flashes, waterproof bodies and other features. But Kodak has also continued to introduce new products such as the Advantix camera, as well as the new range of DC digital cameras, and Ektar, a line of colour films designed specifically for 35mm single-lens reflex cameras. Chapter 10 further explores the development of new products and considers how they can be managed in their various life cycle stages.

Other Product Related Characteristics

When developing products, marketers make many decisions. Some of these decisions involve the physical characteristics of the product; others focus on less tangible support services that are very much a part of the total product.

Physical Characteristics and Product Quality

Quality The core product's ability to achieve the basic functional requirements expected of it

A crucial question that arises during product development is how much **quality** to build into the product. In the core product, quality constitutes the product's ability to achieve the basic functional requirements expected of it. A major dimension of quality is durability. Higher quality often demands better materials and more expensive processing, increasing production costs and, ultimately, the product's price. How much the target market is prepared to pay will affect the level of quality specified. However, a marketer must also set a quality level which is consistent with the company's other products that carry a similar brand. The quality of competing brands is also an important consideration.

A product's physical features require careful consideration by marketers and by those in research and development. For example, product development personnel at Gillette spent considerable resources dealing with the Sensor razor's physical features. Marketers must know what physical features target customers want because the prime basis for decisions about the product features should be the needs and wants of the target market. For example, BT and Rover hold customer clinics offering people the opportunity to examine their product range and comment on desired features. Even a company whose existing products have been designed to satisfy target market desires should continue to assess these desires periodically to determine whether they have changed enough to require alterations in the product.

Supportive Product Related Services

All products, whether they are goods or not, possess intangible qualities. "When prospective customers can't experience the product in advance, they are asked to buy what are essentially promises—promises of satisfaction. Even tangible, testable, feelable, smellable products are, before they're bought, largely just promises."(Levitt)[7] There are many product related services and product intangibles, but three of the most common are guarantees, repairs/replacements and credit.

The type of guarantee a company provides can be a critical issue for buyers, especially when expensive, technically complex goods such as appliances are involved. A **guarantee** specifies what the producer or supplier will do if the product malfunctions. In recent years, guarantors have been legally required to state more simply and specifically the terms and conditions under which the company will take action. Because guarantees must be more precise today, marketers are using them more vigorously as tools to give their brands a competitive advantage. Retailers, such as Dixons, which sells electrical brown goods, including compact disc players and camcorders, are increasingly using guarantees as a competitive tool by providing longer periods of guarantee protection.

Although it is more difficult to provide guarantees for services than for goods, some service marketers do guarantee customer satisfaction. An effective service guarantee should be unconditional, easy to understand and communicate, meaningful, easy to invoke, and quick and easy to collect on. The customer can return a product and get a replacement, a refund or a credit for the returned good. Photographic processors such as SupaSnaps offer free processing on prints not ready within 24 hours. Such guarantees of satisfying the customer are beneficial because they provide clear performance standards, generate feedback from customers on the quality of the service and help build customer loyalty and sales.[8]

A marketer must also be concerned with establishing a system to provide replacement parts and repair services. This support service is especially important for expensive, complex industrial products that buyers expect to last a long time. For example, builders expect construction machinery manufacturers like Caterpillar to be able to provide replacement parts quickly and without fuss. Sometimes these services are provided directly to buyers, in other cases regional service centres or middlemen may be used.

Finally, a company must sometimes provide credit services to customers. Even though credit services place a financial burden on a business, they can yield several benefits. For instance, a company may acquire and maintain a stable market share. Many major oil companies, for example, have competed effectively against petrol discounters by providing credit services. For marketers of relatively expensive items such as furniture, offering credit services enables a larger number of people to buy the product, thus enlarging the market for the item. Another reason for offering credit services is to earn interest income from customers. The types of credit services offered depend on the characteristics of target market members, the company's financial resources, the type of products sold and the types of credit services that competitors offer.

Guarantee An agreement specifying what the producer or supplier will do if the product malfunctions

Marketing must aim to satisfy customers. In the context of products, this goal demands an understanding of the *core* product requirement. However, it depends on marketers identifying and providing the *actual* product features expected and—with ever increasing importance—aspects of the *augmented* product such as customer service, warranty, delivery and credit, personnel, installation and after sales support. Product quality is a subject fundamentally linked to both customer satisfaction and a business's ability to compete. The question that taxes the brand manager of a range of video recorders is not just what features the machines should incorporate but how long the machines should last and with what level of reliability.

Differential advantage An attribute of a product or service highly desired by targeted customers and not currently offered by rival companies or products

A **differential advantage** is an attribute of a product or service highly desired by targeted customers and not currently offered by rival companies or products: it is a unique differentiator, if utilised in that business's sales and marketing activity (see Chapter 7). Invariably, differential advantages are difficult to identify, particularly in crowded and mature markets with a plethora of similar product offers from rival companies. Even when a differential advantage exists, it is rarely sustainable in the medium term as envious competitors copy and follow suit. Nevertheless, a differential advantage does provide a competitive edge. For many years stunning off-road performance combined with the luxury of a limousine gave the Range Rover an edge over its rivals. The Shogun and Jeep now match Range Rover on both counts. In 1999 BP launched an environmentally friendly diesel fuel with 90 per cent reduced emissions. Now all rivals offer similar clean diesels. As businesses strive to derive a differential advantage over rivals, they look not just to the actual product but also, increasingly, to aspects of product quality and the augmented product features.[9]

S U M M A R Y

A *product* is everything, both favourable and unfavourable, that is received in an exchange. It is a complex set of tangible and intangible attributes, including functional, social and psychological utilities or benefits. A product can be an *idea*, a *service*, a *good* or any combination of these three. When consumers purchase a product, they are buying the benefits and satisfaction that they think the product will provide.

Products can be classified on the basis of the buyer's intentions. Thus *consumer products* are those purchased to satisfy personal and family needs. *Industrial* or *business-to-business products,* on the other hand, are purchased for use in a company's operations or to make other products. Because products are classified according to use, the same product may be classified as both a consumer product and an industrial product. Consumer products can be sub-divided into *convenience, shopping, speciality* and *unsought products.* Industrial products can be divided into *raw materials, major equipment, accessory equipment, component parts, process materials, consumable supplies (MRO items)* and *industrial services.*

It is important to remember that a product has three levels: core, actual and augmented. The purchaser buys a core benefit or service (the *core product*) in addition to the product's brand name, features, capabilities, quality, packaging and design (the *actual product*). Increasingly, aspects of the *augmented product* are important considerations for purchasers of consumer goods, services and industrial goods. Warranties, delivery and credit, personnel, installation, after sales support and customer service are integral to the actual product's appeal and perceived benefits. The role of personnel in particular is of fundamental concern to marketers; people now form a central part of the marketing mix.

A *product item* is a specific version of a product that can be designated as a distinct offering among a business's products. A *product line* is a group of closely related product items that are considered a unit because of marketing, technical or end use considerations. The composite, or total, group of products that a company makes available to customers is called the *product mix*. The *depth* of a product mix is measured by the number of different products offered in each product line. The *width* of the product mix is measured by the number of product lines a company offers.

The *product life cycle* describes how product items in an industry move through four major stages: (1) *introduction stage*, (2) *growth stage*, (3) *maturity stage* and (4) *decline stage*. The life cycle concept is used to make sure that the introduction, alteration and termination of a product are timed and executed properly. The sales curve is at zero on intro-duction, rises at an increasing rate during growth, peaks at maturity and then declines. Profits peak towards the end of the growth stage of the product life cycle. The life expectancy of a product is based on buyers' wants, the availability of competing products and other environmental conditions. Most businesses have a composite of life cycle patterns for various products. It is important to manage existing products and develop new ones to keep the overall sales performance at a desired level.

When creating products, marketers must take into account other product related considerations, such as physical characteristics and less tangible support services. Specific physical product characteristics that require attention are the level of *quality* and product features, such as textures, colours and sizes. Support services that may be viewed as part of the total product include *guarantees,* repairs/replacements and credit. The desire to establish a *differential advantage* over rivals is an important consideration for marketers. Product or service attributes are important for this aim, but so too are product quality and aspects of the augmented product.

Important Terms

Product
Good
Service
Ideas
Consumer products
Industrial or business-to-business products
Convenience products
Shopping products
Speciality products
Unsought products
Raw materials

Major equipment
Accessory equipment
Component parts
Process materials
Consumable supplies
MRO items
Industrial services
Core product
Actual product
Augmented product
Product item
Product line

Product mix
Depth (of product mix)
Width (of product mix)
Product life cycle
Introduction stage
Growth stage
Maturity stage
Decline stage
Quality
Guarantee
Differential advantage

Discussion and Review Questions

1. List the tangible and intangible attributes of a spiral notebook. Compare the benefits of the spiral notebook with those of an intangible product such as life insurance.
2. A product has been referred to as a "psychological bundle of satisfaction". Is this a good definition of a product? Why or why not?
3. Is a roll of carpet in a shop a consumer product or an industrial product? Defend your answer.
4. How do convenience products and shopping products differ? What are the distinguishing characteristics of each type of product?
5. Would a hi-fi system that sells for £400 be a convenience, shopping or speciality product?

6. In the category of industrial products, how do component parts differ from process materials?
7. How does a company's product mix relate to its development of a product line? When should a company add depth to its product lines rather than width to its product mix?
8. How do industry profits change as a product moves through the four stages of its life cycle?
9. What is the relationship between the concepts of product mix and product life cycle?
10. What factors must marketers consider when deciding what quality level to build into a product? What support services can be offered to back up product quality?
11. What are aspects of the augmented product for a new car?
12. Why is the augmented product increasingly important when determining a differential advantage?

Recommended Readings

R. J. Calantone, C.A. Di Benedetto and T. Haggblom, "Principles of new product management: exploring the beliefs of product practitioners", *Journal of Product Innovation Management,* vol. 12, no. 3, 1995, pp. 235–247.
A. Craig and S. Hart, "Where to now in new product development research?", *European Journal of Marketing,* vol. 26, no. 11, 1992, pp. 1–49.

P. Doyle, *Marketing Management and Strategy* (London: Prentice-Hall, 1998).
G. Rifkin, "Product development: the myth of short life cycles", *Harvard Business Review,* vol. 72, no. 4, 1994, p. 11.
Y. J. Wind, *Product Policy: Concepts, Methods and Strategy* (Reading, Mass.: Addison-Wesley, 1982).

 C A S E S

8.1 Heineken's Portfolio of Brands

Heineken is Europe's largest brewer. While more than half of its sales are European, world-wide, Heineken is second only to US based Anheuser-Busch. Heineken beer is recognised around the globe. With a presence in 170 countries and more than three quarters of sales originating outside the domestic Dutch market, Heineken has been described as the most international beer brand.

Despite its activities in the US, South East Asia and Asia, Heineken recognises the significance of its strength in Europe—a particularly important market, which accounts for over 40 per cent of world beer sales. Here, despite the mass appeal of the Heineken brand, to stay ahead of the competition the company has to adjust its product mix to suit the needs of different countries, fitting in with local cultures and tastes. In general, Heineken achieves this goal by offering a choice of three core brands in each European country:

- A local brand, aimed at the standard and largest market segment. In Italy this is Dreher, in France "33" and in Spain Aguila Pilsener.
- A brand targeted at the "upper" end of the market. Sometimes this is a locally produced brand, such as the Spanish Aguila Master; in other cases a newer Heineken brand, Amstel, is preferred.
- The Heineken brand itself, aimed at the premium market segment. The beer offered may be manufactured locally or it may be exported from the Netherlands. Either way, the Dutch head office works hard to maintain product quality and brand image.

Chairman Karel Vuursteen believes that it is the proven combination of the Heineken brand with local mainstream brands that creates the successful level of distribution in the market and adequate economies of scale in production. Heineken has a share in over 60 brewing companies around the globe to help facilitate this strategy. The company also keeps up with trends, including Murphy's, iced beers and non-alcoholic brews such as Buckler.

Branding policy in the UK differs slightly from that implemented in other parts of Europe. The standard Heineken brand there is a lower strength version of the beer offered in Europe. The lower strength lager first became popular in pubs across the UK in the 1960s. Now, with the increasing sophistication of the UK beer drinker, the company has introduced the Heineken Export Strength brand—more closely akin to the "standard" Heineken offered throughout Europe.

The competition was caught unawares, however, in 1996 when Heineken re-launched its standard, original Heineken brand, with new packaging and heavy promotional support. Heineken deliberately ambushed arch rival Carlsberg, high profile sponsors of the Euro '96 football championships. The Heineken brand re-launch was successful in its own right but additionally proved an interesting spoiling tactic against Carlsberg's football sponsorship.

SOURCES: Caroline Farquhar, Warwick MBA, 1991–92; "The Netherlands trade review—the beverage market", Economic Intelligence Unit, *Marketing in Europe*, no. 347, October 1991, p. 36; Heineken annual report and accounts, 1991, 1994 and 1996; David Benardy, "Heineken Euro '96 plot", *Marketing Week*, 23 February 1996, p. 7; Nina Munk, "Make mine Hoegaarden", *Forbes*, 18 December 1995, pp. 124–126; Havis Dawson, "Brand brewing", *Beverage World*, October 1995, pp. 50–60; "Heineken stresses sponsorship in marketing non-alcoholic beer", *Crossborder Monitor*, 11 January 1995, p. 9.

Questions for Discussion

1. Why was the UK's version of Heineken lager weaker than its counterpart in the rest of Europe? What problems has this product variation caused Heineken?
2. Why does Heineken opt for a mix of internationally known brands marketed alongside local beers?
3. In what ways is Heineken continuously up-dating its product portfolio and its marketing mix?

8.2 Disney Expands Its Product Mix

After the death of its founder Walt Disney in 1966, the Walt Disney Company seemed to lose its creative edge. As other studios diversified into television and video, Disney seemed content with its library of feature films and animated classics. The company was producing only three or four new films a year, most of which failed at the box office. Disney also pulled out of television after 29 years of network programming. By the mid-1980s, Disney was dependent on theme parks and property development for about 75 per cent of its revenues.

Today, however, Disney executives are intent on re-capturing—and building on—the old Disney magic. Company executives say that the Disney name, culture, films and library are the company's biggest resources, and Disney's plan is to rejuvenate old assets and simultaneously develop new ones. While continuing its traditional appeal to the family segment of the film market, Disney, through its Touchstone Pictures division, is turning out films for adult audiences as well. The company is releasing both old and new programmes for television syndication and testing new promotional and licensing projects. In addition, the Disney theme park has been exported. The Tokyo Disneyland is

attracting millions of people a year, and a $2 billion Disneyland Paris opened in 1992. Disney's overall strategy is to channel the company's revived creativity into improved theme parks, to use the parks to generate interest in Disney films and to promote both parks and merchandise through Disney television shows.

The year 1995 proved a watershed and emphasised the company's turnaround: a blockbuster merger with Capital Cities/ABC, a management coup in hiring Hollywood superagent Michael Ovitz, a turnaround at EuroDisney near Paris, two smash movies—*Pocahontas* and *Toy Story*—and the headhunting of Nickelodeon executive Geraldine Laybourne. The ABC link is perhaps the most significant aspect; never before has a company with the marketing, merchandising and management expertise of Disney owned a television network. ABC is expected to become a powerful promotional vehicle for Disney.

Disney received its new lease on life a few years ago when threats of a corporate takeover prompted the company to replace its top executives. The new management moved quickly to tap the resources of the Disney television and film library. About two hundred Disney films and cartoon packages are now available on video cassette; other classic films, such as *Snow White,* will now be released to theatres every five years instead of every seven. The studio plans to release one new animated film for children every 18 months and about a dozen adult films a year.

Disney is back on network television as well, with the return of the *Disney Sunday Movie.* The company also produces the comedy show *The Golden Girls,* now in syndication, along with two top rated Saturday morning cartoon shows. Following the lead of other studios, Disney has moved into television syndication by marketing packages of feature films, old cartoons and *Wonderful World of Disney* programmes. The company is syndicating *The Disney Afternoon,* a block of children's cartoons that will run from 3 p.m. to 5 p.m. New shows are also being produced for syndication. They include the popular game show *Win, Lose or Draw,* a business news programme and film reviews by Roger Ebert. In an otherwise flat cable television market, the number of subscribers to the family oriented Disney Channel has jumped dramatically—to 4 million. The channel now offers 24 hour features and more original programming than any other pay service. Disney has even signed an agreement with the Chinese government to broadcast a weekly television series starring Mickey Mouse and Donald Duck. The company may license the Chinese to produce Disney merchandise as well.

In the United States, too, marketing of Disney characters is receiving considerable emphasis. Recently, Mickey, Donald and others visited hospital wards and marched in parades in a 120 city tour. Snow White and all seven dwarfs made a special appearance on the floor of the New York Stock Exchange to promote the celebration of Snow White's 50th birthday. Minnie Mouse now has a trendy new look and appears on clothing and watches and in a fashion doll line. Disney is also working with toy companies to develop new characters, such as Fluppy Dogs and Wuzzles, both of which will be sold in stores and featured in television shows. In addition, the company has opened non-tourist retail outlets. Located primarily in shopping malls, Disney Stores carry both licensed products and exclusive theme park merchandise. Disney Stores are now found in most large cities

across Europe. The latest generation opened in Las Vegas and San Francisco, providing an inventive and colourful display of wizardry and entertainment far beyond the traditional retail store.

Disney's revitalised market presence has been credited with increasing attendance at the Disney theme parks to more than 50 million people. In Florida, Disney has recently completed new hotels and a movie studio/tour attraction. Moreover, Disney is constructing a 50 acre water park and adding $1.4 billion worth of new attractions to Walt Disney World. The company is also considering regional centres that would combine restaurants and shopping with evening entertainment. In a recent move, Disney announced plans to extend its expertise into the European time-share business by launching the Disney Vacation Club. The new concept offers holidaymakers accommodations in purpose built facilities at Florida's Disney World. The price is a once only payment of £7,000, which will give club members access to accommodation at Disney World, or over 100 other destinations around the world. It is not yet clear whether the company plans to build vacation clubs at other Disney sites.

Disney intends eventually to reduce the company's financial dependence on parks and hotels. The strategy is to triple the proportion of company profits from films and television and to acquire such distribution outlets as cinemas, television stations and record companies. Recent business deals with Procter & Gamble, McDonald's, Coca-Cola, Time, M&M/Mars, and Sears will help increase Disney's profits and market presence still further.

SOURCES: Stanley Bing, "More magic from Mickey's and Michael's kingdom", *Fortune,* 15 January 1996, p. 51; "Disney's ABC buy creates media co of the future", *Brandweek,* 7 August 1995, p. 4; Marianne Wilson, "Disney's one-two punch", *Chain Store Executive,* July 1995, pp. 92–93; Dudley Clendinen, "Disney's mouse of marketing", *New York Times,* 22 November 1986, pp. 41–L; Pamela Ellis-Simon, "Hi ho, hi ho", *Marketing & Media Decisions,* September 1986, pp. 52–54; Andrea Gabor and Steve L. Hawkins, "Of mice and money in the magic kingdom", *U.S. News & World Report,* 22 December 1986, pp. 44–46; Ronald Grover, "Disney's magic", *Business Week,* 9 March 1987, pp. 62–65; Scott Hume, "Sears gains exclusivity with Disney contract", *Advertising Age,* 23 November 1987, p. 63; Stephen Koepp, "Do you believe in magic?", *Time,* 25 April 1988, pp. 66–76; Marcy Magiera, "Disney tries retailing", *Advertising Age,* 1 June 1987, p. 80; Myron Magnet, "Putting magic back in the kingdom", *Fortune,* 5 January 1987, p. 65;

Raymond Roel, "Disney's marketing touch", *Direct Marketing,* January 1987, pp. 50–53; Stephen J. Sansweet, "Disney Co. cartoons are going to China in commercial foray", *Wall Street Journal,* 23 October 1986, p. 19; Susan Spillman, "Animation draws on its storied past", *USA Today,* 15 November 1989, pp. 1B–2B; Wayne Walley, "Disney enlists Time Inc., Mars to honor Mickey", *Advertising Age,* 6 June 1988, pp. 3, 110; Wayne Walley, "P & G, Disney link videos, products", *Advertising Age,* 18 January 1988, p. 1; and Wayne Walley, "Roger Rabbit makes splash", *Advertising Age,* 27 June 1988, pp. 3, 110; "Disney hunts marketer for Euro timeshare club", *Marketing Week,* 19 February 1993, p. 5; Disney Stores, Walsgrave Triangle, Coventry, 1999; Disneyland Paris, 1999.

Questions for Discussion

1. Disney's product mix consists of many products. Does Disney have product lines? If so, what are they?
2. Disney labels many of its new films for adults as Touchstone Pictures. With a famous name like Disney, why does the company not use the Disney name?
3. Do the products in the Disney product mix have product life cycles? Explain.

9 Branding and Packaging

OBJECTIVES

- To recognise the importance of brands and brand equity
- To understand the types and benefits of brands and how to select, name, protect and license them
- To become aware of the major packaging functions and design considerations and of the way in which packaging is used in marketing strategies
- To examine the functions of labelling and the legal issues associated with labelling

"Brands are at the very heart of marketing. When a company creates a strong brand it attracts customer preference and builds a defensive wall against competition."

Peter Doyle, Warwick Business School

At a factory in York, each day a mountain of thumb-nail sized tyre-shaped white mints is deemed slightly imperfect: chipped, broken or not properly moulded. The sight is awe inspiring, but gives a clue as to the volume of perfectly formed Polo mints manufactured: millions are produced, packaged and shipped daily. With Nestlé's take-over of Rowntree, the world domination of Polo—"the mint with the hole"—was assured. Polo is the UK's top selling mint, with sales of £30 million pa, and has established leadership in many other countries, too. It was not too long before trial flavours and strengths were tried by the product developers in Nestlé. However, the end of 1998 saw one of the most successful spin-offs from the original Polo concept, the sugar-free Polo Supermint, for "instant refreshment". This was not only a masterly extension of the Polo name but proved to be also an inspired packaging execution.

The Polo Supermint from Nestlé Rowntree has even been awarded *Millennium Products* status by the Design Council, an accolade reserved for only a few new designs. The new mini-mints "with the hole" weigh only a tenth of the original, yet contain four times the amount of peppermint oil in relation to their size. The super strength mint not only has appealed to traditional Polo mint buyers, but also has enabled the brand to compete head-to-head with the plethora of extra strong mints produced by rival manufacturers such as Trebor.

The new size and extra strong Polo would inevitably have caught the eye of confectionery buyers on the back of the Polo heritage and the extensive distribution network established by the mighty Nestlé. The marketers of Nestlé wanted to ensure a successful launch and were determined to make the new item distinctive and appealing in its own right. The innovative packaging design and eye catching styling of the new item made an immediate impact in a rather crowded marketplace. The Supermints are packed in plastic dispensers, developed by RPC Market Rasen, which are themselves shaped as giant versions of the original and very familiar Polo mint. The pack houses a pop-up hatch which enables it to dispense individual mini-Polos and to be easily resealed. The regular user soon develops the ability to dispense one-handed and in suitable quantities to appease friends also requiring a refreshing treat. The plastic dispenser is itself packaged in a cool blue square container with eye catching graphics, permitting easy stocking and shelf displays.

Nestlé says that while the mini-Polos were launched to celebrate the Polo brand's 50th birthday, the new item has emerged as one of the company's greatest successes ever. Nestlé believes this demonstrates it is possible to innovate with a 50 year brand. The new item, though, matched the brand values and positioning of the original Polo mint, reflected competitor moves and responded to consumer tastes. The combination of astute branding and clever packaging has certainly created a very successful product for Nestlé and a welcome alternative for Polo fans.

Polo Supermint: revolutionary designed dispenser has helped invigorate a 50-year-old brand

SOURCES: Nestlé Rowntree, York, 1999; Dillons Ltd, 1999; *Marketing,* 4 February 1999, p. 22. *Advertisement:* Courtesy of Nestlé Rowntree.

Brands and packages are part of a product's tangible features, the verbal and physical cues that help customers identify the products they want and influence their choices when they are unsure. For Nestlé's Polo Supermints, branding and packaging have been central to the product's success. A good brand is distinct and memorable; without one, companies could not differentiate their products, and shoppers' choices would essentially be arbitrary. A good package design is cost effective, safe, environmentally responsible and valuable as a promotional tool.

The first part of this chapter defines branding and explains its benefits to customers and sellers, and then examines the importance of brand equity and the various types of brands. The next section explores how companies choose brands, how they protect them, the various branding policies that companies employ and brand licensing. The chapter goes on to discuss how businesses manage brands and ensure that they contribute effectively to the company's fortunes. It then examines the critical role of packaging as part of the product and how it is marketed. The following section explores the functions of packaging, issues to consider in packaging design, how the package can be a major element in marketing strategy and packaging criticisms. The chapter concludes with a discussion of labelling and other product related features, including the product's physical characteristics and supportive product related services.

Branding

Brand A name, term, design, symbol or any other feature that identifies one seller's good or service as distinct from those of other sellers

In addition to making decisions about actual products, marketers must make many decisions associated with branding, such as brands, brand names, brand marks, trademarks and trade names. A **brand** is a name, term, design, symbol or any other feature that identifies one seller's good or service as distinct from those of other sellers. A brand may identify one item, a family of items or all items of

269

Brand name That part of a brand that can be spoken, including letters, words and numbers

Brand mark The element of a brand that cannot be spoken—often a symbol or design

Trademark Legal designation indicating that the owner has exclusive use of a brand

Trade name The full and legal name of an organisation

that seller.[1] A **brand name** is that part of a brand that can be spoken—including letters, words and numbers—such as Coca-Cola. A brand name is often a product's only distinguishing characteristic. Without the brand name, a company could not identify its products. To consumers, brand names are as fundamental as the product itself. Brand names simplify shopping, guarantee a specific level of quality and allow self-expression.[2] Table 9.1 details the world's most valuable brands. For many marketers, establishing a distinctive brand, which is easily remembered and recognised by targeted customers, is one of the primary activities of effective marketing management.

The element of a brand that is not made up of words but is often a symbol or design is called a **brand mark**. One example is the symbol of a baby on Procter & Gamble's Fairy Liquid detergent. Occasionally brand marks are modified for local markets. For example, Microsoft tops its brand name with a butterfly in France, a fish in Portugal and a sun in Spain. A **trademark** is a legal designation indicating that the owner has exclusive use of a brand or a part of a brand and that others are prohibited by law from using it. To protect a brand name or brand mark a company must register it as a trademark with the appropriate patenting office. Finally, a **trade name** is the full and legal name of an organisation, such as Ford Motor Company or Safeway Stores, rather than the name of a specific product.

Benefits of Branding

Branding provides benefits for both buyers and sellers.[3] Brands help buyers identify specific products that they do and do not like, a process that in turn facilitates the purchase of items that satisfy their needs and reduces the time required to purchase the product. Without brands, product selection would be quite random, because buyers could have no assurance that they were purchasing what they preferred. Imagine the chaos in a supermarket if every shopper entered not knowing which products and brands to purchase! Research indicates, however, that the bulk of supermarket shoppers are highly brand loyal. So much so, that in-store redesigns and new shelf-space allocations cause significant distress and generate high levels of customer complaints. A brand also helps buyers evaluate the quality of a product, especially when they are unable to judge its characteris-

Table 9.1 The world's most valuable brands

Brand	Brand Value (in millions)
Coca-Cola	$47,978
Marlboro	47,635
IBM	23,701
McDonald's	19,939
Disney	17,069
Sony	14,464
Kodak	14,442
Intel	13,274
Gillette	11,992
Budweiser	11,985

SOURCE: Kurt Bradenhausen, "Most Valuable Brands", *Financial World*, September/October 1997, p. 62.

tics. In other words, a purchaser for whom a brand symbolises a certain quality level will transfer that perception of quality to the unknown item. A brand thus helps to reduce a buyer's perceived risk of purchase. In addition, it may offer the psychological reward that comes from owning a brand that symbolises status. Certain brands of watches (Rolex) and cars (Rolls Royce) fall into this category.[4]

Sellers benefit from branding because each company's brands identify its products, which makes repeat purchasing easier for consumers. Branding helps a company introduce a new product that carries the name of one or more of its existing products, because buyers are already familiar with the company's existing brands. For example, Heinz regularly introduces new tinned products. Because consumers are used to buying the brand and have a high regard for its quality, they are likely to try the new offerings. Branding also facilitates promotional efforts because the promotion of each branded product indirectly promotes all other products that are similarly branded.

Brand loyalty A strongly motivated and long standing decision to purchase a particular product or service

Branding also helps sellers by fostering brand loyalty. **Brand loyalty** is a strongly motivated and long standing decision to purchase a particular product or service. To the extent that buyers become loyal to a specific brand, the company's market share for that product achieves a certain level of stability, allowing the company to use its resources more efficiently.[5] Loyal customers are highly desirable and much marketing activity is aimed at re-assuring existing customers and canvassing their ongoing support and interest. When a company succeeds in fostering some degree of customer loyalty to a brand, it can charge a premium price for the product. For example, brand loyal buyers of Anadin aspirin are willing to pay two or three times more for Anadin than for a generic brand of aspirin with the same amount of pain relieving agent. However, brand loyalty is declining, partly because of marketers' increased reliance on discounted sales, coupons and other short term promotions and partly because of the sometimes overwhelming array of similar new products from which consumers can choose. In the brand dominated US, a *Wall Street Journal* survey found that 12 per cent of consumers are not loyal to any brand, whereas 47 per cent are brand loyal for one to five product types. Only 2 per cent of the respondents were brand loyal for more than 16 product types (see Figure 9.1). To stimulate loyalty to their brands, some marketers are stressing image advertising, mailing personalised catalogues and magazines to regular users, and creating membership clubs for brand users, for example, Tesco's Club Card or Sainsbury's Reward points.[6] Sometimes consumers make repeat purchases of products for reasons other than brand loyalty. Spurious loyalty is not stable and may result from non-availability of alternative brands or the way in which products are displayed in retail outlets.

Brand recognition A customer's awareness that a brand exists and is an alternative to purchase

There are three degrees of brand loyalty: recognition, preference and insistence. **Brand recognition** exists when a customer is aware that a brand exists and views it as an alternative to purchase if the preferred brand is unavailable or if the other available brands are unfamiliar to the customer. This is the mildest form of brand loyalty. The term *loyalty* clearly is being used very loosely here. One of the initial objectives of a marketer introducing a new brand is to create widespread awareness of the brand in order to generate brand recognition. This theme is re-considered in Part V—Promotion Decisions.

Brand preference The degree of brand loyalty in which a customer prefers one brand over competitive offerings

Brand preference is a stronger degree of brand loyalty in which a customer definitely prefers one brand over competitive offerings and will purchase this brand if it is available. However, if the brand is not available, the customer will accept a substitute brand rather than expend additional effort finding and purchasing the preferred brand. A marketer is likely to be able to compete effectively in a

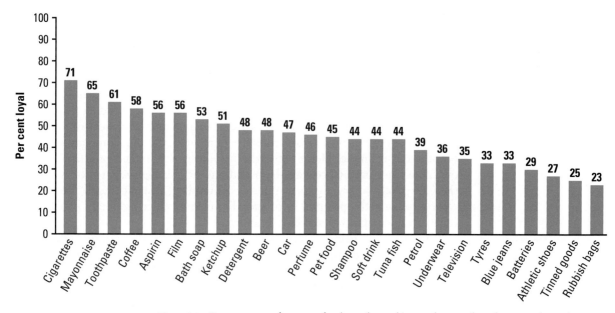

Figure 9.1 Percentage of users of selected products who are loyal to one brand.
SOURCE: Republished by permission of Dow Jones, Inc. via Copyright Clearance Center, Inc.
© 1989 Dow Jones and Company, Inc. All rights reserved worldwide.

market when a number of customers have developed brand preference for its specific brand.

Brand insistence is the degree of brand loyalty in which a customer strongly prefers a specific brand, will accept no substitute and is willing to spend a great deal of time and effort to acquire that brand. If a brand insistent customer goes to a store and finds the brand unavailable, rather than purchasing a substitute brand the customer will seek the brand elsewhere. Brand insistence is the strongest degree of brand loyalty. It is a marketer's dream. However, it is the least common type of brand loyalty. Customers vary considerably regarding the product categories for which they may be brand insistent.

Brand insistence The degree of brand loyalty in which a customer strongly prefers a specific brand and will accept no substitute

Brand Equity

Brand equity The marketing and financial value associated with a brand's strength in a market

A well managed brand is an asset to an organisation. The value of this asset is often referred to as brand equity. **Brand equity** is the marketing and financial value associated with a brand's strength in a market. Besides the actual proprietary brand assets, such as patents and trademarks, four major elements underlie brand equity. These components are brand name awareness, brand loyalty, perceived brand quality and brand associations, as shown in Figure 9.2.[7]

Being aware of a brand leads to brand familiarity, which in turn results in a level of comfort with the brand. A familiar brand is more likely to be selected than an unfamiliar brand because the familiar brand often is viewed as reliable and of acceptable quality compared to the unknown brand. The familiar brand is likely to be in a customer's evoked set whereas the unfamiliar brand is not.

Brand loyalty is a valued component of brand equity because it reduces a brand's vulnerability to competitors' actions. Brand loyalty allows an organisation to keep its existing customers and not have to spend enormous amounts of resources gaining new customers. Loyal customers provide brand visibility and re-assurance to potential new customers. And because customers expect their

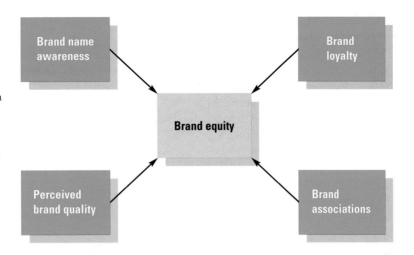

Figure 9.2 Major elements of brand equity. SOURCE: Adapted with the permission of The Free Press, a division of Simon & Schuster, Inc., from *Managing Brand Equity: Capitalizing on the Value of a Brand Name* by David A. Aaker. Copyright © 1991 by David A. Aaker.

brand to be available when and where they shop, retailers strive to carry the brands known for their strong customer following.

Customers associate a certain level of perceived overall quality with a brand. A brand name itself actually stands for a certain level of quality in a customer's mind and is used as a substitute for actual judgement of quality. In many cases customers can't actually judge the quality of the product for themselves and instead must rely on the brand as a quality indicator. Perceived high brand quality helps to support a premium price, allowing a marketer to avoid severe price competition. Also, favourable perceived brand quality can ease the introduction of brand extensions, as the high regard for the brand will likely translate into high regard for the related products.

The set of associations linked to a brand is another key component of brand equity. At times a marketer works to connect a lifestyle, or in some instances a certain personality type, with a particular brand. For example, customers associate Volvo cars with protecting family members, a De Beers diamond with a loving, long lasting relationship (*A diamond is forever*), and Drambuie Liqueur with a unique taste. These types of brand associations contribute significantly to the brand's equity.

Although difficult to measure, brand equity represents the value of a brand to an organisation. An organisation may buy a brand from another company at a premium price because outright brand purchase may be less expensive and less risky than creating and developing a brand from scratch, for example, IKEA's purchase of Habitat. Brand equity helps to give a brand the power to capture and maintain a consistent market share, which provides stability to an organisation's sales volume. The top ten brands with the highest economic value are shown in Table 9.1. The values were determined by multiplying a brand's net profits by the brand's strength index.[8] Any company that owns a brand listed in Table 9.1 would agree that the economic value of that brand is likely to be the greatest single asset in the organisation's possession. A brand's overall economic value rises and falls with the brand's profitability, brand awareness, brand loyalty, perceived brand quality and strength of positive brand associations.

Types of Brands There are three categories of brands: manufacturer brands, own label brands (also called private brands, store brands or dealer brands) and generic brands.

Manufacturer brands are initiated by producers and ensure that producers are identified with their products at the point of purchase—for example, Green Giant, Apple Computer and Wall's ice cream. A manufacturer brand usually requires a producer to become involved in distribution, promotion and, to some extent, pricing decisions. Brand loyalty is encouraged by promotion, quality control and guarantees; it is a valuable asset to a manufacturer. The producer tries to stimulate demand for the product, which tends to encourage middlemen to make the product available. Figure 9.3 shows UDV appealing to its trade distributors.

Own label brands are initiated and owned by resellers—wholesalers or retailers. The major characteristic of own label brands is that the manufacturers are

Figure 9.3 Types of brands. UDV appeals to its trade distributors.
SOURCE: Courtesy of UDV.

not identified on the products. Retailers and wholesalers use these brands to develop more efficient promotion, to generate higher gross margins and to improve store images. Own label brands give retailers or wholesalers freedom to purchase products of a specified quality at the lowest cost without disclosing the identity of the manufacturer. Wholesale brands include Roca, Family Choice, Happy Shopper and Lifestyle. Familiar retailer brand names include St. Michael (Marks & Spencer), Yessica (C & A) and George (Asda). Many successful own label brands are distributed nationally. Matsui domestic appliances (Currys) are as well known as most name brands. Sometimes retailers with successful distributor brands start manufacturing their own products to gain more control over product costs, quality and design in the hope of increasing profits. While one might think that store brands appeal most strongly to lower income shoppers or to up-market shoppers who compare labels, studies indicate that buyers of own label brands have characteristics that match those of the overall population.[9]

Generic brand A brand that indicates only the product category and does not include the company name or other identifying terms

Some marketers of products that have traditionally been branded have embarked on a policy of not branding, often called generic branding. A **generic brand** indicates only the product category (such as aluminum foil) and does not include the company name or other identifying terms. Usually generic brands are sold at prices lower than those of comparable branded items. Although at one time generic brands may have represented as much as 10 per cent of all retail grocery sales, today they account for less than 1 per cent.[10] They are popular for pharmaceuticals and in some discount grocery stores.

Competition between manufacturer brands and own label brands (sometimes called "the battle of the brands") is intensifying in several major product categories, particularly tinned foods, breakfast cereal, sugar and soft drinks. Own label brands now account for around 40 per cent of all supermarket sales.[11] Both men and women are quite favourable towards own label brands of food products, with women (still the major grocery purchasers) even more favourable than men. For manufacturers, developing multiple manufacturer brands and distribution systems has been an effective means of combating the increased competition from own label brands. By developing a new brand name, a producer can adjust various elements of a marketing mix to appeal to a different target market. For example, Scott Paper has developed lower priced brands of paper towels; it has tailored its new products to a target market that tends to purchase own label brands.

Manufacturers find it hard to ignore the marketing opportunities that come from producing own label brands for resellers. If a manufacturer refuses to produce an own label brand for a reseller, a competing manufacturer will. Moreover, the production of own label brands allows the manufacturer to use excess capacity during periods when its own brands are at non-peak production. The ultimate decision whether to produce an own label or a manufacturer brand depends on a company's resources, production capabilities and goals.

Choosing a Brand Name

Marketers should consider a number of factors when they choose a brand name. The name should be easy for customers—including foreign buyers, if the company intends to market its products in other countries—to say, spell and recall. Short, one syllable names such as Mars or Tide satisfy this requirement. The brand name should indicate the product's major benefits and, if possible, should suggest in a positive way the product's uses and special characteristics: negative or offensive references should be avoided. For example, a deodorant should be branded with a name that signals freshness, dryness or long lasting protection, as do Sure, Right Guard and Arrid Extra Dry. The brand should be distinctive, to set it apart from competing brands. If a marketer intends to use a brand for a product line, it must be compatible with all products in the line. Finally, a brand should be designed so that it can be used and recognised in all of the various types of media. Finding the right brand name has become a challenging task, because many obvious product names have already been used. Marketing Insight 9.1 outlines the role played by brand name consultancies in the naming process.

How are brand names derived? Brand names can be created from single or multiple words—for example, Bic or Findus Lean Cuisine. Initials, numbers or sometimes combinations are used to create brands such as IBM PC. At times, words, numbers and initials are combined to yield brand names such as Mazda MX5 or Mitsubishi 3000GT. To avoid terms that have negative connotations, marketers sometimes use fabricated words that have absolutely no meaning at the point when they are created—for example, Kodak and Esso. Occasionally, a brand is simply brought out of storage and used as is or modified. Companies often maintain banks of registered brands, some of which may have been used in the past. Cadillac, for example, has a bank of approximately 360 registered trademarks. The LaSalle brand, used in the 1920s and 1930s, may be called up for a new Cadillac model soon to be introduced.[12] Possible brand names are sometimes tested in focus groups or in other settings to assess customers' reactions.

Who actually creates brand names? Brand names can be created internally by the organisation. Sometimes a name is suggested by individuals who are close to the development of the product. Some organisations have committees that participate in brand name creation and approval. Large companies that introduce numerous new products annually are likely to have a department that develops brand names. Increasingly, outside consultants are used in the process of developing brand names. An organisation may also hire a company that specialises in brand name development.

Even though most of the important branding considerations apply to both goods and services, services branding has some additional dimensions. The brand of the service is usually the same as the company name. For example, American Express, Vidal Sassoon, ProntoPrint and Sheraton are names of companies and the services that they provide. Whereas companies that produce tangible goods (such as Procter & Gamble) can use separate brand names for separate products (such as Daz, Head & Shoulders, Flash and Camay), service providers (such as British Airways) are perceived by customers as having one brand name, even though they offer multiple products (first class, business class and economy). Because the service brand name and company name are so closely interrelated, a service brand name must be flexible enough to encompass a variety of current services, as well as new ones that the company might offer in the future. For example, British Airways—BA—has Club World or Eurotraveller (economy) services, each separately branded, but both strongly branded as BA. Geographical references like "western" and descriptive terms like "trucking" limit the scope of associations that can be made with the brand name. "Northwest Airlines" is not a good name as the company begins flying south and east.[13] Frequently, a service marketer will employ a symbol along with its brand name to make the brand distinctive and to communicate a certain image.

Protecting a Brand Marketers need to design brands that can be protected easily through registration. Amongst the most difficult to protect are generic words, such as aluminum foil, surnames and descriptive geographic or functional names.[14] Because of their

Who Thought of That Name!

Burger King, Coca-Cola, JCB, Nike, Sony or Virgin—no matter what the brand, someone, somewhere and sometime created the names now recognised instantly by millions of loyal customers. David Rivett of Design Bridge, responsible for many new product development projects and the creation of brand names, believes that all too often clients focus on the physical properties of their new products—features, size, colours, quality, operation—at the expense of name consideration, which is "tacked on" to the new product development process just prior to launch. Branding consultancies believe that creating the right atmosphere and having a very clear understanding of both client culture and target market characteristics are fundamental to the creation of a suitable brand name. Very often a "creative workshop" is used by the consultancy to probe the minds of the client personnel in order to establish buzz words or emotive trigger descriptions for the new product which may be incorporated in the brand name. The name for Anchor's So Soft new spreadable butter was so created.

The real difficulty comes not from creating a suitable name, but in registering the preferred choice. Intellectual property lawyers now specialise in trademark registration and searching. Qualitative research, such as focus groups, often throws up many brand names consumers believe might be appropriate. Marketing strategy workshops amongst managers in a company frequently do the same. The result is that some organisations compile extensive lists of names with potential for their types of products, which are then registered even though at the time there is no expectation of using these names. Companies such as Cadbury or Ford have large lists of already registered brand names which at some time they might use but which are no longer available to any other company. This is not "sharp practice", but merely a logical extension of marketers hearing good suggestions from colleagues, distributors and consumers and marking them down for future use.

Another consideration for branding consultancies is how the new product's name will work alongside the client's umbrella brand. For example, Novon is given independence from owner Sainsbury's and Cap Colombie from Nescafé, whereas the Focus, Mondeo and Maverick names are very much tied to the Ford umbrella brand. There is no right or wrong in this dilemma. Some companies, such as Sainsbury's with Novon, want to create sub-brands which in the eyes of target consumers are apparently free-standing. For Ford, the logic of cross-promotion and economies of scale in creating brand awareness have persuaded senior marketers to always utilise the Ford brand alongside the individual model name.

Most brand names are at some point in the creation process tested out on consumers, but according to leading branding consultancy Interbrand Newell & Sorrell, such tests have to be carefully constrained so as not to allow consumer suggestions to set the process back to square one. The research, argues Interbrand, should identify profoundly wrong name suggestions, rather than present consumers with a blank sheet of paper for totally new suggestions. Interbrand's Nometrics testing methodology is well respected in the branding fraternity. First, names are tested in isolation of any product or service. Consumers are invited to nominate likely products to be associated with the suggested names. In the second stage of the Nometrics process, names are overtly linked to specific products and the research gauges the views of consumers and their likelihood for purchasing such named products. Ultimately, a good name cannot overcome product deficiencies, poor distribution, ineffectual promotion, incorrect pricing or inferior customer service, or combat the superiority of a competitor's marketing strategy. A poor, inappropriate, confusing, unmemorable or misleading name can, though, do much harm to an otherwise good product offering.

SOURCES: Tom Blackett, Interbrand Newell & Sorrell; Deborah Carter, Dragon; David Rivett, Design Bridge; Colin Mechan, FLB; Paul Gander, "Generation Game", *Marketing Week*, 22 October 1998, pp. 45–48.

designs, some brands can be legally infringed upon more easily than others. Although registration provides trademark protection, a company should develop a system for ensuring that its trademarks will be renewed as needed. To protect its exclusive rights to a brand, the company must make certain that the selected brand is not likely to be considered an infringement on any existing brand already registered with the relevant patent office. This task may be complex because infringement is determined by the courts, which base their decisions on whether a brand causes consumers to be confused, mistaken or deceived about the source of the product. McDonald's is one company that aggressively protects its trademarks against infringement; it has brought charges against a number of companies with "Mc" names because it fears that the use of the "Mc" will give consumers the impression that these companies are associated with or owned by McDonald's. In Figure 9.4, LEGO includes a symbol within its logo to enhance the recognition of its brand.

If possible, marketers must guard against allowing a brand name to become a generic term used to refer to a general product category.[15] Generic terms cannot

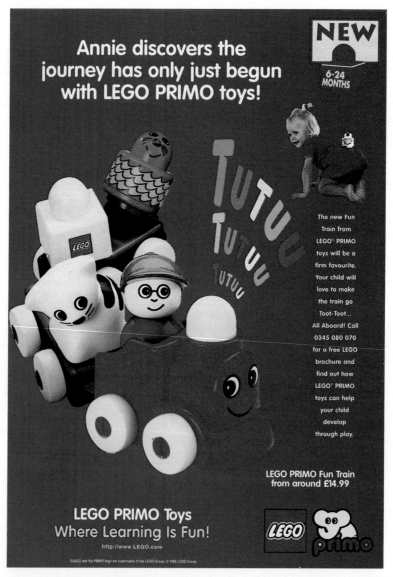

Figure 9.4 Using a symbol with a brand name. LEGO uses a symbol within its logo to make its brand distinctive. SOURCE: This visual is reproduced by special permission of the LEGO Company. The LEGO name is a registered trademark.

Part III Product, Branding, Packaging and Service Decisions

be protected as exclusive brand names. For example, names such as aspirin, escalator and shredded wheat—all brand names at one time—were eventually declared generic terms that refer to product classes; thus they no longer could be protected. To keep a brand name from becoming a generic term, the business should spell the name with a capital letter and use it as an adjective to modify the name of the general product class, as in Kellogg's Rice Krispies.[16] Including the word *brand* just after the brand name is also helpful. An organisation can deal with this problem directly by advertising that its brand is a trademark and should not be used generically. The company can also indicate that the brand is a registered trademark by using the symbol ®.

Companies that try to protect a brand in a foreign country frequently encounter problems. In many countries, brand registration is not possible; the first company to use a brand in such a country has the rights to it. In some instances, a company has actually had to buy its own brand rights from a company in a foreign country because the foreign company was the first user in that country.

Marketers trying to protect their brands must also contend with brand counterfeiting. In many countries, for instance, it is possible to buy fake General Motors parts, fake Rolex watches, fake Chanel perfume, fake Microsoft software, fake Walt Disney character dolls and a host of other products illegally marketed by manufacturers that do not own the brands. Many counterfeit products are manufactured overseas—in South Korea, Italy, Taiwan or China, for example—but some are counterfeited in the countries in which they are sold. The International Anti-Counterfeiting Coalition estimates that roughly $70 billion in annual world trade involves counterfeit merchandise. The sale of this merchandise obviously reduces the brand owners' revenues from marketing their own legitimate products.

Brand counterfeiting is particularly harmful because the usually inferior counterfeit product undermines consumers' confidence in the brand and their loyalty to it. After unknowingly purchasing a counterfeit product, the buyer may blame the legitimate manufacturer if the product is of low quality or—even worse—if its use results in damage or injury. Since counterfeiting has become such a serious problem, many companies are taking legal action against counterfeiters. Others have adopted such measures as modifying the product or the packaging to make counterfeit items easier to detect, conducting public awareness campaigns and monitoring distributors to ensure that they stock only legitimate brands.[17]

Branding Policies

Before it establishes branding policies, a company must first decide whether to brand its products at all. If a company's product is homogeneous and similar to competitors' products, it may be difficult to brand. Raw materials—such as coal, salt, sand and milk—are hard to brand because of the homogeneity of such products and their physical characteristics. Marketers must also consider the degree to which consumers differentiate among brands of a product. For example, while brand may be an important factor in the purchase of coffee, snacks and frozen foods, it is not usually so important a consideration in buying light bulbs, cheese and cling film.

If a company chooses to brand its products, it may opt for one or more of the following branding policies: individual, overall family, line family and brand extension branding. **Individual branding** is a policy of naming each product differently. Procter & Gamble relies on an individual branding policy for its line of fabric washing products, which includes Tide, Bold, Daz and Dreft.

Individual branding   A policy of naming each product differently

A major advantage of individual branding is that if an organisation introduces a poor product, the negative images associated with it will not contaminate the company's other products. An individual branding policy may also facilitate market segmentation when a company wishes to enter many segments of the same market. Separate, unrelated names can be used, and each brand can be aimed at a specific segment.

Overall family branding A policy of branding all of a company's products with the same name or at least part of the name

In **overall family branding**, all of a company's products are branded with the same name or at least part of the name, such as Kraft, Heinz, Microsoft or Ford. In some cases, a company's name is combined with other words to brand items. Heinz uses its name on its products along with a generic description of the item, such as Heinz Salad Cream, Heinz Baked Beans, Heinz Spaghetti and Heinz Tomato Soup. The quality image of its products increases consumer confidence in what they are buying. This brand consistency is stressed in Heinz advertisements (see Figure 9.5). Unlike individual branding, overall family branding means that the promotion of one item with the family brand promotes the company's other products.

Line family branding A policy of using family branding only for products within a single line

Sometimes an organisation uses family branding only for products within a single line. This policy is called **line family branding**. Colgate-Palmolive, for example, produces a line of cleaning products that includes a cleanser, a powdered detergent and a liquid cleaner—all with the name Ajax. Colgate also produces several brands of toothpaste, none of which carries the Ajax brand.

Brand extension branding A company's use of one of its existing brand names as part of an improved or new product, usually in the same product category as the existing brand

Brand extension branding occurs when a company uses one of its existing brand names as part of a brand for an improved or new product that is usually in the same product category as the existing brand. The makers of Timotei Shampoo extended the name to hair conditioner and skin care products. There is one major difference between line family branding and brand extension branding. With line family branding, all products in the line carry the same name, but

Figure 9.5 Overall family branding. Heinz uses its name on its products, along with a generic description of the item. SOURCE: Courtesy of Heinz.

with brand extension branding this is not the case. The producer of Arrid deodorant, for example, also makes other brands of deodorants.

An organisation is not limited to a single branding policy. Instead, branding policy is influenced by (1) the number of products and product lines the company produces, (2) the characteristics of its target markets, (3) the number and types of competing products available and (4) the size of its resources. Anheuser-Busch, for example, uses both individual and brand extension branding. Most of the brands are individual brands; however, the Michelob Light brand is an extension of the Michelob brand. Sometimes companies must up-date brands so that they remain fresh and interesting.

Brand Licensing

A recent trend in branding strategies involves the licensing of trademarks. By means of a licensing agreement, a company may permit approved manufacturers to use its trademark on other products for a licensing fee. Royalties may be as low as 2 per cent of wholesale revenues or higher than 10 per cent. The licensee is responsible for all manufacturing, selling and advertising functions and bears the costs if the licensed product fails. Not long ago, only a few companies licensed their corporate trademarks but today the licensing business is worth billions of pounds and is growing. Harley-Davidson, for example, has authorised the use of its name on non-motorcycle products such as cologne, wine coolers, gold rings and shirts. Disney also licenses its brand for use on a range of products. JCB and Coca-Cola both now license ranges of clothing sold in high street stores.

The advantages of licensing range from extra revenues and low cost to free publicity, new images and trademark protection. For example, Coca-Cola has licensed its trademark for use on glassware, radios, trucks and clothing in the hope of protecting its trademark. Similarly, Jaguar has licensed a range of leisure wear. However, brand licensing is not without drawbacks. The major disadvantages are a lack of manufacturing control, which could hurt the company's name, and the undesirability of bombarding consumers with too many unrelated products bearing the same name. Licensing arrangements can also fail because of poor timing, inappropriate distribution channels or mismatching of product and name.

Managing Brands

With the need for brands to create product differentiation, assist in establishing a competitive edge and encourage product awareness, marketers must manage their brands with care.[18] As explained in detail in the next chapter, this involves understanding when a brand requires re-positioning, modifying, deleting or simply being left alone. Most companies operate with a portfolio of separate brands and products and must make difficult decisions in terms of which are to receive support and the bulk of a business's marketing resource and which are to be killed off or given only minimal support. Chapter 21 explores these strategic choices. As explained in Chapter 4's discussion of consumer buying behaviour, without an understanding of brand loyalty and brand switching, it is difficult to manage a business's brands effectively. It is essential, therefore, for companies to make an effort to research brand loyalty and brand perceptions to help them make sensible decisions that accurately reflect consumers' views.

Research shows that to create **successful brands,** a company must:

Successful brands Brands for which a company must prioritise quality, offer superior service, get there first, differentiate brands, develop a unique positioning concept, have a strong communications programme and be consistent and reliable

- Prioritise quality—the top brands are all high quality in their product fields
- Offer superior service—less easily copied by competitors than pure product attributes
- Get there first—not necessarily technologically, but in the minds of targeted customers, by

1. Exploiting new technology (Rank Xerox, Sony)
2. New positioning concepts (Body Shop, First Direct)
3. New distribution channels (Argos, Direct Line)
4. New market segments (Amstrad, Orange)
5. Using gaps resulting from environmental change (Ecover, Daz Ultra)

- Differentiate its brands—so that consumers perceive the brands on offer as being different
- Develop a unique positioning concept—making the brand and its differentiating characteristics stand out with a clear image and positioning message against rival brands
- Support the brand and its positioning with a strong communications programme—so that target consumers are aware of the brand and its positioning proposition
- Deliver consistency and reliability over time—keeping the brand's values trust-worthy as perceived by target consumers.

Levels of brands The tangible product, the "basic" brand, the "augmented" brand and the "potential" of the brand

Branding expert Peter Doyle[19] states that to build effective brands it is essential for a business to understand that there is more to a brand than simply a catchy name and visible logo. There are, in fact, four **levels of brands:** the tangible product, the "basic" brand, the "augmented" brand and the "potential" of the brand. Level 1, the tangible product, is the degree of quality, performance, features and actual attributes. Level 2, the "basic" brand, is the identity, differentiation and positioning. Level 3, the "augmented" brand, is the aggregated impact from including supplementary products and service support. Level 4, the "potential" of the brand, is reached when customers will not willingly accept substitutes and are unhappy to switch to rival brands; psychological benefits and barriers in the minds of target customers are important determinants of brand potential. There are three essential acid tests for determining whether a brand is successful. Although most companies consider only the overall profit contribution to the end-of-year financial annual report and accounts, when determining a brand's success they should ask the following three fundamental questions:

1. Has the brand captured the leading share in its market segment or distribution channel?
2. Does the brand command prices sufficiently high enough to produce a high profit margin?
3. Will the brand sustain its strong share of profits when rival and generic versions of the product enter the market?

Using these core criteria, many brands are relatively unsuccessful. For marketers, managing brands must include knowing when a brand is succeeding, when it is faltering but may be saved, and when a brand is a lost cause and should be deleted from the company's range of brands. Chapter 21, "Marketing Strategy", examines this difficult issue in more detail.

Packaging

Packaging The development of a product's container and label, complete with graphic design

Packaging involves the development of a container and label, complete with graphic design for a product. A package can be a vital part of a product, making it more versatile, safer or easier to use. Like a brand name, a package can influence customers' attitudes towards a product and thus affect their purchase decisions. For example, several producers of sauces, salad dressings and ketchups have packaged their products in squeezable containers to make use and storage more convenient. Package characteristics help shape buyers' impressions of a product at the time of purchase or during use. This section examines the main functions of packaging and considers several major packaging decisions. The role of the package in marketing strategy is also analysed.

Packaging Functions

Effective packaging means more than simply putting products into containers and covering them with wrappers. First of all, packaging materials serve the basic purpose of protecting the product and maintaining its functional form. Fluids such as milk, orange juice and hair spray need packages that preserve and protect them; the packaging should prevent damage that could affect the product's usefulness and increase costs. Since product tampering has become a problem for marketers of many types of goods, several packaging techniques have been developed to counter this danger. Some packages are also designed to foil shoplifters.

Another function of packaging is to offer convenience for consumers. For example, small, sealed packages—individual sized boxes or plastic bags that contain liquids and do not require refrigeration—strongly appeal to children and young adults with active lifestyles. The size or shape of a package may relate to the product's storage, convenience of use or replacement rate. Small, single serving tins of fruit, such as Del Monte's Fruitinni, may prevent waste and make storage easier. Low, regular-shaped packets may be easier to stack and use cupboard space more efficiently. A third function of packaging is to promote a product by communicating its features, uses, benefits and image. At times, a re-usable package is developed to make the product more desirable. For example, some ice cream containers can be used again as food storage containers.

Major Packaging Considerations

When developing packages, marketers must take many factors into account. Some of these factors relate to consumers' needs; others relate to the requirements of resellers. Obviously, one major consideration is cost. Although a variety of packaging materials, processes and designs are available, some are rather expensive. In recent years buyers have shown a willingness to pay more for improved packaging, but there are limits. Marketers should try to determine, through research, just how much customers are willing to pay for packages.

Developing tamper resistant packaging is very important. Although no package is totally tamper proof, marketers can develop packages that are difficult to tamper with and that also make any tampering evident to resellers and consumers. Because new, safer packaging technologies are being explored, marketers should be aware of changes in packaging technology and legislation and be prepared to make modifications that will ensure consumer safety. One packaging innovation includes an inner pouch that displays the word *open* when air has entered the pouch after opening. Marketers also now have an obligation to inform consumers of the possibilities and risks of product tampering by educating them to recognise possible tampering and by placing warnings on packaging.[20] For example, the tops of many sauce and condiment bottles now have plastic seals around them, so that consumers can be confident that they have not been opened. Baby food manufacturers such as Cow & Gate and Heinz have taken this protection method one step further by using special metal jar tops with pop-up discs showing when a jar has been opened. This move followed cases of tampering in which foreign bodies were introduced into baby foods. Now the special tops expressly warn consumers to watch out for tampering. Although effective tamper resistant packaging may be expensive to develop, when balanced against the costs of lost sales, loss of consumer confidence and a company's reputation, and potentially expensive product liability lawsuits, the costs of ensuring consumer safety are minimal.[21]

Marketers should consider how much consistency is desirable in a company's package designs. The best policy may be not to attempt consistency, especially if a company's products are unrelated or aimed at vastly different target markets. To promote an overall company image, a company may decide that all packages are to be similar or include one major element of the design. This approach is called **family packaging**. Sometimes it is used only for lines of products, as with Campbell's soups, Weight Watchers foods and Planters nuts.

A package's promotional role is an important consideration. Through verbal and non-verbal symbols, the package can inform potential buyers about the product's content, features, uses, advantages and hazards. A company can create desirable images and associations by its choice of colour, design, shape and texture. Many cosmetics manufacturers, for example, design their packages to create impressions of richness, luxury and exclusiveness. A package performs a promotional function when it is designed to be safer or more convenient to use, if such characteristics help stimulate demand.

To develop a package that has a definite promotional value, a designer must consider size, shape, texture, colour and graphics.[22] Beyond the obvious limitation that the package must be large enough to hold the product, a package can be designed to appear taller or shorter. For instance, thin vertical lines make a package look taller; wide horizontal stripes make it look shorter. A marketer may want a package to appear taller because many people perceive something that is taller as being larger.

Colours on packages are often chosen to attract attention. People associate specific colours with certain feelings and experiences. Red, for example, is linked with fire, blood, danger and anger; yellow suggests sunlight, caution, warmth and vitality; blue can imply coldness, sky, water and sadness.[23] When selecting packaging colours, marketers must decide whether a particular colour will evoke positive or negative feelings when it is linked to a specific product. Rarely, for example, do processors package meat or bread in green materials, because customers may associate green with mould. However, recent concern about the state of the environment has, in general, led to an increase in the use of green coloured packaging. Marketers must also decide whether a specific target market will respond favourably or unfavourably to a particular colour. Cosmetics for women are more likely to be sold in pastel packaging than are personal care products for men. Packages designed to appeal to children often use primary colours and bold designs.

Packaging must also meet the needs of resellers. Wholesalers and retailers consider whether a package facilitates transportation, storage and handling. Packages must allow these resellers to make maximum use of storage space, both in transit and in the shops. Products should be packed so that sales staff can transfer them to the shelves with ease. Shape and weight of packaging are also important. Resellers may refuse to carry certain products if their packages are cumbersome. Figure 9.6 shows how these factors have been taken into consideration in developing Cuprinol's Castlepak™ woodcare varnish container.

A final consideration is whether to develop packages that are environmentally responsible. A Cable News Network report on the growing refuse disposal problem in the US stated that nearly 50 per cent of all rubbish consists of discarded plastic packaging, such as polystyrene containers, plastic soft drink bottles, carrier bags and other packaging.[24] Plastic packaging material does not biodegrade,

Family packaging An approach in which all of a company's packages are similar or include one major element of the design

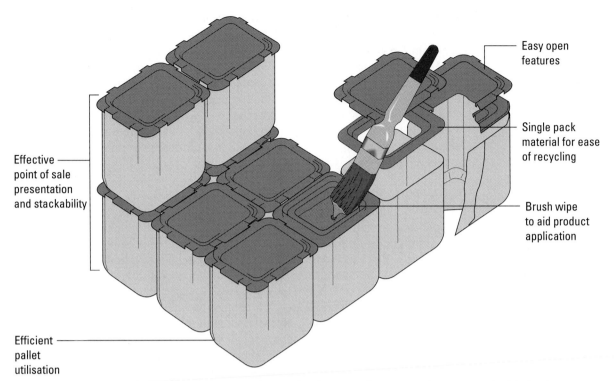

Effective point of sale presentation and stackability

Easy open features

Single pack material for ease of recycling

Brush wipe to aid product application

Efficient pallet utilisation

Figure 9.6 Cuprinol's Castlepak™ woodcare varnish container highlights how environmental consumer usage and operation needs can be incorporated into a single packaging solution. SOURCE: Courtesy of *Marketing Magazine*, London.

and using paper requires the destruction of valuable forest lands. Consequently, a number of companies are recycling more materials and exploring packaging alternatives, helped by packaging experts such as Tetra Pak. H.J. Heinz, for example, is looking for alternatives to its plastic ketchup squeeze bottles. Case 9.2 examines some of the latest packaging innovations.

Companies that decide to develop environmentally responsible packaging have not always received a positive response. For example, customers' responses to Wendy's new paper plates and coffee cups have been mixed; some customers prefer the old non-biodegradable foam packaging. Other companies searching for alternatives to environmentally harmful packaging have experienced similar problems.[25] Thus marketers must carefully balance society's desires to preserve the environment against consumers' desires for convenience.

Packaging and Marketing Strategy

Packaging can be a major component of a marketing strategy. A new cap or closure, a better box or wrapping, or a more convenient container may give a product a competitive edge. The right type of package for a new product can help it gain market recognition very quickly. In the case of existing brands, marketers should periodically re-evaluate packages. Especially for consumer convenience products, marketers should view packaging as a major strategic tool. This section examines ways in which packaging can be used strategically.

Altering the Package At times, a marketer changes a package because the existing design is no longer in style, especially when compared with competitive products. Smith and Nephew redesigned its Simple range of toiletries to show that the products have evolved with the times. A package also may be redesigned because new product features need to be highlighted on the package, or because new packaging materials have become available. A company may decide to change a product's packaging to make the product more convenient or safer to use, or to re-position the product. A major redesign of a simple package costs about £15,000, and the redesign for a line of products may cost up to £200,000.[26] Choosing the right packaging material is an important consideration when redesigning. Different materials vary in popularity at different times. For example, glass is becoming more popular as views on the environment and the need for recyclability come to the fore.[27]

Secondary Use Packaging   A secondary use package is one that can be re-used for purposes other than its initial use. For example, a margarine container can be re-used to store left overs, a jam jar can be used as a drinking glass and short-bread tins can be re-used for storing cakes and biscuits. Secondary use packages can be viewed by customers as adding value to products. If customers value this type of packaging, then its use should stimulate unit sales.

Category Consistent Packaging   Category consistent packaging means that the product is packaged in line with the packaging practices associated with a particular product category. Some product categories—for example, mayonnaise, mustard, ketchup and jam—have traditional package shapes. Other product categories are characterised by recognisable colour combinations—red and white for soup; red and yellow for tea; red, white and blue for Ritz-like crackers. When a company introduces a brand in one of these product categories, marketers will often use traditional package shapes and colour combinations to ensure that customers will recognise the new product as being in that specific product category.

Innovative Packaging   Sometimes, a marketer will employ a unique cap, design, applicator or other feature to make the product competitively distinctive, as illustrated in Figure 9.7. Such packaging can be effective when the innovation makes the product safer or easier to use, or when the unique package provides better protection for the product. In some instances, marketers use innovative or unique packages that are inconsistent with traditional packaging practices to make the brand stand out relative to its competitors. Procter & Gamble, for example, used an innovative, crush proof cylinder to package its Pringles potato crisps. Innovative packaging generally requires considerable resources, not only for the package design itself but also to make customers aware of the unique package and its benefit. Sometimes, innovative packaging can change the way in which consumers use a product. The introduction of cardboard boxed, single serving soft drinks made it easier for consumers to have a drink while travelling by car, train and plane. Even cyclists can drink with ease while on the move!

Multiple Packaging   Rather than packaging a single unit of a product, marketers sometimes use twin packs, tri-packs, six-packs or other forms of **multiple packaging.** For certain types of products, multiple packaging is used to increase demand because it increases the amount of the product available at the point of consumption (in consumers' houses, for example). However, multiple packaging does not work for all types of products. Consumers would not use additional table salt simply because an extra box is in the pantry. Multiple packaging can make products easier to handle and store, as in the case of six-packs for soft drinks; it can also facilitate special price offers, such as two-for-one sales. In addi-

Secondary use package   A package that can be re-used for purposes other than its initial use

Category consistent packaging   The packaging of a product according to the packaging practices associated with a particular product category

Multiple packaging   Packaging that includes more than one unit of a product, such as twin packs, tri-packs and six-packs

Figure 9.7 Innovative packaging. The importance of packaging design cannot be underestimated.
SOURCE: *top*: Courtesy of Van den Bergh Foods; *bottom*: Courtesy of Kalon Group PLC.

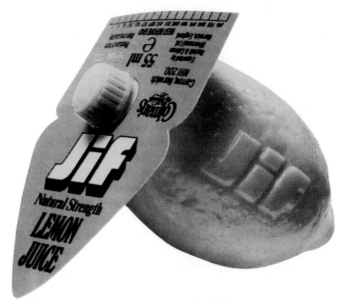

tion, multiple packaging may increase consumer acceptance of the product by encouraging the buyer to try the product several times.

Handling Improved Packaging Packaging of a product may be changed to make it easier to handle in the distribution channel—for example, changing the outer carton, special bundling, shrink wrapping or palletising. In some cases the shape of the package may need to be changed. For example, an ice cream producer may change from a cylindrical package to a rectangular one to facilitate handling. In addition, at the retail level the ice cream producer may be able to get more shelf facings with a rectangular package as opposed to a round one. Outer containers for products are sometimes changed so that they will proceed more easily through automated warehousing systems.

As package designs improve, it becomes harder for any one product to dominate because of packaging. However, marketers still attempt to gain a competitive edge through packaging. Case 9.2 looks at the benefits offered by new types of packaging. Skilled artists and package designers who have experience in marketing research, test packaging to see what sells well, not just what is aesthetically appealing. Since the typical large store stocks 15,000 items or more, products that stand out are more likely to be bought.

Criticisms of Packaging

The last few decades have seen a number of improvements in packaging. However, some packaging problems still need to be resolved. Marketing Insight 9.2 highlights how leading packaging company Tetra Pak has responded to complaints about the ease of use of its containers.

Some packages simply do not work well. The packaging for flour and sugar is, at best, not much better than poor. Both grocers and consumers are very much aware that these packages leak and are easily torn. Can anyone open and close a bag of flour without spilling at least a little bit? Certain packages such as biscuit tins, milk cartons with fold-out spouts and potato crisp bags are frequently difficult to open. The traditional shapes of packages for products such as ketchup and salad dressing make the products inconvenient to use. Have you ever questioned when tapping on a ketchup bottle why the producer didn't put ketchup in a mayonnaise jar?

As discussed earlier, certain types of packaging are being questioned in regard to recyclability and biodegradability. For example, throw-away bottles take considerably more resources to produce than do re-usable glass bottles.

Although many steps have been taken to make packaging safer, critics still focus on health and safety issues. Containers with sharp edges and easily broken glass bottles are sometimes viewed as a threat to safety. Certain types of plastic packaging and aerosol containers represent possible health hazards.

At times, packaging is viewed as being deceptive. Package shape, graphic design and certain colours may be used to make a product appear larger than it actually is. The inconsistent use of certain size designations—such as "giant", "economy", "family", "king" and "super"—can certainly lead to customer confusion. Although customers have traditionally liked attractive, effective, convenient packaging, the cost of such packaging is high. For some products, such as cosmetics, the cost of the package is higher than the cost of the product itself.

Labelling

Labelling Packaging information that can be used for a variety of promotional, informational and legal purposes

Labelling is very closely related to packaging and can be used for a variety of promotional, informational and legal purposes. The label can be used to facilitate the identification of a product by presenting the brand and a unique graphic design. For example, Heinz's ketchup is easy to identify on a supermarket shelf because the brand name is easy to read and is coupled with a distinctive, crown-like graphic design. Labels have a descriptive function. For certain types of products, the label indicates the grade of the product, especially for tinned fruit. Labels can describe the source of the product, its contents and major features, how to use the product, how to care for the product, nutritional information, type and style of the product, and size and number of servings. The label can play a promotional function through the use of graphics that attract attention. The food and drug administrations and consumer protection agencies in different countries have varying requirements concerning warnings, instructions, certifications and manufacturers' identifications. Increasingly, however, the EU is demanding similar standards in all member countries. Despite the fact that consumers have responded favourably to the inclusion of this type of information on labels, evi-

Tetra Pak's Designers Reflect the Ageing Population

Packaging giant Tetra Pak came in for much criticism from consumers and retailers alike during the mid-1990s. For more than two decades, consumers have struggled to open cardboard cartons of milk, juice and soups with flaps that had to be pulled down, then apart, then . . . well, they were not the easiest of items with which to do battle! The alarm bells rang when supermarket giants Sainsbury's and Tesco responded to consumer views and opted for plastic containers with screw caps for milk and juice, threatening to de-stock Tetra Pak cartons totally. Tetra Pak responded by mounting a successful publicity campaign to persuade the media that its cartons were simple to use and indeed were well loved by consumers. The company also modified its packaging design, adding a pop-open spout and top to the traditional carton for easy opening. For a one-product company with 16,000 employees operating in 117 countries and shipping 70 billion cartons annually, the negative consumer reaction had to be addressed speedily and with care.

The consumer backlash against the difficult to open cartons occurred across all types of shoppers. But what about those with disabilities? If consumers with no physical limitations have problems with packaging, then what of those with disabilities? As the 1990s drew to a close, more and more companies were redesigning their packaging to reflect ease of opening and use. Charity Age Concern ran a programme called *Through Other Eyes* for marketing and sales directors. Dressed in rubber gloves, goggles, armbands and ankle weights, those attending the workshop were helped to understand the problems faced by the elderly and disabled.

As Roger Saunders, responsible for the campaign, explained, "How often have you struggled to open a carton of orange juice or a jar of jam, or unwrap the cellophane from around a compact disc? It is often frustrating and ends in broken nails and lost tempers. If you have arthritis or Parkinson's disease, for example, then it is doubly difficult." The Royal College of Art has advised the programme and has indeed developed many innovative packaging applications. One good design is the new flip-top toothpaste tube, which prevents the top from being dropped or lost.

Tetra Pak came in for significant criticism during the *Through Other Eyes* campaign, particularly for its milk cartons. However, Ulf Brasen, Tetra Pak's managing director, was a keen participant in the workshops. "Wearing view-restricting goggles, armbands and ankle weights made simple tasks such as reading the cooking instructions on a food package significantly harder than I would ever have considered possible," he commented. Those involved in this particular awareness campaign universally acknowledge the significant strides made by Tetra Pak to eliminate some of the most common problems. The Tetra Pak ring-pull tops on cartons are significantly better. As Ulf Brasen explained, "We have been looking at this issue for a number of years and are introducing easy-open packaging designs. If disabled people can safely and readily open, pour and reclose our cartons, then so can the rest of the community." Of course, the packaging companies are looking into this issue for economic reasons, too. In light of the ageing population, more and more consumers will find easier-to-open packaging appealing, and manufacturers and retailers will have to supply merchandise in more user friendly containers and packaging. Companies like Tetra Pak are responding to both the needs of the community and the requirements stipulated by their immediate customers, the manufacturers and supermarket chains.

SOURCES: Helen Jones, "It's open war with the Pack", *Independent on Sunday,* 17 December 1995; "Veryfine tuning", *Adweek,* 13 November 1995, p. 6; Liz Dunning, "Design choice: Tetra Pak", *Marketing,* 3 August 1995, p. 11; Emma Hall, "KLD to counter image problem for Tetra Pak", *Campaign,* 28 April 1995, p. 4; Helen Slingsby, "Leader of the Pak", *Marketing Week,* 8 July 1994, pp. 36–37.

dence as to whether they actually use it has been mixed. Several studies indicate that consumers do not use nutritional information, whereas other studies indicate that the information is considered useful. Labels can also promote a manufacturer's other products or encourage proper use of products, resulting in greater customer satisfaction with them.

The label for many products includes a **universal product code (UPC)** or **barcode**—a series of thick and thin lines that identifies the product and provides inventory and pricing information that can be read by an electronic scanner. The

Universal product code (UPC) or barcode A series of thick and thin lines that identifies the product and provides inventory and pricing information readable by an electronic scanner

UPC is read electronically at the retail check-out counter. This information is used by retailers and producers for price and inventory control purposes.

Colour and eye catching graphics on labels overcome the jumble of words—known to designers as "mouse print"—that have been added to satisfy government regulations. Because so many similar products are available, an attention-getting device or "silent salesperson" is needed to attract interest. As one of the most visible parts of a product, the label is an important element in a marketing mix.

● S U M M A R Y

A *brand* is a name, term, design, symbol or any other feature that identifies one seller's good or service as distinct from those of other sellers. A *brand name* is that part of a brand that can be spoken, including letters, words and numbers; the element that cannot be spoken—often a symbol or design—is called a *brand mark*. A *trademark* is a legal designation indicating that the owner has exclusive use of a brand or part of a brand and that others are prohibited by law from using it. A *trade name* is the legal name of an organisation.

Branding helps buyers identify and evaluate products, helps sellers facilitate repeat purchasing and product introduction, and fosters *brand loyalty*—a customer's strongly motivated and long standing decision to purchase a particular product or service. The three degrees of brand loyalty are recognition, preference and insistence. *Brand recognition* exists when a customer is aware that a brand exists and views it as an alternative to purchase if the preferred brand is unavailable. *Brand preference* is the degree of brand loyalty in which a customer prefers one brand over competing brands and will purchase it if it is available. *Brand insistence* is the degree of brand loyalty in which a customer will accept no substitute. *Brand equity* is the marketing and financial value associated with a brand's strength in a market. It represents the value of a brand to an organisation. The four major elements underlying brand equity are brand name awareness, brand loyalty, perceived brand quality and brand associations.

A *manufacturer brand*, initiated by the producer, makes it possible to associate the company more easily with its products at the point of purchase. An *own label brand* is initiated and owned by a reseller, such as a retailer. A *generic brand* indicates only the product category and does not include the company name or other identifying terms. Manufacturers combat the growing competition from own label brands by developing multiple brands.

When selecting a brand name, a marketer should choose one that is easy to say, spell and recall, and that alludes to the product's uses, benefits or special characteristics. Brand names are created inside an organisation by individuals, committees or branding departments, or by outside consultants. Brand names can be devised from words, initials, numbers, nonsense words or a combination of these. Services as well as products are branded, often with the company name and an accompanying symbol that makes the brand distinctive or conveys a desired image.

Producers protect ownership of their brands through patent and trademark offices. Marketers at a company must make certain that their selected brand name does not infringe on an already registered brand by confusing or deceiving consumers about the source of the product. In many countries, brand registration is on a first-come, first-served basis, making protection more difficult. Brand counterfeiting, increasingly common, has potential for undermining consumer confidence in and loyalty to a brand.

Companies brand their products in several ways. *Individual branding* designates a unique name for each of a company's products; *overall family brand-*

ing identifies all of a company's products with the same name; *line family branding* assigns all products within a single line the same name; and *brand extension branding* applies an existing name to a new or improved product. Trademark licensing enables producers to earn extra revenue, receive low cost or free publicity, and protect their trademarks. Through a licensing agreement, and for a licensing fee, a company may permit approved manufacturers to use its trademark on other products.

Strong brands usually create product differentiation, help establish a competitive edge, encourage product awareness and demand a significant amount of management and control. *Successful brands* tend to prioritise quality, offer superior service, get to market or the targeted segment first, be clearly differentiated from rival brands, have a unique positioning concept supported by a strong communications programme and be consistent over time. Four *levels of brands* need to be addressed: the tangible product, the "basic" brand, the "augmented" brand and the "potential" of the brand. To be successful, a brand should capture the leading share in its market segment or distribution channel, command prices sufficiently high to offer high profit margins and be likely to maintain its profit position after more brands and generic versions enter the market. Many companies should be more effective in managing their brands, many of which do not live up to these success criteria.

Packaging involves the development of a container and label, complete with graphic design for a product. Effective packaging offers protection, economy, safety and convenience. It can influence the customer's purchase decision by promoting a product's features, uses, benefits and image. When developing a package, marketers must consider costs relative to how much the target market is willing to pay. Other considerations include how to make the package tamper resistant; whether to use *family packaging, secondary use packaging, category consistent packaging* or *multiple packaging;* how to design the package as an effective promotional tool; how best to accommodate resellers; and whether to develop environmentally responsible packaging.

Packaging can be a major component of a marketing strategy. Companies choose particular colours, designs, shapes and textures to create desirable images and associations. Producers alter packages to convey new features or to make them safer or more convenient. If a package has a secondary use, the product's value to the consumer may be increased. Category consistent packaging makes products more easily recognised by consumers, and innovative packaging enhances a product's distinctiveness. Consumers may criticise packaging that doesn't work well, is not biodegradable or recyclable, poses health or safety problems or is deceptive in some way.

Labelling is an important aspect of packaging that can be used for promotional, informational and legal purposes. Because labels are attention-getting devices, they are significant features in the marketing mix. Various regulatory agencies can require that products be labelled or marked with warnings, instructions, certifications, nutritional information and the manufacturer's identification. Increasingly, most products—even cars—have a *universal product code (UPC)* or *barcode.*

Important Terms

Brand	Brand equity	Levels of brands
Brand name	Manufacturer brands	Packaging
Brand mark	Own label brands	Family packaging
Trademark	Generic brand	Secondary use package
Trade name	Individual branding	Category consistent packaging
Brand loyalty	Overall family branding	Multiple packaging
Brand recognition	Line family branding	Labelling
Brand preference	Brand extension branding	Universal product code (UPC)
Brand insistence	Successful brands	or barcode

Discussion and Review Questions

1. What is the difference between a brand and a brand name? Compare and contrast the terms *brand mark* and *trademark*.
2. How does branding benefit customers and organisations?
3. What are the advantages associated with brand loyalty?
4. What are the distinguishing characteristics of own label brands?
5. Given the competition between own label brands and manufacturer brands, should manufacturers be concerned about the popularity of own label brands? How should manufacturers fight back in the brand battle?
6. Identify and explain the major considerations consumers take into account when selecting a brand.
7. The brand name Xerox is sometimes used generically to refer to photocopying machines. How can Xerox Corporation protect this brand name?
8. Identify and explain the four major branding policies and give examples of each. Can a company use more than one policy at a time? Explain your answer.
9. What are the major advantages and disadvantages of licensing?
10. Why is there more to a brand than its name? Explain your response.
11. What are the most commonly found foundations for successful brands? Illustrate your response with brand examples.
12. What are the three core criteria for assessing the success of a brand?
13. Describe the functions that a package can perform. Which function is most important? Why?
14. When developing a package, what are the major issues that a marketer should consider?
15. In what ways can packaging be used as a strategic tool?
16. What are the major criticisms of packaging?
17. What are the major functions of labelling?

Recommended Readings

P. Doyle, "Building successful brands: the strategic options", *The Journal of Consumer Marketing*, vol. 7, no. 2, 1993, pp. 5–20.

P. Doyle, *Marketing Management and Strategy* (London: Prentice-Hall, 1998).

G. S. Low and R. A. Fullerton, "Brands, brand management and the brand manager system: a critical-histori-cal evaluation", *Journal of Marketing Research*, vol. 31, no. 2, 1994, pp. 173–190.

C. Macrae, *The Brand Chartering Handbook* (London: EIU and Addison-Wesley, 1996).

C. Macrae, S. Parkinson and J. Sheerman, "Managing marketing's DNA: the role of branding", *Irish Marketing Review*, vol. 8, 1995, pp. 13–20.

● C A S E S

9.1 KP Heads for Market Leadership

Snack giant KP has its sights set on half of the snacks, crisps and nuts markets. The company gave itself until the year 2000 to achieve a 50 per cent share of this £1.5 billion market in the UK. Such a goal did not seem unreasonable considering that between 1982 and 1995 KP managed to increase its market share by 10 per cent to 40 per cent.

The threat to KP comes from giant PepsiCo, which the company managed to topple from mar-ket leadership for the first time in 1990. In a closely fought contest for market share, PepsiCo disputes the figures that put KP on top. While KP bases its market share on volume tonnes sold (19.2 per cent of KP's business comes from its production of own-label products for supermarkets), PepsiCo says that branded sales are what matters and calculates its success using figures for branded products only—putting it at 42.6 per cent—ahead by around 14 per cent. PepsiCo merged its Smiths and Walkers subsidiaries to strengthen its branding further, a move that KP hopes will distract PepsiCo's attention from the battle for market supremacy.

New products provide the key to KP's strategy. According to the company's marketing director, around two-thirds of growth will be centred on new products. As new products are added to the range, the company will consider rationalising its existing portfolio. Those snacks and crisps that fail to reach the £20 million level are likely to be dropped. Currently, the values of KP's top four nibbles are £95 million for Hula Hoops, followed by £90 million for KP Nuts, followed by The Real McCoys and Skips, worth £48 million and £45 million respectively.

The merger between Walkers and Smiths resulted in changes for the PepsiCo range. Monster Munch and Smiths Quavers were re-launched as Walkers Quavers and Walkers Monster Munch. This is part of a PepsiCo move, backed by £6.5 million marketing spend, to use the Walkers brand to support its key products. Other changes include the introduction of salt and vinegar flavoured Quavers (to attract children) and mixed cheese to appeal to "housewives".

KP's launch of Roysters Steam Nuts is indicative of the company's drive for innovative products. Representing the company's first move to extend a brand into a new sector, the product follows naturally on from the 1992 introduction of Roysters. The extra large peanuts are available in three tempting flavours: Kentucky Smoke, Louisiana Hot Spice and New York Smoke. KP hopes that the move will provide it with a 5 per cent stake of the £136 million nuts market. According to KP's

---

Core Snack Brands

KP

Hula Hoops	KP Nuts
The Real McCoys	Skips
Solo Lower Fat Crisps	Frisps
Roysters	Discos
Brannigans	Roysters Steam Nuts

PepsiCo

Walkers Crisps	Walkers Quavers
Walkers Monster Munch	Tudor Crisps
French Fries	Ruffles
Looney Tunes	Planters Nuts
Tuba Loops	Crinkles
Frazzles	Sticks
Big D Nuts	

Marketing Director, the Steam Nuts brand has connotations of tradition and intrigue, which should boost a flagging market.

SOURCES: Suzanne Bidlake, "Snack attack by KP demands a crisp reply", *Marketing*, 21 January 1993; "KP extends Roysters to grab 5% of market", *Marketing*, 21 January 1993; Juliana Koranteng, "Quavers revamp for battle with Hula Hoops", *Marketing*, 21 January 1993.

Questions for Discussion

1. To what category of consumer products do snacks, crisps and nuts belong?
2. Is branding important in this market? Why?
3. What is meant by "brand extension"? Why might KP engage in brand extension?

9.2 3D and Environmentally Friendly Packaging Design

Three-dimensional packaging does much more than protect products and make them easy to distribute, handle and use. For marketers, 3D packaging can help differentiate a brand, add value or simply aid consumer recognition. The distinctive shape of the Coca-Cola bottle, recognised worldwide, is synonymous with the brand. The importance of creative packaging design is well established. Maximising packaging design benefits requires an integrated approach that considers financial, manufacturing, distribution and marketing requirements. In some companies this total business approach is achieved by forming staff teams with representatives from all business areas. The teams will consider all aspects of packaging design—materials, size and shape, opening and closure features, material conversion efficiency, retail storage and display, transportability, disposability, filling speed and costs.

Research shows that for some products, innovative packaging is seen to add value in the eyes of target consumers. There is the sensual pleasure of handling the product, a perception of creativity and added prestige from the purchase, as well as the implication that the manufacturer "cares" about the consumer.

Growing consumer concern about the environment and government targets for recycling are putting new pressures on packaging design and development, in addition to all the other marketing and operational requirements of the process. As they look for ways to increase the environmental friendliness of their packaging, companies need to ask a series of questions:

- Can the amount of material in the package be reduced?
- Can the size of the package be reduced?
- Is recyclable material a possibility?
- Are the necessary recycling processes available?
- Are the raw materials used easy to replenish?

Environmental concerns are causing companies to reconsider the appropriateness of traditional packaging materials. For example, glass is coming back to supermarket shelves, while new developments in the use of plastics and paper/board are leading to improvements in recyclability. Even when companies are able to move towards more ecologically sympathetic packaging, there may be hidden problems. For example, the process of recycling itself may waste energy and create pollution. To ensure that the disadvantages of changing packaging design do not outweigh the benefits, a company should undertake a "cradle to grave" analysis of the proposed packaging, looking at all aspects of its manufacture, distribution, use and disposal.

In the rush to meet consumer demands and regulatory requirements, companies are in danger of introducing ineffective packaging solutions. For example, manufacturers have recently introduced flexible re-fill pouches as a replacement for plastic bottles. To the consumer, who sees rigid plastic bottles as bulky and difficult to dispose of, this seems to be a positive step. The lightweight alternative may look better but in practice is awkward to distribute, problematic to stock, hard to open and difficult to recycle. Packaging must be sensible and capable of adding to the brand's image.

These concerns led to Lever Brothers adopting a novel packaging solution for its best selling Comfort fabric conditioner. In 1998 it launched crushable re-fill containers which are easier to stock, display and keep at home than the re-fill pouches. On-pack instructions explain to consumers that the concentrated liquid and thinner packaging save 60 per cent of packaging material versus regular fabric conditioner bottles and that this bottle "is crushable and can be recycled". With BMW setting up plants to recycle and dispose of old BMW cars, PC World retailing re-used inkjet cartridges and Sainsbury's encouraging the re-use of carrier bags, Lever Brothers is not alone in seeking and promoting environmental solutions. Packaging is increasingly a concern, though, for "green" consumers. For Lever Brothers, it does appear that the crushable fabric container has overcome consumer aversion to the flimsy re-fill pouches tried out in the mid-1990s. As ever, packaging is an evolutionary process and no doubt by the time this book hits the bookshops, a more innovative technique will have been deployed.

SOURCES: Lever Brothers, 1999; CGM, *Marketing Guide 14: 3D Packaging Design*, Haymarket Publishing Services Ltd, 1992; John S. Blyth, "Packaging for competitive advantage", *Management Review*, May 1990, p. 64; Dagmar Mussey and Juliana Kanteng, "Packaging strict green rules", *Advertising Age*, 2 December 1991, p. S-10; Katrina Carl, "Good package design helps increase consumer loyalty", *Marketing News*, 19 June 1995, p. 4; Andy Gilgrist, "The shape of things to come", *Marketing Week*, 16 September 1994, pp. 43–47; DTI, 1999.

Questions for Discussion

1. What are the functions and benefits of 3D packaging?
2. How does innovative packaging add value to products?
3. In what ways are companies such as Lever Brothers addressing environmental concerns regarding packaging materials?

10 Developing and Managing Products

"In the globally competitive world, product and brand management represents the most important resource responsibility in the portfolio of the marketing manager's job."

Michael J. Thomas, University of Strathclyde

OBJECTIVES

- To become aware of organisational alternatives for managing products
- To understand how businesses develop a product idea into a commercial product
- To understand the importance and role of product development in the marketing mix
- To acquire knowledge of the management of products during the various stages of a product's life cycle
- To become aware of how existing products can be modified
- To learn how product deletion can be used to improve product mixes

Government forecasters predict that by 2020, a quarter of the population in most EU member states will be over the age of 65. Marketers must anyway strive to predict future consumer needs and anticipate competitors' innovative product developments, but with a changing consumer profile, the challenges in the new millennium are even more demanding. Add in a falling birth rate, more single person households owing to rising divorce rates, an increase in life expectancy, women's growing financial independence, the marked tendency for couples to settle down later in life, a greater propensity to travel, multiplying media influences, harmonisation of EU trade and consumer regulations, more working women and a growth in consumer self-confidence, and it is evident that new product development managers have a dramatically changing environment to address and work within.

The changing face of the consumer has already prompted some brewers to test out "chameleon" bars which change their offerings as the day passes: coffee in the mornings, bistro style lunches, and different lighting, sound systems and drinks menus in the evenings. Some experts believe that retailers will similarly have to alter the ambience and merchandising of their stores, either to reflect changing footfall patterns during the day or to address the different shop-ping styles witnessed weekdays versus the weekends. It is widely expected that the shopping experience will become just as important to the consumer as the goods to be purchased. On-line Internet shopping is going to be increasingly important as this decade unfolds and will further add to the challenges facing retailers and manufacturers of consumer goods.

Indeed, technology is likely to be the single biggest factor as the new millennium commences. Hewlett-Packard expects a new generation of smart consumer electronics. Servers in the home will control heating, lighting and security systems. Self-diagnostic medical kits will become more popular. Super computers—"personalised intelligence agents"—enabling the convergence of digital technologies are the vision of the London Business School. These domestic computers will recognise individual family members, read e-mails aloud, order groceries, give directions in the car, sort out family finances and even specify which movie to watch. Philips predicts that we could eventually wear washable electronic clothing containing tiny implants replacing the need to carry mobile phones. The next generation of mobile phones will anyway soon arrive, enabling convergent technologies to become mobile. Nokia says it will be possible to find out which movies are showing where and to download clips onto hand-held "communication devices".

The counter-balance to all of this may be a social backlash in which consumers feel out of control or intimidated by technology and changing leisure patterns. Some social spotters believe the growth of feng shui is one example of this. Consumers may turn for solace to their "rose-coloured" past, to alternative remedies and beliefs, or to "instant soul" products—*Prozac for the soul* bought off the shelf! Health and beauty products will continue to emerge, including nutriceuticals—food with added health benefits—and cosmeceuticals—cosmetics combined with pharmaceuticals. Functional foods including health benefits, such as low cholesterol margarine, will also grow significantly. Health-delicious food, for example vitamin-enriched chocolate, will also emerge. While all of these "trends" are, at the time of writing, no more than notions, they indicate the rapidly changing marketplace facing many marketers as they develop new products.

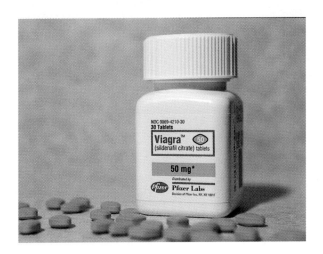

SOURCES: The Henley Centre; London Business School; McCann-Erickson; Retail Futures; Fitch Design; Hewlett-Packard; Philips; Nokia; Young & Rubicam; Cato Consulting; Leatherhead Food Research Association; Oxford Institute of Retail Management; plus the excellent "Star Chart", *Marketing Week,* 7 January 1999, pp. 22–26. *Photo:* Richard Epstein/Photo Edit.

To compete effectively and achieve their goals, companies such as Nokia must be able to adjust their product mix in response to changes in buyers' preferences. A company often has to modify existing products, introduce new products or eliminate products that were successful perhaps only a few years ago. For companies such as Hewlett-Packard, this may include quite a radical change to an existing, well known brand. Sometimes, as in the chapter opener, product alterations are required to keep pace with changing consumer demographics and new technologies. Whatever the reasons for altering products, the product mix must be managed. For example, a marketer may need to delete a product from the mix because a competitor dominates the market. In other circumstances it may be appropriate to expand a company's product mix to take advantage of excess marketing and production capacity. The product portfolio approach, which is reviewed in Chapter 21, tries to create specific marketing strategies to achieve a balanced mix of products that will maximise a company's long term profits. This chapter is more concerned with the management of the resulting product mix. It begins by considering how businesses are organised to develop and manage products. Next, several ways to improve a company's product mix, including new product development from idea generation to commercialisation, are reviewed. The chapter then considers issues and decisions associated with managing a product through the growth, maturity and declining stages of its life cycle. Different types of product modifications are also examined. Finally, the deletion of weak products from the product mix, often one of the hardest decisions for a marketer, is examined.

A company must often manage a complex set of products, markets or both. Often, too, it finds that the traditional functional form of organisation—in which managers specialise in business functions such as advertising, sales and distribution—does not fit its needs. Consequently, management must find an organisational approach that accomplishes the tasks necessary to develop and manage products. Alternatives to functional organisation include the product or brand manager approach, the marketing manager approach and the venture or project team approach.

A **product manager** is responsible for a product, a product line or several distinct products that make up an interrelated group within a multi-product organisation. A **brand manager,** on the other hand, is responsible for a single brand, for example, Lipton's Yellow Label tea or Virgin Cola. A product or brand manager operates cross-functionally to co-ordinate the activities, information and strategies involved in marketing an assigned product. Product managers and brand managers plan marketing activities to achieve objectives by co-ordinating a mix of place/distribution, promotion (especially sales promotion and advertising) and price. They must consider packaging and branding decisions and work closely with research and development, engineering and production departments. The product manager or brand manager approach is used by many large, multiple product companies in the consumer goods business. Increasingly it is a popular approach adopted by marketers responsible for services brands and business-to-business markets.

A **marketing manager** is responsible for managing the marketing activities that serve a particular group or class of customers. This organisational approach is particularly effective when a company engages in different types of marketing activities to provide products to diverse customer groups. A company might have one marketing manager for industrial markets and another for consumer markets. These broad market categories might be broken down into more limited market responsibilities.

A **venture** or **project team** is designed to create entirely new products that may be aimed at new markets. Unlike a product or marketing manager, a venture team is responsible for all aspects of a product's development: research and development, production and engineering, finance and accounting, and marketing. Venture teams work outside established divisions to create inventive approaches to new products and markets. As a result of this flexibility, new products can be developed to take advantage of opportunities in highly segmented markets.

The members of a venture team come from different functional areas of an organisation. When the commercial potential of a new product has been demonstrated, the members may return to their functional areas, or they may join a new or existing division to manage the product. The new product may be turned over to an existing division, a marketing manager or a product manager. Innovative organisational forms such as venture teams are especially important for well established companies operating in mature markets. These companies must take a dual approach to marketing organisation. They must accommodate the management of mature products and also encourage the development of new ones.[1]

Product manager The person responsible for a product, a product line or several distinct products that make up an interrelated group within a multi-product organisation

Brand manager The person responsible for a single brand

Marketing manager The person responsible for managing the marketing activities that serve a particular group or class of customers

Venture or **project team** The group that creates entirely new products, perhaps aimed at new markets, and is responsible for all aspects of the products' development

New Product Development

Developing and introducing new products is frequently expensive and risky. The development of Gillette's Sensor razor took over eight years and resulted in a

£150 million investment.[2] Thousands of new consumer products are introduced annually, and, as indicated in Chapter 8, anywhere from 60 to 90 per cent of them fail. Lack of research, technical problems in design or production and errors in timing the product's introduction are all causes of failure. Although developing new products is risky, so is failing to introduce new products. For example, the makers of Timex watches gained a large share of the watch market through effective marketing strategies during the 1960s and early 1970s. By 1983, Timex's market share had slipped considerably, in part because the company had failed to introduce new products. Timex has since regained market share by introducing a number of new products.

The term *new product* can have more than one meaning. It may refer to a genuinely new product—such as the digital watch once was—offering innovative benefits. But products that are merely different and distinctly better are also often viewed as new. The following items (listed in no particular order) are product innovations of the last 30 years: Post-It notes, birth control pills, personal computers, felt tip pens, anti-ulcer drugs, video cassette recorders, deep fat fryers, compact disc players, soft contact lenses and telephone banking. Thus, a new product can be an innovative variation of an existing product, such as shown in Figure 10.1. It can also be a product that a given company has not marketed previously, although similar products may be available from other companies. The first company to introduce a video cassette recorder clearly was launching a new product, yet if Boeing introduced its own brand of video cassette recorder, this

Figure 10.1 A new product. These Dr. Scheller Cosmetics items are examples of new products. SOURCE: Courtesy of Dr. Scheller Cosmetics AG.

would also be viewed as a new product for Boeing, because it has not previously marketed such products.

Before a product is introduced, it goes through the seven phases of **new product development** shown in Figure 10.2: (1) idea generation, (2) screening ideas, (3) concept testing, (4) business analysis, (5) product development, (6) test marketing and (7) commercialisation. A product may be dropped, and many are, at any of these stages of development. This section examines the process through which products are developed from the inception of an idea to a product offered for sale. Table 10.1 shows how companies can improve their new product success rate.

Idea Generation **Idea generation** involves businesses and other organisations seeking product ideas that will help them achieve their objectives. This task is difficult because only a few ideas are good enough to be commercially successful. Although some organisations get their ideas almost by chance, companies trying to manage their product mixes effectively usually develop systematic approaches for generating new product ideas. At the heart of innovation is a purposeful, focused effort to identify new ways to serve a market. Unexpected occurrences, incongruities, new needs, industry and market changes, and demographic changes may all indicate new opportunities.[3] The forces of the marketing environment (see Chapter 2) often create new opportunities—as well as threats to combat.

New product ideas can come from several sources. They may come from internal sources—marketing managers, researchers, sales personnel, engineers or

Figure 10.2 Phases of new product development

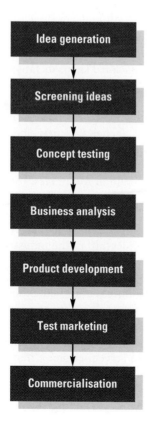

Table 10.1 How to improve new product success

1. Talk with consumers; don't introduce a product just because you have the technology to make it.
2. Set realistic sales goals. Unrealistic goals can result in potentially successful products being terminated.
3. Make all parts of the company (research, manufacturing, marketing and distribution) work together for customer orientation.
4. At each stage of development, the product should have consumer acceptance, the ability to be manufactured at an acceptable cost and sales support.
5. Test market a product long enough to get an accurate assessment. Some products fail because consumers buy them early as a novelty only.
6. Carefully evaluate all product failures to provide information for future product introductions.
7. Monitor competitor developments—a new product must not merely replicate a rival.
8. Keep internal colleagues up-to-date and explain new developments to them.

SOURCE: Christopher P. Power, Kathleen Kerwin, Ronald Grover, Keith Alexander and Robert D. Hof, "Flops: too many new products fail. Here's why—and how to do better", from *Business Week,* 16 August 1993, pp. 78–79.

other organisational personnel. Brainstorming and incentives or rewards for good ideas are typical intra-organisation devices for stimulating the development of ideas. The company 3M is well known for encouraging the generation of new ideas. The idea for 3M's Post-It adhesive backed yellow notes came from an employee. As a church choir member, he used slips of paper for marking songs in his hymn book. Because the pieces of paper fell out, he suggested developing an adhesive backed note.[4] Hewlett-Packard keeps its labs open to engineers 24 hours a day to help generate ideas; it also encourages its researchers to devote 10 per cent of company time to exploring their own ideas for new products.[5]

New product ideas may also arise from sources outside the company—customers, competitors, advertising agencies, management consultants and private research organisations. Johnson & Johnson, for example, acquired the technology for its new, clear orthodontic braces through a joint venture with Saphikon, the developer of the technology behind the braces.[6] Sometimes ideas come from potential buyers of a product. Asking weekend fishermen what they wanted in a sonar fish finder led Techsonic to develop its LCR (liquid crystal recorder) fish finder. The practice of asking customers what they want from its products has helped Techsonic maintain its leadership in the industry.[7]

Screening ideas The process by which a company assesses whether product ideas match its organisational objectives and resources

Screening Ideas Screening ideas involves first assessing whether they match organisational objectives and resources and then choosing the best ideas for further review. Next the company's overall ability to produce and market the product is analysed. Other aspects of an idea that should be weighed are the nature and wants of buyers and possible environmental changes. More new product ideas are rejected during the idea screening phase than during any other phase.

Sometimes a checklist of new product requirements is used to ensure that the screening process is as systematic as possible. If a critical factor on the checklist remains unclear, the type of formal marketing research described in Chapter 6 may be needed. To screen ideas properly, it may be necessary to test product concepts; a product concept and its benefits can be described or shown to consumers. Several product concepts may be tested to discover which might appeal most to a particular target market.

Concept testing   Seeking potential buyers' responses to a product idea

Concept Testing   Concept testing is a phase in which a small sample of potential buyers is presented, often in focus groups, with a product idea through a written or oral description (and perhaps a few drawings) to determine their attitudes and initial buying intentions regarding the product. For a single product idea, an organisation can test one or several concepts of the same product. Concept testing is a low cost procedure that lets a company determine customers' initial reactions to a product idea before it invests considerable resources in research and development. The results of concept testing can be used by product development personnel to better understand which product attributes and benefits are most important to potential customers.

Business analysis   A company's evaluation of a product idea to determine its potential contribution to the company's sales, costs and profits

Business Analysis   During the business analysis phase, the product idea is evaluated to determine its potential contribution to the company's sales, costs and profits. In the course of a business analysis, evaluators ask a variety of questions: Does the product fit in with the company's existing product mix? Does the company have the right expertise to develop the new product? Is demand strong enough to justify entering the market and will the demand endure? What types of environmental and competitive changes can be expected and how will these changes affect the product's future sales, costs and profits? Are the organisation's research, development, engineering and production capabilities adequate? If new facilities must be constructed, how quickly can they be built and how much will they cost? Is the necessary financing for development and commercialisation on hand or obtainable at terms consistent with a favourable return on investment? Will the new product or idea benefit the company's existing portfolio of products? Is there any danger that existing products or services will be cannibalised?

In the business analysis stage, companies seek market information. The results of consumer surveys, along with secondary data, supply the specifics needed for estimating potential sales, costs and profits. At this point, a research budget should explore the financial objectives and related considerations for the new product. Table 10.2 addresses key questions to consider in new product development.

Product development   The phase in which the organisation determines if it is technically and financially feasible to produce a new product

Product Development   Product development is the phase in which the organisation determines if it is technically feasible to produce the product and if it can be produced at costs low enough to make the final price reasonable. To test its acceptability, the idea or concept is converted into a prototype, or working model. Concept cars are used in the development of new vehicles (see Case 10.1). The prototype should reveal tangible and intangible attributes associated with the product in consumers' minds. The product's design, mechanical features and intangible aspects must be linked to wants in the marketplace. This includes the service aspects of the product, which, as Marketing Insight 10.1 shows, are a vital component of many products. Failure to determine how consumers feel about the product and how they would use it may lead to the product's failure. For example, the Sinclair C5 electric buggy was developed as a serious on-road, single seater car for city or country use. However, drivers felt unsafe in the buggy, and campus students ended up using the remaining stocks as on-pavement runabouts.

Table 10.2 Key questions to address in new product development

Concept/Product

1. Do consumers understand your product and is it unique?
2. Is the product perceived as good value?
3. Does your product perform at an acceptable level?
4. What promotion methods are appropriate?
5. What are the sales projections?
6. What is the perceived profitability of the product?

Company

7. Does this product fit the company's product portfolio?
8. Does this product give the company the advantage to move in a new direction or strengthen current positioning?
9. Is current technology being maximised?
10. What are the capital investment requirements?

Target Market

11. Who is the target market for the product?
12. Is there a perception of long term demand for the product?
13. What are the perceived benefits to the customer?
14. What are the requirements to gain distribution?
15. When is the product launch scheduled and what market tests are required?

Competition

16. Who is your primary competition?
17. How do you expect the competition to react to the product?

Final Considerations

18. Where do you derive your information and do you trust the sources?
19. What are the unanswered questions related to new product success?
20. What is the probability of success after considering the above questions?

(Note: In practice, questions 16 and 17 should be tackled much earlier in the process.)
SOURCE: Adapted from Larry A. Constantineau, "The twenty toughest questions for new product proposals", *Journal of Consumer Marketing*. Spring 1992, pp. 51–53. © 1992 MCB University Press, Ltd. Used by permission.

The development phase of a new product is frequently lengthy and expensive; thus a relatively small number of product ideas are put into development. If the product appears sufficiently successful during this phase to merit testing, then during the latter part of the development phase marketers begin to make decisions regarding branding, packaging, labelling, pricing and promotion for use in the test marketing phase.[8]

Test Marketing   A limited introduction of a product in geographic areas chosen to represent the intended market is called **test marketing**. Its aim is to determine the reactions of probable buyers. For example, after McDonald's developed fried chicken products for its fast food menu, it test marketed the idea in certain McDonald's restaurants to find out how those customers felt about eating chicken at McDonald's.[9] The company followed a similar strategy for test

Test marketing   The limited introduction of a product in geographic areas chosen to represent the intended market

Customer Service—Becoming Part of the Product?

A Bug's Life: *new from Walt Disney Pictures, this computer-generated animated fantasy features an all-star line-up of vocal talent including Julia Louis-Dreyfus, David Hyde Pierce, Roddy McDowall, Kevin Spacey and Jonathon Harris.*

Disney's creepy-crawlie computer-animated classic thrilled parents and children alike, as Flik's ants defended their colony against Hopper's grasshoppers. Memorable songs by Randy Newman, plenty of humour, a good plot and state-of-the-art graphics combined to deliver a critically acclaimed movie. *A Bug's Life* was the "product", but for cinema-goers visiting a National Amusements' Showcase multiplex cinema, the experience involved more than the movie.

People visit cinemas to watch a movie for many reasons: to catch the latest release, because friends are going, to be entertained, to go courting, to occupy the kids, to escape from the kids, to be with people, to have an emotional experience, to "kill" time, to have a rest, or "just because it's somewhere to go". The choice of which movie may often be the first decision, but these days, with the growth of multiplex complexes and record cinema attendances, the choice may be which multiplex: Virgin, MGM, UCI or Showcase? For rival operators, the "augmented" product is becoming increasingly important as they seek to develop a competitive edge and to encourage customer loyalty. For example, Showcase strongly emphasises many once secondary or minor features in an attempt to add to the appeal of its cinemas:

State-of-the-art film projection
Acres of free, illuminated car parking
Best seats in town—exclusive rocking loungers
Bargain matinees daily
Freshly popped popcorn
Cinema hire and special group rates
On main coach/bus routes
Dolby stereo equipped auditoria
Air conditioning
Excellent facilities for the disabled
Late night shows every Friday and Saturday
Efficient, courteous service
Gift certificates always available
Art gallery with prints for sale

Car giant Daewoo entered the European market spectacularly in 1995 with an innovative, mould breaking proposition and marketing strategy: selling directly to customers, rather than through franchised garages, and without commission paid sales staff. Daewoo's entire proposition was intended to identify customers' "pet hates" in car buying and to eliminate them from Daewoo's sales and marketing. Daewoo's used car operation received a similar treatment. The company's intention was to re-assure its customers and to reduce the stress and uncertainty inherent in purchasing a second-hand car. While it is still ultimately the car that the Daewoo customer buys, the company has put together an impressive package of additional benefits:

12 month comprehensive Daewoo guarantee
116 point AA approved inspection
Independent mileage check
12 months' AA roadside assistance
Free MOT tests for as long as you own the car
An HPI check to make sure the car hasn't been stolen or written off and that it has no outstanding hire purchase agreements
30 day exchange or money back guarantee
Full service to manufacturer's specification
Where possible, direct contact with all previous owners
6 months' road tax
Free mobile phone
Menu priced servicing with free courtesy car in mainland UK

For many companies, not only Showcase or Daewoo, the augmented product is an increasingly important element in marketing strategy and the search for customer satisfaction. The new product development process increasingly includes the required customer service attributes desired by targeted customers to accompany the purchased product.

SOURCES: Showcase Cinema, Coventry; Daewoo UK; *Coventry Evening Telegraph*, 5 April 1996, p. 64; Disney's press office, 1999; Showcase Cinemas, Walsgrave, Coventry, 1999.

marketing its range of salads and pizza. Test marketing is *not* an extension of the development phase; it is a sample launching of the entire marketing mix and should be conducted only after the product has gone through development and after initial plans regarding the other marketing mix variables have been made.

Companies of all sizes use test marketing to lessen the risk of product failure. The dangers of introducing an untested product include undercutting already profitable products and, should the new product fail, loss of credibility with distributors and customers. When Lever Brothers launched Wisk—previously only a washing powder—in liquid form in 1986, the company had misjudged consumer usage. Many blocked washing machines later, P&G offered liquid Ariel with Arielettes, containers to be placed inside the machines together with the clothes. Re-formulations have now overcome these problems.

Test marketing provides several benefits. It lets marketers expose a product a natural marketing environment to gauge its sales performance. While the product is being marketed in a limited area, the company can seek to identify weaknesses in the product or in other parts of the marketing mix. Corrections can be made more cheaply than if the product had already been introduced nationwide. Test marketing also allows marketers to experiment with variations in advertising, price and packaging in different test areas and to measure the extent of brand awareness, brand switching and repeat purchases that result from alterations in the marketing mix.

The accuracy of test marketing results often hinges on where the tests are conducted. Selection of appropriate test areas is very important. The validity of test marketing results depends heavily on selecting test sites that provide an accurate representation of the intended target market. The criteria used for choosing test cities or television regions depend on the product's characteristics, the target market's characteristics and the company's objectives and resources.

Test marketing can be risky because it is expensive and a company's competitors may try to interfere. A competitor may invalidate test results in an attempt to "jam" the test programme by increasing advertising or promotions, lowering prices or offering special incentives—all to combat the recognition and purchase of a new brand. Sometimes, too, competitors copy the product in the testing stage and rush to introduce a similar product. It is therefore desirable to move quickly and commercialise as soon as possible after testing.

To avoid these risks, companies may use alternative methods to gauge consumer preferences. One such method is simulated test marketing. Typically, consumers at shopping centres are asked to view an advertisement for a new product and are given a free sample to take home. These consumers are subsequently interviewed over the phone and asked to rate the product. The major advantages of simulated test marketing are lower costs, tighter security and, consequently, a reduction in the flow of information to competitors and the elimination of jamming. Scanner based test marketing is another, more sophisticated version of the traditional test marketing method.[10] Some marketing research companies, such as A. C. Nielsen, offer test marketing services to help provide independent assessment of products.

Commercialisation The process of refining and settling plans for full scale manufacturing and marketing

Commercialisation During the **commercialisation** phase, plans for full scale manufacturing and marketing must be refined and settled, and budgets for the project must be prepared. Early in the commercialisation phase, marketing management analyses the results of test marketing to find out what changes in the marketing mix are needed before the product is introduced. For example, the results of test marketing may tell the marketers to change one or more of the product's physical attributes, modify the distribution plans to include more retail outlets, alter promotional efforts or change the product's price. During this phase, the company also has to gear up for production and may therefore face sizeable capital expenditure and personnel costs.

The product enters the market during the commercialisation phase. One study indicates that only 8 per cent of new product projects started by major companies reach this stage.[11] When introducing a product, marketers often spend enormous sums of money for advertising, personal selling and other types of promotion. These expenses, together with capital outlays, can make commercialisation extremely costly; such expenditures may not be recovered for several years. For example, when Ford introduced its new Focus model, the company spent millions of pounds on advertising to communicate the new car's attributes.

Commercialisation is easier when customers accept the product rapidly, which they are more likely to do if marketers can make them aware of its benefits.

Line Extensions

Line extension A product that is closely related to existing products in the line, but meets different customer needs

A **line extension** is the development of a product that is closely related to one or more products in the existing product line but is designed specifically to meet somewhat different needs of customers. For example, Fairy Liquid washing-up detergent was used as a springboard for various detergent based Fairy products including washing powder for automatic washing machines. Many of the so-called new products introduced each year by organisations are in fact line extensions. Line extensions are more common than new products because they are a less expensive, lower risk alternative for increasing sales. A line extension may focus on a different market segment or may be an attempt to increase sales within the same market segment by more precisely satisfying the needs of people in that segment. For example, Nestlé launched an extra strong variant of its Polo mints, Supermints, aimed at lovers of strong peppermints.

Product Adoption Process

Product adoption process The stages buyers go through in accepting a product: awareness, interest, evaluation, trial and adoption

The following stages of the **product adoption process** are generally recognised as those that buyers go through in accepting a product:

1. *Awareness*—The buyer becomes aware of the product.
2. *Interest*—The buyer seeks information and is generally receptive to learning about the product.
3. *Evaluation*—The buyer considers the product's benefits and determines whether to try it.
4. *Trial*—The buyer examines, tests or tries the product to determine its usefulness relative to his or her needs.
5. *Adoption*—The buyer purchases the product and can be expected to use it when the need for this general type of product arises again.[12]

In the first stage, when individuals become aware that the product exists, they have little information about it and are not concerned about obtaining more. Consumers enter the interest stage when they are motivated to get information about the product's features, uses, advantages, disadvantages, price or location. During the evaluation stage, individuals consider whether the product will satisfy certain criteria that are crucial for meeting their specific needs. In the trial stage, they use or experience the product for the first time, possibly by purchasing a small quantity, by taking advantage of a free sample or demonstration, or by borrowing the product from someone. Supermarkets, for instance, frequently offer special promotions to encourage consumers to taste products. During this stage, potential adopters determine the usefulness of the product under the specific conditions for which they need it.

Individuals move into the adoption stage by choosing the specific product when they need a product of that general type. However, the fact that a person enters the adoption process does not mean that she or he will eventually adopt the new product. Rejection may occur at any stage, including adoption. Both product adoption and product rejection can be temporary or permanent.

This adoption process model has several implications for the commercialisation phase. First, the company must promote the product to create widespread awareness of its existence and its benefits. Samples or simulated trials should be arranged to help buyers make initial purchase decisions. Marketers should also emphasise quality control and provide solid guarantees to reinforce buyer opinion during the evaluation stage. Finally, production and physical distribution must be linked to patterns of adoption and repeat purchases. (The product adoption process is also discussed in Chapter 15.) When launching a new product, companies should be aware that buyers differ in the speed with which they adopt a product. Identifying buyers who are most open to new products can help expedite this process. Consumers do not always pass through all stages of the product adoption process as formally as may have been implied thus far. A minor upgrade to a familiar brand may not cause consumers much concern, whereas an innovative product launched by an unknown supplier will give rise to much more extensive consumer decision-making. On the whole, though, marketers would do well to remember the importance of all five stages in this important concept. Consumers must be aware of, have interest in, and be prepared to evaluate and try out a product or service if they are to adopt it—that is, to buy and consume it. The marketing task does not end with first-time adoption, however. The ongoing requirement for marketers is to ensure customer loyalty and repeat purchase.

Products are not usually launched nationwide overnight but are introduced through a process called a roll out. In a roll out, a product is introduced in stages, starting in a set of geographic areas and gradually expanding into adjacent areas. Thus, Cadbury's Wispa bar appeared initially in the North East of England. It may take several years to market the product nationally. Sometimes the test cities are used as initial marketing areas, and the introduction becomes a natural extension of test marketing. Gradual product introduction reduces the risks of introducing a new product. If the product fails, the company will experience smaller losses. Furthermore, it may take some time for a company to develop a suitable distribution network. Also, the number of units needed to satisfy the national demand for a successful product can be enormous, and a company usually cannot produce the required quantities in a short time.

Despite the good reasons for introducing a product gradually, marketers realise that this approach creates some competitive problems. A gradual introduction allows competitors to observe what a company is doing and to monitor results, just as the company's own marketers are doing. If competitors see that the newly introduced product is successful, they may enter the same target market quickly with similar products. Avoiding competition is critical when a company introduces a brand into a market in which it already has one or more brands. Marketers usually want to avoid cannibalising sales of their existing brands, unless the new brand generates substantially larger profits. When Coca-Cola reintroduced Tab, it attempted to position the cola so as to minimise the adverse effects on Diet Coke sales. Similarly, when KP introduces a new snack brand, it must take care to ensure that sales of other KP brands do not suffer.

If a product has been planned properly, its attributes and brand image will give it the distinctive appeal needed. Style, shape, construction, quality of work and colour help create the image and the appeal. Of course buyers are more likely to purchase the product if they can easily identify the benefits. When the new product does not offer some preferred attributes, there is room for another new product or for re-positioning an existing product.[13]

Product Life Cycle Management

Most new products start off slowly and seldom generate enough sales to produce profits immediately. As buyers learn about the new product, marketers should be alert for weaknesses and ready to make corrections quickly, in order to prevent the product's early demise. Computer software companies expect to modify "bugs" when launching new software products. Consumers must be informed quickly and efficiently of any difficulties if damage to the brand image is to be avoided. Marketing strategy should be designed to attract the segment that is most interested in and has the fewest objections to the product. If any of these factors need adjustment, this action, too, must be taken quickly to sustain demand. As the sales curve moves upwards and the break even point is reached, the growth stage begins. (See Figure 8.5 in Chapter 8 for an explanation of the product life cycle concept.)

Marketing Strategy in the Growth Stage

As sales increase, management must support the momentum by adjusting the marketing strategy. The goal is to establish the product's position and to fortify it by encouraging brand loyalty. As profits increase, the company must brace itself for the entrance of aggressive competitors, who may make specialised appeals to selected market segments.

During the growth stage, product offerings may have to be expanded. To achieve greater penetration of an overall market, segmentation may have to be used more intensely. That would require developing product variations to satisfy the needs of customers in several different market segments. Marketers should analyse the product position regarding competing products and correct weak or omitted attributes. Further quality, functional or style modifications may be required.

Gaps in the marketing channels should be filled during the growth period. Once a product has won acceptance, new distribution outlets may be easier to obtain. Sometimes marketers tend to move from an **exclusive** or **selective distribution** to a more **intensive distribution** of dealers to achieve greater market penetration. Marketers must also make sure that the physical distribution system is running efficiently and delivering supplies to distributors before their inventories are exhausted. Because competition increases during the growth period, good service and an effective mechanism for handling complaints are important.

Advertising expenditure may be lowered slightly from the high level of the introductory stage but still needs to be quite substantial. As sales increase, promotion costs should drop as a percentage of total sales. A falling ratio between promotion expenditure and sales should contribute significantly to increased profits. The advertising messages should aim to stress brand benefits and emphasise the product's position. Coupons and samples may be used to increase market share.

Exclusive distribution Market coverage in which only one outlet is used in a geographic area

Selective distribution Market coverage in which only some available outlets in an area are chosen to distribute a product

Intensive distribution Market coverage in which all available outlets are used for distributing a product

After recovering development costs, a business may be able to lower prices. As sales volume increases, efficiencies in production can result in lower costs. These savings may be passed on to buyers. If demand remains strong and there are few competitive threats, prices tend to remain stable. If price cuts are feasible, they can improve price competition and discourage new competitors from entering the market. For example, when compact disc players were introduced in the early 1980s, they carried an £800 price tag. Primarily because of the price, the product was positioned as a "toy for audiophiles"—a very small market segment. To generate mass market demand, compact disc player manufacturers dropped their prices to around £150, and the cost of discs also dropped. The price is now at a point where the margin is low but the turnover is high, and more homes are now investing in compact disc players. A similar pattern has emerged in the sale of mobile phones.

Marketing Strategy for Mature Products

As many products are in the maturity stage of their life cycles, marketers must always be ready to improve the product and marketing mix. During maturity, the competitive situation stabilises and some of the weaker competitors drop out. It has been suggested that as a product matures, its customers become more experienced and their requirements more diverse, so that market segmentation opportunities increase. As customers' needs change, new marketing strategies for mature products may be called for.[14] For example, in the wake of competition from Eurotunnel, ferry operator P&O now stresses its excellent on-board shopping facilities, catering facilities and spacious accommodation in its advertising. Marketers may also need to modify the product. Symptoms of a mature product include price cutting, increased competitive action and shifting from a product orientation to a non-product orientation (price, promotion and place/distribution adaptation); in addition, market growth slows.[15]

Product modification The alteration of one or more characteristics of a company's product

Product modification means changing one or more characteristics of a company's product. This strategy is most likely to be used in the maturity stage of the product life cycle to give a company's existing brand a competitive edge. Case 10.2 shows how even well established brands such as Sellotape must be modified from time to time. Altering a product mix in this way entails less risk than developing a new product because the product is already established in the market. For example, publishers may launch new editions of popular reference books updated with the latest information.

If certain conditions are met, product modification can improve a company's product mix. First, the product must be modifiable. Second, existing customers must be able to perceive that a modification has been made (assuming that the modified item is still aimed at them). Third, the modification should make the product more consistent with customers' desires so that it provides greater satisfaction. If these conditions are not met, it is unlikely that the product modification, however innovative, will be successful. Marketing Insight 10.2 describes several successful modifications to personal banking that have been (and are still being) developed due to emerging technology. Product modifications fall into three major categories: quality, functional and style modifications.

Quality modifications Changes that affect a product's dependability and durability

Quality Modifications Changes concerning a product's dependability and durability are called **quality modifications**. Usually, they are executed by altering the materials or the production process. Reducing a product's quality may allow a company to lower its price and direct the item at a larger target market.

E-Banking Modifies the Current Account

Marketers must constantly look at ways to keep their products "fresh" and up-to-date, modifying existing products as appropriate or bringing out new ones. Personal banking has gone through many phases. Many readers will remember the days when high street banks were open only until mid-afternoon Monday to Friday and there were no ATMs for easy cash withdrawals. Queuing at ageing tills in austere branches was the primary means of operating current bank accounts. Direct debits and standing orders helped, but the real revolution came in the late 1970s with the growth of ATMs—cash dispensers—and then in the early 1990s as most leading banks extended their opening hours and range of services aimed at private customers. Technology has emerged as a driving force for change via other banking services in addition to ATMs. HSBC's First Direct broke ranks by launching as a telephone only, 365 days a year, 24-hour full service personal banking provider. The rapid take-off of First Direct encouraged its traditional high street competitors to offer their own 24-hour telephone banking services—such as Barclays' BarclayCall—based on heavy investment in call centres.

As the new millennium commences, Internet banking is set to change the way in which many customers interact with their banks. Barclays launched a limited service owing to security fears. The company is holding back on a full service launch until its systems can offer greater security to users and until customer concerns about hackers have been allayed. The Royal Bank of Scotland, Lloyds TSB and Nationwide have led the way in launching Internet banking to their customers. It is not only the major high street banking giants that have turned to technology. The Prudential has also turned to e-banking with its Egg brand of e-commerce financial services. Sixty-five thousand people enquired about this intriguing product departure in the first five days after its launch, more than double the number anticipated by the Pru.

Another departure from the traditional high street bank branch is the launch of TV banking. NatWest joined with Microsoft to provide an interactive banking service on Microsoft's WebTV network. The service includes information about mortgages, travel insurance, currency rates, plus standard current account banking, based on NatWest's PC banking package already established on-line. NatWest has its own On-Line division which has focused on high security access for its PC based customers using only a direct dial service rather than any Internet server or third party host. This is in response to customer fears about hackers being able to access their financial dealings via Internet links. A trial in 1998 showed that many of NatWest's personal and small business account holders found the direct dial on-line service highly useful and a popular means of managing their accounts. Although there is a nominal fee, telephone access is charged at local rates and the bank provides the required software free. Telephones, Internet-hooked home PCs, even TVs with set-top boxes are all emerging as means by which personal bankers can avoid traipsing into their local branch in order to execute financial transactions and manage their accounts. No doubt other technological solutions will emerge as the decade unfolds. The traditional high street bank branch current account has very much been modified courtesy of these technological break-throughs.

SOURCES: "Banks can no longer count on consumer inertia for survival", George Pitcher, *Marketing Week*, 22 October 1998, p. 37; "NatWest tests out TV banking", Steve Bell, *Marketing*, 28 January 1999, p. 14; "NatWest offers banking via PC", Steve Bell, *Marketing*, 10 December 1998, p. 5.

By contrast, increasing the quality of a product may give a company an advantage over competing brands. During the last 20 years, marketers have been forced by increased global competition, technological change and more demanding customers to improve product integrity.[16] Higher quality may enable a company to charge a higher price by creating customer loyalty and by lowering customer sensitivity to price. However, higher quality may require the use of more expensive components, less standardised production processes and other manufacturing and management techniques that force a company to charge higher prices.[17] At the beginning of the 1990s, concern for quality increased significantly, with many companies, such as Tesco, Volvo and Caterpillar, finding ways to both increase quality and reduce costs.

Functional modifications Changes that affect a product's versatility, effectiveness, convenience or safety

Functional Modifications   Changes that affect a product's versatility, effectiveness, convenience or safety are called **functional modifications;** they usually require the product to be redesigned. Typical product categories that have undergone considerable functional modifications include home computers, audio equipment and cleaning products. Functional modifications can make a product useful to more people, thus enlarging its market, or improve the product's competitive position by providing benefits competing items do not offer. Functional modifications can also help a company achieve and maintain a progressive image. For example, washing machine manufacturers such as Whirlpool or AEG have developed appliances that use less heat and water. At times, too, functional modifications are made to reduce the possibility of product liability claims.

Style modifications Changes that alter a product's sensory appeal—taste, texture, sound, smell or visual characteristics

Style Modifications   **Style modifications** change the sensory appeal of a product by altering its taste, texture, sound, smell or visual characteristics. Such modifications can be important, because when making a purchase decision a buyer is swayed by how a product looks, smells, tastes, feels or sounds. As illustrated in Figure 10.3, even successful products such as Tango may benefit from this kind of modification.

Although style modifications can be used by a company to differentiate its product from competing brands, their major drawback is that their value is highly subjective. A company may strive to improve the product's style, but customers may actually find the modified product less appealing. Some companies try to minimise these problems by altering product style in subtle ways. For example, Mattel's Barbie Doll has gradually changed over the years to reflect changing fashions.

During the maturity stage of the cycle, marketers actively encourage dealers to support the product, perhaps by offering promotional assistance or help in lowering their inventory costs. In general, marketers go to great lengths to serve dealers and to provide incentives for selling the manufacturer's brand, partly because own label or retailer brands are a threat at this time. As discussed in Chapter 9, own label brands are both an opportunity and a threat to manufacturers, who

Figure 10.3   Style modification. The new look Tango has undergone style modification. SOURCE: Courtesy of Tango.

may be able to sell their products through recognised own label or retailer brand names as well as their own. However, own label or retailer brands frequently undermine manufacturers' brands.

Maintaining market share during the maturity stage requires moderate and sometimes heavy advertising expenditure. Advertising messages focus on differentiating a brand from numerous competitors, and sales promotion efforts are aimed at both consumers and resellers.

A greater mixture of pricing strategies is used during the maturity stage. In some cases, strong price competition occurs and price wars may break out. Sometimes marketers develop price flexibility to differentiate offerings in product lines. Mark-downs and price incentives are more common, but prices may rise if distribution and production costs increase. Marketers of mature products also often alter packaging and even positioning strategies. For example, in the US, Heinz re-packaged and re-positioned its vinegar as an all natural cleaning product.

Marketing Strategy for Declining Products

As a product's sales curve turns downwards, industry profits continue to fall. A business can justify maintaining a product as long as it contributes to profits or enhances the overall effectiveness of a product mix. In this stage, marketers must determine whether to eliminate the product or seek to re-position it in an attempt to extend its life. Usually, a declining product has lost its distinctiveness because similar competing products have been introduced. Competition engenders increased substitution and brand switching as buyers become insensitive to minor product differences. For these reasons, marketers do little to change a product's style, design or other attributes during its decline. New technology, product subtitutes or environmental considerations may also indicate that the time has come to delete a product. For example, the ill-fated Betamax video cassette technology was quickly pushed out by the VHS format.

During a product's decline, outlets with strong sales volumes are maintained and unprofitable outlets are weeded out. An entire marketing channel may be eliminated if it does not contribute adequately to profits. Sometimes a new marketing channel, such as a factory outlet, will be used to liquidate remaining inventory of an obsolete product. Advertising expenditure is at a minimum. Advertising or special offers may slow the rate of decline. Sales promotions, such as coupons and premiums, may temporarily regain buyers' attention. As the product continues to decline, the sales staff shifts its emphasis to more profitable products.

To have a product return a profit may be more important to a company than to maintain a certain market share. To squeeze out all possible remaining profits, marketers may maintain the price despite declining sales and competitive pressures. Prices may even be increased as costs rise if a loyal core market still wants the product. In other situations, the price may be cut to reduce existing inventory so that the product can be deleted. Severe price reductions may be required if a new product is making an existing product obsolete.

Deleting Products

Product deletion The process of eliminating a product that no longer satisfies a sufficient number of customers

Product deletion is the process of eliminating a product that no longer satisfies a sufficient number of customers. Products usually cannot contribute to an organisation's goals indefinitely, and a declining product reduces a company's profitability, draining resources that could be used to modify other products or develop new ones. A marginal product may require shorter production runs, which can increase per unit production costs. Finally, when a dying product completely loses favour with customers, the negative feelings may transfer to some of the company's other products.

Most companies find it difficult to delete a product. It was probably a hard decision for IPC to drop magazine *Options* and admit that it was a failure. A decision to drop a product may be opposed by management and other employees who feel that the product is necessary in the product mix, or by salespeople who still have some loyal customers. Considerable resources and effort are sometimes spent in trying to improve the product's marketing mix enough to increase sales and thus avoid having to delete it.

Some companies delete products only after they have become heavy financial burdens. Robert Maxwell's London newspaper the *Daily News* closed after only a few weeks, having lost £25 million. A better approach is to institute some form of systematic review to evaluate each product and monitor its impact on the overall effectiveness of the company's product mix. Such a review should analyse a product's contribution to the company's sales for a given period and should include estimates of future sales, costs and profits associated with the product. It should also gauge the value of making changes in the marketing strategy to improve the product's performance. A systematic review allows a company to improve product performance and to ascertain when to delete products. Although many companies do systematically review their product mixes, one research study found that few companies have formal, written policies concerning the process of deleting products. The study also found that most companies base their decisions to delete weak products on poor sales and profit potential, low compatibility with the company's business strategies, unfavourable market outlook and historical declines in profitability.[18]

Phase out An approach that lets the product decline without a change in marketing strategy

Run out A policy that exploits any strengths left in the product

Basically, there are three ways to delete a product: (1) phase it out, (2) run it out, or (3) drop it immediately (see Figure 10.4). A **phase out** approach lets the product decline without a change in the marketing strategy. No attempt is made to give the product new life. A **run out** policy exploits any strengths left in the

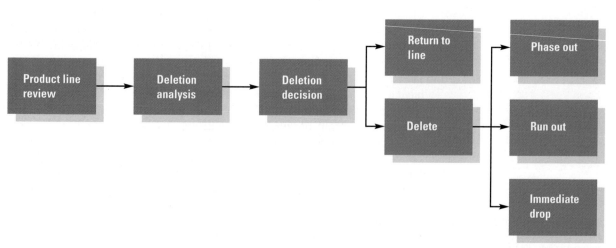

Figure 10.4 Product deletion process. SOURCE: Martin L. Bell, *Marketing: Concepts and Strategies,* 3rd ed., p. 267; copyright © 1979, Houghton Mifflin Company. Reproduced by permission of Mrs. Martin L. Bell.

product. Intensifying marketing efforts in core markets or eliminating some marketing expenditures, such as advertising, may cause a sudden profit increase. This approach is commonly taken for technologically obsolete products, such as older models of camcorders or computers, and is often accompanied by a price reduction. Some car manufacturers use a run out approach to dispose of certain models just before a new launch. The third option, an **immediate drop** of an unprofitable product, is the best strategy when losses are too great to prolong the product's life.

Immediate drop An option that drops an unprofitable product immediately

● S U M M A R Y

To maximise the effectiveness of a product mix, a company usually has to alter its mix through modification of existing products, deletion of a product or new product development. Developing and managing products is critical to a company's survival and growth. The various approaches available for organising product management share common activities, functions and decisions necessary to guide a product through its life cycle. A *product manager* is responsible for a product, a product line or several distinct products that make up an interrelated group within a multi-product organisation. A *brand manager* is responsible for a single brand. *Marketing managers* are responsible for managing the marketing activities that serve a particular group or class of customers. A *venture* or *project team* is sometimes used to create and develop entirely new products that may be aimed at new markets.

A new product may be an innovation that has never been sold by any organisation, or it can be a product that a given company has not marketed previously, although similar products have been available from other organisations. Before a product is introduced, it goes through the seven phases of *new product development*. (1) In the *idea generation* phase, new product ideas may come from internal or external sources. (2) In the process of *screening ideas,* those with the greatest potential are selected for further review. (3) *Concept testing* presents a small number of potential buyers with the concept idea in order to ascertain early approval indicators. (4) During the *business analysis* stage, the product idea is evaluated to determine its potential contribution to the company's sales, costs and profits. (5) *Product development* is the phase in which the organisation determines if it is technically feasible to produce the product and if it can be produced at costs low enough for the final price to be reasonable. (6) *Test marketing* is a limited introduction of a product in geographic areas chosen to represent the intended market. (7) The decision to enter the *commercialisation* phase means that full scale production of the product begins and a complete marketing strategy is developed.

Not all "new" products are genuinely new! Many product introductions are in fact a *line extension*— the development of a product that is closely related to products in the existing product line, but designed to meet different customer needs. The *product adoption process* that buyers go through in accepting a product includes awareness, interest, evaluation, trial and adoption.

As a product moves through its life cycle, marketing strategies will require continual adaptation. In the growth stage, it is important to develop brand loyalty and a market position. Marketers may move from an *exclusive* or *selective distribution* to a more *intensive distribution* of dealers. In the maturity stage, a product may be modified or new market segments may be developed to rejuvenate its sales.

Product modification involves changing one or more characteristics of a company's product. This approach to altering a product mix can be effective when the product is modifiable, when customers can perceive the change and when customers want the modification. *Quality modifications* are changes that relate to a product's dependability and durability. Changes that affect a product's versatility, effectiveness, convenience or safety are called *functional modifications*. *Style modifications* change the sensory appeal of a product.

A product that is declining may be maintained as long as it makes a contribution to profits or enhances the product mix. Marketers must determine whether to eliminate the declining product or to re-position it to extend its life.

Product deletion is the process of eliminating a product that is unprofitable, consumes too many resources and no longer satisfies a sufficient number of customers. *Phase out*, *run out* and *immediate drop* are three ways to delete a product. A product mix should be systematically reviewed to determine when to delete products.

Important Terms

Product manager
Brand manager
Marketing manager
Venture or project team
New product development
Idea generation
Screening ideas
Concept testing
Business analysis

Product development
Test marketing
Commercialisation
Line extension
Product adoption process
Exclusive distribution
Selective distribution
Intensive distribution
Product modification

Quality modifications
Functional modifications
Style modifications
Product deletion
Phase out
Run out
Immediate drop

Discussion and Review Questions

1. What organisational alternatives are available to a company with two product lines, each consisting of four product items?
2. When is it more appropriate to use a product manager than a marketing manager?
3. What type of company might use a venture team to develop new products? What are the advantages and disadvantages of such a team?
4. Do small companies that manufacture one or two products need to be concerned about developing and managing products? Why or why not?
5. Why is product development a cross-functional activity within an organisation? That is, why must finance, engineering, manufacturing and other functional areas be involved?
6. Develop a list of information sources for new product ideas for the car industry.
7. What are the advantages and disadvantages of test marketing?
8. Compare and contrast three ways of modifying a product.
9. What are the stages of the product adoption process, and how do they affect the commercialisation phase?
10. How can a company pro-long the life of a mature product? What actions should be taken to try to stem the product's decline?
11. Give several reasons why a company might be unable to eliminate an unprofitable product.

Recommended Readings

L. de Chernatony and M. H. B. McDonald, *Creating Powerful Brands* (Oxford: Butterworth-Heinemann, 1998).

P. Doyle, "Product life cycle management", in *Companion Encyclopaedia of Marketing*, M. J. Baker, ed. (London: International Thomson Business Press, 2000).

C. Macrae, *The Brand Chartering Handbook* (London: EIU and Addison-Wesley, 1997).

S. Majaro, "Product planning", in *Gower Handbook of Marketing*, 4th edn, M. J. Thomas, ed. (Aldershot: Gower Press, 1995).

M. J. Thomas, "Product development and management", in *The Marketing Book*, 3rd edn, M. J. Baker, ed. (Oxford: Butterworth-Heinemann, 1994).

 C A S E S

10.1 *New Product Development and the Concept Car*

Car manufacturers are well used to the stresses associated with new product development. The costs and difficulties of the process must be vigorously tackled by companies wishing to generate high sales and remain in the forefront of technological development. In spite of recessionary pressures and falling car sales, the industry is investing in the future with a host of new and revised model designs. Recently there have been GM's Frontera up-date, Alfa Romeo's gorgeous 166, the Lupo and Bova from VW, the Yaris supermini from Toyota, Mitsubishi's Space Star, Suzuki's Jimmy off-roader and the Octavia from Skoda, to name but a few launches. Even those manufacturers not launching new models in the near future are seeking to improve and upgrade their existing portfolios.

For many manufacturers, developing so-called concept cars is an important part of the new product development process, which helps new techniques, technologies, materials and production processes to be tested and evaluated. Renault's striking model, the Racoon, described by the company as a "freedom car of tomorrow", is just one example of the concept cars that appear at motor shows around the world. The four wheel drive vehicle is amphibious, has a telephone, fax machine and computer based navigation aids, and was designed using revolutionary product development techniques. Although the vehicle may look unusual to today's consumers, precedents show that today's concept cars do sometimes appear in showrooms in the future. The "ladybird" shaped Ford Ghia Saetta is either Ford's most extravagant test car camouflage ever, or a wacky roadster concept car—or both. According to *Autocar*'s Peter Robinson, the Saetta is basically a two-seater version of Ford's £7,000 city car, the Ka. The Saetta roadster concept car enables Ford to show buyers and management what is possible.

When it was introduced at the Geneva motor show, the Aston Martin Lagonda Vignale created quite a sensation. However, despite the high performance, excellent standards of accommodation and obvious good looks of the model, this too is a concept car. The company's reason for developing the Vignale was to test the future potential for producing hand-built cars by investigating a range of design and production techniques and materials. According to Aston Martin's Lagonda chief executive, Walter Haynes, "There is a place for the handmade luxury car in the future but it has to be fuel efficient and innovative and capable of being a car for life." While the company does not intend to begin commercial production of the Vignale, the development of the car is considered to have been very beneficial to the company's plans for new product development.

Aston Martin is not alone in trying to predict the changes that the twenty-first century will bring. According to the UK Motor Industry Research Association (MIRA), a move towards electrically powered vehicles is likely. It is estimated that by 2010 there may be over 10 million electric cars worldwide, with annual sales running as high as 2 million. The growth seems likely, given increasing concerns about the harmful impact of petrol driven vehicles on the environment. If European companies are to maintain their stake in car production, inevitably they must direct more attention towards developing low emission, electrical vehicle technology. Such programmes will no doubt be accompanied by the development of further concept cars, vehicle trials and long run testing.

Already, the Japanese government is doing much to encourage the development of such technology. So far there has been less activity in Europe, where only the French government displays a similar degree of commitment. According to MIRA's head of automotive services, Dr. Martin White, "People believe the well publicised problems of pollution in Los Angeles are unique to that city and its suburbs sitting as they do in a geographic bowl. But even our own inner-city areas, with their tower blocks and poor air circulation, can suffer the consequences of a similar and relatively effective pollution trap."

Whatever developments the future may bring for car manufacturing, the use of product and concept testing will continue to play an important role in the changing face of car design.

SOURCES: Stewart Smith, "Peugeot keeps it in the family", Telegraph Motoring, *Coventry Evening Telegraph*, 16 March 1993, p. 23; "Face of the future", Telegraph Motoring, *Coventry Evening Telegraph*, 16 March 1993, p. 24; "Luxurious Lagonda", Fast Lane 93, *Coventry Evening Telegraph*, February 1993, p. 11; "The shape of things to come", Fast Lane 93, *Coventry Evening Telegraph*, February 1993, p. 11; *What Car?* magazine, 1996, 1997; Peter Robinson, "Saetta shows how far Ka can go", *Autocar*, 22 May 1996, pp. 26–29.

Questions for Discussion

1. Why is it important for car manufacturers to develop concept cars?
2. What other forms of research and testing are relevant to the launch of a new model?
3. How can consumers' views of concept cars displayed at motor shows feed into the new product development process for production cars?

10.2 Sellotape or Mustard? Increasing Market Penetration

Just as *JCB* is a generic term for backhoe diggers in the construction industry, *Hoover* for vacuum cleaners, *Post-It* for those useful sticky stationery tags, and *Bic* for disposable pens, for many decades *Sellotape* has been the term applied to sticky transparent tape. Over the years, however, many other brands and suppliers have entered the market and eaten away Sellotape's once dominant market share. So where next for Sellotape?

At the end of 1995, following nearly two years of research and planning, Sellotape enjoyed a £2 million re-launch. This represented the "most significant change in the brand's 60 year history", according to Neil Ashley, executive director of the company, re-named the Sellotape Company. The name Sellotape has been the company's core marketing asset for many decades, with nine out of ten consumers familiar with the brand. However, the company has for some time sold a wider range of products than its sticky tape association implies. Michael Peters of the branding specialist Identica, responsible for the Sellotape re-think, was more fervent in his view: "While it is a very famous trademark, it's a grey one." Qualitative marketing research revealed that although well known, hardly any consumer asked for Sellotape by name. Worse, they readily accepted other brands because they could see no obvious product or brand features that gave Sellotape a competitive edge.

The re-launch aimed to address the inherent weakness in becoming a generic name for a product by re-establishing a new brand identity alongside existing core brand values. Rival products not using cellulose are cheaper, so alongside its traditional tape, the Sellotape Company now offers a range of tape made from other source materials. Elephant Tape, for example, is a heavy duty fabric tape that is targeted at the do-it-yourself (DIY) market.

Under the sub-brand Sellotape Office, a range of products aimed at office use has been launched. Ranges have also been targeted at the children's market and the home security market. The view that there are in effect three distinct markets—retail, DIY and office—has led to the development of novel product applications and totally separate ranges.

The key problem to overcome has been "the Colman's mustard dilemma". Colman's, the market leader, had tremendously high brand awareness, and consumers perceived its mustards to be of high quality. Unfortunately, these consumers usually bought only one type of mustard, English; and that one jar lasted for years! Colman's had to increase usage. It achieved this by (1) demonstrating in advertisements and cookery supplements that mustard could be used in a variety of ways, particularly as an additional ingredient in many sauces, just like a herb or spice, and (2) bringing out a range of different mustards, each with unique strengths, flavours and applications: French, Italian and American mustards, along with the traditional English. Consumers were encouraged to have several jars in their cupboards.

For Sellotape, research showed that most customers bought only one roll of sticky tape each year, often around Christmas. The launch of ranges designed for different target audiences—retail, DIY and office—and for various applications—children's activities and home security uses—emulated the brand extension principles so well deployed by Colman's.

Sellotape's strong brand awareness and identity mean that the company does not need to advertise heavily. Instead, the Sellotape Company is relying on direct marketing and point-of-sale promotion to create awareness of its new sub-brands and their applications. A core task for the company has been to break down traditional views of the product and its customers held by employees and to establish additional channels of distribution through toy shops and garden centres to reflect the extended and additional product ranges. It is away from the once core stationery retailers that the Sellotape Company expects to see the strongest growth, particularly in the DIY sector. There, pan-European sales are rising by around 8 per cent each year and now amount to £60 million.

If the Sellotape Company can, like Colman's, encourage its customers to buy two products annually instead of just one and to look for its branded products by name, the heritage of the brand and the re-organisation of the company will reap significant rewards.

SOURCES: "Sellotape acts to avoid getting stuck in a rut", *Independent on Sunday*, 26 November, 1995, IB8; the Sellotape Company, 1996; B&Q, 1996; Sainsbury's Homebase, 1996. With grateful thanks to Meg Carter.

Questions for Discussion

1. At what stages in their product life cycle are the different Sellotape products, and what are the management implications?
2. Why has it been necessary for the Sellotape Company to re-launch its Sellotape range?
3. How might new lines help Sellotape to develop its competitive position in this market?

11 The Marketing of Services

OBJECTIVES

- To understand the nature and characteristics of services
- To classify services
- To understand the development of marketing strategies for services
- To understand the problems involved in developing a differential advantage in services
- To examine the crucial concept of service quality
- To explore the concept of marketing in non-business situations
- To understand the development of marketing strategies in non-business organisations
- To describe methods for controlling non-business marketing activities

"Delivering services is people's business: only great customers and great employees can guarantee great service quality."

Hans Kasper
Rijksuniversiteit Limburg, Maastricht

For several weeks in 1998, TV viewers were surprised to find the commercial break in between segments of their favourite ITV or C4 drama starting and ending with a simple blue screen, at the centre of which was a small "b^2" symbol. This teaser campaign eventually transpired to be for the launch of Barclays' b^2, an all-new financial services brand for a highly innovative long term savings proposition. Barclays' research had identified that relatively few members of the public regularly invested in the stock market for fear of losing their savings. For many consumers, the high street building society proved a safer bet.

b^2 argues that the stock market has always been the key to growing money. The difference is that with b^2, the investor's money is in a fund which tracks the top companies on the stock market: the b^2 Market Track 350 account tracks the top 350 companies, combining established names with medium sized companies that have a diversity of market coverage, creating a spread for any risk. There is no charge for setting up the account, paying in or taking out money. Barclays charges a straight 1 per cent per year for managing the investor's money. The whole proposition is aimed to be clear, simple and "straightforward".

This proposition reflects the feedback from marketing research: consumers are uncertain of the stock market, risk adverse and loathing of financial institutions' bureaucracy. In fact, the developers of the b^2 brand exacted a swift and immediate punishment on members of the Barclays' project team who took their eyes off the target market and customer needs during brainstorming sessions: a swear box was placed on the table for fines to penalise those becoming too obscure, divorced from target market needs or obsessed with technical details!

To ensure acceptance of the b^2 brand and proposition, throughout the product development phase, agency Banks Hoggins O'Shea ran a rolling programme of qualitative research in which ideas were bounced off prospective customers. The key finding was that the whole concept and its marketing message had to be simple. UK consumers rarely want to plan 20 years ahead. They just need to know how much a scheme will cost per month and for how many years: three, five or seven. The research enabled the agency and Barclays to carefully hone the product specification, branding and promotional ideas to reflect the target customer expectations, perceptions, needs and angsts. Once the concept was clear and refined following the qualitative discussion groups and interviews, quantitative research was used to model the likely market size, likely customer up-take and anticipated volume of customer savings. Marketing research was utilised throughout the product development process to ensure b² matched target market expectations and Barclays' commercial targets.

Not all products and brands are so well researched. Many companies have to withdraw failed product launches or embark on extensive product modification in order to properly reflect consumer demand. Ultimately, however good the marketing programme and promotional hype, in order to satisfy customers and gain an edge over competitors, a business must ensure it has the "right" product and branding in the first place.

SOURCES: Barclays plc; Richenda Wilson, "Test for Success", *Marketing Week,* 15 October 1998, pp. 77–78; Steven Hastings of Banks Hoggins O'Shea & Partners; *Radio Times,* 12–18 December 1998, p. 67; b² direct mail, 1999. *Advertisement:* Courtesy of Barclay's b².

This chapter presents concepts that apply specifically to the marketing of services. Services marketing involves marketing in non-profit organisations such as education, healthcare, charities and government, as well as for profit making areas such as entertainment, tourism, finance, personal services and professional services. As detailed in the chapter opener, Barclays has designed a highly innovative marketing programme to launch its new b² brand—a cutting edge, long term savings proposition which allows consumers to use the stock market in a low risk manner.

The chapter begins by considering the contribution of service industries to the economy. It then addresses the unique characteristics of services and the problems they present to marketers. Next, it presents various classification schemes that can help services marketers develop marketing strategies. In addition, it discusses a variety of marketing mix considerations, along with the associated problems of creating and sustaining a differential advantage (competitive edge). The important concept of service quality is then explored. Finally, the chapter defines non-business marketing and examines the development of non-business marketing strategies and the control of non-business marketing activities.

The Nature and Characteristics of Services

Service An intangible product involving a deed, a performance or an effort that cannot be physically possessed

As mentioned in Chapter 8, all products—goods, services and ideas—possess a certain amount of intangibility. A **service** is an intangible product involving a deed, a performance or an effort that cannot be physically possessed.[1] It should be noted that few products can be classified as a pure good or a pure service. Consider, for example, the purchase of a personal computer. When consumers buy a computer, they take ownership of a physical item which they might house in a study at their home, but the maintenance contract linked with the purchase is a service. Similarly, a helpline facility offering software support is providing a service. Most products, such as computers and other brown goods, contain both tangible and intangible components. One component, however, will dominate, and it is this dominant component that leads to the classification of goods, services and ideas.

Figure 11.1 illustrates the tangibility concept by placing a variety of "products" on a continuum of tangibility and intangibility. Tangible dominant products are typically classified as goods, and intangible dominant products are typically considered services. An airline seat or hotel bed may be tangible and physical, but the airline or hotel operator is in fact providing a service: transportation or temporary accommodation. Thus, as defined in Chapter 8, services are intangible dominant products that involve the application of human and mechanical efforts to people or objects.

Growth and Importance of Services

Consumer services Services such as education, healthcare, leisure, catering, tourism, financial, entertainment, home maintenance and other services to help consumers

Business services Services such as repairs and maintenance, consulting and professional advice, installation, equipment leasing, marketing research, advertising, temporary office personnel and caretaking services

In the UK and in Europe, as in the United States, the importance of services in the economy is increasing (see Tables 11.1 and 11.2), employing 67 per cent of the workforce in the UK and 61 per cent in the rest of the European Union. Service industries encompass trade, communications, transport, leisure, food and accommodation, financial and medical services, education, government and technical services. There are services intended for consumers—**consumer services**—and those designed to satisfy businesses—**business services.**

Economic prosperity has been a major catalyst for consumer services growth, leading to an increase in financial services, travel, entertainment and personal care. Lifestyle changes have similarly encouraged expansion of the service sector. Smaller families result in more free time and relatively higher disposable income. Consumers are keener than ever to "buy in" outside services. With the number of women in the workforce more than doubling in the last 40 years, consumers want to avoid tasks such as meal preparation, house cleaning, home maintenance and preparation of tax returns. Furthermore, Europeans have become more fitness and recreation oriented, and with greater leisure time, the demand for fitness and recreational facilities has escalated. In terms of demographics, the population is growing older, and this change has promoted tremendous expansion of healthcare services. Finally, the number and complexity of goods needing servicing have spurred demand for repair services.

Goods (tangible) — Bananas, Jewellery, Compact disc player, Cars/maintenance, Fast food restaurants, Airlines, Beauty salons, Financial services, Telephone services, Education — **Services (intangible)**

Figure 11.1   A continuum of product tangibility and intangibility

Standard Industrial Classification, 1992	June 1985 '000s	%	March 1998 '000s	%
Agriculture, hunting, forestry and fishing	366	1.7	289	1.2
Mining and quarrying, supply of electricity, gas and water	560	2.6	221	1.0
Manufacturing industries	5,002	23.4	4,114	17.7
Construction	1,058	4.9	994	4.3
Wholesale and retail trade and repairs	3,355	15.7	4,033	17.4
Hotels and restaurants	1,004	4.7	1,334	5.7
Transport and storage	879	4.1	854	3.7
Post and telecommunication	450	2.1	512	2.2
Financial intermediation	870	4.1	1,059	4.6
Real estate	154	0.7	284	1.2
Renting, research, computer and other business activities	1,736	8.1	2,697	11.6
Public administration and defence	1,479	6.9	1,348	5.8
Education	1,629	7.6	1,870	8.1
Health and social work activities	2,021	9.4	2,585	11.1
Other community, social and personal activities	851	4.0	1,025	4.4
All industries and services	**21,413**	**100.0**	**23,219**	**100.0**

SOURCE: From *Marketing Pocket Book 1999*. Reprinted by permission of NTC Publications, Ltd.

Table 11.1   Analysis of employee jobs by industry, UK

Not only have consumer services grown in the economy, business services have prospered as well. Business or industrial services include repairs and maintenance, consulting and professional advice, installation, equipment leasing, marketing research, advertising, temporary office personnel and caretaking services. Expenditures for business and industrial services have risen even faster than expenditures for consumer services. This growth has been attributed to the increasingly complex, specialised and competitive business environment.[2]

There are three key reasons behind the growth of business-to-business services:

- *Specialisation*—the delegation of non-care tasks such as advertising, executive recruitment and car fleet management.
- *Technology*—the increase in sophistication leading to the "buying in" of expert knowledge and skills such as IT computing consultants.
- *Flexibility*—the need in many organisations to avoid fixed overhead costs. Marketing research, maintenance and cleaning are frequently brought in only on an ad hoc basis.

Characteristics of Services

The marketing of services is distinct from goods marketing.[3] To understand the nature of services marketing, it is necessary to appreciate the particular characteristics of services. Services have four basic characteristics: (1) intangibility, (2) inseparability of production and consumption, (3) perishability and (4) heterogeneity.[4] Table 11.3 summarises these characteristics and the marketing problems they entail.

			Manufacturing and Production					Services				
Country	Labour Force '000s	As % of Population	Agriculture, forestry, fishing	Mining, quarrying	Manufacturing	Electricity, gas, water	Construction	Wholesale, retail, restaurants, hotels	Transport, storage, communications	Finance, insurance, real estate, business services	Community, social, personal services	Not defined
Austria	3,884	48.1	6.6	0.2	14.6	1.0		21.8	6.2	10.2	24.4	
Belgium	4,214	41.3	2.7	0.3	19.7	0.9	6.6	17.7	7.4	10.6	33.5	0.7
Czech Republic	4,990	48.4	5.5	1.6	28.5	1.7	8.7	19.4	6.9	9.6	18.0	
Denmark	2,822	53.6	4.0	0.1	19.7	0.7	6.6	16.5	7.1	10.5	34.7	0.2
Estonia	707	64.2	9.9		25.5	2.5		16.0	9.6	6.3	14.7	
Finland	2,531	49.4	7.1	0.2	20.7	1.1	5.6	15.0	7.6	10.1	32.3	0.3
France	25,613	43.9	4.7	0.3	18.8	0.9	6.5	16.8	6.3	10.6	35.0	
Germany	39,294	48.0	3.3	0.7	27.0	1.1	8.7	15.1	6.1	8.9	29.1	
Greece	4,294	48.5	19.8	0.4	14.5	1.1	6.5	22.6	6.4	6.7	22.0	
Hungary	3,975	39.2	8.5	0.4	23.6	2.4	5.3	17.4	8.4	6.9	11.6	
Ireland	1,517	41.4	8.8	0.4	17.9	0.8	6.4	13.3	5.5	18.5		
Italy	23,385	40.8	7.0	0.4	22.8	0.9	7.9	21.3	5.4	8.4	25.4	
Latvia	1,168	47.1	18.5		19.2		6.0	16.0	8.8	6.3		
Lithuania	1,653	44.7	24.1		17.6	2.5	7.0	14.0	5.7	3.2	6.2	6.4
The Netherlands	7,517	48.5	3.9	0.2	15.5	0.6	6.1	20.3	6.1	13.8	31.1	2.4
Norway	2,192	49.6	4.8	1.1	15.1	1.0	6.2	18.2	7.5	9.8	36.2	0.1
Portugal	4,332	43.5	13.6	0.4	21.5	0.8	9.0	18.8	3.9	7.6	24.4	
Romania	9,379	41.3	35.4	2.7	24.5	2.0	5.1	9.5	5.8	3.5	9.6	1.9
Spain	16,159	42.1	8.7	0.6	18.9	0.7	9.5	21.2	6.1	7.0	27.4	
Sweden	4,310	48.4	2.9	0.2	19.4	0.9	5.7	15.2	6.6	11.6	37.6	
Switzerland	3,905	55.1	4.5	0.7	19.7		7.4	19.2	6.0	13.0	29.5	
Turkey	22,736	36.3	41.3	0.8	13.5	0.4	5.6	11.6	3.9	2.1	12.8	
United Kingdom	27,137	46.0	1.2		17.7	1.0	4.3	23.1	5.9	17.4	29.4	

Additional Country-Specific Categories

Estonia: Public authorities—5.3%
Hungary: Other services—8.6%, Public administration and defence—6.8%
Ireland: Public administration and defence—4.9%
Latvia: Public authorities—4.7%; Science, education, culture—8.8%; Healthcare and social—6.2%
Lithuania: Public authorities—4.1%; Science, education and culture—9.2%

SOURCE: *The European Marketing Pocket Book*, 1999; Young & Rubicam/The Media Edge with NTC Publications, Henley.

Table 11.2 Labour force composition: services versus manufacturing and production

Table 11.3 Services characteristics and marketing problems

Unique Services Features	Resulting Marketing Problems
Intangibility	Cannot be stored
	Cannot be protected through patents
	Cannot be readily displayed or communicated
	Prices difficult to set
Inseparability	Consumer involved in production
	Other consumers involved in production
	Centralised mass production difficult
Perishability	Services unable to be stockpiled
Heterogeneity	Standardisation and quality difficult to control

SOURCE: Valarie A. Zeithaml, A. Parasuraman and Leonard L. Berry, "Problems and strategies in services marketing", *Journal of Marketing*, Spring 1985, pp. 33–46. Used by permission of the American Marketing Association.

Intangibility An inherent quality of services that are performed and therefore cannot be tasted, touched, seen, smelled or possessed

Search qualities The tangible attributes of a service that can be viewed prior to purchase

Experience qualities Attributes that can be assessed only after purchase and consumption, including satisfaction and courtesy

Credence qualities Attributes that cannot be assessed even after purchase and consumption

Inseparability In relation to production and consumption, a characteristic of services that means they are produced at the same time as they are consumed

Intangibility stems from the fact that services are performances. They cannot be seen, touched, tasted or smelled; nor can they be possessed. Intangibility also relates to the difficulty that consumers may have in understanding service offerings.[5] Services have a few tangible attributes, called **search qualities**, that can be viewed prior to purchase, such as the cleanliness of a doctor's waiting room or the array of tools in a car mechanic's shop. When consumers cannot view a service product in advance and examine its properties, they may not understand exactly what is being offered. Even when consumers do gain sufficient knowledge about service offerings, they may not be able to evaluate the possible choices. On the other hand, services are rich in experience and credence qualities. **Experience qualities** are those qualities that can be assessed only after purchase and consumption (satisfaction, courtesy, pleasure). Restaurants and holidays are examples of services that are high in experience qualities. **Credence qualities** are those qualities that cannot be assessed even after purchase and consumption.[6] An appendix operation, car repairs, consulting and legal representation are examples of services high in credence qualities. How many consumers are knowledgeable enough to assess the quality of an appendectomy, even after the surgery has been performed?

A Volvo car can be test driven before being purchased. It can be viewed in the dealer's showroom and on the streets. It can—to an extent—be consumed prior to the risk taking purchase. The same is not true of a meal in a top restaurant or a theatre seat. The meal may be disappointing, as may the play, but by the time the disappointment is recognised it is too late; the service has been—at least partially—consumed and paid for.

Related to intangibility, therefore, is **inseparability** of production and consumption. Services are normally produced at the same time as they are consumed. A medical examination is an example of simultaneous production and consumption. In fact, the doctor cannot possibly perform the service without the patient's presence, and the consumer is actually involved in the production process. With other services, such as holidaying in a resort hotel, many consumers are simultaneously involved in production. Because of high consumer involvement in most services, standardisation and control are difficult to maintain. Marketing Insight 11.1 illustrates how Dutch banking giant ABN AMRO addresses this difficulty.

Perishability A characteristic of services whereby unused capacity on one occasion cannot be stockpiled or inventoried for future occasions

Because production and consumption are simultaneous, services are also characterised by **perishability**. The consumer of a service generally has to be present and directly involved in the consumption of the service at the time of its production. This means that unused capacity in one time period cannot be stockpiled or inventoried for future time periods. This is a problem which hotel operators face every day. Each operator engages in an ongoing struggle to maintain room occupancy levels. Empty rooms mean lost business. In order to maximise occupancy, the operators may offer "last minute" cut-price deals or specially priced packages to reduce numbers of unused rooms. Some operators also insist on payments of non-refundable deposits when rooms are booked. The hotels' dilemma illustrates how service perishability presents problems very different from the supply and demand problems encountered in the marketing of goods.[7] While an empty hotel room one night is a sale lost for ever, cans of soup remaining on the supermarket shelf or a Nintendo computer game left unsold in a dealer's showroom at the close of business will be available for sale the following day.

Heterogeneity Variability in the quality of service because services are provided by people, and people perform inconsistently

Finally, because most services are labour intensive, they are susceptible to **heterogeneity**. For the service to be provided and consumed, the client generally meets and deals directly with the service provider's personnel; direct contact and interaction are distinguishing features of services. People typically perform services, and people do not always perform consistently. There may be variation from one service to another within the same organisation or variation in the service that a single individual provides from day to day and from customer to customer. A good branch manager is crucial for a company such as Café Rouge or KFC. Poor customer reaction and branch performance can often be traced back to a poor branch manager.[8] Queuing times in McDonald's can vary greatly, often due to teamwork, speed and efficiency variations between branches. A hotel general manager has a significant impact on the attitude of the hotel's staff and thus on the running of the hotel. This may result in varying guest satisfaction, for example, between one Hilton and another. Thus standardisation and quality are extremely difficult to control. However, it is also true that the characteristics of services themselves may make it possible for marketers to customise their offerings to consumers. In such cases, services marketers often face a dilemma: how to provide efficient, standardised service at some acceptable level of quality while simultaneously treating each customer as a unique person.

Classification of Services

Services are a very diverse group of products, and an organisation may provide more than one kind. Examples of services include car hire, maintenance services, healthcare, hair dressing, health centres, child care, domestic services, legal advice, banking, insurance, air travel, education, entertainment, catering, business consulting, dry cleaning and accounting. Nevertheless, services can be meaningfully analysed by using a **five category classification** scheme: (1) type of market, (2) degree of labour intensiveness, (3) degree of customer contact, (4) skill of service provider and (5) goal of the service provider. Table 11.4 summarises this scheme.

Five category classification A method of analysing services according to five criteria: type of market, degree of labour intensiveness, degree of customer contact, skill of service provider and goal of the service provider

Services can be viewed in terms of the market or type of customer they serve—consumer or industrial.[9] The implications of this distinction are very similar to those for all products and therefore are not discussed here. Figure 11.2 illustrates two kinds of marketing services which brand design company jkr and marketing research business AC Nielsen offer to their clients.

Dutch Bankers Build Relationships—ABN AMRO Leads through Services

The 1991 merger between Algemene Bank Nederland and Amsterdam-Rotterdam Bank to create Dutch based ABN AMRO Bank produced the dominant financial institution in the Netherlands, the third largest bank in Europe and one of the world's top 20. With branches throughout Benelux, and over 2,600 branches in 77 other countries, ABN AMRO deals daily with thousands of customers face to face or through telecommunications.

The company's policy is to buy relatively small banking operations around the globe and integrate them fully within its existing business. It does not seek mega-mergers with other large international banks. ABN AMRO North America agreed to buy Chicago Corp which merged with ABN AMRO Securities Inc., resulting in the addition of 20,000 staff outside the Netherlands and a significant New York based operation destined for rapid growth. Hoare Govett has already been so integrated, creating the seventeenth largest insurance broker in the world. Nordic Alfred Berg is now also part of the network.

Significant alliances have been established in South East Asia, with China now seen to be an important market. The strategy is recognised as successful well beyond the banking fraternity; ABN has received many prestigious awards for the competitive success of its global operation.

To facilitate this growth, the bank is one of the world's leading spenders on information systems, maintaining that today's technology helps it to offer an efficient and reliable service to its most valuable asset—its customer base. Customers are kept to the fore through the company's policy of relationship management, a core strategy since 1980. The bank targets only a small number of clients, who are subsequently handled by a large team of relationship managers.

Many consumers find banks' history and formal procedures intimidating and view them as powerful institutions with which they can enjoy little personal interaction. ABN AMRO has tackled this perception head-on, recognising that as fundamentally a service provider dealing with people, its success depends on the attitude and ability of the bank's own personnel. In this respect, ABN AMRO realises it must behave as a service provider and adopt the practices of services marketing.

ABN AMRO places significant emphasis on its employees, who are integral to its products, marketing and the services it provides. The bank's internal marketing focuses on training and motivating its staff worldwide to deliver a consistent, friendly, proficient and superior service to ABN AMRO's many customers. ABN AMRO acknowledges that it is only as good as its personnel—those people who to many customers epitomise the bank's products and services. Its human resource and marketing executives highlight these employees' skills in handling customer contact and delivering the bank's services.

SOURCES: "European 100", *Information Week*, 11 December 1995, pp. 32–41; Yvette Kantrow, "ABN AMRO/Chicago Corp will expand 'significantly' in N.Y.", *Investment Dealers' Digest*, 2 October 1995, pp. 8–9; "Jan Kalff, chairman, ABN AMRO", *Euromoney*, September 1995, p. 64; John Anderson et al., "The 1995 industry all stars", *Independent Energy*, September 1995, pp. 24–30; Matthew Ball, "ABN AMRO aims for 380 of the best", *Corporate Finance*, July 1995, p. 40; "Berg sale raises broking stakes", *Euroweek*, June 1995, p. 45; Caroline Farquhar; ABN AMRO annual report and accounts; Barclays de Zoete Wedd Securities; Credit Suisse First Boston; Financial Times Analysis; "Banking industry report", Salomon Brothers, April 1992; ABN AMRO Utrecht, 1999.

A second way to classify services is by degree of labour intensiveness. Many services, such as child care, education and hair dressing, rely heavily on human labour. Other services, such as telecommunications, fitness centres and public transport, are more equipment intensive.

Labour (people) based services are more susceptible to heterogeneity than are most equipment based services. Marketers of people based services must recognise that the service providers are often viewed as the service itself. Therefore, strategies relating to selecting, training, motivating and controlling employees are very important to the success of most service businesses. A bad attitude from British Airways' ground staff would colour the customer's view not just of the

Table 11.4 Classification of services

Category	Examples
Type of Market	
Consumer	Child care, legal advice, entertainment
Industrial	Consulting, caretaking services, installation
Degree of Labour Intensiveness	
Labour based	Education, haircuts, dentistry
Equipment based	Telecommunications, fitness centres, public transport
Degree of Customer Contact	
High	Healthcare, hotels, air travel
Low	Home deliveries, postal service
Skill of the Service Provider	
Professional	Legal advice, healthcare, accountancy
Non-professional	Domestic services, dry cleaning, public transport
Goal of the Service Provider	
Profit	Financial services, insurance, tourism
Non-profit	Healthcare, education, government

employee concerned but also of the company and all of its service products. A customer who has flown quite happily with British Airways for many years may be prompted to consider taking his or her business to a rival company.

The third way in which services can be classified is by degree of customer contact. High contact services include healthcare, hotels, estate agencies and restaurants; low contact services include home deliveries, theatres, dry cleaning and spectator sports.[10] Note that high contact services generally involve actions that are directed towards individuals. Because these services are directed at people, the consumer must be present during production. Sometimes, for example in the case of a car valeting service, it is possible for the service provider to go to the consumer. However, high contact services typically require that the consumer goes to the production facility. Thus the physical appearance and ambience of the facility may be a major component of the consumer's overall evaluation of the service. The enjoyment of an evening out in a restaurant stems not just from the taste of the food but also from the decor and furnishings, general ambience, and the ability and attitude of the staff. Because the consumer must be present during production of a high contact service, the process of production may be just as important as its final outcome. For example, open plan banks, quick queue systems and ATM facilities aim to improve the transaction process and make the service more enjoyable for the consumer.

Low contact service, in contrast, commonly involves actions directed at things. Although consumers may not need to be present during service delivery, their presence may be required to initiate or terminate the service. The Post Office maintains a network of branches, sorting offices and vehicles. The process of sending a parcel from Cardiff to London or Lille is lengthy. Although they must be present to initiate the service, consumers need not be present during the

Part III   Product, Branding, Packaging and Service Decisions

Figure 11.2 Marketing of services to business users. Marketing research company AC Nielsen and brand design business jkr offer a range of marketing services to their clients.   SOURCES: *left:* Courtesy of AC Nielsen. *right:* Courtesy of jkr.

process. The appearance of the production facilities and the interpersonal skills of actual service providers are thus not as critical in low contact services as they are in high contact services.[11]

Skill of the service provider is a fourth way to classify services. Professional services tend to be more complex and more highly regulated than non-professional services. In the case of legal advice, for example, consumers often do not know what the actual service will involve or how much it will cost until the service is completed, because the final product is very situation-specific. Additionally, solicitors are regulated both by law and by professional associations.

Finally, services can be classified according to the goal of the service provider— profit or non-profit. The second half of this chapter examines non-business marketing, that is, marketing by not-for-profit organisations, such as the public sector and charities. Most non-business organisations provide services rather than goods.

Developing Marketing Strategies for Services

Strategic Considerations In developing marketing strategies, the marketer must first understand what benefits the customer wants, how the company's service offer and brand are perceived relative to the competition and what services consumers buy.[12] In other words, the marketer must develop the right service for the right people at the right price, in the right place with the right positioning and image. The marketer must then communicate with consumers so that they are aware of the need satisfying services available to them. The key aspects of effective target marketing—as explained in Chapter 7—and of managing the implementation of the determined marketing strategy—as detailed in Chapters 20 and 23—apply strongly to the marketing of services.[13]

One of the unique challenges service marketers face is matching supply and demand. Price can be used to help smooth out demand for a service. There are other ways, too, in which marketers can alter the marketing mix to deal with the problem of fluctuating demand. Through price incentives, advertising and other promotional efforts, marketers can remind consumers of busy times and encourage them to come for service during slack periods. Additionally, the product itself can be altered to cope with fluctuating demand. Restaurants, for example, may change their menus, vary their lighting and decor, open or close the bar and add or delete entertainment. A historical tourist destination may stage musical events and firework displays to attract customers in low season. Finally, distribution can be modified to reflect changes in demand. For example, some libraries have mobile units that travel to different locations during slack periods.[14]

The strategies which services marketers implement are contingent upon a good understanding of the pattern and determinants of demand. Does the level of demand follow a cycle? What are the causes of this cycle? Are the changes random?[15] An attempt to use price decreases to shift demand for public transport to off-peak periods would achieve only limited success because of the cause of the cyclical demand for public transport: employment hours. Employees have little control over working hours and are therefore unable to take advantage of pricing incentives.

Table 11.5 summarises a range of marketing and non-marketing strategies which service businesses may use to deal with fluctuating demand. Non-marketing strategies essentially involve internal, employee related actions.[16] They may be the only available choices when fluctuations in demand are random. For example, a strike or natural disaster may cause fluctuations in consumer demand for public transport.

Creating a Differential Advantage in Services

Differential advantage Something desired by the customer that only one company—not its rivals—can offer

The aim of marketing is to satisfy customers, achieving product or brand differentiation with an advantage over competitors' products. This **differential advantage,** sometimes termed a *competitive edge,* is determined by customers' perceptions. A differential advantage is something desired by the customer that only one company—not its rivals—can offer. If the targeted customers do not perceive an advantage, in marketing terms the product offers no benefit over rival products.

Table 11.5 Strategies for coping with fluctuations in demand for services

Marketing Strategies	Non-marketing Strategies
Use different pricing	Hire extra staff/lay off employees
Alter product	Work employees overtime/part time
Change place/distribution	Cross-train employees
Use promotional efforts	Use employees to perform non-vital tasks during slack times
Modify customer service levels	Sub-contract work/seek sub-contract work
Alter branding and positioning	Slow the pace of work
	Turn away business

For any product, achieving and sustaining a differential advantage is difficult, but for services the challenge is even greater. The intangibility of the service product and the central role of people in its delivery are the prime causes of this difficulty, but there are also others:

- Intangibility minimises product differentiation.
- No—or little—patent protection exists.
- Few barriers to entry enable competitors to set up and copy successful initiatives.
- The interface with customers is difficult to control.
- Growth is hard to achieve, particularly since key personnel can only be spread so far.
- Service quality is irregular.
- It is difficult to improve productivity and lower the cost to the consumer.
- Innovation leads to imitation.
- Restrictive regulations abound, particularly in the professions.

The difficulty encountered in creating a differential advantage in services underscores the importance of many of the fundamental steps in marketing. In services it is increasingly important for businesses to identify well defined target market segments in order to bring service products and the marketing mix into line with consumers' exact requirements, to evaluate competitors' service offerings and marketing programmes, and to research customers' satisfaction levels. Branding, supported with well constructed promotional campaigns, is even more central to the reinforcement and communication of any differential advantage for services.

The Extended Marketing Mix for Services

Extended marketing mix for services
In addition to the standard "4Ps" marketing mix—product, promotion, price and place/distribution—there are 3 Ps: process, physical evidence (ambience) and people

The standard marketing mix comprises the "4Ps": product, promotion, price and place/distribution. The discussion about the classification of services has emphasised the importance of three additional elements: process, physical evidence (ambience) and people. Collectively, these seven elements—sometimes called the "7Ps"—form what is termed the **extended marketing mix for services** (see Figure 11.3), which is discussed in detail in Chapter 20. It is essential for services marketers to recognise the importance of these additional "3Ps."

Figure 11.3 The extended marketing mix for services

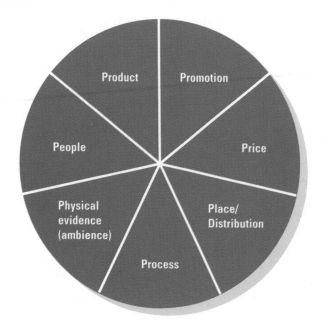

The delivery of high quality services is one of the most important and most difficult tasks that any service organisation faces. Because of their unique characteristics, services are very difficult to evaluate. Hence customers must look closely at service quality when comparing services. **Service quality** is defined as customers' perception of how well a service meets or exceeds their expectations.[17] Note that service quality is judged by customers, not the organisation. This distinction is critical because it forces services marketers to examine their quality from the customer's viewpoint. For example, a bank may view service quality as having friendly and knowledgeable employees. However, the customers of this bank may be more concerned with waiting time, ATM access and security, as well as statement accuracy. Thus it is important for service organisations to determine what customers expect and then develop service products that meet or exceed those expectations.

Service quality Customers' perception of how well a service meets or exceeds their expectations

Customer Evaluation of Service Quality

The biggest obstacle for customers in evaluating service quality is the intangible nature of the service. How can customers evaluate something that they cannot see, feel, taste or hear? Most consumers lack the knowledge or the skills to evaluate the quality of many types of services. Consequently, they must place a great deal of faith in the integrity and competence of the service provider. Despite the difficulties in evaluating quality, service quality may be the only way customers can choose one service over another. For this reason, services marketers live or die by understanding how consumers judge service quality. Table 11.6 defines five dimensions that consumers use when evaluating service quality: tangibles, reliability, responsiveness, assurance and empathy. All of these have links to employee performance. Of the five, reliability is the most important in determining customer evaluations of service quality.[18]

Services marketers pay a great deal of attention to the tangibles dimension of service quality. Tangible attributes, or search qualities, such as the appearance of facilities and employees, are often the only aspects of a service that can be viewed before purchases and consumption. Therefore, services marketers must ensure that these tangible elements are consistent with the overall image of the service product.

Except for the tangibles dimension, the criteria that customers use to judge service quality are intangible. For instance, how does a customer judge reliability? Since dimensions such as reliability cannot be examined with the senses, consumers must rely on other ways of judging service criteria. One of the most important factors in customer judgements of service quality is **service expectations.** These are influenced by past experiences with the service, word-of-mouth communication from other customers and the service company's own advertising. For example, customers are usually eager to try a new restaurant, especially when friends recommend it. These same customers may have also seen advertisements placed by the restaurant. As a result, these customers have an idea of what to expect when they visit the restaurant for the first time. When they finally dine at the restaurant, the quality they experience will change the expectations they have for their next visit and their own comments to friends and colleagues. That is why providing consistently high service quality is important. If the quality of a restaurant, or any services marketer, begins to deteriorate, customers will alter their own expectations and word-of-mouth communication to others accordingly.

Service expectations A factor used in judging service quality involving impressions from past experiences, word-of-mouth communication and the company's advertising

Dimension	Evaluation Criteria	Examples
Tangibles: Physical evidence of the service	Appearance of physical facilities Appearance of service personnel Tools or equipment used to provide the service	A clean and professional looking office A clean and well dressed lecturer The quality of food in a restaurant The equipment used in a medical examination
Reliability: Consistency and dependability in performing the service	Accuracy of billing or record keeping Performing services when promised	An accurate bank statement A confirmed hotel reservation An airline flight departing and arriving on time
Responsiveness: Willingness or readiness of employees to provide the service	Returning customer phone calls Providing prompt service Handling urgent requests	A waiter re-filling a customer's glass of wine without being asked An ambulance arriving within three minutes
Assurance: Knowledge/competence of employees and ability to convey trust and confidence	Knowledge and skills of employees Company name and reputation Personal characteristics of employees	A highly trained financial adviser A known and respected service provider A doctor's bedside manner
Empathy: Caring and individual attention provided by employees	Listening to customer needs Caring about the customer's interests Providing personalised attention	A store employee listening to and trying to understand a customer's complaint A nurse counselling a heart patient

SOURCES: Adapted from Leonard L. Berry and A. Parasuraman, *Marketing Services: Competing Through Quality* (New York: Free Press, 1991); Valarie A. Zeithaml, A. Parasuraman and Leonard L. Berry, *Delivering Quality Service: Balancing Customer Perceptions and Expectations* (New York: Free Press, 1990); and A. Parasuraman, Leonard L. Berry and Valarie A. Zeithaml, "An empirical examination of relationships in an extended service quality model", *Marketing Science Institute Working Paper Series*, report no. 90–122 (Cambridge, Mass.: Marketing Science Institute, 1990), p. 29.

Table 11.6 Dimensions of service quality

Delivering Exceptional Service Quality

Service quality factors Factors that increase the likelihood of providing high quality service: understanding customer expectations, service quality specifications, employee performance, managing service expectations

Providing high quality service on a consistent basis is very difficult. All consumers have experienced examples of poor service: long checkout lines in a supermarket, late airline departures and arrivals, inattentive waiters in a restaurant, or rude bank employees. Obviously, it is impossible for a service organisation to ensure exceptional service quality 100 percent of the time. However, there are many steps that an organisation can take to increase the likelihood of providing high quality service. First, though, the service company must understand the four **service quality factors.** As shown in Figure 11.4 they are (1) understanding customer expectations, (2) service quality specifications, (3) employee performance and (4) managing service expectations.[19]

Figure 11.4 Service quality model. SOURCE: Adapted from A. Parasuraman, Leonard L. Berry and Valarie A. Zeithaml, "An empirical examination of relationships in an extended service quality model", *Marketing Science Institute Working Paper Series, Report No. 90–122.*

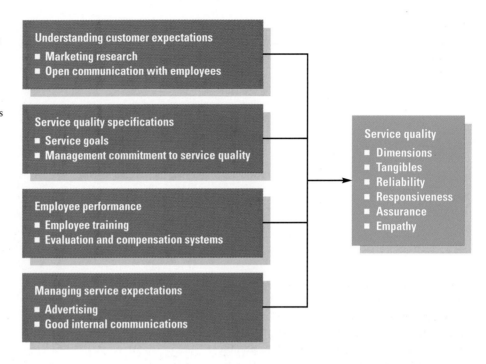

Understanding customer expectations
- Marketing research
- Open communication with employees

Service quality specifications
- Service goals
- Management commitment to service quality

Employee performance
- Employee training
- Evaluation and compensation systems

Managing service expectations
- Advertising
- Good internal communications

Service quality
- Dimensions
- Tangibles
- Reliability
- Responsiveness
- Assurance
- Empathy

Customer's zone of tolerance The difference between the customer's desired level of expectations and the customer's acceptable level of expectations

Understanding Customer Expectations Providers need to understand customer expectations when designing a service to meet or exceed those expectations. Only then can they deliver good service. Customers usually have two levels of expectations—desired and acceptable. The desired level of expectations is what the customer really wants. If this level of expectations is provided, the customer would be very satisfied. The acceptable level is viewed as a reasonable level of performance that the customer considers as being adequate. The difference between these two levels of expectations is called the **customer's zone of tolerance**.[20]

Service companies sometimes use marketing research, such as surveys and focus groups, as a means of discovering customer needs and expectations. Other services marketers, especially restaurants, use comment cards, on which customers can complain or provide suggestions. Another approach is to ask employees. Because customer contact employees interact daily with customers, they are in a good position to know what customers want from the company. Service managers should regularly interact with their employees by asking their opinions on how to best serve customers.

Service Quality Specifications Once an organisation understands its customers' needs, it must establish goals to help ensure good service delivery. These goals, or service specifications, are typically set in terms of employee or machine performance. For example, a bank may require its employees to conform to a dress code. Likewise, the bank may require that all incoming phone calls be answered by the third ring. Specifications like these can be very important in providing quality service as long as they are tied to the needs expressed by customers.

Perhaps the most critical aspect of service quality specifications is managers' commitment to service quality. Service managers who are committed to quality become role models for all employees in the organisation.[21] Such commitment motivates customer contact employees to comply with service specifications. It is also crucial that all managers within the organisation embrace this commitment—especially front line managers, who are much closer to customers than higher level managers.

Employee Performance   Once an organisation sets service quality standards and managers are committed to them, the organisation must find ways to ensure that customer contact employees perform their jobs well. Contact employees in most service industries—bank tellers, flight cabin crew, waiters, sales assistants—are often the least trained and lowest paid members of the organisation. What service organisations must realise is that contact employees are the most important link to the customer, and thus their performance is critical to customer perceptions of service quality.[22] The means to ensure that employees perform well is to recruit and to train them well so that they understand how to do their jobs. Providing information about customers, service specifications and the organisation itself during the training promotes this understanding.[23]

The evaluation and remuneration system used by the organisation also plays a part in employee performance. Many service employees are evaluated and rewarded on the basis of output measures such as sales volume (car salespeople) or the lack of errors during work (bank tellers). But systems using output measures over look other major aspects of job performance: friendliness, teamwork, effort and customer satisfaction. Thus customer oriented measures of performance may be a better basis of evaluation and reward. For example, Dun & Bradstreet has tied employee commissions to customer satisfaction surveys rather than sales volume.[24] This type of system stimulates employees to take care of customer needs rather than focus solely on sales or profits.

Managing Service Expectations   Because expectations are so significant in customer evaluations of service quality, service companies recognise that they must set realistic expectations about the service they can provide. They can set these expectations through advertising and good internal communication. In their advertisements, service companies make promises about the kind of service they will deliver. In fact, a service company is forced to make promises since the intangibility of services prevents it from showing them in the advertisement. However, the advertiser should not promise more than it can deliver; doing otherwise may mean disappointed customers.

To deliver on promises made, a company needs to have good internal communication among its departments—especially management, advertising and operations. Assume, for example, that a restaurant's radio advertisements guaranteed service within five minutes or the meal would be free. If top management or the advertising department failed to inform operations about the five minute guarantee, the restaurant very likely would not meet its customers' service expectations. Even though customers might appreciate a free meal, the restaurant would lose some credibility and revenue.

Word-of-mouth communication from other customers also shapes customer expectations. However, service companies cannot manage this "advertising" directly. The best way to ensure positive word-of-mouth communication is to provide exceptional service quality. It has been estimated that customers tell four times as many people about bad service as they do about good service. Consequently, services marketers must provide four good service experiences for every bad experience just to break even.

Non-business Marketing

Marketing was broadly defined earlier as a set of individual and organisational activities aimed at facilitating and expediting satisfying exchanges in a dynamic environment through the creation, distribution, promotion and pricing of goods, services and ideas. Most of the previously discussed concepts and approaches to managing marketing activities also apply to non-business situations such as the public sector and charities. Of special relevance is the material offered in the first half of this chapter, because many non-business organisations provide services. As a discipline, marketing is becoming increasingly important in the non-business sector. Marketing Insight 11.2 focuses on the changing role of marketing in charities.

Non-business marketing Activities conducted by individuals and organisations to achieve some goal other than ordinary business goals of profit, market share or return on investment

Non-business marketing includes marketing activities conducted by individuals and organisations to achieve some goal other than ordinary business goals of profit, market share or return on investment. However, although a non-business organisation has primary goals which are non-economic, it may be required to become involved in profit making in order to achieve those goals.[25] Thus a charity, such as the Red Cross, must raise funds to support its charitable work. Non-business marketing can be divided into two categories: non-profit organisation marketing and social marketing. Non-profit organisation marketing is the application of marketing concepts and techniques to organisations such as hospitals and colleges. Social marketing is the development of programmes designed to influence the acceptability of social ideas, such as getting people to recycle more newspapers, plastics and aluminium or promoting the regeneration of a deprived inner city area.[26]

Negotiation Mutual discussion or communication of terms and methods in an exchange situation

Persuasion The act of prevailing upon someone by argument to facilitate an exchange

As discussed in Chapter 1, an exchange situation exists when individuals, groups or organisations possess something that they are willing to give up in an exchange. In non-business marketing, the objects of the exchange may not be specified in financial terms. Usually, such exchanges are facilitated through **negotiation** (mutual discussion or communication of terms and methods) and **persuasion** (convincing and prevailing upon by argument). Often negotiation and persuasion are conducted without reference to or awareness of the role that marketing plays in transactions. The discussion here concerns non-business performance of marketing activities, whether exchange takes place or not.

The rest of this chapter first examines the concept of non-business marketing to determine how it differs from marketing activities in business organisations. Next it explores the overall objectives of non-business organisations, their marketing objectives and the development of their marketing strategies. The discussion closes by illustrating how a marketing audit can control marketing activities and promote marketing awareness in a non-business organisation.

Why Is Non-business Marketing Different?

Traditionally and mistakenly, people have not thought of non-business exchange activities as marketing. But consider the following example. Warwick Business School used to promote its degree courses solely through the University of Warwick's prospectuses. In the early 1980s, its main programmes received small advertising budgets. As courses were improved, the wider use of advertising increased awareness of the school and its programmes. A new corporate identity was developed by Coley Porter Bell of London, and each programme, led by the MBA, developed its own full marketing mix and more extensive promotional strategy—all in line with the school's new mission statement. Even when in the 1990s the corporate identity was updated, the school continued to ensure a good fit between the marketing mixes for its different programmes and its overall strategy. Many university departments and state maintained schools are now engaging in marketing strategy.

The Pattern of Charity Participation Changes

Marketing is not an activity which consumers automatically associate with charities. Instead they link advertising and sales promotion with big brands such as Coca-Cola, McDonald's and Virgin. In reality, while commercial organisations such as these seek high returns and profits, charities must find ways to increase their revenues to fund their laudable causes. In recent years, the fund raising activities of charities have become characterised by an increasing professionalism, often involving the appointment of marketing managers, strategists and public relations executives. This has resulted in a greater variety of fund raising methods than ever before. This variety is important in a climate in which all forms of charity participation are thriving but the public's preferences for methods of collecting are changing.

Recent research shows that a massive 87 per cent of UK adults have participated in charitable activities in the last 12 months. For 82 per cent this has taken the form of giving money, while 32 per cent have taken part in a special charity activity or event and 16 per cent have organised or worked for a charity. However, such consumers apparently dislike the use of direct marketing methods, such as direct mail and telephone calls, to solicit funds. Overall, it seems that the traditional personal approaches to collecting funds, such as the use of collecting tins in shopping malls and high streets, are declining in effectiveness. Instead, the public's imagination has been captured by a host of media based activities. For example, specially organised events and television appeals and programmes have been shown to be particularly effective ways of attracting funds. The use of high profile individuals in such appeals, such as royalty, television personalities, well known actors or sports stars, is particularly popular. In a recent survey, 80 per cent of consumers questioned also supported the use of commercial and promotional schemes, such as the sale of products through gift shops and catalogues. A similar percentage stated that they like to buy products that involve the manufacturer making a contribution to charity.

The Imperial Cancer Research Fund is one charity that has sought an innovative approach to fund raising. Recent programmes involve targeting specific commercial businesses to become involved in joint fund raising initiatives. Using its popular support with the public as a springboard, the charity is engaging in a range of joint projects. For example, by joining together with two other charities, the Imperial Cancer Research Fund is linked to the Halifax Visa Charity Card. Since it was launched in 1988 this charity affinity credit card, which is the most successful of its kind, has raised more than £5 million for the charity. Other initiatives include teaming up with leading UK insurer CGU in a deal that sees 10 per cent of new insurance premiums donated to cancer charities. Meanwhile, international swimwear brand Speedo has become linked with the charity to raise sales of its children's sun protection suits. For each suit sold, the company promises a donation to the Imperial Cancer Research Fund. The charity also helps raise awareness of cancer among companies' employees and stakeholders. In a recent move, the charity helped supermarket group Tesco prepare literature about testicular cancer, which was aimed at staff and customers.

Although charitable donations are coping well with the pressures of compassion fatigue and recession, continued success cannot be guaranteed. A decline in legacy income is one area which has already encountered problems. With five other charities (Blue Cross, NSPCC, Oxfam, The RSPB and Shelter), the Imperial Cancer Research Fund is creating a TV commercial which specifically encourages the public to bequeath funds to charity in their wills. These charities are taking such action because they recognise the need to respond to changing expectations about the most appropriate forms of fund raising. In a television age, the charities understand that this involves a willingness to use the full range of media based approaches available.

SOURCES: "Charities unite in donor appeal", *Marketing,* 14 January 1999, p. 4; "Spotlight: charity", *Marketing Week,* 17 December 1998, pp. 28–29; Daz Valladares, "Charities find relief in targeted advertising", *Marketing Week,* 27 November 1992, p. 16; Elaine Hunt, The Human Factor; Tony Lees, NOP Research Group; Imperial Cancer Research Fund; Group http://pitch.phon.ucl.ac.uk /home/dave/TOC_H/charities/.

Many non-business organisations strive for effective marketing activities. Charitable organisations and supporters of social causes are major non-business marketers. Political parties, unions, religious groups and student organisations also perform marketing activities, yet they are not considered businesses. Whereas the chief beneficiary of a business enterprise is whoever owns or holds shares in it, in theory the only beneficiaries of a non-business organisation are its clients, its members or the public at large.

Non-businesses have a greater opportunity for creativity than most business organisations, but trustees or board members of non-businesses are likely to have trouble judging performance when services can be provided only by trained professionals. It is harder for administrators to evaluate the performance of doctors, lecturers or social workers than it is for sales managers to evaluate the performance of salespeople in a for-profit organisation.

Another way in which non-business marketing differs from for-profit marketing is that non-business organisations are sometimes quite controversial. Amnesty International, the RSPCA and Greenpeace spend lavishly on lobbying efforts to persuade government and even the courts to support their interests, in part because acceptance of their aims is not always guaranteed. However, marketing as a field of study does not attempt to define an organisation's goals or debate the issue of non-business versus business goals. Marketing attempts only to provide a body of knowledge to further an organisation's goals. Individuals must decide whether they approve of an organisation's goal orientation. Most marketers would agree that profit and consumer satisfaction are appropriate goals for business enterprises, but there probably would be considerable disagreement about the goals of a controversial non-business organisation.

Non-business Marketing Objectives The basic aim of non-business organisations is to obtain a desired response from a target market. The response could be a change in values, a financial contribution, the donation of services or some other type of exchange. Non-business marketing objectives are shaped by the nature of the exchange and the goals of the organisation. BBC sponsored Children in Need and Comic Relief telethons have raised millions of pounds. Telethons have three specific marketing objectives: (1) to raise funds to support programmes, (2) to plead a case on behalf of disadvantaged groups and (3) to inform the public about the organisation's programmes and services. Tactically, telethons have received support by choosing good causes; generating extensive grass-roots support; portraying disadvantaged people in a positive and dignified way; developing national, regional and local support; and providing quality entertainment.[27] Figure 11.5 illustrates how the exchanges and the purpose of the organisation can influence marketing objectives. (These objectives are used as examples and may or may not apply to specific organisations.)

Non-business marketing objectives should state the rationale for an organisation's existence. An organisation that defines its marketing objective merely in terms of providing a product can be left without a purpose if the product becomes obsolete. However, serving and adapting to the perceived needs and wants of a target public, or market, enhances an organisation's chance to survive and achieve its goals.

Developing Non-business Marketing Strategies Non-business organisations must also develop marketing strategies by defining and analysing a target market and creating and maintaining a marketing mix that appeals to that market.

Target Markets The concept of target markets needs to be revised slightly to apply to non-business organisations. Whereas a business is supposed to have target

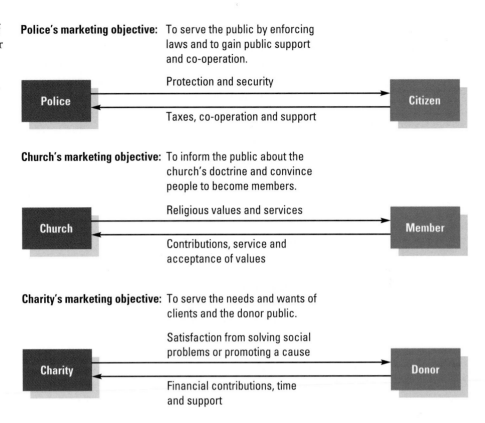

Figure 11.5 Examples of marketing objectives for different types of exchanges. SOURCE: Philip Kotler, *Marketing for Non-profit Organisations*, 2nd edn, © 1982, p. 38. Adapted by permission of Prentice-Hall, Inc., Englewood Cliffs, N.J.

Police's marketing objective: To serve the public by enforcing laws and to gain public support and co-operation.

Police → Protection and security → Citizen
Police ← Taxes, co-operation and support ← Citizen

Church's marketing objective: To inform the public about the church's doctrine and convince people to become members.

Church → Religious values and services → Member
Church ← Contributions, service and acceptance of values ← Member

Charity's marketing objective: To serve the needs and wants of clients and the donor public.

Charity → Satisfaction from solving social problems or promoting a cause → Donor
Charity ← Financial contributions, time and support ← Donor

Target public A collective of individuals who have an interest in or concern about an organisation, a product or a social cause

Client publics In non-business organisations, direct consumers of a product

General publics In non-business organisations, indirect consumers of a product

groups that are potential purchasers of its product, a non-business organisation may attempt to serve many diverse groups. A **target public** is broadly defined as a collective of individuals who have an interest in or concern about an organisation, a product or a social cause. The terms *target market* and *target public* are difficult to distinguish for many non-business organisations. The target public for campaigns promoting healthy eating is adults and teenagers of all ages. However, the target market for many of the advertisements may be individuals currently suffering from a weight problem. When an organisation is concerned about changing values or obtaining a response from the public, it views the public as a market.[28]

In non-business organisations, direct consumers of a product are called **client publics** and indirect consumers are called **general publics**.[29] For example, the client public for a university is its student body, and its general public includes parents, graduates, employers and the University Senate. The client public usually receives most of the attention when an organisation develops a marketing strategy. The techniques and approaches to segmenting and defining target markets discussed in Chapter 7 also apply to non-business target markets.

Developing a Marketing Mix A marketing mix strategy limits choices and directs marketing activities towards achieving organisational goals. The strategy should outline or develop a blueprint for making decisions about product, place/distribution, promotion, price and personnel. These decision variables should be blended to serve the target market.

When considering the product variable, it is important to recognise that non-business organisations deal more often with ideas and services than with goods.

This means it is crucial for organisations to have clearly defined exactly what they are providing. For example, what products do the Women's Institute or a work's social club provide? They offer a forum for social gatherings, courses, outings and a sense of co-operation. Their products are more difficult to define than the average business product. As indicated in the first part of this chapter, the intangibility of services means that the marketing of ideas and concepts is more abstract than the marketing of tangibles, and it requires considerable effort to present benefits.

Because most non-business products are ideas and services, distribution decisions relate to how these ideas and services will be made available to clients. If the product is an idea, selecting the right media (the promotional strategy) to communicate the idea will facilitate distribution. The availability of services is closely related to product decisions. By nature, services consist of assistance, convenience and availability. Availability is part of the total service. For example, making a product such as health services available calls for knowledge of such retailing concepts as site location analysis and logistics management.

Developing a channel of distribution to co-ordinate and facilitate the flow of non-business products to clients is a necessary task, but in a non-business setting the traditional concept of the marketing channel may need to be reviewed. The independent wholesalers available to a business enterprise do not exist in most non-business situations. Instead, a very short channel—non-business organisation to client—is prevalent, because production and consumption of ideas and services are often simultaneous. For example, local government departments often deal directly with householders. Charities generally pitch their fund raising activities directly to their target customers/householders/donors.

Making promotional decisions may be the first sign that non-business organisations are performing marketing activities. Non-business organisations use advertising and publicity to communicate with clients and the public. Direct mail remains the primary means of fund raising for services such as those provided by Christian Aid or UNICEF. In addition to direct mail, organisations such as these use press advertising, public relations and sponsorship. Many non-business organisations are now setting up web sites on the Internet to promote their cause. Personal selling is also used by non-business organisations, although it may be called something else. Churches and charities rely on personal selling when they send volunteers to recruit new members or request donations. The armed forces use personal selling when recruiting officers attempt to persuade men and women to enlist. Special events to obtain funds, communicate ideas or provide services are sales promotion activities. Contests, entertainment and prizes offered to attract donations resemble the sales promotion activities of business enterprises. Amnesty International, for example, has held worldwide concert tours, featuring artists such as Sting and Phil Collins, to raise funds and increase public awareness of political prisoners around the world.

The number of advertising agencies that are donating their time for public service announcements (PSAs) or public information films is increasing, and the quality of print PSAs is improving noticeably. Not-for-profit groups are becoming more interested in the impact of advertising on their organisations, and they realise that second rate PSAs can cause a credibility loss.[30] For example, each year the UK government's "don't drink and drive" campaign is a high spending, hard-hitting programme of advertisements designed to attract as much attention as possible.

Although product and promotion techniques might require only slight modification when applied to non-business organisations, pricing is generally quite different and the decision-making more complex. The different pricing concepts that the non-business organisation faces include pricing in user and donor markets. There are two types of monetary pricing: *fixed* and *variable*. Membership fees, such as the amount paid to become a member of an amateur operatic society, represent a fixed approach to pricing, whereas fund raising activities that lead to donations which help with the society's running costs represent a variable pricing structure.[31]

The broadest definition of price (valuation) must be used when considering non-business products or services. Financial price, an exact monetary value, may or may not be charged for a non-business product. Economists recognise the giving up of alternatives as a cost. **Opportunity cost** is the value of the benefit that is given up by selecting one alternative rather than another. This traditional economic view of price means that if a non-business organisation can persuade someone to donate time to a cause or to change his or her behaviour, the alternatives given up are a cost to (or a price paid by) the individual. Volunteers who answer phones for a university counselling service or suicide hotline, for example, give up the time they could have spent studying or doing other things, as well as the income they might have earned from working in a business organisation.

For other non-business organisations, financial price is an important part of the marketing mix. Non-business organisations today are raising money by increasing the prices of their services or starting to charge for services if they have not done so before. For example, many museums and art galleries, which traditionally allowed free entry into their exhibits, are now charging nominal entrance fees. Organisations like these often use marketing research to determine for what kinds of products people will pay.[32] Pricing strategies of non-business organisations often stress public and client welfare over equalisation of costs and revenues. If additional funds are needed to cover costs, then donations, contributions or grants may be solicited.

The additional elements of the marketing mix for services are also important in non-business marketing. The physical environment quite often poses problems: subscribers and donors want an organisation with the appearance of business-like efficiency without any extravagance. It is important that funds do not appear to have been wasted on luxuries. The process for transactions is increasingly important: regular donors are offered direct debits, automatic payment methods and regular information packs or leaflets detailing the recipient organisation's activities, expenditures and plans. People, too, are of importance: capable administrators, sympathetic helpers, trustworthy fund raisers—they too, must project a caring yet efficient image to the client and general publics.

Opportunity cost The value of the benefit that is given up by selecting one alternative instead of another

Controlling Non-business Marketing Activities

To control marketing activities in non-business organisations, managers use information obtained in the marketing audit to make sure that goals are achieved (see Chapter 22). Table 11.7 lists several summary statistics that are useful for both planning and control. Control is designed to check that the activities outlined in the marketing strategy have taken place and to take corrective action where any deviations are found. The purpose of control is not only to point out errors but to revise organisational goals and marketing objectives as necessary. One way to measure the impact of an advertisement is to audit the number of requests for information or applications, such as those received by Amnesty International, the Army or the WWF (see Figure 11.6).

1. Product mix offerings	B. Number of employees
A. Types of product or services	1. By organisation
B. Number of organisations offering	2. Total industry wide
the product or service	C. Number of volunteers
2. Financial resources	1. By organisation
A. Types of funding used	2. Total industry wide
1. Local government grants	D. Number of customers serviced
2. Government grants	1. By type of service
3. Foundations	2. By organisation
4. Public appeals	3. Total industry wide
5. Fees/charges	**4. Facilities**
B. Number using each type of funding	A. Number and type
C. Number using combinations of	1. By organisation
funding sources	2. Total industry wide
3. Size	B. Location
A. Budget (cash flows)	1. By address
	2. By postcode

SOURCE: Adapted from Philip D. Cooper and George E. McIlvain, "Factors influencing marketing's ability to assist non-profit organizations", John H. Summey and Ronald D. Taylor, eds., *Evolving Marketing Thought for 1980, Proceedings of the Southern Marketing Association* (19–22 November 1980), p. 315. Used by permission.

Many potential contributors decide which charities to support based on the amount of money actually used for charitable purposes. Charities are more aggressively examining their own performance and effectiveness. For example, compared with other charities, the Salvation Army contributes the most of every pound it receives to the needy; its employees are basically volunteers who work for almost nothing. Charities are making internal changes to increase their effectiveness, and many are hiring professional managers and fund raisers to help with strategic planning in developing short term and long range goals, marketing strategies and promotional plans.

To control non-business marketing activities, managers must make a proper inventory of activities performed and prepare to adjust or correct deviations from standards. Knowing where and how to look for deviations and knowing what types of deviations to expect are especially important in non-business situations. Because non-business marketing activities may not be perceived as marketing, managers must clearly define what activity is being examined and how it should function.

It may be difficult to control non-business marketing activities, because it is often hard to determine whether goals are being achieved. A support group for victims of childhood abuse that wants to inform community members of its services may not be able to find out whether it is communicating with people who need assistance. Surveying to discover the percentage of the population that is aware of the assistance which the group offers can show whether the awareness objective has been achieved, but it fails to indicate what percentage of victims of abuse has been assisted. The detection and correction of deviations from standards are certainly major purposes of control, but standards

Figure 11.6 Measuring the impact of advertising. Bose can measure the impact of its advertising by keeping count of the number of requests for information. SOURCE: Courtesy of Bose Corporation.

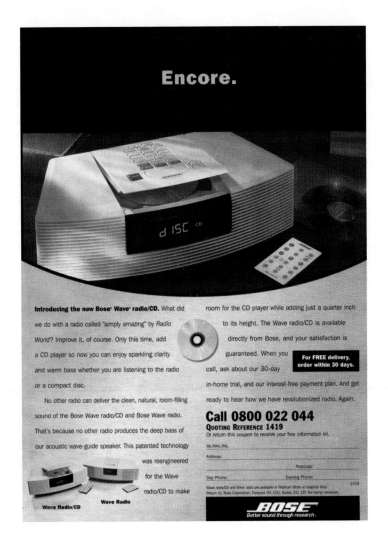

must support the organisation's overall goals. Managers can refine goals by examining the results that are being achieved and analysing the ramifications of those results.

Techniques for controlling overall marketing performance must be compatible with the nature of an organisation's operations. Obviously, it is necessary to control the marketing budget in most non-business organisations, but budgetary control is not tied to standards of profit and loss; responsible management of funds is the objective. Central control responsibility can facilitate orderly, efficient administration and planning. For example, most universities evaluate graduating students' progress to control and improve the quality of education provided. The audit phase typically relies on questionnaires sent to students and eventual employers. The employer completes a questionnaire to indicate the former student's progress; the graduate completes a questionnaire to indicate what additional concepts or skills were needed to perform duties. In addition, a number of faculty members may interview certain employers and former students to obtain information for control purposes. Results of the audit are used to develop corrective action if university standards have not been met. Corrective action might include an evaluation of the deficiency and a revision of the curriculum.

S U M M A R Y

ervices are intangible dominant products that cannot be physically possessed—the result of applying human or mechanical efforts to people or objects. The importance of services in the economy is increasing. There are *consumer services* and *business services*. Services have four distinguishing characteristics: (1) *intangibility*, (2) *inseparability* of production and consumption, (3) *perishability* and (4) *heterogeneity*. Intangibility places greater importance on *search, experience* and *credence qualities*. Because services include a diverse group of industries, classification schemes are used to help marketers analyse their products and develop the most appropriate marketing mix. Services can be viewed in terms of a *five category classification:* type of market, degree of labour intensiveness, degree of customer contact, skill of the service provider and goal of the service provider.

Fluctuating demand is a major problem for most service organisations. Marketing strategies (the marketing mix) as well as non-marketing strategies (primarily internal, employee based actions) can be used to deal with the problem. Before attempting to undertake any such strategies, however, services marketers must understand the patterns and determinants of demand.

The intangibility of the service product, together with the importance of the people component of the extended marketing mix for services, leads to significant difficulties in creating—and sustaining—a *differential advantage* or competitive edge. Increasingly, strong branding and associated promotional strategy are playing more of a role in the marketing strategy for services. The basic marketing mix is augmented for services through the addition of people, physical evidence (ambience) and the process of transaction in order to produce the "7Ps" or the *extended marketing mix for services*.

Service quality is the perception of how well a service meets or exceeds customer expectations. Service quality is very difficult for customers to evaluate due to the intangible nature of the service. When competing services are very similar, service quality may be the only way for customers to distinguish between them. It is crucial for marketers to comprehend *service expectations,* a factor by which customers judge service quality. To increase the quality of their services, services marketers must understand the four *service quality factors*. To achieve customer satisfaction, a service must fall within the *customer's zone of tolerance*.

Non-business marketing includes marketing activities conducted by individuals and organisations to achieve goals other than normal business goals. Non-business marketing uses most of the concepts and approaches applied to business situations. The chief beneficiary of a business enterprise is whoever owns or holds shares in the business, but the beneficiary of a non-business enterprise should be its clients, its members or its public at large. The goals of a non-business organisation reflect its unique philosophy or mission. Some non-business organisations have very controversial goals, but many organisations exist to further generally accepted social causes.

The marketing objective of non-business organisations is to obtain a desired response from a target market, often through *negotiation* or *persuasion*. Developing a non-business marketing strategy consists of defining and analysing a target market and creating and maintaining a marketing mix. *Target, client* and *general publics* must all be identified. In non-business marketing, the product is usually an idea or service. Distribution is involved not so much with the movement of goods as with the communication of ideas and the delivery of services, which results in a very short marketing channel. Promotion is very important in non-business marketing; personal selling, sales promotion, advertising and publicity are all used to communicate ideas and inform people about services. Price is more difficult to define in non-business marketing because of *opportunity costs* and the difficulty of quantifying the values exchanged.

It is important to control marketing strategies in non-business situations. Control is designed to identify what activities have occurred in conformity with marketing strategy and to take corrective action where deviations are found. The standards against which performance is measured must support the non-business organisation's overall goals.

Important Terms

Service
Consumer services
Business services
Intangibility
Search qualities
Experience qualities
Credence qualities
Inseparability
Perishability

Heterogeneity
Five category classification
Differential advantage
Extended marketing mix for
  services
Service quality
Service expectations
Service quality factors
Customer's zone of tolerance

Non-business marketing
Negotiation
Persuasion
Target public
Client publics
General publics
Opportunity cost

Discussion and Review Questions

1. Identify and discuss the distinguishing characteristics of services. What problems do these characteristics present to marketers?
2. What is the significance of "tangibles" in service industries?
3. Use the five category classification scheme to analyse a car valeting service and discuss the implications for marketing mix development.
4. How do search, experience and credence qualities affect the way consumers view and evaluate services?
5. What additional elements must be included in the marketing mix for services? Why?
6. Why is it difficult to create and maintain a differential advantage in many service businesses?
7. Analyse the demand for the hire of sun beds and discuss ways to cope with fluctuating demand.

8. What is the most important dimension in determining customer evaluation of service quality?
9. Compare and contrast the controversial aspects of non-business versus business marketing.
10. Relate the concepts of product, place/distribution, promotion and price to a marketing strategy aimed at preventing drug abuse.
11. What are the differences between clients, publics and consumers? What is the difference between a target public and a target market?
12. What is the function of control in a non-business marketing strategy?
13. Discuss the development of a marketing strategy for a university. What marketing decisions should be made in developing this strategy?

Recommended Readings

L. Berry, *On Great Service* (New York: The Free Press, 1995).
B. Edvardsson, B. Thomasson and J. Ovretveit, *Quality of Service, Making It Really Work* (London: McGraw Hill, 1994).
W. J. Glynn and J. G. Barnes, *Understanding Services Management, Integrating Marketing, Organisational Behaviour, Operations and Human Resource Management* (Chichester: John Wiley and Sons, 1995).
C. Grönroos, *Service Management and Marketing* (Lexington, Mass.: Lexington Books, 1990).
C. H. Lovelock, *Principles of Services Marketing and Management* (Englewood Cliffs, N.J.: Prentice-Hall, 1999).

11.1 Multiplex Cinemas: The Promise of UCI

In 1991 over 107 million cinema seats were sold in Germany. In the UK the number was 91 million, a significant rise from 72 million in 1985. Now around 11 per cent of the population claim to be "regular" film-goers. Despite additional television channels and transmitting hours, relaxed regulations in terms of television censorship, the introduction of more cable and satellite television services and the increasing range of competing activities for leisure time, the cinema industry is booming. This boom can be attributed mainly to two factors: better, more attractive cinemas in more accessible locations and a regular stream of US made "block-buster" movies.

United Cinemas International (UCI), a joint venture between MCA and Paramount, leads the development of the new generation of cinemas: the multiplex. Each multiplex has 8 to 10 screens offering a wide choice of movies for all social groups and ages. In addition to the mainstream releases there are children's clubs, late night adult clubs and showings of critically acclaimed "art" films. The luxuriously appointed auditoria have air conditioning, extra leg room, comfortable seating, wide screens and Dolby stereo Surroundsound. All multiplexes offer extensive refreshment facilities and some, such as the Milton Keynes complex "The Point", house restaurants, a nightclub and an amusement area.

These large, often out-of-town developments are quite different from the traditional Victorian Regal or Roxy with one screen and limited amenities. The consumer of the 1980s came to expect more comfortable, glitzy surroundings, with easy car parking and access. The boom in cinema attendance, though, has also benefited the older, traditional town centre cinemas. High street chains are reporting increased ticket sales, as are the remaining independent cinemas.

MGM, Showcase and UCI have brought a new generation of cinemas to Europe with plans for expansion throughout the EU and Scandinavia. The UCI ethos is well defined:

> It is the philosophy of United Cinemas International to offer a complete cinematic entertainment package to every member of the family, and, in so

doing, become an important part of the community. Through the concept of the multiplex cinema this philosophy will be "screened" worldwide, with UCI acting as the catalyst which will bring people back to the cinema—truly recreating the magic of the movies.

From the first UK UCI in 1985, the company now operates over 50 sites. Each, whether it has 6 or 18 screens, aims to present a wide choice of films, with top picture and sound quality based on the latest technology in luxurious, clean and well maintained surroundings. High management and staff service levels, the convenience of easily accessible sites in or near shopping and leisure complexes that have easy public transport links and ample parking, and value for money complete the UCI offer.

The goal of becoming part of the community is central to UCI's marketing. Months before a new cinema opening, UCI liaises with community leaders to discuss ways in which the cinema and the company can help with special events or activities. Links with local arts festivals, charity fund raising, sponsorship of events, special interest films for the community, exhibitions and publicity are just a few of the activities in which UCI becomes involved. Opening galas are always staged in aid of a prominent local charity and involve people from all sectors of the local community. Celebrities turn out and often a spectacular event is staged free for everyone—perhaps a fireworks display or one-off Drive-In movie, an event pioneered in Europe by UCI.

UCI believes that staff training "provides the essential foundation upon which all successful organisations base their business". A smart appearance and friendly personality are essential qualities, but "attitude" is of central importance. New recruits are taught basic skills in each main area—box office, refreshment, usher, health and hygiene, fire safety and first aid. They take written and oral exams, gaining in status and pay as they pass each stage. The very best employees reach the coveted "Top Gun" status and receive the opportunity to enter management posts. For managers, training is equally rigorous and includes orientation programmes for the UCI and multiplex philosophies and courses at UCI's Manchester training department in employment law, cinema administration, discipline and grievance procedures, communication and training skills, leadership and teamwork. Ultimately, the individual cinema can be run efficiently and for the consumers' benefit only if the manager is caring and well versed in UCI's philosophy, which is reiterated in UCI's "promise":

Thank You for Choosing a UCI Cinema

We promise that when you visit one of our cinemas,

Our staff will be friendly, courteous and helpful.

The foyers, corridors and auditoriums will be clean and tidy.

The toilets will be clean and fully stocked.

Refreshment areas will be clean, and refreshments will be served hot or cold as intended.

The film presentation will be of the highest quality, with crystal clear pictures and top quality sound.

If for any reason your visit is not up to our promise or your expectations, please see one of our duty managers, and let us know your views.

We value your impressions as much as we do your custom.

The attention to detail highlighted by UCI's charter is important given the increasing competition from home entertainment systems and services, as well as from the growing chains of rival multiplex operators. For example, the 120 strong MGM chain was bought by the ever expanding leisure force Virgin in a £200 million deal. Virgin developed a more aggressive and varied marketing strategy. Promotional spend has been increased to over £5 million and activity will move away from the traditional newspaper "what's on" advertisements. With the launch of *Take 2*, a cinema concept showing second run blockbuster films at bargain prices, MGM is fighting the triple onslaught of multiplex cinemas, in-home entertainment and consumer spending on the National Lottery. Ten years ago, cinema attendances stood at half today's level and the video age seemed set to wipe out the industry. The multiplex turned the situation round, but in a maturing market major players such as UCI must endeavour to maintain service standards and to seek an edge over their rivals.

SOURCES: David Teather, "Virgin to cinema's rescue", *Marketing*, 13 July 1995, p. 10; "MGM ditches 'listings' approach", *Marketing*, 10 November 1994, p. 5; "MGM fends off rivals with Take 2 cinema launch", *Marketing*, 18 August 1994, p. 1; "Movies eclipse films", *The Economist*, 5 February 1994, pp. 95–96; *Screen Digest*, August 1990; "The cinema industry", *Key Note*, 1990; Kok Bon; "General household survey", HMSO; UCI, "Projecting a philosophy"; "Bright lights, big picture show", *Marketing Week*, 6 February 1993, p. S6; UCI information pack.

Questions for Discussion

1. What has led to the "re-birth" of the cinema industry?
2. Compared with its numerous competitors, what advantages are offered by the multiplex concept?
3. How do the core lessons of services marketing reveal themselves in UCI's trading formula?

11.2 Expansion of Healthcare Marketing: PPP and BUPA Fight for Leadership

Private healthcare is far removed from the marketing of Sony Walkmans or Caterpillar earthmovers. What is the product? The consultation with a specialist? The treatment? Perhaps the speed from diagnosis to operation? The en suite, comfortable facilities? Or the improved condition and lifestyle of the patient? In the UK, BUPA is a leader in the provision of private (non-government provided) healthcare and has recruited a team of marketers in order to re-kindle its marketing.

Although there are dozens of healthcare companies—and more from Europe entering the UK market each year—only a handful offer the complexity of products available from BUPA. The insurance operation sells health cover policies, which to many consumers represent the most visible side of BUPA. There is much more, however. BUPA owns its own hospitals, operating theatre units, care homes and health clinics. The organisation both buys and sells healthcare provision and increasingly works in localised partnerships with the state run national health service (NHS). The company is thus far more than an insurance broker; as a result, it has many publics. These include companies that subscribe for insurance cover on behalf of their employees as a "perk"; suppliers of medical equipment and drugs; the medical profession, which recommends its hospitals and facilities; NHS trust managers; insurance brokers, who recommend policies to their clients; the general and specialist media; and consumers as private purchasers of policies and as patients.

Private medical insurer PPP was founded in 1940 and now has two million members worldwide. PPP pays out £2.4 million each day for medical treatment: neuro, cardiac and vascular surgery, oncology and transplants are all included in a wide range of treatments covered by PPP's policies. Now part of insurance giant Guardian Royal Exchange, PPP is striving to overtake arch rival BUPA and has developed a tightly honed target market strategy in order to achieve this goal.

The principal market for BUPA and PPP insurance is the corporate sector; they therefore target sales activity at companies taking out policies for their employees. In addition, BUPA and PPP are now devoting more attention to promoting their services directly to consumers in order to increase membership and enlarge their customer base. Television advertisements emphasise the relatively low cost of private health cover "from as little as £17 per month". With *fund holding* GPs taking a fresh look at private medicine, BUPA and PPP are also publicising their facilities and locations to the general medical profession.

In the recent rapid expansion of the private healthcare sector, Nuffield Hospitals and AMI have taken market share from BUPA. PPP now has 30 per cent of the market, with BUPA's share down from 60 per cent to 40 per cent. BUPA's marketing used to be handled regionally, but with over 30 hospitals, 30 health screening clinics, homes for the elderly and an occupational health service, BUPA feels the need for a formal marketing strategy and centralised control. Already the enhanced marketing activity has turned a £63 million loss at the end of the 1980s into a pre-tax profit to be reinvested in BUPA's facilities.

BUPA's actions coincided with the launch of a new rival, Firstchoice, led by ex-BUPA executives. Claiming to be the UK's first health insurance broker, Firstchoice develops tailor made insurance packages and sells services from over 20 healthcare companies. It has established agreements with all of the market's major players, except with BUPA. Whereas most competitors target the corporate sector primarily, Firstchoice believes there is growing consumer interest in private healthcare cover and services. Firstchoice is segmenting the marketplace and developing marketing programmes aimed at specific target audiences, employing many tools created by the marketers of the consumer goods giants.

Towards the end of 1995, however, PPP launched a £30 million drive to close the gap on rival BUPA, commencing with a branding campaign featuring its first ever mainstream advertising campaign, designed to distance the company from the insurance industry's "uncaring image". The £15 million year long campaign began with a 60 second brand building and awareness generating advertisement, followed by a series of product feature and cost benefit commercials. PPP became the biggest spending healthcare advertiser in the UK, although this expenditure was indicative primarily of the overall growth of the sector. Private medical insurance is now worth £2 billion per annum in the UK, and volume is rising sharply as consumers strive to safeguard their families' medical provision in the light of strained resources in the state funded NHS. BUPA now pays out over £2 million each day in benefits to its policy holders requiring medical treatment or consultation. Despite the efforts of Firstchoice as a broker, PPP as a rival insurer, or Nuffield with competing private hospitals, BUPA is still the market leader. In the insurance operation alone, it has 40 per cent of the market. Its unique mix of activities, from insurance to hospital and screening clinic owner to purchaser and provider of healthcare, provides a good base in this highly competitive marketplace, but also a highly complex organisation to market.

SOURCES: Liz Fisher, "Careful nursing in the private bag", *Accountancy,* July 1995, pp. 34–36; John Owen, "PPP challenges BUPA with £15 million blitz", *Campaign,* 13 October 1995, p. 8; David Teather, "PPP plans push on health rival", *Marketing,* 12 October 1995, p. 5; "Firstchoice claims new line in health insurance", *Marketing Week,* 26 February 1993, p. 9; PPP website, 1999; Claire Murphy, "BUPA looks for better health", *Marketing,* 3 December 1998, p. 21.

Questions for Discussion

1. Why are leading private medical insurance companies such as BUPA and PPP turning more to the marketing tactics deployed by consumer goods companies?
2. To which groups of people must BUPA appeal? Will this mix impact on the marketing strategy BUPA follows? Use specific examples to explain your answers.
3. What exactly is the product BUPA offers its customers? How can BUPA define this product for its target customers?

Having identified marketing opportunities, a business should recommend a marketing strategy that involves selecting the target market, determining the required positioning and developing a differential advantage. For the recommended target market strategy to be implemented, a marketing mix must be developed. The marketing mix centres on the "5Ps" of product, people, place/distribution, promotion and pricing decisions.

Part III of *Marketing: Concepts and Strategies* has addressed the product ingredient of the marketing mix and its integral component, the people ingredient. It has also examined the associated aspects of customer service, branding, packaging, labelling and services. Special consideration has been given to the role of marketing in non-business or not-for-profit organisations.

Before progressing, readers should be confident that they are now able to:

Describe the basic product decisions

• What are the definitions and classifications of products adopted by marketers? • What distinguishes product items, product lines and product mixes? • Why is the product life cycle so important? • What organisational structures are available to manage products? • Why are the different levels of a product so important in determining a competitive edge over rivals' products?

Explain the importance of branding and packaging

• Why are brands and brand equity important? • What are the types of brands, their benefits and the ways in which they can be selected, named, protected and licensed? • What are the functions and design considerations of packaging? • What is the role of packaging in marketing strategy? • What are the functions of labelling and the associated legal issues?

Outline the requirements for developing and managing products

• What alternatives are there for managing products? • How does a business develop a product idea into a commercial product? • What is the role of product development in the marketing mix? • Why must products be managed differently in the various stages of the product life cycle? • How can product modification or product deletion benefit the marketing mix?

Understand the special requirements for the marketing of services

• What are the nature and characteristics of services? • How can services be classified? • How can marketing strategies be developed for services? • Why are there difficulties in creating a differential advantage for services?

Marketing Opportunity Analysis	Chapters
• The marketing environment	2
• Marketing in international markets	3
• Consumer buying behaviour	4
• Organisational markets and business-to-business buying behaviour	5
• Marketing research and information systems	6

Target Market Strategy	Chapters
• Market segmentation and prioritisation	7, 21
• Product and brand positioning	7, 21
• Competitive advantage	7, 21

Marketing Mix Development	Chapters
• Product, branding, packaging and service decisions	8–11
• Place (distribution and channel) decisions	12–14
• Promotion decisions	15–17
• Pricing decisions	18, 19
• Supplementary decisions	3, 20, 23, 24

Marketing Management	Chapters
• Strategic marketing and competitive strategy	21, 22
• Marketing planning and forecasting sales potential	22
• Implementing strategies and internal marketing relationships and measuring performance	23
• Marketing ethics and social responsibility	24

• Why is the concept of service quality crucial? • Why is marketing in non-business situations unique? • How can marketing strategies be developed and marketing activities be controlled for non-business organisations?

IV Place (Distribution and Channel) Decisions

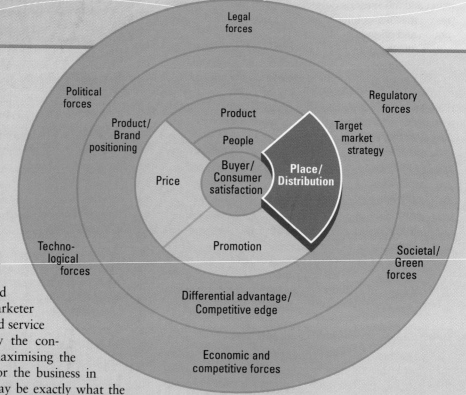

Legal forces

Political forces

Regulatory forces

Product/Brand positioning

Product

People

Target market strategy

Price

Buyer/Consumer satisfaction

Place/Distribution

Technological forces

Promotion

Societal/Green forces

Differential advantage/Competitive edge

Economic and competitive forces

Having identified a marketing opportunity and selected a target market, the marketer must design a product and service package that will satisfy the consumers targeted while maximising the marketing opportunity for the business in question. The product may be exactly what the targeted consumers desire, but if it is not made available to them, they will not be able to adopt the product. The place ingredient of the marketing mix addresses the distribution and marketing channel decisions that are necessary to provide the target market with convenient and ready access to the product or service, but in a manner that is beneficial to the supplier of the product or service. **Part IV of** *Marketing: Concepts and Strategies* examines the nature of marketing channels, wholesalers and distributors, the physical distribution of products and services, plus retail marketing.

Chapter 12, "Marketing Channels", explains the marketing channel concept and the functions and different types of marketing channels. The chapter considers channel integration and the levels of market coverage, and then examines the selection of dis-

tribution channels, including the increasingly popular option of direct marketing. Behavioural aspects of channels, particularly the concepts of co-operation and relationship building, conflict and leadership, are then explored. The chapter concludes by examining legal issues in channel management.

Chapter 13, "Wholesalers, Distributors and Physical Distribution", presents a description of the nature of wholesaling in its broadest forms in the marketing channel, explains wholesalers' activities and their classification, examines agencies that facilitate wholesaling and explores some changing patterns in wholesaling and distribution. The chapter then moves on to discuss physical distribution management and objectives. It explains order processing, materials handling, and different types of warehousing and their objectives. The chapter then examines inventory management and concludes with an analysis of different methods of transportation.

Chapter 14, "Retailing", explains the purpose and function of retailing in the marketing channel, provides an overview of retail locations and major store types, and describes non-store retailing and franchising. The chapter highlights the many strategic issues concerning modern retailing and concludes with a look at current trends in retailing.

By the conclusion of Part IV of *Marketing: Concepts and Strategies*, readers should understand the essential place decisions concerning marketing channels and distribution required in the marketing mix.

12 Marketing Channels

OBJECTIVES

- To understand the marketing channel concept and the nature of marketing channels
- To discuss the functions of marketing channels
- To examine different types of channels
- To examine channel integration and levels of market coverage
- To consider the selection of distribution channels and the emergence of direct marketing
- To explore the behavioural aspects of channels, especially the concepts of co-operation, relationship building, conflict and leadership
- To examine legal issues in channel management

"Effective management of manufacturer-dealer relationships is formidably problematic but strategically imperative."

David Shipley
Trinity College, University of Dublin

The Internet is changing the way in which consumers shop. In the past, those seeking to replenish their kitchen cupboards, fridges and freezers would usually visit their local supermarket or hypermarket. Now, these same consumers can visit the Internet and order their groceries for direct delivery to their homes. The concept is seen to be particularly attractive to professional, high earning, ABC1 men and women who work long hours and have limited leisure time. The Tesco Direct concept is one service which allows customers to buy their groceries directly over the Internet. Consumers can access the Tesco web site and select their purchase items. Their orders are then compiled by a team of in-store sales assistants for next day delivery to consumers' homes.

Initially, the Tesco Direct concept was trialled in 11 stores in two major UK cities. The company's preliminary research showed that around two hundred thousand consumers were using the service offered by these 11 stores and that this was increasing by ten thousand every week. Before long, the obvious popu-

larity of Internet shopping prompted Tesco to roll out Tesco Direct to other parts of the UK. By the end of the first year, the company aimed to be offering the service from one hundred Tesco stores. Careful consideration has been given to the marketing of the Internet shopping service. The sight of the Tesco Direct logo displayed by the company's delivery vans is already becoming familiar to those living in the areas where the service is offered. In addition, the retailer is using a combination of local poster and in-store advertising, direct mail and an Internet campaign to promote the Tesco Direct operation.

It seems as if the home shopping concept is enjoying a new wave of popularity among consumers. Major competitors Asda and Sainsbury's have also been testing Internet shopping facilities, while Somerfield is engaged in a national roll out of its home shopping operation. Frozen food retailer Iceland is already enjoying considerable success with its service. Estimates suggest that by early 1999, more than one-tenth of the company's turnover was being generated from the home shopping operation.

Increasing familiarity with shopping on the Internet looks set to increase the demand for services like Tesco Direct. How substantial a part of Tesco's business the service will become remains to be seen. However, Tesco management clearly understands that retaining its leading position means being ready to respond to changing shopping needs. Even so, industry experts are warning that the new shopping trend could be harmful for supermarket giants, providing considerable opportunities for their smaller rivals. For such smaller businesses, the Internet could offer important additional sales. By contrast, for the likes of Tesco and Sainsbury's, the danger is that existing sales will be cannibalised. Furthermore, a substantial shift in grocery shopping from the supermarkets to the Internet could damage scale advantages and affect profitability. Some experts even suggest that the trend could alter the way consumers make their purchase decisions. Current research suggests that 80 per cent of purchase decisions are made in store. If the buying process takes place at home instead, the control which retailers can exert may be radically reduced, thus altering the brand and product choices which consumers make.

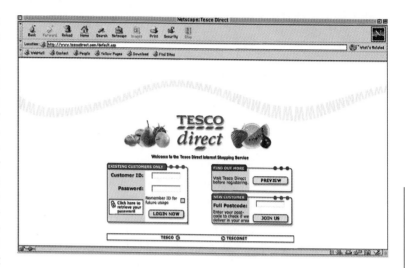

SOURCES: "Tesco to roll out Internet shopping service", *Marketing Week*, 15 April 1999, p. 6; Alexandra Jardine, "Tesco Direct rolls out to 100 outlets", *Marketing*, 15 April 1999, p. 1; Alan Mitchell, "Home shopping boom a threat to market leaders", *Marketing Week*, 1 April 1999, pp. 26–27; Gordon Ellis-Brown, "Inspiring new users is key to home shopping survival", *Marketing Week*, 25 March 1999, p. 14; Ben Rosier, "Web TV ties with Tesco for interactive TV tests", *Marketing*, 1 April 1999, p. 15; Michael Kavanagh, "Tangled in the Net", *Marketing Week*, 28 January 1999, pp. 53–55; Lisa Campbell, "Tesco in Excite tie-up", *Marketing*, 18 February 1999, p. 12; **www.tesco.co.uk**. *Advertisement:* Courtesy of Tesco Direct.

Distribution involves activities that make products available to customers when and where they want to purchase them. It is sometimes referred to as the *place* element in the marketing mix of the *Ps*: product, place/distribution, promotion, price and people. Choosing which channels of distribution to use is a major decision in the development of marketing strategies, as in the case of Tesco's new on-line shopping concept. Changes in the manner in which products are distributed have a major impact on customers. For example, the moves by food retailers to sell petrol from sites adjacent to their supermarkets has affected the UK petrol market in a number of important ways. Reducing petrol prices and increasing promotional activity are damaging margins to a point where profitability is severely threatened. In the long term this may force small suppliers out of business, thus reducing consumer choice (see Marketing Insight 12.1 on page 361). Internet retailing is a new channel which for some products and services increasingly cuts out the need for wholesalers and retail stores. It is forecast that soon the bulk of music sales and banking transactions will be via e-commerce. Such direct marketing negates the need for high street shops and bank branches.

This chapter focuses on the description and analysis of marketing channels, first discussing the nature of channels and their functions and then explaining the main types of channels and their structures. These sections are followed by a review of several forms of channel integration. Consideration is given to how marketers determine the appropriate intensity of market coverage for a product and to the factors that are considered when selecting suitable channels of distribution. After examining behavioural patterns within marketing channels and the relationships that develop between channel members, the chapter concludes by looking at several legal issues affecting channel management. Subsequent chapters further explore the roles of channel members or intermediaries and of physical distribution management.

The Nature of Marketing Channels

Channel of distribution (or **marketing channel**) A group of individuals and organisations that direct the flow of products from producers to customers

Marketing intermediary A middleman who links producers to other middlemen or to those who ultimately use the products

Merchants Intermediaries who take title to products and re-sell them

Functional middlemen Intermediaries who do not take title to products

A **channel of distribution** (sometimes called a **marketing channel**) is a group of individuals and organisations that direct the flow of products from producers to customers. Providing customer satisfaction should be the driving force behind all marketing channel activities. Buyers' needs and behaviour are therefore important concerns of channel members. Channels of distribution make products available at the right time, in the right place and in the right quantity by providing such product-enhancing functions as transport and storage.[1]

Most, but not all, channels of distribution have marketing intermediaries, although there is currently a growth of direct marketing with some suppliers interacting with consumers without the use of intermediaries (see Chapter 17). A **marketing intermediary,** or middleman, links producers to other middlemen or to those who ultimately use the products. Marketing intermediaries perform the activities described in Table 12.1. There are two major types of intermediaries: merchants and functional middlemen (agents and brokers). **Merchants** take title to products and re-sell them, whereas **functional middlemen** do not take title to products. Both types facilitate the movement of goods and services from producers to consumers.

Both retailers and wholesalers are intermediaries. Retailers purchase products for the purpose of re-selling them to users. Merchant wholesalers re-sell products to other wholesalers and to retailers. Functional wholesalers, such as agents and brokers, expedite exchanges among producers and resellers and are compensated by fees or commissions. For purposes of discussion in this chapter, all wholesalers are considered merchant middlemen unless otherwise specified.

Channel members share certain significant characteristics. Each member has different responsibilities within the overall structure of the distribution system, but mutual profit and success can be attained only if channel members co-operate in delivering products to the market. The area of relationship management has recently received a great deal of attention in marketing circles. This is increasingly important in delivering adequate customer service to target market customers. A supplier desires an ongoing and lucrative relationship with its customers. It recognises the importance of the various channel members in maintaining this relationship and strives for mutually beneficial relationships with its channel intermediaries.

Although distribution decisions need not precede other marketing decisions, they do exercise a powerful influence on the rest of the marketing mix. Channel decisions are critical because they determine a product's market presence and buyers' accessibility to the product. The strategic significance of these decisions is further heightened by the fact that they entail long term commitments. For example, it is much easier for a company to change prices or packaging than to change existing distribution systems.

It may be necessary for companies to use different distribution paths in different countries or for different target market segments. The links in any channel, however, are the merchants (including producers) and agents who oversee the movement of products through that channel. Marketing channels are

Table 12.1 Marketing channel activities performed by intermediaries

Category of Marketing Activities	Possible Activities Required
Marketing information	Analyse information such as sales data; perform or commission marketing research studies
Marketing management	Establish objectives; plan activities; manage and co-ordinate financing, personnel and risk taking; evaluate and control channel activities
Facilitating exchange	Choose and stock product assortments that match the needs of buyers
Promotion	Set promotional objectives; co-ordinate advertising, personal selling, sales promotion, publicity, sponsorship, direct mail and packaging
Price	Establish pricing policies and terms of sales
Physical distribution	Manage transport, warehousing, materials handling, inventory control and communication
Customer service	Provide channels for advice, technical support, after sales back-up and warranty provision
Relationships	Facilitate communication, products and parts, financial support and credit, inventory levels, after market needs, on-time delivery and customer service to maintain relationships with other marketing intermediaries and between suppliers and their targeted customers

commonly classified into channels for consumer products or channels for industrial, business-to-business products.

Functions of Marketing Channels

Marketing channels serve many functions. Although some of these functions may be performed by a single channel member, most functions are accomplished through both independent and joint efforts of channel members. These functions include creating utility, facilitating exchange efficiencies, alleviating discrepancies, standardising transactions and providing customer service.

Creating Utility

Marketing channels create four types of utility: time, place, possession and form. (1) *Time utility* is having products available when the customer wants them. (2) *Place utility* is created by making products available in locations where customers wish to purchase them. (3) *Possession utility* is created by giving the customer access to the product to use or to store for future use. Possession utility can occur through ownership or through arrangements such as lease or rental agreements that give the customer the right to use the product. (4) Channel members sometimes create *form utility* by assembling, preparing or otherwise refining the product to suit individual customer needs.

Facilitating Exchange Efficiencies

Marketing intermediaries can reduce the costs of exchanges by efficiently performing certain services or functions. Even if producers and buyers are located in the same city, there are costs associated with exchanges. As Figure 12.1 shows, when four buyers seek products from four producers, sixteen transactions

Figure 12.1 Efficiency in exchanges provided by an intermediary

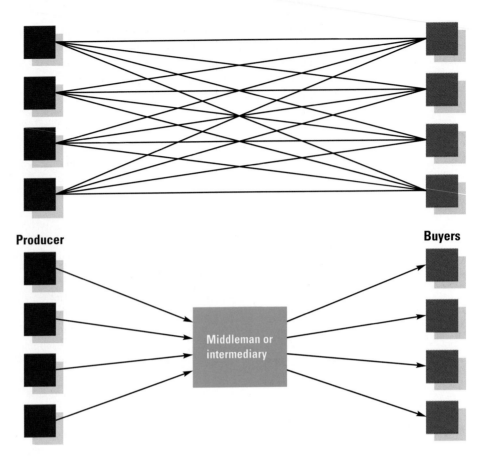

Producer

Buyers

Middleman or intermediary

are possible. If one intermediary serves both producers and buyers, the number of transactions can be reduced to eight. Intermediaries are specialists in facilitating exchanges. They provide valuable assistance because of their access to, and control over, important resources used in the proper functioning of marketing channels.

Nevertheless, the press, consumers, public officials and other marketers freely criticise intermediaries, especially wholesalers (retail wholesalers, dealers, distributors). In a US survey of the general public, 74 per cent believed that "wholesalers frequently make high profits, which significantly increase prices that consumers pay".[2] Critics accuse wholesalers of being inefficient and parasitic. Consumers often wish to make the distribution channel as short as possible, assuming that the fewer the intermediaries, the lower the price. For example, Virgin's financial services operation aims to offer competitive prices by cutting out brokers. Because suggestions to eliminate them come from both ends of the marketing channel, wholesalers must be careful to perform only those marketing activities that are truly desired. To survive, they must be more efficient and more customer focused than alternative marketing institutions.

Critics who suggest that eliminating wholesalers would lower consumer prices do not recognise that doing so would not remove the need for services that wholesalers provide. Although wholesalers can be eliminated, in many markets the functions they perform cannot. Other channel members would have to perform those functions, and customers would still have to fund them. In addition, all producers would have to deal directly with retailers or consumers, so that every producer would have to keep voluminous records and hire enough personnel to deal with a multitude of customers. Customers might end up paying a great deal more for products because prices would reflect the costs of less efficient channel members. Direct customer-supplier marketing is possible in some markets. For instance, web based Boxman has a successful direct relationship with its music-buying customers. JCB, on the other hand, would find it difficult to sell directly and depends on its dealers for parts and maintenance provision to its construction equipment customers. Heinz, Kellogg's, Sony, Ford and BA all depend on channel members—retailers, dealers or travel agents—in order to sell their products and services. These companies may well use direct mail to contact their existing or potential customers, but channel members play an important role in their marketing programmes.

To illustrate wholesalers' efficient services, assume that all wholesalers have been eliminated. Because there are more than 1.5 million retailers, a widely purchased consumer product—say, toilet paper—would require an extraordinary number of sales contacts, possibly more than a million, to maintain the current level of product exposure. For example, Scott would have to deliver its paper products, establish warehouses all over Europe and maintain fleets of trucks. Selling and distribution costs for Scott's products would rocket. Instead of a few contacts with food brokers, large retail businesses and merchant wholesalers, such manufacturers would face thousands of expensive contacts with and shipments to smaller retailers. Such an operation would be highly inefficient, and costs would be passed on to consumers. Wholesalers are often more efficient and less expensive.

Alleviating Discrepancies

The functions performed within marketing channels help to overcome two major distribution problems: discrepancies in quantity and discrepancies in assortment. With respect to discrepancies in quantity, consider a company that manufactures jeans. The company specialises in goods it can produce most efficiently, denim clothing. To make jeans most economically, the producer turns out a hundred thousand pairs of jeans each day. Few people, however, want to buy a hundred thousand pairs of jeans; they just want a few pairs. Thus the quantity of jeans the company can produce efficiently is more than the average customer wants. This is called *discrepancy in quantity*.

Assortment A combination of products put together to provide customer benefits

An **assortment** is a combination of products put together to provide customer benefits. Consumers create and hold an assortment. The set of products made available to customers is a company's assortment. Most consumers want a broad assortment of products. Besides jeans, they want to buy shoes, food, cars, hi-fi systems, soft drinks and many other products. Yet the jeans manufacturer has a narrow assortment because it makes only jeans and a few other denim clothes. A *discrepancy in assortment* exists because consumers want a broad assortment, but an individual manufacturer produces a narrow assortment.

Sorting activities Functions that let channel members divide roles and separate tasks

Sorting out Separating products into uniform, homogeneous groups

Quantity and assortment discrepancies are resolved through sorting activities of channel members. **Sorting activities** are functions allowing channel members to divide roles and separate tasks; they include sorting out, accumulation, allocation and assorting of products (see Figure 12.2).[3] (1) **Sorting out,** the first step in developing an assortment, is separating conglomerates of heterogeneous products into relatively uniform, homogeneous groups based on product characteristics such as size, shape, weight or colour. Sorting out is especially common in the marketing of agricultural products and other raw materials, which vary widely in size, grade and quality and would be largely unusable in an undifferentiated

Figure 12.2 Sorting activities conducted by channel members

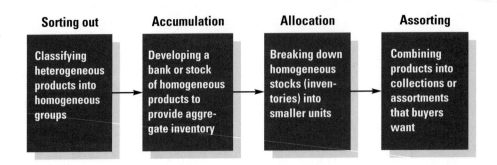

Sorting out	Accumulation	Allocation	Assorting
Classifying heterogeneous products into homogeneous groups	Developing a bank or stock of homogeneous products to provide aggregate inventory	Breaking down homogeneous stocks (inventories) into smaller units	Combining products into collections or assortments that buyers want

Accumulation The development of a bank of homogeneous products with similar production or demand requirements

Allocation The breaking down of large homogeneous inventories into smaller lots

Assorting The grouping of products that buyers want to have available in one place

mass. A grape crop, for example, must be sorted into grapes suitable for making wine, those best for turning into grape juice and those to be sold by food retailers. (2) **Accumulation** is the development of a bank, or inventory, of homogeneous products with similar production or demand requirements. Farmers who grow relatively small quantities of grapes, for example, transport their sorted grapes to central collection points, where they are accumulated in large lots for movement into the next level of the channel. Accumulation lets producers continually use up stocks and replenish them, thus minimising losses from interruptions in the supply of materials. (3) **Allocation** is the breaking down of large homogeneous inventories into smaller lots. This process, which addresses discrepancies in quantity, enables wholesalers to buy efficiently in lorry loads or railway car loads and apportion products by cases to other members. A food wholesaler, for instance, serves as a depot, allocating products according to market demand. The wholesaler may divide a single lorry load of Del Monte canned tomatoes among several retail food stores. (4) **Assorting** is the process of combining products into collections or assortments that buyers want to have available in one place. Assorting eliminates discrepancies in assortment by grouping products in ways that satisfy buyers. Assorting is especially important to retailers, for they strive to create assortments matching the demands of consumers who patronise their stores. Although no single customer is likely to buy one of everything in the store, retailers must anticipate the probability of purchase and provide a satisfactory range of product choices. For example, the same food wholesaler that supplies supermarkets with Del Monte tomato products may also buy canned goods from competing food processors so that the grocery store can choose from a wide assortment of canned fruit and vegetables.

Standardising Transactions

Marketing channels help to standardise the transactions associated with numerous products. In many purchase situations, the price is not negotiable; it is predetermined. Although there may be some variation in units of measure, package sizes, delivery schedules and location of the exchange, marketing channel members tend to limit customers' options with respect to these types of issues. When a customer goes to a supermarket to purchase a loaf of bread, it is unlikely that the individual will be able to buy a half loaf of bread, buy a loaf sliced lengthwise, negotiate the price, obtain a written warranty or return an unused portion of the loaf. Many of the details associated with the purchase of a loaf of bread are standardised.

Providing Customer Service

Channel members participate in providing customer service. Retailers of durable goods are expected to provide in-store advice and demonstrations, technical know-how, delivery, installation, repair services, parts and perhaps instruction or training. Channel members above the retailers are responsible for supporting retailers' efforts to provide end-user service and satisfaction even though they may not come into direct contact with ultimate customers. To gain and maintain a differential advantage, channel members make decisions and take actions to provide excellent customer service and support.

In mature markets with relatively little product differentiation between rival brands—such as packaged holidays, audio/hi-fi systems, conference venues or replacement car exhausts/tyres—and in newly emerging markets with innovative products and inexperienced consumers, it is often the customer service provided through the distribution channel that provides marketers with an edge over their competitors. In many markets—from cars, financial services, grocery retailing to PCs—it is the service provided by channel members which maintains an ongoing, mutually satisfactory relationship between supplier and consumer and which may be responsible for maintaining brand loyalty.

Types of Channels

Because marketing channels appropriate for one product may be less suitable for others, many different distribution paths have been developed. The various marketing channels can be classified generally as channels for consumer products or channels for industrial, business-to-business products.

Channels for Consumer Products Figure 12.3 illustrates several channels used in the distribution of consumer products. Besides the channels listed, a manufacturer may use sales branches or sales offices.

Figure 12.3 Typical marketing channels for consumer products

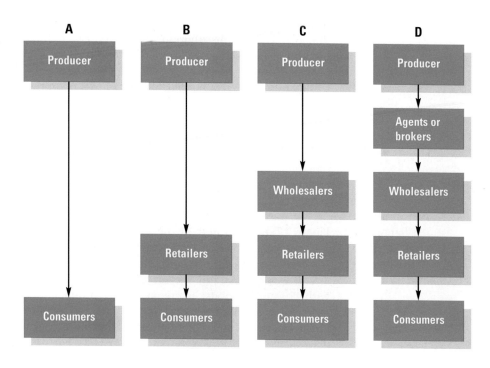

Channel A describes the direct movement of goods from producer to consumers. Customers who pick their own fruit from commercial orchards or buy cosmetics from door-to-door salespeople are acquiring products through a direct channel. A producer who sells goods directly from the factory to end users and ultimate consumers is using a direct marketing channel. Although this channel is the simplest, it is not necessarily the cheapest or the most efficient method of distribution. As explored in Chapter 17, e-commerce—the use of the Internet for marketing communications, selling and purchasing—has in recent years led to a growth in direct marketing for a variety of products, notably travel tickets, books, videos and CDs, financial services and merchandise retailed by the traditional mail order catalogue operators. Channel A, the direct approach, is no longer the preserve of farm shops and factory outlets.

E-commerce The use of the Internet for marketing communications, selling and purchasing

Channel B, which moves goods from producer to retailers and then to consumers, is often used by large retailers that can buy in quantity from a manufacturer. Such retailers as Marks & Spencer, Sainsbury's, Aldi and Carrefour, for example, sell clothing, food and many other items they have purchased directly from the producers. Cars are also commonly sold through this type of marketing channel.

A long standing distribution channel, especially for consumer products, channel C takes goods from producer to wholesalers, then to retailers and finally to consumers. This option is very practical for a producer who sells to hundreds of thousands of consumers through thousands of retailers. A single producer finds it hard to do business directly with thousands of retailers. For example, consider the number of retailers that stock Coca-Cola. It would be extremely difficult, if not impossible, for Coca-Cola to deal directly with all the retailers that sell its brand of soft drink. Manufacturers of tobacco products, confectionery, some home appliances, hardware and many convenience goods sell their products to wholesalers, who then sell to retailers, who in turn do business with individual consumers.

Channel D—through which goods pass from producer to agents to wholesalers to retailers, and only then to consumers—is frequently used for products intended for mass distribution, such as processed food. For example, to place its biscuit line in specific retail outlets, a food processor may hire an agent (or a food broker) to sell the biscuits to wholesalers. The wholesalers then sell the biscuits to supermarkets, vending machine operators and other retail outlets.

Contrary to popular opinion, a long channel may be the most efficient distribution channel for certain consumer goods. When several channel intermediaries are available to perform specialised functions, costs may be lower than if one channel member is responsible for all the functions in all territories. Some manufacturers opt for all or most of these four channels in order to cater for the needs and buying processes of the different customers which make up their various targeted market segments.

Channels for Industrial, Business-to-Business Products

Figure 12.4 shows four of the most common channels for industrial products. Like their consumer products counterparts, manufacturers of industrial products sometimes work with more than one level of wholesalers.

Channel E illustrates the direct channel for industrial products. In contrast with consumer goods, many industrial products—especially expensive equipment, such as steam generators, aircraft and mainframe computers—are sold directly to the buyers. For example, Airbus Industries sells aircraft directly to airlines such as British Airways and Air France. The direct channel is most feasible for many manufacturers of industrial goods because they have fewer customers, and those customers may be clustered geographically as explained in Chapter 5.

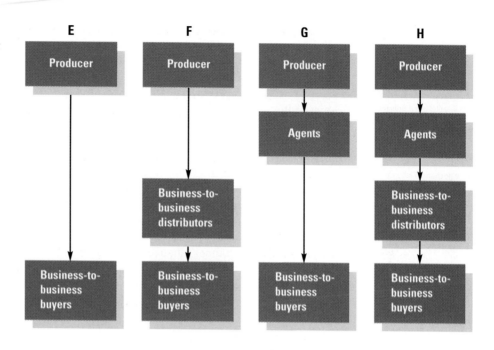

Figure 12.4 Typical marketing channels for industrial, business-to-business products

E	F	G	H
Producer	Producer	Producer	Producer
		Agents	Agents
	Business-to-business distributors		Business-to-business distributors
Business-to-business buyers	Business-to-business buyers	Business-to-business buyers	Business-to-business buyers

Buyers of complex industrial products can also receive technical assistance from the manufacturer more easily in a direct channel. In some cases the provision of such information may continue for the life time of the product. As with consumer markets, e-commerce and the desire to develop one-to-one direct relationships have led to a growth in the use of channel E.

If a particular line of industrial products is aimed at a larger number of customers, the manufacturer may use a marketing channel that includes **industrial distributors,** merchants who take title to products and carry inventory (channel F). Construction products made by Case or JCB, for example, are sold through industrial or business-to-business distributors as are building materials, operating supplies and air conditioning equipment. Industrial distributors can be most effectively used when a product has broad market appeal, is easily stocked and serviced, is sold in small quantities and is needed rapidly to avoid high losses.[4]

Channel G—from producer to agents to industrial or business-to-business buyers—may be chosen when a manufacturer without a marketing department needs market information, when a company is too small to field its own salesforce or when a company wants to introduce a new product or to enter a new market without using its own salespeople. Thus a large soya bean producer might sell its product to animal food processors through an agent.

Channel H is a variation of channel G: goods move from producer to agents to industrial distributors and then to industrial buyers. A manufacturer without a salesforce may rely on this channel if its industrial customers purchase products in small quantities or if they must be re-supplied frequently and therefore need access to decentralised inventories. Japanese manufacturers of electronic components, for example, work through export agents who sell to industrial distributors serving small producers or dealers overseas.

Multiple Marketing Channels

When aiming at diverse target markets, it may be appropriate for a manufacturer to use several marketing channels simultaneously, with each channel involving a different group of intermediaries. For example, a manufacturer turns to multiple channels when the same product is directed to both consumers and

Industrial distributor An independent business that takes title to industrial products and carries inventories

industrial customers. When Procter & Gamble sells cleaning products for household use, the products are sold to supermarkets through grocery wholesalers or, in some cases, directly to the larger retailers, whereas the cleaning products going to restaurants or institutions follow a different distribution channel. In some instances, a producer may prefer **dual distribution:** the use of two or more marketing channels for distributing the same products. Villeroy & Boch is a respected supplier of fine china and glassware to households across the world. The company also has ranges for the catering industry, sold and promoted through a separate marketing channel.

Dual distribution A channel practice whereby a producer distributes the same products through two or more different channels

A **strategic channel alliance** exists when the products of one organisation are distributed through the marketing channels of another organisation. The products are often similar with respect to target markets or product uses, but they are not direct competitors. For example, a brand of bottled water might be distributed through a marketing channel for soft drinks, or a US cereal producer might form a strategic channel alliance with a European food processor. Alliances can provide benefits both for the organisation that owns the marketing channel and for the company whose brand is being distributed through the channel.

Strategic channel alliance Arrangement for distributing the products of one organisation through the marketing channels of another

Channel Integration

Channel functions may be transferred among intermediaries, to producers and even to customers. This section examines how channel members can either combine and control most activities or pass them on to another channel member. Remember, though, that the channel member cannot eliminate functions; unless buyers themselves perform the functions, they must pay for the labour and resources needed for the functions to be performed. The statement that "you can eliminate middlemen but you can't eliminate their functions" is an accepted principle of marketing.

Many marketing channels are determined by consensus. Producers and intermediaries co-ordinate their efforts for mutual benefit. Some marketing channels, however, are organised and controlled by a single leader, which can be a producer, a wholesaler or a retailer, depending on the industry. The channel leader may establish channel policies and co-ordinate the development of the marketing mix. Marks & Spencer and IKEA, for example, are channel leaders for several of the many products they sell, exerting significant pressure on suppliers to adhere to their production, delivery and pricing standards. The various links or stages of the channel may be combined under the management of a channel leader either horizontally or vertically. Integration may stabilise supply, reduce costs and increase co-ordination of channel members.

Vertical Channel Integration

Vertical channel integration The combination of two or more stages of the channel under one management

Combining two or more stages of the channel under one management is **vertical channel integration.** One member of a marketing channel may purchase the operations of another member or simply perform the functions of the other member, eliminating the need for that intermediary as a separate entity. For example, changes in the regulations controlling the UK electricity industry have led to an increase in vertical channel integration, as some companies controlling the supply and distribution of electricity have merged (see Case 12.2). Total vertical integration encompasses all functions from production to ultimate buyer; it is exemplified by oil companies that own oil wells, pipelines, refineries, terminals and service station forecourts. Marketing Insight 12.1 examines the plight of the major petrol producers.

All Hands to the Pump

The distribution of petrol has entered a period of change as fuel companies Esso, Shell and BP are challenged by food retailers offering cut-price petrol from forecourts adjacent to their supermarket outlets. For food retailers such as Tesco and Sainsbury's, which purchase petrol at the lowest prices on the world oil markets, the fuel sales are treated as a loss leader aimed at drawing customers in to buy groceries. Meanwhile, the vertically integrated fuel companies are realising that petrol sales may no longer be profitable on their own. In such an environment the ability to generate business away from the core area of fuel sales is essential; new ways must therefore be found to encourage customers to visit petrol forecourts. For this reason, most of the fuel companies have given considerable attention to the stocking and pricing of other goods offered by their petrol forecourts.

It is perhaps ironic that in the longer term these pressures look likely to reduce consumer choice. Some industry experts believe that as petrol prices spiral downwards, smaller and more remote petrol outlets will be forced out of business, with sales becoming focused on fewer, higher volume sites. This view seems to be at odds with research results, which suggest that 55 per cent of consumers are unaware of petrol prices, choosing their petrol forecourt on the basis of location.

The challenge to the fuel giants does not end with low prices. Since Tesco rolled out its Clubcard scheme for its national network of petrol stations, the 6.5 million customers who hold a card can enjoy cost saving benefits to their fuel as well as their grocery bills. The Clubcard allows customers to collect points as they spend; these are later exchanged for money-off coupons. Asda's Fill and Save card offers similar benefits.

Not surprisingly, the fuel companies have responded quickly to the competitive attack from the supermarkets. Esso's Pricewatch scheme has involved first reducing prices to win customers back and then offering to match supermarket prices within a three mile radius. In its first two months, the company spent £4.1 million promoting the campaign. Shell has adopted a different approach, that of aggressively promoting its Smart Card, which allows customers to collect points that can be exchanged for a wide range of gifts. Yet despite these efforts, the supermarkets' share of the market has risen to well over a third.

BP and Mobil announced a joint venture in Europe aimed at achieving greater economies of scale and providing access to over three thousand more forecourts around Europe. In the UK, the combined forces of BP and Mobil moved the venture into second place behind Esso. In other markets in Europe it became market leader. The main benefits to the companies revolve around supply efficiencies, as the companies share costs and cut down on duplication. The move entailed switching over Mobil's outlets to BP's green livery and shedding between two and three thousand jobs from the European network. Yet despite the fact that the joint venture enjoyed a 15 per cent market share in the UK, it remains to be seen whether the sites will be profitable.

SOURCES: Julian Lee, "Clubcard move fuels price war", *Marketing*, 29 February 1996, p. 1; Martin Payne and Phillip Wisson, "Retailscan: ads fuel petrol's risky price war", *Marketing Week*, 19 April 1996, pp. 30–31; Claire Murphy, "Why sites are key to fuel fight", *Marketing*, 7 March 1996, p. 16; Ken Gofton, "Coupons flourish as distribution shifts", *Marketing*, 7 March 1996, p. 12; Conoco, 1999.

Whereas members of conventional channel systems work independently and seldom co-operate, participants in vertical channel integration co-ordinate their efforts to reach a desired target market.[5] This more progressive approach to distribution enables channel members to regard other members as extensions of their own operations. Vertically integrated channels are often more effective against competition because they result in increased bargaining power, the ability to inhibit competitors and the sharing of information and responsibilities.[6] At one end of an integrated channel, for example, a manufacturer might provide advertising and training assistance, and the retailer at the other end would buy the manufacturer's products in quantity and actively promote them.

Figure 12.5 Comparison of a conventional marketing channel and a vertical marketing system. SOURCE: Adapted from *Strategic Marketing*, by D. J. Kollat et al. Copyright © 1972. Reprinted by permission.

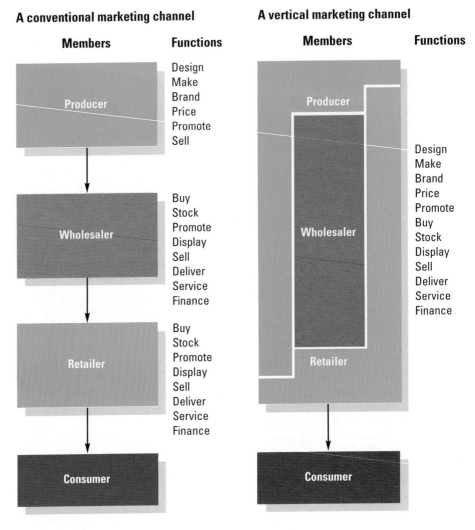

A conventional marketing channel

Members	Functions
Producer	Design Make Brand Price Promote Sell
Wholesaler	Buy Stock Promote Display Sell Deliver Service Finance
Retailer	Buy Stock Promote Display Sell Deliver Service Finance
Consumer	

A vertical marketing channel

Members	Functions
Producer	
Wholesaler	Design Make Brand Price Promote Buy Stock Display Sell Deliver Service Finance
Retailer	
Consumer	

Vertical marketing system (VMS)
Marketing channel in which a single channel member co-ordinates or manages channel activities to achieve efficient, low cost distribution aimed at satisfying target market customers

In the past, integration has been successfully institutionalised in marketing channels called vertical marketing systems. A **vertical marketing system (VMS)** is a marketing channel in which a single channel member co-ordinates or manages channel activities to achieve efficient, low cost distribution aimed at satisfying target market customers. Because the efforts of individual channel members are combined in a VMS, marketing activities can be co-ordinated for maximum effectiveness and economy, without duplication of services. Vertical marketing systems are also competitive, accounting for a growing share of retail sales in consumer goods.

Most vertical marketing systems today take one of three forms: corporate, administered or contractual. The *corporate* VMS combines all stages of the marketing channel, from producers to consumers, under a single ownership. Supermarket chains that own food processing plants and large retailers that purchase wholesaling and production facilities are examples of corporate VMSs. Figure 12.5 contrasts a conventional marketing channel with a VMS, which consolidates marketing functions and institutions.

In an *administered* VMS, channel members are independent, but a high level of inter-organisational management is achieved by informal co-ordination.

Members of an administered VMS may agree, for example, to adopt uniform accounting and ordering procedures and to co-operate in promotional activities. Although individual channel members maintain their autonomy, as in conventional marketing channels, one channel member (such as the producer or a large retailer) dominates the administered VMS, so that distribution decisions take into account the system as a whole. Because of its size and power as a retailer, Marks & Spencer exercises a strong influence over the independent manufacturers in its marketing channels, as do Kellogg's (cereals) and BMW (cars).

Under a *contractual* VMS, the most popular type of vertical marketing system, inter-organisational relationships are formalised through contracts. Channel members are linked by legal agreements that spell out each member's rights and obligations. For instance, franchise organisations such as McDonald's and KFC are contractual VMSs. Other contractual VMSs include wholesaler sponsored groups such as SPAR, Mace or IGA (Independent Grocers' Alliance) stores, in which independent retailers band together under the contractual leadership of a wholesaler.

Horizontal Channel Integration

Horizontal channel integration
The combination of institutions at the same level of channel operation under one management

Combining institutions at the same level of channel operation under one management constitutes **horizontal channel integration.** An organisation may integrate horizontally by merging with other organisations at the same level in a marketing channel. For example, the owner of a bistro may buy another bistro and then re-brand it in the same way as the existing business. Horizontal integration may enable a business to generate sufficient sales revenue to integrate vertically as well.

Although horizontal integration permits efficiencies and economies of scale in purchasing, marketing research, advertising and specialised personnel, it is not always the most effective method of improving distribution. The increase in size may result in decreased flexibility, difficulties in co-ordination, and the need for additional marketing research and large scale planning. Unless distribution functions for the various units can be performed more efficiently under unified management than under the previously separate managements, horizontal integration will not reduce costs or improve the competitive position of the integrating company.

Different Levels of Market Coverage

The kind of coverage that is appropriate for different products is determined by the characteristics and behaviour patterns of buyers. Chapter 8 divides consumer products into three categories—convenience products, shopping products and speciality products—according to how the purchase is made. In considering products to buy, consumers take into account replacement rate, product adjustment (services), duration of consumption, time required to find the product and similar factors.[7] Three major levels of market coverage are intensive, selective and exclusive distribution.

Intensive Distribution

Intensive distribution The use of all available outlets for distributing a product

In **intensive distribution,** all available outlets are used for distributing a product. Intensive distribution is appropriate for convenience products such as bread, chewing gum, beer and newspapers. To consumers, availability means a store located nearby and minimal time necessary to search for the product at the store. Sales may have a direct relationship to availability. The successful sale of bread and milk at service stations or of petrol at convenience grocery stores has shown that the availability of these products is more important than the nature of the outlet. Convenience products have a high replacement rate and require almost no service. To meet these demands, intensive distribution is necessary, and multiple channels may be used to sell through all possible outlets. Marketing Insight 12.2 describes how Games Workshop has adopted a mix of distribution channels to support rapid growth.

Producers of packaged consumer items rely on intensive distribution. In fact, intensive distribution is one of Procter & Gamble's key strengths. It is fairly easy for this company to formulate marketing strategies for many of its products (soaps, detergents, food and juice products, and personal care products) because consumers want availability provided quickly and intensively.

Selective Distribution

Selective distribution   The use of only some available outlets in an area to distribute a product

In **selective distribution,** only some available outlets in an area are chosen to distribute a product. Selective distribution is appropriate for shopping products. Durable goods such as electrical appliances and exclusive fragrances usually fall into this category. Such products are more expensive than convenience goods. Consumers are willing to spend more searching time, visiting several retail outlets to compare prices, designs, styles and other features.

Selective distribution is desirable when a special effort—such as customer service from a channel member—is important. Shopping products require differentiation at the point of purchase. To motivate retailers to provide adequate pre-sale service, selective distribution and company owned stores are often used. Many industrial products are sold on a selective basis to maintain a certain degree of control over the distribution process. For example, agricultural herbicides are distributed on a selective basis because dealers must offer services to buyers, such as instructions about how to apply the herbicides safely or the option of having the dealer apply the herbicide.

Exclusive Distribution

Exclusive distribution   The use of only one outlet in a relatively large geographic area to distribute a product

In **exclusive distribution,** only one outlet is used in a relatively large geographic area. Exclusive distribution is suitable for speciality products that are purchased rather infrequently, are consumed over a long period of time, or require service or information to fit them to buyers' needs. Exclusive distribution is not appropriate for convenience products and many shopping products. It is often used as an incentive to sellers when only a limited market is available for products. For example, cars such as the Rolls Royce are sold on an exclusive basis. Royal Copenhagen's premium china is retailed through carefully selected, exclusive retail outlets (see Figure 12.6). A producer who uses exclusive distribution generally expects a dealer to be very co-operative with respect to carrying a complete inventory, sending personnel for sales and service training, participating in promotional programmes and providing excellent customer service. Exclusive distribution gives a company tighter image control because the types of distributors and retailers that distribute the product are closely monitored.[8]

Choosing Distribution Channels

Choosing the most appropriate distribution channels for a product can be complex. Producers must choose specific intermediaries carefully, evaluating their sales and profit levels, performance records, other products carried, clientele, availability and so forth. In addition, producers must also examine other factors that influence distribution channel selection, including organisational objectives

Games Workshop: Multiple Distribution Channels

As the name suggests, Games Workshop manufactures and sells games, but these are no ordinary games and this is no ordinary business. With a turnover of £70 million, this fast growing company employs more than two thousand people and has over 250 retail outlets in Australia, Canada, Germany, Hong Kong, Spain, the US and the UK, with the growing Italian market still being serviced from the UK. In 1999 the company opened its two-hundredth store, in Amsterdam. The fantasy games produced by Games Workshop take place in one of two settings: (1) a fantasy world filled with Dwarfs, Elves, rat-like Scaven, green Orcs and Goblins; (2) the future of a war-torn universe in the forty-first millennium. This setting is occupied by the enigmatic Eldar, genetically enhanced Space Marines and an alien race called the Tyranids, who are all battling for survival. Games Workshop enthusiasts can buy from a range of boxed games, containing the rule book, charts and templates, dice and miniature figures needed to begin their fantasy battle. The basics can then be added to from the extensive range of Games Workshop troops, special squads and war machines. As enthusiasts develop their armies and paint them in colours of their choice, they begin to build their own personalised version of their game of choice.

For those unfamiliar with the fantasy game concept, the uncharted territory of the retail outlets can feel like alien territory. Wall space is stacked high with numerous games, figures, paints, magazines, books and tee-shirts. In the centre is a gaming table, which is usually covered with the remains of an ongoing battle. At other times, the shops are full of teenagers and children, conducting a closely fought Warhammer contest. On some days the outlets resemble a crèche for big kids, with staff carefully orchestrating activities. The battles organised in-store are an important part of the weekly itinerary. The featured game varies on different days, so that enthusiasts of Warhammer, Warhammer 40,000, Necromunda and the other Games Workshop products can all get their turn. These games induct newcomers into the gaming experience, while for "old hands" they showcase new product launches.

The shop staff, always Games Workshop enthusiasts, are vital to the success of the retail outlets. They must be able to maintain an enthusiasm for the brand, keeping up to date with all of the latest new product launches. The ability to handle customers of all ages and backgrounds—from the young teenagers who regularly "hang out" at the stores to the uninitiated visiting the outlets for the first time—is also essential. Nonplussed parents clutching "Christmas lists" or birthday present suggestions experience a friendly welcome from staff who will happily search among the reams of Games Workshop packaging to retrieve some unlikely named item.

As well as its network of retail stores, Games Workshop has agencies—typically specialist modelling shops—distributing its figures and games, while even the likes of Toys "R" Us have been known to stock the popular gaming sets. In addition, there is a mail order operation which can be accessed through the retail stores as well as directly by telephone or the Internet. This £3+ million mail order operation has 40 staff and a database of 150,000 contacts. The aim is to provide a fast and efficient service, despatching all orders within 24 hours. This facility handles up to one thousand calls daily and can deal with enquiries in a range of languages. While the stores are an integral feature of the Games Workshop "experience", the company has been quick to recognise the value of adopting a mix of distribution channels to support its rapid expansion plans.

SOURCES: Jervis Johnson and Chris Prentice of Games Workshop; The Games Workshop web site, **www.games-workshop.co.uk**; James Dibb-Simkin; Sally Dibb and Lyndon Simkin, *The Marketing Casebook*, 2nd edn (London: ITBP, 2000).

and resources, market characteristics, buying behaviour, product attributes and environmental forces. In some markets, such as the distribution of insurance products, these factors may indicate that multiple channels should be used.[9]

Organisational Objectives and Resources

Producers must carefully consider their objectives and the cost of achieving them in the marketplace. A company's objectives may be broad—such as higher profits, increased market share and greater responsiveness to customers—or narrow,

ROYAL COPENHAGEN

Blue Fluted, half lace.
Hand-painted since 1775.

Figure 12.6   Using exclusive distribution. Royal Copenhagen china controls its choice of retail outlets.   SOURCE: Courtesy of Royal Copenhagen.

such as replacing an intermediary that has left the channel. The organisation may possess sufficient financial and marketing clout to control its distribution channels, for example, by engaging in direct marketing or by operating its own fleet of lorries. On the other hand, an organisation may have no interest in performing distribution services or may be forced by lack of resources and experience to depend on middlemen.

Companies must also consider how effective their past distribution relationships and methods have been and question their appropriateness in regard to current objectives. One business might decide to maintain its basic channel structure but add members for increased coverage in new territories. Another company might alter its distribution channel so as to provide same-day delivery on all orders.

Market Characteristics Beyond the basic division between consumer markets and industrial markets, several market variables influence the design of distribution channels. Geography is one factor; in most cases, the greater the distance between the producer and its markets, the less expensive is distribution through intermediaries rather than through direct sales. Market density must also be considered; when customers tend to be clustered in several locations, the producer may be able to eliminate middlemen. Figure 12.7 shows how warehouses are often promoted on the basis of location. Transport, storage, communication and negotiation are specific functions performed more efficiently in high density markets. Market size—measured by the number of potential customers in a consumer or industrial market—is yet

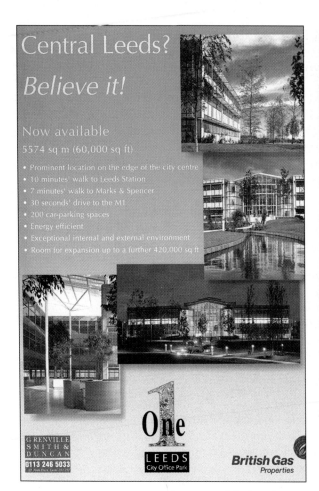

Figure 12.7 Market characteristics. Warehouses are often promoted on the basis of location. SOURCE: *left:* Courtesy of Central Leeds; *right:* Courtesy of Quayside.

another variable. Direct sales may be effective if a producer has relatively few buyers for a product, but for larger markets the services of middlemen may be required.[10] As explored in Chapter 17, e-commerce is encouraging many suppliers to deal directly with customers, even when they are geographically spread or diverse in nature. There is no doubt that the growing popularity of direct marketing and web based marketing is forcing marketers to re-appraise their market characteristics and deployment of channel intermediaries. Direct customer-supplier relationships are the result in channels where wholesaler/retailer channel members once dominated, such as CDs, books, holidays and financial services.

Buying Behaviour

Buying behaviour is a crucial consideration in selecting distribution channels. To be able to match intermediaries with customers, the producer must have specific, current information about customers who are buying the product and how, when and where they are buying it.[11] A manufacturer might find direct selling economically feasible for large volume sales but inappropriate for small orders.

The producer must also understand how buyer specifications vary according to whether buyers perceive products as convenience, shopping or speciality items (see Chapter 8). Customers for magazines, for example, are likely to buy the product frequently (even impulsively) from a variety of outlets. Buyers of home computers, however, carefully evaluate product features, dealers, prices and after sales services.

Buyers may be reached most effectively when producers are creative in opening up new distribution channels. In the UK, effective distribution, the essential tool in the highly competitive soft drinks sector, is forcing brand leader Coca-Cola and Schweppes Beverages to find creative ways of extending distribution. Schweppes launched a company, Vendleader, to increase penetration of sales through vending machines.

Product Attributes Another variable in the selection of distribution channels is the product itself. Because producers of complex industrial products must often provide technical services to buyers both before and after the sale, these products are usually shipped directly to buyers. Perishable or highly fashionable consumer products with short shelf lives are also marketed through short channels. In other cases, distribution patterns are influenced by the product's value; the lower the price per unit, the longer the distribution chain. Additional factors to consider are the weight, bulkiness and relative ease of handling the products. Producers may find wholesalers and retailers reluctant to carry items that create storage or display problems.[12] For example, manufacturers of breakfast cereals such as Kellogg's and Nabisco must use packaging that retailers find easy to handle and display.

Environmental Forces Finally, producers making decisions about distribution channels must consider the broader forces in the total marketing environment—that is, the political, legal, regulatory, societal/green, technological, economic and competitive forces. Technology, for example, has made possible electronic scanners, computerised inventory systems such as EPOS (electronic point-of-sale) and electronic shopping devices, all of which are altering present distribution systems and making it harder for technologically unsophisticated companies to remain competitive. Internet access has led to a growth in home shopping and direct marketing. Changing family patterns and the emergence of important minority consumer groups are driving producers to seek new distribution methods for reaching market segments. Interest rates, inflation and other economic variables affect members of distribution channels at every level. Environmental forces are numerous and complex and must be taken into consideration if distribution efforts are to be appropriate, efficient and effective (see Chapter 2). For example, EU regulation changes have impacted on the retailing of cars, resulting in a power shift away from the car manufacturers to the independently owned showrooms, which can now source vehicles from a variety of manufacturers to sell at a single location.

Behaviour of Channel Members

The marketing channel is a social system with its own conventions and behaviour patterns. Each channel member performs a different role in the system and agrees (implicitly or explicitly) to accept certain rights, responsibilities, rewards and sanctions for non-conformity. Channel members have certain expectations of other channel members. Retailers, for instance, expect wholesalers and manufacturers to maintain adequate inventories and to deliver goods on time. For their part, wholesalers expect retailers to honour payment agreements and to keep them informed of inventory needs. This section discusses several issues related to channel member behaviour, including co-operation and relationship building, conflict and leadership. Marketers need to understand these behavioural issues to make effective channel decisions and to maintain relationships with facilitating channel members and loyal customers.

Channel Co-operation and Relationship Building

Channel co-operation is vital if each member is to gain something from other members.[13] Without co-operation, neither overall channel goals nor member goals can be realised. Policies must be developed that support all essential channel members; otherwise, failure of one link in the chain could destroy the channel.

There are several ways to improve channel co-operation. A marketing channel should consider itself a unified system, competing with other systems. This way, individual members will be less likely to take actions that would create disadvantages for other members. Similarly, channel members should agree to direct their efforts towards a common target market so that channel roles can be structured for maximum marketing effectiveness, which in turn can help members achieve their individual objectives. It is crucial to define precisely the tasks that each member of the channel is to perform. This definition provides a basis for reviewing the intermediaries' performance and helps reduce conflicts because each channel member knows exactly what is expected of it. As explained in Chapter 5, it is often in the interests of channel members to build long term relationships. These relationships can improve channel co-operation and help individual channel members better adapt to the needs of the others.[14]

Channel Conflict

Although all channel members work towards the same general goal—distributing goods and services profitably and efficiently—members may sometimes disagree about the best methods for attaining this goal.[15] Each channel member wants to maximise its own profits while maintaining as much autonomy as possible.[16] However, if this self-interest creates misunderstanding about role expectations, the end result is frustration and conflict for the whole channel. For individual organisations to function together in a single social system, each channel member must clearly communicate and understand role expectations. Communication difficulties are a potential form of channel conflict and can lead to frustration, misunderstandings and poorly co-ordinated strategies.[17]

Channel conflict often arises when a given channel member does not conduct itself in the manner expected by other channel members. Wholesalers expect producers to monitor quality control and production scheduling, and they expect retailers to market products effectively. Producers and retailers expect wholesalers to provide co-ordination, functional services and communication. But if members do not fulfil their roles—for example, if wholesalers or producers fail to deliver products on time or the producers' pricing policies cut into the margins of down-stream channel members—conflict may ensue.

Channel conflicts also arise when dealers over emphasise competing products or diversify into product lines traditionally handled by other, more specialised intermediaries. In some cases, conflict develops because producers strive to increase efficiency by circumventing intermediaries, as is happening in marketing channels for microcomputer software and video games. Many software-only stores are establishing direct relationships with software producers, bypassing wholesale distributors altogether. Some dishonest retailers are also pirating software or making unauthorised copies, thus cheating other channel members

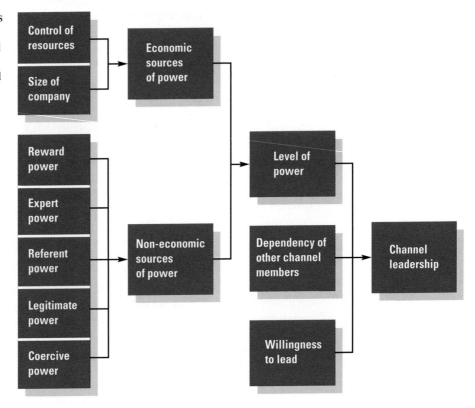

Figure 12.8 Determinants of channel leadership.
SOURCE: R. D. Michman and S. D. Sibley, *Marketing Channels and Strategies*, 2nd edn (Worthington, Ohio: Publishing Horizons, Inc., 1980), p. 413. Reproduced by permission.

out of their due compensation. Consequently, suspicion and mistrust are heightening tensions in software marketing channels.[18]

Although there is no single method for resolving conflict, an atmosphere of co-operation can be re-established if two conditions are met. First, the role of each channel member must be specified. To minimise misunderstanding, all members must be able to expect unambiguous, agreed-on levels of performance from one another. Second, channel members must institute certain measures of channel co-ordination, a task that requires leadership and the benevolent exercise of control.[19] To prevent channel conflict, producers or other channel members may provide competing resellers with different brands, allocate markets among resellers, define direct sales policies to clarify potential conflict over large accounts, negotiate territorial issues between regional distributors and provide recognition to certain resellers for the importance of their role in distributing to others. Hallmark, for example, distributes its Ambassador greetings card line in discount stores and its name brand Hallmark line in up-market department and specialist card stores, thus limiting the amount of competition among retailers carrying its products.[20]

Channel Leadership

Channel power The ability to influence another channel member's goal achievement

The effectiveness of marketing channels hinges on channel leadership, which may be assumed by producers, retailers or wholesalers. To become a leader, a channel member must want to influence and direct overall channel performance. Furthermore, to attain desired objectives, the leader must possess **channel power,** which is the ability to influence another channel member's goal achievement. As Figure 12.8 shows, the channel leader derives power from seven sources, two of them economic and five non-economic.

Part IV   Place (Distribution and Channel) Decisions

The five non-economic sources of power—reward, expert, referent, legitimate and coercive—are crucial for establishing leadership. (1) A channel leader gains reward power by providing financial benefits. (2) Expert power exists when other channel members believe that the leader provides special expertise required for the channel to function properly. (3) Referent power emerges when other members strongly identify with and emulate the leader. (4) Legitimate power is based on a superior-subordinate relationship. (5) Coercive power is a function of the leader's ability to punish other channel members.[21]

In many countries, producers assume the leadership role in marketing channels. A manufacturer—whose large scale production efficiency demands increasing sales volume—may exercise power by giving channel members financing, business advice, ordering assistance, advertising and support materials.[22] For example, BMW and Mercedes-Benz control their dealers totally, specifying showroom design and layout, discount levels and quotas of models. Coercion, though, causes dealer dissatisfaction that is stronger than any impact from rewards, so the use of coercive power can be a major cause of channel conflict.[23]

Retailers can also function as channel leaders, and with the domination of national chains and own label merchandise they are increasingly doing so. For example, Sainsbury's challenged Coca-Cola with its own label of cola, which was similarly packaged to that of the market leader. Small retailers, too, may share in the leadership role when they command particular consumer respect and patronage in local or regional markets. Among large retailers, Carrefour, IKEA, Marks & Spencer and Tesco base their channel leadership on wide public exposure to their products. These retailers control many brands and sometimes replace uncooperative producers. IKEA exercises power by dictating manufacturing techniques, lead times, quality levels and product specifications.

Wholesalers assume channel leadership roles as well, although they were more powerful decades ago, when most manufacturers and retailers were small, underfinanced and widely scattered. Today, wholesaler leaders may form voluntary chains with several retailers, which they supply with bulk buying or management services or which market their own brands. In return, the retailers shift most of their purchasing to the wholesaler leader. In Scandinavia, buying groups act as wholesalers, with bulk ordering price advantages, expert advertising and purchasing. Other wholesaler leaders such as Intersport or SPAR might also help retailers with store layouts, accounting and inventory control.

Legal Issues in Channel Management

The multitude of laws governing channel management are based on the general principle that the public is best served when competition and free trade are protected. Under the authority of such national legislation as the UK's Competition Commission, Fair Trading Act, Prices Act, Trade Descriptions Act and Consumer Protection Act, or EU Competition Laws and dictates, the courts and regulatory agencies determine under what circumstances channel management practices violate this underlying principle and must be restricted and when these practices may be permitted. Although channel managers are not expected to be legal experts, they should be aware that attempts to control distribution functions may have legal repercussions. The following practices are among those frequently subject to legal restraint.

Restricted Sales Territories

Restricted sales territories System by which a manufacturer tries to prohibit intermediaries from selling its products outside designated sales territories

To tighten its control over the distribution of its products, a manufacturer may try to prohibit intermediaries from selling its products outside designated sales territories, creating **restricted sales territories.** The intermediaries themselves often favour this practice, because it lets them avoid competition for the producer's brands within their own territories. Many companies have long followed the policy of restricting sales in this fashion. In recent years, the courts have adopted conflicting positions in regard to restricted sales territories. Although they have deemed restricted sales territories a restraint of trade among intermediaries handling the same brands (except for small or newly established companies), the courts have also held that exclusive territories can actually promote competition among dealers handling different brands. At present, the producer's intent in establishing restricted territories and the overall effect of doing so on the market must be evaluated for each case individually.

Tying Contract

Tying contract Arrangement whereby a supplier (usually a manufacturer or franchiser) furnishes a product to a channel member with the stipulation that the channel member must purchase other products as well

When a supplier (usually a manufacturer or franchiser) furnishes a product to a channel member with the stipulation that the channel member must purchase other products as well, a **tying contract** exists.[24] Suppliers, for instance, may institute tying arrangements to move weaker products along with more popular items. To use another example, a franchiser may tie the purchase of equipment and supplies to the sale of franchises, justifying the policy as necessary for quality control and protection of the franchiser's reputation. A related practice is full-line forcing. In this situation, a supplier requires that channel members purchase the supplier's entire line to obtain any of the products. Manufacturers sometimes use full-line forcing to ensure that intermediaries accept new products and that a suitable range of products is available to customers.

The courts accept tying contracts when the supplier alone can provide products of a certain quality, when the intermediary is free to carry competing products as well and when a company has just entered the market. Most other tying contracts are considered illegal.

Exclusive Dealing

Exclusive dealing System by which a manufacturer forbids an intermediary to carry products of competing manufacturers

When a manufacturer forbids an intermediary to carry products of competing manufacturers, the arrangement is called **exclusive dealing.** A manufacturer receives considerable market protection in an exclusive dealing arrangement and may cut off shipments to an intermediary that violates such an agreement.

An exclusive dealing contract is generally legally permitted if dealers and customers in a given market have access to similar products or if the exclusive dealing contract strengthens an otherwise weak competitor.

Refusal to Deal

Refusal to deal Situation in which suppliers will not do business with wholesalers or dealers simply because these wholesalers or dealers have resisted policies that are anti-competitive or in restraint of trade

Producers have the right to choose the channel members with whom they will do business (and the right not to choose others). Within existing distribution channels, however, suppliers may not refuse to deal with wholesalers or dealers just because these wholesalers or dealers have resisted policies that are anti-competitive or in restraint of trade. Suppliers are further prohibited from organising some channel members in **refusal to deal** actions against other members who choose not to comply with illegal policies.[25]

Distribution refers to activities that make products available to customers when and where they want to purchase them. A *channel of distribution* (or *marketing channel*) is a group of individuals and organisations that direct the flow of products from producers to customers. In most channels of distribution, producers and customers are linked by *marketing intermediaries* or middlemen, called *merchants* if they take title to products and *functional middlemen* if they do not take title. Channel structure reflects the division of responsibilities among members. Ongoing relationships with customers are seen as increasingly important via relationship marketing. Effective distribution channels and deployment of channel intermediaries are central to the development of mutually satisfactory ongoing relationships between intermediaries and between producers and their customers.

Marketing channels serve many functions that may be performed by a single channel member but are mostly accomplished through both independent and joint efforts of channel members. These functions include creating utility, facilitating exchange efficiencies, alleviating discrepancies, standardising transactions and providing customer service. Although intermediaries can be eliminated, their functions are vital and cannot be dropped; these activities must be performed by someone in the marketing channel or passed on to customers. Because intermediaries serve both producers and buyers, they reduce the total number of transactions that would otherwise be needed to move products from producer to ultimate users. Intermediaries' specialised functions also help keep down costs.

An *assortment* is a combination of products assembled to provide customer benefits. Intermediaries perform *sorting activities* essential to the development of product assortments. Sorting activities allow channel members to divide roles and separate tasks. Through the basic tasks of *sorting out, accumulation, allocation* and *assorting* products for buyers, intermediaries resolve discrepancies in quantity and assortment. The number and characteristics of intermediaries are determined by the assortments and the expertise needed to perform distribution activities.

Channels of distribution are broadly classified as channels for consumer products or channels for industrial (business-to-business) products. Within these two broad categories, different marketing channels are used for different products. Although some consumer goods move directly from producer to consumers, consumer product channels that include wholesalers and retailers are usually more economical and efficient. Industrial goods move directly from producer to end users more frequently than do consumer goods. Channels for industrial products may also include agents, *industrial distributors* or both. Most producers use *dual distribution* or multiple channels so that the distribution system can be adjusted for various target markets. Sometimes *strategic channel alliances* are used so that the products of one organisation can be distributed through the marketing channels of another. Direct marketing, aided by *e-commerce*, has recently encouraged many marketers to cut out channel intermediaries in both consumer and business-to-business transactions.

Integration of marketing channels brings various activities under the management of one channel member. *Vertical integration* combines two or more stages of the channel under one management. In the *vertical marketing system (VMS)* a single channel member co-ordinates or manages channel activity for the mutual benefit of all channel members. Vertical marketing systems may be corporate, administered or contractual. *Horizontal integration* combines institutions at the same level of channel operation under a single management.

A marketing channel is managed so that products receive appropriate market coverage. In *intensive distribution*, producers distribute a product using all available outlets. In *selective distribution*, outlets are screened to use those most qualified for exposing a product properly. *Exclusive distribution* usually uses one outlet to distribute a product in a large geographic area when there is a limited market for the product.

When selecting distribution channels for products, manufacturers evaluate potential channel members carefully. Producers consider the organisation's objectives and available resources; the location, density and size of a market; buying behaviour in the target market; product attributes; and external forces in the marketing environment. Technology, notably e-commerce, has recently played a major role in certain markets in the selection of distribution channels.

A marketing channel is a social system in which individuals and organisations are linked by a common goal: the profitable and efficient distribution of goods and services. The positions or roles of channel members are associated with rights, responsibilities and rewards, as well as sanctions for non-conformity. Channels function most efficiently when members co-operate; when they deviate from their roles, channel conflict can arise. Effective marketing channels are usually a result of channel leadership and of relationship building between channel members.

Channel leaders can facilitate or hinder other channel members' goal achievement, deriving this *channel power* from seven sources, two of them economic and five non-economic. Producers are in an excellent position to structure channel policy

and to use technical expertise and consumer acceptance to influence other channel members. Retailers gain channel control through consumer confidence, wide product mixes and intimate knowledge of consumers. Wholesalers and buying groups become channel leaders when they have expertise that other channel members value and when they can co-ordinate functions to match supply with demand.

Channel management is governed by a variety of legal issues. These are based on the principle that the public is best served when competition and free trade are protected. Various practices may be subject to legal restraint. To tighten their distribution control, manufacturers may try to operate *restricted sales territories,* where intermediaries are barred from selling products outside designated areas. A *tying contract* occurs when a supplier stipulates that another channel member must purchase other products in addition to the one originally supplied. *Exclusive dealing* occurs when a manufacturer forbids an intermediary to carry products of competing manufacturers. *Refusal to deal* means that a producer will not do business with a wholesaler or dealer that has resisted policies that are anti-competitive or in restraint of trade.

Important Terms

Channel of distribution
   (or marketing channel)
Marketing intermediary
Merchants
Functional middlemen
Assortment
Sorting activities
Sorting out
Accumulation

Allocation
Assorting
E-commerce
Industrial distributor
Dual distribution
Strategic channel alliance
Vertical channel integration
Vertical marketing system
   (VMS)

Horizontal channel integration
Intensive distribution
Selective distribution
Exclusive distribution
Channel power
Restricted sales territories
Tying contract
Exclusive dealing
Refusal to deal

Discussion and Review Questions

1. Compare and contrast the four major types of marketing channels for consumer products. Through which type of channel is each of the following products most likely to be distributed: (a) new cars, (b) cheese biscuits, (c) cut-your-own Christmas trees, (d) new text books, (e) sofas, (f) soft drinks?

2. "Shorter channels are usually a more direct means of distribution and therefore are more efficient." Comment on this statement.

3. Describe an industrial distributor. What types of products are marketed through industrial distributors?

4. Under what conditions is a producer most likely to use more than one marketing channel?

5. Why do consumers often blame intermediaries for distribution inefficiencies? List several reasons.

6. How do the major functions that intermediaries perform help resolve discrepancies in assortment and in quantity?

7. How does the number of intermediaries in the channel relate to the assortments retailers need?

8. Can one channel member perform all channel functions?

9. Identify and explain the major factors that influence decision-makers' selection of marketing channels.

10. Name and describe companies that use (a) vertical integration and (b) horizontal integration in their marketing channels.

11. Explain the major characteristics of each of the three types of vertical marketing systems (VMSs).

12. Explain the differences among intensive, selective and exclusive methods of distribution.

13. What impact has the growing popularity of e-commerce had on marketing channels?

14. "Channel co-operation requires that members support the overall channel goals to achieve individual goals." Comment on this statement.

15. How do power bases within the channel influence the selection of the channel leader?

Recommended Readings

J. C. Anderson and J. A. Narus, "A model for distributor firm and manufacturing firm working relationships", *Journal of Marketing*, vol. 54, no. 1, 1990, pp. 42–58.

M. Christopher, *Logistics and Supply Chain Management* (London: Pitman, 1998).

S. D. Hunt, M. M. Ray and V. R. Wood, "Behavioural dimensions of channels of distribution: review and synthesis", *Journal of the Academy of Marketing Science,* vol. 13, no. 3, 1985, pp. 1–24.

B. Rosenbloom, *Marketing Channels: A Management View* (Fort Worth: Dryden, 1999).

D. Shipley and C. Egan, "Power, conflict and co-operation in brewer-tenant distribution channels", *International Journal of Service Industry Management*, vol. 3, no. 4, 1992, pp. 44–62.

● C A S E S

12.1 First Direct Innovative Banking Channels

With First Direct you can do your banking when it suits you, not when it suits us. We're open every hour, of every day, 365 days a year. So, if you want to transfer cash on a Sunday or set up a standing order late at night, you just ring up. And yes, you always talk to a real person. Because everything's done by phone, you can also bank from wherever you are . . . at home or in the office. And all calls are charged at local rate.

Most consumers have a bank cheque account from which cash is drawn, bills are paid and cheques written, and into which salaries, pensions or grant cheques are paid. For many consumers, the bank is a high street or shopping mall office—imposing, formal and often intimidating. Whether it's National Westminster, Barclays or Lloyds TSB in the UK, or ABN AMRO or Rabobank in the Netherlands, each high street bank is fairly alike, with similar products and services, personnel, branch layouts, locations and opening hours. Differentiation has been difficult to achieve and generally impossible to maintain over any length of time as competitors have copied rivals' moves. Promotional strategy and brand image have been the focus for most banking organisations, supported with more minor tactical changes in, for example, opening hours or service charges. For the majority of bank account holders, however, the branch—with its restricted openings, formal ambience and town centre location—is the only point of contact for the bulk of transactions.

First Direct, owned by HSBC (Midland), but managed separately, broke the mould in 1989. Launched with a massive £6 million promotional campaign, First Direct bypassed the traditional marketing channel. First Direct has no branches and no branch overhead and operating costs. It provides free banking, unlike its high street competitors with their system of bank charges combined with interest paid on positive balances. First Direct is a telephone banking service that offers full current and deposit account facilities, cheque books, automatic bill payment and ATM "hole in the wall" cash cards through HSBC's international service-till network.

HSBC has established a purpose built administrative centre for First Direct in Leeds, guaranteeing immediate, personal response to calls 24 hours a day. All normal banking transactions can be completed over the telephone. Initial reactions were positive, with many non-HSBC (Midland) account holders switching to the innovative new style of banking. The more traditional consumer—who equates the marbled halls of the Victorian branches with heritage, security and traditional values—has been less easily converted. For the targeted, more financially aware and independent income earner, First Direct is proving very popular.

First Direct's services and products are not new, but the chosen marketing channel—no branches, only telephone call centres—is innovative. Customers no longer have to reach inaccessible, parked-up, town centre branches with queues and restricted opening hours. First Direct has introduced a service, alien to some more traditional tastes perhaps, which is more readily available and with fewer costs. Hundreds of thousands of consumers have welcomed the launch of this new option, but millions have preferred to bank the traditional way. The start for First Direct was highly encouraging.

First Direct innovated and major rivals have all launched their own telephone and Internet based banking services in response to the consumers' positive view of this telephone banking proposition.

SOURCES: "Midland fails to bank on a third successive win", *Marketing*, 19 July 1990, p. 7; Mat Toor, "Taxis fare well with First Direct", *Marketing*, 19 April 1990, p. 1; "Banking industry report", Salomon Brothers, 1992; First Direct advertising, 1993; First Direct fact file, 1993; Beverly Crany, "Reading your MIND", *Marketing*, 22 February 1996, pp. 33–34; HSBC, 1999; Barclays, 1999.

Questions for Discussion

1. Why is innovation in marketing channels generally difficult to achieve?
2. Why was First Direct different from its rivals? What gave it differentiation when it first launched?
3. Why might some potential customers of First Direct have reservations about the innovative nature of the service?

12.2 Deregulation and Distribution Changes for the Utilities

In 1990 the British government began the process of privatising the state owned electricity industry. The aims of the scheme, which followed the privatisation of the telephone, water and gas industries, were clear: greater efficiency, more choice and lower prices for consumers. The UK's 12 regional electricity companies (RECs) experienced the first stage of privatisation in 1994, when the business market (those customers spending more than £12,000 annually on electricity) was opened up to competition. For the first time the RECs were able to compete for customers away from their own geographic area. For some, the impact was devastating. According to a senior marketing manager at one of the RECs, "In London, it was a huge shock. Almost overnight we lost 30 per cent of our business." Deregulation in the domestic market was originally set for 1998, but IT teething problems put this back to the present. The RECs are now faced with balancing their desire to retain existing customers with their ambitions for capturing new business.

An important characteristic of the privatisation approach was to separate electricity generation, distribution and supply. The intent of this move away from vertical integration was to ensure that the large generators (such as National Power and PowerGen) were kept apart from those supplying businesses and consumers (the RECs). This, it was stated, would reduce the power of the generators to control prices by making them compete to find buyers of their electricity. The government was also responding to criticism of its privatisation of the gas industry, which resulted in a vertically integrated distribution system from the gas field through to the end consumer.

In practice, anticipation of the market changes resulted in a host of merger and acquisition activity involving gas, electricity and water companies. With Scottish Power being allowed to buy REC Manweb and Hanson's acquisition of Eastern Electricity, it seemed inevitable that the industry would soon consist of a small number of vertically integrated businesses. US and French utility companies bought into UK electricity, gas and water businesses, in some instances making large corporations. Yet the government then surprised industry experts by refusing to allow generators PowerGen and National Power to bid for the RECs Midland Electric and Southern Electric. Meanwhile, US companies Houston Industries, Texas-Utilities and Pacific Gas and Electric have all acquired RECs.

An interesting aspect of the privatisation of the utilities has been the degree to which supply companies may re-position themselves as total providers of utility services. According to Rick Peel, a consultancy expert in the field, "The benefits of such an arrangement include access to a partner's markets, a stronger brand, new technology or simply bundling one product with another." Not surprisingly, considerable interest in this approach has already been shown. For example, some of the RECs have participated in the South West gas trial. This was a test market experiment run in 1996 to allow half a million residential customers to "shop around" for their gas supply from a range of competing companies. It was hoped that the pilot scheme would allow testing of the complex distribution and billing mechanisms in a relatively controlled manner.

While many questions about how suppliers will differentiate their products and how the practicalities of billing and meter reading systems will be handled remain unanswered, the biggest unknown is how the change in distribution will really affect consumers and what their reaction will be to the changes.

Now free to shop around between traditional and new entrant gas and electricity suppliers, consumers are faced with a multitude of brands, pricing packages, marketing campaigns and channel member allies. Even supermarkets and forecourts are selling electricity pre-payment cards. For some consumers, this choice has led to savings. For others, the marketplace appears highly confusing. For the marketers in the RECs, choices are still being made. It seems certain new channels to market will emerge. Virgin, Tesco or RAC electricity? Only time will tell.

SOURCES: "Britain's electricity shocker", *Economist,* 13 April 1996, p. 15; "Britain: short circuit", *Economist,* 13 April 1996, pp. 27–29; Meg Carter, "The mains attraction", *Marketing Week,* 8 December 1995, pp. 36–39; George Pitcher, "MMC's change of heart turns privatisation policy on its head", *Marketing Week,* 19 April 1996, p. 27; PowerGen, 1998; Midlands Electricity and East Midlands Electricity, 1999.

Questions for Discussion

1. How and why may consumers soon deal with new marketing channel members in seeking electricity supplies?
2. Why are strategic alliances likely to be important in the distribution of electricity?
3. How and why does the distribution of electricity and insurance differ?

13 Wholesalers, Distributors and Physical Distribution

OBJECTIVES

- To understand the nature of wholesaling in its broadest forms in the marketing channel

- To learn about wholesalers' activities and how wholesalers are classified

- To examine agencies that facilitate wholesaling and explore changing patterns in wholesaling

- To understand how physical distribution activities are integrated into marketing channels and overall marketing strategies, and to examine physical distribution objectives

- To learn about order processing, materials handling and different types of warehousing and their functions

- To appreciate the importance of inventory management and the development of adequate assortments of products for target markets

- To gain insight into different transportation methods and how they are selected and co-ordinated

"One of the most neglected, yet potentially most powerful, elements of the marketing mix is the way we reach and service the customer."

Martin Christopher
Cranfield University School of Management

Technological advances and faster, more reliable transportation that make it possible for companies to operate with much smaller inventories are transforming the nature of warehousing. To survive in today's competitive marketplace, traditional warehouses are making radical changes to become effective supply chain members.

For example, one significant trend is the increased use of cross-docking, an approach whereby products received at a warehouse are immediately shipped out without ever being put into storage. With computerised information systems, warehouses can pre-assign a shipping door for each in-bound carton. When the shipment arrives, a receiving dock employee can quickly apply a bar coded shipping label that includes destination data, and place the carton directly on an out-bound vehicle. Cross-docking greatly reduces labour and time associated with han-dling materials. Cross-docking is even changing the configuration of the warehouse. Although traditional warehouses are square, with truck doors on one side and rail/truck doors on the other, combination storage/cross-dock warehouses look more like a modified *U* with storage at either end and cross-docking areas in the centre. Goods are received through the cross-dock area and moved directly to shipping doors or, if necessary, to short term storage, which minimises the distance goods have to travel within the warehouse.

Warehouses are also providing more value added services such as packaging, assembly, consolidation, end-aisle display creation, labelling, barcoding and automatic shipment notifications. Warehouses can often provide these services to manufacturers at a lower cost than the manufacturers could manage themselves. For many public warehouses, these services comprise as much as 50 per cent of their activities.

With more and more companies eliminating inventory, warehouses are performing fewer storage functions. Instead, they are growing adept at keeping products moving quickly and accurately. This requires sophisticated computer information systems (and computer literate warehouse employees) to minimise storage costs and time while maximising quality service to warehouse customers. The best warehouses are therefore re-inventing their role as supply chain members by becoming expertly managed "flow through" centres.

SOURCE: Lisa H. Harrington, "Taking Stock of Warehousing", *Inbound Logistics*, July 1995, pp. 24–28. *Photo:* Courtesy of John Zoine/Uniphoto.

This chapter addresses wholesalers' and distributors' activities within a marketing channel, plus the importance of physical distribution management. Wholesaling is viewed here as *all* exchanges among organisations and individuals in marketing channels, except transactions with ultimate consumers. The focus is on (1) merchant wholesalers and distributors, (2) agents and brokers, and (3) manufacturers' own branches and offices—the "middlemen" in many marketing channels. This chapter examines the importance of wholesalers and their functions, noting the services they render to producers and retailers alike; it then classifies various types of wholesalers and facilitating agencies. Changing patterns in wholesaling are explored. The chapter then turns to physical distribution, its concepts, objectives and techniques. Order processing, materials handling, warehousing, inventory management and transportation are discussed. As explained in the chapter opener, technology plays an increasingly significant role in distribution. Physical distribution is essential to customer satisfaction and the exchange process at the heart of marketing.

The Nature and Importance of Wholesaling

Wholesaling Intermediaries' activity in the marketing channel between producers and business-to-business customers to facilitate the exchange—buying and selling—of goods

Wholesaling comprises all transactions in which the purchaser intends to use the product for re-sale, for making other products or for general business operations. It does not include exchanges with ultimate consumers. Wholesaling establishments are engaged primarily in selling products directly to industrial, reseller (e.g. retailers), government and institutional users. This is a broader definition than that applied by the retail trade for cash and carry suppliers. The term **wholesaling** is used in its broadest sense: intermediaries' activity in the marketing channel between producers and business-to-business customers to facilitate the exchange—buying and selling—of goods.

379

A **wholesaler** is an individual or business engaged in facilitating and expediting exchanges that are primarily wholesale transactions. Only occasionally does a wholesaler engage in retail transactions, which are sales to ultimate consumers.

The Activities of Wholesalers

In the United States and in Europe more than 50 per cent of all products are exchanged, or their exchange is negotiated, through wholesaling institutions. Owing to the strength of large, national retailers, in the UK wholesaling is not as important in consumer markets. There are also far fewer wholesalers. For example, just 27 wholesale companies and buying groups account for 85 per cent of the grocery wholesale market. In Scandinavia, Iberia and much of eastern Europe, wholesaling companies (or buying groups) account for the bulk of exchanges. Of course, it is important to remember that the distribution of all goods requires wholesaling activities, whether or not a wholesaling institution is involved. Table 13.1 lists the major activities wholesalers perform. The activities are not mutually exclusive; individual wholesalers may perform more or fewer activities than Table 13.1 shows. Wholesalers provide marketing activities for organisations above and below them in the marketing channel.

Services for Producers Producers, above wholesalers in the marketing channel, have a distinct advantage when they use wholesalers. Wholesalers perform specialised accumulation and

Table 13.1 Major wholesaling activities

Activity	Description
Wholesale management	Planning, organising, staffing and controlling wholesaling operations
Negotiating with suppliers	Serving as the purchasing agent for customers by negotiating supplies
Promotion	Providing a salesforce, advertising, sales promotion, publicity and other promotional mix activity
Warehousing and product handling	Receiving, storing and stockkeeping, order processing, packaging, shipping outgoing orders and materials handling
Transport	Arranging and making local and long distance shipments
Inventory control and data processing	Controlling physical inventory, bookkeeping, recording transactions, keeping records for financial analysis
Security	Safeguarding merchandise
Pricing	Developing prices and providing price quotations
Financing and budgeting	Extending credit, borrowing, making capital investments and forecasting cash flow
Management and marketing assistance to clients	Supplying information about markets and products and providing advisory services to assist customers in their sales efforts

Part IV   Place (Distribution and Channel) Decisions

allocation functions for a number of products, thus allowing producers to concentrate on developing and manufacturing products that match consumers' wants.

Wholesalers provide services to producers as well. By selling a manufacturer's products to retailers and other customers and by initiating sales contacts with the manufacturer, wholesalers serve as an extension of the producer's salesforce. Wholesalers also provide four forms of financial assistance: (1) they often pay the costs of transporting goods; (2) they reduce a producer's warehousing expenses and inventory investment by holding goods in inventory; (3) they extend credit and assume the losses from buyers who turn out to be poor credit risks; and (4) when they buy a producer's entire output and pay promptly or in cash, they are a source of working capital. In addition, wholesalers are conduits for information within the marketing channel, keeping manufacturers up to date on market developments and passing along the manufacturers' promotional plans to other middlemen in the channel.

Ideally, many producers would like more direct interaction with retailers, as close contact with major retail chains may lead to greater shelf-space allocation and higher margins for a producer's goods, there being no middlemen to take a cut. Wholesalers, however, usually have closer contact with retailers because of their strategic position in the marketing channel. Besides, even though a producer's own salesforce is probably more effective in its selling efforts, the costs of maintaining a salesforce and performing the activities normally done by wholesalers are usually higher than the benefits received from better selling. Wholesalers can also spread their costs over many more products than most producers, resulting in lower costs per product unit. For these reasons, many producers have chosen to control promotion and influence the pricing of products and have shifted transport, warehousing and financing functions to wholesalers. It must be remembered that the close relationship in the UK between manufacturers and the large retail groups is not typical of much of Europe where wholesalers tend to act as the manufacturer-retailer interface.

Services for Retailers
Wholesalers help their retailer customers select inventory. In industries where obtaining supplies is important, skilled buying is essential. A wholesaler that buys is a specialist in understanding market conditions and an expert at negotiating final purchases. For example, based on its understanding of local customer needs and market conditions, a building supply wholesaler purchases inventory ahead of season so that it can provide its retail customers with the building supplies they want when they want them.[1] A retailer's buyer can thus avoid the responsibility of looking for and co-ordinating supply sources. Moreover, if the wholesaler makes purchases for several different buyers, expenses can be shared by all customers. A manufacturer's salespeople can offer retailers only a few products at a time, but independent wholesalers have a wide range of products always available, often from a variety of producers.

By buying in large quantities and delivering to customers in smaller lots, a wholesaler can perform physical distribution activities—such as transport, materials handling, stock planning, communication and warehousing—more efficiently and can provide more service than a producer or retailer would be able to do with its own physical distribution system. Furthermore, wholesalers can provide quick and frequent delivery even when demand fluctuates. They are experienced in providing fast delivery at low cost, thus allowing the producer and the wholesalers' customers to avoid risks associated with holding large product inventories.[2]

Because they carry products for many customers, wholesalers can maintain a wide product line at a relatively low cost. Often wholesalers can perform storage and warehousing activities more efficiently, permitting retailers to concentrate on other marketing activities. When wholesalers provide storage and warehousing, they generally take on the ownership function as well, an arrangement that frees retailers' and producers' capital for other purposes.

Wholesalers are very important in reaching global markets. Approximately 85 per cent of all prescription drugs sold in Europe go through wholesalers that are within national borders. In the future, it is anticipated that more wholesalers will operate across borders, particularly as changing EU regulations and the movement towards European monetary union reduce EU restrictions.[3]

Classifying Wholesalers

Many types of wholesalers meet the different needs of producers and retailers. In addition, new institutions and establishments develop in response to producers and retail organisations that want to take over wholesaling functions. Wholesalers adjust their activities as the contours of the marketing environment change.

Wholesalers are classified along several dimensions. Whether a wholesaler is owned by the producer influences how it is classified. Wholesalers are also grouped according to whether they take title to (actually own) the products they handle. The range of services provided is another criterion used for classification. Finally, wholesalers are classified according to the breadth and depth of their product lines. Using these dimensions, this section discusses three general categories, or types, of wholesaling establishments: (1) merchant wholesalers, (2) agents and brokers, and (3) manufacturers' sales branches and offices. Remember that the term *wholesaling* is used here in its broader context: intermediaries' activity in the marketing channel between producers and business-to-business customers.

Merchant Wholesalers

Merchant wholesalers Wholesalers that take title to goods and assume the risks associated with ownership

Merchant wholesalers (see Figure 13.1) take title to goods and assume the risks associated with ownership. They are independently owned businesses, buying and re-selling products to industrial or retailer customers. Some are involved with packaging and developing their own label brands for their retailer customers. Merchant wholesalers account for over half of all wholesale revenues.[4] Industrial product merchant wholesalers tend to be better established and earn higher profits than consumer goods wholesalers and are likely to have selective distribution arrangements with manufacturers. These wholesalers enable producers to service customers if they have inadequate selling resources to sell directly. Wholesalers provide the producer with market coverage, making sales contacts, storing stock, handling orders, collecting marketing intelligence and providing customer service.[5] Merchant wholesalers are referred to by various names: wholesaler, jobber, distributor, assembler, exporter and importer. They fall into two categories: full service or limited service.

Full service wholesalers Middlemen who offer the widest possible range of wholesaling functions

Full Service Merchant Wholesalers Full service wholesalers are middlemen who offer the widest possible range of wholesaling functions. Their business-to-business customers rely on them for product availability, suitable assortments, bulk breaking of larger quantities into smaller orders, financial assistance and

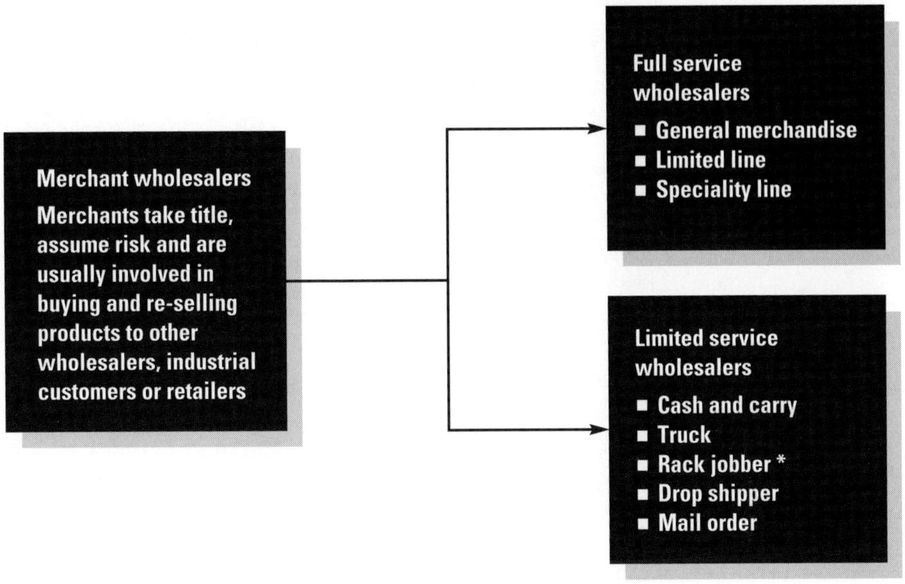

Figure 13.1 Types of merchant wholesalers. *Rack jobbers, in many cases, provide such a large number of services that they can be classified as full service, speciality line wholesalers.

Merchant wholesalers
Merchants take title, assume risk and are usually involved in buying and re-selling products to other wholesalers, industrial customers or retailers

Full service wholesalers
- General merchandise
- Limited line
- Speciality line

Limited service wholesalers
- Cash and carry
- Truck
- Rack jobber *
- Drop shipper
- Mail order

Limited service wholesalers
Middlemen who provide only some marketing services and specialise in a few functions

General merchandise wholesalers
Middlemen who carry a wide product mix but offer limited depth within the product lines

Distributors Companies that buy and sell on their own account but tend to deal in the goods of only certain specified manufacturers

Limited line wholesalers
Wholesalers that carry only a few product lines but offer an extensive assortment of products within those lines

Speciality line wholesalers
Middlemen who carry the narrowest range of products, usually a single product line or a few items within a product line

Rack jobbers Speciality line wholesalers that own and maintain their own display racks in supermarkets and chemists

credit lines, technical advice and after sales service. Full service wholesalers often provide their immediate customers with marketing support. Grocery wholesalers help smaller retailers with store design and layout, site selection, personnel training, financing, merchandising, advertising, coupon redemption and scanning. Gross margins are high, but so are operating expenses.

Limited Service Merchant Wholesalers Limited service wholesalers provide only some marketing services and specialise in few functions. The other functions are provided by producers, other middlemen or even by customers. Limited service merchant wholesalers take title to merchandise, but often do not deliver the merchandise, grant credit, provide marketing intelligence, carry stocks or plan ahead for customers' future needs. They earn smaller profit margins than full service merchant wholesalers. Relatively few in number, these wholesalers are important for speciality foods, perishable items, construction supplies and coal.

Table 13.2 summarises the different categories of full service and limited service merchant wholesalers: **general merchandise wholesalers**, including **distributors, limited line wholesalers, speciality line wholesalers**, including **rack jobbers; cash and carry wholesalers; truck wholesalers; drop shippers;** and **mail order wholesalers.**

Agents and Brokers

Functional middlemen
Intermediaries who perform a limited number of marketing activities in exchange for a commission

Agents Middlemen who represent buyers or sellers on a permanent basis

Brokers Middlemen employed temporarily by either buyers or sellers

Agents and brokers (see Figure 13.2) negotiate purchases and expedite sales but do not take title to products. They are **functional middlemen,** intermediaries who perform a limited number of marketing activities in exchange for a commission, which is generally based on the products' selling price. **Agents** are middlemen who represent buyers or sellers on a permanent basis. **Brokers** are usually middlemen whom either buyers or sellers employ temporarily.

Although agents and brokers perform even fewer functions than limited service wholesalers, they are usually specialists in particular products or types of customer and can provide valuable sales expertise. They know their markets well and often form long lasting associations with customers. Agents and brokers enable manufacturers to expand sales when resources are limited, to benefit from

Categories of Full Service Merchant Wholesalers

1. General Merchandise Wholesalers

Middlemen who carry a wide product mix but offer limited depth within product lines. Medicines, hardware, non-perishable foods, cosmetics, detergents, tobacco. Develop strong, mutually beneficial relationships with local retail stores, who often buy all their needs from these wholesalers.

For industrial customers these wholesalers provide all supplies and accessories and are often called *industrial distributors* or *mill supply houses*. **Distributors** are companies which buy and sell on their own account but tend to deal in the goods of only certain specified manufacturers.

2. Limited Line Wholesalers

Wholesalers that carry only a few product lines, such as groceries, lighting fixtures, drilling equipment, construction equipment, but offer an extensive assortment of products within these lines. They provide similar services to general merchandise wholesalers.

In industrial markets they serve large geographic areas and provide technical expertise. In consumer goods markets, they often supply single or limited line retailers. Some computer limited line wholesalers provide customers with the products of only four or five manufacturers, but for only a limited number of their lines.

3. Speciality Line Wholesalers

These middlemen carry the narrowest range of products, often only a single product line or a few items within a product line. Shellfish, fruit or cheese wholesalers are speciality line wholesalers.

Categories of Limited Service Merchant Wholesalers

1. Cash and Carry Wholesalers

Their customers are retailers or small industrial businesses who provide their own transport and collect from wholesale depots. Some full service wholesalers also set up cash and carry depots in order to reduce their operating costs and boost margins when supplying smaller retailer or industrial customers.

Cash and carry middlemen generally handle a limited line of products with a high turnover rate, such as groceries, building materials, electrical supplies, office supplies. For example, Booker has a network of cash and carry warehouse depots stocking fresh and frozen foods, cigarettes, wines and spirits, meats and provisions. Selling only to the trade, Booker offers bulk discounts to hotels, restaurants, the catering industry and local small shops.

Cash and carry operators have little or no expenditures for outside sales staff, marketing, research, promotion, credit or delivery. Their business-to-business customers benefit from lower prices and immediate access to products.

2. Truck Wholesalers

These wholesalers, sometimes called *truck jobbers*, transport a limited line of products directly to customers for on-the-spot inspection and selection. Often small operators who own and drive their own trucks or vans, they tend to have regular routes, calling on retailers and businesses to determine their needs. They may carry items, such as perishables, which other wholesalers do not stock. Meat, service station supplies and tobacco lines are often carried by truck jobbers.

Truck jobbers sell, promote and transport goods, but tend to be classified as limited service merchant wholesalers because they do not provide credit lines. Low volume sales and relatively high levels of customer service result in high operating costs. In eastern and southern Europe, truck jobbers are common marketing channel intermediaries.

3. Drop Shippers

These intermediaries, also known as *desk jobbers*, take title to goods and negotiate sales, but never take actual possession of products. They forward orders from retailers, industrial buyers or other wholesalers to manufacturers and arrange for large shipments of items to be delivered directly from producers to customers. The drop shipper assumes

(Continued)

Table 13.2 Types of full and limited service merchant wholesalers

Table 13.2 Types of full and limited service merchant wholesalers (cont.)

Categories of Full Service Merchant Wholesalers	Categories of Limited Service Merchant Wholesalers
They understand the particular requirements of the ultimate buyer and offer their customers detailed product knowledge and depth of choice. To assist retailers, they may set up displays and arrange merchandise. In industrial markets, they are often better placed than the manufacturer to offer customers technical advice and service. *Rack jobbers* are speciality line wholesalers who own and maintain their display racks in supermarkets and pharmacies. They specialise in non-food items, notably branded, widely advertised products sold on a self-service basis, which retailers prefer not to order or stock themselves because of inconvenience or risk. Health and beauty aids, toys, books, magazines, videos and CDs, hardware, housewares and stationery are typical products handled by rack jobbers. They send out delivery personnel who set up displays, mark merchandise, stock shelves and keep billing records. The retailer customer only has to provide the space. Most rack jobbers operate on a pay and display basis, taking back any unsold stock from the retailer.	responsibility for products during the entire transaction, including the costs of any unsold goods. Drop shippers are involved most commonly in the large volume purchases of bulky goods such as coal, coke, oil, chemicals, timber and building materials. Normally sold in wagon loads, these products are expensive to handle and ship relative to their unit value, so it is sensible to minimise unloading. One facet of drop shipping is its use by the large supermarket retailers, direct from manufacturers to the larger supermarket stores. These large supermarkets can each sell an entire lorry load of certain produce. Drop shippers incur no stockholding costs and provide only minimal customer assistance, leading to low operating costs which can be passed on to customers. They do provide planning, credit and personal selling services. **4. Mail Order Wholesalers** These wholesalers use catalogues instead of salesforces to sell to retail, institutional and industrial buyers. Customers use telecommunications, the Internet or post to send orders which are often despatched through courier companies or the postal service. This enables customers in remote, inaccessible areas to be serviced. As explained in Chapters 14 and 17, mail order in general is growing, and is particularly important for cosmetics, speciality foods, hardware, sporting goods, business and office supplies, car parts, clothing and music. Payment is usually expected up-front by cash or credit card, but discounts may be offered for bulk orders. Mail order wholesalers hold stocks but provide little other service.

SOURCES: Louis W. Stern, Barton A. Weitz, "The revolution in distribution: challenges and opportunities", (Special Issue: The Revolution in Retailing), *Long Range Planning*, December 1997, vol. 30, no. 6, p. 823(7); Leonard J. Kistner, C. Anthony Di Benedetto, Sriraman Bhoovaraghavan, "An integrated approach to the development of channel strategy", *Industrial Marketing Management*, October 1994, vol. 23, no. 4, p. 315(8); Elizabeth Jane Moore, "Grocery distribution in the UK: recent changes and future prospects", *International Journal of Retail & Distribution Management*, 19 July 1991, pp. 18–24; "Drop-shipping grows to save depot costs", *Supermarket News*, 1 April 1985, pp. 1, 17.

Figure 13.2 Types of agents and brokers

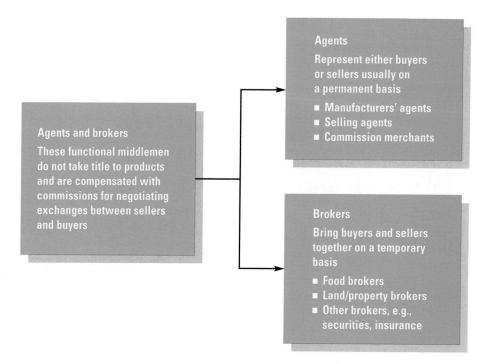

Agents and brokers
These functional middlemen do not take title to products and are compensated with commissions for negotiating exchanges between sellers and buyers

Agents
Represent either buyers or sellers usually on a permanent basis
- Manufacturers' agents
- Selling agents
- Commission merchants

Brokers
Bring buyers and sellers together on a temporary basis
- Food brokers
- Land/property brokers
- Other brokers, e.g., securities, insurance

Cash and carry wholesalers
Middlemen whose customers will pay cash and furnish transport

Truck wholesalers Limited service wholesalers that transport products directly to customers for inspection and selection

Drop shippers Intermediaries who take title to goods and negotiate sales but never take actual possession of products

Mail order wholesalers Wholesalers that use catalogues instead of sales forces to sell products to retail, industrial and institutional buyers

Manufacturers' agents
Independent middlemen or distributors who represent two or more sellers and usually offer customers complete product lines

the services of a trained salesforce and to hold personal selling costs down. However, despite the advantages they offer, agents and brokers face increased competition from merchant wholesalers, manufacturers' sales branches and offices, and direct sales efforts, including the growing use of the Internet.

This section concentrates on three types of agents: manufacturers' agents, selling agents and commission merchants, as well as examining the brokers' role in bringing about exchanges between buyers and sellers. Table 13.3 summarises services provided by wholesalers including limited service merchant wholesalers, agents and brokers.

Agents Manufacturers' agents—who account for over half of all agent wholesalers—are independent middlemen or distributors who represent two or more sellers and usually offer customers complete product lines. They sell and take orders year round, much as a manufacturer's sales office does. Restricted to a particular territory, a manufacturers' agent handles non-competing and complementary products. The relationship between the agent and each manufacturer is governed by written agreements explicitly outlining territories, selling price, order handling and terms of sale relating to delivery, service and warranties. Manufacturers' agents are commonly used in the sale of clothing and accessories, machinery and equipment, iron, steel, furniture, automotive products, electrical goods and certain food items.

Although most manufacturers' agents run small enterprises, their employees are professional, highly skilled salespeople. The agents' major advantages, in fact, are their wide range of contacts and strong customer relationships. These intermediaries help large producers minimise the costs of developing new sales territories and adjust sales strategies for different products in different locations. Agents are also useful to small producers who cannot afford outside salesforces of their own, because they incur no costs until the agents have actually sold some-

a. Various services provided by limited service merchant wholesalers

	Cash and Carry	Truck Wholesaler[a]	Drop Shipper[b]	Mail Order
Physical possession of merchandise	Yes	Yes	No	Yes
Personal sales calls on customers	No	Yes	No	No
Information about market conditions	No	Yes	Yes	Yes
Advice to customers	No	Yes	Yes	No
Stocking and maintenance of merchandise in customers' stores	No	Yes	No	No
Credit to customers	No	No	Yes	Some
Delivery of merchandise to customers	No	Yes	No	No

b. Various services agents and brokers provide

	Brokers	Manufacturers' Agents	Selling Agents	Commission Merchants
Physical possession of merchandise	No	Some	No	Yes
Long term relationship with buyers or sellers	No	Yes	Yes	Yes
Representation of competing product lines	Yes	No	No	Yes
Limited geographic territory	No	Yes	No	No
Credit to customers	No	No	Yes	Some
Delivery of merchandise to customers	No	Some	Yes	Yes

[a]Also called truck jobber.
[b]Also called desk jobber.

Table 13.3 Services provided by wholesalers

thing. By concentrating on a limited number of products, agents can mount an aggressive sales effort that would be impossible with any other distribution method except producer owned sales branches and offices. In addition, agents are able to spread operating expenses among non-competing products and thus offer each manufacturer lower prices for services rendered.

The chief disadvantage of using agents is the higher commission rate (usually 10 to 15 per cent) they charge for new product sales. When sales of a new product begin to build, total selling costs go up, and producers sometimes transfer the selling function to in-house sales representatives. For this reason, agents try to avoid depending on a single product line; most work for more than one manufacturer.

Manufacturers' agents have little or no control over producers' pricing and marketing policies. They do occasionally store and transport products, assist with planning and provide promotional support. Some agents help retailers advertise and maintain a service support organisation. The more services offered, the higher the agents' commission.

Selling agents market either all of a specified product line or a manufacturer's entire output. They perform every wholesaling activity except taking title to products. Selling agents usually assume the sales function for several producers at a time and are often used in place of a marketing department. In contrast to other agent wholesalers, selling agents generally have no territorial limits and

Selling agents Agents who market either all of a specified product line or a manufacturer's entire output

have complete authority over prices, promotion and distribution. They play a key role in the advertising, marketing research and credit policies of the sellers they represent, at times even advising on product development and packaging.

Selling agents, who account for about 1 per cent of the wholesale trade, are used most often by small producers or by manufacturers who find it difficult to maintain a marketing department because of seasonal production or other factors. A producer having financial problems may also engage a selling agent. By so doing, the producer relinquishes some control of the business but may gain working capital by avoiding immediate marketing costs.

To avoid conflicts of interest, selling agents represent non-competing product lines. The agents play an important part in the distribution of textiles, and they also sometimes handle canned foods, household furnishings, clothing, timber and metal products. In these industries, competitive pressures increase the importance of marketing relative to production, and the selling agent is a source of essential marketing and financial expertise.

Commission merchants are agents who receive goods on consignment from local sellers and negotiate sales in large central markets. Most often found in agricultural marketing, commission merchants take possession of commodities in lorry loads, arrange for any necessary grading or storage and transport the commodities to auction or markets where they are sold. When sales have been completed, an agent deducts a commission plus the expense of making the sale and then turns over the profits to the producer.

Sometimes called factor merchants, these agents may have broad powers regarding prices and terms of sale, and they specialise in obtaining the best price possible under market conditions. Commission merchants offer planning assistance and sometimes extend credit, but they do not usually provide promotional support. Because commission merchants deal in large volumes, their per unit costs are usually low. Their services are most useful to small producers who must get products to buyers but choose not to field a salesforce or accompany the goods to market themselves. In addition to farm products, commission merchants may handle textiles, art, furniture or seafood products. Businesses—including farms—that use commission merchants have little control over pricing, although the seller can specify a minimum price. Generally, the seller is able to supervise the agent's actions through a check of the commodity prices published regularly in newspapers. Large producers, however, need to maintain closer contact with the market and so have limited need for commission merchants.

Brokers Brokers seek out buyers or sellers and help negotiate exchanges. In other words, brokers' primary purpose is to bring buyers and sellers together. Thus brokers perform fewer functions than other intermediaries. They are not involved in financing or physical possession, have no authority to set prices and assume almost no risks. Instead, they offer their customers specialised knowledge of a particular commodity and a network of established contacts.

Brokers are especially useful to sellers of certain types of products who market those products only occasionally. Sellers of used machinery, seasonal food products, financial securities and land/property may not know of potential buyers. A broker can furnish this information. The party who engages the broker's services—usually the seller—pays the broker's commission when the transaction is completed. Many consumers these days deal with insurance brokers when insuring a car or house contents, or with a mortgage broker when buying a house or moving. It is likely that energy brokers will set up to market gas and electricity supplies in the recently deregulated marketplace for utilities.

Commission merchants Agents who receive goods on consignment from local sellers and negotiate sales in large central markets

Food brokers Intermediaries who sell food and general merchandise items to retailer owned and merchant wholesalers, grocery chains, industrial buyers and food processors.

Food brokers—the most common type of broker—are intermediaries who sell food and general merchandise items to retailer owned and merchant wholesalers, grocery chains, industrial buyers and food processors. Food brokers enable buyers and sellers to adjust to fluctuating market conditions. They also aid in grading, negotiating and inspecting foods, and in some cases they store and deliver products. Because of the seasonal nature of food production, the association between broker and producer is temporary—though many mutually beneficial broker-producer relationships are resumed year after year. Because food brokers provide a range of services on a somewhat permanent basis and in specific geographic territories, they can more accurately be described as manufacturers' agents.

Manufacturers' Sales Branches and Offices

Sometimes called manufacturers' wholesalers, manufacturers' sales branches and offices resemble merchant wholesalers' operations. These producer owned middlemen account for about 9 per cent of wholesale establishments and generate approximately one-third (31 per cent) of all wholesale sales.[6]

Sales branches Manufacturer owned middlemen selling products and providing support services to the manufacturer's salesforce, especially in locations where large customers are concentrated and demand is high

Sales branches are manufacturer owned middlemen selling products and providing support services to the manufacturer's salesforce, especially in locations where large customers are concentrated and demand is high. They offer credit, deliver goods, give promotional assistance and furnish other services. In many cases, they carry inventory, although this practice often duplicates the functions of other channel members and is now declining. Customers include retailers, industrial buyers and other wholesalers. Branch operations are common in the electrical supplies, plumbing, timber and car parts industries.

Sales offices Manufacturer owned operations that provide support services normally associated with agents

Sales offices are manufacturer owned operations that provide support services which are normally associated with agents. Like sales branches, they are located away from manufacturing plants, but unlike branches, they carry no inventory. A manufacturer's sales offices or branches may sell products that enhance the manufacturer's own product line. For example, Hiram Walker, a distiller, imports wine from Spain to increase the number of products that its sales offices can offer wholesalers. Most large manufacturers have their own networks of sales branches and sales offices.

Manufacturers may set up sales branches or sales offices so that they can reach customers more effectively by performing wholesaling functions themselves. Daewoo opted for this approach as detailed in Marketing Insight 13.1. A manufacturer may also set up these branches or offices when required specialised wholesaling services are not available through existing middlemen. In some situations, however, a manufacturer may bypass its wholesaling organisation entirely: for example, in the case of Daewoo's showrooms or if the producer decides to serve large retailer customers directly. One major distiller bottles own label spirits for a UK grocery chain and separates this operation completely from the company's sales office, which serves other retailers.

Facilitating Agencies

Facilitating agencies Organisations such as transport companies, insurance companies, advertising agencies, marketing research agencies and financial institutions that perform activities that enhance channel functions

The total marketing channel is more than a chain linking the producer, intermediary and buyer. **Facilitating agencies**—transport companies, insurance companies, advertising agencies, marketing research agencies and financial institutions—may perform activities that enhance channel functions. Note, however, that any of the functions these facilitating agencies perform may be taken over by the regular marketing intermediaries in the marketing channel.

The basic difference between channel members and facilitating agencies is that channel members perform the negotiating functions (buying, selling and taking title), whereas facilitating agencies do not: they perform only the various tasks that are detailed below.[7] In other words, facilitating agencies assist in the operation of the channel, but they do not sell products. The channel manager may view the facilitating agency as a sub-contractor to which various distribution tasks can be farmed out according to the principle of specialisation and division of labour.[8]

Channel members (producers, wholesalers, distributors or retailers) may rely on facilitating agencies because they believe that these independent businesses will perform various activities more efficiently and more effectively than they themselves could. Facilitating agencies are functional specialists that perform special tasks for channel members without getting involved in directing or controlling channel decisions. Public warehouses, finance companies, transport companies, and trade shows and trade markets are facilitating agencies that expedite the flow of products through marketing channels.

Public Warehouses

Public warehouses Storage facilities available for a fee

Public warehouses are storage facilities available for a fee. Producers, wholesalers and retailers may rent space in a warehouse instead of constructing their own facilities or using a merchant wholesaler's storage services. Many warehouses also order, deliver, collect accounts and maintain display rooms where potential buyers can inspect products.

To use goods as collateral for a loan, a channel member may place products in a bonded warehouse. If it is too impractical or expensive to transfer goods physically, the channel member may arrange for a public warehouser to verify that goods are in the channel member's own facilities and then issue receipts for lenders.[9] Under this arrangement, the channel member retains possession of the products but the warehouser has control. Many field public warehousers know where their clients can borrow working capital and are sometimes able to arrange low cost loans.

Finance Companies

Wholesalers and retailers may be able to obtain financing by transferring ownership of products to a sales finance company or bank while retaining physical possession of the goods. Often called "floor planning", this form of financing enables wholesalers and retailers—especially car and electrical appliance dealers—to offer a greater selection of products for customers and thus increase sales. Loans may be due immediately upon sale, so products financed this way are usually well known, sell relatively easily and present little risk.

Other financing functions are performed by factors—organisations that provide clients with working capital by buying their accounts receivable or by lending money, using the accounts receivable as collateral. Most factors minimise their own risks by specialising in particular industries, in order to better evaluate individual channel members within those industries. Factors usually lend money for a longer time than banks. They may help clients improve their credit and collection policies and may also provide management expertise.

Transport Companies

Rail, road, air and other carriers are facilitating agencies that help manufacturers and retailers transport products. Each form of transport has its own advantages. Railways ship large volumes of bulky goods at low cost; in fact, outside the UK, a "unit train" is the cheapest form of over-land transport for ore, grain or other commodities. Air transport is relatively expensive but is often preferred for shipping high value or perishable goods. Trucks, which usually carry short haul, high

Daewoo's Innovative Distribution

When Korean Daewoo entered the European car market, it was an unknown brand. The company makes everything from fork lift trucks to electrical appliances, aeroplanes to earthmovers, but it is for its competitively priced family cars that Daewoo is now best known. In its first six months of operation in the UK it sold an incredible 14,000 cars. With South Korea now ranked the sixth largest producer of cars in the world, but with slow domestic sales, such a successful launch into Europe should come as no surprise. The company has established sales operations in most of northern Europe and bought into Austrian and Polish manufacturers in order to capitalise on market opportunities in eastern Europe.

The launch marketing blitz itself was innovative and inspired. The company's marketing research revealed all the aspects of car buying that consumers mistrust or despise: dealers on commission, hard-sell aggressive sales personnel, over exaggerated promotional campaigns and poor after service. The promotional executions used the following themes to explain how Daewoo is different: good value, reliable cars with ABS brakes, door impact protection and power steering, non-commission sales advisers, three year warranties, courtesy cars or pick up and collection for services, AA road cover, no-fuss guarantees. More important, in a market known for its hype, all these features have been shown to be true.

Daewoo has also managed to differentiate itself and to be innovative in its choice of distribution. Most car manufacturers opt for a network of franchised dealerships: independent companies that operate a particular manufacturer's franchise. Such franchises are often notoriously over hungry for business: sales staff, paid on commission, traditionally pounce on customers as they enter showrooms, and they have poor reputations for looking after customers who have their cars serviced there after making a purchase.

Daewoo avoided this traditional distribution channel. Instead it owns its own dealerships and sells direct. These are genuinely places for showing rather than selling cars. Personnel are sales advisers earning full salaries rather than commissions on hard-fought sales, and they are trained to respond to queries with helpful information rather than "foot-in-the-door" sales tactics. The showrooms have crèches and children's play areas, plus café facilities. Cars are serviced not at the same location, but by carefully trained technicians at Halfords, the do-it-yourself out-of-town service centres. The innovative choice of channel to market is intended to take the pressure off consumers as they make what is generally their hardest and most expensive purchasing decision after buying a house.

SOURCES: *What Car?*, February 1996, p. 27; Andy Fry, "Channels of communication", *Marketing*, 5 October 1995, pp. III–V; Tony Taylor, "Campaign of the week: Daewoo", *Marketing*, 3 August 1995, p. 8; Michael Newman, "Driving for exports", *Far Eastern Economic Review*, 158 (25), 1995, pp. 54–55; Neil Merrick, "Putting pushy salespeople out of commission", *People Management*, 1 (9) 1995, pp. 10–11, *What Car?*, March 1999; Daewoo, 1999.

value goods, now carry more and more products because factories are moving closer to their markets. As a result of technological advances, pipelines now transport powdered solids and fluidised solid materials, as well as petroleum and natural gas.

Transport companies sometimes take over the functions of other middlemen. Because of the ease and speed of using air transport for certain types of products, parcel express companies (see Figure 13.3) can eliminate the need for their clients to maintain large stocks and branch warehouses. In other cases, freight forwarders perform accumulation functions by combining less than full shipments into full loads and passing on the savings to customers—perhaps charging a wagon rate rather than a less than wagon rate.

Trade Shows and Trade Markets   Trade shows and trade markets enable manufacturers or wholesalers to exhibit products to potential buyers and thus help the selling and buying functions.

Figure 13.3 Facilitating agencies. Parcel express companies such as DHL, FedEx, UPS and Securicor Omega Express facilitate and sometimes perform functions of marketing channel members.
SOURCE: Courtesy of Securicor.

Trade shows Industry exhibitions that offer both selling and non-selling benefits

Trade shows are industry exhibitions that offer both selling and non-selling benefits.[10] On the selling side, trade shows let vendors identify prospects; gain access to key decision-makers; disseminate facts about their products, services and personnel; and actually sell products and service current accounts through contacts at the show.[11] Trade shows also allow a company to reach potential buyers who have not been approached through regular selling efforts. In fact, research indicates that most trade show visitors have not been contacted by a sales representative of any company within the past year, and many are therefore willing to travel several hundred miles to attend trade shows to learn about new goods and services.[12] The non-selling benefits include opportunities to maintain the company image with competitors, customers and the industry; gather information about competitors' products and prices; and identify potential channel members.[13] Trade shows have a positive influence on other important marketing variables, such as maintaining or enhancing company morale, product testing and product evaluation.

Trade shows can permit direct buyer-seller interaction and may eliminate the need for agents. Companies exhibit at trade shows because of the high concentration of prospective buyers for their products. Studies show that it takes, on average, 5.1 sales calls to close an industrial sale but less than 1 sales call (0.8) to close a trade show lead. The explanation for the latter figure is that more than half of the customers who purchase a product based on information gained at a trade show order the product by mail or by phone after the show. When customers use these more impersonal methods to gather information, the need for major sales calls to provide such information is eliminated.[14]

Trade markets are relatively permanent facilities that businesses can rent to exhibit products year round. At these markets, such products as furniture, home decorating supplies, toys, clothing and gift items are sold to wholesalers and retailers. In the United States, trade markets are located in several major cities, including New York, Chicago, Dallas, High Point (North Carolina), Atlanta and Los Angeles. The Dallas Market Center, which includes the Dallas Trade Mart, the Home Furnishing Mart, the World Trade Center, the Decorative Center, Market Hall, InfoMart and the Apparel Mart, is housed in six buildings designed specifically for the convenience of professional buyers. Paris, Rotterdam and London all have centres similar in scale to Birmingham's National Exhibition Centre (NEC), which offers a 240 hectare (600 acre) site, with open display areas, plus 125,000 square metres (156,000 square yards) of covered exhibition space, hotels, parking for thousands of cars, plus rail and air links. Each year there are toy, fashion, giftware, antique trade fairs at the NEC, when trade customers can select merchandise for their next sales seasons.

Trade markets Relatively permanent facilities that businesses can rent to exhibit products year round

Changing Patterns in Wholesaling

The nature of the wholesaling industry is changing. The distinction between wholesaling activities that any business can perform and the traditional wholesaling establishment is becoming blurred. Changes in the nature of the marketing environment itself have transformed various aspects of the industry. For instance, they have brought about an increasing reliance on computer technology to expedite the ordering, delivery and handling of goods. The trend towards globalisation of world markets has resulted in other changes to which astute wholesalers are responding. The predominant shifts in wholesaling today are (1) the consolidation of the wholesaling industry and (2) the development of new types of retailers.

Wholesalers Consolidate Power

Like most major industries, the wholesale industry is experiencing a great number of mergers. Wholesaling businesses are acquiring or merging with other businesses primarily to achieve more efficiency in the face of declining profit margins.[15] Consolidation also gives larger wholesalers more pricing power over producers. Some analysts have expressed concern that wholesalers' increased price clout will increase the number of single source supply deals, which may reduce competition among wholesalers as well as retailers and producers. Nevertheless, the trend towards consolidation of wholesaling businesses appears to be continuing.[16] It is also crossing national borders, as many European companies take advantage of the EU's cross-border trade and regulatory improvements.

One of the results of the current wave of consolidation in the wholesale industry is that more wholesalers are specialising. For example, McKesson once distributed chemicals, wines and spirits but now focuses only on medicines. The new larger wholesalers can also afford to purchase and use more modern technology to manage inventories physically, provide computerised ordering services and even help manage their retail customers' operations.[17]

New Types of Wholesalers

The trend towards larger retailers (discussed in Chapter 14) will offer opportunities as well as dangers for wholesaling establishments. Opportunities will develop from the expanded product lines of these mass merchandisers. A merchant wholesaler of groceries, for instance, may want to add other low cost, high volume products sold in superstores. On the other hand, some limited function merchant wholesalers may no longer have a role to play. For example, the volume of sales may eliminate the need for rack jobbers, who usually handle slow moving products that are purchased in limited quantities. The future of independent wholesalers, agents and brokers depends on their ability to delineate markets and furnish desired services. The trend is also towards large global groups such as Makro, now present throughout Latin America, Asia and the Pacific as well as its European heartland (see Case 13.1).

The Importance of Physical Distribution

Physical distribution A set of activities—consisting of order processing, materials handling, warehousing, inventory management and transportation—used in the movement of products from producers to consumers, or end users

Wholesalers, in their various guises, are essential "players" in many businesses' marketing channels. Also important is the ability to physically deliver products to customers. **Physical distribution** is a set of activities—consisting of order processing, materials handling, warehousing, inventory management and transportation—used in the movement of products from producers to consumers, or end users. Planning an effective physical distribution system can be a significant decision in developing a marketing strategy. A company that has the right goods in the right place at the right time in the right quantity and with the right support services is able to sell more than competing businesses that fail to accomplish these goals. Physical distribution is an important variable in a marketing strategy because it can decrease costs and increase customer satisfaction. In fact, speed of delivery, along with service and dependability, is often as important to buyers as cost. In some situations, for example the emergency provision of a spare part for vital production line machinery, it may even be the single most important factor. For most companies, physical distribution accounts for about one-fifth of a product's retail price.

Physical distribution deals with physical movement and inventory holding (storing and tracking inventory or stock until it is needed) both within and among marketing channel members. Often one channel member will arrange the movement of goods for all channel members involved in exchanges. For example, a packing company ships fresh salmon and champagne (often by air) to remote markets on a routine basis. Frequently, buyers are found while the goods are in transit.

The physical distribution system is often adjusted to meet the needs of a channel member. For example, an agricultural equipment dealer who keeps a low inventory of replacement parts requires the fastest and most dependable service when parts not in stock are needed. In this case, the distribution cost may be a minor consideration when compared with service, dependability and promptness. Grocery retailers such as Aldi or Asda receive some deliveries to central and regional warehouses, whereas other deliveries from manufacturers such as Heinz or Kellogg's go directly to individual stores as required, and insisted upon, by the retail companies. Failure to deliver products to customers where, when and how customers demand is likely to lose orders, diminish customer loyalty and provide opportunities for competing suppliers, and is not going to afford a mutually satisfying relationship between supplier and customer.

Physical Distribution Objectives

Objective of physical distribution
Decreasing costs while increasing customer service

For most companies, the main **objective of physical distribution** is to decrease costs while increasing customer service.[18] In the real world, however, few distribution systems manage to achieve these goals in equal measure. The large stock inventories and rapid transport essential to high levels of customer service drive up costs. On the other hand, reduced inventories and slower, cheaper shipping methods cause customer dissatisfaction because of stock-outs or late deliveries. Physical distribution managers strive for a reasonable balance of service, costs and resources. They determine what level of customer service is acceptable yet realistic, develop a "system" outlook of calculating total distribution costs and trade higher costs at one stage of distribution for savings in another. In this section these three performance objectives are examined more closely.

Customer Service

Customer service   In terms of physical distribution: availability, promptness and quality

In varying degrees, all businesses attempt to satisfy customer needs and wants through a set of activities known collectively as **customer service.** Many companies claim that service to the customer is their top priority. These companies see service as being as important in attracting customers and building sales as the cost or quality of the companies' products.

Customers require a variety of services. At the most basic level, they need fair prices, acceptable product quality and dependable deliveries.[19] There are many facets of service as described throughout *Marketing: Concepts and Strategies*, but in the physical distribution area, availability, promptness and quality are the most important dimensions of customer service. These are the main factors that determine how satisfied customers are likely to be with a supplier's physical distribution activities.[20] Customers seeking a higher level of customer service may also want sizeable inventories, efficient order processing, availability of emergency shipments, progress reports, post-sale services, prompt replacement of defective items and warranties. Customers' inventory requirements influence the level of physical distribution service they expect. For example, customers who want to minimise inventory storage and shipping costs may require that suppliers assume the cost of maintaining inventory in the marketing channel, or the cost of premium transport.[21] Because service needs vary from customer to customer, companies must analyse—and adapt to—customer preferences. Attention to customer needs and preferences is crucial to increasing sales and obtaining repeat sales. A company's failure to provide the desired level of service may mean the loss of customers. Without customers there can be no profit.

Companies must also examine the service levels competitors offer and match those standards, at least when the costs of providing the services can be balanced by the sales generated. For example, companies may step up their efforts to identify the causes of customer complaints or institute corrective measures for billing and shipping errors. In extremely competitive businesses, such as the market for vehicle parts, businesses may concentrate on product availability. To compete effectively, manufacturers may strive for inventory levels and order processing speeds that are deemed unnecessary and too costly in other industries.[22]

Services are provided most effectively when service standards are developed and stated in terms that are specific, measurable and appropriate for the product: for example, "Guaranteed delivery within 48 hours". Standards should be communicated clearly to both customers and employees and rigorously enforced. In many cases, it is necessary to maintain a policy of minimum order size to ensure that transactions are profitable; that is, special service charges are added to orders smaller than a specified quantity. Many carrier companies operate on this basis. Many service policies also spell out delivery times and provisions for back ordering, returning goods and obtaining emergency shipments. The overall objective of any service policy should be to improve customer service just to the point beyond which increased sales would be negated by increased distribution costs.

Total Distribution Costs

Although physical distribution managers try to minimise the costs of each element in the system—order processing, materials handling, inventory, warehousing and transportation—decreasing costs in one area often raises them in another. By using a total cost approach to physical distribution, managers can view the distribution system as a whole, not as a collection of unrelated activities. The emphasis shifts from lowering the separate costs of individual functions to minimising the total cost of the entire distribution system.

The total cost approach calls for analysing the costs of all possible distribution alternatives, even those considered too impractical or expensive. Total cost analyses weigh inventory levels against warehousing expenses, materials handling costs against various modes of transport and all distribution costs against customer service standards. The costs of potential sales losses from lower performance levels are also considered. In many cases, accounting procedures and statistical methods can be used to calculate total costs. Where hundreds of combinations of distribution variables are possible, computer simulations may be helpful. In no case is a distribution system's lowest total cost the result of using a combination of the cheapest functions; instead, it is the lowest overall cost compatible with the company's stated service objectives.

Cost Trade-offs

Cost trade-offs The offsetting of higher costs in one area of the distribution system by lower costs in another area, to keep the total system cost effective

A distribution system that attempts to provide a specific level of customer service for the lowest possible total cost must use **cost trade-offs** to resolve conflicts about resource allocations. That is, higher costs in one area of the distribution system must be offset by lower costs in another area if the total system is to remain cost effective.

Trade-offs are strategic decisions to combine (and re-combine) resources for greatest cost effectiveness. When distribution managers regard the system as a network of interlocking functions, trade-offs become useful tools in a unified distribution strategy. The furniture retailer IKEA uses a system of trade-offs. To ensure that each store carries enough inventory to satisfy customers in the area, IKEA groups its retail outlets into regions, each served by a separate distribution centre. In addition, each IKEA store carries a five week back stock of inventory. Thus IKEA has chosen to trade higher inventory warehousing costs for improved customer service.[23] The remainder of the chapter focuses on order processing, materials handling, warehousing, inventory management and transportation, all of which are essential physical distribution activities.

Order Processing

Order processing The receipt and transmission of sales order information

Order processing—the first stage in a physical distribution system—is the receipt and transmission of sales order information. Although management sometimes overlooks the importance of these activities, efficient order processing facilitates product flow. Computerised order processing, used by many businesses, speeds the flow of information from customer to seller.[24] Indeed, in many industries key suppliers are linked "live" to retailers' or distributors' tills and order books. They are thus able to replenish or supply exactly in line with demand and actual sales. When carried out quickly and accurately, order processing contributes to customer satisfaction, repeat orders and increased profits.

Generally, there are three main tasks in order processing: (1) order entry, (2) order handling and (3) order delivery.[25] Order entry begins when customers or salespeople place purchase orders by mail, telephone, fax or computer. In some companies, sales service representatives receive and enter orders personally and also handle complaints, prepare progress reports and forward sales order information.[26]

The next task, order handling, involves several activities. Once an order has been entered, it is transmitted to the warehouse, where the availability of the product is verified, and to the credit department, where prices, terms and the customer's credit rating are checked. If the credit department approves the purchase, the warehouse begins to fill the order. If the requested product is not in stock, a production order is sent to the factory or the customer is offered a substitute item.

When the order has been filled and packed for shipment, the warehouse schedules pick up with an appropriate carrier. If the customer is willing to pay for express service, priority transport, such as overnight courier, is used. The customer is sent an invoice, inventory records are adjusted and the order is delivered.

Order processing can be done manually or electronically, depending on which method provides greater speed and accuracy within cost limits. Manual processing suffices for a small volume of orders and is more flexible in special situations; electronic processing is more practical for a large volume of orders and lets a company integrate order processing, production planning, inventory, accounting and transport planning into a total information system.[27] Many leading retail groups, with products from groceries to electrical goods, have their stores networked to the head office. Suppliers are also electronically linked to the retailers' head offices, so that stock can be ordered electronically.

Materials Handling

Materials handling The physical handling of products

Materials handling, or the physical handling of products, is important for efficient warehouse operations, as well as in transport from points of production to points of consumption. The characteristics of the product itself often determine how it will be handled. For example, fresh dairy produce has unique characteristics that determine how it can be moved and stored.

Materials handling procedures and techniques should increase the usable capacity of a warehouse, reduce the number of times a good is handled, improve service to customers and increase their satisfaction with the product. Packaging, loading, movement and labelling systems must be co-ordinated to maximise cost reduction and customer satisfaction.

In Chapter 9 it was noted that the protective functions of packaging are important considerations in product development. Appropriate decisions about packaging materials and methods allow for the most efficient physical handling; most companies employ packaging consultants or specialists to accomplish this important task. Materials handling equipment is used in the design of handling systems.

Unit loading Grouping one or
more boxes on a pallet or skid,
permitting movement of efficient
loads by mechanical means

Containerisation The practice of
consolidating many items into a single
large container that is sealed at its point
of origin and opened at its destination,
greatly increasing efficiency and security
in shipping

Unit loading is grouping one or more boxes on a pallet or skid; it permits movement of efficient loads by mechanical means, such as fork lifts, trucks or conveyor systems. **Containerisation** is the practice of consolidating many items into a single large container that is sealed at its point of origin and opened at its destination. The containers are usually 2.5 metres (8 feet) wide, 2.5 metres (8 feet) high, and 3, 6, 7.5 or 12 metres (10, 20, 25, or 40 feet) long. They can be conveniently stacked and sorted as units at the point of loading. Because individual items are not handled in transit, containerisation greatly increases efficiency and security in shipping.

Warehousing

Warehousing The design and
operation of facilities for storing and
moving goods

Warehousing, the design and operation of facilities for storing and moving goods, is an important physical distribution function. Warehousing provides time utility by enabling companies to compensate for dissimilar production and consumption rates. That is, when mass production creates a greater stock of goods than can be sold immediately, companies may warehouse the surplus goods until customers are ready to buy. Warehousing also helps stabilise the prices and availability of seasonal items. Following is a description of the basic functions of warehouses and the different types of warehouses available. Distribution centres, special warehouse operations designed so that goods can be moved rapidly, are also examined.

Warehousing Functions

Private warehouse A warehouse
operated by a company for shipping and
storing its own products

Public warehouses Warehouses that
rent storage space and related physical
distribution facilities to other companies
and sometimes provide distribution services such as receiving and unloading
products, inspecting, re-shipping, filling
orders, financing, displaying products and
co-ordinating shipments

Field public warehouse A warehouse established by a public warehouse
at the owner's inventory location

Bonded storage A warehousing
arrangement by which imported or
taxable products are not released until
the owners of the products have paid
customs duties, taxes or other fees

Distribution centre A large,
centralised warehouse that receives
goods from factories and suppliers,
regroups them into orders and quickly
ships them to customers

Warehousing is not limited simply to the storage of goods. When warehouses receive goods by wagon loads or lorry loads, they break the shipments down into smaller quantities for individual customers; when goods arrive in small lots, the warehouses assemble the lots into bulk loads that can be shipped out more economically.[28] Warehouses perform these basic distribution functions:

1. *Receiving goods*—The merchandise is accepted, and the warehouse assumes responsibility for it.
2. *Identifying goods*—The appropriate stockkeeping units are recorded, along with the quantity of each item received. The item may be marked with a physical code, tag or other label; or it may be identified by an item code (a code on the carrier or container) or by physical properties.
3. *Sorting goods*—The merchandise is sorted for storage in appropriate areas.
4. *Despatching goods to storage*—The merchandise is put away so that it can be retrieved when necessary.
5. *Holding goods*—The merchandise is kept in storage and properly protected until needed.
6. *Recalling and picking goods*—Items customers have ordered are efficiently retrieved from storage and prepared for the next step.
7. *Marshalling the shipment*—The items making up a single shipment are brought together and checked for completeness or explainable omissions. Order records are prepared or modified as necessary.
8. *Despatching the shipment*—The consolidated order is packaged suitably and directed to the right transport vehicle. Necessary shipping and accounting documents are prepared.[29]

Types of Warehouses

A company's choice of warehouse facilities is an important strategic consideration. By using the right warehouse, a company may be able to reduce trans-

Part IV   Place (Distribution and Channel) Decisions

portation and inventory costs or improve its service to customers; the wrong warehouse may drain company resources. For example, a company that produces processed foods must locate its warehousing close to main transport routes to facilitate delivery to supermarkets in different parts of the country. Besides deciding how many facilities to operate and where to locate them, a company must determine which type of warehouse will be most appropriate. Warehouses fall into two general categories: private and public. In many cases, a combination of private and public facilities provides the most flexible approach to warehousing. Table 13.4 summarises the basic types of warehouses: **private warehouse; public warehouses,** including **field public warehouse** and **bonded storage warehouse;** and **distribution centre.**

Inventory Management

Inventory management The development and maintenance of adequate assortments of products to meet customers' needs

Inventory management involves developing and maintaining adequate assortments of products to meet customers' needs. Because a company's investment in inventory usually represents 30 to 50 per cent of its total assets, inventory decisions have a significant impact on physical distribution costs and the level of customer service provided. When too few products are carried in inventory, the result is **stock-outs,** or shortages of products, which result in fewer sales and customers switching to alternative brands. But when too many products (or too many slow moving products) are carried, costs increase, as do the risks of product obsolescence, pilferage and damage. The objective of inventory management, therefore, is to minimise inventory costs while maintaining an adequate supply of goods. Marketing Insight 13.2 shows how staff at Benetton use high technology equipment to ensure that the company's inventory is managed efficiently.

Stock-outs Shortages of products resulting from a lack of products carried in inventory

There are three types of inventory costs. (1) *Carrying costs* are holding costs; they include expenditures for storage space and materials handling, financing, insurance, taxes and losses from spoilage of goods. (2) *Replenishment costs* are related to the purchase of merchandise. The price of goods, handling charges and expenses for order processing contribute to replenishment costs. (3) *Stock-out costs* include sales lost when demand for goods exceeds supply and the clerical and processing expenses of back ordering. A company must control all the costs of obtaining and maintaining inventory in order to achieve its profit goals. Management must therefore have a clear idea of the level of each type of cost incurred. Customers' expectations of product availability and tolerable delivery lead times will vary between target market segments.

Inventory managers deal with two issues of particular importance. They must know when to re-order and how much merchandise to order. For example, many high street banks no longer require current account customers to order new cheque books. Once a certain cheque number is reached, a new book is automatically sent to the customer. The **re-order point** is the inventory level that signals that more inventory should be ordered. Three factors determine the re-order point: (1) the expected time between the date an order is placed and the date the goods are received and made ready for re-sale to customers; (2) the rate at which a product is sold or used up; and (3) the quantity of **safety stock** on hand, or inventory needed to prevent stock-outs. The optimum level of safety stock depends on the general demand and the standard of customer service to be provided. If a business is to avoid shortages without tying up too much capital in inventory, some systematic method for determining re-order points is essential.

Re-order point The inventory level that signals the need to order more inventory

Safety stock Inventory needed to prevent stock-outs

Private Warehouses

Are operated by a company for the purpose of storing and distributing its own products. Leased or purchased when a business builds up sales to warrant a long term physical presence in a territory, they are important for businesses requiring specialised storage and handling, such as JCB or Ford for after-market parts. The large retail chains such as Aldi, Carrefour or Marks & Spencer are the biggest users of private warehouses. Private warehouses face fixed costs such as land rents, insurance, taxes, maintenance and debt expense and should only be considered if sales levels are sufficient and stable over time. They also tie up capital and resources and require expert management. Private warehouses give companies more control over the distribution of their products and may offer secondary benefits such as property appreciation.

Public Warehouses

Rent storage space and related physical distribution facilities to other companies, sometimes providing distribution services such as receiving and unloading products, inspecting, re-shipping, filling orders, financing, displaying products and co-ordinating shipments. Public warehouses are very useful to businesses (a) experiencing seasonal demand for their products, (b) with low volume storage needs, (c) needing to maintain stocks at various locations, (d) testing new markets or operations, (e) with private warehouses needing additional storage space. There are no fixed costs to the user, who only rents space as and when required. There are two specialised types of public warehouses: field and bonded.

Field Public Warehouse A warehouse established by a public warehouser at the owner's inventory location. The warehouser becomes the custodian for the products and issues a receipt which can be used as collateral for a loan by the products' producer.

Bonded Storage A warehousing arrangement under which imported or taxable products are not released until the product owners have paid customs duties, taxes or other fees. Bonded warehouses are used by some businesses to defer tax payments until products are delivered to customers.

The Distribution Centre

Receives goods from factories and suppliers, regroups them into orders and quickly ships them to customers. These large, centralised warehouses can be seen at many motorway intersections and are used by most large manufacturers. The focus is on rapid active movement rather than passive storage. One storey, large buildings adjacent to major transport arteries, they are highly automated with computer controlled robots, fork lifts and hoists collecting and moving products to loading docks. Most distribution centres are privately owned. They serve customers in regional markets or supply the company's smaller branch warehouses. The core benefit is the enhancement of customer service by ensuring product availability, full product lines and quick turnaround, with reduced costs. Factories can ship large quantities at bulk load rates, reducing transport costs. Rapid turnaround reduces stock holding costs. Some distribution centres also facilitate production by receiving and consolidating raw materials and providing final assembly for some products.

SOURCES: James C. Johnson and Donald F. Wood, *Contemporary Physical Distribution & Logistics,* 2nd edn (Tulsa, Okla.: Penn Well Publishing Company, 1982), p. 356; Carl M. Guelzo, *Introduction to Logistics Management* (Englewood Cliffs, N.J.: Prentice-Hall, 1986), p. 102.

Table 13.4 Basic types of warehouses

The inventory manager faces several trade-offs when re-ordering merchandise. Large safety stocks ensure product availability and thus improve the level of customer service; they also lower order processing costs because orders are placed less frequently. Small safety stocks, on the other hand, cause frequent re-orders and high order processing costs but reduce the overall cost of carrying inventory. Figure 13.4 illustrates two order systems involving different order

Benetton's New "Sell Direct" Policy Benefits from Its International Electronic Data Interchange System

How important can eight people be to a multinational clothing manufacturer and retailer? To Benetton, the Italian causal wear company, the eight people who run the warehouse that handles the distribution of 50 million pieces of clothing a year are extremely important. These eight people are responsible for processing 230,000 articles of clothing a day to serve 6,500 stores in 110 countries, of which 1,500 are located in Italy, 800 in the United States and 400 in the UK. Though sales in the garment industry have sagged recently, Benetton is still moving tremendous amounts of knit and cotton clothing. After their small clothing business expanded into an international fashion sensation, executives at Benetton realised that highly efficient physical distribution methods were a must.

Benetton has linked its sales agents, factory and warehouse together using an international electronic data interchange (EDI) system managed by General Electric Information Services. Suppose a student in Maastricht wants to buy a Benetton sweater identical to his older brother's. He goes to a Benetton store and searches for it, only to be disappointed when he finds that the sweater is not there. The salesperson assures him that the sweater will arrive in a month. The salesperson then calls a Benetton sales agent, who places the sweater order on a personal computer. Three times a day, this information is collected and sent to the company's mainframe system in Italy, where the computer searches inventory data to find out if the requested item is in stock. If not, an order automatically travels to a machine that cuts the materials

and immediately starts to knit the sweater. Workers put the finished sweater in a box with a barcoded label and send it to the warehouse. In the warehouse, a computer commands a robot to retrieve the sweater and any other merchandise that needs to be transported to the same store.

In the mid-1990s, Benetton surprised the rag trade (the clothing industry) by announcing that it was to launch a "direct sell" operation—home shopping via catalogues and courier delivery firms. Benetton in the UK was the first high street store based retailer to opt for direct home shopping since Next launched its *Next Directory* in 1986. Effective stock control and distribution will now be even more important for Italy's Benetton.

Through efficient management of physical distribution activities and the use of technologically advanced equipment, Benetton ensures that its products are available to consumers when and where they want them. Close attention to physical distribution activities has helped the company achieve its objectives and become a major competitor in the fashion industry. With the addition of a home shopping operation, it is essential for Benetton's logistical support to be "state-of-the-art".

SOURCES: Barbara DePompa, "More power at your fingertips", *Information Week*, 23 December 1991, p. 22; Lory Zottola, "The united systems of Benetton", *Computerworld*, 2 April 1990, p. 70; Harriet Fox, "Benetton opts for direct sell", *Marketing*, 16 March 1995, p. 5; Tom O'Sullivan and David Benady, "Unravelling of Benetton?", *Marketing Week*, 3 February 1995, pp. 21–22; Fiorenza Belussi, "The Italian job", *RDM*, Summer 1994, pp. ix–x.

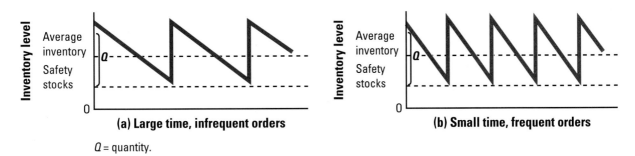

(a) Large time, infrequent orders   (b) Small time, frequent orders

Q = quantity.

Figure 13.4   Effects of order size on an inventory system

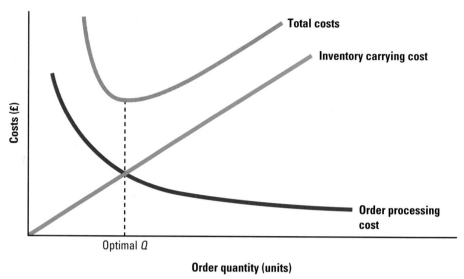

Figure 13.5 Economic order quantity (EOQ) model

Total costs

Inventory carrying cost

Costs (£)

Order processing cost

Optimal *Q*

Order quantity (units)

quantities but the same level of safety stocks. Figure 13.4(a) shows inventory levels for a given demand of infrequent orders; Figure 13.4(b) illustrates the levels needed to fill frequent orders at the same demand.

Economic order quantity (EOQ) The order size that minimises the total cost of ordering and carrying inventory

To quantify this trade-off between carrying costs and order processing costs, a model for an **economic order quantity (EOQ)** has been developed (see Figure 13.5); it specifies the order size that minimises the total cost of ordering and carrying inventory.[30] The fundamental relationships underlying the widely accepted EOQ model are the basis of many inventory control systems. Keep in mind, however, that the objective of minimum total inventory cost must be balanced against the customer service level necessary for maximum profits. Therefore, because increased costs of carrying inventory are usually associated with a higher level of customer service, the order quantity will often lie to the right of the optimal point in the figure, leading to a higher total cost for ordering and larger carrying inventory.

Fluctuations in demand, for example in times of economic recession, mean that it is not always easy to predict changing inventory levels. When management miscalculates re-order points or order quantities, inventory problems develop. Warning signs include an inventory that grows at a faster rate than sales, surplus or obsolete inventory, customer deliveries that are consistently late or lead times that are too long, inventory that represents a growing percentage of assets, and large inventory adjustments or write-offs.[31] However, there are several tools for improving inventory control. From a technical standpoint, an inventory system can be planned so that the number of products sold and the number of products in stock are determined at certain checkpoints. The control may be as simple as tearing off a code number from each product sold so that the correct sizes, colours and models can be tabulated and re-ordered. Many bookshops insert re-order slips of paper into each item of stock, which can be removed at the checkout. A sizeable amount of technologically advanced electronic equipment is available to assist with inventory management. In many larger stores, such as Tesco and Toys "R" Us, checkout terminals connected to central computer systems instantaneously up-date inventory and sales records. For continuous, automatic up-dating of inventory records, some companies use pressure sensitive circuits installed under ordinary industrial shelving to weigh inventory, convert the weight to units and display any inventory changes on a video screen or computer printout.

Various techniques have also been used successfully to improve inventory management. The just-in-time concept, widely used in Japan, calls for companies to maintain low inventory levels and purchase products and materials in small quantities, just at the moment they are needed for production. Ford, for example, sometimes receives supply deliveries as often as every two hours.[32] Just-in-time inventory management depends on a high level of co-ordination between producers and suppliers, but the technique enables companies to eliminate waste and reduce inventory costs significantly. When Polaroid implemented just-in-time techniques as part of its zero base pricing programme to reduce the overall cost of purchased materials, equipment and services, it saved an average of £15 million per year.[33]

Another inventory management technique, the 80/20 rule, holds that fast moving products should generate a higher level of customer service than slow moving products, on the theory that 20 per cent of the items account for 80 per cent of the sales. Thus an inventory manager attempts to keep an adequate supply of fast selling items and a minimal supply of the slower moving products. ABC sales: contribution analysis strives to maintain inventory levels while maximising financial returns to the business (see Figure 21.11).

Transportation

Transportation The process of moving a product from where it is made to where it is purchased and used

Transportation adds time and place utility to a product by moving it from where it is made to where it is purchased and used.[34] Because product availability and timely deliveries are so dependent on transport functions, a company's choice of transport directly affects customer service and satisfaction. A business may even build its distribution and marketing strategy around a unique transport system if the system ensures on-time deliveries that will give the business a competitive edge. This section considers the principal modes of transport, the criteria companies use to select one mode over another and several methods of co-ordinating transport services.

Transport Modes

Transport modes Methods of moving goods; these include railways, motor vehicles, inland waterways, airways and pipelines

There are five major **transport modes,** or methods of moving goods: railways, motor vehicles, inland waterways, airways and pipelines. Each mode offers unique advantages; many companies have adopted physical handling procedures that facilitate the use of two or more modes in combination. Table 13.5 summarises the core transport modes.

Criteria for Selecting Transport

Marketers select a transport mode on the basis of costs, transit time, reliability, capability, accessibility, security and traceability.[35] Table 13.6 summarises various cost and performance considerations that help determine the selection of transport modes. It is important to remember that these relationships are approximations and that the choice of a transport mode involves many trade-offs. These attributes all have a significant impact on a customer's perception of customer service levels.

Costs One consideration that helps determine transportation mode, involving comparison of alternative modes to determine whether the benefits of a more expensive mode are worth the higher costs

Costs Marketers compare alternative means of transport to determine whether the benefits from a more expensive mode are worth the higher **costs.** Air freight

Motor Vehicles

Provide the most flexible schedules and routes of all transport modes because they can go almost anywhere. Uniquely can transport goods from factory or warehouse directly to customer. Other modes, such as rail or air freight, often depend on trucks and vans to complete the journey for goods being transported. More expensive than rail and prone to bad weather disruption. Restricted in terms of weight and size of loads. Often criticised for damage and pilferage of goods in transit. In response, new technology now tracks shipments and eases loading/handling. Computerised route planning is now the norm, with companies ensuring goods are delivered efficiently.

Planning distribution routes

Area routes connect customers in concentratred areas.

Arc (circumferential) routes link customers in arcs at different distances from the distribution centre.

Radial routes link customers in radial groups to and from the distribution centre.

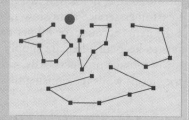 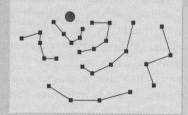 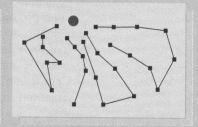

The figure above shows three types of routes which can be used, depending on vehicle capacity, order size, geographic characteristics and existence of suitable major routes. Road haulage dominates within Europe: quick, flexible and relatively cost efficient, it has overtaken rail.

Rail

Used for heavy, bulky freight that must be transported over land for long distances: minerals, sand, timber, pulp, chemicals, farm products, cars, low value manufactured goods. Efficient for transporting full wagon car loads with little handling, not for smaller quantities. Some factories and warehouses are purposively located adjacent to rail links. The opening of the Channel Tunnel has encouraged businesses to locate near the new Euro-hubs for cross-Channel rail freight. This trend may reverse the steady decline in rail freight tonnage. High fixed costs, shortages of wagons at peak times, poor track investment and increased competition from road and air hauliers have plagued European rail operators.

Inland Waterways

The cheapest method of shipping heavy, low value, non-perishable goods such as coal, grain, sand, petroleum. Considerable capacity: barges on inland rivers, canals and navigation systems can haul many times the weight of one railway wagon, but much more slowly. Require links with road and rail and can be hampered by harsh winters freezing waterways or summer droughts drying up channels. Although only of peripheral importance for freight in the UK, the inland waterways are very important in Germany and Benelux. Very fuel efficient haulage. Seen by many as an environmentally friendly transport solution. Observers believe tonnages will increase.

Air Freight

The fastest growing and most expensive form of shipping. Helped by the rapid growth in airport locations, flights and acceptance of this mode of transport. Generally deployed for perishable goods; high value, low

(Continued)

Table 13.5 Major transport modes

Table 13.5 Major transport modes (cont.)

bulk items; and products to be delivered long distances quickly, such as emergency products or replacement parts. Capacity is limited only by the size and number of aircraft. A medium-ranged jet carries about 18,000 kilos (40,000 pounds) of freight, but purpose built cargo planes can now carry up to 90,000 kilos (200,000 pounds). Most freight is carried on passenger aircraft, along with mail. Despite its expense, air freight reduces stockholding costs and in-transit losses from theft and damage. Ground transport for pick up and final delivery adds time and cost to the air freight bill.

Pipelines

The most automated of transport modes, usually belong to the shipper and carry the shipper's products, typically petroleum or chemicals. The Trans-Alaska Pipeline, owned by a consortium of oil companies such as Exxon, Mobile and BP, transports crude oil from remote drilling sites to shipping terminals on the coast. Slurry pipelines have been developed to transport pulverised coal, grain or wood chips suspended in water. Pipelines move products slowly but continuously at relatively low cost. They are reliable and reduce damage to goods in transit and theft. However, their goods suffer from evaporation shrinkage, sometimes by up to 1 per cent, and minimum quantities of 25,000 barrels are required for efficient pipeline operation. North Sea oil and gas in Scandinavia, the Netherlands and the UK depend on pipelines. Installation leaks worry environmentalists, but oil tankers leak, too.

SOURCES: Carl M. Guelzo, *Introduction to Logistics Management* (Englewood Cliffs, N.J.: Prentice-Hall, 1986), pp. 50-52; John Gattorna, *Handbook of Physical Distribution Management* (Aldershot: Gower Publishing Co. Ltd, 1983), pp. 263–266; Charles A. Taff, *Management of Physical Distribution and Transportation* (Homewood, Ill.: Irwin, 1984), p. 126.

carriers provide many benefits, such as high speed, reliability, security and traceability, but at higher costs relative to other transport modes. When speed is less important, marketers prefer lower costs.

Recently, marketers have been able to cut expenses and increase efficiency. Railways, airlines, road hauliers, barges and pipeline companies have all become more competitive and more responsive to customers' needs. Surveys reveal that in recent years transport costs per tonne and as a percentage of sales have declined, now averaging 7.5 per cent of sales. This figure varies by industry, of course: electrical machinery, textiles and instruments have transport costs of only 3 or 4 per cent of sales, whereas timber products, chemicals and food have transport costs close to 15 per cent of sales.

Table 13.6 Ranking of transport modes by selecting criteria, highest to lowest

	Costs	Transit Time	Reliability	Capability	Accessibility	Security	Traceability
Most	Air	Water	Pipeline	Water	Road	Pipeline	Air
	Pipeline	Rail	Rail	Road	Rail	Water	Road
	Rail	Pipeline	Road	Rail	Air	Rail	Rail
	Road	Road	Air	Air	Water	Air	Water
Least	Water	Air	Water	Pipeline	Pipeline	Road	Pipeline

SOURCE: Selected information adapted from J. L. Heskett, Robert Ivie and J. Nicholas Glaskowsky, *Business Logistics* (New York: Ronald Press, 1973). Reprinted by permission of John Wiley & Sons, Inc.

Transit Time Transit time is the total time a carrier has possession of goods, including the time required for pick up and delivery, handling and movement between the points of origin and destination. Closely related to transit time is frequency, or number of shipments per day. Transit time obviously affects a marketer's ability to provide service, but there are some less obvious implications as well. A shipper can take advantage of transit time to process orders for goods en route, a capability especially important for agricultural and raw materials shippers. Some railways also let shipments already in transit be re-directed, for maximum flexibility in selecting markets.

Transit time The total time a carrier has possession of goods

Reliability The total **reliability** of a transport mode is determined by the consistency of service provided. Marketers must be able to count on their carriers to deliver goods on time and in an acceptable condition. Along with transit time, reliability affects a marketer's inventory costs, which include sales lost when merchandise is not available. Unreliable transport necessitates maintaining higher inventory levels to avoid stock-outs. Reliable delivery service, on the other hand, enables customers to save money by reducing inventories; for example, if pharmacists know that suppliers can deliver drugs within hours of ordering, they can carry a smaller inventory.

Reliability The consistency of service provided

Capability Capability is the ability of a transport mode to provide the appropriate equipment and conditions for moving specific kinds of goods. For example, many products must be shipped under controlled temperature and humidity. Other products, such as liquids or gases, require special equipment or facilities for their shipment.

Capability The ability of a transport mode to provide the appropriate equipment and conditions for moving specific kinds of goods

Accessibility A carrier's **accessibility** refers to its ability to move goods over a specific route or network (rail lines, waterways or roads).

Accessibility The ability to move goods over a specific route or network

Security A transport mode's **security** is measured by the physical condition of goods upon delivery. A business does not incur costs directly when goods are lost or damaged, because the carrier is usually held liable in these cases. Nevertheless, poor service and lack of security will indirectly lead to increased costs and lower profits for the company, since damaged or lost goods are not available for immediate sale or use. In some cases, companies find it necessary to transport products using courier companies such as TNT or Omega.

Security The measure of the physical condition of goods upon delivery

Traceability Traceability is the relative ease with which a shipment can be located and transferred (or found if it is lost). Quick traceability is a convenience that some businesses value highly. Shippers have learned that the ability to trace shipments, along with prompt invoicing and processing of claims, increases customer loyalty and improves a company's image in the marketplace.[36] Courier companies now offer clients Internet tracking of goods in transit.

Traceability The relative ease with which a shipment can be located and transferred

Co-ordinating Transport Services

To take advantage of the benefits various types of carriers offer, and to compensate for their deficiencies, marketers often must combine and co-ordinate two or more modes of transport. In recent years, **intermodal transport,** as this integrated approach is sometimes called, has become easier because of new developments within the transport industry.

Several kinds of intermodal shipping are available, all combining the flexibility of road haulage with the low cost or speed of other forms of transport.

Intermodal transport The combination and co-ordination of two or more modes of transport

Containerisation facilitates intermodal transport by consolidating shipments into sealed containers for transport by piggyback (shipping that combines truck trailers and railway flatcars), fishyback (truck trailers and water carriers), and birdyback (truck trailers and air carriers). As transport costs increase, intermodal services gain in popularity. Intermodal services have been estimated to cost 25 to 40 per cent less than all-road transport in the US, where they account for about 12 to 16 per cent of total transport business.[37]

Freight forwarders Specialised agencies that co-ordinate and combine shipments from several businesses into efficient lot sizes

Specialised agencies, **freight forwarders**, provide other forms of transport co-ordination. These agencies combine shipments from several businesses into efficient lot sizes. Small loads—less than 225 kilos (500 pounds)—are much more expensive to ship than full lorry loads and frequently must be consolidated. The freight forwarder takes small loads from various shippers, buys transport space from carriers and arranges for the goods to be delivered to their respective buyers. The freight forwarder's profits come from the margin between the higher, less than car load rates charged to each shipper and the lower car load rates the agency pays. Because large shipments require less handling, the use of a freight forwarder can speed transit time. Freight forwarders can also determine the most efficient carriers and routes and are useful for shipping goods to foreign markets.

Megacarriers Freight companies that provide several methods of shipment, such as rail, road and air service

One other transport innovation is the development of **megacarriers**, freight companies that provide several methods of shipment, such as rail, road and air service. Air carriers have increased their ground transport services. As they have expanded the range of transport alternatives, carriers have also put greater stress on customer service.

Strategic Issues in Physical Distribution

The physical distribution functions discussed in this chapter—order processing, materials handling, warehousing, inventory management and transportation—account for about one-third of all marketing costs. Moreover, these functions have a significant impact on customer service and satisfaction, which are of prime importance to marketers.[38] Effective marketers accept considerable responsibility for the design and control of the physical distribution system. They work to ensure that the business's overall marketing strategy is enhanced by physical distribution, with its dual objectives of decreasing costs while increasing customer service. Remember, to ensure that customers are satisfied, they must be able to obtain within reason the product or service when and where they want it.

The strategic importance of physical distribution is evident in all elements of the marketing mix. Product design and packaging must allow for efficient stacking, storage and transport; decisions to differentiate products by size, colour and style must take into account the additional demands that will be placed on warehousing and shipping facilities. Competitive pricing may depend on a company's ability to provide reliable delivery or emergency shipments of replacement parts; a company trying to lower its inventory costs may offer quantity discounts to encourage large purchases. Promotional campaigns must be co-ordinated with distribution functions so that advertised products are available to buyers; order processing departments must be able to handle additional sales order information efficiently. Distribution planners must consider warehousing and transportation costs, which may influence—for example—the company's policy on stock-outs or its choice to centralise (or decentralise) its inventory.

No single distribution system is ideal for all situations, and any system must be evaluated continually and adapted as necessary. For instance, pressures to adjust service levels or reduce costs may lead to a total restructuring of the marketing channel relationships; changes in transportation, warehousing, materials handling and inventory may affect speed of delivery, reliability and economy of service. Marketing strategists must consider customers' changing needs and preferences and recognise that changes in any one of the major distribution functions will necessarily affect all other functions. Consumer oriented marketers will analyse the various characteristics of their target markets and *then* design distribution systems to provide products at acceptable costs.

● S U M M A R Y

Wholesaling includes all transactions in which the purchaser intends to use the product for resale, for making other products or for general business operations. It does *not* include exchanges with the ultimate consumers. The term *wholesaling* is used in its broadest sense: intermediaries' activity in the marketing channel between producers and business-to-business customers to facilitate the exchange—buying and selling—of goods. *Wholesalers* are individuals or businesses that facilitate and expedite primarily wholesale transactions between producers and business-to-business customers.

Except in the UK consumer markets, where large multiple retailers dominate, more than half of all goods are exchanged through wholesalers, although the distribution of any product requires that someone must perform wholesaling activities, whether or not a wholesaling institution is involved. For producers, wholesalers perform specialised accumulation and allocation functions for a number of products, letting the producers concentrate on developing and manufacturing the products. For retailers, wholesalers provide buying expertise, wide product lines, efficient distribution, and warehousing and storage services.

Various types of wholesalers serve different market segments. How a wholesaler is classified depends on whether the wholesaler is owned by a producer, whether it takes title to products, the range of services it provides, and the breadth and depth of its product lines. The three general categories of wholesalers are merchant wholesalers, agents and brokers, and manufacturers' sales branches and offices.

Merchant wholesalers are independently owned businesses that take title to goods and assume risk; they account for over half of all wholesale revenues. They are either full service wholesalers, offering the widest possible range of wholesaling functions, or limited service wholesalers, providing only some marketing services and specialising in a few functions. *Distributors* buy and sell on their own account but tend to deal in the goods of only certain manufacturers. *Full service wholesalers* include (1) *general merchandise wholesalers,* which offer a wide but relatively shallow product mix; (2) *limited line wholesalers,* which offer extensive assortments in a few product lines; and (3) *speciality line wholesalers,* which offer great depth in a single product line or in a few items within a line. *Rack jobbers* are speciality line wholesalers that own and service display racks in supermarkets and chemists. There are four types of *limited service wholesalers.* (1) *Cash and carry wholesalers* sell to small businesses, require payment in cash and do not deliver. (2) *Truck wholesalers* transport a limited line of products directly to customers for inspection and selection. (3) *Drop shippers* own goods and negotiate sales but never take possession of products. (4) *Mail order wholesalers* sell to retail, industrial and institutional buyers through direct mail catalogues.

Agents and brokers, sometimes called *functional middlemen,* negotiate purchases and expedite sales but do not take title to products. They are usually specialists and provide valuable sales expertise. *Agents* represent buyers or sellers on a permanent basis. *Manufacturers' agents* offer customers the complete product lines of two or more sellers; *sell-*

ing agents market a complete product line or a producer's entire output and perform every wholesaling function except taking title to products; *commission merchants* receive goods on consignment from local sellers and negotiate sales in large central markets. *Brokers*, such as *food brokers*, negotiate exchanges between buyers and sellers on a temporary basis.

Manufacturers' sales branches and offices are vertically integrated units owned by manufacturers. *Sales branches* sell products and provide support services for the manufacturer's salesforce in a given location. *Sales offices* carry no inventory and function much as agents do.

Facilitating agencies do not buy, sell or take title but perform certain activities that enhance channel functions. They include *public warehouses*, finance companies, transport companies, and *trade shows* and *trade markets*. In some instances, these organisations eliminate the need for a wholesaling establishment.

The nature of the wholesaling and distribution industry is changing in response to changes in the marketing environment. The predominant changes are the increasing consolidation of the wholesaling industry and the growth of new types of wholesalers.

Physical distribution is a set of activities that moves products from producers to consumers, or end users. These activities include order processing, materials handling, warehousing, inventory management and transportation. An effective physical distribution system can be an important component of an overall marketing strategy, because it can decrease costs and lead to higher levels of customer satisfaction. Physical distribution activities should be integrated with marketing channel decisions and should be adjusted to meet the unique needs of a channel member. For most companies, physical distribution accounts for about one-fifth of a product's retail price.

The main *objective of physical distribution* is to decrease costs while increasing customer service. Physical distribution managers therefore try to balance service, distribution costs and resources. Companies must adapt to customers' needs and preferences, offer service comparable to—or better than—that of their competitors, and develop and communicate desirable *customer service* policies.

The costs of providing service are minimised most effectively through the total cost approach, which evaluates the costs of the system as a whole rather than as a collection of separate activities. *Cost trade-offs* must often be used to offset higher costs in one area of distribution against lower costs in another area.

Order processing, the first stage in a physical distribution system, is the receipt and transmission of sales order information. Order processing consists of three main tasks. (1) Order entry is the placement of purchase orders from customers or salespeople by mail, telephone, fax or computer. (2) Order handling involves checking customer credit, verifying product availability and preparing products for shipping. (3) Order delivery is provided by the carrier most suitable for a desired level of customer service. Order processing may be done manually or electronically, depending on which method gives greater speed and accuracy within cost limits.

Materials handling, or the physical handling of products, is an important element of physical distribution. Packaging, loading, movement and labelling systems must be co-ordinated to maximise cost reduction and customer requirements. Basic handling systems include *unit loading* on pallets or skids, permitting movement by mechanical devices, and *containerisation*, the practice of consolidating many items into a single large container.

Warehousing involves the design and operation of facilities for storing and moving goods. It is important for companies to select suitable warehousing conveniently located close to main transport routes. *Private warehouses* are owned and operated by a company for the purpose of storing and distributing its own products. *Public warehouses* rent storage space and related physical distribution facilities to other companies. Public warehouses may furnish security for products that are being used as collateral for loans by establishing *field public warehouses*. They may also provide *bonded storage* for companies wishing to defer tax payments on imported or taxable products. *Distribution centres* are large, centralised warehouses specially designed to facilitate the rapid movement of goods to customers. In many cases, a combination of private and public facilities provides the most flexible approach to warehousing.

The objective of *inventory management* is to minimise inventory costs while maintaining a supply of goods adequate for customers' needs. All inventory costs—carrying, replenishment and stock-out costs—must be controlled if profit goals are to be met. To avoid *stock-outs* without tying up too much capital in inventory, a business must have a systematic method of determining a *re-order point,* the inventory level at which more inventory is ordered. The trade-offs between the costs of carrying larger average *safety stocks* and the costs of frequent orders can be quantified using the *economic order quantity (EOQ)* model. Inventory problems may take the form of surplus inventory, late deliveries, write-offs and inventory that is too large in proportion to sales or assets. Methods for improving inventory management include systems that continuously monitor stock levels and techniques such as just-in-time management and the 80/20 rule.

Transportation adds time and place utility to a product by moving it from where it is made to where it is purchased and used. The five major *transport modes* are motor vehicles, railways, inland waterways, airways and pipelines. Marketers evaluate transport modes with respect to *costs, transit time, reliability, capability, accessibility, security* and *traceability;* final selection of a transport mode involves many trade-offs. *Intermodal transport* allows marketers to combine the advantages of two or more modes of transport; this method is facilitated by containerisation, *freight forwarders*—who co-ordinate transport by combining small shipments from several businesses into efficient lot sizes—and *megacarriers*—freight companies that offer several methods of shipment.

Physical distribution affects every element of the marketing mix: product, price, promotion, place/distribution and personnel/customer service. To give customers products at acceptable prices, marketers consider consumers' changing needs and any shifts within the major distribution functions. They then adapt existing physical distribution systems for greater effectiveness. Physical distribution functions account for about one-third of all marketing costs and have a significant impact on customer satisfaction. Therefore, effective marketers are actively involved in the design and control of physical distribution systems.

Important Terms

Wholesaling
Wholesaler
Merchant wholesalers
Distributors
Full service wholesalers
General merchandise
  wholesalers
Limited line wholesalers
Speciality line wholesalers
Rack jobbers
Limited service wholesalers
Cash and carry wholesalers
Truck wholesalers
Drop shippers
Mail order wholesalers
Functional middlemen
Agents
Brokers
Manufacturers' agents
Selling agents

Commission merchants
Food brokers
Sales branches
Sales offices
Facilitating agencies
Public warehouses
Trade shows
Trade markets
Physical distribution
Objective of physical distribution
Customer service
Cost trade-offs
Order processing
Materials handling
Unit loading
Containerisation
Warehousing
Private warehouse
Field public warehouse
Bonded storage

Distribution centre
Inventory management
Stock-outs
Re-order point
Safety stock
Economic order quantity (EOQ)
Transportation
Transport modes
Costs
Transit time
Reliability
Capability
Accessibility
Security
Traceability
Intermodal transport
Freight forwarders
Megacarriers

Discussion and Review Questions

1. Is there a distinction between wholesalers and wholesaling? If so, what is it?
2. What services do wholesalers provide to producers and retailers?
3. Drop shippers take title to products but do not accept physical possession. Commission merchants take physical possession of products but do not accept title. Defend the logic of classifying drop shippers as wholesale merchants and agents as commission merchants.
4. What are the advantages of using agents to replace merchant wholesalers? What are the disadvantages?
5. Why are manufacturers' sales offices and branches classified as wholesalers? Which independent wholesalers are replaced by manufacturers' sales branches? Which independent wholesalers are replaced by manufacturers' sales offices?
6. "Public warehouses are really wholesale establishments." Is this correct?
7. Discuss the role of facilitating agencies. Identify three facilitating agencies and explain how each type performs this role.
8. Discuss the cost and service trade-offs involved in developing a physical distribution system.
9. What factors must physical distribution managers consider when developing a customer service mix?
10. What is the advantage of using a total cost approach to distribution?
11. What are the main tasks involved in order processing?
12. Discuss the advantages of using an electronic order processing system. Which types of businesses are most likely to use such a system?
13. How does a product's package affect materials handling procedures and techniques?
14. Explain the major differences between private and public warehouses. What is a field public warehouse?
15. In what circumstances should a company use a private warehouse instead of a public one?
16. Describe the costs associated with inventory management.
17. Explain the trade-offs inventory managers face when re-ordering merchandise.
18. How can managers improve inventory control? Give specific examples of techniques.
19. Compare the five major transport modes in terms of costs, transit time, reliability, capability, accessibility, security and traceability.
20. Discuss how marketers can combine or co-ordinate two or more modes of transport. What advantage do they gain by doing this?
21. Discuss how the elements of the marketing mix affect physical distribution strategy.

Recommended Readings

M. Christopher, *Marketing Logistics* (Oxford: Butterworth-Heinemann, 1997).

J. Fernie, "International comparisons of supply chain management in grocery retailing", *Service Industries Journal,* vol. 15, no. 4, 1995, pp. 134–147.

J. Gattorna, ed., *Strategic Supply Chain Alignment: Best Practices in Supply Chain Management* (Aldershot: Gower, 1998).

D. M. Lambert and J. R. Stock, *Strategic Logistics Management* (Homewood, Ill.: Richard D. Irwin, 1993).

R. C. Laming, *Beyond Partnership—Strategies for Innovation and Lean Supply* (New York: Prentice-Hall, 1993).

D. Shipley, ed., "Industrial distribution channel management", special edition, *European Journal of Marketing,* vol. 23, no. 2, 1989.

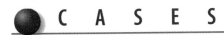

C A S E S

13.1 New Directions for Traditional Wholesalers

Heinz boss Tony O'Reilly heads Fitzwilton group, a major Irish motor, cash and carry, and industrial group, trading as M6 Cash and Carry in Britain. Despite the sector's worth of close to £8.5 billion in

1992, O'Reilly described UK cash and carry trading conditions as the "toughest in recent years, with volumes and sales just keeping pace with inflation". The boom years of the mid-1980s encouraged numerous new entrants, but now there is over capacity, with declining numbers of depots and increasing liquidations. This squeeze has hit the smaller operators most; the largest companies are consolidating their grip on the sector: Booker, Landmark, Nurdin & Peacock, and NISA-Today's have over 70 per cent of the market. This concentration replicates the grocery retailing scene of the late 1960s, when supermarket groups merged to produce a handful of dominant players.

Although price remains a core trading proposition, service and brand image are increasingly important. Indeed, the cash and carry sector has been shaken up by the entry of Holland's Makro, a self-service wholesaler. Makro is part of SHV Holdings, a large international distribution and energy company and the sixth largest company in the Netherlands. With sales of £7 billion, the company is now active throughout Europe. In the UK, Makro has 7,000 employees and 21 UK sites, and has quickly moved into fifth place with around 8 per cent of the cash and carry market and sales around £800 million.

Makro's latest two openings in Aberdeen and Croydon are, at over 3,000 square metres (about 100,000 square feet), more than twice the average size of a cash and carry warehouse. These depots have the latest computer systems, customer service points and in-store displays. Makro serves the trade as a cash and carry wholesaler of groceries, fresh foods, wines, spirits, beer and cigarettes, household goods, clothing, toys and sports equipment. The company retails a clutch of own label brands in these categories, including Aro, Louis Chevalier and Roca.

In a relatively traditional sector dominated by four long standing companies, Dutch Makro has had a major impact in a short time. Its mix of merchandise is more comprehensive than that of its competitors, forcing several, such as Booker and Landmark, to re-think their merchandising strategies. Because depth and breadth of stock within individual product categories are not as extensive as those of UK rivals, the industry has been prompted to re-think, and most companies have reduced the number of lines stocked. Although not the first wholesaler with own label products, Makro's promotion of its own ranges has encouraged its com-

petitors to divert more attention to this area, which now accounts for 20 per cent of all sales in the cash and carry sector.

Perhaps Makro's biggest impact has been in the sales and marketing techniques it has brought to the UK. Cash and carry warehouses used to be dowdy depots that paid little attention to layout, up-keep, design or ambience, and demonstrated even less regard for customer service and satisfaction. Price was the name of the game: customers could buy in bulk at a discount but were offered few additional benefits. Makro's philosophy brings to the cash and carry sector the retailing techniques of the hypermarket: carefully controlled branch designs and lay-outs, high levels of staff training and a significant emphasis on building ongoing relationships with customers.

Makro's philosophy is encouraging other whole-salers to follow suit. Now customers are being offered better service, together with assistance in building their own company image through local press and television advertising. The leading cash and carry companies are offering marketing support to their key accounts not just to stimulate sales but also to build up those customers' loyalty to their nearby warehouse. These changes have been accompanied by a rise in average sales per depot from £9.2 million in 1986 to £14.9 million in 1991.

Depots have been up-rated by the leading groups, with new equipment, better stocking systems and improved physical distribution. They have also initiated sales promotions campaigns and incentive programmes. Computerisation has helped lower costs and improve efficiency. With Germany's Siemens Nixdorf, Booker has created MIDAS (management information depot application system), giving each of its depots a comprehensive invoicing, mailing, sales data, customer information and stock control system. This system has improved Booker's ability to target customers and monitor stock needs. Systems such as MIDAS have enabled the leading companies to reduce their product lines. For example, Nurdin & Peacock used to carry 60,000 lines but has now reduced its coverage to 40,000 and is aiming to reach 30,000 without alienating customers.

Branches are being rationalised, both to respond to economic downturns and to benefit from cost economies and enhanced computer systems. For example, companies are either consolidating three out-dated neighbouring depots into one central, spacious, service oriented depot, or they are closing a branch while extending and refurbishing a neighbouring one. Own label lines are taking up to 20 per cent of cash and carry sales; among the most popular are Booker's grocery Family Choice label and its catering Chef's Larder range, Landmark's Lifestyle, and Nurdin & Peacock's Happy Shopper. There are own label brands in most of the key product areas: grocery, catering (for the catering trade), confectionery, wines, spirits, lager and beer, and cigarettes. Own label brands are even available for some fresh foods, shirts and sports equipment (Makro), and garden products (Nurdin & Peacock). Companies have also established specialist sales teams to provide expert advice and service. For example, Nurdin & Peacock has separate teams handling independent grocers, garage forecourts and newsagents, and the catering trade.

Significant investment has gone into staff training, new stores, computer systems, sales teams and the development of own label products. The overriding aim has been to provide customers with a better service that is closely in tune with their needs,

even down to offering marketing advice and support for customers' promotional campaigns. As the sector has evolved, customer service and modernised operations have taken a prime position. The cash and carry sector now involves much more than pure discounting.

SOURCES: "Cash & carry outlets", Key Note, 1992; IGD Research Services; Harvest; Booker promotional material; Nick Higham, "Independent—at any price?", *Marketing Week*, 11 February 1994, p. 19; Makro Leicester; *Marketing Pocket Book* (NTC Publications, 1996); Charles Thurston, "Testing Latin waters", *Global Finance*, June 1995, p. 25; Ian Fraser, "Retailer to the world", *Director*, June 1994, pp. 48–52.

Questions for Discussion

1. How are the major cash and carry companies responding to changing customer needs?
2. How are computerised retailing systems contributing to improved customer service?
3. Why are cash and carry companies offering marketing and promotional advice to their customers?

Company	Market Share (%)	Number of Depots	
		1989	1992
Booker	22.0	171	166
Today's	15.5	86	90
Landmark	17.0	75	90
Nurdin & Peacock	15.0	38	50
Sterling	4.7	31	39
Mojo	1.4	25	24
Makro	7.6	15	21
Watson & Philip	2.0	14	12
Batleys	5.0	11	11

SOURCE: Key Note, 1992.

13.2 New Solutions for Packaging Transportation

Businesses which transport products are facing a dilemma in their choice of cushioning materials to protect their products during distribution. The use of polystyrene peanuts, the most common cushioning material, is provoking increasing criticism from both consumers and environmentalists for several reasons. First, polystyrene peanuts are made from petroleum, a non-renewable resource. Second, the

peanuts are not biodegradable; they remain in the environment anywhere from 400 to 1,000 years. Third, some peanuts contain chlorofluorocarbons (CFCs) that are released during incineration. CFCs are widely known for their damaging effects on the earth's ozone layer. Finally, the peanuts produce static electricity, making them useless for cushioning sensitive electronic equipment.

The purpose of any cushioning material is to protect a package's contents from harm during the distribution process. Internal packaging is important because if it fails to do its job, the quality of the package's contents becomes a secondary concern. However, in the face of increased environmental awareness, many companies are discovering that their choice of packaging materials is fast becoming an important issue with their customers.

There are several alternatives to polystyrene peanuts, each having advantages and disadvantages. One of the cleverest alternatives is popcorn, which many industry experts say could be the answer to the dilemma. Popcorn is attractive because it is biodegradable and costs one quarter as much as polystyrene peanuts. Likewise, unpopped popcorn is less expensive to ship and store before it is needed. However, in some countries popcorn is not an option at present because it is considered a food, not a packaging material. Many countries forbid the use of popcorn as a cushioning material until a method can be found to prevent people from eating it after it has been used for shipping purposes.

Billed as a direct alternative to polystyrene peanuts, Eco-Foam is made from a special hybrid corn and is composed of 95 per cent cornflour, making it fully biodegradable and less prone to static electricity. Eco-Foam, which looks a lot like polystyrene peanuts, is attractive because it can be used with the same dispensing equipment as peanuts. Thus a company that currently uses peanuts can switch to Eco-Foam with very little inconvenience. However, Eco-Foam is more expensive and has one major drawback: it fully disintegrates when it gets wet. This makes Eco-Foam impractical for use in shipping liquid-filled containers or in situations in which the threat of water damage is high. In addition, Eco-Foam has a tendency to shrink when exposed to high heat and humidity, which is always a possibility in a vehicle trailer or on a train.

Quadra-Pak, a third choice, is fully biodegradable and recyclable, contains no CFCs and is produced totally from refuse materials. Quadra-Pak is made by stacking heavyweight paper in layers that are then cut into strips 10 centimetres (4 inches) long and 0.3 centimetres (0.125 inches) wide. The cut lengths are then compacted into an accordion shape that makes them act as if spring loaded. The finished product measures about 2.5 centimetres (1 inch) long but expands when it is jostled. The result is a packing material that protects from all sides

while preventing a carton's contents from moving about. Although Quadra-Pak possesses superior cushioning properties to peanuts, it is more expensive to manufacture and cannot be used with current dispensing equipment.

Other options include Bio-Puffs—a loose-fill foam packaging peanut that biodegrades within weeks or months—and vermiculite, a naturally occurring mineral that was used by the military to ship munitions in Operation Desert Storm. With so many alternatives and the relentless pressure of environmentalists to use more environmentally friendly packing materials, the Polystyrene Packaging Council (PPC) is crying foul. PPC admits that CFCs were once a problem, but even then, it argues, only 2 per cent of all polystyrene contained CFCs, and their use was phased out of polystyrene production in 1989. To curb negative publicity, the PPC—along with four producers of poly-styrene peanuts—is creating a peanut recycling programme.

While many packaging options exist, there is no perfect answer to the current dilemma. All of the options have good and bad characteristics. For the most part, companies currently choose a packing material on the basis of cost and performance. Thus SAS Cargo Systems, an air freight firm, transports perishables such as seafood and fruit from the United States to Scandinavia. SAS uses CoolGuard, a foil-backed insulation material, to maintain the required temperature. Ultimately, however, for companies like SAS the choice of material will depend more and more upon the needs of the customer and the material's impact on the environment.

SOURCES: Jerry Drisaldi, "Protective packaging: it's your responsibility", *Inbound Logistics,* November 1991, p. 39; Walter L. Weart, "Packaging dilemmas: the sequel", *Inbound Logistics,* June 1991, pp. 27–29; Bob Freiday, "Popcorn, peanuts, and Quadra-Paks", *Inbound Logistics,* February 1991, pp. 25–28; "Environmental concerns influence packaging", *Inbound Logistics,* June 1990, p. 4; Patricia B. Demetrio, "A race against time", *Inbound Logistics,* June 1994, pp. 40–48.

Questions for Discussion

1. What are the advantages and disadvantages of each of the packaging options discussed above?
2. How does a company's choice of packaging materials affect its ability to serve customer needs?
3. Overall, which packaging material would you choose? Why? How would your decision change if you were shipping electronic equipment? Glass? Liquid-filled containers?

14 Retailing

"The power, prestige and proactivity of major retailers now exceeds that of their manufacturer suppliers."

Peter J. McGoldrick
Manchester Business School

OBJECTIVES

- To understand the purpose and function of retailing in the marketing channel
- To describe and distinguish retail locations and major store types
- To understand non-store retailing and franchising
- To learn about strategic issues and current trends in retailing

Future prospects are looking great for electrical retailer Dixons. As the company's share price continues to grow, retail analysts are praising the way that Dixons has sought out new opportunities. The retailer has shown particular interest in computer hardware and software opportunities. At a time when the UK PC market has seen a 67 per cent growth in just four years, the attractions of the sector seem obvious. What is more interesting is the retailer's willingness to spot trends and, if necessary, move into new and innovative areas. According to John Clare, Dixons' Chief Executive, "We're in the business of planting seeds, and when we've a seed that has started to flourish and grow, then we're ready to pump a lot of money into it."

Thus the company's PC World and The Link chains continue to expand their high street and out-of-town presence. In addition, Dixons has recently launched @jakarta, a national chain of electronic game shops which the company hopes will become a major high street brand. Retail analysts have been particularly impressed by the launch of Freeserve, Dixons' bold move into Internet service provision. As an early entrant into this burgeoning sector, the company could gain considerable advertising revenue. Already Dixons is credited with developing a major presence in the market, attracting many new consumers to the Internet.

At the beginning of the 1990s, the retailer's future looked much bleaker than today. Problems with Silo,

DIXONS' BUSINESS DIVISIONS

High Street

Consists of Dixons (brown electrical goods), The Link (mobile phones), airport trading and @jakarta

Out-of-Town

Currys (white/brown electrical goods)

PC World

Includes PC World, PC World Business Direct and Mastercare after sales service

Freeserve

Internet and e-commerce interests

the company's US electrical retailer, were resulting in mounting losses. In 1993, in order to extricate the business from the situation, management made the painful decision to sell its US operation. At the same time, Dixons was finding that its presence in the high street was increasingly isolated. The trend for electrical retailing to move to out-of-town locations meant that Dixons and its white goods chain Currys were left with a large number of relatively small town centre stores at a time when the competition was moving away to out-of-town sheds and retail parks.

Dixons learnt important lessons as a result of these difficulties. These lessons have shaped the company's future strategy. Now the company is wary about overseas opportunities, choosing instead to focus on acquiring outlets from small retailers and regional electricity companies. This helped support the company's strategy of organic growth for its Dixons, PC World, Currys and The Link retail brands. Dixons has also decided to focus its expansion on areas which are synergistic with its core business interests. Thus the company has divided its main retailing areas of business into three divisions, high street, out-of-town and PC World, with a separate division, Freeserve, looking after its Internet and e-commerce interests.

The future for Dixons' business divisions is impossible to predict. However, it is clear that Dixons' tenacity in overcoming its difficulties and its eye for innovative opportunities have put the company in good shape for the millennium.

SOURCES: Paul Edwards, "Computer power play", *Marketing Week,* 15 April 1999, pp. 37–38; Julian Lee, "How Dixons reinvented itself", *Marketing,* 1 April 1999, pp. 26–27; Philip Buxton, "Dixons expands buoyant @jakarta computer arm", *Marketing Week,* 14 January 1999, p. 10. *Photo:* Courtesy of Dixons.

Marketing research has enabled Dixons to develop retail concepts in line with consumers' wishes and a marketing strategy that has enhanced its profits. Marketing methods that satisfy consumers serve well as the guiding philosophy of retailing. Retailers are an important link in the marketing channel because they are both marketers and customers for producers and wholesalers. They perform many marketing activities, such as buying, selling, grading, risk taking and developing information about consumers' wants. Of all marketers, retailers are the most visible to ultimate consumers. They are in a strategic position to gain feedback from consumers and to relay ideas to producers and intermediaries in the marketing channel. Retailing is an extraordinarily dynamic area of marketing.

This chapter examines the nature of retailing and its importance in supplying consumers with goods and services. It discusses retail locations and the major types of retail stores and describes several forms of non-store retailing, such as in-home retailing, telemarketing, automatic vending and mail order retailing.

With the recent growth in direct marketing (see Chapter 17), mail order, in-home retailing and telemarketing have all become more active. This chapter also looks at franchising, a retailing form that continues to grow in popularity. Finally, it presents several strategic issues in retailing: location, property ownership, product assortment, retail positioning, atmospherics, store image, scrambled merchandising, the wheel of retailing, the balance of retailing, retail technology and the impact of the deregulation of the European Union.

The Nature of Retailing

Retailing All transactions in which the buyer intends to consume the product through personal, family or household use

Retailer A business that purchases products for the purpose of re-selling them to ultimate consumers, the general public, often from a shop or store

Retailing includes all transactions in which the buyer intends to consume the product through personal, family or household use. The buyers in retail transactions are ultimate consumers. A **retailer,** then, is a business that purchases products for the purpose of re-selling them to ultimate consumers, the general public, often from a shop or store. As the link between producers and consumers, retailers occupy an important and highly demanding position in the marketing channel. It is complicated, too: retailers sell other companies' products, yet have to devise their own product/service mixes. They devise their own target market strategies and conduct analyses of marketing opportunities. The merchandise they sell derives from producers that have undertaken their own analysis of marketing opportunities and developed their own target market strategies and brand positionings. These strategies—producers' and retailers'—have, to a degree, to mesh in order for all channel members to make adequate financial returns, while ultimately striving to give satisfaction to the consumer. Although most retailers' sales are to consumers, non-retail transactions occasionally occur when retailers sell products to other businesses. Retailing activities usually take place in a store or in a service establishment, but exchanges through telephone selling, vending machines, mail order retailing and the Internet occur outside stores.

It is common knowledge that retailing is important to the economy, being a large employer and major service sector component. Table 14.1, for example, shows the level of retail sales in the UK. Also, most personal income is spent in retail stores.

By providing assortments of products to match consumers' wants, retailers create place, time, possession and form utilities. (1) *Place utility* means moving products from wholesalers or producers to a location where consumers want to buy them. (2) *Time utility* involves maintaining specific business hours to make products available when consumers want them. (3) *Possession utility* means facilitating the transfer of ownership or use of a product to consumers. (4) In the case of services such as hairdressing, dry cleaning, restaurants and car repairs, retailers themselves develop most of the product utilities. The services of such retailers provide aspects of *form utility* associated with the production process. Retailers of services usually have more direct contact with consumers and more opportunity to alter the product in the marketing mix (see Chapter 11).

Retail Locations

Central Business District

The traditional hub of most cities and towns is the **central business district (CBD),** the focus for shopping, banking and commerce and hence the busiest part of the whole area for traffic, public transport and pedestrians. Examples are London's Oxford and Regent streets, the Champs Elysées in Paris and Berlin's

Table 14.1 Retail sales by type of business, UK

Kind of Business	Number of Businesses	Number of Outlets	Retail Turnover[1] £m
Total Retail Trade	206,964	320,624	193,236
Food, drink & tobacco retailers	**58,321**	**74,134**	**14,566**
Fruit & vegetables	6,841	8,979	1,279
Meat & meat products	10,662	12,459	2,464
Fish	1,997	2,551	245
Bread, cakes, flour or sugar confectionery	4,931	9,506	1,463
Alcoholic & other drinks	6,313	11,172	3,773
Tobacco products	17,127	18,537	3,940
Other sales of food, drink & tobacco	10,450	10,931	1,400
Pharmaceutical & medical goods retailers[2]	**7,321**	**13,789**	**7,375**
Dispensing chemists	6,643	11,537	6,043
Medical & orthopaedic goods	194	514	128
Cosmetics & toilet articles	484	1,738	1,203
Other specialised retailers (new goods)	**90,291**	**153,796**	**70,488**
Textiles	1,592	3,019	847
Clothing	15,274	33,133	24,398
Footwear & leather goods	6,265	13,865	3,783
Furniture, lighting & household articles	9,941	14,616	6,764
Electrical household appliances, radio & television goods	7,447	13,245	8,280
Hardware, paints & glass	6,124	8,231	6,345
Books, newspapers & stationery	9,590	16,650	4,542
Floor coverings	1,988	3,016	1,463
Photographic, optical & precision equipment, office supplies & equipment (including computers, etc.)	5,330	8,513	3,047
Other retailers	26,739	39,506	11,019
Second-hand goods retailers	**5,146**	**7,014**	**1,511**
Repair businesses	**2,005**	**2,649**	**438**
Non-specialised retailers	**37,559**	**59,509**	**89,658**
Food, drink & tobacco retailers	22,157	37,556	71,968
Other retailers	15,402	21,953	17,687
Retail sales not in stores	**6,321**	**9,735**	**9,204**
Mail order houses	2,102	3,053	7,199
Stalls & markets	1,031	2,961	301
Other retailers	3,188	3,720	1,704

Notes: [1]Inclusive of VAT. [2]Including cosmetics and toilet articles.
SOURCE: *The Retail Pocket Book 1999*, p. 73. Reprinted by permission of NTC Publications, Ltd.

Central business district (CBD) The traditional hub of most cities and towns; the focus for shopping, banking and commerce and hence the busiest part of the whole area

Kurfürstendamm.[1] The CBD is sub-divided into zones: generally, retailers are clustered together in a zone; banking and insurance companies locate together; legal offices occupy neighbouring premises; municipal offices and amenities are built on adjoining plots (town hall, library, law courts, art galleries).

Within the shopping zone certain streets at the centre of the zone will have the main shops and the highest levels of pedestrian footfall. In this area, known as

BAA's Retailing Initiative Takes Off

BAA owns and operates seven airports in the UK, including Heathrow, Gatwick and rapidly expanding Stanstead. BAA's 80 million passengers account for 70 per cent of the UK's air passenger traffic. The company, privatised in 1987, builds and manages terminals and runways and handles security. Chief Executive Sir John Egan, former champion of Jaguar Cars, intends to keep London as the "hub of Europe", ahead of challengers Paris, Frankfurt, Amsterdam and Vienna.

A few years ago Egan instigated a policy review emphasising a commitment to quality service, on-site competition and the introduction of branded operations and concessions. All proposals followed extensive marketing research. Three tax-free operators currently compete for the available business: Allders, Forte and Harrods. SAS, Häagen-Dazs and Garfunkels compete for catering business, along with big names such as Upper Crust, Granary, Casey Jones and Burger King. The BAA Skyshop brand disappeared and was replaced with Forte bookshops and market leaders W. H. Smith and John Menzies. Only well known retail brands are now welcome.

With the EU having phased out intra-community duty-free trade, Egan sees retail operations as the way to continue BAA's impressive profits record. Already 10 per cent of terminal space—46,000 square metres (500,000 square feet)—is devoted to retailing. Egan intends to expand space significantly, with the help of retailing director Barry Gibson, whose record of senior positions at Littlewoods, Burton Group and Jean Machine have well equipped him for the task. Some 90,000 square metres (1 million square feet) of new shopping space opened in 1998, and pre-tax profits reached £450 million.

BAA has taken restless passengers waiting for flights and put them into shops selling well known brands and a variety of merchandise. Research from 120,000 interviews each year has shown that retail outlets are a high priority for passengers. The following are now offered: Bally, Benetton, Body Shop, Sock Shop, Aquascutum, Burberry, Harrods, Thomas Cook. The captive audience is appreciative of the changes, as are the retailers. Tie Rack's sales at Heathrow are £27,000 per square metre (£3,000 per square foot) annually, 10 times the ratio the company's high street stores achieve. Heathrow's Terminal 4 houses BAA's first "serious" shopping mall, with 20 retailers, natural daylight, shopping trolleys and big brands. Other malls are now in development.

SOURCES: BAA press office; Bunhill, *The Independent on Sunday*, 21 February 1993, p. IB40; Clare Sambrook, "BAA talks shop on airport retailing", *Marketing*, 29 October 1992, pp. 25–30; *The Independent on Sunday*, 11 February 1996, p. IB5; "It's not easy being green", *The Economist*, 6 January 1995, p. 29.; BAA, 1999.

Prime pitch The area at the centre of the shopping zone with the main shops and the highest levels of pedestrian footfall

the **prime pitch**, the key traders or magnets (Marks & Spencer, Boots or major department stores) will occupy prominent sites, so generating much of the footfall. Other retailers vie to be located close to these key traders so as to benefit from the customer traffic they generate. The highest rents are therefore paid for such sites. The CBD shopping centre—the city or town centre—generally offers shopping goods and some convenience items. Clothing, footwear, jewellery, cosmetics and financial services dominate the CBD. For the most part, grocers have moved out of town, along with furniture and DIY* stores.

Property developers build shopping malls or centres in and around the CBD. Each development has one or more magnets (big name variety or department stores) both to attract shoppers and to encourage other retailers to locate within the development. Most city centres now have one covered shopping centre development (Eldon Square in Newcastle, Arndale Centre in Manchester).[2] As discussed in Marketing Insight 14.1, not only city centres have covered shopping malls. On streets adjacent to this area of prime pitch, rents are lower but so is footfall. These secondary sites are suitable for speciality retailers or discounters,

*DIY (do-it-yourself) merchandise includes building materials, hardware, plumbing and electrical goods, kitchen units and gardening requirements.

which have either lower margins or lower **customer thresholds** (the number of customers required to make a profit). Figure 14.1 shows the composition of a typical central business district (CBD).

Suburban Centres

Historically, as urban areas expanded during the early part of the twentieth century, they joined and subsequently swallowed up neighbouring towns and villages. The shopping centres of these settlements survived to become **suburban centres** of the now larger city or town. Where the expansion of the town was planned, suburban centres were created at major road junctions to cater for local shopping needs and reduce demands and congestion in the CBD.[3] Suburban centres tend to offer convenience goods (frequently demanded, cheaper items such as groceries and drugs) and some shopping goods (clothing and footwear). Apart from a supermarket or limited range variety store (such as Woolworth), the shops tend to be small store outlets from 150 to 250 square metres (1,650 to 2,750

Figure 14.1 The composition of a typical central business district (CBD). SOURCE: Lyndon Simkin and Sally Dibb

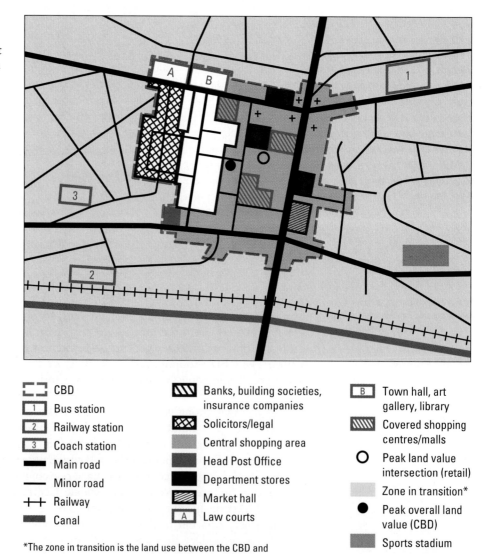

⌐⌐ CBD	▨ Banks, building societies, insurance companies	B Town hall, art gallery, library
1 Bus station	▧ Solicitors/legal	▨ Covered shopping centres/malls
2 Railway station	Central shopping area	
3 Coach station	Head Post Office	O Peak land value intersection (retail)
▬ Main road	Department stores	Zone in transition*
— Minor road	▨ Market hall	● Peak overall land value (CBD)
┼┼ Railway	A Law courts	Sports stadium
▬ Canal		+ Cinema/theatre

*The zone in transition is the land use between the CBD and suburban housing areas: light manufacturing, transport termini, wholesaling, garages, medical, multi-family residences.

square feet); many are privately owned—unlike those in the CBD, which tend to be owned by national retail chains.

Edge of Town Sites

During the 1970s, as rents in the CBD rose and sites sufficient for large, open-plan stores became harder to obtain, retailers looked to the green fields adjacent to outer ring roads for expansion. The superstore era had dawned as the major grocery, carpets and furniture, electrical and DIY retailers opened free-standing "sheds". Needing more space to display stock and sell their goods than they could afford or obtain in the CBD or even suburban centre, but still requiring high traffic levels, they sought sites adjacent to major road arteries into the CBD. Initially, planning authorities protected green belt and undeveloped land, so the retailers occupied disused warehouses and factory units in once thriving industrial and commercial areas.

The planners then began to realise that stylish retail outlets could brighten up areas, create employment, attract traffic and rejuvenate decaying zones. Major retail chains such as the grocery retailers with their frequently purchased convenience goods attracted large volumes of traffic. Relocating these stores to non-retail areas of the city, and particularly to **edge of town sites,** helped redistribute traffic volumes and make use of the latest infrastructure. Retailers no longer had to occupy run down warehouses; they could acquire undeveloped land on the edge of built up areas and provide purpose built stores, parking facilities and amenities for their customers.[4]

Edge of town sites Retail locations on undeveloped land, providing purpose built stores, parking facilities and amenities for their customers on the edge of a built up area

Retail Parks

The progression of the out-of-town concept and relaxation of planning regulations by local authorities led to the mid-1980s initiation of **retail parks,** in which free-standing superstores, each over 2,500 square metres (27,500 square feet) are grouped together to form retail villages or parks. Located close to major roads, they offer extensive free parking. Most of the stores offer one floor shopping with wide ranges. Grocery superstores locate so as to be easily accessible to their consumers, as do the retailers of large, expensive shopping goods: carpets, furniture, electrical goods, toys. The extensive ranges and displays of DIY retailers make such locations viable.

Retail parks Groupings of free-standing superstores, forming a retail village

Increasingly, planners are for the first time allowing clothing and footwear retailers to locate out of town. They initially feared the demise of the CBD, but forecasts now show that both CBD and out-of-town centres can survive serving the same town or city.

Most retail parks provide only superstores, but some have shopping malls of speciality and chain stores, such as Birmingham's Merry Hill or Gateshead's Metro Centre. Many shoppers now visit the CBD and retail parks for a leisure activity as much as a purchasing activity. The time is past when "serious" shopping took place just once a week: many consumers shop several times each week, aided by the now commonplace Sunday opening of many retail stores. Leisure facilities are frequently incorporated to cater for a family day out: ice skating rinks, cinemas, children's play areas, restaurants, fast food outlets and food courts (see Figure 14.2).

Major Store Types

Department and Variety Stores

Retail stores are often classified according to width of product mix and depth of product lines. **Department stores** are physically large—around 25,000 square metres (275,000 square feet)—and occupy prominent positions in the traditional

Figure 14.2 The out-of-town shopping mall has reached Europe. Gateshead's Metro Centre offers the major retail chains plus extensive leisure amenities and catering facilities. SOURCE: Courtesy of The Metro Centre.

Department stores Physically large stores that occupy prominent positions in the traditional heart of the town or city or as anchor stores in out-of-town malls

heart of the town or city, the central shopping centre. Out-of-town shopping malls, such as Manchester's Trafford Park or Kent's Blue Water, include leading department stores as anchor stores to attract consumers and smaller retail store tenants. Department stores are characterised by wide product mixes in considerable depth for most product lines. Most towns have at least one such store; larger towns and cities have the population size to support several. The smaller town's department store is generally independently owned, whereas the larger store groups—Debenhams, House of Fraser, John Lewis or Allders in the UK; AuHPrintemps in France; El Corte Ingles in Spain; or Karlstadt in Germany—have stores in many cities. Within a department store, related product lines are organised into separate departments such as cosmetics, men's and women's fashions and accessories, housewares, home furnishings, haberdashery and toys. Each department functions as a self-contained business unit, and the buyers for individual departments are fairly autonomous. Financial services, hairdressing and restaurants or coffee shops act as additional "pulls" to attract customers into the store.

Quite often concessionaires operate shops within shops. Brides has its own bridal shops and agencies in secondary locations but also operates the bridal departments in many Debenhams and House of Fraser department stores. Concessionaires either pay a fixed rental per square metre of space occupied in the host department store or pay a percentage commission on the volume of business. In department stores, concessions or shops-within-shops are typical for fashion clothing, cosmetics and housewares.

Throughout the 1970s and 1980s, with the growth of shopping malls and covered centres, the explosion in the number of speciality shops and the move to out-of-town shopping, the demise of department stores was predicted. Yet they are still at the heart of many CBD shopping centres. With new management teams and investment, most department store groups are once again thriving and expanding, building new stores in towns where they were not previously represented and in out-of-town retail parks, as well as refurbishing existing outlets.

Variety stores tend to be slightly smaller and often are more specialised, offering a reduced range of merchandise. Their appeal tends to be middle market, price points are more critical and the selection of additional services is limited, compared with a department store, usually just coffee shops. C&A focuses on men's, women's and children's clothing; Marks & Spencer on clothing and food; BhS and Littlewoods on clothing and housewares; Woolworth on housewares, records and tapes, children's clothing and confectionery. Variety stores are characterised by low cost facilities, self-service shopping, central payment points and multiple purchases; they appeal to large, heterogeneous target markets, especially price-conscious customers.

Grocery Supermarkets, Superstores and Hypermarkets

In the 1960s, grocery retailers, led by Sainsbury's, Tesco and Fine Fare, expanded into 1,000 square metre (11,000 square foot) supermarkets, either in the city centre or within suburban centres. As product ranges grew, self-service requirements called for more space; and as city centre rents rose, the age of the superstore arrived. Size requirements grew further still, and there was an exodus from the city centre. In the 1980s the average grocery superstore grew from 2,500 square metres to 5,500 square metres (27,500 to 61,000 square feet) and moved away from the suburban centre to either free-standing superstore sites or out-of-town retail parks.

Supermarkets and grocery **superstores** are large, self-service stores that carry a complete line of food products as well as other convenience items—cosmetics, non-prescription drugs and kitchenwares. Some, such as Asda or Tesco, sell clothing and small electrical appliances. Grocery superstores are laid out in departments for maximum efficiency in stocking and handling products but have central checkout facilities by the exits to the ample, free parking. Prices are considerably lower than in the independently owned supermarkets based in suburban shopping centres or in neighbourhood grocery shops. An increase in the number of price-conscious consumers demanding greater choice, improved packaging and refrigeration, as well as the advent of widespread car ownership, spurred the huge growth of major grocery superstore retailers Sainsbury's, Tesco, Asda, Somerfield and Safeway.

Of the top retailers in Europe (Table 14.2), many are superstore trading grocery companies. They are at the forefront of retail technology—barcode scanning EPOS (electronic point-of-sale) tills, shelf allocation modelling, robotised warehouse stacking—and of monitoring changes in customer attitudes and expectations. Increasingly, to gain an edge over the competition, they are launching more own label products with attributes equal to, if not better than, the manufacturers' brands also on sale. In some leading supermarkets, own label lines and non-branded fresh produce now account for 50 per cent of sales. The grocery retailers have led the transition in Europe, crossing national borders to trade in many countries. This move was initiated by the discounters, such as Aldi, Netto and Carrefour.

Asda, based in Leeds and now part of the mighty Wal-Mart group, began as a discount retailer of grocery products in the northern industrial regions of the UK. Needing large premises but unable to gain planning permission to build on green field sites, the company operated initially from redundant cinemas and converted

Table 14.2 The top 20 west European retailers

Rank	Company	Country	Core Retail Activity	Sales £m	Year End
1	Metro	Germany	Multi-sector	29,982[1]	31/12/97
2	Rewe	Germany	Grocery	18,691[1]	31/12/97
3	Tengelmann	Germany	Multi-sector	17,842[2]	1995/96
4	Carrefour	France	Grocery	17,698[2]	31/12/97
5	Auchan	France	Grocery	16,960[1]	31/12/97
6	Aldi Group	Germany	Grocery	16,015[1]	31/12/97
7	Intermarché	France	Grocery	14,821[3]	31/12/97
8	Edeka Group	Germany	Grocery	14,769[1]	31/12/97
9	Centres Leclerc	France	Grocery	14,336[1]	31/12/97
10	Tesco plc	UK	Grocery	13,887[2]	22/2/97
11	J Sainsbury	UK	Grocery	13,395[2]	8/3/97
12	Promodès	France	Grocery	11,610[4]	31/12/97
13	Karstadt	Germany	Grocery	11,299[5]	31/12/96
14	Lidl & Schwartz	Germany	Grocery	9,495[5]	31/12/96
15	Migros	Switzerland	Grocery	9,107[5]	31/12/96
16	Casino	France	Grocery	7,960[4]	31/12/97
17	Co-operative Society	UK	Variety	7,948[6]	31/12/96
18	Marks & Spencer	UK	Variety	7,841[2]	31/3/97
19	Safeway plc	UK	Grocery	7,066[2]	29/3/97
20	ASDA	UK	Grocery	6,952[2]	3/5/97

Notes: Sources of information: [1]Turnover, Eurodata 1997. [2]Sales, Annual Accounts 1997. [3]La Tribune, February 1998. [4]Sales, Retail Newsletter, March 1998. [5]Turnover, Eurodata 1996. [6]Sales, Annual Accounts 1996/97.

SOURCE: *The Retail Pocket Book 1999.* Reprinted by permission of NTC Publications, Ltd.

industrial warehouses. As the superstore era blossomed, Asda was a guiding force. Today the company is a leader in superstore grocery retailing, with over 250 purpose built free-standing superstores offering manufacturer and Asda branded goods. The stores have over 4,500 square metres (50,000 square feet) of one floor retail space, pleasing ambience and additional amenities such as cafés, crèche facilities and ample free parking. The company has a new distribution network, fully computerised and centralised, with on-line EPOS systems monitoring the exact stock requirements of each store.

Hypermarkets take the benefits of the superstore even further, using their greater size—over 9,000 square metres (100,000 square feet)—to give the customer a wider range and depth of products. They are common in the US, France and Germany, but there are few genuine hypermarkets in the UK, except perhaps for Sainsbury's Savacentre.

Hypermarkets Stores that take the benefits of the superstore even further, using their greater size to give the customer a wider range and depth of products

Discount Sheds, Superstores and Category Killers

The move away from the city or town centre was not confined to multiple grocery retailers. Furniture, carpets and electrical appliances require large display areas, ranges with strength in depth and, if possible, one floor shopping. The concentration of retailers in the city centre led to limited store opening opportunities (large enough sites were hard to find) and to high rents. When the electrical retailer Comet and furniture retailers Queensway and MFI sought out-of-town sites, they too were initially forced by the planning authorities to occupy disused warehouses and industrial units along arteries into the city centre. As the planners reviewed their regulations, these companies, along with the major DIY and toy retailers, developed purpose built discount "sheds" or retail warehouses. Originally free-standing, these 2,000 to 3,500 square metre (22,000 to 39,000 square foot) stores are increasingly found in out-of-town retail parks.

Discount sheds Cheaply constructed, one storey retail stores with no window displays and few add-on amenities; oriented towards car-borne shoppers

The **discount sheds** are cheaply constructed, one storey retail stores with no window displays and few add-on amenities. Oriented towards car-borne shoppers, they have large, free car parks and spacious stock facilities to enable shoppers to take delivery of their purchases immediately. Checkout points and customer services are kept to a minimum. As major retail groups have seen the cost benefits of locating out of town, more companies have opened out-of-town, free-standing or retail park superstores. Many customers would not tolerate the minimalist approach to ambience and service levels. Construction is still basic, but more resources are devoted to shop fitting expertise and customer service. US Toys "R" Us and Sweden's IKEA typify the new generation of superstores. Most retail groups selling electrical goods, carpets, furniture, toys, groceries or DIY goods, not just the discounters, now operate superstores. Increasingly, major variety store companies, departmental store groups, and clothing and footwear retailers are developing superstores: Marks & Spencer, Debenhams and Sears are among them.

Category killers Large stores, tending to be superstore sized, that specialise in a narrow line of merchandise

Often categorised separately, **category killers** are large stores, tending to be superstore sized, that specialise in a narrow line of merchandise. They are known as category killers—an "Americanism"—because they have a huge selection within a narrow category of merchandise and "kill off" the smaller stores retailing similar lines of merchandise. They require high footfall to be viable and tend to be located in large towns and cities on edge of town sites. The large DIY operators such as B&Q or Homebase have led to the closure of many small, traditional hardware stores. Currys (electrical goods), Office World (office supplies) and the new superstores being opened by JJB Sports or Allsports (sporting goods) are category killers.

Warehouse Clubs

Warehouse clubs Large scale, members only selling operations combining cash and carry wholesaling with discount retailing

A rapidly growing form of mass merchandising, **warehouse clubs** are large scale, members only selling operations combining cash and carry wholesaling with discount retailing. For a nominal annual fee, small retailers purchase products at wholesale prices for business use or for re-sale. Warehouse clubs also sell to ultimate consumers affiliated with credit unions, schools, hospitals and banks, but instead of paying a membership fee, individual consumers pay about 5 per cent more on each item than do business customers.

Sometimes called buying clubs, warehouse clubs offer the same types of products as discount stores but in a limited range of sizes and styles. Warehouse clubs offer a broad product mix, including non-perishable foods, beverages, books, appliances, housewares, car parts, hardware and furniture. Their facilities, often located in industrial areas, have concrete floors and aisles wide enough for fork lifts. Merchandise is stacked on pallets or displayed on pipe racks. All payments must be in cash, and customers must transport purchases themselves. Warehouse clubs appeal to many price-conscious consumers and small retailers unable to obtain wholesaling services from larger distributors. CostCo was the first US-style warehouse club to enter the UK.

Speciality Shops

Most shopping centres and towns have a major department store. At the other end of the spectrum is the traditional corner shop. Few small shops these days retail a variety of product groups. In suburban areas such shops tend to specialise in retailing one convenience product category—newsagents with cigarettes and newspapers, greengrocers, chemists, hair salons, etc. In the town centre (CBD) few retailers of convenience goods, with their low margins, can afford the rents and business tax. Instead, the small store retailers—250 square metres (2,750 square feet) and under—in the CBD town centre specialise in shopping or comparison items: clothing, footwear, CDs and tapes, cosmetics, jewellery. Ownership of such retail outlets is increasingly concentrated in the hands of a few major retail groups (see Table 14.3), some of which also have retail brands that operate as department stores or out-of-town superstores. **Speciality shops** offer self-service but a greater level of assistance from store personnel than department stores and carry a narrow product mix with deep product lines. A typical 300 square metre (3,300 square feet) footwear or clothing retail store will have window displays to entice passing pedestrians, one or two checkout points and three or four assistants. Such stores depend on the town centre's general parking facilities and on proximity to a key trader, such as Boots or Marks & Spencer, which will generate pedestrian traffic.

Speciality shops Stores that offer self-service but a greater level of assistance from store personnel than department stores and carry a narrow product mix with deep product lines

Convenience Stores

As the number of neighbourhood grocery stores declined in the 1960s and 1970s with the expansion of the superstore based national grocery chains, a niche

Arcadia (fashion clothing shops, mail order)	Burton, Top Man, Principles/Principles for Men, Top Shop, Evans, Dorothy Perkins, Hawkshead, Racing Green, Miss Selfridge, Outfit, Wallis, Warehouse
Boots (chemists, opticians, car accessories)	Boots, Halfords
Dixons (electricals, computers, mobile phones, computer games)	Dixons, Currys, PC World, The Link, @jakarta
Kingfisher (variety stores, chemists, electricals, DIY, music, office supplies)	Woolworth, Superdrug, Comet, B&Q, Staples, MVC
J. Sainsbury (grocery, DIY)	Sainsbury, Savacentre; Homebase
Sears (jewellery, mail order, discounters)	Hornes, Your Price; Milletts Leisure; Freemans; Stage 1, Stage 2
Storehouse (fashion clothing, children's wear)	Blazer, Mothercare, One Up
Thorn EMI (TV rental, books, records, household goods)	Radio Rentals; Dillons; HMV; Crazy George's; Waterstone's
W. H. Smith (newsagency, books, CDs/tapes)	W. H. Smith, Waterstone's, Paperchase, Our Price, Virgin, Wee Three Records (US), Playhouse, John Menzies

Table 14.3 Large retail groups

Convenience stores Shops that sell essential groceries, alcoholic drinks, drugs and newspapers outside the traditional shopping hours

emerged in the market to be filled by **convenience stores.** These shops sell essential groceries, alcoholic drinks, drugs and newspapers outside the traditional 9.00 a.m. to 6.00 p.m. shopping hours. The major superstores extended their opening hours to 8.00 p.m. to facilitate after work shopping, but no major retailers catered for "emergency" or top-up shopping. There was a resurgence of the traditional corner shop located in suburban housing estates, offering limited ranges but extended opening hours. Consumers pay a slight price premium but receive convenience in terms of location and opening hours. In the 1970s and 1980s, the voluntary groups (Spar, Mace, VG) and national retail groups such as Dillons, Circle K and 7-Eleven re-positioned their brands into the "open all hours" top-up or emergency shopping niche. Although they now face competition from the increasing number of 24 hour supermarkets and forecourt shops, convenience stores are on the increase.

Discounters

Discounters Operations that take short term leases in un-let units in malls, selling such items as stationery, toys, confectionery and gifts at deeply discounted prices

An emerging trend is for un-let units in malls and the CBD to be taken on very short term leases, sometimes even weekly, by "pile it high, sell it cheap" **discounters** selling items such as stationery, toys, confectionery, gifts—often at "everything under a £1!!". Understandably, these operations invest little in shop fitting, promotion or staff training. For their landlords, such tenants may not be ideal, but they do generate rental income in what would otherwise be empty shop units. There are national chains of discounters, such as Poundstretcher or What Everyone Wants, which do invest in shop fitting and local press advertising and which do intend long term occupancy of sites. These operations also are no frills, low service, low price trading concepts. Marketing Insight 14.2 discusses the importance of value-for-money retailing propositions in more mainstream categories of stores.

Factory Outlet Villages

Factory outlet villages Converted rural buildings or purpose built out-of-town retail parks for manufacturers' outlets retailing branded seconds, excess stocks and last season's lines or trialling new lines

These retail villages initially sold seconds—imperfect new merchandise—similar to the lines stocked in many factory shops in converted mills or rural locations, in some instances with eight to ten shop units clustered together. Now developers are designing and building out-of-town **factory outlet villages** for major manufacturers' and branded goods, with up to twenty mini-superstores grouped together, such as Cheshire Oaks on Merseyside. Increasingly, major manufacturers and retailers are using these stores to off-load last season's lines, excess stocks and branded seconds or to trial new lines. These outlets are very popular for designer label clothing, linens, crockery and homewares.

Markets and Cash and Carry Warehouses

Markets Halls where fresh foods, clothing and housewares are sold, catering for budget-conscious shoppers who typically have a middle and down-market social profile

Cash and carry warehouses Outlets that retail extensive ranges of groceries, tobacco, alcohol, beverages and confectionery to newsagents, small supermarkets and convenience stores, and the catering trade

In most towns there are wholesale **markets** selling meat, greengrocery, fruit, flowers and fish from which speciality retailers make their inventory purchases. Traditional, too, is the general retail market selling to the general public, either in recently refurbished Victorian market halls or in council provided modern halls adjacent to the town centre shopping malls. Such market halls sell fresh foods, clothing and housewares, and they cater for budget-conscious shoppers who typically have a middle and down-market social profile.

Cash and carry warehouses, such as Booker or Makro, retail extensive ranges of groceries, tobacco, alcohol, beverages and confectionery to newsagents, small supermarkets and convenience stores, and the catering trade (hotels, guest houses, restaurants and cafés). By purchasing from manufacturers in bulk, cash and carry companies can offer substantial price savings to their customers, who in turn can add a retail margin without alienating their customers. Many countries, particularly Scandinavia, have hybrid outlets that combine the speciality shop, convenience store and cash and carry warehouse. Buying groups link small, often privately owned local retailers with similar shops; collectively their purchasing power is enhanced, and they increasingly operate their own wholesale warehouses and offer own label brands.

Catalogue Showrooms

Catalogue showroom Outlets in which one item of each product class is on display and the remaining inventory is stored out of the buyers' reach

In a **catalogue showroom** one item of each product class is on display and the remaining inventory is stored out of the buyers' reach. Using catalogues that have been mailed to their homes or are on counters in the store, customers order the goods at their leisure. Shop assistants usually complete the order form and then collect the merchandise from the adjoining warehouse. Catalogue showrooms, such as Argos or Index, regularly sell goods below the manufacturers' list price and often provide goods immediately. Higher product turnover, fewer losses through damage or shoplifting and lower labour costs lead to their reduced retail prices. Jewellery, luggage, photographic equipment, toys, small appliances, housewares, sporting goods, garden furniture and power tools are the most commonly available items, listed by category and brand in the company's catalogue.

Categories

Table 14.1 summarised the sales of the major categories of retailing. It is worth noting that the categories with the most stores do not necessarily top the league for highest turnover or profitability. The superstore and department store retailers have relatively few outlets, but they account for large floor areas and include many of the main retail groups. European, and UK in particular, retail statistics are notoriously poor, being based on infrequent estimates rather than regular censuses. Agencies such as AGB, Euromonitor, Jordans, Mintel and Verdict produce regular reports on retail sectors and consumer expectations based on commissioned marketing research surveys. These are available by subscription or occasionally, for the newest versions, through business libraries. These agencies tend to use categories similar to those discussed by the retail trade itself rather than the stilted, amalgamated official classification:

Food/grocery • CTN (confectionery, tobacco, news) • Off-licence beverages
Men's/women's wear • Children's wear • Footwear/leather goods
Furniture/carpets/soft furnishings
Electrical (small appliances, brown and white goods)
Hardware • DIY
Chemist/druggist
Books/greeting cards
Jewellers
Toys
Mixed retail businesses
Mail order
Restaurants/cafés/catering • Hotels
Banking/financial services

It is clear from this extensive list of retail categories just how important retailing is in the marketing channel for the bulk of consumer purchases and consumption. Producers require retailers in order to implement their marketing strategies and to satisfy targeted consumers. They must also strive to satisfy their immediate customers, the retailers. Retailers themselves require marketing strategies and programmes in order to satisfy their targeted consumers, sell their supplying producers' wares and meet financial performance targets.

Supermarkets Discover That Good Value Can Be Expensive

At a time when supermarket retailing is at its most sophisticated, with more effort than ever devoted to store layout, atmospherics and customer service, it may seem surprising that leading UK supermarkets are engaged in a pricing battle. Tesco, Kwik Save, Asda and Sainsbury's have all been promoting price cutting activities. It seems that the leading retailers all agree that customer loyalty can be bought and that value for money is what it requires. In the words of one retailing expert, "We have moved from the phase of cheap and nasty, through cheap and cheerful, to cheap and chic, as personified by IKEA. Now we are in the age of cheap and clever, best illustrated by the example of EasyJet."

Even Tesco, the market leader, is not averse to cutting its prices. Although Tesco has systematically moved its brand away from a "cheap and cheerful" image, the company still believes that price is an important aspect of its offer. Over the years the retailer has frequently used the concept of value in its marketing. This was illustrated when in 1993 Tesco launched its so-called "Value" items. Nowadays, the importance of value continues, with the retailer employing pricing specialists, who make decisions about which products to discount. Tesco has a stated policy of using value to earn the long term loyalty of its customer base, and senior managers believe that this will continue to be crucial to the company's leading position.

Any business that attempts to compete on price must keep a careful watch on its profitability. For Tesco, the risks associated with cost cutting are carefully balanced by achieving savings elsewhere. However, management is quick to point out that these savings are not made at the customers' expense. For example, in five years, Tesco reduced the costs of building new outlets by one-third. The retailer also considerably reduced its supply chain costs. Meanwhile, it became the most successful retailer in the UK in terms of market share and profitability gains.

However, the kind of price competition in which the supermarkets are engaging is not without difficulties.

Indeed, as the Office of Fair Trading (OFT) sets out to investigate profit margins and competition among the largest supermarkets, some experts believe that the prices on offer are not the bargain they seem. If the OFT decides to refer the matter to the Competition Commission, the market leaders, which have already endured considerable negative publicity, may have more public scrutiny to endure. In general, the media believes that supermarkets have been slow to react to criticisms of high prices. Whatever the eventual findings of the OFT, it is clear that unwillingness to respond to media criticism may leave the supermarkets looking guilty.

Another danger of a price cutting approach is that the supermarket chains will damage customer perceptions. For example, Sainsbury's experience of price cutting has not been a happy one. Its widely promoted *Value to Shout About* campaign failed to bring about the up turn in fortunes it hoped for and was unpopular with customers. The problem was that the campaign moved too far away from Sainsbury's traditional quality and choice positioning. The result was that Sainsbury's axed its advertising agency and created a new communications programme which maintained the notion of value, but within the context of the retailer's existing quality/service-led positioning. Pricing is notoriously problematic as the basis for a strategy. Supermarketers' value oriented strategies are carefully constructed, but must be managed with care. Tesco appears to have effectively incorporated value within its overall brand positioning, while arch rival Sainsbury's has utilised value less successfully.

SOURCES: Alexandra Jardine, "Price stays at heart of UK retailing", *Marketing,* 11 March 1999, p. 18; Sue Beenstock, "UK supermarkets insist their price is right", *Marketing,* 8 April 1999, p. 15; Philip Buxton, "Sainsbury's makes AMV pay for 'Value' failure", *Marketing Week,* 1 April 1999, p. 12; Alexandra Jardine, "Sainsbury's set for more Cleese", *Marketing,* 11 February 1999, p. 5.

Non-store Retailing

Non-store retailing The selling of goods or services outside the confines of a retail facility

Non-store retailing is the selling of goods or services outside the confines of a retail facility. This form of retailing accounts for an increasing percentage of sales (see Table 14.4) and includes personal sales methods, such as in-home retailing

Table 14.4 Trends in non-store retailing

	Mail Order Sales Value £ million	Annual Growth (%)	Mail Order Business vs. All Retailer Business		Mail Order % of Total Retail Sales
			Index 1990 = 100		
			Mail Order	All Retailers	
1990	5,355	5.3	100	100	4.2
1991	5,516	3.0	103	105	4.1
1992	5,676	2.9	106	109	4.1
1993	6,051	6.6	113	114	4.1
1994	6,373	5.3	119	120	4.2
1995	6,158	−3.4	115	124	3.9
1996	6,319	2.6	118	131	3.8
1997	6,801	7.6	127	139	3.8

SOURCE: *The Retail Pocket Book 1999*, p. 103. Reprinted by permission of NTC Publications, Ltd.

and telemarketing, and non-personal sales methods, such as automatic vending and mail order retailing (which includes catalogue retailing). A growing form of non-store retailing is the use of the Internet to promote and sell goods and services; orders can be placed using a credit card via a home based PC.

Certain non-store retailing methods are in the category of **direct marketing**: the use of non-personal media, the Internet or telesales to introduce products to consumers, who then purchase the products by mail, telephone or the Internet. In the case of telephone orders, salespeople may be required to complete the sales. Telemarketing, mail order and catalogue retailing are all examples of direct marketing, as are sales generated by coupons, direct mail and Freephone, bell gratis 0800 numbers and the Internet.

Direct marketing The use of non-personal media, the Internet or telesales to introduce products to consumers, who then purchase the products by mail, telephone or the Internet.

In-Home Retailing

In-home retailing Selling via personal contacts with consumers in their own homes

In-home retailing is selling via personal contacts with consumers in their own homes. Companies such as Avon, Amway and Betterware send representatives to the homes of pre-selected prospects. Traditionally, in-home retailing relied on a random, door-to-door approach. Some companies now use a more efficient approach. They first identify prospects by reaching them by phone, mail or the Internet or by intercepting them in shopping malls or at consumer trade fairs. These initial contacts are limited to a brief introduction and the setting of appointments.

Some in-home selling, however, is still undertaken without information about sales prospects. Door-to-door selling without a pre-arranged appointment represents a tiny proportion of total retail sales, less than 1 per cent. Because it has so often been associated with unscrupulous and fraudulent techniques, it is illegal in some communities. Generally, this method is regarded unfavourably because so many door-to-door salespeople are under trained and poorly supervised. A big disadvantage of door-to-door selling is the large expenditure, effort and time it demands. Sales commissions are usually 25 to 50 per cent (or more) of the retail price; as a result, consumers often pay more than a product is worth. Door-to-door selling is used most often when a product is unsought—for instance, encyclopaedias or double glazed windows, which most consumers would not be likely to purchase in a store.

A variation of in-home retailing is the home demonstration or party plan, which such companies as Tupperware, Ann Summers and Mary Kay Cosmetics use successfully. One consumer acts as host and invites a number of friends to view merchandise at his or her home, where a salesperson is on hand to demonstrate the products. The home demonstration is more efficient for the sales representative than contacting each prospect door-to-door, and the congenial atmosphere partly overcomes consumers' suspicions and encourages them to buy. Home demonstrations also meet the buyers' needs for convenience and personal service. Commissions and selling costs make this form of retailing expensive, however. Additionally, successful party plan selling requires both a network of friends and neighbours who have the time to attend such social gatherings and a large number of effective salespeople. With so many household members now holding full time jobs, both prospects and sales representatives are harder to recruit. The growth of interactive telephone-computer home shopping and the growing use of the Internet may also cut into party plan sales.

Telemarketing

Telemarketing The direct selling of goods and services by telephone based on either a cold canvass of the telephone directory or a pre-screened list of prospective clients

More and more organisations—IBM, Merrill Lynch, Avis, Ford, Quaker Oats, Time and American Express, to name a few—are using the telephone to strengthen the effectiveness of traditional marketing methods. **Telemarketing** is the direct selling of goods and services by telephone based on either a cold canvass of the telephone directory or a pre-screened list of prospective clients. (In some areas, certain telephone numbers are listed with an asterisk to indicate the people who consider sales solicitations a nuisance and do not want to be bothered.) Telemarketing can generate sales leads, improve customer service, speed up collection of over-due accounts, raise funds for not-for-profit groups and gather market data.[5]

In some cases, telemarketing uses advertising to encourage consumers to initiate a call or to request information about placing an order. Such advertisements will include "a call to action" to prompt target consumers to dial an 0800 Freephone number. This type of retailing is only a small part of total retail sales, but its use is growing. Research indicates that telemarketing is most successful when combined with other marketing strategies, such as direct mail or advertising in newspapers, radio and television.

Automatic Vending

Automatic vending The use of coin operated self-service machines to sell small, standardised, routinely purchased products such as chewing gum, sweets, newspapers, cigarettes, soft drinks and coffee

Automatic vending makes use of coin operated self-service machines and accounts for less than 1 per cent of all retail sales. In the UK there are approximately 1.2 million vending machines. Locations and the percentage of sales each generates are as follows:[6]

Plants and factories	38%
Public locations (e.g. stores)	26
Offices	16
Colleges and universities	6
Government facilities	3
Hospitals and nursing homes	3
Primary and secondary schools	2
Others	6

Video game machines provide an entertainment service, and many banks now offer machines that dispense cash or offer other services, but these uses of vending machines are not reported in total vending sales volume.

Automatic vending is one of the most impersonal forms of retailing. Small, standardised, routinely purchased products (chewing gum, sweets, newspapers, cigarettes, soft drinks, coffee) can be sold in machines because consumers usually buy them at the nearest available location. Machines in areas of heavy traffic provide efficient and continuous services to consumers. The elimination of sales personnel and the small amount of space necessary for vending machines give this retailing method some advantages over stores. The advantages are partly offset by the expense of the frequent servicing and repair needed.

Mail Order Retailing

Mail order retailing   Selling by description because buyers usually do not see the actual product until it arrives in the mail

Mail order retailing involves selling by description because buyers usually do not see the actual product until it arrives in the mail. Sellers contact buyers through direct mail, catalogues, television, radio, magazines and newspapers, and increasingly via the Internet. A wide assortment of products such as compact discs, books and clothing is sold to consumers through the mail. Placing mail orders by telephone and e-mail is increasingly common. The advantages of mail order selling include efficiency and convenience. Mail order houses, such as Freemans, Otto Versand or La Redoute, can be located in remote, low cost areas and avoid the expenses of store fixtures. Eliminating personal selling efforts and store operations may result in tremendous savings that can be passed along to consumers in the form of lower prices. On the other hand, mail order retailing is inflexible, provides limited service and is more appropriate for speciality products than for convenience products. As shown in Table 14.4, mail order is on the increase.

Catalogue retailing   A type of mail order retailing in which customers receive their catalogues by mail, or pick them up if the catalogue retailer has stores

When **catalogue retailing** (a specific type of mail order retailing) is used, customers receive their catalogues by mail, or they may pick them up if the catalogue retailer has stores, as does Littlewoods. Although in-store visits result in some catalogue orders, most are placed by mail, telephone or the Internet. In the US, General Foods created Thomas Garroway Ltd., a mail order service supplying gourmet pasta, cheese, coffee and similar items. Other packaged goods manufacturers involved in catalogue retailing include Hanes, Nestlé, Thomas J. Lipton, Sunkist and Whitman Chocolates.[7] These catalogue retailers are able to reach many two income families who have more money and less time for special shopping. In the UK, manufacturers and store focused retail groups tend not to be involved with catalogue or home shopping. The specialist mail order companies such as GUS and Freemans dominate this sector. Recently, though, Arcadia (with over two thousand shops) bought over various mail order brands, indicating the growing importance of this channel of distribution. The UK mail order market is worth over £7 billion, having grown by 27 per cent since 1990.[8]

Franchising

Franchising   An arrangement whereby a supplier (franchisor) grants a dealer (franchisee) the right to sell products in exchange for some type of consideration

Franchising is an arrangement whereby a supplier, or franchisor, grants a dealer, or franchisee, the right to sell products in exchange for some type of consideration. For example, the franchisor may receive some percentage of total sales in exchange for furnishing equipment, buildings, management know-how, marketing assistance and branding to the franchisee. The franchisee supplies labour and capital, operates the franchised business and agrees to abide by the provisions of the franchise agreement. This next section looks at the major types of retail franchises, the advantages and disadvantages of franchising and trends in franchising.

Major Types of Retail Franchises

Retail franchise arrangements can ordinarily be classified as one of three general types. (1) In the first arrangement, a manufacturer authorises a number of retail stores to sell a certain brand name item. This franchise arrangement, one of the oldest, is common in the sales of cars and trucks, farm equipment, earthmoving equipment and petroleum. The majority of all petrol is sold through franchised independent retail service stations, and franchised dealers handle virtually all sales of new cars and trucks. (2) In the second type of retail franchise, a producer licenses distributors to sell a given product to retailers. This franchising arrangement is common in the soft drinks industry. Most international manufacturers of soft drink syrups—Coca-Cola, Pepsi-Cola—franchise independent bottlers, which then service retailers. (3) In the third type of retail franchise, a franchisor supplies brand names, techniques or other services, instead of a complete product. The franchisor may provide certain production and distribution services, but its primary role in the arrangement is the careful development and control of marketing strategies. This approach to franchising, which is the most typical today, is used by many companies, including Holiday Inn, McDonald's, Avis, Hertz, KFC, Body Shop, Holland & Barrett, Pronuptia and Benetton.

Advantages and Disadvantages of Franchising

Advantages and Disadvantages of Franchising

Franchising offers several advantages to both the franchisee and the franchisor. It enables a franchisee to start a business with limited capital and to make use of the business experience of others. Moreover, an outlet with a nationally advertised name, such as Body Shop or Burger King, is often assured of customers as soon as it opens. If business problems arise, the franchisee can obtain guidance and advice from the franchisor at little or no cost. Franchised outlets are generally more successful than independently owned businesses: only 5 to 8 per cent of franchised retail businesses fail during the first two years of operation, whereas approximately 54 per cent of independent retail businesses fail during that period.[9] The franchisee also receives materials to use in local advertising and can take part in national promotional campaigns sponsored by the franchisor.

The franchisor gains fast and selective distribution of its products through franchise arrangements without incurring the high cost of constructing and operating its own outlets. The franchisor therefore has more capital available to expand production and to use for advertising. At the same time, it can ensure, through the franchise agreement, that outlets are maintained and operated to its own standards. The franchisor also benefits from the fact that the franchisee, being a sole proprietor in most cases, is likely to be very highly motivated to succeed. The success of the franchise means more sales, which translate into higher royalties for the franchisor.

Despite their numerous advantages, franchise arrangements also have several drawbacks. The franchisor can dictate many aspects of the business: decor, the design of employees' uniforms, types of signs and numerous details of business operations. In addition, franchisees must pay to use the franchisor's name, products and assistance. Usually, there is a one-time franchise fee and continuing royalty and advertising fees, collected as a percentage of sales. In addition, franchisees often must work very hard, putting in 10 and 12 hour days, six days a week. In some cases, franchise agreements are not uniform: one franchisee may pay more than another for the same services. The franchisor also gives up a certain amount of control when entering into a franchise agreement. Consequently, individual establishments may not be operated exactly as the franchisor would operate them.

Trends in Franchising

Franchising has been used since the early 1950s, primarily for service stations and car dealerships. However, it has grown enormously since the mid-1960s.[10] This growth has generally paralleled the expansion of the fast food industry—the industry in which franchising is widely used. Of course, franchising is not limited to fast foods. Franchise arrangements for health clubs, pest control, hair salons and travel agencies are widespread. The estate agency industry has also experienced a rapid increase in franchising. The largest franchising sectors, ranked by sales, are: car and truck dealers (52 per cent), service stations (14 per cent), restaurants (10 per cent) and non-food retailing (5 per cent).[11] Many internationally known brands, such as Burger King, McDonald's, Benetton and Body Shop, use franchising as their core means of rapid global expansion. Table 14.5 lists the top ten international franchises.

Strategic Issues in Retailing

Consumers often have vague reasons for making a retail purchase. Whereas most industrial, business-to-business purchases are based on economic planning and necessity, consumer purchases often result from social influences and psychological factors. Because consumers shop for a variety of reasons—to search for specific items, to escape boredom or to learn about something new—retailers must do more than simply fill space with merchandise; they must make desired products available, create stimulating environments for shopping and develop marketing strategies that increase sales and store patronage. Research indicates that for many consumers, shopping is far more than the task of purchasing and collecting goods: it is a social, leisure oriented activity. This section discusses how store location, property ownership, product assortment, retail positioning, atmospherics, store image, scrambled merchandising, the wheel of retailing, the balance of retailing power, retail technology and EU deregulation affect these retailing objectives.[12]

Location

Location The strategic retailing issue that dictates the limited geographic trading area from which a store must draw its customers

Location, the least flexible of the strategic retailing issues, is one of the most important, because location dictates the limited geographic trading area from which a store must draw its customers.[13] Thus retailers consider a variety of factors when evaluating potential locations, including the location of the company's target customers within the trading area, the economic climate in the region, the kinds of products being sold, the availability of public transport, customer characteristics and competitors' locations.[14] The relative ease of movement to and from the site is important, so pedestrian and vehicular traffic, parking and transport must all be taken into account. Most retailers prefer sites with high pedestrian traffic; preliminary site investigations often include a pedestrian count to determine how many of the passers-by are truly prospective customers. Similarly, the nature of the area's vehicular traffic is analysed. Certain retailers, such as service stations and convenience stores, depend on large numbers of car-borne customers but try to avoid overly congested locations. In addition, parking space must be adequate, and transport networks (major thoroughfares and public transport) must be able to accommodate customers and delivery vehicles.

Retailers also evaluate the characteristics of the site itself: the other stores in the area, particularly the proximity of key traders or magnets; the size, shape and visibility of the plot or building under consideration; and the rental, leasing or ownership terms under which the building may be occupied. Retailers also look for compatibility with nearby retailers because stores that complement one another draw more customers for everyone. This is particularly true for clothing, footwear and jewellery retailers.[15] When making site location decisions, retailers must select from among several general types of location: free-standing structures, traditional business districts, neighbourhood/suburban shopping centres, out-of-town superstores and retail parks. In recent years retailers have been moving away from the traditional store assessment procedure of pedestrian counts and "eyeballing" the site's immediate location. Various agencies—notably CACI and SAMI—have detailed databases examining each shopping centre. Computer modelling, such as SLAM (Store Location Assessment Model), has become more widespread, bringing a basis of objectivity to what was previously an intuitive decision-making process based on few hard facts.[16]

Property Ownership

Property ownership is perpetually an issue in retailing. Some companies, such as Marks & Spencer, invest heavily to own the majority of their property portfolio. This gives security of tenure, saves on rents and lease negotiations, and adds to the book value of the company. To release operating funds, companies often engage in "sale and lease-back" deals. Property companies buy the freehold to add to their assets but immediately give a favourable lease to the retailer. In recent years companies that once held the freehold for most of their stores have sold off property to make available operating funds for new computer systems, store refurbishment or new store openings. Companies such as Arcadia or Next argue that they are primarily retailers and should not tie up funds in property ownership. Retailers that locate mainly in covered shopping centres and in retail parks generally have to accept lease agreements as the centre's developer maintains ownership of the property.

Product Assortment

Table 14.5 Top 10 International Franchises

1. McDonald's
2. Yogen Früz Worldwide
3. Subway
4. KFC
5. Kumon Math & Reading Centers
6. Wendy's Int'l. Inc.
7. TCBY Treats
8. Taco Bell Corp.
9. Blockbuster Video
10. Mail Boxes Etc.

SOURCE:
"*Entrepreneur*'s 1999 Top 200 International Franchises", www.entrepreneurmag.com/international/200intl.hts, accessed 2000.

The product assortments that retailers develop vary considerably in breadth, depth and quality. Retail stores are often classified according to their product assortments. Conversely, a store's type affects the breadth and depth of its product offerings as shown in Figure 14.3. Thus a speciality store has a single product line but considerable depth in that line. Tie Rack stores and Fannie May Candy Shops, for example, carry only one line of products but many items within that line. In contrast, discount stores may have a wide product mix, such as housewares, car products, clothing and food. Department stores may have a wide product mix with different product line depths. Nevertheless, it is usually difficult to maintain both a wide and a deep product mix because of the inventories required. In addition, some producers prefer to distribute through retailers that offer less variety so that their products gain more exposure and are less affected by the presence of competing brands. Discounters like Everything Under £1 have a wide product mix with little depth. The limited line grocery chains, led by Netto and Aldi, have a moderate product mix with restricted depth—an approach that has brought them significant success as they target the budget-conscious.[17]

Issues of product assortment are often a matter of what and how much to carry. When retailers decide what should be included in their product assortments, they consider an assortment's purpose, status and completeness.[18] *Purpose* relates to how well an assortment satisfies consumers and at the same time furthers the retailer's goals. *Status* identifies by rank the relative importance of each product in an assortment: for example, motor oil might have low status in a store that sells convenience foods. *Completeness* means that an assortment includes the products necessary to satisfy a store's customers; the assortment is incomplete when some products are missing. An assortment of convenience foods must include milk to be complete because most consumers expect to be able to buy milk when purchasing other food products. New products are added to (and

Figure 14.3 Relationships between merchandise breadth and depth for a typical discount store, department store and speciality store. SOURCE: Robert F. Hartley, *Retailing: Challenge and Opportunity*, 3rd edn, p. 118. Copyright © 1984 by Houghton Mifflin Company. Used by permission.

Discount store

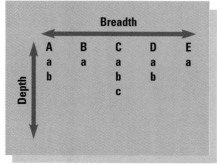

Department store

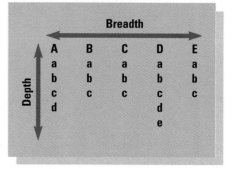

Speciality store

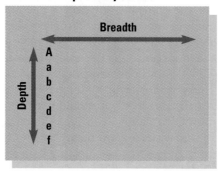

The capital letters represent the number of product lines, and the small letters depict the choices in any one product line. Thus it can be seen that discount stores are wide and shallow in merchandise assortment. Speciality stores, at the other extreme, have few product lines, but much more depth in the few they carry. The typical department store falls in between, having a broad assortment with many merchandise lines and medium depth in each line.

declining products are deleted from) an assortment when they meet (or fail to meet) the retailer's standards of purpose, status and completeness.

The retailer also considers the quality of the products to be offered. The store may limit its assortments to expensive, high quality goods for upper income market segments; it may stock cheap, low quality products for low income buyers; or it may try to attract several market segments by offering a range of quality within its total product assortment.

How much to include in an assortment depends on the needs of the retailer's target market. A discount store's customers expect a wide and shallow product mix, whereas speciality store shoppers prefer narrow and deep assortments. If a retailer can increase sales by increasing product variety, the assortment may be enlarged. If a broader product mix ties up too much floor space or creates storage problems, however, the retailer may stock only the products that generate the greatest sales. Other factors that affect product assortment decisions are personnel, store image, inventory control methods and the financial risks involved.[19]

Retail Positioning

Retail positioning The strategy of identifying a highly attractive market segment and serving it in a way that distinguishes the retailer from others in the minds of consumers in that segment

Because of the emergence of new types of stores (discount sheds, warehouse clubs, superstores, hypermarkets) and the expansion of product offerings by traditional stores, competition among retailers is intense. Thus it is important for management to consider the retail business's market positioning.[20] **Retail positioning** involves identifying an unserved or under-served market niche, or a highly attractive market segment, and serving it through a strategy that distinguishes the retailer from others in the minds of consumers in that segment.[21] The retailer must have a proposition, trading concept, brand image or merchandise policy that is visibly different from its competitors.

There are several ways in which retailers position themselves.[22] A retailer may position itself as a seller of high quality, premium priced products providing many services. A store such as Selfridges, which specialises in expensive high fashion clothing and jewellery, sophisticated electronics and exclusive home furnishings, might be expected to provide wrapping and delivery services, personal shopping consultants and restaurant facilities. Fortnum & Mason, for example, emphasises superlative service and even hires pianists to play in the entrance of its store.[23] Dixons, the electrical retailer, is often referred to as "the grown man's toy shop". Another type of retail company, such as IKEA, may be positioned as a marketer of reasonable quality products at low prices.

Atmospherics

Atmospherics The physical elements in a store's design that appeal to consumers' emotions and encourage them to buy

Atmospherics are often used to help position a retailer. **Atmospherics** are the physical elements in a store's design that appeal to consumers' emotions and encourage them to buy. Exterior and interior characteristics, layout and displays all contribute to a store's atmosphere. Department stores, restaurants, hotels, service stations and shops combine these elements in different ways to create specific atmospheres that may be perceived as warm, fresh, functional or exciting.

Exterior atmospheric elements include the appearance of the store front, the window displays, store entrances and degree of traffic congestion. Exterior atmospherics are particularly important to new customers, who tend to judge an unfamiliar store by its outside appearance and may not enter the store if they feel intimidated by the building or inconvenienced by the car park. Because consumers form general impressions of shopping centres and business districts, the businesses and neighbourhoods surrounding a store will affect how buyers perceive the atmosphere of a store.

Interior atmospheric elements include aesthetic considerations such as lighting, wall and floor coverings, changing rooms and store fixtures. Interior sensory elements also contribute to atmosphere. Colour, for example, can attract shoppers to a retail display. Many fast food restaurants use bright colours such as red and yellow because these have been shown to make customers feel hungrier and eat faster, thus increasing turnover. Sound is another important sensory component of atmosphere and may consist of silence, soft music or even noisiness. Scent may be relevant as well; within a store, the odour of perfume suggests an image different from that suggested by the smell of prepared food. A store's layout— arrangement of departments, width of aisles, grouping of products and location of cashiers—is yet another determinant of atmosphere. Closely related to store layout is the element of crowding. A crowded store may restrict exploratory shopping, impede mobility and decrease shopping efficiency. An apparently empty store, however, may imply unpopularity and deter shoppers from entering.

Once the exterior and interior characteristics and store layout have been determined, displays are added. Displays enhance the store's atmosphere and give customers information about products. When displays carry out a store-wide theme, during the Christmas season, for instance, they attract customers' attention and generate sales. So do displays that present several related products in a group, or ensemble. Interior displays of products stacked or hanging neatly on racks create one kind of atmosphere; marked down items grouped together on a bargain table produce a different kind.

Retailers must determine the atmosphere that the target market seeks and then adjust atmospheric variables to encourage the desired awareness and action in consumers. High fashion boutiques generally strive for an atmosphere of luxury and novelty; discount stores must not seem too exclusive and expensive. To appeal to multiple market segments, a department store retailer may create different atmospheres for different operations within the store; for example, the discount basement, the sports department and the women's shoe department may each have a distinctive atmosphere.

Store Image

Image A functional and psychological picture in the consumer's mind

To attract customers, a retail store must project an **image**—a functional and psychological picture in the consumer's mind—that is acceptable to its target market. Although heavily dependent on atmospherics and design, a store's image is also shaped by its reputation for integrity, the number of services offered, location, merchandise assortments, pricing policies, promotional activities, community involvement and the retail brand's positioning.[24]

Characteristics of the target market—social class, lifestyle, income level and past buying behaviour—help form store image as well. How consumers perceive the store can be a major determinant of store patronage. Consumers from lower socio-economic groups tend to patronise small, high margin, high service food stores and prefer small, friendly building societies/loan companies over large, impersonal banks, even though these companies charge high interest. Affluent consumers look for exclusive, high quality establishments that offer prestige products and labels.

Retailers should be aware of the multiple factors that contribute to store image and recognise that perceptions of image vary. For example, one study found that in the United States consumers perceived Wal-Mart and Kmart differently, although the two sold almost the same products in stores that looked quite similar, offered the same prices and even had similar names. Researchers discovered that Wal-Mart shoppers spent more money at Wal-Mart and were more satisfied with the store than Kmart shoppers were with Kmart, in part because of differences in the retailers' images. For example, Wal-Mart employees wore waistcoats; Kmart employees did not. Wal-Mart purchases were packed in paper bags while Kmart used plastic bags. Wal-Mart had wider aisles, recessed lighting and carpeting in some departments. Even the retailers' logos affected consumers' perceptions: Wal-Mart's simple white and brown logo appeared friendly and "less blatantly commercial", while Kmart's red and turquoise blue logo conveyed the impression that the stores had not changed much since the 1960s. These atmospheric elements gave consumers the impression that Wal-Mart was more "up-market", warmer and friendlier than Kmart.[25]

Scrambled Merchandising

Scrambled merchandising The addition of unrelated products and product lines, particularly fast moving items that can be sold in volume, to an existing product mix

When retailers add unrelated products and product lines, particularly fast moving items that can be sold in volume, to an existing product mix, they are practising **scrambled merchandising**. For example, a convenience store might start selling lawn fertiliser. Retailers adopting this strategy hope to accomplish one or more of the following: (1) to convert their stores into one-stop shopping centres, (2) to generate more traffic, (3) to realise higher profit margins, (4) to increase impulse purchases.

In scrambling merchandise, retailers must deal with diverse marketing channels and thus may reduce their own buying, selling and servicing expertise. The practice can also blur a store's image in consumers' minds, making it more difficult for a retailer to succeed in today's highly competitive, saturated markets. Finally, scrambled merchandising intensifies competition among traditionally distinct types of stores and forces suppliers to adjust distribution systems so that new channel members can be accommodated. Asda is predominantly a grocery retailer; however, most Asda stores carry the "George" clothing ranges. The company retails small electrical appliances, DIY goods and car accessories in some stores but not in others. During the summer months, gardening supplies and equipment are sold. In the months leading up to Christmas, that floor space is given over to children's toys and gifts.

The Wheel of Retailing

Wheel of retailing The hypothesis that new retailers often enter the marketplace with low prices, margins and status and eventually emerge at the high end of the price/cost/services scales to compete with newer discount retailers

As new types of retail businesses come into being, they strive to fill niches in the dynamic environment of retailing. One hypothesis regarding the evolution and development of new types of retail stores is the **wheel of retailing**.[26] According to this theory, new retailers often enter the marketplace with low prices, margins and status. The new competitors' low prices are usually the result of innovative cost cutting procedures, and they soon attract imitators. Gradually, as these businesses attempt to broaden their customer base and increase sales, their operations and facilities become more elaborate and more expensive. They may move to more desirable locations, begin to carry higher quality merchandise or add customer services. Eventually, they emerge at the high end of the price/cost/services scales, competing with newer discount retailers who are following the same evolutionary process.[27]

For example, supermarkets have undergone many changes since their introduction in the 1920s. Initially, they provided limited services in exchange for lower food prices. However, over time they developed a variety of new services, including free coffee, gourmet food sections and children's play areas. Now traditional town centre supermarkets are being challenged by superstores and hypermarkets, which offer more product choices than the original supermarkets and have under-cut supermarket prices.

Figure 14.4 illustrates the wheel of retailing for department stores and discounters. Department stores such as Debenhams started out as high volume, low cost merchants competing with general stores and other small retailers; out-of-town discount sheds developed later, in response to the rising expenses of services in department stores. Many out-of-town discount sheds now appear to be following the wheel of retailing by offering more services, better locations, high quality inventories and, therefore, higher prices. Some out-of-town discount sheds are almost indistinguishable from department stores.

Like most hypotheses, the wheel of retailing may not fit every case. For example, it does not adequately explain the development of convenience stores, speciality stores, department store branches and vending machine operations. Another major weakness of the theory is that it does not predict what retailing innovations will develop, or when. Still, the hypothesis works reasonably well in many industrialised, expanding economies.

Current Trends

Balance of retailing power The balance of negotiating and buying power between retailers and their suppliers

In addition to the strategic issues highlighted above, mention must also be made of some current trends with strategic implications. The **balance of retailing power** is a well documented subject: the balance of negotiating and buying power between retailers and their suppliers.[28] As more retailers devote shelf space to their own label branded goods, the major manufacturers find themselves squeezed out.[29] In the clothing market nearly all chain retailers now give precedence to their own label goods. Marks & Spencer takes the situation to the extreme: only St. Michael (Marks & Spencer's own label) goods are on sale. The company dictates quality levels, lead times, packaging and delivery conditions, and often the price it will pay to its suppliers![30] A few years ago retailer Sainsbury's threatened to de-stock Kellogg's cereals totally and Kellogg's refused to supply Sainsbury's. Two giant brands were locked in a power struggle.

Figure 14.4 The wheel of retailing, which explains the origin and evolution of new types of retail stores. SOURCE: Adapted from Robert F. Hartley, *Retailing: Challenge and Opportunity*, 3rd edn, p. 42. Copyright © 1984 by Houghton Mifflin Company. Used by permission.

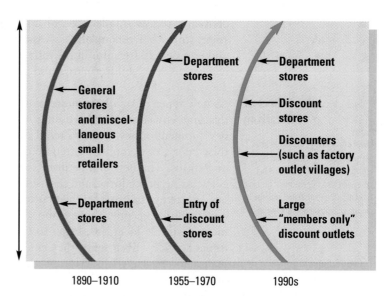

High prices and mark-ups, many services, expensive surroundings

Low prices and mark-ups, few services, austere surroundings

General stores and miscellaneous small retailers

Department stores

Department stores

Entry of discount stores

Department stores

Discount stores

Discounters (such as factory outlet villages)

Large "members only" discount outlets

1890–1910   1955–1970   1990s

If the "wheel" is considered to be turning slowly in the direction of the arrows, then the department stores around 1900 and the discounters later can be viewed as coming on the scene at the low end of the wheel. As it turns slowly, they move with it, becoming higher price operations, and in doing so they leave room for lower price retailers to gain entry at the low end of the wheel.

Increasingly compromise and negotiation are leading to deals beneficial to both sides of the equation: retailers receive preferential treatment and buying terms while manufacturers receive contracts to supply major retail chains exclusively with their own label needs, often alongside their own manufacturer brands.[31] Certainly for most of the large retail chains, the power is in the hands of the retailers, not the manufacturers.

Retail technology Systems that increase retailers' efficiency and productivity and often create a competitive edge

EPOS Electronic point-of-sale scanning of barcodes for inventory management

Technology Retailers are turning to **retail technology** for improved efficiency and productivity and often to create a competitive edge.[32] Table 14.6 shows the current levels of electronic systems penetration in retailing. Barcode scanning and **EPOS** (electronic point-of-sale) systems enable companies to monitor exact consumer spending patterns on a store-by-store basis, to prevent stock-outs and to have detailed sales data to add weight to negotiations with suppliers. EFTPOS (electronic funds transfer at point of sale) equipment facilitates speedy payment for goods, thereby reducing checkout queues; the rapid debiting of customer accounts is to the benefit of the retailer's bank account and cash flow. Video screens and video walls bring a new medium for the promotion of goods and services, as well as for the transfer of information. Retailers such as Tesco are already using sites on the Internet to promote ranges and even to take home delivery orders. The spread of computer systems has enabled consultants to develop computer graphic tools for the modelling of store location choice, customer demographics and shelf space allocation.[33]

Retail technology is not cheap—£80,000 to bring a typical shoe shop on-line with an EPOS system—but it allows decision-makers to be fully aware of sales trends and customer needs. When linked to the warehouse network, the EPOS process brings increased speed and efficiency to the physical distribution process. Most national retail groups have centralised their distribution.[34] The grocery

a. Number of grocery scanning stores by group, Great Britain, December 1998

Group	Number of Stores Scanning	% of Stores	% of All Commodity Volume Scanned
Kwik Save	883	100.0	100.0
Tesco	596	100.0	100.0
Somerfield	503	92.8	97.9
Safeway	438	100.0	100.0
Sainsbury	393	100.0	100.0
Alldays	248	100.0	100.0
ASDA	220	100.0	100.0
Dillons	166	32.8	32.8
Waitrose	117	100.0	100.0
Netto	117	100.0	100.0
Budgens	101	58.1	51.4
Lidl	126	100.0	100.0
Wm Morrison	85	100.0	100.0
Jacksons	69	98.6	98.2
Healds Day & Nite	71	100.0	100.0
Europa Foods	43	100.0	100.0
Presto	16	100.0	100.0
Lawrence Hunt Spar	22	100.0	100.0
Savacentre	13	100.0	100.0
Rusts	11	100.0	100.0
Walter Wilson	6	12.5	27.3
One Stop	6	3.2	3.2
Freshways	4	12.5	12.6
Nevins	4	22.2	22.2
Aldi	3	1.5	1.5
Dawn Til Dusk	3	5.6	5.6
Morning, Noon & Night	3	9.7	9.7
Bells Stores	1	3.0	1.9
GT Smith	1	8.3	11.0
Tates Lateshopper	1	0.7	0.6
All Multiples	4,270	74.2	96.4
Co-Operatives	1,680	75.0	88.7
Independents	2,445	9.0	15.0
Total	8,395	23.9	90.4

b. Trend in the number of grocery scanning stores, Great Britain

Year	Number of Stores Scanning	Year	Number of Stores Scanning	Year	Number of Stores Scanning
April 1988	535	June 1992	2,695	December 1995	6,525
January 1989	972	June 1993	3,710	December 1996	7,580
January 1990	1,497	December 1993	3,932	December 1997	8,276
January 1991	1,894	December 1994	4,864	December 1998	8,395

(Continues)

Table 14.6 Current levels of electronic systems penetration in retailing *(cont.)*

c. International comparisons: grocery stores equipped with scanners, 1996*

Country	Turnover Scanned (%)	Country	Turnover Scanned (%)	Country	Turnover Scanned (%)
New Zealand	99	Spain	79	Argentina	41
Sweden	98	Chile	78	Switzerland	39
France	95	Austria	74	Taiwan	34
Australia	93	Portugal	71	Singapore	30
Denmark	93	Netherlands	66	Brazil	27
Belgium	89	Puerto Rico	65	Malaysia	25
Great Britain	88	Hong Kong	60	South Korea	18
Japan	87	Mexico	55	Thailand	18
Canada	87	Ireland	55	Greece	16
Finland	86	Germany	47	Turkey	12
USA	86	Italy	46	South Africa	10
Norway	81	Colombia	43		

*Ranked by percentage of food turnover scanned.

SOURCE: *The Retail Pocket Book 2000* (NTC Publications in association with ACNielsen, 200), pp.168–169. E-mail: info@ntc.co.uk. Reprinted with permission.

companies, for instance, have one or two huge, centrally located warehouses close to the heart of the motorway network. Through EPOS data, each store's exact requirements are despatched from the central warehouse to match actual daily or weekly sales patterns. Often the warehouse is automated, with robotised handling. This reduces stockholdings in both the store itself and centrally, and minimises safety stocks (the "extra" stock held to cater for surges in demand or supplier delays).[35]

Dixons and Currys have two major warehouses that receive most of their deliveries from manufacturers. Small appliances are despatched to individual stores—to match each store's sales patterns—but white goods (too large to occupy branch space productively) are held at regional warehouses, each of which serves 30 or 40 branches and delivers directly to customers rather than to the shops. Prior to the introduction of EPOS and the move to warehouse centralisation, such fine-tuning would not have been possible.

As discussed in Chapter 17, technology is advancing the growth of direct marketing and in-home shopping. Direct retailing via mail order catalogues, Internet selling and teleselling is increasing rapidly, bringing more choice for the consumer in terms of when, where and how to shop; greater competition to some retailers; and additional channels to manage for those retailers adding direct selling operations to their armoury.

Deregulation Deregulation of the European Community in 1992/93 has had various implications for European retailers.[36] Market leaders in the UK, for example, once perceived as unassailable, are relatively small on a European scale. A grocery retailer with 12 per cent of the UK market may have 0.5 per cent of the European market. Large UK groups that previously bought out smaller regional UK retailers now find themselves being targeted for takeover by French and German retail groups. More non-UK based companies are establishing footholds in the UK market, which was previously relatively free from Continental

European competition. Increasingly, the major French, German, Italian and Scandinavian retailers operate throughout Europe.[37] Even these large national companies, however, are becoming targets for acquisition by larger international businesses or facing new entrant competition as these businesses set up operations in new countries. For many years, particularly in more affluent South East England, retailers have found it difficult to attract high calibre sales assistants and managers in competition for employment with other industrial sectors. Current research is anticipating an exaggeration of the problem as many UK residents move across the English Channel to find employment in France and beyond.

● S U M M A R Y

Retailing includes all transactions in which the buyer intends to consume the product through personal, family or household use. *Retailers*, businesses that purchase products for the purpose of reselling them to ultimate consumers, are important links in the marketing channel because they are customers for wholesalers and producers. Most retailing takes place inside stores or service establishments, but retail exchanges may also occur outside stores through telemarketing, vending machines, mail order catalogues and the Internet. By providing assortments of products to match consumers' wants, retailers create place, time, possession and form utilities.

Retail stores locate in the *central business district (CBD)*—the traditional centre of the town or the *prime pitch*—or in locations that provide an adequate *customer threshold*—in *suburban centres*, in *edge of town sites* or in *retail parks*. The national chains occupy the prime pitch sites in the CBD and the edge of town sites. Locally based independent retailers tend to dominate in the suburbs and focus on convenience and some comparison goods.

Retail stores are often classified according to width of product mix and depth of product lines. The major types of retail stores are *department stores, variety stores, superstores* and *supermarkets, hypermarkets, discount sheds, category killers, warehouse clubs, speciality shops, convenience stores, discounters, factory outlet villages, markets, cash and carry warehouses* and *catalogue showrooms*. Department stores are characterised by wide product mixes in considerable depth for most product lines. Their product lines are organised into separate departments that function much as self-contained businesses do. Speciality retailers offer substantial assortments in a few product lines. They include traditional speciality shops which carry narrow product mixes with deep product lines.

Non-store retailing is the selling of goods or services outside the confines of a retail facility. *Direct marketing* is the use of non-personal media, the Internet or telesales to introduce products to consumers, who then purchase the products by mail, telephone or the Internet. The Internet is becoming increasingly important in direct marketing. Forms of non-store retailing include: *in-home retailing* (selling via personal contacts with consumers in their own homes), *telemarketing* (direct selling of goods and services by telephone based on either a cold canvass of the telephone directory or a pre-screened list of prospective clients), *automatic vending* (selling through machines), *mail order*, the Internet, and *catalogue retailing* (selling by description because buyers usually do not see the actual product until it arrives in the mail).

Franchising is an arrangement whereby a supplier grants a dealer the right to sell products in exchange for some type of consideration. Retail franchises are of three general types: (1) a manufacturer may authorise a number of retail stores to sell a certain brand name item; (2) a producer may license distributors to sell a given product to retailers; or (3) a franchisor may supply brand names, techniques or other services, instead of a complete product. Franchise arrangements have a number of advantages and disadvantages over traditional business forms, and their use is increasing.

To increase sales and store patronage, retailers must consider several strategic issues. *Location* determines the trading area from which a store must draw its customers and should be evaluated carefully. When evaluating potential sites, retailers take into account a variety of factors, including the location of the company's target market within the trading area, the economic climate in the region, the kinds of products being sold, the availability of public transport, customer characteristics and competitors' locations. Retailers can choose from among several types of locations: free-standing structures, traditional business districts, neighbourhood/suburban shopping centres, out-of-town superstores and retail parks. The retailer must decide whether to invest heavily in owning freeholds or to negotiate leases. The breadth, depth and quality of the product assortment should be of the kind that can satisfy the retailer's target market customers.

Retail positioning involves identifying an unserved or under-served market niche, or a highly attractive market segment, and serving the segment through a strategy that distinguishes the retailer from others in consumers' minds. *Atmospherics* are the physical elements in a store's design that can be adjusted to appeal to consumers' emotions and thus induce them to buy. Store *image* derives not only from atmospherics but also from location, products offered, customer services, prices, promotion and the store's overall reputation. *Scrambled merchan-dising* adds unrelated product lines to an existing product mix and is being used by a growing number of stores to generate sales.

The *wheel of retailing* hypothesis holds that new retailers start as low status, low margin and low price operators. As they develop, they increase services and prices and eventually become vulnerable to newer discount retailers, which enter the market and repeat the cycle. However, the hypothesis may not apply in every case. There is an ever changing *balance of retailing power* between retailers and their suppliers, emphasised by the growth of retailers' own label brands, which compete with manufacturers' brands. *EPOS* (electronic point of sale) and other *retail technology* systems have revolutionised retailing and—when coupled with new, often centralised warehouse networks—have reduced stockholdings, improved efficiency and productivity, and minimised the risk of stock-outs, often creating a competitive edge. The reduction of European Union border controls and regulations is making the retailing environment much more fluid and dynamic: it holds new opportunities for expansion or strategic alliances in other countries, but it also carries the risk of takeover and increased competition in domestic markets.

Important Terms

Retailing	Category killers	Automatic vending
Retailer	Warehouse clubs	Mail order retailing
Central business district (CBD)	Speciality shops	Catalogue retailing
Prime pitch	Convenience stores	Franchising
Customer threshold	Discounters	Location
Suburban centres	Factory outlet villages	Retail positioning
Edge of town sites	Markets	Atmospherics
Retail parks	Cash and carry warehouses	Image
Department stores	Catalogue showroom	Scrambled merchandising
Variety stores	Non-store retailing	Wheel of retailing
Supermarkets and superstores	Direct marketing	Balance of retailing power
Hypermarkets	In-home retailing	Retail technology
Discount sheds	Telemarketing	EPOS

Discussion and Review Questions

1. What are the major differences between speciality shops and department stores?
2. How does a superstore differ from a supermarket?
3. Evaluate the following statement: "Direct marketing and non-store retailing are roughly the same thing."
4. Why is door-to-door selling a form of retailing? Some consumers feel that direct mail orders skip the retailer. Is this true?

5. If you were to open a retail business, would you prefer to open an independent store or to own a store under a franchise arrangement? Explain your preference.

6. What major issues should be considered when determining a retail location?

7. Describe the major types of shopping centres. Give examples of each type in your area.

8. How does atmosphere add value to products sold in a store? How important are atmospherics for convenience stores?

9. How should one determine the best retail store atmosphere?

10. Discuss the major factors that help determine a retail store's image.

11. Is it possible for a single retail store to have an overall image that appeals to sophisticated shoppers, extravagant shoppers and bargain hunters? Why or why not?

12. In what ways does the use of scrambled merchandising affect a store's image?

13. In what ways has technology improved retailing productivity?

14. What are the likely effects of EU deregulation on retailing in the EU?

Recommended Readings

S. Brown, *Retail Location: A Micro-Scale Perspective* (Aldershot: Avebury, 1992).

D. Cook and R. D. Walters, *Retail Marketing* (London: Prentice-Hall, 1991).

A. Ghosh, *Retail Management* 2nd edn (Orlando: Dryden Press, 1997).

P. J. McGoldrick, *Retail Marketing*, 2nd edn (London: McGraw-Hill, 1997).

P. J. McGoldrick and G. Davies, *International Retailing: Trends and Strategies* (London: Pitman, 1995).

● C A S E S

14.1 Dutch Retailer Ahold's Global Ambitions

Leading Dutch retailer Royal Ahold, like many large companies in the Netherlands, has pursued a range of international expansion opportunities. The relatively small size of the Netherlands market means that companies wishing to expand their operations must often seek new business further afield. In the case of Ahold, this has involved successful expansion into central and southern Europe, the US, Latin America and Asia.

Ahold has demonstrated a considerable interest in global expansion. Using a variety of market entry strategies, the retailer has recently entered a range of new markets. In 1977 Ahold arrived in the US. This was achieved through the company's acquisition of six supermarket chains, which are grouped into four operating companies. Stop & Shop operates 200 supermarkets and superstores in the New England and New York areas. BI-LO is responsible for more than 250 outlets in North and South Carolina, Tennessee and Georgia. Giant Food Stores has around 150 stores in a variety of different locations. The 230 stores of TOPS Markets can be found in the New York and Ohio regions.

Ahold's expansion interests have not been restricted to the US. The company's move into Portugal came in 1992 through a joint venture with local partner Jerônimo Martins, while entry into the Czech Republic was achieved through a wholly owned subsidiary in 1995. In 1996, the retailer was able to enter the Latin American market by forming a new joint venture with Bompreço, a large Brazilian retailer.

Ahold has chosen markets for two distinct sets of reasons. The US market was deemed attractive because of its size and established market structure. The characteristics of this well developed, competitive environment meant that in order to survive Ahold had to adopt a low cost leadership strategy. By choosing an entry strategy of growth by acquisition, Ahold was able to quickly achieve the desired economies of scale. The company dealt with its unfamiliarity with the US market by giving autonomy to the different operating companies which it formed.

The retailer had rather different reasons for entering its other markets. In many cases, such as in Latin America and Asia, Ahold was entering retail markets which were relatively poorly developed.

Country	Local Partner	Legal Form	Participation	Stores
Portugal	Jerônimo Martins	Joint venture	49%	Pingo Doce — 131
				Feira Nova — 15
Spain	Caprabo	Joint venture	50%	17
Czech Republic	Euronova	Subsidiary	100%	Mana — 76
				Sesam — 38
				Prima — 8
Poland	Euronova	Joint venture	50%	Sesam — 45
				Supermarkets — 6
				Hypermarkets — 2
Thailand	Central Group	Joint venture	49%	TOPS — 39
China	Zhonghui	Joint venture	50%	TOPS — 40
Singapore	Kuok Group	Joint venture	60%	TOPS — 13
Malaysia	Kuok Group	Joint venture	60%	TOPS — 5
Indonesia	PSP Group	Technical assistance	N.A.	TOPS — 7
Brazil	Bompreço S.A.	Joint venture	50%	Bompreço — 93
Argentina	Velox*	Joint venture	50%	Disco — 109
Chile	Velox	Joint venture	50%	Santa Isabel — 68
Peru	Velox	Joint venture	50%	Santa Isabel — 15
Paraguay	Velox	Joint venture	50%	Santa Isabel — 5
Ecuador	Velox	Joint venture	50%	Santa Isabel — 1

SOURCE: Adapted from Royal Ahold, annual report, 1998.

*Joint venture owns 50.35 per cent of Argentinean Disco, 65 per cent of Chilean Santa Isabel.

Ahold clearly saw opportunities in these markets, due to a lower level of competitive activity than in mature European markets, and the prospects of high economic growth. Not surprisingly, for these markets Ahold's strategy was different from that pursued in the US. In countries where the retail sector was under-developed there was the opportunity to enter the market through a partnership with a local company or by developing a green field operation. In most cases, the preferred approach was for Ahold to enter into joint ventures with a local business. This allowed important local market knowledge to be acquired as quickly as possible. This quick entry into the market was also attractive to Ahold because it gave the company the opportunity to establish a first mover advantage and to have early influence over the way in which the retail sector developed.

The prospects for Ahold look good. The retailer is already the second largest food and grocery retailer in the US. In the other markets in which it is trading, Ahold expects to achieve profitability quickly. However, management knows that its ultimate success will be affected by its ability to co-ordinate its global operation and by the pace of economic recovery in some of its more vulnerable markets.

SOURCES: Marcelo Rocha, "The globalisation of supermarkets: a case study approach", MBA project, University of Warwick; T.M. Robinson and C.M. Clarke-Hill, "Directional growth by European retailers", *International Journal of Retail and Distribution Management*, 18 (5), 1990; Royal Ahold, 1997 annual report, 1998; D. Orgel, "Ahold-ing its course: careful steering through the rough waters of acquisitions and realignments has left Ahold USA headed toward continued growth", *Supermarket News*, 48 (14), 6 April 1998; B. Smit, "Shopkeeper with a taste for expansion", *The European*, 13 February 1997; www.ahold.nl.

Questions for Discussion

1. Why has Ahold not simply deployed its Dutch trading concept in North and South American markets?
2. What marketing strengths may emerge from Ahold's global growth?
3. Why might a national market leader such as Tesco fear a global player such as Ahold?

14.2 Technology to Increase Home Shopping: Catalogue Retailer Littlewoods Stays Ahead

Throughout the 1970s and 1980s, pundits were predicting the demise of the traditional home catalogue shopping companies such as Littlewoods, Freemans, Great Universal Stores and Otto Versand's Grattan. Instead, Next's Directory and a whole host of specialist operators such as Innovations entered a market that turned out to be far from obsolete. One in three consumers now buys goods at home through catalogue retailing, a market set for important technological changes. Internet shopping is adding to the interest in buying from home and receiving goods via courier or the Post Office. Even high street retailers, such as Arcadia, have acquired mail order businesses as the sector grows.

John Moores started his mail order business from one office, a little warehouse, with one secretary. Already a millionaire from his football pools operation, Moores wanted to see if he could "make another million from nothing". Pools customers were recruited as customers for mail order, and they in turn persuaded relatives, friends and neighbours to buy from Moores' catalogues. In its first year, the Littlewoods catalogue division had sales of £100,000. In 1936, sales hit £4 million. Today Littlewoods accounts for 16 per cent of the home shopping market and 25 per cent of the mail order sector, a market worth £6.8 billion; the company deals with £2 million worth of orders each working day and despatches 40 million parcels annually to UK homes.

Sixty years of Littlewoods' catalogue sales have echoed consumer changes. When it all began in the 1930s, most people had never travelled more than 50 miles from their birthplace, there was an economic slump, women "slaved" as housewives, few houses had electricity, even large towns had only a few shops, and there was no such entity as a supermarket. In the 1940s Littlewoods joined the war effort, supplying 13,000 food packs daily for troops in Burma, 12 million shells, 750 Wellington bomber bodies, 50,000 rubber dinghies and 5 million parachutes. A fireside chair cost £2, a three-piece suite £8, a double bed or vacuum cleaner £3, a diamond ring £1.50 and gas irons 50p. By the present Queen's coronation in 1953, half the population crammed into bars and lucky neighbours' houses to watch the ceremony on television. Tea, sugar, butter and cheese were still rationed, an electric iron cost £2.40 and a ballpoint pen £1.74 in the still austere 1950s.

The swinging 1960s ushered in a credit driven society seeking consumer durables and more stylish merchandise: transistor radios for £12.60, cine cameras at £55, a sewing machine for £38. In the 1970s inflation soared to 15.9 per cent and Britain joined the European Common Market. A radio cost £6.65 or 20 weeks at 33p; a superior three-piece suite £75.75 or £1.51 a week for 50 weeks. A Hotpoint washing machine cost £131.29 and a Hoovermatic £103.85. The 1980s, the decade of Margaret Thatcher, heralded increased consumer spending and prosperity, rising unemployment and crime, and inner city riots. The microchip arrived in nearly every household, and the yuppies wheeled and dealed their way to inherit the land! Health foods and non-smoking grew in popularity, home ownership rocketed and nearly all households had a television set, a fridge and central heating. AIDS imposed its tragic effects on society, and people worried more about the world's starving millions and under-privileged.

Throughout all of these evolving, and at times dramatic, consumer changes, Littlewoods led the catalogue sector. In retailing, the burgeoning of retail chains nationwide and even internationally created a shopping-conscious consumer happy to see increased choice and rapid development of new shopping centres, malls and retail parks. With the adoption of the US superstore concept and out-of-town retailing, many analysts predicted the demise of high street retailers and home catalogue shopping. Sears, Freemans, Grattan, GUS and Little-woods all suffered during the early 1980s, but the adoption of sound marketing principles led to rekindled fortunes.

These companies monitored changing consumer tastes and trends more closely, altering their merchandise ranges and prices accordingly. They created new identities for separate catalogues, each targeted at slightly different groups of customers. For example, German-acquired Grattan trades through several catalogues: Grattan—a household name—Kaleidoscope, Scotcade, You & Yours, Look Again, Curiosity Shop, Class and Mode. Freemans operates as Freemans, Face Values, Editions, Complete

a. Home shopping: market shares

Company	Market Share (%)
GUS	24.2
Littlewoods	16.1
Freemans	7.4
Grattan	7.4
Empire	4.6
N. Brown	4.2
Fine Art	3.2
Next	3.1
Direct selling	13.2
Other	16.6
Total	100.0

SOURCE: Verdict Research.

b. Some mail order houses

Great Universal Stores: incl. Great Universal; Choice; Family Album; Fashion Extra; Marshall Ward; Kays; Accolade; Kit; Style Plus; Innovations; Racing Green; Hawkshead; McCord; Home Free; Stocking Fillas. Over 50 Catalogue Bargain Shop outlets.

Littlewoods Organisation: incl. John Moores; Brian Mills; Burlington; Littlewoods; Janet Frazer; Peter Craig; All of Us; Index Extra. 151 Index Catalogue shops (many within chain stores); 15 Hitchens catalogue surplus shops.

Freemans (Sears): incl. Freemans; Face Values; Christmas Clothing; Summer Selection.

Grattan (Otto Versand): incl. Grattan; Kaleidoscope; Scotcade; Look Again; Curiosity Shop; Class; Mode.

Empire Stores (La Redoute): incl. Empire; La Redoute; Vert Baudet; Daxon.

SOURCES: Companies concerned, 1999; *The Retail Pocket Book 1999* (Henley, Oxon: NTC Publications, 1999), p. 134. Reprinted by permission. Verdict.

Essentials, Clothkits, We Are, Direct Collection and the Jan Harvey Collection. Each catalogue has a different mix of styles and merchandise, price points and sourcing, giving each its own positioning in a highly competitive marketplace. In addition to the clothing and household goods dominated catalogues of the major companies, there are niche specialists offering narrowly focused ranges, including perfumes and cosmetics, toys and novelty goods, home/office stationery and equipment, photographic products, car accessories and speciality foods.

The sector is far from in decline (see Table 14.4). Littlewoods believes that leisure trends and the increasing use of in-home technology favour the continued success of catalogue retailing. The company expects technology to make it possible to buy almost anything while sitting in an armchair at home. Already, personal financial business from insurance to current account banking can be conducted over the telephone or through home computers. Catalogues can be made available on home computers or displayed through video discs on television screens. Investments in such technologies are high, but the differential advantage is potentially great so long as consumers accept the innovations. In the interim, Littlewoods has kept its options open; in addition to its catalogue business, the company operates a chain of high street variety stores, Littlewoods and over one hundred Index catalogue stores in town centres and retail parks. In mail order, though, Littlewoods and its rivals anticipate the dawning of a whole new era of catalogue retailing and home shopping.

SOURCES: Littlewoods; Freemans; Grattan; *The Marketing Pocket Book 1993* (Henley-on-Thames: NTC), p. 60; Barbara Argument, "Rise and rise of mail order shopping", *Coventry Evening Telegraph*, 1 September 1992, pp. L2–3; with grateful thanks to the *Coventry Evening Telegraph* and Littlewoods; "Great Universal Stores", *Retail Business*, September 1994, pp. 70–76, 82–87; David Martin, "Catalogues face some home truths", *Marketing Week*, 9 September 1994, pp. 21–22; David Benady, "Retail dinosaurs go on a revival course", *Marketing Week*, 9 June 1995, p. 20; Littlewoods 1999; *The Marketing Pocket Book 1999*.

Questions for Discussion

1. What threats have faced the catalogue retailers? How have these been addressed?
2. What are the current trends in the home shopping sector?
3. Why does Littlewoods anticipate the dawning of a whole new era?

The place ingredient of the marketing mix addresses the distribution and marketing channel decisions necessary to provide the target market with convenient and ready access to a product or service. The place specification developed in the marketing mix must be beneficial to the supplier of the product or service if it is to remain in business and be commercially viable. Part IV of *Marketing: Concepts and Strategies* has examined the nature of marketing channels, wholesalers and distributors, the physical distribution of products and services, plus the nuances of retail marketing.

Before progressing, readers should be confident that they are now able to:

Explain the concept of the marketing channel

• What is the marketing channel? • What are the functions and types of marketing channels? • What is meant by channel integration and levels of market coverage? • What issues determine the selection of a marketing channel and what impact is the emergence of direct marketing having? • Why are the concepts of co-operation, relationship building, conflict and leadership important in marketing channel management? • What legal issues concern marketers as they manage marketing channels?

Describe the functions of wholesalers, distributors and physical distribution management

• What is meant, in its broadest sense, by wholesaling? • What activities do wholesalers undertake and how can wholesalers be classified? • What agencies facilitate wholesaling? • What are the changing patterns in wholesaling? • How are physical distribution activities integrated into marketing channels and overall marketing strategies? • What are the objectives of physical distribution? • What are the roles of order processing, materials handing, warehousing, inventory management and transportation in effective physical distribution?

Outline the nature of retailing and the specialist requirements for retail marketers

• What is the function of retailing in the marketing channel? • What are the principal retail locations and major store types? • What are non-store retailing and franchising? • What are the strategic issues and current trends in retailing?

Marketing Opportunity Analysis	Chapters
• The marketing environment	2
• Marketing in international markets	3
• Consumer buying behaviour	4
• Organisational markets and business-to-business buying behaviour	5
• Marketing research and information systems	6

Target Market Strategy	Chapters
• Market segmentation and prioritisation	7, 21
• Product and brand positioning	7, 21
• Competitive advantage	7, 21

Marketing Mix Development	Chapters
• Product, branding, packaging and service decisions	8–11
• Place (distribution and channel) decisions	12–14
• Promotion decisions	15–17
• Pricing decisions	18, 19
• Supplementary decisions	3, 20, 23, 24

Marketing Management	Chapters
• Strategic marketing and competitive strategy	21, 22
• Marketing planning and forecasting sales potential	22
• Implementing strategies and internal marketing relationships and measuring performance	23
• Marketing ethics and social responsibility	24

V Promotion Decisions

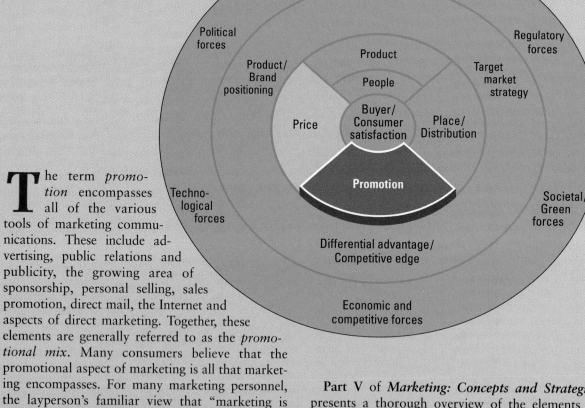

Legal forces

Political forces

Regulatory forces

Product/Brand positioning

Product

People

Target market strategy

Price

Buyer/Consumer satisfaction

Place/Distribution

Promotion

Techno-logical forces

Societal/Green forces

Differential advantage/Competitive edge

Economic and competitive forces

The term *promotion* encompasses all of the various tools of marketing communications. These include advertising, public relations and publicity, the growing area of sponsorship, personal selling, sales promotion, direct mail, the Internet and aspects of direct marketing. Together, these elements are generally referred to as the *promotional mix*. Many consumers believe that the promotional aspect of marketing is all that marketing encompasses. For many marketing personnel, the layperson's familiar view that "marketing is advertising" is a tiresome but frequently encountered attitude. It must be emphasised that promotion is just another ingredient of the marketing mix, the tactical toolkit marketers use to implement marketing strategies. Nevertheless, it is a very important ingredient, one that accounts for the vast proportion of most businesses' marketing budgets, employs millions of people in Europe alone and constitutes an essential aspect of communicating an organisation's product or service proposition and its associated brand positioning strategy.

Part V of *Marketing: Concepts and Strategies* presents a thorough overview of the elements of promotion and how the promotional mix fits into marketing strategy.

Chapter 15, "Promotion: An Overview", discusses the role of promotion in the marketing mix, the process of communication *per se* and the way in which the concept of the product adoption process relates to promotional activity. The chapter goes on to explain the aims of promotion and the elements of the promotional mix. The chapter concludes by examining the factors that influence the selection of promotional mix ingredients.

Chapter 16, "Advertising, Public Relations and Sponsorship", takes these three aspects of the promotional mix and explores their use in more detail. The chapter commences by describing the nature and uses of advertising and then examines the steps and personnel involved in developing an advertising campaign. The emphasis then switches to the nature of publicity and public relations; following this discussion, the chapter highlights some of the current trends in the spheres of advertising and public relations (PR). Finally, it explores the rapidly evolving specialist area of sponsorship.

Chapter 17, "Personal Selling, Sales Promotion, Direct Mail, the Internet and Direct Marketing", begins by examining the nature and major purposes of personal selling, along with the basic steps in the personal selling process. It identifies the types of salesforce personnel and goes on to explore the nature of sales management. The chapter then explains the uses of sales promotion and the wide range of related activities, and then focuses on the role of direct mail in the promotional mix. The chapter concludes with an overview of the Internet and direct marketing, and looks at the growing popularity of these promotional methods.

By the conclusion of Part V of *Marketing: Concepts and Strategies,* readers should understand the essential promotion decisions and composition of the promotional mix within the marketing mix.

15 Promotion: An Overview

O B J E C T I V E S

- To understand the role of promotion in the marketing mix
- To examine the process of communication
- To understand the product adoption process and its implications for promotional efforts
- To understand the aims of promotion
- To explore the elements of the promotional mix
- To acquire an overview of the major methods of promotion
- To explore factors that influence the selection of promotional mix ingredients

> *"Marketing communication is the art of seducing a consumer on his way to your competitor."*
>
> Patrick De Pelsmacker
> University of Antwerp

In a multi-media campaign, the National Society for the Prevention of Cruelty to Children (NSPCC) pledged to raise £300m in just 12 months. This figure was six times more than the charity's usual target of £50m. Through its *Full Stop* campaign, the NSPCC hopes to bring an end to child cruelty within a generation.

Following the trend for provocative charity advertising, the campaign began with an unsettling series of television advertisements. These depicted various toys and other children's icons, such as Action Man, Rupert Bear and the Spice Girls, covering their eyes against a soundtrack of shouting parents

and crying children. At the same time, 3,500 posters carrying the same message appeared, with the NSPCC web site offering support (**www.nspcc.org.uk**). The mailing of leaflets to every UK household bearing the

---

The Campaign Time Scale

- *Early March:* Start of PR campaign, which continues through to Easter, when public address systems at airports and railway stations will be used to broadcast reminders.
- *March 9:* "Early warning" letter to the NSPCC's 160,000 "best donors", alerting them to the campaign and seeking their support.
- *March 15:* Updated web site goes live, encouraging people to sign the NSPCC pledge on-line.
- *March 16:* Three week TV and poster campaign begins. Sixty second adverts in first week followed by 30 and ten second versions. Forty-eight sheet posters on 3,500 sites designed to deliver 55 per cent coverage with 21 opportunities to see. Some 4,000 sites for 6-sheet posters will also be used.
- *March 22:* Personalised letters to just under one million existing donors. Delivery of door-drop letter and pledge document to 23 million homes begins. Press advertisements appear, offering an alternative vehicle for signing the pledge.
- *March 27–28:* Call to action weekend, with volunteers manning 2,000 sites.

SOURCE: Adapted from "NSPCC aims to convert abuse anger into cash", *Marketing*, 25 March 1999, pp. 37–38.

message "Together we can stop cruelty to children once and for all" followed. The intention was to capitalise on the awareness created by the advertising campaign. Through this mass targeting, the NSPCC was making clear its intention to mobilise everyone. At the centre of the campaign was a pledge document, through which the public and businesses were invited to donate funds to the charity.

The charity intended for 20 per cent of its target donations to come from businesses. There were many ways in which businesses could become involved. The NSPCC developed a special toolkit which explained some of the sponsorship opportunities and cause related marketing possibilities. Microsoft, which sponsors NSPCC advertising and holds fund raisers for the charity, is one company that already had links with the charity. The software business states it is happy to be associated with a cause which supports child welfare, particularly in view of its increasing emphasis on developing educational software for families and the young.

At the beginning of the NSPCC's campaign it was unclear whether or not the £300m target could be met. However, the key was in the scale of the appeal and the fact that it combined a carefully constructed mix of different promotional tools and techniques.

SOURCES: "NSPCC aims to convert abuse anger into cash", *Marketing*, 25 March 1999, pp. 37–38; Jade Garrett, "Charities snub

shock tactics for subtle approach", *Campaign*, 26 March 1999, p. 10; "Spotlight charity", *Marketing Week*, 17 December 1998, pp. 28–29; "Charities unite in donor appeal", *Marketing*, 14 January 1999, p. 4. *Advertisement:* Courtesy of the National Society for the Prevention of Cruelty to Children.

O rganisations use various promotional approaches to communicate with target markets, as NSPCC did with its *Full Stop* campaign. This chapter looks at the general dimensions of promotion, defining promotion in the context of marketing and examining the roles which it plays. Next, to understand how promotion works, the chapter analyses the meaning and process of communication, as well as the product adoption process. The remainder of the chapter discusses the major types of promotional methods and the factors that influence an organisation's decision to use specific methods of promotion: advertising, personal selling, publicity and public relations, sales promotion, sponsorship, direct mail, the Internet and direct marketing.

The Role of Promotion

People's attitudes towards promotion vary. Some hold that promotional activities, particularly advertising and personal selling, paint a distorted picture of reality because they provide the customer with only selected information.[1] Proponents of this view often suggest that promotional activities are unnecessary and wasteful and that promotion costs are too high, resulting in higher prices.

They may also argue that too much promotion has caused changes in social values, such as increased materialism. Others take a positive view. They believe that advertising messages often project wholesome values—such as affection, generosity or patriotism[2]—or that advertising, as a powerful economic force, can free countries from poverty by communicating information.[3] It has also been argued that advertising of consumer products was a factor in the decline of communism and the move towards a free enterprise system in eastern Europe. However, none of these impressions is completely accurate.

Promotion Communication with individuals, groups or organisations in order to facilitate exchanges by informing and persuading audiences to accept a company's products

The role of **promotion** in a company is to communicate with individuals, groups or organisations with the aim of directly or indirectly facilitating exchanges by informing and persuading one or more of the audiences to accept the company's products.[4] PepsiCo, for example, recruited pop star Michael Jackson to communicate the benefits of its cola drink. Rock Against Drugs (RAD), a not-for-profit organisation, employs popular rock musicians, such as Lou Reed, to communicate its anti-drug messages to teenagers and young adults. Like PepsiCo and RAD, marketers try to communicate with selected audiences about their company and its goods, services and ideas in order to facilitate exchanges. Marketing Insight 15.1 describes how Kodak used promotion in the launch of its new Advantix range of cameras.

Exchanges are facilitated by marketers ensuring that information is targeted at appropriate individuals and groups: potential customers, interest groups (such as environmental and consumer groups), current and potential investors and regulatory agencies. Some marketers use *cause related marketing,* which links the purchase of their products to philanthropic efforts for a particular cause. Cause related marketing often helps a marketer boost sales and generate goodwill through contributions to causes that members of its target markets want to support. For example, as the chapter opener explains, the NSPCC encourages businesses such as Microsoft to become involved in joint initiatives to raise funds. Similarly, Procter & Gamble has tied promotional efforts for some of its products with contributions to the Special Olympics.

Viewed from this wider perspective, promotion can play a comprehensive communications role.[5] Some promotional activities, such as publicity and public relations, can be directed towards helping a company justify its existence and maintain positive, healthy relationships between itself and various groups in the marketing environment.

Although a company can direct a single type of communication—such as an advertisement—towards numerous audiences, marketers often design a communication precisely for a specific target market. A company frequently communicates several different messages concurrently, each to a different group. For example, McDonald's may direct one communication towards customers for its Big Mac, a second message towards investors about the company's stable growth and a third communication towards society in general regarding the company's Ronald McDonald Houses, which provide support to families of children suffering from cancer.

To gain maximum benefit from promotional efforts, marketers must make every effort to properly plan, implement, co-ordinate and control communications. Effective promotional activities are based on information from the marketing environment (see Chapter 2), often obtained from an organisation's marketing information system (see Chapter 6). How effectively marketers can use promotion to maintain positive relationships depends largely on the quantity and quality of information an organisation takes in. For example, concerns about

Kodak's Challenge: Revitalising a Market through Innovation

When mighty Kodak launched its Advantix range, it faced quite a dilemma. To recoup its significant development costs, the promotional message at the heart of its launch and brand building campaigns had to appeal to both the dedicated photographer and the "happy snapper". Large sales volumes were essential. By using some technical information in its advertising within a simple, memorable execution, Kodak's advertising proved a successful ingredient in the marketing mix for the Advantix.

Five of the biggest players in the photographic market spent five years and £750 million developing a new mass consumer system: the Advanced Photo System (APS). As the products came to the market in the summer of 1996, two intriguing issues attracted the attention of observers: which company would gain market leadership and whether consumers would really want this innovation. As with the development of the CD player and video recorder, rival manufacturers were forced to pool technical resources in order to develop the new technology. Once it was created, the erstwhile partners divided, each to launch competing products. The market for cameras and films had declined in the core European, American and Japanese markets: APS was intended to revitalise a slumbering market, just as CD players and video cameras had done previously in the brown goods market.

APS has a film that drops into the camera like a battery into a Walkman. The cameras permit three different picture sizes to be selected, and more expensive models enable the user to switch a film mid-roll and re-use it later. Because the films are 24mm—as opposed to the currently dominant 35mm format—they allow for smaller and lighter cameras. The films are priced similarly to their 35mm counterparts, although the cameras cost around 20 per cent more than 35mm models. Developed jointly by Kodak, Fujifilm, Minolta, Nikon and Canon, the new technology is already being used by over 50 licensees. In year one, the combined marketing spend of the five creators was thought to be around £100 million.

Kodak believes that for Advantix to succeed, consumers must trust in the technology and the quality of the product. To help communicate the credentials of its Advantix brand, Kodak UK has doubled its advertising spend to nearly £10 million, much of which is promoting the new product. To re-assure customers, Kodak's advertising plays on the company's reputation, record of constant product innovation and position as the most established name in the market. A good reputation is not enough, however, as Kodak knows. Its campaign includes advertising with 30 and 60 second executions, supported by sales promotion and point-of-sale activity. Fuji entered the market first with a range of six cameras, film and a photo player enabling customers to view their holiday snaps on their television screens. This launch gave Fuji an initial 60 per cent of the fledging APS market. Kodak's promotional activity quickly helped to knock Fuji back, although the APS market has yet to take off in a manner that will give the major players adequate returns.

Sources: Roger Baird, "Stakes high in bid to boost photo sector", *Marketing Week,* 28 June 1996, p. 23; Loredana Roberts, "Kodak Advantix", *Marketing,* 22 February 1996, p. 9; Mark Maremont, "Will a new film click?", *Business Week,* 5 February 1996, p. 46; Amy Dunkin, "The next great leap for Shutterbugs", *Business Week,* 22 April 1996, pp. 150–152.

genetically modified (GM) foods have led certain supermarkets to improve in-store labeling, so that consumers are better informed about those products affected. Because the basic role of promotion is to communicate, it is important to analyse what communication is and how the communication process works.

The Communication Process

Communication can be viewed as the transmission of information.[6] For communication to take place, however, both the sender and the receiver of the information must share some common ground. They must share an understanding of the symbols used to transmit information, usually pictures or words. For instance, an individual transmitting the following message may believe he or she is communicating with readers of *Marketing: Concepts and Strategies:*

在工廠吾人製造化粧品，在商店吾人銷售希望。

However, communication has not taken place, because few readers understand the intended message.[7] Thus **communication** is defined here as a sharing of meaning.[8] Implicit in this definition is the notion of transmission of information, because sharing necessitates transmission.

As Figure 15.1 shows, communication begins with a source. A **source** is a person, group or organisation that has an intended meaning it attempts to share with an audience. For example, a source could be a political party wishing to recruit new members or an organisation that wants to send a message to thousands of consumers through an advertisement. A **receiver** is the individual, group or organisation that decodes a coded message. A **receiving audience** is two or more receivers who decode a message. The intended receivers, or audience, of an advertisement for MBA courses might be junior business executives wishing to broaden their managerial skills. The source may be a European business school such as INSEAD.

To transmit meaning, a source must convert the meaning into a series of signs that represent ideas or concepts. This is called the **coding process,** or *encoding.* When encoding meaning into a message, a source must take into account certain characteristics of the receiver or receiving audience. First, to share meaning, the source should use signs that are familiar to the receiver or receiving audience. Marketers who understand this fact realise how important it is to know their target market and to make sure that an advertisement, for example, is written in language that the target market can understand. Thus when Lever Brothers advertises its Persil washing powder, it makes no attempt to explain the chemical reactions involved when the product removes dirt and grease, because this would not be meaningful to consumers. There have been some notable problems in the language translation of advertisements. For example, a beer advertisement translated from English to Spanish using the tag line *"Sueltate"* was supposed to mean "Let go!" but actually invited readers to "Get diarrhoea!".[9] Thus it is important that people fully understand the language used in promotion.

Communication A sharing of meaning through the transmission of information

Source A person, group or organisation that has an intended meaning it attempts to share with an audience

Receiver An individual, group or organisation that decodes a coded message

Receiving audience Two or more receivers who decode a message

Coding process The process of converting meaning into a series of signs that represent ideas or concepts; also called *encoding*

Figure 15.1 The communication process

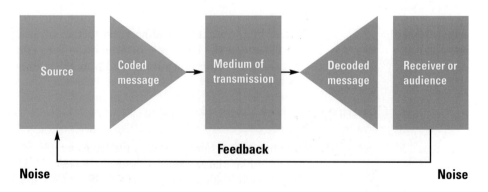

Part V   Promotion Decisions

Second, when encoding a meaning, a source should try to use signs that the receiver or receiving audience uses for referring to the concepts the source intends. Marketers should generally avoid signs that can have several meanings for an audience. For example, an international advertiser of soft drinks should avoid using the word *soda* as a general term for soft drinks. Although in some places soda is taken to mean "soft drink", in others it may connote bicarbonate of soda, an ice cream drink, or something that one mixes with Scotch whisky.

To share a coded meaning with the receiver or receiving audience, a source must select and use a medium of transmission. A **medium of transmission** carries the coded message from the source to the receiver or receiving audience. Transmission media include ink on paper, vibrations of air waves produced by vocal cords, chalk marks on a chalkboard and electronically produced communication, as in radio, television, mobile phones and the Internet.

Sometimes a source chooses an inappropriate medium of transmission. A coded message may reach some receivers, but not the right ones. For example, suppose a local theatre group spends most of its advertising budget on radio advertisements. If theatre-goers depend mainly on newspapers for information about local drama, then the theatre group will not reach its intended target audience. Coded messages may also reach intended receivers in an incomplete form because the intensity of the transmission is weak. For example, radio signals can be received effectively over a limited range that may vary depending on climatic conditions. Members of the target audience who live on the fringe of the broadcasting area may receive only a weak signal.

In the **decoding process**, signs are converted into concepts and ideas. Seldom does a receiver decode exactly the same meaning that a source encoded. When the result of decoding is different from what was encoded, **noise** exists. Noise has many sources and may affect any or all parts of the communication process. When a source selects a medium of transmission through which an audience does not expect to receive a message, noise is likely to occur. Noise sometimes arises within the medium of transmission itself. Radio static, faulty printing processes and laryngitis are sources of noise. Interference on viewers' television sets during an advertisement is noise and lessens the impact of the message. Noise also occurs when a source uses a sign that is unfamiliar to the receiver or that has a different meaning from the one the source intended. Noise may also originate in the receiver. As Chapter 4 discusses, a receiver may be unaware of a coded message because his or her perceptual processes block it out or because the coded message is too obscure.

The receiver's response to a message is **feedback** to the source. The source usually expects and normally receives feedback, although it may not be immediate. During feedback, the receiver or receiving audience is the source of a message that is directed towards the original source, which then becomes a receiver. Feedback is encoded, sent through a medium of transmission (for example, a survey questionnaire) and then decoded by the receiver, the source of the original communication. It is logical, then, to think of communication as a circular process.

During face-to-face communication, such as in personal selling or product sampling, both verbal and non-verbal feedback can be immediate. Instant feedback lets communicators adjust their messages quickly to improve the effectiveness of their communication. For example, when a salesperson realises through feedback that a customer does not understand a sales presentation, he or she adapts the presentation to make it more meaningful to the customer. In interpersonal communication, feedback occurs through talking, touching, smiling, nodding, eye movements and other body movements and postures.

Medium of transmission The tool used to carry the coded message from the source to the receiver or receiving audience

Decoding process The process in which signs are converted into concepts and ideas

Noise A condition that exists when the decoded message is different from what was encoded

Feedback The receiver's response to a message

When mass communication such as advertising is used, feedback is often slow and difficult to recognise. If Disneyland Paris increased its advertising in order to increase the number of visitors, it might be 6 to 18 months before the theme park could recognise the effects of the expanded advertising. Although it is harder to recognise, feedback does exist for mass communication. Figure 15.2 illustrates a unique programme developed by Playstation to obtain feedback on whether its message was received by its target market. Advertisers, for example, obtain feedback in the form of changes in sales volume or in consumers' attitudes and awareness levels, monitored through tracking research.

Each communication channel has a limit on the volume of information it can handle effectively. This limit, called **channel capacity**, is determined by the least efficient component of the communication process. Communications that depend on vocal speech provide a good illustration of this. An individual source can talk only so fast, and there is a limit to how much an individual receiver can take in aurally. Beyond that point, additional messages cannot be decoded; thus meaning cannot be shared. Although a radio announcer can read several hundred words a minute, a one minute advertising message should not exceed 150 words because most announcers cannot articulate the words into understandable messages at a rate beyond 150 words per minute. This figure is the limit for both source and receiver, and marketers should keep this in mind when developing radio advertisements. At times, a company creates a television advertisement that contains several types of visual material and several forms of audio messages, all transmitted to viewers at the same time. Such communication may not be totally effective, because receivers cannot decode all the messages simultaneously.[10]

Now that the basic communication process has been explored, it is worth considering more specifically how promotion is used to influence individuals, groups or organisations to accept or adopt a company's products. Although the product adoption process was briefly touched upon in Chapter 10, it is discussed more

Channel capacity The limit on the volume of information that a particular communication channel can handle effectively

Figure 15.2 Getting feedback. With this direct response press advertisement, the impact of the campaign for Playstation can be judged. SOURCE: Courtesy of Playstation.

fully in the following section in order to provide a better understanding of the conditions under which promotion occurs.

Promotion and the Product Adoption Process

Marketers do not promote simply to inform, educate and entertain; they communicate to facilitate satisfying exchanges—products or services for money or donations. One long run purpose of promotion is to influence and encourage buyers to accept or adopt goods, services and ideas. At times, an advertisement may be informative or entertaining, yet it may fail to get the audience to purchase the product. For example, some advertisements seem to be weak in communicating benefits—they focus instead on getting customers to feel good about the product. The ultimate effectiveness of promotion is determined by the degree to which it affects product adoption among potential buyers or increases the frequency of current buyers' purchases.

To establish realistic expectations about what promotion can do, product adoption should not be viewed as a one-step process. Rarely can a single promotional activity cause an individual to buy a previously unfamiliar product. The acceptance of a product involves many steps. Although there are several ways to look at the **product adoption process,** it is commonly divided into five stages (see Figure 15.3): (1) awareness, (2) interest, (3) evaluation, (4) trial and (5) adoption.[11]

In the **awareness stage,** individuals become aware that the product exists, but they have little information about it and are not concerned about obtaining more. When Barclays launched b^2 financial services, it used a provocative b^2 flash teaser advertisement. Later, longer advertisements fully detailed the new portfolio of products. In Figure 15.4 JCB's teaser advertisement (left) did not reveal its

Product adoption process   A series of five stages in the acceptance of a product: awareness, interest, evaluation, trial and adoption

Awareness stage   The beginning of the product adoption process, when individuals become aware that the product exists but have little information about it

Figure 15.3   Effective promotional tools for reaching consumers in various stages of the product adoption process

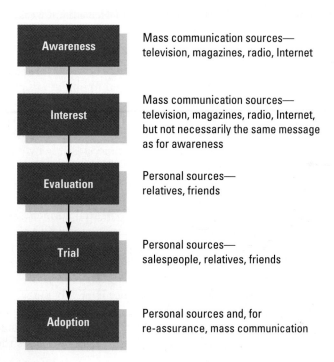

Awareness	Mass communication sources—television, magazines, radio, Internet
Interest	Mass communication sources—television, magazines, radio, Internet, but not necessarily the same message as for awareness
Evaluation	Personal sources—relatives, friends
Trial	Personal sources—salespeople, relatives, friends
Adoption	Personal sources and, for re-assurance, mass communication

Some of these features are optional extras.

SEATBELT

ROPS/FOPS CANOPY STRUCTURE · BEACON · POLYCARBONATE SCREEN · REAR EMERGENCY EXIT

EXTERNAL REAR VIEW MIRROR · SINGLE LOADER ARM · FLAT, UNCLUTTERED FLOOR · SERVO CONTROLS · LEFT HAND DOOR · REVERSE ALARM

FRONT AND REAR WORKLIGHTS · FINGERTIP ATTACHMENT CONTROL · RESTRAINT ACTIVATED BRAKE · SIDE ACCESS

GRAB HANDLES FOR CAB ACCESS · SCREEN GUARD · RESTRAINT ISOLATED HYDRAULICS · ADJUSTABLE OPERATOR RESTRAINT · NON-SLIP STEP FOR ACCESS · REAR ROAD LIGHTS

EXCELLENT VISIBILITY · TWIN LEVER QUICKHITCH · LOCKABLE FILLER CAPS · "GREEN" ENGINE

FULL CAB OPTION · SELF-LEVELLING BUCKET · LIFT ARM SAFETY STRUT · LOGICAL CONTROL PATTERNS · LOW NOISE LEVELS · 6mm LOCKABLE STEEL REAR DOOR

YOU'RE LOOKING AT THE WORLD'S SAFEST SKID STEER.

In our view, no other skid steer has so many features contributing to operational safety. As you can clearly see.

JCB

IT PAYS TO SPECIFY JCB.

For the full picture contact the JCB Information Centre, P.O. Box 444, Clifton, Nottingham NG11 6FR or phone free on 0800 581761.

Figure 15.4 Building awareness. JCB launched its skid steer initially with this teaser advertisement (left) before running the second advertisement, which revealed the actual product (right). SOURCE: Client John Bradley, JCB Sales Ltd. Agency: CB Brookes Advertising, Ltd.

Interest stage The stage of the product adoption process when customers are motivated to obtain information about the product's features, uses, advantages, disadvantages, price or location

Evaluation stage The stage of the product adoption process when customers decide whether the product will satisfy certain criteria that are crucial for meeting their specific needs

Trial stage The stage of the product adoption process when individuals use or experience the product for the first time

Adoption stage The final stage of product acceptance, when customers choose the specific product when they need a product of that type

innovative single arm skid steer; later adverts did (right). Consumers enter the **interest stage** when they are motivated to obtain information about the product's features, uses, advantages, disadvantages, price or location. During the **evaluation stage,** individuals consider whether the product will satisfy certain criteria that are crucial for meeting their specific needs. In the **trial stage,** they use or experience the product for the first time, possibly by purchasing a small quantity, by taking advantage of a free sample or demonstration or by borrowing the product from someone. Supermarkets, for example, frequently offer special promotions to encourage consumers to taste products such as cheese, cooked meats, snacks or pizza. During this stage, potential adopters determine the usefulness of the product under the specific conditions for which they need it.

Individuals move into the **adoption stage** by choosing the specific product when they need a product of that general type. It cannot be assumed, however, that because a person enters the adoption process she or he will eventually adopt the new product. Rejection may occur at any stage, including adoption. Both product adoption and product rejection can be temporary or permanent.

For the most part, people respond to different information sources at different stages of the adoption process. Figure 15.3 illustrates the most effective sources

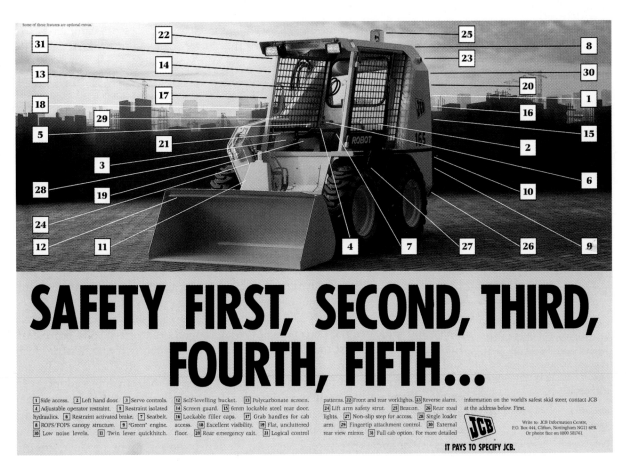

Some of these features are optional extras.

SAFETY FIRST, SECOND, THIRD, FOURTH, FIFTH...

1 Side access. 2 Left hand door. 3 Servo controls. 4 Adjustable operator restraint. 5 Restraint isolated hydraulics. 6 Restraint activated brake. 7 Seatbelt. 8 ROPS/FOPS canopy structure. 9 "Green" engine. 10 Low noise levels. 11 Twin lever quickhitch.

12 Self-levelling bucket. 13 Polycarbonate screen. 14 Screen guard. 15 6mm lockable steel rear door. 16 Lockable filler caps. 17 Grab handles for cab access. 18 Excellent visibility. 19 Flat, uncluttered floor. 20 Rear emergency exit. 21 Logical control

patterns. 22 Front and rear worklights. 23 Reverse alarm. 24 Lift arm safety strut. 25 Beacon. 26 Rear road lights. 27 Non-slip step for access. 28 Single loader arm. 29 Fingertip attachment control. 30 External rear view mirror. 31 Full cab option. For more detailed

information on the world's safest skid steer, contact JCB at the address below. First.

JCB

Write to: JCB Information Centre, P.O. Box 444, Clifton, Nottingham NG11 6PR. Or phone free on 0800 581761.

IT PAYS TO SPECIFY JCB.

Figure 15.4 *(Continued)*

for each stage. Mass communication sources, such as television advertising, are often effective for moving large numbers of people into the awareness stage. Producers of consumer goods commonly use massive advertising campaigns when introducing new products. They do so to create product awareness as quickly as possible within a large portion of the target market.

Mass communication sources may also be effective for people in the interest stage who want to learn more about a product. During the evaluation stage, individuals often seek information, opinions and reinforcement from personal sources—relatives, friends and associates. In the trial stage, individuals depend on salespeople for information about how to use the product properly to get the most out of it. Marketers must use advertising carefully when consumers are in the trial stage. If advertisements greatly exaggerate the benefits of a product, the consumer may be disappointed when the product does not meet expectations.[12] It is best to avoid creating expectations that cannot be satisfied, because rejection at this stage will prevent adoption. Friends and peers may also be important sources during the trial stage. By the time the adoption stage has been reached, both personal communication from sales personnel and mass communication through advertisements may be required. Even though the particular stage of the adoption process may influence the types of information sources consumers use, marketers must remember that other factors—such as the product's characteristics, price and uses, as well as the characteristics of customers—also affect the types of information sources that buyers desire and believe.

Because people in different stages of the adoption process often require different types of information, marketers designing a promotional campaign must determine what stage of the adoption process a particular target audience is in before they can develop the message. Potential adopters in the interest stage will need different information from people who have already reached the trial stage. Often a campaign will include several different advertisements and promotional mix tools in order to appeal simultaneously to different consumers who are at different stages in the product adoption process.

When a company introduces a new product, people do not all begin the adoption process at the same time and they do not move through the process at the same speed. Of those people who eventually adopt the product, some enter the adoption process rather quickly, whereas others start considerably later. For most products, too, there is a group of non-adopters who never begin the process.

Product Adopter Categories

Adopter categories Five groups into which customers can be divided according to the length of time it takes them to adopt a product: innovators, early adopters, early majority, late majority and laggards

Innovators The first people to adopt a new product

Early adopters People who choose new products carefully and are often consulted by people from the remaining adopter categories

Early majority People who adopt products just prior to the average person

Late majority People who are quite sceptical about new products but eventually adopt them because of economic necessity or social pressure

Laggards The last people to adopt a new product, suspicious of new products and oriented towards the past

Depending on the length of time it takes them to adopt a new product, people can be divided into five major **adopter categories**: innovators, early adopters, early majority, late majority and laggards.[13] Figure 15.5 shows each adopter category and indicates the percentage of total adopters that it typically represents. **Innovators** are the first to adopt a new product. They enjoy trying new products and tend to be venturesome. **Early adopters** choose new products carefully and are viewed as "the people to check with" by those in the remaining adopter categories. People in the **early majority** adopt just prior to the average person; they are deliberate and cautious in trying new products. **Late majority** people, who are quite sceptical about new products, eventually adopt them because of economic necessity or social pressure. **Laggards**, the last to adopt a new product, are oriented towards the past. They are suspicious of new products or are unable to easily afford them, and when they finally adopt the innovation, it may already have been replaced by a newer product. When microwave ovens first appeared, only technocrats or food boffins—the innovators—bought them. Then "trend setters", the early adopters, came into the market. After several years and prompted by many frozen food manufacturers' new product launches, many more consumers—the early majority—decided to adopt the microwave oven. Eventually, the rest of the masses—the late majority—decided that they, too, should have a microwave oven "given that most people have one now". There are, though, some households only now deciding to buy one—the laggards; and some—the non-adopters—never will. When developing promotional efforts, a marketer

Figure 15.5 Distribution of product adopter categories. SOURCE: Reprinted with the permission of The Free Press, a division of Simon & Schuster, Inc., from *Diffusion of Innovations*, Third Edition by Everett M. Rogers. Copyright © 1962, 1971, 1983 by The Free Press.

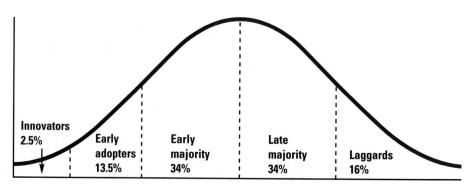

Innovators 2.5%

Early adopters 13.5%

Early majority 34%

Late majority 34%

Laggards 16%

should bear in mind that people in different adopter categories often need different forms of communication and different types of information.

Aims of Promotion Communication

Five communication effects Communication aims that include category need, brand awareness, brand attitude, brand purchase intention and purchase facilitation

Category need The consumer's perception of his or her need for a product in a certain category

Product adoption is a major focus for any promotional activity. There are, though, five basic communications aims, known as the **five communication effects,** which are defined as follows.[14]

Category Need The consumer must realise he or she wants a particular product—particularly for innovative new category product launches—and must perceive a **category need** in order to be motivated even to consider a product. When compact disc players were launched, many consumers had perfectly adequate album and/or cassette based hi-fi systems and did not see any need to purchase a compact disc player. CD producers had to create a category need.

Brand awareness The consumer's ability to identify a manufacturer's or retailer's brand in sufficient detail to distinguish it from other brands

Brand Awareness The consumer must be able to identify (recognise or recall) a manufacturer's or retailer's brand within the category in sufficient detail to make a purchase. **Brand awareness** means that the manufacturer or retailer must make its brand stand out, initially through product attributes supported by distinctive promotional activity. Sony wants consumers to be aware of *its* compact disc players rather than Aiwa or Amstrad players.

Brand attitude A consumer's particular impression of a brand, formed by emotions and logic or cognitive beliefs

Brand Attitude Emotions and logic or cognitive beliefs combine to give the consumer a particular impression of a product. This **brand attitude** directs consumer choice towards a particular brand. Companies need customers to have a positive view of their brands.

Brand purchase intention The consumer's decision and efforts to purchase the particular product

Brand Purchase Intention Once a category need and brand awareness are established, if the consumer's brand attitude is favourable, he or she will decide to purchase the particular product and take steps to do so, showing **brand purchase intention.**

Purchase facilitation Circumstances that make it possible for the consumer to purchase the product: availability, location, price and familiarity of vendor

Purchase Facilitation Having decided to buy, the consumer requires the product to be readily available at a convenient location, at a suitable price and from a familiar dealer: **purchase facilitation.** The manufacturer must ensure that other marketing mix factors (product, people, place/distribution and price) do not hinder the purchase. Sony customers expect wide distribution from reputable retailers, with no budget pricing. Sony produces high quality goods, but it has several well respected competitors and must ensure product availability and continued product improvement to prevent brand switching.

To provide a better understanding of how promotion can move people closer to the acceptance of goods, services and ideas, the next section focuses on the major promotional methods available to an organisation—the promotional mix.

The Promotional Mix

Several types of promotional methods can be used to communicate with individuals, groups and organisations. When an organisation combines specific ingredients to promote a particular product, that combination constitutes the

Promotional mix The specific combination of ingredients an organisation uses to promote a product, traditionally including four ingredients: advertising, personal selling, publicity and public relations, and sales promotion

promotional mix for that product. The four traditional ingredients of a **promotional mix** are advertising, personal selling, publicity and public relations, and sales promotion. Increasingly, sponsorship and direct mail are elements of the promotional mix in their own right (see Figure 15.6).[15] The Internet and direct marketing are recent additions to the promotional mix. For some products, businesses use all of these ingredients; for other products, two or three will suffice. This section analyses the major ingredients of a promotional mix and the chief factors that influence an organisation to include specific ingredients in the promotional mix for a specific product. Chapters 16 and 17 examine the promotional mix ingredients in greater detail.

Promotional Mix Ingredients

At this point consideration is given to some general characteristics of advertising, personal selling, publicity and public relations, sales promotion, sponsorship, direct mail, the Internet and direct marketing.

Advertising A paid form of non-personal communication about an organisation and its products that is transmitted to a target audience through a mass medium

Advertising Advertising is a paid form of non-personal communication about an organisation and its products that is transmitted to a target audience through a mass medium such as television, radio, newspapers, magazines, direct mail, public transport, outdoor displays, catalogues or the Internet. Individuals and organisations use advertising to promote goods, services, ideas, issues and people. Because it is highly flexible, advertising offers the options of reaching an extremely large target audience or focusing on a small, precisely defined segment of the population. For instance, McDonald's advertising focuses on a large audience of potential fast food consumers, ranging from children to adults, whereas advertising for DeBeers' diamonds focuses on a much smaller and specialised target market.

Advertising offers several benefits. It can be an extremely cost efficient promotional method because it reaches a vast number of people at a low cost per person. For example, if the cost of a four colour, one page advertisement in the *Sunday Telegraph* magazine is £7,000, and the magazine reaches 700,000 readers, the cost of reaching 1,000 subscribers is only £10 per person. Advertising also lets the user repeat the message a number of times. Unilever advertises many

Figure 15.6 Possible ingredients of an organisation's promotional mix

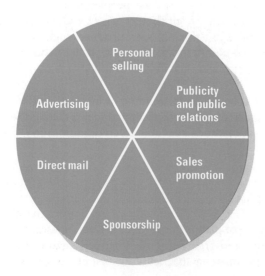

of its products (cleaning products, foods, cosmetics) on television, in magazines and through outdoor advertising. In addition, advertising a product in a certain way can add to its value. For example, BMW cars are advertised as having more sophistication, style and technical innovation than Honda, Toyota and other Japanese companies' vehicles. The visibility that an organisation gains from advertising enhances the company's public image.

Advertising also has several disadvantages. Even though the cost per person reached may be low, the absolute monetary outlay can be extremely high, especially for advertisements shown during popular television programmes. These high costs can limit, and sometimes prevent, the use of advertising in a promotional mix. Moreover, advertising rarely provides rapid feedback. Measuring its effect on sales is difficult, and it ordinarily has a less persuasive impact on customers than, for example, personal selling.[16]

Personal Selling   Selling that involves informing customers and persuading them to purchase products through personal communication in an exchange situation is called **personal selling**. The phrase *to purchase products* should be interpreted broadly to encompass the acceptance of ideas and issues. **Telemarketing,** described in Chapter 14 as direct selling over the telephone, relies heavily on personal selling.

Personal selling has both advantages and limitations when compared with advertising. Advertising is general communication aimed at a relatively large target audience, whereas personal selling involves more specific communication aimed at one person or several people. Reaching one person through personal selling costs considerably more than doing so through advertising, but personal selling efforts often have a greater impact on customers. Personal selling also provides immediate feedback, which allows marketers to adjust their message to improve communication. It helps them determine and respond to customers' needs for information.

When a salesperson and customer meet face to face, they use several types of interpersonal communication. Obviously, the predominating communication form is language—both speech and writing. In addition, a salesperson and customer frequently use **kinesic communication,** or body language, by moving their heads, eyes, arms, hands, legs or torsos. Winking, head nodding, hand gestures and arm motions are forms of kinesic communication. A good salesperson can often evaluate a prospect's interest in a product or presentation by watching for eye contact and head nodding. **Proxemic communication,** a less obvious form of communication used in personal selling, occurs in face-to-face interactions when either person varies the physical distance that separates the two people. When a customer backs away from a salesperson, for example, that individual may be indicating that he or she is not interested in the product or may be expressing dislike for the salesperson. Touching, or **tactile communication,** can also be used; shaking hands is a common form of tactile communication in many countries.

Publicity and Public Relations   Publicity refers to non-personal communication in news story form about an organisation or its products, or both, that is transmitted through a mass medium at no charge. Examples of publicity include magazine, newspaper, radio and television news stories about new retail stores, new products or personnel changes in an organisation. Although both advertising and publicity are transmitted through mass communication, the sponsor does not pay the media costs for publicity and is not identified. Nevertheless, publicity should

Personal selling   The use of personal communication in an exchange situation to inform customers and persuade them to purchase products

Telemarketing   Direct selling over the telephone, relying heavily on personal selling

Kinesic communication   Body language, including winking, head nodding, hand gestures and arm motions

Proxemic communication   A subtle form of communication used in face-to-face interactions when either person varies the physical distance that separates the two

Tactile communication   Interpersonal communication through touching, including shaking hands

Publicity   Non-personal communication in news story form about an organisation and/or its products that is transmitted through a mass medium at no charge

never be viewed as free communication. There are clear costs associated with preparing news releases and encouraging media personnel to broadcast or print them. A business that uses publicity regularly must have employees to perform these activities or obtain the services of a public relations consultancy or an advertising agency. Either way, the company bears the costs of the activities.

Publicity must be planned and implemented so that it is compatible with, and supportive of, other elements in the promotional mix.[17] However, publicity cannot always be controlled to the extent that other elements of the promotional mix can be. For example, just as Perrier's contamination problems (see Case 16.2 on pages 519–520) appeared to be easing, a BBC television programme showed that the "bottled at source" packaging was misleading because the bubbles were added during the bottling process. Sainsbury's, the UK's major grocery retailer, refused for many months to re-stock Perrier until the wording on the packaging was altered, creating further adverse publicity for the French company. The **public relations** mechanism manages and controls the process of effectively using publicity (see Chapter 16).[18] As noted in Marketing Insight 15.2, public relations is increasingly being used not only in its own right but also as a complementary tool to the rest of the promotional mix.

Public relations Managing and controlling the process of using publicity effectively

Sales promotion An activity or material that acts as a direct inducement by offering added value to or incentive for the product to resellers, salespeople or consumers

Sales Promotion   A **sales promotion** is an activity or material that acts as a direct inducement by offering added value to or incentive for the product to resellers, salespeople or consumers.[19] Examples of sales promotion include coupons, on-pack deals, trade shows, bonuses and contests used to enhance the sales of a product. The term *sales promotion* should not be confused with *promotion;* sales promotion is but a part of the more comprehensive area of promotion that encompasses advertising, personal selling, publicity and public relations, sponsorship, direct mail, the Internet and direct marketing. Some sales promotions, however, are closely associated with additional elements of the promotional mix (see Chapter 16). Currently, marketers spend about half as much on sales promotion as they do on advertising. Sales promotion appears to be growing in use more than advertising.

Marketers frequently rely on sales promotion to improve the effectiveness of other promotional mix ingredients, especially advertising and personal selling. For example, some businesses allocate 25 per cent of their annual promotional budget to trade shows in order to introduce new products, meet key industry personnel and identify likely prospects.[20]

Marketers design sales promotion to produce immediate, short run sales increases. For example, the major brewers such as Heineken and Whitbread use a continuous programme of sales promotion techniques to boost sales in the highly competitive beer and lager market: free drinks and prize competitions, scratch cards and trade incentives.

Generally, if a company employs advertising or personal selling, it either depends on them continuously or turns to them cyclically. However, a marketer's use of sales promotion tends to be irregular. Many products are seasonal. For example, Thomas Cook and Lunn Poly promote summer package holidays predominantly in the winter and spring months. Qualcast pushes its lawn mowers and other gardening equipment from Easter onwards. On the whole, sales promotions are infrequent, ad hoc campaigns.

Sponsorship   The financial or material support of an event, activity, person, organisation or product by an unrelated organisation or donor is called

There's More to PR Than Handling Bad Publicity

Advocates of public relations (PR) are quick to point to the many different uses to which this aspect of the promotional mix can be put. Although traditionally PR is associated with handling the effects of negative publicity, its uses are becoming ever more diverse. The application of PR in product launches is just one example. The application of PR as an aid to handling publicity is widely recognised. This was aptly illustrated by the battle between Greenpeace and Royal Dutch Shell. For weeks, Greenpeace, one of the world's best known environmental groups, had been protesting Royal Dutch Shell's plan to dispose of the Brent Spar oil rig by sinking it deep into the Atlantic. Greenpeace warned that the rig's toxic and radioactive sludge would wreak havoc on the ocean's environment. Then television viewers around the world saw a band of Greenpeace activists trying to land on the rig in the North Sea. To fend off this small band of eco-warriers, mighty Shell Oil blasted them with high powered water cannons. These pictures left viewers with the negative image of a huge multinational oil company bullying a squad of brave environmentalists. Losing what became a public opinion battle, Shell was forced to halt its dumping plans. Greenpeace's victory over Shell illustrates the power of effective public relations and Greenpeace's ability to use publicity well.

While advertising has been traditionally viewed as the primary promotional tool in launching new products, PR is playing a greater role than ever before. Some businesses are even choosing to use PR instead of advertising, seeing it as better value for money. For example, when the classic film *The Sting* was released on home video to mark its twenty-fifth anniversary, around two hundred journalists were sent teaser mailings of tiny silver bees in little jewellery boxes, with the message, "You could still get stung after 25 years." The clear intention in targeting the journalists was to attract as much publicity as possible to the launch. In addition, fashion designer Ben de Lisi was invited to design an outfit which drew inspiration from the film. This attracted considerable attention on a high profile day time television show.

In many cases, businesses launching new products are seeing PR as a useful complementary promotional tool to traditional advertising and sales promotion activities. One particular advantage is that consumers are more inclined to trust the third party endorsement which PR offers. Another advantage is that PR can be used to highlight other marketing mix components. For instance, when Diamond White cider was recently re-launched in new cobalt and blue packaging, PR was used to draw attention to a sales promotion which offered consumers the chance to win a weekend in Ibiza. In a separate product launch, Reebok capitalised on the popularity of the Spice Girls to promote its new football shirts for Liverpool Football Club. The agency concerned approached Sporty Spice, an ardent Liverpool fan, who agreed to wear the shirt for no charge. It was not long before teenage fans were also sporting the Reebok kit. The message for the future seems to be that PR has an important role to play in its own right and in conjunction with the rest of the promotional mix. PR can do much more than overcome adverse publicity in times of crisis.

SOURCES: Robert Gray, "PR in the driving seat", *Marketing*, 26 November 1998, pp. 29–33; George Pitcher, "God help those who confuse advertising and PR disasters", *Marketing Week*, 14 January 1999, p. 33; Robert Gray, "Does PR measure up?", *Marketing*, 17 December 1998, pp. 27–31; Bhushau Bahree, Kyle Pope and Allanna Sullivan, "How Greenpeace sank Shell's plan to dump big oil rig in Atlantic", *Wall Street Journal*, 7 July 1995, pp. A1, A3; "Greenpeace Brent Spar protest in the North Sea", World Wide Web, **http://www.greenpeace.org/comms/brent/brent.html**, 10 October 1995; and Anastasia Toufexis, "It's not easy being Greenpeace", *Time*, 16 October 1995, p. 86.

Sponsorship The financial or material support of an event, activity, person, organisation or product by an unrelated organisation or donor

sponsorship. Funds are made available to the recipient of the sponsorship in return for prominent public recognition of the benefactor's generosity and display of the sponsor's name, products and brands. Sponsorship is no longer confined to the arts or the sporting world, although many galleries, theatrical companies, sports events and teams could not survive without sponsorship. Research and development, buildings, degree courses, charitable events—all often benefit from sponsorship. The donor or sponsor gains the benefits of enhanced company, brand or individual reputation and awareness, as well as possibly improved morale and employee relations. Note the number of prestigious or well known brands sponsoring the Olympics or World Cup.

Direct Mail   The direct mail industry takes a significant slice of the promotional budgets for many companies and organisations. Few households and companies fail to receive direct mail solicitations. **Direct mail** is used to entice prospective customers or charitable donors to invest in products, services or worthy causes. Throughout Europe, direct mail is used as a pre-sell technique prior to a sales call, to generate orders, qualify prospects for a sales call, follow up a sale, announce special or localised sales and raise funds for charities and not-for-profit organisations. Good database management is essential, and the material must be carefully targeted to overcome the growing public aversion to "junk mail".

The Internet   From humble beginnings as a "talk shop" for boffins and computer buffs, the **Internet**—a network of computer networks stretching across the world, linking computers of different types—is now firmly established in many office workers' daily routines and accessed in millions of households. Marketers have been quick to identify this additional medium as an opportunity for providing existing and potential customers with company, product and brand information. Most large companies now have their own web sites, while the major Internet servers such as Microsoft and Yahoo are targeting small businesses and providing e-commerce capability at affordable prices.[21] Use of the Internet is not uniform across all parts of society, although there is evidence to suggest that it is no longer the pastime of only the young, affluent and well educated. Scrambling of confidential information such as credit card and bank account details has enabled the recent explosion in the number of purchases made on-line.

As a promotional mix ingredient, the Internet provides a tool which can be quickly up-dated or modified and which can produce material aimed at very tightly defined target groups or even individual consumers. From Interflora to Tesco to JCB, the Internet is increasingly part of the promotional mix, and for direct marketers, the actual point of the sales transaction. Few television and press advertisements for services or consumer goods do not now direct their target audience to associated web sites for additional information. Consumers can then interact with these hosts, in many instances, via e-mail and interactive web page information request facilities. Web sites must be tailored to match the target customer buying behaviour and expectations, and must be informative but not mesmerising, while reflecting the existing branding and product positioning already established by a business's marketers. They require expert design and up-dating, as with any ingredient in the promotional mix. The intranet—internal in-company Internet networks—has improved communications within many organisations, becoming an important facet of internal marketing (see Chapter 23).

Direct Marketing   First used in the 1960s, until its recent popularity direct marketing described the most common direct marketing approaches: direct mail and mail order. Currently experiencing a surge in popularity, direct marketing now encompasses all the communications tools which enable a marketer to deal directly with targeted customers: direct mail, telemarketing, direct response television advertising, door-to-door/personal selling and the Internet. **Direct marketing** is a decision by a company's marketers to (1) select a marketing channel which avoids dependence on marketing channel intermediaries, and (2) focus

Direct mail   A method of communication used to entice prospective customers or charitable donors to invest in products, services or worthy causes

Internet   A network of computer networks stretching across the world, linking computers of different types

Direct marketing   A decision by a company's marketers to select a marketing channel which avoids dependence on marketing channel intermediaries and to focus marketing communications activity on promotional mix ingredients which deal directly with targeted customers

marketing communications activity on promotional mix ingredients which deal directly with targeted customers. Direct marketing is now adopted by a host of businesses ranging from fast moving consumer goods companies, business-to-business marketers, charities and even government departments.[22] Of all elements of the promotional mix, it is reported to be the fastest growing, but this is partly a reflection of the large number of promotional mix ingredients which it includes.[23]

In terms of the promotional mix, there are several key implications. Direct mail is on the increase. Telemarketing has grown and will continue to do so with more businesses turning to the direct marketing toolkit aided by advances in automated call centres. Door-to-door selling and leaflet dropping, visible forms of direct marketing encountered by most householders, are also on the increase. Direct response advertising—containing a call for action within the advertisement either by coupon or telephone—is now close to a third of all advertising as marketers turn to direct marketing and as the growth in satellite and cable television channels enables more direct response television advertising. The Internet, too, is used by direct marketers to communicate with current and prospective customers. The deployment of any direct marketing campaign must strive to reflect targeted customer behaviour, needs and perceptions; provide a plausible proposition which is clearly differentiated from competitors' propositions; and match an organisation's corporate goals and trading philosophy. Direct marketing is not a substitute for the traditional promotional mix. Direct marketing is an increasingly popular deployment of marketing, resulting from marketers' choices regarding their preferred marketing channel and selection of promotional mix ingredients.

Now that the basic components of an organisation's promotional mix have been discussed, it is important to consider how that mix is created. The factors and conditions that affect the selection of the promotional methods a specific organisation uses in its promotional mix for a particular product need to be examined.

| Selecting Promotional Mix Ingredients | Marketers vary the composition of promotional mixes for many reasons. Although all ingredients can be included in a promotional mix, frequently a marketer chooses not to use them all. In addition, many businesses that market multiple product lines use several promotional mixes simultaneously. |

Marketers vary the composition of promotional mixes for many reasons. Although all ingredients can be included in a promotional mix, frequently a marketer chooses not to use them all. In addition, many businesses that market multiple product lines use several promotional mixes simultaneously.

An organisation's promotional mix (or mixes) is not an unchanging part of the marketing mix. Marketers can and do change the composition of their promotional mixes. The specific promotional mix ingredients employed and the intensity with which they are used depend on a variety of factors, including the organisation's promotional resources, objectives and policies; characteristics of the target market; characteristics of the product; and cost and availability of promotional methods.

Promotional Resources, Objectives and Policies The quality of an organisation's promotional resources affects the number and relative intensity of promotional methods that can be included in a promotional mix. If a company's promotional budget is extremely limited, the business is likely to rely on personal selling because it is easier to measure a salesperson's contribution to sales than to measure the effect of advertising. A business must have a sizeable promotional budget if it is to use regional or national advertising and sales promotion activities. Organisations with extensive promotional resources can usually include more ingredients in their promotional mixes. However, larger promotional budgets do not necessarily imply that the companies will use a greater number of promotional methods.

An organisation's promotional objectives and policies also influence the types of promotion used. If a company's objective is to create mass awareness of a new convenience good, its promotional mix is likely to lean heavily towards advertising, sales promotion and possibly publicity. If a company hopes to educate consumers about the features of durable goods, such as home electrical appliances, its promotional mix may combine a moderate amount of advertising, possibly some sales promotion efforts designed to attract customers to retail stores and a great deal of in-store personal selling, this being an excellent way to inform customers about these types of products. If a company's objective is to produce immediate sales of consumer non-durables, such as paper products and many grocery goods, the promotional mix will probably stress advertising and sales promotion efforts. Business-to-business marketers often use detailed trade advertising, personal selling through sales representatives, sales promotions—often in the guise of bulk discounts and trade show exhibits—and direct mail of brochures and price lists.

Characteristics of the Target Market   The size, geographic distribution and socio-economic characteristics of an organisation's target market also help dictate the ingredients to be included in a product's promotional mix. To some degree, market size determines the composition of the mix. If the size is quite limited, the promotional mix will probably emphasise personal selling, which can be quite effective for reaching small numbers of people. Organisations that sell to industrial markets and companies that market their products through only a few wholesalers frequently make personal selling the major component of their promotional mixes. When markets for a product consist of millions of customers, organisations use advertising and sales promotion because these methods can reach masses of people at a low cost per person. The Coca-Cola Company attempted to reach consumers through a non-traditional vehicle when it placed a commercial for Diet Coke in the introduction to the home video version of the 1989 blockbuster *Batman*. Warner Home Video, the distributor of *Batman*, believed that it would sell more than 10 million copies of the video cassette, exposing millions of consumers to the Diet Coke message at a low cost per person.[24]

The geographic distribution of a company's customers can affect the combination of promotional methods used. Personal selling is more feasible if a company's customers are concentrated in a small area than if they are dispersed across a vast region. When the company's customers are numerous and dispersed, advertising may be more practical.

The distribution of a target market's socio-economic characteristics, such as age, income or education, may dictate the types of promotional techniques that a marketer selects. For example, personal selling may be much more successful than print advertisements for communicating with poorly educated people, because it allows meaning or product attributes to be explained face to face.

Characteristics of the Product   Generally, promotional mixes for industrial products concentrate on personal selling. In promoting consumer goods, on the other hand, advertising plays a major role. This generalisation should be treated cautiously, however. Industrial goods producers do use some advertising to promote their goods, particularly in the trade press. Advertisements for computers, road building equipment and aircraft are not altogether uncommon, and sales promotion is used to promote industrial goods. Personal selling is used extensively for services and consumer durables, such as insurance, leisure and education, home appliances, cars and houses, and consumer convenience items are promoted mainly through advertising and sales promotion. Publicity appears in promotional mixes for industrial goods, consumer goods and services. Many organisations use direct mail, and more are now examining the growing use of corporate sponsorship. Most organisations are also developing web sites.

Marketers of highly seasonal products are often forced to emphasise advertising, and possibly sales promotion, because off-season sales will not support an extensive year round salesforce. Although many toy producers have salesforces to sell to resellers, a number of these companies depend to a large extent on advertising to promote their products.

The price of a product also influences the composition of the promotional mix. High priced products call for more personal selling because consumers associate greater risk with the purchase of such products and usually want the advice of a salesperson. Few consumers, for example, would be willing to purchase a refrigerator or personal computer from a self-service establishment. For low priced convenience items, marketers use advertising rather than personal selling at the retail level. The profit margins on many of these items are too low to justify the use of salespeople, and most customers do not need advice from sales personnel when buying such products.

A further consideration in creating an effective promotional mix is the stage of the product life cycle (see Chapter 8). During the introduction stage, a good deal of advertising may be necessary for industrial, business-to-business and consumer products to make potential users aware of a new product. For many products, personal selling and sales promotion are helpful as well at this stage. In the case of consumer non-durables, the growth and maturity stages call for a heavy emphasis on advertising. Industrial and business-to-business products, on the other hand, often require a concentration of personal selling and some sales promotion efforts during these stages. In the decline stage, marketers usually decrease their promotional activities, especially advertising. Promotional efforts in the decline stage often centre on personal selling and sales promotion efforts.

The intensity of market coverage is still another factor affecting the composition of the promotional mix. When a product is marketed through intensive distribution, the business depends strongly on advertising and sales promotion. A number of convenience products, such as lotions, cereals and coffee, are promoted through samples, coupons and cash refunds. Where marketers have opted for selective distribution, marketing mixes vary considerably as to type and amount of promotional methods. Items handled through exclusive distribution frequently demand more personal selling and less advertising. Expensive watches, furs and high quality furniture are typical products that are promoted heavily through personal selling. Intensive, selective and exclusive distribution are discussed in Chapter 12.

A product's use also affects the combination of promotional methods. Manufacturers of highly personal products, such as non-prescription contraceptives, feminine hygiene products and hemorrhoid treatments, count on advertising for promotion because many users do not like to talk to sales personnel about such products.

Cost and Availability of Promotional Methods The cost of promotional methods is a major factor to analyse when developing a promotional mix. National advertising and sales promotion efforts require large expenditures. For example, some detergent brands have annual advertising budgets of £10 to £15 million. However, if the efforts are effective in reaching extremely large numbers of people, the cost per individual reached may be quite small, possibly a few pennies per person. Moreover, not all forms of advertising are expensive. Many small, local businesses advertise their products through local newspapers, magazines, radio stations, outdoor signs and public transport.

Another consideration that marketers must explore when formulating a promotional mix is the availability of promotional techniques. Despite the tremendous number of media vehicles, a company may find that no available advertising medium effectively reaches a certain market. For example, a product may be banned from being advertised on television, as cigarettes are in many countries. A stockbroker may find no suitable advertising medium for investors in Manchester United Football Club: should the stockbroker use financial publications, sports magazines or general media? The problem of media availability becomes even more pronounced when marketers try to advertise in other countries. Some media, such as television, simply may not be available to advertisers. Television advertising in Scandinavia is minimal. In the UK only seven and a half minutes of advertising are permitted per average hour of terrestrial television, with a maximum of twelve minutes in any one "real" hour.[25] The media that are available may not be open to certain types of advertisements. For example, in Germany, advertisers are forbidden to make brand comparisons in television advertisements. Other promotional methods have limitations as well. An organisation may wish to increase the size of its salesforce but be unable to find qualified personnel. In the United States, some state laws prohibit the use of certain types of sales promotion activities, such as contests. Such prohibited techniques are thus "unavailable" in those locations.

Push Policy versus Pull Policy

Push policy A promotional policy in which the producer promotes the product only to the next institution down the marketing channel

Pull policy A promotional policy in which a business promotes directly to consumers in order to develop a strong consumer demand for its products

Another element that marketers should consider when they plan a promotional mix is whether to use a push policy or a pull policy. With a **push policy,** the producer promotes the product only to the next institution down the marketing channel. For instance, in a marketing channel with wholesalers and retailers, the producer promotes to the wholesaler, in this case the channel member just below the producer (see Figure 15.7). Each channel member in turn promotes to the next channel member. A push policy normally stresses personal selling. Sometimes sales promotion, direct mail and advertising are used in conjunction with personal selling to push the products down through the channel.

As Figure 15.7 shows, a company using a **pull policy** promotes directly to consumers with the intention of developing a strong consumer demand for the products. It does so through advertising, sales promotion, direct mail, sponsorship and packaging that helps manufacturers build and maintain market share.[26] Because consumers are persuaded to seek the products in retail stores, retailers will in turn go to wholesalers or the producer to buy the products. The policy is thus intended to "pull" the goods down through the channel by creating demand at the consumer level.

A push policy can be combined with a pull policy. Mars, for example, has a pull policy aimed at the consumer: sponsorship of events and advertising create awareness; packaging, sales promotions—such as competitions or discounts— and direct mail prompt product trial and adoption. Simultaneously, the company's push policy of trade advertising, sales promotions and personal selling persuades channel members to stock and retail its products.

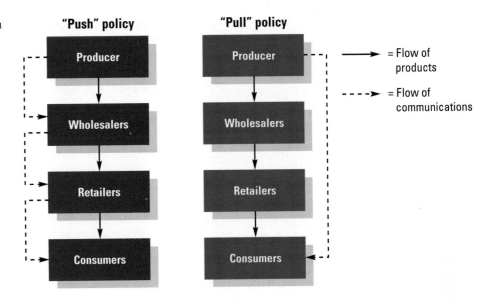

Figure 15.7 Comparison of push and pull promotional policies

"Push" policy

Producer → Wholesalers → Retailers → Consumers

"Pull" policy

Producer → Wholesalers → Retailers → Consumers

→ = Flow of products

- - → = Flow of communications

● S U M M A R Y

The primary role of *promotion* is to communicate with individuals, groups or organisations in the environment with the aim of directly or indirectly facilitating exchanges.

Communication is a sharing of meaning through the transmission of information. The communication process involves several steps. Using the *coding process*, the *source* first converts the meaning into a series of signs that represent concepts. The source should employ signs that are familiar to the *receiver* or *receiving audience* and choose signs that the receiver or receiving audience uses for referring to the concepts or ideas being promoted. The coded message is sent through a *medium of transmission* to the receiver or receiving audience. The receiver or receiving audience then uses the *decoding process* to convert the signs into concepts and usually supplies *feedback* to the source. When the decoded message differs from the encoded one, a condition called *noise* exists. Occasionally, *channel capacity* is reached when the volume of information can no longer be handled effectively.

One long run purpose of promotion is to influence and encourage customers to accept or adopt goods, services and ideas. The ultimate effectiveness of promotion is determined by the degree to which it affects product adoption or increases the frequency of current buyers' purchases. The *product adoption process* consists of five stages. (1) In the *awareness stage*, individuals become aware of the product. (2) People move into the *interest stage* when they seek information about the product. (3) In the *evaluation stage*, individuals decide whether the product will meet certain criteria that are crucial for satisfying their specific needs. (4) During the *trial stage*, the consumer actually uses or experiences the product for the first time. (5) In the *adoption stage*, the consumer decides to use the product on a regular basis. Product rejection may occur at any stage. People can be divided into five major adopter categories—*innovators, early adopters, early majority, late majority* and *laggards*—according to how long it takes them to start using a new product.

There are *five communication effects*. A manufacturer or retailer must establish a *category need* for a product. Consumers must have *brand awareness* and a favourable *brand attitude* towards the products. If the consumer decides to make a purchase—*brand purchase intention*—the company's overall marketing policy must guarantee distribution, suitable product quality and attributes, and set the relevant price points—*purchase facilitation*.

The *promotional mix* for a product may include the four major promotional methods—advertising, personal selling, publicity and public relations, and sales promotion—as well as the growing areas of sponsorship and direct mail. The Internet and direct marketing are currently very popular additions to companies' promotional mixes. *Advertising* is a paid form of non-personal communication about an organisation and its products that is transmitted to a target audience through a mass medium. *Personal selling* is a process of informing customers and persuading them to purchase products through personal communication in an exchange situation. *Kinesic, proxemic* and *tactile communication* are important in personal selling. *Telemarketing* often supports personal selling. *Publicity* is non-personal communication in news story form about an organisation or its products, or both, that is transmitted through a mass medium at no charge, controlled by the *public relations* mechanism. *Sales promotion* is an activity or material that acts as a direct inducement by offering added value to or incentive for the product to resellers, salespeople or consumers. *Sponsorship* involves financial or material support of an event, activity, person, organisation or product in return for prominent public recognition and display of the sponsor's name, products and brands. The *Internet,* networked independent computers, through organisations' web sites is a growing part of promotional activity. Many businesses are turning to *direct marketing* which is a decision to avoid the use of marketing channel intermediaries and to focus marketing communications activity on promotional unit ingredients which deal directly with targeted customers, such as personal selling, direct mail, direct response advertising, telemarketing and the Internet. *Direct mail* is used to entice prospective customers or charitable donors to invest in products, services or worthy causes.

There are several major determinants of what promotional methods to include in a promotional mix: the organisation's promotional resources, objectives and policies; the characteristics of the target market; the characteristics of the product; and the cost and availability of promotional methods. Marketers must also consider whether to use a push policy or a pull policy, or a combination of the two. With a *push policy,* the producer promotes the product only to the next institution down the marketing channel. Normally, a push policy stresses personal selling. A company that uses a *pull policy* promotes directly to consumers with the intention of developing a strong consumer demand for the products. Once consumers are persuaded to seek the products in retail stores, retailers in turn go to wholesalers or the producer to buy the products.

Important Terms

Promotion
Communication
Source
Receiver
Receiving audience
Coding process
Medium of transmission
Decoding process
Noise
Feedback
Channel capacity
Product adoption process
Awareness stage
Interest stage
Evaluation stage

Trial stage
Adoption stage
Adopter categories
Innovators
Early adopters
Early majority
Late majority
Laggards
Five communication effects
Category need
Brand awareness
Brand attitude
Brand purchase intention
Purchase facilitation
Promotional mix

Advertising
Personal selling
Telemarketing
Kinesic communication
Proxemic communication
Tactile communication
Publicity
Public relations
Sales promotion
Sponsorship
Direct mail
Internet
Direct marketing
Push policy
Pull policy

Discussion and Review Questions

1. What is the major task of promotion? Do businesses ever use promotion to accomplish this task and fail? If so, give several examples.
2. What is communication? Describe the communication process. Is it possible to communicate without using all of the elements in the communication process? If so, which ones can be omitted?
3. Identify several causes of noise. How can a source reduce noise?
4. Describe the product adoption process. In certain circumstances, is it possible for a person to omit one or more of the stages in adopting a new product? Explain your answer.
5. Describe a product that many people are in the process of adopting. Have you begun the adoption process for this product? If so, what stage have you reached?
6. What is category need? Illustrate your answer with examples.
7. Identify and briefly describe the major promotional methods that can be included in an organisation's promotional mix. How does publicity differ from advertising?
8. What forms of interpersonal communication in addition to language can be used in personal selling?
9. List the communications tools that direct marketing encompasses and explain the recent surge in popularity of this promotional tool.
10. How do target market characteristics determine which promotional methods to include in a promotional mix? Assume that a company is planning to promote a cereal to both adults and children. Along what major dimensions would these two promotional efforts have to be different?
11. How can a product's characteristics affect the composition of its promotional mix?
12. Evaluate the following statement: "Appropriate advertising media are always available if a company can afford them."
13. Explain the difference between a pull policy and a push policy. Under what conditions should each policy be used?

Recommended Readings

J. J. Burnett, *Promotion Management* (Boston, Mass.: Houghton Mifflin, 1993).

J. Engel, M. Warshaw and T. Kinnear, *Promotional Strategy: Managing the Marketing Communications Process*, 8th edn (Boston, Mass.: Irwin, 1994).

C. R. Evans, *Marketing Channels—Infomercials and the Future of Televised Marketing* (London: Prentice-Hall, 1994).

M. FitzGerald and D. Arnott, *Marketing Communications Classics* (London: International Thomson Publishing, 2000).

M. M. Mirabito, *The New Communication Technologies* (Stoneham, Mass.: Focal Press, 1997).

C. Petersen and A. Toer, *Sales Promotion in Post-Modern Marketing* (Aldershot: Gower, 1995).

● C A S E S

15.1 Cause Related Marketing

Cause related marketing is enjoying an upsurge in popularity. At a time when consumer groups are pushing for business to behave in an ethical and socially responsible manner, fostering links with charities and other good causes is one avenue to follow. Many businesses believe that there are long term benefits in supporting good causes. In particular, they hope that consumer perceptions of the business and its brands will be enhanced by such connections. Perhaps the company will be seen as more caring or socially responsible as a result.

Communicating the link between a company and its sponsorship of charitable causes needs to be handled carefully. Consumers can be suspicious if the chosen cause is not obviously linked to the business concerned. Many businesses avoid this difficulty by carefully selecting a relevant theme for their cause related marketing. For example, BT focuses on the area of communication. One of the causes that the company supports is Winston's Wish, an organisation helping children to talk about and deal with the death of a loved one. Meanwhile baby equipment manufacturer Mamas & Papas also themes its support through links with four different baby charities, including the NSPCC and BLISS (Baby Life Support Systems). British Gas, via its links with Help the Aged, has focused efforts on helping to reduce the number of elderly people dying from illnesses and difficulties related to cold temperatures in the home. Senior managers at British Gas realise that the company must demonstrate its commitment to the cause, and accordingly a long term approach has been planned. This began with a home insulation programme targeted at older consumers and included offering those at risk help with their heating bills, plus the funding of heating for daycare centres.

Of course, it is difficult to measure the effectiveness of a cause related campaign. However, research by Business in the Community suggests that the potential is good. Eighty-six per cent of consumers indicate that they are likely to have a more positive perception of a business which is doing something to make the world a better place. The same percentage suggests that if quality and price are equal, they are more likely to choose a product which is linked with a good cause. Slightly less, 61 per cent, say that they would change their chosen retail outlet for the same reason. Of course, it is never certain if people really do behave in the way they say they will. However, it is clear that to be taken seriously, businesses becoming involved in cause related marketing must demonstrate a long term commitment to a relevant charity. It is also crucial that such businesses avoid the impression that their charitable support is simply another facet of the marketing programme. An expert on cause related marketing explains: "We are moving away now from the 'buy our product and we'll give 10 pence to this charity' kind of approach. A relationship between a company and charity has to be more than just a fling. It's not just the latest marketing tool which can be shoved on to the most junior member of the marketing team to handle."

Businesses' reasons for becoming involved in cause related marketing vary. The family-run R Griggs Group, which manufactures the world famous Dr Martens brand of footwear, has always tried to contribute positively to social causes because it believes this is the right approach for the business. The company supports the homeless charity Shelter because homelessness and unemployment are issues which concern its key customer group. Similarly, cosmetics company Avon developed links with breast cancer charities because this was an area which concerned its customers, primarily middle aged women at home. Although the business has been involved with promoting this particular cause for some years, Avon has only recently sought to communicate the connection more publicly. Senior managers hope that consumers will view the association in a positive way and will appreciate that Avon cares about its customers and what they think. In some circumstances, there are also internal reasons for involvement. When supermarket giant Sainsbury's became involved in Comic Relief (a fund raising effort for a range of good causes, principally African, which is based around a telethon organised by well known comedians), managers suggested that an important benefit was the sense of team building among company employees.

Whatever the reasons for becoming involved in cause related marketing, like any aspect of a marketing programme, careful planning is essential. Various guidelines are available for businesses seeking to develop their marketing in this way.

For the charities themselves, the reasons for fostering links with businesses are well defined. Competition for the public's cash is greater than ever. The number of charities is increasing, and consumers are apparently becoming fatigued with traditional methods of collecting, such as door-to-door envelope drops and street collections. Older consumers, traditionally an important group of donors, are anxious about being able to support themselves into their old age. This means that the major charities are increasingly trying to educate younger consumers into donating manageable and regular amounts. Now, more than ever, charities are turning to marketing to help them in their fund raising battle. Many are now employing professional marketers in an attempt to ensure that programmes are

appropriately planned and executed. The use of e-mail lists, hard hitting television advertising and links between charities and commercial products are just a few of the resulting initiatives.

Within this environment, the benefits of joining forces with businesses are obvious and are leading to a host of innovative fund raising opportunities. In many cases, this involves becoming linked with products—such as credit cards and insurance—which support the charity. According to Anthony Boumann, head of fund raising for the animal charity RSPCA: "The trick is to provide appropriate offers. We are a large, general charity appealing mainly to BC1s and C2s, so we need small amounts of cash from large numbers. That's why RSPCA credit cards work well for us."

SOURCES: Julia Bird, "Harder times mean smarter marketing", *Marketing*, 25 March 1999, p. 45; Ken Gofton, "NSPCC aims to convert abuse anger into cash", *Marketing*, 25 March 1999, pp. 37–38; Claire Murphy, "Brand values can build on charity ties", *Marketing*, 25 March 1999, pp. 41–42; Jade Garrett, "Charities snub shock tactics for subtle approach", *Campaign*, 26 March 1999; "Charities unite in donor appeal", *Marketing*, 14 January 1999, p. 4; "Spotlight: charity", *Marketing Week*, 17 December 1998, pp. 28–29; Daz Valladares, "Charities find relief in targeted advertising", *Marketing Week*, 27 November 1992, p. 16.

Questions for Discussion

1. Why might businesses turn to fostering good causes?
2. Were they to do so, what are the risks for a business such as Shell and a charity such as Oxfam in teaming up together?
3. How is cause related marketing adding a new slant to the promotional mix?

15.2 Häagen-Dazs: Promoting an Adult Ice Cream

Häagen-Dazs makes the best selling superpremium ice cream in North America. Its luscious ingredients include chocolate from Benelux, vanilla from Madagascar, coffee from Brazil, strawberries from Oregon and nuts from Hawaii and Switzerland—and the text on the packaging serenely asserts that it is the world's best ice cream. Since Grand Metropolitan's take-over of Pillsbury, Häagen-Dazs has come to Europe in a big way. In less than a decade, sales in Britain, France and Germany have climbed from £3 million to £70 million, with con-

sumers happily paying two or three times the cost of rival, traditional brands for this premium product.

London's Leicester Square shop served close to one million ice cream lovers in its first year. The success of the Victor Hugo Plaza shop in Paris, now the company's second busiest, led to the establishment of its first European factory in France. Häagen-Dazs shops have opened in Italy, Spain, Benelux and Scandinavia. The appealing flavours can now be found not only in the company's shops but also at airports, in cafés and in carefully selected delicatessens, with rapidly growing popularity.

The product's high quality has been essential in maintaining a loyal customer following, but it was promotional work that led to the successful take-off of what was previously an unheard-of brand in Europe. Free tasting was a major prong of attack; over 5 million free cupfuls of ice cream were given away during the company's European launch. Thousands of retailers, cafés and delis were supplied with branded freezers both to display and carefully look after the new premium ice cream. Häagen-Dazs spent £30 million on advertising, stressing the de luxe ingredients, unusual flavours and novelty of the product. Europeans currently eat 25 per cent of the 3 billion gallons of ice cream consumed worldwide. Häagen-Dazs plans to increase consumption by appealing to more than traditional ice cream lovers.

The summer afternoon stroll with an ice cream cornet, the family trip to a fun park or beach, a snack during a film or concert, the sticky climax of a birthday party feast had long been the core market for Wall's and Lyons Maid (now Nestlé). Ice Cream Mars changed all that by creating an ice cream bar suitable for any occasion and particularly attractive to adults. Häagen-Dazs goes further! Award winning press adverts, artistically shot, often in black and white, feature lithe, semi-nude couples entwined in exotic poses while feeding each other Häagen-Dazs ice cream. The appeal of vanilla ice cream bars hand-dipped in Belgian chocolate and rolled in roasted almonds now seems hard to resist for adults everywhere. The advertising imagery promotes an adult, up-market, glamorous positioning for this superpremium ice cream. The Häagen-Dazs range has been expanded to include frozen yogurts, sorbets and now ice cream novelties, such as the ice cream sandwich made with cookies.

SOURCES: "Dairy produce", *Campaign*, 15 March 1996, p. 34; "Häagen-Dazs cinema first", *Campaign*, 26 March 1995, p. 5; "Pillsbury's global training plan", *Crossborder Monitor*, 19 April 1995, p. 9; G. Mead, "Sex, ice and videod beer", *Financial Times*, 26 September 1992, p. 5; "Saucy way to sell a Knickerbocker Glory—Häagen-Dazs' new ice cream campaign", *Financial Times*, 8 August 1991, p. 8; "Häagen-Dazs is using sex to secure an up market niche in Britain's £400m ice cream market", *Observer*, 4 August 1991, p. 25; M. Carter, "The luxury ice cream market", *Marketing Week*, 22 May 1992, p. 30.

Questions for Discussion

1. Why did the London launch of Häagen-Dazs utilise so many stunts and such a mix of promotional activity?
2. Why did Häagen-Dazs target the adult market rather than families or children?
3. Was the "adult" positioning and promotional execution risky? Why did Häagen-Dazs deploy this positioning strategy?

16 Advertising, Public Relations and Sponsorship

"The strengths and weaknesses of publicity provide a mirror image to those of advertising which, when combined, complement one another synergistically."

Norman Hart

OBJECTIVES

- To explore the nature and uses of advertising
- To become aware of the major steps involved in developing an advertising campaign
- To find out who is responsible for developing advertising campaigns
- To gain an understanding of publicity and public relations
- To be aware of current trends in advertising and public relations
- To examine the nature of sponsorship

The Internet connects a rapidly growing number of homes, businesses and schools across the globe to a huge array of information and, increasingly, to the sales particulars of many companies' products and services. In its early years, the Internet was purely a vehicle for communicating information. Now, with scrambling techniques to safeguard credit card details, the Internet can be used as an interactive advertising, product information, ordering and payment tool within the marketing mix. Experts believe that within a few years, the Internet could be taking a staggering £200 billion in orders for all types of products and services, notably banking and financial services, which are predicted to be the fastest growing sector of the Internet for promoting and selling products, as well as for small firms with limited advertising budgets.

German car giant BMW has used the Internet to create a service only available on-line, the BMW Approved Used Car Directory. This service is interactive, providing a search and find facility, as well as general BMW information support. Users may either specify a desired model/colour/specification/age/price combination for the BMW system to locate or scroll through comprehensive lists of used BMWs for sale through the dealer network. All local BMW dealers are on the Internet, promoting their site through local media and press advertising.

To work, a "good" Internet site must attract target customers' attention and fulfil their expectations, just as any other product or service should. The information being offered by BMW and its dealers must be of interest to target BMW customers and relevant users of the Internet. The site should be interactive, offering users the chance to become involved. The Internet site must be interesting and of high quality. It should be promoted; otherwise either users will not track it down, or it will be swamped by the plethora of sites being set up. It must pay for itself: a good Internet site costs around £30,000 to set up. The Internet site will need to be staffed, particularly if users are likely to seek responses to very specific queries or to place an order. Above all, advertisers need to remember that the imagery and message used on the Internet must be consistent and fully integrated with the rest of their promotional mix.

Whether it is for Newcastle United Football Club, Condé Nast's *Vogue* and *Tatler* or Richard Branson's Virgin, the Internet is playing an increasingly significant role in many businesses' promotional activity. The Internet is a growing part of the promotional mix and indeed also of the overall marketing mix. Most TV and press advertising directs consumers to web sites for additional information. The Internet is very much part of the advertising executive's toolkit. The recent growth of direct marketing has enhanced significantly the role of the Internet in promotional strategy.

SOURCES: *Marketing Guides:* "The Internet", 27 June 1996; C. Lloyd, "On a quest to bring the Internet to the masses", *Sunday Times,* 26 November 1995; "Innovation", *Sunday Times,* 19 and 26 November, 31 December 1995; "Scramble to build a super showroom in cyberspace", *Independent on Sunday,* 4 February 1996, p. IB 8; "Pay by plastic plan on internet", *Evening Telegraph,* 3 February 1996, p. 15. *Screen capture:* Courtesy of Eurostar Co.

T his chapter explores the many dimensions of advertising, publicity and public relations, and sponsorship. Initially focusing on how advertising is used, it goes on to examine the major steps by which an advertising campaign is developed, describing who is responsible for developing such campaigns. After analysing publicity and public relations and comparing their characteristics with those of advertising, the chapter explores the different forms publicity may take. The following section considers how publicity is used and what is required for an effective public relations programme. After discussing negative publicity and some problems associated with the use of publicity, the chapter examines some of the current trends in advertising and public relations, as typified by the growing use of the Internet in marketing. It concludes with a look at the increasing use of sponsorship in the promotional mix.

The Nature of Advertising

Advertising permeates everyone's daily lives.[1] It may be perceived positively or as an annoyance, encouraging channel hopping during advertising breaks or fast forwarding of video recordings.[2] Some advertising informs, persuades or entertains; some of it bores, even offends. For example, consumer groups have been whitewashing billboards advertising tobacco products because they believe such advertisements encourage children to smoke.[3]

Advertising is a paid form of non-personal communication that is transmitted through mass media such as television, radio, newspapers, magazines, direct mail, public transport vehicles, outdoor displays and now also the Internet.

Advertising   A paid form of non-personal communication that is transmitted through mass media such as television, radio, newspapers, magazines, direct mail, public transport vehicles, outdoor displays and the Internet

Ambient Advertising Seeks Out New Sites

When did you last spot an advertisement in a surprising place? Perhaps it was a Volkswagen promotion on the handle of a petrol pump, an advert on a bus ticket or even the promotion of clean air in Wales on the back of a dirty van. The industry refers to the use of such media as ambient advertising. According to outdoor advertising agency Concord, which claims to be the first to define the form, ambient advertising is "non-traditional out-of-home advertising". For example, at the Atlanta Olympic games, sprinter Linford Christie promoted Puma by wearing contact lenses featuring the sportswear brand. Finding new and creative ways of advertising using the outdoor world represents a move away from the traditional media of television, radio, cinema press and posters. Advocates of the new approach believe that ambient advertising has huge potential.

Companies commissioning promotional work involving ambient media have been pleased to discover that considerable free press coverage can result. Ben and Jerry's, the American ice cream business, attracted considerable publicity when it hired cows to act as mobile advertising hoardings. The animals, which were grazing alongside a major motorway, were fitted with coats sporting an ice cream advertisement. Meanwhile Beck's beer was promoted using an advertisement grown (mown) in a 30 acre field sited alongside a heavily used railway line.

In addition to identifying new surfaces as replacement billboards, ambient advertising makes use of existing objects as promotional sites. Elida Fabergé recently advertised its Vaseline Intensive Care deodorant by attaching fake roll-on containers to the hanging grab-straps on the London Underground. The aim was to draw attention to the product at a time when commuters might be particularly amenable to considering its benefits. Meanwhile Unilever targeted consumers' sense of smell by impregnating the scent of Radion washing powder onto the reverse of bus tickets.

Views about the effectiveness of ambient advertising vary. "Ambient campaigns don't always target a specific audience. The Beck's advert was successful because of the press coverage it generated but as an ad it didn't target the correct demographic spread. It targeted a whole commuter train of people only a small number of whom like to drink Beck's." So is some of the new ambient advertising just a novel public relations stunt? Not according to Alan Greaney, director of the Media Initiatives Agency who believes that ambient is appropriate in certain circumstances. He does, however, stress the importance of linking the product with an appropriate medium. For example, the decision to advertise breath mints Clorets on the lids of curry takeaway boxes was clearly an appropriate one.

With just 12 per cent of outdoor spend devoted to ambient advertising, it remains a relatively small part of the industry. However, growth of this novel area is considerable, with some estimates suggesting growth of around 70 per cent in 1998. Questions about effectiveness will no doubt remain. The failure of advertising on eggs (so-called "eggverts") was well publicised, while some in the industry believe that consumers will become so over-loaded by commercial images that even the impact of those spotted in unexpected places will lessen in time.

SOURCES: Sian Phillips, "Space invaders", *Hotline*, Winter 1998/99, pp. 16–19; David Reed, "Fuel injection", *Marketing Week*, 4 February 1999, pp. 37–42.

Marketing Insight 16.1 presents some innovative advertising forms. An organisation can use advertising to reach a variety of audiences, ranging from small, precise groups, such as the stamp collectors of the major conurbations, to large audiences, such as all the buyers of fax machines in Sweden.

When people are asked to name major advertisers, most immediately mention business organisations. However, many types of organisations—including governments, churches, universities, civic groups and charitable organisations—take advantage of advertising. For example, the UK government is one of the largest advertisers: "Heroin Screws You Up", Employment Training, the euro campaign and the DTI Enterprise Initiative are just a few examples. So even though advertising is analysed here in the context of business organisations, it should be borne in mind that much of the discussion applies to all types of organisations. See Table 16.1 for details of advertising in Europe.

Marketers sometimes give advertising more credit than it deserves. This attitude causes them to use advertising when they should not. For example, manufacturers of basic products such as sugar, flour and salt often try to differentiate their products, with minimal success. Under certain conditions, advertising can work effectively for an organisation. The questions in Table 16.2 raise some general points that a marketer should consider when assessing the potential value of advertising as an ingredient in a product's promotional mix. The list is not all-inclusive. Numerous factors have a bearing on whether advertising should be used at all, and if so, to what extent.

The Uses of Advertising

Advertising can serve a variety of purposes. Individuals and organisations use it to promote products and organisations, to stimulate demand, to off-set competitors' advertising, to make sales personnel more effective, to educate a market's customers and dealers, to increase the uses of a product, to remind and reinforce customers, and to reduce sales fluctuations (see Figure 16.1).[4]

Promoting Products and Organisations

Institutional advertising The type of advertising that promotes organisational images, ideas or political issues

Product advertising The type of advertising that promotes goods and services

Advertising is used to promote goods, services, ideas, images, issues, people and indeed anything that the advertiser wants to publicise or foster. Depending on what is being promoted, advertising can be classified as institutional or product advertising. **Institutional advertising** promotes organisational images, ideas or political issues. For example, some of Seagram's advertising promotes the idea that drinking and driving do not mix, in order to create and develop a socially responsible image. **Product advertising** promotes goods and services. Business, government and private non-business organisations turn to it to promote the uses, features, images and benefits of their products. When Monsanto introduced a new pesticide to help farmers clean up weeds in post-harvest stubble, it used press advertising to tout the benefits of Sting CT, including a competition (for a trip to Italy) and a coupon to mail in for further technical details of the product. It is this type of advertising that readers, as consumers, will be familiar with, be it the advertisements for Ford cars, Kellogg's cereals or Barclays Bank's services.

Stimulating Primary and Selective Demand

Pioneer advertising The type of advertising that informs people about a product: what it is, what it does, how it can be used and where it can be purchased

When a specific business is the first to introduce an innovation, it tries to stimulate *primary demand*—demand for a product category rather than a specific brand of the product—through pioneer advertising. This is often referred to as creating category need. **Pioneer advertising** informs people about a product: what it is, what it does, how it can be used and where it can be purchased. Because pioneer advertising is used in the introductory stage of the product life cycle when there are no competitive brands, it neither emphasises the brand name nor compares brands. The first company to introduce the compact disc player, for instance, initially tried to stimulate primary demand (create category need) by emphasising the benefits of compact disc players in general rather than the benefits of its brand. Product advertising is also used sometimes to stimulate primary demand for an established product. Occasionally, an industry trade group, rather than a single company, sponsors advertisements to stimulate primary demand.

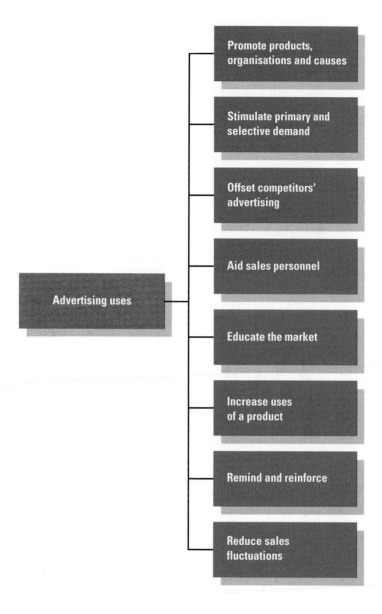

Figure 16.1 Major uses of advertising

Advertising uses

- Promote products, organisations and causes
- Stimulate primary and selective demand
- Offset competitors' advertising
- Aid sales personnel
- Educate the market
- Increase uses of a product
- Remind and reinforce
- Reduce sales fluctuations

Competitive advertising The type of advertising that points out a brand's uses, features and advantages that may not be available in competing brands

Comparative advertising The type of advertising that compares two or more brands on the basis of one or more product attributes

For example, to stimulate demand for milk, the old Milk Marketing Board sponsored advertisements that demonstrated how healthy and pleasant milk is to drink. In Figure 16.2, advertising promotes the use of potatoes.

To build *selective demand,* or demand for a specific brand, an advertiser turns to competitive advertising. **Competitive advertising** points out a brand's uses, features and advantages that benefit consumers but may not be available in competing brands. For example, BMW heavily promotes the technical abilities and innovative features of its cars in its advertising.

Another form of competitive advertising is **comparative advertising,** in which two or more brands are compared on the basis of one or more product attributes. Companies must not, however, misrepresent the qualities or characteristics of the comparison product.

Figure 16.2 Stimulating primary demand. This advertisement aims to stimulate demand for potatoes in general, rather than for a specific brand. SOURCE: Courtesy of the British Potato Marketing Board.

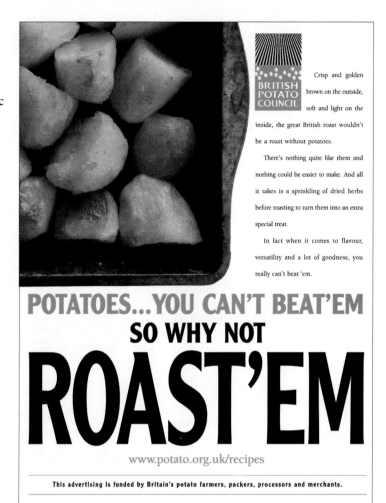

BRITISH POTATO COUNCIL

Crisp and golden brown on the outside, soft and light on the inside, the great British roast wouldn't be a roast without potatoes.

There's nothing quite like them and nothing could be easier to make. And all it takes is a sprinkling of dried herbs before roasting to turn them into an extra special treat.

In fact when it comes to flavour, versatility and a lot of goodness, you really can't beat 'em.

POTATOES...YOU CAN'T BEAT'EM
SO WHY NOT
ROAST'EM

www.potato.org.uk/recipes

This advertising is funded by Britain's potato farmers, packers, processors and merchants.

Off-setting Competitors' Advertising

Defensive advertising The type of advertising that aims to off-set or lessen the effects of a competitor's promotional programme

When marketers advertise to off-set or lessen the effects of a competitor's promotional programme, they are using **defensive advertising.** Although defensive advertising does not necessarily increase a company's sales or market share, it may prevent a loss in these areas. For example, when McDonald's first test marketed pizza, Pizza Hut countered with defensive advertising to protect its market share and sales. Pizza Hut advertised both on television and in newspapers in the two test cities, emphasising that its product is made from scratch, whereas McDonald's uses frozen dough.[5] Defensive advertising is used most often by companies in extremely competitive consumer product markets, such as the fast food industry.

Making Sales Personnel More Effective

Business organisations that stress personal selling often use advertising to improve the effectiveness of sales personnel. Advertising created specifically to support personal selling activities tries to pre-sell a product to buyers by informing them about its uses, features and benefits and by encouraging them to contact local dealers or sales representatives. This form of advertising helps salespeople find good sales prospects. Advertising is often designed to support personal selling efforts for industrial products, insurance and consumer durables, such as cars and major household appliances. For example, advertising may bring a prospec-

	Y&R	McCann-Erickson	O&M	BBDO Group	Grey	Bates	APL	Publicis	JWT	Saatchi
UK	7	4	3	8	9	1	16	14	5	6
Germany	4	5	2	1	3	14	7	6	8	19
France	5	6	7	8	12	13	10	4	14	11
Italy	1	4	8	16	9	10	14	3	5	7
Spain	7	3	2	6	4	1	13	15	5	17
Netherlands	1	5	3	2	11	21	12	4	6	18
Switzerland	1	2	7	—	8	14	9	5	13	15
Sweden	1	2	7	5	6	4	8	13	14	11
Finland	12	3	8	15	1	7	6	4	10	—
Norway	12	3	6	10	4	2	—	9	—	13
Denmark	1	4	7	5	2	3	8	17	12	11
Belgium	9	2	1	3	8	16	7	10	11	5
Austria	14	8	5	10	11	13	6	9	12	3
Greece	9	4	2	3	16	12	7	20	1	5
Portugal	3	1	7	11	15	17	2	5	6	10
Turkey	5	3	15	7	1	2	10	9	11	8
Poland	10	3	11	8	9	4	6	13	5	4
Hungary	4	1	2	8	9	3	6	14	12	3
Czech Rep.	2	3	6	1	7	10	8	13	9	10
Russia	6	2	4	3	8	7	5	12	9	7
Romania	9	1	4	5	11	3	6	8	10	3
Countries	21	21	21	20	21	21	20	21	20	20
Average	5.9	3.3	5.6	6.8	7.8	8.4	8.3	9.9	8.9	9.3

Notes: Irish figures are unavailable. Ranking is for highest billing office in each country. Average ranking is average of those countries where an office exists.

SOURCE: *The Retail Pocket Book 1999*, p. 18. Reprinted by permission of NTC Publications, Ltd.

Table 16.1 Advertising in Europe

tive buyer to a showroom, but usually a salesperson plays a key role in actually closing the sale.

Educating the Market
A change to a business's strategy may lead to it entering new markets or introducing innovative products. This will require an orientation programme for targeted customers and required channel intermediaries. Part of this communications task may entail advertising. Even if a company modifies its marketing mix in existing markets—new product specifications, after sales policies or pricing, for example—it may need to educate the market—customers and dealers—regarding the changes.

Increasing the Uses of a Product
The absolute demand for any product is limited because people in a market will consume only so much of it. Given both this limit on demand and competitive conditions, marketers can increase sales of a specific product in a defined geographic market only to a certain point. To improve sales beyond this point, they

Table 16.1 Advertising in Europe (cont.)

b. ADVERTISING EXPENDITURE BY COUNTRY AND MEDIUM (US$m), 1997

Country	Total	Newspapers	Magazines	TV	Radio	Cinema	Outdoor/ Transport
Germany	19,168.9	9,240.8	3,570.7	4,766.0	753.5	195.7	642.3
UK	15,718.6	6,365.9	2,892.2	5,101.5	585.7	118.2	655.1
France	9,258.0	2,218.9	2,139.4	3,149.9	610.8	52.8	1,086.2
Italy	5,875.0	1,205.4	938.8	3,378.3	207.6	—	144.9
Spain	4,417.8	1,382.4	677.7	1,690.5	428.0	36.5	202.7
Netherlands	3,314.7	1,629.2	744.6	629.3	181.9	11.8	117.9
Switzerland	2,317.9	1,248.5	436.2	235.7	62.7	26.9	308.0
Sweden	1,855.4	1,092.9	241.0	373.3	54.5	10.7	83.0
Belgium	1,626.9	401.3	370.4	559.5	137.5	24.0	134.2
Austria	1,593.2	711.2	270.1	362.3	142.1	3.0	104.5
Denmark	1,433.8	881.7	192.6	282.7	26.3	10.0	40.4
Norway[1]	1,138.7	665.0	121.1	210.5	116.3	5.6	20.3
Finland	1,057.6	602.9	170.6	215.3	34.9	1.3	32.7
Greece	1,000.5	203.1	260.7	465.4	49.3	—	22.0
Portugal	883.7	134.9	160.5	421.2	62.3	2.9	101.9
Ireland	697.1	440.4	20.8	149.9	44.2	4.7	37.0

Notes: Data are net of discounts; they include agency commission and press classified advertising but exclude production costs. Data are ranked on total adspend. [1]Data for Norway are estimates.

SOURCE: *The Retail Pocket Book 1999*, p. 22. Reprinted by permission of NTC Publications, Ltd.

must either enlarge the geographic market and sell to more people or develop and promote a larger number of uses for the product. If a business's advertising convinces buyers to use its products in more ways, the sales of the products go up. For example, Nabisco used advertising to inform consumers that its Shredded Wheat cereal contains no added sugar and is high in natural fibre, which is essential to a healthy, balanced diet. The company is thus attempting to position Shredded Wheat as part of a wholesome diet, as well as a popular children's cereal. When promoting new uses, an advertiser attempts to increase the demand for its own brand without driving up the demand for competing brands.

Reminding and Reinforcing Customers

Reminder advertising The type of advertising that reminds customers of the uses, characteristics and benefits of an established brand

Reinforcement advertising The type of advertising that tries to assure current users that they have made the right choice and tells them how to get the most satisfaction from the product

Marketers sometimes employ **reminder advertising** to let consumers know that an established brand is still around and that it has certain uses, characteristics and benefits. Procter & Gamble, for example, reminds consumers that its Crest toothpaste is still the best one for preventing cavities. **Reinforcement advertising,** on the other hand, tries to assure current users that they have made the right choice and tells them how to get the most satisfaction from the product. Both reminder and reinforcement advertising aim to prevent a loss in sales or market share. Much of Ford's range focused advertising is designed to re-assure existing Ford owners that the company is forward thinking and customer oriented. The advertising for Head and Shoulders is as much concerned with reminding existing users of the shampoo's virtues as it is about building awareness for potential new users.

Table 16.1 Advertising in Europe (cont.)

c. PER CAPITA ADVERTISING and ADVERTISING GROWTH, 1997

Country	Adspend Per Capita			Real Year on Year Change (%)		
	Local Currency	US$	Index Europe = 100	94/95	95/96	96/97
Switzerland	473.8	326.5	176.3	5.8	−3.5	−0.5
Denmark	1,789.9	271.0	146.4	9.4	2.3	5.9
United Kingdom	165.5	271.0	146.4	4.8	5.1	6.4
Norway[1]	1,813.7	256.4	138.5	10.0	7.8	6.8
Germany	404.5	233.3	126.0	4.3	0.1	2.1
Netherlands	414.9	212.6	114.8	5.0	4.9	7.0
Sweden	1,600.7	209.7	113.3	4.2	−0.1	7.8
Finland	1,066.0	205.3	110.9	10.6	1.9	8.6
Ireland	127.6	193.6	104.6	13.6	8.5	13.9
Austria	2,020.1	165.5	89.4	−0.7	3.1	8.4
Belgium	5,683.3	158.9	85.8	9.9	2.3	8.6
France	927.0	158.8	85.8	2.3	0.9	2.6
Spain	16,437.4	112.3	60.7	−1.0	−0.3	4.2
Italy	173,981.9	102.2	55.2	−0.5	5.5	5.9
Greece	25,968.8	95.1	51.4	29.0	−35.3	10.8
Portugal	15,711.6	89.6	48.4	3.5	9.3	13.0

Notes: Growth rates are based on total advertising expenditure at constant (1990) prices. Data are net of discounts; they include agency commission and press classified advertising but exclude production costs. Data are ranked by adspend per capita (US$).

[1]Data for Norway for 1996 and 1997 are estimates.

SOURCE: *The Retail Pocket Book 1999*, p. 23. Reprinted by permission of NTC Publications, Ltd.

Reducing Sales Fluctuations

The demand for many products varies from month to month because of such factors as climate, holidays, seasons and customs. A business, however, cannot operate at peak efficiency when sales fluctuate rapidly. Changes in sales volume translate into changes in the production or inventory, personnel and financial resources it requires. To the extent that marketers can generate sales during slow periods, they can smooth out the fluctuations. When advertising reduces fluctuations, a manager can use the business's resources more efficiently. Business traveller oriented hotels such as Holiday Inn or Hilton promote discounted rooms for weekend leisure breaks in order to utilise otherwise unused facilities.

Advertising is often designed to stimulate business during sales slumps. For example, advertisements promoting price reductions of lawncare equipment or package holidays can increase sales during the winter months. On occasion, a business advertises that customers will get better service by coming in on certain days rather than others. During peak sales periods, a marketer may refrain from advertising to prevent over stimulating sales to the point where the company cannot handle all the demand. For example, coupons for the delivery of pizza are often valid only from Monday to Thursday, not Friday to Sunday, which are the peak delivery days.

1. **Does the product possess unique, important features?**

   Although homogeneous products such as cigarettes, petrol and beer have been advertised successfully, they usually require considerably more effort and expense than other products. On the other hand, products that are differentiated on physical rather than psychological dimensions are much easier to advertise. Even so, "being different" is rarely enough. The advertisability of product features is enhanced when buyers believe that those unique features are important and useful.

2. **Are "hidden qualities" important to buyers?**

   If by viewing, feeling, tasting or smelling the product buyers can learn all there is to know about the product and its benefits, advertising will have less chance of increasing demand. Conversely, if not all product benefits are apparent to consumers on inspection and use of the product, advertising has more of a story to tell, and the probability that it can be profitably used increases. The "hidden quality" of vitamin C in oranges once helped explain why Sunkist oranges could be advertised effectively, whereas the advertising of lettuce has been a failure.

3. **Is the general demand trend for the product favourable?**

   If the generic product category is experiencing a long term decline, it is less likely that advertising can be used successfully for a particular brand within the category. For example, CDs virtually extinguished the demand for turntables.

4. **Is the market potential for the product adequate?**

   Advertising can be effective only when there are sufficient actual or prospective users of the brand in the target market.

5. **Is the competitive environment favourable?**

   The size and marketing strength of competitors and their brand shares and loyalty will greatly affect the possible success of an advertising campaign. For example, a marketing effort to compete successfully against Kodak film, Heinz baked beans, or McDonald's restaurants would demand much more than simply advertising.

6. **Are general economic conditions favourable for marketing the product?**

   The effects of an advertising programme and the sales of all products are influenced by the overall state of the economy and by specific business conditions. For example, it is much easier to advertise and sell luxury leisure products (hi-fi systems, sailing boats, video cameras, exotic holidays) when disposable income is high.

7. **Is the organisation able and willing to spend the money required to launch an advertising campaign?**

   As a general rule, if the organisation is unable or unwilling to undertake an advertising expenditure that as a percentage of the total amount spent in the product category is at least equal to the market share it desires, advertising is not likely to be effective.

8. **Does the company possess sufficient marketing expertise to market the product?**

   The successful marketing of any product involves a complex mixture of product and consumer research, product development, packaging, pricing, financial management, promotion, customer service and distribution. Weakness in any area of marketing is an obstacle to the successful use of advertising.

SOURCE: Adapted from Charles H. Patti, "Evaluating the role of advertising", *Journal of Advertising*, Fall 1977, pp. 32–33. Reprinted by permission of the *Journal of Advertising*.

Table 16.2   Some issues to consider when deciding whether to use advertising

A company's use of advertising depends on the company's objectives and resources and on environmental forces. The degree to which advertising accomplishes the marketer's goals depends in large part on the advertising campaign.

Developing an Advertising Campaign

Advertising campaign An attempt to reach a particular target market by designing a series of advertisements and placing them in various advertising media

An **advertising campaign** involves designing a series of advertisements and placing them in various advertising media to reach a particular target market. As Figure 16.3 indicates, the general steps in developing and implementing an advertising campaign are (1) identifying and analysing the advertising target, (2) defining the advertising objectives, (3) creating the advertising platform, (4) determining the advertising budget, (5) developing the media plan, (6) creating the advertising message, (7) executing the campaign and (8) evaluating the effectiveness of the advertising. The number of steps and the order in which they are carried out may vary according to an organisation's resources, the nature of its product, the types of target markets or audiences to be reached and the advertising agency selected.[6] These general guidelines for developing an advertising campaign are appropriate for all types of organisations.

Identifying and Analysing the Advertising Target

Advertising target The group of people at which advertisements are aimed

The **advertising target** is the group of people at which advertisements are aimed. For example, the target audience for Special K and All-Bran cereals is health-conscious adults. Identifying and analysing the advertising target are critical processes; the information they yield helps determine the other steps in developing the campaign. The advertising target often includes everyone in a company's target market. Marketers may, however, seize some opportunities to slant a campaign at only a portion of the target market.

Advertisers analyse advertising targets to establish an information base for a campaign. Information commonly needed includes the location and geographic distribution of the target group; the distribution of age, income, ethnic origin, sex and education; and consumer attitudes regarding the purchase and use of both the advertiser's products and competing products. It is important to be able to profile the targeted consumers, but also to be able to understand their views—likes/dislikes, uses, angsts, peer expectations—of the product being advertised. It is crucial to know how consumers perceive the standing and brand positioning of

Figure 16.3 General steps for developing and implementing an advertising campaign

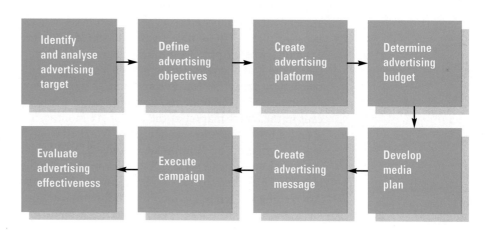

the product vis-à-vis competitors' propositions. Qualitative marketing research is very important in this process, particularly the use of focus group discussions.[7] The exact kinds of information that an organisation will find useful depend on the type of product being advertised, the characteristics of the advertising target, and the type and amount of competition. Generally, the more advertisers know about the advertising target, the more likely they are to develop an effective advertising campaign. When the advertising target is not precisely identified and properly analysed, the campaign may not succeed.

Defining the Advertising Objectives

The advertiser's next step is to consider what the company hopes to accomplish with the campaign. Because advertising objectives guide campaign development, advertisers should define their objectives carefully to ensure that the campaign will achieve what they want. Advertising campaigns based on poorly defined objectives seldom succeed.

Advertising objectives should be stated clearly, precisely and in measurable terms. Precision and measurability allow advertisers to evaluate advertising success: to judge, at the campaign's end, whether the objectives have been met, and if so, how well. To provide precision and measurability, advertising objectives should contain benchmarks—the current condition or position of the business—and indicate how far and in what direction the advertiser wishes to move from these benchmarks. For example, the advertiser should state the current sales level (the benchmark) and the amount of sales increase that is sought through advertising. Brand awareness should be assessed prior to the campaign, during its run and at its conclusion to ascertain progress. An advertising objective also should specify a timeframe, so that advertisers know exactly how long they have to accomplish the objective. Thus an advertiser with average monthly sales of £450,000 (the benchmark) might set the following objective: "Our primary advertising objective is to increase average monthly sales from £450,000 to £540,000 within 12 months." Another company might set the following objective: "We have 12 per cent brand awareness in our core target market. At the end of 15 months, we wish this percentage to match that of our key rival." This also tells the advertiser when evaluation of the campaign should begin.

If an advertiser defines objectives by sales, the objectives focus on raising absolute monetary sales, increasing sales by a certain percentage or increasing the company's market share. However, even though an advertiser's long run goal is to increase sales, not all campaigns are designed to produce immediate sales. Some campaigns are designed to increase product or brand awareness, make consumers' attitudes more favourable or increase consumers' knowledge of a product's features. These objectives are stated in terms of communication. For example, when Apple Computers introduced home computers, its initial campaign did not focus on sales but on creating brand awareness and educating consumers about the features and uses of home computers. A specific communication objective might be to increase product feature awareness from 0 to 40 per cent in the target market at the end of six months. The RAC's £5 million annual spend aims to increase membership, while Rolling Rock, the premium bottled lager distributed by Whitbread, spends £3 million annually to boost sales and increase brand awareness.[8] Objectives must be realistic. An advertising agency must be prepared to let a client know when its goals are not attainable. Advertising is merely a communications tool: it cannot overcome product deficiencies or a poorly developed marketing strategy.

Creating the Advertising Platform

Advertising platform The basic issues or selling points that an advertiser wishes to include in the advertising campaign

Before launching a political campaign, party leaders develop a political platform, which states the major issues that will be the basis of the campaign. Like a political platform, an **advertising platform** consists of the basic issues or selling points that an advertiser wishes to include in the advertising campaign. A single advertisement in an advertising campaign may contain one or several issues in the platform. Although the platform sets forth the basic issues, it does not indicate how they should be presented.

A marketer's advertising platform should consist of issues that are important to consumers. One of the best ways to determine what those issues are is to survey consumers about what they consider most important in the selection and use of the product involved. For example, Procter & Gamble has developed re-fill packages for some of its cleaning products. The re-fill packages provide a unique benefit by not adding to solid waste disposal problems.[9] Environmentally conscious consumers consider this a positive selling feature. The selling features of a product must not only be important to consumers; if possible, they should also be features that competitive products do not have.

Although research is the most effective method for determining the issues of an advertising platform, it is expensive. As a result, the advertising platform is most commonly based on the opinions of personnel within the business and of individuals in the advertising agency, if an agency is used. Qualitative research, typically focus groups, is often used to test the validity of these insiders' views before the campaign is produced. This trial and error approach generally leads to some successes and some failures.

Because the advertising platform is a base on which to build the message, marketers should analyse this step carefully. A campaign can be perfect in the selection and analysis of its advertising target, the statement of its objectives, its media strategy and the form of its message. But the campaign will still fail if the advertisements communicate information that consumers do not consider important when they select and use the product.

Determining the Advertising Budget

Advertising budget The total amount of money that a marketer allocates for advertising over a period of time

The **advertising budget** is the total amount of money that a marketer allocates for advertising over a period of time. It is difficult to determine this amount because there is no way to measure the precise effects of spending a certain amount of money on advertising.

Many factors affect a business's decision about how much to spend for advertising. The geographic size of the market and the distribution of buyers within the market have a great bearing on this decision. Both the type of product being advertised and a business's sales volume relative to competitors' sales volumes play a part in determining what proportion of a business's revenue is spent on advertising. Advertising budgets for industrial products are usually quite small relative to the sales of the products—more is spent on personal selling, direct mail and trade shows—whereas consumer convenience items, such as soft drinks, soaps and cosmetics, generally have large budgets. Sega's pan-European campaign, through agency WCRS, for its Dreamcast games console was worth £60 million.[10]

Objective and task approach A technique for determining an advertising budget that involves determining campaign objectives and then attempting to list the tasks required to accomplish them

Of the many sales promotion techniques used to determine the advertising budget, one of the most logical is the **objective and task approach.** Using this approach, marketers initially determine the objectives that a campaign is to achieve and then attempt to list the tasks required to accomplish them. The costs of the tasks are then calculated and added to arrive at the amount of the total budget. This approach has one main problem: marketers usually find it hard to estimate the level of effort needed to achieve certain objectives. A coffee marketer, for example, might find it extremely difficult to determine by what amount it should increase national television advertising in order to raise a brand's market share from 8 to 12 per cent. As a result of this problem, advertisers do not often use the objective and task approach.

In the more widely used **percentage of sales approach,** marketers simply multiply a company's past sales, plus a factor for planned sales growth or decline, by a standard percentage based on both what the business traditionally spends on advertising and what the industry averages. This approach has one major flaw: it is based on the incorrect assumption that sales create advertising, rather than the reverse. Consequently, a marketer using this approach at a time of declining sales will reduce the amount spent on advertising. But such a reduction may further diminish sales. Though illogical, this technique has gained wide acceptance because it is easy to use and less disruptive competitively; it stabilises a company's market share within an industry. However, in times of declining sales, many businesses do increase their contribution to advertising in the hope of reversing the decline.

Another way to determine the advertising budget is the **competition matching approach.** Marketers who follow this approach try either to match their major competitors' budgets or to allocate the same percentage of sales for advertising as their competitors do. Although a wise marketer should be aware of what competitors spend on advertising, this technique should not be used by itself, because a company's competitors probably have different advertising objectives and different resources available for advertising. Many companies and advertising agencies engage in quarterly competitive spending reviews, comparing competitors' expenditures in print, radio and television with their own spending levels. Competitive tracking of this nature occurs at both the national and regional levels.

At times, marketers use the **arbitrary approach:** a high level executive in the business states how much can be spent on advertising for a certain time period. The arbitrary approach often leads to under-spending or over spending. Although hardly a scientific budgeting technique, it is expedient.

Establishing the advertising budget is critically important. If it is set too low, the campaign cannot achieve its full potential for stimulating demand. When too much money is allocated for advertising, the over spending that results wastes financial resources. An advertising agency being briefed must know the budget size to be able to plan the campaign effectively.

Developing the Media Plan

As Table 16.3 shows, advertisers spend tremendous amounts of money on advertising media. These amounts have grown rapidly during the past two decades. To derive the maximum results from media expenditures, a marketer must develop an effective media plan. A **media plan** sets forth the exact media vehicles to be used for advertising (specific magazines, television channels, newspapers, radio programmes, movies, billboards, web sites and so forth) and the dates and times when the advertisements will appear. The effectiveness of the plan determines how many people in the advertising target will be exposed to the message. It also determines, to some degree, the effects of the message on those individuals. Media planning is a complex task that requires thorough analysis of the advertising target, as well as of any legal restrictions that might apply. For example, the EU has strict regulations pertaining to the advertising of tobacco, foods and pharmaceuticals and to comparative advertising. More regulations are coming in

---

Percentage of sales approach   A budgeting technique that involves multiplying a company's past sales, plus a factor for planned sales growth or decline, by a standard percentage based on both what the business traditionally spends on advertising and what the industry averages

Competition matching approach A budgeting technique in which marketers either match their major competitors' budgets or allocate the same percentage of sales for advertising as their competitors

Arbitrary approach   A budgeting technique in which a high level executive in the business states how much can be spent on advertising over a certain time period

Media plan   The process of establishing the exact media vehicles to be used for advertising, and the dates and times when the advertisements will appear

---

a. THE TOP 20 ADVERTISERS, 1997

			Advertising Ex penditure			
Rank	Advertiser	Total £ '000s	TV %	Radio %	Press %	Other %
1	BT plc	129,286	75.0	4.2	17.3	3.4
2	Procter & Gamble Ltd	91,504	96.3	0.9	2.2	0.6
3	Ford Motor Company Ltd	72,683	63.9	5.6	22.1	8.4
4	Vauxhall Motors Ltd	66,298	55.4	5.3	32.8	6.5
5	Kellogg Company of GB Ltd	61,249	81.2	1.4	9.1	8.3
6	Procter & Gamble Health & Beauty	60,174	90.6	0.9	6.1	2.3
7	Renault UK Ltd	59,476	64.7	6.4	21.4	7.5
8	Elida Fabergé Ltd	54,511	77.8	0.8	10.6	10.8
9	Van den Bergh Foods Ltd	54,162	82.5	1.3	9.2	7.0
10	Mars Confectionery	51,871	85.3	0.4	6.8	7.4
11	Nissan Motor GB Ltd	47,741	71.5	0.8	15.6	12.1
12	Central Office of Information	44,562	51.2	11.5	29.2	8.1
13	Volkswagen UK Ltd	43,504	68.9	2.9	20.0	8.2
14	Rover Group Ltd	42,806	42.7	3.7	43.3	10.4
15	Lever Brothers Ltd	41,615	84.6	1.4	8.1	5.8
16	Peugeot Motor Co plc	40,947	63.5	0.5	27.7	8.3
17	Boots Company plc	39,198	59.6	0.3	28.9	11.1
18	Coca-Cola Great Britain & Ireland	37,885	80.4	7.4	4.1	8.2
19	McDonald's Restaurants Ltd	36,075	70.3	13.7	0.9	15.1
20	L'Oréal Golden Ltd	35,901	85.3	0.1	14.3	0.4

SOURCE: *The Marketing Pocket Book 1999*, p. 113. Reprinted by permission of NTC Publications, Ltd.

Table 16.3   UK advertising

connection with alcohol, financial services, cars, environmental labelling and the portrayal of women.

To formulate a media plan, the planner selects the media for a campaign and draws up a time schedule for each medium. As Marketing Insight 16.1 details, there are some innovative media choices. The media planner's primary goal is to reach the largest possible number of people in the advertising target for the amount of money spent on media. In addition, a secondary goal is to achieve the appropriate message reach and frequency for the target audience while staying within the budget. **Reach** refers to the percentage of consumers in the advertising target actually exposed to a particular advertisement in a stated time period. **Frequency** is the number of times these targeted consumers are exposed to the advertisement.

Media planners begin with rather broad decisions; eventually, however, they must make very specific choices. A planner must first decide which kinds of media to use: radio, television, newspapers, magazines, direct mail, outdoor displays, public transport, the Internet,[11] or a combination of two or more of these. After making the general media decision, the planner selects specific sub-classes within each medium. Estée Lauder, for example, might advertise its Clinique cosmetic line in women's magazines, as well as during daytime, prime time and late-night television.

Reach The percentage of consumers in the advertising target actually exposed to a particular advertisement in a stated time period

Frequency The number of times targeted consumers are exposed to a particular advertisement

Table 16.3   UK advertising (cont.)

b. TOTAL ADVERTISING EXPENDITURE BY MEDIUM AND BY TYPE

	£ million						Percentage of Total					
	1992	1993	1994	1995	1996	1997	1992	1993	1994	1995	1996	1997
By Medium												
National newspapers, incl. col. suppl.	1,155	1,220	1,336	1,433	1,510	1,650	14.6	14.8	14.7	14.6	14.2	14.2
Regional newspapers, incl. free sheets	1,640	1,715	1,871	1,963	2,061	2,237	20.7	20.8	20.6	19.9	19.4	19.3
Consumer magazines	466	448	499	533	583	660	5.9	5.4	5.5	5.4	5.5	5.7
Business and professional magazines	746	714	785	897	1,018	1,106	9.4	8.7	8.6	9.1	9.6	9.5
Directories	523	551	589	639	692	737	6.6	6.7	6.5	6.5	6.5	6.4
Press production costs	427	438	472	514	550	577	5.4	5.3	5.2	5.2	5.2	5.0
Total Press	4,957	5,085	5,552	5,979	6,413	6,967	62.6	61.8	61.1	60.7	60.4	60.1
Television, incl. prod. costs	2,472	2,604	2,888	3,125	3,363	3,651	31.2	31.6	31.8	31.7	31.7	31.5
Outdoor and transport, incl. prod. costs	284	300	350	378	426	500	3.6	3.6	3.9	3.8	4.0	4.3
Cinema, incl. prod. costs	45	49	53	69	73	88	0.6	0.6	0.6	0.7	0.7	0.8
Radio, incl. prod. costs	157	194	243	296	344	393	2.0	2.4	2.7	3.0	3.2	3.4
Total	7,915	8,232	9,086	9,846	10,619	11,599	100.0	100.0	100.0	100.0	100.0	100.0
By Type												
Display advertising												
Press[1]	2,951	3,008	3,241	3,463	3,645	3,860	37.3	36.5	35.7	35.2	34.3	33.3
Television	2,472	2,604	2,888	3,125	3,363	3,651	31.2	31.6	31.8	31.7	31.7	31.5
Other media[2]	486	543	646	743	843	981	6.2	6.6	7.2	7.5	7.9	8.5
Total display	5,908	6,154	6,775	7,331	7,851	8,492	74.7	74.8	74.6	74.5	73.9	73.2
Classified advertising[3]	2,006	2,078	2,311	2,515	2,768	3,107	25.3	25.2	25.4	25.5	26.1	26.8
Total	7,915	8,232	9,086	9,846	10,619	11,599	100.0	100.0	100.0	100.0	100.0	100.0

Notes: [1]Including financial notices and display advertising in business and professional journals, but not advertising in directories.
[2]Outdoor and transport, cinema and radio.
[3]Including all directory advertising.

SOURCE: *The Marketing Pocket Book 1999*, p. 119. Reprinted by permission of NTC Publications, Ltd.

Media planners take many factors into account as they devise a media plan. They analyse the location and demographic characteristics of people in the advertising target because the various media appeal to particular demographic groups in particular locations. For example, there are radio stations directed mainly at teenagers, magazines for men in the 18 to 34 age group and television programmes aimed at adults of both sexes. Media planners should also consider the size and type of audiences that specific media reach. Several data services collect and periodically publish information about the circulations and audiences of various media. The cost of media is an important but troublesome consideration. Planners try to obtain the best coverage possible for the amount of money spent, yet there is no accurate way of comparing the cost and impact of a television advertisement with the cost and impact of a newspaper advertisement.

The content of the message sometimes affects the choice of media. Print media can be used more effectively than broadcast media to present many issues or numerous details. The makers of Tartare Light Fromage Frais produce wordy magazine advertisements, including recipes as well as product details, to boost demand and educate consumers about the product's uses. The advertisements appear in most women's and food magazines. If an advertiser wants to promote beautiful colours, patterns or textures, media that offer high quality colour reproduction—magazines or television—should be used instead of newspapers. For example, cosmetics can be far more effectively promoted in a full colour magazine advertisement than in a black and white newspaper advertisement.

Table 16.1 provides data on the amounts of advertising expenditure in Europe by media. The data indicate that different countries give greater priority to certain types of advertising media. The medium selected is determined by the characteristics, advantages and disadvantages of the major media available (see Table 16.4).

Given the variety of vehicles within each medium, media planners must deal with a vast number of choices. The multitude of factors that affect media rates obviously adds to the complexity of media planning. A **cost comparison indicator** lets an advertiser compare the costs of several vehicles within a specific medium (such as two newspapers) in relation to the number of people reached by each vehicle. For example, the "milline rate" is the cost comparison indicator for newspapers; it shows the cost of exposing a million people to a space equal to one agate line.[*]

Cost comparison indicator A measure that allows an advertiser to compare the costs of several vehicles within a specific medium in relation to the number of people reached by each vehicle

Creating the Advertising Message

The basic content and form of an advertising message are a function of several factors. The product's features, uses and benefits affect the content of the message. Characteristics of the people in the advertising target—their sex, age, education, ethnic origin, income, occupation and other attributes—influence both the content and form. When Procter & Gamble promotes its Crest toothpaste to children, the company emphasises the importance of daily brushing and decay control. When it markets Crest to adults, it discusses tartar and plaque. To communicate effectively, an advertiser must use words, symbols and illustrations that are meaningful, familiar and attractive to the people who constitute the advertising target—the target audience.

The objectives and platform of an advertising campaign also affect the content and form of its messages. For example, if a company's advertising objectives

[*] An agate line is one column wide and the height of the smallest type normally used in classified newspaper advertisements. There are fourteen agate lines in one column inch.

Medium	Types	Unit of Sale	Factors Affecting Rates	Cost Comparison Indicator	Advantages	Disadvantages
Newspaper	National Local Morning Evening Sunday Sunday supplement Weekly Special Local free sheets	Column cms/inches Counted words Printed lines Agate lines	Volume and frequency discounts Number of colours Position charges for preferred and guaranteed positions Circulation level	Milline rate = cost per agate line × 1,000,000 divided by circulation Cost per column cm/inch	Almost everyone reads a newspaper; purchased to be read; selective for socio-economic groups; national geographic flexibility; short lead time; frequent publication; favourable for co-operative advertising; merchandising services	Short life; limited reproduction capabilities; large advertising volume limits exposure to any one advertisement; plethora of local free sheets annoys some householders
Magazine	Consumer Farm Business Sports Travel	Pages Partial pages Column cms/inches	Circulation level Cost of publishing Type of audience Volume discounts Frequency discounts Size of advertisement Position of advertisement (covers) Number of colours Regional issues	Cost per thousand (CPM) = cost per page × 1,000 divided by circulation	Socio-economic selectivity; good reproduction; long life; prestige; geographic selectivity when regional issues are available; read in leisurely manner	High absolute monetary cost; long lead time; long user life
Direct mail	Letters Catalogues Price lists Calendars Brochures Coupons Circulars Newsletters Postcards Booklets Samples	Not applicable	Cost of mailing lists Postage Production costs	Cost per contact	Little wasted circulation; highly selective; circulation controlled by advertiser; few distractions; personal; stimulates action; use of novelty; easy to measure performance; hidden from competitors	Expensive; no editorial matter to attract readers; considered junk mail by many; criticised as invasion of privacy; increasingly regulated

(Continues)

Table 16.4 Characteristics, advantages and disadvantages of major advertising media

Table 16.4 Characteristics, advantages and disadvantages of major advertising media (cont.)

Medium	Types	Unit of Sale	Factors Affecting Rates	Cost Comparison Indicator	Advantages	Disadvantages
Radio	AM FM	Programme types Spots: 5, 10, 20, 30, 60 seconds	Time of day Audience size Length of spot or programme Volume and frequency discounts	Cost per thousand (CPM) = cost per minute × 1,000 divided by audience size	Highly mobile; low cost broadcast medium; message can be quickly changed; geographic selectivity; socio-economic selectivity	Little national radio advertising; provides only audio message; has lost prestige; short life of message; listeners' attention limited because of other activities while listening
Television	ITV/C4/C5 Satellite Cable	Programme types Spots: 15, 20, 30, 60 seconds	Time of day Length of spot Volume and frequency discounts Audience size	Cost per thousand (CPM) = cost per minute × 1,000 divided by audience size	Reaches large audience; low cost per exposure; uses both audio and video; highly visible; high prestige; geographic and socio-economic selectivity	High monetary costs; highly perishable message; size of audience not guaranteed; prime time limited; increasing channel hopping during commercial breaks and zapping through advertisements on video recordings
Inside public transport	Buses Underground	Full, half and quarter showings are sold on a monthly basis	Number of passengers Multiple-month discounts Production costs Position	Cost per thousand passengers	Low cost; "captive" audience; geographic selectivity	Does not secure quick results
Outside public transport	Buses Taxis	Full, half and quarter showings; space also rented on per unit basis	Number of advertisements Position Size	Cost per 100 exposures	Low cost; geographic selectivity; reaches broad, diverse audience	Lacks socio-economic selectivity; does not have high impact on readers

(Continues)

Table 16.4 Characteristics, advantages and disadvantages of major advertising media (cont.)

Medium	Types	Unit of Sale	Factors Affecting Rates	Cost Comparison Indicator	Advantages	Disadvantages
Outdoor	Papered posters/billboards Painted displays Spectaculars Poster vans	Papered posters: sold on monthly basis in multiples Painted displays and spectaculars; sold on per unit basis	Length of time purchased Land rental Cost of production Intensity of traffic Frequency and continuity discounts Location	No standard indicator	Allows for repetition; low cost; message can be placed close to the point of sale; geographic selectivity; works 24 hours a day	Message must be short and simple; no socio-economic selectivity; seldom attracts readers' full attention; criticised for being traffic hazard and blight on country-side
Internet	Corporate web sites	Home pages Menu pages on company's *own* web sites	In-house or out-sourced web site development Web master's overheads	"Free" for media, but costs of developing web site and specific pages must be budgeted	Rapid growth in Internet use; quickly up-dated messages; interactive messages; interactive contact via e-mail links; ability to link to detailed editorial; multi-media messages	Skewed take-up amongst certain consumer groups; resistance by some to seeking web based advertisements; slow access speeds and variable reproductive quality; poorly pre-pared material; infancy of technique

SOURCES: Some of the information in this table is from S. Watson Dunn and Arnold M. Barban, *Advertising: Its Role in Modern Marketing*, 6th edn (Hinsdale, Ill.: Dryden Press, 1986); and Anthony F. McGann and J. Thomas Russell, *Advertising Media* (Homewood, Ill.: Irwin, 1981).

involve large sales increases, the message demands hard hitting, high impact language and symbols. When campaign objectives aim at increasing brand awareness, the message may use much repetition of the brand name and words and illustrations associated with it. Thus the advertising platform is the foundation on which campaign messages are built. Agencies strive to develop platforms with longevity in order to foster long term brand building. For example, JWT's Andrex puppies have represented the toilet tissue in nearly thirty years of advertising; BA still uses the Saatchi brothers' "World's favourite airline" and its globe image; Cogent's "The Jewson lot" continues almost twenty years later to inform DIYers and jobbing builders that Jewson caters for their every need.

The choice of media obviously influences the content and form of the message. Effective outdoor displays and short broadcast spot announcements require concise, simple messages. Magazine and newspaper advertisements can include more detail and long explanations. Because several different kinds of media offer geographic selectivity, a precise message can be tailored to a particular geographic section of the advertising target. Some magazine and national newspaper publishers produce **regional issues**: for a particular issue, the advertisements and editorial content of copies appearing in one geographic area differ from those appearing in other areas. A clothing manufacturer might decide to use one message in London and another in the rest of the UK. A company may also choose to advertise in only a few regions. Such geographic selectivity lets a business use the same message in different regions at different times.

The basic components of a print advertising message are shown in Figure 16.4. The messages for most advertisements depend on the use of copy and artwork.

Copy   The verbal portion of an advertisement is **copy**. It includes headlines, subheadlines, body copy and the signature (see Figure 16.4). When preparing advertising copy, marketers attempt to move the target audience through a persuasive sequence called **AIDA**: attention, interest, desire and action. Consumers will not visit a store, trial a product or make a purchase of an unfamiliar product unless marketers first grab their attention, gain their interest and make the product appear desirable. Emotive and persuasive advertising plays a key role in this process. Not all copy need be this extensive, however.

The headline is critical because often it is the only part of the copy that people read. It should attract readers' attention and create enough interest to make them want to read the body copy. The sub-headline, if there is one, links the headline to the body copy. Sometimes it helps explain the headline.

Body copy for most advertisements consists of an introductory statement or paragraph, several explanatory paragraphs and a closing paragraph. Some copywriters have adopted a pattern or set of guidelines to develop body copy systematically: (1) identify a specific desire or problem of consumers, (2) suggest the good or service as the best way to satisfy that desire or solve that problem, (3) state the advantages and benefits of the product, (4) indicate why the advertised product is the best for the buyer's particular situation, (5) substantiate the claims and advantages, and (6) ask the buyer for action.[12]

The signature identifies the sponsor of the advertisement. It may contain several elements, including the company's trademark, logo, name and address. The signature should be designed to be attractive, legible, distinctive and easy to identify in a variety of sizes.

Because radio listeners often are not fully "tuned in" mentally, radio copy should be informal and conversational to attract their attention and achieve greater impact. The radio message is highly perishable. Thus radio copy should

Regional issues   Versions of a magazine or newspaper that differ across geographic regions in their advertising and editorial content

Copy   The verbal portion of an advertisement

AIDA   A persuasive sequence used in advertisements: attention, interest, desire and action

Figure 16.4 Copy and artwork elements of printed advertisements. This advertisement clearly differentiates the basic elements of print advertising. SOURCE: Courtesy of Lufthansa German Airlines.

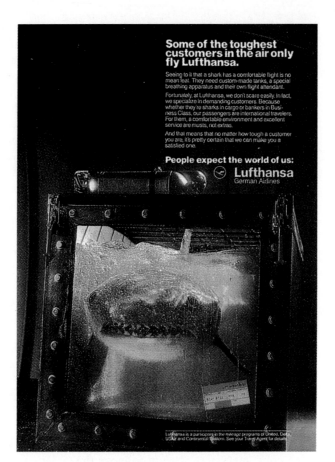

Headline

Body Copy

Sub-headline
Signature

Illustration

consist of short, familiar terms. Its length should not require a delivery rate exceeding approximately two and a half words per second.

In television copy, the audio material must not over power the visual material and vice versa. However, a television message should make optimal use of its visual portion. Copy for a television advertisement is initially written in parallel script form. The video is described in the left column and the audio in the right column. When the parallel script is approved, the copywriter and the artist combine the copy with the visual material through use of a **storyboard,** which depicts a series of miniature television screens showing the sequence of major scenes in the advertisement. During the creative thinking phase, storyboards tend to be cartoon sketches. Once an idea is deemed worthy of production, a more polished storyboard is produced (see Figure 16.5). Technical personnel use the storyboard as a blueprint when they produce the advertisement.

Storyboard A series of miniature television screens or cartoons used to show the sequence of major scenes in the advertisement

Artwork The illustration and layout of the advertisement

Illustrations Photographs, drawings, graphs, charts or tables used in advertisement artwork

Artwork Artwork consists of the illustration and layout of the advertisement (see Figure 16.4). Although **illustrations** are often photographs, they can also be drawings, graphs, charts or tables. Illustrations are used to attract attention, to encourage the audience to read or listen to the copy, to communicate an idea quickly or to communicate an idea that is difficult to put into words.[13] They are especially important because consumers tend to recall the visual portion of advertisements better than the verbal portions. Advertisers use a variety of illustration techniques, which are identified and described in Table 16.5.

Figure 16.5 Storyboard for Ferrero Rocher advertisement. SOURCE: Courtesy of *Lansdown Conquest*.

Layout The physical arrangement of the illustration, headline, sub-headline, body copy and signature of an advertisement

The **layout** of an advertisement is the physical arrangement of the illustration, headline, sub-headline, body copy and signature. The arrangement of these parts in Figure 16.4 is only one possible layout. These same elements could be arranged in many ways. The final layout is the result of several stages of preparation. As it moves through these stages, the layout helps people involved in developing the advertising campaign exchange ideas. It also provides instructions for production personnel.

Executing the Campaign

The execution of an advertising campaign requires an extensive amount of planning and co-ordination. Regardless of whether or not an organisation uses an advertising agency, many people and organisations are involved in the execution of a campaign.[14] Production companies, research organisations, media houses, printers, photo engravers and commercial artists are just a few of the people and organisations that contribute to a campaign.

Implementation requires detailed schedules to ensure that various phases of the work are done on time. Advertising management personnel must evaluate the quality of the work and take corrective action when necessary. In some instances, changes have to be made during the campaign so that it meets campaign objectives more effectively or responds to consumer research feedback.

Evaluating the Effectiveness of the Advertising

Pre-tests Evaluations performed before an advertising campaign that attempt to assess the effectiveness of one or more elements of the message

There are various ways to evaluate the effectiveness of advertising. They include measuring achievement of advertising objectives; gauging the effectiveness of copy, illustrations or layouts; and assessing certain media.

Advertising can be evaluated before, during and after the campaign. Evaluations performed before the campaign begins are called **pre-tests** and usually attempt to evaluate the effectiveness of one or more elements of the message. To pre-test advertisements, marketers sometimes use a **consumer focus group,** a semi-structured discussion, led by a moderator, involving actual or potential buyers of the advertised product. Members are asked to judge one or several

Illustration Technique	Description
Product alone	Simplest method; advantageous when appearance is important, when identification is important, when trying to keep a brand name or package in the public eye, or when selling through mail order
Emphasis on special features	Shows and emphasises special details or features as well as advantages; used when product is unique because of special features
Product in setting	Shows what can be done with product; people, surroundings or environment hint at what product can do; often used in food advertisements
Product in use	Puts action into the advertisement; can remind readers of benefits gained from using product; must be careful not to make visual cliché; should not include anything that will divert attention from product; used to direct readers' eyes towards product
Product being tested	Uses test to dramatise product's uses and benefits versus competing products
Results of product's use	Emphasises satisfaction from using product; can liven up dull product; useful when nothing new can be said
Dramatising headline	Appeal of illustration dramatises headline; can emphasise appeal but dangerous to use illustrations that do not correlate with headlines
Dramatising situation	Presents problem situation or shows situation in which problem has been resolved
Comparison	Compares product with "something" established; the something must be positive and familiar to audience
Contrast	Shows difference between two products or two ideas or differences in effects between use and non-use; before and after format is a commonly used contrast technique
Diagrams, charts and graphs	Used to communicate complex information quickly; may make presentations more interesting
Phantom effects	X-ray or internal view; can see inside product; helpful to explain concealed or internal mechanism
Symbolic	Symbols used to represent abstract ideas that are difficult to illustrate; effective if readers understand symbol; must be a positive correlation between symbol and idea
Testimonials	Actually shows the testifier; should use famous person or someone to whom audience can relate

SOURCES: Dorothy Cohen, *Advertising* (New York: Wiley, 1972), pp. 458–464; and S. Watson Dunn and Arnold M. Barban, *Advertising: Its Role in Modern Marketing*, 6th edn (Hinsdale, Ill.: Dryden Press, 1986), pp. 497–498.

Table 16.5 Illustration techniques for advertisements

Consumer focus group A semi-structured discussion, led by a moderator, involving actual or potential buyers of advertised products who are asked to judge one or several dimensions of the advertisements

dimensions of two or more advertisements. Such tests are based on the belief that consumers are more likely than advertising experts to know what will influence them.

To measure advertising effectiveness during a campaign, marketers usually take advantage of "enquiries". In the initial stages of a campaign, an advertiser may use several direct response advertisements simultaneously, each containing a coupon or an 0800 contact number or a form requesting information. The advertiser records the number of coupons or calls that are returned from each type of advertisement. If an advertiser receives 78,528 coupons from advertisement A, 37,072 coupons from advertisement B and 47,932 coupons from advertisement C, advertisement A is judged superior to advertisements B and C. For advertisements that do not demand action—coupon returning or dialling an 0800 Freephone number—enquiries are difficult to monitor.

Evaluation of advertising effectiveness after the campaign is over is called a **post-campaign test** or **post-test.** Advertising objectives often indicate what kind of post-test will be appropriate. If an advertiser sets objectives in terms of communication—product awareness, brand awareness or attitude change—then the post-test should measure changes in one or more of these dimensions. Typically, qualitative marketing research (focus groups or depth interviews) is used before, during and after a campaign to monitor shifts in consumers' perceptions. It is hoped that brand awareness will have improved following the running of a particular advertising campaign. Advertisers sometimes use consumer surveys or experiments to evaluate a campaign based on communication objectives. These methods are costly, however.

For campaign objectives that are stated in terms of sales, advertisers should determine the change in sales or market share that can be attributed to the campaign. Unfortunately, such changes brought about by advertising cannot be measured precisely;[15] many factors independent of advertisements affect a company's sales and market share. Competitive actions, government actions and changes in economic conditions, consumer preferences and weather are only a few factors that might enhance or diminish a company's sales or market share. However, by using data about past and current sales and advertising expenditures, an advertiser can make gross estimates of the effects of a campaign on sales or market share.

Because consumer surveys and experiments are expensive, and because it is so difficult to determine the direct effects of advertising on sales, many advertisers evaluate print and television advertisements according to the degree to which consumers can remember them. The post-test methods based on memory include recognition and recall tests. Such tests are usually performed by research organisations through consumer surveys. If a **recognition test** is used, individual respondents are shown the actual advertisement and asked whether they recognise it. If they do, the interviewer asks additional questions to determine how much of the advertisement each respondent read, heard or viewed. When recall is evaluated, the respondents are not shown the actual advertisement but instead are asked about what they have seen or heard recently. Recall can be measured through either unaided or aided recall methods. In an **unaided** or **spontaneous recall test,** subjects are asked to identify advertisements that they have seen recently but are given no clues to help them remember. A similar procedure is used in an **aided** or **prompted recall test,** except that subjects are shown a list of products, brands, company names or trademarks to jog their memory. Several research organisations, such as AC Nielsen, Audience Selection and Gallup, provide research services that test recognition and recall of advertisements (see Table 16.6).

The major justification for using recognition and recall methods is that people are more likely to buy a product if they can remember an advertisement about it than if they cannot. However, recalling an advertisement does not necessarily lead to buying the product or brand advertised. Research shows that the more "likeable" an advertisement is, the more it will influence consumers. People who enjoy an advertisement are twice as likely to be persuaded that the advertised brand is best. Of about 16 per cent of those who liked an advertisement, a significant number increased their preference for the brand. Only a small percentage of those who were neutral about the advertisement felt more favourable

Post-campaign test or **post-test**
The evaluation of advertising effectiveness after a campaign

Recognition test A test in which an actual advertisement is shown to individual respondents, who are then asked whether they recognise it

Unaided or **spontaneous recall test** A test in which subjects are asked to identify advertisements that they have seen recently but are given no clues to help them remember

Aided or **prompted recall test** A test in which subjects are asked to identify advertisements while being shown a list of products, brands, company names or trademarks to jog their memory

Q: Which of the following TV commercials do you remember seeing recently?

	Last Week	Account	Agency/TV Buyer	%
1	(1)	Walkers Crisps	*Abbott Mead Vickers BBDO/Media Vest*	81
2	(2)	BT	*Abbott Mead Vickers BBDO/The Allmond Partnership*	79
3	(3)	McDonald's	*Leo Burnett*	73
4	(2)	Andrex	*Banks Hoggins O'Shea FCB/MindShare*	72
5	(4)	Specsavers	*In-house/CIA Medianetwork*	68
6=	(6)	Thomas Cook	*TBWA GGT Simons Palmer/Booth Lockett Makin*	67
6=	(−)	Mr Muscle Kitchen Cleaner	*Banks Hoggins O'Shea FCB/Optimedia*	67
8	(−)	Cadbury's Creme Egg	*TBWA GGT Simons Palmer/Carat*	65
9=	(−)	Kellogg's Crunchy Nut Cornflakes	*J Walter Thompson/MindShare*	62
9=	(5)	One 2 One	*Bartle Bogle Hegarty/Motive*	62
11	(−)	Batchelors Pasta 'n' Sauce	*Mother/Initiative Media*	56
12=	(−)	Kinder Surprise	*In-house/Initiative Media*	51
12=	(−)	J&J Baby Protective Moisturiser	*Ammirati Puris Lintas/BMP OMD*	51
14	(−)	Army Recruitment	*Saatchi & Saatchi/MediaVest*	48
15	(−)	Alfa Romeo	*Lansdown Conquest/MediaVest*	45
16	(−)	Daz	*Leo Burnett/P&G Buying Unit*	43
17	(−)	Vanish Laundry Tablets	*WCRS/BMP OMD*	39
18	(−)	Nestlé Shreddies	*McCann-Erickson/Universal McCann*	38
19=	(−)	The Equitable Life	*TBWA GGT Simons Palmer/New PHD*	35
19=	(−)	E45 Skin Confidence	*DMB&B/BMP OMD*	35

Adwatch research was conducted from February 5 to February 7 by **NOP Research Group** (0171–890 9445) as part of a weekly telephone omnibus survey among more than 1000 adults. Copies of the Adwatch data and analysis are available from Liz Price at NOP. Advertisements were selected by **The Register** (0171–343 3030) and **CIA Medianetwork** (0171–633 9999).

SOURCE: Reprinted with permission from *Marketing Magazine*, 18 February 1999.

Table 16.6   Results of tested recall of advertisements

towards the brand as a result of the advertisement.[16] The type of television programme in which the product is advertised can also affect consumers' feelings about the advertisement and the product it promotes. Viewers judge advertisements placed in happy programmes as more effective and recall them somewhat better.[17]

Researchers are also using a sophisticated technique called *single source data* to help evaluate advertisements. With this technique, individuals' behaviour is tracked from television sets to the checkout counter. Monitors are placed in preselected homes, and microcomputers record when the television set is on and which channel is being viewed. At the supermarket checkout, the individual in the sample household presents an identification card. The cashier records the purchases by scanner, and the data are sent to the research facility. This technique is bringing more insight into people's buying patterns than ever before. The use of technology and scanning techniques is discussed in more detail in Chapter 6.

An advertising campaign may be handled by (1) an individual or a few people within the company, (2) an advertising department within the organisation or (3) an advertising agency.

In very small businesses, one or two individuals are responsible for advertising and many other activities as well. Usually these individuals depend heavily on personnel at local newspapers and broadcasting stations for copywriting, artwork and advice about scheduling media.

In certain types of large businesses—especially in larger retail organisations—advertising departments create and implement advertising campaigns. Depending on the size of the advertising programme, an advertising department may consist of a few multi-skilled people or a sizeable number of specialists, such as copywriters, artists, media buyers and technical production co-ordinators. An advertising department sometimes obtains the services of independent research organisations and also hires freelance specialists when they are needed for a particular project.

When an organisation uses an advertising agency, such as Ogilvy & Mather or JWT, the organisation and the agency usually develop the advertising campaign jointly. How much each party participates in the campaign's total development depends on the working relationship between the client marketers and the agency. Ordinarily, a company relies on the agency for copywriting, artwork, technical production and formulation of the media plan.

An advertising agency can assist a business in several ways. An agency, especially a larger one, supplies the client company with the services of highly skilled specialists—not only copywriters, artists and production co-ordinators but also media experts, researchers and legal advisers. Agency personnel have often had broad experience in advertising and are usually more objective than a client's employees about the organisation's products. Figure 16.6 outlines the structure of a typical advertising agency.

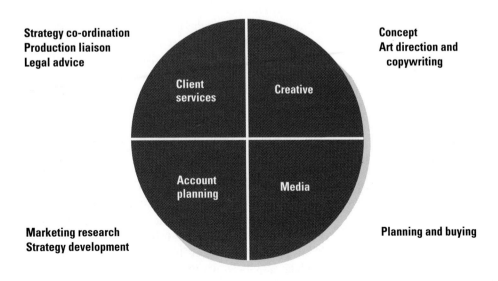

Figure 16.6 A typical advertising agency structure

Strategy co-ordination
Production liaison
Legal advice

Concept
Art direction and
    copywriting

Client services

Creative

Account planning

Media

Marketing research
Strategy development

Planning and buying

Because an agency traditionally receives most of its income from a 15 per cent commission on media purchases, marketers can obtain some agency services at a low or moderate cost. For example, if an agency contracts for £400,000 of television time for a client, it typically receives a commission of £60,000 from the television company. Although the traditional compensation method for agencies is changing and now includes other factors, the media commission still off-sets some costs of using an agency. Some agencies are considering breaking the mould; the agency would be paid by results. Clients would pay a bonus to the agency for meeting targets or receive a payback (refund) if the advertising failed to deliver.[18]

Now that advertising has been explored as a potential promotional mix ingredient, it is time to consider a related ingredient, publicity, and its controlling mechanism, public relations.

Publicity and Public Relations

Publicity Communication in news story form about an organisation and/or its products that is transmitted through a mass medium at no charge

Publicity is communication in news story form about an organisation, its products or both that is transmitted through a mass medium at no charge (although the publicity activity will incur production and personnel costs). Publicity can be presented through a variety of vehicles, several of which are examined here.

Within an organisation, publicity is sometimes viewed as part of public relations—a larger, more comprehensive communications function. **Public relations** is a planned and sustained effort to establish and maintain goodwill and mutual understanding between an organisation and its **target publics:** customers, employees, shareholders, trade bodies, suppliers, government officials and society in general.[19]

Public relations A planned and sustained effort to establish and maintain goodwill and mutual understanding between an organisation and its target publics

Target publics An organisation's target audience: customers, employees, shareholders, trade bodies, suppliers, government officials and society in general

For example, core publics for Barclays Bank include customers, potential customers, staff and unions, other businesses, suppliers, shareholders, the Treasury, Bank of England and city journalists. For the Boy Scouts Association, publics include boys(!), young boy Cubs destined to become Scouts, the community, business sponsors, adults as potential Scout Leaders, adults as parents, adults as former members whose views will influence others, adults as teachers, plus local press journalists.

Publicity is the result of various public relations efforts. For example, when Tesco decided to make a special effort to stock environmentally safe products and packaging, its public relations department sent out press releases to various newspapers, magazines and television contacts, as well as to its suppliers. The result was publicity in the form of magazine articles, newspaper acknowledgements and television coverage. There are three broad categories of public relations: (1) the **PR event**—one-shot, ad hoc affairs concerned with a specific purpose such as an open day or VIP visit; (2) the **PR campaign**—a period of PR activity involving several events and techniques but with definite start and end dates; (3) the **PR programme**—ongoing, lengthy duration, awareness building or awareness maintaining multi-technique PR activity. From the end of the 1980s, public relations has been the fastest growing element in the promotional mix.[20]

PR event A public relations event concerned with a specific purpose such as an open day or VIP visit

PR campaign A period of PR activity involving several events and techniques but with definite start and end dates

PR programme An ongoing, lengthy duration, awareness building or awareness maintaining multi-technique PR activity

Publicity and Advertising Compared

Although publicity and advertising both depend on mass media, they differ in several respects. Advertising messages tend to be informative or persuasive, whereas publicity is primarily informative. Advertisements are sometimes designed to have an immediate impact on sales; publicity messages are more subdued. Publicity releases do not identify sponsors; advertisements do. The sponsor pays for media time or space for advertising, but not for publicity, and there is therefore no guarantee of inclusion. Communications through publicity are usually included as part of a television programme or a print story, but advertisements are normally separated from the broadcast programmes or editorial portions of print media so that the audience or readers can easily recognise (or ignore) them. Publicity may have greater credibility than advertising among consumers because as a news story it may appear more objective. Finally, an organisation can use advertising to repeat the same messages as many times as desired; publicity is generally not subject to repetition.

Kinds of Publicity

Press (news) release A publicity mechanism, usually consisting of a single page of typewritten copy

Feature article A manuscript longer than a press release (up to 3,000 words) that is usually prepared for a specific publication

Captioned photograph A photograph with a brief description explaining its content

There are several types of publicity mechanisms.[21] The most common is the **press (news) release** which is usually a single page of typewritten copy containing fewer than 300 words. A press release, sometimes called a news release, also gives the company's or agency's name, its address and phone number, and the contact person.[22] Car makers often use press releases to introduce new products. Figure 16.7 is an example of a press release. A **feature article** is a longer manuscript (up to 3,000 words) that is usually prepared for a specific publication. A **captioned photograph** is a photograph with a brief description explaining the picture's content. Captioned photographs are especially effective for illustrating a new or improved product with highly visible features.

Figure 16.7 Example of a press release. Advertising agency Lansdown Conquest, part of WPP, trumpets its winning of a new client's account.
SOURCE: Courtesy of Lansdown Conquest.

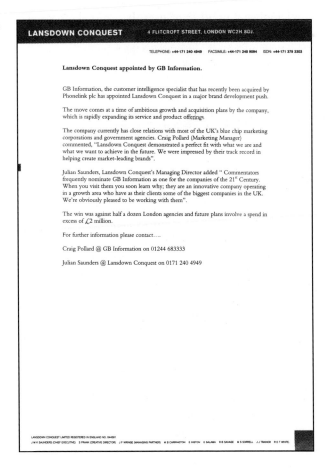

There are several other kinds of publicity. A **press conference** is a meeting called to announce a major news event. Media personnel are invited and are usually supplied with written materials and photographs. In addition, letters to the editor and editorials are sometimes prepared and sent to newspapers and magazines. However, newspaper editors frequently allocate space on their editorial pages to local writers and national columnists. Finally, films and tapes may be distributed to broadcasting companies in the hope that they will be aired. The broader remit of public relations also includes training personnel to meet and handle the media (journalists); arranging interviews; establishing links with VIPs and influential bodies; managing visits, seminars and meetings; and maintaining information flows within the organisation. Increasingly, PR consultants utilise the Internet and help clients set up their web sites.

A marketer's choice of specific types of publicity depends on considerations that include the type of information being transmitted, the characteristics of the target audience, the receptivity of media personnel, the importance of the item to the public, and the amount of information that needs to be presented. Sometimes a marketer uses a single type of publicity in a promotional mix. In other cases, a marketer may use a variety of publicity mechanisms, with publicity being the primary ingredient in the promotional mix. **Third party endorsement**—for example, from a trade body, VIP or media personality—increases the credibility of publicity and public relations. This is a recommendation (written, verbal or visual) from an opinion leader or respected personality.

Third party endorsement A recommendation from an opinion leader or respected personality used to increase the credibility of publicity and public relations

Uses of Publicity

Publicity has a number of uses. It can make people aware of a company's products, brands or activities; help a company maintain a certain level of positive public visibility; and enhance a particular image, such as innovativeness or progressiveness. Companies also try to overcome negative images through publicity. Some businesses seek publicity for a single purpose and others for several purposes. As Table 16.7 shows, publicity releases can tackle a multitude of specific issues. It must be remembered that an organisation has a number of audiences—customers, suppliers, distributors, shareholders, journalists—as well as its internal market: its employees and management. Publicity needs to target all of these publics.

Requirements of a Publicity Programme

For maximum benefit, a business should create and maintain a systematic, continuous publicity programme.[23] A single individual or department—within the organisation or from its advertising agency or public relations consultancy—should be responsible for managing the programme. Relationships must be maintained with the media, particularly to facilitate crisis management public relations. Effective public relations is impossible without well developed ongoing contacts with newspaper, television and radio journalists. It is important to establish and maintain good working relationships with these media personnel. Often personal contact with editors, reporters and other news personnel is essential; without their input a company may find it hard to design its publicity programme so as to facilitate the work of newspeople. Media personnel reject a great deal of publicity material because it is poorly written or not newsworthy. To maintain an effective publicity programme, a company must strive to avoid these flaws. Guidelines and checklists can aid it in this task. Material submitted must match the particular newspaper's style, for example in length, punctuation and layout.

Finally, an organisation has to evaluate its publicity efforts.[24] Usually, the effectiveness of publicity is measured by the number of releases actually published or

Marketing Developments	Reports on Current Developments
New products	Reports on experiments
New uses for old products	Reports on industry conditions
Research developments	Company progress reports
Changes of marketing personnel	Employment, production and sales statistics
Large orders received	Reports on new discoveries
Successful bids	Tax reports
Awards of contracts	Speeches by principals
Special events	Analyses of economic conditions
	Employment gains
Company Policies	Financial statements
New guarantees	Organisation appointments
Changes in credit terms	Opening of new markets
Changes in distribution policies	Government trade awards
Changes in service policies	
Changes in prices	**Personalities—Names Are News**
	Visits by famous people
News of General Interest	Accomplishments of individuals
Annual election of directors	Winners of company contests
Meetings of the board of directors	Employees' and directors' advancements
Anniversaries of the organisation	Interviews with company officials
Anniversaries of an invention	Company employees serving as judges for
Anniversaries of the senior directors	contests
Holidays that can be tied to the organisation's	Interviews with employees
activities	**Slogans, Symbols, Endorsements**
Annual banquets	
Conferences and special meetings	Company's slogan—its history and development
Open house to the community	A tie-in of company activities with slogan
Athletic events	Creation of a slogan
Awards of merit to employees	The company's trademark
Laying of cornerstone	The company's name plate
Opening of an exhibition	Product endorsements

SOURCE: Albert Wesley Frey, ed., *Marketing Handbook,* Second Edition (New York: Ronald Press, 1965), pp. 19–35. Copyright © 1965. Reprinted by permission of John Wiley & Sons, Inc.

Table 16.7 Possible topics for publicity releases

broadcast. To monitor print media and determine which releases are published and how often, an organisation can hire a cuttings service—a business that cuts out, counts and sends published news releases to client companies. To measure the effectiveness of television publicity, a company can enclose a card with its publicity releases and request that the television company record its name and the dates when the news item is broadcast, but companies do not always comply. Though some television and radio tracking services do exist, they are costly. Many leading exponents of public relations believe there must be four facets to an effective PR programme: (1) *research*—on the problem opportunity; (2) *action*—that includes assessment and planning; (3) *communication*—of key messages to the relevant publics; (4) *evaluation*—of the effects of these messages.

Dealing with Unfavourable Publicity

Up to this point publicity has been discussed as a planned promotional mix ingredient. However, companies may have to deal with unfavourable publicity regarding an unsafe product, an accident, the actions of a dishonest employee or some other negative event. For example, when British Airways' Lord King had to apologise publicly to a rival airline, Virgin Atlantic Airways, and its boss, Richard Branson, for a "dirty tricks campaign", BA's credibility was severely damaged and seat reservations reportedly declined significantly.[25] The BSE beef crisis and the up-roar over GM Foods forced government departments, farming bodies, meat producers, supermarket companies and consumer associations to deal with unfavourable publicity.

Such unfavourable publicity can arise quickly and dramatically. A single negative event that produces unfavourable publicity can wipe out a company's favourable image and destroy consumer attitudes that took years to build through promotional efforts. Moreover, the mass media today can disseminate information faster and to larger audiences than ever before, and bad news generally receives much attention in the media. Thus the negative publicity surrounding an unfavourable event now reaches more people.[26] By dealing effectively with a negative situation, an organisation can minimise the damage from unfavourable publicity.

To protect an organisation's image, it is important to avoid unfavourable publicity or at least to lessen its effects. First and foremost, the organisation can directly reduce negative incidents and events through safety programmes, inspections and effective quality control procedures. However, because organisations obviously cannot eliminate all negative occurrences, they need to establish policies and procedures for the news coverage of such events. These policies and procedures should aim at reducing negative impact.

In most cases, organisations should expedite news coverage of negative events rather than try to discourage or block it. The expediting approach not only tends to diminish the fall out from negative events but also fosters a positive relationship with media personnel. Such a relationship is essential if news personnel are to co-operate with a company and broadcast favourable news stories about it. Facts are likely to be reported accurately, but if news coverage is discouraged, rumours and misinformation may be passed along. An unfavourable event can easily be blown up into a scandal or a tragedy. It can even cause public panic.

Crisis management A process in which a company responds to negative events by identifying key targets (publics) for which to provide publicity, developing a well rehearsed contingency plan, reporting facts quickly and providing access for journalists

Crisis management involves (1) the identification of key targets (publics) for which to provide material or publicity; (2) the need for a well rehearsed contingency plan and public relations exercise; (3) the ability and skills of the organisation to report quickly and accurately details of the crisis itself; and (4) the provision of immediate access by journalists to information and personnel. Above all, the organisation must remain in control of the situation and the material being published or broadcast. See Case 16.2 for a text book example of crisis management.

Limitations in Using Publicity

Free media publicity is a double-edged sword: the financial advantage comes with several drawbacks. If company messages are to be published or broadcast, media personnel must judge them newsworthy. Consequently, messages must be timely, interesting and accurate. Many communications simply do not qualify. It may take time and effort to convince media personnel of the news value of publicity releases. Even a top public relations consultancy achieves a hit rate of only one out of every four press releases being published in the press.

Although marketers usually encourage media personnel to air a press release at a certain time, they control neither the content nor the timing of the communication. Media personnel alter the length and content of publicity releases to fit publishers' or broadcasters' requirements and may even delete the parts of the message that the business's marketers deem most important. Furthermore, media personnel use publicity releases in time slots or positions that are most convenient for them; thus the messages often appear at times or in locations that may not reach the business's target audiences. These limitations can be frustrating. Nevertheless, properly managed publicity offers an organisation substantial benefits at relatively low cost.

Trends Impacting on Advertising and Public Relations

The world of advertising is facing significant changes. Briefly, these include a mixture of market trends and client-induced pressures. For example, a growing number of agencies are having to offer pan-European capabilities as major advertisers believe they must consider pan-European campaigns. The major international agencies already have widespread office networks, but for the smaller agencies there is a need to establish links with small agencies in other countries. With the concentration of media ownership across borders, agencies and clients have to be able to negotiate package deals across countries.[27] Rupert Murdoch's media empire, which covers newspapers, magazines, radio, satellite and terrestrial television all the way from the Pacific Rim through North America and across Europe, is a prime illustration. There is increasing pressure on advertising agencies and public relations consultancies to justify the value of their activities and campaigns. Simple qualitative research into the visual appeal of a particular campaign is not seen as sufficient by major advertisers. These clients have short term sales gains as a motivation for advertising; many advertising personnel, however, believe that the role of advertising is also critical for longer term **brand building,** as a brand's image and standing are developed with intended long term benefits for brand awareness and brand value.[28]

Brand building Developing a brand's image and standing with a view to creating long term benefits for brand awareness and brand value

Senior advertising agency figures are also aware that the recession of the early 1990s caused many clients to downgrade their advertising budgets and to re-evaluate their promotional spend. The result has been the rationalisation of agencies, leading to mergers, even closures, and an urgency among agencies to seek competitive edges over their rivals. There are now also far fewer medium sized advertising agencies, the field having polarised into major international advertising agencies and numerous local or regional small agencies.[29] This trend has also affected public relations. There is now an increasing tendency for clients and agencies to develop closer and longer term relationships, as tight budgets require a close, mutual understanding of what the advertising and public relations must achieve for a particular brand or product.

The sphere of public relations is also undergoing significant change. Clients are demanding pan-European and international services. Through the development of technology—such as the Internet and interactive television—plus new advertising formats—such as the growing use of mini-documentary style, lengthy "advertorials" and infomercials—there is a move to more overt competition between public relations consultancies and advertising agencies. Advertising agencies perceive these developments to be part of their toolkit, whereas public relations consultancies have begun to include these innovations in their armoury. In addition, the public relations industry believes it is maturing and accordingly needs to become more professional, recruiting higher calibre personnel and providing better training, while ensuring that their output is assessed in terms of client goals and expectations.[30] These enhancements require time and high budgets in an ever more competitive market. With all these changes, there is little doubt that both the marketing environment and client requirements are significantly affecting the nature of the services offered by advertising agencies and public relations consultancies.

This chapter concludes with an overview of corporate sponsorship—an element of the promotional mix that is increasingly apparent to many consumers and a promotional tool now used by many organisations.

Sponsorship

Sponsorship The financial or material support of an event, activity, person, organisation or product by an unrelated organisation or donor

Sponsorship is the financial or material support of an event, activity, person, organisation or product by an unrelated organisation or donor. Generally, funds will be made available to the recipient of the sponsorship deal in return for the prominent exposure of the sponsor's name or brands.[31]

Increasing Popularity of Sponsorship

A decade or so ago sponsorship in the arts became an established form of funding for individual performances, tours, whole seasons or exhibitions; indeed some theatrical companies and galleries came to depend on it.[32] Many orchestras, ballet, opera or theatre companies, museums and art galleries would not have survived in the face of declining government subsidies for the arts had it not been for corporate sponsorship. Sports were soon to follow, as numerous football teams found that gate receipts and pitch advertising revenues were no longer adequate to cover wage bills and operating costs. While the larger clubs earn seven figure revenues from shirt sponsorship by companies such as Sony, JVC or Heineken, deals for as little as £20,000 are not uncommon in the lower leagues; either way, this form of financial support is becoming essential to guarantee the survival of many clubs.

The popularity of corporate sponsorship has grown dramatically: few leading sports or arts events are without corporate sponsorship, as detailed in Table 16.8 and Marketing Insight 16.2.[33] Sponsors believe there are two key benefits to the company and its products. First and foremost, media coverage is unbridled. Volvo estimates that its £2 million investment in tennis sponsorship has been worth the equivalent of £15 million spent on advertising. Its banners are displayed at its tournaments, as are examples of its model range. Volvo advertisements and publicity appear in the programmes. The Volvo brand appears in advertising for the event, and usually the company's cars transport the celebrity players during the tournaments. Not only does the public see the company's advertisements, they cannot fail to see its brand name displayed extensively. In addition, the product is on hand for demonstration, while television coverage of the events takes the Volvo name into every tennis fan's home; radio and press coverage prominently features Volvo's name.

Few spectators at the Olympics or World Cup football championships can fail to notice the identities of the leading sponsors. To many sports enthusiasts, the leading competitions become generically known as the Gillette Cup, NatWest Trophy, Prudential Series or Coca-Cola Cup. In equestrian events, the horses' names often include the name of the sponsoring company. Visitors to the Royal Shakespeare Company's performances are clearly informed of the support given by leading sponsors. Montserrat Caballe's performance at Birmingham's prestigious Symphony Hall was made possible largely by the sponsorship of Forward

Football Sponsorship

Sports sponsorship is a multi-million pound business (see Table 16.8). The ongoing revolution in broadcasting media is further increasing the myriad of opportunities available to businesses wishing to promote their brands through these means. Football sponsorship has proved particularly attractive to would-be sponsors. The reasons for this popularity are not difficult to judge. For example, the UK football industry has grown by a staggering 20 per cent in a little over six years. Only the UK's computer sector has fared better.

The costs of buying high profile football sponsorship are considerable. Nationwide Building Society, which has committed resources to football sponsorship over a number of years, has recently become involved in a four year £15m deal to sponsor the England national team. Even though Green Flag, the first England sponsor, paid a mere £4m for a similar time period, Nationwide believes that the investment is justified and will be paid for by building its brand values among the 24 million football-loving consumers who enjoy watching the sport. This brand building includes advertisement signage at home games, ticketing and broadcasting rights as well as the use of the Nationwide logo on the team's training kit. Ultimately, the company believes that the benefits will be measured in an increased customer base and better returns for investors.

Nationwide is not alone in its belief in the benefits of football sponsorship. Bass Brewers has recently renewed its sponsorship of the UK's FA Premier League, which has run since 1993. AXA, Umbro, Walkers, Coca-Cola and One 2 One are some of the other businesses which have chosen to pursue opportunities in the game. Umbro's involvement is as England shirt sponsor in a five year deal worth £50m. The launch of the new kit in 1999 was accompanied by an advertising campaign featuring England players such as Alan Shearer and Michael Owen.

Despite the perceived benefits of such sponsorship, investment is not without risks. In a rapidly changing and increasingly commercial environment, sponsors need to ensure that they maintain a reasonable level of control over their interests. Recent bad publicity surrounding former England team manager Glenn Hoddle provided a stark illustration of just one potential problem. On that occasion, Nationwide moved fast to protect its brand by distancing itself from comments which the England coach was alleged to have made about disabled people. Sponsors also need to question which other brands may become involved in sponsoring their chosen sport, and what effect the resulting clutter may have on their own brand image. In the words of broadcasting expert Richard Foster, "I still find it a little odd to watch the FA Carling [lager] Premiership on Sky, sponsored by Ford [cars]. Or the Nationwide [building society] Division One Championship, in association with Duckhams [oils]. As a result of such deals, the event sponsors are quite rightly seeking assurances prior to agreement, as to who could or should be the broadcast sponsor."

The increasing commercial interest in sports sponsorship is being matched by a variety of new broadcasting opportunities, such as those provided by the launch of digital television. This suggests a bright future for sports sponsorship and the organisations which benefit from it. Only a decade ago, most broadcast sports were televised by the BBC with strict rules limiting sponsors' brand exposure. Now consumers and viewers take for granted the variety of logos and brand names accompanying most major sporting events.

SOURCES: "England sponsorship", *Marketing*, 18 February 1999, p. 11; "The winning circle", *Marketing Week*, 22 October 1998, pp. 51–54; Richard Foster, "Why sponsors need to renegotiate the rule book", *Marketing Week*, 25 February 1999, p. 16; Ian Darby, "Can the FA meet its goals?", *Marketing*, 14 January 1999, p. 14; "Umbro backs England kit with TV ad", *Marketing*, 18 March 1999, p. 7.

Trust Group, a fact made clear in all promotional material—leaflets, advertising and publicity—and in the concert's programme.

The second benefit of corporate sponsorship is internal. Many organisations believe that their sponsorship of events helps improve the morale of their workforce. On one level, high profile, brand building sponsorship, such as AXA Insurance's involvement with cricket, re-assures the workforce and re-affirms the

Table 16.8 Expenditure on sponsorship

Sports Sponsorship: Total Expenditure

	1991	1992	1993	1994	1995	1996	1997
Market size, £m	238	239	250	265	285	302	322
No. of sponsorships	759	659	745	818	946	987	995

Corporate Sponsorship of Sport, 1996/97

	1996	1997		Number of Involvements 1996	1997
Alcoholic drinks	106	123	Communications	42	57
Cars/allied trades	87	85	Grocery	43	44
Sports goods/clothing	125	84	Media	27	41
Banks/finance	65	79	Soft drinks/water	40	40
Insurance	58	76	Tobacco	34	29

Corporate Sponsorship of the Arts[1], 1996/97

	%		Expenditure by Art Form %
Music	18.3	Film/video	2.7
Festival	13.7	Heritage	2.2
Museums	12.6	Dance	2.0
Drama/theatre	11.0	Arts centres	1.6
Visual arts/photography/craft	7.4	Community arts	1.1
Opera	4.5	Literature/poetry	0.6

Note: [1]Based on Business Sponsorship Incentive Scheme (BSIS). Total corporate sponsorship in 1996/97 was £86.1m (£48.0m from sponsorship, £15.3m from corporate membership and donations and £22.9m from capital projects and support in kind).

SOURCE: *The Marketing Pocket Book 1999*, p. 122. Reprinted by permission of NTC Publications, Ltd.

company's leading position in its marketplace. On a more human level, sponsorship for altruistic projects, such as worthy community causes, helps give employees a "warm", positive feeling towards their employer. McDonald's support of Ronald McDonald Houses close to children's hospitals and its sponsorship of local school events not only help the community but also make its employees feel more positive towards the company.

Applications for Sponsorship

Sponsorship used to be a tool of public relations and the domain of public relations consultancies. Increasingly, it is a specialist area and a separate component of the promotional mix. Public relations consultancies still handle many sponsorship deals, but a growing number of specialist sponsorship advisers now introduce sponsors to appropriate recipients. It should not be thought that sponsorship is prominent only in the sports and arts worlds. It is an activity of growing importance in many fields. Universities and colleges seek sponsorship for students, technical equipment, buildings and even degree programmes. Hospitals receive and welcome the sponsorship of buildings, operating theatres and fund raising events. Engineering and scientific research, particularly in universities and "research clubs", benefit from the sponsorship of research and development, often from organisations in completely unrelated fields of business.

No matter what the area, if a company believes its brand reputation will be enhanced and its brand awareness improved by its involvement with an organisation or an event, sponsorship becomes an important element in its promotional mix. Sponsorship can be for events or competitions, equipment or buildings, ideas or research, learning or development, animals or people, commercial or charitable causes, television programmes, products or services, single activities or ongoing programmes.

Reputable Partnerships

Reputable partnerships Reputable and ethical dealings between a recognised, welcome and acceptable recipient organisation and a sponsoring organisation

There are ground rules to be considered by the prospective sponsor. As with any promotional activity, the sponsor must ensure that the recipient organisation, event or product is recognised by the sponsor's target audience, that it is welcome and acceptable to its target audience and that it is reputable and ethical in its dealings. **Reputable partnerships** are essential. The sponsor does not want to invest its promotional budget in activities not recognised by its own target market. The sponsor cannot risk becoming involved with an event or organisation which has a risqué reputation and unprofessional management; such a situation threatens the sponsor's reputation and brands. Consider the effect on a prestigious brand if an athlete sponsored by that brand failed a dope test or was found guilty of cheating. The recipient, too, needs to be wary of the donor's image and reputation.

● S U M M A R Y

*A*dvertising is a paid form of non-personal communication that is transmitted to consumers through mass media, such as television, radio, newspapers, magazines, direct mail, public transport vehicles, outdoor displays and now the Internet. Both non-business and business organisations use advertising. Advertising has many uses: to create awareness of products, organisations and causes; to stimulate primary and selective demand; to off-set competitors' advertising; to aid sales personnel; to educate the market; to increase uses of a product; to remind and reinforce; to reduce sales fluctuations.

Marketers use advertising in many ways. *Institutional advertising* promotes organisational images and ideas, as well as political issues. *Product advertising* focuses on the uses, features, images and benefits of goods and services. To make people aware of a new or innovative product's existence, uses and benefits, marketers rely on *pioneer advertising* in the introductory stage to stimulate primary demand for a general product category—often referred to as creating category need. Then they switch to *competitive advertising* to boost selective demand by promoting a particular brand's uses, features and advantages that may not be available in competing brands. *Comparative advertising* is a form of competitive advertising in which two or more brands are compared on the basis of one or more product attributes.

Through *defensive advertising,* a company can sometimes lessen the impact of a competitor's promotional programme. A company can also make its own salesforce more effective through advertising designed to support personal selling. A business modifying its marketing mix uses advertising to educate the market regarding the changes. To increase market penetration, an advertiser sometimes focuses a campaign on promoting a greater number of uses for the product. *Reminder advertising* for an established product lets consumers know that the product is still around and that it has certain characteristics, benefits and uses. Marketers may use *reinforcement advertising* to assure current users of a particular brand that they have selected the best brand. Marketers also use advertising to smooth out fluctuations in sales.

Although marketers may vary in how they develop *advertising campaigns,* they should follow a general pattern. First, they must identify and analyse the *advertising target.* Second, they should establish what they want the campaign to accomplish by defining the advertising objectives. The third step is creating the *advertising platform,* which contains the basic issues to be presented in the campaign. Fourth, advertisers must decide on the *advertising budget,* that is, how much money will be spent on the campaign; they arrive at this decision through the *objective and task approach,* the *percentage of sales approach,* the *competition matching approach,* or the *arbitrary approach.* Fifth, they must develop the *media plan* by selecting and scheduling the media to be used in the campaign, taking into account the desired *reach* and *frequency* as well as *cost comparison indicators.* In the sixth step, advertisers use *copy, artwork* and *illustrations* to create the message, with the aid of *storyboards* and careful *layouts,* bearing in mind *AIDA,* the persuasive sequence of attention, interest, desire and action. *Regional issues* of magazines and newspapers allow messages to be tailored to geographic areas. In the seventh step, marketers execute their advertising campaign, after extensive planning and co-ordination. Finally, advertisers must devise one or more methods for evaluating the effectiveness of the advertisements, including *pre-tests,* the use of *consumer focus groups,* direct response coupons or 0800 contact numbers, *post-campaign tests, recognition tests,* and *unaided* or *aided recall tests.* The single source data technique uses technology to track buying behaviour and evaluate advertisements.

Advertising campaigns can be developed by personnel within the organisation or in conjunction with advertising agencies. When a campaign is created by the organisation's personnel, it may be developed by only a few people, or it may be the product of an advertising department within the organisation. The use of an advertising agency may be advantageous to a client company because an agency can provide highly skilled, objective specialists with broad experience in the advertising field at low to moderate costs to the client company.

Publicity is communication in news story form about an organisation, its products or both, transmitted through a mass medium at no charge. Generally, publicity is part of the larger, more comprehensive communications function of *public relations.* There are three broad categories of public relations: the *PR event,* the *PR campaign,* and the *PR programme.* Publicity is mainly informative and usually more subdued than advertising. There are many types of publicity, including *press (news) releases, feature articles, captioned photographs, press conferences,* editorials, films and tapes. In addition, public relations includes training managers to handle journalists and publicity, establishing links with influential bodies and VIPs, managing visits and seminars, and providing information to employees. Increasingly, PR consultants utilise the Internet and help clients set up web sites. *Third party endorsement,* in which a VIP, trade body or celebrity publicly endorses a product or a brand, is particularly effective. *Target publics* include consumers, suppliers, distributors, journalists, trade bodies, government officials and shareholders, as well as employees and managers inside the business, and society in general. Effective public relations depends on thorough identification of target publics. To have an effective publicity programme, someone—either in the organisation or in the business's agency—must be responsible for creating and maintaining systematic and continuous publicity efforts. Effective PR programmes require research, action, communication of key messages to relevant publics, plus evaluation.

An organisation should avoid negative publicity by reducing the number of negative events that result in unfavourable publicity or at least lessen its effects. To diminish the impact of unfavourable publicity, an organisation should institute policies and procedures for implementing *crisis management*—identifying key targets, developing a contingency plan and providing access for journalists—when negative events do occur. Problems that organisations confront when seeking publicity include the reluctance of media personnel to print or broadcast releases and a lack of control over the timing and content of messages.

There are significant client-induced pressures and market trends affecting advertising agencies and public relations consultancies. These include client demands for international and pan-European service, concentration of media ownership, accountability over the effectiveness of the promotional activity, short term goals versus longer term *brand building*, reduced client budgets, rationalisation in terms of the number and size of agencies, the growing use of technology such as the Internet, conflict between advertising agencies and public relations consultancies over advertorials and infomercials, and the need to offer an increasingly professional service.

Sponsorship is the financial or material support of an event, activity, person, organisation or product by an unrelated organisation or donor in return for the prominent exposure of the sponsor's name and brands. An additional benefit can be to raise the morale of employees within the donor organisation. Once the domain of arts and sports, sponsorship applications are broadening. Universities, colleges, hospitals and engineering and scientific research institutes also seek sponsorship. Sponsorship recipients and donors must be certain of each other's ethics, image and reputation. *Reputable partnerships* are essential.

Important Terms

Advertising
Institutional advertising
Product advertising
Pioneer advertising
Competitive advertising
Comparative advertising
Defensive advertising
Reminder advertising
Reinforcement advertising
Advertising campaign
Advertising target
Advertising platform
Advertising budget
Objective and task approach
Percentage of sales approach
Competition matching approach
Arbitrary approach

Media plan
Reach
Frequency
Cost comparison indicator
Regional issues
Copy
AIDA
Storyboard
Artwork
Illustrations
Layout
Pre-tests
Consumer focus group
Post-campaign test or post-test
Recognition test
Unaided or spontaneous
   recall test

Aided or prompted recall test
Publicity
Public relations
Target publics
PR event
PR campaign
PR programme
Press (news) release
Feature article
Captioned photograph
Press conference
Third party endorsement
Crisis management
Brand building
Sponsorship
Reputable partnerships

Discussion and Review Questions

1. What is the difference between institutional and product advertising?
2. When should advertising be used to stimulate primary demand? When should advertising be used to stimulate selective demand?
3. What are the major steps in creating an advertising campaign?
4. What is an advertising target? How does a marketer analyse the target audience after it has been identified?
5. Why is it necessary to define advertising objectives?
6. What is an advertising platform, and how is it used?
7. What factors affect the size of an advertising budget? What techniques are used to determine this budget?
8. Describe the steps required in developing a media plan.

9. What is the role of copy in an advertising message?
10. What role does an advertising agency play in developing an advertising campaign?
11. Discuss several ways to post-test the effectiveness of an advertisement.
12. What is publicity? How does it differ from advertising?
13. How do organisations use publicity? Give several examples of press releases that you have observed recently in local media.
14. What are target publics? Why must they be carefully identified and handled by a public relations department?
15. How should an organisation handle negative publicity? Identify a recent example of a company that received negative publicity. Did the company deal with it effectively?
16. Explain the problems and limitations associated with using public relations. How can some of these limitations be minimised?
17. How can sponsorship enhance brand awareness for a sponsoring organisation?
18. What factors must an organisation consider before selecting a sponsor or recipient organisation?

Recommended Readings

C. L. Bovee and J. V. Thill, *Excellence in Business Communication* (Englewood Cliffs, N.J.: Prentice-Hall, 1998).

C. L. Bovee, J. V. Thill, G. P. Dovel and M. B. Wood, *Advertising Excellence* (New York: McGraw-Hill, 1995).

N. A. Hart, *Industrial Marketing Communications* (London: Kogan Page, 1993).

N. A. Hart, *Strategic Public Relations* (London: Macmillan Press, 1995).

T. Hunt and J. E. Grunig, *Public Relations Techniques* (Fort Worth: Harcourt Brace, 1997).

D. E. Parente and A. Barban, *Advertising Campaign Strategy* (Fort Worth: Harcourt Brace, 1997).

● C A S E S

16.1 British Airways' Evolving Promotion

In the late 1970s British Airways (BA) had lost its way as the UK's national airline. The merger of BOAC and BEA had not gone smoothly, financial performance was poor and travel surveys showed customer satisfaction to be low. The 1979 election of a Conservative government gave new impetus to improve, as the government wished to privatise the state owned airline. Lord King was appointed chairman in 1983, and under him the airline quickly became operationally sound, although customers had not perceived the change.

The subsequent promotional strategy can be divided into three distinct phases. From 1983 to 1985 the global campaigns of Saatchi & Saatchi aimed "to make the airline feel proud again". Employees were to feel valued and part of a successful organisation, customers were to believe BA was superior to competitors and financial institutions were to see the turnaround in BA as a prelude to privatisation. The now famous "Manhattan Landing" commercial made no attempt to demonstrate product benefits, create category need or purchase intention. The message was that BA was large and "the world's favourite airline". The campaign was hugely successful in the UK and US—BA's main markets. Sales increased by 28 per cent in the US and 13 per cent elsewhere; the US voted the commercial the best of all airlines' promotion in 1984. Perceptions of BA changed.

By 1985, awareness of BA had grown. The objective then was to alter customer attitudes, particularly in the lucrative business class sector. Stressing service and comfort, advertisements were targeted at business travellers, particularly in the United

States; "Superclub Seats", "Supercare", and "Putting People First" are examples of such advertisements. The campaign was influenced by Colin Marshall, who had recently joined BA from Avis and believed in service as a means of differentiation. Training programmes improved service levels so that the reality of the product offer matched the message of BA's promotion.

Since 1987, BA's advertising has concentrated on its "pillar" brands. BA had previously promoted a recognisable corporate image but had only haphazardly promoted its various services, such as Club Class and the Shuttles. Mike Batt joined the airline from Mars and brought marketing techniques that focused on the product rather than on the company or corporate image. He introduced the concept of pillar brands, the key products that supported the global and corporate branding already in place. The corporate identity remained part of the promotion, but the focus turned to selling specific products to particular market segments using distinctive brands—for example, Club World, Saver Shuttle, Executive Shuttle, Euro Traveller. The "Boardroom" advertisement sold Club World—a long haul service providing comfort and convenience and enabling passengers to arrive fit for work—to businesspeople. Following these branding and promotion exercises, the number of business class passengers increased by 31 per cent worldwide and 12 per cent in Europe.

Through M&C Saatchi, BA still spends over £70 million annually on its global advertising account, one of the most prestigious accounts in the world of advertising. The result is very high brand awareness and an image for being an ultra-high service provider at competitive fare rates. The latest advertising has executions aimed separately at business and leisure users, concentrating on the hopes and dreams of BA's passengers. The message, though, is consistent with the platform adopted throughout the 1980s: BA is big, convenient, friendly and looks after its customers—"The World's Favourite Airline".

SOURCES: John Tylee, "BA confirms M&C Saatchi's position", *Campaign,* 12 April 1996, p. 1; Douglas Nelms, "Imaging's new demands", *Air Transport World,* April 1996, pp. 34–38; Noreen O'Leary, "Limits of illusion", *Adweek,* 15 January 1996, pp. 14–18; Laurel Wentz, "BA's $150m campaign makes worldwide debut", *Advertising Age,* 8 January 1996, p. 33; John Tylee, "M&C Saatchi unveils new look ads in BA branding drive", *Campaign,* 5 January 1996, p. 1; Saatchi & Saatchi directors; *Sunday Times,* 27 May 1990; John Francis, "BA promotions in the 1980s", University of Warwick, 1990.

Questions for Discussion

1. How important is a strong corporate identity in the successful advertising of services?
2. Creating a successful platform is difficult. Keeping it fresh is more so. Discuss the problems of building on BA's powerful and innovative "Manhattan Landing" advertisement.

16.2 Public Relations and Perrier's Crisis

On 10 February 1990, in North Carolina, bottles of Perrier were found to be contaminated with benzene. For the best selling brand of mineral water in the world this meant a huge crisis. "Once a critical situation arises the most vital task is to do everything you can to reduce damage to the absolute minimum. We were fortunate that we had agreed procedures in advance and these procedures were followed absolutely", stated Perrier spokesperson Wenche Marshall Foster. "From the very beginning we were determined to keep everyone fully informed."

Perrier's crisis team in the UK moved quickly; senior executives of Perrier, its PR agency Infoplan and advertising agency Leo Burnett had been briefed before the contamination scare on the needs of crisis management. Within hours of the contamination announcement, Perrier had set up tests with independent consultant Hydrotechnica so as to have accurate information to give out. The crisis team knew it had to be truthful throughout. Infoplan immediately set up a telephone information service, which dealt with 1,700 calls each day from distributors, retailers and consumers. Within three days of the crisis breaking, shelves worldwide had been cleared and all stocks returned to Perrier. The company achieved goodwill by moving so decisively. No press conferences were given. Instead, the five members of the crisis team individually met journalists for in-depth, head-to-head interviews to give precise and clear information and to minimise poor publicity.

Perrier risked competitors moving to take advantage of the crisis, since retailers would not leave shelves empty. Perrier, though, was the clear brand leader with the only established image worldwide. Competitors would take time to develop such strength, and their stocks were not high. Evian and others had nothing to gain from drawing further attention to Perrier's crisis, which was damaging the industry as a whole.

Perrier handled the crisis in PR text book fashion. With 85 per cent of the American and 60 per cent of the UK market, it had a great deal to lose. The company informed its publics of its difficulties, tackled the contamination problems and re-launched the product with new packaging and bottle sizes—clearly to be seen as new stock—with a "Welcome Back" promotional campaign. Within months, Perrier's market share was climbing back and shelf space had been regained. The company did not hide anything, it identified the various audiences to brief and it tackled its production to ensure that there were no repeat problems. Consumers, distributors, public health bodies and the media were made to feel part of Perrier's solution through the effective use of PR.

Perrier handled its crisis very efficiently, but never fully regained its domination of the bottled mineral water market—the fastest expanding sector of the beverages market in the 1990s. Perrier's success had been noted by major beverage suppliers; the removal of its bottles from shelves and the contamination scare gave rivals the opportunity to move in. Despite re-packaging, fresh designs and a new advertising agency, Publicis, Perrier struggled to re-kindle its former glory days and was taken over by the mighty Swiss company, Nestlé. Today, supermarket shelves have a multitude of rival mineral water brands, many mixed with exotic fruit flavours or energy enhancing ingredients. Nevertheless, Perrier still has very high brand awareness, significant market share and a loyal customer base.

SOURCES: John Tylee, "Publicis extends 'eau' theme for Perrier blitz", *Campaign,* 19 May 1995, p. 7; Greg Prince, "In hot water", *Beverage World,* March 1995, pp. 90–95; "Perrier aims to recapture lost young drinkers", *Marketing,* 24 March 1994, p. 1; *Marketing Week,* 2 March 1990; *Personally Speaking,* 27 March 1990; *Fortune,* 23 April 1990.

Questions for Discussion

1. How important is it to have an ongoing commitment to public relations in the event of a crisis?
2. Could Perrier's competitors have taken more advantage of the crisis?
3. Did the same publicity message go out to all of Perrier's publics or target audiences?

17 Personal Selling, Sales Promotion, Direct Mail, the Internet and Direct Marketing

"If we are what we do, then we all of us, are salespeople."

Antonis Simintiras, The Open University

OBJECTIVES

* To understand the nature and major purposes of personal selling
* To learn the basic steps in the personal selling process
* To identify the types of salesforce personnel
* To gain insight into sales management decisions and activities
* To become aware of what sales promotion activities are and how they can be used
* To become familiar with specific sales promotion methods
* To understand the role of direct mail in the promotional mix
* To be aware of the growing importance of the Internet in marketing communications
* To appreciate direct marketing's use of the promotional mix

Since its launch in 1914, International Business Machines (IBM) has transformed the public's perception of "salesman" from shady character to knowledgeable professional. IBM sales personnel understood their customers' needs and worked with them to show how computers could solve their business problems. On the strength of its technology and its salesforce, IBM became an international computer powerhouse. During the 1980s, however, IBM began selling hardware rather than solutions, and its prominence began to fade. When GTE, one of IBM's top customers, wanted to switch from a mainframe system to a less expensive network of personal computers, IBM representatives tried to dissuade the company from changing. GTE switched not only systems but also suppliers, opting for Hewlett-Packard. After suffering a number of such staggering losses, IBM re-engineered its 35,000 person salesforce to better meet its customers' needs.

What IBM recognised is that having talented and hard-working salespeople isn't enough to maintain a differential advantage. To help its sales staff win and keep customers, the company re-organised its field force by industry instead of by geography. In what industry experts call IBM's biggest restructuring in decades, the company established 14 industry areas—banking, retail, travel, insurance and others. Instead of selling a huge and confusing array of IBM products to all customers within a geographic area, salespeople specialise in specific industries, developing expertise in the businesses they serve. They know their customers better and are more familiar with the specific products that satisfy their needs. According to the company's CEO, re-engineering has transformed IBM sales personnel from order takers into business advisers.

It appears that the changes are beginning to pay off. IBM's work station sales grew by 47 per cent in one year, taking business away from market leader Sun Microsystems, Inc. One of IBM's large customers recently reported that the IBM people calling on them are more attuned to what the business does and what it needs. Stated the company's president, "We don't have to explain to them what's going on."

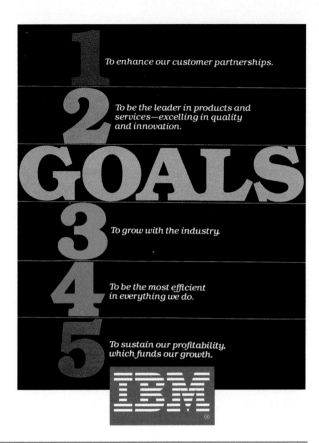

1 To enhance our customer partnerships.

2 To be the leader in products and services—excelling in quality and innovation.

GOALS

3 To grow with the industry.

4 To be the most efficient in everything we do.

5 To sustain our profitability, which funds our growth.

IBM

SOURCES: Based on information from Laurie Hays, "IBM chief unveils top-level shake-up, consolidating sales arm, software line", *Wall Street Journal,* 10 January 1995, p. B6; Craig Stedman, "Users laud IBM reorganization—for now", *Computerworld,* 30 January 1995, p. 57; "Reengineering: is there a doctor in the house?", *Sales & Marketing Management.* April 1995, p. S17; Chuck Paustian, "Icons Michael Jordan, IBM journey the comeback trail", *Business Marketing,* April 1995, p. 8; James Kaczman, "Just fix it, your sales process, that is", *Sales & Marketing Management,* September 1995, pp. 39–44; and Ira Sager, "The few, the true, the blue", *Business Week,* 30 May 1994, pp. 124–126. *Advertisement:* Courtesy of IBM.

A s indicated in Chapter 15, personal selling, sales promotion, direct mail, the Internet and direct marketing are possible ingredients in a promotional mix. Personal selling is the most widely used. Sometimes it is a company's sole promotional tool, although it is generally used in conjunction with other promotional mix ingredients. Personal selling is becoming more professional and sophisticated, with sales personnel acting more as consultants and advisers. Sales promotion, direct mail and the Internet are also playing an increasingly important role in marketing strategies.[1] Direct marketing, a term frequently now cited by marketers, is also a growing tool. Although partly an aspect of marketing channel selection—in this case opting not to utilise some of the services of channel intermediaries—there are implications for marketers' promotional strategies, as discussed in this chapter.

This chapter examines the purposes of personal selling, its basic steps, the types of salespeople involved in personal selling and how they are selected. It also discusses the major sales management decisions and activities, which include setting objectives for the salesforce and determining its size; recruiting, selecting, training, compensating and motivating salespeople; managing sales territories; and controlling sales personnel, as with IBM in the chapter opener. The discussion then goes on to explore several characteristics of sales promotion, the reasons for using sales promotion and the sales promotion methods available for use in a promotional mix. Use and types of direct mail are then examined. The chapter concludes with a look at the role of the Internet and the growing use of direct marketing.

The Nature of Personal Selling

Personal selling The process of using personal communication in an exchange situation to inform customers and persuade them to purchase products

Personal selling is the process of informing customers and persuading them to purchase products through personal communication in an exchange situation. For example, a salesperson describing the benefits of a Braun shaver to a customer in a Boots store is using personal selling. Personal selling gives marketers the greatest freedom to adjust a message to satisfy customers' information needs. In comparison with all other promotional methods, personal selling is the most precise, enabling marketers to focus on the most promising sales prospects. Other promotional mix ingredients are aimed at groups of people, some of whom may not be prospective customers. A major disadvantage of personal selling is its cost. Generally, it is the most expensive ingredient in the promotional mix, owing to the associated costs of salaries, cars and expenses. Personal selling costs are increasing faster than advertising costs.

Businesses spend more money on personal selling than on any other promotional mix ingredient. Millions of people, including increasing numbers of women, earn their living through personal selling. In the UK it is estimated that 600,000 people are directly employed as salespeople.[2] A selling career can offer high income, a great deal of freedom, a high level of training and a high level of job satisfaction.[3] Unfortunately, consumers often view personal selling negatively. A study of marketing students' perceptions of personal selling showed that approximately 25 per cent of the survey group associated it directly with door-to-door selling. In addition, 59 per cent of all students surveyed had a negative impression of personal selling. Major businesses, professional sales associations and academic institutions are making an effort to change the negative stereotypes associated with salespeople.[4] Ethical standards of selling practice are a major part of this enhancement, prompted by EU, government and consumer groups.

Personal selling goals vary from one company to another. However, they usually involve finding prospects, persuading prospects to buy and keeping customers satisfied. Identifying potential buyers who are interested in an organisation's products is critical. Because most potential buyers seek information before they make a purchase, salespeople must ascertain prospects' information needs and then provide the relevant information. To do so, sales personnel must be well trained, both in regard to their products and in regard to the selling process in general.[5]

Salespeople need to be aware of their competitors. They need to monitor new products being developed, and they should be aware of all competitors' sales activities in their sales territories. Salespeople must emphasise the advantages their products provide when their competitors' products do not offer that specific advantage.[6] Sales personnel are a useful source of marketing intelligence, often ignored by their marketing colleagues.

Few businesses survive solely on profits from one-sale customers. For long run survival, most marketers depend on repeat sales. This notion is at the core of relationship marketing, as described in Chapter 1. A company has to keep its customers satisfied to obtain repeat purchases. Besides, satisfied customers help attract new ones by telling potential customers about the organisation and its products. Even though the whole organisation is responsible for providing customer satisfaction, much of the burden falls on salespeople. The salesperson is almost always closer to customers than anyone else in the company and often provides buyers with information and service after the sale. Such contact not only gives salespeople an opportunity to generate additional sales but also offers them a good vantage point from which to evaluate the strengths and weaknesses of the company's products and other marketing mix ingredients. Their observations are helpful in developing and maintaining a marketing mix that better satisfies both customers and the business.

A salesperson may be involved in achieving one or more of the three general goals. In some organisations, there are people whose sole job is to find prospects. This information is relayed to salespeople, who then contact the prospects. After the sale, these same salespeople may do the follow up work, or a third group of employees may have the job of maintaining customer satisfaction. In many smaller organisations, a single person handles all these functions. No matter how many groups are involved, several major sales tasks must be performed to achieve these general goals.

Elements of the Personal Selling Process

The exact activities involved in the selling process vary from one salesperson to another and differ for particular selling situations. No two salespeople use exactly the same selling methods. Nonetheless, many salespeople—either consciously or unconsciously—move through a general selling process as they sell products. This process consists of seven elements, or steps: (1) prospecting and evaluating, (2) preparing, (3) approaching the customer, (4) making the presentation, (5) overcoming objections, (6) closing and (7) following up, as shown in Figure 17.1.

Prospecting and Evaluating

Prospecting Developing a list of potential customers

Developing a list of potential customers is called **prospecting.** A salesperson seeks the names of prospects from the company's sales records, referrals, trade shows, newspaper announcements (of marriages, births, deaths and so on), public records, telephone directories, trade association directories, telemarketing lists[7] and many other sources. Sales personnel also use responses from advertisements that encourage interested people to send in an information request form. Seminars and meetings may produce good leads. Seminars may be targeted at particular types of clients, such as solicitors, accountants, the over-55s or specific business people.

After developing the prospect list, a salesperson evaluates whether each prospect is able, willing and authorised to buy the product. On the basis of this evaluation, some prospects may be deleted, while others are deemed acceptable and ranked according to their desirability or potential.

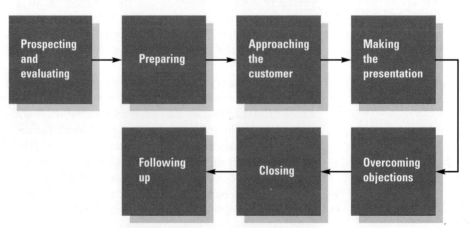

Figure 17.1 Elements of personal selling

Part V Promotion Decisions

Preparing

Before contacting acceptable prospects, a salesperson should find and analyse information about each prospect's specific product needs, current use of brands, feelings about available brands and personal characteristics. The most successful salespeople are thorough in their preparation. They prepare by identifying key decision-makers, reviewing account histories and reports, contacting other clients for information, assessing credit histories and problems, preparing sales presentations, identifying product needs and obtaining all relevant literature.[8] Being well informed about a prospect makes a salesperson better equipped to develop a presentation that precisely communicates with the prospect.

For example, Xerox developed an automated sales process to help sales personnel prepare for complex sales situations after discovering that its salespeople spent half their time on sales inhibiting activities, such as looking for forms and gathering information. Preparing an order required 5 to 13 forms, and one-third of all orders were rejected because of mistakes on the forms. To overcome the problem, Xerox developed computer work stations to assist its salesforce in shaping proposals, prospecting and preparing, and to link salespeople throughout the company without a piece of paper having to be touched.[9]

Approaching the Customer

Approach The manner in which a salesperson contacts a potential customer

The **approach,** the manner in which a salesperson contacts a potential customer, is a critical step in the sales process. In more than 80 per cent of initial sales calls, the purpose is to gather information about the buyer's needs and objectives. Creating a favourable impression and building rapport with the prospective client are also important tasks in the approach, because the prospect's first impression of the salesperson is usually a lasting one, with long run consequences. During the initial visit, the salesperson strives to develop a relationship rather than just push a product. The salesperson may have to call on a prospect several times before the product is considered.[10]

One type of approach is based on referrals. The salesperson approaches the prospect and explains that an acquaintance, an associate or a relative, suggested the call. The salesperson who uses the cold canvass method calls on potential customers without their prior consent. Repeat contact is another common approach; when making the contact, the salesperson mentions a prior meeting. The exact type of approach depends on the salesperson's preferences, the product being sold, the business's resources and the characteristics of the prospect.

Making the Presentation

During the sales presentation, the salesperson must attract and hold the prospect's attention to stimulate interest and stir up a desire for the product. The salesperson should have the prospect touch, hold or actually use the product. If possible, the salesperson should demonstrate the product and get the prospect more involved with it to stimulate greater interest. Audio-visual materials may be used to enhance the presentation.

During the presentation, the salesperson must not only talk but also listen. The sales presentation gives the salesperson the greatest opportunity to determine the prospect's specific needs by listening to questions and comments and observing responses. Even though the salesperson has planned the presentation in advance, she or he must be able to adjust the message to meet the prospect's information needs.

Overcoming Objections

An effective salesperson usually seeks out a prospect's objections in order to address them. If they are not apparent, the salesperson cannot deal with them, and they may keep the prospect from buying. One of the best ways to overcome a prospect's objections is to anticipate and counter them before the prospect has an opportunity to raise them. However, this approach can be risky because the salesperson may mention some objections that the prospect would not have raised. If possible, the salesperson should handle objections when they arise. They can also be dealt with at the end of the presentation.

Closing

Closing The step in the selling process in which the salesperson asks the prospect to buy the product or products

Closing is the step in the selling process in which the salesperson asks the prospect to buy the product or products. During the presentation, the salesperson may use a "trial close" by asking questions that assume the prospect will buy the product. For example, the salesperson might ask the potential customer about financial terms, desired colours or sizes, delivery arrangements or the quantity to be purchased. The reactions to such questions usually indicate how close the prospect is to buying. A trial close allows prospects to indicate indirectly that they will buy the product without having to say those sometimes difficult words, "I'll take it".

A salesperson should try to close at several points during the presentation, because the prospect may be ready to buy. One closing strategy involves asking the potential customer to take a trial order. The sales representative should either guarantee a refund if the customer is not satisfied or make the order a free offer.[11] Often an attempt to close the sale will result in objections. Thus closing can be an important stimulus that uncovers hidden objections, which can then be addressed.

Following Up

After a successful closing, the salesperson must follow up the sale. In the follow up stage, the salesperson should determine whether the order was delivered on time and installed properly, if installation was required. He or she should contact the customer to learn what problems or questions have arisen regarding the product. The follow up stage can also be used to determine customers' future product needs. This step provides both information and ideas which may prove helpful in selling to other likely customers, and the opportunity to cement relationships with existing customers.

Types of Salespeople

To develop a salesforce, a marketer must decide which types of salespeople will best sell and represent the business's products. Most companies deploy several types of salespeople. Based on the functions they perform, salespeople generally are classified as order getters, order takers or support personnel. Sometimes the same salesperson performs all three sets of tasks. When recruiting sales personnel, marketers seldom focus on only one type of salesperson: most businesses require a mix of selling skills. A product's uses, characteristics, competitive position, complexity, customer profile, selected marketing channel(s), promotional mix, price and margin influence the kinds and numbers of sales personnel recruited.

Order getters Employees who increase a company's sales by selling to new customers and by increasing sales to existing customers

Order getters are tasked to increase a company's sales by selling to new customers and by increasing sales to existing customers. This entails a process of recognising buyers' needs, informing prospects and persuading them to try, then buy the product. This is often termed *creative selling*. There are two types of order getters: those dealing with current customer sales and those chasing new business sales. (1) *Current customer order getters* call on people who have already purchased a business's products. They seek to sell more to existing customers and to gain sales leads from these customers to contact other customers.

(2) *New business order getters* are crucial for a company's longer term survival as all businesses require additional, new customers. These salespeople locate prospects and convert them into buyers. The time-share industry uses various promotional techniques—direct mail, competitions, road shows, free trial offers—to attract potential buyers to attend seminars or open days at the time-share site. Once on site, it is up to the new business order getters to explain the concept of time-sharing, demonstrate the facilities and close the deal. Without the involvement of sales personnel, it is unlikely prospects would sign up for a time-share. BMW's approved used car Internet service attracts potential buyers but the deal is closed by salespeople at the dealerships.

Order takers Employees who ensure that repeat customers have sufficient quantities of products when and where they are needed in order to maintain and perpetuate ongoing relationships

Taking orders is a repetitive task that sales staff perform to maintain and perpetuate ongoing relationships with customers. **Order takers** seek repeat sales. A major task is to ensure that repeat customers have sufficient quantities of products when and where they are needed. This is particularly important in many business-to-business markets in which manufacturers depend on components for production of their own products. Most order takers handle repeat orders for standardised products that are purchased routinely, minimising the selling effort.[12] IT systems increasingly link suppliers with customers, enabling the relationship to be handled remotely and automatically. There are two types of order takers: inside order takers and field order takers. (1) *Inside order takers* are located in a business's call centre or offices and receive orders by post, fax, e-mail or telephone. They do occasionally deal face to face with customers: for example, sales assistants inside retail stores are classified as inside order takers. (2) *Field order takers*—the field force—are salespeople who travel to customers. Customers often depend on these regular calls to maintain required inventories and keep abreast of any product modifications, while these field based order takers rely on such ongoing relationships and customer loyalty to achieve their sales targets. Neither inside nor field order takers should be thought of as entirely passive functionaries who simply record orders. In many businesses, order takers generate the bulk of sales.

Support personnel Employees who facilitate the selling function but do more than solely participate in selling

Missionary salespeople Support salespeople, usually employed by manufacturers to assist their customers' selling efforts

Trade salespeople Employees who take orders as well as help trade customers promote, display and stock their products

Technical salespeople Employees who give technical assistance to current customers

Support personnel facilitate the selling function but often do more than solely participate in the selling process. Particularly common in industrial or business-to-business markets, support personnel locate prospects, educate customers, build goodwill and provide aftermarket, after sales service. There are three main categories of support personnel. (1) **Missionary salespeople** are employed by manufacturers to assist their customers' selling efforts. For example, pharmaceutical and medical product manufacturers sell to wholesalers but employ missionary salespersonnel to visit retailers to promote retailers' orders being placed with wholesalers. (2) **Trade salespeople** undertake order taking as well as help trade customers promote, display and stock their products. The major manufacturers of alcoholic beverages deploy trade salespeople to ensure prominent shelf displays of their products in off-licences and supermarkets. They re-stock shelves, obtain more shelf space, set up displays, provide in-store demonstrations, distribute samples and arrange joint promotions. (3) **Technical salespeople** give technical assistance to current customers. They advise customers on product characteristics, applications, system designs, installation, plus health and safety issues. Agrochemicals, chemicals and heavy plant are technically advanced products requiring technical salespeople to support order getters and marketers. In markets with standardised products and little product differentiation, marketers may offer superior technical support and customer service as a means of developing a differential advantage over competitors.

The salesforce is directly responsible for generating a business's primary input: sales revenue. Without adequate sales revenue, a business cannot survive long. A company's reputation is often determined by the ethical conduct of its salesforce. On the other hand, the morale and, ultimately, the success of a company's salesforce are determined in large part by adequate compensation, room for advancement, sufficient training and management support—all key areas of sales management. When these elements are not satisfactory, sales staff may leave for more satisfying jobs elsewhere. It is important to evaluate the input of salespeople because effective salesforce management helps to determine a company's success.

This section explores eight general areas of sales management: (1) establishing salesforce objectives, (2) determining salesforce size, (3) recruiting and selecting sales personnel, (4) training sales personnel, (5) compensating sales personnel, (6)

Figure 17.2 Assisting the salesforce. Espace's advertising produces sales leads for the company's salesforce. SOURCE: Courtesy of Espace/Cebeco Seed Innovations.

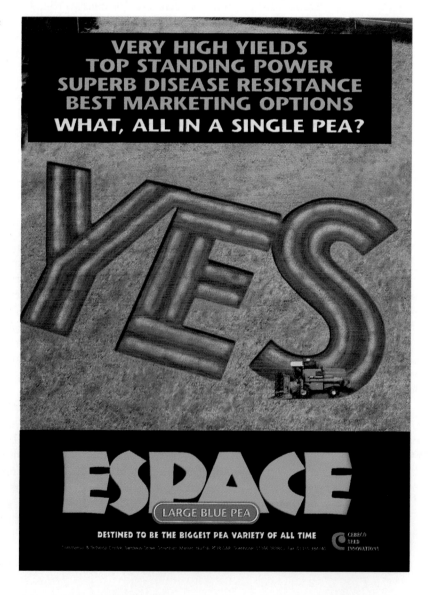

VERY HIGH YIELDS
TOP STANDING POWER
SUPERB DISEASE RESISTANCE
BEST MARKETING OPTIONS
WHAT, ALL IN A SINGLE PEA?

ESPACE
LARGE BLUE PEA

DESTINED TO BE THE BIGGEST PEA VARIETY OF ALL TIME

motivating salespeople, (7) managing sales territories and (8) controlling and evaluating salesforce performance.

Establishing Salesforce Objectives

To manage a salesforce effectively, a sales manager must develop sales objectives. Sales objectives tell salespeople what they are expected to accomplish during a specified time period. These objectives give the salesforce direction and purpose and serve as performance standards for the evaluation and control of sales personnel. For example, in Figure 17.2, Espace uses advertising to produce leads and thereby help salespeople meet their sales goals. As with all types of objectives, sales objectives should be stated in precise, measurable terms and should specify the time period, customer type and geographic areas involved.

Sales objectives are usually developed for both the total salesforce and each salesperson. Objectives for the entire force are normally stated in terms of sales volume, market share or profit. Volume objectives refer to a quantity of money or sales units. For example, the objective for an electric drill manufacturer's salesforce might be to sell £6 million worth of drills annually or 600,000 drills annually. When sales goals are stated in terms of market share, they usually call for an increase in the proportion of the company's sales relative to the total number of products sold by all businesses in that particular industry. When sales objectives are based on profit, they are generally stated in terms of monetary amounts or in terms of return on investment. Sales objectives, or quotas, for an individual salesperson are commonly stated in terms of monetary or unit sales volume. Other bases used for individual sales objectives include average order size, average number of calls per time period and the ratio of orders to calls.

Determining Salesforce Size

Deciding how many salespeople to use is important because the size of the salesforce influences the company's ability to generate sales and profits. Moreover, salesforce size affects the compensation methods used, salespeople's morale and overall salesforce management. Salesforce size must be adjusted from time to time because a company's marketing plans change, as do markets and forces in the marketing environment. It is dangerous, however, to cut back the size of the salesforce to increase profits by cutting costs. The sales organisation could then lose its strength and resilience, preventing it from rebounding when growth returns or better market conditions prevail. The organisation that loses capacity through cutbacks may not have the energy to accelerate.[13] There are several analytical methods for determining the optimal size of the salesforce. Although marketing managers may use one of these methods, they normally temper their decisions with a good deal of subjective judgement.[14]

Recruiting and Selecting Sales Personnel

Recruiting A process by which the sales manager develops a list of applicants for sales positions

To create and maintain an effective salesforce, a sales manager must recruit the right type of salespeople. **Recruiting** is a process by which the sales manager develops a list of applicants for sales positions. The cost of hiring, training and retaining a salesperson is soaring; currently, costs in the UK can reach £60,000 or more.[15]

To ensure that the recruiting process results in a pool of qualified salespeople from which to choose, a sales manager should establish a set of required qualifications before beginning to recruit. Although for years marketers have attempted to identify a set of traits that characterise effective salespeople, there is currently no such set of generally accepted characteristics. Therefore, a sales manager must develop a set tailored to the sales tasks in a particular company. Two activities can help establish this set of requirements. The sales manager should prepare a job description that lists the specific tasks salespeople are to perform. The manager should also analyse the characteristics of the company's successful salespeople, as well as those of its ineffective sales personnel. From the job description and the analysis of traits, the sales manager should be able to develop a set of specific requirements and be aware of potential weaknesses that could lead to failure.

A sales manager generally recruits applicants from several sources: departments within the business, other companies, employment agencies, educational institutions, respondents to advertisements and individuals recommended by current employees. The specific sources a sales manager uses depend on the type of salesperson required and the manager's experiences with particular sources.

The process of hiring a salesforce varies tremendously from one company to another. One technique used to determine whether potential candidates will be good salespeople is an assessment centre. Assessment centres are intense training environments that place candidates in realistic problem settings in which they must assign priorities to their activities, make decisions and act on their decisions. Candidates are judged by experienced managers or trained observers. Assessment centres have proved to be valuable in helping to select good salespeople.[16]

Sales management should design a selection procedure that satisfies the company's specific needs. The process should include enough steps to yield the information needed to make accurate selection decisions. However, because each step incurs a certain expense, there should be no more steps than necessary. The stages of the selection process should be sequenced so that the more expensive steps, such as physical examination, are near the end. Fewer people will then move through the higher cost stages.

Recruitment should not be sporadic; it should be a continuous activity aimed at reaching the best applicants. The selection process should systematically and effectively match applicants' characteristics and needs with the requirements of specific selling tasks. Finally, the selection process should ensure that new sales personnel are available where and when they are needed. Recruitment and selection of salespeople are not one-off decisions. The market and marketing environment change, as do an organisation's objectives, resources and marketing strategies. Maintaining the proper mix of salespeople thus requires the continued attention of the company's sales management.

Training Sales Personnel

Many businesses have formal training programmes; others depend on informal, on-the-job training. Some systematic training programmes are quite extensive; others are rather short and rudimentary. Regardless of whether the training programme is complex or simple, its developers must consider who should be trained, what should be taught and how the training should occur.

A sales training programme can concentrate on the company, on products or on selling methods. Training programmes often cover all three areas. For experienced company sales staff, training usually emphasises product information, although it also describes new selling techniques and any changes in company plans, policies and procedures.

Training programmes can be aimed at newly hired salespeople, experienced sales staff or both. Ordinarily, new sales personnel require comprehensive training, whereas experienced personnel need both refresher courses about established products and training in new product information. Training programmes can be directed at the entire salesforce or at one segment of it.

Sales training may be done in the field, at educational institutions, in company facilities or in several of these locations. Some businesses train new employees before assigning them to a specific sales position. Other businesses, however, put them into the field immediately and provide formal training only after they have gained a little experience. Training programmes for new personnel can be as short as several days or as long as three years. Sales training for experienced personnel is often scheduled during a period when sales activities are not too demanding. Because training experienced salespeople is usually an ongoing effort, a company's sales management must determine the frequency, sequencing and duration of these activities.

Sales managers, as well as other salespeople, often engage in sales training—whether daily on-the-job or periodically in sales meetings. Salespeople sometimes receive training from technical specialists within their own organisations. In addition, a number of individuals and organisations sell special sales training programmes. Appropriate materials for sales training programmes range from films, texts, manuals and cases to programmed learning devices, audio and video cassettes and CDs. As for teaching methods, lectures, demonstrations, simulation exercises and on-the-job training can all be effective. The choice of methods and materials for a particular sales training programme depends on the type and number of trainees, the programme's content and complexity, its length and location, the size of the training budget, the number of teachers and the teachers' preferences.

Compensating Sales Personnel

To develop and maintain a highly productive salesforce, a business must formulate and administer a compensation or remuneration plan that attracts, motivates and retains the most effective individuals. The plan should give sales management the desired level of control and provide sales personnel with an acceptable level of freedom, income and incentive. It should also be flexible, equitable, easy to administer and easy to understand. Good remuneration programmes facilitate and encourage proper treatment of customers.

Even though these requirements appear to be logical and easily satisfied, it is actually quite difficult to incorporate them all into a simple programme. Some of them will be satisfied, and others will not. Studies evaluating the impact of financial incentives on sales performance indicate four general responses. (1) For price sensitive individuals, an increase in incentives will usually increase their sales efforts, and a decrease in financial rewards will diminish their efforts. (2) Unresponsive salespeople will sell at the same level regardless of the incentive. (3) Leisure sensitive salespeople tend to work less when the incentive system is implemented. (4) Income satisfiers normally adjust their performance to match their income goal. Understanding potential reactions and analysing the personalities of the salesforce can help management evaluate whether an incentive programme might work.[17] Therefore, in formulating a compensation or remuneration plan, sales management must strive for a proper balance of freedom, income and incentives.

The developer of a compensation programme must determine the general level of compensation required and the most desirable method of calculating it. In analysing the required compensation level, sales management must ascertain a salesperson's value to the company on the basis of the tasks and responsibilities associated with the sales position. The sales manager may consider a number of factors, including salaries of other types of personnel in the business, competitors' compensation plans, costs of salesforce turnover and the size of non-salary selling expenses and perks.

Sales compensation programmes usually reimburse salespeople for their selling expenses, provide a certain number of fringe benefits—such as health insurance, company car and pension scheme—and deliver the required compensation level.

Straight salary compensation/ remuneration plan A plan according to which salespeople are paid a specified amount per time period

Straight commission compensation/ remuneration plan A plan according to which salespeople are paid solely on the basis of their sales for a given time period

Combination compensation/ remuneration plan A plan according to which salespeople are paid a fixed salary plus a commission based on sales volume

To do that, a company may use one or more of three basic compensation methods: straight salary, straight commission or a combination of salary and commission. In a **straight salary compensation/remuneration plan**, salespeople are paid a specified amount per time period. This sum remains the same until they receive a pay increase or decrease. In a **straight commission compensation/remuneration plan**, salespeople's compensation is determined solely on the basis of their sales for a given time period. A commission may be based on a single percentage of sales or on a sliding scale involving several sales levels and percentage rates. In a **combination compensation/remuneration plan**, salespeople are paid a fixed salary plus a commission based on sales volume. Some combination programmes require a salesperson to exceed a certain sales level before earning a commission; others offer commissions for any level of sales. Car dealers pay their sales personnel small basic salaries, with sales-linked bonuses making up the bulk of earnings.

Compensation/ Remuneration Method	Frequency of Use (%)*	When Especially Useful	Advantages	Disadvantages
Straight salary	17.4	Compensating new salespeople; company moves into new sales territories that require developmental work; salespeople need to perform many non-selling activities	Gives salesperson maximum amount of security; gives sales manager large amount of control over salesforce; easy to administer; yields more predictable selling expenses	Provides no incentive; necessitates closer supervision of salespeople's activities; during sales declines, selling expenses remain at same level
Straight commission	6.5	Highly aggressive selling is required; non-selling tasks are minimised; company cannot closely control salesforce activities	Provides maximum amount of incentive; by increasing commission rate, sales managers can encourage salespeople to sell certain items; selling expenses relate directly to sales resources	Salespeople have little financial security; sales manager has minimum control over salesforce; may cause salespeople to give inadequate service to smaller accounts; selling costs less predictable
Combination	76.1	Sales territories have relatively similar sales potentials; company wishes to provide incentive but still control salesforce activities	Provides certain level of financial security; provides some incentive; selling expenses fluctuate with sales revenue	Selling expenses less predictable; may be difficult to administer

*The figures are computed from "Alternative sales compensation and incentive plans", *Sales & Marketing Management*, 17 February 1986, p. 57. *Note:* The percentage for Combination includes compensation methods that involved any combination of salary, commission or bonus.

SOURCE: Based on John P. Steinbrink, "How to pay your sales force", *Harvard Business Review*, July/August 1978.

Table 17.1 Characteristics of salesforce compensation/remuneration methods

Traditionally, department stores have paid salespeople straight salaries, but combination compensation plans are becoming popular. Concessionaries in Debenhams, for example, are offering commissions (averaging 6 to 8 per cent) to a large segment of their salesforce. The practice has made the salespeople more attentive to a customer's presence and needs; it has also attracted older, more experienced salespeople, who tend to be in short supply.[18]

Table 17.1 lists the major characteristics of each salesforce compensation method. Note that the combination method is most popular. When selecting a compensation method, sales management weighs the advantages and disadvantages shown in Table 17.1.

Proper administration of the salesforce compensation programme is crucial for developing high morale and productivity among sales personnel. A good salesperson is highly marketable in today's workplace, and successful sales managers switch industries on a regular basis. Basic knowledge and skills related to sales management are in demand, and sometimes new insights can be gained from different work experiences. For example, one of British Steel's best sales managers was recruited from the grocery sector. To maintain an effective compensation programme and retain productive employees, sales management should periodically review and evaluate the plan and make necessary adjustments.

Motivating Salespeople

A sales manager should develop a systematic approach for motivating the salesforce to be productive. Motivating should not be viewed as a sporadic activity reserved for periods of sales decline. Effective salesforce motivation is achieved through an organised set of activities performed continuously by the company's sales management. For example, scheduled sales meetings can motivate salespeople. Periodic sales meetings have four main functions: (1) recognising and reinforcing the performance of salespeople, (2) sharing sales techniques that are working, (3) focusing employees' efforts on matching the corporate goals and evaluating their progress towards achieving these goals, and (4) teaching the sales staff about new products and services.[19]

Although financial compensation is important, a motivational programme must also satisfy non-financial needs. Sales personnel, like other people, join organisations to satisfy personal needs and achieve personal goals. Sales managers must become aware of their sales personnel's motives and goals and then attempt to create an organisational climate that lets their salespeople satisfy their personal needs.

A sales manager can use a variety of positive motivational incentives as well as financial compensation (see Figure 17.3). For example, enjoyable working conditions, power and authority, job security and an opportunity to excel can be effective motivators. Salespeople can also be motivated by their company's efforts to make their job more productive and efficient. For example, Honeywell Information Systems developed a computerised sales support system that increased sales productivity by 31 per cent and reduced salesforce turnover by 40 per cent within a year. This system can track sales leads and provide customer profiles and competitor data.[20]

Sales contests and other incentive programmes can also be effective motivators. Sales contests can motivate salespeople to focus on increasing sales or new accounts, promoting special items, achieving greater volume per sales call, covering territories better and increasing activity in new geographic areas.[21] Some companies have found such incentive programmes to be powerful motivating tools that marketing managers can use to achieve corporate goals. Properly designed, an incentive programme can pay for itself many times over. However,

Figure 17.3 Motivating salesforce performance through an organised set of activities

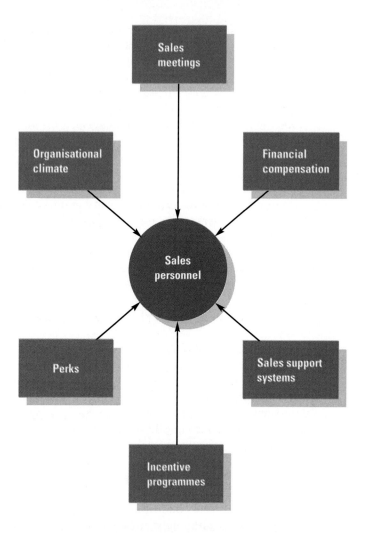

for an incentive system to succeed, the marketing objectives must be accepted by the participants and prove effective in the marketplace. Some organisations also use negative motivational measures: financial penalties, demotions, even terminations of employment.

Managing Sales Territories The effectiveness of a salesforce that must travel to its customers is influenced to some degree by sales management's decisions regarding sales territories. Sales managers deciding on territories must consider the size and shape of sales territories and the routing and scheduling of salespeople.

Size and Shape of Sales Territories Several factors enter into the design of the size and shape of sales territories. First, sales managers must construct the territories so that sales potentials can be measured. Thus sales territories often consist of several geographic units for which market data are obtainable, such as census tracts, cities, counties or regions. Sales managers usually try to create territories that have similar sales potentials or require about the same amount of work. If territories have equal sales potentials, they will almost always be unequal in geographic size. The salespeople who are assigned the larger territories will have to work longer and harder to generate a certain sales volume. Conversely, if sales territories that require equal amounts of work are created, sales potentials for those territories will often vary. If sales personnel are partially or fully compensated through commissions, they will have unequal income potentials. Many sales managers try to balance territorial workload and earnings potential by using differential commission rates. Although a sales manager seeks equity when developing and maintaining sales territories, some inequities will always prevail.

A territory's size and shape should also be designed to enable the salesforce to provide the best possible customer coverage and to minimise selling costs. Sales territory size and shape should take into account the density and distribution of customers.

Routing and Scheduling Salespeople   The geographic size and shape of a sales territory are the most important factors affecting routing and scheduling of sales calls. Next are the number and distribution of customers within the territory, followed by the frequency and duration of sales calls. The person in charge of routing and scheduling must consider the sequence in which customers are called on, the specific roads or transport schedules to be used, the number of calls to be made in a given period and what time of day the calls will occur. In some companies, salespeople plan their own routes and schedules with little or no assistance from the sales manager; in other organisations, the sales manager draws up the routes and schedules. No matter who plans the routing and scheduling, the major goals should be to minimise salespeople's non-selling time (the time spent travelling and waiting) and maximise their selling time. The planners should try to achieve these goals in a way that holds a salesperson's travel and accommodation costs to a minimum. Many companies use agencies, such as SPA Ltd, to construct databases of actual and potential customers and associated sales territories. SPA has a database of car and lorry drive-times, even taking account of road works, which allows sales territories to be delineated. These territories can share out actual and potential customers and allocate the salesforce in relation to the time taken to service them.

| Controlling and Evaluating Salesforce Performance | To control and evaluate salesforce activities properly, sales management needs information. A sales manager cannot observe the field salesforce daily and so relies on call reports, customer feedback and invoices. Call reports identify the customers called on and present detailed information about interaction with those clients. Travelling sales personnel must often file work schedules indicating where they plan to be during specific future time periods. |

The dimensions used to measure a salesperson's performance are determined largely by sales objectives. These objectives are normally set by the sales manager. If an individual's sales objective is stated in terms of sales volume, then that person should be evaluated on the basis of sales volume generated. Even though a salesperson may be assigned a major objective, he or she is ordinarily expected to achieve several related objectives as well. Thus salespeople are often judged along several dimensions. Sales managers evaluate many performance indicators, including average number of calls per day, average sales per customer, actual sales relative to sales potential, number of new customer orders, average cost per call and average gross profit per customer.

To evaluate a salesperson, a sales manager may compare one or more of these dimensions with a pre-determined performance standard. However, sales management commonly compares one salesperson's current performance either with the performance of other employees operating under similar selling conditions or with his or her past performance. Sometimes management judges factors that have less direct bearing on sales performance, such as personal appearance, knowledge of the product and competitors.

After evaluating their salesforce, sales managers must take any corrective action needed, because it is their job to improve the performance of the sales-force. They may have to adjust performance standards, provide additional sales training or try other motivational methods. Corrective action may demand comprehensive changes in the salesforce.

Many industries, especially technical ones, are monitoring their salesforces and increasing productivity through the use of lap-top computers and Internet links. In part, the increasing use of computers in technical sales is a response to customers' greater technical sophistication. Product information—especially information on price, specifications and availability—helps salespeople to be more valuable. Some companies that have provided their salesforces with lap-tops expect a 15 to 20 per cent increase in sales.[22]

Sales Promotion

The Nature of Sales Promotion

Sales promotion An activity or material that acts as a direct inducement and offers added value to or incentive to buy the product

As defined earlier in Chapter 15, **sales promotion** is an activity or material (or both) that acts as a direct inducement and offers added value to or incentive to buy the product to resellers, salespeople or consumers.[23] The sale probably would have taken place without the sales promotion activity, but not for a while; the promotion has brought the sale forward. For example, a consumer loyal to Persil washing powder may purchase a packet every four weeks. If, however, in the third week Sainsbury's or Tesco has Persil on offer or with an on-pack promotion, the consumer will probably buy a week early to take advantage of the deal. Sales promotion encompasses all promotional activities and materials other than personal selling, advertising, publicity and sponsorship. In competitive markets, where products are very similar, sales promotion provides additional inducements to encourage purchases. Sales promotions are designed to generate short term sales and goodwill towards the promoter.

Sales promotion has grown dramatically in the last 20 years, largely because of the focus of business on short term profits and value and the perceived need for promotional strategies to produce short term sales boosts.[24] Current estimates in the UK suggest that consumer sales promotion is worth £2 billion annually. Include price discounting and the figure could be £4 billion higher; include trade sales promotion and the total reaches £8 billion.[25] The most significant change in promotion expenditures in recent years has been the transfer of funds usually earmarked for advertising to sales promotion. Companies now spend 54 per cent of their combined marketing services budgets on advertising and 21 per cent on sales promotion.[26] Fundamental changes in marketing, which have led to a greater emphasis on sales promotion, mean that specialist sales promotion agencies have increased and many major advertising agencies have developed sales promotion departments.

Ratchet effect The stepped impact of using sales promotion and advertising together

An organisation often uses sales promotion activities in conjunction with other promotional efforts to facilitate personal selling, advertising or both.[27] Figure 17.4 depicts what is known as the **ratchet effect**—the stepped impact of using sales promotion (short term sales brought forward) and advertising (longer term build up to generate sales) together. Sales promotion efforts are not always secondary to other promotional mix ingredients. Companies sometimes use advertising and personal selling to support sales promotion activities. For example, marketers frequently use advertising to promote contests, free samples and spe-

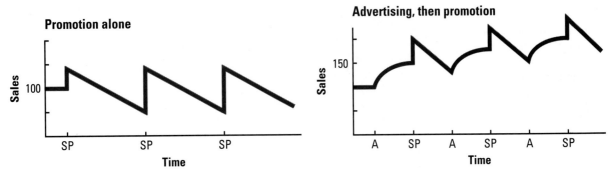

Figure 17.4 The "ratchet effect". Sales promotion (SP) brings forward sales but has an immediate effect. An advertising campaign (A) takes time to take off and to generate sales, but can switch other brand users and non-users. The ratchet effect has been identified in most consumer and service markets. SOURCE: W. T. Moran, "Insights from pricing research", in E. B. Bailey, ed., *Pricing Practices and Strategies* (New York: The Conference Board, 1978), pp. 7 and 13. Used by permission.

cial offers. Manufacturers' sales personnel occasionally administer sales contests for wholesale or retail salespeople. The most effective sales promotion efforts are closely inter-related with other promotional activities. Decisions regarding sales promotion therefore often affect advertising and personal selling decisions, and vice versa.

Sales Promotion Opportunities and Limitations

Sales promotion can increase sales by providing an extra incentive to purchase. There are many opportunities to motivate consumers, resellers and salespeople to take a desired action. Some kinds of sales promotion are designed specifically to identify and attract new customers, to introduce a new product and to increase reseller inventories. Some are directed at increasing consumer demand; still others focus on both resellers and consumers. Regardless of the purpose, marketers need to ensure that the sales promotion objectives are consistent with the organisation's overall objectives, as well as with its marketing and promotion objectives.[28]

Although sales promotion can support a brand image, excessive price reduction sales promotion, such as discount coupons or two-for-one pack offers, can affect it adversely. Companies therefore must decide between short term sales increases and the long run need for a desired reputation and brand image.[29] As already noted, sales promotion has been catching up with advertising in total expenditure; but in the future, brand advertising may become more important relative to sales promotion. Some companies that shifted from brand advertising to sales promotion have lost market share, particularly in consumer markets where advertising is essential to maintain awareness and brand recognition. Advertising does not necessarily work better than sales promotion. There are trade-offs between these two forms of promotion, and the marketing manager must determine the right balance to achieve maximum promotional effectiveness.

Sales Promotion Methods

Most sales promotion methods can be grouped into the categories of consumer sales promotion and trade sales promotion. **Consumer sales promotion techniques** are pitched at consumers: they encourage or stimulate consumers to

patronise a specific retail store or to try a particular product. **Trade sales promotion methods** are aimed at marketing channel intermediaries: they stimulate
wholesalers, retailers or dealers to carry a producer's products and to market
these products aggressively. Figure 17.5 shows how all members of a marketing
channel can be engaged in sales promotion activities with different target audiences and techniques.

Marketers consider a number of factors before deciding which sales promotion
methods to use.[30] They must take into account both product characteristics (size,
weight, costs, durability, uses, features and hazards) and target market characteristics (age, sex, income, location, density, usage rate and shopping patterns).
How the product is distributed and the number and types of resellers may determine the type of method used. The competitive and legal environmental forces
may also influence the choice.

Consumer Sales Promotion Techniques

The principal consumer sales promotion techniques include coupons, demonstrations, frequent user incentives, point-of-sale (POS) materials, free samples,
money refunds, premiums, price-off offers, and consumer contests and sweepstakes.

Coupons are used to stimulate consumers to try a new or established product,
to increase sales volume quickly, to attract repeat purchasers or to introduce new
package sizes or features. Coupons usually reduce the purchase price of an item.
The savings may be deducted from the purchase price or offered as cash. For best
results, coupons should be easy to recognise and state the offer clearly. The
nature of the product (seasonality, maturity, frequency of purchase and so on) is
the prime consideration in setting up a coupon promotion.

Several thousand manufacturers distribute coupons, which are used by approximately 80 per cent of all households. One study found that pride and satisfaction from obtaining savings through the use of coupons and price-consciousness
were the most important determinants of coupon use.[31] Coupons are distributed
through free-standing inserts (FSIs), print advertising, direct mail/leaflet drops
and in stores. Historically, FSIs have been the dominant vehicle for coupons.[32]

Figure 17.5   Uses of sales
promotion in the
marketing channel.
Consumer: Coupons,
free samples,
demonstrations,
competitions. Trade
(aimed at wholesalers,
retailers, salespeople):
Sales competitions, free
merchandise, P-O-S
displays, plus trade
shows and conferences.
SOURCE: John Rossiter and
Larry Percy, *Advertising and
Promotion Management.*
Copyright © 1987 by The
McGraw-Hill Companies,
Inc. Reprinted with
permission of The McGraw-
Hill Companies.

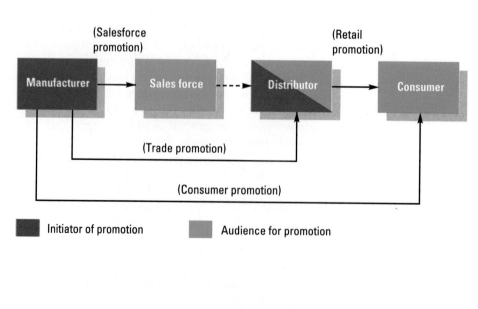

When deciding on the proper vehicle for their coupons, marketers should consider strategies and objectives, redemption rates, availability, circulation and exclusivity. The whole coupon distribution and redemption business has become very competitive. To draw customers to their stores, grocers may double and sometimes even triple the value of the coupons they bring in. But because the practice of doubling and tripling coupons is expensive, many of these retailers have asked manufacturers to reduce the face value of the coupons they offer.[33]

There are several advantages to using coupons. Print advertisements with coupons are often more effective than non-promotional advertising in generating brand awareness. Generally, the larger the coupon's cash offer, the better the recognition generated. Another advantage is that coupons are a good way to reward present users of the product, win back former users and encourage purchases in larger quantities. Coupons also let manufacturers determine whether the coupons reached the intended target market because they get the coupons back.

Coupons also have drawbacks. Fraud and misredemption are possible, and the redemption period can be quite lengthy. Table 17.2 illustrates coupon distribution and redemption rates in the UK. In addition, some experts believe that

Table 17.2 Coupon distribution and redemption rates in the UK

	1993	1994	1995	1996	1997
Distribution (billions)	3.0	4.2	4.4	4.0	4.7
Distribution medium of coupons redeemed (%)					
Newspaper	—	—	—	3.5	3.5
Magazine	—	—	—	7.7	7.7
Door-to-door	—	—	—	10.9	11.6
In-/on-pack	—	—	—	33.4	32.2
In-store	—	—	—	14.6	14.0
Direct mail	—	—	—	23.2	24.2
Others	—	—	—	6.6	6.8
Redemption (millions)	278	193	211	212	272
Average redemption rates by media (%)					
Newspaper	—	—	—	0.9	0.7
Magazine	—	—	—	1.1	1.4
Door-to-door	—	—	—	7.5	7.7
In-/on-pack	—	—	—	26.9	25.1
In-store	—	—	—	4.4	6.2
Direct mail	—	—	—	22.9	22.9
Total redemption value (£m)	91	66	93	70	136
Average face value (pence)	33	34	44	33	50
Manufacturers' average handling allowance[1] to retailers (pence per 100 coupons)	251	251	360	—	360

Note: [1]Excluding retailer tailor-made promotions.

SOURCE: *The Marketing Pocket Book 1995.* Reprinted by permission of NTC Publications, Ltd.

coupons are losing their value because so many manufacturers are offering them, and consumers have therefore learned not to buy without some incentive, whether it be a coupon, a rebate or a refund. There has been a general decline in brand loyalty among heavy coupon users. In addition, many consumers redeem coupons only for products they normally buy. Studies have shown that about 75 per cent of coupons are redeemed by people who already use the brand on the coupon. So, as an incentive to use a new brand or product, coupons have questionable success. Another problem with coupons is that stores often do not have enough of the coupon item in stock. This situation can generate ill-will towards both the store and the product.[34]

Although the use of coupons as a sales promotion technique is expected to grow in the next few years, marketers' concerns about their effectiveness could well diminish their appeal. However, coupons will probably remain a major sales promotion component for stimulating trial of new products. Coupons will also be used to increase the frequency of purchase for established products that show sluggish sales. On the other hand, successful, established products may be reducing their profits if 75 per cent of the coupons are redeemed by brand loyal customers.[35]

Demonstrations of products at dealers, retailers, or trade shows are excellent attention-getters. Manufacturers often use them to show how a product actually works in order to encourage trial use and purchase of the product. Because labour costs can be extremely high, demonstrations are not widely used. They can, however, be highly effective for promoting certain types of products, such as appliances, cosmetics and cars. Cosmetics marketers, such as those for Estée Lauder, sometimes offer potential customers "makeovers" to demonstrate their products' benefits and proper application.

Many companies develop **frequent user incentives** to reward customers who engage in repeat purchases. For example, most major international airlines offer a frequent flier programme through which customers who have flown a specified number of miles are rewarded with free tickets for additional travel. Air Miles takes this concept further, extending it across many products. Supermarket loyalty cards are another popular incentive. A **loyalty card** offers discounts or free merchandise to regular customers. Thus frequent user incentives help foster customer loyalty to a specific company or group of co-operating companies that provides extra incentives for patronage. Marketing Insight 17.1 describes Tesco's very successful loyalty card. Frequent user incentives have also been used by service businesses, such as car hire companies, hotels and credit card companies, as well as by marketers of consumer goods. (See Figure 17.6.)

An older frequent user incentive is trading stamps. **Trading stamps** are dispensed in proportion to the amount of a consumer's purchase and can be accumulated and redeemed for goods. Retailers use trading stamps to attract consumers to specific stores. Stamps are attractive to consumers as long as they do not drive up the price of goods. They are effective for many types of retailers. Trading stamps were very popular in the 1960s, but their use as a sales promotion method declined dramatically in the 1970s. However, Green Shield stamps made a comeback, and petrol retailers are now offering in-house stamps redeemable for limited collections of goods.

Point-of-sale (P-O-S) materials include such items as outside signs, window displays, counter pieces, display racks and self-service cartons. Innovations in P-O-S displays include sniff teasers, which give off a product's aroma in the store as consumers walk within a radius of four feet, and computerised interactive displays, which ask a series of multiple choice questions and then display informa-

---

Demonstrations Occasions at which manufacturers show how a product actually works in order to encourage trial use and purchase of the product

Frequent user incentives Incentive programmes that reward customers who engage in repeat purchases

Loyalty card A mechanism whereby regular customers who remain loyal to a particular company are rewarded with discounts or free merchandise

Trading stamps Stamps, dispensed in proportion to the amount of a consumer's purchase, that can be accumulated and redeemed for goods

Point-of-sale (P-O-S) materials Enhancements designed to increase sales and introduce products, such as outside signs, window displays, counter pieces, display racks and self-service cartons

Tesco Moves Ahead with the Help of Clubcard

Not too long ago Green Shield trading stamps were the most widely encountered frequent user sales promotion. Today, it is the loyalty card. The current wave was instigated by the petrol forecourts, which offer points with petrol towards prizes or catalogue merchandise. In 1995 supermarket giant Tesco introduced its loyalty card, the Tesco Clubcard, to ridicule by competitors. Tremendously successful, the cards have accordingly increased the number of Tesco shoppers, and in 1996 the company overtook arch rival Sainsbury's as the number one grocery retailer in the UK. Not resting on its laurels, Tesco surprised many of its rivals—including Sainsbury's—which by then had introduced their own loyalty cards, by launching Clubcard Plus.

Within a year the original Clubcard had 6.5 million regular customers who used their cards to earn discounts against their spending. Clubcard Plus goes further: it offers holders interest paid on their balances and can be used like any other debit card. This move into financial services is not new. Marks & Spencer has a very successful division handling its payment card, which now also sells PEPs and pensions. Once a music business, now a hotelier and airline, Virgin sells life insurance and other financial services on the back of its highly visible and reputable brand name. The difference with Tesco is that instead of using its brand name to sell financial services, it is using its loyalty card based financial product to sell its brand name and successful chain of supermarkets.

Tesco's Clubcard has enabled the company to overtake its rivals and has, analysts believe, increased the frequency of shopping visits to Tesco stores. Within twelve months of being launched, the Clubcard had become the most popular loyalty scheme in the UK, ahead of the more established schemes run by companies such as Esso and Air Miles. Thanks also to operators like Shell with its Smart Card and the widely accepted Air Miles, it is expected that by the start of the millennium, most UK consumers will be enrolled in one or more of the leading loyalty card schemes, making available to the schemes' marketers a wealth of demographic, lifestyle and spending data. The opportunities for more carefully honed target marketing are thereby much increased.

The loyalty card has proved to be a major success story and not only as a sales promotion tool, particularly for Tesco. By 1999, Tesco's stores accounted for over 15 per cent of all UK grocery shopping, and the company held a 4 per cent lead over its closest competitor, Sainsbury's. Moves into direct home delivery and web based shopping reflect the continued innovative approach taken by Tesco's marketers. Some research reveals that shoppers' wallets are over spilling, with too many loyalty cards causing some dissonance. As with all products, it will be the most appropriately targeted and defined loyalty cards—such as Clubcard—which retain customer loyalty.

SOURCES: David Benardy, "Tesco plays its Clubcard right", *Marketing Week*, 3 November 1995, pp. 30–31; "Tesco's Clubcard tops loyalty", *Marketing*, 25 May 1995, p. 4; Martin Croft, "It's all in the cards", *Marketing Week*, 24 March 1995; Anthony Bailey, "There's lolly in your trolley", *Independent on Sunday*, 9 June 1996, p. IB18.; Tesco Annual Report, 1999.

tion on a screen to help consumers make a product decision.[36] IKEA stores offer interactive monitors on which room layouts and colour combinations may be tested prior to purchases. These items, which are often supplied by producers, attract attention, inform customers and encourage retailers to carry particular products. A retailer is likely to use point-of-sale materials if they are attractive, informative, well constructed and in harmony with the store. With two-thirds of all purchases resulting from in-store decisions, P-O-S materials can help sustain incremental sales if a brand's essential components—brand name, positioning and visual image—are the basis of the P-O-S display.[37]

A survey of retail store managers indicated that almost 90 per cent believed that P-O-S materials sell products. The retailers surveyed also said that P-O-S is essential for product introductions. Different forms of display materials are carried by different types of retailers. Convenience stores, for example, favour window banners and "shelf talkers" (on-the-shelf displays or signs), whereas chain chemists prefer floor stands and devices that provide samples.[38]

Figure 17.6 Sales promotion. Examples of sales promotions, including competitions, loyalty schemes and discount coupons.

Free samples Give-aways used to stimulate trial of a product, to increase sales volume in the early stages of a product's life cycle or to obtain desirable distribution

Free samples of merchandise are used for several reasons: to stimulate trial of a product, to increase sales volume in the early stages of a product's life cycle or to obtain desirable distribution. The sampling programme should be planned as a total event, not merely a give-away.[39] Sampling is the most expensive of all sales promotion methods; production and distribution through such channels as mail delivery, door-to-door delivery, in-store distribution and on-package distribution entail very high costs. In designing a free sample, marketers should consider factors such as the seasonality of the product, the characteristics of the market and prior advertising. Free samples are not appropriate for mature products and products with a slow turnover.

Money refunds A specific amount of money mailed to customers who submit proof of purchase

With **money refunds**, consumers submit proof of purchase and are mailed a specific amount of money. Usually, manufacturers demand multiple purchases of the product before a consumer can qualify for a refund. For example, Panasonic marketed a line of VHS tapes that featured a £1 rebate per tape for up to 12 purchases. A customer had to send in the sales receipt and a proof of purchase from inside each tape package. This method, used primarily to promote trial use of a product, is relatively inexpensive. Nevertheless, because money refunds sometimes generate a low response rate, they have limited impact on sales.

One of the problems with money refunds or rebates is that many people perceive the redemption process as too complicated. Consumers also have negative perceptions of manufacturers' reasons for offering rebates. They may believe that these are new, untested products or products that have not sold well. If these perceptions are not changed, rebate offers may degrade the image and desirability of the product being promoted. If the promotion objective in the rebate offer is to increase sales, an effort should be made to simplify the redemption process and proof of purchase requirements.[40]

Premiums Items offered free or at minimum cost as a bonus for purchasing a product

Premiums are items offered free or at minimum cost as a bonus for purchasing a product. Vidal Sassoon offered a free, on-pack 50 ml "travel size" container of shampoo with its 200 ml size of Salon Formula shampoo. Kellogg's offered easy art books with its Variety Packs. Premiums can attract competitors' customers, introduce different sizes of established products, add variety to other promotional efforts and stimulate loyalty. Inventiveness is necessary, however; if an offer is to stand out and achieve a significant number of redemptions, the premium must be matched to both the target audience and the brand's image.[41] To be effective, premiums must be easily recognisable and desirable. Premiums are usually distributed through retail outlets or the mail, but they may also be placed on or in packages. Case 17.2 relates the sorry tale of Hoover's free flight promotion.

Price-off offers give buyers a certain amount off the regular price shown on the label or package. Similar to coupons, this method can be a strong incentive for trying the product; it can stimulate product sales, yield short lived sales increases and promote products in off-seasons. It is an easy method to control and is used frequently for specific purposes. However, if used on an ongoing basis, it reduces the price to customers who would buy at the regular price and frequent use of price-off offers may cheapen a product's image. In addition, the method often requires special handling by retailers.

Consumer contests encourage individuals to compete for prizes based on their analytical or creative skill. This method generates traffic at the retail level. Marriott and Hertz co-sponsored a scratch-card contest with a golf theme to boost sales during the slow winter travel season. Contestants received game cards when they checked in at a Marriott hotel or hired a Hertz car and scratched off spots to see if they had won prizes, such as cars, holidays or golf clubs.[42] However, marketers should exercise care in setting up a contest. Problems or errors may anger consumers or result in legal action. Contestants are usually more involved in consumer contests than they are in sweepstakes (see below), even though the total participation may be lower. Contests may be used in conjunction with other sales promotion methods, such as coupons.

The entrants in a **consumer sweepstake** submit their names for inclusion in a draw for prizes. Sweepstakes are used to stimulate sales and, as with contests, are sometimes teamed with other sales promotion methods. Sweepstakes are used more often than consumer contests and tend to attract a greater number of participants. The cost of a sweepstake is considerably less than the cost of a contest.[43] Successful sweepstakes or competitions can generate widespread interest and short term increases in sales or market share.

Trade Sales Promotion Methods

Producers use sales promotion methods to encourage resellers, especially retailers and dealers, to carry their products and promote them effectively. The methods include buy back allowances, buying allowances, counts and re-counts, free merchandise, merchandise allowances, co-operative advertising, dealer listings, premium or push money, sales contests and dealer loaders.

A **buy back allowance** is a certain sum of money given to a purchaser for each unit bought after an initial deal is over. This method is a secondary incentive in which the total amount of money that resellers can receive is proportional to their purchases during an initial trade deal, such as a coupon offer. Buy back allowances foster co-operation during an initial sales promotion effort and stimulate re-purchase afterwards. The main drawback of this method is its expense.

A **buying allowance** is a temporary price reduction to resellers for purchasing specified quantities of a product. A soap producer, for example, might give retailers £1 for each case of soap purchased. Such offers may be an incentive to handle a new product, achieve a temporary price reduction or stimulate the purchase of an item in larger than normal quantities. The buying allowance, which takes the form of money, yields profits to resellers and is simple and straightforward to

Price-off offers A method of encouraging customers to buy a product by offering a certain amount off the regular price shown on the label or package

Consumer contests Contests designed to generate traffic at the retail level in which consumers compete for prizes based on their analytical or creative skill

Consumer sweepstakes A method of stimulating sales in which consumers submit their names for inclusion in a draw for prizes

Buy back allowance A certain sum of money given to a purchaser for each unit bought after an initial deal is over

Buying allowance A temporary price reduction given to resellers who purchase specified quantities of a product

use. There are no restrictions on how resellers use the money, which increases the method's effectiveness.

The **count and re-count** promotion method is based on the payment of a specific amount of money for each product unit moved from a reseller's warehouse in a given time period. Units of a product are counted at the start of the promotion and again at the end to determine how many have moved from the warehouse. This method can reduce retail stock-outs by moving inventory out of warehouses and can also clear distribution channels of obsolete products or packages and reduce warehouse inventories. The count and re-count method might benefit a producer by decreasing resellers' inventories, making resellers more likely to place new orders. However, this method is often difficult to administer and may not appeal to resellers who have small warehouses.

Free merchandise is sometimes offered to resellers who purchase a stated quantity of the same or different products. Occasionally, free merchandise is used as payment for allowances provided through other sales promotion methods. To avoid handling and bookkeeping problems, the usual method of giving away merchandise free is by reducing the invoice.

A **merchandise allowance** is a manufacturer's agreement to pay resellers certain amounts of money for providing special promotional efforts, such as advertising or displays. This method is best suited to high volume, high profit, easily handled products. One major problem with using merchandise allowances is that some retailers or dealers perform their activities at a minimally acceptable level simply to obtain the allowances. Before paying retailers or dealers, manufacturers usually verify their performance. Manufacturers hope that the retailers' or dealers' additional promotional efforts will yield substantial sales increases.

Co-operative advertising is an arrangement whereby a manufacturer agrees to pay a certain amount of a retailer's or dealer's media costs for advertising the manufacturer's products. The amount allowed is usually based on the quantities purchased. Before payment is made, a retailer or dealer must show proof that advertisements did appear. These payments give retailers or dealers additional funds for advertising. They can, however, put a severe burden on the producer's advertising budget. Some retailers or dealers exploit co-operative advertising programmes by crowding too many products into one advertisement. Some retailers or dealers cannot afford to advertise; others can afford it but do not want to advertise. Still others actually put out advertising that qualifies for an allowance but are not willing to undertake the paperwork required for reimbursement from producers.[44]

A **dealer listing** is an advertisement that promotes a product and identifies the names of participating retailers or dealers who sell the product. Dealer listings can influence retailers or dealers to carry the product, build traffic at the retail level and encourage consumers to buy the product at participating dealers.

Premium or **push money** is used to push a line of goods by providing additional compensation/remuneration to salespeople. This promotion method is appropriate when personal selling is an important part of the marketing effort; it is not effective for promoting products that are sold through self-service. Although this method often helps a manufacturer obtain commitment from the salesforce, it can also be very expensive.

Sales contests are designed to motivate distributors, retailers and sales personnel by recognising and rewarding outstanding achievements. The Colt Car Company, importer of Japanese made Mitsubishi cars, designed a sales contest that offered dealers an incentive trip for two to Barbados if they improved their

---

Count and re-count A promotion method based on the payment of a specific amount of money for each product unit moved from a reseller's warehouse in a given time period

Free merchandise Give-aways sometimes offered to resellers who purchase a stated quantity of the same or different products

Merchandise allowance A manufacturer's agreement to pay resellers certain amounts of money for providing special promotional efforts, such as advertising or displays

Co-operative advertising An arrangement whereby a manufacturer agrees to pay a certain amount of a retailer's or dealer's media costs for advertising the manufacturer's products

Dealer listing An advertisement that promotes a product and identifies the names of participating retailers or dealers who sell it

Premium or **push money** Additional compensation/remuneration provided to salespeople in order to push a line of goods

Sales contest A way to motivate distributors, retailers and sales personnel by recognising and rewarding outstanding achievements

sales figures by 10 to 12 per cent. Approximately 50 per cent of the dealers met this sales goal and won the trip.[45] To be effective, this method must be equitable for all sales personnel involved. One advantage of the method is that it can achieve participation at all levels of distribution. However, the results are temporary and prizes are usually expensive.

Dealer loader A gift to a retailer or dealer who purchases a specified quantity of merchandise

Dealer loaders are gifts to a retailer or dealer who purchases a specified quantity of merchandise. Often dealer loaders are used to obtain special display efforts from retailers by offering essential display parts as premiums. For example, a manufacturer might design a display that includes a sterling silver tray as a major component and give the tray to the retailer. Marketers use dealer loaders to obtain new distributors and push larger quantities of goods.

Direct Mail

Direct mail Printed advertising material delivered to a prospective customer's or donor's home or work address

Direct mail and telephone selling are part of the direct marketing category described in Chapter 14. Direct mail is the delivery to the target's home or work address of printed advertising material to contact prospective customers or donors. The use of direct mail to contact prospective customers and to solicit interest in products or services is not new.[46] Advertising agencies, public relations consultancies and in particular sales promotions houses have been using mail shots for several decades. With approximately 6 per cent of all promotional budgets in consumer goods and services, its own professional bodies and trade associations, and the growing sophistication of consumer databases, the direct mail industry believes it warrants recognition as a separate element of the promotional mix alongside advertising, sales promotion, personal selling, publicity and public relations, and sponsorship.[47]

Uses for Direct Mail

Direct mail is not confined to consumers; it is an important promotional activity in many business-to-business markets. Direct mail delivers the promotional message—and sometimes the product—through the postal service, private delivery businesses and the expanding network of in-home fax machines. Direct mail is used to create brand awareness and stimulate product adoption.[48] There is even the growth of direct mail via e-mail addresses. Throughout Europe, direct mail is widely used to generate orders, pre-sell prior to a sales call, qualify prospects for a sales call, screen out non-prospects, follow up a sale, announce special sales and localised selling initiatives, and raise funds for charities and non-profit organisations. In the UK, the average household receives 166 items of direct mail each year (see Table 17.3).

Attention-Seeking Flashes

Junk mail Unwanted mail often binned unread by uninterested recipients

Flashes Headers printed on a direct mail package to gain the recipients' attention

Direct mail packages must prompt the recipient to open them, rather than treat them as **junk mail**—unwanted mail often binned unread by uninterested recipients. "Prize inside", "Your opportunity to win", "Not a circular", "Important documentation enclosed" are just some of the popular headers or **flashes** printed prominently on the address labels to gain the recipients' attention. In some markets, these are sufficient at least to persuade the recipient to open the package. With the boom in direct mail and the growing adverse reaction to junk mail, however, persuasive phrases are often not enough. Packaging design is becoming more important in enticing recipients, through attractive or unusual shapes and designs, to examine the details of the direct mail shot.

Table 17.3 The direct mail industry

a. Direct Mail Advertising—Volume and Expenditure, UK

	Volume Items (million)			Expenditure, £m		
	Consumer Items	Business Items	Total Items	Production Costs	Postage Costs	Total Costs
1986	976	425	1,401	325	149	474
1987	1,161	465	1,626	300	183	483
1988	1,221	545	1,766	326	204	530
1989	1,445	672	2,117	485	273	758
1990	1,544	728	2,272	633	297	930
1991	1,435	687	2,122	605	290	895
1992	1,658	588	2,246	603	342	945
1993	1,772	664	2,436	552	352	904
1994	2,015	715	2,730	646	404	1,050
1995	2,198	707	2,905	673	462	1,135
1996	2,436	737	3,173	904	500	1,404
1997	2,626	794	3,420	984	556	1,540

b. Direct Mail Costs, UK

The average British household receives 12.8 items of direct mail every four weeks. Direct mail is defined as personally addressed advertising that is delivered through the post. Direct mail suppliers will provide quotations on request. Prices can vary dramatically with volume and type of material. Specimen charges range as follows:

Service	Approx. Cost per '000
List rental cost by type:	
Consumer list (responders/purchasers)	£90
Consumer lifestyle database	£90
Electoral register—geodemographic selection	£90
Named subscribers to business magazines	£150
Companies classified by SIC code	£90
Laser printing	£12–£20
Inserting: 1–2 items by machine	£9–£14
3–4 items by machine	£14–£20

c. Senders of Consumer Direct Mail, 1997

	Percentage of Total Consumer Volume		Percentage of Total Consumer Volume
Mail order	14.6	Book clubs	3.5
Retail/store cards	11.1	Magazines/papers	3.0
		Readers Digest	2.0
Insurance	10.9	Building societies	1.9
Banks	10.7	Government/ local authorities	1.0
Charities	8.3		
Manufacturers	5.7	Education	0.4
Utilities	5.5	Others[1]	21.4

Note: [1]Includes entertainment and travel.

SOURCE: *The Marketing Pocket Book 1996* and *The European Marketing Pocket Book 1999*, pp. 125, 153. Reprinted by permission of NTC Publications, Ltd.

The Package

Direct mail package A mix of mailing envelope, covering or explanatory letter, circular, response device and return device

The **direct mail package** is more than just the envelope. Often it is a mix of mailing envelope, covering or explanatory letter, circular, response device and return device. The mailing envelope has to overcome the recipients' inertia, often through catchy flashes and design flair. The letter needs to be personalised and clear, appeal to the beliefs and lifestyle of the recipients and elicit interest in the product or service in question. The circular contains the service or product details and specifications: colour, sizes, capabilities, prices, photographs or illustrations, and guarantees and endorsements from satisfied customers or personalities. The circular is the primary selling tool in the pack and often takes the form of a booklet, broadsheet, jumbo folder, brochure or flyer. The response device is typically an order form, which must be legally correct, must repeat the selling message and product benefits, must be simple to read and fill out and comprehensive in the information requested. Alternatively, the response device can be an 0800 Freephone telephone number or credit card hotline. The return device is any mechanism that enables the recipient to respond with an order or donation. It can be an information request form, order form or payment slip and is usually accompanied by a pre-printed—and often pre-paid—return envelope.

Mailing Lists

Mailing lists Directories of suitable, relevant recipients or targets

Eighty per cent of direct mail is opened: only 63 per cent is partially read; less still leads to an order or donation. Depending on the scale of the targeted audience, however, the costs are relatively low: design, printing, postage and the purchase or compilation of **mailing lists**—directories of suitable, relevant recipients or targets. To be effective, appropriate targeting of direct mail is essential. Mailing lists must be as up-to-date as possible. There is a rule of thumb in the industry that one-third of addresses on a list change each year owing to deaths and re-locations. Within a year or two a list can be obsolete. Internal lists are those compiled in-house from customer addresses, account details and records of enquiries. External lists are produced by list brokers or mailing houses and are bought—or rented—at commercial rates.

The suppliers of these external lists often undertake the complete direct mail operation for clients, from identification of recipients and compilation of lists to production of printed material, postage and even receipt of response devices. External lists can be either addresses of product category customers, including those of competing businesses if available, or general lists of targets with apparently suitable demographic profiles and lifestyles. Many of the leading geodemographic databases, such as ACORN or MOSAIC, were originally developed to assist in the targeting of direct mail. The Post Office can also be a good data source (see Figure 17.7).

Copy Writing

Copy writing The creation and wording of the promotional message

The targeting does not stop with the acquisition of a mailing list. The printed and product material included in the direct mail package must be written, designed and produced to appeal to the targets. The material must be prepared by people who understand the emotions and attitudes of the prospective customers. **Copy writing**, the creation and wording of the promotional message, is an important skill in the promotional mix, especially in the production of direct mail. The text must appeal to the target audience; sell the product; re-assure the reader; be informative, clear and concise; and lead to a positive response.

Strengths and Weaknesses of Direct Mail

There are many advantages associated with direct mail. The medium offers a wide variety of styles and formats—more than offered by a radio or press advertisement, for example. The package can be personalised and customised. Often it will be received and read alone, not in competition with other promotions from

Figure 17.7 Collecting data. The Royal Mail promotes a range of services to the marketing research and direct mail industries, emphasising its comprehensive and up-to-date databases.
SOURCE: Courtesy of Royal Mail/Bates UK.

other products and services. Extensive and detailed information can be included, much more than with advertising, and product samples may be integral to the direct mail package. Marketing research and database management can lead to accurate targeting of direct mail. Sending material directly to people's homes and workplaces can hit targets otherwise inaccessible to promotional activity.

The primary disadvantage is the growing consumer view that direct mail is junk mail that should be consigned to the dustbin without even being opened. If used on a large scale, direct mail can prove costly—perhaps less so than a sales-force or television advertising, but more expensive than many public relations activities and some local or trade advertising. The direct mail packages and campaigns need to be up-dated to remain fresh in the fight against the junk mail image. In many countries, the paucity of up-to-date mailing lists increases the cost of direct mail, reduces the response rates and adds to consumer dislike of the concept of unsolicited direct selling through the post.

For organisations as diverse as retailer Marks & Spencer, financial services group American Express, catalogue retailer GUS, charity Oxfam, consumer goods manufacturer Unilever or British Airways, direct mail is an important, everyday component of the promotional mix. Whether it is on behalf of the starving in the

Third World, double glazing for windows, fast food or book clubs, direct mail is familiar to consumers in most countries. For office supplies, maintenance services, security, computing products, and raw materials and components, in business-to-business markets direct mail is another important promotional tool, often supporting trade advertising and personal selling campaigns.

The Internet

Internet A network of computer networks stretching across the world, linking computers of different types

A few years ago only computer buffs had accessed the **Internet**—a network of computer networks stretching across the world, linking computers of different types—on a regular basis and mostly for on-line discussions or searches for information. Although these are still popular activities, the information superhighway is currently a major focus of attention for marketers of consumer goods, services, charities and industrial products. As more and more businesses hook up to the Internet and thousands of households daily subscribe to Internet services provided by hosts such as MSN, AOL, CompuServe or BT, the opportunities for interacting with prospective and current customers are immense. By the mid-1990s companies as diverse as Ford, Sony and JCB were providing product and company details on their web pages. A **web site** is a coherent document readable by a web browser, containing simple text or complex hypermedia presentations. At first, these sites tended to be for information purposes rather than overtly promotional tools or selling opportunities. BMW was one of the first businesses to spot the opportunity for selling on the web, creating a directory of used cars available from its network of independent dealerships. A major hindrance to on-line sales and marketing of consumer goods and services was consumer concern about the security of making purchases on-line. Web hosts and credit card companies had to invest in technology that allowed scrambling and coding of confidential credit card or bank account information before consumers were prepared to make on-line purchases.

Web site A coherent document readable by a web browser, containing simple text or complex hypermedia presentations

E-commerce The use of the Internet for commercial transactions

By 1998, five million purchases were made on-line in the UK, worth an estimated £500 million.[49] This figure is likely to be the start of a massive increase in **e-commerce,** the use of the Internet for commercial transactions. Arch rivals Microsoft and Yahoo are both now targeting the small business sector. BizTalk from Microsoft and Fusion Marketing Online from Yahoo offer small businesses a ready-made one-stop e-commerce platform to enable businesses too small to create their own web sites and e-commerce departments to communicate and sell via the web.

As more and more households connect to the Internet through increasing numbers of connections worldwide (see Table 17.4), confidence in using this medium for transactions is growing. This is not uniform across all consumers. Just as with any new product (see Chapter 15), there are innovators, early adopters and the early majority, while others are resistant to this new way of conducting business or simply do not have the equipment, expertise or available resources to hook up. Research indicates that there are signs that older consumers, the less affluent and the less educated are now accessing the web. Leading research company NOP predicted that "Internet use will clearly be a mass market activity by the beginning of the millennium". In 1997, seven million people in Britain accessed the Internet, a figure which rose to 11 million in 1998.[50]

As an ingredient in the promotional mix, there is no doubt that the Internet is of growing importance. While this is not yet true for all countries—see Table

		Connections Worldwide (Adjusted)	Domain	Replied to Ping[1]
1995	January	5,846,000	71,000	970,000
	July	8,200,000	120,000	1,149,000
1996	January	14,352,000	240,000	1,682,000
	July	16,729,000	488,000	2,569,000
1997	January	21,819,000	828,000	3,392,000
	July	26,053,000	1,301,000	4,314,410
1998	January	29,670,000	—	5,331,640
	July	36,739,000	—	6,529,000

Notes: In August 1981 there were 213 Internet connections. [1]Estimated by pinging 1% of all hosts.

SOURCE: *Marketing Pocket Book 1999* (Henley-on-Thames: NTC Publications, 1998), p. 156. Reprinted by permission.

Number of Internet hosts by country

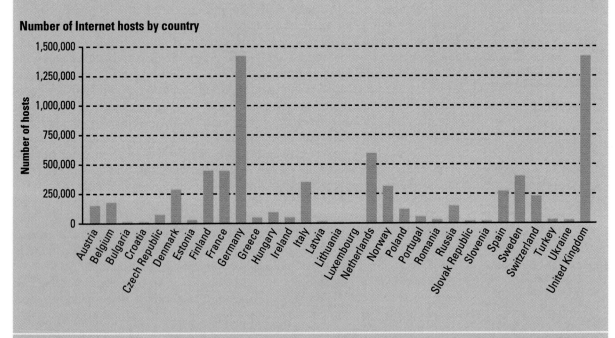

Note: Survey is based on domain name country codes (.uk,.de, etc.), There is not necessarily any correlation between this code and where a host is actually located.

SOURCE: *European Marketing Pocket Book, 1999*, p. 20. Reprinted by permission of NTC Publications, Ltd.

Table 17.4 The growth of the Internet

17.4—it is a trend most observers expect to continue with the associated rapid growth of e-commerce. Few major brands do not have their own web pages. Most television and press advertisements direct consumers to web addresses for further information or ordering facilities. Packaging for many consumer products signals the presence of a web site. CD retailer Boxman launched in 1999 with a fanfare of publicity announcing the arrival of this on-line music retailer (see

Marketing Insight 17.2). Boxman has opted to trade entirely via the Internet. Television advertisements told the story of how time consuming and inconvenient it is to leave home to purchase the latest chart hit from a traditional city centre music store. Instead, music lovers were encouraged to log on and buy via Boxman's web site. Publisher Random House used its web site to offer discount vouchers for its titles, redeemable in branches of bookseller Waterstone's. Florist Interflora promoted its on-line booking service ahead of Mother's Day.

The Internet enables frequent and customised changes of messages targeted at specific consumers. If linked to e-mail access, it also enables the consumer to have ready access to the site host, leading to an ongoing and evolving relationship between marketer and customer.[51] Internal marketing has also befriended the web, with **intranet** in-company Internet networks facilitating routine communications, fostering group communications, providing uniform computer applications, distributing the latest software, or informing colleagues of marketing developments and new product launches.

There is a clear process for developing a web site, from the planning of the site's goals, analysis of the required content, design and build of the site, implementation using hypertext mark-up language (HTML) and development to ensure that once up and running the site reflects user views and is regularly updated.[52] To be effective, a web site must contain information perceived relevant and interesting by a company's targeted customers. Marketers should ensure that their particular targeted customers are in fact prepared and able to access the Internet. The pages of the site need to be stylish and eye catching but easy to interpret. Web site branding and imagery must be consistent with the brand positioning of existing products, the product's packaging and other promotional mix executions such as advertising and sales promotion materials. The web site's ethos should not contradict the work of the rest of the marketing mix or the product's heritage. The information on the web site should be regularly and accurately up-dated and tailored carefully to reflect the buying behaviour of the targeted customer. As with any marketing activity, the web site needs to be designed to be memorable and distinctive. Far from being a minor task, marketers have realised recently that web site design is a specialised activity which requires the skills of a qualified web master and the careful design of material to reflect the characteristics of the product, the brand and of the intended consumer.

> **Intranet** Internal, in-company Internet networks for routine communications, fostering group communications, providing uniform computer applications, distributing the latest software, or informing colleagues of marketing developments and new product launches

Direct Marketing

So far this chapter has examined personal selling, sales promotion, direct mail and the Internet. To conclude, the chapter turns to one of the "in" concepts: direct marketing. First used in the 1960s, until its recent popularity direct marketing described the most common direct marketing approaches: direct mail and mail order. Now direct marketing encompasses all the communications tools which enable a marketer to deal directly with targeted customers: direct mail, telemarketing, direct response television advertising, door-to-door/personal selling and the Internet. Increasingly marketers are utilising the direct marketing toolkit to do more than simply generate sales, although sales generation remains the foremost task for direct marketers.

Direct marketing is a decision by a company's marketers to (1) select a marketing channel which avoids dependence on marketing channel intermediaries, and (2) focus marketing communications activity on promotional mix ingredients which deal directly with targeted customers. The American Direct Marketing

> **Direct marketing** A decision by a company's marketers to select a marketing channel which avoids dependence on marketing channel intermediaries and to focus marketing communications activity on promotional mix ingredients which deal directly with targeted customers

Association defines direct marketing as "an interactive system of marketing which uses one or more 'advertising' media to effect a measurable response and/or transaction at any location". This definition raises some important aspects. (1) Direct marketing is an interactive system. Advertising communicates via a mass medium such as television or the press. Direct marketing contacts targeted consumers directly, can tailor messages to the individual and solicits direct feedback. This interactive, one-to-one communication is essential to the definition of direct marketing. (2) The American Direct Marketing Association's definition uses the term *advertising*. It really should be *communication*[53] in its broader sense, as direct marketing utilises personal selling, direct mail, technology—telephone, fax and the Internet—plus direct response advertising containing coupon response or Freephone elements. (3) Most ingredients of the promotional mix, particularly advertising and public relations, find it difficult to accurately measure responses and effectiveness. This is not the case with direct marketing: the interactive nature of the communication enables individual consumer responses to be tracked. (4) Direct marketers do not utilise retail outlets, wholesale depots or industrial distributors. They do not depend on potential customers visiting their own retail outlet or depot: they can contact consumers at home or at work via direct mail, telephone or fax, and increasingly via Internet links.

Direct marketing evolved from those mail order businesses—Littlewoods, GUS, Grattan—which developed catalogues and mail shots to customers in order to sell directly from their warehouses, negating the need for retail outlets and showrooms.[54] They were joined by a diverse mix of businesses—from factory outlets, to machine tool companies to specialist food producers—which wished to sell directly to consumers. In order to achieve these aims, these businesses had to devise marketing communications tools which attracted sufficient numbers of the right types of customers who would choose to deal directly with them, rather than buying from the more traditional marketing intermediaries in the marketing channel. The agents, brokers, dealers, distributors, wholesalers and retailers were cut out of the choice of distribution channel. Although mail order sales declined in the 1980s, towards the end of that decade the major operators revitalised their fortunes and were joined by mail order operations from major retailers such as Marks & Spencer—with its home furnishings catalogue—and the Next Directory. Ubiquitous telephone access has helped facilitate mail order operations, and the recent rapid growth in home computer Internet access has provided a further growth spurt.

Direct marketing is now adopted by a host of businesses ranging from fast moving consumer goods companies, business-to-business marketers, charities and even government departments.[55] Of all elements of the promotional mix, it is reported to be the fastest growing, but this is partly a reflection of the large number of promotional mix ingredients which it includes,[56] such as direct mail, teleselling and the Internet. Various factors have contributed to this growth, as detailed in Figure 17.8. A desire by marketers to identify alternative media and promotional tools, the need to improve targeting of potential customers, improvements in marketing data and databases, advances in technology and systems permitting cost effective direct and interactive contact with certain types of consumers—all have encouraged the growth of direct marketing.

In terms of the promotional mix, there are several key implications. (1) Direct mail is on the increase. Eighty-three per cent of the largest 1,500 UK companies expect to deploy more direct mail in the new millennium, with the bulk focusing on prospecting for sales rather than responding to direct response advertising

Boxman Takes Music Sales to the Internet

Marketers all over the world are getting to grips with selling over the Internet. Current estimates by Webdo Geneva indicate that by the year 2000 this exciting new medium had between 300 million and one billion users accessing 1.5 million different web sites. More importantly, a recent study by American investment bank Morgan Stanley has suggested that in the next five years or so, approximately 5 per cent of world retail trade and 11 per cent of business-to-business transactions will be conducted on the Internet.

The best Internet selling opportunities look likely to be in the areas of financial services, travel, books and software, but sales of video and music products also have considerable potential. Globally, the sector is already buoyant, with thousands of different sites selling on-line CDs. In 1997, Internet sales accounted for around £17.6m, just 0.1 per cent of the global market. According to Market Tracking International, by 2005 the figure will have reached £2.4bn, over 7 per cent of the global market. This follows a time when growth for the music industry generally has flattened out. In 1997 worldwide music sales of £23.3bn had increased a mere 2 per cent on the previous year. With many emerging markets hitting economic crisis and the massive US market experiencing a 3 per cent fall, future prospects were not particularly encouraging.

Boxman is one of the music companies which aims to capitalise on Internet selling opportunities. According to its web site, Boxman is a music retail company which intends "to sell more music to more people, faster, cheaper and more conveniently through the new possibility provided by the Internet". Boxman sees the Internet as a means for reaching a mass market through mass communications to sell mass products. The company hopes that it will be able to satisfy the needs of consumers with a diverse mix of musical tastes, whether or not they are currently familiar with the Internet. Boxman believes that in the longer term all consumers will become accustomed to using the Internet and that it will capture sales by offering six key values:

- *Simplicity:* the web site is easy to navigate and simple to use, so that consumers can find, pay for and receive their requirements with ease.

- *Speed:* Boxman is sympathetic to the relatively high costs of Internet connections in Europe, so use of the site and receipt of the music are high speed.
- *Ease of use:* through its technical collaboration with IBM, Boxman has provided a site which is easily accessible and which communicates effectively with even the most inexperienced Internet user.
- *Value:* savings achieved by avoiding the usual distribution costs associated with the sale of music are shared with Boxman customers. For example, a chart product sold in the high street for £14.00, is available for just £10.00 from Boxman.
- *Security:* the company is aware of consumer concerns about security, particularly in relation to Internet sites. Boxman offers consumers security in the sophisticated payment system it uses and also by being a local service located in the UK which complies with required legal and fiscal obligations, through its innovative and credible brand name and by ensuring delivery in a short time and using excellent packing conditions.
- *Real added value:* Boxman has a clearly stated intention of offering the consumer access to a diverse mix of music at competitive prices from the comfort of home. According to the web site, "Boxman is an attitude, a clever way of life, which is simple, practical and current".

The Internet is a new and relatively untried media so estimates of the size of marketing opportunities on offer vary. Whether or not Boxman will be able to maintain its leading position in the European on-line market remains to be seen. However, most sources agree that for Internet music sales, the only way to go is up.

SOURCES: Matthew Reed, "Online sales go uptempo", *Marketing,* 7 January 1999, pp. 23–24; Philip Rooke, "Production must take backseat on the Internet", *Marketing Week,* 11 March 1999, p. 30; "Why Net music is poised to hit the high notes", *Marketing Week,* 25 February 1999, p. 40; **www.boxman.co.uk**.

Figure 17.8 Catalysts of change behind the growth of direct marketing. SOURCE: Lisa O'Malley, Maurice Patterson, and Martin Evans, *Exploring Direct Marketing*. Copyright © 1999. Reprinted with permission.

requests for brochures or catalogues. (2) Telemarketing has grown and will continue to do so as more businesses turn to the direct marketing toolkit aided by advances in automated call centres. (3) Personal selling has suffered in the past from poorly identified sales targeting, but better geodemographic targeting and improved analysis of direct marketing responses are enabling more focused use of personal selling. (4) Door-to-door selling and leaflet dropping are also on the increase and are visible forms of direct marketing encountered by most householders. (5) In 1989 direct response advertising—containing a call for action within the advertisement either by coupon or telephone—accounted for less than one-fifth of advertising revenue. Now the figure is closer to one-third as marketers increasingly jump on the direct marketing "band wagon" and as the growth in satellite and cable television channels enables more direct response television advertising. (6) The most obvious implication is for use of the Internet to communicate with current and prospective customers. As more and more consumers hook up to the Internet either at home or at work, the opportunity is growing for marketers to communicate directly with consumers with increasingly bespoke messages. Table 17.5 presents an indication of the growth of direct marketing promotional activity.

It is important to remember, however, that—as with all marketing propositions and promotional mix executions—to be welcomed by targeted customers and effective in terms of generating sales, the deployment of any direct marketing

Table 17.5 Direct marketing expenditure and responses

EXPENDITURE ON DIRECT MARKETING

	1992	1993	1994	1995	1996	1997
						£ million
Direct mail[1]	945	904	1,050	1,135	1,404	1,540
Door-to-door distribution	300	310	317	327	—	—
Telemarketing	62	75	90	108	—	—
Total	1,307	1,289	1,457	1,570	—	—

Note: [1]At current prices.

DIRECT MARKETING RESPONSE RATES

	Response Rate (%)	Cost per Item (pence)	Number of Campaigns	Average Campaign Size, '000s
Consumer campaigns				
Direct mail	7.4	49	554	206
Door drops	0.9	9	39	1,165
Inserts	0.6	4	60	482
Press	0.3	3	23	1,348
Business campaigns				
Direct mail	4.0	66	577	26
Door drops	0.1	6	9	407
Inserts	0.8	7	28	56
Press	0.3	23	19	80

Note: All data weighted by volume mailed.

SOURCE: *Marketing Pocket Book 1999*, pp. 124, 155. Reprinted by permission of NTC Publications, Ltd.

campaign must strive to reflect targeted customer behaviour, needs and perceptions; provide a plausible proposition which is clearly differentiated from competitors' propositions; and match an organisation's corporate goals and trading philosophy. Direct marketing is not a substitute for marketing practice *per se,* nor for the traditional promotional mix. Direct marketing is an increasingly popular deployment of marketing. It stems from certain marketers' strategic choices in terms of marketing channel and the selection of which promotional mix tactics will best facilitate contact with prospective customers.

● S U M M A R Y

P ersonal selling is the process of informing customers and persuading them to purchase products through personal communication in an exchange situation. Personal selling is the most precise promotional method, but also the most expensive. The three general purposes of personal selling

are finding prospects, convincing them to buy and keeping customers satisfied.

Many salespeople—either consciously or unconsciously—move through a general selling process as they sell products. In *prospecting,* the salesperson develops a list of potential customers. Before contacting acceptable prospects, the salesperson prepares by finding and analysing information about the prospects and their needs. The *approach* is the manner in which a salesperson contacts a potential customer. During the sales presentation, the salesperson must attract and hold the prospect's attention to stimulate interest and desire for the product. If possible, the salesperson should handle a prospect's objections when they arise. *Closing* is the step in the selling process in which the salesperson asks the prospect to buy the product or products. After a successful closing, the salesperson must follow up the sale.

In developing a salesforce, a marketer must decide which types of salespeople will sell the company's products most effectively. The three classifications of salespeople are *order getters, order takers* and *support personnel.* Current customer order getters deal with people who have already purchased a business's products. New business order getters locate prospects and convert them into buyers. Order takers seek repeat sales and fall into two categories: inside order takers and field order takers. Sales support personnel facilitate the selling function, but their duties usually extend beyond making sales. The three types of support personnel are *missionary, trade* and *technical salespeople.*

The effectiveness of salesforce management is an important determinant of a company's success because the salesforce is directly responsible for generating a business's sales revenue. The major decision areas and activities on which sales managers must focus are establishing salesforce objectives, determining salesforce size, recruiting and selecting sales personnel, training sales personnel, compensating/remunerating sales personnel, motivating salespeople, managing sales territories, and controlling and evaluating salesforce performance.

Sales objectives should be stated in precise, measurable terms and should specify the time period, customer type and geographic areas involved. The size of the salesforce must be adjusted from time to time because a business's marketing plans change, as do markets and forces in the marketing environment.

The task of *recruiting* and selecting sales personnel involves attracting and choosing the right type of salespeople to maintain an effective salesforce. When developing a training programme, managers must consider a variety of dimensions, such as who should be trained, what should be taught and how the training should occur. Compensation of salespeople involves formulating and administering a compensation/remuneration plan that attracts, motivates and holds the right types of salespeople for the business. Choices include a *straight salary compensation/remuneration plan,* a *straight commission compensation/remuneration plan* and a *combination compensation/remuneration plan.* Motivation of salespeople should allow the company to attain high productivity. Managing sales territories, another aspect of salesforce management, focuses on such forces as the size and shape of sales territories and the routing and scheduling of salespeople. To control and evaluate salesforce performance, the sales manager must use information obtained through sales personnel's call reports, customer feedback and invoices.

Sales promotion is an activity or material (or both) that acts as a direct inducement and offers added value to or incentive to buy the product to resellers, salespeople or consumers. Marketers use sales promotion to increase sales, to identify and attract new customers, to introduce a new product and to increase reseller inventories. Sales promotion methods fall into two general categories: consumer and trade. *Consumer sales promotion techniques* encourage consumers to buy from specific retail stores or dealerships or to try a specific product. These techniques include *coupons, demonstrations, frequent user incentives*—such as *loyalty cards* or *trading stamps—point-of-sale (P-O-S) materials, free samples, money refunds, premiums, price-off offers,* and *consumer contests* and *sweepstakes. Trade sales promotion methods* stimulate wholesalers, retailers or dealers to carry a producer's products and to market these products aggressively. These techniques include *buy back allowances, buying allowances, counts and re-counts, free merchandise, merchandise allowances, co-operative advertising, dealer listings, premium* or *push money, sales contests* and *dealer loaders.* The *ratchet effect* is the stepped impact of using sales promotion and advertising together.

Direct mail uses the postal service to contact prospective customers or donors and to solicit interest in products or services. The main problem facing the direct mail industry is the growing adverse reaction to it as *junk mail*. Nevertheless, direct mail is widely used for consumer goods and services and also in business-to-business marketing. Increasingly, it is also important to non-profit organisations and charitable fund raising. Direct mail must be carefully designed with an attention-seeking *flash*, good *copy writing* and a well constructed *direct mail package*. *Mailing lists* quickly become obsolete, and good database management is essential for the effective targeting of direct mail shots.

The *Internet*, networked independent computers, is no longer the focus of only computer buffs. Users are multiplying daily, including both consumers and businesses seeking to interact with prospective and current customers. Most businesses now have *web sites* and recognise the potential for *e-commerce*. Scrambling and coding of credit card information has helped build consumer confidence in on-line purchase transactions. Web sites are clearly flagged on much television and print advertising. In-company Internet networks—*intranets*—are enabling rapid dissemination of routine communications, group communications, uniform computer applications, the latest software and information about product developments, and are assisting with internal marketing. Enabling frequent up-dating of messages, individually targeted communications and sales ordering, the Internet now features in many businesses' promotional mixes.

Direct marketing is a decision to do without marketing channel intermediaries and to focus most promotional resources on activities which deal directly with targeted customers, such as personal selling, telemarketing and direct mail. Now adopted by consumer goods producers, services, business-to-business companies, charities and even government departments, direct marketing has recently enjoyed rapid growth. This is likely to continue, with more direct mail, automated call centres, personal selling, door-to-door selling and leaflet dropping, direct response television advertising and use of the Internet to contact potential customers. As with Internet sites, direct marketing must be tailored to suit the behaviour and expectations of the target audience, while reflecting existing branding and other promotional mix designs.

Important Terms

Personal selling
Prospecting
Approach
Closing
Order getters
Order takers
Support personnel
Missionary salespeople
Trade salespeople
Technical salespeople
Recruiting
Straight salary compensation/ remuneration plan
Straight commission compensation/ remuneration plan
Combination compensation/ remuneration plan
Sales promotion
Ratchet effect

Consumer sales promotion techniques
Trade sales promotion methods
Coupons
Demonstrations
Frequent user incentives
Loyalty card
Trading stamps
Point-of-sale (P-O-S) materials
Free samples
Money refunds
Premiums
Price-off offers
Consumer contests
Consumer sweepstakes
Buy back allowance
Buying allowance
Count and re-count

Free merchandise
Merchandise allowance
Co-operative advertising
Dealer listing
Premium or push money
Sales contest
Dealer loader
Direct mail
Junk mail
Flashes
Direct mail package
Mailing lists
Copy writing
Internet
Web site
E-commerce
Intranet
Direct marketing

Discussion and Review Questions

1. What is personal selling? How does personal selling differ from other types of promotional activities?
2. What are the primary purposes of personal selling?
3. Identify the elements of the personal selling process. Must a salesperson include all of these elements when selling a product to a customer? Why or why not?
4. How does a salesperson find and evaluate prospects? Do you find any of these methods ethically questionable?
5. Are order getters more aggressive or creative than order takers? Why or why not?
6. Identify several characteristics of effective sales objectives.
7. How should a sales manager establish criteria for selecting sales personnel? What are the general characteristics of a good salesperson?
8. What major issues or questions should be considered when developing a salesforce training programme?
9. Explain the major advantages and disadvantages of the three basic methods of compensating salespeople. In general, which method do you prefer? Why?
10. What major factors should be taken into account when designing the size and shape of a sales territory?
11. How does a sales manager—who cannot be with each salesperson in the field on a daily basis—control the performance of sales personnel?
12. What is sales promotion? Why is it used?
13. Does sales promotion work well in isolation from the other promotional mix elements?
14. For each of the following, identify and describe three techniques and give several examples: (a) consumer sales promotion techniques, and (b) trade sales promotion methods.
15. What types of sales promotion methods have you observed recently?
16. How does direct mail gain the interest of its recipients?
17. What are the problems facing users of direct mail?
18. Marketers initially viewed the Internet primarily as a means to disseminate product and manufacturer information. What technological advances had to be made before the Internet could be used for selling opportunities?
19. In what ways is direct marketing an "interactive" system? Which marketing channel intermediaries are bypassed due to the nature of this system?

Recommended Readings

D. Bird, *Commonsense Direct Marketing*, 3rd edn (London: Kogan Page, 1999).

J. Cummins, *Sales Promotion: How to Create and Implement Campaigns That Really Work*, 2nd edn (London: Kogan Page, 1998).

G. Lancaster and D. Jobber, *Selling and Sales Management*, 3rd edn (London: Pitman, 1994).

A. C. Semintiras, J. W. Cadogan and G. A. Lancaster, "Salesforce behaviour: in search of motivational determinants", *Industrial Marketing Management*, vol. 25, no. 5, 1996, pp. 1–17.

T. A. Shimp, *Advertising, Promotion, and Supplemental Aspects of Integrated Marketing Communication*, 4th edn (Fort Worth: Dryden Press, 1997).

● C A S E S

17.1 Nintendo Competes through Sales Promotion Efforts

When Hiroshi Yamauchi was 21 years old, he inherited his grandfather's playing card company, Nintendo, Inc., and built it into a videogame empire. By the beginning of the 1990s, Nintendo owned 90 per cent of the videogame business and recorded annual sales of £2.9 billion. For many children, Nintendo's Super Mario character had become more popular than Mickey Mouse. Then, videogame company Sega Systems stormed into the United States and Europe with products and promotions that challenged rival Nintendo head on. In just a few years, Nintendo lost half of its European and American market shares to Sega. The once dominant videogame marketer also found itself scrapping with Sony, PC software developers and the Internet for a piece of the £9½ billion electronic fun industry. To reverse its downward trend, Nintendo turned to numerous sales promotions designed to increase sales and retail visibility and to attract new customers through hands on play.

Billed as the "largest videogame competition in history", Nintendo's *Powerfest* was the company's most lavish sales promotion event ever. The videogame tour—which included 38 free play sampling stations where participants could try new Nintendo games and in-store attractions with premium give-aways and sweepstakes—included cities all over the United States and culminated in a world championship tournament.

From time to time, Nintendo does stage grand scale promotions such as *Powerfest,* but its fundamental strategy is to link specific sales promotions to specific products. To interest kids in the new brightly coloured edition of its hand-held video system, the "Play It Loud" Game Boy, Nintendo held a national promotion called *Made in the Shade.* At company sponsored body painting contests using the game's red, yellow, green and black signature colours, participants sampled the Game Boy system. Those who purchased a Play It Loud Game Boy during the promotion received free Terminator-style sunglasses and an opportunity to buy logo bearing tank tops, caps and beach towels at reduced prices.

To launch its Donkey Kong Country II videogame, Nintendo joined Kellogg's to create a £9½ million promotion that included sweepstakes and premiums. Packages of breakfast cereals contained entries for the Donkey Kong Sweepstakes offering ten thousand prizes, including Nintendo systems and games. Cereal buyers could also find free premiums inside boxes of Corn Flakes, Raisin Bran, and four other Kellogg's cereals. To maintain interest in the game after its introduction, Nintendo unveiled *Banana Bucks,* a sales promotion offering a variety of premiums such as Donkey Kong figurines, clothing and CDs in exchange for points earned when buying Donkey Kong Country. Many retailers offered special Donkey Kong Land phone cards good for 10 minutes of free calls to Nintendo's game tips hotline.

Although Nintendo strongly believes in sales promotions that feature premiums and sweepstakes, company executives are convinced that a videogame's most powerful sales promotion tool is sampling. A teenager who plays a game at a mall display is much more likely to want to own it than a teenager who sees a picture of the game in a magazine ad or on a TV commercial. In the case of Virtual Boy, Nintendo's new portable three-dimensional game system, hands on sampling is essential. Print ads can't display the technology, and even television can't adequately convey the 3-D experience. To give videogame lovers experience with Virtual Boy, Nintendo teamed up with Blockbuster Entertainment for a £3 million sales promotion aimed at offering customers the opportunity to try the Virtual Boy System.

Recent studies indicate that interest in videogames is still high, but with so many competitors battling for market share, experts predict that some companies will not survive. To remain a contender in the industry it almost single handedly created, Nintendo continues to count on successful sales promotion efforts.

SOURCES: World Wide Web, **http://www.nintendo,** 30 January 1996; Terry Lefton, "NBC, Nintendo set fall blockbuster", *Brandweek,* 22 May 1995, p. 6; Joe Mandese and Kate Fitzgerald, "'Virtual' promotion", *Advertising Age,* 22 May 1995, p. 40; Kate Fitzgerald, "Just playing along", *Advertising Age,* 17 July 1995, p. 24; Kate Fitzgerald, "Videogame struggle is mortal combat", *Advertising Age,* 10 October 1995, p. 46; Terry Lefton, "Nintendo flanks competitors with title loyalty program," *Brandweek,* 6 Mar 1995, p. 13; Erin Flynn, "Kellogg, Nintendo re-tie promo knot", *Brandweek,* 21 January 1995, p. 19; Geoffrey Smith, "Scary stuff", *Financial World,* 21 February 1995, p. 8; Judith Abrams, "Next-generation hardware", *Dealerscope Merchandising,* May 1995, p. 20; and Kathleen Morris, "Nightmare in the funhouse", *Financial World,* 21 February 1995, pp. 32–35.

Questions for Discussion

1. What types of sales promotion methods has Nintendo employed?
2. In what ways do Nintendo's specific sales promotion efforts provide benefits to the company?
3. Evaluate Nintendo's practice of using product-specific sales promotion efforts rather than linking a sales promotion effort to a broader product line or its total product mix.

17.2 Promoting Free Flights: Hoover Comes Unstuck

Whether it's Sainsbury's and Boots with BA, Boots and railways, Sony and Thomas Cook, or Bird's Eye Menumaster and National Express Coaches, retailers and manufacturers have frequently negotiated with carriers to offer free travel or holidays to boost sales. The depressed holiday industry has welcomed the opportunity to use excess capacity and increase demand. It was not too surprising when consumer electronics giant Hoover joined the ranks of manufacturers offering free trips in order to stimulate demand for its white goods, first by offering free tickets to Europe with purchases of more than £100, then by extending the promotion to include free tickets to the US. What was not predictable was the adverse publicity the scheme brought for Hoover.

The second promotion was supported by a high profile £1 million television campaign. The offer included two free flights to either Orlando or New York for every purchase over £100, with an additional £60 towards car hire and accommodation for purchases over £300. Hoover claimed that the tickets into Europe had constituted its most successful promotion ever, putting its £130 vacuum cleaner ahead of its £100 model and making its £380 washing machine more popular than its £300 model.

In November 1992 a *Daily Record* story, "Hoover's flight shocker", started the trouble. This story alleged that none of the airlines Hoover claimed was involved in the US deal had any knowledge of the scheme and that Hoover had yet to reserve a single airline seat. The article also stated that the sales promotion company behind the offer was £500,000 in debt. In response, Hoover launched a major damage limitation exercise, including full page adverts assuring people that there was no mystery, that the offer was genuine and that free flights were available. Hoover's problems did not end there, however. Media attention increased, as did stories of disgruntled consumers.

From BBC consumer affairs programme *Watchdog* to the House of Commons, questions were asked about the ethics of the deal and the apparently unfair treatment of hundreds of annoyed consumers who, having purchased a Hoover product and received their vouchers, had actually attempted to claim their prizes. Many potential holidaymakers could not get first or even second choices of dates or destination. Many were refused their choices so often that Hoover's promotions company refused to permit any travel! Over 70 MPs demanded a Parliamentary investigation. Eventually, the Office of Fair Trading was brought in to investigate.

Hoover had intended neither to mislead nor to disappoint its customers, but the promotion nevertheless severely affected the company's reputation. Circumstances combined in several well publicised cases to make a deteriorating situation even worse for the company. What began as a sales boosting, attention-grabbing sales promotion rapidly turned into a damaging public relations nightmare for Hoover. Key directors were dismissed and the US parent company had to shell out millions of pounds to meet travellers' demands for their prizes. Twelve months later, disputes had still to be settled.

US parent Maytag Corp. had bought Britain's Hoover for $320 million in 1989. In 1995, Maytag sold its European operation to an Italian company at a loss of $135 million. The free flights promotion was, as described in many newspapers, "a fiasco", damaging not just this type of promotional activity but, more severely, the Hoover brand name and even the viability of the company. High profile court cases led by disgruntled consumers only made matters worse. Almost a decade later, consumers and retailers still remember this disastrous marketing communications campaign.

SOURCES: Clare Sambrook, "Do free flights really build brands?", *Marketing*, 15 October 1992, p. 11; Mat Toor, "Hoover retaliates over flights offer", *Marketing*, 3 December 1992, p. 3; Robert Dwek, "Hoover extends its free flights deal", *Marketing*, 29 October 1992, p. 16; BBC and ITN television news broadcasts, March and April 1993; Chris Knight, "Direct route", *Marketing Week*, 8 September 1995, pp. 58–59; Marcia Berss, "Whirlpool's bloody nose", *Forbes*, 11 March 1996, pp. 90–92.

Questions for Discussion

1. How damaging to the Hoover name and reputation was this sales promotion campaign?
2. How could Hoover have avoided these problems?
3. How, in the light of this promotional disaster, should Hoover have utilised the public relations toolkit to overcome the adverse publicity?

The promotion ingredient of the marketing mix addresses how a business promotes itself and its products to its target publics and target audiences. The decisions made by marketers concerning promotion affect how an organisation communicates with its target markets; how consumers are made aware of its products, services and activities; and how marketers expect to explain their determined brand positioning strategies. The chapters in Part V of Marketing: Concepts and Strategies have explained the core aspects of the promotional mix—advertising, publicity and public relations, sponsorship, personal selling, sales promotion and direct mail—and many of the key current trends and developments in the sphere of marketing communications, such as use of the Internet and direct marketing.

Before progressing, readers should be confident that they are now able to:

Explain the role of promotion and communication in marketing

· What is the role of promotion in the marketing mix? · What is the process of communication? · How does the product adoption process relate to promotional activity? · What are the aims of promotion? · What are the elements of the promotional mix? · How do businesses select which promotional mix ingredients to use?

Describe the use of advertising, publicity and sponsorship

· What are the uses of advertising? · What are the steps involved in developing an advertising campaign and whom does it involve? · What is publicity? · What is the nature of public relations? · What current trends are altering the work of advertising agencies and public relations consultancies? · What is meant by sponsorship in marketing terms? · How is sponsorship used by marketers?

Describe the use of personal selling, sales promotion, direct mail, the Internet and direct marketing

· What are the purposes, steps and types of personal selling? · What are the principal tasks of sales management? · What are the uses of sales promotion? · What are the methods and tools of sales promotion? · What does direct mail involve? · What is the role of direct mail within the promotional mix? · How are marketers using the Internet in promotional strategies? · What is direct marketing? · Which ingredients of the promotional mix are utilised by direct marketers?

Marketing Opportunity Analysis	Chapters
• The marketing environment	2
• Marketing in international markets	3
• Consumer buying behaviour	4
• Organisational markets and business-to-business buying behaviour	5
• Marketing research and information systems	6

Target Market Strategy	Chapters
• Market segmentation and prioritisation	7, 21
• Product and brand positioning	7, 21
• Competitive advantage	7, 21

Marketing Mix Development	Chapters
• Product, branding, packaging and service decisions	8–11
• Place (distribution and channel) decisions	12–14
• Promotion decisions	15–17
• Pricing decisions	18, 19
• Supplementary decisions	3, 20, 23, 24

Marketing Management	Chapters
• Strategic marketing and competitive strategy	21, 22
• Marketing planning and forecasting sales potential	22
• Implementing strategies and internal marketing relationships and measuring performance	23
• Marketing ethics and social responsibility	24

VI Pricing Decisions

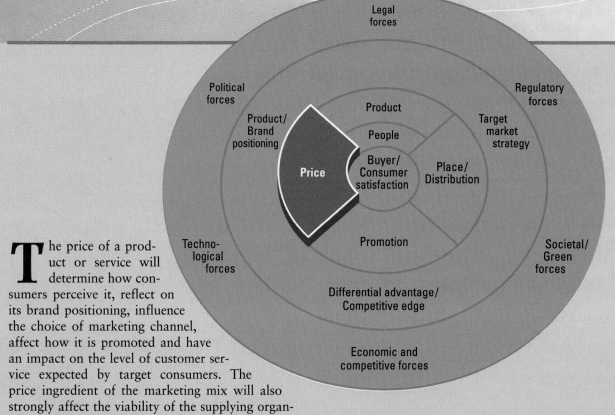

Legal forces

Political forces

Regulatory forces

Product/ Brand positioning

Product

People

Target market strategy

Price

Buyer/ Consumer satisfaction

Place/ Distribution

Techno- logical forces

Promotion

Societal/ Green forces

Differential advantage/ Competitive edge

Economic and competitive forces

The price of a product or service will determine how consumers perceive it, reflect on its brand positioning, influence the choice of marketing channel, affect how it is promoted and have an impact on the level of customer service expected by target consumers. The price ingredient of the marketing mix will also strongly affect the viability of the supplying organisation. The pricing decisions for a business must take into account consumers' notion of value. The concept of pricing is complex, but as a marketing mix ingredient it is of fundamental importance to the successful implementation of a marketing strategy. **Part VI** of *Marketing: Concepts and Strategies* explains the principal concepts of pricing and the setting of prices.

Chapter 18, "Pricing Concepts", explains the characteristics and role of price in marketing, outlines the differences between price and non-price competition, examines different pricing objectives and explores key factors that affect marketers' pricing decisions. The chapter then discusses perceived

value for money before turning to the complex aspect of pricing in industrial or business-to-business markets. The chapter concludes by analysing the concept of economic value to the customer.

Chapter 19, "Setting Prices", presents a detailed examination of the eight major stages in the process used to establish prices. In doing so, the chapter explores various activities that must be addressed: selecting pricing objectives; assessing the target market's evaluation of price and ability to buy; determining the demand for a product; and analysing the relationships between demand, costs and profits. The chapter next considers evaluating competitors' prices and examines different pricing policies. The chapter concludes with a look at pricing methods—including cost oriented, demand oriented, competition oriented and marketing oriented pricing—and discusses the need to determine a specific price and the "pricing balance".

By the conclusion of Part VI of *Marketing: Concepts and Strategies,* readers should understand the essential pricing decisions required in the formulation of the marketing mix.

18 Pricing Concepts

O B J E C T I V E S

- To understand the characteristics and role of price
- To be aware of the differences between price and non-price competition
- To examine different pricing objectives
- To explore key factors that affect pricing decisions
- To understand perceived value for money and how it affects consumers' decisions
- To consider issues unique to the pricing of products for industrial or business-to-business markets
- To analyse the concept of economic value to the customer

"The task of setting a price is one of the most important decisions in determining the marketing mix."

Peter Leeflang, Rijksuniversiteit Groningen

At the Third Empire hotel in France, the cheapest room costs around £200 a night, and dinner for two with wine can run as high as £300. The next morning, boiled and scrambled eggs with chives, marinated raw salmon, smoked ham, salami, a platter of cheeses, fresh and preserved fruits, and bread costs £22 a person. On the other hand, at a little diner in Montreal a breakfast platter of two eggs, bacon, toast, hash brown potatoes and juice costs around £1. From country to country and city to city around the world, the price of breakfast varies dramatically, even for the same food.

A recent study compared the price of a breakfast consisting of toast, cereal, eggs and milk in eleven countries. To get each item separately at the lowest price would require travelling around the world. Bread is least expensive in London, eggs in Bangkok and milk in Mexico. To buy all of the ingredients for this breakfast in the United States, grocery shoppers pay about £5.50. Breakfast in Rome or Tokyo costs more. For the same items in Rome, the cash register receipt totals £7 and in Tokyo a very expensive £13.85. Shoppers in Mexico City and London, however, get breakfast for the bargain price of under £4.20.

To make breakfast more interesting, several US cereal makers are using ingredients such as pecans, almonds, dried blueberries, cherries and exotic grains. Packaged elegantly with gold foil in boxes adorned with water-colour art, some up-market varieties cost breakfast eaters about £3 for a 340–454g package. Although this price seems high to Americans, Tokyo residents have to pay almost £4.80 for a 454g box of plain old corn flakes or boring bran. In Manila and Singapore as well, shoppers pay premium prices for ordinary cereals. Paying only £1.10 for a 454g box, Londoners get the best cereal deal of all the cities surveyed.

Why does the price of a simple meal range from affordable to outrageous depending on where you eat it? Several factors affect the price of breakfast in different countries. First, the exchange rate affects prices. For US cereal manufacturers selling goods in Europe, when the dollar's value fell, the price of breakfast in Brussels rose about £1.80. Second, a locale's cost of living in general influences the cost of specifics such as breakfast food. Finally, breakfast costs are determined by supply and demand. In Japan, for example, because milk and cereal are not popular foods, supplies of these breakfast staples are limited and prices are high.

SOURCES: Jennifer Fulkerson, "The continental breakfast", *American Demographics,* July 1995, pp. 18–20: Jonathan Dahl, "Travel: shop around to avoid Europe's high prices", *Wall Street Journal,* 14 April 1995, p. B9; Betsy Spethmann, "Cereal chic", *Brandweek,* 7 August 1995, pp. 26–28; Anthony Marshall, "It doesn't take a fool to spy erratic pricing", *Hotel & Motel Management,* 24 April 1995, p. 13; Jacqueline Simmons. "Travel: Canada, a welcome break for Americans", *Wall Street Journal,* 23 June 1995, p. B11; and Paul Levy, "The Mobile Guide: three stars, three figures", *Wall Street Journal,* 17 May 1995, p. A18. *Photo:* Gamma Liaison.

Companies such as Kellogg's which produce breakfast cereals use price, along with other elements, to distinguish their products from competitive brands. For these companies, as for most businesses, pricing is a crucial element in the marketing mix. This chapter begins by considering the characteristics of price before exploring the crucial role which it plays in determining a business's profitability. The chapter then looks at some of the differences between price and non-price competition. The different types of pricing objectives that marketers may establish are explored, followed by a detailed examination of the numerous factors that can affect pricing decisions. The chapter then discusses perceived value for money before examining selected issues related to the pricing of products for industrial or business-to-business markets. The chapter concludes by analysing the concept of economic value to the customer.

The Characteristics and Role of Price

Price The value placed on what is exchanged

To a buyer, **price** is the value placed on what is exchanged. Something of value—usually buying power—is exchanged for satisfaction or utility. As described in Chapter 2, buying power depends on a buyer's income, credit and wealth, yet price does not always involve a financial exchange. In fact, trading of products—barter—is the oldest form of exchange. Money may or may not be involved. Many organisations, however, adopt a narrow view of pricing, seeing this element of the marketing mix as a means of setting monetary price points and levels. In fact, a much broader view is desirable which takes into account issues such as target customers' perceptions of value for money and requirements for easy payment terms.

Buyers' interest in price stems from their expectations about the usefulness of a product or the satisfaction they may derive from it. Buyers have limited resources so they must weigh up the utility of a product against its cost to decide whether the exchange is worthwhile. In most societies **financial price** is the basis of market exchanges. This can be used to quantify almost anything of value that is exchanged, including ideas, services, rights and goods. Thus the financial value of a Paris penthouse might be 50 million French francs.

Financial price The basis of market exchanges; the quantified value of what is exchanged

Terms Used to Describe Price

Price is expressed in different terms for different exchanges. For instance, motor insurance companies charge a *premium* for protection from the cost of injuries or repairs stemming from a car accident. A police officer who stops a motorist for speeding writes a ticket that requires a *fine* to be paid. A lawyer charges a *fee*, and a *fare* is charged for a railway or taxi. A *toll* is sometimes charged for the use of bridges. *Rent* is paid for the use of equipment or for a flat. An estate agent receives a *commission* on the sale of a property. A *deposit* is made to reserve merchandise. A *tip* helps pay waitresses or waiters for their services. *Interest* is charged for loans, and *taxes* are paid for government services. The value of many products is called *price*.

Although price may be expressed in a variety of ways, it is important to remember that the purpose of this concept is to quantify and express the value of the items in a market exchange.

The Importance of Price to Marketers

As pointed out in Chapter 10, developing a product may be a lengthy process. It takes time to plan promotion and to communicate benefits. Distribution usually requires a long term commitment to dealers who will handle the product. Often price is the only aspect a marketer can change quickly to respond to changes in demand or to the actions of competitors. This does not mean, though, that the price variable is flexible in all situations. Distributors and/or consumers may be alienated by significant price changes.[1]

Price is also a key element in the marketing mix because it relates directly to the generation of total revenue.[2] The following equation is an important one for the entire organisation:

Profits = Total Revenues − Total Costs
or
Profits = (Price × Quantities Sold) − Total Costs

Prices can have a dramatic impact upon a company's profits. Price affects the profit equation in several ways. It directly influences the equation because it is a major component. It has an indirect impact because it can be a major determinant of the quantities sold. Even more indirectly, price influences total costs through its impact on quantities sold.

The example from Table 18.1 clearly illustrates the link between price and a company's profitability. As the table demonstrates, for a business with a 40 per cent contribution margin and a 10 per cent net profit, even a relatively small change in the prices set can have a major impact on the level of profit enjoyed. Thus a 10 per cent reduction in price would cause profits to fall to zero, while a 10 per cent rise would double the level of profitability. By contrast, it is also important to consider that a 10 per cent increase or decrease in volume would have a rather smaller impact on profits. It is vital that marketers are fully aware

Table 18.1 The importance of price change on profitability

Income statement: Alpha Products

		£ million
Turnover		200
Discounts and allowances	30	
Materials	30	
Direct labour	40	
Other variable costs	20	—
Profit contribution		80
Marketing and advertising	10	
Research and development	10	
Fixed costs	40	—
Net profit		20

Sensitivity analysis: Effect of 10% changes in price and costs on varying assumptions about volume losses.

	Change in profits £m (+ %)		
	Volume loss		
Change in	0%	−10%	−15%
Price (+10%)	20 (100)	10 (50)[1]	5 (25)
Total overhead (−10%)	6 (30)	−2 (−10)[2]	−6 (−30)
R & D (−10%)	1 (5)	−7 (−35)	−11 (−55)
Marketing and advertising (−10%)	1 (5)	−7 (−35)	−11 (−55)
Fixed costs (−10%)	4 (20)	−7 (−35)	−11 (−55)
Volume (+10%)	8 (40)	—	—

---

[1]For example, if prices are increased by 10% and volume falls as a result by 10%, then profits rise by £10m (or +50%).

[2]If total overhead costs are cut by 10% (£6m) and volume falls as a result by 10%, then profits fall by £2m (−10%).

SOURCE: P. Doyle, *Marketing Management and Strategy*. Copyright © 1998 Prentice-Hall Europe.

---

of these stark relationships when setting prices. In particular, this example illustrates the difficulty faced by businesses attempting to build a differential advantage based on low prices.

Because price has a psychological impact on customers, marketers can use it symbolically. By raising a price, they can emphasise the quality of a product and try to increase the status associated with its ownership. The example of Chevas Royal Scotch whisky is one which is often quoted. The declining fortunes of this brand were reversed following a substantial price rise. Lowering a price can also have a dramatic impact on demand, attracting bargain-hunting customers who are prepared to spend extra time and effort to save a small amount.

Figure 18.1 Price competition. SOURCE: Courtesy Halfords/Abbot Mead Vickers, BBDO Limited.

Price and Non-price Competition

A product offering can compete on either a price or a non-price basis. The choice will affect not only pricing decisions and activities but also those associated with other marketing mix decision variables.

Price Competition

Price competition A policy whereby a marketer emphasises price as an issue and matches or beats the prices of competitors

When **price competition** is used, a marketer emphasises price as an issue and matches or beats the prices of competitors (see Figure 18.1). Bic engages in price competition by pricing its perfume or pens low and emphasising price in its advertisements. To compete effectively on a price basis, a company should be the low cost producer of the product. If all companies producing goods in an industry charge the same price, the company with the lowest costs is the most profitable. Companies that stress low price as a key element in the marketing mix tend to produce standardised products. For example, in many countries suppliers of domestic electricity and gas use price competition. Sellers using this approach may change prices frequently or at least must be willing and able to do so, particularly in response to competitors changing their prices. In many countries, the postal service and United Parcel Service or DHL engage in direct price competition in their pricing of overnight air express services.

Price competition gives a marketer flexibility. Prices can be altered to account for changes in the company's costs, or in demand for the product, or when competitors cut prices. However, a major drawback of price competition is that competitors also have the flexibility to adjust their prices and can quickly match or beat an organisation's price cuts. A price war may result. Furthermore, if a user of price competition is forced to raise prices, competing companies that are not under the same pressures may decide not to raise their prices. As the 1990s drew to a close, the supermarket giants were locked into a spiral of price competition. Sainsbury's was promoting low prices across hundreds of popular product lines in an attempt to claw back market share from Tesco. Tesco's response was to launch a low price promotion of its own.[3] EDLP[4] (everyday low pricing) is a recent variation on price competition. Companies like Procter & Gamble hope to strengthen consumer loyalty by permanently cutting prices of key brands. The first two categories to benefit were the core markets of dishwashing liquids, such as Fairy Liquid, and nappies, such as Pampers. EDLP is funded by reducing promotions budgets so that retail prices can be cut while retailers' margins remain static.

EDLP   Everyday low pricing; budget savings passed on by the manufacturer to the consumer through reduced prices

Non-price Competition

Non-price competition   A policy in which a seller elects not to focus on price but to emphasise other factors instead

In **non-price competition**, a seller elects not to focus on price but instead emphasises distinctive product features, service, product quality, promotion, packaging or other factors to distinguish the product from competing brands. Organisations which use non-price competition aim to increase unit sales through means other than changing the brand's price. For example, Galway Irish Crystal stresses heritage and product quality rather than competitive price. One major advantage of non-price competition is that a company can build customer loyalty towards its brand. If customers prefer a brand because of non-price issues, they may not be easily lured away by competing companies and brands. Indeed, such customers might become confused or alienated if price cuts were offered. Customers whose primary attraction to a store is based on non-price factors are less likely to leave their regular store for a lower competitive price. Price is not the most durable factor from the standpoint of maintaining customer loyalty.[5] But when price is the primary reason that customers buy a particular brand, the competition can attract such customers through price cuts.

Non-price competition is workable under the right conditions. A company must be able to distinguish its brand through unique product features, higher quality, customer service, promotion, packaging and the like (see Figure 18.2). The brand's distinguishing features should be difficult, if not impossible, for a competitor to copy. Buyers must not only be able to perceive these distinguishing characteristics but must also view them as desirable. Marketing Insight 18.1 looks at how Parker uses its brand image in non-price competition. Finally, the organisation must extensively promote the distinguishing characteristics of the brand to establish its superiority and to set it apart from competitors in the minds of buyers.

Many European companies put less emphasis on price than do their American counterparts. They look for a competitive edge by concentrating on promotion, research and development, marketing research and marketing channel considerations. In a study of pricing strategy, many companies stated specifically that they emphasise research and development and technological superiority; competition based on price was seldom a major marketing consideration.[6]

Figure 18.2 Non-price competition. In this advertisement, Procter & Gamble stresses the cleaning power and gentleness of Fairy washing powder rather than its price.
SOURCE: ©The Proctor and Gamble Company. Used by permission.

A marketer attempting to compete on a non-price basis is still not able simply to ignore competitors' prices, however. The business must be aware of competitors' prices and will probably price its brand near or slightly above competing brands. As an example, Sony sells television sets in a highly competitive market and charges higher prices for its sets; but it is successful nonetheless. Sony's emphasis on high product quality both distinguishes it from its competitors and allows it to set higher prices. Therefore, price remains a crucial marketing mix component in situations that call for non-price competition.

Pricing Objectives

Pricing objectives Overall goals that describe what a company wants to achieve through its pricing efforts

Pricing objectives are overall goals that describe what a company wants to achieve through its pricing efforts. Because pricing objectives influence decisions in most functional areas—including finance, accounting and production—the objectives must be consistent with the company's overall mission and purpose. Banking is an area where pricing is a major concern. As competition has intensified, bank executives have realised that their products must be priced to meet not only short term profit goals but also long term strategic objectives.[7] Because of the

Parker Targets Its Pricing

Status symbols are expensive by nature—sleek European sports cars, 18-carat gold watches and ostrich skin briefcases are all very costly. Though smaller and less expensive, fancy fountain pens have become a common sight in the hands of influential business people. Such pens have high price tags and are much more difficult to maintain than ballpoints, felt tip pens or roller ball pens. However, recent sales figures indicate that the semi-obsolete fountain pen is making a comeback as the writing instrument of choice for status minded individuals.

Of the premium priced fountain pens, Montblanc pens are probably the most prestigious. Named after the highest mountain in Europe, these German made fountain pens cost from about £100 to £5,000 (for a solid gold one). The most popular model costs about £300. Prestige pricing has worked well for Montblanc, placing the pen in the same category as Rolex watches, Porsche sunglasses, BMW cars and Gucci luggage. Former US president Ronald Reagan, ex–Prime Minister Margaret Thatcher and fictional super spy James Bond all use Montblanc pens.

Parker also makes high priced "power" pens, including its revived Duofold model, which was popular during the 1920s. The Duofold comes in a blue and maroon marbled finish and sells for about £175. Waterman and S.T. Dupont also sell fine fountain pens. The Waterman Le Man series, which comes in seven sizes, is priced at around £160. Dupont pens have a distinctive Chinese lacquer finish and are priced from £200 to £300 (for the gold flecked models).

Consumers can pay just 20 pence to write with a disposable biro pen, yet many thousands choose to spend £20, £50 or even £150 on a pen. Why? The product's image and the individual consumer's own aspirations dictate that such pens must do more than simply write. For Parker, this psychological pricing influence is not to be ignored. The company has developed a comprehensive approach to determining pricing for its various ranges. This involves a rigorous process of target market identification and analysis—per target market—of desired product and brand attributes for writing instruments. Various pricing algorithms are then applied, taking into account brand image and qualitative issues in addition to straightforward cost analyses. The approach concludes with an exhaustive investigation to determine customer willingness to pay a premium for the company's de luxe products.

SOURCES: Chuck Tomkovick and Kathryn Dobie, "Apply hedonic pricing models and factorial surveys at Parker Pen to enhance new product success", *Journal of Product Innovation Management*, 12 (4), 1995, pp. 334–335; Allen Norwood, "Pen offers status", *Charlotte Observer*, 20 November 1988, pp. 1c–3c; Parker Pen Co. sales literature, 1996.

many areas involved, a marketer often uses multiple pricing objectives. This section looks at a few of the typical pricing objectives that companies might set for themselves.

Survival A fundamental pricing objective is survival. Most businesses will tolerate difficulties such as short run losses and internal upheaval if they are necessary for survival. Because price is a flexible and convenient variable to adjust, it is sometimes used to increase sales volume to levels that match the company's expenses.

Profit Although businesses may claim that their objective is to maximise profits, in practice this objective is difficult to measure. Because of this difficulty, profit objectives tend to be set at levels that are viewed as satisfactory. Specific profit objectives may be stated in terms of actual monetary amounts or in terms of percentage change relative to the profits of a previous period.

Return on Investment Pricing to attain a specified rate of return on the company's investment is a profit related pricing objective. Most pricing objectives based on return on investment

(ROI) are achieved by trial and error, because not all cost and revenue data needed to project the return on investment are available when prices are set.

The objective of return on investment may be used less as managers and marketers in diversified companies stress the creation of shareholder value. When shareholder value is used as a performance objective, strategies—including those involving price—are evaluated on the basis of the impact they will have on the value investors perceive in the company.[8]

Market Share Many companies establish pricing objectives to maintain or increase a product's market share in relation to total industry sales. For example, Volkswagen AG cut prices on its Jettas, Golfs, Cabriolets and Carats by 5 to 14 per cent and introduced two new models—the Corrado and Passat—at unexpectedly lower prices to boost its share of the car market.[9]

Maintaining or increasing market share need not depend on growth in industry sales. Remember that a company can increase its market share even though sales for the total industry are decreasing. On the other hand, assuming that the overall market is growing, a business's sales volume may actually increase as its market share within the industry decreases.

Cash Flow Some companies set prices to recover cash as fast as possible, especially when a short product life cycle is anticipated. Financial managers are understandably interested in quickly recovering capital spent to develop products. However, although it may sometimes be desirable, the use of cash flow and recovery as an objective over simplifies the value of price in contributing to profits. A disadvantage of this pricing objective could be high prices, which might allow competitors with lower prices to gain a large share of the market.

Status Quo In some cases, a business may be in a favourable position and may simply wish to maintain the status quo. Such objectives can focus on several dimensions—maintaining a certain market share, meeting (but not beating) competitors' prices, achieving price stability or maintaining a favourable public image. A status quo pricing objective can reduce a company's risks by helping to stabilise demand for its products. The use of status quo pricing objectives sometimes minimises pricing as a competitive tool, leading to a climate of non-price competition in an industry.

Product Quality A company might have the objective of product quality leadership in the industry. For example, the construction equipment manufacturer JCB aims to be ranked as one of the leading companies in its industry in terms of product quality and customer satisfaction.[10] Having such a goal normally dictates a relatively high price to cover the high product quality and, in some instances, the high cost of research and development.

Factors Affecting Pricing Decisions

Pricing decisions are affected by many factors. Frequently there is considerable uncertainty about the reactions to price on the part of buyers, channel members, competitors and others. Price is also an important consideration in marketing planning, market analysis and sales forecasting. It is a major issue when assessing a brand's position relative to competing brands. Most factors that affect pricing decisions can be grouped into one of the nine categories shown in Figure 18.3.

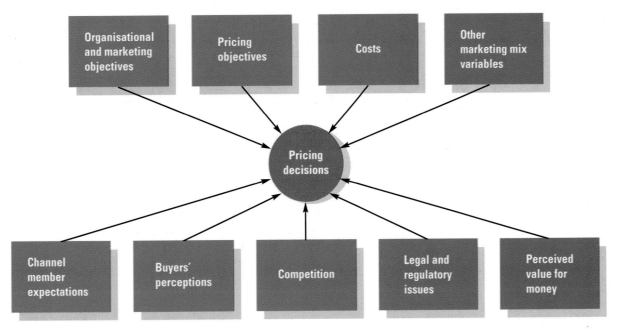

Figure 18.3 Factors that affect pricing decisions

This section explores how each of these nine groups of factors enters into price decision-making.

Organisational and Marketing Objectives

Marketers should set prices that are consistent with the organisation's goals and mission. For example, cosmetic brands such as Chanel and Helena Rubenstein are positioned at the exclusive end of the market, and have high price tags to match. Marketers in these organisations know that discounting prices on these brands would not be in line with the overall organisational goal.

Decision-makers should also make pricing decisions that are compatible with the organisation's marketing objectives. Say, for instance, that one of a producer's marketing objectives is a 12 per cent increase in unit sales by the end of the next year. Assuming that buyers are price sensitive, increasing the price or setting a price above the average market price would not be in line with the company's sales objective. A case in point: GM (Vauxhall) has introduced high performance, well specified model variants to the top of each of its model ranges, for example, the £20,000 Vectra V6 GSi and the £32,000 Omega 3.0i V6 Elite. Such prices ensure that these particular models have only limited appeal. GM's stated objective, however, is to be market leader in terms of sales volume. The company, therefore, is careful to price the great majority of its cars in line with the price expectations of the bulk of the car buying public and fleet operators—far below these £20,000 Vectra and £32,000 Omega levels.[11]

Pricing Objectives

As already explained, the type of pricing objectives a marketer uses will have considerable bearing on the determination of prices.[12] Thus a market share pricing objective usually causes a company to price a product below competing brands of similar quality to attract competitors' customers to the company's brand. This type of pricing can lead to lower profits. A marketer sometimes uses temporary price reductions in the hope of gaining market share. By contrast, a cash flow pricing objective may cause a company to set a relatively high price, which can place the product at a competitive disadvantage. Paradoxically, a cash flow pricing objective sometimes results in a low price sustained in the long term. However, this type of objective is more likely to be addressed by using temporary price reductions, such as sales, refunds and special discounts.

Costs　Obviously, costs must be an issue when establishing price. A business may temporarily sell products below cost to match the competition, to generate cash flow or even to increase market share; but in the long run it cannot survive by selling its products below cost. A marketer should be careful to analyse all costs so that they can be included in the total costing associated with a product.

Marketers must also take into account the costs that a particular product shares with other products in the product line, particularly the costs of research and development, production and distribution. Services are especially subject to cost sharing. For example, the costs of a bank building are spread over the costs of all services the bank offers.[13] Most marketers view a product's cost as a minimum, or floor, below which the product cannot be priced. Cost analysis is discussed in more detail in the next chapter.

Other Marketing Mix Variables　All marketing mix variables are closely interrelated. Pricing decisions can influence decisions and activities associated with product, place/distribution, promotion and customer service variables. A product's price frequently affects the demand for the item. A high price, for instance, may result in low unit sales, which in turn may lead to higher production costs per unit. Conversely, lower per unit production costs may result from a low price. For many products, buyers associate better product quality with a high price and poorer product quality with a low price. This perceived price-quality relationship influences customers' overall image of products or brands. Thus consumers may be prepared to pay a high price for a designer watch because they believe it is a high status item.

Pricing decisions influence the number of competing brands in a product category. When a company introduces a product, sets a relatively high price and achieves high unit sales, competitors may be attracted to this product category. If a company uses a low price, the low profit margin may be unattractive to potential competition.

The price of a product is linked to several dimensions of its distribution. Premium priced products are often marketed through selective or exclusive distribution; lower priced products in the same product category may be sold through intensive distribution. For example, Cross pens are distributed through selective distribution and Bic pens through intensive distribution. The manner in which a product is stored and transported may also be associated with its price. As Figure 18.4 shows, when a producer is developing the price of a product, the profit margins of marketing channel members such as wholesalers and retailers must be considered. It is important that channel members be adequately compensated for the functions they perform.

The way a product is promoted can be affected by its price. Bargain prices are often included in advertisements, whereas premium prices are less likely to appear in advertising messages. The issue of a premium price is sometimes included in advertisements for up-market items, such as luxury cars or fine jewellery. Higher priced products are more likely to require personal selling efforts than lower priced ones. A customer may purchase an inexpensive watch in a self-service environment but hesitate to buy an expensive watch in the same store, even if it is available there. Indeed, there may be an expectation that a high price is accompanied by enhanced levels of customer service.

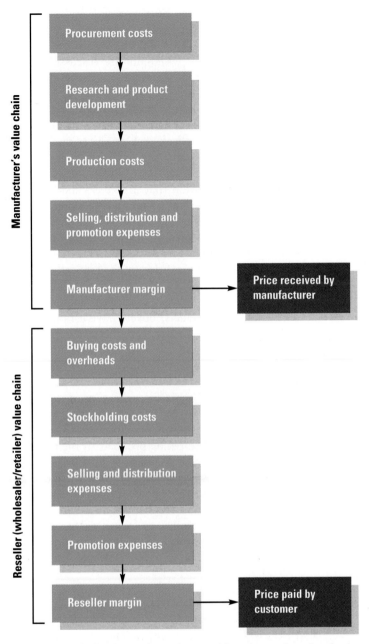

Figure 18.4 Wholesaler and retailer considerations when developing price

The price structure can affect a salesperson's relationship with customers. A complex pricing structure takes longer to explain to customers, is more likely to confuse the buyer and may cause misunderstandings that result in long term customer dissatisfaction. For example, the pricing structures of many airlines are complex and frequently confuse ticket sales agents and travellers alike.

Channel Member Expectations When making price decisions, a producer must consider what distribution channel members (such as wholesalers, retailers and dealers) expect. A channel member certainly expects to receive a profit for the functions performed. The amount of profit expected depends on the amount of time and resources expended and on an assessment of what would be gained by handling a competing product instead.

Channel members often expect producers to provide discounts for large orders and quick payment. (Discounts are discussed later in this chapter.) At times, resellers expect producers to provide several support activities, such as sales training, service training, repair advisory service, co-operative advertising, sales promotions and perhaps a programme for returning unsold merchandise to the producer. These support activities clearly incur associated costs and are expressly required by some resellers, so a producer must consider these costs when determining prices.

Buyers' Perceptions

One important question that marketers should assess when making price decisions is, "How important is the price to people in the target market?" The importance of price is not absolute; it can vary from market segment to market segment and from person to person. Members of one market segment may be more sensitive to price than members of a different target market. Moreover, the importance of price will vary across different product categories. Price may be a more important factor in the purchase of bread than in the purchase of a pair of shoes, because buyers may be more sensitive to the price of a frequently purchased item.

For numerous products, buyers have a range of acceptable prices. This range can be fairly narrow in some product categories but wider in others. (This issue and related ones are discussed in more detail in the next chapter.) Consumers' perceptions of price may also be influenced by the price of other products in a company's product line or by the price of competing products. Exposure to a range of prices in a product line affects the consumers' expectations and perceptions of acceptable prices.[14] Buyers' perceptions of a product relative to competing products may allow or encourage a company to set a price that differs significantly from the prices of competing products. If the product is deemed superior to most of the competition, a premium price may be feasible. Strong brand loyalty sometimes makes it possible for the company to charge a premium price for its product. There is a considerable body of research on the relationship between price and consumers' perceptions of quality. Consumers use price as an indicator of quality when brands are unfamiliar and when the perceived risk of making unsatisfactory choices is high. They also rely on price as an indicator if there is little information available and judging a product's attributes is difficult.[15]

Competition

A marketer needs to know competitors' prices so that a company can adjust its own prices accordingly.[16] This does not mean that a company will necessarily match competitors' prices; it may set its price above or below theirs. It is also important for marketers to assess how competitors will respond to price adjustments. Will they change their prices (some, in fact, may not), and if so, will they raise or lower them? For example, it is likely that as Hertz stresses its keen pricing, competitors will adjust their pricing.

Chapter 2 describes several types of competitive market structures which impact upon price setting. When a company operates as a monopoly and is unregulated, it can set whatever prices the market will bear. However, the company may avoid pricing the product at the highest possible level for fear of inviting government regulation or because it wants to penetrate a market by using a lower price. If the monopoly is regulated, it normally has less pricing flexibility; the regulatory body lets it set prices that generate a reasonable, but not excessive, return. A government-owned monopoly may price products below cost to make them accessible to people who otherwise could not afford them. However, government-owned monopolies sometimes charge higher prices to control demand.

In an oligopoly, only a few sellers operate, and there are high barriers to competitive entry. A business in such an industry, for example, telecommunications, drugs or steel, can raise its price, hoping that its competitors will do the same. Very little can be gained through price cuts because when an organisation cuts its price to gain a competitive edge, other companies are likely to follow suit.

A market structure characterised by monopolistic competition means numerous sellers with differentiated product offerings. The products are differentiated by physical characteristics, features, quality and brand images. The distinguishing characteristics of its product may allow a company to set a different price from its competitors. However, businesses engaged in a monopolistic competitive market structure are likely to practice non-price competition, discussed earlier in this chapter.

Under conditions of perfect competition, there are many sellers. Buyers view all sellers' products as the same. All companies sell their products at the going market price, and buyers will not pay more than that. This type of market structure, then, gives a marketer no flexibility in setting prices.

Legal and Regulatory Issues

At times government action sways marketers' pricing decisions. To curb inflation, the government may invoke price controls, "freeze" prices at certain levels or determine the rates at which prices can be increased. With the privatisation of once public utilities, the UK government set up regulatory bodies that stressed minimum and maximum charges (for example, OFWAT for water).

Many regulations and laws affect pricing decisions and activities. Not only must marketers refrain from fixing prices, they must also develop independent pricing policies and set prices in ways that do not even suggest collusion. Over the years, legislation has been established to safeguard consumers and businesses from the sharp practices of other companies. In the UK, the Monopolies and Mergers Commission prevents the creation of monopolistic situations. The consumer is protected by the Trade Descriptions Act, the Fair Trading Act, the Consumer Protection Act and many more. All countries have similar legislation, and the European Union legislates to protect consumers within the community.

Perceived Value

Perceived value for money The benefit consumers perceive to be inherent in a product or service, weighed against the price demanded

Most discussions about pricing revolve around the actual monetary value—the *price*—to be charged for the good or service. However, marketers must not lose sight of the **perceived value for money**—the benefit consumers perceive to be inherent in a product or service, weighed against the price demanded—which consumers have of a particular brand. Sometimes, particularly in consumer markets, these benefits are more psychological than tangible. In other circumstances, the benefits are real and can be measured. For instance, interest free credit, maintenance contracts and extended warranties are all features which may affect a consumer's perception of value for money. Consumers will not pay more than they value the benefit inherent in a product or service. Consumers balance the price demanded, typically in monetary terms, against the anticipated level of use and satisfaction to be gained from buying and using the specific product. Various factors will influence this equation: the consumers' previous experience of the brand and similar products, the perceived quality of the product in question, its brand image, purpose, anticipated usage, overall appeal and the nature of competing offers. These emotive issues are often difficult to quantify, but through qualitative marketing research, most businesses are able to assess their target market's views of value.

Industrial markets consist of individuals and businesses that purchase products for re-sale, for use in their own operations or for producing other products. Establishing prices for this category of business-to-business buyers is sometimes different from setting prices for consumers. Industrial marketers have experienced much change because of economic uncertainty, sporadic supply shortages and an increasing interest in service. Differences in the size of purchases, geographic factors and transport considerations require sellers to adjust prices. This section discusses several issues unique to the pricing of industrial products and business-to-business markets—including discounts, geographic pricing, transfer pricing and price discrimination. The section concludes by considering the concept of economic value to the customer (EVC), which is also explored in Marketing Insight 18.2.

Price Discounting

Producers commonly provide intermediaries with discounts off list prices. Although there are many types of discounts, they usually fall into one of five categories: trade, quantity, cash and seasonal discounts, and allowances.

Trade or **functional discount**   A reduction off the list price given by a producer to an intermediary for performing certain functions

Trade Discounts   A reduction off the list price given by a producer to an intermediary for performing certain functions is called a **trade** or **functional discount**. The functions for which intermediaries are compensated may include selling, transporting, storing, final processing and perhaps providing credit services. The level of discount can vary considerably from one industry to another.

Quantity discounts   Reductions from the list price that reflect the economies of purchasing in large quantities

Quantity Discounts   Reductions from the list price that reflect the economies of purchasing in large quantities are called **quantity discounts**. Cost savings usually occur in four areas. First, fewer but larger orders reduce per unit selling costs. Second, fixed costs, such as invoicing and sales contracts, remain the same or go down. Third, costs for raw materials are lower, because quantity discounts are often available to the seller. Fourth, longer production runs mean no increases in holding costs.[17] In addition, a large purchase may shift some of the storage, finance and risk taking functions to the buyer.

Cumulative discounts   Quantity discounts aggregated over a stated period of time

Non-cumulative discounts   One-off quantity discounts

Quantity discounts can be either cumulative or non-cumulative. **Cumulative discounts** are aggregated over a stated period of time. Purchases of £10,000 in a three month period, for example, might entitle the buyer to a 5 per cent, or £500, rebate. Such discounts are supposed to reflect economies in selling and encourage the buyer to purchase from one seller. **Non-cumulative discounts** are one-off reductions in prices based on the number of units purchased, the monetary value of the order or the product mix purchased.

Cash discount   A simple price reduction given to a buyer for prompt payment or payment in cash

Cash Discounts   A **cash discount**, or simple price reduction, is given to a buyer for prompt payment or payment in cash. A policy to encourage prompt payment is a popular practice in setting prices. Such discounts are based on cash payments or cash paid within a stated time. For example, "2/10 net 30" means that a 2 per cent discount will be allowed if the account is paid within 10 days. However, if the buyer does not pay within the 10 day period, the entire balance is due within 30 days without a discount. If the account is not paid within 30 days, interest may be charged.

Seasonal discount   A price reduction given to buyers who purchase goods or services out of season

Seasonal Discounts   A price reduction given to buyers who purchase goods or services out of season is a **seasonal discount**. These discounts let the seller main-

Business-to-Business Pricing Using EVC Analysis

Analysing economic value to the customer (EVC) is a useful aid to setting prices for business-to-business organisations. This example concerns the pricing of panel presses, which are supplied to the car parts business. The analysis focuses on the market leader and two other competitors.

The analysis begins by considering a reference product against which the costs of competing products are compared. In this case, the market leader is used as the reference product. In this example, a car parts company buying the panel press from the market leader would expect to pay the following costs. The purchase price of the press is £60,000. Start up costs such as installation charges, staff training and lost production during installation are £20,000, and post-purchase costs including operating costs such as labour, servicing/maintenance and power are £130,000. This means that over its life cycle, the panel press will cost the car parts company a total of £210,000.

Companies competing with the market leader present the customer with a different profile of costs. Company A has, by incorporating a number of new design features, managed to cut the start up costs for a comparable panel

press to £10,000 and reduced post-purchase costs to £105,000. This means that the total costs for the press are £35,000 less than those for the market leader. The result is that Company A's press offers the customer an EVC of £210,000 less £115,000 = £95,000. Assuming that Company A charged a purchase price of £95,000 for the panel press, the customer would face total life cycle costs which were equivalent with the market leading product. If, however, Company A decided to offer the panel press at a purchase price of only £80,000, the lower life cycle costs of the product would give the customer a considerable financial incentive to buy.

Consider the position of a second competitor, Company B, with similar start up and post-purchase costs to the market leader. This company has, through certain technological advances, increased the rate at which the press can be operated, potentially increasing productivity and therefore revenue for the customer. As a result, the press has the potential to offer an additional £50,000 profit contribution over the presses of the market leader and Company A. The EVC associated with this is £110,000, because this is the highest price which the customer might be expected to pay.

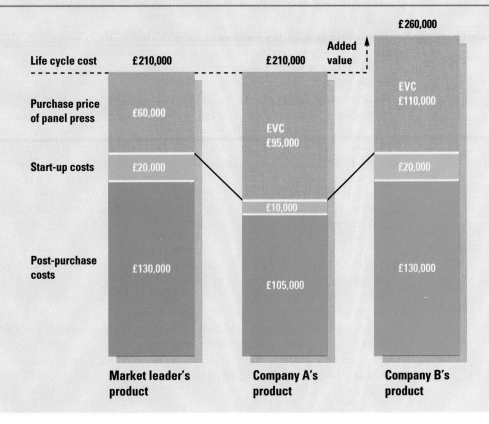

tain steadier production during the year. For example, hotels in holiday resorts offer seasonal discounts at times of year when the weather is poor.

Allowances Another type of reduction from the list price is an **allowance**—a concession in price to achieve a desired goal. Trade-in allowances are price reductions granted for turning in a used item when purchasing a new one. For example, £50 for an old fridge or freezer is credited against the purchase of a new machine. Allowances help give the buyer the ability to make the new purchase. Another example is promotional allowances, which are price reductions granted to dealers for participating in advertising and sales support programmes intended to increase sales of a particular item.

Geographic Pricing

Geographic pricing involves reductions for transport costs or other costs associated with the physical distance between the buyer and the seller. Prices may be quoted as being F.O.B. (free-on-board) factory or destination. An **F.O.B. factory price** indicates the price of the merchandise at the factory before it is loaded onto the carrier vehicle; it thus excludes transport costs. The buyer must pay for shipping. An **F.O.B. destination price,** which means that the producer absorbs the costs of shipping the merchandise, may be used to attract distant customers.

To avoid the problems involved in charging different prices to each customer, **uniform geographic pricing,** sometimes called *postage stamp pricing,* may be used. The same price is charged to all customers regardless of geographic location, and the price is based on average shipping costs for all customers. Petrol, paper products and office equipment are often priced on a uniform basis.

Zone prices are regional prices that take advantage of a uniform pricing system; prices are adjusted for major geographic zones as the transport costs increase. For example, the prices of a manufacturer located in the northern French town of Lille may be higher for buyers in the south of France than for buyers in Paris.

Base point pricing is a geographic pricing policy that includes the price at the factory, plus freight charges from the base point nearest the buyer. This policy, which is now rarely used, can result in all buyers paying freight charges from one location, regardless of where the product was manufactured!

When the seller absorbs all or part of the actual freight costs, **freight absorption pricing** is being used. The seller might choose this method because it wishes to do business with a particular customer or to get more business; more business will cause the average cost to fall and counter-balance the extra freight cost. This strategy is used to improve market penetration and to retain a hold in an increasingly competitive market.

Transfer Pricing

When one unit in a company sells a product to another unit within the same company, **transfer pricing** occurs. The price is determined by one of the following methods:

Actual full cost—calculated by dividing all fixed and variable expenses for a period into the number of units produced.
Standard full cost—calculated on what it would cost to produce the goods at full plant capacity.
Cost plus investment—calculated as full cost, plus the cost of a portion of the selling unit's assets used for internal needs.
Market based cost—calculated at the market price less a small discount to reflect the lack of sales effort and other expenses.

The choice of a method of transfer pricing depends on the company's management strategy and the nature of the units' interaction. The company might initially choose to determine price by the actual full cost method. But later price changes could result in a market based method or another method that the management of the company decides is best for its changed business situation.[18]

Price Discrimination

A policy of **price discrimination** results in different prices being charged in order to give a group of buyers a competitive edge. In some countries, price discrimination is regarded as illegal in certain circumstances. For example, in the US price differentials are legal only when customers are not in competition with one another. The EU is also keen to stamp out price discrimination.

Price differentiation is a form of market segmentation that companies use to provide a marketing mix that satisfies different segments. Because different market segments perceive the value of a particular product differently, depending on the product's importance and value to the industrial buyer, marketers may charge different prices to different market segments. Price discrimination can also be used to modify demand patterns, support sales of other products, help move obsolete goods or excessive inventories, fill excess production capacity and respond to competitors' activities in particular markets.[19] Table 18.2 shows the principal forms of price discrimination. For price discrimination to work, several conditions are necessary:

1. The market must be segmentable.
2. The cost of segmenting should not exceed the extra revenue from price discrimination.
3. The practice should not breed customer discontent.
4. Competition should not be able to steal the segment that is charged the higher price.
5. The practice should not violate any applicable laws.

Table 18.2 Principal forms of price discrimination

Bases of Discrimination	Examples
Buyers' income	Low priced admission to leisure and recreation facilities for the unemployed
Buyers' age	Children's haircuts, lower admission charges for students and senior citizens
Buyers' location	Zone prices and season ticket reductions for bus and train travel
Buyers' status	Lower prices to new customers, quantity discounts to big buyers
Use of product	Eat-in and take-away prices for fast foods
Qualities of products	Relatively higher prices for de luxe models
Labels on products	Lower prices for unbranded products
Sizes of products	Relatively lower prices for larger sizes (e.g. the "giant economy" size)
Peak and off-peak services	Lower prices for off-peak services (excursion rates on public transport, off-season rates at resorts, holiday and evening telephone rates)

The relationship between price and profitability is considered briefly at the start of this chapter and will be examined in more detail in Chapter 19. It is already clear that the ability to charge a higher price can have a major and positive impact upon profitability. It is also apparent that in order to achieve higher prices, businesses must be able to offer the customer some kind of differential advantage. In industrial markets, this advantage must usually be measurable in economic terms because businesses are driven by the need to reduce costs and increase revenue. Thus a manufacturer of switch gears may be prepared to switch to a more expensive supplier of fork lift trucks if the products supplied have lower running costs. The concept of economic value to the customer encapsulates this notion and is a useful aid to determining prices in industrial markets. The underlying principle of **economic value to the customer** (EVC) is that a premium price can be charged while still offering the customer better value than the competition.

There are various reasons why a costly product may provide good economic value to the customer, including lower set-up or running costs, the provision of superior servicing or other after sales support, or a better warranty deal. It is even possible that the life of the product may be longer or that its productivity may be greater than lower priced alternatives. Whatever the reason behind the value on offer, if EVC is to be demonstrated, the initial high price of the product must be justified by an overall lower life time cost. Marketing Insight 18.2 provides a worked example which illustrates how EVC works in practice.

Economic value to the customer (EVC) The underlying principle that a premium price can be charged while still offering the customer better value than the competition

● S U M M A R Y

Price is the value placed on what is exchanged. The buyer exchanges buying power—which depends on the buyer's income, credit and wealth—for satisfaction or utility. Price does not always involve a financial exchange; barter, the trading of products, is the oldest form of exchange. Price is a key element in the marketing mix because it relates directly to the generation of total revenue. The profit factor can be determined mathematically by first multiplying price by quantities sold to calculate total revenues and then subtracting total costs. Price is often the only variable in the marketing mix that can be adjusted quickly and easily to respond to changes in the external environment. *Financial price* is the basis of market exchanges—the quantified value of what is exchanged.

A product offering can compete on either a price or a non-price basis. *Price competition* emphasises price as the product differential. Prices fluctuate frequently, and sellers must respond to competitors changing their prices. *EDLP*, everyday low pricing, is a budget saving passed on from the manufacturer to the consumer. *Non-price competition* emphasises product differentiation through distinctive product features, services, product quality or other factors. Establishing brand loyalty by using non-price competition works best when the product can be physically differentiated and when the customer can recognise these distinguishing characteristics and views them as desirable.

Pricing objectives are overall goals that describe what a company wants to achieve through its pricing efforts. The most fundamental pricing objective is the business's survival. Price can be easily adjusted to increase sales volume to levels that match the company's expenses. Profit objectives, which are usually stated in terms of actual monetary amounts or percentage change, are normally set at a satisfactory level rather than at a level designed for profit maximisation. Pricing for return on investment (ROI) sets a specified rate of return as its objective. A pricing objective to maintain or increase market share is established in relation to total industry sales. Other types of pricing objectives include cash flow, status quo and product quality.

A group of nine factors enters into pricing decisions: (1) organisational and marketing objectives, (2) pricing objectives, (3) costs, (4) other marketing mix variables, (5) channel member expectations, (6) buyers' perceptions, (7) competition, (8) legal and regulatory issues, and (9) perceived value. When setting prices, marketers should make decisions consistent with the organisation's goals and mission. Pricing objectives heavily influence price setting decisions. Most marketers view a product's cost as the floor below which a product cannot be priced. Due to the inter-relation of the marketing mix variables, price can affect product, promotion, place/distribution and service level decisions. The revenue that channel members expect for the functions they perform must also be considered when making price decisions.

Buyers' perceptions of price vary. Some consumer segments are sensitive to price, but others may not be; before determining the price, therefore, a marketer needs to be aware of its importance to the target market. Knowledge of the prices charged for competing brands is essential so that a company can adjust its prices relative to those of competitors. Government regulations and legislation can also influence pricing decisions through laws to enhance competition and by invoking price controls—for example, to curb inflation.

Perceived value for money is an important consideration when setting prices. Consumers do not regard price purely as the monetary value being demanded in exchange for a good or a service. The quality of the item, its brand image, purpose, usage and overall appeal—along with the consumers' previous experiences and certain tangible benefits such as interest free credit and warranties—dictate the consumers' view of value for money.

Unlike consumers, industrial or business-to-business buyers purchase products to use in their own operations or for producing other products. When adjusting prices, industrial sellers take into consideration the size of the purchase, geographic factors and transport requirements. Producers commonly provide *trade* or *functional discounts* off list prices to intermediaries. The five categories of discounts include (1) trade, (2) quantity, (3) cash and (4) seasonal discounts, and (5) allowances. A trade discount is a price reduction for performing such functions as storing, transporting, final processing or providing credit services. If an intermediary purchases in large enough quantities, the producer gives a *quantity discount,* which can be either *cumulative* or *non-cumulative*. A *cash discount* is a price reduction for prompt payment or payment in cash. Buyers who purchase goods or services out of season may be granted a *seasonal discount*. A final type of reduction from the list price is an *allowance,* such as a trade-in allowance.

Geographic pricing involves reductions for transport costs or other costs associated with the physical distance between the buyer and the seller. An *F.O.B. factory price* means that the buyer pays for shipping from the factory; an *F.O.B. destination price* means that the producer pays for shipping the merchandise. When the seller charges a fixed average cost for transport, the practice is known as *uniform geographic pricing*. *Zone prices* take advantage of a uniform pricing system adjusted for major geographic zones as the transport costs increase. *Base point pricing* involves prices being adjusted for shipping expenses incurred by the seller from the base point nearest the buyer. A seller who absorbs all or part of the freight costs is using *freight absorption pricing*. *Transfer pricing* occurs when one unit in a company sells a product to another unit within the same company.

When a *price discrimination* policy is adopted, different prices are charged in order to give a group of buyers a competitive edge. In some countries, price differentials are legal only in circumstances where competition is not damaged.

The concept of *economic value to the customer (EVC)* is sometimes used in industrial markets to aid price setting. The underlying principle is that a premium price can be charged while still offering better value than the competition. This is because industrial, business-to-business companies are driven by the need to reduce costs and increase revenue.

Important Terms

Price	Quantity discounts	F.O.B. destination price
Financial price	Cumulative discounts	Uniform geographic pricing
Price competition	Non-cumulative discounts	Zone prices
EDLP	Cash discount	Base point pricing
Non-price competition	Seasonal discount	Freight absorption pricing
Pricing objectives	Allowance	Transfer pricing
Perceived value for money	Geographic pricing	Price discrimination
Trade or functional discount	F.O.B. factory price	Economic value to the customer (EVC)

Discussion and Review Questions

1. Why are pricing decisions so important to a business?
2. Compare and contrast price and non-price competition. Describe the conditions under which each form works best.
3. How does a pricing objective of return on investment (ROI) differ from a pricing objective to increase market share?
4. Why is it crucial to consider both marketing objectives and pricing objectives when making pricing decisions?
5. In what ways do other marketing mix variables affect pricing decisions?
6. What types of expectations may channel members have about producers' prices, and how do these expectations affect pricing decisions?
7. How do legal and regulatory forces influence pricing decisions?
8. Why must marketers consider consumers' perceptions of value for money when setting prices?
9. Compare and contrast a trade discount and a quantity discount.
10. What is the difference between a price discount and price discrimination?
11. What is EDLP (everyday low pricing)? How does it work?
12. Why is the concept of EVC (economic value to the customer) important when setting prices in business-to-business markets?

Recommended Readings

E. Gijsbrechts, "Pricing and pricing research in consumer marketing: some recent developments", *International Journal of Research in Marketing*, vol. 10, 1993, pp. 15–115.

B. K. Monroe, *Pricing: Making Profitable Decisions*, 2nd edn (New York: McGraw-Hill, 1990).

M. H. Morris, "Separate prices as a marketing tool", *Industrial Marketing Management*, vol. 16, 1987, pp. 79–86.

T. Nagle and R. K. Holden, *The Strategy and Tactics of Pricing* (Englewood Cliffs: Prentice-Hall, 1995).

J. Winckler, *Pricing for Results* (Oxford: Butterworth-Heinemann, 1983).

● C A S E S

18.1 *Pricing Risks to Brand Positioning: Mumm Champagne*

As the Christmas 1992 festivities died down and revellers looked to New Year's Eve celebrations, few realised the significant changes occurring throughout the European Community. Britain's then Prime Minister John Major lit one of hundreds of beacons to mark the dawning of a new era in intra-European trade and co-operation. The customs posts had a new, more limited focus: travellers entering the EU from other parts of the world. For EU business people and tourists alike, the formalities of passport checks and duty-free allowances when passing from country to country in the EU had changed beyond recognition. Passport checks were few, and car-borne travellers could load more goods in their cars than—according to leading motoring organisations and the police—their vehicles could safely transport.

Many EU consumers noticed no changes until their annual holidays took them into Europe. For some more alert consumers, the changes in EU regulations had an immediate impact. Car ferry operators reported brisk business and above average passenger levels as UK consumers headed for the French coastal hypermarkets to load up with cut-price wines and spirits. Coach operators from the South of England were joined by operators from the Midlands and the North running "away days" to the French hypermarkets. For the hypermarkets, extra stocks were brought in and English language signage became more prominent.

There had been much talk about 1992's EU deregulation. Governments had been preparing companies and trade organisations for several years, but the low cost wines of France were the first concrete manifestation of the changes for many UK consumers. Not only the French hypermarkets were facing new and changing opportunities. The new regulations were to cause upheaval for many companies, including Seagram's, makers of Mumm champagne.

Seagram's decided to sell its Mumm brand in the UK at prices similar to Mumm's French prices. Why? "We had to align our prices with those charged in France, to prevent the French coming over and buying it cheaper from here [the UK]", explained Seagram's. The price per case to the trade was to increase £23, pushing the wholesale price per bottle up from £14.33 to £16.25. The retail price to the consumer was £17.99 but rose to over £20, pushing Mumm ahead of arch rivals Moet Chandon, Mercier and Piper Heidsieck. "We are trying to re-position Mumm with a more premium image because the current positioning is not enough to support the new bottle price."

Seagram's had to re-think its pricing differential between France and the UK for its Mumm brand as trade barriers altered and consumers had an incentive to travel further to purchase, even potentially crossing the English Channel. The existing press advertising for Mumm, through Ogilvy & Mather, had to be shelved as Mumm was re-positioned. Seagram's second champagne marque, Perrier Jouet, also received additional marketing attention to reduce any loss to the re-positioned Mumm brand.

The French hypermarkets, UK coach operators, car ferry companies and alcoholic beverages giant Seagram's were not the only companies to notice changes caused by the macro marketing environment: EU deregulation. In Seagram's case, the pricing policies of major brands had to be altered and brand positioning re-assessed.

SOURCES: Paul Meller, "Mumm price follows in French fashion", *Marketing*, 28 January 1993, p. 6; the Automobile Association; BBC and ITN television news broadcasts, 1 and 2 January 1993; Paul Meller, "Champagne: missing the marque?", *Marketing*, 17 December 1992, pp. 16–19; Seagram's 1995; Oddbins, 1996.

Questions for Discussion

1. In raising prices for Mumm, what considerations influenced Seagram's decision? Why did these complicate the issue for Seagram's?
2. What was the impact on Mumm's positioning? What are the risks of a radical price revision to positioning? Explain your answer.

18.2 Perfume Discounting—Pricing Policies to Rattle the Leading Brands

For decades the leading perfume houses of Paris, London and New York have sought exclusive, premium brand positioning: Joy, Chanel No. 5 and Givenchy have been marketed as high priced, de luxe lines available only from carefully selected retailers: leading department stores, fragrance houses and only those chemists with a genuine perfumery. Even a company as reputable as Boots has failed to gain Chanel's permission to retail Chanel fragrances throughout its chain of stores. Chanel permits only the larger, more exclusive branches of Boots to stock its brands, sometimes giving preference to an independent specialist fragrance house in a town to retail its products.

While these up-market brands have controlled distribution, they have also prevented price discounting. The more mass market brands, such as Revlon, Max Factor or Boots' own No. 7, have been left to take the bulk of the market on volume, pricing way below Joy, Chanel No. 5 or Givenchy. In this way, these more expensive, selectively distributed brands have nurtured an exclusive, premium image to support their higher prices.

Kingfisher, owners of Woolworths and B&Q DIY, has created the UK's leading chain of discount drugstores. Kingfisher's Superdrug chain caught the marketplace by surprise. It brought in full in-store pharmacies to rival Boots but kept its discounting focus by reducing prices of proprietary medicines by around 10 per cent. Superdrug also looked to the perfume market, reducing the prices of the more mass market brands it stocked. Why, though, should Superdrug not create full perfumery sections in its larger branches and stock the more up-market, exclusive brands? More importantly, why should Superdrug not discount the prices of these leading exclusive brands of perfume, in line with the chain's general trading philosophy as a discounter?

Shock waves were felt throughout the industry. The perfume producers had spent decades creating premium priced, exclusive brands. Discounting by a retail chain was the antithesis of this strategy. Independent perfume retailers had been able to occupy prime pitch sites with high staffing levels and glamorous shop fittings on the basis of the higher margins offered by the slower selling exclusive brands. The pricing and images of these brands had for decades protected them from the national retail chains and buying groups. The large department stores were less dependent on maintaining the premium pricing, but they similarly saw their sales decline as Superdrug followed through with its plans. EU and UK trading laws and anti-price fixing legislation seemed to be on Superdrug's side, too.

It was not easy going for Superdrug. Along with the other discounters, Superdrug was refused supplies from the perfume manufacturers; the company had to source from "the grey market", mainly overseas wholesalers. The producers' PR mechanisms mobilised many industry players against the moves. Superdrug's first press advertising campaign for its discounting of fine fragrances was rejected by a string of up-market colour supplements and publishing houses. According to the marketing press, the colour supplements of *The Independent on Sunday, The Sunday Times* and *The Observer* refused to carry the Superdrug advertisements for

fear of provoking repercussions from the up-market perfume houses, all leading advertisers in these newspapers' supplements.

Prior to Christmas, the peak selling season for all perfumes—including brands such as Joy, Chanel and Givenchy—leading department store operator House of Fraser, which owns Harrod's and stores in most large cities in the UK, reduced prices of many leading perfumes. Boots, too, retaliated against Superdrug's move. For example, in branches of Boots permitted to sell Chanel, a smaller Chanel No. 5 perfume dropped from around £28 to £21, a price still well ahead of the more mass market brands, but the largest discount for such a brand seen in one of its core retail outlets. Boots and House of Fraser admitted they were "reviewing daily" their pricing policies.

Years of brand building and image cultivation were in jeopardy. More to the point, the retailers were to risk reducing sales of these still lucrative brands. Superdrug wanted to enter the upper echelons of the fragrance market, but not to let discounting devalue the worth of stocking some of these brands. There were no intentions to replicate the price discounting and tit-for-tat retaliations in the DIY or grocery sectors of retailing, or in the holiday industry. The fragrance market, though, witnessed quite dramatic upheavals in a very conservative market. The entry of Superdrug, with its aggressive pricing policy and discounting, caused changes in strategies throughout the industry, by perfume producers, retailers and the media.

SOURCES: "Superdrug finds refuge in women's magazines", *Marketing Week*, 13 November 1992, p. 6; Helen Slingsby, "House of Fraser reviews scent pricing", *Marketing Week*, 18 December 1992, p. 5; "Stop press", *Marketing*, 19 November 1992, p. 7; "Eau Zone expands with new name", *Marketing Week*, 6 November 1992, p. 8; Suzanne Bidlake, "Givenchy TV ads 'plug' discounters", *Marketing*, 17 December 1992, p. 6, Suzanne Bidlake, "Perfume firms fear wrath of retailers", *Marketing*, 29 October 1992, p. 5; Suzanne Bidlake, "Asda apes Superdrug with discount scent", *Marketing*, 22 October 1992, p. 5.

Questions for Discussion

1. What were the pricing objectives of perfume manufacturers such as Chanel and Givenchy? Explain.
2. What impact could a price war have on brand loyalty in this market? Why?
3. On what criteria had competition in this market previously been based? Was the new focus on price a sensible development?

19 Setting Prices

"Price is the most dangerous marketing weapon a firm can use. It should be handled with great care."

Eric Waarts

Erasmus University, Rotterdam

OBJECTIVES

- To understand the eight major stages of the process used to establish prices
- To explore issues connected with selecting pricing objectives
- To grasp the importance of assessing the target market's evaluation of price and its ability to buy
- To learn about demand for a product and to analyse the relationships between demand, costs and profits
- To learn how to evaluate competitors' prices and to investigate the different types of pricing policies
- To examine the major kinds of pricing methods and to understand how to determine a specific price
- To consider the "pricing balance"

Traditionally a consumer favourite, towards the end of the 1990s Kellogg's market share was being eroded by strong competition from rival General Mills and retailers' own label brands. It seems that one reason for the company's falling sales was that consumers believed the breakfast cereal brand to be expensive when compared with competitors' offerings. A second problem was the declining popularity of pre-sweetened cereals, an area in which Kellogg's had traditionally been strong. Consumers began to demand healthier breakfast options, leading to a decline in the overall market size. The scale of Kellogg's problems required radical action from the business, which responded by cutting prices on some of its most popular brands. The company also moved to emphasise the health benefits and nutritional value of eating breakfast cereal. It hoped that such action would help improve the growth of the sector.

The company ensured that consumers heard about its price cutting strategy by pouring an additional £20m into its UK advertising budget. This 40 per cent increase in spend was focused on a TV and press campaign which stressed that Kellogg's cereals are good value for money. The campaign began with a number of 20 second television advertisements informing the consumer about price cuts on brands such as Rice Krispies and Frosties. The advertisements featured mums and children in the supermarket and were accompanied by a sympathetic voiceover, saying that "Juggling the family shop isn't easy, especially when you want them to have their favourite. Now with Kellogg's help you can".

This was a radical departure from Kellogg's usual positioning as a premium brand. Traditionally, the company stressed the quality of its popular breakfast cereal brands, distancing itself from own labels by stating that "we don't make cereals for anyone else". Such a change in direction was brought about by a period of stagnation in the breakfast cereal market, during which retailers' own label brands made considerable inroads into Kellogg's market share. Families all over the country were electing to buy the cheaper retail brands, saving an average of 33 per cent in the process. Overall, during the period between 1996 and 1998, the market share of retailers' own label brands

587

increased almost 10 per cent up to nearly 33 per cent.

Although Kellogg's change in stance was drastic, it seems that the business may have had little option. Senior managers at Kellogg's believed that decisive action was needed to improve sales and encourage the market to grow. According to one food analyst: "This was Kellogg's UK being realistic. Although it has lost share to private label, until now the market has been growing so it hasn't been a problem in terms of volume. Now Kellogg's feels responsible for kicking the market into action." All marketers face difficult pricing decisions. Kellogg's market leading position and long term branding had protected it from frequent price-led initiatives. Even for Kellogg's, though, price became a very important aspect of its marketing mix programmes.

SOURCES: Anne-Marie Crawford, "Kellogg looks at branded TV slot", *Marketing*, 11 February 1999, p. 4; Danny Rogers, "Kellogg blitz to push price cuts", *Marketing*, 17 December 1998, p. 1; Robert McLuhan, "Kellogg push targets mums", *Marketing*, 4 March 1999, p. 21. *Photo*: Greg Meadows/Stock Boston.

I n the breakfast cereals market, a decline in market growth and increasing competition from retailer own label brands have increased the importance of price as a marketing tool. Major player Kellogg's has been forced to defend its market leading position by instigating price cuts. Setting prices of products requires careful analysis of numerous issues. This chapter examines the eight stages of a process that marketers can use when setting prices.

Figure 19.1 illustrates these eight stages. Stage 1 is the selection of a pricing objective that is congruent with the company's overall objectives and its marketing objectives. In stage 2, both the target market's evaluation of price and the ability of these consumers to buy must be assessed. Stage 3 requires marketers to determine the nature and price elasticity of demand. Stage 4, which consists of analysing demand, cost and profit relationships, is necessary for estimating the economic feasibility of alternative prices. Evaluation of competitors' prices, which constitutes stage 5, helps determine the role of price in the marketing strategy. Stage 6 is the selection of a pricing policy, or the guidelines for using price in the marketing mix. Stage 7 involves developing a method for calculating the price charged to customers. Stage 8, the determination of the final price, depends on environmental forces and marketers' understanding and use of a systematic approach to establishing prices. These stages are not rigid steps that all marketers must follow but rather guidelines that provide a logical sequence for establishing prices. In some situations, additional stages may need to be included in the price setting process: in others, certain stages may not be necessary.

Figure 19.1 Stages for establishing prices

Stages for Establishing Prices

In considering the stages for establishing prices, it is important for marketers to grasp target customers' evaluation of price and perceived value for money, as well as understand market trends and competitors' pricing moves.[1] The "economics" of pricing—demand curves and price elasticity, plus the relationship in the market in question between demand, costs and profits—must also be addressed. The marketer must ultimately choose from a variety of pricing policies and specific pricing methods. In reviewing the eight stages for establishing prices, the remainder of this chapter examines these issues in greater depth. The final section explains that in the reality of day-to-day operational situations, many marketers are forced to take a broader look at pricing concerns and to exercise a degree of pragmatism in determining the price element of the marketing mix.

Selection of Pricing Objectives (Stage 1)

Chapter 18 considered the various types of pricing objectives. Pricing objectives must be explicitly stated because they form the basis for decisions about other stages of pricing.[2] The statement of pricing objectives should include the time within which the objectives are to be accomplished.

Marketers must be certain that the pricing objectives they set are consistent with the company's overall and marketing objectives. Marketing Insight 19.1 shows that Waterford priced its new range deliberately low to enable its corporate goals to be achieved. Inconsistent objectives cause internal conflicts and confusion and can prevent the business from achieving its overall goals. Furthermore, such inconsistency may cause marketers to make poor decisions during the other stages in the price setting process.

Businesses normally have multiple pricing objectives, some short term and others long term. For example, the pricing objective of gaining market share is normally short term in that it often requires the company to price its product quite low relative to competitors' prices. A business should have one or more pricing objectives for each product. For the same product aimed at different market segments, marketers sometimes choose different pricing objectives. A marketer typically alters pricing objectives over time.

Assessing the Target Market's Evaluation of Price and Its Ability to Buy (Stage 2)

Although it is generally assumed that price is a significant issue for buyers, the importance of price depends on the type of product, the type of target market and the purchase situation. For example, most buyers are more sensitive to petrol prices than to the cost of a new passport. With respect to the type of target market, the price of an airline ticket is much more important to a tourist than to a business traveller. The purchase situation also has a major impact. Thus motorists would not normally be prepared to pay the inflated prices which motorway service areas charge for canned drinks and food. By assessing the target market's evaluation of price, a marketer is in a better position to know how much emphasis to place on price. This also allows the marketer to determine how far above the competition a company can set its prices.

As discussed in Chapter 7, the people who make up a market must have the ability to buy a product. This ability to buy, like buyers' evaluation of price, has direct consequences for marketers. It involves such resources as money, credit, wealth and other products that could be traded in an exchange. Understanding customers' buying power and knowing how important a product is to them in comparison with other products helps marketers correctly assess the target market's evaluation of price. As outlined in the previous chapter, it is also important to understand the consumers' view of actual price versus perceived value for money.

Determining Demand (Stage 3)

Determining the demand for a product is the responsibility of marketing managers, who are aided in this task by marketing researchers and forecasters. Marketing research and forecasting techniques yield estimates of sales potential or the quantity of a product that could be sold during a specific period. (Chapter 22 describes such techniques as surveys, time series analyses, correlation methods and market tests.) These estimates are helpful in establishing the relationship between a product's price and the quantity demanded.

The Demand Curve

For most products, the quantity demanded goes up as the price goes down and goes down as the price goes up. Thus there is an inverse relationship between price and quantity demanded. As long as the marketing environment and buyers' needs, ability (purchasing power), willingness and authority to buy remain stable, this fundamental inverse relationship will continue.

Figure 19.2 illustrates the effect of one variable—price—on the quantity demanded. The classic **demand curve** (D1) is a graph of the quantity of products expected to be sold at various prices, if other factors remain constant.[3] It illustrates that as price falls, the quantity demanded usually increases. Demand depends on other factors in the marketing mix, including product quality, promotion and distribution. An improvement in any of these factors may cause a shift to, say, demand curve D2. In such a case, an increased quantity (Q2) will be sold at the same price (P). For example, if a manufacturer of engine oil improves the quality of its product, customers may be prepared to pay more for it because they do not need to change it as frequently.

Demand curve A graph of the quantity of products expected to be sold at various prices, if other factors remain constant

Waterford: Crystal Maker Moves "Downscale"

Irish crystal manufacturer Waterford Glass Group acquired the famous chinaware manufacturer Josiah Wedgwood in 1986. The china division became profitable, but the crystal operation suffered a 73 per cent drop in profits. Gradually, there has been an overall recovery, and Waterford Wedgwood is now the world's leading manufacturer of high quality china and glassware. The company is particularly strong in North America, with expanding markets in Japan and Europe. Its products, premium priced giftware, are bought for special occasions or as notable gifts—emotional purchases supported by its strong, reputable brand names of Waterford and Wedgwood. The declining fortunes for the company in the late 1980s/early 1990s forced the company to re-examine its ranges and price levels.

With its new Marquis line, initially targeted at the North American market, the venerable crystal maker took a new approach to manufacturing and marketing. Waterford moved its production into Europe and scaled down its price points, which now start at $30 for smaller pieces, on average 30 per cent cheaper than traditional Waterford lines. Seen by some observers as risky, this new line for "the less well heeled", manufactured in Germany, Portugal and parts of the former Yugoslavia, has brought crystal to a more youthful target market.

In the US, where Waterford has 28 per cent of the luxury crystal market, "Marquis by Waterford Crystal" is positioned in the $30 to $40 niche (although larger platters and bowls retail at $135) in order to compete more directly with crystal suppliers Mikasa, Lenox, Miller Rogasks and Gorham. The 1991 launch into 30 stores proved immediately profitable. Marquis was a huge gamble; it moved the company away from the "finest hand-crafted Irish" traditions and the Waterford brand heritage, which in the US and Japan puts it alongside names such as Rolls Royce and Rolex. Marquis has been rolled out successfully globally.

The traditional Wedgwood and Waterford ranges are not generally intended to be day-to-day functional lines. They are premium priced and intended as "special", lasting purchases. This is an image well cultivated by the company's advertising and public relations and its refusal to become involved with discounting and retailer promotions. Carefully controlled distribution through only leading china/crystal showrooms and department stores further enhances the exclusive branding. Premium priced modern designs by John Rocha cemented Waterford's prestige positioning. The core market is the giftware sector, which its ceramics and glassware share with cutlery, jewellery (by far the dominant gift category), toys and games, and leather goods. Within crystal giftware there are five distinct segments: general giftware, weddings, investment giftware, business gifts/incentives and specials such as sporting trophies.

The giftware market depends on emotions. The selection of a gift, no matter what the occasion, is a personal, subjective and often risky action. Nowhere are individual consumer tastes and social influences more to the fore. Innovative, individually crafted, expensive crystal is a difficult purchase over which buyers agonise. High ticket prices and the very "personal" nature of the merchandise often extend the buying process as family and friends' opinions are sought. Will the choice be liked? Is it right for the intended home? Is it correct for the occasion? Is it value for money?

Waterford's enviable worldwide reputation is built upon a heritage of hand-crafted superior workmanship at its Irish birthplace. The company has been able to command premium prices in expanding international markets. The giftware market is idiosyncratic and very much consumer driven. In an economic recession, premium priced crystal is not at the top of every consumer's shopping list. Waterford is striving to build on its roots, while taking its wares into more countries and to a wider audience with its new lines, designer ranges and lower pricing with Marquis. In each segment, customers have specific needs and expectations, not always matched by the premium priced Waterford products. To expand the appeal and sales of a de luxe product without alienating the core target market is no easy task, particularly for such an emotive product as crystal.

SOURCES: Waterford Company statements, 1992–1999; Harvest; Warwick University's Business Information Service; Caroline Farquhar; Sally Dibb and Lyndon Simkin, *The Marketing Casebook* (ITP: London, 2000); Robert Gray, "A green and pleasant brand", *Marketing*, 20 July 1995, pp. 22–23; "Gifts galore", *Incentive*, 169 (4), 1995, pp. 77–86; "Give 'em a hand", *Incentive*, 168 (6), 1994, pp. 79–82.

Figure 19.2 Demand curve illustrating the price-quantity relationship and an increase in demand. SOURCE: Reprinted from *Dictionary of Marketing Terms*, Peter D. Bennett, ed., 1988, p. 54, published by the American Marketing Association. Used by permission.

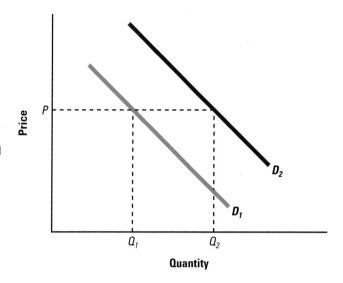

There are many types of demand, and not all conform to the classic demand curve shown in Figure 19.2. Prestige products, such as exclusive fragrances, designer clothes and jewellery, seem to sell better at high prices than at low ones. These products are desirable partly because their cost makes buyers feel superior. If their price fell drastically and many people owned them, they would lose some of their appeal.

The demand curve in Figure 19.3 shows the relationship between price and quantity for prestige products. Demand is greater, not less, at higher prices. For a certain price range—from P1 to P2—the quantity demanded (Q1) goes up to Q2. After a point, however, raising the price back-fires. If the price of a product goes too high, the quantity demanded goes down. The figure shows that if the price is raised from P2 to P3, quantity demanded goes back down from Q2 to Q1.

Demand Fluctuations

Changes in buyers' needs, variations in the effectiveness of other marketing mix variables, the presence of substitutes and dynamic environmental factors can influence demand. Restaurants and utility companies experience large fluctuations in demand daily. Holiday companies, fireworks suppliers, and air conditioning and heating contractors also face demand fluctuations because of the seasonal nature of these items. The demand for mobile phones, leaded fuels and fur coats has changed significantly over the last few years. In some cases, demand fluctuations are predictable and in others they are not. Some companies cope with unpredictable demand fluctuations by correlating demand for a specific product with demand for the total industry or with some other economic variable.

Gauging Price Elasticity of Demand

Up to this point, the discussion has considered how marketers identify the target market's evaluation of price and its ability to purchase and how they examine whether price is related inversely or directly to quantity. The next stage in the process is to gauge price elasticity of demand. **Price elasticity of demand** provides a measure of the sensitivity of demand to changes in price. It is formally defined as the percentage change in quantity demanded relative to a given percentage change in price (see Figure 19.4).[4] The percentage change in quantity demanded

Price elasticity of demand A measure of the sensitivity of demand to changes in price

Figure 19.3 Demand curve illustrating the relationship between price and quantity for prestige products

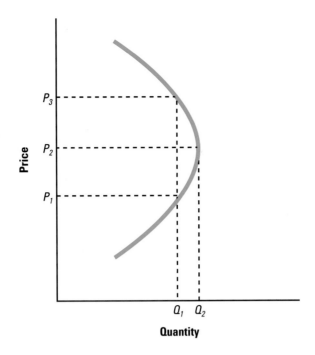

caused by a percentage change in price is much greater for elastic demand than for inelastic demand. For products such as electricity, gas and water, demand is relatively inelastic. When its price is increased, say from P1 to P2, quantity demanded goes down only a little, from Q1 to Q2. For products such as movie tickets, demand is relatively elastic. When price rises sharply, from P1 to P2, quantity demanded goes down a great deal, from Q1 to Q2.

If marketers can determine price elasticity of demand, it is much easier for them to set a price. By analysing total revenues as prices change, marketers can determine whether a product is "price elastic". Total revenue is price times quantity: thus 10,000 rolls of wallpaper sold in one year at a price of £10 per roll equals £100,000 of total revenue. If demand is *elastic,* a change in price causes an opposite change in total revenue—an increase in price will decrease total revenue, and a decrease in price will increase total revenue. An *inelastic* demand

Figure 19.4 Elasticity of demand. SOURCE: Adapted from *Dictionary of Marketing Terms*, Peter D. Bennett, ed., 1988, p. 54, published by the American Marketing Association. Used by permission.

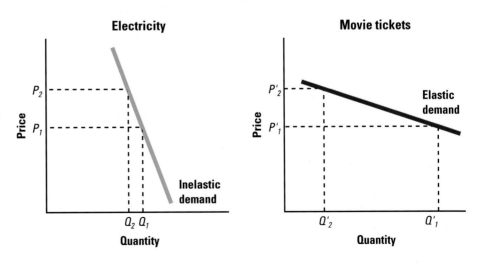

results in a change in the same direction in total revenue—an increase in price will increase total revenue, and a decrease in price will decrease total revenue. The following formula determines the price elasticity of demand:

$$\text{Price Elasticity of Demand} = \frac{\% \text{ Change in Quantity Demanded}}{\% \text{ Change in Price}}$$

For example, if demand falls by 8 per cent when a seller raises the price by 2 per cent, the price elasticity of demand is -4 (the negative sign indicating the inverse relationship between price and demand). If demand falls by 2 per cent when price is increased by 4 per cent, then elasticity is $-\frac{1}{2}$. The less elastic the demand, the more beneficial it is for the seller to raise the price. Products for which substitutes are not readily available and for which consumers have strong needs (for example, electricity or petrol) usually have inelastic demand.

Marketers cannot base prices solely on elasticity considerations. They must also examine the costs associated with different volumes and see what happens to profits.

Analysis of Demand, Cost and Profit Relationships (Stage 4)

The previous section examined the role of demand in setting prices and the various costs and their relationships; this section explores the relationships between demand, costs and profits. There are two approaches to understanding demand, cost and profit relationships: (1) marginal analysis and (2) break even analysis.

Marginal Analysis

Fixed costs Those costs that do not vary with changes in the number of units produced or sold

Average fixed cost The fixed cost per unit produced, calculated by dividing fixed costs by the number of units produced

Variable costs Those costs that vary directly with changes in the number of units produced or sold

Average variable cost The variable cost per unit produced, calculated by dividing the variable costs by the number of units produced

Total cost The sum of average fixed costs and average variable costs multiplied by the quantity produced

Average total cost The sum of the average fixed cost and the average variable cost

Marginal cost (MC) The extra cost a company incurs when it produces one more unit of a product

Marginal analysis is the examination of what happens to a company's costs and revenues when production (or sales volume) is changed by one unit. Both production costs and revenues must be evaluated. To determine the costs of production, it is necessary to distinguish between several types of costs. **Fixed costs** do not vary with changes in the number of units produced or sold. The cost of renting a factory does not change because production increases from one shift to two shifts a day, or because twice as much wallpaper is sold. Rent may go up, but not because the factory has doubled production or revenue. **Average fixed cost,** the fixed cost per unit produced, is calculated by dividing fixed costs by the number of units produced.

Variable costs vary directly with changes in the number of units produced or sold. The wages for a second shift and the cost of twice as much paper are extra costs that occur when production is doubled. Variable costs are usually constant per unit; that is, twice as many workers and twice as much material produce twice as many rolls of wallpaper. **Average variable cost,** the variable cost per unit produced, is calculated by dividing the variable costs by the number of units produced.

Total cost is the sum of average fixed costs and average variable costs multiplied by the quantity produced. The **average total cost** is the sum of the average fixed cost and the average variable cost. **Marginal cost (MC)** is the extra cost a company incurs when it produces one more unit of a product. Table 19.1 illustrates various costs and their relationships. Notice that the average fixed cost declines as the output increases. The average variable cost follows a U shape, as does the average total cost. Because the average total cost continues to fall after the average variable cost begins to rise, its lowest point is at a higher level of out-

1	2	3	4	5	6	7
Quantity	Fixed Cost	Average Fixed Cost (2) ÷ (1)	Average Variable Cost	Average Total Cost (3) + (4)	Total Cost (5) × (1)	Marginal Cost
1	£40	£40.00	£20.00	£60.00	£60	£10
2	40	20.00	15.00	35.00	70	5
3	40	13.33	11.67	25.00	75	15
4	40	10.00	12.50	22.50	90	20
5	40	8.00	14.00	22.00	110	30
6	40	6.67	16.67	23.33	140	40
7	40	5.71	20.00	25.71	180	

Table 19.1 Costs and their relationships

put than that of the average variable cost. The average total cost is lowest at 5 units at a cost of £22, whereas the average variable cost is lowest at 3 units at a cost of £11.67. As shown in Figure 19.5, marginal cost equals average total cost at the latter's lowest level. In Table 19.1 this occurs between 5 and 6 units of production. Average total cost decreases as long as the marginal cost is less than the average total cost, and it increases when marginal cost rises above average total cost.

Marginal revenue (MR) is the change in total revenue that occurs when a company sells an additional unit of a product. Figure 19.6 depicts marginal revenue and a demand curve. Most businesses in Europe face downward sloping demand curves for their products. In other words, they must lower their prices to sell additional units. This situation means that each additional product sold provides the business with less revenue than the previous unit sold. MR then becomes less than average revenue, as Figure 19.6 shows. Eventually, MR reaches zero, and the sale of additional units merely hurts the company.

However, before the company can determine whether a unit makes a profit, it must know its cost, as well as its revenue, because profit equals revenue minus cost. If MR is a unit's addition to revenue and MC is a unit's addition to cost, then MR minus MC tells whether the unit is profitable or not. Table 19.2 illustrates the relationships between price, quantity sold, total revenue, marginal revenue, marginal cost and total cost. It indicates where maximum profits are possible at various combinations of price and cost.

Profit is maximised where MC = MR (see Table 19.2). In this table MC = MR at 4 units. The best price, therefore, is £33.75 and the profit is £45. Up to this point, the additional revenue generated from an extra unit of sale exceeds the additional total cost. Beyond this point, the additional cost of another unit sold exceeds the additional revenue generated, and profits decrease. If the price was based on minimum average total cost—£22 (Table 19.1)—it would result in less profit: only £40 (Table 19.2) or 5 units at a price of £30 versus £45 for 4 units at a price of £33.75.

Graphically combining Figures 19.5 and 19.6 into Figure 19.7 shows that any unit for which MR exceeds MC adds to a company's profits, and any unit for which MC exceeds MR subtracts from a company's profits. The company should produce at the point where MR equals MC, because this is the most profitable level of production.

Marginal revenue (MR) The change in total revenue that occurs when a company sells an additional unit of a product

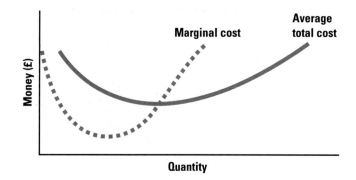

Figure 19.5 Typical marginal cost and average cost relationships

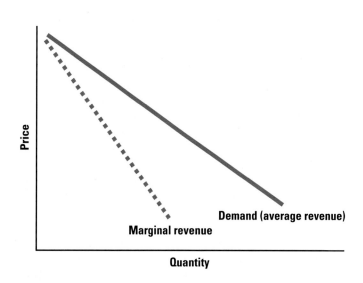

Figure 19.6 Typical marginal revenue and demand (average revenue) relationships

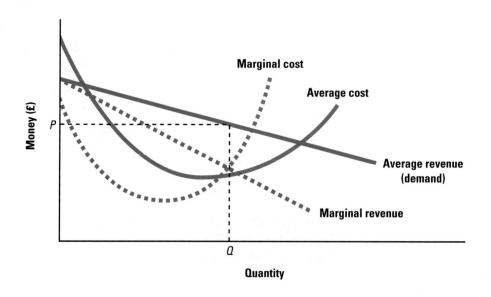

Figure 19.7 Combining the marginal cost and marginal revenue concepts for optimal profit

Table 19.2 Marginal analysis: method of obtaining maximum profit producing price

1	2	3	4	5	6	7
Price	Quantity Sold	Total Revenue (1) × (2)	Marginal Revenue	Marginal Cost	Total Cost	Profit (3)−(6)
£57.00	1	£ 57	£57	£—	£ 60	£−3
55.00	2	110	53	10	70	40
40.00	3	120	10	5	75	45
33.75*	4	135	15	15	90	45
30.00	5	150	15	20	110	40
27.00	6	162	12	30	140	22
25.00	7	175	13	40	180	−5

*Boldface indicates best price-profit combination.

This discussion of marginal analysis may give the false impression that pricing can be highly precise. If revenue (demand) and cost (supply) remained constant, then prices could be set for maximum profits. In practice, however, cost and revenue change frequently. The competitive tactics of other companies or government action can quickly undermine a company's expectations of revenue. Thus marginal analysis is only a model from which to work. It offers little help in pricing new products before costs and revenues are established. On the other hand, in setting prices of existing products, especially in competitive situations, most marketers can benefit by understanding the relationship between marginal cost and marginal revenue.

Break Even Analysis

Break even point The point at which the costs of producing a product equal the revenue made from selling the product

The point at which the costs of producing a product equal the revenue made from selling the product is the **break even point.** If a pet food manufacturer has total annual costs of £100,000 and in the same year sells £100,000 worth of pet food, then the company has broken even: no profits, no losses.

Figure 19.8 illustrates the relationships of costs, revenue, profits and losses involved in determining the break even point. Knowing the number of units necessary to break even is important in setting the price. If a product priced at £100 per unit has an average variable cost of £60 per unit, then the contribution to fixed costs is £40. If total fixed costs are £120,000, here is the way to determine the break even point in units:

$$\text{Break Even Point} = \frac{\text{Fixed Costs}}{\text{Per Unit Contribution to Fixed Costs}}$$

$$\frac{\text{Fixed Costs}}{\text{Price-Variable Costs}}$$

$$\frac{£120,000}{£40}$$

$$= 3{,}000 \text{ Units}$$

To calculate the break even point in terms of cash sales volume, multiply the break even point in units by the price per unit. In the preceding example, the break even point in terms of cash sales volume is 3,000 (units) times £100, or £300,000.

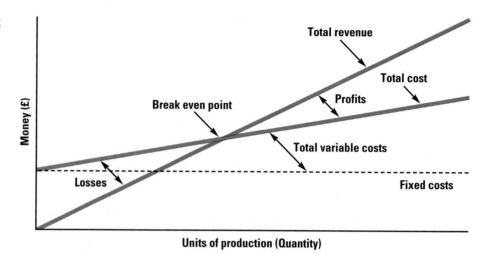

Figure 19.8 Determining the break even point

To use break even analysis effectively, a marketer should determine the break even point for each of several alternative prices. This allows the marketer to compare the effects on total revenue, total cost and the break even point for each price under consideration. Although this comparative analysis may not tell the marketer exactly what price to charge, it will identify highly undesirable price alternatives that should definitely be avoided.

Break even analysis is simple and straightforward. It does assume, however, that the quantity demanded is basically fixed (inelastic) and that the major task in setting prices is to recover costs. It focuses more on how to break even than on how to achieve a pricing objective, such as percentage of market share or return on investment. Nonetheless, marketing managers can use this concept to determine whether a product will achieve at least a break even volume. In other words, it is easier to answer the question "Will we sell at least the minimum volume necessary to break even?" than the question "What volume of sales will we expect to sell?"

Evaluation of Competitors' Prices (Stage 5)

Marketers are generally in a better position to establish prices when they know the prices charged for competing brands. Learning competitors' prices may be a regular function of marketing research. Some grocery and department stores, for example, have full time comparative shoppers who systematically collect data on prices. Companies may also purchase price lists, sometimes weekly, from syndicated marketing research agencies.

Finding out what prices competitors are charging is not always easy, especially in producer and reseller markets. Even if a marketer has access to price lists, they may not reflect the actual prices at which competitive products are sold because those prices may be established through negotiation.

Competitors' prices and the marketing mix variables that they emphasise partly determine how important price will be to customers. Marketers in an industry in which non-price competition prevails need competitive price information to ensure that their company's prices are the same as its competitors' prices. In some instances, a company's prices are designed to be slightly above competitors' prices to give its products an exclusive image. Alternatively, another company may use price as a competitive tool and attempt to set its prices below those of competitors. DFS, Toys "R" Us and Superdrug, for example, have all acquired a large market share through aggressive competitive prices.

Selection of a Pricing Policy (Stage 6)

Pricing policy A guiding philosophy or course of action designed to influence and determine pricing decisions

A **pricing policy** is a guiding philosophy or course of action designed to influence and determine pricing decisions. Pricing policies set guidelines for achieving pricing objectives and are an important component of an overall marketing strategy. Generally, pricing policies should answer this recurring question: "How will price be used as a variable in the marketing mix?" This question may relate to the effects of (1) introducing new products, (2) competitive situations, (3) government pricing regulations, (4) economic conditions or (5) implementing pricing objectives. Pricing policies help marketers solve the practical problems of establishing prices. This section examines the most common pricing policies: pioneer pricing, psychological pricing, professional pricing and promotional pricing.

Pioneer Pricing Policies

Pioneer pricing The setting of a base price for a new product

Pioneer pricing—setting the base price for a new product—is a necessary part of formulating a marketing strategy and a fundamental marketing mix decision. The base price is easily adjusted and can be set high to recover development costs quickly or to provide a reference point for developing discount prices to different market segments. When marketers set base prices, they also consider how quickly competitors will enter the market, whether they will mount a strong campaign on entry and what effect their entry will have on the development of primary demand. If competitors will enter quickly with considerable marketing force and with limited effect on the primary demand, a company may adopt a base price that will discourage their entry.[5]

Price skimming A pricing policy whereby a company charges the highest possible price that buyers who most desire the product will pay

Price Skimming Price skimming is charging the highest possible price that buyers who most desire the product will pay. This pioneer approach provides the most flexible introductory base price. Demand tends to be inelastic in the introductory stage of the product life cycle (for example, as with digital television and the pocket calculator).

Price skimming can provide several benefits, especially when a product is in the introductory stage of its life cycle. A skimming policy can generate much needed initial cash flows to help off-set sizeable developmental costs. When introducing a new model of camera, Polaroid initially uses a skimming price to defray large research and development costs. Price skimming can be particularly important when a company introduces a product because its production capacity may be limited. A skimming price can help keep demand consistent with a company's production capabilities. Sometimes the use of a skimming price may attract competition into an industry because the high price makes that type of business appear to be quite lucrative.

Penetration pricing A pricing policy of setting a price below the prices of competing brands in order to penetrate a market and produce a larger unit sales volume

Penetration Pricing Penetration pricing is setting a price below the prices of competing brands in order to penetrate a market and produce a larger unit sales volume. When introducing a product, a marketer sometimes uses penetration pricing to gain a large market share quickly. As shown in Figure 19.9, penetration pricing is popular even for well known products. This approach places the

Figure 19.9 Pricing.
Many advertisements
place great emphasis on
apparently keen pricing.
Source: Courtesy Bodum
AG.

marketer in a less flexible position than price skimming because it is more difficult to raise a penetration price than to lower or discount a skimming price. It is not unusual for a company to use a penetration price after having skimmed the market with a higher price.

Penetration pricing can be especially beneficial when marketers suspect that competitors could enter the market easily. First, if penetration pricing lets one marketer gain a large market share quickly, competitors might be discouraged from entering the market. Second, entering the market may be less attractive to competitors when penetration pricing is used, because the lower per unit price results in lower per unit profit; this may cause competitors to view the market as not being especially lucrative.

Penetration pricing is particularly appropriate when demand is highly elastic. Highly elastic demand means that target market members would purchase the product if it was priced at the penetration level but that few would buy the item if it was priced higher. A marketer should consider using penetration pricing when a lower price would result in longer production runs, increasing production significantly and reducing per unit production costs.

Psychological Pricing

Psychological pricing A pricing method designed to encourage purchases that are based on emotional rather than rational responses

Psychological pricing encourages purchases that are based on emotional rather than rational responses. Used most often at the retail level, psychological pricing includes odd-even pricing, customary pricing, prestige pricing and price lining. Psychological pricing has limited use for industrial products.

Odd-even pricing A pricing method that tries to influence buyers' perceptions of the price or the product by ending the price with certain numbers

Odd-Even Pricing   Through **odd-even pricing**—that is, ending the price with certain numbers—marketers try to influence buyers' perceptions of the price or the product. Odd pricing assumes that more of a product will be sold at £99.95 than at £100. Supposedly, customers will think, or at least tell friends, that the product is a bargain—not £100, mind you, but £99, plus a few insignificant pence. Also, customers are supposed to think that the store could have charged £100 but instead cut the price to the last penny or so, to £99.95. Some claim, too, that certain types of customers are more attracted by odd prices than by even ones. However, no substantial research findings support the notion that odd prices produce greater sales. Nonetheless, even prices are far more unusual today than odd prices. Even prices are used to give a product an exclusive, high quality or up-market image. A tie manufacturer, for example, may print on a premium silk tie packet a suggested retail price of £42 instead of £41.95; the even price of the tie is used to enhance its up-market image.

Customary pricing A pricing method whereby goods are priced primarily on the basis of tradition

Customary Pricing   In **customary pricing**, certain goods are priced primarily on the basis of tradition. Recent economic uncertainties have caused most prices to fluctuate fairly widely, but the classic example of the customary, or traditional, price is the telephone call. Until the mid-1980s, UK public telephones were geared to the use of particular coins. For years the 2p and, later, the 10p slots were widely recognised. BT's initial response to rising prices was to alter the cost of units so that less call time was allowed for the same money. Since then, demands for greater flexibility of use have seen public call boxes altered to accept most British coins.

Prestige pricing A pricing method whereby prices are set at an artificially high level to provide prestige or a quality image

Prestige Pricing   In **prestige pricing**, prices are set at an artificially high level to provide prestige or a quality image. In the United States, pharmacists report that some consumers complain if a prescription does not cost enough because they associate a drug's price with its potency. Businesses in Europe often associate the quality of service provided by a management consultant with price. Prestige pricing is used especially when buyers associate a higher price with higher quality. Typical product categories in which selected products are given prestige prices include perfumes, cars, alcoholic beverages, jewellery, cameras, and electrical appliances. Dramatically lowering the prices of products with prestige prices would be inconsistent with the perceived images of such products.

Price lining A pricing method whereby a business sets a limited number of prices for selected groups or lines of merchandise

Price Lining   When a business sets a limited number of prices for selected groups or lines of merchandise, it is using **price lining**. A retailer may have various styles and brands of men's shirts of similar quality that sell for £10. Another line of higher quality shirts may sell for £20. Price lining simplifies consumers' decision-making by holding constant one key variable in the final selection of style and brand within a line. In product line pricing, the company should look at the prices of the overall product line to ensure that the price of the new model lies within the range of existing prices for that line. Failure to consider the impact of the new model's price relative to the existing product line may change buyers' perceptions of all the models in the line.[6]

The basic assumption in price lining is that the demand is inelastic for various groups or sets of products. If the prices are attractive, customers will concentrate their purchases without responding to slight changes in price. Thus a women's dress shop that carries dresses priced at £85, £55 and £35 might not attract many more sales with a drop to, say, £83, £53 and £33. The "space" between the prices

Figure 19.10 Price lining

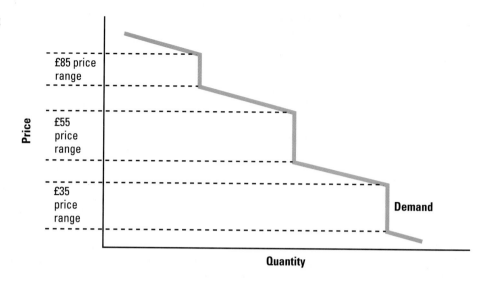

of £55 and £35, however, can stir changes in consumer response. With price lining, the demand curve looks like a series of steps, as shown in Figure 19.10.

Professional Pricing

Professional pricing Pricing used by people who have great skill or experience in a particular field or activity

Professional pricing is used by people who have great skill or experience in a particular field or activity. Some professionals who provide such products as medical services feel that their fees (prices) should not relate directly to their time and involvement in specific cases; rather, they charge a standard fee regardless of the problems involved in performing the job. Some estate agents' and solicitors' fees are prime examples: 2 per cent of a house sale price, plus VAT, and £500 for house conveyancing. Other professionals set prices in other ways.

The concept of professional pricing carries with it the idea that professionals have an ethical responsibility not to over charge unknowing customers. In some situations, a seller can charge customers a high price and continue to sell many units of the product. Medicine offers several examples. If a patient with high blood pressure requires four tablets a day to survive, the individual will pay for the prescription whether it costs £5 or £50 per month. In fact, the patient would purchase the pills even if the price went higher. In these situations sellers could charge exorbitant fees. Drug companies claim that despite their positions of strength in this regard, they charge "ethical" prices rather than what the market will bear.[7] However, in parts of Europe the high cost of the new impotence drug Viagra has recently attracted criticism among medical professionals.

Promotional Pricing

Promotional pricing Pricing related to the short term promotion of a particular product

Price is an ingredient in the marketing mix, and it is often co-ordinated with promotion. The two variables sometimes are so inter-related that the pricing policy is promotion oriented. **Promotional pricing** is a pricing policy whereby pricing is related to the short term promotion of a particular product. Examples of promotional pricing include (1) **price leaders**, (2) **special event pricing**, (3) **everyday low pricing (EDLP)** and (4) **experience curve pricing**. These types of pricing are illustrated in Table 19.3, which also explains the circumstances in which they can be used.

Misleading Pricing

Misleading pricing Pricing policies that intentionally confuse or dupe consumers

Many countries have legislation controlling the use of **misleading pricing**—pricing policies that intentionally confuse or dupe consumers. The UK Consumer Protection Act (1987), which makes it illegal to mislead customers about the price at which products or services are offered for sale, is typical. This Act con-

Table 19.3 Types of promotional pricing

Price leaders Products sold below the usual mark-up, near cost or below cost

Special event pricing Advertised sales or price cutting that is linked to a holiday, season or event to increase sales volume

Everyday low pricing (EDLP) The reduction of retail prices of leading brands for a prolonged period

Experience curve pricing A pricing policy in which a company expands its market share by fixing a low price that high cost competitors cannot match

• Price Leaders	Products sold below the usual mark-up, near cost or below cost. Used most often in supermarkets and department stores to attract consumers by giving low prices on just a few items. The intention is that while in store they will buy other full priced items.
• Special Event Pricing	Advertised sales or price cutting that is linked to a holiday, season or event to increase sales volume. If the pricing objective is survival, special sales events may help generate the necessary operating capital. Marketers can use this pricing to generate revenue when there is a sales lag.
• Everyday Low Pricing (EDLP)	The reduction of retail prices of leading brands for a prolonged period. EDLP is usually given high visibility in a store. Reduced promotional budgets and improvements in logistics are used to create financial savings that are used to support such price cuts.
• Experience Curve Pricing	A pricing policy in which a company expands its market share by fixing a low price that high cost competitors cannot match. This practice is possible when a company gains cumulative production experience and is able to reduce manufacturing costs at a predictable rate through improved methods, materials, skills and machinery. The so called experience curve depicts the inverse relationship between production costs per unit and cumulative production quantity.

SOURCES: Amanda Richards, "P&G price cuts to hit own label", *Marketing*, 15 February 1996, p. 1; "P&G censures press over memo coverage", *Marketing Week*, 23 February 1996, pp. 8–9; Allan Mitchell, "Two sides of the same argument", *Marketing Week*, 16 February 1996, pp. 26–27; Stephen Hoch, Xavier Dreze and Mark Purk, "EDLP—hi-lo, and margin arithmetic", *Journal of Marketing*, 58 (4), 1994, pp. 16–27.

tains a code of practice which, although not legally binding, encourages companies to offer explanations whenever price comparisons or reductions are made. According to the *Which?* handbook of consumer law, "Unexplained reductions from a store's own prices should be used only if the goods have been on sale at the same store for 28 days in the preceding six months, and if the price quoted was the last price at which the goods were on sale."[8] South Korean car manufacturer Daewoo is mounting a campaign against the asterisk, common in most rivals' advertisements. These state a list price for a car model, yet the "small print", as referenced by the asterisk, reveals additional costs for delivery, number plates and road tax that may be as much as £450. Daewoo argues that hiding these extra charges is misleading.[9]

Pricing method   A mechanical procedure for assigning prices to specific products on a regular basis

After selecting a pricing policy, a marketer must choose a **pricing method**, a mechanical procedure for assigning prices to specific products on a regular basis. The pricing method structures the calculation of the actual price. The nature of a product, its sales volume or the amount of product the company carries will determine how prices are calculated. For example, a procedure for pricing the thousands of products in a supermarket must be simpler and more direct than that for calculating the price of a limited edition ceramic figurine made by Wedgwood or Royal Doulton. This section examines four types of pricing methods: cost oriented, demand oriented, competition oriented and marketing oriented pricing.

Cost Oriented Pricing

Cost oriented pricing   A pricing method whereby a monetary amount or percentage is added to the cost of a product

In **cost oriented pricing**, a monetary amount or percentage is added to the cost of a product. The method thus involves calculations of desired margins or profit margins. Cost oriented pricing methods do not necessarily take into account the economic aspects of supply and demand, nor do they necessarily relate to a specific pricing policy or ensure the attainment of pricing objectives. They are, however, simple and easy to implement. Two common cost oriented pricing methods are cost plus and mark-up pricing.

Cost plus pricing   A pricing method based on adding a specified amount or percentage to the seller's cost after that cost is determined

Cost Plus Pricing   In **cost plus pricing**, the seller's costs are determined and the price is then set by adding a specified amount or percentage of the cost to the seller's cost. Cost plus pricing is appropriate when production costs are difficult to predict or production takes a long time. Custom made equipment and commercial construction projects are often priced by this method. The government frequently uses cost oriented pricing in granting defence contracts. One pitfall for the buyer is that the seller may increase costs to establish a larger profit base. Furthermore, some costs, such as overheads, may be difficult to determine.

In periods of rapid inflation, cost plus pricing is popular, especially when the producer must use raw materials that are fluctuating in price. For industries in which cost plus pricing is common and sellers have similar costs, price competition may not be especially intense.

Mark-up pricing   A pricing method whereby a product's price is derived by adding a pre-determined percentage of the cost, called *mark-up*, to the cost of the product

Mark-Up Pricing   A common pricing method among retailers is **mark-up pricing**. In mark-up pricing, a product's price is derived by adding a pre-determined percentage of the cost, called *mark-up*, to the cost of the product. Although the percentage mark-up in a retail store varies from one category of goods to another (35 per cent of cost for hardware items and 100 per cent of cost for greeting cards, for example), the same percentage is often used to determine the price of items within a single product category, and the same or similar percentage mark-up may be standardised across an industry at the retail level. Using a rigid percentage mark-up for a specific product category reduces pricing to a routine task that can be performed quickly.

Mark-up can be stated as a percentage of the cost or as a percentage of the selling price. The following example illustrates how percentage mark-ups are determined and points out the differences between the two methods. Assume that a retailer purchases a tin of new potatoes at 45p, adds 15p to the cost, and then prices the potatoes at 60 pence. Here are the figures:

$$\text{Mark-Up as a Percentage of Cost} = \frac{\text{Mark-Up}}{\text{Cost}} = \frac{15}{45} = 33\frac{1}{3}\%$$

$$\text{Mark-Up as a Percentage of Selling Price} = \frac{\text{Mark-Up}}{\text{Selling Price}} = \frac{15}{60} = 25\%$$

Obviously, when discussing a percentage mark-up, it is important to know whether the mark-up is based on cost or selling price.

Mark-ups normally reflect expectations about operating costs, risks and stock turnovers. Wholesalers and manufacturers often suggest standard retail mark-ups that are considered profitable. An average percentage mark-up on cost may be as high as 100 per cent or more for jewellery or as low as 20 per cent for this text book.

Demand Oriented Pricing

Demand oriented pricing A pricing method based on the level of demand for a product, resulting in a high price when demand is strong and a low price when demand is weak

Price differentiation A pricing method used when a company wants to use more than one price in the marketing of a specific product

Rather than basing the price of a product on its cost, marketers sometimes use a pricing method based on the level of demand for a product: **demand oriented pricing.** This method results in a high price when demand for a product is strong and a low price when demand is weak. Admission to the theatre often operates on this basis, with higher prices when demand is highest at weekends and during peak holiday periods. To use this method, a marketer must be able to estimate the amounts of a product that consumers will demand at different prices. The marketer then chooses the price that generates the highest total revenue.

A marketer may favour a demand oriented pricing method called **price differentiation** when a company wants to use more than one price in the marketing of a specific product. Price differentiation can be based on such considerations as type of customer, type of distribution channel or the time of the purchase. Here are several examples. Football clubs charge higher admission prices for high profile cup matches. Red roses are much more expensive on Valentine's Day than at other times of the year. London hotel accommodation is more expensive in the summer than in the winter.

For price differentiation to work properly, the marketer must be able to segment a market on the basis of different strengths of demand and then keep the segments separate enough so that segment members who buy at lower prices cannot then sell to buyers in segments that are charged a higher price.

Price differentiation is often facilitated in international marketing by the geographic distance between markets. For example, the price Matsushita Electric Co. charges for cordless Panasonic telephones in Japan is eight times the price charged for cordless telephones of slightly lower quality in the United States. When a Japanese trading company re-imported the US cordless phones and sold them for $80 instead of the Japanese model, which cost $657, consumers lined up to buy the cheaper telephone. To combat the re-importation, Matsushita bought up all the unsold, made for export Panasonic telephones it could find to eliminate the wide price differential.[10] The removal of trade barriers in the EU means that consumers are able, for the first time, to overcome the effects of price discrimination. They are free, for example, to shop around in different member states for the best deal on a new car or mortgage.

Price differentiation can also be based on employment in a public service position. For example, many music shops offer a 15 per cent discount to musicians.

Compared with cost oriented pricing, demand oriented pricing places a company in a better position to reach higher profit levels, assuming that buyers value the product at levels sufficiently above its actual cost. To use demand oriented pricing, however, a marketer must be able to estimate demand at different price levels, which is often difficult to do accurately.

Competition Oriented Pricing

In using **competition oriented pricing,** a business considers costs and revenue to be secondary to competitors' prices. The importance of this method increases if competing products are almost homogeneous and the company is servicing markets in which price is the key variable of the marketing strategy.[11] A business that uses competition oriented pricing may choose to be below competitors' prices, above competitors' prices or at the same level. The price of this text book paid by the bookshop to the publishing company was determined using competition oriented pricing. Competition oriented pricing should help attain a pricing objective to increase sales or market share. Competition oriented pricing methods may be combined with cost approaches to arrive at price levels necessary to generate a profit.

Marketing Oriented Pricing

More complex than cost or competition oriented pricing, **marketing oriented pricing** takes into account a wide range of factors:

- Marketing strategy
- Competition
- Value to the customer
- Price-quality relationships
- Explicability
- Costs
- Product line pricing
- Negotiating margins
- Political factors
- Effect on distributors/retailers

The price set must reflect the product's marketing strategy: its target market profile, brand positioning, sales targets. The price point—the actual ticket or displayed price—must also mesh with the other marketing mix ingredients. For example, an up-market premium priced restaurant will not work if located in a seedy area of town. Marketing Insight 19.2 shows how retailer Marks & Spencer is co-ordinating changes in a number of aspects of its marketing mix to tie in with price reductions. Marketers must be aware of competing products' prices and the product's value as perceived by the targeted customer. The customer in question has to be receptive to the determined price. This customer focused view is also reflected in two other criteria to consider: the price-quality relationship of the product and the explicability of the finalised prices. Just how plausible to the customer is the recommended price? If the product is part of a range, its price point will affect the other product lines on offer, and the whole range must be priced to avoid an individual product harming the achieved price and image of related lines. While a business must ensure that its costs of production, distribution and marketing are covered, it also has to recognise that its dealers and distributors must make an adequate margin on units sold and set its prices to its distribution channel partners accordingly. These channel members and the ultimate customer may expect to negotiate over price—very common in business-to-business markets—so the price must be set to permit such negotiating and discounting. Trade and government regulations may affect the flexibility a business has in establishing prices. For example, EU anti-dumping laws forbid hefty price discounting for certain markets. The intention of marketing oriented pricing is to take account of external factors as seen by the customer and experienced by channel members, in addition to the internal cost and performance drivers for so long central to management's thinking when setting prices.

M&S Emphasises Value for Money

As the 1990s drew to a close, global retailer Marks & Spencer hit a crisis. In one year alone the company's profit forecasts were cut almost in half to between £625m and £675m. The retailer's clothing lines were particularly heavily hit. Sales of M&S clothing were down, with some consumers describing the ranges as dowdy and of poor value. This equated to a 6 per cent reduction in clothing sales in the important Christmas period. M&S reacted by using its immense buying power to force suppliers to cut their prices so that M&S could in turn reduce prices in store without further damaging its profit margins.

As a result of its problems, M&S undertook a major overhaul of its marketing activity. Traditionally, the company had played down the importance of marketing, adopting the view that quality products at reasonable prices helped to clearly state what M&S and its in-store St Michael brand represented. Senior managers had placed greater emphasis on making the right buying decisions than on the use of advertising and other marketing tools. Thus M&S had a typical media spend of only one-tenth of supermarket chain Sainsbury's. Indeed, until recently, the retailer did not even have a dedicated marketing department.

In response to its problems, and following a lengthy strategic review, M&S made some wide ranging changes, including the appointment of its first marketing director. At the time, a company spokesperson claimed that this important development would "enable us to present our customers our full range of products and services in a co-ordinated way. It will also allow us to understand the aspirations of individual customers in much greater depth". Whatever the precise motivations behind the emergence of marketing at M&S, the retailer was quick to launch a spate of advertising.

As a result of the changes, new IT systems were introduced to help improve supply, and extra emphasis was placed on customer service, with around three thousand extra shop floor staff put in place. In addition, and perhaps most significantly, M&S decided to actively position itself as a value for money retailer. This was accompanied by reductions in prices amid criticisms that the brand had become too expensive. The significance of these criticisms should not be under-estimated for a brand which consumers traditionally believed to be more about quality than price. While M&S had always set prices which were reasonable, rather than low, consumers had grown to expect that these would be matched by good quality.

In seeking to emphasise the notion of value for money, M&S will need to steer a careful course. In particular, the business must not damage the image of a quality brand which many consumers hold dear. Analysts suggest that the first step for M&S is to merchandise more prudently to put better product ranges in its stores. According to one expert: "Marketing can only cover for bad products so far. Even with the best marketing in the world, it is still going to be hard to shift them. That's what M&S has to get right first." The components of the marketing mix do not work in isolation. M&S might be devoting greater resources to promotional activity, but it recognises the need to improve in-store customer service and ambience, while balancing keen prices with good quality to offer consumers value for money merchandise.

SOURCES: "'Expensive' M&S to reposition as value for money", *Marketing*, 25 February 1999, p. 5; Alexandra Jardine, "Time for M&S to follow Tesco", *Marketing*, 28 January 1999, p. 17; Philip Buxton, "Can marketing save falling retail giants?", *Marketing Week*, 28 January 1999, pp. 19–20; Alexandra Jardine, "M&S rescue job goes to insider", *Marketing*, 21 January 1999, p. 1; George Pitcher, "Reality forces UK retail giants to check out their strategic options", *Marketing Week*, 21 January 1999, p. 23; George Pitcher, "Supermarkets build defences for battle with the regulators", *Marketing Week*, 4 March 1999, p. 23.

Determining a Specific Price (Stage 8)

Pricing policies and methods should direct and structure the selection of a final price. If they are to do so, it is important for marketers to establish pricing objectives, to know something about the target market and to determine demand, price elasticity, costs and competitive factors. In addition to those economic factors, the manner in which pricing is used in the marketing mix will affect the final price.

Although a systematic approach to pricing is suggested here, in practice prices are often finalised after only limited planning; or they may be set just by trial and error. Later on marketers then determine whether the revenue minus costs yields a profit. This approach to pricing is not recommended, because it makes it difficult to discover pricing errors.

In the absence of government price controls, pricing remains a flexible and convenient way to adjust the marketing mix. In most situations, prices can be adjusted quickly—in a matter of minutes or over a few days. This flexibility and freedom do not characterise the other components of the marketing mix.

The "Pricing Balance"—The Need for Pragmatism

This chapter has presented a sequence of the stages a marketer must address in determining a price that will reflect customer expectations, match market developments and still produce a suitable financial return for the company in question. These eight stages identified for establishing prices must be tackled. However, in the reality of many markets, the external trading environment can change quickly and constantly: consumers are relatively fickle and revise their expectations, market developments alter the pattern of the market, and competitors are always modifying their marketing mix—a price cutting campaign, a new model launch, a high profile advertising campaign or, perhaps, a customer service initiative. To respond to such quick-fire events, marketers may be forced to react pragmatically by modifying their own pricing policy and method.

In the context of the marketing mix, price is, after all, an element that in most cases can be altered relatively quickly, that is, when compared with the time and resources required to launch a new product, modify a channel of distribution, improve customer service or create and run a new advertising campaign. Even in this context, however, the shrewd marketer should endeavour to minimise price cutting and discounting. Generally, the only beneficiary of a price war in the short term is the consumer, not the business, its distributors, the brand or the long term flexibility of the marketing mix. The car industry is a current example of how pricing incentives, such as discounts, cheap credit facilities and trade-in deals, can become an entrenched part of pricing. The marketer, then, should make pricing decisions on the basis of marketing intelligence, market trends, customer perceptions and competitor activity. Pragmatism must never lose sight of the "economics" of pricing and the fundamental relationship between demand, costs and profits: there must be a sensible trade-off or "pricing balance" between economic analysis and pragmatism.

● S U M M A R Y

The eight stages in the process of establishing prices are as follows: (1) selecting pricing objectives; (2) assessing the target market's evaluation of price and its ability to buy; (3) determining demand; (4) analysing demand, cost and profit relationships; (5) evaluating competitors' prices;

(6) selecting a pricing policy; (7) developing a pricing method; and (8) determining a specific price.

The first stage, selecting pricing objectives, is critical because pricing objectives form a foundation on which the decisions of subsequent stages are based. Businesses may use numerous pricing objectives: short term and long term ones, and different ones for different products and market segments.

The second stage in establishing prices is an assessment of the target market's evaluation of price and its ability to buy. This stage tells a marketer how much emphasis to place on price and may help the marketer determine how far above the competition the company can set its prices. Understanding customers' buying power and knowing how important a product is to them in comparison with other products helps marketers correctly assess the target market's evaluation of price.

In the third stage, a business must determine the demand for its product. The classic *demand curve* is a graph of the quantity of products expected to be sold at various prices, if other factors are held constant. It illustrates that, as price falls, the quantity demanded usually increases. However, for prestige products, there is a direct positive relationship between price and quantity demanded: demand increases as price increases—up to a certain point. Next, *price elasticity of demand*—the percentage change in quantity demanded relative to a given percentage change in price—must be determined. If demand is elastic, a change in price causes an opposite change in total revenue. Inelastic demand results in a change in the same direction in total revenue when a product's price is changed.

Analysis of demand, cost and profit relationships—the fourth stage of the process—can be accomplished through marginal analysis or break even analysis. Marginal analysis is the examination of what happens to a company's costs and revenues when production (or sales volume) is changed by one unit. Marginal analysis combines the demand curve with a company's costs to develop an optimum price for maximum profit. *Fixed costs* do not vary with changes in the number of units produced or sold; *average fixed cost* is the fixed cost per unit produced. *Variable costs* vary directly with changes in the number of units produced or sold. *Average variable cost* is the variable cost per unit produced. *Total cost* is the sum of average fixed costs and average variable costs multiplied by the quantity produced. *Average total cost* is the sum of the average fixed cost and average variable cost. The optimum price is the point at which *marginal cost* (the extra cost associated with producing one more unit of a product) equals *marginal revenue* (the change in total revenue that occurs when one additional unit of a product is sold). Marginal analysis is only a model; it offers little help in pricing new products before costs and revenues are established.

Break even analysis—determining the number of units necessary to break even—is important in setting the price. The point at which the costs of producing a product equal the revenue made from selling the product is the *break even point*. To use break even analysis effectively, a marketer should determine the break even point for each of several alternative prices, so that the effects on total revenue, total cost and the break even point for each price can be considered. However, this approach assumes that the quantity demanded is basically fixed and that the major task is to set prices to recover costs.

A marketer needs to be aware of the prices charged for competing brands. This awareness allows a company to keep its prices the same as competitors' prices when non-price competition is used. If a company uses price as a competitive tool, it can price its brand below competing brands.

A *pricing policy* is a guiding philosophy or course of action designed to influence and determine pricing decisions. Pricing policies help marketers solve the practical problems of establishing prices. Two types of *pioneer pricing* policies are price skimming and penetration pricing. With *price skimming*, a company charges the highest price that buyers who most desire the product will pay. *Penetration pricing* sets a price below the prices of competing brands in order to penetrate the market and produce a larger unit sales volume. Another pricing policy, *psychological pricing*, encourages purchases that are based on emotional rather than rational responses. It includes *odd-even pricing, customary pricing, prestige pricing* and *price lining*. A third pricing policy, *professional pricing*, is used by people who have great skill or experience in a particular field. *Promotional pricing* is a pricing policy in which pricing is related to the short term promotion of a particular product. *Price leaders* and *special event pricing* are examples of promotional pricing, as is *everyday low pricing (EDLP)*. *Experience curve pricing* fixes a low price that high cost competitors cannot match. Experience curve pricing is possible when experience reduces manufacturing costs at a predictable rate. *Misleading pricing*—in which consumers are intentionally misled about the true cost or value of a product or service—is increasingly monitored and tackled through consumer protection legislation.

A *pricing method* is a mechanical procedure for assigning prices to specific products on a regular basis. Four types of pricing methods are cost oriented, demand oriented, competition oriented and marketing oriented pricing. In using *cost oriented pricing*, a company determines price by adding a monetary amount or percentage to the cost of the product. Two common cost oriented pricing methods are *cost plus pricing* and *mark-up pricing*. *Demand oriented pricing* is based on the level of demand for a product. To use this method, a marketer must be able to estimate the amounts of a product that buyers will demand at different prices,

particularly if the company wishes to use *price differentiation* for the marketing of a specific product. Demand oriented pricing results in a high price when demand for a product is strong and a low price when demand is weak. In the case of *competition oriented pricing,* costs and revenues are secondary to competitors' prices. Competition oriented pricing and cost approaches may be combined to arrive at price levels necessary to generate a profit. *Marketing oriented pricing* is a pricing method whereby a company takes into account a wide range of factors including marketing strategy, competition, value to the customer, price-quality relationships, explicability, costs, product line pricing, negotiating margins, political factors and the effect on distributors/retailers.

Pricing policies and methods should direct and structure the selection of a final price. For the most part, pricing remains a flexible and convenient way to adjust the marketing mix. Pragmatism may require the marketer to revise pricing on an ad hoc basis in response to market developments. While such reactions are to some extent inevitable, marketers must never lose sight of the longer term implications for the brand or the fundamental relationship between demand, costs and profits.

Important Terms

Demand curve	Pioneer pricing	Everyday low pricing (EDLP)
Price elasticity of demand	Price skimming	Experience curve pricing
Fixed costs	Penetration pricing	Misleading pricing
Average fixed cost	Psychological pricing	Pricing method
Variable costs	Odd-even pricing	Cost oriented pricing
Average variable cost	Customary pricing	Cost plus pricing
Total cost	Prestige pricing	Mark-up pricing
Average total cost	Price lining	Demand oriented pricing
Marginal cost (MC)	Professional pricing	Price differentiation
Marginal revenue (MR)	Promotional pricing	Competition oriented pricing
Break even point	Price leaders	Marketing oriented pricing
Pricing policy	Special event pricing	

Discussion and Review Questions

1. Identify the eight stages that make up the process of establishing prices.
2. Why do most demand curves demonstrate an inverse relationship between price and quantity?
3. List the characteristics of products that have inelastic demand. Give several examples of such products.

4. Explain why optimum profits should occur when marginal cost equals marginal revenue.
5. The Chambers Company has just gathered estimates in preparation for a break even analysis for a new product. Variable costs are £7 a unit. The additional plant will cost £48,000. The new product will be charged £18,000 a year for its share of general overheads. Advertising expenditure will be £80,000, and £55,000 will be spent on distribution. If the product sells for £12, what is the break even point in units? What is the break even point in sales volume?
6. Why should a marketer be aware of competitors' prices?
7. For what type of products would a pioneer price skimming policy be most appropriate? For what type of products would penetration pricing be more effective?
8. Why do consumers associate price with quality? When should prestige pricing be used?
9. What factors must be taken into consideration when adopting a marketing oriented approach to pricing?
10. In setting prices, why must marketers take a "balanced" view of a broad set of issues?

Recommended Readings

M. Campanelli, "The price to pay", *Sales & Marketing Management,* vol. 146, no. 10, 1994, pp. 96–102.

M. V. Marn and R. L. Rosiello, "Managing price, gaining profit", *Harvard Business Review,* vol. 70, no. 5, 1992, pp. 84–94.

T. Nagle, *Strategy and Tactics of Pricing: A Guide to Profitable Decision-Making* (Hemel Hempstead: Prentice-Hall, 1994).

H. Simon, "Pricing opportunities—and how to exploit them", *Sloan Management Review,* vol. 33, no. 2, 1992, pp. 55–65.

K. Steward, "Fixing the price", in *Effective Industrial Marketing,* N. Hart, ed. (London: Kogan Page, 1994).

C A S E S

19.1 Cheap Beans Means Own Label for Heinz

For decades Heinz has built up an enviable range of products—far more than the old positioning statement of "57 varieties"—and significant brand reputation. Rarely in any marketing research do consumers voice complaints about Heinz products. Apart from soups, tomato ketchup and salad cream, the company is perhaps best known for its baked beans in tomato sauce. Few observers thought the baked bean market, already differentiated with the addition of sausages and burgers, would see any development. Then came the budget lines. At a time when an average branded tin of humble baked beans retailed at around 30p, the own label budget lines were priced at 16p. They eventually fell to as low as 6p a can, becoming loss leaders for the supermarket chains and the cause of real problems for the big brands. Nestlé reacted by withdrawing its long standing Crosse & Blackwell branded baked beans totally from the marketplace.

The major brands' traditional defence in such situations has been to declare that such budget priced products could not possibly have been sourced from them: Coca-Cola and Kellogg's frequently use advertising to state that they do not manufacture own label or budget brands for supermarket chains. In the baked bean battle, however, the situation has been destabilised by Heinz's very determined entry into the supply of own label beans. Heinz claims that the downward price spiral was instigated by the retailers well before it decided to supply own label brands. Heinz uses own label supply contracts, which account for only 3 per cent of its output, to utilise spare capacity in its factories.

For the consumer, the situation is uncertain: did Heinz produce those discounted own label baked beans or not? As word spreads that some own label beans are originating from Heinz sites, the risk is that consumers will come to believe that all low cost baked beans are in fact Heinz products so there is no reason to pay more to purchase Heinz branded cans. The share of own label baked beans moved up from 28.6 per cent in 1994 to 33.7 per cent in 1995, with predictions that it would achieve 40 per cent by the end of the decade. The growth has not all been at Heinz's expense by any means, as the departure of Crosse & Blackwell created a void into which many retailers pushed their own label lines. However, Heinz's share has dropped from 41.2 per cent to 40.3 per cent.

Heinz refuses to supply its "standard" recipes to the retailers as own label budget priced lines, thereby sustaining differentiation of its branded product. Heinz believes it will maintain its domination of the baked bean market while enhancing its scale economies by utilising excess capacity to supply a limited number of supermarket chains with own label brands. In a market in which the retail price has dropped from around 30p a can to only 5p or 6p, the risks for Heinz are nevertheless great.

Its balancing act in supplying some budget lines to Tesco, Sainsbury's and Kwik Save therefore poses an even greater dilemma. For the consumer, the sensational price reductions are very welcome, but the longer term effects on brand values are far from clear.

SOURCES: Stephanie Bentley, "Heinz own label hits supply snag", *Marketing Week*, 16 February 1996, p. 9; Stephanie Bentley, "Budget brands cook up trouble for Heinz", *Marketing Week*, 1 March 1996, p. 24; Julian Lee and Claire Murphy, "Cracking the lookalike code", *Marketing*, 29 February 1996, p. 12.

Questions for Discussion

1. What factors have caused Heinz to move into producing own label products?
2. How important has price traditionally been to Heinz's marketing? Is price alone a basis for competing in this market? Why or why not?
3. What are the long term dangers for Heinz, if any, of a price war?

19.2 Toys "R" Us—Sweden Faces Stiff Price Competition

Toys "R" Us, which leads the US toy market with its chain of over 400 warehouse-style toy supermarkets spread across the country, is expanding rapidly in Europe and the Pacific Rim. In Europe its growth is fast bringing a new style and scale of toy retailing to the UK (50 branches), Germany (40), France (25), Spain (12) and Austria (5). The company has long been an innovator in both its pricing policies and its toy supermarket design. Toys "R" Us brings customers into the store by discounting such baby care products as buggies and disposable nappies below cost. The strategy is that once parents are in the store, they will spend on toys the money they saved on the discounted baby goods.

Toys "R" Us stores are usually located along road arteries, well away from central business district (CBD) shopping malls, to keep down costs and prevent customers from being distracted by other toy merchants. Isolation from shopping malls also means that customers will load up their shopping trolleys because they do not have to lug their purchases through crowded malls.

The first Toys "R" Us store was opened in 1957 as the Children's Supermarket (the "Rs" are printed backwards to encourage name recognition), offering brand name toys and baby goods below normal retail prices. Today, it still offers brand name toys at 20 to 50 per cent below retail price. Each store has a full stock of thousands of different toys and baby goods tracked by a computer system that almost eliminates stock-outs. Managers don't place orders for toys, the toys just arrive on time, thus averting the Toys "R" Us definition of a major disaster—not having a certain toy on display and ready to sell.

Toys "R" Us sets its price for a particular item based on how much it projects customers will pay for it. The company then determines the price at which it is willing to purchase the toy from the manufacturer and negotiates fiercely with the manufacturer to get the toy at that price. The company has a definite advantage in negotiations because it buys in such large volume. Toy manufacturers also treat Toys "R" Us well because the company is often a testing ground for new toys. Price is so important to the Toys "R" Us strategy that even when demand for a toy is high and supplies are short, the company will not raise its price on the toy to make a quick profit.

Market share is the Toys "R" Us main pricing objective; and at present it is the number one toy store in the United States. In the UK, local independent toy shops still account for the bulk of the toy market share, but in only a few years Toys "R" Us has become the leading national chain. The company says it is willing to cut prices to retain its leading position. Other toy stores are scrambling to meet the competition from Toys "R" Us; those that do not change their strategies wind up out of the toy market altogether. Many stores, such as Kmart, or Asda in the UK, expand their toy lines only for the six week Christmas season and bring customers in with sales. Although Toys "R" Us never holds sales, it maintains its huge selection and discount prices year round. Customers who found good buys at Toys "R" Us at Christmas will also shop there for children's birthdays and other special days, when other retail stores have a limited selection. Even new parents who drop in to Toys "R" Us for discounted baby products tend to return to buy toys. The company also sells sporting goods "toys", such as footballs and bicycles, suitable for teens, young adults and family members of almost any age.

Some competitors (in the UK, Mothercare owned Mothercare World) have adopted the Toys "R" Us supermarket approach and have tried to meet Toys "R" Us prices throughout the year. Other stores are trying non-price competition by offering educational and babysitting services. However, Toys "R" Us intends to rely on its non-price attributes of convenience, selection and inventory, as well as price competition, to hold its position.

Toys "R" Us has expanded internationally, into Europe, Canada, Japan and other parts of Asia with close to 200 stores outside the US. The company has plans for many more stores overseas to take advantage of the world toy market, which is nearly double that of the United States. Additionally, it opened Kids "R" Us in the United States, a chain of children's clothing stores similar to the toy stores. The latest country to receive the famous reversed R logo is Sweden. Much to the chagrin of the Swedish Federation of Toy Retailers, Toys "R" Us announced that a chain of 15 toy superstores would be operational in Sweden.

Toys "R" Us has customer loyalty behind it. Customers know that they can find *the* toy that a child wants, at the best price, at Toys "R" Us. And if the child does not like the toy, the purchaser may return it for a full refund with no questions asked.

SOURCES: Robert J. Cole, "Toys "R" Us to open stores in Japan within two years", *The New York Times,* 27 September 1989, pp. D1, D6; Dan Dorfman, "Toys "R" Us: Mattel play?", *USA Today,* 28 June 1987, p. 2B; Trish Hall, "Finding gold in overalls and bibs", *The New York Times,* 25 December 1988, pp. F1, F10; Mark Maremont, Dori Jones Yang and Amy Dunkin, "Toys "R" Us goes overseas—and finds that toys 'R' them, too", *Business Week,* 26 January 1987, pp. 71–72; David Owen, "Where toys come from", *Atlantic Monthly,* October 1986, pp. 64–78; Jesus Sanchez, "Toymakers make a play for market", *USA Today,* 10 February 1987, pp. 1B–2B; Toys "R" Us UK HQ, 1993; "Toys "R" Us launches UK loyalty, credit card", *Marketing Week,* 6 October 1995, p. 11; Claes Philipson, "Toys embarks on important initiative", *European Retail,* 30 August 1994, p. 12.

Questions for Discussion

1. What are the major pricing objectives of Toys "R" Us?
2. Assess the Toys "R" Us practice of not raising the prices of products that are scarce and in high demand.
3. A major disadvantage of using price competition is that competitors can match prices. Or can they? Evaluate this potential threat for Toys "R" Us.

The price of a product or service is the value placed on what is exchanged by the supplying business and the consumer. There is much more to pricing, however, than the setting of a specific monetary figure. The price of a product or a service will affect how it is perceived by consumers, how it is distributed and promoted, the level of customer service expected and the brand positioning strategy to be pursued. The pricing strategy developed by a business will also fundamentally relate to its performance and even to its viability. Pricing is not one of the more "glamorous" ingredients of the marketing mix, such as product development or promotional activity, but it is very important and relatively easy to manipulate.

Before progressing, readers should be confident that they are now able to:

Outline the central concepts of pricing

• What are the characteristics and role of price in marketing? • What are the differences between price and non-price competition? • What are the different pricing objectives? • What factors affect marketers' pricing decisions? • Why is it important to consider the consumers' view of value versus price? • What is required in setting prices in business-to-business markets? • What is meant by the concept of economic value to the customer?

Explain the requirements of setting prices

• What are the eight major steps of the process used to establish prices? • What issues are faced when selecting pricing objectives? • Why must marketers assess the target market's evaluation of price? • How is demand for a product determined, and what are the relationships between demand, costs and profits? • Why must marketers evaluate competitors' pricing? • What are the different pricing policies and methods and how do they help to determine a specific price? • What is the "pricing balance"?

Marketing Opportunity Analysis	Chapters
• The marketing environment	2
• Marketing in international markets	3
• Consumer buying behaviour	4
• Organisational markets and business-to-business buying behaviour	5
• Marketing research and information systems	6

Target Market Strategy	Chapters
• Market segmentation and prioritisation	7, 21
• Product and brand positioning	7, 21
• Competitive advantage	7, 21

Marketing Mix Development	Chapters
• Product, branding, packaging and service decisions	8–11
• Place (distribution and channel) decisions	12–14
• Promotion decisions	15–17
• Pricing decisions	18, 19
• Supplementary decisions	3, 20, 23, 24

Marketing Management	Chapters
• Strategic marketing and competitive strategy	21, 22
• Marketing planning and forecasting sales potential	22
• Implementing strategies and internal marketing relationships and measuring performance	23
• Marketing ethics and social responsibility	24

VII Manipulating the Marketing Mix

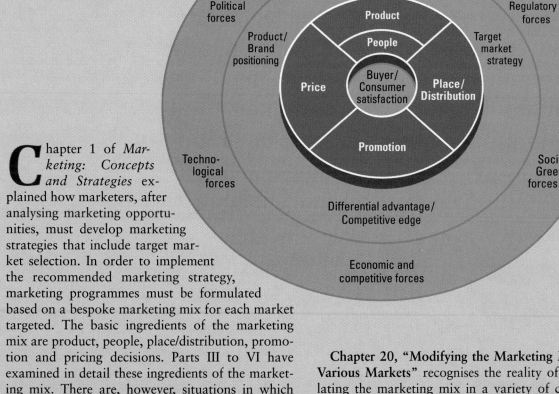

Legal forces

Political forces

Regulatory forces

Product/Brand positioning

Product

People

Target market strategy

Price

Buyer/Consumer satisfaction

Place/Distribution

Technological forces

Promotion

Societal/Green forces

Differential advantage/Competitive edge

Economic and competitive forces

Chapter 1 of *Marketing: Concepts and Strategies* explained how marketers, after analysing marketing opportunities, must develop marketing strategies that include target market selection. In order to implement the recommended marketing strategy, marketing programmes must be formulated based on a bespoke marketing mix for each market targeted. The basic ingredients of the marketing mix are product, people, place/distribution, promotion and pricing decisions. Parts III to VI have examined in detail these ingredients of the marketing mix. There are, however, situations in which market characteristics or the nature of the product require the standard marketing mix to be modified. These situations occur most notably in business-to-business markets and the marketing of services, and when companies are engaged in marketing in international markets.

Part VII of *Marketing: Concepts and Strategies* explores the manipulation of the marketing mix to cater for business-to-business markets, the marketing of services and marketing in international markets.

Chapter 20, "Modifying the Marketing Mix for Various Markets" recognises the reality of formulating the marketing mix in a variety of complex business situations. The chapter commences by explaining why in many situations the basic marketing mix requires modification. It examines the nature of the marketing mix for business-to-business markets and presents the complex and extended marketing mix required for services. To conclude, the chapter highlights the many additional issues considered by marketers involved with global markets and relates them to the development of the marketing mix.

615

By the conclusion of Part VII of *Marketing: Concepts and Strategies,* readers should understand why in certain circumstances the standard marketing mix requires modification and manipulation. Chapter 20 should be read in conjunction with Chapters 3, 5 and 11.

20 Modifying the Marketing Mix for Various Markets

"Expanding the traditional boundaries of the marketing mix is imperative for international and services contexts."

Constantine Katsikeas
Cardiff Business School

OBJECTIVES

- To recognise that in many situations the basic marketing mix requires modification
- To examine the nature of the marketing mix for business-to-business markets
- To understand the more complex and extended marketing mix required for services
- To recognise that for marketers involved with global marketing, the marketing mix requires consideration of additional issues

For many employees a benefit offered by employers is private health insurance. Until the 1980s, BUPA dominated this market in Britain with health insurance policies and a network of private hospitals and clinics. The primary benefits to customers are speedy consultations and treatment—beating the state hospital queues—and hotel-like facilities in hospitals for patients and their relatives. In recent years, demand has stagnated with around 12 per cent of the population buying private health cover. However, the competitive arena has been far from static. Private hospital operators have proliferated and many new sites have opened, while many mainstream insurance companies have launched their own private health insurance schemes. Norwich Union, Legal & General, Royal and Sun Alliance, and now Abbey National's Abbey Healthcare have combined to erode BUPA's market share from 60 per cent to 40 per cent. Direct rival PPP has made significant inroads, capturing 30 per cent of the £2 billion market.

For all companies operating in this market, the fundamental problem is the complexity of the "product" being offered. BUPA's group marketing director Pat Stafford believes that—as with all financial services—consumers are not sure what they have bought. Healthcare policies must be simplified and claims pro-

cedures curtailed if consumer resistance is to be overcome. BUPA has invested £50 million into developing Call BUPA First, its paperless system of claims. Customer service has been a priority with better training of personnel, new procedures and a responsive attitude to customer requirements. A brand-building initiative has commenced with the aim of "getting more people to see the benefit of BUPA's health services and, crucially, see them as worth paying for". The strapline *You're Amazing* is at the centre of this brand building, emphasising the importance of customers being able to deal quickly with any ailments or medical concerns without undue inconvenience or delay.

To ensure BUPA is fully customer oriented, the business has been divided into five distinct divisions: healthcare, nursing homes, hospitals, the Spanish subsidiary Sanitas, plus dental/travel insurance. Each has been allocated top level marketers from consumer goods and services backgrounds. Research has revealed that the general public is largely cynical about health insurance, creating a significant challenge for BUPA's expanding team of marketers. The situation is additionally complicated for BUPA because it has both consumer and business-to-business target market segments. A growing number of householders

617

the personal health service

are being enticed into the private healthcare market by seductive television advertising, direct mail and offers "piggybacking" on existing contents, motor or home insurance schemes. The core market remains, though, the corporate sector with large and small businesses providing policies for their employees along with pension schemes and company cars. The marketing package required to entice a private consumer at home into protecting his or her family and the proposition necessary to persuade ICI or JCB to buy into a scheme for thousands of their employees are both quite different. This adds to the number of BUPA products to be marketed and the manner in which they are packaged, promoted and sold to target customers.

BUPA hopes that through more efficient systems, innovative products and services, hefty investment in facilities—210 care homes were recently purchased from Care First—the establishment of a customer service oriented culture and enhanced supportive IT systems, not only will the business effectively defend its position against the growing band of competitors, but it will also successfully attract new category users into the private health sector.

SOURCES: BUPA; Claire Murphy, "BUPA looks for better health", *Marketing*, 3 December 1998, p. 21; Lisa Campbell, "BUPA axes O&M for direct focus", *Marketing*, 26 November 1998, p. 1. *Advertisement*: Courtesy of BUPA.

The core ingredients of the marketing mix—the marketing manager's tactical toolkit—have been examined in detail in Parts III to VI of *Marketing: Concepts and Strategies*. While these chapters have broadly covered consumer, business-to-business, service and not-for-profit markets, inevitably there has been some bias towards the marketing of consumer goods. In part this reflects the plethora of consumer brands and their coverage in the media, while in part it has been deliberate: all readers of this text, as consumers themselves, will be familiar with many of the products and services featured so far. It is important to acknowledge, however, that the marketing of services and business-to-business products is moderately different from the marketing of consumer goods, as BUPA has recognised. Those companies involved in international marketing, trading across national borders and cultures, are faced with additional issues that have an impact on their marketing activity.

These differences are not major: "marketing is marketing", and the approach outlined in this text holds true across consumer, business-to-business, services and not-for-profit markets. The marketing environment must be analysed, as must consumer behaviour and customer needs, the competitive situation and general trends. A marketing strategy must be determined that identifies segments, prioritises target markets, judges the ability to compete and defines a desired brand or product positioning. Once the analysis and strategy stages are complete, programmes must be developed that—through the marketing mix—implement the recommended target market strategy.[1] Control mechanisms must be in place to ensure effective implementation of both the marketing strategy and the associated marketing mix programmes. This is true no matter what the market in question.

Nevertheless, there are differences in the characteristics of the respective markets for consumer, business-to-business and service products. These are evident in the practices of business-to-business marketers, but particularly for those responsible for the marketing of services. This chapter presents a summary of some of the most important, if at times subtle, differences encountered when marketing business-to-business products and marketing services. The chapter concludes by suggesting how international marketing requires consideration of additional issues in formulating a marketing mix.

Characteristics of Business-to-Business Marketing Mixes

As with consumer marketers, business-to-business marketers must also create a marketing mix that will satisfy the customers in the target market. In many respects, the general concepts and methods involved in developing a business-to-business marketing mix are similar to those used in consumer product marketing as outlined in Parts III to VI of this text. In this section the focus is on the features of business-to-business marketing mixes that differ from the marketing mixes for consumer products. Each of the main components in a business-to-business marketing mix is examined: product, place/distribution, promotion, price and people. Personnel are not particularly part of the product, but they are integral to the selling and promotional activity in all markets, and are important in developing ongoing relationships in many industrial markets.

Product
After selecting a target market, the business-to-business marketer has to decide how to compete. Production oriented managers may fail to understand the need to develop a distinct appeal for their product to give it a differential advantage. Positioning the product (discussed in Chapters 7 and 10) is necessary to serve a market successfully, whether it is consumer or business-to-business.[2]

Compared with consumer marketing mixes, the product ingredients of business-to-business marketing mixes often include a greater emphasis on services, both before and after sales. Services, including on-time delivery, quality control, custom design (see Figure 20.1) and a comprehensive parts distribution system, may be important components of the product. Marketing Insight 20.1 reveals the importance of a service "package" in the truck market.

Before making a sale, business-to-business marketers provide potential customers with technical advice regarding product specifications, installation and applications. Many business-to-business marketers depend heavily on long term customer relationships that perpetuate sizeable repeat purchases.[3] Therefore, business-to-business marketers also make a considerable effort to provide services after the sale. Because business-to-business customers must have products available when needed, on-time delivery is another service included in the product component of many business-to-business marketing mixes. A business-to-business marketer unable to provide on-time delivery cannot expect the marketing mix to satisfy business-to-business customers. Availability of parts must also be included in the product mixes of many business-to-business marketers in order to prevent costly production delays. The business-to-business marketer that includes availability of parts within the product component has a competitive edge over one that fails to offer this service. Furthermore, customers whose average purchases are large often desire credit; thus some business-to-business marketers include credit services in their product mixes. When planning and developing a business-to-business product mix, a business-to-business marketer

Figure 20.1 Business-to-business services. Beton offers its services to the building industries. SOURCE: Courtesy of Beton.

of component parts and semi-finished products must realise that a customer may decide to make the items instead of buying them. In some cases, then, business-to-business marketers compete not only with one another, but also with their own potential customers.

Frequently, industrial products must conform to standard technical specifications that business-to-business customers want. Thus business-to-business marketers often concentrate on functional product features rather than on marketing considerations. This fact has important implications for business-to-business salespeople. Rather than concentrating just on selling activities, they must assume the role of consultants, seeking to solve their customers' problems and influencing the writing of specifications.[4] For example, salespeople for computer hardware often act as consultants for software as well as the basic computer kit. Most customers now expect this level of service. Many suppliers have gone out of business because of their inability to offer such a service.

Because industrial products are rarely sold through self-service, the major consideration in package design is protection. There is less emphasis on packaging as a promotional device.

Research on business-to-business customer complaints indicates that such buyers usually complain when they encounter problems with product quality or delivery time. On the other hand, consumers' complaints refer to other problems,

Volvo Trucks Fights Back—Aftermarket Opportunities Help Recovery

Volvo Trucks is a wholly owned subsidiary of Volvo. It is the division that handles the importing, manufacturing, sales and marketing, and after sales support for all Volvo heavy goods vehicles. Throughout the 1990s, truck sales declined in most key markets, but some manufacturers performed better owing to their exposure to the stronger US market. In western Europe, sales at the end of the decade were down from 100,000 in 1992 to 80,000 vehicles in the light/medium category, and in the heavy category from 150,000 to 120,000. Italy, Germany and France saw sales decline by 20 per cent, Spain by 40 per cent, but there was recently a recovery in the UK, where sales increased by 8 per cent. Mercedes-Benz, Volvo Trucks and Renault have been the dominant players in an increasingly competitive marketplace.

For most of the major players in the European truck market, two major trends are dictating current marketing strategies. The decline in new vehicle sales is leading to an increased focus on the aftermarket. The market for replacement parts is more stable and offers some degree of cushioning against the more extreme fluctuations in demand for new vehicles. Similarly, tyres, fuels and lubricants continue to sell steadily even when there is a downturn in truck sales. Most truck manufacturers are devoting more of their marketing effort to servicing, maintenance and provision of parts.

The second trend has been a move by hauliers and large companies with their own transport fleets away from purchasing new vehicles outright. There has been a switch to leasing and contract hire, whereby the truck manufacturer ultimately retains ownership of the vehicle and has to off-load the vehicles when they are returned by the haulier. This development has forced marketers to learn a variety of new financial skills. They have to set leasing and contract hire rates sufficiently high to make an operating profit, bearing in mind the increased competition in the market. They must also be prepared to take back and re-sell large numbers of used vehicles.

For the business-to-business marketer working in the truck business, the task is no longer simply one of marketing and selling new vehicles—the provision of after sales services and parts and the negotiating of complex leasing and contract hire agreements are becoming increasingly important. The pattern, however, differs country by country, causing problems for Volvo's marketers and necessitating prudent marketing planning that takes into account each country's trading characteristics.

SOURCES: "Looking up, looking down—tracing an entire chain", *Works Management,* July 1995, pp. 37–41; "The West European truck sector: recovery in prospect?", *European Motor Business,* 4th quarter, 1994, pp. 90–130; Jim Mele, "Volvo builds a city truck for the future", *Fleet Owner,* October 1995, p. 16. "Heavy going", *Automotive Management,* 13 September 1990; John Griffiths, "Truck sales suffer fall in September of nearly 40%", *Financial Times,* 17 October 1990; Richard Longworth, "Glitter shadows and lights at the ends of tunnels", *Transport Week,* 22 September 1990, pp. 40–41.

such as customer service and pricing. This type of buyer feedback allows business-to-business marketers to gauge marketing performance. It is important that business-to-business marketers respond to valid complaints because the success of most industrial products depends on repeat purchases. Because buyer complaints serve a useful purpose, many industrial companies facilitate this feedback by providing customer service departments and call centres.[5]

If a business-to-business marketer is in a mature market, growth can come from attracting market share from another business; alternatively, a company can look at new applications or uses for its products. JCB dominates the backhoe digger market in Europe, but the economic recession, which resulted in reduced construction of buildings and infrastructure, hit its key customers hard. The company used its existing skills and facilities to design an innovative range of very safe, single arm skid-steer machines. These nimble, compact "mini-diggers" are now appearing on most building sites and are entering the hire market, proving very successful for JCB. Putting user safety and environmental concerns to the fore, they lend themselves particularly well to buyer needs for smaller construction equipment in Germany and Scandinavia. JCB's success, managed by a well qualified team of business-to-business marketers, stems from winning sales from its competitors, seeking new applications for its products and designing innovative products.

Place/Distribution

The place/distribution ingredient in business-to-business marketing mixes differs from that for consumer products with respect to the types of channels used, the kinds of intermediaries available, and the transport, storage and inventory policies. Nonetheless, the primary objective of the physical distribution of industrial products is to ensure that the right products are available when and where needed.

Distribution channels tend to be shorter for industrial products than for consumer products. (Figure 20.2 shows the four commonly used industrial distribution channels that were described in Chapter 12). Although **direct distribution channels,** in which products are sold directly from producers to users, are not used frequently in the distribution of consumer products, they are the most widely used for industrial products. More than half of all industrial products are sold through direct channels (channel E in Figure 20.2). Industrial or business-to-business buyers like to communicate directly with producers, especially when expensive or technically complex products are involved. For this reason business-to-business buyers prefer to purchase expensive and highly complex mainframe and mini-computers directly from the producers. In these circumstances, an industrial customer wants the technical assistance and personal assurances that only a producer can provide.

A second industrial distribution channel involves an industrial or business-to-business distributor to facilitate exchanges between the producer and customer (channel F in Figure 20.2). A **business-to-business distributor** is an independent business that takes title to products and carries inventories. Such distributors are

Direct distribution channels
Distribution channels in which products are sold directly from producers to users

Business-to-business distributor
An independent business that takes title to products and carries inventories

Figure 20.2 Typical marketing channels for industrial products/ business-to-business markets

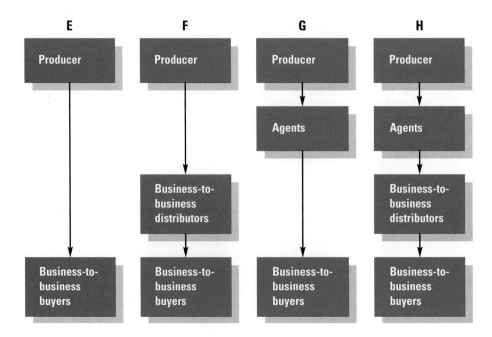

merchant wholesalers; they assume possession and ownership of goods, as well as the risks associated with ownership. Business-to-business distributors usually sell standardised items, such as maintenance supplies, production tools and small operating equipment. Some carry a wide variety of product lines; others specialise in one or a small number of lines. Industrial distributors can be used most effectively when a product has broad market appeal, is easily stocked and serviced, is sold in small quantities and is needed rapidly to avoid high losses (such as a part for an assembly line machine).[6]

Business-to-business distributors or dealers offer sellers several advantages. They can perform the needed selling activities in local markets at relatively low cost to a manufacturer. They can reduce a producer's financial burden by providing their customers with credit services. Because industrial distributors usually maintain close relationships with their customers, they are aware of local needs and can pass on market information to producers. By holding adequate inventories in their local markets, these distributors reduce the producers' capital requirements.

There are, though, several disadvantages to using business-to-business distributors. They may be difficult to control because they are independent companies. Because they often stock competing brands, an industrial producer cannot depend on them to sell a specific brand aggressively. Furthermore, industrial distributors maintain inventories, for which they incur numerous expenses; consequently, they are less likely to handle bulky items or items that are slow sellers relative to profit margin, need specialised facilities or require extraordinary selling efforts. In some cases, business-to-business distributors lack the technical knowledge necessary to sell and service certain industrial items.

In the third business-to-business distribution channel (channel G in Figure 20.2), a manufacturer's agent is employed. As described in Chapter 12, a manufacturer's agent or representative is an independent business person who sells complementary products of several producers in assigned territories and is compensated through commissions. Unlike an industrial distributor, a manufacturer's agent does not acquire title to the products and usually does not take possession. Acting as a salesperson on behalf of the producers, a manufacturer's agent has no latitude, or very little, in negotiating prices or sales terms.

Using manufacturers' agents can benefit a business marketer. These agents usually possess considerable technical and market information and have an established set of customers. For an industrial seller with highly seasonal demand, a manufacturer's agent can be an asset because the seller does not have to support a year round salesforce. The fact that manufacturers' agents are paid on a commission basis may also make them an economical alternative for a company that has extremely limited resources and cannot afford a full time salesforce.

Certainly, the use of manufacturers' agents is not problem-free. Even though straight commissions may be cheaper for an industrial seller, the seller may have little control over manufacturers' agents. Because of the compensation method, manufacturers' agents generally want to concentrate on their larger accounts. They are often reluctant to spend adequate time following up sales, to put forward special selling efforts or to provide sellers with market information when such activities reduce the amount of productive selling time. Because they rarely maintain inventories, manufacturers' agents have a limited ability to provide customers quickly with parts or repair services.

The fourth business-to-business distribution channel (channel H in Figure 20.2) has both a manufacturer's agent and an industrial distributor between the producer and the business-to-business customer. This channel may be appropriate when the business marketer wishes to cover a large geographic area but maintains no salesforce because demand is highly seasonal or because the company cannot afford one. This type of channel can also be useful for a business-to-business marketer that wants to enter a new geographic market without expanding the company's existing salesforce.

So far, this discussion has implied that all channels are equally available and that an industrial producer can select the most desirable option. However, in a number of cases, only one or perhaps two channels are available for the distribution of certain types of products. An important issue in channel selection is the manner in which particular products are normally purchased. If customers ordinarily buy certain types of products directly from producers, it is unlikely that channels with intermediaries will be effective. Other dimensions that should be considered are the product's cost and physical characteristics, the costs of using various channels, the amount of technical assistance customers need and the size of product and parts inventory needed in local markets.

Physical distribution decisions regarding transport, storage and inventory control are especially important for business-to-business marketers. Some raw materials and other industrial products may require special handling; for example, toxic chemicals used in the manufacture of some products must be shipped, stored and disposed of properly to ensure that they do not harm people or the environment. In addition, the continuity of most business-to-business buyer-seller relationships depends on the seller having the right products available when and where the customer needs them. This requirement is so important that business-to-business marketers must sometimes make a considerable investment in order processing systems, materials handling equipment, warehousing facilities and inventory control systems. Tioxide holds extensive stocks of TiO_2 for distribution to a variety of business markets—ranging from PVC, paint to inks—worldwide. Without high stocks and a quickly responsive distribution system, rivals would gain an edge.

Many industrial purchasers are moving away from traditional marketing exchange relationships—in which the buyer purchases primarily on price from multiple suppliers—to more tightly knit, relational exchanges, which are long lasting, less price driven agreements between manufacturers and suppliers.[7] Just-in-time inventory management systems are providing the rationale underlying these new types of relationships. In order to reduce inventory costs and to eliminate waste, buyers purchase new stock just before it is needed in the manufacturing process. To make this system effective, they must share a great deal of information with their suppliers, since these relationships are collaborative.

Promotion

The combination of promotional efforts used in business-to-business marketing mixes generally differs from those for consumer products, especially convenience goods. The differences are evident in the emphasis on various promotional mix ingredients and the activities performed in connection with each promotional mix ingredient.

For several reasons, most business-to-business marketers rely on **personal selling,** informing and persuading customers to purchase through personal communication, to a much greater extent than do consumer product marketers (except, perhaps, marketers of consumer durables). Because an industrial seller often has fewer customers, personal contact with each customer is more feasible. Some industrial products have technical features that are too numerous or too complex to explain through non-personal forms of promotion. Moreover, business-to-business purchases are frequently high in value and must be suited to the job and

Personal selling The task of informing and persuading customers to purchase through personal communication

TRUE RELAXATION CAN BE ACHIEVED BY A STATE OF MIND THAT DEMANDS NO THOUGHT AT ALL.

EXACTLY.

Close your eyes. Breathe gently. Free your being from negativity. Feel stress slipping from your shoulders as you discover Toyota's reliability. Let unforeseen expenses fall away with a warranty that brings you three years or 60,000 miles of tranquillity. Become enlightened by our Whole Life Costs. On the lean-burn Avensis 1.8 GS, for example, they're 1.5p per mile less than the Passat and over 2.0p less than the Mondeo and Vectra.* Yes, by comparison, it seems there's little to running a Toyota fleet. But there's everything to our range, including sports models and 4x4s. Call our Fleet Business Centre. For uncluttering your mind from the pressures of management, the car in front is a Toyota.

Toyota Fleet Business Centre 0845 271 2712 www.toyota.co.uk

*SOURCE: CARCOST FOR 3 YEARS/60,000 MILES INC. FUEL. FOR FULL DETAILS OF COMPARISON, PLEASE CONTACT EMMOX 01494 442001.

TOYOTA FLEET

Figure 20.3 A typical business-to-business advertisement. In industrial selling, advertising often supplements personal selling efforts. SOURCE: Courtesy Toyota/Saatchi and Saatchi/Justin Pomfrey.

available where and when needed; thus business buyers want reinforcement and personal assurances from industrial sales personnel. Because business marketers depend on repeat purchases, sales personnel must follow up sales to make certain that customers know how to use the purchased items effectively, as well as to ensure that the products work properly. Personal selling is often supported with advertising activity (see Figure 20.3).

Salespeople need to perform the role of educators, showing buyers clearly how the product fits their needs. When the purchase of a product is critical to the future profitability of the business-to-business buyer, buying decision-makers gather extensive amounts of information about all alternative products. To deal with such buyers successfully, the seller must have a highly trained salesforce that is knowledgeable not only about its own company's products but also about competitors' offerings. Besides, if sales representatives offer thorough and reliable information, they can reduce the buyer's uncertainty, as well as differentiate their company's product from the competition. Finally, the gathering of information lengthens the decision-making process. Thus it is important for salespeople to be patient; to avoid pressuring their clients as they make important, new and complex decisions; and to continue providing information to their prospects throughout the entire process.[8]

As Table 20.1 illustrates, the average cost of an industrial sales call varies from industry to industry. Selling costs comprise salaries, commissions, bonuses, and

Industry	Number of Business-to-Business Companies Reporting	Average Daily Number of Sales Calls Per Salesperson	Average Cost of Business-to-Business Sales Call	Average Daily Sales Call Costs[b] Per Sales-Person
Printing and publishing	18	3.2	$148.60	$ 475.52
Chemicals and allied products	41	4.0	$155.20	$ 620.80
Petroleum and coal products	12	5.3	$ 99.10	$ 525.23
Primary metal industries	15	3.9	$363.90	$1,419.21
Fabricated metal products	113	3.9	$186.10	$ 725.79
Machinery, except electrical	275	3.5	$257.30	$ 900.55
Electronic computing equipment (computer hardware)	17	4.2	$452.60	$1,900.92
Electrical and electronic equipment	137	3.5	$238.40	$ 834.40
Transport equipment	41	2.9	$255.90	$ 742.11
Instruments and related products	73	3.9	$209.50	$ 817.05
Wholesale trade-durable goods	29	5.1	$139.80	$ 712.98
Business services	30	2.8	$227.20	$ 636.16

[a] No comparable UK/EU statistics available.

[b] This cost is determined by multiplying the average daily number of calls per salesperson by the average cost per sales call for each industry.

SOURCE: Laboratory of Advertising Performance (LAP), report no. 8052.3 (date unavailable). Reprinted by permission of McGraw-Hill, Inc.

Table 20.1 The average cost of a business-to-business sales call between selected industries in the United States[a]

travel and entertainment expenses. Some business-to-business sales are very large. A Boeing salesperson, for instance, closed a sale with Delta Air Lines for commercial aircraft worth $3 billion.[9] But on average, only 350 aircraft are sold each year, resulting in sales of $105 billion. Generally, aircraft salespeople work hardest in the three to five years before a sale is made.[10]

Because of the escalating costs of advertising and personal selling, telemarketing—the creative use of the telephone to enhance the salesperson's function—is on the increase. Some of the activities in telemarketing include Freephone 0800 phone lines and personal sales workstations—assisted by data terminals—that take orders, check stock and order status, and provide shipping and invoicing information.

Although not all business-to-business sales personnel perform the same sales activities, they can generally be grouped into the following categories, as described in Chapter 17: technical, missionary, and trade or inside order takers. An inside order taker could effectively use telemarketing. Regardless of how sales personnel are classified, industrial selling activities differ from consumer sales efforts. Because business-to-business sellers are frequently asked for technical advice about product specifications and uses, they often need technical backgrounds and are more likely to have them than consumer sales personnel. Compared with typical buyer-seller relationships in consumer product sales, the interdependence that develops between industrial buyers and sellers is likely to be stronger. Sellers count on buyers to purchase their particular products, and buyers rely on sellers to provide information, products and related services when and where needed. Although business-to-business salespeople do market their products aggressively, they almost never use "hard sell" tactics because of their role as technical consultants and the interdependence between buyers and sellers.

Advertising is emphasised less in business sales than in consumer transactions. Some of the reasons given earlier for the importance of personal selling in business-to-business promotional mixes explain why. However, advertising often supplements personal selling efforts. Because the cost of a business-to-business sales call is high and continues to rise, advertisements that allow sales personnel to perform more efficiently and effectively are worthwhile for business-to-business marketers. Advertising can make business customers aware of new products and brands; inform buyers about general product features, representatives and organisations; and isolate promising prospects by providing enquiry forms or the addresses and phone numbers of company representatives. To ensure that appropriate information is sent to a respondent, it is crucial for the enquiry to specify the type of information desired, the name of the company and respondent, the company's SIC (Standard Industrial Classification) number and the size of the organisation.

Because the demand for most business-to-business products is derived demand—for example, demand for construction equipment stems from consumer demand for more new houses, which in turn prompts building companies to require more plant and equipment—marketers can sometimes stimulate demand for their products by stimulating consumer demand. Thus a business-to-business marketer occasionally sponsors an advertisement promoting the products sold by the marketer's customers.

When selecting advertising media, business-to-business marketers primarily choose print media such as trade publications and direct mail; they seldom use broadcast media. Trade publications and direct mail reach precise groups of industrial customers and avoid wasted circulation. In addition, they are best suited for advertising messages that present numerous details and complex product information (which are frequently the types of messages that business-to-business advertisers wish to convey).

Compared with consumer product advertisements, industrial advertisements are usually less persuasive and more likely to contain a large amount of copy and detail. In contrast, marketers that advertise to reach ultimate consumers sometimes avoid extensive advertising copy because consumers are reluctant to read it. Whereas consumers desire emotional, attention-grabbing messages in advertising, business-to-business advertisers believe that industrial purchasers with any interest in their products will search for information and read long messages.

Sales promotion activities, too, can play a significant role in business-to-business promotional mixes. They encompass such efforts as catalogues, trade shows and trade sales promotion methods, including merchandise allowances, buy back allowances, displays, sales contests and the other methods discussed in Chapter 17. Business-to-business marketers go to great lengths and considerable expense to provide catalogues that describe their products to customers.

Customers refer to various sellers' catalogues to determine specifications, terms of sale, delivery times and other information about products. Catalogues thus help buyers decide which suppliers to contact.

Trade shows can be effective vehicles for making many customer contacts in a short time. One study found that business-to-business marketers allocate 25 per cent of their annual promotional budgets to trade shows in order to communicate with their current and potential customers, promote their corporate image, introduce new products, meet key account executives, develop mailing lists, identify sales prospects and find out what their competitors are doing. Although trade shows take second place to personal selling, they rank above print advertising in influencing business-to-business purchases, particularly as the business buyers reach the stages in the buying process of need recognition and supplier evaluation (see Chapter 5).

Many companies that participate in trade shows lack specific objectives regarding what they hope to accomplish by such participation. Companies with the most successful trade show programmes have written objectives for the tasks they wish to achieve, and they carefully select the type of show in which to take part so that those attending match the company's target market.[11]

The way in which business marketers use publicity in their promotional mixes may not be much different from the way in which marketers of consumer products use it. As described in Chapter 16, more companies are incorporating public relations automatically into their promotional mixes.

Price   Compared with consumer product marketers, industrial or business-to-business marketers face many more price constraints from legal and economic forces. With respect to economic forces, an individual industrial company's demand is often highly elastic, requiring the company to approximate competitors' prices. This condition often results in non-price competition and a considerable amount of price stability (see Chapter 18).

Today's route to sustainable *differential advantage* (competitive edge) lies in offering customers something that the competition does not offer—something that helps them increase their productivity and profitability. Companies achieve high market share not by offering low prices but by offering their customers superior value and product quality.[12] Customers are willing to pay higher prices for quality products.[13] Companies such as Caterpillar Tractor, Hewlett-Packard and 3M have shown that a value based strategy can win a commanding lead over competition. Such companies emphasise the highest quality products at slightly higher prices.

Many industrial companies are devoting increased resources to training, so that their personnel are better qualified and more willing to provide full customer service. Corporate image, reliability and flexibility in production and delivery, technical innovation and well executed promotional activity also present opportunities to create a differential advantage. Price used to be the basis for differentiation in industrial markets, but price can be reduced only so far if companies are to remain viable. Although cost is still important, in most markets companies have attempted to move away from a selling proposition based purely on low price. They have realised that *value* is not necessarily equal to a low price. Service, reliability, payment terms, image and design are just a few factors in addition to price that influence many sales. Today, value—keen price coupled with a product/service offer—and not raw, low price is often the deciding factor for many business-to-business customers.

Administered pricing A pricing method in which the seller determines the price for a product and the customer pays the specified price

Although there are various ways to determine prices of industrial products, the three most common are administered pricing, bid pricing and negotiated pricing. With **administered pricing,** the seller determines the price (or series of prices) for a product and the customer pays that specified price. Marketers who use this approach may employ a one price policy in which all buyers pay the same price, or they may set a series of prices that are determined by one or more discounts. In some cases, list prices are posted on a price sheet or in a catalogue. The list price is a beginning point from which trade, quantity and cash discounts are deducted. Thus the actual (net) price a business-to-business customer pays is the list price less the discount(s). When a list price is used, the business-to-business marketer sometimes specifies the price in terms of list price times a multiplier. For example, the price of an item might be quoted as "list price $\times$ .78", which means the buyer can purchase the product at 78 per cent of the list price. Simply changing the multiplier lets the seller revise prices without having to issue new catalogues or price sheets.

Bid pricing Determination of prices through sealed or open bids submitted by the seller to the buyer

With **bid pricing,** prices are determined through sealed or open bids. When a buyer uses sealed bids, selected sellers are notified that they are to submit their bids by a certain date. Normally, the lowest bidder is awarded the contract, as long as the buyer believes that the company is able to supply the specified products when and where needed. In an open bidding approach, several, but not all, sellers are asked to submit bids. In contrast to sealed bidding, the amounts of the bids are made public. Finally, a business purchaser sometimes uses negotiated bids. Under this arrangement, the customer seeks bids from a number of sellers and screens the bids. Then the customer negotiates the price and terms of sale with the most favourable bidders, until either a final transaction is consummated or negotiations are terminated with all sellers.

Sometimes a buyer will be seeking either component parts to be used in production for several years or custom built equipment to be purchased currently and through future contracts. In such instances, an industrial seller may submit an initial, less profitable bid to win "follow on" (subsequent) contracts. The seller that wins the initial contract is often substantially favoured in the competition for follow on contracts. In such a bidding situation, a business-to-business marketer must determine how low the initial bid should be, the probability of winning a follow on contract and what combination of bid prices on both the initial and the follow on contract will yield an acceptable profit.[14]

Negotiated pricing Determination of prices through negotiations between the seller and the buyer

For certain types of business markets, a seller's pricing component may have to allow for **negotiated pricing.** That is, even when there are stated list prices and discount structures, negotiations may determine the actual price a business customer pays. Negotiated pricing can benefit both seller and buyer because price negotiations frequently lead to discussions of product specifications, applications and perhaps product substitutions. Such negotiations may give the seller an opportunity to provide the customer with technical assistance and perhaps sell a product that better fits the customer's requirements; the final product choice might also be more profitable for the seller. The buyer benefits by gaining more information about the array of products and terms of sale available and may acquire a more suitable product at a lower price.

Some business-to-business marketers sell in markets in which only one of these general pricing approaches prevails. Such marketers can simplify the price components of their marketing mixes. However, a number of business marketers sell to a wide variety of business customers and must maintain considerable flexibility in pricing.

People

This chapter has already emphasised the importance of people in the marketing of business-to-business products. The role of personal selling is especially important in many business markets, particularly those in which the purchase is deemed risky because of its size, value or complexity. For many technologically advanced products, the need to have face-to-face explanation and guidance is fundamental to the customers' perceived level of satisfaction. The development of long term **relationships**—regular, ongoing contacts—with business-to-business customers, is increasingly a driving factor in the development of marketing mixes for businesses supplying other businesses. Where products are high value or complex, customers often expect such relationships. Even in commodity markets—for example, basic components, computer consumerables or the provision of electricity—relationships are seen as a means of maintaining contact with customers, ensuring re-orders and enabling a supplying business to differentiate itself through customer service rather than price alone. More attention is being given to the effective recruitment, training and motivation of personnel who are often in regular contact with a business's immediate customers, typically other businesses in the marketing channel.

Amending the Marketing Mix for Services

The original marketing mix defined by McCarthy included the now well known "4Ps" of product, promotion, price and place (distribution/channels). Most authors now mention an additional ingredient of the marketing mix: people. Originally suggested by services marketers who acknowledged that consumers often view the personnel providing a service as part and parcel of the service "product" being offered, the people aspect of the marketing mix has become an accepted part of most businesses' marketing programmes, not only for organisations marketing services. The nature of services, however, as described in Chapter 11, has led marketers to further adapt the marketing mix.[15] The intangibility of service products, inseparability of production and consumption, perishability and heterogeneity—the key characteristics of services—force the marketing mix to be amended in two ways: (1) the traditional 4Ps of product, promotion, price and place/distribution have some important extra dimensions unique to the marketing of services, and (2) the marketing mix is itself modified to include the additional core ingredients of process, physical evidence (ambience) and people, thereby creating the "7Ps" of what is termed the **extended marketing mix for services**.[16] Figure 20.4 presents this revised marketing mix for services. This section examines in more detail the amendments required when determining a marketing mix for services, commencing with the traditional 4Ps, before reviewing the additional ingredients of the extended marketing mix.[17]

Product

Goods can be defined in terms of their physical attributes, but services, because of their **intangibility**—that is, their inability to be perceived by the senses—cannot. It is often difficult for consumers to understand service offerings and to evaluate possible service alternatives. The gas and electricity companies, for example, offer schemes to spread bill payments and to assist the financially disadvantaged, plus several methods for making payments. These services are explained in the companies' advertisements.

There may also be tangibles (such as facilities, employees or communications) associated with a service. These tangible elements help form a part of the product and are often the only aspects of a service that can be viewed prior to pur-

Figure 20.4 The
extended marketing mix
for services

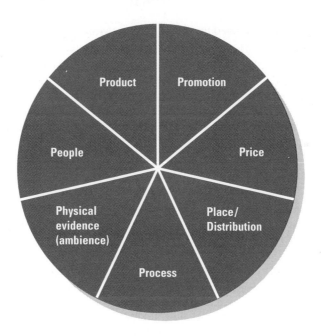

Service provider A person who
offers a service, such as a bank clerk or
hair stylist

Service product quality The
consumer's perception of the quality
of service he or she receives

chase. Consequently, marketers must pay close attention to associated tangibles and make sure that they are consistent with the selected image of the service product.[18] For example, consumers perceive public transport at night as plagued by crime and therefore hesitate to use it. Improvements in the physical appearance of tube stations and reductions in the time between trains are tangible cues that consumers can use to judge public transport services.

The service product is often equated with the **service provider,** for example, the bank clerk or the hair stylist becomes the service a bank or a beauty salon provides. Because consumers tend to view services in terms of service personnel and because personnel are inconsistent in their behaviour, it is imperative that service providers effectively select, train, motivate and control contact people.

After testing many variables, the Strategic Planning Institute (SPI) in the United States developed an extensive database on the impact of various business strategies on profits. The institute found that "relative perceived product *quality*" is the single most important factor in determining long term profitability. In fact, because there are generally no objective measures to evaluate the quality of professional services (medical care, legal services and so forth), the customer is actually purchasing confidence in the service provider.[19] The strength or weakness of the service provided often affects consumers' perceptions of **service product quality.** Of the companies in the SPI database, businesses that rate low on service lose market share at the rate of 2 per cent a year and average a 1 per cent return on sales. Companies that score high on service gain market share at the rate of 6 per cent a year, average a 12 per cent return on sales and charge a significantly higher price.[20] These data indicate that companies having service dominant products must score high on service quality.

Because services are performances rather than tangible goods, the concept of service quality is difficult to grasp. However, price, quality and value are important considerations of consumer choice and buying behaviour for both goods and services.[21] It should be noted that it is not objective quality that matters, but the consumer's subjective perceptions. Instead of quality meaning conformity to a set of specifications—which frequently determine levels of product quality—service quality is defined by customers.[22] Moreover, quality is frequently determined through a comparison—in the case of services, by contrasting what the consumer expected of a service with her or his actual experience.[23]

Service providers and service consumers may have quite different views of what constitutes service quality. Consumers frequently enter service exchanges with a set of pre-determined expectations. Whether a consumer's actual experiences exceed, match or fall below these expectations will have a great effect on future relationships between the consumer and the service provider. To improve service quality, a service provider must adjust its own behaviour to be consistent with consumers' expectations or re-educate consumers so that their expectations will parallel the service levels that can be achieved.[24]

A study of doctor-patient relationships proposed that when professional service exceeds client expectations, a true person-to-person bonding relationship develops. However, the research also revealed that what doctors viewed as being quality service was not necessarily what patients perceived as quality service. Although interaction with the doctor was the primary determinant of the overall service evaluation, patients made judgements about the entire service experience, including factors such as the appearance and behaviour of receptionists, nurses and technicians; the decor; and even the appearance of the building.[25]

Other product concepts discussed in Chapters 9 and 10 are also relevant here. Management must make decisions regarding the product mix, positioning, branding and new product development of services. It can make better decisions if it analyses the organisation's service products in terms of **complexity** and **variability**. Complexity is determined by the number of steps required to perform a service. Variability reflects the amount of diversity allowed in each step of service provision. In a highly variable service, every step in performing the service may be unique, whereas in cases of low variability, every performance of the service is standardised.[26] For example, services provided by doctors are both complex and variable. Patient treatment may involve many steps, and the doctor has considerable discretion in shaping the treatment for each individual patient. In general, to decrease costs and widen the potential market and to better control quality, service providers seek to limit both complexity and variability.

An examination of the complete service delivery process, including the number of steps and decisions, enables marketers to plot their service products on a complexity/variability grid, such as the one in Figure 20.5. The position of a service on the grid has implications for its positioning in the market. Furthermore, any alterations in the service delivery process that shift the position of the service on the complexity/variability grid have an impact on the positioning of the service in

Complexity In services marketing, the number of steps required to perform a service

Variability The amount of diversity allowed in each step of service provision

Figure 20.5
Complexity/variability grid for medical services. SOURCE: Adapted from Lynn Shostack, 1985 American Marketing Association Faculty Consortium on Services Marketing, Texas A&M University, 7–11 July. Reprinted by permission of the American Marketing Association.

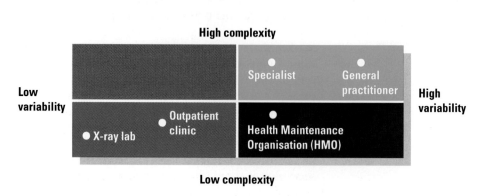

Table 20.2 Effects of shifting positions on the complexity/variability grid

Downgrading Complexity/Variability	Upgrading Complexity/Variability
Standardises the service	Increases costs
Requires strict operating controls	Indicates higher margin/lower volume strategy
Generally widens potential market	
Lowers costs	Personalises the service
Indicates lower margin/higher volume strategy	Generally narrows potential market
Can alienate existing markets	Makes quality more difficult to control

SOURCE: Adapted from Lynn Shostack, 1985 American Marketing Association Faculty Consortium on Services Marketing, Texas A&M University, 7–11 July. Reprinted by permission of the American Marketing Association.

the marketplace. Table 20.2 details the effects of such changes. When structuring the service delivery system, marketers should consider the organisation's marketing goals and target market.

Promotion   As intangible dominant products, services are not easily promoted. The intangible is difficult to depict in advertising, whether the medium is print or broadcast. Service advertising should thus emphasise tangible cues that will help consumers understand and evaluate the service. The cues may be the physical facilities in which the service is performed or some relevant tangible object that symbolises the service itself.[27] For example, restaurants may stress their physical facilities—clean, elegant, casual and so on—to provide clues as to the quality or nature of the service. Insurance firms, such as Legal and General, use objects as symbols to help consumers understand their services. Legal and General's umbrella symbol reflected an image of paternalistic protection. Midland (HSBC) Bank's old slogan *The Listening Bank* gave the impression of understanding, helpfulness and service. Service providers may also focus their advertising on the characteristics they believe customers want from their services. National Westminster Bank's promotion stressed its ability to offer unbiased, independent advice about pensions. Commercial Union Assurance—*We won't make a drama out of a crisis*—emphasised speed of service in dealing with insurance claims and the provision of assistance in sorting out the problem.

The symbols, catch lines and imagery common to most financial organisations reflect the increasing importance of branding in services.[28] Differentiation between rival services is difficult, as is effective promotion. Branding is helping to distinguish competing services and to provide a platform for promotional activity.[29]

To be successful, organisations must not only maximise the difference between the value of the service to the customer and the cost of providing it; they must also design the service with employees in mind. Contact personnel are critical to the perception of quality service. They must be provided with sufficient tools and knowledge to furnish the type of service that the customer desires. Because service industries are information driven, they can substitute knowledgeable, highly trained personnel for the capital assets used in more product oriented businesses.[30]

Thus employees in a service organisation are an important secondary audience for service advertising. Variability in service quality, which arises from the labour intensive nature of many services, is a problem for service marketers, because consumers often associate the service with the service provider. Advertising can have a positive effect on customer contact personnel. It can shape employees' perceptions of the company, their jobs and how management expects them to perform. It can be a tool for motivating, educating and communicating with employees.[31] For example, British Airways' famous strapline on its advertising throughout the 1980s and 1990s, "the world's favorite airline", was designed not just to remind air travellers that more people flew with BA than with any other airline but also to develop a sense of pride among BA's flight and ground personnel.

Personal selling is potentially powerful in services because this form of promotion lets consumers and salespeople interact. When consumers enter into a service transaction, they must, as a general rule, interact with the service organisation's employees. Customer contact personnel can be trained to use this opportunity to reduce customer uncertainty, give re-assurance, reduce dissonance and promote the reputation of the organisation.[32] Once again, therefore, properly managing contact personnel is important.

Although consumer service organisations have the opportunity to interact with actual customers and those potential customers who contact them, they have little opportunity to go out into the field and solicit business from all potential consumers. The very large number of potential customers and the high cost per sales call rule out such efforts. On the other hand, marketers of industrial services, like the marketers of industrial goods, are dealing with a much more limited target market and may find personal selling the most effective way of reaching their customers.

Sales promotions, such as contests, are feasible for service providers, but other types of promotions are more difficult to implement. How does an organisation display a service? How does it provide a free sample without giving away the whole service? A complimentary visit to a health club or a free skiing lesson could possibly be considered a free sample to entice a consumer into purchasing a membership or taking lessons. Although the role of publicity and the implementation of a public relations campaign do not differ significantly in the goods and service sectors, service marketers appear to rely on publicity much more than goods marketers do.[33] Customers are receptive to stories of good (and bad!) service, plus public relations is highly cost effective (see Chapter 16).

Consumers tend to value word-of-mouth communications more than company sponsored communications. This preference is probably true for all products, but especially for services, because they are experiential in nature. For this reason, service organisations should attempt to stimulate word-of-mouth communications.[34] They can do so by encouraging consumers to tell their friends about satisfactory performance. Many businesses, for instance, prominently display signs urging customers to tell their friends if they like the service and to tell the business if they do not. Some service providers, such as hairdressers, give their regular customers discounts or free services for encouraging friends to come in for a haircut. Word-of-mouth can be simulated through communications messages that feature a testimonial—for example, television advertisements showing consumers who vouch for the benefits of a service a particular organisation offers.

One final note should be made in regard to service promotion. The promotional activities of most professional service providers, such as doctors, lawyers and accountants, are severely limited. Until recently, all these professionals were prohibited by law from advertising. Although these restrictions have now been lifted in many countries, there are still many obstacles to be overcome. Not used to seeing professionals advertise, consumers may reject the advertisements of those who do. Furthermore, professionals are not familiar with advertising and consequently do not always develop advertisements appropriate for their services. In many countries, lawyers are being forced to consider advertising, both because many potential clients do not know that they need legal services and because there is an over supply of lawyers. Consumers want more information about legal services, and lawyers have a very poor public image.[35] On the other hand, doctors and dentists are more sceptical about the impact of advertising on their image and business. Despite the trend towards professional services advertising, the professions themselves exert pressure on their members to advertise or promote only in a limited way because such activities are still viewed as somewhat risqué.

Price

Price plays both an economic and a psychological role in the service sector, just as it does with physical goods. However, the psychological role of price in respect to services is magnified; after all, consumers must rely on price as the sole indicator of service quality when other quality indicators are absent. In its economic role, price determines revenue and influences profits. Knowing the real costs of each service provided is vital to sound pricing decisions (see Chapters 18 and 19).[36]

Services may also be bundled together and then sold for a single price. Service bundling is a practical strategy, because in many types of services there is a high ratio of fixed to variable costs and high cost sharing amongst service offerings. Moreover, the demand for certain services is often inter-dependent. For example, banks offer packages of banking services—current and savings accounts and credit lines that become active when customers overdraw their other accounts. Price bundling may help service marketers cross-sell to their current customers or acquire new customers. The policy of price leaders also may be used by discounting the price of one service product when the customer purchases another service at full price.[37] Visitors to a safari park may be offered discounted entry to the attached fairground and amusements.

Service intangibility may also complicate the setting of prices. When pricing physical goods, management can look to the cost of production (direct and indirect materials, direct and indirect labour, and overheads) as an indicator of price. It is often difficult, however, to determine the cost of service provision and thus identify a minimum price. Price competition is severe in many service areas characterised by standardisation. Usually, price is not a key variable when marketing is first implemented in an organisation. Once market segmentation and specialised services are directed to specific markets, specialised prices are set. Next comes comparative pricing as the service becomes fairly standardised. Price competition is quite common in the hotel and leisure sectors, banking and insurance.

Many services, especially professional services, are situation-specific. Thus neither the service provider nor the consumer knows the extent of the service prior to production and consumption. Once again, because cost is not known beforehand, price is difficult to set. Despite the difficulties in determining cost, many service providers use cost plus pricing. Others set prices according to the competition or market demand.

Pricing of services can also help smooth out fluctuations in demand. Given the perishability of service products, this is an important function. A higher price may be used to deter or off-set demand during peak periods, and a lower price may be used to stimulate demand during slack periods. The railways offer cheap day returns and savers to minimise sales declines in slack periods. Airlines rely heavily on price to help smooth out their demand, as do many other operations, such as pubs and entertainment clubs, cinemas, resorts and hotels.

Place/Distribution

In the service context, distribution is making services available to prospective users. Marketing intermediaries are the entities between the actual service provider and the consumer that make the service more available and more convenient to use.[38] The distribution of services is very closely related to product development. Indirect distribution of services may be made possible by a tangible representation or a facilitating good, for example, a bank credit card.[39]

Almost by definition, service industries are limited to direct channels of distribution. Many services are produced and consumed simultaneously; in high contact services in particular, service providers and consumers cannot be separated. In low contact services, however, service providers may be separated from customers by intermediaries. Dry cleaners, for example, generally maintain strategically located retail stores as drop-off centres, and these stores may be independent or company owned. Consumers go to the branch to initiate and terminate service, but the actual service may be performed at a different location. The separation is possible because the service is directed towards the consumer's physical possessions, and the consumer is not required to be present during delivery.

Other service industries are developing unique ways to distribute their services. To make it more convenient for consumers to obtain their services, airlines, car hire companies and hotels have long been using intermediaries: travel agencies. In financial services marketing, the two most important strategic concerns are the application of technology and the use of electronic product delivery channels—such as automatic cash dispensers and electronic funds transfer systems—to provide customers with financial services in a more widespread and convenient manner.[40] Consumers no longer have to go to their bank for routine transactions; they can now receive service from the nearest cash dispenser or conduct transactions via telephone or fax. Indeed, HSBC's First Direct banking operation is managed entirely through telecommunications: there is no bank branch network (see Case 12.1 in Chapter 12). Most banks now offer Internet access for customers wishing to conduct their financial transactions from the comfort of their homes, negating the need to visit branches. Bank credit cards have enabled banks to extend their credit services to consumers over widely dispersed geographic areas through an international network of intermediaries, namely, the retailers who assist consumers in applying for and using the cards.

Process

The acts of purchasing and consumption are important in all markets—consumer, industrial or service. The direct involvement of consumers in the production of most services and the perishability of these services place greater emphasis on the process of the transaction for services. Friendliness of staff and flows of information affect the customer's perception of the service product offer. Appointment or queuing systems become part of the service. Ease or difficulty of payment can enhance or spoil the consumption of a service. Diners in a TGI Friday's or Pizza Hut expect prompt service, informative menus, no waiting and no delays in paying their bills at the conclusion of their meals. These are operational issues that *directly* affect customer perceptions and satisfaction: they are important aspects of the marketing of services.[41]

Physical Evidence (Ambience)   The environment in which a service is offered, and consumed, is central to the consumer's understanding of the service and to her or his enjoyment or satisfaction. The "feel" is very much part of the service offer. Whether in a restaurant, hospital, sports club or bank, the appearance and ambience matter. Layout, decor, up-keep; noise and aroma; general ease of access and use—all become part of the service product. Even tyre depots have recognised this aspect of the extended marketing mix for services, providing comfortable customer waiting areas with seating, drinks machines, TV and newspapers.

People   The nature of most services requires direct interaction between the consumer and personnel representing the service provider's organisation. In many services, customers interact with one another, and the organisation's staff also interact with one another. This level of human involvement must be given maximum attention if customers are to maximise their use of the service and, ultimately, their satisfaction.[42] Employee selection, training and motivation are central considerations. A restaurant may have a superb operation, but if the chef or waiters become demoralised and unmotivated, they will begin to deliver low quality meals and inefficient service, resulting in a poor product from the consumer's point of view. Operational staff often help "produce" the service product, sell it and assist in its consumption. Many service businesses are totally dependent on their personnel, as Leo Burnett, founder of the international advertising agency that bears his name, summed up: "Every evening all our assets go down the elevator"—people!

Strategic Adaptation of Marketing Mixes for International Markets

As explained in Chapter 3, marketing in non-domestic markets requires an understanding of the marketing environment and a specifically devised strategy. Once a company determines overseas market potential and understands the foreign environment, it develops and adapts its marketing mix(es). Creating and maintaining the marketing mix are the final steps in developing the international marketing strategy. Only if foreign marketing opportunities justify the risk will a company go to the expense of adapting the marketing mix. Of course, in some situations new products are developed for a specific country. In these cases, there is no existing marketing mix and no extra expense to consider in serving the foreign target market: new marketing programmes must be designed.

Product and Promotion   As Figure 20.6 shows, there are five possible strategies for adapting product and promotion across national boundaries: (1) keep product and promotion the same worldwide, (2) adapt promotion only, (3) adapt product only, (4) adapt both product and promotion and (5) invent new products.[43]

Keep Product and Promotion the Same Worldwide   This strategy attempts to use in the foreign country the product and promotion developed for the home market, an approach that seems desirable wherever possible because it eliminates the expenses of marketing research and product re-development. American companies PepsiCo and Coca-Cola use this approach in marketing their soft drinks. Although both translate promotional messages into the language of a particular country, they market the same product and promotional messages around the

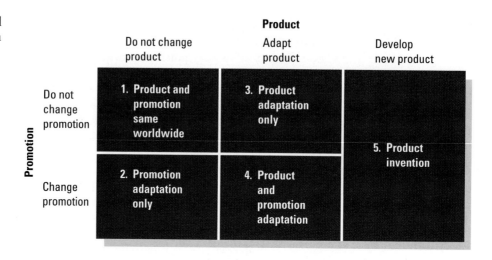

Figure 20.6 International product and promotion strategies. SOURCE: Adapted from Warren J. Keegan, *Global Marketing Management*, 4th edn, (Englewood Cliffs, N.J.: Prentice-Hall, 1989), pp. 378–382. Used by permission.

world. Despite certain inherent risks that stem from cultural differences in interpretation, exporting advertising copy does provide the efficiency of international standardisation, or globalisation. As the following examples imply, not all brands/products are suitable for export in their existing forms: *Zit* fizzy drink (Greece), *Bum's* biscuits (Sweden), *Krapp* toilet paper (Sweden), *Grand Dick* red wine (France), and *Sor Bits* mints (Denmark).[44] Global advertising embraces the same concept as global marketing, discussed in Chapter 3. An advertiser can save hundreds of thousands of pounds by running the same advertisement worldwide.

Adapt Promotion Only This strategy leaves the product basically unchanged but modifies its promotion. For example, McDonald's provides similar products throughout the world but may modify the media for its advertising messages. This approach may be necessary because of language, legal or cultural differences associated with the advertising copy. When Polaroid introduced its SX-70 camera in Europe, for example, it used the same television and print advertisements featuring the same "celebrities" that it had used in the United States. However, because the personalities featured were in fact not well known in Europe, the advertisements were not effective, and sales of the SX-70 were initially low. Only when Polaroid adapted its promotion to appeal to regional needs and tastes did the SX-70 begin to achieve success.[45] Promotional adaptation is a low cost modification compared with the costs of re-developing engineering and production and physically changing products.

Generally, the strategy of adapting only promotion infuses advertising with the culture of the people who will be exposed to it (see Figure 20.7). Often promotion combines thinking globally and acting locally. At company headquarters, a basic global marketing strategy is developed, but promotion is modified to fit each market's needs, often using locally based advertising agencies.

Adapt Product Only The basic assumption in modifying a product without changing its promotion is that the product will serve the same function under different conditions of use. Soap and washing powder manufacturers have adapted their products to local water conditions and washing equipment without changing their promotions. Household appliances also have been altered to use different power voltages.

TR EAU PHÄE

Treauphy.

EIGEN L EAU B

Bleau your own trumpet.

PR EAU PAGANDE

Preaupaganda.

FEAU REVER

Figure 20.7 Adapting promotion across national boundaries. Source: Courtesy Perrier Exports.

A product may have to be adjusted for legal reasons. Japan, for example, has some of the most stringent car emission requirements in the world. European cars that fail emission standards cannot be marketed in Japan. Sometimes, products must be adjusted to overcome social and cultural obstacles. American Jell-O introduced a powdered jelly mix that failed in Britain because Britons were used to buying jelly in cube form. Resistance to a product is frequently based on attitudes and ignorance about the nature of new technology. It is often easier to change the product than to overcome technological, social or cultural biases.

Adapt Both Product and Promotion When a product serves a new function or is used differently in a foreign market, then both the product and its promotion need to be altered. For example, when Procter & Gamble marketed its Cheer washing powder in Japan, it promoted the product as being effective in all temperatures. Most Japanese, however, wash clothes in cold water and therefore do not care about all temperature washing. Moreover, the Japanese often add a lot of fabric softener to the wash, and Cheer did not produce many suds under those conditions. Procter & Gamble thus reformulated Cheer so that it would not be affected by the addition of fabric softeners and changed the promotion to emphasise "superior" cleaning in cold water. Cheer then became one of Procter & Gamble's most successful products in Japan.[46] Adaptation of both product and promotion is the most expensive strategy discussed so far, but it should be considered if the foreign market appears large enough and competitively attractive.

Invent New Products This strategy is selected when existing products cannot meet the needs of a non-domestic market. General Motors developed an all purpose, jeep-like motor vehicle that can be assembled in developing nations by mechanics with no special training. The vehicle is designed to operate under varied conditions; it has standardised parts and is inexpensive. Colgate-Palmolive developed an inexpensive, all plastic, hand-powered washing machine that has the tumbling action of a modern automatic machine. The product, marketed in less developed countries, was invented for households that have no electricity. Strategies that involve the invention of products are often the most costly, but the pay-off can be great. The clockwork radio was designed as a low cost and effective educational medium for poor regions of southern Africa. It proved a success in this context, but surprisingly also in the United States and developed economies, where it took on cult status and sold for a high price as an up-market, trendy status symbol.

Place/Distribution and Pricing Decisions about the distribution system and pricing policies are important in developing an international marketing mix. Figure 20.8 illustrates different approaches to these decisions.

Distribution A company can sell its product to an intermediary that is willing to buy from existing marketing channels, or it can develop new international marketing channels. Obviously, some service companies, such as Citicorp or ABN AMRO, need to develop their own distribution systems to market their products. However, many products, such as toothpaste, are distributed through intermediaries and brokers. The company must consider distribution both between countries and within the foreign country. Marketing Insight 20.2 reveals how confectionery giant Suchard seeks to acquire local companies in order to

Pan-European Suchard Thinks Globally, Operates Locally

The chocolate confectionery business of US-Swiss Kraft Jacob Suchard represents 65 per cent of its Sw. fr. 9 billion turnover. Suchard has been gearing up for global markets since the late 1960s by developing global brands, such as Milka and Toblerone, and undertaking a number of strategically important acquisitions. In taking over other European confectionery companies, such as Du Lac (Italian), Pavlides (Greek) and Terry's (UK), Suchard has sought established distribution and retail channels in areas where it was not traditionally strong. This has helped the company to develop its own global brands alongside smaller, local products. The acquisition of the West German cocoa trader Van Houten in 1987 gave Suchard closer control over its raw materials.

At the pan-European level, global brands are now assisted by the EU single market allowing unrestricted flow of goods between EU countries. Companies with pan-European brands, including Suchard, benefit from the advertising opportunities offered by European satellites, which are less exploited by national brands. It is probable that over several years preferences and eating habits within Europe will gradually converge as communication of this type increases. Companies such as Suchard have evolved from operating within a domestic market to being international players. As such, they must now seek additional marketing intelligence and data, re-think strategies and modify their marketing mixes.

In the UK, Terry's of York was a major player, though relatively small next to the mighty Cadbury's and Rowntree's (now owned by Nestlé). It did, however, have many well known brands and products, good distribution coverage and modern production facilities. Acquisition by Suchard immediately increased the company's share of the UK confectionery market and improved distribution coverage for the existing range of Suchard products. Suchard is currently focusing on eastern Europe. An automated logistics centre in Fallingbostel caters for retail and wholesale customers throughout Germany. The company has a 99.2 per cent stake in Rumania's state confectionery maker, Poiana SA, and promised to invest £30 million by the end of the 1990s. In Lithuania, Suchard has acquired production facilities from Kaunas, rather than supplying the market with imported chocolate. Kaunas's sales have doubled since the 1993 takeover. While mainstream brands are taken into these new markets, Suchard prefers to acquire locally based production and to supply existing national brands alongside those international "best sellers" it believes have local potential.

SOURCES: Terry's of York;" "Krafting' bar code and EDI technology", *Automatic ID News*, December 1995, p. 22;"KJS to put further $17m in confectioner", *Finance East Europe*, 6 October 1995, p. 12;"Chocolate maker stirs pot in Lithuania", *Crossborder Monitor*, 4 October 1995, p. 8;"Making a marque", *Corporate Location*, September/October 1995, pp. 42–43.

gain both ready-made production facilities and the acquired companies' distribution networks.

In determining distribution alternatives, the existence of retailers and wholesalers that can perform marketing functions between and within countries is one major factor. If a country has a segmented retail structure consisting primarily of one-person shops or street sellers, it may be difficult to develop new marketing channels for products such as packaged goods and prepared foods. Quite often in Third World countries, certain channels of distribution are characterised by ethnodomination. *Ethnodomination* occurs when an ethnic group occupies a majority position within a marketing channel. Indians, for example, own approximately 90 per cent of the cotton gins in Uganda; the Hausa tribe in Nigeria dominates the trade in kola nuts, cattle and housing; and Chinese merchants dominate the rice economy in Thailand. Marketers must be sensitive to ethnodomination and recognise that the ethnic groups operate in sub-cultures with a unique social and economic organisation.[47]

Figure 20.8 Strategies for international distribution and pricing

Distribution

	No effort to establish new marketing channels	Establish new marketing channels
Do not change price policies	1. Same price policies; no control over distribution	3. Establish new channels and use same price policies
Change price policies	2. Price policies changed for international markets; no control over distribution	4. Develop new channels and change price policies

Price policies

If the product being sold across national boundaries requires service and information, then control of the distribution process is desirable. Caterpillar, for example, sells more than half its construction and earthmoving equipment outside its native US. Because it must provide services and replacement parts, Caterpillar has established its own dealers in foreign markets. Regional sales offices and technical experts are also available to support local dealers. A manufacturer of paint brushes, on the other hand, would be more concerned about agents, wholesalers or other manufacturers (for example, of paint) that would facilitate the product's exposure in a foreign market. Control over the distribution process would not be so important for that product because services and replacement parts are not needed.

Research suggests that international companies use independently owned marketing channels when they market in countries perceived to be highly dissimilar to their home markets. However, when they market complex products, they develop vertically integrated marketing channels to gain control of distribution. To manage the distribution process from manufacturer to customer contact requires an expert salesforce that must be trained specifically to sell the company's products. Moreover, when products are unique or highly differentiated from those of current competitors, international companies also tend to design and establish vertically integrated channels.[48]

It is crucial to realise that a country's political instability can jeopardise the distribution of goods. For example, when the United States invaded Panama in late 1989, the Panama Canal was closed for several days, delaying shipments of goods through the canal. Similarly, during the political unrest in China, military activity and fighting made it difficult to move goods into and out of certain areas. Instability centering on Iraq and the Persian Gulf had a similar effect. Thus it must be stressed again how important it is to monitor the environment when engaging in international marketing. Companies that market products in unstable regions may need to develop alternative plans to allow for sudden unrest or hostility and to ensure that the distribution of their products is not jeopardised.

It is important to have the "right" product or service to appeal to the target market in an international market. A significant impediment to effective international marketing, however, is distribution. It is not always easy to grasp how marketing channels operate in an alien territory. Companies setting up in Russia find the channels, bureaucracy and corruption difficult to manage. It is never easy to identify the most suitable channel members and players with which to do business, or to find those that should be permitted to sell a company's products.

Pricing   The domestic and non-domestic prices of products are usually different. For example, the prices charged for Walt Disney videos in the UK, Germany and Spain will all vary, as well as being different from US prices. The increased costs of transport, supplies, taxes, tariffs and other expenses necessary to adjust a company's operations to international marketing can raise prices. A key decision is whether the basic pricing policy will change (as discussed in Chapter 19). If it is a company's policy not to allocate fixed costs to non-domestic sales, then lower foreign prices could result.

It is common practice for EU countries to sell off foodstuffs and pharmaceuticals at knock down prices to eastern European and African states respectively. This kind of sale of products in non-domestic markets—or vice versa—at lower prices than those charged in domestic markets (when all the costs have not been allocated or when surplus products are sold) is called **dumping.** Dumping is illegal in some countries if it damages domestic companies and workers.

A cost plus approach to international pricing is probably the most common method used because of the compounding number of costs necessary to move products from their country of origin. Of course, as the discussion of pricing policies in Chapter 19 points out, understanding consumer demand and the competitive environment is a necessary step in selecting a price.

The price charged in other countries is also a function of foreign currency exchange rates. Fluctuations in the international monetary market can change the prices charged across national boundaries on a daily basis. There has been a trend towards greater fluctuation (or float) in world money markets. For example, a sudden variation in the exchange rate, which occurs when a nation devalues its currency, can have wide ranging effects on consumer prices.

There are also pricing issues that stem from transfer pricing practices and the problems of parallel imports. **Transfer pricing** is the price charged between profit centres, for example, a manufacturing company and its foreign subsidiary. Company policies can force subsidiaries to sell products at higher prices than the local competition, even though the true costs of their manufacture may be no different. The manufacturer tries to make a profit even from its "internal" customer, its own subsidiary.[49] **Parallel imports,** that is, goods exported from low price to high price countries, are an increasing problem. For example, French and Belgian beer producers export to the UK at set price levels, but consumers and small independent retailers cross by car ferry to Calais and stock up with similar brands at much lower prices than those the manufacturers "officially" offer to UK customers. Independent operators have set up import/export businesses to take well known beer brands into the UK to be sold at prices higher than in their native markets, but still lower than those offered by the manufacturers' official export agents. A similar trade in new cars is also now evident, under-cutting UK dealers' prices.

There are also important price ramifications to consider stemming from product or brand positioning and any differences between countries. For example, in the UK Stella Artois beer is marketed as "re-assuringly expensive", whereas in its native Belgium it is more of a commodity, mass market brand competing against brands such as Duval or the specialist "Trappist monk" beers. Pricing, in any market, must reflect the brand positioning adopted.[50]

Dumping   The sale of products in non-domestic markets at lower prices than those charged in domestic markets, when all costs are not allocated or when surplus products are sold

Transfer pricing   The price charged between profit centres, for example, between a manufacturing company and its foreign subsidiary

Parallel imports   Goods that are imported through "non-official" channels from low price to high price countries

People As noted earlier, great importance is now attached to the people ingredient of the marketing mix. The nature of many business-to-business markets and the form of most service products often lead businesses to determine formally the role of people within their marketing mixes. In the context of international marketing, the people ingredient is also important. Chapter 3 highlighted how marketers performing across national boundaries must be aware of often striking differences, country by country or region by region, in the marketing environment. Often, cultural and social forces are the most varied—and also the most difficult for marketers based in another country and culture to understand. Companies must deploy people with the "right" skills to address such issues either from their own ranks or from third parties in the territories under scrutiny. Channel members such as agents can often assist in this respect. Having personnel who understand the nuances of an international market is a fundamental requirement for effective marketing, but so too is the need for those personnel with the cultural and local knowledge to be able to implement a marketing mix, which itself may well have been modified to reflect the nuances of the relevant marketing environment.

● S U M M A R Y

This chapter explains why and how the marketing mix must be manipulated differently for business-to-business markets, services marketing and international markets.

Business-to-business marketing is a set of activities directed at facilitating and expediting exchanges involving industrial products and customers in industrial, business-to-business markets. Like marketers of consumer products, business-to-business marketers must develop a marketing mix that satisfies the needs of customers in the industrial target market. Personnel are not generally seen as integral to the product itself, but perhaps more than in consumer marketing they are central to the selling process and are a key part of promotional activity. The product component frequently emphasises services, which are often of primary interest to business customers. The marketer must also consider that the customer may elect to make the product rather than buy it. Industrial products must meet certain standard specifications that business users want.

The distribution of business-to-business products differs from that of consumer products in the types of channels used, the kinds of intermediaries available, and the transport, storage and inventory policies. A *direct distribution channel*, in which products are sold directly from producers to users, is common in business marketing. Also used are channels containing manufacturers' agents, *business-to-business distributors* or both agents and distributors. Channels are chosen on the basis of several variables, including availability and the typical mode of purchase for a product.

Personal selling is a primary ingredient of the promotional component in business-to-business marketing mixes. Sales personnel often act as technical advisers both before and after a sale. Advertising is sometimes used to supplement personal selling efforts. Business-to-business marketers generally use print advertisements containing more information but less persuasive content than consumer advertisements. Other promotional activities include catalogues and trade shows.

The price component for business marketing mixes is influenced by legal and economic forces to a greater extent than it is for consumer marketing mixes. *Administered*, *bid* and *negotiated pricing* are additional possibilities in many business-to-business markets. Pricing may be affected by competitors' prices, as well as by the type of customer who buys the product. Increasingly, though price is still important, many companies are seeking new ways of creating a differential advantage. Value for money is important in most markets, but low price is not an effective differential advantage except in the very short term. Flexibility and reliability in production and delivery can be differentiating factors, as can technical innovation, personnel and customer service, promotional activity and even payment terms. People, important in the context of personal selling, are also often required to establish ongoing long term *relationships* with key customers.

The basic marketing mix is augmented for services through the addition of people, physical evidence (ambience) and the process of transaction in order to produce the "7Ps" or the *extended marketing mix for services*. When developing a marketing mix for services, several aspects deserve special consideration. Regarding product, service offerings are often difficult for consumers to understand and evaluate. The tangibles associated with a service may be the only visible aspect of the service, and marketers must manage these scarce tangibles with care. Because services are often viewed in terms of the *service providers*, service providers must carefully select, train, motivate and control employees, particularly to guarantee *service product quality*. Consumers determine the quality of services subjectively, often by contrasting what was expected of a service with the actual experience. Service providers need to meet these expectations or re-educate consumers. Service marketers are selling long term relationships as well as performance. It is important to understand the *complexity* of the service product and to seek to limit its *variability*.

Promoting services is problematic because of their *intangibility*. Advertising should stress the tangibles associated with the service or use some relevant tangible object. Branding is used to distinguish competing services. Personnel in direct contact with customers should be considered an important secondary audience for advertising. Personal selling is very powerful in service organisations because customers must interact with personnel; some forms of sales promotion, however, such as displays and free samples, are difficult to implement. The publicity component of the promotional mix is vital to many service organisations. Because customers value word-of-mouth communications, messages should

attempt to stimulate or simulate word-of-mouth. Many professional service providers, however, are severely restricted in their use of promotional activities.

Price plays three major roles in the service sector. It plays a psychological role by indicating quality and an economic role by determining revenues. Price is also a way to help smooth out fluctuations in demand.

Service distribution channels are typically direct because of simultaneous production and consumption. However, innovative approaches such as drop-off points, intermediaries and electronic distribution—such as the Internet—are being developed.

International marketing requires careful planning. Marketing activities performed across national boundaries are usually significantly different from domestic marketing activities. International marketers must have a profound awareness of the foreign environment and of social and cultural differences. The international marketing strategy is ordinarily adjusted to meet the needs and desires of markets across national boundaries.

After a country's environment has been analysed, marketers must develop a marketing mix and decide whether to adapt product or promotion. There are five possible strategies for adapting product and promotion across national boundaries: (1) keep product and promotion the same worldwide, (2) adapt promotion only, (3) adapt product only, (4) adapt both product and promotion and (5) invent new products. Foreign distribution channels are nearly always different from domestic ones. Identifying and understanding channels in foreign markets are not easy tasks. Distribution channels can become a major impediment in international marketing. The allocation of costs, transport considerations or the costs of doing business in foreign markets will affect pricing. *Transfer pricing* and *parallel imports* are important considerations, as are the regulations pertaining to *dumping*. It is also necessary to set pricing levels that reflect the nuances of a product's brand positioning in a particular market: the same brand may occupy distinctly different positions in separate territories.

Important Terms

Direct distribution channels
Business-to-business distributor
Personal selling
Administered pricing
Bid pricing
Negotiated pricing

Relationships
Extended marketing mix
  for services
Intangibility
Service provider
Service product quality

Complexity
Variability
Dumping
Transfer pricing
Parallel imports

Discussion and Review Questions

1. How do business-to-business marketing mixes differ from those of consumer products?
2. What are the major advantages and disadvantages of using industrial distributors?
3. Why do business-to-business marketers rely on personal selling more than consumer products marketers?
4. Why would a business-to-business marketer spend resources on advertising aimed at stimulating consumer demand?
5. Compare three methods of determining the price of industrial products.
6. Why must a differential advantage be based on more than just low prices?
7. Discuss the role of promotion in services marketing.
8. What additional elements must be included in the marketing mix for services? Why?
9. Why is it difficult to create and maintain a differential advantage in many service businesses?
10. Why do the marketers of services place so much emphasis on the people ingredient of the marketing mix?
11. What are the principal choices a company can make when manipulating the marketing mix for international markets?
12. How and why can the place/distribution ingredient of the marketing mix cause problems for international marketers?
13. What additional factors determine a company's pricing policy in foreign markets?

Recommended Readings

F. Bradley, *International Marketing Strategy,* 3rd edn (Hemel Hempstead: Prentice-Hall, 1998).

C. Lovelock, *Principles of Services Marketing and Management* (Englewood Cliffs, N.J.: Prentice-Hall, 1999).

C. Lovelock, *Services Marketing* (Englewood Cliffs, N.J.: Prentice-Hall, 1996).

A. Payne, *The Essence of Services Marketing* (Hemel Hempstead: Prentice-Hall, 1993).

A. Payne and M. H. B. McDonald, *Marketing Planning for Services* (Oxford: Butterworth-Heinemann, 1997).

T. L. Powers, *Modern Business Marketing* (St. Paul, Minn.: West, 1990).

● C A S E S

20.1 *Porsche AG: Striving for Recovery*

Founded in 1930 by Dr Ferdinand Porsche, the company known today as Porsche AG began as a research and development organisation. The original company accepted contracts from individuals and businesses to design new cars, aeroplanes and ships. The company built prototypes of each design and thoroughly tested them. If the business that commissioned the work approved the design, the product was then produced by one of the large manufacturing companies in Germany. After World War II, the Porsche family experienced a period of hardship, disappointment and personal tragedy. Porsche's son, Dr Ferry Porsche, began a company to manufacture family designed sports cars in 1948. Despite depressed economic conditions, the company persevered and prospered. By 1973, Porsche AG had built and sold some 200,000 Porsches, gaining worldwide recognition for its cars and their promise of "driving in its purest form".

Porsche today is organised into three divisions located in three suburbs of Stuttgart: the factory, in Zuffenhausen; testing, engineering and design, in Weissach; and marketing, in Ludwigsburg. The Porsche Research and Development Centre has produced the 959 race car, an aircraft engine, the TAG motor and designs for ambulances, mobile surgery units, gliders, fire engines and fork lift trucks. The company holds more than 2,000 patents, and innovations developed by Porsche are in several manufacturers' car models.

Despite Porsche's reputation for excellence, the company fell on hard times. It was forced to raise prices on cars sold in the US because of changes in the dollar exchange rate. Because of the price increases, a weakening US dollar, and lower priced Japanese imitations, sales in the United States dropped significantly in the late 1980s. Roughly 60 per cent of all Porsches were sold in the United States. Production dropped from 50,000 cars annually to 20,000.

Porsche is successful in markets where the social climate favours people who want to demonstrate their success and where the economic climate is conducive to the entrepreneur. Recessions have caused Porsche major problems. Porsche management believes that its customers have high personal goals, are ambitious, do not like to compromise and give their best efforts every time. Although not averse to risk, they prepare thoroughly for new ventures. Porsche customers are apparently goers and doers, but not show-offs. To succeed, Porsche AG must exhibit some of its customers' traits. Customers must be able to identify with the company—to see in it the same characteristics they see in themselves.

Wendelin Wiedeking became chairman in 1993. After six years of deteriorating sales, by 1995 the company was at last breaking even. Sales recovered to 30,000 units and Japanese consultants re-engineered the whole manufacturing operation, bringing significant cost savings. Close to £1 billion was invested in re-vamping the model range to include a two-seater roadster and the next generation 911. To reduce the company's dependence on the ever more crowded market for high performance sports cars, Wiedeking has returned to the company's roots and is seeking more engineering and design contracts through Weissach, Porsche's legendary research and development arm.

Work for VW Seat and development of the first mainstream Chinese family car are supported by the production of designer sun glasses, audio equipment and tableware. The main business of manufacturing and selling cars is not taking a back seat, however. Aside from introducing new models, the company has revolutionised customer databases to take account of national buying characteristics and loyalty levels. In the UK and US, this effort has helped dealers boost the proportion of repeat buyers to close to three out of four Porsche drivers. The databases, supplemented by extensive marketing research, have helped the company to re-define its customer groups into "top guns", "elitists", "proud owners", "bon vivants" and "fantasists", each with a bespoke marketing mix.

SOURCES: Porsche UK, Reading; *Marque* magazine, 1996; Dyan Machan, "Salvation in Stuttgart", *Forbes,* 11 September 1995, pp. 154–155; Regina Eisman, "Porsche", *Incentive,* June 1995, pp. 54–55; Alex Taylor, "Porsche slices up its buyers", *Fortune,* 16 January 1995, p. 24; "Japan to the rescue", *German Brief,* 6 May 1994, pp. 4–5.

Questions for Discussion

1. Why has the Porsche company broadened its product portfolio by encouraging Weissach to undertake more design contracts? What benefits or disadvantages does this policy bring to Porsche?

2. Recessions in various parts of Porsche's global operation have brought the company problems. In developing an international marketing strategy, how can Porsche take account of various economic trends?

3. Porsche undertakes projects for rival car manufacturers, most notably VW Seat. What are the benefits of such ventures for these clients? Are there any potential problems in following this strategy for Porsche's own car marketers?

20.2 Aer Lingus—A Programme for a Better Airline

Since the 1930s Aer Lingus has carried the flag as Ireland's state airline. Now an independent company, the airline has gone from strength to strength, winning countless awards for its business and tourist class services to and from Ireland. It competes in four distinct markets: the transatlantic long haul sector against such giants as American Airlines and British Airways; within the European Union against a plethora of national carriers such as Lufthansa or TAP; in the London/provincial UK market, against British Airways, British Midland, Ryan Air and a host of smaller airlines; and domestically within Ireland, where Aer Lingus competes with small Irish airlines, road and rail. Aer Lingus's marketing programmes must reflect the nuances and requirements of its international and national markets, while acknowledging that as a service provider its marketing mix is complex and difficult to control. Aer Lingus is a "people business", and as such believes its future depends on its ability to satisfy its target customers in a way which gives it an edge over its competitors.

The Board is on record as stating that "Aer Lingus is in the service business, not a supplier of seats on aircraft—a traditional international organisational focus of many airlines—but as a supplier of a total travel experience". To compete successfully, the airline knows it must increase its already strong emphasis on service and quality. The Aer Lingus brand is strong in its core markets and can only be strengthened by the company's desire to be ever more customer focused. This emphasis inevitably leads to a focus on the airline's personnel; their recruitment, training, attitudes, ability and motivation ensure that they give "good service". It also extends to any environment—terminal, aircraft, the Internet or booking point—in which customers encounter Aer Lingus, as well as the ease with which customers can book seats, travel and experience the airline's service product.

Towards the end of the 1990s, turnover (over £800 million pa) and operating profits (£47 million in 1997) rose, as carefully honed business strategies were implemented. Aer Lingus argues its success stems from the considerable effort it has put into analysing its markets and defining tightly its business proposition and from "developing necessary new skills and brand values to meet the ever changing needs of customers, while retaining an emphasis on core strengths, such as friendliness and Irish identity, which have been important factors in our success in the past". Aer Lingus's current strategy centres on increased differentiation in the marketplace with the right package of service and product at competitive prices. The market is becoming polarised between low priced, no frills, point-to-point service providers and, at the other extreme, full service, added value airlines such as Aer Lingus. The full service operators seek to provide comprehensive service levels and flexible travel options throughout the business and leisure markets at all price points. This "top end" market remains the mainstream, despite the inroads of Go or EasyJet, and comprises customers who wish to travel with an airline which offers a top quality, reliable product and service at competitive prices. According to Aer Lingus, the market is "not intrinsically price sensitive, but is highly 'value sensitive' ".

Recently, Aer Lingus launched internally its *Programme for a Better Airline*, to ensure it effectively continues to identify and meet its customers' needs. Marketing analysis revealed where the company was positioned within its chosen target markets, and ongoing contact with customers helps to develop a customer oriented culture. The *Programme for a Better Airline* is an articulation of how the airline is focusing on its customers, with clear structures, priorities and empowered actions. It also has led to specific improvements for customers based on feedback revealing their key concerns: punctuality, queuing, in-flight experience, baggage delivery and airport facilities. Aer Lingus established minimum performance standards in each of these prime areas, which were communicated to customers. The airline is now one of the most punctual in Europe and is consistently more punctual than its rivals on every route it flies. To reduce the length of queues, dedicated check-in facilities have been created at Dublin and London Stanstead. At London Heathrow a new fast track security channel saves passengers time between check-in and departure points, while new baggage delivery systems and airport lounges have improved the passenger experience at most airports used by the airline. More customer service staff have been deployed and in-flight cabin crew have been encouraged to build on the airline's well perceived friendliness and helpfulness. In order to achieve the company's over riding objective—to remain the preferred choice for customers flying into and out of Ireland—Aer Lingus continues to build alliances with other airlines through code sharing agreements and joint marketing programmes. More than half a dozen times in recent years, these initiatives have resulted in Aer Lingus being voted the best airline on transatlantic and London routes by business commuters and tourists travelling to and from Ireland. Market share and profitability have accordingly risen.

The over riding emphasis is nicely summed up by the company:

> Behind every strategic and tactical decision—including aircraft acquisition—there must be a single, unwavering commitment to enhancing customer value. We live in an age when customer demand and awareness are growing rapidly. Paying lip service to the concept of putting the customer first is easy. The real work is ensuring that it is more than an attractive business theory and that we make it a practical, every day objective of everyone in the airline in everything they do.

The results have been impressive:

- Transatlantic routes into Dublin and Shannon airports saw an increase of 14 per cent in flights and 16 per cent in passenger numbers to close to three quarters of a million people each year.
- Traffic on London routes increased by 8 per cent.
- Continental Europe witnessed new, larger aircraft, extra destinations and greater frequency of departures, notably serving Finland (with Finnair), Spain, Italy, France and Germany.
- Over one and a half million passengers use Aer Lingus Commuter each year, with the sub-brand's eight destinations in Britain and five Irish airports feeding into Dublin. Despite fierce price competition on these routes, passenger numbers rose by 8 per cent, supported by cost saving ticket books for frequent fliers, upgraded ground services, a new bespoke Aer Lingus Commuter check-in facility at Dublin Airport and the introduction of the business oriented Premier service.

- Cargo has risen by 10 per cent to 42,000 tonnes, with the load factor improving 2 per cent to 72 per cent of capacity. This has been supported with the introduction of an interactive tracking and schedule information service via the Internet.

Aer Lingus is seeking to build a reputation for being "world class" in managing customer relationships with special emphasis on three core values: professionalism, intuition and intimacy. Standards of *professionalism* are rising throughout the business community and this is being reflected in Aer Lingus's activities. *Intuition* is the utilisation of staff experience to see beyond first appearances and to understand the customer. *Intimacy* involves establishing empathy with customers, to see situations from the customers' view.

SOURCES: Jimmy Ang; Aer Lingus; Aer Lingus report and accounts; T. McEnaney, "Aer Lingus set to profit on Dublin/London route", *The Times*, 19 January 1995; D. Churchill, "Cabin pressures", *Management Today*, 4 October 1994; "A fighting chance—Aer Lingus", *Airline Business*, 1 June 1995; Bernie Cahill, Chairman of Aer Lingus; Aer Lingus Annual Reports 1998/9; Aer Lingus media relations, 1999.

Questions for Discussion

1. How has Aer Lingus attempted to put its customers at the forefront of its business development?
2. In what ways has the role of personnel become central to the airline's operations?
3. Why must the airline's marketing mix focus on more than the traditional 4Ps?

PART VII   P O S T S C R I P T

The marketing mix is the tactical toolkit deployed by marketers to implement their marketing strategy and to take their product or service offering to their target market. The basic ingredients of the marketing mix are the "5Ps" of product, people, place/distribution, promotion and price, described in Parts III to VI of *Marketing: Concepts and Strategies*. There are, however, situations in which either market characteristics or the nature of the product requires modification of the standard marketing mix—most notably, for business-to-business markets, services marketing and international markets. Part VII of *Marketing: Concepts and Strategies* has explored how the marketing mix must be manipulated in these situations. Chapter 20 should be read in conjunction with Chapters 3, 5 and 11.

Before progressing, readers should be confident that they are now able to:

Explain why, when and how the basic marketing mix requires additional manipulation

• In what situations does the standard marketing mix require modification? • What is the nature of the marketing mix for business-to-business markets? • What is the extended marketing mix for services? • Why does the marketing of services require additional ingredients in the marketing mix? • What issues do marketers encounter in international markets? • Why must the marketing mix be manipulated for international markets?

Marketing Opportunity Analysis	Chapters
• The marketing environment	2
• Marketing in international markets	3
• Consumer buying behaviour	4
• Organisational markets and business-to-business buying behaviour	5
• Marketing research and information systems	6

Target Market Strategy	Chapters
• Market segmentation and prioritisation	7, 21
• Product and brand positioning	7, 21
• Competitive advantage	7, 21

Marketing Mix Development	Chapters
• Product, branding, packaging and service decisions	8–11
• Place (distribution and channel) decisions	12–14
• Promotion decisions	15–17
• Pricing decisions	18, 19
• Supplementary decisions	3, 20, 23, 24

Marketing Management	Chapters
• Strategic marketing and competitive strategy	21, 22
• Marketing planning and forecasting sales potential	22
• Implementing strategies and internal marketing relationships and measuring performance	23
• Marketing ethics and social responsibility	24

VIII Marketing Management

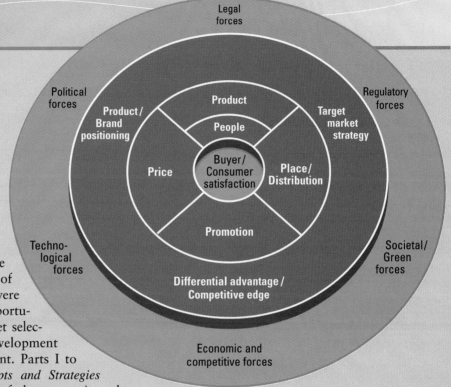

I n Chapter 1, Figure 1.4, the generic tasks of marketing strategy were identified as marketing opportunity analysis, target market selection, marketing mix development and marketing management. Parts I to VII of *Marketing: Concepts and Strategies* examined the first three of these generic tasks, while target market selection was discussed in detail in Chapter 7. There are, however, additional concepts to be addressed when developing a marketing strategy. These are explained at the beginning of Part VIII of *Marketing: Concepts and Strategies*. The focus then becomes the management, implementation and control of marketing strategy and marketing activity, in particular the popular and important technique of marketing planning. Finally, of growing concern to marketers and consumers are the topics of ethics and social responsibility in marketing. These issues must be of central concern to marketers when they determine marketing strategies and then strive to implement these strategies. **Part VIII** of *Marketing: Concepts and Strategies* explores further the central issues of marketing strategy, marketing planning and forecasting sales potential, implementing strategies and measuring performance, and the role of ethics and social responsibility in marketing.

Chapter 21, "Marketing Strategy", presents an overview of marketing strategy and the strategic planning process. The chapter begins by defining marketing strategy and evaluating a company's organisational mission, goals and corporate strategy. The discussion next focuses on assessing organisational opportunities and resources and considers strategic objectives and strategic focus. Target market strategy and brand positioning are analysed, along with the roles that competitive positions and differential advantage play in the competitive marketplace. The chapter then explores marketing objectives and marketing mix tactical programmes, as well as the importance of implementation and performance monitoring. The chapter concludes with a detailed look at several tools for strategic market planning.

Chapter 22, "Marketing Planning and Forecasting Sales Potential", examines the marketing planning process and presents an overview of the marketing plan. The chapter then highlights the important relationship between marketing analysis—including the SWOT analysis—marketing strategy and marketing programmes for implementation. The discussion turns to the related issues of the assessment of market and sales potential and to the principal sales forecasting methods. Finally, the major components of a marketing audit are described.

Chapter 23, "Implementing Strategies, Internal Marketing Relationships and Measuring Performance", commences by describing how marketing activities are organised within a company's structure and explains the various ways of organising a marketing unit. The chapter then examines the marketing implementation process, various approaches to marketing implementation and the importance of internal marketing. The discussion next focuses on implementing and controlling marketing activities. The chapter closes with a look at popular methods

and criteria for evaluating marketing strategies and performance.

Chapter 24, "Marketing Ethics and Social Responsibility", defines marketing ethics and explains the importance of this concept in today's marketing world. The chapter explores the factors that influence ethical decision-making, discussing some of the important ethical issues marketers face. Next it presents ways of improving ethical decisions in marketing. The focus of the chapter then switches to social responsibility: explaining the concept, exploring important issues and describing strategies for dealing with social dilemmas. Finally, the concepts of social responsibility and marketing ethics are compared and contrasted.

By the conclusion of Part VIII of *Marketing: Concepts and Strategies,* readers should understand more about the complexities of developing marketing strategies, the importance of competition, the role of marketing planning and forecasting sales potential, ways of implementing marketing strategy and measuring performance, and the significant influence of ethics and social responsibility in marketing.

21 Marketing Strategy

> *"A proper analysis of the strategic aspects of any competitive marketplace may not result in certain success, but it almost always helps to avoid failures."*
>
> Robin Wensley, Warwick Business School

O B J E C T I V E S

- To define marketing strategy and to evaluate a company's organisational mission, goals and corporate strategy
- To assess organisational opportunities and resources and to consider strategic objectives and strategic focus
- To analyse target market strategy and brand positioning
- To examine competitive positions and differential advantage
- To explore marketing objectives and marketing mix tactical programmes
- To understand implementation and performance monitoring and to examine tools for strategic market planning

Drinks giant the Coca-Cola Company is moving into the fashion business with the global launch of "Coca-Cola Ware". So why is the company extending the well known brand for soft drinks into new territory? In general, Coca-Cola has enjoyed the effects of massive growth in global soft drinks sales. However, towards the end of 1998, for the first time in many years, the company failed to hit its expected 7 to 8 per cent volume growth. Following its disappointing performance, senior managers were quick to deny that the core soft drinks business had reached maturity, blaming economic problems in key markets for the difficulties. The launch of Coca-Cola Ware was not, they stated, because of difficulties with the core business. Instead, the company sees the clothing as a promotional activity, an extension of Coca-Cola's licensing programme which raises the profile of the brand around the world and is a core ingredient of the brand's strategy. The new range will certainly add an extra dimension to the company's existing licensing activities. With 250 licensees offering some 10,000 different items in 40 different countries, the precedent for such an arrangement is well established.

The new clothing range, which comprises casual clothing and accessories, will be test marketed prior to being launched globally. The target market for the jeans, woven clothing and knitwear will initially be teenagers and the young, but in the future may include other age groups. According to US spokeswoman Susan McDermott, "This is an integrated approach to create a fashion line with a cohesive feel and a sense of lifestyle." Coca-Cola Ware will be sold through department stores and specialist "active" wear shops. The company is quick to stress that the range will be used to support and communicate Coca-Cola brand values, rather than to detract from the soft drinks' business. This is a similar brand-building approach to that adopted by construction equipment giants CAT and JCB, whose footwear and clothing ranges have done much to raise the profile of their brands. However, some industry experts warn about the dangers of de-valuing the core brand, suggesting that the fashion market is notoriously difficult to enter.

One of the difficulties that Coca-Cola may face is that consumers are already over exposed to promotional clothing. Cigarette companies Marlboro and Camel, construction equipment manufacturers Caterpillar and JCB, and travel and music business Virgin are just a few of those which have extended their brands into this area. Not all have been successful. Jaguar is one of the latest to enter the fray, with a

653

range of men's clothing which will compete with the likes of Boss and Armani. The appearance of the Jaguar suits, shirts, ties, shorts and sweaters coincides with the launch of the new Jaguar S-Type car. The clothing is sold through department stores and is supported by an advertising campaign. The rationale for the move is linked to the company's desire to target its cars at younger consumers. The Jaguar S-Type is the first of a series of models which Jaguar hopes will appeal to the younger market, and the company believes that this appeal may be reflected in a desire to purchase fashion items carrying the same brand.

The extension of familiar brands into clothing is not a new trend. However, in a highly competitive market already saturated with well known fashion house labels, success is difficult to achieve. One brand extension expert believes that brands seeking such a move must exhibit three crucial strengths: expertise, image and reputation. Few would deny that the classic and timeless brand of Coca-Cola possesses these qualities. Yet even so, how consumers will respond to Coca-Cola

Ware remains difficult to predict. All marketers strive to promote their brands. Coca-Cola's marketers hope Coca-Cola Ware will lead to thousands of walking "adverts" raising the profile of this already ubiquitous and successful brand. It is a strategy yet to be proven.

SOURCES: Amanda Wilkinson, "Is Coke hip?", *Marketing Week,* 28 January 1999, pp. 26–29; Julia Day, "Coke plans global clothing brands", *Marketing Week,* 21 January 1999, pp. 37–42; "Jaguar drives in UK men's clothing market", *Marketing Week,* 18 March 1999, p. 7. *Photo*: Lincoln Potter/Gamma Liaison.

P arts I and II of this text explored the analysis of marketing opportunities, in particular the need to understand the moves and trends in a marketplace, customer buying behaviour and needs, and the importance of targeting the right market segments. Parts III to VII focused on the tactical marketing mix ingredients that ultimately take a product or service into a marketplace to reach the targeted consumers. This chapter aims to highlight which strategic marketing considerations help to ensure that the product or service is marketed for the benefit of the organisation as well as its targeted customers, and differently enough from its competitors' marketing programmes to give the organisation's product or service a perceived advantage over these competitors that will lead to success in the marketplace. These core components of marketing strategy are illustrated in Figure 21.1 and are clearly of great concern to the business described in this chapter's opener, Coca-Cola. Although for simplicity's sake this text has deliberately discussed the tactics of marketing first (Parts III to VII), it is important to realise that marketers must have developed a clearly thought out marketing strategy *before* specifying the marketing mix issues of product/service/people, place/distribution, promotion and pricing. This strategy must reflect the organisation's corporate goals, market trends, opportunities and the competitive situation, while aiming to give the targeted customers satisfaction.

The chapter first explores how to develop marketing strategies and then discusses strategic market planning, stressing the importance of organisational

Figure 21.1 The components of marketing strategy

mission, goals and corporate strategy. The discussion next turns to assessing organisational opportunities and resources, as well as identifying strategic objectives and strategic focus. The chapter addresses the pivotal role of identifying market segments, targeting and brand positioning in marketing strategy: the development of clear target market priorities. The analysis then focuses on competitive strategies for marketing: the role of competition, its ramifications for strategy, competitive positions and warfare strategies. The link between marketing objectives and marketing mix tactical programmes is examined, along with implementation and performance monitoring. The chapter concludes with a look at some of the related analytical tools associated with the planning of a marketing strategy: the product portfolio analysis, the market attractiveness-business position model, Profit Impact on Marketing Strategy (PIMS), the ABC sales: contribution analysis and the product life cycle concept. Other aspects of the strategic marketing management process—marketing planning, forecasting sales potential, implementing strategies, internal marketing relationships and measuring performance—are covered in subsequent chapters.

Marketing Strategy Defined

Marketing strategy   A strategy indicating the specific target markets and the types of competitive advantages that are to be developed and exploited

Marketing strategy indicates the specific markets towards which activities are to be targeted and the types of competitive advantages that are to be developed and exploited.[1] Implicitly, as described in Figure 21.1, the strategy requires clear objectives and a focus in line with an organisation's corporate goals; the "right" customers must be targeted more effectively than they are by its competitors, and associated marketing mixes should be developed into marketing programmes that successfully implement the marketing strategy.[2]

Strategic market plan   An outline of the methods and resources required to achieve an organisation's goals within a specific target market

A **strategic market plan** is an outline of the methods and resources required to achieve an organisation's goals within a specific target market. It takes into account not only marketing but also all the functional aspects of a business unit that must be co-ordinated. These functional aspects include production, finance and personnel. Environmental issues are an important consideration as well. The concept of the strategic business unit is used to define areas for consideration in a specific strategic market plan. Each **strategic business unit** (SBU) is a division, product line or other profit centre within a parent company. Each sells a distinct set of products to an identifiable group of customers, and each competes with a well defined set of competitors. Each SBU's revenues, costs, investments and strategic plans can be separated and evaluated apart from those of the parent company. SBUs operate in a variety of markets, which have differing growth rates, opportunities, degrees of competition and profit making potential. Construction giant JCB, for example, includes the Compact Division for smaller machines, a strategic business unit (see Figure 21.2). Strategic planners therefore must recognise the different performance capabilities of each SBU and carefully allocate resources. They must also ensure that the SBUs complement each other for the greater good of the overall business.

Strategic business unit (SBU) A division, product line or other profit centre within a parent company

Strategic market planning A process that yields a marketing strategy that is the framework for a marketing plan

Marketing plan   The written document that includes the framework and set of activities for implementing and controlling an organisation's marketing activities

The process of **strategic market planning** yields a marketing strategy that is the framework for a marketing plan. A **marketing plan** (see Chapter 22) includes the framework and entire set of activities to be performed; it is the written document or blueprint for implementing and controlling an organisation's marketing activities. Thus a strategic market plan is *not* the same as a marketing plan—it is a plan of *all* aspects of an organisation's strategy in the marketplace.[3] A marketing plan, in contrast, deals primarily with implementing the marketing strategy as it relates to target markets and the marketing mix.[4]

Figure 21.3 shows the components of strategic market planning. The process is based on the establishment of an organisation's overall goals, and it must stay within the bounds of the organisation's opportunities and resources. When the business has determined its overall goals and identified its resources, it can then assess its opportunities and develop a corporate strategy. Marketing objectives must be designed so that their achievement will contribute to the corporate strategy and so that they can be accomplished through efficient use of the company's resources.

Figure 21.2 An SBU in operation. JCB's Compact Division caters for users of construction equipment requiring small machines. SOURCE: Client: John Bradley, JCB Sales Ltd. Agency: CD Brooks Advertising Ltd.

To achieve its marketing objectives, an organisation must develop a marketing strategy, or a set of marketing strategies, as shown in Figure 21.3. The set of marketing strategies that are implemented and used at the same time is referred to as the organisation's **marketing programme.** Most marketing programmes centre around a detailed marketing mix specification and include internal controls and procedures to ensure that they are implemented effectively. Through the process of strategic market planning, an organisation can develop marketing strategies that, when properly implemented and controlled, will contribute to the achievement of its marketing objectives and its overall goals. To formulate a marketing strategy, the marketer identifies and analyses the target market and develops a marketing mix to satisfy individuals in that market. Marketing strategy is best formulated when it reflects the overall direction of the organisation and is coordinated with all the company's functional areas.

As indicated in Figure 21.3, the strategic market planning process is based on an analysis of the broader marketing environment, by which it is very much affected. As detailed in Chapter 2, marketing environment forces can place constraints on an organisation and possibly influence its overall goals; they also affect the amount and type of resources that a business can acquire. However,

Figure 21.3
Components of
strategic market
planning

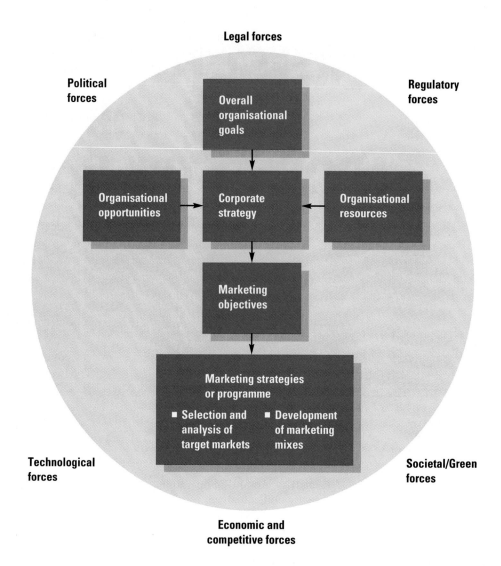

these forces can create favourable opportunities as well—opportunities that can
be translated into overall organisational goals and marketing objectives. For
example, when oil prices declined during the second half of the 1980s, consumers
viewed cars with high petrol consumption more favourably. This situation
created an opportunity for manufacturers of large vehicles, such as BMW and
Volvo.

Marketers differ in their viewpoints concerning the effect of marketing environment variables on marketing planning and strategy. Some take a determinis-
tic perspective, believing that companies must react to external conditions and
tailor their strategies and organisational structures to deal with these conditions.
According to others, however, companies can influence their environments by
choosing in which markets to compete, lobbying regulators and politicians, striving to modify social views, joining forces with trade bodies for campaigning purposes and so forth. They can also change the structures of their industries,
engaging in activities such as mergers and acquisitions, demand creation or technological innovation.[5]

Regardless of which viewpoint is adopted, marketing environment variables play a part in the creation of a marketing strategy. When environment variables affect an organisation's overall goals, resources, opportunities or marketing objectives, they also affect its marketing strategies, which are based on these factors. Marketing environment forces more directly influence the development of a marketing strategy through their impact on consumers' needs and desires and their effect on competitors' plans. In addition, these forces have a bearing on marketing mix decisions. For instance, competition strongly influences marketing mix decisions. The organisation must diagnose the marketing mix activities it performs, taking into account competitors' marketing mix decisions, and develop some differential advantage to support a strategy. Thus as Honda and Toyota entered the luxury car market with the Acura and Lexus models, European car makers BMW, Mercedes and Jaguar had to change their marketing strategies to maintain their market shares. They did so by lowering prices, introducing new models and creating brand building marketing communications campaigns to compete with the new Japanese models.

Organisational Mission, Goals and Corporate Strategy

Mission The broad, long term tasks that the organisation wants to accomplish

Central to the strategic market plan is a clear view of the organisational mission, goals and corporate strategy. A company's organisational goals should be derived from its **mission,** the broad, long term tasks that the organisation wants to accomplish. IBM, for example, has stated that its mission is helping business people make decisions. When a company decides on its mission, it really answers two questions: (1) What is the company's core business/area of activity? (2) What should this be?[6] Although these questions seem very simple, they are in fact two of the hardest yet most important questions that any business can answer.

Creating or revising a mission statement is very difficult because of the many complex variables that must be examined. However, having a mission statement can greatly benefit the organisation in at least five ways.[7]

- A mission statement gives the organisation a clear purpose and direction, keeping it on track and preventing it from drifting.
- A mission statement describes the unique aim of the organisation that helps to differentiate it from similar competing organisations.
- A mission statement keeps the organisation focused on customer needs rather than its own abilities. This ensures that the organisation remains externally rather than internally focused.
- A mission statement provides specific direction and guidelines to top managers for selecting alternative courses of action. It helps them decide which business opportunities to pursue, as well as which opportunities not to pursue.
- A mission statement provides guidance to all employees and managers of an organisation, even if they work in different parts of the world. As a result, the mission statement acts like glue to hold the organisation together.

A company's mission and overall organisational goals should guide all its planning efforts. Its goals should specify the ends, or results, that are sought. Examples of organisational goals include profit, return on investment, an increase in market shares or an increase/decrease in the number of active markets. Organisations can also have short term and long term goals. Companies experiencing financial difficulty may be forced to focus solely on the short term results necessary to stay in business, such as increasing cash flow by lowering prices or selling off parts of the business. Other organisations may have more optimistic, long term goals. In many cases, companies that pursue long term goals have to sacrifice short term results to achieve them. Businesses which are successful over time tend to have a longer term, market share driven strategy, rather than a short term, "profits only" emphasis.

A business in serious financial trouble may be concerned solely with short run results needed for staying in business. There usually is an airline or major retailer being forced by cash shortages to take drastic action to stay in business. Lowndes Queensway, once the UK's largest retailer of carpets and furniture, had to re-negotiate its financing several times with city institutions, alter payment and credit lines and terms with its suppliers, and ultimately identify which of its five hundred superstores should be closed to save costs. The company went into receivership despite all its efforts. On the other hand, some companies have more optimistic goals. Often manufacturers such as General Motors have goals that relate to return on investment. A successful company, however, may want to sacrifice the current year's profits for the long run and at the same time pursue other goals, such as increasing market share.

Corporate strategy A strategy that determines how resources are to be used to meet the organisation's goals in the areas of production, finance, research and development, personnel and marketing

Corporate strategy determines the means for utilising resources in the areas of production, finance, research and development, personnel and marketing to reach the organisation's goals. A corporate strategy determines not only the scope of the business but also its resource deployment, differential advantages and overall co-ordination of R & D, production, finance, distribution, sales, marketing and other functional areas. The term *corporate* in this context does not apply only to corporations; corporate strategy is used by all organisations, from the smallest sole proprietorship to the largest multinational corporation.

Corporate strategy planners are concerned with issues such as diversification, competition, differentiation, inter-relationships among business units and environmental issues. Strategic planners attempt to match the resources of the organisation with the various opportunities and risks in the external environment. Corporate strategy planners are also concerned with defining the scope and role of the strategic business units of the organisation so that they are co-ordinated to reach the ultimate goals desired.

While not the focus of *Marketing: Concepts and Strategies,* it is important to recognise that the marketing strategy, marketing plan and tactical marketing mix programmes actioned by a business's marketers must reflect the aims and ethos of the overall corporate plan. Unfortunately, in some instances those empowered to deliver marketing programmes are unaware or unconcerned with the nuances of the organisation's overall corporate plan and may even be pursuing a course of action which is at odds with the Board's sense of purpose. In some businesses this reflects the paucity of analysis behind corporate planning and the failure to involve senior marketers in such strategy development. In most businesses, the forces of the external marketing environment, competitors' strategies and evolving customer expectations are poorly assessed. In other cases, only a business's marketers are aware of these issues and have the relevant marketing intelligence to be able to suggest likely scenarios. It is, therefore, essential that those responsible for establishing corporate plans tap into this expertise and knowledge within the marketing function, just as it is necessary for marketers to devise target market strategies and marketing mix programmes which properly reflect the direction desired by the corporate strategy.

Deregulation: A Bright Future for Regional Electricity Companies?

As they still are in many European countries, Britain's utilities used to be state owned and operated. The Central Electricity Generating Board generated and the National Grid physically distributed the energy to both domestic and business users, with regional electricity boards acting as the customer interface, connecting supplies, determining consumption through meter reading and billing customers for the electricity consumed. In the mid-1980s the government decided to continue its privatisation programme and create a commercially run electricity supply industry with shareholders and competition as in most other industries. The sale raised over £10 billion in equity and debt for the government and created over 12 million shareholders. The entire privatisation scheme lasted four years and cost an estimated £1 billion to facilitate. Upon its dissolution in 1990 the Central Electricity Generating Board employed 47,000 people. The new look industry employs only 25,000.

Before the break up of the state run electricity industry, a household or factory in one part of the country would have dealt primarily with just one regional electricity board: YEB (Yorkshire Electricity Board) in Yorkshire, MEB (Midlands Electricity Board) in Birmingham, EMEB (East Midlands Electricity Board) in Leicester and so on. To all intents and purposes, customers would have had no dealings with a generator, which in any case was the same organisation throughout the country. Privatisation divided the generating side of the industry among five new and publicly quoted companies, such as PowerGen and National Power. The regional electricity boards became regional electricity companies, still with a focus on their own geographic region, but with shareholders and a renewed profit making motivation.

Then came deregulation in earnest. First, customers using more than 100kW of electricity per annum were told that they could "shop around" to seek better tariffs from suppliers other than their local regional electricity company (REC). In practice, this enabled large companies, institutions and retail groups, whose consumption beat the 100kW threshold, to seek alternative quotes from other RECs and even, at times, directly from some generators. The infrastructure did not alter. There remained only one network of cables and pylons. The customer interface with a particular REC might have changed, as might the tariff agreed and the logo on the bill. From 1999, this freedom of competition extended to consumers of less than 100kW—small businesses and residential households. Even if a customer lives in YEB's traditional geographic territory, he or she is contacted by the other 11 RECs, perhaps by some generators, and even by businesses as diverse as BP, Currys, Direct Line, Tesco or Virgin, which may choose to enter the retail end of the electricity supply market by buying in bulk from the RECs, the generators or private generators entering the marketplace.

In a market where previously there was no competition, this situation is highly confusing to customers. It is also a major shift in orientation for the RECs. They must determine which customers they should target; where in the country they should target them; what proposition and levels of customer service, pricing, payment terms and promotional support they should offer; and what channels of distribution they should use. The need to identify a differential advantage over rivals in a commodity market and to develop a distinctive and plausible positioning strategy is taxing all of the RECs as they strive to come to terms with a rapidly evolving market and stiff competition. It remains to be seen whether customers will genuinely benefit or whether bills will rise to cover the huge sales and marketing expenditure suddenly required. There is no doubt, though, that throughout every REC, a tremendous amount of research and strategic thinking is currently under way as the companies operate now in a deregulated market.

Sources: "Energy market report: electricity", *Energy Economist*, October 1995, pp. 29–32; "Energy market report: electricity", *Energy Economist*, January 1995, pp. 30–31; Nick Hasell, "Power bargaining", *Management Today*, July 1994, pp. 68–70; Alex Henney, "Challenging the status quo", *Fortnightly*, 15 July 1994, pp. 26–31; Margaret McKinlay, "100kW users test the water in the electricity pool", *Purchasing & Supply Management*, February 1994, pp. 20–21; PowerGen, 1999; East Midlands Electricity, 1999.

There are three major considerations in assessing opportunities and resources: (1) evaluating marketing opportunities, (2) environmental scanning (discussed in Chapter 2) and (3) understanding the business's capabilities and assets. An appreciation of these elements is essential if an organisation is to build up a sustainable differential advantage or competitive edge.

Marketing Opportunities

Marketing opportunity
Circumstances and timing that allow an organisation to take action towards reaching a target market

A **marketing opportunity** arises when the right combination of circumstances occurs at the right time to allow an organisation to take action towards reaching a target market. Marketing Insight 21.1 describes an opportunity in the electricity supply market owing to government deregulation. An opportunity provides a favourable chance or opening for the business to generate sales from identifiable markets. For example, in reaction to the overwhelming growth in cereals and other foods containing oat bran (which some researchers believe helps lower cholesterol levels), the Quaker Oats Company developed an advertising campaign to remind consumers that Quaker porridge oats have always contained oat bran. The advertisements told consumers that eating porridge is "the right thing to do" and helped boost sales of Quaker Oats dramatically.[8] Increasing concerns about cancer and heart disease gave Quaker a marketing opportunity to reach consumers who are especially health-conscious by touting the health benefits of its oats. Kellogg's also took advantage of the popularity of oat bran by creating its Common Sense™ Oat Bran cereal. Interestingly, in 1990 a study published in a leading medical journal questioned the effectiveness of oat bran in lowering cholesterol, concluding that it was the elimination of high cholesterol animal products that really lowered cholesterol. Therefore, some of the oat bran mystique vanished overnight. The term **strategic window** has been used to describe what are often temporary periods of optimum fit between the key requirements of a market and the particular capabilities of a company competing in that market.[9]

Strategic window   A temporary period of optimum fit between the key requirements of a market and the particular capabilities of a company competing in that market

The attractiveness of marketing opportunities is determined by market factors such as size and growth rate; by political, legal, regulatory, societal/green, economic and competitive, and technological marketing environment forces; and by internal capital, plant, and human and financial resources.[10] Because each industry and product are somewhat different, the factors that determine attractiveness tend to vary.

Market requirements
Requirements that relate to customers' needs or desired benefits

Market requirements relate to customers' needs or desired benefits. Market requirements are satisfied by components of the marketing mix that provide buyers with these benefits. Of course, buyers' perceptions of what requirements fulfil their needs and provide the desired benefits determine the success of any marketing effort. Marketers must devise strategies to out-perform competitors by finding out what product attributes buyers use to select products. An attribute must be important and differentiating if it is to be useful in strategy development. As discussed in Chapters 4 and 5, when marketers fail to understand buyers' perceptions and market requirements, the result may be failure. For example, prior to its takeover by Sears, Freemans launched its by mail "Specialogue" for yuppie men. What the company failed to realise was that its target customers wanted branded goods from prestigious speciality retail outlets; they just did not perceive mail order shopping to be suitable for them.

Environmental Scanning

In Chapter 2 **environmental scanning** was defined as the process of collecting information about the marketing environment to help marketers identify opportunities and assist in planning. Some companies have derived substantial benefits

Environmental scanning The process of collecting information about the marketing environment to help marketers identify opportunities and assist in planning

from establishing an "environmental scanning (or monitoring) unit" within the strategic planning group or from including line management in teams or committees to conduct environmental analysis. This approach engages management in the process of environmental forecasting and enhances the likelihood of successfully integrating forecasting efforts into strategic market planning.[11] Results of forecasting research show that even simple quantitative forecasting techniques out-perform the unstructured intuitive assessments of experts.[12] Many builders and property developers in the UK believe that the house buying public is unwilling to pay the increased cost of energy efficient new housing. However, research suggests that consumers *are* happy to pay extra, within reason, for the increased comfort levels and reduced fuel bills associated with such property.[13]

Environmental scanning to detect changes in the environment is extremely important if a business is to avoid crisis management. A change in the external marketing environment can suddenly alter a business's opportunities or resources. Re-formulated, more effective strategies may then be needed to guide marketing efforts. For example, after the UK government legislated against heavy emissions from cars and gave unleaded fuel tax advantages, petrol suppliers and vehicle manufacturers had to re-formulate their strategies and marketing programmes.[14] Because car manufacturers had engaged in environmental scanning and were aware that such legislation might indeed be enacted because of social and political concerns, most had already begun developing plans for cars powered by clean fuel. Ford Motor Company, for example, is testing a car that can run on methanol, ethanol, petrol or any combination of those fuels.[15] Environmental scanning should identify new developments and determine the nature and rate of change.

Capabilities and Assets

Capabilities A company's distinctive competencies to do something well and efficiently

Marketing assets Capabilities that managers and the marketplace view as beneficially strong

A company's **capabilities** relate to *distinctive competencies* that it has developed to do something well and efficiently. A company is likely to enjoy a *differential advantage* (see page 669) over its rivals in an area where its competencies out-do those of its potential competitors.[16] Often a company may possess manufacturing or technical skills that are valuable in areas outside its traditional industry. For example, BASF, known for its manufacture and development of audio and video tapes, produced a new type of lightweight plastic that has uses in other industries. **Marketing assets** highlight capabilities that managers and the marketplace view as beneficially strong. These capabilities can then be stressed to the company's advantage. *Customer based assets* include brand image and reputation; *distribution based assets* may involve density of dealers and geographic coverage; *internal marketing assets* include skills, experience, economies of scale, technology and resources.[17] It is essential for a business to take time to assess its capabilities and assets and to map these alongside identified opportunities. The SWOT—Strengths, Weaknesses, Opportunities, Threats—analysis integral to most marketing planning processes is one means for addressing this need, as detailed in Chapter 22. Today marketing planners are especially concerned with external resource constraints.

Strategic Objectives and Strategic Focus

Having evaluated the overall corporate vision, those responsible for devising the marketing strategy must build on their analysis of opportunities and internal capabilities by analytically assessing the most promising directions for their business and marketing activity. Ansoff developed a well known tool, the market/product matrix to assist in this decision-making, as depicted in Figure 21.12 on page 681. A business may choose one or more competitive strategies, including intense growth, diversified growth and integrated growth. This matrix can help in determining growth that can be implemented through marketing strategies.

Intense Growth

Intense growth Growth that occurs when current products and current markets have the potential for increasing sales

Market penetration A strategy of increasing sales of current products in current markets

Market development A strategy of increasing sales of current products in new markets

Product development A strategy of increasing sales by improving present products or developing new products for current markets

Intense growth can take place when current products and current markets have the potential for increasing sales. There are three main strategies for intense growth: market penetration, market development and product development.

Market penetration is a strategy of increasing sales in current markets with current products. For example, Coca-Cola and PepsiCo try to achieve increased market share through aggressive advertising.

Market development is a strategy of increasing sales of current products in new markets. For example, a European aircraft manufacturer was able to enter the US market by offering Eastern Airlines financing that Boeing could not match. Evian devised a new use for its mineral water by developing its "Brumisateur", an atomiser spray for the skin.

Product development is a strategy of increasing sales by improving present products or developing new products for current markets. PepsiCo and Coca-Cola both have new container sizes, low calorie/low sugar versions and vending machine services.

Diversified Growth

Diversified growth Growth that occurs when new products are developed to be sold in new markets

Horizontal diversification A process that occurs when new products not technologically related to current products are introduced into current markets

Concentric diversification A process that occurs when new products related to current products are introduced into new markets

Conglomerate diversification A process that occurs when new products unrelated to current technology, products or markets are introduced into new markets

Diversified growth occurs when new products are developed to be sold in new markets. Companies have become increasingly diversified since the 1960s. Diversification offers some advantages over single business companies, because it allows companies to spread their risk across a number of markets. More important, it allows companies to make better and wider use of their management, technical and financial resources. For example, marketing expertise can be used across businesses, which may also share advertising themes, distribution channels, warehouse facilities or even salesforces.[18] The three forms of diversification are horizontal, concentric and conglomerate.

Horizontal diversification results when new products that are not technologically related to current products are introduced to current markets. Sony, for example, diversified from electronics to movie production through its purchase of Columbia Pictures. The purchase gave Sony a library of 2,700 films, including *Ghostbusters 2* and *When Harry Met Sally*, as well as 23,000 television episodes, which it has used to establish its line of video tapes.[19]

In **concentric diversification,** the marketing and technology of new products are related to current products, but the new ones are introduced into new markets. For instance, Dow Chemical has diversified into agricultural chemicals and pharmaceuticals through joint ventures in those industries.[20]

Conglomerate diversification occurs when new products are unrelated to current technology, products or markets and are introduced into markets new to the company. For example, Bass, the British brewer, acquired the American Holiday Inn hotel chain, and Laura Ashley, the UK clothing and furnishings company, has moved into the fragrance market with Laura Ashley No. 1.

Integrated Growth

Integrated growth Growth that occurs in three possible directions: forwards, backwards or horizontally

Integrated growth can occur in the same industry that the company is in and in three possible directions: forwards, backwards or horizontally. A company growing through forward integration takes ownership or increased control of its distribution system. For example, a shoe manufacturer might start selling its products through wholly owned retail outlets.

In backward integration, a company takes ownership or increased control of its supply systems. A newspaper company that buys a paper mill is integrating backwards. Horizontal integration occurs when a company takes ownership or control of some of its competitors. For example, prior to its financial collapse, Polly Peck International, the British/Cypriot fruit grower and distributor, purchased Del Monte's fresh fruit division.[21]

In developing strategies, an organisation must consider the competitive positions in the marketplace and formulate marketing strategies and tactics accordingly. Some authors have adopted warfare analogies to describe the strategic options for competing in a market.[22] This chapter later examines the concept of competitive positions—as distinct from product or brand positionings, discussed in Chapter 7.

Target Market Strategy and Brand Positioning

Central to achieving a company's corporate vision is the need to build up a loyal customer base of satisfied customers. Tesco did not overtake Sainsbury's by chance: it developed a clear marketing strategy based on a desire to fully satisfy a carefully targeted set of market segments. Tesco is continuously upgrading its stores, adding new services and product lines, and innovating with channels of distribution through Tesco Metro and Tesco Direct, with the aim of addressing its targeted segment customer needs. Market segmentation is at the core of robust marketing strategy development. As explained in Chapter 7, this involves identifying customer needs, expectations, perceptions and buying behaviour so as to group together homogeneous customers who will be satisfied and marketed to in a similar manner. One segment will differ from another in terms of customer profile and buying behaviour, and also with regard to the sales and marketing activity likely to satisfy these customers. Having sufficient knowledge of these customers is fundamental.

Taking the time to objectively and sensibly group a market's customers into meaningful market segments is a discipline many businesses are only now discovering. The fast movers, market leaders and successful brands in a marketplace all base their marketing strategies on carefully honed market segmentation analyses. In the newly deregulated domestic electricity market, marketers have identified segments of low income households desperate to save 50p per week on their electricity bills, suburban households with large fuel bills but little interest in small energy savings in their overall extensive monthly spending, environmentalists keen to have wave power or hydro electricity, amongst many others. Not all of these segments are attractive to target.

It is important to remember that the process of market segmentation involves more than simply grouping customers into segments. Shrewd targeting of certain segments and the development of a clear brand positioning are part and parcel of the market segmentation process. The basis of Chapter 7's coverage—identifying segments, targeting, positioning and developing a differential advantage over rivals—is the foundation of a marketing strategy.

Business must identify priority target markets that are worthwhile targeting with bespoke marketing mix programmes: product, price, place/distribution, promotion and people. Even the mighty Ford or General Motors has to decide which segments in the car and van market to pursue, opting not to have models aimed at all buyers in the market. It is important to balance current core target markets with those offering future viability. Once determined, in each target market the business must strive to emphasise to those targeted customers the relevance and applicability of its product and marketing mix proposition. This is achieved through all ingredients of the marketing mix, but specifically through developing a distinctive, plausible and memorable brand positioning, such as BMW's *The Ultimate Driving Machine*. This positioning imagery is communicated to targeted customers primarily through the promotional mix, packaging and design. The remaining marketing mix ingredients must be specified so as to support this brand positioning and communication. An up-market restaurant, for example, requires a suitably lavish ambience, slick service, quality food and befitting price to match its branding and promotional campaigns. It is important to finalise the target market strategy of priority target market segments and required brand positioning before developing the marketing mix tactics of the marketing programmes destined to implement this strategy. These tactical programmes must reflect the marketing analyses and target market strategy requirements rather than being merely a continuation of previous marketing mix activities.

Competitive Positions and Differential Advantage

Competitive Positions As detailed in Chapters 2 and 7, it is important to understand the nature of competition. This involves more than a cursory examination of like-for-like major rivals. Most organisations consider only similar companies or brands to be their competitors. As shown in Figure 21.4, there are other facets of competition which must be evaluated. What of the smaller players which may one day emerge as dominant in a market or specific segment? Why not pre-empt such an outcome by developing a strategy to knock them back while still only a small rival? What about the new entrant into the marketplace? Could its appearance have been foreseen? What actions are required to minimise its threat? How did Rover or Citroën fend off the entry of Daewoo in the small car sector? Did they even antic-

Figure 21.4 The five competitive forces determining industry competition. SOURCE: Michael E. Porter, *Competitive Advantage* (New York: The Free Press, 1985).

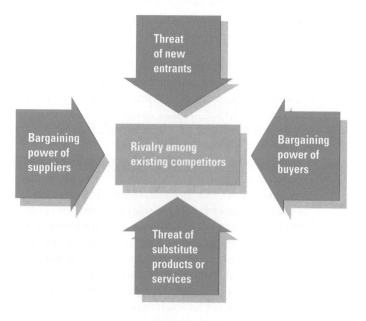

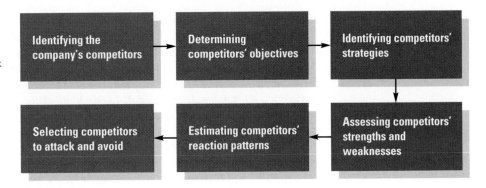

ipate Daewoo's entry? What of innovative solutions to customers' problems? JCB produces construction equipment which digs trenches for pipes and cables. Micro-bore tunnelling moles lay pipes without the need for a trench. Not manufactured by the construction equipment companies, such moles—substitute competition—could be missed by JCB's marketers as a competitive threat without a rigorous analysis of the competitive arena. The power of suppliers and of consumers can also vary per company and act as a competitive force, particularly if one business encounters greater supply problems or more severe customer bargaining than its rivals face from their suppliers and customers. These competitor categories are in addition to the like-for-like rivals considered by most businesses to be their competitors. The full competitor arena should be assessed.

In addition to realising the importance of examining all categories of competitors, it is necessary to understand what must be known. Most companies can describe their competitors: who, where, with what and at what price. Few businesses genuinely understand their rivals' strategies or endeavour to predict their rivals' reaction to moves they themselves may make. Very few companies attempt to identify those individual competitors it is sensible to avoid in a head-to-head marketing campaign or those most likely to be vulnerable to attack at low risk to the company's resource base. It is prudent to avoid head-to-head conflict with a similarly sized and resourced adversary. It is more desirable to identify the weaknesses of more vulnerable competitors and address these through the business's proposed marketing mix programmes. Figure 21.5 identifies the essential stages in a robust competitor analysis. No marketing strategy should be formulated without the shrewd analysis of competitors.

Many marketers view their marketplace as a battlefield, opting to compete on only certain fronts, engaging with carefully selected opponents, where there is a perceived differential advantage over the enemy. This warfare analogy has become increasingly popular and hinges on identifying the competitive positions of the various businesses competing in a market segment.[23] The categories of **competitive positions**—roles in the competitive marketplace that organisations assume, which influence their marketing strategies and tactics—include the market leader, market challengers, fast movers, market followers and market nichers. These should be identified within each target market segment.

In the world of market shares, there has to be one—and only one—**market leader**: the player enjoying individually the largest slice of the market. In some business-to-business markets, a market leader can have a majority of industry sales, particularly when patent protection or technical innovation gives it an

Competitive positions Roles in the competitive marketplace that organisations assume, which influence their marketing strategies and tactics

Market leader The single player enjoying the largest individual share in the market

advantage over competitors. In most markets, however, the market leader may have only 10 to 20 per cent of the market's sales. The market leader has the highest market share and retains its competitive position by expanding the total market or expanding market share at the expense of its rivals, while protecting or defending current market share by retaining its customer base. In this context, the market leader, although successful, perhaps has the most difficult task: it must find strategies to increase market size and market share, as well as maintaining strategies to defend its current share.

Market challengers   Non-market leaders that aggressively try to capture market share from their rivals

Behind the market leader are competing companies, which are market challengers, fast movers, market followers or market nichers. **Market challengers** are non-market leaders that aggressively attack rivals, including the market leader, to take more market share. In most instances, these players are number two, three and perhaps four in a market, aspiring to market leadership. It is important to remember, though, that to qualify as challengers these companies must be proactive and aggressive in their sales and marketing rather than passively reinforcing the existing hierarchy. **Fast movers** are smaller rival companies not yet destined to be major challengers, but growing rapidly on a smaller scale. A new entrant may have only 2 per cent of the market, but what is to stop it from increasing its share to 8 per cent within two years? A business may only have 4 per cent of the market, but three years ago it only had 2 per cent. What is to prevent it from having 8 per cent in three years' time?

Fast movers   Smaller rival companies not yet destined to be major challengers, but growing rapidly on a smaller scale.

Market followers   Low share competitors without the resources, market position, research and development, or commitment to challenge for extra sales and market share

Market followers are low share competitors without the resources, market position, research and development, or commitment to challenge for extra sales and market share. These companies tend to be the "plodders" or "me-toos" in a market, whose raison d'être is to do as before and survive. In boom times these players can latch onto the success of their larger rivals, but in recession—or when faced with rivals' product innovation—they often struggle for sales. Most markets also contain **market nichers**: companies that specialise by focusing on only a very narrow range of products such as Sock Shop or Saab, or on a select band of consumers such as Body Shop or Porsche. Nichers survive by finding a safe, small, profitable market segment—often apparently too small to attract the market leaders and challengers. Nichers specialise and can genuinely gear up a marketing mix that exactly matches their target customers' needs. They are vulnerable to market down turns, the entry of rival nichers and the sudden attention of the major players in the marketplace, as happened to Porsche when the North American target market hit a recession and Japanese rivals appeared with cheaper two-seat sports coupés.

Market nichers   Companies that specialise by focusing on only a very narrow range of products or on a select band of consumers

Defensive warfare   A policy of striking a balance between waiting for market developments or competitor activity and proactively parrying competitors' actions

A market leader must defend its position, while simultaneously seeking more market share. Only a market leader should consider **defensive warfare** as a strategic foundation. Strong defence involves striking a balance between waiting for market developments or competitor activity and proactively parrying competitors' actions. As market leader, the company must remember that a false sense of security and passive inactivity lead to disaster: the best defensive strategy is the courage to attack; and strong moves by competitors should always be blocked, never ignored. To defend its market share, a market leader must treat existing customers well and attentively and never take them for granted. The marketing mix must be continually up-dated and target customers' needs regularly considered. New markets, products and opportunities should always be sought and evaluated. Occasionally, if faced by a strong challenger in a small or declining market, a market leader should consider divesting and concentrating resources in its other markets. Others may have to turn to defensive warfare when attacked by the market leader or challengers, but only the market leader should build a strategy around the desire to defend its current position.

A challenger has to attack for market share, but on what basis? The leader, and perhaps other challengers, will be strong and rich in resources. A challenger's attack must be well thought out and not suicidal in terms of the company's medium term future. Few observers could accept the logic in Sainsbury's attacking leader Tesco on the basis of price. This was not the core facet of Sainsbury's service-led culture, nor was Tesco the weakest of rivals to choose to fight! In **offensive warfare,** the main consideration is the market leader's strength: where are there any chinks in the leader's armour? A challenger seeking market share must identify a weakness in the leader's marketing mix and develop a genuine corresponding strength. With such a differential advantage or competitive edge, the challenger's resources may well be sufficient to steal ground successfully from the leader. Any attack, however, should be on a narrow front, where the challenger is perceived by the target customers to have an advantage and where resources can be focused. If no real weakness in the market leader exists, a challenger may attack head-on. Such an attack can be successful only if there are numerous, very weak market followers, if the leader is slow to react and if a price cutting war does not result. In the last situation, the leader's resource base may "kill off" the challenger's attack.

Followers are vulnerable, but careful monitoring of market segments, marketing environment forces and competitive trends can help ensure their survival. They must serve exactly only a few market segments, specialising rather than diversifying in terms of products and markets and making prudent use of what research and development resources are available. Nichers must watch for signs of competitor threats and possible changes in target segment customers' needs, and they may need to consider product development and, ultimately, diversification. Their marketing mixes must be tailored exactly to meet the expectations of their target segment.

All organisations should know, for all their markets and target segments, which companies occupy these competitive positions. They must alter their strategies and marketing programmes accordingly. Organisations should also review their rivals' marketing strategies and marketing programmes: many companies are surprisingly predictable. Response to rivals' pricing policies, frequency of new product launches, entry into new markets and timing of promotional campaigns, for example, can often be accurately anticipated. In this way, thorough **competitor scanning**—the monitoring of competitive positions and competitors' strategies—helps to establish more realistic marketing goals, develop successful strategies and programmes, and pre-empt nasty shocks caused by competitors' actions.[24] It is essential to understand competitors' strategies, their strengths and weaknesses, and any differential advantages they hold which must be combatted.[25]

Differential Advantage

If a marketing mix is developed that matches target market needs and expectations and is superior to those offered by competitors, there is a real—or perceived—**differential advantage**. A differential advantage is an attribute of a brand, product, service or marketing mix which is desired by the targeted customer and provided by only one supplier: it is a unique edge over rivals in satisfying this customer. If successful, a business is likely to have its differential

Offensive warfare A policy whereby challengers aggressively seek market share by identifying any weakness in the leader's marketing mix and developing a genuine corresponding strength

Competitor scanning The monitoring of competitive positions and competitors' strategies

Differential advantage An attribute of a brand, product, service or marketing mix which is desired by the targeted customer and provided by only one supplier

advantage copied by rivals. Direct Line innovated in selling car insurance over the telephone, cutting out the broker. This more convenient and cheaper service was very popular with customers, gaining market leadership for Direct Line. Very high profits followed. Rivals caught up, offering their own telephone based direct selling of car insurance. Nevertheless, Direct Line developed a sizeable and successful customer base which is still proving difficult for competitors to win back.

Achieving a differential advantage—or competitive edge—requires an organisation to make the most of its opportunities and resources while offering customers a satisfactory mix of tangible and intangible benefits.[26] When striking a balance between customer requirements on the one hand and company resources on the other, competitor activity must also be monitored. For example, there is little sense in promoting speedy distribution to customers if several large competing organisations offer a faster service. An understanding of competitors and customers' perceptions of companies' propositions is an essential part of identifying a differential advantage. Once determined, it is sensible to maximise the use of any differential advantage in marketing mix programmes, particularly in the promotional mix.

There are many different sources of differential advantage that companies can pursue. It is important to ensure that the promoted differential advantage is (1) unique, (2) desirable to the targeted customer, (3) not simply the expected marketing mix taken for granted by the target market and (4) not simply an internal perception. For example, a new range may be superior to its predecessor, but compared to competitors' products offer few benefits to the customer. The marketers could be guilty of identifying the new range's advantages over the former range, wrongly believing these to offer a differential advantage.

Low price should also be avoided as a differential advantage at the centre of a marketing strategy unless a business genuinely has the scale economies to maintain a low cost base and offer low price leadership. Only one company in any market can occupy this platform. Others are vulnerable to being under-cut and losing their apparent differential advantage. Jet's lowest price proposition was undermined by Esso's highly effective Tigerwatch lowest price guarantee. Low price can be utilised as a short term tactic—for example, to off-load excessive stocks—but should not form a differential advantage unless it can be defended against all comers.

If there is no observable differential advantage, a business must look to its strengths over its rivals. While not unique, these will still form the foundation for its ability to compete effectively. The SWOT analysis, which examines strengths, is discussed in the next chapter. The composite of any differential advantage with any strengths is a company's **basis for competing**, which should form the leading edge of the business's marketing strategy. For some companies, such as 3M, innovativeness is the focus, while for others, like Vidal Sassoon hair salons, image plays an important part. The Body Shop concentrates on environmentally friendly cosmetics, whereas for multiplex cinemas the differential advantage is the choice of multiple screens at one location. Some of these ways of gaining an edge are easier to sustain than others. For example, many UK companies that have traditionally focused on low price have found this advantage difficult to maintain in the long term.[27] The airline industry is just one to be plagued by periodic price wars, with many companies turning instead to flexibility and customer service as the basis for competing.

Basis for competing A business's combined strengths as identified in a SWOT analysis and any differential advantage, which should form the leading edge of the business's marketing strategy

Marketing Objectives

A marketing strategy must specify its core marketing objectives. These are typically defined in terms of market segments, market shares, customer satisfaction or brand awareness measures, profitability and financial contribution—or in retailing as sales per square metre of selling space—plus various product and market developments. These developments may include the assessment of new product launch outcomes, new territory or market segment entry. Without specification of these expectations it is difficult to ensure a fit with the determined overall corporate strategy. It is impossible, too, to monitor ongoing performance or benchmark the effectiveness of the recommended marketing strategy against competitors' strategies. This theme is explored further in the following chapters.

Marketing Mix Tactical Programmes

Parts III to VII of *Marketing: Concepts and Strategies* have explored in detail the ingredients of the marketing mix, the tactical toolkit utilised by marketers in striving to implement their recommended marketing strategy and target market strategy. These product, place/distribution, promotion, price and people issues should be determined only after the marketing strategy has been produced. The marketing strategy itself should be developed only after the core marketing analyses have been undertaken: trends, marketing environment forces, customer buying behaviour, competition, opportunities and capabilities. The marketing process requires analysis, strategy formulation and then the specification of tactical marketing mix programmes to facilitate the implementation of the desired target market strategy.

Implementation and Performance Monitoring

Marketing programmes depend on detailed marketing mix specification: product, place/distribution, promotion, price and people issues. In addition, marketing programmes require the specification of budgets for actioning the desired marketing mix recommendations. These budgets must reflect the anticipated sales from the sales forecast (see Chapter 22) and the trends inherent in the targeted market segments. Sales and marketing personnel must know of their responsibilities in implementing the recommended marketing programmes. There may be a requirement on colleagues outside the sales and marketing functions or on senior executives. Schedules must be determined so that it is clear when specific marketing mix activities are expected to occur.

It is essential that the implementation of a marketing strategy be facilitated. This involves specifying by whom, when, how and at what cost the desired marketing mix programmes will be actioned. There may be internal marketing issues to address, such as those connected with the sharing of marketing intelligence and strategies, communication channels within the business, hierarchical support and resources. Finally, marketing must demonstrate its worth. The marketing programmes should be evaluated against pre-determined performance measures to ensure their effective implementation and success in terms of the desired marketing objectives detailed within the marketing strategy. These themes are explored in the following chapters of *Marketing: Concepts and Strategies*.

A number of tools have been developed to aid marketing managers in their planning efforts. Based on ideas used in the management of financial portfolios, several models that classify an organisation's product portfolio have been proposed. These models allow strategic business units (SBUs) or products to be classified and visually displayed according to the attractiveness of various markets and a business's relative market share within those markets. Four of these tools are the Boston Consulting Group (BCG) product portfolio analysis, the market attractiveness-business position model, the Profit Impact on Marketing Strategy (PIMS) and the ABC sales: contribution analysis. In addition, the product life cycle concept explored in Chapter 8 is an important tool often utilised in determining future strategies for brands and products. This assessment—based on the notion of introduction, growth, maturity and decline stages in the life of a product or market—is useful in recommending marketing strategy. As described in Chapter 10, the options are quite different for marketers facing growth or mature stages, and markedly so for the introduction versus the decline stages. The Boston Consulting Group matrix described next builds on this suggestion.

The Boston Consulting Group (BCG) Product Portfolio Analysis

Product portfolio analysis A strategic planning tool that takes a product's market growth rate and its relative market share into consideration in determining a marketing strategy

Just as financial investors have different investments with varying risks and rates of return, businesses have a portfolio of products characterised by different market growth rates and relative market shares. **Product portfolio analysis,** the Boston Consulting Group approach, is based on the philosophy that a product's market growth rate and its relative market share are important considerations in determining its marketing strategy. All the company's products should be integrated into a single, overall matrix and evaluated to determine appropriate strategies for individual SBUs and the overall portfolio strategies. However, a balanced product portfolio matrix is the end result of a number of actions—not just the analysis alone. Portfolio models can be created on the basis of present and projected market growth rates and proposed market share strategies. These strategies include four options: build share, maintain share, harvest share or divest business. Managers can use these models to determine and classify each product's expected future cash contributions and future cash requirements.

Generally, managers who use a portfolio model must examine the competitive position of a product—or product line—and the opportunities for improving that product's contribution to profitability and cash flow.[28] The BCG analytical approach is more of a diagnostic tool than a guide for making strategy prescriptions.

Figure 21.6, which is based on work by the BCG, enables the marketing manager to classify a company's products into four basic types: stars, cash cows, dogs and problem children.[29] **Stars** are products with a dominant share of the market and good prospects for growth. However, they use more cash than they generate to finance growth, add capacity and increase market share. **Cash cows** have a dominant share of the market but low prospects for growth. Typically, they generate more cash than is required to maintain market share. Cash cows generate much needed funds to support the stars and problem children. **Dogs** have a subordinate share of the market and low prospects for growth. These are struggling products. They are frequently found in mature markets and often should be phased out or withdrawn immediately. **Problem children,** sometimes called "question marks", have a small share of a growing market and generally require a large amount of cash to build share. The question is, are they capable of becoming star products or are they destined to be dogs?

Stars Products with a dominant share of the market and good prospects for growth

Cash cows Products with a dominant share of the market but low prospects for growth

Dogs Products that have a subordinate share of the market and low prospects for growth

Problem children Products that have a small share of a growing market, generally requiring a large amount of cash to build share

Figure 21.6 Illustrative growth-share matrix developed by the Boston Consulting Group.
Source: *Perspectives*, No. 66, "The product portfolio". Reprinted by permission from The Boston Consulting Group, Inc., Boston, MA. Copyright © 1970.

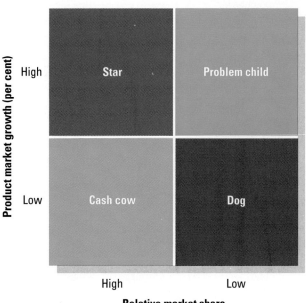

The growth-share matrix in Figure 21.6 can be expanded to show a company's whole portfolio by providing for each product (1) its cash sales volume, illustrated by the size of a circle on the matrix; (2) its market share relative to competition, represented by the horizontal position of the product on the matrix; and (3) the growth rate of the market, indicated by the position of the product in the vertical direction. It should be noted that relative market share is a company's own market share relative to the biggest competitor's. Figure 21.7, suggests marketing strategies appropriate for cash cows, stars, dogs and problem children.

The long term health of an organisation depends on having some products that generate cash and provide acceptable profits, plus others that use cash to support growth. Among the indicators of overall health are the size and vulnerability of the cash cows, the prospects for the stars, if any, and the number of problem children and dogs. Particular attention must be paid to those products with large cash appetites. Unless the company has an abundant cash flow, it cannot afford to sponsor many such products at one time. If resources, including debt capacity, are spread too thinly, the company will end up with too many marginal products and will be unable to finance promising new product entries or acquisitions in the future.

Market Attractiveness-Business Position Model

Market attractiveness-business position model   A two dimensional matrix that helps determine which SBUs have an opportunity to grow and which should be divested

The **market attractiveness-business position model,** illustrated in Figure 21.8, is another two-dimensional matrix. However, rather than using single measures to define the vertical and horizontal dimensions of the matrix, the model employs multiple measurements and observations. It is an increasingly popular tool, particularly in businesses producing detailed annual marketing plans. The vertical dimension—*market attractiveness*—includes all the strengths and resources that relate to the market, such as seasonality, economies of scale, competitive intensity, industry sales and the overall cost and feasibility of entering the market. The horizontal axis—*business position*—is a composite of factors such as sales, relative market share, research and development, price competitiveness, product quality and market knowledge as they relate to the product in building market

Stars	Problem children
Characteristics	**Characteristics**
■ Market leaders	■ Rapid growth
■ Fast growing	■ Poor profit margins
■ Substantial profits	■ Enormous demand for cash
■ Require large investment to finance growth	
	Strategies
Strategies	■ Invest heavily to get a disproportionate share of new sales
■ Protect existing share	■ Buy existing market shares by acquiring competitors
■ Re-invest earnings in the form of price reductions, product improvements, providing better market coverage, production efficiency and so on	■ Divestment (see Dogs)
	■ Harvesting (see Dogs)
■ Obtain a large share of the new users	■ Abandonment (see Dogs)
	■ Focus on a definable niche where dominance can be achieved

Cash cows	Dogs
Characteristics	**Characteristics**
■ Profitable products	■ Greatest number of products fall in this category
■ Generate more cash than needed to maintain market share	■ Operate at a cost disadvantage
	■ Few opportunities for growth at a reasonable cost
Strategies	■ Markets are not growing; therefore, little new business
■ Maintain market dominance	
■ Invest in process improvements and technological leadership	**Strategies**
■ Maintain price leadership	■ Focus on a specialised segment of the market that can be dominated and protected from competitive inroads
■ Use excess cash to support research and growth elsewhere in the company	■ Harvesting—cut back all support costs to a minimum level; support cash flow over the product's remaining life
	■ Divestment—sale of a growing concern
	■ Abandonment—deletion from the product line

Product market growth (per cent): High / Low

Relative market share: High / Low

Figure 21.7 Characteristics and strategies for the four basic product types in the growth-share matrix. SOURCE: Concepts in this figure adapted from George S. Day, "Diagnosing the product portfolio", *Journal of Marketing*, April 1977, pp. 30–31. Reprinted by permission of the American Marketing Association.

share. Each company deploying this tool selects its own criteria, but uses these same ones over time to analyse changes. A slight variation of this matrix is called General Electric's Strategic Business Planning Grid because General Electric is credited with extending the product portfolio planning tool to examine market attractiveness and business strength. Marketing Insight 21.2 on page 679 explains how the chemicals giants deploy this tool.

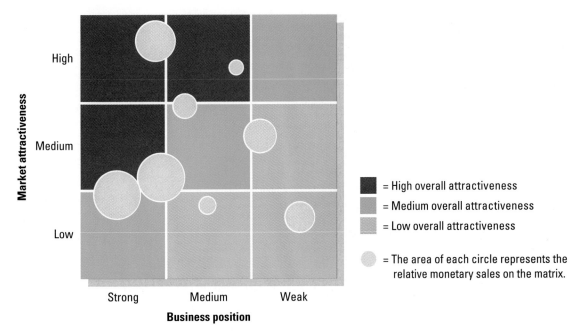

High overall attractiveness

Medium overall attractiveness

Low overall attractiveness

The area of each circle represents the relative monetary sales on the matrix.

Figure 21.8 Market attractiveness-business position model. SOURCE: Adapted from Derek F. Abell and John S. Hammond, *Strategic Market Planning: Problems and Analytical Approaches* (Englewood Cliffs, N.J.: Prentice-Hall, 1979), p. 213. Used by permission.

The best situation for a company is to have a strong business position in an attractive market. The upper left area in Figure 21.8 represents the opportunity for an invest/grow strategy, but the matrix does not indicate how to implement this strategy. The purpose of the model is to serve as a diagnostic tool to highlight SBUs that have an opportunity to grow or that should be divested or approached selectively.[30] SBUs that occupy the invest/grow position can lose their position through faulty marketing strategies.

Decisions on allocating resources to SBUs of medium overall attractiveness should be arrived at on a basis relative to other SBUs that are either more or less attractive. The lower right area of the matrix is a low growth harvest/divest area. Harvesting is a gradual withdrawal of marketing resources on the assumption that sales will decline at a slow rate but profits will still be significant at a lower sales volume. Harvesting and divesting—even abandonment, or deletion from the product line—may be appropriate strategies for SBUs characterised by low overall attractiveness.

Profit Impact on Marketing Strategy (PIMS)

Profit Impact on Marketing Strategy (PIMS) A research programme that compiled a databank of information on 3,000 strategic business units of 200 different businesses in order to assist in analysing marketing performance and formulating marketing strategies

The US Strategic Planning Institute (SPI) developed a databank of information on 3,000 strategic business units of 200 different businesses during the period 1970 to 1983 for the **Profit Impact on Marketing Strategy (PIMS)** research programme.[31] The sample is somewhat biased because it is composed primarily of large, profitable manufacturing companies marketing mature products; service organisations and distribution companies are under-represented. However, 19 per cent of the sample is composed of international businesses.[32] The member organisations of the Institute provided confidential information on successes, failures and marginal products. Figure 21.9 shows a PIMS data form. The data have been analysed to provide members with information about how similar

Figure 21.9 Sample page from PIMS data form. SOURCE: PIMS Data Form reproduced by permission of the Strategic Planning Institute (PIMS programme), Cambridge, Mass., 1979.

103: "LIFE CYCLE" STAGE OF PRODUCT CATEGORY

How would you describe the stage of development of the types of products or services sold by this business during the last three years? *(Check one)*

... Introductory Stage: Primary demand for product just starting to grow; products or services still unfamiliar to many potential users ☐ 1

... Growth Stage: Demand growing at 10% or more annually in real terms: technology or competitive structure still changing ☐ 2

... Maturity Stage: Products or services familiar to vast majority of prospective users; technology and competitve structure reasonably stable ☐ 3

... Decline Stage: Products viewed as commodities: weaker competitors beginning to exit ☐ 4

104: What was this business's first year of commercial sales? *(Check one)*

Prior to 1930	1930–1949	1950–1954	1955–1959	1960–1964	1965–1969	1970–1974	1975–
☐ 0	☐ 1	☐ 2	☐ 3	☐ 4	☐ 5	☐ 6	☐ 7

105: At the time this business first entered the market, was it ... *(Check one)*

... One of the pioneers in first developing such products or services? ☐ 1

... An early follower of the pioneer(s) in a still growing, dynamic market? ☐ 2

... A later entrant into a more established market situation? ☐ 3

106–07: PATENTS AND TRADE SECRETS

Does this business benefit *to a significant degree* from patents, trade secrets, or other proprietary methods of production or operation ...

106: Pertaining to products or services?   NO ☐ 0   YES ☐ 1   **107:** Pertaining to processes?   NO ☐ 0   YES ☐ 1

108: STANDARDISATION OF PRODUCTS OR SERVICES

Are the products or services of this business .. *(Check one)*

... More or less standardised for all customers? ☐ 0

... Designed or produced to order for individual customers? ☐ 1

109: FREQUENCY OF PRODUCT CHANGES

Is it typical practice for the business and its major competitors to change all or part of the line of products or services offered ... *(Check one)*

... Annually (for example, annual model changes)? ☐ 1

... Seasonally? ☐ 2

... Periodically, but at intervals longer than one year? ☐ 3

... No regular, periodic pattern of change? ☐ 4

110: TECHNOLOGICAL CHANGE

Have there been major technological changes in the products offered by the business or its major competitors, or in methods of production, during the last 8 years? *(If in doubt about whether a change was "major," answer NO.)*   NO ☐ 0   YES ☐ 1

organisations performed under a given set of circumstances and about the factors that contributed to success or failure in given market conditions.

The unit of observation in PIMS is the SBU. Table 21.1 shows the types of information provided on each business in the PIMS database. The PIMS database includes both diagnostic and prescriptive information to assist in analysing marketing performance and formulating marketing strategies. The analysis focuses on options, problems, resources and opportunities. The PIMS project has identified more than 30 factors that affect the performance of businesses. These factors can be grouped into three sets of variables: (1) those relating to the structure of the marketplace in which the company competes; (2) those that describe the company's competitive position within that market; and (3) those that relate to the strategy chosen by the company.[33] These factors may interact, as well as directly affect performance and profitability. Some of the main findings of the PIMS project are discussed briefly below.

Strong Market Position   Market position refers to the relative market share that a company holds in relation to its competition. Companies that have a large share

Characteristics of the Business Environment	Structure of the Production Process
Long run growth rate of the market Short run growth rate of the market Rate of inflation of selling price levels Number and size of customers Purchase frequency and magnitude	Capital intensity (degree of automation, etc.) Degree of vertical integration Capacity utilisation Productivity of capital equipment Productivity of people Inventory levels
Competitive Position of the Business Share of the served market Share relative to largest competitors Product quality relative to competitors Prices relative to competitors Pay scales relative to competitors Marketing efforts relative to competitors Pattern of market segmentation Rate of new product introductions	**Discretionary Budget Allocations** Research and development budgets Advertising and promotion budgets Salesforce expenditures **Strategic Moves** Patterns of change in the controllable elements above **Operating Results** Profitability results Cash flow results Growth results

SOURCE: Reproduced by permission of the Strategic Planning Institute [PIMS programme], Cambridge, Mass.

Table 21.1 Types of information provided on each business in the PIMS database

of a market tend to be the most profitable. However, it should be noted that market share does not necessarily create profitability. Business strategies, such as the marketing of high quality products, and the provision of good service result in profitability.

High Quality Products Organisations that offer products of higher quality tend to be more profitable than their competitors. They are able to demand higher prices for those products. Moreover, high quality offerings instil customer loyalty, foster repeat purchases, insulate companies from price wars and help build market share. In Figure 21.10, Bounce promotes its ongoing commitment to quality. It appears impossible for companies to overcome inferior offerings with high levels of marketing expenditures. Advertising is no substitute for product quality.

Lower Costs Companies achieve lower costs through economies of scale, ability to bargain with suppliers or backward integration. Low costs heighten profitability levels.

Investment and Capital Intensity The higher the required investment to compete in an industry, the more pressure there is on a company to use fully its production capacity. Moreover, these factors tend to have a negative impact on profitability.

Figure 21.10 A commitment to quality. Fabric conditioner Bounce promotes a quality image. SOURCE: © The Procter and Gamble Company. Used by permission.

The ABC Sales: Contribution Analysis

ABC sales: contribution analysis
An approach that examines the financial worth to a company of its products, product groups or customers

The **ABC sales: contribution analysis** can be conducted at either product group or product line level; for the total market, territories or sub-markets; for customer groups/market segments; or for individual customer accounts. The aim is to show both the amount of sales and the financial contribution from these sales—that is, the financial worth—to the company's fortunes. Financial success, after all, is not confined to sales volume figures; a business must have an adequate level of contribution (sales revenue minus all variable costs) from its sales. This analysis helps companies to identify the relative value of different products, markets or even individual customer accounts, assisting with the allocation of resources.

An example of an ABC sales: contribution analysis chart is shown in Figure 21.11. The 45 degree diagonal line from bottom left to top right is the optimum. It is a straightforward rule, not a regression line, however. Ideally, the dots on the chart would be located on the line (good sales and contribution) and be at the top right of the graph (high sales and high contribution). These "sell a lot, make a lot" are the "A" class. Typically, however, this is not the case. The majority of customers or markets fall at the bottom left of the graph (low sales and low contribution: the "C" class), or they have average sales and average contributions (the "B" class).

To Market Waste—ICI's Strategists Hit on the Right Formula

Although recently sold off by ICI and broken up between various new owners, including former arch rival Du Pont, Tioxide managed to establish market leadership through shrewd planning and well conceived strategies. Tioxide Group vied head to head with the US's Du Pont organisation for leadership worldwide of the TiO_2, titanium dioxide, market. This innocuous powder appears in all paints, inks, PVCs and plastics. As a commodity it is predominantly sold on price, although for certain applications the purity of the pigment is important. With some customers, such as car manufacturers, a significant level of technical expertise and laboratory support is required too.

Although TiO_2 is a commodity, the major players such as Du Pont, Kemira, Kerr McGee, Kronos, SCM and Tioxide do attempt in certain markets to create a differential advantage over their rivals. This may be based on the purity of the pigment from a particular plant, the volume of production, guaranteeing supplies to customers dependent on TiO_2 to finish their products, innovative distribution through tankers or variable pack sizes, delivery times, expertise in the customers' technical needs or long term relationships permitting the sharing of both technical product and market knowledge.

Because there are relatively few competitors—perhaps only 20 major production sites around the world—there is significant rivalry to secure supplies of the raw materials used to produce TiO_2. In addition to the occasional but inevitable production failures and plant closings, this market endures significant cyclical hitches in the supply of TiO_2 to customers. The dilemma then for the major operators is which customers to continue to supply. Should those that take the largest tonnages be given priority? In terms of cash flow, perhaps; but as these customers exercise huge purchasing power, they often buy at the lowest profit margins for companies such as Du Pont or Tioxide. However, to alienate such large customers as ICI Paints or BMW would jeopardise a TiO_2 supplier's long term viability. There has to be a balance between guaranteeing to supply long standing, large customers—particularly those that also operate globally and may well buy from a network of a TiO_2 supplier's plants—and supporting smaller but highly profitable accounts. In times of restricted supply, the use of portfolio models, such as the market attractiveness-business position model or the ABC sales: contribution analysis, plays an active role in these chemicals giants' decision-making.

For the strategists in Du Pont or Tioxide, a persistent problem has been what to do with the waste slurry left from the production of TiO_2 in its purest forms for the major ink, packaging or paint companies. Tioxide tackled this dilemma head-on. Chairman Alan Pedder set up a management group to investigate the possibilities for marketing the waste slurry (or "co-product") in its own right. To the surprise of some industry observers, this effort has proved highly successful, both in finding existing applications and customers that could easily tolerate a lower grade pigment (i.e. with some co-product included) and in identifying totally new applications and customers for the slurry product. In 1994, Tioxide sold more tonnes of co-products from the production of titanium dioxide production than TiO_2 itself.

Sources: Peter Fairly, "Tioxide grows materials group", *Chemical Week*, 5 July 1995, p. 18; Sean Milmo, "Tioxide embraces TiO_2 by-products", *Chemical Marketing Reporter*, 12 June 1995, p. 9; Marjorie Coeyman, "Du Pont, Tioxide plan capacity hike", *Chemical Week*, 19 October 1994, p. 14; Brent Shearer, "TiO_2 producers mull new plants", *Chemical Marketing Reporter*, 9 January 1995, p. 3.

Three important conclusions can be drawn from an ABC analysis. (1) It can identify highly attractive customers, markets or products (depending on the chosen unit of analysis) in terms of the associated contributions, but where sales are relatively low. For such accounts, an increase in sales (no matter how slight), with associated high prices and good financial returns, will be highly rewarding. (2) It can determine accounts with high sales figures but low or pitiful contributions. Cash flow may be good, but profitability is not helped. Even a slight increase in

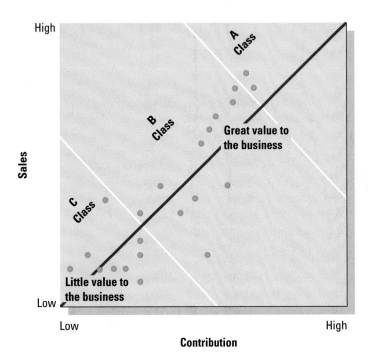

The dots could be products, product groups, market territories, segments or even individual customer accounts depending on the chosen level of analysis

Figure 21.11   Example of ABC sales: contribution chart

contribution is most desirable. (3) It can challenge the historical perspective that often clouds judgement as to what constitutes a good product, market or customer. Every business has its historically most rewarding customers and products that are no longer performing in sales terms, contribution or both! Often, managers still believe the historical rhetoric rather than recognise that the situation has moved on; new priorities must benefit from the available resources and marketing effort. The ABC analysis generally unearths a few such instances and identifies the rump of unrewarding accounts or customers not worth pursuing.

Significance of Strategic Market Planning Approaches

The approaches presented here provide an overview of the most popular analytical methods used in strategic market planning. However, the Boston Consulting Group's portfolio analysis, the market attractiveness-business position model, the Profit Impact on Marketing Strategy research programme, the ABC sales: contribution analysis and the product life cycle concept are used not only to diagnose problem areas or to recognise opportunities but also to facilitate the allocation of resources among business units. They are not intended to serve as formulae for success or prescriptive guides, which lay out cut-and-dried strategic action plans.[34] These approaches are supplements to, not substitutes for, the marketing manager's own judgement. The real test of each approach, or any integrated approach, is how well it helps management diagnose the company's strengths and weaknesses and prescribe strategic actions for maintaining or improving performance. The emphasis should be on making sound decisions with the aid of these analytical tools.[35]

Another word of caution regarding the use of portfolio approaches is necessary. The classification of SBUs into a specific portfolio position hinges on four

Figure 21.12 Ansoff's competitive strategies. SOURCE: H. I. Ansoff, *The New Corporate Strategy* (New York, N.Y.: John Wiley & Sons, 1988), p. 83. Reproduced by permission of the author.

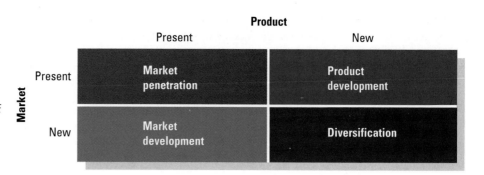

factors: (1) the operational definition of the matrix dimensions; (2) the rules used to divide a dimension into high and low categories; (3) the weighting of the variables used in composite dimensions, if composite dimensions are used; and (4) the specific model used.[36] In other words, changes in any of these four factors may well result in a different classification for a single SBU.

The key to understanding the tools for strategic market planning described in this chapter is recognition that strategic market planning takes into account all aspects of a company's strategy in the marketplace. Most of *Marketing: Concepts and Strategies* is about functional decisions and strategies of marketing as a part of business. This chapter focuses on the recognition that all functional strategies, including marketing, production and finance, must be co-ordinated to reach organisational goals. Results of a survey of top industrial companies sponsored by the *Harvard Business Review* indicate that portfolio planning and other general planning techniques help managers strengthen their planning process and solve the problems of managing diversified companies. However, the results also indicate that analytical techniques alone do not result in success. Management must blend these analyses with managerial judgement to deal with the reality of the existing situation.

There are other tools that aid strategic market planning and the development of marketing strategies besides those examined here. Many businesses have their own approaches to planning that incorporate, to varying degrees, some of the approaches discussed here. All strategic planning approaches have some similarity in that several of the components of strategic market planning outlined in Figure 21.3—especially competitive strategies regarding market/product relationships as illustrated in Figure 21.12—are related to a plan of action for reaching objectives.

● S U M M A R Y

Marketing strategy indicates the specific markets towards which activities are to be targeted and the types of competitive advantages that are to be developed and exploited. A marketing strategy aims to target customer segments of most benefit to an organisation in a manner that provides a differential advantage over competitors and matches the organisation's corporate goals.

A *strategic market plan* is an outline of the methods and resources required to achieve an organisation's goals within a specific target market; it takes into account all the functional areas of a business unit that must be co-ordinated. A *strategic business unit (SBU)* is a division, product line or other profit centre within a parent company and is used to define areas for consideration in a specific strategic market plan. The process of *strategic market planning* yields a marketing strategy that is the framework for a marketing plan. A *marketing plan* includes the framework and entire set of activities to be performed; it is the written document or blueprint for implementing and controlling an organisation's marketing activities.

Through the process of strategic market planning, an organisation can develop marketing strategies that, when properly implemented and controlled, will contribute to achieving the organisation's overall goals. The set of marketing strategies that are implemented and used at the same time is referred to as the organisation's *marketing programme*. Most marketing programmes centre around a detailed marketing mix specification and include internal controls and procedures to ensure that they are implemented effectively. Marketing environment forces are important in—and profoundly affect—the strategic market planning process. These forces imply opportunities and threats that influence an organisation's overall goals.

Central to the marketing strategy is a clear view of the corporate mission and goals. These may well be developed separately to the marketing strategy but the marketing strategy must aim to reflect the overall corporate vision. A business's organisational goals should be derived from its *mission,* that is, the broad, long term tasks that the organisation wants to achieve. These goals should guide planning efforts and specify the ends, or results, that are sought. *Corporate strategy* determines the means for utilising resources in the areas of production, finance, research and development, personnel and marketing to reach the organisation's goals.

There are three major considerations in assessing opportunities and resources: (1) evaluating marketing opportunities, (2) environmental scanning, and (3) understanding the company's capabilities and assets. A *marketing opportunity* arises when the right combination of circumstances occurs at the right time, allowing an organisation to take action towards reaching a target market. An opportunity offers a favourable chance for the company to gen-

erate sales from identifiable markets. A *strategic window* is a temporary period of optimum fit between the key requirements of a market and the particular capabilities of a company competing in that market. *Market requirements* relate to customers' needs or desired benefits. Market requirements are satisfied by components of the marketing mix that provide buyers with these benefits. *Environmental scanning* is the process of collecting information about the marketing environment to help marketers identify opportunities and assist in planning. A company's *capabilities* relate to distinctive competencies that it has developed to do something well and efficiently. A company is likely to enjoy a differential advantage in an area in which its competencies and *marketing assets* out-do those of its potential competition.

Having evaluated the overall corporate vision, those responsible for devising the marketing strategy must build on their analysis of opportunities and internal capabilities by analytically assessing the most promising directions for their business and its marketing activity. Competitive strategies that can be implemented through marketing include *intense growth, diversified growth* and *integrated growth*. Intense growth includes *market penetration, market development* or *product development*. Diversified growth includes *horizontal, concentric* and *conglomerate diversification*. Integrated growth includes forwards, backwards and horizontal integration.

Integral to achieving a company's corporate vision is the need to develop a loyal customer base of satisfied customers. It is essential to continuously improve the company's proposition so as to address evolving target market customer needs and expectations. The market segmentation process of segmentation, targeting and positioning is the core element of the recommended marketing strategy.

It is important to understand the nature of competition and to utilise this knowledge in determining a marketing strategy. Aspects of the strategy should be purposively designed to maximise any weaknesses in competitors' activities and pre-empt any impending moves from rivals. Competitors should not be viewed only as like-for-like rivals: new entrants, substitute products or services, and the bargaining power of suppliers and of buyers can all form competitive threats or opportunities. In developing strategies, an organisation must consider the *competitive positions* in the marketplace. The *market leader* must both defend its position and seek new sales opportunities. Attack may prove the best form of defence. *Market challengers* must aggressively seek market share gains but carefully select the basis on which to attack: a chink in the leader's armour or a quick response to changing consumer needs. *Fast movers* may be small but they have the potential to win market share from rivals and should be combatted. *Market followers* are the "plodders" or "me-toos", prone to be squeezed in times of recession or in response to challengers' aggression. *Market nichers* specialise in terms of product and customer segment. They can very successfully tailor their marketing to their customers' needs but are vulnerable to competitors' entry into their target segments. To compete successfully, any organisation needs to consider the principles of *offensive* and *defensive warfare* and to understand its competitors' strategies through *competitor scanning*.

An organisation should strive for a *differential advantage* or competitive edge in its markets. A differential advantage is an attribute of a brand, product, service or marketing mix which is desirable to targeted customers and provided by only one supplier. Marketing mix programmes should emphasise desirable attributes of a company's marketing mix that its target customers consider unmatched by competitors. The combined strengths as identified in a SWOT analysis and any differential advantage make up the *basis for competing*, which should form the leading edge of a business's marketing strategy.

A marketing strategy must specify its core marketing objectives, typically defined in terms of market segments, market shares, customer satisfaction or brand awareness measures, profitability and financial contribution, plus various product and market developments. Without specification of objectives it is difficult to assess the performance of the marketing strategy or to ensure its fit with the overall corporate strategy.

The tactical ingredients of the marketing mix—product, place/distribution, promotion, price and people issues—should be determined only after a marketing strategy has been specified. The marketing strategy must be decided only after the essential

analyses of marketing—trends, the marketing environment forces, customer buying behaviour, competition, opportunities and capabilities—have been undertaken. Analysis should come first, then strategic thinking and finally determination of tactical implementation programmes.

Marketing programmes depend on detailed marketing mix specifications, but also on the determination of budgets for implementing these marketing mix requirements. These budgets must reflect the sales forecast and trends in the targeted market segments. Sales and marketing personnel should take responsibility for implementing the marketing plan's recommendations, and schedules for marketing mix activity must be established. Implementation of a marketing strategy has to be facilitated, which involves specifying by whom, when, how and at what cost the desired marketing mix programmes will be implemented. These programmes must be evaluated against pre-determined performance measures.

A number of tools have been developed to aid marketing managers in their planning efforts, including the Boston Consulting Group (BCG) *product portfolio analysis*, the market attractiveness-business position model, the Profit Impact on Marketing Strategy (PIMS) and the ABC sales: contribution analysis. The product life cycle concept is also important in determining marketing strategies. The BCG approach is based on the philosophy that a product's market growth rate and its relative market share are key factors influencing marketing strategy. All the company's products are integrated into a single, overall matrix—including *stars, cash cows, dogs* and *problem children*—and are evaluated to determine appropriate strategies for individual SBUs and the overall portfolio strategies.

The *market attractiveness-business position model* is a two-dimensional matrix. The market attractiveness dimension includes all the sources of strength and resources that relate to the market, such as seasonality, economies of scale, competitive intensity, industry sales and the cost of competing. The business position axis measures sales, relative market share, research and development, and other factors that relate to building a market share for a product.

The *Profit Impact on Marketing Strategy (PIMS)* research programme of the US Strategic Planning

Institute developed a databank of confidential information on the successes, failures and marginal products of more than 3,000 strategic business units of 200 different businesses. The unit of observation in PIMS is an SBU. The results of PIMS include both diagnostic and prescriptive information to assist in analysing marketing performance and formulating marketing strategies. The analysis focuses on options, problems, resources and opportunities. The *ABC sales: contribution analysis* examines the financial worth to a company of its products, product groups or customers.

Tools for strategic market planning are used only to diagnose problem areas or recognise opportunities. They are supplements to, not substitutes for, the marketing manager's own judgement. The real test of each approach, or any integrated approach, is how well it helps management diagnose the company's strengths and weaknesses and prescribe strategic actions for maintaining or improving performance.

Important Terms

Marketing strategy
Strategic market plan
Strategic business unit (SBU)
Strategic market planning
Marketing plan
Marketing programme
Mission
Corporate strategy
Marketing opportunity
Strategic window
Market requirements
Environmental scanning
Capabilities
Marketing assets
Intense growth

Market penetration
Market development
Product development
Diversified growth
Horizontal diversification
Concentric diversification
Conglomerate diversification
Integrated growth
Competitive positions
Market leader
Market challengers
Fast movers
Market followers
Market nichers
Defensive warfare

Offensive warfare
Competitor scanning
Differential advantage
Basis for competing
Product portfolio analysis
Stars
Cash cows
Dogs
Problem children
Market attractiveness-business
   position model
Profit Impact on Marketing
   Strategy (PIMS)
ABC sales: contribution analysis

Discussion and Review Questions

1. Why should an organisation develop a marketing strategy? What is the difference between strategic market planning and the strategy itself?
2. Identify the major components of strategic market planning and explain how they are inter-related.
3. In what ways do marketing environment forces affect strategic market planning? Give some specific examples.
4. What is a mission statement? Why must marketing strategists understand their business's corporate strategy?
5. What are some of the issues that must be considered in analysing a business's opportunities and resources? How do these issues affect marketing objectives and marketing strategy?
6. Why is marketing opportunity analysis necessary? What are the determinants of marketing opportunity?
7. In relation to resource constraints, how can environmental scanning affect a company's long term strategic market planning? Consider product costs and benefits affected by the environment.
8. Why do you think more companies are diversifying? Give some examples of diversified businesses.

9. Target marketing—the market segmentation process—is at the heart of a marketing strategy. Why must this be so?
10. Why should companies attempt to understand the strategies of their competitors? Explain your views.
11. How can a market leader best defend its competitive position?
12. What are the strengths of a market nicher? In what way is a nicher vulnerable?
13. Why must a marketing strategy include detailed marketing objectives?
14. In what ways should implementation of a marketing strategy be facilitated?
15. What are the major considerations in developing the product portfolio matrix? Define and explain the four basic types of products suggested by the Boston Consulting Group.
16. When should marketers consider using PIMS for strategic market planning?

Recommended Readings

D. A. Aaker, *Strategic Marketing Management* (New York: Wiley, 1998).

M. J. Baker, *The Marketing Manual* (Oxford: Butterworth-Heinemann, 1998).

D. Littler and D. Wilson, eds, *Marketing Strategy* (Oxford: Butterworth-Heinemann, 1995).

J. O'Shaughnessy, *Competitive Marketing: A Strategic Approach* (London: Unwin-Hyman, 1995).

M. E. Porter, *Competitive Advantage: Creating and Sustaining Superior Performance* (New York: Free Press, 1998).

M. E. Porter, *Competitive Strategy: Techniques for Analyzing Industries and Competitors* (New York: Free Press, 1998).

 # C A S E S

21.1 Ireland: Marketing a Country

During the 1960s and 1970s, Ireland's economy lagged behind those of its European neighbours. The Irish government realised it needed to create more employment opportunities in industries of the future in order to establish a more affluent, outward looking basis to the country's economy. Today Ireland has a trade surplus in excess of 12.6 per cent of GNP, a balance of payments surplus equivalent to 6.2 per cent of GNP and one of the lowest inflation rates in Europe. Membership in the EU has brought significant benefits to the country, including grants for infrastructure enhancements and improved international links. Over one thousand international companies have been encouraged to invest in factories, distribution centres or office complexes.

From its previous dependence on agriculture, the economy has become far more balanced. Industry accounts for 35 per cent of GDP; distribution, transport and communication for 18 per cent; services for 31 per cent; and agriculture for just 10 per cent. Although not solely responsible for this change, the Industrial Development Authority (IDA) has figured prominently in Ireland's economic transformation. Established to promote industrial development, the IDA has encouraged overseas companies to locate in Ireland, creating close to 100,000 jobs by 1996, an incredible 10,000 per annum; 400 US companies alone have settled on an Irish base as a gateway into the huge EU market of over 360 million consumers. As many as 180 German companies have set up in Ireland, attracted by its skilled workforce, tax base and culture. Household names including IBM, Microsoft, Lotus, Norwich, Union, Siemens, CIGNA, McGraw-Hill, Massachusetts Mutual, Ericsson, Philips, Fujitsu, Northern Telecom, Pratt & Whitney, Merck Sharp & Dohme, Braun, Coca-Cola and Nestlé are important investors and employers.

The IDA has succeeded not by good luck but through the development of an evolving business strategy. First, it identified specific sectors of economic activity for international growth. Ireland wanted to attract the growth companies of the future, not yesteryear. Financial services, electronics, high tech engineering, consumer products, branded food and drinks, and healthcare were earmarked to lead the economy into the twenty-first century. The US, Pacific, Asia, Britain, Germany, Benelux and Scandinavia were home to these growth industries, so the IDA set up a network of 20 offices in these territories to push the Irish message.

Having targeted the growth industries, the IDA knew it had to offer benefits in order to attract any interest in locating and investing in Ireland. Research revealed several negative perceptions of the country and its people as impoverished, rural, agricultural and poorly educated. The facts paint a far different picture, and through glossy printed publicity, seminars, press involvement and various road shows, IDA personnel, politicians and leading Irish industrialists sought to convey the real story.

The message was carefully honed to reflect the target companies' concerns and to offer tangible rewards for investing in Ireland:

- A young, English speaking, highly educated workforce superior to most in Europe.
- A 10 per cent corporate tax rate up to the year 2010 and freedom to repatriate profits.
- A state-of-the-art digital and satellite telecommunications system.
- Generous capital, employment, research and development, and training grants.
- A stable currency and low inflation rate.
- Duty-free access to the EU market.
- Return on investment (29.9 per cent) more than three times the EU (9.4 per cent) and world (8.6 per cent) averages.
- Most European cities within two hours' flying time.
- A vigorous sub-contracting and component supply industry.

- A unique, historic culture and quality of life with superb recreational and leisure facilities.

The pliable, capable, young workforce has been a significant attraction, as has the cultural and recreational base. The stable economy and hefty financial incentives for many companies simply helped close the deal for re-location. With extensions to Shannon International Airport, the creation of the associated duty-free zone trading estate—the first in the world—significant investment from both the private and public sectors and the recent development of the superb waterfront financial services centre in Dublin, the Irish strategy has worked.

An opportunity existed to create a rationale for overseas companies to put Ireland at the top of their location and investment lists. Advantages were created and existing benefits reinforced to establish a clear basis for companies to choose Ireland. Careful targeting of industries and companies, supported by comprehensive promotion, led to the establishment of operations in Ireland by over one thousand companies. The IDA and its partner organisations have successfully marketed a country.

SOURCES: Irish Embassy, London; Industrial Development Authority (IDA); IDA promotional material: "Dublin: the international financial services centre", "Ireland: put yourself in our hands in the 90s"; Shannon Development promotional literature; "Facts about Ireland", IDA, 1995, 1996, 1999.

Questions for Discussion

1. Why was targeting central to the IDA strategy?
2. What problems had to be overcome to attract overseas investors to locate in Ireland?
3. What benefits were offered by the IDA? How did this varied package communicate the Irish message?

21.2 Creative Marketing Is Crucial to Cadbury's Strategy

The Cadbury story began in 1824, in the Midlands of England, when Quaker John Cadbury opened a small grocery shop business. Several years later, the foundations for the manufacturing business of today were put in place when John Cadbury began producing cocoa and drinking chocolate. The business soon grew and in 1879 production was moved to a new site, which became known as Bournville. Following the formation of Cadbury Brothers Limited in 1899, the company was on its way to becoming one of the world's best loved brands. Soon after, Cadbury launched Dairy Milk chocolate, the brand that was to become the UK's favourite moulded bar.

Today, Cadbury is market leader in the UK and a major global confectionery player, offering a variety of famous brands to consumers around the world. In 1969, Cadbury joined forces with drinks business Schweppes. The Cadbury Schweppes empire which was formed now uses some of the most up-to-date and sophisticated production techniques and managerial approaches to support its manufacturing and sales operation. For example, the changes seen at Bournville's design department, which employs a large team of designers to prepare packaging and a full range of sales materials, are typical of those which have affected the company. At the current time, the Cadbury design function uses a wide variety of computer graphics and information technology to assist its work. For example, the potential impact of new pack designs can be assessed by generating computer images of the product in different kinds of shelf display.

Despite the changes that the company has seen over its 175 year history, the Cadbury commitment to quality has remained consistent. Early promotions for the Cadbury brand highlighted the quality of the ingredients used. Today, this emphasis on quality continues to be reflected in all aspects of the company's production and marketing processes. For example, the following extract from the Cadbury web site highlights the importance which quality plays in the development of packaging for the company's products:

1. Cadbury is well known for the good quality of its products, a reputation which must be maintained.
2. The quality of confectionery is judged by two factors—the appearance of the product before purchase and, most important, the taste.
3. Cadbury produces vast quantities of chocolates and sweets which must sell themselves off the shelves of supermarkets and a wide range of other retail outlets.

The market for Cadbury's products remains buoyant. The market value of confectionery continues to increase year-on-year, with sales of chocolate

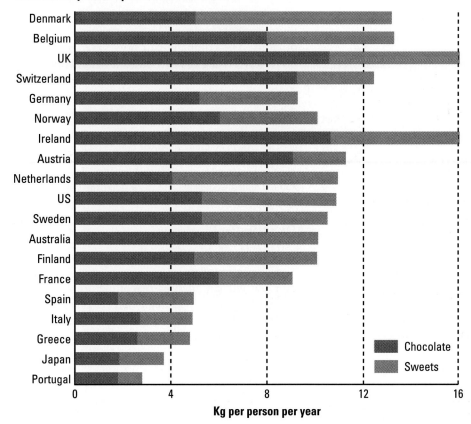

Confectionery consumption around the world

Kg per person per year

making up around 70 per cent of it. Annual sales of Cadbury's chocolate brands are worth approximately £1.3bn. In just ten years, the UK confectionery market, which is one of the largest in the world, has seen growth of some 16 per cent. With confectionery continuing to dominate the snack food market, the average Briton eats his or her way through almost 16kg of confectionery each year (or one chocolate bar or container of sweets each day). This compares with 9kg in France and a mere 3kg in Japan.

Cadbury faces a keen competitive environment in its home market, with the likes of Mars and Nestlé vying for market share. Current estimates suggest that Cadbury and Trebor Bassett hold a combined market share of around 30 per cent, with Mars on 20 per cent and Nestlé having 18 per cent. Effective new product development has played a vital role in supporting Cadbury's strong market position. Research indicates that the company has been responsible for some 60 per cent of successful new product launches in the last 10 years. In particular, the company is keen to develop more filled bar products, an area of the market where Mars and Nestlé have dominated. The profitability of these products, which usually incorporate a mere coating

Filled Bars Market Share

Brand	Value sales	%
Nestlé Kit Kat	£163.7m	14.3
Mars Bar	£132.4m	11.5
Twix (Mars)	£88.6m	7.7
Snickers (Mars)	£75.5m	6.6
Nestlé Aero	£60.5m	5.3
Bounty (Mars)	£42.1m	3.7
Cadbury's Crunchie	£37.4m	3.3
Cadbury's Time Out	£36.0m	3.1
Milky Way (Mars)	£30.9m	2.7
Cadbury's Caramel	£30.5m	2.7
Total	£1.14bn	

(Value sales to year ending Nov. 98) All outlets (Grocery and Impulse) SOURCE: Information Resources

of chocolate, also attracts Cadbury. For this reason, the company has already put a major marketing effort behind the launch of its recently developed Fuse bar.

Creative marketing has also played an important role in helping Cadbury to retain its market leading position. In 1990, the company opened Cadbury World, the chocolate theme park located at Bournville. Since its opening, the attraction has become a favourite with visitors, and is regularly featured as one of the country's most visited tourist attractions. Six years later the company innovated again, signing a deal to sponsor leading television soap *Coronation Street*. The rationale for the sponsorship was that it would allow the company to promote the overall Cadbury brand. Since 1997, a change in sponsorship rules means that Cadbury has also been able to add various product-specific messages, which it changes at different times of year. For example, Crème Eggs are promoted in the run up to Easter.

The desire for efficient marketing spending also lies behind a more recent move in which Cadbury has created an over-arching family brand for six of its children's confectionery products. The Cadbury Land brand allows Buttons, Curly Wurly, Taz, Chomp, Fudge and Wildlife bars to be marketed under a single banner. The financial advantages are obvious. The company can now save substantially on its advertising costs as one television commercial can be used to promote all six brands at once.

SOURCES: Claire Murphy, "Cadbury's quiet revolution", *Marketing*, 11 February 1999, pp. 24–25; Ian Darby, "Cadbury goes for growth as it imports Yowie brand", *Marketing*, 22 April 1999, p. 4; Lisa Campbell, "Cadbury returns to base", *Marketing*, 17 December 1998, p. 7; "Cadbury Schweppes Public Limited Company", Hoover's Company Capsules, 1997, Hoover's, Inc., Austin, TX; **www.cadbury.co.uk**.

Questions for Discussion

1. Why, as a market leader, must Cadbury continue to innovate?
2. How will an analysis of competitors' strategies assist Cadbury's strategic market planning?
3. Why must Cadbury have a carefully constructed target market strategy?

22 Marketing Planning and Forecasting Sales Potential

"The overall purpose of marketing planning and its principal focus is the identification and creation of sustainable competitive advantage."

Malcolm McDonald
Cranfield University School of Management

O B J E C T I V E S

- To understand the marketing planning process
- To gain an overview of the marketing plan
- To examine the relationship between marketing analysis, marketing strategy and marketing programmes for implementation
- To examine the role of the SWOT analysis in marketing planning
- To become familiar with market and sales potential and sales forecasting methods
- To analyse the major components of a marketing audit

Throughout the 1980s, the retail developers could do no wrong. It seemed that most towns and cities at some point woke up to new shopping centres and office developments. Retailers demanded more sites in the main shopping areas, so the developers used any available land or building opportunity to deliver more retail space. Once this was constructed, it was not unusual for there to be waiting lists of eager retailers for each of the empty units. The developers simply had to persuade the municipal planning authorities to grant planning permission to build and then entice one of the leading magnet retail groups—Marks & Spencer or a department store such as Debenhams—to take an anchor unit to guarantee pedestrian footfall as an inducement to other tenant retailers. Burton Group (Acacia), one of the UK's leading retail groups, went one stage further, establishing the Burton Property Trust to act as a property developer and commissioning five major shopping centre developments. Retailers such as British Shoe Corporation had site assessors touring the streets, responding within hours to a letting agent's notification of a vacant unit. If a speedy decision was not forthcoming, the shoe retailer knew a rival multiple retailer would sign up the site.

Today a different story prevails in most towns. There is far more shop space than there are retailers able and willing to pay the required rents and agree to the lengthy leases. The developers must now market their centres, malls and precincts. Some have opted for the "any tenant" approach simply to guarantee lease income, leading to a confused mix and style of retail units co-existing with one another: up-market fashion adjacent to an "Anything for a £" discounter, or a department store next to an impromptu budget market. The result in such cases is often a dissatisfied mix of tenants and alienated shoppers attempting to understand just who are the targets of the shopping centre development and what the marketing proposition is. For major insurance companies such as the Prudential, which owns and manages many of Europe's leading shopping centres, a need has arisen for more prudent business planning and marketing expertise.

A manager of a major development in the Prudential's portfolio of shopping centres is no longer responsible only for signing up tenants and dealing with legal issues of leases, nor just for instigating security arrangements, negotiating cleaning contracts and setting car parking charges. Such managers now have to analyse the catchment population of the town centre: the types of people, where they come from, how frequently they come, what their spending power is, and what their likes, tastes and needs are. Where else do they shop? Why there? What are the underlying trends and patterns of shopping? Where are the competitive shopping centres? What do they offer? What additional amenities? How do such centres promote themselves? What is their brand proposition and positioning? The Prudential's managers plan for their shopping centre as if they were developing a range of Ford cars. While short term needs must be addressed, so must the longer term requirements of underlying trends and evolving customer expectations. These will have ramifications for the optimum tenant mix, the selection of retailers present, relationships with the municipal authorities, the provision of amenities and car parking. Indeed, modifications will be required in terms of refurbishment, access and tenant mix that require many years of careful planning

and budgeting. In such cases, the formality of marketing planning acts as a welcome framework and guiding managerial process.

SOURCES: "UK steers retailing back to centre of city", *ENR*, 13 November 1995, pp. 22–23; John Fernie, "The coming of the fourth-wave", *International Journal of Retail & Distribution Management*, 23 (1), 1995, pp. 4–11; Jonathan Duckworth, centre manager, West Orchards Shopping Centre, 1996. *Photo*: Rhoda Sidney/Stock Boston.

Manipulation of the marketing mix to match target market needs and expectations constitutes a daily activity for most marketing personnel. However, as explained in the previous chapter and as illustrated in the chapter opener, fundamental strategic decisions need to be addressed before the marketing mix(es) are formulated. To expedite this process and link the strategic decision-making to the development of actionable marketing programmes, many organisations turn to formal marketing planning. Some companies conduct a marketing audit as a preliminary analysis to gain a realistic understanding of the organisation, its personnel and its market. This chapter examines the nature of marketing planning. Like all business activities, marketing needs to have goals; often these are sales targets and market share objectives. To set the right goals, marketers must be able to forecast future sales and market size trends.

This chapter begins with a discussion of the marketing planning process and an overview of the marketing plan. It then discusses the relationship between marketing analysis—including the SWOT analysis—marketing strategy and marketing programmes for implementation. The chapter examines in detail market and sales potential and forecasting techniques for predicting sales before concluding with a discussion of the major components of a marketing audit. Marketing planning is a systematic process involving the assessment of marketing opportunities and resources, the determination of marketing objectives and the development of a plan for implementation and control. A sales forecast is an estimation of the amount of a service or product that an organisation expects to sell during a specific period at a specified level of marketing activities. Market potential is a prediction of industrywide market size, everything else being equal, over a specified time period.

The marketing audit, where applied, is a systematic examination of the objectives, strategies, organisation and performance of a company's marketing unit.

Marketing Planning

Marketing planning A systematic process of assessing marketing opportunities and resources, determining marketing objectives and developing a thorough plan for implementation and control

Marketing plan A document or blueprint detailing requirements for a company's marketing activity

Marketing planning cycle A circular process that runs in two directions, with planning running one way and feedback the other

Marketing planning is a systematic process that involves assessing marketing opportunities and resources, determining marketing objectives and developing a thorough plan for implementation and control. A core output of marketing planning is the **marketing plan,** a document or blueprint that details requirements for a company's marketing activity. The marketing planning process involves analysing the marketplace, modifying the recommended marketing strategy accordingly and developing detailed marketing mix programmes designed to implement the specified marketing strategy.[1]

Figure 22.1 illustrates the **marketing planning cycle.** Note that marketing planning is a circular process. As the dotted feedback lines in the figure indicate, planning is not one way. Feedback is used to co-ordinate and synchronise all the stages of the planning cycle. Most businesses produce marketing plans annually. Once up and running, this process involves revising the previous year's plan by up-dating the essential marketing analyses, revising the recommended strategy

Figure 22.1 The marketing planning cycle

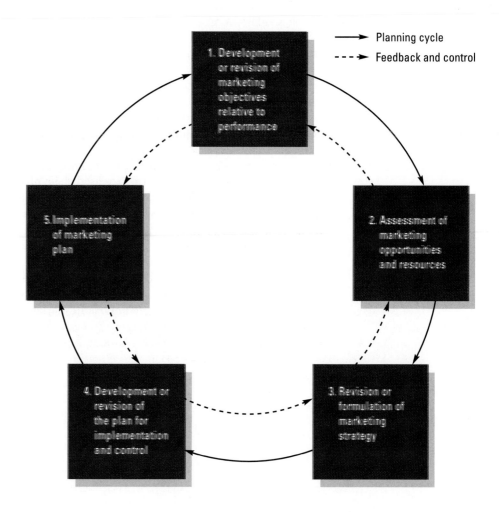

accordingly, before determining detailed marketing mix action plans. The resulting plan normally is presented to the Board for approval before becoming the documented set of actions for sales and marketing personnel to follow.

The duration of marketing plans varies. Plans that cover a period of one year or less are called **short range plans. Medium range plans** are usually for two to five years. Marketing plans that extend beyond five years are generally viewed as **long range plans.** These plans can sometimes cover a period of up to 20 years. Marketing managers may have short, medium and long range plans all at the same time. Long range plans are relatively rare. However, as the marketing environment continues to change and business decisions become more complex, profitability and survival will depend more and more on the development of long range plans.[2] Most marketing plans are revised annually with a detailed three years' perspective.[3] Organisations choose to up-date fully and revise their marketing plans, modifying their marketing programmes and changing the detail of their marketing mix(es) as a result. Overall strategic market planning as described in the previous chapter is unlikely to face annual changes of such magnitude, although strategy modifications will always be needed to respond to changes in customer needs, the marketing environment and competitors' activities.

The extent to which marketing managers develop and use plans also varies. Although planning provides numerous benefits, some managers do not use formal marketing plans because they spend almost all their time dealing with daily problems, many of which would be eliminated by adequate planning. However, planning is becoming more important to marketing managers, who realise that planning is necessary to develop, co-ordinate and control marketing activities effectively and efficiently.[4] When formulating a marketing plan, a new enterprise or a company with a new product does not have current performance to evaluate or an existing plan to revise. Therefore, its marketing planning centres on analysing available resources and options to assess opportunities. Managers can then develop marketing objectives and a strategy. In addition, many businesses recognise the need to include information systems in their plans so that they can have continuous feedback and keep their marketing activities oriented towards objectives. One research study, which examined 207 different companies, found that those that had maintained or increased their planning departments during the past five years and had increased their allocation of resources to planning activities out-performed those whose planning departments had become smaller.[5] Sound marketing planning enabled Citroën to establish its Xantia range in the fleet car market: the company's first significant success in this highly competitive segment (see Figure 22.2).

To illustrate the marketing planning process, consider the decisions that went into the planning in the United States of the national newspaper *USA Today.* Table 22.1 lists several of the more important marketing decisions. Of course, to reach the objective, a detailed course of action was communicated throughout the organisation. In short, specific marketing plans should do the following:

1. Specify expected results so that the organisation can anticipate what its situation will be at the end of the current planning period.
2. Identify the resources needed to carry out the planned activities so that a budget can be developed.
3. Describe in sufficient detail the activities that are to take place so that responsibilities for implementation can be assigned and schedules determined.

Short range plans   Plans that cover a period of one year or less

Medium range plans   Plans that usually cover two to five years

Long range plans   Plans that extend beyond five years

Figure 22.2 The importance of marketing planning. Shrewd marketing planning enabled Citroën's Xantia to compete effectively in the fleet car market.
Source: Courtesy of Citroën/Euro/RSCG.

4. Provide for the monitoring of activities and the results so that control can be exerted.[6]
5. Lead to the implementation of the organisation's marketing strategy.
6. Be in line with customer needs and market developments.
7. Emphasise any differential advantage or business strength over rivals.

There is a logical and relatively straightforward approach to the process of marketing planning:

1. Analysis of markets and the trading environment.
2. Determination of core target markets.
3. Identification of a differential advantage (competitive edge).
4. Statement of specific goals and desired product or service positioning.
5. Development of marketing mixes to implement plans.
6. Determination of required budgets and allocation of marketing tasks.
7. Monitoring of performance and evolving market conditions.

Objective: Achieve 1 million in circulation by reaching an up-market segment, primarily of males who hold professional and managerial positions and who made at least one trip of 200 miles or more within the last year.

Opportunity: Paper tends to be a second newspaper purchase for readers. *USA Today* is not in competition directly with local papers, and it is not positioned against other national newspapers/magazines.

Market: Circulation within a 200 mile radius of 15 major markets, representing 54 per cent of the US population, including such cities as Chicago, Houston, New York, Los Angeles and Denver.

Product: Superior graphic quality; appeal to the television generation through short news items, a colour weather map and other contemporary features.

Price: Competitive.

Promotion: Pedestal-like vending machines with attention grabbing design and a higher position than competitors to differentiate the paper and bring it closer to eye level. Outdoor advertising and some print advertising promotes the paper.

Distribution: News stands, vending machines in busy locations, direct mail and hotel distribution.

Implementational and Control: Personnel with experience in the newspaper business who can assist in developing a systematic approach for implementing the marketing strategy and design, as well as an information system to monitor and control the results.

SOURCE: Kevin Higgins, "*USA Today* nears million reader mark", *Marketing News*, 15 April 1983, pp. 1, 5. Reprinted by permission of the American Marketing Association.

Table 22.2 illustrates these aspects of the marketing planning process in more detail. A good marketing plan addresses each of these aspects thoroughly and objectively, ensuring its heart is truly customer focused.

Obviously, the marketing plan document needs to be carefully written to attain these objectives. The next section of this chapter takes a closer look at the marketing plan itself.

The Marketing Plan

The marketing plan is the written document or blueprint governing all of a business's marketing activities, including the implementation and control of those activities.[7] A marketing plan serves a number of purposes:

1. It offers a "road map" for implementing a company's strategies and achieving its objectives.
2. It assists in management control and monitoring of implementation of strategy.
3. It informs new participants in the plan of their role and function.
4. It specifies how resources are to be allocated.
5. It stimulates thinking and makes better use of resources.
6. It assigns responsibilities, tasks and timing.
7. It makes participants aware of problems, opportunities and threats.
8. It assists in ensuring that an organisation is customer focused, aware of market and competitive movements, realistic in its expectations and prudent in its use of resources.

Table 22.2 The core steps of the marketing planning process

Analysis

The marketing environment and trends

Company's Strengths, Weaknesses, Opportunities and Threats (SWOT)

Customers' needs, buying behaviour and perceptions; market segmentation and brand positioning

Competition and competitors' strategies

Marketing opportunities

The balance of the product portfolio and ABC sales: contribution analysis

Strategy

Determination of core target markets; basis for competing/differential advantage; desired product/brand positioning; marketing objectives and sales targets

Programmes for Implementation

Specification of sales targets and expected results

Specification of plans for marketing mix programmes:

- products
- promotion
- place/distribution
- people (service) levels
- pricing

Specification of tasks/responsibilities; timing; costs; budgets

Ongoing work

Monitoring progress and benchmarking performance

SOURCE: Sally Dibb and Lyndon Simkin, *The Marketing Planning Workbook* (London: Routledge, 1996). Reprinted with permission.

A company should have a plan for each marketing strategy it develops. Because such plans must be changed as forces in the company and in the environment change, marketing planning is a continuous process.

Organisations use many different formats when devising marketing plans. Plans may be written for strategic business units, product lines, individual products or brands, or specific markets. Most plans share some common ground, however, by including an executive summary; a statement of objectives; background to the market; market analysis and examination of realistic marketing opportunities (a description of environmental forces, customers' needs, market segments and internal capabilities); competitor activity; an outline of marketing strategy, target market priorities, differential advantage, brand and product positioning; a statement of expected sales patterns; the detail of marketing mixes required to implement the marketing plan; controls; financial requirements and budgets; and any operational considerations that arise from the marketing plan (see Table 22.3). The following sections consider the major parts of a typical marketing plan, as well as the purpose that each part serves.

Management or Executive Summary

The *management summary,* or *executive summary* (often only one or two pages) should be a concise overview of the entire report, including key aims, overall strategies, fundamental conclusions and salient points regarding the suggested marketing mix programmes. Not many people read an entire report, tending to dip in here and there, so the management summary should be comprehensive and clear.

Table 22.3   Parts of a
marketing plan

1. **Management or Executive Summary**
2. **Marketing Objectives**
   a. Company mission statement
   b. Detailed company objectives
   c. Product group goals
3. **Product/Market Background**
   a. Product range and explanation
   b. Market overview and sales summary
   c. ABC sales: contribution financial performance assessment
   d. Directional policy matrix evaluation of the product portfolio
4. **Marketing Analyses**
   a. Marketing environment and trends
   b. Customers' needs and segments
   c. Competition and competitors' strategies
   d. Strengths, Weaknesses, Opportunities, Threats (SWOT) analysis
5. **Marketing Strategies**
   a. Core target markets (segments)
   b. Basis for competing/differential advantage
   c. Desired product/brand positioning
6. **Statement of Expected Sales Forecasts and Results**
7. **Marketing Programmes for Implementation**
   a. Marketing mixes
   b. Tasks and responsibilities
8. **Controls and Evaluation: Monitoring of Performance**
9. **Financial Implications/Required Budgets**
   a. Delineation of costs
   b. Expected returns on investment for implementing the marketing plan
10. **Operational Considerations**
    a. Personnel and internal marketing relationships and communications
    b. Research and development/production needs
    c. Marketing information system
11. **Appendices**
    a. SWOT analysis details
    b. Background data and information
    c. Marketing research findings

SOURCE: Sally Dibb and Lyndon Simkin, *The Marketing Planning Workbook* (London: Routledge, 1994). Reprinted with permission.

Marketing Objectives

Marketing objective   A statement of what is to be accomplished through marketing activities

Objectives are for the benefit of the reader, such as senior executives, to give perspective to the report. Aims and objectives should be stated briefly but should include reference to the organisation's mission statement (corporate goals), objectives and any fundamental desires for core product groups or brands. This section describes the objectives underlying the plan. A **marketing objective** is a statement of what is to be accomplished through marketing activities. It specifies the results expected from marketing efforts. A marketing objective should be expressed in clear, simple terms so that all marketing personnel understand exactly what they are trying to achieve. It should be written in such a way that its accomplishment can be measured accurately. If a company has an objective of increasing its market share by 12 per cent, the company should be able to measure changes in its market share accurately. A marketing objective should also [specify a ti]meframe for accomplishing the objective. For example, a company [with an o]bjective of introducing three new products should state the time [by whic]h this is to be done.

[An objective] may be stated in terms of degree of product introduction or inno[vation, sales v]olume, profitability per unit, gains in market share or improve[ment in cust]omer satisfaction or awareness of the company's products and [brands. It] must also be consistent with the company's overall organisational [goals.]

[The marke]t background is a necessary section. Not everyone will be fully [aware of t]he products and their markets. This section "scene sets", helping [everyone—f]or example, a chief executive or advertising manager—to under[stand the mark]eting plan.

[This sec]tion is the heart of the marketing planning exercise: if incomplete [or defe]ctive, the recommendations are likely to be based on an inaccurate [view of the ma]rket and the company's potential. Marketing Insight 22.1 exam[ines how Sainsb]ury has utilised analysis to modify its whole marketing strategy. [Analysis gi]ves a sound foundation to the recommendations and market[ing strategie]s. It includes analyses of the marketing environment, market [trends, buye]rs, competitors, competitive positions and competitors' strategies, [a review o]f the business's product portfolio and the financial performance [of products,] market segments and even certain customers. The market attractiveness-business position model and the ABC sales: contribution analysis detailed in the previous chapter are popular tools employed by marketers to assess portfolio and performance.

The marketing environment section of the marketing plan describes the current state of the marketing environment, including the legal, political, regulatory, technological, societal/green, and economic and competitive forces, as well as ethical considerations. It also makes predictions about future directions of those forces. For example, the retailer Safeway was among the first to respond to consumer concern about the use of artificial fertilisers and pesticides. It offered its customers a choice of either regular fruit and vegetables or organically grown produce at a higher price.

As mentioned in Chapter 2, environmental forces can hamper an organisation in achieving its objectives. This section of the plan also describes the possible impact of these forces on the implementation of the marketing plan. Most marketing plans include extensive analyses of competitive, legal and regulatory forces, perhaps even creating separate sections for these influential forces of the marketing environment. It is important to note here that because the forces of the marketing environment are dynamic, marketing plans should be reviewed and modified periodically to adjust to change.

Marketing exists to enable an organisation to meet customers' needs properly. This is particularly true in the marketing planning process. The views, needs and expectations of current and potential customers are important as a basis for formal marketing planning. Without such an understanding and analysis of likely changes in customer requirements, it is impossible to safely target those markets of most benefit to the organisation's fortunes. It is also impossible to specify a correct marketing mix (or mixes).

The analysis of the marketing environment includes competitive forces and trends. As explained in the previous chapter, however, a meaningful marketing plan and associated programmes for implementation necessitate a prior comprehensive analysis of an organisation's competitive position in its markets and territories, together with an understanding of rival organisation's marketing strategies. The failure to understand or anticipate competitors' likely actions is a major weakness in most businesses.[8]

The *SWOT analysis* is an important foundation for any marketing plan, helping to produce realistic and meaningful recommendations. The section in the main body of the report should be kept to a concise overview, with detailed market-by-market or country-by-country SWOTS—and their full explanations—kept to the appendices. Many marketers conduct a **SWOT analysis:** Strengths, Weaknesses, Opportunities, Threats. The first half of this analysis—strengths and weaknesses—examines the company's position, or that of its product, vis-à-vis customers, competitor activity, environmental trends and company resources. The second half of the SWOT takes this review further to examine the opportunities and threats identified and to make recommendations that feed into marketing strategy and the marketing mix. The marketing environment analysis often reveals probable opportunities and threats. The result of the SWOT analysis should be a thorough understanding of the organisation's status and its standing in its markets. A SWOT analysis must be objective, with evidence provided to support the points cited. The focus should be on issues likely to concern customers.

SWOT analysis Analysis that determines a company's position by examining four factors: Strengths, Weaknesses, Opportunities and Threats

Marketing Strategies

Strategies should be self-evident if the analyses have been objective and thorough: which target markets are most beneficial to the company, what is to be the basis for competing and differential advantage or competitive edge in these markets, and what is the desired product or brand positioning. This strategy statement must be realistic and detailed enough to act upon.

This section of the marketing plan provides a broad overview of the plan for achieving the marketing objectives and, ultimately, the organisational goals. Marketing strategy focuses on defining a target market and developing a marketing mix to gain long run competitive and consumer advantages. There is a degree of overlap between corporate strategy and marketing strategy. Marketing strategy is unique in that it has the responsibility to assess buyer needs and the company's potential for gaining competitive advantage, both of which ultimately must guide the corporate mission.[9] In other words, marketing strategy guides the company's direction in relationships between customers and competitors. The bottom line is that a marketing strategy must be consistent with consumer needs, perceptions and beliefs. Thus this section should describe the company's intended target market and how product, people, promotion, place/distribution and price will be used to develop a product or brand positioning that will satisfy the needs of members of the target market.

Michael Porter[10] describes three **generic competitive strategies,** which he maintains help companies to achieve industry success (see Figure 22.3). The first is *cost leadership,* in which low cost producers exploit experience curve effects to achieve market penetration. The key is the development of a low cost structure allowing high returns even when competition is intense. Amstrad, Aldi and Texas Instruments have successfully operated as cost leaders. *Differentiation,* the sec-

Generic competitive strategies Strategies that help companies achieve industry success, including cost leadership, differentiation and focus

Cadbury's Managing for Value Programme

Cadbury Schweppes, one of the world's leading manufacturers of soft drinks and confectionery, has been re-appraising its marketing approach. Through the Managing for Value (MFV) Programme, the business is changing the way it prioritises its marketing budget. In simple terms, the MFV approach is designed to ensure that promotion is focused on the most profitable brands and that marketing investment generally is aimed only at profitable new and existing products.

At Cadbury, the chocolate arm of the Cadbury Schweppes business, the MFV programme is changing the way that marketers within the business work. The notion of *return on capital employed* has become an important maxim for all. For example, it is no longer sufficient for marketing managers to justify promotional spend on the basis that it wins market share from the likes of Mars or Nestlé. Now they must also understand the cost and production implications of their proposals and be able to show how expenditure contributes to market share and earnings.

Throughout the 1980s and the start of the 1990s, Cadbury Schweppes had a clear strategy of increasing market share. In order to achieve the kind of global dominance it was seeking, the company engaged in a series of high profile acquisitions. However, shareholders became uneasy as the value of shares was reduced. As a result, in 1997, the company set up its MFV programme. The CEO described the initiative as "the most comprehensive and group-wide commitment to strategic change and management process ever undertaken in Cadbury Schweppes".

According to one business analyst: "In the short term, Managing for Value may mean that Cadbury loses market share. But the process of identifying and then supporting only those brands which will make Cadbury profitable will yield it more value in the long term." Already there have been a number of casualties of the MFV approach. Production of Trebor Bassett Wiggley Worms, a jelly based product targeted at children, has already been halted. The problem was that the profit potential of the product was insufficient to justify the amount of shelf space it took up.

Meanwhile, the fortunes of some of the company's lower profile products have been restored as a result of MFV. Fry's Turkish Delight, a major brand in the 1970s, is one of the winners from the new strategy. Many consumers were delighted to see the return of the "Touch of Paradise" advertisements, which last ran in the 1970s. Cadbury decided to invest in a major promotional push for the brand because analysis highlighted its excellent profit potential. This is due to the relatively low chocolate content (and therefore low ingredient cost) of the Turkish Delight bar.

In general, Cadbury produces block chocolate brands such as Dairy Milk, Fruit and Nut and Whole Nut. These products are costly to manufacture because they use a great deal of cocoa beans, which are expensive. Now the MFV programme has encouraged the company to produce new products which have a thinner covering of chocolate. Competitors like Mars, which produces filled bars such as Mars, Bounty and Snickers, have been following this approach for many years. Cadbury's new Fuse bar, like Turkish Delight, is an example of a low chocolate product which the company hopes will prove successful in this area of the market. Despite the success of this new product launch and the good record which Cadbury has in developing new offerings, managers know that the company needs to focus particularly on the filled bar market.

Although it is clear that MFV will make the decisions associated with new product launches more complex, the company believes that this is justified. Ultimately, managers hope that the result will be a greater chance of success in the marketplace.

SOURCES: Claire Murphy, "Cadbury's quiet revolution", *Marketing,* 11 February 1999, pp. 24–25; Lisa Campbell, "Cadbury returns to base", *Marketing,* 17 December 1998, p. 7; Cadbury Schweppes Public Limited Company, Hoover's Company Capsules, 1997, Hoover's, Inc., Austin, TX; **www.cadbury.co.uk**.

ond generic competitive strategy, involves companies developing a product or service that is unique or superior in some way. Products with this quality, whether in terms of features, image or design, often have higher than average prices. Sony stereos and Raleigh bicycles are both examples of products for which a high price can be demanded. Indeed, the price of items like these is part of the products'

Figure 22.3 Generic routes to competitive advantage. SOURCE: Based on M. E. Porter, *Competitive Strategy: Techniques for Analysing Industries and Competitors* (New York: Free Press, 1980). From *Distance Learning MBA Notes,* Warwick Business School, 1987.

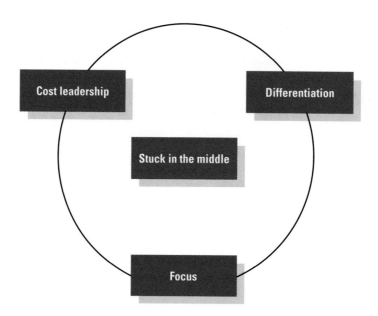

character and ethos. The final generic competitive strategy is *focus,* in which companies concentrate their efforts on particular segments of the market. In some instances this is because there are insufficient resources to compete on a larger scale. Focus allows companies like Rolex and Porsche to service particular sub-groups of customers in the watch and car markets. Although focusing has its attractions in terms of gearing the marketing mix to a quite specific and narrow customer target, the associated risks are high. The danger is that, if attacked head-on, such highly specialised companies may find it difficult to develop alternative competencies. Porter warns against companies becoming "stuck in the middle" of the three strategies. If this happens, he argues, customers may not have a good reason for purchasing a company's products or services.

Expected Results

Having highlighted the strategic thrust and intention, it is important to explain the *expected results* and sales volumes to show why the strategies should be followed. These forecasts should be quantified—typically as expected units of sales and possible market shares. This stage is important if the required marketing mix budgets are to be approved by senior managers.

Marketing Programmes for Implementation

Marketing programme recommendations are the culmination of the various analyses and statements of strategies: exactly what needs to be done, how and why. This is the detailed presentation of the proposed marketing mixes to achieve the goals and implement the strategies. In poor marketing plans, there is a lack of analysis and strategy, with the focus falling on the tactical marketing mix recommendations. Robust planning requires the recommendation of detailed marketing mixes, but only after time has been taken to thoroughly address the core marketing analyses and determine a detailed marketing strategy.

Each market segment to be targeted may require its own, tailor made marketing mix. This section of the marketing plan is of paramount importance, as it gives the specific details of the marketing activity required to implement the marketing plan and to achieve the organisation's strategic goals. Each element of the marketing mix should be discussed in turn, with specific recommendations explained in sufficient detail to enable managers to put them into action. Product, people (service), pricing, place/distribution and promotion must all be addressed. Associated tasks should be allocated to personnel and responsibilities for action clearly identified. This is the core output of marketing planning: the detailed plan of action for the business's marketing programmes.

Controls and Evaluation

It is essential that *controls* be established along with measures to assess the on-going implementation of the marketing plan. This section details how the results of the plan will be measured. For example, the results of an advertising campaign designed to increase market share may be measured in terms of increases in sales volume or improved brand recognition and acceptance by consumers. Next, a schedule for comparing the results achieved with the objectives set forth in the marketing plan is developed. Finally, guidelines may be offered outlining who is responsible for monitoring the programme and taking remedial action. Financial measures such as sales volumes, profitability and market shares will be included. "Softer" issues such as brand awareness and customer satisfaction should also be monitored.[11]

Financial Implications/Required Budgets

The full picture may not be known, but an indication of required resources and the *financial implications* must be given. The financial projections and budgets section outlines the returns expected through implementation of the plan. The costs incurred will be weighed against expected revenues. A budget must be prepared to allocate resources in order to accomplish marketing objectives. It should contain estimates of the costs of implementing the plan, including the costs of advertising, salesforce training and remuneration, development of distribution channels and marketing research.

Operational Considerations

These strategies and marketing programmes may have ramifications for other product groups, sectors or territories, for research and development, for engineering or production and so on. The *operational implications* must be highlighted, but too much detail may be inappropriate and politically sensitive within the organisation.

Appendices

The main body of the report should be as concise as possible. The document must, though, tell the full story and include evidence and statistics that support the strategies and marketing programmes being recommended. The use of *appendices*—so long as they are fully cross-referenced in the main body of the report—helps to keep the report concise and well focused.

Market and Sales Potential and Sales Forecasting

Unfortunately, many organisations' sales and marketing activities are reactions to changes in the marketplace, particularly the actions of competitors, rather than planned and carefully orchestrated activities that anticipate consumer needs and expectations. In such reactive organisations, predictions of future changes in market size and potential tend to be rudimentary or non-existent. Estimations of their own likely sales are often based only on the hunches of managers or on the status quo. The forecasting of market potential and expected sales is problematic but must be undertaken thoroughly and with as much objectivity as marketing intelligence and information permit. Forecasts are integral to robust marketing planning. They are also pivotal to shrewd budgeting and the allocation of promotional mix budgets. As explored in Chapter 23, monitoring performance is an essential part of the marketing process. Without an assessment of likely sales, it is difficult to evaluate performance. This section focuses on market and sales potential and on sales forecasting techniques.

Market and Sales Potential

Market potential The total amount of a product that customers will purchase within a specified period of time at a specific level of industry-wide marketing activity

Market potential is the total amount of a product that customers will purchase within a specified period of time at a specific level of industry-wide marketing activity. Market potential can be stated in terms of monetary value or units and can refer to a total market or to a market segment. As shown in Figure 22.4, market potential depends on economic, social and other marketing environment factors. When analysing market potential, it is important to specify a timeframe and to indicate the relevant level of industry marketing activities. One airline determined that in one year 3,300,000 customers travelled to Europe on its aircraft—more customers than any other airline had. Based on this finding, its marketers were able to estimate the market potential for European travel in the following year, taking into account other environmental factors and market trends. Before investing heavily on new rides, theme park leader Alton Towers carefully assesses likely sales (see Marketing Insight 22.2).

Marketers have to assume a certain general level of marketing effort in the industry when they estimate market potential. The specific level of marketing effort certainly varies from one company to another, but the sum of all companies' marketing activities equals industry marketing efforts. A marketing manager must also consider whether and to what extent industry marketing efforts will change. For instance, in estimating the market potential for the spreadsheet software industry, Microsoft must consider changes in marketing efforts by Lotus and other software producers. If marketing managers at Microsoft know that

Figure 22.4 The relationship between market potential, sales potential and sales forecast.
SOURCE: Based on M. E. Porter, *Competitive Strategy: Techniques for Analysing Industries and Competitors* (New York: Free Press, 1980). From *Distance Learning MBA Notes*, Warwick Business School, 1987.

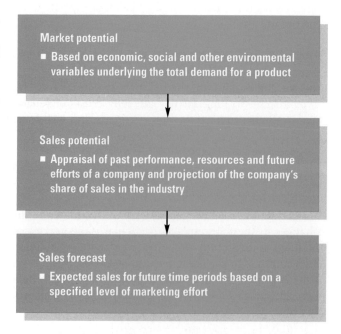

Market potential
- Based on economic, social and other environmental variables underlying the total demand for a product

Sales potential
- Appraisal of past performance, resources and future efforts of a company and projection of the company's share of sales in the industry

Sales forecast
- Expected sales for future time periods based on a specified level of marketing effort

Planning for More Than a Day Out—Alton Towers

The theme park is a leisure park consisting of rides and attractions built around a central theme or themes. Walt Disney created the concept in the United States, and the Disney Corporation has since taken the concept to Japan and now to France. The UK theme park industry really took off in the early 1980s. By 1989, 9.5 million visitors had spent £105 million. Current figures estimate that by 2000, 16 million visitors would have spent £250 million in the UK, although the opening of the Paris Disney World and of the Channel Tunnel would have some bearing on these figures. The top five theme parks in the UK are listed below:

	Per Cent of Day Trippers
Museums and galleries	33.0
Historic properties	22.5
Wildlife attractions	10.0
Theme parks	5.5
Gardens	4.0
Other (seaside resorts, holiday centres, etc.)	25.0

	Visitors (millions)
Alton Towers	2.65
Chessington World of Adventure	1.3
Thorpe Park	1.3
Frontierland	1.3
The American Adventure	0.7

Not only do theme parks compete with one another, though geographically many cater for purely local markets, they also compete with a whole range of day trip activities (see table in right column).

Despite various economic blips and global troubles such as those in Iraq, the Balkans and parts of Africa, all economic indicators point to an increase in leisure time and in discretionary income. Alton Towers aims to maintain its market leadership and continually invests in new rides and facilities. It opened a £20 million holiday village next to the park (for the leisure and business conference markets) and spent £10 million on the leading white knuckle Oblivion ride. The strategy is to attract new visitors in the UK and from Continental Europe, while encouraging repeat visits from current users. Key targets are young adults aged 15 to 24, families with children, school parties and, increasingly, the corporate sector for sales incentive schemes and corporate events (AGMs, product launches, salesforce parties and so on). The corporate sector was a leading reason for developing good quality on-site hotel accommodation. Each segment has its own marketing mix and strategy: separate price policies, promotional tactics and even product offerings. Originally conceived as a day tripper, family oriented park, Alton Towers has monitored demographic changes and competitor activity and is planning to cater for its key segments' differing needs well into the next century, with more hotels, entertainment, under-cover rides, events and improved access. Even rock concerts are now staged in the park's open air arena. No changes to the site are made without researching visitors' needs and market trends or thorough marketing planning.

SOURCES: British Tourist Authority, 1999; "Visits to tourist attractions", Alton Towers' promotional material, 1996; "CCSB names its Nemesis after roller coaster", *Marketing*, 10 March 1994, p. 6; "Santa's thoughtful sackful", *Professional Engineering*, 7 (21), 1994, p. 9.; Alton Towers, 1999; Bryan Adams web site, 1999.

Lotus is planning to introduce a new version of the Lotus 1-2-3 spreadsheet product with a new advertising campaign, this fact will contribute to Microsoft's estimate of the market potential for computer software.

Sales potential is the maximum percentage of market potential that an individual company within an industry can expect to obtain for a specific product or service (see Figure 22.4). Several general factors influence a company's sales potential. First, the market potential places absolute limits on the size of the

Sales potential The maximum percentage of market potential that an individual company can obtain for a specific product or service

company's sales potential. Second, the magnitude of industry-wide marketing activities has an indirect but definite impact on the company's sales potential. Those activities have a direct bearing on the size of the market potential. When Pizza Hut advertises home delivered pizza, for example, it indirectly promotes pizza in general; its advertisements may, in fact, also help sell competitors' home delivered pizza. Third, the intensity and effectiveness of a company's marketing activities relative to those of its competitors affect the size of the company's sales potential. If a company is spending twice as much as any of its competitors on marketing efforts and if every unit of currency spent is more effective in generating sales, the company's sales potential will be quite high compared with that of its competitors.

There are two general approaches to measuring sales potential: break down and build up. In the **break down approach,** the marketing manager first develops a general economic forecast for a specific time period. Next, market potential is estimated on the basis of this economic forecast. The company's sales potential is then derived from the general economic forecast and the estimate of market potential.

In the **build up approach,** an analyst begins by estimating how much of a product a potential buyer in a specific geographic area, such as a sales territory, will purchase in a given period. Then the analyst multiplies that amount by the total number of potential buyers in that area. The analyst performs the same calculation for each geographic area in which the company sells products and then adds the totals for each area to calculate the market potential. To determine the sales potential, the analyst must estimate, by specific levels of marketing activities, the proportion of the total market potential that the company can obtain.

For example, the marketing manager of a regional paper company with three competitors might estimate the company's sales potential for bulk gift wrapping paper using the build up approach. The manager might determine that each of the 66 paper buyers in a single sales territory purchases an average of 10 rolls annually. For that sales territory, then, the market potential is 660 rolls annually. The analyst follows the same procedure for each of the business's other nine sales territories and then totals the market potential for each sales territory (see Table 22.4). Assuming that this total market potential is 6,000 rolls of paper (the quantity expected to be sold by all four paper companies), the marketing manager would estimate the company's sales potential by ascertaining that it could sell about 33 per cent of the estimated 6,000 rolls at a certain level of marketing effort (2,000 rolls). The marketing manager might develop several sales potentials, based on several levels of marketing effort.

Whether marketers use the break down or the build up approach, they depend heavily on sales estimates. To gain a clearer idea of how these estimates are derived, it is essential to understand sales forecasting.

Developing Sales Forecasts

A **sales forecast** is the amount of a product that the company actually expects to sell during a specific period of time at a specified level of marketing activities (see Figure 22.4). The sales forecast differs from the sales potential: it concentrates on what the actual sales will be at a certain level of marketing effort, whereas the sales potential assesses what sales are possible at various levels of marketing activities, based on certain environmental conditions. Businesses use the sales forecast for planning, organising, implementing and controlling their activities. The success of numerous activities depends on the accuracy of this forecast. Forecasts help to estimate market attractiveness, monitor performances, allocate resources effectively and efficiently, and gear up production to meet demand.

Break down approach An approach that derives a company's sales potential from the general economic forecast and the estimate of market potential

Build up approach An approach that measures the sales potential for a product by first calculating its market potential and then estimating what proportion of that potential the company can expect to obtain

Sales forecast The amount of a product that the company actually expects to sell during a specific period of time at a specific level of marketing activities

Table 22.4 The market potential calculations for bulk wrapping paper

Territory	Number of Potential Customers	Estimated Purchases	Total
1	66	10 rolls	660 rolls
2	62	10	620
3	55	5	275
4	28	25	700
5	119	5	595
6	50	20	1,000
7	46	10	460
8	34	15	510
9	63	10	630
10	55	10	550
		Total market potential	6,000 rolls

Excess stocks are wasteful and cost money; but production set too low leads to missed sales, and perhaps customer or distributor unease.[12]

A sales forecast must be time-specific. Sales projections can be short (one year or less), medium (one to five years) or long (longer than five years). The length of time chosen for the sales forecast depends on the purpose and uses of the forecast, the stability of the market, and the company's objectives and resources.

To forecast sales, a marketer can choose from a number of forecasting methods. Some of them are arbitrary; others are more scientific, complex and time consuming. A business's choice of method or methods depends on the costs involved, the type of product, the characteristics of the market, the time span of the forecast, the purposes of the forecast, the stability of the historical sales data, the availability of required information and the forecasters' expertise and experience.[13] The common forecasting techniques fall into five categories: executive judgement, surveys, time series analysis, correlation methods and market tests.[14]

Executive Judgement At times, a company forecasts sales chiefly on the basis of **executive judgement**, which is the intuition of one or more executives. This approach is highly unscientific but expedient and inexpensive. Executive judgement may work reasonably well when product demand is relatively stable and the forecaster has years of market related experience. However, because intuition is swayed most heavily by recent experience, the forecast may be overly optimistic or overly pessimistic. Another drawback to intuition is that the forecaster has only past experience as a guide for deciding where to go in the future.

Executive judgement A way of forecasting sales based on the intuition of one or more executives

Surveys A second way to forecast sales is to use **surveys**, questioning customers, sales personnel or experts regarding their expectations about future purchases.

Through a **customer forecasting survey**, marketers can ask customers what types and quantities of products they intend to buy during a specific period of time. This approach may be useful to a business that has relatively few customers. For example, a computer chip producer that markets to less than a hundred computer manufacturers could conduct a customer survey. PepsiCo, though, has millions of consumers and cannot feasibly use a customer survey to forecast future

Surveys A method of questioning customers, sales personnel or experts regarding their expectations about future purchases

Customer forecasting survey A method of asking customers what types and quantities of products they intend to buy during a specific period of time

sales, unless its sampling is known to reflect the entire market, which is hard to verify, or it is polling the views of its main distributors.

Customer surveys have several drawbacks. Customers must be able and willing to make accurate estimates of future product requirements. Although industrial buyers can sometimes estimate their anticipated purchases accurately from historical buying data and their own sales forecasts, many cannot make such estimates. In addition, for a variety of reasons, customers may not want to take part in a survey. Occasionally, a few respondents give answers that they know are incorrect, making survey results inaccurate. Moreover, customer surveys reflect buying intentions, not actual purchases. Customers' intentions may not be well formulated, and even when potential purchasers have definite buying intentions, they do not necessarily follow through with them. A common marketing research problem is probing consumers about their actual purchasing and consumption behaviour as opposed to their perceptions or anticipated behaviour. Finally, customer surveys consume much time and money.

Salesforce forecasting survey
A method of asking members of a company's salesforce to estimate the anticipated sales in their territories for a specified period of time

In a **salesforce forecasting survey**, members of the company's salesforce are asked to estimate the anticipated sales in their territories for a specified period of time. The forecaster combines these territorial estimates to arrive at a tentative forecast. (See Figure 22.5.)

A marketer may survey the sales staff for several reasons. The most important one is that the sales staff are closer to customers on a daily basis than other company personnel; therefore they should know more about customers' future product needs. Moreover, when sales representatives assist in developing the forecast,

Figure 22.5 Graphical presentations of forecasts and sales. Visual depictions of sales and profits are popular in marketing plan documents.

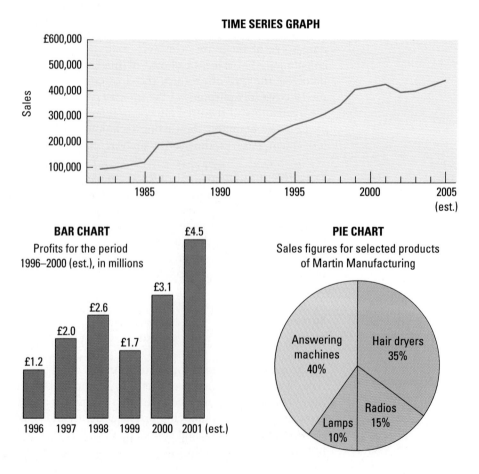

they are more likely to work towards its achievement. Another advantage of this method is that forecasts can be prepared for single territories, for divisions consisting of several territories, for regions made up of multiple divisions and then for the total geographic market. Thus the method readily provides sales forecasts from the smallest geographic sales unit to the largest.

Despite these benefits, a salesforce survey has certain limitations. Salespeople can be too optimistic or pessimistic because of recent experiences. In addition, salespeople tend to under-estimate the sales potential in their territories when they believe that their sales goals will be determined by their forecasts. They also dislike paperwork because it takes up the time that could be spent selling. If the preparation of a territorial sales forecast is time consuming, the sales staff may not do the job adequately.

Nonetheless, salesforce surveys can be effective under certain conditions. If, for instance, the salespeople as a group are accurate—or at least consistent—estimators, the over estimates and under-estimates should balance each other out. If the aggregate forecast is consistently over or under actual sales, then the marketer who develops the final forecast can make the necessary adjustments. Assuming that the survey is well administered, the salesforce can have the satisfaction of helping to establish reasonable sales goals. It can also be assured that its forecasts are not being used to set sales quotas.

The **Delphi method** is very popular: managers' and sales personnel's views are validated centrally, and the resulting forecasts are returned to those involved for further comment. Participants—such as field managers—make separate, individual forecasts. A central analyst independently aggregates and modifies their forecasts. This revised forecast is returned to the separate participants, who can then amend their forecasts in the context of the consolidated picture. The central analyst then collates the up-dated forecasts to produce the company's overall final forecast. The Delphi technique avoids many weighting and judgemental problems; the median of the group's overall response will tend to be more accurate; and the approach is useful for short, medium and long term forecasts, as well as for new product development, for which there is no historical information on which to base a forecast.

When a company wants an **expert forecasting survey**, it hires experts to help prepare the sales forecast. These experts are usually economists, management consultants, advertising executives, academics or other people outside the company who have solid experience in a specific market. Drawing on this experience and their analyses of available information about the company and the market, the experts prepare and present their forecasts or answer questions regarding a forecast. Using experts is expedient and relatively inexpensive. However, because they work outside the company, experts may not be as motivated as company personnel to do an effective job.

Time Series Analysis The technique by which the forecaster, using the company's historical sales data, tries to discover a pattern or patterns in the company's sales over time is called **time series analysis**. If a pattern is found, it can be used to forecast sales. This forecasting method assumes that the past sales pattern will continue in the future. The accuracy, and thus the usefulness, of time series analysis hinges on the validity of this assumption.

In a time series analysis, a forecaster usually performs four types of analysis: trend, cycle, seasonal and random factor.[15] **Trend analysis** focuses on aggregate sales data, such as a company's annual sales figures, over a period of many years to determine whether annual sales are generally rising, falling or staying about

Delphi method A centralised forecasting method that takes into account the views of managers, sales personnel and individual participants; aggregates them; and modifies them

Expert forecasting survey A survey prepared by outside experts such as economists, management consultants, advertising executives or academics

Time series analysis A forecasting technique that uses a company's historical sales data to discover a pattern or patterns in the company's sales over time

Trend analysis Analysis that focuses on aggregate sales data over a period of many years to determine whether annual sales are generally rising, falling or constant

the same. Through **cycle analysis,** a forecaster analyses sales figures (often monthly sales data) over a period of three to five years to ascertain whether sales fluctuate in a consistent, periodic manner. When performing **seasonal analysis,** the analyst studies daily, weekly or monthly sales figures to evaluate the degree to which seasonal factors, such as climate and holiday activities, influence the company's sales. **Random factor analysis** is an attempt to attribute erratic sales variations to random, non-recurring events, such as a regional power failure, a natural disaster or political unrest in a foreign market. After performing each of these analyses, the forecaster combines the results to develop the sales forecast.

Time series analysis is an effective forecasting method for products with reasonably stable demand, but it is not useful for products with highly erratic demand. Seagram, the importer and producer of spirits and wines, uses several types of time series analysis for forecasting and has found them quite accurate. For example, Seagram's forecasts of industry sales volume have proved correct within ± 1.5 per cent, and the company's sales forecasts have been accurate within ± 2 per cent.[16] However, time series analysis is not always so dependable.

Correlation Methods Like time series analysis, correlation methods are based on historical sales data. When using **correlation methods,**[17] the forecaster attempts to find a relationship between past sales and one or more variables such as population, per capita income or gross national product. To determine whether a correlation exists, the forecaster analyses the statistical relationship between changes in past sales and changes in one or more variables—a technique known as *regression analysis.*[18] The object of regression analysis is a mathematical formula that accurately describes a relationship between the company's sales and one or more variables; however, the formula indicates only an association, not a causal relationship. Once an accurate formula has been established, the analyst plugs the necessary information into the formula to derive the sales forecast.

Correlation methods are useful when a precise relationship can be established. However, a forecaster seldom finds a perfect correlation. Furthermore, this method can be used only when the available historical sales data are extensive and reliable. Ordinarily, then, correlation techniques are futile for forecasting the sales of new products, or in markets where changes are frequent and extensive.

Market Tests Conducting a **market test** involves making a product available to buyers in one or more test areas and measuring purchases and consumer responses to distribution, promotion and price. Even though test areas are often cities with populations of 200,000 to 500,000, test sites can be larger metropolitan areas or towns with populations of 50,000 to 200,000, or ITV regions. A market test provides information about consumers' actual purchases rather than about their intended purchases. In addition, purchase volume can be evaluated in relation to the intensity of other marketing activities—advertising, in-store promotions, pricing, packaging, distribution and the like. On the basis of customer response in test areas, forecasters can estimate product sales for larger geographic units. For example, Cadbury's Wispa first appeared in the Tyne Tees area of North East England. Sales showed management that the company had to build more production capacity to cope with a national roll out of the brand and full launch.

Because it does not require historical sales data, a market test is an effective tool for forecasting the sales of new products or the sales of existing products in new geographic areas. The test gives the forecaster information about customers' real actions rather than intended or estimated behaviour. A market test also gives a marketer an opportunity to test various elements of the marketing mix. But these tests are often time consuming and expensive. In addition, a marketer cannot be certain that the consumer response during a market test represents the total market response or that such a response will continue in the future.

Using Multiple Forecasting Methods

Although some businesses depend on a single sales forecasting method, most companies use several techniques. A company is sometimes forced to use several methods when it markets diverse product lines, but even for a single product line several forecasts may be needed, especially when the product is sold in different market segments. Thus a producer of car tyres may rely on one technique to forecast tyre sales for new cars and on another to forecast the sales of replacement tyres. Variation in the length of the needed forecasts may call for several forecast methods. A company that employs one method for a short range forecast may find it inappropriate for long range forecasting. Sometimes a marketer verifies the results of one method by using one or several other methods and comparing results.[19] No matter which technique—or mix of approaches—is deployed, it is essential that marketers produce accurate and useful sales forecasts and assessments of market potential.

The Marketing Audit

Marketing audit A systematic examination of the marketing group's objectives, strategies, organisation and performance

A **marketing audit** is a systematic examination of the marketing group's objectives, strategies, organisation and performance. Its primary purpose is to identify weaknesses in ongoing marketing operations and plan the necessary improvements to correct these weaknesses. The marketing audit does not concern itself with the company's marketing position; that is the purpose of the company's marketing plan. Rather, the marketing audit evaluates how effectively the marketing organisation performed its assigned functions.[20]

Like an accounting or financial audit, a marketing audit should be conducted regularly instead of just when performance control mechanisms show that the system is out of control. The marketing audit is not a control process to be used only during a crisis, although a business in trouble may use it to isolate problems and generate solutions. It is a useful diagnostic tool for correcting marketing activity.

A marketing audit may be specific and focus on one or a few marketing activities, or it may be comprehensive and encompass all of a company's marketing activities. Table 22.5 lists many possible dimensions of a marketing audit. An audit might deal with only a few of these areas, or it might include them all. Its scope depends on the costs involved, the target markets served, the structure of the marketing mix and environmental conditions. The results of the audit can be used to re-allocate marketing effort and to re-examine marketing opportunities. For example, after the rise in consumer interest in buying unleaded petrol during the 1980s, the oil companies realised that many customers were still using leaded fuel, because the engine performance of their cars was better. Launching the new "super" unleaded brands late in the 1980s helped to counter these problems.

The marketing audit should aid evaluation by doing the following:

1. Describing current activities and results to sales, costs, prices, profits and other performance feedback.

Part I.   The Marketing Environment Audit

Marketing Environment Forces

A. Economic
1. What does the company expect in the way of inflation, material shortages, unemployment and credit availability in the short run, medium run and long run?
2. What effect will forecast trends in the size, age distribution and regional distribution of population have on the business?

B. Technological
1. What major changes are occurring in product technology? In process technology?
2. What are the major generic substitutes that might replace this product?

C. Political/Legal/Regulatory
1. What laws are being proposed that may affect marketing strategy and tactics?
2. What national and local government actions should be watched? What is happening with pollution control, equal opportunity employment, product safety, advertising, price controls and so on that is relevant to marketing planning?

D. Societal/Green
1. What attitude is the public taking towards business and the types of products produced by the company?
2. What changes in consumer lifestyles and values have a bearing on the company's target markets and marketing methods?
3. Will the cost and availability of natural resources directly affect the company?
4. Are there public concerns about the company's role in pollution and conservation? If so, what is the company's reaction?

Task Environment

A. Markets
1. What is happening to market size, growth, geographic distribution and profits?
2. What are the major market segments and their expected rates of growth? Which are high opportunity and low opportunity segments?

B. Customers
1. How do current customers and prospects judge the company and its competitors on reputation, product quality, service, salesforce and price?
2. How do different classes of customers make their buying decisions?
3. What evolving needs and satisfactions are the buyers in this market seeking?

C. Competitors
1. Who are the major competitors? What are the objectives and strategy of each major competitor? What are their strengths and weaknesses? What are the sizes and trends in market shares?
2. What trends can be foreseen in future competition and substitutes for this product?

D. Distribution and Dealers
1. What are the main trade channels bringing products to customers?
2. What are the efficiency levels and growth potentials of the different trade channels?

E. Suppliers
1. What is the outlook for the availability of key resources used in production?
2. What trends are occurring among suppliers in their patterns of selling?

F. Facilitators and Marketing Organisations
1. What is the outlook for the cost and availability of transport services?
2. What is the outlook for the cost and availability of warehousing facilities?
3. What is the outlook for the cost and availability of financial resources?
4. How effectively is the advertising agency performing? What trends are occurring in advertising agency services?

G. Publics
1. Where are the opportunity areas or problems for the company?
2. How effectively is the company dealing with publics?

(Continues)

Table 22.5   Dimensions of a marketing audit

Table 22.5 Dimensions of a marketing audit (cont.)

Part II. Marketing Strategy Audit

A. Business Mission

1. Is the business mission clearly focused with marketing terms and is it attainable?

B. Marketing Objectives and Goals

1. Are the corporate goals clearly stated? Do they lead logically to the marketing objectives?
2. Are the marketing objectives stated clearly enough to guide marketing planning and subsequent performance measurement?
3. Are the marketing objectives appropriate, given the company's competitive position, resources and opportunities? Is the appropriate strategic objective to build, hold, harvest, divest or terminate this business?

C. Strategy

1. What is the core marketing strategy for achieving the objectives? Is it sound?
2. Are the resources budgeted to accomplish the marketing objectives inadequate, adequate or excessive?
3. Are the marketing resources allocated optimally to prime market segments, territories and products?
4. Are the marketing resources allocated optimally to the major elements of the marketing mix, i.e. product quality, service, salesforce, advertising, promotion and distribution?

Part III. Marketing Organisation Audit

A. Formal Structure

1. Is there a high level marketing manager with adequate authority and responsibility over those company activities that affect customer satisfaction?
2. Are the marketing responsibilities optimally structured along functional, product, end use and territorial lines?

B. Functional Efficiency

1. Are there good communications and working relations between marketing and sales?
2. Is the product management system working effectively? Are the product managers able to

plan profits or only sales volume?
3. Are there any groups in marketing that need more training, motivation, supervision or evaluation?

C. Interface Efficiency

1. Are there any problems between marketing and manufacturing, research and development, purchasing, finance, accounting and legal departments that need attention?

Part IV. Marketing Systems Audit

A. Marketing Information System

1. Is the marketing intelligence system producing accurate, sufficient and timely information about developments in the marketplace?
2. Is marketing research being adequately used by company decision-makers?
3. Is available marketing intelligence properly shared/accessed by managers?

B. Marketing Planning System

1. Is the marketing planning system well conceived and effective?
2. Is sales forecasting and measurement of market potential soundly carried out?
3. Are sales quotas set on a proper basis?

C. Marketing Control System

1. Are the control procedures (monthly, quarterly, etc.) adequate to ensure that the annual plan's objectives are being achieved?
2. Is provision made to analyse periodically the profitability of different products, markets, territories and channels of distribution?
3. Is provision made to examine and validate periodically various marketing costs?

D. New Product Development System

1. Is the company well organised to gather, generate and screen new product ideas?
2. Does the company do adequate concept research and business analysis before investing heavily in a new idea?
3. Does the company carry out adequate product and market testing before launching a new product?

(Continues)

Table 22.5 Dimensions of a marketing audit   (cont.)

Part V.   Marketing-Productivity Audit

A. Profitability Analysis

1. What is the profitability of the company's different products, served markets, territories and channels of distribution?
2. Should the company enter, expand, contract or withdraw from any business segments, and what would be the short and long run profit consequences?

B. Cost Effective Analysis

1. Do any marketing activities seem to have excessive costs? Are these costs valid? Can cost reducing steps be taken?

Part VI.   Marketing Function Audits

A. Products and Service

1. What are the product line objectives? Are these objectives sound? Is the current product line meeting these objectives?
2. Are there particular products that should be phased out?
3. Are there new products that are worth adding?
4. Are any products able to benefit from quality, feature or style improvements?
5. Is adequate customer service provided?
6. Is there an aftermarket support package—warranty, parts and servicing, dealer network?

B. Price

1. What are the pricing objectives, policies, strategies and procedures? Are prices set on sound cost, demand and competitive criteria?
2. Do the customers see the company's prices as being in or out of line with the perceived value of its products?
3. Does the company use price promotions effectively?

C. Distribution

1. What are the distribution objectives and strategies?
2. Is there adequate market coverage and service?
3. How effective are the following channel members: distributors, manufacturers' reps, brokers, agents and so on?

4. Should the company consider changing its distribution channels?

D. Promotional Mix

1. What are the organisation's advertising objectives? Are they sound?
2. Is the right amount being spent on advertising? How is the budget determined?
3. Are the ad themes and copy effective? What do customers and the public think about the advertising?
4. Are the advertising media well chosen?
5. Is the internal advertising staff adequate?
6. Is the sales promotion budget adequate? Is there effective and sufficient use of sales promotion tools, such as samples, coupons, displays and sales contests?
7. Is the publicity budget adequate? Is the public relations staff competent and creative?
8. Is use of the Internet appropriate? If so, is the web site well designed?
9. What of sponsorship? Is it relevant? Are associated bodies appropriate and reputable?
10. Is direct marketing possible? Through what media and with what proposition?

E. Salesforce

1. What are the organisation's salesforce objectives?
2. Is the salesforce large enough to accomplish the company's objectives?
3. Is the salesforce organised along the proper principle(s) of specialisation (territory, market, product)? Are there enough (or too many) sales managers to guide the field sales reps?
4. Does the sales compensation level and structure provide adequate incentive and reward?
5. Does the salesforce show high morale, ability and effort?
6. Are the procedures for setting quotas and evaluating performance adequate?
7. How does the company's salesforce compare with the salesforces of competitors?

SOURCE: Philip Kotler, *Marketing Management: Analysis, Planning, and Control,* 6th edn (Englewood Cliffs, N.J.: Prentice-Hall, 1988), pp. 748–751. Used by permission.

2. Gathering information about customers, competition and environmental developments that may affect the marketing strategy and the effective implementation of marketing mix programmes.
3. Exploring opportunities and alternatives for improving the marketing strategy.
4. Providing an overall database to be used in evaluating the attainment of organisational goals and marketing objectives.
5. Diagnosing reasons for the successes and failures experienced by a company's marketers and their analyses, strategies and tactical marketing mix programmes.

Marketing audits can be performed internally or externally. An internal auditor may be a top level marketing executive, a company-wide auditing committee or a manager from another office or of another function. Although it is more expensive, an audit by outside consultants is usually more effective; external auditors have more objectivity, more time for the audit and greater experience.

There is no single set of procedures for all marketing audits. However, companies should adhere to several general guidelines. Audits are often based on a series of questionnaires administered to the company's personnel. These questionnaires should be developed carefully to ensure that the audit focuses on the right issues. Auditors should develop and follow a step-by-step plan to guarantee that the audit is systematic. When interviewing company personnel, the auditors should strive to talk to a diverse group of people from many parts of the company. The auditor should become familiar with the product line, meet staff from headquarters, visit field organisations, interview customers, interview competitors and analyse information for a report on the marketing environment.[21] The audit framework and associated questionnaires should remain consistent over time, so that improvements and problems can be noted between audits.

To achieve adequate support, the auditors normally focus first on the company's top management and then move down through the organisational hierarchy. The auditor looks for different points of view within various departments of the organisation or a mismatch between the customers' and the company's perception of the product as signs of trouble in an organisation.[22] The results of the audit should be reported in a comprehensive written document, which should include recommendations that will increase marketing productivity and determine the company's general direction. The marketing audit lets an organisation change tactics or alter day-to-day activities as problems arise. For example, marketing auditors often wonder whether a change in budgeted sales activity is caused by general market conditions or is due to a change in the company's market share.

Although the concept of auditing implies an official examination of marketing activities, many organisations audit their marketing activities informally. Any attempt to verify operating results and to compare them with standards can be considered an auditing activity. Many smaller businesses probably would not use the word *audit,* but they do perform auditing activities. Several problems may arise in an audit of marketing activities. Marketing audits can be expensive in time and money. Selecting the auditors may be difficult because objective, qualified personnel may not be available. Marketing audits can also be extremely disruptive because employees sometimes fear comprehensive evaluations, especially by outsiders. The benefits, though, are significant. The audit reveals successes and also problem areas that need to be addressed.

S U M M A R Y

In order to manipulate the marketing mix to match target market needs and achieve organisational goals, a company must address fundamental strategic decisions. To expedite this process and to set appropriate goals, many companies use marketing planning.

Marketing planning is a systematic process that involves assessing marketing opportunities and resources, determining marketing objectives and developing a full plan for implementation and control. A core output of marketing planning is the *marketing plan,* a document or blueprint containing the requirements for a company's marketing activity. The marketing planning process involves (1) analysing the marketplace, (2) modifying the recommended marketing strategy accordingly and (3) developing detailed marketing mix programmes designed to implement the specified marketing strategy. The *marketing planning cycle* is a circular process of planning and feedback that allows for revision. Most companies up-date their plans annually, typically with a three year focus. There are *short, medium* and *long range plans* available, however.

A key part of the marketing plan is the *marketing objective,* a statement of what is to be accomplished through marketing activities. Objectives should be measurable, indicate a timeframe and be consistent with a company's overall organisational goals.

The heart of the marketing plan is the analysis section. The elements analysed include the marketing environment and market trends, customers, competitive positions and competitors' strategies, plus the company's capabilities to respond to marketing opportunities, the appropriateness of its product and brand portfolio and an ABC sales: contribution analysis of financial performance. A *SWOT analysis,* which identifies Strengths, Weaknesses, Opportunities and Threats, helps to produce realistic and meaningful marketing recommendations.

The strategy recommendations within the marketing plan examine target market priorities, the basis for competing, differential advantage, and desired brand and product positioning. Marketing strategy guides the company's direction in relationships between customers and competitors. It is important to have a clearly defined *generic competitive strategy:* cost leadership, differentiation or focus. Marketing programmes implement the recommended marketing strategy. They discuss each element of the marketing mix in detail—including allocation of schedules and tasks, personnel, budgets, responsibilities and monitoring of ongoing performance—in order to implement the marketing plan and achieve the organisation's strategic goals.

Sales and marketing activities should be carefully planned activities that anticipate consumer needs and expectations. Whether using a total market or a market segmentation approach, a marketer must be able to measure the sales potential of the target market or markets. *Market potential* is the total amount of a product that customers will purchase within a specified period of time at a specific level of industry-wide marketing activity. *Sales potential* is the maximum percentage of market potential that an individual company within an industry can expect to obtain for a specific product or service. There are two general approaches to measuring sales potential: *break down* and *build up*. A *sales forecast* is the amount of a product that the company actually expects to sell during a specific period of time and at a specified level of marketing activities. Several methods are used to forecast sales: *executive judgement, surveys (customer, salesforce* and *expert forecasting surveys,* including the *Delphi method), time series analysis (trend analysis, cycle analysis, seasonal analysis, random factor analysis), correlation methods* and *market tests.* Although some businesses may rely on a single sales forecasting method, most companies employ several different techniques. It is an essential part of the marketing process to develop objective and reliable sales forecasts and assessments of market potential.

To identify weaknesses in ongoing marketing operations and plan the necessary improvements to correct these weaknesses, it is sometimes necessary to audit marketing activities. A *marketing audit* is a systematic examination of the marketing group's objectives, strategies, organisation and performance. A marketing audit attempts to identify what a marketing unit is doing, to evaluate the effectiveness of these activities and to recommend future marketing activities. It is a useful diagnostic tool for correcting marketing activity.

Important Terms

Marketing planning	Sales potential	Expert forecasting survey
Marketing plan	Break down approach	Time series analysis
Marketing planning cycle	Build up approach	Trend analysis
Short range plans	Sales forecast	Cycle analysis
Medium range plans	Executive judgement	Seasonal analysis
Long range plans	Surveys	Random factor analysis
Marketing objective	Customer forecasting survey	Correlation methods
SWOT analysis	Salesforce forecasting survey	Market test
Generic competitive strategies	Delphi method	Marketing audit
Market potential		

Discussion and Review Questions

1. What is marketing planning? How does it help companies better target their marketplaces?
2. In what ways do marketing environment forces affect marketing planning? Give some examples.
3. What is a SWOT analysis? How does it lead to an understanding of realistic market opportunities?
4. What issues *must* be thoroughly analysed during marketing planning prior to the formulation of a marketing mix programme?
5. Why is it important to determine a differential advantage?
6. Porter's generic competitive strategies warn against being "stuck in the middle". Why?
7. Why is a marketer concerned about sales potential when trying to find a target market?
8. What is a sales forecast, and why is it important?
9. What is the Delphi method to forecasting? Why is it a popular tool?
10. Why would a company use a marketing audit?

Recommended Readings

S. Dibb, L. Simkin and J. Bradley, *The Marketing Planning Workbook* (London: International Thomson Business Press, 1996).

M. McDonald, *Marketing Plans: How to Prepare Them: How to Use Them* (Oxford: Butterworth-Heinemann, 1999).

M. McDonald, *Marketing Plans That Work: Targeting Growth and Profitability* (Oxford: Butterworth-Heinemann, 1997).

J. Saunders, ed. "Exploring marketing planning", special issue, *Journal of Marketing Management,* vol. 12, nos. 1–3, 1996.

L. Simkin, "Addressing organisational pre-requisites in marketing planning", *Marketing Intelligence and Planning,* vol. 14, no. 5, 1996, pp. 39–46.

L. Simkin, "People and processes in marketing planning: the benefits of controlling implementation", *Journal of Marketing Management,* vol. 12, no. 5, 1996, pp. 375–390.

● C A S E S

22.1 Denmark's Carlsberg Capitalises on Regional Brands

In 1992 there was a revolution in the UK brewing industry as Allied Domecq's Allied Breweries, responsible for such established beer brands as Tetley's Bitter, Castlemaine XXXX and Skol, merged with Carlsberg A/S to form Carlsberg-Tetley. Carlsberg A/S was formed in 1970 with the merger of the Tuborg and Carlsberg breweries, has a turnover of over 15 billion Dkr, employs over 15,000 people and brews in more than 40 countries. With six major breweries around the country, the new Carlsberg-Tetley joint venture certainly had the production capacity to take on the industry to try to become the number one player in the UK. Castlemaine had already become a leading lager brand and with Carlsberg—second only to the Dutch Heineken—the portfolio was even stronger. Indeed, only four beer brands can genuinely claim pan-European coverage: Heineken, Carlsberg, Stella Artois and Guinness.

Unlike rival Whitbread, which now focuses on the leisure industry by operating hotels, entertainment centres and numerous restaurant chains in addition to its beer brands, Carlsberg-Tetley sees itself primarily as a brewer. It has an impressive estate of pubs and inns, plus a wide range of trade and wholesale customers. New product development, an integral aspect of the company's strategy, includes Carlsberg Ice Beer and draught Tetley's Bitter in a can, as well as the revival of the Samuel Allsopp Brewery Company in Burton, which produces small quantities of high quality, speciality beers. The brands are heavily promoted, with sponsorship playing a key role in the promotional mix. Tetley sponsors the England cricket team; Carlsberg has supported Liverpool FC since 1992 and in 1996 co-sponsored the European Football Championships. Carlsberg also is a leading supporter of the Phoenix, Monsters of Rock and Reading music festivals. Skol's Golden Cue has been the premier amateur pool tournament for several years. Various Rugby League and Rugby Union clubs benefit from sponsorship by Carlsberg-Tetley's regional brands.

The regional nature of the company is its core strength and also its key weakness. Rivals Scottish Courage—formed from the merger of Scottish & Newcastle with Courage—Bass, Whitbread and Guinness have all endeavoured to move away from historical regional markets, with local brands brewed in traditional brewery centres serving only an immediate geographic territory. Whitbread's Boddington's, Heineken and Murphy's are available throughout the UK and beyond. For Carlsberg-Tetley, its regional breweries all produce brands with local heritage and long standing sales records in their own hinterlands: Wrexham Lager in Wrexham; Burton Ale and Ansell's at the Inde

Coope site in Burton; Tetley's in Leeds; Walker's and Greenall's in Warrington; Archibald Arrol's and Calder's in Alloa. Several of these breweries now also produce and bottle the truly national brands: Carlsberg, Castlemaine XXXX, Skol, Tuborg and Tetley's.

In Northampton, where it has brewed to its Danish standards since 1972, Carlsberg now produces the complete mix of lagers in the Carlsberg-Tetley line-up: Carlsberg Pilsner, Carlsberg Export, Carlsberg Special Brew, Tuborg Gold, Skol and—for both the British and Danish markets—Carlsberg Ice. With this relative newcomer, the company has pooled the might of its resources: Carlsberg Ice is produced in Northampton, iced in Wrexham and bottled in Burton.

Carlsberg-Tetley's desire is to retain the traditional regional strengths and extensive distribution based on decades of brewing in the various major brewery centres, while emulating direct rivals such as Whitbread by creating national brands with full marketing and promotional support. This balancing act and support of such an extensive portfolio of well known and regional brands cannot be undertaken without very shrewd marketing planning and prudent use of resources.

SOURCES: The Corporate Communications Office, Carlsberg-Tetley; Tom Wright, "New view at Carlsberg-Tetley", Campaign, 15 December 1995, p. 14; "Carlsberg-Tetley creates NPD team to launch 'new age' alcoholic drinks", Marketing Week, 27 October 1995, p. 8; George Pitcher, "Breaking the charmed circle", Marketing Week, 4 August 1995, p. 25; Emma Hall, "Carlsberg sets off £10 million ad overhaul", Campaign, 14 July 1995, p. 1; David Benady and Tom O'Sullivan, "Danes force pace of change at Carlsberg", Marketing Week, 7 July 1995, p. 20.

Questions for Discussion

1. How has Carlsberg used its marketing mix to cater for differences in regional tastes?
2. What ways does Carlsberg have available to create a differential advantage over its rivals?
3. How can marketing planning help Carlsberg to capitalise upon its regional brands?

22.2 Binney & Smith Brightens Marketing Strategy for Crayola Crayons

While Nintendo and Playstation games and MTV music videos have captured children's attention, Crayola Crayons have languished on store shelves. Now Binney & Smith, a division of Hallmark

Cards, is fighting back with a new marketing strategy for the venerable crayon. The company launched a huge MTV-style campaign, which targets children rather than parents.

Traditionally Binney & Smith targeted Crayola Crayons at parents, using educational themes. But after recognising that children's purchasing power and influence on family purchases have increased in recent years, the company decided to change the crayon's image as an old fashioned toy to an exciting way for kids and teens to express themselves. To this end, the company developed new advertisements featuring rock music, "hip" kids and soaring colours for showing during television programmes seen by children. In-store videos provided to toy stores and retailers of children's clothing followed up the theme.

After marketing research indicated that children prefer brighter colours, the company decided to retire blue grey, green blue, lemon yellow, maize, orange red, orange yellow, raw umber and violet blue to the Crayola Hall of Fame and to replace them with the more vivid cerulean, dandelion, fuchsia, jungle green, royal purple, teal blue, vivid tangerine and wild strawberry. This decision was controversial, however. The company was inundated with phone calls, letters and petitions from people who missed the old colours. Protesters marched on the company, carrying placards with slogans like "We hate the new 8!" and "They call it a retirement, I call it a burial." RUMPS, the Raw Umber and Maize Preservation Society, finally got its way. The company issued a commemorative tin containing the 64 crayon box and a special pack of the eight colours dropped one year earlier. Even though kids liked the new colours, parents liked the old eight colours. The company issued a statement saying that the old colours were revived partly because the company is in the business of providing what the consumer wants.

Along with new advertisements and colours, the company introduced ColourWorks, a line of erasable crayon sticks and retractable coloured pencils and pens. The company brought out Silver Swirls, crayons that have twirls of silver mixed in with the wax colours. Pictures coloured with Silver Swirls can be buffed to a high sheen with tissue. The new line was not only tested by children but also named by them. The company has licensed its brand to Concord Cameras for a range of brightly coloured single use cameras aimed at children under 12. Several software companies have recognised the Crayola brand appeal: Micrografx offers the Crayola Amazing Art Adventure and the Crayola Art Studio—software games that encourage art and design a long way from the traditional wax crayon. A range of PC interactive software products has emerged, still focusing on drawing and creativity, but not based purely on the familiar wax crayon. The latter remains the company's core line, though it now features as part of making kits—Badge Bonanza or Crayola Jewellery—and a whole host of design sets. Clearly, the Crayola brand is still very popular with children, parents and toy stores.

Despite its new focus on children, Binney & Smith did not forget who actually holds the purse strings; the company continues to target parents with advertisements in women's and parents' magazines. The company hopes that its new strategy will lead more children to reach for Crayola Crayons instead of the Nintendo joystick or LEGO bricks.

So far, the revised strategy for Crayola seems to be working. Sales are up; shelf space in toy stores could not be better, despite stiff competition from a host of rival products and toys; and deals with airlines, fast food outlets and restaurant chains to provide "time filler" packs for children have boosted brand awareness.

SOURCES: Ellen Neuborne, "Crayola crayons have old colors back", *USA Today*, 2 October 1991, p. 2B; Ken Riddle, "Crayola draws brighter lines in the market", *Marketing*, 21 January 1991, p. 4; Beefeater Restaurants, 1993; Toys "R" Us, Leicester, 1996; Loretta Roach, "Single use explosion", *Discount Merchandiser*, September 1995, pp. 28–30; Robyn Parets, "Children's edutainment titles vie for shelf space", *Discount Store News*, 19 June 1995, pp. C6–C9; Binney & Smith UK, 1999; Toys "R" Us, 1999.

Questions for Discussion

1. Why did Binney & Smith have to up-date its marketing of Crayola and change its strategy?
2. What are Crayola's target audiences? Why did the company need to approach them differently?
3. Why has the company negotiated with airlines and restaurants to offer give-aways?

23 Implementing Strategies, Internal Marketing Relationships and Measuring Performance

OBJECTIVES

- To understand how marketing activities are organised within a company's structure
- To become familiar with ways of organising a marketing unit
- To examine the marketing implementation process
- To learn about approaches to marketing implementation and to grasp the importance of internal marketing
- To explore implementing and controlling marketing activities
- To learn how sales and marketing cost analysis can be used as methods of evaluating performance
- To explain the popular criteria for measuring marketing performance

"The real strategic problem in marketing is not strategy, it is managing implementation and change."

Nigel Piercy
Cardiff Business School

As hotel companies prepare their businesses for the new millennium, many are paying greater attention than ever to their long term marketing strategy. In particular, the need to develop strong brands has come to the fore. Behind this emphasis lies the pressure for hotels to differentiate themselves from their competitors. In the past, hotels were generally differentiated on the basis of the service and facilities being offered. Nowadays, as the product and service mix provided by three and four star hotels becomes increasingly standardised, this form of differentiation is becoming more difficult. At the same time, there is also a growing awareness that the short term tactical marketing approach which many hotel chains have adopted must be replaced with a longer term strategic focus.

Stakis is just one of the many hotel companies which have been revising their marketing strategy. Following a major branding review, the company has decided to overhaul its corporate identity. Now the chain is aiming for a softer, more emotional appeal. The hotel division of Granada Group, Forte, has also recently changed its marketing strategy. As a result, the company's individual brands will each be marketed separately. In the move, which is designed to ensure the development of each individual brand, the marketing department has been restructured so that Posthouse, Heritage, Le Meridien and London Signature Hotels will each have their own marketing head. Operationally, it is hoped each hotel brand will be more tightly controlled, with uniformity of offer and service guaranteed to match target market expectations.

Bass Hotels & Resorts is another player which has given careful thought to brand development. This major hotel company—with close to 3,000 hotels and over 460,000 bedrooms around the world—is clear about the role which well defined brands play in its success. The company has paid particular attention to its branding strategy, developing and investing in five different hotel brands (see table).

Each hotel brand is carefully defined in terms of hotel attributes, target marketing and internal operational characteristics. Members of staff are carefully focused on their brand's proposition and expectations.

The hotel business was a victim of recession in the early 1990s. Now industry experts are concerned that a new downturn in business might be about to follow the period of growth which the industry has recently enjoyed. So far, the decline in room occupancy figures is only small, but hoteliers want to ensure that proactive steps are taken to stave off future difficulties. For many, marketing looks set to play an important role. However, the short term tactical marketing culture of the past is being overhauled. Instead, more careful consideration than ever is being given to long term strategy, with an emphasis on brand development and on internal controls to ensure effective delivery to targeted customers of the brand concept. The hotel industry has recognised that marketing not only promotes a brand externally: it must also control the uniformity of the proposition internally.

SOURCES: Lucy Killgren, "Hotel chains wake up to power of brands", *Marketing Week*, 21 January 1999, p. 20; Lucy Barrett, "Forte axes role in brand review", *Marketing*, 4 February 1999, p. 2; *Directory of Hotels and Services*, Bass Hotels & Resorts, July 1998; **http://www.holiday-inn.com**. *Images*: Courtesy Bass Hotels & Resorts.

Inter-Continental	Provides up-scale accommodation for leisure and business travellers. Business rooms offer large desks; printer/copier/fax machines, surge protected outlets, voice mail. Large conference rooms.
Crowne Plaza	Located in key cities/airports, offering superior comfort and facilities. Spacious rooms with mini bar/tea and coffee making, trouser press, modem point. Meeting facilities, fully equipped gym.
Holiday Inn	Full range of services for leisure and business guests. Comfortable, well appointed rooms with room service. Fitness, leisure and business facilities. Meeting rooms.
Holiday Inn Express	Designed for business and leisure travellers who want great value and don't need full restaurant, leisure or large meeting facilities. Modern, well equipped rooms with business communication point and dataport. One price per room. Free Continental breakfast. Restaurant nearby.
Staybridge Suites by Holiday Inn	Hotels offering extended stay of four days plus. Spacious studios or suites have voice mail, computer point and desk. Business, fitness and leisure services. Convenience store and free buffet breakfast and laundry.

This chapter focuses first on the marketing unit's position in the organisation and the ways the unit itself can be organised. It goes on to examine several issues regarding the implementation of marketing strategies, particularly *relationship marketing*, *internal marketing* and *total quality management*. The next section considers the basic components of implementing and controlling marketing activities. The chapter then discusses the use of cost and sales analyses to evaluate the effectiveness of marketing strategies and to measure the company's performance before concluding with an examination of popular marketing performance measures.

Organising Marketing Activities

The organisation of marketing activities involves the development of an internal structure for the marketing unit, including relationships and lines of authority and responsibility that connect and co-ordinate individuals. This section first looks at the place of marketing within an organisation and examines the major alternatives available for organising a marketing unit. The hotel industry, as described in the chapter's opener, has recognised the importance of marketing and of communicating the message within the business. This section then shows how marketing activities can be structured to fit into an organisation so as to contribute to the accomplishment of overall objectives.

The Place of Marketing in an Organisation

Because the marketing environment is so dynamic, the position of the marketing unit within the organisation has risen during the past 25 years. Companies that truly adopt the marketing concept develop a distinct organisational culture—a culture based on a shared set of beliefs that makes the customers' needs the pivotal point of a company's decisions about strategy and operations.[1] Instead of developing products in a vacuum and then trying to persuade consumers to buy them, companies using the marketing concept begin with an orientation towards their customers' needs and desires. If the marketing concept serves as a guiding philosophy, the marketing unit will be closely co-ordinated with other functional areas, such as production, finance and personnel. Figure 23.1 shows the organisation of a marketing unit by types of customers. This form of internal organisation works well for organisations having several groups of customers whose needs differ significantly.

Marketing must interact with other functional departments in a number of key areas. It needs to work with manufacturing in determining the volume and variety of the company's products. Those in charge of production often rely on marketers for accurate sales forecasts. Research and development departments depend heavily on information gathered by marketers about product features and benefits desired by consumers, as well as details of complaints concerning current products. Decisions made by the physical distribution department hinge on information about the urgency of delivery schedules and cost/service trade-offs.[2] For example, at Honda, all departments have worked together for a long time, whereas at Chrysler the manufacturing group was not even on the product design committee until 1981. With rapid market segmentation forcing companies to design cars even faster than in the past, co-ordination between engineering, production, marketing and finance is essential.[3]

Marketing oriented organisation
A company that concentrates on discovering what buyers want and providing it in a way that lets the company achieve its objectives

A **marketing oriented organisation** concentrates on discovering what buyers want and providing it in a way that lets the company achieve its objectives. Such a company has an organisational culture that effectively and efficiently produces a sustainable differential advantage.[4] It focuses on customer analysis, competitor analysis and the integration of the business's resources to provide customer value and satisfaction, as well as long term profits.[5] As Figure 23.2 shows, the marketing director's position is at the same level as those of the financial, production and personnel directors. Thus the marketing director takes part in top level decision-making. Note, too, that the marketing director is responsible for a variety of activities. Some of them—sales forecasting and supervision and product planning—would be under the jurisdiction of other functional managers in production or sales oriented organisations.

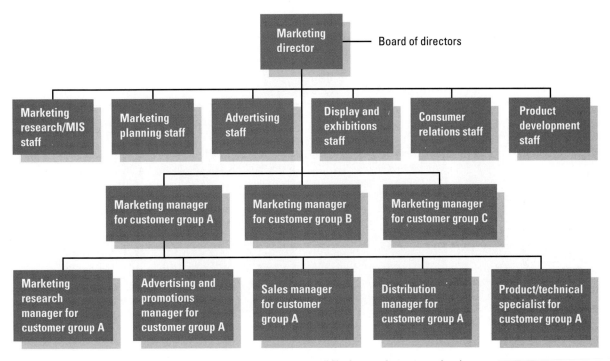

Note: In some organisations, each marketing manager would have responsibility for a product group rather than a customer group, and would be termed a product manager.

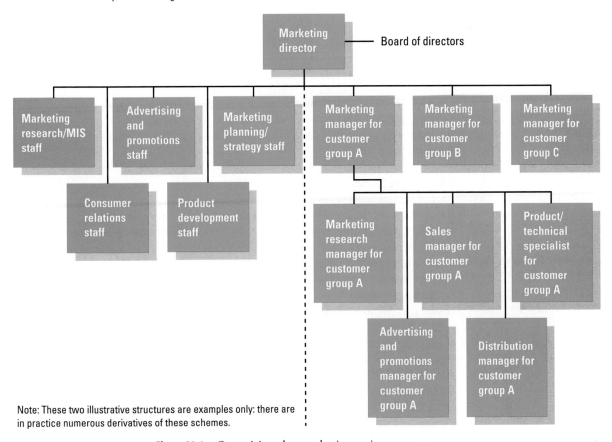

Note: These two illustrative structures are examples only: there are in practice numerous derivatives of these schemes.

Figure 23.1 Organising the marketing unit

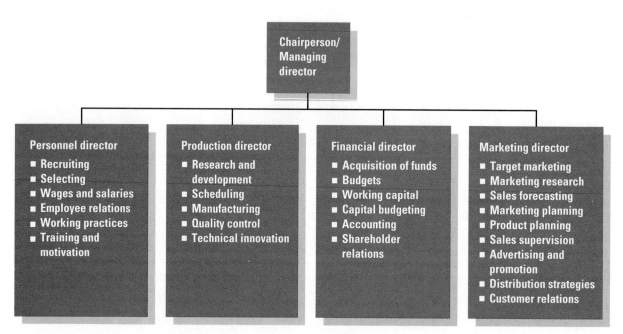

Figure 23.2   Organisational chart of a marketing oriented company

Both the links between marketing and other functional areas (such as production, finance and personnel) and the importance of marketing to management evolve from the organisation's basic orientation. Marketing encompasses the greatest number of business functions and occupies an important position when a company is marketing oriented; it has a limited role when the company views the role of marketing as simply selling products that it makes. However, a marketing orientation is not achieved simply by re-drawing the organisational chart; management must also adopt and use the marketing orientation as a management philosophy.

Centralisation versus Decentralisation

Centralised organisation   A company in which top level managers delegate very little authority to the lower levels of the organisation

Decentralised organisation   A company in which decision-making authority is delegated as far down the chain of command as possible

The organisational structure that a company uses to connect and co-ordinate various activities affects its success. Basic decisions relate to how various participants in the company will work together to make important decisions, as well as to co-ordinate, implement and control activities. Top managers create corporate strategies and co-ordinate lower levels. A **centralised organisation** is one in which the top level managers delegate very little authority to lower levels of the organisation. In a **decentralised organisation,** decision-making authority is delegated as far down the chain of command as possible. The decision to centralise or decentralise directly affects marketing in the organisation.

In a centralised organisation, major marketing decisions originate with top management and are transmitted to lower levels of management. A decentralised structure gives marketing managers more opportunity for making key strategic decisions. IBM has adopted a decentralised management structure so that its marketing managers have a chance to customise strategies for customers. On the other hand, Hewlett-Packard and 3M have become more centralised by consolidating functions or eliminating divisional managers.[6] Although decentralising may foster innovation and a greater responsiveness to customers, a decentralised company may be inefficient or appear to have a blurred marketing strategy when dealing with larger customers. A centralised organisation avoids confusion among the marketing staff, vagueness in marketing strategy and autonomous decision-makers who are out of control. Of course, overly centralised companies often become dependent on top management and respond too slowly to be able to solve problems or seize new opportunities. Obviously, finding the right degree of centralisation for a particular company is a difficult balancing act.

While many highly centralised organisations are quite successful, the overall trend is for companies to decentralise. This trend is partly caused by the need for organisations to remain very flexible, given the ever changing marketing environment. For some companies, the need to adapt to changing customer needs is of critical importance. These organisations often use an extreme form of decentralisation: **empowerment**. This involves giving front line employees the authority and responsibility to make marketing decisions without seeking the approval of their supervisors.[7] The following examples illustrate empowerment:

Empowerment Giving front line employees the authority and responsibility to make marketing decisions without seeking the approval of their supervisors

- A car salesperson is allowed to negotiate the price or financing arrangement with a customer without speaking with the sales manager.
- A retail sales assistant decides, without seeking the approval of a manager, whether to refund customers' money on products they return.
- A receptionist at a hotel gives one night's free accommodation to a dissatisfied guest who complains about poor service.
- A retail store manager is permitted to lower prices on merchandise in order to match a competitor without asking the regional manager.

Although employees at any level in an organisation can be empowered to make decisions, empowerment is used most often at the front line, where employees interact daily with customers. Service and retail marketers practise empowerment quite extensively because of the interactive nature of these businesses. However, empowerment can work in a manufacturing organisation as well.

One of the characteristics of empowerment is that employees can perform their jobs the way they see fit, as long as their methods and outcomes are consistent with the mission of the organisation.[8] However, the effectiveness of empowerment is tied to the organisation's culture. Empowerment works best when the corporate culture is guided by a sense of shared direction, which ensures that employees make the right decisions.[9] Obviously, creating this type of culture does not happen overnight. The corporate vision must be communicated to employees so that they understand how their job affects the vision. Employees must also be trained and persuaded to accept the corporate vision and to become part of the organisation's culture.[10]

Major Alternatives for Organising the Marketing Unit

How effectively a company's marketing management can plan and implement marketing strategies depends on how the marketing unit is organised. Effective organisational planning can give the company a competitive edge. The organisational structure of a marketing department establishes the authority relationships between marketing personnel and specifies who is responsible for making certain decisions and performing particular activities. This internal structure is the vehicle for directing marketing activities.

In organising a marketing unit, managers divide the work into specific activities and delegate responsibility and authority for those activities to people in various positions within the unit. These positions include, for example, the sales manager, the research manager and the advertising manager.

No single approach to organising a marketing unit works equally well in all businesses. A marketing unit can be organised according to (1) functions, (2) products, (3) regions or (4) types of customer. The best approach or approaches depend on the number and diversity of the company's products, the characteristics and needs of the people in the target market and many other factors.

Businesses often use some combination of organisation by functions, products, regions or customer types. Product features may dictate that the marketing unit be structured by products, whereas customers' characteristics require that it be organised by geographic region or by type of customer. Construction equipment leader JCB has organised by product types (crawler excavators, backhoe diggers, compact equipment and so on), but many financial institutions organise by customers, because personal banking needs differ from commercial ones. By using more than one type of organisation, a flexible marketing unit can develop and implement marketing plans to match customers' needs precisely. To develop organisational plans that give a company a differential advantage, four issues should be considered:

1. Which jobs or levels of jobs need to be added, deleted or modified? For example, if new products are important to the success of the business, marketers with strong product development skills should be added to the organisation.
2. How should reporting relationships be structured to create a competitive edge? This question is discussed further in the following descriptions of organisational structure.
3. To whom should the primary responsibility for accomplishing work be assigned? Identifying primary responsibility explicitly is critical for effective performance appraisal and reward systems.
4. Should any committees or task forces be organised?[11]

Organising by Functions Some marketing departments adopt a structure known as **organising by functions,** such as marketing research, product development, distribution, sales, advertising and customer relations. The personnel who direct these functions report directly to the top level marketing executive. This structure is fairly common because it works well for some businesses with centralised marketing operations, such as Ford and General Motors. In more decentralised companies, such as some retailers or giants Procter & Gamble and Unilever, functional organisation can raise severe co-ordination problems. The functional approach may, however, suit a large, centralised company whose products and customers are neither numerous nor diverse.

Organising by functions A way of structuring a marketing department in which personnel directing marketing research, product development, distribution, sales, advertising and customer relations report to the top level marketing executive

Organising by Products A business that produces and markets diverse products may find the functional approach inadequate. The decisions and problems related to a single marketing function for one product may be quite different from those related to the same marketing function for another product. As a result, businesses that produce diverse products sometimes organise their marketing units according to product groups. **Organising by products** gives a company the flexibility to develop special marketing mixes for different products.

The product management system, which was introduced by Procter & Gamble, operates in about 85 per cent of companies in the consumer packaged goods industry. In this structure, the product manager oversees all activities related to his or her assigned product. He or she develops product plans, sees that they are implemented, monitors the results and takes corrective action as necessary. The

Organising by products A way of structuring a marketing department so that the company has the flexibility to develop special marketing mixes for different products

product manager is also responsible for acting as a liaison between the company and its marketing environment, transmitting essential information about the environment to the company.[12] The product manager may also draw on the resources of specialised staff in the company. **Category management,** currently popular in supermarkets, off-licences, CTNs and forecourt shops, takes this notion further, with marketers becoming responsible for categories of product lines—such as fresh foods or tobacco—or for categories of distributors—such as all alcoholic beverage departments in supermarkets or off-licences, for a specific brand of alcohol.

Category management A variation of organising by products whereby marketers are responsible for categories of product lines or categories of distributors

Organising by Regions   A large company that markets products nationally (or internationally) may adopt a structure for its marketing activities known as **organising by regions.** Managers of marketing functions for each region report to their regional marketing manager; all the regional marketing managers report directly to the executive marketing manager. Companies often adopt this regional structure to put more senior management personnel into the field, get closer to customers and enable the company to respond more quickly and efficiently to regional competitors. This form of organisation is especially effective for a business whose customers' characteristics and needs vary greatly from one region to another.

Organising by regions A way of structuring a marketing department, used by large national or international companies, that requires managers of marketing functions for each region to report to their regional marketing manager

A company with marketing managers for each separate region has a complete marketing staff at its headquarters to provide assistance and guidance to regional marketing managers. The major UK brewers had national headquarters and marketing centres, often in London, but regional brands, each with their own marketing department, in major provincial conurbations. The regional office controlled the marketing and promotion of its brand within guidelines specified by the head office. However, not all companies organised by regions maintain a full marketing staff at their head offices. Businesses that try to penetrate the national market intensively sometimes divide regions into sub-regions.

Organising by type of customer A way of structuring a marketing department suitable for a business that has several groups of customers with very different needs and problems

Organising by Type of Customer   Sometimes the marketing unit opts for **organising by type of customer.** This form of internal organisation works well for a business that has several groups of customers whose needs and problems differ significantly. For example, Bic may sell pens to large retail stores, wholesalers and institutions. Retailers may want more rapid delivery of small shipments and more personal selling by the producer than do either wholesalers or institutional buyers. Because the marketing decisions and activities required for these two groups of customers differ considerably, the company may find it efficient to organise its marketing unit by type of customer.

In an organisation with a marketing department broken down by customer group, the marketing manager for each group reports to the top level marketing executive and directs most marketing activities for that group. A marketing manager controls all activities needed to market products to a specific customer group.

The planning and organising functions provide purpose, direction and structure for marketing activities. However, until marketing managers implement the marketing plan, exchanges cannot occur. In fact, organisers of marketing activities can become excessively concerned with planning strategy while neglecting implementation. Before John Harvey-Jones joined ICI, some analysts believed that its management's preoccupation with procedures and plans caused the company's business to suffer. Obviously, implementation of plans is important to the

Figure 23.3 Implementing plans involves co-operation. Aerospatiale's teamwork message supports the idea that co-operation is needed to implement marketing strategies. SOURCE: Courtesy Aerospatiale.

success of any organisation as described in Marketing Insight 23.1 for McDonald's. Proper implementation of a marketing plan depends on internal marketing to employees, the motivation of personnel who perform marketing activities, effective communication within the marketing organisation and the co-ordination of marketing activities. In Figure 23.3, Aerospatiale promotes its teamwork philosophy in business with other countries and internally.

The Marketing Implementation Process

Marketing implementation
A process that involves activities to put marketing strategies into action

Marketing implementation is the "how?" of marketing strategy; it involves activities directed at putting marketing strategies into action. Although implementation is often neglected in favour of strategic planning, the implementation process itself can determine whether a marketing strategy is successful. Marketing planning used to result in tactical marketing mix recommendations. Now, a robust plan is not deemed complete until the how, by whom and when issues are addressed: allocation of budgets, personnel, schedules and performance measures to the specific marketing mix recommendations. In short, good marketing strategy combined with bad marketing implementation is a guaranteed recipe for failure. Marketing has to be made to happen!

McDonald's Keeps Tight Control

Mighty McDonald's, famous for its golden arches, was established in 1940 when Dick and Mac McDonald opened up in San Bernadino, California. Ray Kroc, credited with the chain's global ambitions, bought the rights to develop the brand in 1955 and created McDonald's Corporation. Every day, from Moscow to Hong Kong, McDonald's serves over 38 million people, including a million in the UK where the company enjoys a 75 per cent share of the hamburger market. Nearest rival Burger King, despite massive recent expansion, can manage only 15 per cent. There are 23,000 McDonald's restaurants in 109 countries producing sales in 1998 of £22.13 billion and profits of £1.09 billion. Strongest growth is currently in Europe. Leading branding consultancy Interbrand ranked McDonald's as the most recognised brand in the world, beating even Coca-Cola.

Whether in Lisbon, Chicago or Manchester, a McDonald's restaurant is instantly evident, with a homogeneous layout, ambience, design and ethos that are the envy of most services marketers. The menus change slightly to reflect local tastes, but for the most part there is consistency in the product the world over. Alcohol is available in Lousanne, while incredible ice cream concoctions are on offer in Porto, but everywhere the core dishes are the same—The Big Mac, chicken nuggets and Filet-O-Fish—to eat in or, at many locations, available as a drive through take-away. Single adults snacking, business representatives lunching, children partying or teenagers dining before taking in a movie: McDonald's caters for a wide range of customers.

When McDonald's first came to the UK, it had to educate its customers to expect unbuttered rolls, no knives or forks and no table service. This may seem strange to a generation that has grown up in fast food restaurants, but it was a major marketing task. Staff, too, had to be trained and managed to perform their duties effectively. Despite being in Lisbon, Portugal, for years, when McDonald's opened in Porto in northern Portugal, it advertised the concept of the hamburger and explained that it could be eaten for lunch or dinner and even as a snack any time of the day. Behind the scenes, internal marketing programmes ensured that staff also grasped the fundamentals of the McDonald's trading concept and ideals.

Controls are central to the trading practices of the company. Every customer ordering a Big Mac must receive a similar meal every time: cooked identically, with similar relish, wrapping, pricing and a smile. With 70 per cent of McDonald's restaurants franchised to independently owned companies and operators, such uniformity does not occur by accident. Country managers are allowed to source locally but must conform to well established ingredients and standards. While Burger King emphasises its food, McDonald's promotes the whole restaurant experience and establishes performance standards to maintain a consistent customer offer. As the company continues to grow, with innovative outlets on ferries, at football grounds and even in Guy's Hospital, internal operational controls are just as important to its success as is the hefty promotional activity—£44 million in the UK in 1998—designed to keep the brand in the target audience's mind. McDonald's understands the importance of maintaining high standards and of integrating the brand, people, design, ambience, technology and food to create a winning experience. Not everyone is a McDonald's fan, but millions daily are happy to return to the trusted golden arches.

SOURCES: "Progressive not McDesperate", Letters, *Marketing Week*, 22 April 1999, p. 32; "Aroma therapy", *Marketing Week*, 8 April 1999, pp. 28–29; Ian Darby, "Big Mac blunder hits McDonald's", *Marketing*, 7 January 1999, p. 1; Claire Murphy, "How McDonald's conquered the UK", *Marketing*, 18 February, pp. 30–31.

An important aspect of the implementation process is understanding that marketing strategies almost always turn out differently than expected. In essence, all organisations have two types of strategy: intended strategy and realised strategy.[13] **Intended strategy** is the strategy that the organisation decided on during the planning phase and wants to use. **Realised strategy,** on the other hand, is the strategy that actually takes place; it comes about during the process of implementing the intended strategy. The realised strategy is not necessarily any better than the intended strategy, though it is often worse.

Intended strategy The strategy on which the company decides during the planning phase

Realised strategy The strategy that actually takes place

**Problems in
Implementing
Marketing Activities**

Why do marketing strategies sometimes turn out differently than expected? The most common reason is that managers fail to realise that marketing implementation is just as important as marketing strategy.[14] Both strategy and implementation are important to strategic planning. The relationship between strategic planning and implementation creates a number of problems for managers when they plan implementation activities. Three of the most important problems are:[15]

- *Marketing strategy and implementation are related.* Companies that experience this problem typically assume that strategic planning always comes first, followed by implementation. In reality, marketing strategies and implementation activities should be developed simultaneously. The content of the marketing strategy determines how it will be implemented. Likewise, implementation activities may require that changes be made in the marketing strategy. Thus it is important for marketing managers to understand that strategy and implementation are really two sides of the same coin.
- *Marketing strategy and implementation are constantly evolving.* This second problem refers to how strategy and implementation are both affected by the marketing environment. Since the environment is constantly changing, both marketing strategy and implementation must remain flexible enough to adapt. The relationship between strategy and implementation is never fixed; it is always evolving to accommodate changes in customer needs, government regulation or competition.
- *The responsibilities for marketing strategy and implementation are separated.* This problem is often the biggest obstacle in implementing marketing strategies. Typically, marketing strategies are developed by the top managers in an organisation. However, the responsibility for implementing those strategies rests at the front line of the organisation. This separation can impair implementation in two ways (see Figure 23.4). First, because top managers are separated from the front line, where the company interacts daily with customers, they may not grasp the unique problems associated with implementing marketing activities. Second, people, not organisations, implement

Figure 23.4 The separation of strategic planning and marketing implementation.
SOURCE: From O. C. Ferrell, George H. Lucas and David J. Luck, *Strategic Marketing Management: Text and Cases*, Copyright © 1994, p. 183. Reprinted with permission.

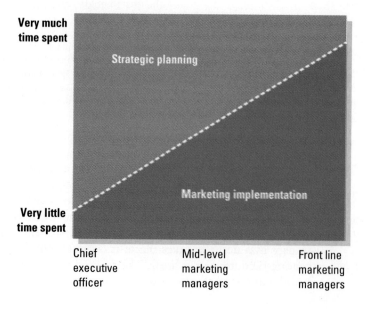

Figure 23.5 Elements of marketing implementation.
SOURCE: Lawrence R. Jauch and William F. Glueck, *Strategic Management and Business Policy*, Third Edition. Copyright © 1988 by The McGraw-Hill Companies. Reprinted with permission of The McGraw-Hill Companies.

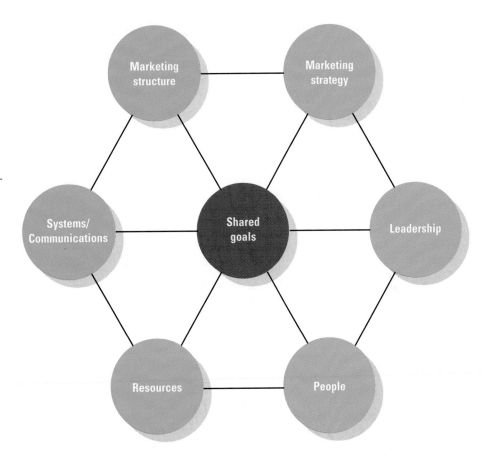

strategies. Front line managers and employees are often responsible for implementing strategies, even though they had no voice in developing them. Consequently, these front line employees may lack motivation and commitment.[16]

Components of Marketing Implementation

The marketing implementation process has several components, all of which must mesh if the implementation is to succeed. These components are shown in Figure 23.5. The systems component refers to work processes, procedures and the way in which information is structured—elements ensuring that the organisation's day-to-day activities are carried out. Typical organisational systems include marketing information systems, strategic planning systems, marketing planning processes, budgeting and accounting systems, manufacturing and quality control systems, and performance measurement systems.

The people component in Figure 23.5 refers to the importance of employees in the implementation process. It includes such factors as the quality, diversity and skills of the workforce within the organisation and also covers the human resources function. Issues like employee recruitment, selection and training have great bearing on the implementation of marketing activities.[17] Closely linked to the people component is leadership, or the art of managing people. It involves such issues as employee motivation, communication and reward policies.

At the centre of marketing implementation are shared goals, which draw the entire organisation together into a single, functioning unit. These goals may be simple statements of the company's objectives. On the other hand, the goals may be detailed mission statements, outlining corporate philosophy and direction. Shared goals appear in the centre of Figure 23.5 because they hold all the other components together to ensure successful marketing implementation.[18] Without shared goals, different parts of the organisation might work toward different goals or objectives, thus limiting the success of the entire organisation.

Approaches to Marketing Implementation

Once they grasp the problems and recognise the components of marketing implementation, marketing managers can decide on an approach for implementing marketing activities. Just as organisations can achieve their goals by using different marketing strategies, they can also implement their marketing strategies by using different approaches. This section discusses three general approaches to marketing implementation: relationship marketing, internal marketing and total quality management. These approaches, which represent mindsets that marketing managers can adopt when organising and planning marketing activities, are not mutually exclusive. Indeed, many companies adopt a combination of these approaches when designing marketing activities.

Relationship Marketing

Relationship marketing Places emphasis on the interaction between buyers and sellers and is concerned with winning and keeping customers by maintaining links between marketing, quality and customer service

The five markets model of relationship marketing In addition to customer markets, the core audiences of influencers, referrals, employee recruitment markets, suppliers and internal markets

Relationship marketing has recently attracted considerable attention in the marketing literature.[19] It focuses on the interaction between buyers and sellers and is concerned with winning and keeping customers by maintaining links between marketing, quality and customer service.[20] The term *relationship marketing* has been defined as attracting, maintaining and—in multi-service organisations— enhancing customer relationships.[21] The notion hinges on selling organisations taking a longer term view of customer relationships to ensure that those customers converted are also retained. There has been a shift from transaction based marketing towards a relationship focus, as explained by leading exponent Payne: "Transaction marketing of the 1980s placed the emphasis on the individual sale. Relationship marketing of the 1990s placed the emphasis on individual customers and seeks to establish a long term relationship between customer and company".[22]

The fundamental message is that ongoing, longer term relationships are essential for a business's viability and market performance. While marketers are encouraged to devote greater resources to developing such customer relationships, the relationship marketing literature explains that such long term commitment stems not only from treating customers differently, but also from addressing other audiences. As detailed in the **five markets model of relationship marketing** in Figure 23.6, these audiences include (1) referral markets, such as insurance brokers and advisers, (2) suppliers, (3) employee recruitment markets, (4) influencer markets, such as government bodies, EU officials and the central bank, and finally (5) internal markets.

In highlighting this final "market" of the five markets model, relationship marketers are acknowledging the damage which can be done if employees do not understand their role in ensuring that marketing recommendations are adequately actioned. In order to effectively exploit this internal market, thought

Figure 23.6 The five markets model of relationship marketing. SOURCE: M. Christopher, A. Payne and D. Ballantyne, *Relationship Marketing* (Oxford: Butterworth-Heinemann, 1991).

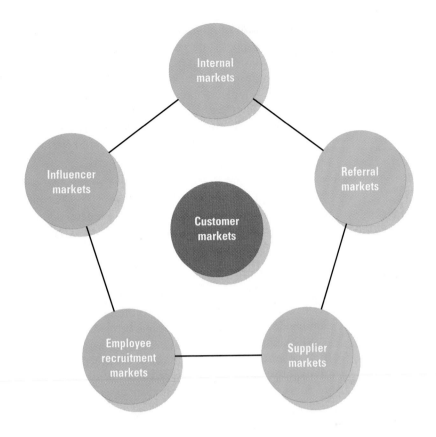

must be devoted to the establishment of communication channels; leadership qualities and people skills; associated resources; information content, access and sharing; IT support systems; management controls; clear internally focused propositions and messages; plus priorities for which employees are primary targets.

Internal Marketing

Internal marketing The application of marketing internally within the company, with programmes of communication and guidance targeted at internal audiences to develop responsiveness and a unified sense of purpose among employees

So much appears to hinge on **internal marketing,** which is the application of marketing internally within the company, with programmes of communication and guidance targeted at internal audiences. It plays a vital role in developing a customer focused organisation and helps ensure coherent relationship marketing.[23] Internal marketing is based on communication, the development of responsiveness and a unified sense of purpose among employees. It aims to develop internal and external customer awareness and to remove functional or human barriers to organisational effectiveness. Internal marketing centres on the notion that every member of the organisation has a "supplier" and a "customer". Long term, ongoing relationships require improved customer service. High levels of service depend on individuals ensuring that their suppliers and customers are happy. The concept also requires that all members of staff work together, in tune with the organisation's mission, strategy and goals. The aim is to ensure that all staff represent the business in the best possible way in all transactions they have with suppliers, customers and other staff. Internal marketing is a philosophy for managing human resources with a marketing perspective.[24]

In order to achieve this internal cohesiveness, internal marketers propose six steps:[25]

1. The creation of internal awareness
2. Identification of internal "customers" and "suppliers"
3. Determination of internal customers' expectations
4. Communication of these expectations to internal suppliers
5. Internal suppliers' modifications to their activities to reflect internal customers' views
6. A measure of internal service quality and feedback to ensure a satisfactory exchange between internal customers and suppliers.

The exponents of marketing planning have for many years realised that internal organisational barriers are likely to impede or restrict the implementation of marketing plans and marketing strategies.[26] They propose that senior managers address the people and cultural concerns detailed in Figure 23.7 before embarking on developing marketing plans, new market segmentation schemes or marketing strategies. These issues reflect the importance of addressing the internal market in effectively pursuing the implementation of marketing strategies and the deployment of recommended marketing mix programmes. Failure to control internal audiences and develop suitable control strategies will reduce the viability of the marketing function's recommended strategies and marketing plan recommendations in the external marketplace.

Marketing activities cannot be effectively implemented without the cooperation of employees. Employees are the essential ingredient in increasing productivity, providing customer service and beating the competition. Thus, in addition to marketing activities targeted at external customers, companies use internal

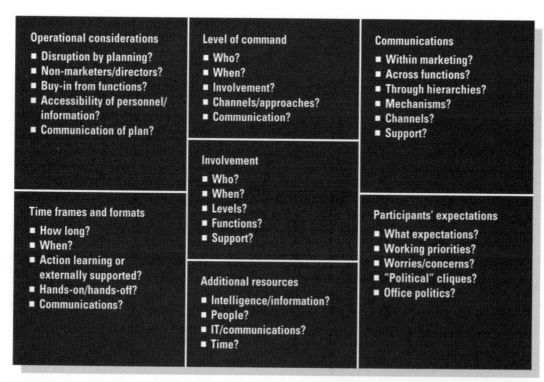

Figure 23.7 People and culture pre-requisites to effective marketing and marketing planning programmes. SOURCE: L. Simkin.

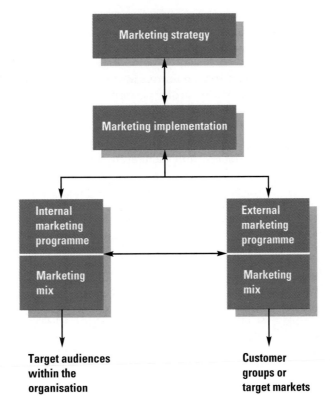

Figure 23.8 The internal marketing framework. SOURCE: Reprinted by permission from Nigel F. Piercy, *Market-Led Strategic Change*. Copyright © 1992.

marketing to attract, motivate and retain qualified internal customers (employees) by designing internal products (jobs) that satisfy employees' wants and needs. Generally speaking, internal marketing refers to the managerial actions necessary to make all members of the marketing organisation understand and accept their respective roles in implementing the marketing strategy. This means that all of them, from the chairperson of the company to the hourly workers on the shop floor, must understand the role they play in carrying out their jobs and implementing the marketing strategy. Everyone must do his or her part to ensure that customers are satisfied. All personnel within the company, both marketers and those who perform other functions, must recognise the tenet of customer orientation and service that underlies the marketing concept.

Like external marketing activities, internal marketing may involve market segmentation, product development, research, distribution, and even public relations and sales promotion.[27] The internal marketing framework is shown in Figure 23.8. As in external marketing, the marketing mix is used in the internal marketing approach to satisfy the needs of employees. For example, an organisation may sponsor sales competitions to encourage sales personnel to boost their selling efforts. Some companies encourage employees to work for their companies' customers for a period of time, often while continuing to receive their regular salaries. This helps the employees (and ultimately the company) to understand better customers' needs and problems, lets them learn valuable new skills and heightens their enthusiasm for their regular jobs. In addition, many companies use planning sessions, workshops, letters, formal reports and personal conversations as tools of internal distribution to ensure that employees understand the corporate mission, the organisation's goals and the marketing strategy. The ultimate result is more satisfied employees and improved customer relations.

Total Quality Management

Total quality management (TQM) Co-ordinated efforts directed at improving all aspects of a business—from product and service quality to customer and employee satisfaction

A primary concern today in some organisations is total quality management. Major reasons for this concern about quality are competition, more demanding customers and poorer profit performance due to reduced market shares and higher costs. **Total quality management (TQM)** is the co-ordination of efforts directed at improving all aspects of a business: enhancing customer satisfaction, increasing employee participation and empowerment, forming and strengthening supplier partnerships, and facilitating an organisational culture of continuous quality improvement. Customer satisfaction can be improved through higher quality products and better customer service, such as reduced delivery times, faster responses to customer inquiries and treatment of customers that shows caring on the company's part.

As a management philosophy, TQM relies heavily on the talents of employees to continually improve the quality of the organisation's goods and services. The TQM philosophy is founded on three basic principles: empowered employees, continuous quality improvement and quality improvement teams.[28]

Empowered Employees   Ultimately, TQM succeeds or fails because of the efforts of the organisation's employees. Thus employee recruitment, selection and training are critical to the success of marketing implementation. Empowerment means giving employees the authority to make decisions in order to satisfy customer needs. However, empowering employees is successful only if the organisation is guided by an overall corporate vision, shared goals and a culture that supports the TQM effort.[29] Such a system cannot spring up overnight. A great deal of time, effort and patience are needed to develop and sustain a quality oriented culture in an organisation. Three years of training workshops and evolution were required at JCB before TQM became firmly established as a managerial philosophy.

Continuous Quality Improvement   The continuous improvement of an organisation's products and services is built around the notion that quality is free: not having high quality goods and services can be very expensive, especially in terms of dissatisfied customers.[30] The continuous improvement of quality also means more than simple quality control, or the screening out of bad products during production. Rather, continuous improvement means building in quality from the very beginning—totally redesigning the product, if necessary. Continuous improvement is a slow, long term process of creating small improvements in quality. Companies that adopt TQM realise that the major advancements in quality occur because of an accumulation of these small improvements over time.

Benchmarking The process of comparing the quality of an organisation's goods, services or processes with that of its best performing competitors

A primary tool of the continuous quality improvement process is **benchmarking,** or the measurement and evaluation of the quality of an organisation's goods, services or processes as compared with the best performing companies in the industry.[31] Benchmarking lets an organisation know where it stands competitively in its industry, thus giving the company a goal to aim for over time. This goal is usually to be the best in the industry.

Quality Improvement Teams   The idea behind the team approach is to get the best and brightest people from a wide variety of perspectives working on a quality improvement issue simultaneously. Team members are usually selected from a cross-section of jobs within the organisation, as well as from among suppliers and customers. Customers are included in the quality improvement team because they are in the best position to know what they and other customers want from the company. Suppliers, too, understand the market.

Total quality management can provide several benefits. Overall financial benefits include lower operating costs, a higher return on sales and investment, and an improved ability to use premium pricing rather than competitive pricing. Additional benefits include faster development of innovations, improved access to global markets, higher levels of customer retention and an enhanced reputation.[32] Despite these advantages, only a handful of companies use the TQM approach, although the numbers are growing. The reason is that putting the TQM philosophy into practice requires a great deal of organisational resources: time, effort, money and patience on the part of the organisation. However, companies with the resources necessary to implement TQM gain an effective means of achieving major competitive advantages in their respective industries.

Although many factors can influence the effectiveness of the internal marketing and total quality management approaches, two issues are crucial. First, top management must be totally committed to internal marketing or TQM and must make either one or both of the approaches their top priority. Committed top managers serve as role models for other managers and employees.[33] It is naive for managers to expect employees to be committed to an approach when top managers are not. Second, management must co-ordinate the specific elements of these approaches to ensure that they work in harmony with each other. Over emphasising one aspect of relationship marketing, internal marketing or TQM can be detrimental to the other components, thus limiting the success of the overall programme.

Implementing Marketing Activities

Motivating Marketing Personnel

An important element in implementing the marketing plan, and in internal marketing, is motivating marketing personnel to perform effectively. People work to satisfy physical, psychological and social needs. To motivate marketing personnel, managers must discover their employees' needs and then develop motivational methods that help them satisfy those needs. It is crucial that the plan for motivating employees be fair, ethical and well understood by them. Additionally, rewards to employees must be tied to organisational goals. In general, to improve employee motivation, companies need to find out what workers think, how they feel and what they want. Some of this information can be obtained from an employee attitude survey. A business can motivate its workers by directly linking pay with performance, by informing workers how their performance affects department and corporate results, by following through with appropriate compensation, by promoting or implementing a flexible benefits programme and by adopting a participative management approach.[34]

Consider the following example. Suppose a salesperson can sell product A or B to a particular customer, but not both products. Product A sells for £200,000 and contributes £20,000 to the company's profit margin. Product B sells for £60,000 and has a contribution margin of £40,000. If the salesperson receives a commission of 3 per cent of sales, he or she would obviously prefer to sell product A, even though the sale of product B contributes more to the company's profits. If the salesperson's commission was based on contribution margin instead of sales and the company's goal was to maximise profits, both the company and the salesperson would benefit more from the sale of product B.[35] By tying rewards to organisational goals, the company encourages behaviour that meets organisational goals.

Besides tying rewards to organisational goals, managers must motivate individuals by using different motivational tools, based on each individual's value system. For example, some employees value recognition more than a slight pay increase. Managers can reward employees with money, plus additional fringe benefits, prestige or recognition, or even non-financial rewards such as job autonomy, skill variety, task significance and increased feedback. A survey of Fortune 1000 companies found that "the majority of organisations feel that they get more for their money through non-cash awards, if given in addition to a basic compensation plan".

Communicating within the Marketing Unit

With good communication, marketing managers can motivate personnel and co-ordinate their efforts. Marketing managers must be able to communicate with the company's high level management to ensure that marketing activities are consistent with the company's overall goals. Communication with top level executives keeps marketing managers aware of the company's overall plans and achievements. It also guides what the marketing unit is to do and how its activities are to be integrated with those of other departments—such as finance, production or personnel—with whose management the marketing manager must also communicate to co-ordinate marketing efforts. For example, marketing personnel must work with the production staff to help design products that customers want. To direct marketing activities, marketing managers must communicate with marketing personnel at the operations level, such as sales and advertising personnel, researchers, wholesalers, retailers and package designers.

To facilitate communication, marketing managers should establish an information system within the marketing unit. The marketing information system (discussed in Chapter 6) should allow for easy communication among marketing managers, sales managers and sales personnel. Marketers need an information system to support a variety of activities, such as planning, budgeting, sales analyses, performance evaluations and the preparation of reports. An information system should also expedite communications with other departments in the organisation and minimise destructive competition between departments for organisational resources. Managers must be encouraged to communicate freely, sharing ideas, insights, marketing intelligence, strategies and tactical recommendations. Such channels of communication should be across business functions and hierarchies. Stone-walling, gatekeeping, ring-fencing and misinformation—all facets of petty "office politics"—offer no benefits.

Co-ordinating Marketing Activities

Because of job specialisation and differences related to marketing activities, marketing managers must synchronise individuals' actions to achieve marketing objectives. In addition, they must work closely with managers in research and development, production, finance, accounting and personnel to see that marketing activities mesh with other functions of the company. In Figure 23.9, Sony's advertisement is the outward indication of a highly co-ordinated and carefully planned strategy. Marketing managers must co-ordinate the activities of market-

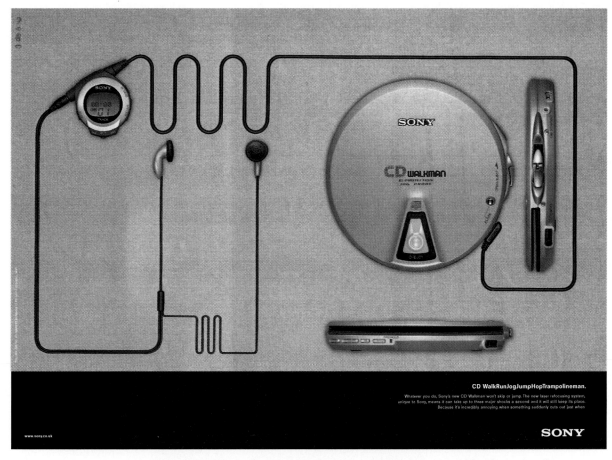

Figure 23.9   Co-ordinating marketing activities. Sony's worldwide success hinges on thorough marketing planning and comprehensive implementation of strategies across national borders.   SOURCE: Courtesy of Sony Europa.

ing staff within the business and integrate those activities with the marketing efforts of external organisations—advertising agencies, resellers (wholesalers, retailers and dealers), researchers and shippers, among others. Marketing managers can improve co-ordination by using internal marketing activities to make each employee aware of how his or her job relates to others and how his or her actions contribute to the achievement of marketing plans.

Controlling Marketing Activities

Marketing control process   One that establishes performance standards, evaluates actual performance and reduces the differences between desired and actual performance

To achieve marketing objectives as well as general organisational goals, marketing managers must effectively control marketing efforts. The **marketing control process** consists of establishing performance standards, evaluating actual performance by comparing it with established standards and reducing the differences between desired and actual performance, using corrective action, if necessary. This process helped Xerox to recover ground lost to competitors. Dunkin'

Donuts has developed a programme to ensure consistency throughout its franchises. Dunkin' Donuts controls the quality of operations in its franchised units by having franchisees attend Dunkin' Donuts University. Owners and managers of Dunkin' Donuts are required to take a six week training course, covering everything from customer relations and marketing to production, including a test of making 140 dozen doughnuts in eight hours. As part of the test, an instructor randomly selects six of the 1,680 doughnuts made to ascertain that they weigh around 350 grammes (12 ounces) and measure just under 20 centimetres (8 inches) when stacked. The Dunkin' Donuts University was opened to guarantee uniformity in all aspects of the business operations throughout the 1,700 franchise units.[36] Kodak's and 3M's efforts to implement and control their marketing strategies are discussed in Marketing Insight 23.2.

Although the control function is a fundamental management activity, it has until recently received little attention in marketing. There are both formal and informal control systems in organisations. The formal marketing control process involves performance standards, evaluation of actual performance and corrective action to remedy shortfalls (see Figure 23.10). The informal control process, however, involves self-control, social or group control, and cultural control through acceptance of a company's value system. Which type of control system dominates depends on the environmental context of the business.[37]

Figure 23.10 The marketing control process

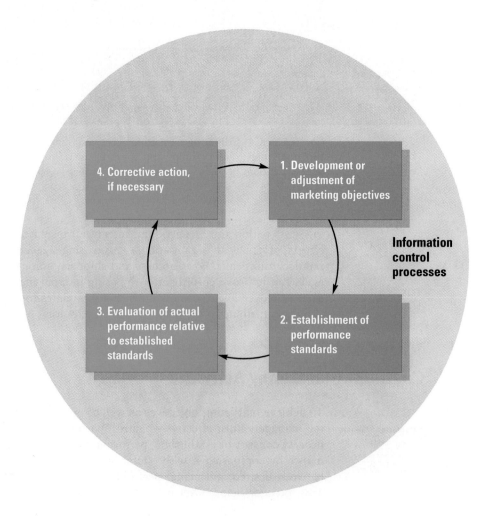

Kodak and 3M Plan for the Future by Targeting Youth Market

To the purist camera buff or photographic enthusiast, the growth in single use cameras is an unwelcome phenomenon. By the mid-1990s, over one million single use, "point and shoot", cheap and relatively disposable cameras were being sold each year. 3M introduced its second generation, Slimline. Kodak continued to introduce more and more single use cameras: the Kodak Wedding camera is tipped to be the largest growing member of the Kodak range, and by specifically targeting such a large market—weddings—the company expected the overall market to more than double in size. The Kodak Fun Saver Pocket cameras are even smaller and cheaper, aimed at children. Concord Camera has gone one further. Licensing the Crayola brand name—famous for crayons and colouring pens—from Hallmark Cards, Concord's single use cameras are very colourfully decorated and are designed to appeal to children under 12. Kalimar has linked up with the Barbie Doll, producing Barbie-branded single use cameras aimed at girls aged 5 to 15. Japanese giant Fuji is also active in the single use market, with its Quick Snap range aimed at the holiday season and tourists.

For the manufacturers, the purpose of the single use camera is to encourage people hesitant to use cameras or those unlikely to purchase an expensive Pentax or Ricoh model to enter the market. By targeting youngsters, the camera and film manufacturers are investing in the potential heavy users of the future—the next generation of snap-happy consumers, who make up the bulk of film sales and income from film processing. Companies such as 3M and Kodak have devoted a great deal of time, thought and resources to developing all facets of the photographic market.

It is important for companies to have developed shrewd target market strategies such as those deployed in the Crayola or Barbie tie-ins, and it is essential for them to have clearly identified a customer need and to be able to satisfy it. In marketing terms, however, that is not the complete picture. 3M and Kodak have not only developed carefully honed customer propositions and marketing strategies. In addition, they have devoted a great deal of time and resources to managing the implementation of their determined marketing strategies, recognising that without thorough and careful planning inside their businesses, it is unlikely that their chosen marketing strategies will ever be effectively or successfully actioned.

In many cases markets have been analysed, strategies developed and marketing mix programmes formulated—only to be made redundant by inadequate internal resources, ineffective managerial processes, poor communications, low morale or poor understanding. Implementation is just as important as marketing strategy. Implementation must itself be well planned, carefully controlled and effectively managed to ensure that a business's recommended strategy is put into practice and to facilitate the smooth instigation of the required marketing mix programmes. Both Kodak and 3M expend a significant amount of effort managing the implementation of their marketing activities.

SOURCES: Dixons plc, 1999; Loretta Roach, "Single use explosion", *Discount Merchandiser,* September 1995, pp. 28–30; Boots UK, 1996; Kodak UK, 1996; Pete Hisey, "Photo industry focuses on kids", *Discount Store News,* 20 March 1995, p. 47; Childrensworld store catalogue, 1996; Toys "R" Us, Coventry, 1999.

Establishing Performance Standards

Performance standard An expected level of performance against which actual performance can be compared

Planning and controlling are closely linked because plans include statements about what is to be accomplished. For purposes of control, these statements function as performance standards. A **performance standard** is an expected level of performance against which actual performance can be compared. Examples of performance standards might be the reduction of customers' complaints by 20 per cent, a monthly sales quota of £150,000, a 10 per cent increase per month in new customer accounts or an increased measure of brand awareness.

Performance standards are also given in the form of budget accounts; that is, marketers are expected to achieve a certain objective without spending more than a given amount of resources. Performance standards can relate to product quality and should be tied to organisational goals.

Evaluating Actual Performance

To compare actual performance with performance standards, marketing managers must know what marketers within the company are doing and must have information about the activities of external organisations that provide the business with marketing assistance. Information is required about the activities of marketing personnel at the operations level and at various marketing management levels. Most businesses obtain marketing assistance from one or more external individuals or organisations, such as advertising agencies, middlemen, marketing research organisations and consultants. To maximise benefits from external sources, a company's marketing control process must monitor their activities. Although it may be difficult to obtain the necessary information, it is impossible to measure actual performance without it.

Records of actual performance are compared with performance standards to determine whether and how much of a discrepancy exists. For example, a salesperson's actual sales are compared with his or her sales quota. If there is a significant negative discrepancy, the sales manager takes corrective action.

Taking Corrective Action

Marketing managers have several options for reducing a discrepancy between established performance standards and actual performance. They can take steps to improve actual performance, can reduce or totally change the performance standard or do both. Changes in actual performance may require the marketing manager to use better methods of motivating marketing personnel or to find more effective techniques for co-ordinating marketing efforts.

Sometimes performance standards are unrealistic when they are written. In other cases, changes in the marketing environment make them unrealistic. For example, a company's annual sales goal may become unrealistic if several aggressive competitors enter the market. In fact, changes in the marketing environment may force managers to change their marketing strategy completely.

Requirements for an Effective Control Process

A marketing manager should consider several requirements in creating and maintaining effective marketing control processes.[38] Effective control hinges on the quantity and quality of information available to the marketing manager and the speed at which it is received. The control process should be designed so that the flow of information is rapid enough to allow the marketing manager to detect quickly differences between actual and planned levels of performance. A single control procedure is not suitable for all types of marketing activities, and internal and environmental changes affect an organisation's activities. Therefore, control procedures should be flexible enough to adjust to both varied activities and changes in the organisation's situation. For the control process to be usable, its costs must be low relative to the costs that would arise if controls were lacking. Finally, the control process should be designed so that both managers and subordinates can understand it and its requirements.

Problems in Controlling Marketing Activities

When marketing managers attempt to control marketing activities, they frequently run into several problems. Often the information required to control marketing activities is unavailable or is available only at a high cost. Even though marketing controls should be flexible enough to allow for environmental changes, the frequency, intensity and unpredictability of such changes may hamper effective control. In addition, the time lag between marketing activities and their effects limits a marketing manager's ability to measure the effectiveness of marketing activities.

Consider the problems of demand fluctuation in the video games industry. By failing to control the number of video game products offered, Nintendo, Atari and Sega glutted the market with so many video game titles that consumers were confused and disappointed with the numerous look-alike products. Companies are avoiding past mistakes by carefully analysing the success of video games and deleting older games that are no longer profitable. For example, Nintendo withdrew 18 of its 36 games to make room for new product introductions. This careful analysis and control of product offerings has helped home video games make a comeback from being a spectacular but short lived fad of the early 1980s.[39] It is estimated that one out of two homes has either a Nintendo, Sega or Sony system.

Because marketing and other business activities overlap, marketing managers cannot determine the precise cost of marketing activities. Without an accurate measure of marketing costs, it is difficult to know if the effects of marketing activities are worth their expense. Finally, marketing control may be difficult because it is very hard to develop exact performance standards for marketing personnel.

Methods of Evaluating Performance

There are specific methods for assessing and improving the effectiveness of a marketing strategy. A marketer should state in the marketing plan what a marketing strategy is supposed to accomplish. These statements should set forth performance standards, which are usually stated in terms of profits, sales, market share, brand awareness, customer satisfaction levels or costs. Actual performance must be measured in similar terms so that comparisons are possible. This section describes sales analysis and marketing cost analysis, two general ways of evaluating the actual performance of marketing strategies. "Softer" measures such as brand awareness and customer satisfaction levels are also important and feature in the performance measures utilised by marketing-led businesses.

Sales Analysis

Sales analysis The use of sales figures to evaluate a business's current performance

Sales analysis uses sales figures to evaluate a company's current performance. It is probably the most common method of evaluation, because sales data partially reflect the target market's reactions to a marketing mix and are often readily available, at least in aggregate form.

Marketers use current sales data to monitor the impact of current marketing efforts. However, that information alone is not enough. To provide useful analyses, current sales data must be compared with forecast sales, industry sales, specific competitors' sales or the costs incurred to achieve the sales volume. For example, knowing that a store attained a £600,000 sales volume this year does not tell management whether its marketing strategy has been successful. However, if managers know that expected sales were £550,000, they are then in a better position to determine the effectiveness of the company's marketing efforts. In addition, if they know that the marketing costs needed to achieve the £600,000 volume were 12 per cent less than budgeted, they are in an even better position to analyse their marketing strategy precisely.

Sales Measurements   Although there are several types of **sales measurements**, the basic unit of measurement is the sales transaction. A sales transaction results in a customer order for a specified quantity of an organisation's product sold under specified terms by a particular salesperson or sales group on a certain date. Many organisations record these bits of information about their transactions. With such a record, a company can analyse sales in terms of cash or sales volume or market share.

Companies frequently use cash volume sales analysis because currency is a common denominator of sales, costs and profits. However, price increases and decreases affect total sales figures. For example, if a company increased its prices by 10 per cent this year and its sales volume is 10 per cent greater than last year, it has not experienced any increase in unit sales. A marketing manager who uses cash volume analysis should factor out the effects of price changes.

A company's market share is the company's sales of a product stated as a percentage of industry sales of that product. For example, KP, Golden Wonder and Walkers account for around 70 per cent of the UK savoury snacks market. In the carbonated drinks sector, Coca-Cola has a leading 16 per cent share by volume.[40] Market share analysis lets a company compare its marketing strategy with competitors' strategies. The primary reason for using market share analysis is to estimate whether sales changes have resulted from the company's marketing strategy or from uncontrollable environmental forces. When a company's sales volume declines but its share of the market stays the same, the marketer can assume that industry sales declined—because of some uncontrollable factors—and that this decline was reflected in the company's sales. However, if a company experiences a decline in both sales and market share, it should consider the possibility that its marketing strategy is not effective.

Even though market share analysis can be helpful in evaluating the performance of a marketing strategy, the user must interpret results cautiously. When attributing a sales decline to uncontrollable factors, a marketer must keep in mind that such factors do not affect all companies in the industry equally. Not all companies in an industry have the same objectives, and some change their objectives from one year to the next. Changes in the objectives of one company can affect the market shares of one or all companies in that industry. For example, if a competitor significantly increases promotional efforts or drastically reduces prices to increase market share, a company could lose market share despite a well designed marketing strategy. Within an industry, the entrance of new companies or the demise of established ones also affects a specific business's market share, and market share analysts should attempt to account for these effects. Kentucky Fried Chicken (KFC), for example, probably re-evaluated its marketing strategies when McDonald's introduced its own fried chicken product.

Whether it is based on sales volume or market share, sales analysis can be performed on aggregate sales figures or on disaggregated data. Aggregate sales analysis provides an overview of current sales. Although helpful, aggregate sales analysis is often insufficient, because it does not bring to light sales variations within the aggregate. It is not uncommon for a marketer to find that a large proportion of aggregate sales comes from a small number of products, geographic

Sales measurements   Data regarding sales transactions that are used to analyse performance, usually in terms of cash volume or market share

areas or customers. This is sometimes called the "iceberg principle" because only a small part of an iceberg is visible above the water. To find such disparities, total sales figures are usually broken down by geographic unit, salesperson, product, customer type or a combination of these categories.

In sales analysis by geographic unit, sales data can be classified by city, county, region, country or any other geographic designation for which a marketer collects sales information. Actual sales in a geographic unit can be compared with sales in a similar geographic unit, with last year's sales or with an estimated market potential for the area. For example, if a company finds that 18 per cent of its sales are coming from an area that represents only 8 per cent of the potential sales for the product, then it can be assumed that the marketing strategy is successful in that geographic unit.

Because of the cost associated with hiring and maintaining a salesforce, businesses commonly analyse sales by salesperson to determine the contribution each member of the salesforce makes. Performance standards for each salesperson are often set in terms of sales quotas for a given time period. Evaluation of actual performance is accomplished by comparing a salesperson's current sales with a pre-established quota or some other standard, such as the previous period's sales. If actual sales meet or exceed the standard and the sales representative has not incurred costs above those budgeted, that person's efforts are acceptable.

Sales analysis is often performed according to product group or specific product item. Marketers break down their aggregate sales figures by product to determine the proportion that each contributed to total sales. Columbia Pictures, for example, might break down its total sales figures by box office figures for each film produced. A company usually sets a sales volume objective—and sometimes a market share objective—for each product item or product group, and sales analysis by product is the only way to measure such objectives. A marketer can compare the breakdown of current sales by product with those of previous years. In addition, within industries for which sales data by product are available, a company's sales by product type can be compared with industry averages. To gain an accurate picture of where sales of specific products are occurring, marketers sometimes combine sales analysis by product with sales analysis by geographic area or salesperson.

Analyses based on customers are usually broken down by type of customer. Customers can be classified by the way they use a company's products, their distribution level (producer, wholesaler, retailer), their size, the size of orders or other characteristics. Sales analysis by customer type lets a company ascertain whether its marketing resources are allocated in a way that achieves the greatest productivity. For example, sales analysis by type of customer may reveal that 60 per cent of the salesforce is serving a group that accounts for only 15 per cent of total sales.

A considerable amount of information is needed for sales analyses, especially if disaggregated analyses are desired. The marketer must develop an operational system for collecting sales information; obviously, the effectiveness of the system for collecting sales information largely determines the ability of a company to develop useful sales analyses.

Marketing Cost Analysis

Although sales analysis is critical for evaluating the effectiveness of a marketing strategy, it gives only part of the picture. A marketing strategy that successfully generates sales may also be extremely costly. To obtain a complete picture, a company must know the marketing costs associated with using a given strategy to

Marketing cost analysis The break down and classification of costs to determine which are associated with specific marketing activities

achieve a certain sales level. **Marketing cost analysis** breaks down and classifies costs to determine which are associated with specific marketing activities. By comparing costs of previous marketing activities with results generated, a marketer can better allocate the business's marketing resources in the future. Marketing cost analysis lets a company evaluate the effectiveness of an ongoing or recent marketing strategy by comparing sales achieved and costs incurred. By pin-pointing exactly where a company is experiencing high costs, this form of analysis can help isolate profitable or unprofitable customer segments, products or geographic areas.

For example, the market share of Komatsu, a Japanese construction equipment manufacturer, began to decline in the United States when prices increased because of the high yen value. Komatsu responded by developing an equal joint venture with Dresser Industries, making it the second largest company in this industry. The joint venture with Dresser allowed Komatsu to shift a large amount of its final assembly to the United States, to Dresser plants that had been running at 50 per cent capacity. By using Dresser's unused capacity and existing US plants, Komatsu avoided the start up costs of new construction and gained an immediate manufacturing presence in the United States.[41] This cost control tactic has enabled Komatsu to use price more effectively as a marketing variable to compete with industry leader Caterpillar.

In some organisations, personnel in other functional areas—such as production or accounting—see marketers as primarily concerned with generating sales, regardless of the costs incurred. By conducting cost analyses, marketers can counter this criticism and put themselves in a better position to demonstrate how marketing activities contribute to generating profits. Even though hiring a sports figure such as Monica Seles is costly, in many sectors sales goals cannot be reached without large expenditures for promotion. Many advertisers believe that using celebrities helps to increase sales. Research shows that the public are good at identifying which personalities are linked to advertised brands. Ultimately, cost analysis should show if promotion costs are effective in increasing sales. A robust marketing plan is not complete without a detailed budget which, when balanced with the sales forecast, marketing analyses, strategic thinking and detailed marketing mix programmes, explains the required marketing spend.

The task of determining marketing costs is often complex and difficult. Simply ascertaining the costs associated with marketing a product is rarely adequate. Marketers must usually determine the marketing costs of serving specific geographic areas, market segments or even specific customers. The ABC sales: contribution analysis outlined in Chapter 21 is a useful tool in this endeavour.

A first step in determining the costs is to examine accounting records. Most accounting systems classify costs into **natural accounts**—such as rent, salaries, office supplies and utilities—which are based on how the money was actually spent. Unfortunately, many natural accounts do not help explain what marketing functions were performed through the expenditure of those funds. It does little good, for example, to know that £80,000 is spent for rent each year. The analyst has no way of knowing whether the money is spent for the rental of production, storage or sales facilities. Therefore, marketing cost analysis usually requires some of the costs in natural accounts to be reclassified into **marketing function accounts**, which indicate the function performed through the expenditure of funds. Common marketing function accounts are transport, storage, order processing, selling, advertising, sales promotion, marketing research, consultancy and customer credit.

Natural accounts The classification of costs based on how money was actually spent

Marketing function accounts A method of indicating the function performed through the expenditure of funds

Natural accounts can be reclassified into marketing function accounts as shown in the simplified example in Table 23.1. Note that a few natural accounts, such as advertising, can be reclassified easily into functional accounts because they do not have to be split across several accounts. For most of the natural accounts, however, marketers must develop criteria for assigning them to the various functional accounts. For example, the number of square metres of floor space used was the criterion for dividing the rental costs in Table 23.1 into functional accounts. In some instances, a specific marketing cost is incurred to perform several functions. A packaging cost, for example, could be considered a production function, a distribution function, a promotional function or all three. The marketing cost analyst must reclassify such costs across multiple functions.

Three broad categories are used in marketing cost analysis: direct costs, traceable common costs and non-traceable common costs. **Direct costs** are directly attributable to the performance of marketing functions. For example, salesforce salaries might be allocated to the cost of selling a specific product item, selling in a specific geographic area or selling to a particular customer. **Traceable common costs** can be allocated indirectly, using one or several criteria, to the functions that they support. For example, if the company spends £80,000 annually to rent space for production, storage and selling, the rental costs of storage could be determined on the basis of cost per square metre used for storage. **Non-traceable common costs** cannot be assigned according to any logical criteria and thus are assignable only on an arbitrary basis. Interest, taxes and the salaries of top management are non-traceable common costs.

The manner of dealing with these three categories of costs depends on whether the analyst uses a full cost or a direct cost approach. When a **full cost approach** is used, cost analysis includes direct costs, traceable common costs and non-traceable common costs. Proponents of this approach claim that if an accurate profit

Direct costs Costs directly attributable to the performance of marketing functions

Traceable common costs Costs that can be allocated indirectly, using one or several criteria, to the functions they support

Non-traceable common costs Costs that cannot be assigned according to any logical criteria

Full cost approach An approach in which cost analysis includes direct costs, traceable common costs and non-traceable common costs

Profit and Loss Statement							
Sales	£250,000			**Functional Accounts**			
Cost of goods sold	45,000						
Gross profit	205,000		**Personal**			**Marketing**	**Non-**
Expenses (natural accounts)		**Advertising**	**Selling**	**Transport**	**Storage**	**Research**	**Marketing**
Rent	£ 14,000		£ 7,000		£6,000		£ 1,000
Salaries	72,000	£12,000	32,000	£7,000		£1,000	20,000
Supplies	4,000	1,500	1,000			1,000	500
Advertising	16,000	16,000					
Freight	4,000			2,000			2,000
Taxes	2,000				200		1,800
Insurance	1,000				600		400
Interest	3,000						3,000
Bad debts	6,000						6,000
Total	£122,000	£29,500	£40,000	£9,000	£6,800	£2,000	£34,700
Net profit	£ 83,000						

Table 23.1 Reclassification of natural accounts into functional accounts

picture is desired, all costs must be included in the analysis. However, opponents point out that full costing does not yield actual costs, because non-traceable common costs are determined by arbitrary criteria. With different criteria, the full costing approach yields different results. A cost-conscious operating unit can be discouraged if numerous costs are assigned to it arbitrarily. To eliminate such problems, the **direct cost approach,** which includes direct costs and traceable common costs but not non-traceable common costs, is used. Opponents say that this approach is not accurate, because it omits one cost category.

Direct cost approach An approach that includes only direct costs and traceable common costs

Marketers can use several methods to analyse costs. The methods vary in their precision. This section examines three cost analysis methods—analysis of natural accounts, analysis of functional accounts, and analysis by product, geographic area or customer.

Marketers can sometimes determine marketing costs by performing an analysis of natural accounts. The precision of this method depends on how detailed the company's accounts are. For example, if accounting records contain separate accounts for production wages, salesforce wages and executive salaries, the analysis can be more precise than if all wages and salaries are lumped into a single account. An analysis of natural accounts is more meaningful, and thus more useful, when current cost data can be compared with those of previous periods or with average cost figures for the entire industry. Cost analysis of natural accounts frequently treats costs as percentages of sales. The periodic use of cost-to-sales ratios lets a marketer ascertain cost fluctuations quickly.

The analysis of natural accounts may not shed much light on the cost of marketing activities. In such cases, natural accounts must be reclassified into marketing function accounts for analysis. Whether certain natural accounts are reclassified into functional accounts and what criteria are used to reclassify them will depend to some degree on whether the analyst is using direct costing or full costing. After natural accounts have been reclassified into functional accounts, the cost of each function is determined by adding together the costs in each functional account. Once the costs of these marketing functions have been determined, the analyst is ready to compare the resulting figures with budgeted costs, sales analysis data, cost data from earlier operating periods or perhaps average industry cost figures, if these are available.

Although marketers usually obtain a more detailed picture of marketing costs by analysing functional accounts than by analysing natural accounts, some businesses need an even more precise cost analysis. The need is especially great if the businesses sell several types of products, sell in multiple geographic areas or sell to a wide variety of customers. Activities vary in marketing different products in specific geographic locations to certain customer groups. Therefore, the costs of these activities also vary. By analysing the functional costs of specific product groups, geographic areas or customer groups, a marketer can find out which of these marketing entities are the most cost effective to serve. In Table 23.2, the functional costs derived in Table 23.1 are allocated to specific product categories.

A similar type of analysis could be performed for geographic areas or for specific customer groups. The criteria used to allocate the functional accounts must be developed so as to yield results that are as accurate as possible. Use of faulty criteria is likely to yield inaccurate cost estimates, which in turn lead to less effective control of marketing strategies. Marketers determine the marketing costs for various product categories, geographic areas or customer groups and then compare them with sales. This analysis lets them evaluate the effectiveness of the company's marketing strategy or strategies.

Performance Measures

Marketing performance The assessment of the effectiveness of marketing programmes to implement recommended marketing strategies, fulfil corporate financial expectations and achieve the required levels of customer satisfaction.

Sales per square metre A financial measure retailers might use to assess marketing performance

The evaluation of **marketing performance**—the assessment of the effectiveness of marketing programmes to implement recommended marketing strategies, fulfil corporate financial expectations and achieve the required levels of customer satisfaction—is a necessary control mechanism in the marketing process. Table 23.3 describes some popular performance measures adopted by marketers to assess overall markets, specific segments or product lines. Most UK companies are notoriously short term in their thinking, focusing on profitability as their over riding measure. Other financial measures include return on investment, return on capital employed and, for retailers, **sales per square metre** of selling space. Units produced and units sold are included as measures by most manufacturers, leading to an assessment of production capacity utilisation. Market share is a vital

Table 23.2 Functional accounts divided into product group costs

Functional Accounts		Product Groups		
		A	B	C
Advertising	£29,500	£14,000	£ 8,000	£ 7,500
Personal selling	40,000	18,000	10,000	12,000
Transport	9,000	5,000	2,000	2,000
Storage	6,800	1,800	2,000	3,000
Marketing research	2,000		1,000	1,000
Total	£87,300	£38,800	£23,000	£25,500

Table 23.3 Performance measures in marketing

Profitability
  Net profit is the difference between the income from goods sold and all expenses (production, personnel, distribution, marketing, etc.) incurred

Sales Volumes
  $s, £s or ECUs/euros
  Units sold

Market Share
  Brand or product share of the overall market's sales

Return on Investment

$$\text{ROI} = \frac{\text{Net Income}}{\text{Total Investment}}$$

Return on Capital Employed

$$\text{ROE} = \frac{\text{Net Profit}}{\text{Sales}} \times \frac{\text{Sales}}{\text{Assets}}$$

Customer Satisfaction Levels
  Tracked over time through customer surveys

Customers' Brand Awareness
  Monitored over time through customer surveys

criterion for judging performance. While it is without question important for businesses to be financially viable—making adequate profits to be able to fund future investments in production, people, new products, new target markets and so forth—increasingly marketers have accepted the need to evaluate performance on additional, more customer oriented measures.

Marketing aims to satisfy customers, so it is sensible to monitor **customer satisfaction.** Over time, such surveys should reveal an improvement in customer satisfaction levels, otherwise it could be argued that the marketing plan recommendations are failing to fully address target customer needs and expectations. Most hotel companies operate room card surveys of guest satisfaction in order to monitor customers' experiences and improve performance of their staff, services and facilities. A measure of **brand awareness,** as illustrated in Chapter 16's Table 16.6, is also monitored by a growing number of marketers to ensure that their tactical marketing programmes are effectively bringing their brands and products to their target market's attention. While such tracking involves qualitative marketing research, measures of customer satisfaction and brand awareness must be integral to a business's assessment of performance, alongside the important traditional financial performance measures. Ultimately, a well managed, customer oriented company should use a mix of financial and qualitative measures to judge its performance and the effectiveness of its marketing programmes. In addition, performance measures are more meaningful if they attempt to benchmark a business's performance against that of its key competitors.

Performance in the promotional mix has taxed experts for decades and there remain few proven objective solutions to determining the value of promotional spend to the business's overall fortunes. It is possible in public relations to use a **clippings service** to count the frequency of mentions of a specific brand or company in selected media, but this approach fails to assess the positive/negative mix of citations and cannot extrapolate to draw conclusions relating to sales gains resulting specifically from this PR activity. Hits on a company's web site are counted, but do these lead to sales? If an order is placed via the Internet, then a link can be shown, but if not, it is difficult to demonstrate a causal relationship between the web site and sales. Even if an order is placed via the Internet, it is possible that the customer was in fact responding primarily to a press or TV advertisement or to an earlier in-store demonstration. Sponsorship agencies monitor the awareness of clients' brands when linked to sporting events or the performing arts, but cannot prove that such awareness leads directly to increased sales of products, better profitability or rising market share.

Salesforce managers monitor individual sales personnel in terms of the ratio of calls to orders. In addition, the salesforce is directly involved in the selling process and instantly judges its own performance. What stands for a good ratio of orders to calls is still a subjective assessment. Sales promotions are perhaps the safest to measure as they generally require customers to redeem coupons and vouchers or submit competition applications, all of which may be counted. However, subjective judgement is still used in determining what constitutes a "good" redemption rate. Most problematic is the assessment of advertising effectiveness. This is unfortunate as advertising often accounts for the largest proportion of the marketing budget. It is possible, as described in Chapter 16, to monitor target audience awareness of advertising but not to prove that exposure to a specific advertisement has led to a specific sale. At the moment, there are no easy solutions to this dilemma, yet marketers must attempt to assess the performance of their endeavours, seeking to validate their promotional mix spending. The tools

Customer satisfaction A qualitative measure of marketing performance that involves surveying customers over time

Brand awareness A qualitative measure of marketing performance that determines whether a company's brands capture the attention of their target markets

Clippings service A service that counts the frequency of mentions of a specific brand or company in selected media

described here are far from perfect but they demonstrate an effort to assess promotional effectiveness. Many businesses unfortunately fail to utilise even these simplistic tools.[42]

● S U M M A R Y

The organisation of marketing activities involves the development of an internal structure for the marketing unit, including relationships and lines of authority and responsibility that connect and co-ordinate individuals. The internal structure is the key to directing marketing activities. In a *marketing oriented organisation,* the focus is on finding out what buyers want and providing it in a way that lets the company achieve its objectives. A *centralised organisation* is one in which the top level managers delegate very little authority to lower levels of the business. In a *decentralised organisation,* decision-making authority is delegated as far down the chain of command as possible. An extreme form of decentralisation is *empowerment,* in which front line employees are given the authority and responsibility to make marketing decisions without seeking the approval of their supervisors. The marketing unit can be *organised by* (1) *functions,* (2) *products,* (3) *regions* or (4) *types of customer. Category management* is an in-vogue variation of organising by products. An organisation may use only one approach or a combination.

Marketing implementation, a process that involves activities to put marketing strategies into action, is an important part of the marketing management process. To help ensure effective implementation, marketing managers must consider why the intended marketing strategies do not always turn out as expected. *Realised strategies* often differ from the *intended strategies* because of the three problems of implementation: that marketing strategy and implementation are related, that they are constantly evolving and that the responsibility for them is separated. Marketing managers must also consider other vital components of implementation—resources, systems, people, leadership and shared goals—to ensure the proper implementation of marketing strategies.

Approaches organisations use for marketing implementation include *relationship marketing, internal marketing* and *total quality management (TQM).* In relationship marketing, the focus is on winning and keeping customers by maintaining links between marketing, quality and customer service. This requires a company to satisfy not only customers but also those audiences in the *five market model of relationship marketing:* referral, supplier, employee recruitment markets, influencer and internal markets. Internal marketing is the application of marketing internally within the company, with programmes of communication and guidance targeted at internal audiences to develop responsiveness and a unified sense of purpose among employees. It is a philosophy for managing human resources with a marketing perspective so that all members of the marketing organisation understand and accept their respective roles in implementing the marketing strategy.

The TQM approach relies heavily on the talents of employees to continually improve the quality of the organisation's goods and services. The three essentials of the TQM philosophy are empowered employees, continuous quality improvement and the use of quality improvement teams. One of TQM's primary tools is *benchmarking,* or measuring and evaluating the quality of an organisation's goods, services or processes in relation to the best performing companies in the industry. Putting the TQM philosophy into practice requires a great deal of organisational resources. For relationship marketing, internal marketing or TQM to be successful, top management must be totally committed and the specific elements of these programmes must be co-ordinated to ensure that they work in harmony with each other.

Implementation is an important part of the marketing management process. Proper implementation of a marketing plan depends on internal marketing to motivate personnel who perform marketing activities, effective communication within the marketing unit and the co-ordination of marketing activities.

Managers can motivate personnel by tying rewards, both financial and non-financial, to organisational goals. A company's communication system must allow the marketing manager to communicate with high level management, with managers of other functional areas in the company and with personnel involved in marketing activities both inside and outside the organisation. Finally, marketing managers must co-ordinate the activities of marketing personnel and integrate these activities with those in other areas of the company and with the marketing efforts of personnel in external organisations.

The *marketing control process* consists of establishing performance standards, evaluating actual performance by comparing it with established standards and reducing the difference between desired and actual performance. *Performance standards,* which are established in the planning process, are expected levels of performance against which actual performance can be compared. In evaluating actual performance, marketing managers must know what marketers within the business are doing and must have information about the activities of external organisations that provide the company with marketing assistance. Then actual performance is compared with performance standards. Marketers must determine whether a discrepancy exists and, if so, whether it requires corrective action, such as changing the performance standards or improving actual performance.

Effective marketing control hinges on the quantity and quality of information and the speed at which it is received. The control of marketing activities is not a simple task. Problems encountered include environmental changes, time lags between marketing activities and their effects, and difficulty in determining the costs of marketing activities. In addition to these, it may be hard to develop exact performance standards for marketing personnel.

Control of marketing strategy can be achieved through *sales* and *marketing cost analyses. Sales measurements* are usually analysed in terms of either cash volume or market share. For a sales analysis to be effective, it must compare current sales performance with forecast company sales, industry sales, specific competitors' sales or the costs incurred to generate the current sales volume. A sales analysis can be performed on the company's total sales, or the total sales can be disaggregated and analysed by product, geographic area, salesperson or customer type.

Marketing cost analysis involves an examination of accounting records and, frequently, a reclassification of *natural accounts* into *marketing function accounts*. Three broad categories are used in marketing cost analysis: *direct costs, traceable common costs* and *non-traceable common costs*. Such an analysis is often difficult, because there may be no logical, clear cut way to allocate natural accounts into functional accounts. The analyst may choose either a *direct cost approach* or *full cost approach*. Cost analysis can focus on (1) an aggregate cost analysis of natural accounts or functional accounts or (2) an analysis of functional accounts for products, geographic areas or customer groups.

Performance measures popular in evaluating *marketing performance* include assessing overall markets, specific segments or product lines in terms of financial profitability, contribution or return on investment; market share; *customer satisfaction* levels; and qualitative measures of customer *brand awareness*. Retail marketers additionally favour a measure of *sales per square metre* of store selling space. A *clippings service* can be used to count the frequency of mentions of a particular brand or company in the media.

Important Terms

Marketing oriented organisation
Centralised organisation
Decentralised organisation
Empowerment
Organising by functions
Organising by products

Category management
Organising by regions
Organising by type of customer
Marketing implementation
Intended strategy
Realised strategy

Relationship marketing
The five markets model of
 relationship marketing
Internal marketing
Total quality management
 (TQM)

Benchmarking	Natural accounts	Direct cost approach
Marketing control process	Marketing function accounts	Marketing performance
Performance standard	Direct costs	Sales per square metre
Sales analysis	Traceable common costs	Customer satisfaction
Sales measurements	Non-traceable common costs	Brand awareness
Marketing cost analysis	Full cost approach	Clippings service

Discussion and Review Questions

1. What determines the place of marketing within an organisation? Which type of organisation is best suited to the marketing concept? Why?
2. What factors can be used to organise the internal aspects of a marketing unit? Discuss the benefits of each type of organisation.
3. Why might an organisation use multiple bases for organising its marketing unit?
4. What attributes distinguish relationship marketing from transaction based marketing?
5. What is internal marketing? Why is it important in implementing marketing strategies?
6. Total quality management is a growing force in many businesses. What is TQM? How can it help to implement marketing strategies effectively?
7. Why is motivation of marketing personnel important in implementing marketing plans?
8. How does communication help in implementing marketing plans?
9. What are the major steps of the marketing control process?
10. List and discuss the five requirements for an effective control process.
11. Discuss the major problems in controlling marketing activities.
12. What is a sales analysis? What makes it an effective control tool?
13. What performance measures are favoured by marketers?
14. Identify and describe three cost analysis methods. Compare and contrast direct costing and full costing.

Recommended Readings

F. V. Cespedes, *Consurrency Marketing: Integrating Product, Sales and Service* (Cambridge, Mass.: Harvard Business School Press, 1995).

S. Dibb, L. Simkin and J. Bradley, *The Marketing Planning Workbook* (London: International Thomson Business Press, 1996).

W. D. Giles, "Making strategy work", *Long Range Planning,* vol. 24, no. 4, 1991, pp. 75–91.

N. Piercy, *Market-Led Strategic Change* (Oxford: Butterworth-Heinemann, 1997).

L. Simkin, "People and processes in marketing planning: the benefits of controlling implementation", *Journal of Marketing Management,* vol. 12, no. 5, 1996, pp. 375–390.

 C A S E S

23.1 The LEGO Story Carries on Building

The LEGO story began in 1932 when Ole Kirk Christiansen, a carpenter and joiner, began making wooden toys in his small workshop in Billund, Denmark. The LEGO name was devised in 1934, by combining the Danish words "Leg Godt", which means "play well". Right from the start, the founder established a basis of quality, using the motto "Only the best is good enough". Before too long, Ole Kirk Christiansen was selling his toys across Denmark. After realising the potential of plastic as a medium, a primitive version of the LEGO brick was launched. With either four or eight studs, the bricks, which were known as "Automatic Binding Bricks", were the forerunner of today's LEGO brick. In 1954 using the LEGO brick as its basis, the company developed what was to become known as the "LEGO System of Play". This used the kinds of building elements with which LEGO has become synonymous and consisted of a series of boxed construction sets. The first significant sales outside the domestic market followed in 1956, when a new sales company was formed in Germany.

Today, with more than 10,000 employees in 30 different countries, the LEGO Group is one of the largest toy manufacturers in the world. The company is still owned and run by the founding Kirk Christiansen family. LEGO products are made in Denmark, the US, Switzerland and Korea. The company is the only European business to occupy a place in the world's Top Ten toy manufacturers. It is not too difficult to see why. LEGO products are sold through some 60,000 retail outlets in more than 130 countries. Indeed, between 1949 and 1998 the company produced around 203 billion LEGO elements and estimates that 2.3 billion mini figures have been moulded and assembled in that time.

The core LEGO product remains the ubiquitous little brick, popular with children all over the world. However, to keep pace with rivals' copy-cat products, plus the plethora of other types of toys, ranging from Furbies to Barbie, the company must continually appraise children's tastes and up-date its products accordingly. It has done this by launching toddlers' LEGO—larger bricks—and Techno kits of robots and spaceships aimed at older children, plus a host of related products from play tables to dressing-up accessories. Today, the LEGO international range consists of over 400 different sets and incorporates many new products.

The LEGO Group is always on the look-out for new ways to drive its business forward. Indeed, the business sees the continual renewal of its products as one of the LEGO Group hallmarks. LEGO theme parks—profit centres in their own right, but still related to LEGO's core product—are one example of this approach. The 150 acre Legoland built on the site of Windsor Safari Park focuses on family entertainment and on the use of LEGO bricks—both for children to play with by creating monster designs and as the camouflage enveloping the park's buildings and rides. A major theme is the use of giant LEGO bricks to re-create famous buildings such as London's Big Ben and events and personalities from stage and screen. The intention is to establish an oasis of tranquility for children in an increasingly rowdy and violent society, building on LEGO's hallmark belief that children's innocence should be nurtured and cherished. Other Legoland theme parks are sited in Billund, the company's home, and in Carlsbad, southern California.

Examples of the company's pursuit of new ventures include its recent entry into the business of licence agreements and the development of LEGO Media Products. The licence agreements cover products such as children's clothes, watches, games and bedding. In addition, LEGO has incorporated a number of Disney film characters into its range. For example, two to five year olds are being targeted with Winnie the Pooh, Tigger, Piglet and Eeyore characters. The LEGO Media Products initiative offers consumers a range of children's software, videos, books and music. This link with technology and the Internet is further exploited in interactive centres at the company's theme parks.

It seems that a characteristic of LEGO's success has been the business's willingness to pursue new ideas and stretch the LEGO concept into hitherto unexplored areas. Not surprisingly, the company has been quick to enter business on the web, setting up a comprehensive web site. This provides a perfect opportunity for LEGO to introduce the world to its new products, which the company stresses are specifically designed for many different age groups. Thus older enthusiasts are encouraged to set up mock battles with Rock Raiders, an extension of the LEGO SYSTEM range. This is a gang of tough, hard working rock drillers who research alien planets in their hunt for energy crystals. There is danger everywhere and the Rock Raiders have their hands full dealing with boiling hot lava, rapid rivers and rock monsters! Meanwhile, babies and infants are being targeted with new LEGO PRIMO products. There is a new and exciting water theme which includes a range of bath time animals. A playpen activity wall incorporates a number of fun elements for children to play with, while the LEGO Play

House which is aimed at kids between six months and three years, can also be used as a storage container.

Even on the Internet, the LEGO Group has sought ways to innovate. In 1999 the company launched the cyberspace LEGO World Shop (**www.LEGO.com/LEGOWORLDSHOP**). Initially only products from the LEGO MINDSTORMS and LEGO TECHNIC were available on the site, with plans to extend its scope in the future. The site is accessible to all European member states as well as in Norway, Canada, the US, Australia, New Zealand, Iceland and Israel. The LEGO Group is pleased with the simple, secure purchasing approach which the World Shop offers to consumers, which it explains thus:

> It is extraordinarily easy for consumers to buy LEGO products at LEGO World Shop. They simply click on the products they wish to buy and add them to an electronic "shopping basket". The order is completed by entering a credit card number. This is both the simplest and most popular way to shop on the Internet. The LEGO World Shop is using a technology that guarantees a very high level of security, when the customer goes on-line. When the customer has made his transaction, he receives an electronic receipt.

The LEGO Group's willingness to seek new ideas and opportunities has long been part of its strategic approach. However, the company is quick to point out that the need to stimulate children's creativity remains at the heart of its philosophy. This is indicated in the company positioning statement: "Creativity unlimited . . . Just imagine." The LEGO Group's concern for children has also pro-vided the impetus for its involvement in setting up a new global institution—Next Generation Forum—which aims to encourage children's creativity, imagination and learning. Whatever the new millennium will bring for the LEGO Group, its continued commitment to these ideals looks inevitable. This success story has not occurred by chance. LEGO is customer focused, ruthlessly aware of its competitive environment and continually concerned with controlling its R&D, production, sales and marketing activities internally. Managers are carefully briefed to understand the LEGO mentality and marketing strategy. This strategy is implemented through detailed marketing plans which are regularly assessed to enable ongoing modifications as required.

SOURCES: Legoland UK; Charles Darwent, "Lego's billion-dollar brickworks", *Management Today*, September 1995, pp. 64–68; "Legoland rejigs team", *Marketing*, 4 March 1999, p. 5; Richard Morais, "Babes in toyland?", *Forbes*, 3 January 1994, pp. 70–71; "A faint squeak from Euro-Mickey", *The Economist*, 29 July 1995, p. 56; Jeff Ferry and Richard Hooper, "The great game of infant-motion", *Director*, September 1995, pp. 30–38; **www.lego.com**.

Questions for Discussion

1. How has LEGO kept pace with evolving customer expectations?
2. Why does the LEGO Group monitor carefully the implementation of its marketing programmes?
3. What steps should the LEGO Group take to control the marketing of one of its new products?

23.2 Timex Stands the Test of Time

During the 1970s, watches took a technological leap forward from wind-up spring mechanisms to quartz crystals, batteries and digital displays. The Timex Corporation, however, lagged behind other manufacturers in making the changes. When the Swiss made Swatch invaded department stores and convinced customers that their watches were not just time telling devices but fashion statements, Timex was not ready to offer any competition. At Timex, reliability had always been the number one priority, certainly not style and fashion. For years, Timex's sales suffered because of a drab image, especially in contrast with the colourful Swatch.

Then came the 1990s, the decade of value. As value came to take precedence over status, more price-conscious consumers were attracted by quality at moderate prices than by designer labels. Timex took advantage of this trend to revive its 41 year old brand, the old reliable Timex watch. By blending its "value pricing" message with some trendy new designs and diversifying its product for specific niche markets, Timex is making a comeback.

Consumers can still buy an unadorned Timex watch for about £5, and analysts say that these simple styles with easy to read faces are the company's best sellers. To compete in a crowded market, however, Timex is developing stylish special collections for two separate adult divisions, dress watches and sports watches, as well as expanding its children's unit. The company has even set up studios in France and the United States to design Timex renditions of colourful creative watches. In the adult fashion arena, Timex offers women its Images line with neon accented hands, floral patterned watch bands, and over-sized faces, and men the Carriage III collection. For those with poor vision, Timex created the Easy Reader with large clear numbers. Sports watch buyers can choose from models with names like Surf, Brave Wave and Magnum that are shock and water resistant and offer features like compasses, pedometers, chronographs and thermometers. After soliciting educators' advice, the company came up with its Gizmoz watches to help children aged 5 to 9 tell time. Colourful designs are on the band instead of the face, which displays all of the numbers and colour codes hour and minute hands. For example, black faced watches have white hours and hour hands but green minutes and minute hands. There is even a Lefty Gizmoz available. To appeal to parents, whose money really buys the Gizmoz watches, Timex offers a kids' loss protection plan that replaces a watch for only half the purchase price.

Timex's advertising strategy is to appeal to niche markets by reviving its traditional "durable yet inexpensive" positioning and revitalising its powerful brand identity. The famous Timex theme, "It Takes a Licking and Keeps On Ticking", takes a humorous bent in television spots where sumo wrestlers wear Timex watches strapped to their middles as they grapple on the mat and rock musicians use Timex watches to strum their guitars. In a recent print advertising campaign, the company featured real people who, like the Timex watches they wear, have been through rough experiences but survived to tell the tale. On television talk shows, company executives introduced the Timex *Why Pay More* magazine, featuring Timex watches as part of fashion outfits selling for under £50.

With watch sales in most countries declining, most watchmakers are concerned. At Timex, however, executives are celebrating sales and market share increases. The company now controls a larger segment of the market than its four biggest competitors combined. Timex is happy to be shedding its dowdy and boring image. Rising young professional people don't have to put their wrists behind their backs to hide a Timex any more, or announce loudly to colleagues that they are only wearing a Timex while their Rolex is being repaired. Marketing executives have carefully monitored the introduction of this strategy to (1) ensure that early signs of success or failure could be acted upon and (2) modify marketing programmes continually in order to enhance the impact of Timex's new approach. Sales and financial performance are evaluated regularly: so far they reveal a success story. Changing fashions and aggressive competitors such as Swatch caught Timex out once before. The company does not intend to be left behind again, despite its industrial relations problems in Europe.

Timex's European advertising budget is now close to £6 million, through McCann-Erickson. A major £2.2 million blitz in the UK pushed the company's new Indiglo night-light technology before the rest of the watch industry developed rival technology. This campaign, too, was carefully monitored and rivals' reactions assessed. Continual benchmarking of Timex's fortunes is helping the company compete effectively and with great success.

SOURCES: Cara Appelbaum, "High time for Timex", *Adweek's Marketing Week,* 29 July 1991, p. 24; BBC/ITN news broadcasts, Spring 1993; "Timex races for Indiglo profits", *Marketing,* 31 March 1994, p. 3; "Briefs", *Marketing,* 6 January 1994, p. 6; "Rzed opens shop with Timex infomercial", *Campaign,* 19 May 1995, p. 8.

Questions for Discussion

1. Which environmental forces are likely to be of greatest interest to marketing managers at Timex?
2. Identify the target markets towards which Timex is aiming its products.
3. Why must Timex continually assess its performance and the impact of its marketing?

24 Marketing Ethics and Social Responsibility

> *"Virtues such as honesty are not self-evident when applied to complex marketing decisions."*
>
> O. C. Ferrell, University of Memphis

OBJECTIVES

- To define and understand the importance of marketing ethics
- To understand the ethical decision-making process
- To discuss some important ethical issues in marketing
- To identify ways to improve ethical decisions in marketing
- To understand the concept of social responsibility and to explore several important issues of social responsibility
- To describe strategies for dealing with social dilemmas
- To compare and contrast the concepts of social responsibility and marketing ethics

Recent consumer concern about the potential safety of genetically modified foods highlighted the concept of *ethical food* and demonstrated the scale of consumer influence over goods on sale. As a result of the public outcry about the sale of so-called GM (genetically modified) foods, supermarkets and other food retailers were forced to respond. Freezer food retailer Iceland led the way by publicly banning GM ingredients from its own label products, while supermarket retailers Sainsbury's, Asda and Safeway are also phasing out GM own label items. The extent to which this will actually be achieved remains to be seen. The difficulty identifying foods and ingredients in pre-cooked dishes which have been genetically modified is just one of the problems which retailers will face. However, this is just one example of growing consumer interest in the notion of ethical food, which has been defined as food prepared with regard to animal welfare, respect for nature, concern about consumer safety and a fair deal for food producers. According to one food writer, ethical food covers three broad areas: cruelty-free, organic and fairly traded foods.

Cruelty-free food can be defined as food which has been produced in a manner to ensure as little animal cruelty as possible. Consumers have been generally concerned about the standards of animal care, following serious outbreaks of food poisoning and the BSE crisis. In 1994, the RSPCA (Royal Society for the Prevention of Cruelty to Animals) set up the Freedom Food animal welfare label system. This system identifies five freedom areas concerning animal treatment by which those producers receiving the Freedom Food logo must abide. These are freedom from: pain, injury and disease; fear and distress; hunger and thirst; discomfort; and from being prevented from expressing normal behaviour.

Organic food is food that is free from genetic modification, irradiation, pesticides, chemical fertilisers, artificial additives and synthetic dyes. Unfortunately for consumers, many organic foods are more expensive to buy than the alternatives and they may not be as visually appealing. The Soil Association has recently set up a scheme to encourage "organic box schemes". Under these schemes consumers pay a membership fee in return for a weekly box of organic fruit and vegetables. These are usually provided by local farms, approved by The Soil Association, which deliver to households in their proximity a box containing a predetermined value of seasonal, organic fresh produce.

Fairly traded foods ensure that Third World producers receive a better deal for the foods they grow. The Fairtrade Mark, which allows farmers of goods such as tea, coffee and cocoa to continue with their traditional lifestyles, will be six years old in the new millennium. This initiative protects these producers from fluctuations in the market and ensures that they receive a price for commodities which covers costs and provides a basic living wage. Foods which are produced under fair trade schemes, such as those marketed under the Traidcraft label, now appear in most major supermarkets. However, the charity Christian Aid, which supports the fair trade initiative, believes that much more can be done and that "all the supermarkets have yet to turn their good words into real improvements".

The success of cruelty-free and organic foods and fair trade initiatives suggests that consumers are keen to become involved in more ethically produced foods. The intense consumer reaction to publicity about the possible harmful effects of genetically modified foods and the scale of the response from the food industry illustrates the power of public reaction. The extent to which this reaction translates into the availability of organic, cruelty-free and fair trade foods on supermarket shelves remains to be seen. However, recent trends would suggest the dawning of a new era for a

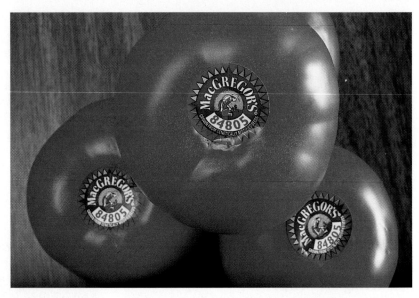

wide range of ethical foods. These foods appeal to certain consumers and have encouraged those major retailers with a concern for social responsibility to introduce new lines to their stores.

SOURCES: Vanessa Berridge, "Ethical food: the next best thing?", *Good Food,* April 1999, pp. 76–77; "How to grow your own", *Coventry Evening Telegraph,* 22 May 1999, p. 2; Alexandra Jardine, "Retailers in retreat on Frankenstein foods", *Marketing,* 1 April 1999, p. 17; Robert McLuhan, "Iceland's new strategy proves popular with customers", *Marketing,* 1 April 1999, p. 24; Alan Mitchell, "GM food row boils down to a question of trust", *Marketing Week,* 4 March 1999, pp. 24–25. *Photo:* Tony Freeman/Photo Edit.

Marketers need to be aware of the ethical and social responsibility issues that may arise out of the marketing of their products and services. As illustrated in the chapter opener, food manufacturers and retailers are currently being forced to respond to consumer pressure for cruelty-free, organic and fairly traded foods, while also taking into account consumer safety. This interest in "ethical food" demonstrates that the issue of ethics in marketing is evolving and set to increase in prominence.

The debate over ethical food illustrates that all marketing activities can be judged as morally right or wrong by society, consumers, interest groups, competitors and others. Although most marketers operate within the limits of the law, some do engage in activities that are not considered acceptable by others. A number of recently publicised incidents in marketing, such as deceptive or objectionable advertising, misleading packaging, questionable selling practices, manipulation, corruption and pollution, have raised questions as to whether specific marketing practices are acceptable and beneficial to society. The limits of acceptable marketing practices and the obligations marketers have to society are issues of marketing ethics and social responsibility.

This chapter gives an overview of the role of ethics and social responsibility in marketing decision-making. The chapter first defines marketing ethics and discusses the factors that influence ethical decision-making in marketing. Next it outlines some specific ethical issues in marketing and explores ways to improve ethics in marketing decisions. The chapter then focuses on the issue of social responsibility, looking at the impact of marketing decisions on society and developing some strategies for dealing with social responsibility dilemmas. The chapter closes by comparing and contrasting the concepts of marketing ethics and social responsibility.

The Nature of Marketing Ethics

No one has yet developed a universally accepted approach for dealing with the controversial and often misunderstood concept of ethics.[1] However, marketing personnel need to examine the issue of marketing ethics to help them make marketing decisions that are acceptable and beneficial to society.[2] This is not always easy, as well intentioned marketing managers are frequently pushed in the wrong direction by organisational pressures.[3] This section considers the meaning of marketing ethics.

Marketing Ethics Defined

Marketing ethics Moral principles that define right and wrong behaviour in marketing

Ethics relate to moral evaluations of decisions and actions as right or wrong on the basis of commonly accepted principles of behaviour. **Marketing ethics** are moral principles that define right and wrong behaviour in marketing. The most basic ethical issues have been formalised through laws and regulations to conform to the standards of society. At the very least, marketers are expected to obey these laws and regulations. However, it is important to realise that marketing ethics go beyond legal issues.

Ethics are individually defined and may vary from one person to another. Some companies, such as Levi Strauss, have been taking more initiative in this area in the belief that consumers are looking more and more to the company behind the product.[4] Although individual marketers often act in their own self-interest, it is important that they operate in accordance with sound moral principles based on ideals such as fairness, justice and trust.[5] Consumers generally regard unethical marketing activities—for instance, deceptive advertising, misleading selling tactics, price fixing and the deliberate marketing of harmful products—as unacceptable and often refuse to do business with marketers that engage in such practices. Thus when marketers deviate from accepted moral principles to further their own interests at the expense of others, continued marketing exchanges become difficult, if not impossible.[6]

Marketing Ethics Are Controversial

Few topics in marketing are more misunderstood or controversial than ethics. Most people can make a judgement as to whether they believe a particular marketing decision to be right or wrong, ethical or unethical, but their ideas depend on the nature of the organisation, their experiences in life and their personal values. Many marketers have such strong convictions about what is morally right or wrong that they deeply resent discussions of alternative ways to make ethical decisions.

If society judges an activity that an organisation undertakes to be wrong or unethical, then this view directly affects the organisation's ability to achieve its goals. Although not all activities deemed unethical by society may be illegal, consumer protests against a particular activity may result in legislation that restricts or bans it. Thus, as Marketing Insight 24.1 shows, the drinks industry was forced to respond to consumer and government pressure regarding the marketing of so-called "alcopops" (alcoholic soft drinks). When an organisation engages in unethical marketing activities, it may not only lose sales as dissatisfied consumers refuse to deal with it, it may also face legal action, fines and even prison for its executives. Manufacturer Hoover ran a now infamous sales promotion in late 1992 offering free flights to anyone purchasing a Hoover product valued over £100 (see Case 17.2). Thousands of consumers purchased Hoover vacuum cleaners and washing machines expressly to take advantage of this offer, but many hundreds were disappointed. The offer was flawed: some of Hoover's agents acted unscrupulously; few people were offered their choice of holiday destination; the BBC programme *Watchdog* showed agents deliberately obstructing consumers attempting to take up the offer. Hoover had not broken any laws but was deemed by the media and consumers to have behaved unethically.[7] Such an example illustrates the importance of understanding marketing ethics and recognising ethical issues.

Because marketing ethics are so controversial, it is important to state that it is not the purpose of this chapter to question anyone's personal ethical beliefs and convictions. Instead, its goal is to highlight the importance of ethical issues and ethical decision-making in marketing. Understanding the impact of ethical decisions in marketing can help people to recognise and resolve ethical issues within an organisation.

Understanding the Ethical Decision-Making Process

To grasp the significance of ethics in marketing decision-making, it is necessary to examine the factors that influence the ethical decision-making process.[8] Individual factors, organisational relationships and opportunity are three factors that interact to determine ethical decisions in marketing (see Figure 24.1).[9]

Individual Factors

Moral philosophies Principles or rules that individuals use to decide what is right or wrong

Utilitarianism A moral philosophy concerned with maximising the greatest good for the greatest number of people

Ethical formalism A rule oriented philosophy that focuses on the intentions associated with a particular behaviour and on the rights of the individual

Ethical conflict arises when people encounter situations they cannot control or resolve in the privacy of their own lives. In such situations, individuals base their decisions on their own concepts of right and wrong and act accordingly in their daily lives. **Moral philosophies**—the principles or rules that individuals use to decide what is right or wrong[10]—are often cited to justify decisions or explain behaviour. People learn these principles and rules through socialisation by family members, social groups, religion and formal education. It is widely believed that ethical decision-making can be enhanced by identifying and improving one's personal moral philosophy.

At least two major types of moral philosophy are associated with marketing decisions, each with its own concept of rightness, or ethicalness, and rules for behaviour. **Utilitarianism** is concerned with maximising the greatest good for the greatest number of people. Utilitarians judge an action or decision by the consequences for all the people affected. In other words, in a situation with an ethical component, utilitarians will compare all possible options and select the one that promises the best results for the most people.

Ethical formalism is a rights or rule oriented philosophy that focuses on the intentions associated with a particular behaviour and on the rights of the individual. Ethical formalism develops specific standards of behaviour by determin-

Consumer Pressure Takes the Fizz out of "Alcopops"

Alcoholic soft drinks took the UK market by storm in the summer of 1995. In a survey of 18 to 24 year olds, 84 per cent of those questioned were aware of the new sector. With names like Hooper's Hooch (Bass), Lemonheads (Carlsberg-Tetley) and Two Dogs (Merrydown), the so-called "alcopops" provided a welcome boost for the brewers and cider makers. Early entrants into the market were quickly followed by a host of others. Even supermarket giant Sainsbury's joined the foray with its own-label brand Piranha.

However, before long the drinks industry was being resoundingly attacked by consumer pressure groups and politicians who claimed that the packaging and marketing of the drinks was appealing too strongly to under-age drinkers. Such was the visibility and success of the campaign that the manufacturers moved quickly to re-package and re-name the brands. The brewer Whitbread, just one of the companies that elected to modify their branding of alcopops, openly stated its intention not to tempt under-age drinkers. As it launched its new range of Shott's Alcoholic Seltzers aimed at adult drinkers, the company shied away from names Lemonade Bomb and Cream Soda Blast because of their association with soft drinks aimed at children. Instead the company went to market with brand names Lemon Jag, Soda Heist and Cranberry Charge. The company also chose not to market the new range in cans, so often associated with soft drinks. Instead, Shott's Alcoholic Seltzers appeared in 330 ml bottles.

As individual manufacturers moved to respond to the concern expressed by the public, the brewers' and cider makers' industry body, the Portman Group, which promotes "sensible drinking", drew up a code of conduct to guide marketing activity in the sector. The underlying rationale for the code is in line with the Advertising Standards Authority's recommendation that drinks should not be advertised to appeal to children. Initial feedback from the Portman Group was that the marketing of the drinks should not lead a "reasonable" individual to say that they are targeted at children. At its peak in December 1996, leading brand Hooper's Hooch sold 370,000 barrels. Hostile public opinion to the whole product category and associated restrictions imposed on sales, marketing and advertising activity saw this fall back to under 150,000 barrels by the end of 1998. In 1999 rival Two Dogs was re-launched, targeting instead male 20 to 30 year olds. The good news for the consumer in all this is that public pressure counts and can persuade businesses to heed their ethical and social responsibilities.

SOURCES: David Benady, "Soft targets", *Marketing Week*, 19 January 1996; David Benady, "Whitbread rejigs alcopop launch for 'adult' appeal", *Marketing Week*, 9 February 1996; Julien Lee, "Sainsbury sinks teeth into 'soft booze' market", *Marketing*, 16 November 1995; Harriet Marsh, " 'Soft booze' focuses spend below-the-line", *Marketing*, 23 November 1995; Sharon Marshall, "Will Cott strike gold with cola?", *Marketing*, 25 January 1996; Ros Snowdon, "New 'alcopops' avoid under-18s", *Marketing*, 8 February 1996; Bass, 1999.

ing whether an action can be taken consistently as a general rule, without considering alternative results.[11] Ethical formalists judge an action or decision on the basis of whether it infringes on individual rights or universal rules. The biblical Golden Rule—do unto others as you would have them do unto you—exemplifies ethical formalism. So does Immanuel Kant's categorical imperative: every action should be based on reasons that everyone could act on, at least in principle, and that action must be based on reasons that the decision-maker would be willing to have others use.[12]

There is no universal agreement on the correct moral philosophy to use in resolving ethical issues. Moreover, research suggests that marketers may use different moral philosophies in different decision situations. Each philosophy could result in a different decision in an ethical dilemma. And, depending on the particular situation, marketers will sometimes change their value structure or moral philosophy when they are making decisions.[13] These changes in individual philosophies are usually based on organisational relationships.

Figure 24.1 Factors that influence the ethical decision-making process

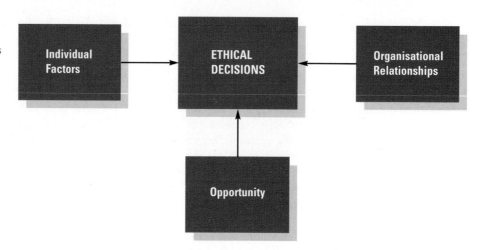

Organisational Relationships

Although it is true that individuals can and do make moral choices pertaining to business affairs, it is also true that people do not operate in a vacuum.[14] Ethical choices in marketing are most often made jointly in work groups and committees or in conversations and discussions with co-workers. Marketers learn to resolve ethical issues not only from their individual backgrounds, but also from people with whom they associate in work groups and in the marketing organisation. The outcome of this learning process depends on the strength of each individual's personal values, opportunity for unethical behaviour, and exposure to others who behave ethically or unethically. **Significant others** include superiors, peers and subordinates in an organisation who influence the ethical decision-making process. Although people outside the organisation, such as family members and friends, also influence decision-makers, organisational structure and culture operate through significant others to influence ethical decisions.

Significant others Superiors, peers and subordinates in an organisation who influence the ethical decision-making process

Organisational, or **corporate, culture** can be defined as a set of values, beliefs, goals, norms and rituals that members or employees of an organisation share. A company's culture may be expressed formally through codes of conduct, memos, manuals and ceremonies, but it is also expressed informally through work habits, dress codes, extra-curricular activities and anecdotes. An organisation's culture gives its members meaning and suggests rules for how to behave and deal with problems within the organisation.

Organisational, or **corporate, culture** A set of values, beliefs, goals, norms and rituals that members or employees of an organisation share

Most experts agree that the chief executive or marketing director sets the ethical tone for the entire organisation. Lower level managers obtain their cues from top managers, but they, too, impose some of their personal values on the company. This interaction between corporate culture and executive leadership helps determine the ethical value system of the company.

The role of co-workers in influencing ethical choices depends on the person's exposure to unethical behaviour in making ethical decisions. Especially in ethical grey areas, the more a person is exposed to unethical activity by others in the organisational environment, the more likely it is that he or she will behave unethically. Most marketers take their cues or learn from co-workers how to solve problems—including ethical problems.[15]

Organisational pressure plays a key part in creating ethical issues. Nearly all marketers face difficult issues when solutions are not obvious or when organisational objectives and personal ethical values may conflict. For example, a salesperson may be asked by a superior to lie to a customer over the phone about a late product shipment. A survey found that almost one-third of those surveyed felt pressure from superiors to violate company policy in order to achieve business objectives. Of the nearly one-third who had witnessed behaviour that they viewed as a violation of company policy or the law, fewer than half said they reported the misconduct to their companies.[16]

Because organisational culture, relationships and pressures influence ethical behaviour, it is suggested that the management of marketing ethics should focus on designing and developing organisations for marketers, who, like all human beings, display the normal range of personal ethical variations and the tendency sometimes to take advantage of opportunities. As mentioned earlier, in some situations it is hard to identify the right or wrong choice, and in other situations individuals may think they know what is right, but competitive or organisational pressures encourage the wrong behaviour.

Opportunity

Opportunity provides another pressure that may determine whether a person will behave ethically. **Opportunity** is a favourable set of conditions that limit barriers or provide rewards. Rewards may be internal or external. Internal rewards are the feelings of goodness and worth a person experiences after carrying out an altruistic action. External rewards are what a person expects to receive from others in terms of values generated and provided on an exchange basis. External rewards are often received from peers and top management in the form of praise, promotions and pay raises.

If a marketer takes advantage of an opportunity to act unethically and is rewarded or suffers no penalty, he or she may repeat such acts as other opportunities arise. For example, a salesperson who receives a pay rise after using a deceptive sales presentation to increase sales is being rewarded for this behaviour and so will probably continue it. Indeed, opportunity to engage in unethical conduct is often a better predictor of unethical activities than personal values.[17]

Besides rewards and the absence of punishment, other elements in the business environment help to create opportunities. Professional codes of ethics and a company policy on ethics also influence opportunity by prescribing what behaviours are acceptable. The larger the rewards and the lesser the punishment for unethical behaviour, the greater the probability that unethical behaviour will be practised.

Ethical Issues in Marketing

Developing awareness of ethical issues is important in understanding and improving marketing ethics. An **ethical issue** is an identifiable problem, situation or opportunity requiring an individual or organisation to choose from among several actions that must be evaluated as right or wrong, ethical or unethical. Any time an activity causes consumers to feel deceived, manipulated or cheated, a marketing ethical issue exists, regardless of the legality of that activity.

Ethical issues typically arise because of conflicts between individuals' personal moral philosophies and the marketing strategies, policies and organisational environment in which they work. Ethical issues may stem from conflicts between a marketer's attempts to achieve organisational objectives and customers' desires for safe, fair and reliable products.[18] For example, a London baker took Barclays Bank plc to court, claiming that the bank had failed to pass on interest rate cuts, thus causing him to pay back too much on a commercial loan. Barclays defended its position by saying that it was not obliged to review repayments when base rates were cut. The court ruled in the baker's favour, opening the way for a host of copy-cat claims from other small businesses dissatisfied with their banks.

Regardless of the reasons behind specific ethical issues, once the issues are identified, marketers and organisations must decide how to deal with them. In marketing many different ethical issues arise, some of which are now considered.

Product Issues

Product related ethical issues generally arise when marketers fail to disclose risks associated with the product or information about its function, value or use. Ethical issues also sometimes arise when marketers fail to inform customers about changes in product quality; this failure is a form of dishonesty about the nature of the product. For example, Lever Brothers launched a new version of its Persil brand of washing powder. Known as Persil Power, the detergent claimed to have particularly outstanding cleaning ability. When Lever's senior managers launched Persil Power, they strongly believed that the accelerator (special ingredient) the product contained would give them a competitive edge over rival detergents. Yet concerns were soon being expressed that the product was causing clothes to rot. Consumer concern was evidenced by a slump in the brand's market share. Before long, the product was being removed from supermarket shelves, yet Lever Brothers failed to respond decisively to the criticisms. For a while the company stood by Persil Power, claiming that the problems were exaggerated. Ultimately though, it was forced to replace the brand.[19]

Many companies, of course, take care to emphasise product safety concerns in their advertising. Such messages send a signal to all employees in the organisation, as well as to customers, concerning a company's ethical standards. Thus frozen food retailer Iceland moved quickly to respond to consumer concerns about GM foods. The company's willingness to deal positively and openly with the issue has proved popular with its customers.[20]

Promotion Issues

The promotion process provides a variety of situations that can create ethical issues: for instance, false and misleading advertising and manipulative or deceptive sales promotions, tactics or publicity efforts. Case 24.1 describes the problems faced by Nestlé following consumer protests about the ethics of its advertising of baby milk. Unethical actions in advertising can destroy the trust customers have in an organisation. Abuses in advertising can range from exaggerated claims and concealed facts to being unfair to a competitor.[21] Exaggerated claims cannot be substantiated; for example, claims that a certain age reversing skin lotion is superior to any other on the market often cannot be verified by consumers or experts. Concealed facts are material facts deliberately omitted from a message. Perrier's packaging implied that the bubbles in its mineral water are natural and are bottled at the source. Many consumers still believe that the bubbles in their mineral water are natural, yet many products have these bubbles added during the bottling process. When consumers learn that promotion messages are untrue, they may feel cheated and refuse to buy the product again; they may also complain to government or other regulatory bodies. For a while Sainsbury's refused to stock brand leader Perrier because it considered the labelling misleading to consumers.

Another form of advertising abuse arises when acceptable levels of decency are broached. The use of children in advertising is one such contentious issue. When Calvin Klein's advertising featured young, scantily clad models in provocative poses, shocked consumers claimed that the line into pornography had been crossed. Although the company refused to reveal the ages of the models appearing in the advertisements, the campaign was brought to an early end.[22]

The ethics of advertising to children is an area which is likely to come under scrutiny from the European Union. In Sweden, TV advertising to children is banned altogether. Support for the Swedes' tough line is forthcoming from Denmark and Greece and raises the possibility that the freedom of advertisers in other countries to promote their products to children may be curtailed. Supporters of the advertising industry's right to develop promotions targeted at children, such as those shown in Figure 24.2, suggest that no harm is done provided the executions are honest and ethical.[23]

A common problem in personal selling is judging what types of sales activities are acceptable. Consumers may perceive salespeople as unethical because of the common belief that sales personnel often pressure customers to purchase products they neither need nor want. Nevertheless, the salesforces of most businesses, such as IBM and Procter & Gamble, are well educated, well trained and professional; they know that they must act ethically or risk losing valuable customers and sales. Although most salespeople are ethical, some do engage in questionable actions. For example, some use very aggressive and manipulative tactics to sell almost worthless gemstones, holidays or other products over the phone.

The use of bribery in personal selling situations is also an ethical issue. Even when a bribe is offered to benefit the organisation, it is usually considered unethical. Because it jeopardises fairness and trust, it harms the organisation in the long run.

Figure 24.2   The ethics of advertising. Companies which promote their products to children must be particularly careful that their approach is ethical.   SOURCES: *left*: This visual is reproduced by special permission of the LEGO Company. The LEGO name is a registered trademark. *right*: Courtesy of Sony.

Pricing Issues   Typical ethical issues in pricing include price fixing, predatory pricing and failure to disclose the full price associated with a purchase. The emotional and subjective nature of price creates many situations in which misunderstandings between the seller and buyer cause ethical problems. Marketers have the right to price their products so that they earn a reasonable profit, but ethical issues may crop up when a company seeks to earn high profits at the expense of its customers. When Richard Branson launched Virgin Cola, he supported its relatively low price by arguing that consumers were effectively paying a brand tax on leading cola brands.

Distribution Issues   Ethical issues in distribution involve relationships and conflicts between producers and marketing middlemen. Marketing middlemen, or intermediaries (wholesalers, retailers and dealers), facilitate the flow of products from the producer to the ultimate consumer. Each intermediary performs a different role and accepts certain rights, responsibilities and rewards associated with that role. For example, producers can expect retailers to honour payment agreements and keep them informed of inventory needs. Failure to make payments in a timely manner may be considered an ethical issue.

Manipulating a product's availability for purposes of exploitation and using coercion to force intermediaries to behave in a specific manner are particularly serious ethical issues in the distribution sphere. For example, a powerful manufacturer can exert undue influence over an intermediary's choice of whether to handle a product or how to handle it.

Other ethical issues in distribution relate to some stores' refusal to deal with some types of middlemen. Some controversy surrounds retailers such as Tesco or Marks & Spencer, which often insist on doing business directly with a producer rather than using an intermediary. Marks & Spencer has been accused of threatening to buy from other producers if companies refuse to sell to it directly. Similar buy direct policies are in effect at B&Q, the largest UK retailer of do-it-yourself building supplies, and at Do It All, the home improvement chain. These retailers, which emphasise low prices, maintain that bypassing intermediaries cuts costs and does not involve any ethical issues. However, some small companies cannot afford to maintain their own salesforces and must rely on intermediaries to sell their products to retailers. The refusal of Tesco or B&Q and others to deal with intermediaries effectively shuts these smaller companies out of the market because they cannot compete with companies that have their own salesforces.

Improving Ethical Decisions in Marketing

Unethical behaviour generally arises because of unethical personnel or problems with the organisation's ethical standards. One way to view an organisation's ethical standards is by considering a "bad apple—bad barrel" analogy. Some people always act in their own self-interest regardless of organisational goals or accepted moral standards; they are sometimes called "bad apples". To eliminate unethical behaviour, an organisation must rid itself of these bad apples, or unethical people. It can attain this goal through screening techniques and through enforcement of ethics codes.[24] However, organisations also sometimes become "bad barrels"—not because the individuals within them are bad, but because the pressures to survive and succeed create conditions that reward unethical behaviour. A way of resolving the problem of the bad barrel is to redesign the organisation's image and culture so that it conforms to industry and societal norms of ethical behaviour.[25]

If top management develops and enforces programmes to encourage ethical decision-making, then they become a force to help individuals make better ethical decisions. When marketers understand the policies and requirements for ethical conduct, they can more easily resolve ethical conflicts. On the other hand, marketers can never fully abdicate their personal ethical responsibility in making decisions. Claiming to be an agent of the business ("the company told me to do it") is not accepted as a legal excuse and is even less defensible from an ethical perspective.[26]

To promote ethical conduct requires teamwork and initiative, which often result in higher quality products. This leads to the potential for an ethical advantage: better reputation, sales, market share and profits. A proactive ethical approach to marketing should consider at least four fundamental values of interpersonal communication: respect, understanding, caring and fairness.[27] Table 24.1 shows one recommended method for developing ethical relationships and promoting integrity in marketing.

Table 24.1 A method to create ethical relationships in marketing

1. **Listen and learn.**
   Recognise the problem or decision-making opportunity that confronts your company, team or unit. Don't argue, criticise or defend yourself—keep listening and reviewing until you are sure you understand others.
2. **Identify the ethical issues.**
   Examine how co-workers and consumers are affected by the situation or decision at hand. Examine how you feel about the situation and understand the viewpoint of those who are involved in the decision or the consequences of the decision.
3. **Create and analyse options.**
   Try to put aside strong feelings such as anger or desire for power and prestige and come up with as many alternatives as possible before developing an analysis. Ask everyone involved for ideas about which options offer the best long term results for you and the company. Which option will increase your self-respect even if, in the long run, things don't work out the way you hope?
4. **Identify the best option from your point of view.**
   Consider it and test it against some established criteria, such as respect, understanding, caring, fairness, honesty and openness.
5. **Explain your decision and resolve any differences that arise.**
   This may require neutral arbitration from a trusted manager or taking "time out" to re-consider, consult or exchange written proposals before a decision is reached.

SOURCE: Used by permission from Tom Rusk, M.D. with D. Patrick Miller, "Doing the Right Thing", *Sky*, August 1993, Reprinted with permission.

Codes of Ethics

Codes of ethics Formalised rules and standards that describe what the company expects of its employees

It is difficult for employees to determine whether behaviour within an organisation is acceptable if the organisation does not have uniform policies and standards. Without standards of behaviour, employees will generally make decisions based on their observations of how their peers and managers behave. **Codes of ethics** are formalised rules and standards that describe what the company expects of its employees. Codes of ethics encourage ethical behaviour by minimising opportunities for unethical behaviour: the company's employees know both what is expected of them and what the punishment is for violating the rules. Codes of ethics also help marketers deal with ethical issues or dilemmas that develop in daily operations by prescribing or limiting certain activities. They do this by providing general guidelines for achieving organisational goals and objectives in a morally acceptable manner. Top management should also provide leadership and guidelines in implementing the codes.

Table 24.2 presents the American Marketing Association's Code of Ethics. The code does not cover every ethical issue, but it is a useful overview of what marketers believe are sound moral principles for guiding marketing activities. This code could be used to help structure an organisation's code of ethics.

Controlling Unethical Behaviour

Ethical behaviour in marketing must be based on a strong moral foundation, including personal moral development and an organisational structure that encourages and rewards ethical action. The impact of competitive pressures on ethical behaviour must be understood. The idea that marketing ethics are learned at home, at school and in family relationships does not recognise the impact of opportunity and the organisation on the ethics of decision-makers.

If a company is to maintain ethical behaviour, its policies, rules and standards must be worked into its control system. If the number of employees making ethical decisions on a regular basis is not satisfactory, then the company needs to determine why and must take corrective action through enforcement of its code of ethics. If codes are mere window dressing and do not relate to what is expected or to what is rewarded in the corporate culture, then they serve no purpose except to give an illusion of concern about ethical behaviour.

The Nature of Social Responsibility

Social responsibility An organisation's obligation to maximise its positive impact and minimise its negative impact on society

The concepts of ethics and social responsibility are often used interchangeably, although each has a distinct meaning. **Social responsibility** in marketing refers to an organisation's obligation to maximise its positive impact and minimise its negative impact on society. Whereas ethics relate to individual decisions, social responsibility concerns the impact of an organisation's decisions on society.

For example, the launch of the UK National Lottery attracted considerable national interest, with top prizes of many millions of pounds on offer. As lottery players became obsessed with the idea of winning a fortune, politicians, community leaders and the clergy became concerned about the possible effects of this new gambling fever on family budgets. While interest groups were divided over a possible solution to this problem, some believed that Camelot, the company that organised the National Lottery, should cut the value of top prizes.[28] Social responsibility, then, can be viewed as a contract with society, whereas ethics relate to carefully thought out rules of moral values that guide individual and group decision-making.

Members of the American Marketing Association (AMA) are committed to ethical professional conduct. They have joined together in subscribing to this Code of Ethics embracing the following topics:

Responsibilities of the Marketer

Marketers must accept responsibility for the consequences of their activities and make every effort to ensure that their decisions, recommendations and actions function to identify, serve and satisfy all relevant publics: consumers, organisations and society. Marketers' professional conduct must be guided by:

1. The basic rule of professional ethics: not knowingly to do harm;
2. The adherence to all applicable laws and regulations;
3. The accurate representation of their education, training and experience; and
4. The active support, practice and promotion of this Code of Ethics.

Honesty and Fairness

Marketers shall uphold and advance the integrity, honour and dignity of the marketing profession by:
1. Being honest in serving consumers, clients, employees, suppliers, distributors and the public;
2. Not knowingly participating in conflict of interest without prior notice to all parties involved; and
3. Establishing equitable fee schedules including the payment or receipt of usual, customary and/or legal compensation for marketing exchanges.

Rights and Duties of Parties

Participants in the marketing exchange process should be able to expect that:
1. Products and services offered are safe and fit for their intended uses;
2. Communications about offered products and services are not deceptive;
3. All parties intend to discharge their obligations, financial and otherwise, in good faith; and others in organisational relationships. They

4. Appropriate internal methods exist for equitable adjustment and/or redress of grievances concerning purchases.

It is understood that the above would include, *but is not limited to,* the following responsibilities of the marketer:

In the Area of Product Development Management:

Disclosure of all substantial risks associated with product or service usage
Identification of any product component substitution that might materially change the product or impact on the buyer's purchase decision
Identification of extra cost added features

In the Area of Promotions:

Avoidance of false and misleading advertising
Rejection of high pressure manipulations, or misleading sales tactics
Avoidance of sales promotions that use deception or manipulation

In the Area of Distribution:

Not manipulating the availability of a product for purpose of exploitation
Not using coercion in the marketing channel
Not exerting undue influence over the resellers' choice to handle a product

In the Area of Pricing:

Not engaging in price fixing
Not practising predatory pricing
Disclosing the full price associated with any purchase

In the Area of Marketing Research:

Prohibiting selling or fund raising under the guise of conducting research
Maintaining research integrity by avoiding misrepresentation and omission of pertinent research data
Treating outside clients and suppliers fairly

Organisational Relationships

Marketers should be aware of how their behaviour may influence or impact on the behaviour of

(Continues)

Table 24.2   The American Marketing Association's Code of Ethics

Table 24.2   The American Marketing Association's Code of Ethics   (cont.)

should not encourage or apply coercion to obtain unethical behaviour in their relationships with others, such as employers, suppliers or customers.

1. Apply confidentiality and anonymity in professional relationships with regard to privileged information.
2. Meet their obligations and responsibilities in contracts and mutual agreements in a timely manner.

3. Avoid taking the work of others, in whole, or in part, and representing this work as their own or directly benefiting from it without compensation or consent of the originator or owner.
4. Avoid manipulation to take advantage of situations to maximise personal welfare in a way that unfairly deprives or damages the organisation or others.

Any AMA members found to be in violation of any provision of this Code of Ethics may have his or her Association membership suspended or revoked.

NOTE: A similar code has yet to be produced in the EU.

SOURCE: Reprinted by permission of the American Marketing Association.

The four dimensions of social responsibility are generally considered to be economic, legal, ethical and philanthropic concerns (see Figure 24.3). The first two have long been acknowledged, but philanthropic and ethical issues have gained recognition more recently. Ethics has already been covered in this chapter because it is essential to social responsibility and is a vital ingredient of trust in both organisational relationships and customer relations. Philanthropic activities are additional responses that may not be required but promote human welfare or goodwill, as do economic, legal and ethical considerations.

In enlightened companies today, social responsibility is a vital factor in major marketing strategy decisions. There has been ample evidence of how ignoring social responsibility can destroy trust with customers and be a stimulus for government regulations. When marketers deviate from socially acceptable activities, they can be held legally responsible; they can also be damaged in terms of economic success. Social responsibility, then, can be viewed as a contract with society, whereas ethics relates to carefully thought out rules of moral values that guide individual and group decision-making.

Impact of Social Responsibility on Marketing

Marketing managers try to determine what accepted relationships, obligations and duties exist between the marketing organisation and society. Increasingly, businesses are recognising that the long term value of conducting business in a socially responsible manner far outweighs short term costs.[29] A recent survey of 1,000 heads of households indicated that 90 per cent of those interviewed were more likely to buy from a company with the best reputation for social responsibility when quality, service and price were equal among competitors.[30]

To preserve socially responsible behaviour while achieving organisational goals, organisations must monitor changes and trends in society's values. For example, retailers around the world are responding to public concerns about the conditions in which animals are reared and are putting pressure on producers to develop more humane farming methods. Control procedures are needed to ensure

Figure 24.3 The pyramid of corporate social responsibility. SOURCE: Reprinted from *Business Horizons,* July/August 1991. Copyright © 1991 by the Foundation for the School of Business at Indiana University. Used with permission.

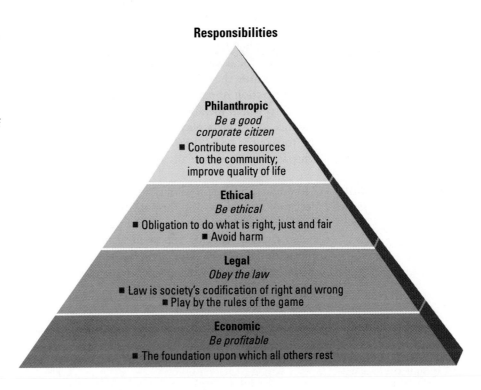

Responsibilities

Philanthropic
Be a good corporate citizen
■ Contribute resources to the community; improve quality of life

Ethical
Be ethical
■ Obligation to do what is right, just and fair
■ Avoid harm

Legal
Obey the law
■ Law is society's codification of right and wrong
■ Play by the rules of the game

Economic
Be profitable
■ The foundation upon which all others rest

that organisations act appropriately; an organisation's top management must assume some responsibility for its employees' conduct by establishing and enforcing policies.

Marketers must determine what society wants and then predict the long run effects of their decisions. Often outside specialists such as doctors, lawyers and scientists are consulted, but there is sometimes a lack of general agreement as to what is an acceptable marketing decision. Forty years ago, for example, tobacco marketers promoted cigarettes as being good for health. Now, years after the discovery that cigarette smoking is linked to cancer and other medical problems, society's attitude towards smoking has changed, and marketers are confronted with new social responsibilities, such as providing a smoke-free atmosphere for customers. Major airlines now operate only non-smoking flights on certain routes, and most major hotel chains reserve at least some of their rooms for non-smokers. Most other businesses within the food, travel and entertainment industries also provide smoke-free areas.

Because society is made up of many diverse groups, finding out what society as a whole wants is difficult, if not impossible. In trying to satisfy the desires of one group, marketers may dissatisfy others. Moreover, there are costs associated with many of society's demands. For example, society wants a cleaner environment and the preservation of wildlife and habitats, but it also wants low priced petrol and heating oil. Shell suffered a spate of bad publicity and negative consumer response following allegations about its environmental record in Nigeria (see Marketing Insight 24.2). Thus companies that market petrol and oil must carefully balance the costs of providing low priced products against the costs of manufacturing and packaging their products in an environmentally responsible manner. Such a balance is difficult to achieve to the satisfaction of all members of society. Shell has recently become engaged in a major drive to improve its reputation by focusing public attention on its interest in environmental projects.[31] This is because the company now recognises the need to respond to negative consumer reaction about its previous actions. Marketers also need to evaluate the extent to which members of society are willing to pay for what they want. For instance, consumers may want more information about a product yet be unwilling to pay the costs the company incurs in providing the data. Thus marketers who want to make socially responsible decisions may find the task difficult.

Social Responsibility Issues
Although social responsibility may seem to be an abstract ideal, managers make decisions related to social responsibility on a daily basis. To be successful, a business must determine what customers, government officials, competitors and society in general want or expect in terms of social responsibility. The success of international retailer Body Shop has been attributed to the company's awareness of the green movement and demonstration of social responsibility. Table 24.3

Issue	Description	Major Societal Concerns
Consumer movement	Activities undertaken by independent individuals, groups and organisations to protect their rights as consumers	The right to safety The right to be informed The right to choose The right to be heard
Community relations	Society anxious to have marketers contribute to its well-being, wishing to know what businesses do to help solve social problems Communities demanding that companies listen to their grievances and ideas	Equality issues Disadvantaged members of society Safety and health Education and general welfare
Green marketing	Consumers insisting not only on the quality of life but also on a healthy environment so that they can maintain a high standard of living during their lifetimes	Conservation Water pollution Air pollution Land pollution
Diversity	Employees and consumers pressing for greater awareness and acknowledgment of demographic and lifestyle diversity issues, which are rising in importance for organisations as diversity in the workforce and general population grows	Equal opportunity in employment Integration Appreciation of how differences can contribute to success

Table 24.3 Social responsibility issues

Social Responsibility: Shell's Onslaught

Oil company Shell faced an onslaught of public criticism following the execution of campaigner and author Ken Saro-Wiwa and eight others in Nigeria. The public outcry focused on two charges against Shell: causing environmental damage, and complicity in the Nigerian government's oppression of the Ogoni people. Concerned groups argued that Shell's economic involvement in the country, where it had been operating for over 50 years, inevitably meant that it was politically involved too. While Shell continued to insist that it would have been inappropriate to have intervened in the case of Ken Saro-Wiwa, the company's decision to announce a $4 billion liquefied natural gas project within days of the executions added fuel to consumers' concerns. The situation in which Shell found itself had important implications for many other multinationals globally, as consumers increasingly demanded that such companies accepted ethical and social responsibility for their business actions.

Shell came under attack from a range of pressure groups such as Amnesty International, Friends of the Earth and Greenpeace. In particular, the company was accused of environmental double standards. In the words of environmental campaigner Jonathan Porritt, "Global companies such as Shell can no longer have it both ways. They cannot on the one hand support a very good environmental record in European markets and on the other wreak environmental devastation in other parts of the world." These concerns were echoed by Friends of the Earth executive director Charles Secrett, who accused Shell executives of only being " . . . concerned about their responsibilities to shareholders and the bottom line. Shell must take its social and environmental responsibilities seriously. Until it does that it will always face difficulties". Meanwhile, the green retailer Body Shop, which supported the Ogoni cause for more than two years, entered the fray by running a newspaper advertisement directly criticising Shell's involvement in Nigeria. In only its third above-the-line promotion ever, Body Shop's spoiler advertisement features the words, "Dear Shell, This is the truth and it stinks." The retailer then went on to exhort consumers to boycott Shell products.

Amidst the flood of accusations, Shell used newspaper advertisements to try to defuse the crisis, arguing that its investment in Nigeria led to the creation of thousands of jobs. While the company accepted that there had been environmental difficulties, it insisted that it had taken responsibility for some of these problems. As 21 other members of the Ogoni people awaited trial in Nigeria on charges similar to those of which Ken Saro-Wiwa was convicted, it seemed likely that the debate would continue. As consumers around Europe continued to protest, publicise and lobby against Shell, the company realised it had a difficult task ahead.

Indeed, ultimately it was consumer rather than political pressure which posed the greatest threat for Shell. More than three years after the Saro-Wiwa affair, Shell was forced to engage in a £20 million drive to repair the damage done to its reputation. This investment followed a MORI survey which showed that 10 per cent of respondents were highly critical of the company's reputation and operations. Shell hopes that its action will encourage debate on environmental issues such as those on which the company has been criticised. However, pressure groups such as Friends of the Earth and Greenpeace are still waiting to be convinced that Shell has done enough to change its image.

SOURCES: Tom O'Sullivan, "Shell needs more than slick solution", *Marketing Week*, 24 November 1995; This Week, "Body Shop joins Shell row with spoiler ad", *Marketing*, 23 November 1995; Alexandra Jardine, "Shell stresses ethical action to salvage brand reputation", *Marketing*, 18 March 1999, p. 9; Alexandra Jardine, "£20m drive to fix Shell image", *Marketing*, 11 March 1999, p. 1.

summarises several major categories of social responsibility issues, which include the consumer movement, community relations, green marketing and diversity in the workforce.

Consumer Movement   One of the most significant social responsibility issues in marketing is the consumer movement, which Chapter 2 defines as the efforts of independent individuals, groups and organisations to protect the rights of consumers. A number of interest groups and individuals have taken actions such as lobbying government officials and agencies, letter writing campaigns, placing advertisements and boycotting companies they consider irresponsible.

A number of high profile consumer activists continue to crusade for consumer rights. Consumer activism has resulted in legislation requiring various safety features in cars: seat belts, padded dashboards, stronger door catches, headrests, shatterproof windscreens and collapsible steering columns. Activists' efforts have furthered the passage of several consumer protection laws, such as the Trade Descriptions Act (1968), the Consumer Protection Act (1987), the Fair Trading Act (1973), the Food Act (1984) and the Weights and Measures Act (1985).

Community Relations   Social responsibility also extends to marketers' roles as community members. Individual communities expect marketers to contribute to the satisfaction and growth of their communities. Thus many marketers view social responsibility as including contributions of resources (money, products, time) to community causes such as education, the arts, recreation, disadvantaged members of the community and others. British Airways' "Change for Good" partnership with UNICEF encourages donations of foreign currency from passengers which can then be used to fund a range of health and educational projects aimed at children around the world. McDonald's, Shell, Ogilvy & Mather and Hewlett Packard all have programmes that contribute funds, equipment and personnel to educational reform. Similarly, Tesco has a scheme that allows shoppers to collect vouchers enabling their local schools to obtain computer equipment. All these efforts, of course, have a positive impact on local communities, but they also indirectly help the organisations in the form of goodwill, publicity and exposure to potential future customers. Thus, although social responsibility is certainly a positive concept, most organisations do not embrace it without the expectation of some indirect long term benefit.

Green marketing The specific development, pricing, promotion and distribution of products that do not harm the environment

Green Marketing   Green marketing refers to the specific development, pricing, promotion and distribution of products that do not harm the environment. An independent coalition of environmentalists, scientists and marketers is one group involved in evaluating products to assess their environmental impact, determining marketers' commitment to the environment and producing *The Green Guide*. For consumers this has been a confusing time, as they are faced by an array of products making a variety of environmental claims. Recently the confusion has been somewhat alleviated by the promotion of two standard labels throughout Europe. Both labels have government backing. The ecolabel is awarded to products that have been judged by independent assessors as better for the environment than the norm in their respective product groups. The energy label provides information about energy consumption and efficiency of white goods. As Figure 24.4 illustrates, the UK Government also encourages labelling to reduce confusion over environmental claims.

Green movement   A movement of consumers committed to increasing environmental awareness and bringing about changes in production, marketing and consumption

As discussed in Chapter 2, perhaps one of the most fundamental changes facing marketers and consumers alike, which began in the 1990s and continues into the new millennium, is the tremendous growth of the **green movement**. Increased environmental awareness has led to changes in production methods—from product design, materials and packaging to promotion and selling messages, and even product disposal—as well as changes in marketing and consumption. Figure 24.5 illustrates a campaign for ecologically sound paints.

Figure 24.4 Ethics in marketing. The UK government supports labelling to reduce consumer confusion over environmental claims. SOURCE: Department of the Environment.

Diversity Diversity in the work environment is the integration and utilisation of an increasingly diverse workforce. Companies that successfully utilise the workforce are finding increases in creativity and motivation and reductions in staff turnover. From a marketing perspective, the more closely the workforce matches the population, the better it understands consumer needs and wants. Levi Strauss recruits and manages a very diverse workforce: more than half of all its US employees come from minority groups. Fourteen per cent of its top management is non-Caucasian, and 30 per cent is female.[32] Xerox also deserves praise for its outstanding workplace diversity. Of its more than 47,000 employees, 32 per cent are women and 26 per cent are minorities. Moreover, about a quarter of the company's corporate officers are women and minorities.[33]

Strategies for Dealing with Social Responsibility Issues

There are four basic strategies for systematically dealing with social responsibility issues: (1) reaction, (2) defence, (3) accommodation and (4) proaction.

Reaction Strategy A business adopting a **reaction strategy** allows a condition or potential problem to go unresolved until the public learns about it. The situation may be known to management (like one car maker's problems with fuel tank combustibility) or it may be unknown. In either case, the business denies responsibility but tries to resolve the problem, deal with its consequences and continue doing business as usual to minimise the negative impact.

Reaction strategy A business's decision to allow a condition or potential problem to go unresolved until the public learns about it

Defence Strategy A business using a **defence strategy** tries to minimise or avoid additional obligations linked to a problem or problems. Commonly used defence tactics include legal manoeuvering and seeking the support of trade unions that

Defence strategy A business's decision to try to minimise or avoid additional obligations linked to a problem or problems

Figure 24.5 Social responsibility. In the Netherlands, the campaign for ecologically safe paints is gathering support from consumers and from industry. Source: Courtesy SNC Neptune Distribution/Thonon.

embrace the company's way of doing business and that support the industry. Businesses often lobby to avoid government action or regulation. For example, the direct mail industry lobbied against an increase in bulk postal rates because it knew it would have to pass on these increases to its clients, advertisers and advertising agencies. Sizeable increases in postal rates could put it at a competitive disadvantage in relation to print media, such as newspaper inserts, which are not carried by mail. Thus the industry took a defensive position to protect its own and its clients' interests.

Accommodation strategy
A business's decision to take responsibility for its actions when it is encouraged by special interest groups or threatened by government intervention

Accommodation Strategy A business using an **accommodation strategy** assumes responsibility for its actions. A business might adopt the accommodation strategy when special interest groups are encouraging a particular action or when the business perceives that if it fails to react, the government will pass a law to ensure compliance.

For example, McDonald's developed a nutrition oriented advertising campaign to appease dietitians and nutritionists who had urged that accurate nutritional information should be provided on all fast food products. However, instead of soothing the interest groups, the McDonald's campaign antagonised them. The groups claimed that its portrayal of McDonald's food as healthy was inaccurate. A McDLT, chips and milkshake contain 1,283 calories, approximately 60 per cent of the entire recommended daily calorie intake for an adult woman. In addition, that meal contains 15 teaspoons of fat, 10 teaspoons of sugar, no fibre, and approximately 70 per cent of the recommended daily allowance of salt. In the US, dietitians and nutritionists petitioned the Food and Drug Administration in the hope that the agency would require nutritional labelling on products to alert consumers to high levels of fat, sodium and sugar, and low levels of starch and fibre.[34] McDonald's chose to take an accommodation strategy to curtail lobbying against nutritional information disclosure when it probably should have adopted a proactive strategy. Figure 24.6 illustrates how GroceryAid is dedicated

Figure 24.6 GroceryAid is dedicated to working with companies in the grocery industry to channel products to charities caring for the disadvantaged. SOURCE: Courtesy Institute of Grocery Distribution.

to working with companies in the grocery industry to channel products to charities caring for the disadvantaged.

Proactive Strategy   A business that uses a **proactive strategy** assumes responsibility for its actions and responds to accusations made against it without outside pressure or the threat of government intervention. A proactive strategy requires management, of its own free will, to support an action or cause. For example, in response to the increasing concerns about green issues in Europe, BMW is setting up plants throughout Europe to recycle its cars when they reach the end of their road life.[35]

Social Responsibility and Marketing Ethics

Although the concepts of marketing ethics and social responsibility are often used interchangeably, it is important to remember that ethics relate to individual moral evaluations—judgements about what is right or wrong in a particular decision-making situation. Social responsibility is the obligation of an organisation to maximise its positive impact and minimise its negative impact on society. Thus social responsibility deals with the total effect of marketing decisions on society. These two concepts work together; a company that supports both socially acceptable moral philosophies and individuals who act ethically is likely to make decisions that have a positive impact on society.

One way to evaluate whether a specific behaviour is ethical and socially responsible is to ask other people in an organisation if they approve of it. For

Table 24.4   Organisational audit of marketing ethics and social responsibility control mechanisms

		Answer True or False for each statement.
T	F	1. No mechanism exists for top management to detect social responsibility and ethical issues relating to employees, customers, the community and society.
T	F	2. There is no formal or informal communication within the organisation about procedures and activities that are considered acceptable behaviour.
T	F	3. The organisation fails to communicate its ethical standards to suppliers, customers and groups that have a relationship with the organisation.
T	F	4. There is an environment of deception, repression and cover-ups concerning events that could be embarrassing to the company.
T	F	5. Remuneration systems are totally dependent on economic performance.
T	F	6. The only concerns about environmental impact are those that are legally required.
T	F	7. Concern for the ethical value systems of the community with regard to the company's activities is absent.
T	F	8. Products are described in a misleading manner, with no information on negative impact or limitations communicated to customers.

True answers indicate a lack of control mechanisms, which, if implemented, could improve ethics and social responsibility.

social responsibility issues, contact with concerned consumer groups and industry or government regulatory groups may be helpful. Checking to see if there is a specific company policy about the activity may also resolve the issue. If other people in the organisation approve of the activity and it is legal and customary within the industry, the chances are that the activity is acceptable from both an ethical and social responsibility perspective. Table 24.4 provides an audit mechanism to control ethics and social responsibilities in marketing.

A rule of thumb for ethical and social responsibility issues is that if they can withstand open discussion and result in agreements or limited debate, an acceptable solution may exist. Still, even after a final decision is reached, different viewpoints on the issue may remain. Openness is not the complete solution to the ethics problem; but it does create trust and facilitate learning relationships.[36]

S U M M A R Y

Marketing ethics are moral principles that define right and wrong behaviour in marketing. Most marketing decisions can be judged as ethical or unethical. Ethics are a very important concern in marketing decisions, yet they may be one of the most misunderstood and controversial concepts in marketing.

Individual factors, organisational factors and opportunity are three important components of ethical decision-making. *Moral philosophies* are principles or rules that individuals use to decide what is right or wrong. People learn these rules through socialisation. Two types of moral philosophy are associated with marketing decisions: utilitarianism and ethical formalism. *Utilitarianism* is concerned with maximising the greatest good for the greatest number of people. *Ethical formalism*, on the other hand, focuses on the intentions associated with a particular behaviour and on the rights of the individual.

Ethical choices in marketing are most often made jointly in work groups and committees or in discussions with co-workers. *Significant others* are superiors, peers and subordinates in an organisation who influence the ethical decision-making process. *Organisational*, or *corporate, culture* is a set of values, beliefs, goals, norms and rituals that members or employees of an organisation share. *Opportunity*—a favourable set of conditions that limit barriers or provide internal or external rewards—to engage in unethical behaviour provides another pressure that may determine whether a person behaves ethically. If an individual uses an opportunity afforded him or her to act unethically and escapes punishment or even gains a reward, that person is more likely to repeat such acts when circumstances favour them.

An *ethical issue* is an identifiable problem, situation or opportunity requiring an individual or organisation to choose from alternatives that must be evaluated as right or wrong. Ethical issues typically arise because of conflicts between individuals' personal moral philosophies and the marketing strategies, policies and organisational environment in which they work. Product related ethical issues may develop when marketers fail to disclose risks associated with the product or information about its function, value or use. The promotion process provides situations that can result in ethical issues, such as false and misleading advertising and deceptive sales tactics. Sales promotions and publicity that use deception or manipulation also create significant ethical issues. The emotional and subjective nature of price creates conditions in which misunderstandings between the seller and buyer lead to ethical problems. Ethical issues in distribution relate to relationships and conflicts among producers and marketing middlemen.

Unethical behaviour generally arises because of unethical personnel or problems with the organisation's ethical standards. To promote ethical conduct requires teamwork and initiative. *Codes of ethics*, which formalise what an organisation expects of its employees, minimise opportunities for unethical behaviour because they provide rules to guide conduct and punishments for violating the rules. If the number of employees making ethical decisions on a regular basis is not satisfactory, the company needs to determine why and to take corrective action through enforcement. Enforcement of standards is what makes codes of ethics effective.

Social responsibility in marketing refers to an organisation's obligation to maximise its positive impact and minimise its negative impact on society. Marketing managers try to determine what accepted relationship, obligations and duties exist between the business organisation and society. The four dimensions of social responsibility are generally considered to be economic, legal, ethical and philanthropic concerns.

To be successful, a business must determine what customers, government officials, competitors and society in general want or expect in terms of social responsibility. Major categories of social responsibility issues include the consumer movement, community relations, green marketing and diversity in the workforce. The consumer movement refers to the activities of independent individuals, groups and organisations in trying to protect the rights of consumers. Communities expect marketers to contribute to the satisfaction and growth of their communities. *Green marketing* refers to the specific development, pricing, promotion and distribution of products that do not harm the environment. The *green movement,* which began in the 1990s and continues into the new millennium, is bringing about tremendous changes in production, marketing and consumption—for marketers and consumers alike. Diversity in the work environment leads to increases in creativity and motivation and reductions in turnover.

Four basic strategies for dealing with social responsibility issues are reaction, defence, accommodation and proaction. A business adopting a *reaction strategy* allows a condition or potential problem to go unresolved until the public learns about it. A business using the *defence strategy* tries to minimise or avoid additional obligations associated with a problem or problems. By using the *accommodation strategy,* a business assumes responsibility for its action when encouraged to do so by special interest groups or threatened by government intervention. A business that uses the *proactive strategy* assumes responsibility for its actions and responds to accusations made against it without outside pressure or the threat of government intervention.

The concepts of marketing ethics and social responsibility work together because a company that supports both socially acceptable moral philosophies and individuals who act ethically will generally make decisions that have a positive impact on society. If other people in the company approve of an activity and it is legal and customary within the industry, chances are the activity is both ethical and socially responsible.

Important Terms

Marketing ethics
Moral philosophies
Utilitarianism
Ethical formalism
Significant others
Organisational, or corporate, culture

Opportunity
Ethical issue
Codes of ethics
Social responsibility
Green marketing

Green movement
Reaction strategy
Defence strategy
Accommodation strategy
Proactive strategy

Discussion and Review Questions

1. Why are ethics an important consideration in marketing decisions?

2. How do the factors that influence ethical or unethical decisions interact?

3. What ethical conflicts could arise if a company's employees chose to fly only on certain airlines in order to accrue personal frequent flier miles?

4. Compare and contrast the moral philosophies of utilitarianism and ethical formalism. How would a proponent of each philosophy react to a manufacturer's claims that genetically modified foods can feed more people using fewer resources?

5. How is ethical behaviour influenced by organisational culture, relationships and pressures?

6. What are some of the areas that result in major ethical issues in marketing?

7. How can ethical decisions in marketing be improved?

8. How can people with different personal values join together to make ethical decisions in an organisation?

9. Explain the difference between ethics and social responsibility and give some examples of each.

10. What are some of the major social responsibility issues?

11. Describe strategies for dealing with social responsibility issues.

Recommended Readings

T. Donaldson, *The Ethics of International Business* (New York: Oxford University Press, 1992).

O. C. Ferrell, J. Fraedrich and L. Ferrell, *Business Ethics,* 4th edn (Boston: Houghton Mifflin, 2000).

G. R. Laczniak and P. E. Murphy, *Ethical Marketing Decisions: The Higher Road* (Boston: Allyn and Bacon, 1993).

W. W. Manley, *Executive's Handbook of Model Business Conduct Codes* (Englewood Cliffs, N.J.: Prentice-Hall, 1991).

Bodo Schlegelmilch, *Marketing Ethics: An International Perspective* (London: International Thomson Learning, 1998).

C. N. Smith, "Marketing strategies for the ethics era", *Sloan Management Review,* vol. 36, no. 4, 1995, pp. 85–97.

● C A S E S

24.1 Nestlé Faces Pressure Groups

In 1995 two university students approached Nestlé for advertising for their alternative student newspaper, the *Oxford Independent*. When the newspaper appeared in 1996, instead of a Kit-Kat advertisement, Nestlé used its copy space to oppose consumer pressure groups boycotting its products because of its marketing of infant formula in developing countries. In 1999 the Advertising Standards Authority (ASA) upheld a complaint made against this advertisement by the pressure group Baby Milk Action, which aims to halt the commercial promotion of bottle feeding and supports breast feeding. For Nestlé, this was simply the latest instalment in an ongoing battle against pressure groups, which

began in 1977 when the US based Infant Formula Action Coalition protested against Nestlé's role in promoting artificial feeding of babies. Consumers were asked to boycott all Nestlé products as a protest against the company's high profile promotion of infant formula and its policy of widely distributing free samples to medical personnel and health centres.

According to a World Health Organisation (WHO) report, up to 1.5 million babies who die each year would survive if the decline in breastfeeding were reversed. The International Code of Marketing of Breast-Milk Substitutes was established in 1981, yet Nestlé didn't sign up to it until

1984. The consumer boycott was suspended, only to be reinstated in 1988 when the International Baby Food Action Network (IBFAN) voiced concern over Nestlé's compliance with the Code. Baby Milk Action complained about the 1996 *Oxford Independent* advertisement, supported by IBFAN.

Nestlé's advertising copy had stated that "even before the WHO International Code of Marketing Breast-Milk Substitutes was introduced in 1981, Nestlé marketed infant formula ethically and responsibly, and has done so ever since". The ASA provisionally ruled that Nestlé could not support this claim and that, indeed, it "went too far". The ASA also objected to the copy claim that Nestlé employees do not provide free samples for hospitals for use with healthy babies. The ASA ruled that the implications that such practices had ceased "a very long time" ago were unacceptable and misleading. Nestlé had admitted to giving out free samples in South Africa until October 1992, in Thailand until July 1988, in Bangladesh until January 1993 and to hospitals in China as recently as April 1994—only two years before the *Oxford Independent* advertisement. ASA also ruled that Nestlé's suggestion that it had complied with the 1981 Code implied long term and consistent agreement, which in fact could not be substantiated by Nestlé. The ASA warned Nestlé not to repeat the three claims in UK advertising.

This has been a public relations nightmare for Nestlé. The students believe Nestlé placed the advertisement as a tester of opinion and probably under-estimated the ongoing hostility of consumer groups to its marketing practices of infant formula. Nestlé itself has refused to comment on its approach. In 1999, Nestlé embarked on a corporate image boosting campaign, emphasising its high quality, reliable products, its endorsement of the 1981 Code and the company's links with developing communities. The company pointed to its 60,000 employees living in developing countries and the extensive measures in place to ensure that the business develops in harmony with changes in the local communities.

Unfortunately for Nestlé, reaction to its "greater good" claims was far from universally positive. Greenpeace has targeted Nestlé chocolate bar Butterfinger in Germany owing to its use of GM labelled packaging. Greenpeace believes Nestlé has an unrealistically "bullish approach to genetic engineering . . . bringing it problems worldwide". The

pressure group argues that this bullish stance is similar to that portrayed in Nestlé's handling of its baby food marketing. Charity Save The Children has endured an ongoing debate with Nestlé over its infant formula marketing drives, stating that it has "had intermittent and unsatisfactory dealings with Nestlé" which has "shown an unwillingness, in our view, to deal fairly with our concerns". Save The Children states that it takes seriously the role of corporate responsibility, particularly concerning the obligations to children in terms of feeding. As the leading producer of infant formula with 40 per cent of the market, Nestlé has an obligation, argues Save The Children, to lead the way in ethical standards and social responsibility in terms of product development and marketing campaigns.

There clearly is a need for infant formula—many mothers are unable or unwilling to provide breast-milk for their children—but the WHO and IBFAN concerns are with aggressive marketing campaigns persuading many mothers to turn immediately to infant formula for their babies at the expense of the nourishing and protective benefits of breast feeding. How should Nestlé have dealt with the issue? Cause Concern, Saatchi & Saatchi's cause related marketing division, argues Nestlé should (a) ignore it, (b) deal with it through the courts, or (c) negotiate with the pressure groups. These three options needed evaluating and one course of action following. In addition, a PR offensive could have promoted Nestlé's extensive donations to charity and involvement with Kids' Clubs, for example.

To overcome the hostility, Nestlé needs to avoid undertaking any unethical marketing activity and to guarantee to comply with the 1981 Code. In addition, it needs to embark on an ethical drive within the business and in terms of its communications with its various target audiences. Increasingly, consumers want a brand which satisfies them, but also they want to know in what the brand believes and for what the supplying company stands. In most markets, particularly mature ones, consumers have a choice of products from competing companies. Whilst product attributes, supporting customer service, branding and marketing communications undoubtedly play a significant role in consumer choice between brands, the ethical reputation of a company increasingly plays a role, too. Benetton, McDonald's, Shell and Nestlé are just some of the more high profile companies that have faced a consumer backlash because of aspects of their trading practices. Many others will follow them in the new millennium as consumers become more aware of organisations' trading and business practices.

SOURCES: Amanda Wilkinson, "Cause for concern", *Marketing Week,* 11 February 1999, pp. 28–31; David Benady and Amanda Wilkinson, "Nestlé acts to boost its corporate image", *Marketing Week,* 13 May 1999, p. 26; Stephanie Bentley, "Nestlé chief fights back over ethics ruling", *Marketing Week,* 18 February 1999, p. 7; Amanda Wilkinson, "Nestlé loses ASA battle", *Marketing Week,* 4 February 1999, p. 5; Letters, *Marketing Week,* 27 May 1999, p. 33.

Questions for Discussion

1. How should Nestlé have addressed the concerns of the pressure groups?
2. Is Save The Children right to complain about its dealings with Nestlé? Are such corporate expectations reasonable?
3. What role could a code of ethical and responsible marketing conduct play in an organisation such as Nestlé?

24.2 McDonald's Social Responsibility

McDonald's Corporation is the largest food service organisation in the world. McDonald's competes on the basis of price and value by offering quality food products with speed and convenience in reliable, clean restaurants. Its brand is one of the most advertised in the world, and the company spends millions of pounds a year on marketing.

Customer satisfaction is the cornerstone of the McDonald's marketing strategy. The company wants to make every customer contact an enjoyable experience by serving quality food at affordable prices and providing fast, accurate, friendly service. Most people reading this case have had the McDonald's experience many times.

The philosophy of Ray Kroc, McDonald's founder, was that McDonald's and its franchises should put something back into the communities in which they do business. In addition, McDonald's believes that being a good corporate citizen means treating people with fairness and integrity and sharing success in the communities where the company operates. This philosophy is implemented in many different ways throughout the McDonald's corporation.

Quality education is a priority for most countries, and McDonald's is committed to making a contribution, whether it's in the US, the UK, France, Switzerland or South East Asia. Many young people who work in McDonald's stores are taught the importance of responsibility, self-discipline and good work habits. McDonald's works with parents, educators and students and believes in supporting education through various programmes that encourage and recognise scholastic achievement. The company allows school fund raising and charitable activities such as car washing days on its sites; it sponsors computer equipment; and it encourages school children to continue into higher education.

McDonald's is concerned about affirmative action and equal opportunity. The company attempts to attract minorities, women, disabled and older people and to develop their potential without regard to race, sex, religion, ethnicity, educational or cultural background. McJobs is an employment programme established to assist mentally and physically challenged individuals to develop their skills and confidence to succeed. The McMasters programme attempts to recruit, train and retain some of McDonald's most valued employees—people aged 55 and over.

As a responsible corporate citizen, McDonald's is committed to protecting the environment. The company has many ongoing efforts to manage solid waste, conserve and protect natural resources, and promote sound environmental practices. Although many studies indicated that foam packaging is environmentally sound, McDonald's phased out this packaging in 1990 because of customer feedback. There are programmes within the McDonald's organisation to reduce the weight and volume of packaging, to recycle, to implement re-usable materials whenever feasible and to purchase a minimum of £65 million worth a year of recycled materials for use in the construction, equipping and operations of restaurants. In addition, McDonald's refuses to purchase beef from companies that destroy tropical rain forests to create cattle grazing lands. This policy is strictly enforced and closely monitored.

Part of the philosophy of giving something back to the communities is dedicated to helping children achieve their fullest potential. Since its founding in 1984 in memory of Ray Kroc, Ronald McDonald Children's Charities (RMCC) has funded thousands of grants totalling tens of millions of pounds to help support programmes in the areas of healthcare and medical research, specially designed rehabilitation facilities and special youth education programmes.

The Ronald McDonald House programme is the cornerstone of RMCC, providing a "home away from home" for families of seriously ill children being treated at nearby hospitals. The first Ronald McDonald House was developed over 20 years ago in Philadelphia, Pennsylvania, when the NFL's Philadelphia Eagles, a children's hospital and owner/operators of McDonald's restaurants decided to establish a place where parents of sick children could be with others who understood their situation and could provide emotional support.

In 1991, the 150th Ronald McDonald House was opened. Houses are now appearing outside America: London's first won praise from all quarters. In total, more than 2,500 bedrooms serve some 4,000 family members each night. Each house is located close to a major medical facility.

Each Ronald McDonald House is run by a local non-profit organisation composed of members of the medical community, McDonald's owner/operators, businesses and civic organisations, and parent volunteers. More than 12,000 volunteers provide the backbone of the programme, helping with all aspects of House operations, including fund raising, renovation, programme development and services to families. Families staying at Ronald McDonald Houses are asked to make a small donation per day. If that is not possible, their stay is free.

McDonald's attempts to contribute to all aspects of community life by supporting education, pursuing equal opportunity and affirmative action in employment practices, operating Ronald McDonald Children's Charities and promoting sound environmental practices. All of these activities combined demonstrate a commitment to putting something back into the communities that spend so much of their disposable income at McDonald's restaurants. Few companies can compete with the high level of commitment McDonald's has made to communities.

SOURCES: McDonald's 1990 annual report; *Ronald McDonald House Fact Sheet*, Ronald McDonald Children's Charities, Kroc Drive, Oakbrook, Ill.; *Ronald McDonald House Backgrounder*, Ronald McDonald Children's Charities; *Ronald McDonald House World*, a newsletter published for the Ronald McDonald House family, Winter 1991; "Ronald McDonald's Children's Charities" video cassette; McDonald's in-store leaflets; McDonald's, London.

Questions for Discussion

1. Why, in your opinion, has McDonald's selected Ronald McDonald Children's Charities as one of its most visible attempts to implement social responsibility?
2. Why are environmental, educational and equal opportunity/affirmative action issues so important to the long term success of McDonald's?
3. Currently, 65 per cent of all future McDonald's owner/operators in training are minorities and women. What impact will this have on McDonald's operations in the future?

Chapter 1 explained that in order to take advantage of any identified marketing opportunities, an organisation must first develop a marketing strategy and then create marketing mix programmes to help implement the recommended strategy. Parts I and II of *Marketing: Concepts and Strategies* examined marketing opportunity analysis. Chapter 7 detailed the principal part of a marketing strategy: target market selection. Part VIII has taken these concepts further, examining in more detail the nature of marketing strategy, planning, implementation and control. In addition, the important issues of ethics and social responsibility have been highlighted.

Readers should be confident that they are now able to:

Describe the key aspects of marketing strategy

• What is marketing strategy? • How does a company determine its organisational mission, goals and corporate strategy? • What are organisational opportunities and resources? • Why are strategic objectives and strategic focus important? • What advantages does a company look for when developing its target market strategy and brand positioning? • What is the importance of understanding competitive positions and differential advantage? • What are marketing objectives and marketing mix tactical programmes? • How can implementation and performance monitoring, along with tools for strategic market planning, help a company achieve its organisational goals?

Explain the process of marketing planning and forecasting sales potential

• What is the marketing planning process? • What are the purposes of the marketing plan? • What is the relationship between marketing analysis—including the SWOT analysis—marketing strategy and marketing programmes for implementation? • How are market and sales potential determined? • What are the principal sales forecasting methods? • What are the major components of a marketing audit?

Understand the issues relating to implementing strategies, internal marketing relationships and measuring performance

• How are marketing activities organised within a company's structure? • What are the ways of organising a marketing unit? • What is the marketing implementation process? • What are some of the approaches to marketing implementation? • Why is internal marketing important to an organisation? • What are implementing and controlling marketing activities? • How can sales and marketing cost analysis be used as methods of evaluating performance? • What are the popular criteria for measuring marketing performance?

Discuss the relevance of ethics and social responsibility in marketing

• What is meant by ethics in marketing? • Why is it an important concept in marketing? • What factors influence the ethical decision-making process? • What are the main ethical issues facing marketers? • How can ethical decision-making be improved? • What is meant by social responsibility? • What are the important social responsibility issues facing marketers? • What strategies exist for dealing with social dilemmas? • How are the concepts of social responsibility and marketing ethics related?

Marketing Opportunity Analysis	Chapters
• The marketing environment	2
• Marketing in international markets	3
• Consumer buying behaviour	4
• Organisational markets and business-to-business buying behaviour	5
• Marketing research and information systems	6

Target Market Strategy	Chapters
• Market segmentation and prioritisation	7, 21
• Product and brand positioning	7, 21
• Competitive advantage	7, 21

Marketing Mix Development	Chapters
• Product, branding, packaging and service decisions	8–11
• Place (distribution and channel) decisions	12–14
• Promotion decisions	15–17
• Pricing decisions	18, 19
• Supplementary decisions	3, 20, 23, 24

Marketing Management	Chapters
• Strategic marketing and competitive strategy	21, 22
• Marketing planning and forecasting sales potential	22
• Implementing strategies and internal marketing relationships and measuring performance	23
• Marketing ethics and social responsibility	24

Marketing in the New Millennium—the Thoughts of Leading Exponents

As the fourth edition of *Marketing: Concepts and Strategies* is destined to hit the bookshelves in the first year of the new millennium, it is opportune to solicit the views of various marketing educator colleagues. What does the future hold for the discipline of marketing?

Well known to several generations of marketing professors—and responsible for well over a dozen leading lights entering the profession—**Michael Baker** has been at the forefront of academic marketing for longer than we can remember. Michael's thoughts challenge the view held in some circles that marketing is in some mid-life crisis. He disagrees also with the notion that marketing will disappear in the customer oriented company of the new twenty-first century. Networks, relationships, partnering and strategic alliances are the future, and marketing will be the co-ordinator of such activities. Templeton's **Keith Blois** intriguingly examines the growing impact of IT and technology, arguing that they won't bring a return to personalised service—automated call centres and cyberspace are pretty faceless!—but they will lead to individualism. Electronic marketing's individualism requires data and consumer trust: quite a challenge for marketers.

Peter Doyle takes the line that marketing's role in top management will grow, but marketers will need to become much more financially literate. Cost cutting, downsizing, re-engineering, all give boosts to shareholder value, but only as "quick-hit fixes". Long term sustainable growth is the real driver for shareholder value. Marketers identify these opportunities for growth, but they must be more financially articulate in determining "good" opportunities. Consumer psychology expert **Gordon Foxall** adopts the stance of the under-siege marketing professor attempting to demystify his university subject. Do we marketers really know what marketing is? Why should others agree? What is its basis? Gordon points a finger at the academic marketing fraternity and asks whether it is time we finally answer these questions. Are marketers akin to astronomers or economists?!

Graham Hooley's piece offers a wonderfully concise overview of many insightful references examining the future trends facing marketing: value migration, with top brands struggling to routinely command loyalty or premiums; cyberspace's borderless world; the blurring of supplier/company/competitor/customer boundaries. Graham argues that marketers must learn quickly and have a culture of learning and rapid response. Longer term relationships are the key, but the marketing function *per se* may not be responsible for managing them. The marketing philosophy will come to pervade the whole organisation and trading ethos of successful businesses. This theme is echoed by former European Marketing Academy President **Hans Kasper**, who focuses on the human side of marketing. Hans expects the service sector to become even more important, with the associated emphasis on people and relationships. IT will dominate personal interactions, so the diminishing bursts of interaction between consumer and service provider personnel will become more decisive.

Leading Dutch marketer **Peter Leeflang** argues that the forces of the marketing environment affecting businesses also impact on the discipline of marketing and all marketers. Social changes, internationalism and IT will dramatically alter the field of marketing. ITC will lead to the full knowledge of *un*met customer needs and *dis*satisfaction. It will permit just-in-time, bespoke, individual marketing.

Customer intimacy will be the key. Existing marketing principles will place marketers in the primary role of handling these evolving challenges. Implementation expert **Nigel Piercy** notes the move from transaction to brand to relationship to value as the guiding philosophy in marketing activity, with the result that value driven strategy processes will dominate. This will entail improved internal marketing, plus the dependency on transparency, integrity, trustworthiness and value in marketing practices. Marketing, Nigel anticipates, will manage these internal and external relationships but will need to improve its marketing communications skills.

Overall Themes

As ever, marketers never fully agree with each other. If each leading text and practitioner body adopts a unique definition of marketing, why should marketers be expected to concur with each other as they debate the future challenges to be addressed by marketing? That said, certain core themes appear throughout the following "guru" pieces:

- Customer intimacy—individualism or one-to-one marketing—will become the focus for many marketers.
- Marketing's principles will pervade throughout the organisation, though not necessarily led by a marketing department.

- Value based strategies will become the core approach for building customer loyalty and differentiation.
- IT and technology will impact on consumers, companies and marketers more and more, bringing the capability for customer intimacy, if marketers can be trusted.
- One-to-one marketing programmes, the increasing role of IT and value-led strategies all demand integrity and trustworthiness in delivery and within the marketing function.
- Relationships will become even more important, though individualism and IT may alter the style of delivery. Marketing will manage these relationships so long as its communications toolkit improves and evolves.

The implication from all of these thoughts is that marketing, as ever, faces many challenges in a dynamic and competitive environment. The challenges are, though, all within marketing's remit and are not too far removed from the principles extolled by the traditional marketing philosophy.

As we champion marketing in the new millennium, we trust you will enjoy the following thoughts of these leading marketers.

Sally Dibb
Lyndon Simkin
Warwick Business School, 2000

Michael J. Baker *Professor of Marketing,*
Strathclyde Business School

Marketing's Disappearance in a Customer Oriented Firm

With the advent of a new millennium the future of marketing as a discipline is a topic which has exercised both academics and practitioners alike. Indeed, it is the subject of the final chapter of the *International Encyclopedia of Marketing* published in May 1999. It was also the subject of a book edited by Donald Lehmann and Catherine Jocz entitled *Reflections on the Futures of Marketing* published by the Marketing Science Institute in 1997.

In the latter book Professor Fred Webster offers the view that "Among the several management functions, marketing has the most difficulty defining its position in the organisation because it is simultaneously culture, strategy and tactics". No doubt this comment was prompted by discussions of "marketing's mid-life crisis" (McKinsey) and the associated view that if marketing is everybody's business then there is no need for a marketing function. If this is the case, then, clearly, marketing has no future.

Against this background Webster's three-fold distinction is useful because it extends the more usual discussion of the marketing concept (culture) as a philosophy of business which should pervade the whole organisation and the marketing function (strategy and tactics) which are concerned with putting the philosophy into practice. Now that the philosophy of serving customer needs has become the dominant culture in business organisations, it is unsurprising that the role of marketing has become blurred. One result is that this common ownership dilutes the claim of marketing to be its sponsor and custodian. Similarly, as the philosophy has become widely accepted so, too, has the need to convert this into a strategy which manages the interface between the organisation and its various constituencies. The result is that strategy, too, becomes a shared activity.

The result of both these changes is that the third element of marketing—its practice—becomes dominant in people's perceptions and confirms their suspicions that marketing is really just a superior form of selling supported by advertising and promotion. On the other hand, if the three dimensions of marketing—culture, strategy and tactics—become truly integrated in the creation of the ultimate objective of a customer oriented firm then there is a possibility that it might result in the disappearance of marketing as a distinguishable discipline.

In my view this is unlikely to happen. While all may share the vision and espouse the culture, the management of the interface and the creation and delivery of customer value will still remain the responsibility of what we currently recognise as marketing. In the process, however, we may achieve a more balanced result in sympathy with my own preferred definition of marketing as being concerned with "the creation and maintenance of mutually satisfying exchange relationships". Such relationships reflect a win-win outcome which must be preferable to either of the currently dominant theories of competition. While Michael Porter's analysis sees the firm as subject to the control of the marketplace, its antithesis, Resource Based theory, sees the firm as controlling the market. Ultimately, the future of marketing must be the reconciliation of these opposing views through collaboration rather than adversarial competition. As such, marketing's focus will be networks, relationships, partnering and strategic alliances.

SOURCE: Reprinted by permission of Michael Baker.

Keith Blois *Templeton College, Oxford*

Impersonalised Customisation?

Peapod will remind its customers to re-order an item. Amazon will inform customers of new books which, given their reading preferences, they might enjoy. This, younger people imply, is a new and amazing level of service. To the elderly such a level of service is not amazing, being no more than the level of service that they once received from their grocery store or their bookseller. Such levels of service disappeared with the demise of the local shop as economies of scale, together with the removal of the legal basis of retail price maintenance, led to increased concentration in the retail trade. The reappearance of these services—though now in an impersonal form—is the result of developments in IT.

There are, in addition, significant developments in manufacturing which may, if linked with IT, create opportunities for the further re-establishment of service to customers. For just as small shops have disappeared from the High Street, so many small manufacturers have disappeared from the towns that they once served because the economics of mass production have left them uncompetitive. However, there are examples of new technologies making localised production once again an economic possibility. Thus small breweries are being re-established in local towns and some mini-breweries now exist within public houses. Instead of being mass produced, individual cans of paint can be mixed to a customer's exact requirement in the local shop (by analogy one would have thought that it would also be technically possible to offer some food products—e.g. yoghurts—as individualised products!). In a similar vein it is also predicted that customers will soon be able to have clothes made to measure by a machine while they wait in the shop.

Thus there is a new age of personalised service and products—or is there? It will not be an age of "personalised" services and products but of "individualised" services and products which will sometimes be extremely impersonal—as is already made apparent by automated call-centres.

The challenge to marketers will be how to utilise this capability to "individualise" their offering. For it to be effective, customers will have to be persuaded to trust providers with information about themselves and allow access to personal financial resources, while providers will have to deliver a quality product. Yet the stated intention of some of these providers is to dominate markets and the behaviour of some has sometimes been surprisingly cavalier. This move towards electronic marketing will throw up new questions about the role of and the nature of brands in both consumer and organisational markets. The brand may have to become a guarantor first of the supplier's trustworthiness and only second of the quality of the supplier's product.

SOURCE: Reprinted by permission of Dr. Keith Blois, Fellow of Templeton College, University of Oxford, and Duty Director, Said Business School, University of Oxford.

Peter Doyle *Professor of Marketing, Warwick Business School, University of Warwick*

Marketing and Shareholder Value

I see marketing in the future playing a much bigger role in top management. This will mean that marketing professionals will have to become much more financially literate in how they present marketing strategies.

Today, the central role of the top management team is seen as maximising shareholder value. Pressures from active investors mean that managers cannot survive unless they are giving good returns to shareholders. But too many companies perceive increasing shareholder value as about cost cutting, downsizing and re-engineering. In fact, such strategies provide only a temporary boost to profits and long-term growth permanently suffers.

What investors recognise is that the key to shareholder value is long term, profitable growth. That is why Internet and pharmaceutical stocks sell at price-earnings ratios four or five times that of slow growth businesses. Chief executives are realising that they cannot generate long run profitability from more cost cutting. Rationalisation has come to the end of the line. For the future they have to look for growth.

Marketing will become more important because it provides the external perspective to identify and capitalise on growth opportunities. The board will look to marketing to develop the ideas and the strategies to grow their business. Marketing professionals have the skills to analyse changing customer needs and to identify the areas where competitive advantage can be built.

But not any growth will do. It has to be "good" growth—that is growth that earns profits above the firm's threshold margin. In the past, marketing managers have been slow to quantify the financial effects of their marketing strategies. They have preferred to rely on qualitative measures such as changes in consumer attitudes, brand awareness or customer satisfaction. But the board knows that such measures have at best only a weak link to financial performance and has not been impressed.

Today's marketers are demonstrating that their strategies not only generate customer satisfaction but also create value for investors. This means that young marketing managers are learning new financial skills, such as shareholder value analysis, and new statistical tools, such as econometrics, in order to isolate the effects of their policies on customer purchasing patterns. In this way marketing is becoming more rigorous, more financially robust and more relevant to the key issues facing top executives in the 21st century.

SOURCE: Reprinted by permission of Peter Doyle.

Gordon Foxall *Professor of Consumer Behaviour and Honorary Professor of Psychology, Keele University*

An Application Area

Some years ago, I fractured my skull and pulverised the bones in my wrist. The first injury threatened no vital organ but the second was serious: it was the hand I write with. As I chatted with the professor of orthopaedics (no less) who was treating me, it emerged that he knew a colleague of mine who was about to take up a chair of marketing in another university. Vocally italicising in the manner of the incredulous, he said: "I hadn't realised that *marketing* was a *university* subject". For once I knew instantly what to say and fully intended to point out that if *bone setting* belonged in a university . . . But the pain in my arm persuaded me that this was no time to question the revealed order.

At some point, however, we must start defending our subject by putting it on the sound intellectual basis it deserves. Perhaps the question most frequently asked of marketing professors is "What *is* marketing?" It is apparently one they have difficulty answering. Confusion is inherent in the very question, eliding function and philosophy, profit-seeking and altruism, consideration and opportunism. Marketing professors are not alone in having failed to come to a definitive view on the substance of their subject matter. Uniquely among the social and business studies, mention of academic marketing raises eyebrows and evokes statements that show the misunderstanding of which only the otherwise-educated are capable. Their surprise is not so much that intelligent people would consider its future but that it ever had a past.

Conventional answers to the questions about what marketing is and why it belongs in a university usually focus on its relevance, its capacity to enhance competitiveness, enlarge wealth and add to human well-being. But such accounts remain simplistic: they reflect the prescriptive stance that first-generation marketing professors could easily assume, the attitude that marketing has technological merits notwithstanding its lack of an established scientific base.

The nature and scope of marketing are described all too often without any assistance from a disciplinary framework. The assumption often seems to be made that marketing is already a discipline, able of itself and in its own terms to explain the phenomena it encompasses as its own. However, marketing is not a discipline; it is an application area *for* disciplines. It is an area of human activity on which the light of several disciplines can be made to shine. It is not coterminous with any of these but is elucidated by them all. As complete an understanding of marketing as we are capable of producing requires the unique viewpoints of all of them as well as their interactions. The strength of marketing in all this is the light it throws on actual human activity, the challenge it presents to the disciplines that attempt its explication.

We shall not understand marketing, let alone justify our positions as people who profess it for a living, by assuming that it is somehow a "practical" subject that defies intellectual analysis. No more can we remain on the surface than astronomers could rest content with the self-evident geocentricism that their unenhanced eyes witnessed, plainly and unambiguously, every day. Nor can we ape those economists who have striven relentlessly to avoid contact with the world of observation. Economists in the 1930s "knew" how marketing operated and why, and they daily imagined that their theories captured the realities of firms and transactions. It took a 21-year old LSE graduate in Commerce, Ronald Coase, whose formal training in economics was minimal, to examine systematically the nature of firms and to point out that they constituted "islands of centralised planning" within the unfettered market, that they came into being in order to reduce costs of which economists had chosen to be oblivious, and that they had implications for economic theory, management and policy which were being ignored.

Marketing, too, waits upon the exercise of disinterested curiosity.

SOURCE: Reprinted by permission of Gordon Foxall, Professor of Consumer Behaviour, Keele University.

Graham Hooley   *Professor of Marketing, Aston Business School*

The Future That Has Already Arrived!

Predicting the future is notoriously hazardous—especially when people will read those predictions in that future and with the benefit of hindsight! As Peter Drucker (1997) has shown, however, it is possible to identify events that have already happened, or trends that are already emerging and that will have continuing effects for the next decade or two. Below are a number of key trends that are already emerging and are likely to continue to impact on marketing practice and theory for the foreseeable future.

Customers are becoming increasingly demanding of the products and services they buy. Customers demand, and expect, reliable and durable products with quick, efficient service at reasonable prices. What is more, there is little long-term stability in customer demand. Competitive positions are achieved through offering superior customer value, and yet without constant improvement "value migration" will occur—buyers will migrate to an alternative value offering (Slywotzky, 1996).

A second major trend looking set to continue is that customers are less prepared to pay a substantial premium for products or services that do not offer demonstrably greater value. While it is undeniable that well-developed and managed brands can command higher prices than unbranded products in many markets, the differentials commanded are now much less than they were and customers are increasingly questioning the extra value they get for the extra expense. The sophisticated customer is less likely to be attracted to cheap products with low quality, and yet is unlikely to be won by purely image-based advertising. The implications are clear—differentiation needs to be based on providing demonstrably superior value to customers.

Technology, of course, continues to develop at a bewildering pace, affecting not just the "high tech" industries such as telecommunications and personal computers but also other industries that make use of the new technologies. Time and distance are shrinking rapidly as firms use the Internet to market their offerings to truly global markets. One result is that cross-national segments are now emerging for products and services from fast foods, to books and toys, to computers and cars. Ohmae's "borderless world" (1990) exists—in cyberspace, at least!

Talking of "boundaries", a further change that will continue to affect marketing is the blurring of the frontiers between firms, their suppliers, their customers and even their competitors. As customers become more demanding in their requirements and the level of competitiveness increases, firms are seeing growing opportunities in collaboration and partnering with others in the supply chain. The process of marketing is becoming far more complicated than it ever was.

In reaction to the above, a number of critical issues are emerging for marketing management and theory. First and central to developing a sustainable competitive advantage in rapidly, and often unpredictably, changing circumstances is the ability to learn fast and adapt quickly (Dickson, 1992). A major challenge for any organisation is to create the combination of culture and climate to maximise learning (Slater and Narver, 1995).

In increasingly demanding, crowded and competitive markets there is no substitute for being market-oriented. This does not, however, imply over-sophisticated marketing operations and elaborate marketing departments. Staying close to the customer, understanding her/his needs and requirements, and marshalling the firm's resources, assets and capabilities to deliver superior value are what count. Here the resource-based view of the firm (see Hamel and Prahalad, 1994) can add important new insights into achieving the necessary fit between firm and market (Day, 1994).

The shift from transaction based marketing to relationship marketing will likely intensify in many markets as firms seek to establish closer bonds with their customers (see Payne, 1995). They will need to realise, however, that for any relationship to last requires benefits on both sides. Too many early attempts at "relationship building" have simply been mechanisms to buy temporary loyalty. Relationship building will need to become far more sophisticated.

Firms will also increasingly practice "multi-mode marketing"—pursuing intense relationship building strategies with some customers, less intense strategies with others and arms length strategies with yet others, depending on the long-term value of the customer and their requirements.

And finally, what role for marketing in the organisation? It is likely that the marketing philosophy will become more important to firms while the marketing department becomes less distinct and even less powerful as an organisational component. Some of the most market-oriented firms don't have marketing departments (see Simon, 1996). They see marketing as the guiding approach to business and the job of everyone—not simply the set of activities carried out by "marketing" personnel.

In the highly demanding and competitive markets envisaged for the foreseeable future, the ability to assimilate data, turn them into knowledge, and act on that knowledge to create strategies leveraging the resources (assets and capabilities) of the firm—through establishing deep relationships with chosen individual customers or market segments—is likely to be the key route to creating sustainable competitive advantage.

SOURCE: Reprinted by permission of Professor Graham Hooley of the Aston Business School.

References

G. S. Day, "The capabilities of market driven organizations", *Journal of Marketing*, 58 (3), 1994, pp. 37–52.

P. R. Dickson, "Towards a general theory of competitive rationality", *Journal of Marketing*, 56 (1), 1992, pp. 69–83.

P. Drucker, "The future that has already happened", *Harvard Business Review*, 75 (5), 1997, pp. 20–24.

G. Hamel and C. K. Prahalad, *Competing for the Future* (Boston: Harvard Business School Press, 1994).

K. Ohmae, *The Borderless World* (New York: Harper Business, 1990).

A. Payne, *Advances In Relationship Marketing* (London: Kogan Page, 1995).

H. Simon, *Hidden Champions* (Boston: Harvard Business School Press, 1996).

S. F. Slater and J. C. Narver, "Market orientation and the learning organization", *Journal of Marketing*, 59 (3), 1995, pp. 63–74.

A. Slywotzky, *Value Migration* (Boston: Harvard Business School Press, 1996).

Hans Kasper *Professor of Services and Retail Management, University of Maastricht*

The Human Side of Marketing

The human side of marketing will become more and more important in the new millennium. Several causes underlie this trend. Service industries will dominate western economies to a large degree. In the service encounter, the personal interaction sets the tone for the final service quality as perceived by customers and employees. Mutual relationships are becoming more important in creating satisfaction and loyalty. Quality, effective commitment and trust are necessary to develop long term relationships which avoid conflict and opportunism. This is very different than focusing on just the exchange of title, monetary values and calculative commitment. The soft side of enterprise will dominate the hard side, especially in mature or saturated markets. This will be hard to understand for those companies focusing on financial goals (return on investment, shareholder value, etc.), especially when short term goals are valued over long term goals. Many of the shareholders are not interested in the company as such, but only in the value of their shares (and managers have to satisfy that need of this target group of "customers" as well). They easily switch when investing in another company will be more profitable. In many firms, those different perspectives of marketing and finance on managing the company may cause conflicts. Our objective is to avoid such clashes and find solutions for these challenges. An integrated view on managing the company may create the mutual benefits that satisfy all parties involved in the company.

Caring about people (employees as well as customers) is typical for the culture of market-oriented organisations, but requires a long term perspective in the firm's corporate culture. The notion of the service profit chain shows the need for integrating HRM, marketing and finance (and the shareholder) in the twenty-first century. Everybody is looking for value in the exchange relationship.

The impact of information technology is growing, not only with respect to gathering and processing market information and disseminating it throughout the organisation, but also in the personal interaction between customer and company. Time for personal interaction will decrease in general. Therefore, the scarce moments of personal interaction will become more and more decisive. This sets high standards for the effective and efficient performance of the company's employees. The moments of truth are diminishing but will be more decisive.

In the new millennium, marketing will become tougher and more challenging than ever before in bringing the whole society to a higher level of welfare and well-being.

SOURCE: Reprinted by permission of Hans Kasper, Professor of Services and Retail Management, University of Maastricht and Director of ETIL bv.

Peter S. H. Leeflang *Professor of Marketing and Dean, University of Groningen and Professor of Marketing, European Institute for Advanced Studies in Management (EIASM), Brussels*

The Future of "Marketing" Is . . .

At the start of the new millennium we face fundamental changes in the marketing environment which make it necessary for existing firms and marketing scientists to reconsider *modus operandi*. The turbulence in the marketing environment is high. Many changes in economic, demographic, cultural, political and legal variables affect supply and demand. Examples are the weak relations between income and expenditure on product categories such as cars, clothing, holidays and household appliances. This trend and the individualisation trend make it hardly possible to identify segments using "a priori" variables. We face a growing number of subcultures penetrating existing subcultures and a more elderly (greying) and less young (degreening) population. We observe a continuing trend of internationalisation of competition among manufacturers and retailers along horizontal and vertical dimensions. Most critical changes occur in the technological realm and more specifically in the area of information and communication technology (ICT). Developments in ICT make it possible for sellers to be truly customer oriented. Information about individual purchase behaviour will soon be widely available; the repeated electronic communication between sellers and buyers facilitates the sellers' collection of data on customer satisfaction and unmet needs. In this way sellers will increasingly recognise customers' heterogeneity in needs, preferences, decision-making criteria, etc., and provide values that truly allow for customers' utility maximisation.

The *"new marketing management"* will be maximally efficient in the exploitation of heterogeneity in customer needs and preferences. The extreme scenario includes the planning, implementation and control of:

- production on order of values that match selected customers' preferences,
- at prices they are willing to pay,
- with exchanges facilitated by two-way communication and just-in-time promotions, and
- values distributed based on customers' specifications, using the traditional channels and outlets and electronic shopping.

In both marketing practice and marketing science, a core concept is the relationship between the firm, its selected customers and other key interest groups such as employees and partners in the value chain. Another core concept is the realisation of customer satisfaction. All firms must make adaptations in their vision; their mission, objectives, strategies, structure and culture; their information systems; their marketing decisions and their reward systems to establish relationships in order to realise customer satisfaction. The choice of the dominant value discipline or core strategy plays a pivotal role in this respect. This choice is largely guided by the organisation's core competencies. Some companies have the knowledge and resources to excel in offering homogeneous products or services in mass markets and adopt a value discipline of *operational efficiency* (Treacy and Wiersema, 1993). Other companies may have emphasised the understanding of customer heterogeneity in preferences, which may favour the choice of a *"customer intimacy"* value discipline. The value discipline of *product leadership* requires core competencies in R & D and/or consumer research. Treacy and Wiersema (1993) argue that successful firms excel in at least one of these three disciplines. In the future we will see more and more firms that adapt one of these disciplines. The role of marketing as a discipline will be most disseminated if the customer intimacy discipline is chosen. This means that the role of marketing becomes more important. Marketing principles, marketing knowledge and marketing information will become more relevant in (nearly) all relevant areas and disciplines. Also, the other value disciplines lead to another and a more prominent role of marketing in organisations. As a consequence, knowledge and information about customers is spread over the whole company. Organisationally we will see diffusion between the existing functional areas. They need to be motivated and empowered to jointly make decisions regarding desirable changes in activities. As a consequence the frontiers of the marketing discipline will become more fuzzy in the future.

These developments also have their consequences for the development of marketing science. The marketing science arena will be dominated by discussions about the establishment of relationships, the measurement of customer satisfaction and the development of condensed information about consumer behaviour which can be spread all over the company. The need to improve the dual relationship between customer and seller will also direct the marketing activities of firms. The measurement of the effectiveness and efficiency of these activities using mathematical models and the creation of appropriate marketing information systems are among the most important research topics in the future.

SOURCE: Part of this text is based on Hoekstra, Leeflang, Wittink (1999). Reprinted by permission of Peter Leeflang.

References

J. C. Hoekstra, P. S. H. Leeflang and D. R. Wittink, "The customer concept: the basis for a new marketing paradigm", *Journal of Market Focused Management*, 4, 1999, pp. 43–75.

M. Treacy and F. Wiersema, "Customer intimacy and other value disciplines", *Harvard Business Review*, vol. 71, January/February 1993, pp. 84–93.

Nigel F. Piercy *Sir Julian Hodge Chair in Marketing and Strategy, Cardiff Business School*

The Future of Marketing Is Strategizing

Marketing as a discipline and business process will transform dramatically in many ways over the coming years. I am convinced that three issues will be prime among the drivers of "new marketing":

- the move in marketing thinking and practice from transaction to brand to relationship and then to value,

- the development of value-driven strategy processes in post-functional marketing, and

- the growing role of internal marketing in managing through alliances and networked organisations of the future.

From Transaction to Brand to Relationship to Value

There are already signs that the enthusiasm of the 1990s for "relationship marketing" will wane, and that a new focus for marketing strategy in an era of sophisticated, marketing-literate customers will be essential. That focus is likely to be provided by value.

Figure 1 below illustrates my logic in seeing marketing strategy—and the search for customer loyalty—progress from transactional and brand approaches to relationship and value-based strategies.

- *Transactional business*—This is where most of us started—the issue was the "deal", the contract or the sale. The customer was the enemy and we used pseudo-military words to describe how to "beat" the customer. This approach works as long as the customer is unsophisticated and as

Figure 1 From transactions, brands and relationships to value.
SOURCE: Nigel F. Piercy, *Tales from the Marketplace: Stories of Revolution, Reinvention and Renewal* (Oxford: Butterworth-Heinemann, 1999).

long as customer loyalty does not matter to the seller.

- *Brand-based competition*—When we realised how much impact customer retention has on profitability, we changed our approach and we did our best to tie customers to a brand (that is, take away their choices—or make them think we had). By adding brand values and associations (anything but cutting price), we tried to take customers hostage. In some cases, this was more blatant than others: a warranty becoming invalidated if the customer uses a competitor's supplies; barriers to interfacing equipment from different suppliers; the sheer hassle involved in changing bank accounts; and so on. The trouble is that ultimately customers tend to see through the bad deals and look for something better.

- *Relationship marketing*—The failure of brands to deliver long term customer loyalty meant we had to emphasise improving customer relationships. The 1990s were awash with customer loyalty programmes, loyalty bonuses, customer satisfaction measurement, customer care policies, complaint response systems and the like. There is nothing wrong with any of these things, and some have been fantastic sales promotion devices—for example, in grocery retailing. However, as customers get smarter, these approaches do not buy loyalty. Smart customers are happy to take all the benefits on offer and report high levels of satisfaction—they just do not give long term loyalty in return.

- *Value-driven business*—Achieving customer loyalty with sophisticated customers is the new challenge and we are only just beginning to realise what it means. It will mean transparency. It will mean integrity and trustworthiness. It will mean innovative ways of doing business. It will mean a focus on value in customers' terms, not ours. It will require new types of organisation and technology to deliver that value.

Value-Driven Strategy

The search for superior customer value and the pay-off in loyalty will lead us in the direction of value-driven strategy. The context for this approach is:

Figure 2 The sources of value-driven strategy. SOURCE: Nigel F. Piercy, *Tales from the Marketplace: Stories of Revolution, Reinvention and Renewal* (Oxford: Butterworth-Heinemann, 1999).

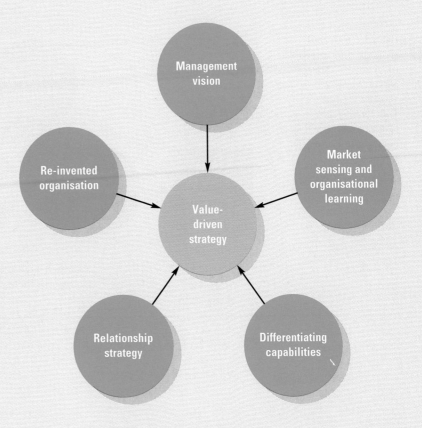

the need for "strategizing" to develop innovative business models, not "planning" to enshrine the models of the past; the decline in the importance of traditional formal marketing functions and systems in many major organisations and their replacement with process-based approaches; and the new types of issues that drive superior customer value. Figure 2 suggests how the agenda for value-driven strategy in marketing is developing.

- *Value-driven strategy*—a total focus on building a winning value proposition for customers that reflects customer priorities and needs
- *Management vision*—clarity in direction and purpose that is effectively communicated throughout the company
- *Market sensing and organisational learning*—understanding the external world by efforts to listen and learn and respond
- *Differentiating capabilities*—using the core competencies of the company to build competitive differentiation
- *Relationship strategy*—recognition and management action to sustain the network of relationships that have to be effective to achieve superior performance

- *Reinvented organisation*—change to organisational form and process to sustain the strategy and renew it

The Role of Marketing in the Internal Marketplace

As organisations develop new and unfamiliar forms—hollow networks, alliances, constellations and modular groups, for example—a critical role for marketing processes will be to manage relationships with employees, partners, allies, outsourcers and other stakeholders to deliver value superiority to the customer marketplace. Rapid market change, new competitive structures, new business models and growing regulatory control, all underline the need for a fresh approach to applying communication skills and relationship building capabilities internally as well as externally. The approach is suggested in Figure 3.

In turn, this suggests the need for marketing to pursue internal alliances in organisations and networks with other process owners, to build value-driven capabilities.

Figure 3 External strategy and internal marketing. SOURCE: Nigel F. Piercy, *Market-Led Strategic Change: Transforming the Process of Going to Market* (Oxford: Butterworth-Heinemann, 1997).

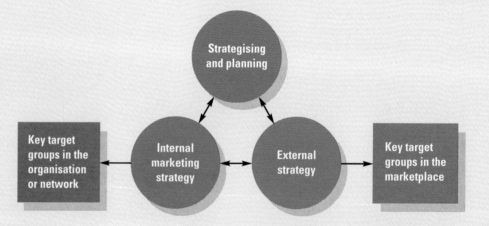

SOURCE: Reprinted by permission of Nigel F. Piercy, Sir Julian Hodge Chair in Marketing and Strategy, Cardiff Business School.

A Case Study Analysis

T his appendix considers how to tackle case study analysis and presents five case studies complete with questions for either classroom discussion or self-tuition. The cases are Colgate-Palmolive, Electrolux, Aer Lingus, Avis and the Walt Disney Company.

How to Tackle Case Study Analysis*

At undergraduate, postgraduate and practitioner level, the case study is a well accepted and widely used learning tool. The popularity of case studies in marketing management education is primarily linked to the technique's ability to bridge the gap between marketing theory and practical situations, thus allowing students to apply the concepts they have learned. Success in providing case study solutions, as in real life, is largely determined by the nature and quality of the analysis carried out. Learning how to make decisions about case studies in a logical, objective and structured way is essential. Such decisions must take into consideration all relevant aspects of the marketing and competitive environment, together with an appreciation of the company's resources. Developing the necessary decision-making and analytical skills promotes an understanding of different corporate structures and philosophies and of the implementation of a range of marketing tools. In addition, the learning process allows the risks and problems associated with managerial decision-making to be experienced first hand.

A popular approach to case study learning is to work in seminar or syndicate groups, which helps develop group as well as individual skills—a very positive contribution, given the extent to which managers in real business situations must work in teams. Developing group skills takes time as individuals learn to cope with the differing opinions and views of colleagues. However, this model closely emulates actual work situations in which a working consensus must be reached. Although preparing cases on an individual basis may appear simpler than taking a range of disparate group views into consideration, a more limited range of

---

* This overview is an abridged version of the guidance offered in Sally Dibb and Lyndon Simkin, *The Marketing Casebook: Cases and Concepts* (International Thomson Business Press: London, 1994).

alternatives may be developed. Nevertheless, tackling cases individually also builds up analytical and decision-making skills.

This appendix is divided into three parts. The first considers the fundamentals of situation analysis, which should be undertaken to give a general overview of the key case issues *prior* to the stages outlined above. The second part reviews the five stages of the case study process, and the third examines the presentation of case study findings.

Situation Analysis

The areas requiring attention are a company's internal position (structure, financial situation, marketing organisation), market analysis, external environment and competition.

Company's Internal Position

An appreciation of the company's internal position, drawing attention to particular capabilities and resources, is vital. This analysis should take into consideration the company structure, financial situation and marketing organisation.

Company Structure The structure of organisations influences operational and managerial decisions. By answering the following questions, students can develop an appropriate overview of company characteristics. This understanding should be used as a basis for assessing how realistic are the various case solutions eventually recommended.

- Is the organisational structure hierarchical or flat?
- Where does the balance of power lie?
- What is the company's mission statement?
- Does the company have particular philosophies?
- What are the key characteristics of the company?
- Is managerial activity delineated by function?
- Who are the key decision-makers for each functional area?
- How do the lines of communication operate?
- What formal and informal decision-making structures operate?

Company Financial Situation Various techniques can be used to assess the financial position of the company. An overview of the financial health of the company can be achieved from the balance sheet and income statement. The web site for *Marketing: Concepts and Strategies*, which can be found by selecting Business and then Text Web Sites from http://college.hmco.com, presents details for marketing related financial analyses. Comparing current figures with those from earlier trading periods is especially informative because it allows changes over time to be mapped.

Financial ratios are calculated using information from the basic balance sheet and income statement (see Table A.1 below). These ratios can be used to achieve greater financial insight into an organisation and can be compared with ratios from competing organisations to allow a better understanding of the company's relative position. Sometimes a break-even analysis is also useful (see Chapter 19).

When using financial ratios, it is important to be aware of the following points. First, ratios represent a snap-shot of a company's financial state at a particular point in time. When comparing the results from more than one ratio, therefore, it is necessary to ensure that the figures applied are from the same time period and calculated according to similar accounting conventions. Second, the way in which ratios are interpreted and used is more important than the figures in isolation. To understand the significance of a particular ratio, it is essential to understand all of the internal and external factors responsible for the financial position reflected in the figures. Once the financial analysis is complete, it is necessary to pull together the different strands of the overall financial picture and identify which issues are likely to have an impact upon the recommended case solutions.

Company Marketing Organisation   Evaluating how the company handles its marketing should systematically cover all aspects of the marketing strategy and programmes: marketing research processes and marketing information systems,

a. Profitability ratios

These ratios measure financial and operating efficiency by assessing the organisation's ability to generate profit from revenue and money invested.

Name of Ratio	Calculated
1. Gross profit margin This shows the total margin available to meet operating expenses and generate a profit.	$\dfrac{\text{Sales} - \text{Cost of goods sold}}{\text{Sales}}$
2. Net profit margin Sometimes called return on sales, this ratio shows after tax profit per £ (pound) spent.	$\dfrac{\text{Profit after taxes}}{\text{Sales}}$
3. Return on assets This ratio measures the company's return on total investment.	$\dfrac{\text{Profit after taxes}}{\text{Total assets}}$
4. Return on net worth Also referred to as return on stockholders' equity, this ratio gives a measure of the rate of return on shareholders' equity.	$\dfrac{\text{Profit after taxes}}{\text{Total shareholders' equity}}$

b. Liquidity ratios

These ratios are used to demonstrate the company's ability to meet current liabilities and to ensure solvency.

Name of Ratio	Calculated
1. Current ratio This demonstrates the company's ability to satisfy short term liabilities.	$\dfrac{\text{Current assets}}{\text{Current liabilities}}$
2. Quick ratio Also referred to as the acid test ratio, this demonstrates the company's ability to meet current liabilities, in the period in which they are due, without resorting to the sale of stock.	$\dfrac{\text{Current assets} - \text{Inventory}}{\text{Current liabilities}}$
3. Inventory to net working capital This indicates the degree to which company working capital is tied up in stock.	$\dfrac{\text{Inventory}}{\text{Current assets} - \text{Current liabilities}}$

(*Continues*)

Table A.1   Key financial ratios

This group of ratios helps in the assessment of the company's responsiveness to debt and ability to meet repayments as scheduled.

Name of Ratio	Calculated
1. Debt to assets ratio This indicates the extent to which borrowed funds have been employed to finance the company's operations.	$\dfrac{\text{Total liabilities}}{\text{Total assets}}$
2. Debt to equity ratio This shows the balance of equity provided by the owners, and funds provided by creditors.	$\dfrac{\text{Total liabilities}}{\text{Total shareholders' equity}}$
3. Long term debt to equity ratio This ratio allows the balance between owners' equity and liabilities to be viewed in context of the company's overall capital structure.	$\dfrac{\text{Long term liabilities}}{\text{Total shareholders' equity}}$

d. Activity ratios

These ratios can show how effectively the company generates sales and profit from assets.

Name of Ratio	Calculated
1. Total assets turnover This ratio, which signals the level of sales productivity and utilisation of total assets, can be compared with the industry average to show whether the volume of business generated justifies the level of asset investment.	$\dfrac{\text{Sales}}{\text{Total assets}}$
2. Fixed assets turnover This measures both sales productivity and utilisation of equipment and plant.	$\dfrac{\text{Sales}}{\text{Fixed assets}}$
3. Inventory turnover This measure of inventory turnover can be compared with the industry norm to show whether the company carries too large or small an inventory.	$\dfrac{\text{Sales}}{\text{Inventory}}$

Table A.1 Key financial ratios (continued)

maintenance of the product portfolio (including new product development), pricing strategies, distribution policy (including the policing and management of distributors), all aspects of marketing communications, personnel, customer and after sales service.

Market Analysis Understanding market structure and customer requirements is a fundamental stage in any case analysis. The following key questions should be addressed:

Market Structure

- What is the market size?
- What are the trends in market size—is it increasing or decreasing? How quickly?
- How is the market structured? What evidence is there of segments?
- Which segment(s) or customer group(s) is the company targeting?

Customers

- Who are the customers?
- What are the customers like?
- For what purpose do they buy the product/service? What are their needs?
- What features do they look for in the product/service?
- What is the buying process?
- Who and what factors influence them as they buy?
- How do they feel about the product/service?
- How do they feel about alternative suppliers?

It is necessary to assess how effectively the company is reaching its target customers and whether it is geared for expected changes in customer needs and/or market structure. This analysis will have an impact on the solution(s) selected.

External Environment

A wide range of factors from the external marketing environment have an impact on the well-being of an organisation. These include economic, political, societal/green, technological, legal and regulatory issues, as discussed in Chapter 2. Monitoring these factors is important, because changes can have a major impact on a company's business dealings. Recognising the significance of such changes early on can help companies to maximise the positive benefits and minimise the detrimental effects. Early warning of the effects of environmental factors can be achieved by assessing the potential opportunities/threats presented by changes. In case study analysis, as in real life, it is often necessary to extrapolate trends and make predictions regarding the level of future change. It is helpful to remember that most potential threats can also be viewed as opportunities should an organisation have the resources and interest to pursue them.

Competition

Understanding the competitive structure of markets helps companies put their marketing options into perspective (see Chapters 2 and 21). From the customers' viewpoint, buying decisions are based on the strengths and weaknesses of a particular player relative to other available choices. Questions to be considered in relation to the competitive situation include the following:

- Who are the key players?
- How is market share divided amongst competing organisations?
- What competitive positions do the players occupy; who is market leader; which companies are challengers, fast movers, followers and nichers?
- How aggressive are the competing organisations and what are the trends? Is it possible to identify fast movers?
- On what basis are key competitors competing? What are their differential advantages—are these sustainable and how are they supported with marketing programmes?
- Are there likely to be new entrants or competition from substitute solutions?

Understanding the answers to these questions allows the case analyst to appreciate fully the relative competitive strengths and weaknesses of the company and to assess whether or not different case solutions are realistic. It may also be possible to use this information to predict how key competitors are likely to respond to different case solutions.

The Case Study Process

Identify and Analyse Case Problem Areas

After the situational analysis has been conducted, a clear view of the problems/key issues set out in the case study must be developed. Although the use of specific case questions will affect exactly where the key areas lie, the company and other analyses undertaken will usually have revealed a range of problem areas that need to be addressed. Any specific questions can be tackled once these problem areas have been identified. *One* way to make this assessment of the case material and the core issues is to carry out a marketing audit. The marketing audit offers a systematic way of considering all aspects of the company's marketing set-up, within a pre-determined structure (see Chapter 23 for a full explanation). For example, it covers the marketing environment, marketing strategy, marketing organisation, marketing systems and marketing programmes. Carrying out a marketing audit should aid the analysis by:

- describing current activities and results: sales, costs, profits, prices, etc.
- gathering data about customers, competitors and relevant environmental developments
- exploring opportunities for improving marketing strategies
- providing an overall database to be used in developing marketing strategies and programmes for implementation.

Not all cases require or have sufficient information for a formal audit. The initial situation analysis may well give adequate focus and understanding. In more complex cases covering dynamic and competitive markets, the marketing audit can assist in sifting through the market and company data to identify more thoroughly the most pertinent issues.

When developing a list of problem areas, it is necessary to distinguish clearly between symptoms of problems and the problems themselves. Symptoms are defined as the outward signs of an underlying problem or problems. For instance, symptoms might include falling sales, declining profits and shrinking market share. The problem may be poor understanding of customers, signalling a need for closer links with customers and regular feedback from the marketplace.

The identification of symptoms and problems should start with the biggest problem(s). The associated symptoms can then be pin-pointed and listed. Minor difficulties, whether or not related to the major problems, should be dealt with after the main problem(s) have been determined. It is helpful to signal whether the problems are affecting the company's position in the short, medium or long term.

Derive Alternative Solutions

Selecting an appropriate case solution is an iterative process that should start by generating a number of alternatives. Each potential solution must relate to the case's key problem area(s) and offer a realistic way of solving it. It is not a good idea to spend time reviewing too many similar solutions. Detailed fine-tuning can be carried out at a later stage, once a selection has been made. In some circumstances it is helpful to frame the generation of alternatives around the following questions:

- Where is the company now?
- How did it get to its current position?
- Where does it want to go/what does it want to achieve?
- How can it achieve what it wants and move to where it wants to go?

An understanding of the organisation's current position should already have been achieved through the situation analysis, but explicitly framing the first two questions helps ensure that these issues from the earlier analysis are not over-looked. At this stage it ought to be possible to exclude the more unrealistic solutions, so that the more likely options can be analysed further.

Analyse Alternative Solutions

The next step is a critical evaluation of the proposed solutions. This should involve a formal assessment of the advantages and disadvantages of every alternative. Each proposal should be considered within the context of the company, market, competitor and environmental analyses that have already been carried out. Conducting "What if . . . ?" analyses—in which attempts are made to predict the likely outcome(s) of alternative solutions—can be useful. It is also helpful to list each advantage and disadvantage formally, if possible, ranking the relative importance of each. This ranking should help identify the best solution.

Recommend the "Best" Alternative

Provided that the case analysis has been thorough, deciding on the best solution should not be too complex. Whichever option is selected, the environmental, competitor and market analyses must be double checked to ensure that the chosen solution is consistent with prevailing market conditions. It is rarely possible to identify a course of action that is ideal in all respects, so it is helpful to consider both the acceptability of the various options and the associated risks. Limited data availability and/or ambiguous market conditions may create problems. However, it should be remembered that managers must often make definitive decisions when only limited information is available.

Once a decision has been made, arguments should be prepared supporting the choice(s). In some circumstances, part of the recommendations may be based on the success of initial actions. Some flexibility will be required in responding to the differing circumstances that may arise.

Implement the Chosen Solution

Ensuring that the recommended plans and marketing programmes can be implemented is as fundamental to case study learning as the analyses and choice of the best solution. Consideration should be given to the following issues:

- At which target groups is the solution aimed?
- How will the company's offering be positioned?
- Will this provide a strong basis for competing and differential advantage?
- Exactly how will the solution be implemented?

Marketing mix considerations (product, people, price, promotion and place/distribution) include the following issues:

- What processes will need to be set up to ensure that implementation occurs?
- Which departments/individuals will take responsibility for the day-to-day implementation?
- When will the solution be implemented?
- What are the likely cost implications of implementing the solution?
- What are the expected benefits of implementing the solution (revenues, cash flow, competitive position, customer perceptions, etc.)?

In real situations, implementation may be affected by a range of interacting factors and unforeseen circumstances. For this reason, it is helpful to recommend a contingency plan, to be followed in the event that the initial recommendations are unsuccessful.

Presenting the Case Study Findings

Various formats can be used to report the findings of case study analysis, among them an informal discussion, a structured formal presentation or a written report. Learning how to present case solutions, like the analysis itself, takes time. While there is a strong personal element in presentational style, the following guidelines are intended to help develop effectiveness in this area. Marketers must be able to make professional presentations and write good reports.

Formal Presentations

Case study presentations can become turgid, clumsy and monotonous, but with care and imagination they can be easily transformed into a lively and interesting forum for debate. The following simple suggestions should assist in this process:

- Keep repetition of the basic case facts to a minimum. After all, other students will probably have read the case study anyway.
- Try to maintain eye contact with the audience. This can be achieved by not addressing the overhead projector screen/overhead projector/board.
- Avoid the use of fully scripted notes. Prompt cards inserted between overhead transparencies or "key word" notes made on paper copies of the transparencies can be helpful.
- Keep visual materials as simple as possible. An audience will have difficulty taking in highly complex tables or slides that are covered in text. Clever use of colour and diagrams can make visual aids easier to follow. Presentation slides or transparencies must *never* be too "wordy" or detailed.
- Use lively material, add the occasional touch of humour and try to involve the audience. Try to vary the presentation format: do not always opt for the formal style of the frontal lecture.
- Avoid using too much material for the presentation time allocated.
- Do not use too many presenters: hand-over time is wasteful and boring for the audience.
- Rehearse! Never be surprised by your own material. Think through in advance the points to be made at each stage of the presentation. Also check any electrical equipment and know how to use it.
- Introduce the presentation, its aims and presenters. Conclude with a brief summary of key points.

Written Reports

The most appropriate structure for writing up a case analysis will depend on the student's or tutor's objectives as well as on individual style and any organisation constraints regarding format. Report writing is a skill that takes practice to develop properly but offers considerable rewards when mastered. The purpose of the case study report is to present analyses and recommendations, demonstrating a full and thorough understanding of the situation. The emphasis should be on reasoned argument that supports the key recommendations rather than a mere reiteration of the information presented in the case.

Much has been written about report structure, which is an area of concern for student and tutor alike. Too often reports are submitted with imperceptible structure, verbose paragraphs and no sense of direction or clear recommendations. Although there is no standard report format that can be applied in all circumstances, certain generalisations are possible. Essentially, the report should contain the following:

Background to the Case Study   This should give a simple overview of the company/industry and may include an indication of the nature of the market.

Understanding of the Underlying Problem(s)   This will probably focus on the areas highlighted by the tutor or in case questions. The problem should be briefly stated at this stage.

Analysis of Case Study Material   The analysis part of the case study will involve the most extensive and detailed discussion. It is here that the student reports on the company and marketing analyses undertaken. The length of this part of the report will probably require a series of sub-headings to add structure and clarity to the discussion.

Recommendations with Justifications   The recommendations represent the outcomes of the case study analysis and should emerge naturally out of the discussion section of the report. The report itself should already have *told the story,* leaving no surprises about the recommended course of action.

Every report is different, but the following simple checklist of section headings may be helpful to consider when structuring the final document:

   I.   Executive/management summary
  II.   Introduction (including objectives)
 III.   Background to the problem
 IV.   Analysis (divided into relevant sections)
  V.   Conclusions and recommendations
 VI.   Bibliography/references
VII.   Appendices (supporting data and facts)

Points to Remember

- The executive summary should provide a succinct, one or two page account of the entire report. It should explain the background to the case, discuss the key issues and themes, report on the analysis and list the recommendations.
- The report should be as user-friendly as possible, with page numbers, a table of contents, numbered sections and sub-headings. References should be sourced within the main body of the report and then listed in full in the bibliography. Diagrams and tables should also be properly labelled and referenced.
- The writing style should be as clear as possible, free of long sentences and jargon. If jargon is unavoidable, a glossary should explain terms not in common usage.
- Arguments should be supported with appropriate sources (references, statistics, quotes, examples, comparisons, etc.) as available to add credibility to the discussion.
- Data from the case should be used with care and, if possible, interpreted; this may involve extrapolating trends or making predictions regarding the likely outcome of certain activities. Only data relevant to the point being made should be included.
- Any relevant material that would clutter the main body of the document should be placed in appendices. Each appendix should be referred to within the main body of the report and listed in the table of contents.

A.1 The Global Adventures of Colgate-Palmolive

Founded in 1806 by William Colgate, New York based Colgate-Palmolive Co, is genuinely a multi-national enterprise, deriving nearly two-thirds of its business from international sales. Having marketed its products in some regions of the world for over 75 years, the company sells its well known brands, such as Colgate (toothpaste), Palmolive (dishwashing liquid), Ajax (cleanser), Irish Spring (soap), Fab (detergent) and Mennen Speed Stick (deodorant), in more than 150 countries in all corners of the globe. In the early 1990s, four areas of particular international interest to the Colgate-Palmolive Company were geographical expansions in the former East Germany, Poland and Mexico, and ongoing association with the Operation Smile programme.

Successful Expansion into the Former East Germany

Once the dust from the fall of the Berlin Wall had settled and East and West Germany were united under a common currency, the shelves of retail outlets in the former East Germany were transformed virtually overnight from small and drab displays of poor quality products into bright, Western-style assortments of high quality goods from around the world. Colgate-Palmolive was one of the first companies to realise success in the new market, both because it was positioned for easy entry—it had operations in neighbouring countries—and because consumers in the former communist nation were eager to try the company's products, which they had seen on West German television but previously had been unable to cross the border to buy. After less than three years in the region, the company was doing 35 per cent of its total German toothpaste business on the eastern side of the crumbled Berlin Wall, even though the region accounted for only 25 per cent of the total German population.

This early success occurred even though Colgate-Palmolive had some initial problems in expanding into the newly liberated country. For example, besides the financial and political risk involved in investing in the region, hiring a salesforce was something of a dilemma. Sales had been a non-existent and unnecessary profession under communist rule; goods were merely produced and then distrib-uted by the all-powerful central government. To overcome this difficulty, Colgate-Palmolive initially brought in experienced West German salespeople but eventually established sales training programmes in the region to teach the "new profession" to local citizens.

The Use of a Joint Venture Approach in Poland

By far the largest potential market in eastern Europe, with a population of 38 million prospective consumers, Poland became a primary target for Colgate-Palmolive when the country began moving to a free market economy in 1990. As soon as the Polish borders opened up to the ways of the Western world, Colgate-Palmolive products were readily available at a range of retail outlets. Open-air street markets were also filled with products brought in by individuals from neighbouring countries. Like consumers in the former East Germany, Polish consumers almost overnight saw radical changes in the types and quality of products available to them.

To promote long term growth in the Polish market, Colgate-Palmolive entered into a joint venture agreement with a local entrepreneur experienced in consumer product sales and distribution. Initially, the company planned to offer only a limited line of its top products—Colgate toothpaste, Palmolive soap and shampoo, and Ajax scouring powder—through the joint venture partner, which was entrusted with the responsibilities of manufacturing and marketing the goods. For its manufacturing facilities, Colgate-Palmolive worked with its joint venture partner to buy a partially completed complex, which was then renovated into a highly modern production facility. To make this joint operating arrangement run smoothly, Colgate-Palmolive appointed a native Pole general manager for the region. The new general manager had previously served the company in a variety of senior marketing management positions in both Belgium and France.

The Revolutionary Use of Video Intelligence in Mexico

To better understand Mexico's large and diverse population, particularly in terms of social and cultural differences, Colgate-Palmolive conducted what it termed a "video anthropological study" of the country's rapidly expanding consumer market. This study had two main objectives: to find out, by observing and talking with Mexican consumers, how certain products were actually used, and to gather general information on the lifestyles of these consumers. Colgate-Palmolive was not interested in product use itself, but rather in the *processes* in which its products *could* be used. Five processes were studied: dishwashing, house cleaning, oral care, hair care, and laundry or fabric care.

An independent team of researchers set out across the country, compiling 60 hours of video taped discussions with consumers. The result of this exercise was a series of video tapes covering each of the five main process areas. Initial analysis showed Colgate-Palmolive marketing managers that Mexican consumers' activities diverged significantly along socio-economic lines. For example, those in the higher socio-economic groups did their laundry and took care of fabrics in the same way as many middle class Europeans, using electric appliances and even the service of maids or housekeepers. But less well off Mexican consumers, for whom in-home water was often a luxury, did their washing manually in tubs using washboards or in local streams using rocks, with a variety of soaps to get their clothes clean.

Marketing managers at Colgate-Palmolive learned a great deal from this revolutionary use of video technology. The information directly affected new product development and the creation of advertising themes for existing products in the Mexican market. For example, marketing managers set out to develop new laundry care products that used less water and advertising messages that showed how Colgate-Palmolive products could be used in situations where little water was available. As a result of these efforts, new laundry pre-soak and spray stain removers were developed specifically for the Mexican market.

Operation Smile

Operation Smile is a volunteer organisation of doctors, dentists and corporate sponsors that travels all over the world, performing reconstructive surgery on children who suffer from cleft palates or cleft lips—facial deformities of the mouth and nasal region. Although these disorders are fairly common and corrective surgery is not considered compli-

cated by Western medical standards, for many children in developing or Third World nations such surgery is either unaffordable or unavailable in their immediate geographic areas. In these cases, Operation Smile goes to the patient and performs the surgery free of charge. Since its inception in 1982, Operation Smile has performed reconstructive surgery or specialised dental treatment on well over 5,000 children. In addition, local doctors have been taught how to perform these corrective procedures, so that they can be done on a regular basis in their particular region.

Colgate-Palmolive has joined forces with Operation Smile in several of the developing countries in which it currently operates or hopes to in the future. In Panama, for example, the company organised and funded a public relations campaign featuring a series of "before and after" photo displays to inform parents in isolated rural regions that cleft lips or palates are in fact treatable. Then the company urged these parents to bring their children to local facilities to have the corrective work done free of charge. In addition, Colgate-Palmolive organised fund raising efforts in the local business community to offset the cost of the services provided. In Panama, the company has been at least partly responsible for the treatment of nearly 200 children.

Colgate-Palmolive's affiliation with Operation Smile not only encompasses organising and funding corrective surgery but also includes extensive oral education programmes for children in many less developed nations. For example, in Kenya the company is well known for its education programmes offered in conjunction with various community organisations in rural areas. The company also stocks the Operation Smile facilities with free toothpaste, soap and other supplies. All in all, Colgate-Palmolive's association with Operation Smile gives it a foundation for future investment and a unique opportunity to link its corporate goals with those of a well known and well regarded global charitable organisation.

International Growth

Colgate-Palmolive's Operation Smile activities and its initiatives in Mexico, Poland and the former East Germany form an integral part of its extensive international marketing programme. The company's aggressive concurrent development and introduction of new products in numerous other countries around the world clearly signal its intention to maintain its international focus. As further evidence of the company's strong commitment to the continuing global expansion, in 1992 Colgate-Palmolive became the first Western company to manufacture toothpaste in China, where a market of 4.2 billion potential customers proved eager for the high quality consumer products that Colgate-Palmolive could provide. These efforts, coupled with others, such as its revolutionary use of video intelligence gathering techniques in Mexico and its association with the Operation Smile programme, ensure that Colgate-Palmolive will continue to serve as a model for other companies hoping to succeed as multinational marketers in the dynamic global marketplace.

SOURCES: Gary Hoover, Alta Campbell and Patrick J. Spain, eds, *Hoover's Handbook of American Business 1993* (Austin, Tex.: Reference Press, 1993), p. 204; Colgate-Palmolive Co., *1992 Annual Report;* and Colgate-Palmolive Co., corporate videos, 1990–1992.

Questions for Discussion

1. Discuss how Colgate-Palmolive has responded to changing social, economic and political forces in the former East Germany. Why should companies use caution when expanding into such regions?
2. What kinds of useful information did Colgate-Palmolive gain from its video anthropological study in Mexico? Why is such knowledge especially important for a company entering international markets?
3. What factors might have played a role in Colgate-Palmolive's decision to enter into a joint venture agreement in the Polish market? Discuss the possible rationale for the company's decision to initially market only a limited number of its products in Poland.

A.2 Sweden's Electrolux Defends Europe from Whirlpool's Customer Oriented Attack

Relatively recently, US white goods giant Whirlpool was a minor player in the European market for dishwashers, cookers, fridge/freezers and washing machines. In the mid-1980s, following a period of mixed fortunes, Whirlpool decided to re-focus on the white goods market with the stated aim of becoming the world's number one manufacturer. In 1989 the company formed a joint venture with Philips of The Netherlands, now wholly owned by Whirlpool. Other joint ventures followed, along with consolidation by continent: the North American Appliance Group brought together Whirlpool's operations in the US, Canada and Mexico; a new Asian strategy centred on rejuvenated regional headquarters based in Tokyo. In much of the world, however, the white goods market bottomed out, with most major manufacturers reporting sluggish sales and deteriorating profits.

American Rivals Targeted Europe

Arch American rivals Whirlpool and Maytag Corporation targeted the expanding European Union with an eye on the associated benefits of growing trade opportunities with the former Eastern Bloc. In 1989 Maytag bought Britain's Hoover for around £200 million; Whirlpool paid £600 million for the appliance division of Philips, adding a further £312 million for re-tooling and upgrading Philips' plants. The Americans have experienced mixed fortunes in Europe. In 1995, following promotional gaffes—problems with promotional offers of free flights caused consumer uproar, adverse media publicity and declining sales—Maytag sold off its European operations, including Hoover, to an Italian business, accepting a loss of £85 million. Whirlpool, though, has decided to battle on, even though its European sales of around 30 per cent of its global total sales remained flat in the 1990s. The European division was blamed for a fall in Whirlpool's earnings per share from £2.75 to £1.75 in 1994. To reverse this decline, the company has been highly active. By focusing on Asia, notably India and China, towards the end of the 1990s, Whirlpool established global leadership for many home appliances. This enabled the company to re-visit its European operation to revive its fortunes.

Pan-European Whirlpool

National designers and researchers have been merged into pan-European teams that work much more closely with Whirlpool's US designers. New products now use common "platforms" enabling different models to be built on the same underlying chassis, with associated development and production economies. Customer service centres, typical of most North American original equipment manufacturers but not the norm in Europe, were established in Germany, the UK, Belgium, Holland and Austria, with plans laid for more Customer Assistance Centres elsewhere, subject to sales levels. The European market is characterised by strong regional and cultural differences. Retail groups with national coverage, such as Currys or Comet, are prevalent in the UK, Benelux, France and Germany, but around the Mediterranean and in eastern Europe, buying groups and independent retailers still dominate. Not all retailers offer the Mastercare warranty support of the Dixons group; in most countries, the onus of aftermarket service still falls on manufacturers' agents. In England, consumers prefer front loading washing machines, whereas their counterparts in France insist on top loading models. In Italy or Portugal, spin speeds are much lower than in Germany, reflecting the general warmth of the climate and preference for drying clothes outdoors. To accommodate these variations, Whirlpool's sales arm accordingly operates 19 sales teams, with 650 representatives liaising with over 40,000 trade partners: retailers, wholesalers and buying groups.

The sales and marketing activities are not set up by country, instead following trade channels and market segments. The marketing strategy centres on building long term relationships with retailers, wholesalers and buying groups, ensuring value added relationships that bring significant financial reward to both Whirlpool and its distributors. The service offer also varies quite distinctly between the various market segments served, with a stated policy of attempting to create a differential advantage through the augmented product: customer service and warranties. This has led to a significant investment in dealer education, electronic data interchange, trade marketing, after sales service, and dealer and strategic trade partnerships.

The Philips-Whirlpool joint venture centred on a strategy of gaining market penetration by building up customer and dealer service levels and by concentrating on the augmented product, as detailed in Figure A2.1. This increased service level guaranteed a replacement machine if product failure occurred in the first 12 months of use, regardless of where in Europe the machine was purchased. Customer care hotlines were established, and customers were offered a 10 year spare part guarantee based on a once only premium payment. If service engineers failed to arrive within two working days, the customer was entitled to a full refund. Dealers' needs were also given priority; Whirlpool Financial Corporation offered a range of financial services to retailers, including extended payment terms and financing of display stock and store inventory. The new look, wholly owned Whirlpool operation in Europe is continuing this service-led, customer focused strategy.

As a result, Whirlpool now occupies the number three slot in Europe, with 13 per cent of the market and leadership in central and eastern Europe. There are 11,000 staff and 11 factories in six countries serving Europe. The company is instigating a branding initiative, transferring the brand heritage and credentials from its American heartland across Europe, supported by a major pan-European advertising drive. The "Fantastic World" campaign aims to establish both the Whirlpool brand identity and key features of a massive programme of new product development and enhancement. In 1995 the new range of faster dryers and washing machines with wider doors and easier access appeared. These new products reflected the findings of a major programme of marketing research, which examined user behaviour and requirements. By the end of 1996, over 60 per cent of sales stemmed from these new products. The strategy is to provide more value without any proportional price increase. New energy efficient refrigerators and dishwashers also reflect growing consumer concerns about the earth's renewable resources and atmospheric pollution, and form the basis of the range aimed at enhancing Whirlpool's position in the new millennium. In a highly competitive marketplace, Whirlpool has demonstrated a commitment to its European ambitions.

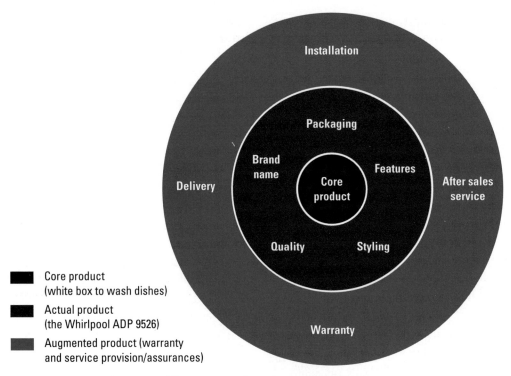

Core product
(white box to wash dishes)

Actual product
(the Whirlpool ADP 9526)

Augmented product (warranty
and service provision/assurances)

Figure A2.1   The augmented product of Whirlpool

Electrolux Attains Global Leadership

For leading rival Electrolux, the Swedish company with most to lose to Whirlpool's European advance, these activities have proved unwelcome but inevitable. Electrolux is Europe's market leader, Bosch-Siemens, Whirlpool and France's Groupe Brandt the leading challengers. Bosch-Siemens has recently made significant progress, raising sales of consumer electrical goods from 7.9 DM billion in 1995 to 11.3 DM billion in 1998. Electrolux has not been idle. In 1995 it publicly re-affirmed its intention to become the world's dominant manufacturer of white goods, setting up a new Asian operation in Singapore and extending its hold over Brazil. It has invested over £65 million in establishing capabilities in the emerging markets of India and China. The global market is still highly fragmented, though, with Japanese suppliers controlling the Asia Pacific market, US giants General Electric and Whirlpool dominating the Americas and the European operations of Sweden's Electrolux and Germany's Bosch-Siemens leading a plethora of national brands in Europe.

In Europe, to fight back against the inroads of Whirlpool, Electrolux is adopting a three-pronged strategy:

- Multi-branding in existing national markets
- Establishing operations in eastern Europe
- Increasing attention to customer service

First, existing markets are being defended by multi-branding: well known names such as Electrolux, Zanussi (Italian based but Electrolux owned) and newly acquired AEG of Germany are marketed alongside a large number of national brands bought up by the Swedish giant over the years. These rival ranges offer a mix of price, feature, distribution and brand value ingredients, which together provide Electrolux with a formidable range of marketing options.

Second, the opening up of trade opportunities in the once communist Eastern Bloc has proved highly attractive. Refrigerators are assembled in Hungary, portable refrigerators in the Czech Republic and washing machines in Poland. Third, Electrolux's marketers have paid special attention to aftermarket, after sales support and warranties as they seek an edge over ever more combative rivals.

Global Economies and Multi-Branding

Electrolux firmly believes that success in the future will depend on global product development to share information on technology, developments, manufacturing material management, component development and purchasing, combined with regional marketing activity that reflects local consumer needs and brand positionings. While local brands are expected to dominate the ethnocentric North American market, a mix of multinational and local brands will continue to dominate in Europe. In this respect Electrolux believes it has a clear advantage over the US-originated single brand Whirlpool. To consumers across Europe, AEG occupies a high price, high quality, premium position; Zanussi, a lower to middle value position (except in the UK, where its famous "Appliance of Science" long standing advertising has established its reputation for technically advanced products); and the name Electrolux is safe, reliable and upper middle market position. Given the plethora of national brands occupying a diversity of niche positions, Electrolux feels it is well placed to provide (1) a highly desirable selection of brand names for customers and dealers seeking the reassurance of internationally recognised brands, (2) Zanussi products or locally produced products for consumers buying on the basis of value for money and (3) AEG products for consumers prepared to pay more for better features and reliability.

There is no doubt that Electrolux is not prepared to sit back on its 23 per cent of the European market. Acquisition of AEG narrowly placed it in the lead worldwide over Whirlpool. The US rival's inroads on Europe, carefully planned and marketing-led, offer an impressive level of customer service. Through a mixture of new product development, new market entry, brand development and customer care, Electrolux intends not only to keep Whirlpool at bay but also to cement its position as the global market leader.

SOURCES: Marcia Berss, "Whirlpool's bloody nose", *Forbes,* 11 March 1996, pp. 90–92; Joe Jancsurak, "Holistic strategy pays off", *Appliance Manufacturer,* February 1996, pp. W3–W18; Patrick Oster and John Rossant, "Call it Worldpool", *Business Week,* 28 November 1994, pp. 98–99; "Dedication to majors", *Appliance Manufacturer,* May 1994, pp. W4–W10; Neal McGrath, "New broom sweeps into Asia", *Asian Business,* March 1996, p. 22; "Electrolux to assemble washing machines", *Finance East Europe,* 6 October 1995, p. 10; Joe Jancsurak, "Global trends for 1995–2005", *Appliance Manufacturer,* June 1995, pp. A3–A6; Joe Jancsurak, "Big plans for Europe's big three", *Appliance Manufacturer,* April 1995, pp. 26–30; Sally Dibb and Lyndon Simkin, *The Marketing Casebook: Cases and Concepts* (London: Routledge, 1994); Whirlpool web site, 1999; Bosch-Siemens web site, 1999; Groupe Brandt web site, 1999.

Questions for Discussion

1. In venturing into eastern Europe, what aspects of the marketing environment must the leading white goods manufacturers consider? Discuss.
2. Why has Whirlpool adopted a customer service oriented strategy based on the augmented product? Why might some customers prefer such a service-led product offering? Explain which customers.
3. Whirlpool and Electrolux have adopted very different branding strategies in their head-to-head global battle. Why? What are the relative advantages and disadvantages of the two companies' respective approaches? Discuss.

A.3 Competing on Nationalistic Fervour and Improving Customer Service—Aer Lingus

The airline industry is unusual: its strategic importance and exacting safety and technical requirements make it highly regulated. People skills, whether those of pilots, ground crews or cabin staff, are specialised and expensive. The cost of leasing or buying aircraft is very high. Routes are highly sought after, particularly into the major international hubs such as London, Amsterdam or Paris.

The much vaunted freedom of the skies policy, central to the harmonisation of European deregulation and the creation of the European Union, has yet to materialise, with major carriers still defending relative monopoly conditions on certain routes. Few airlines are as profitable as British Airways, yet every government strives to have a "national" carrier of which its population can be proud. Most states in the EU have a host of smaller airlines attempting to emulate Air France, British Airways, KLM and Lufthansa. A significant development has been the emergence of low price, no frills operators such as pioneer EasyJet, BA's Go and Virgin Express based in Brussels.

Ireland's Growth

The situation in Ireland is no different, except that the country has recently enjoyed tremendous success in economic growth and in attracting investment from an impressive and diverse list of international corporations that includes Dell, IBM, Siemens, CIGNA, McGraw-Hill, ABN AMRO, Chase Manhattan, Deutsche Bank, General Electric, Grand Metropolitan, Sumitomo, Ericsson, Hitachi, Sandoz, Schering-Plough, Fruit of the Loom, Glen Dimplex, Krups, Heineken, Nestlé and the ubiquitous Coca-Cola. As a result, good communications are crucial. For the government and people of Ireland as well as the expanding international business community, air travel has increasingly become a necessity. The Shannon duty-free zone and continued prosperity of Dublin have added to the volume of freight traffic heading to Ireland. For the quasi state airline Aer Lingus, these growing demands have provided a welcome boost to business; they are also the reason more and more rival airlines are seeking slots for flights into Dublin.

Complex Competitive Situation

The highly competitive airline industry is characterised by four strategic groups:

- Global carriers with truly global networks, such as American Airlines, British Airways, KLM, Qantas and United.
- Medium size international carriers, with significant international routes but less global reach, such as Cathay Pacific, SAS and Virgin.
- Regional carriers focused on regional networks and destinations, such as British Midland, Iberia and Swissair.
- Local carriers serving domestic short hop, intercity destinations, such as Deutsche BA, Ryanair and TAT.

In addition, there are numerous charter operators, such as Air 2000 or Caledonian, plus businesses dealing only with air freight and couriers.

Aer Lingus is a regional carrier with a few key international routes emanating from Dublin, an impressive network with most major British regional airports and a growing selection of European destinations. As such the company competes with rivals in all four strategic groups, contending with the Club branding and high service levels offered by British Airways, the cut-price deals of Ryanair and the high promotional spends of most major European airlines. In addition, Ireland's proximity to the Welsh coast forces Aer Lingus to consider the ferry operators as competitors for much business to and from the UK.

High Expectations

A lot is expected of Aer Lingus, until recently Ireland's official national carrier. In terms of sales, it is Ireland's thirteenth largest company, and by number of employees (12,000) it is ranked third. Now standing on its own commercial platform, the company has a monumental mission. According to former marketing director Maurice Coleman, it is tough for the airline because "we have to compete with several of the really big players on the transatlantic routes, the large airlines in the European Union as well as the smaller, 'no frills' operators within certain UK and Irish domestic routes. So while we have to be commercially competitive with other major carriers in different segments of the free market, back home in Ireland and as a major employer, people expect us to take an accommodating attitude to labour relations, work practices and to provide long term employment".

The official, publicly stated mission statement is equally demanding:

> The Aer Lingus mission is to be a strong niche airline, primarily carrying passengers and freight into and out of Ireland, capable of sustained profitability through commercially viable products and practices and a keen customer focus, delivered by committed and well motivated staff. It will strive to attain a position in which its subsidiaries are profitable and viable within themselves, are strategic to the core airline business and the ownership of which enhances the achievability of the airline's objectives.

For the core business, the airline, there is stiff and varied competition. On its transatlantic routes, American Airlines, British Airways, Delta, KLM,

Northwest and Singapore offer premium service competition, while Virgin and Air India provide value for money rivalry. Principal competition on its European routes stems from the trimmer regional carriers—notably Air UK, British Midlands, Maersk Air and SAS. On the London and UK provincial routes, BA's stronger franchises, especially CityFlyer Express and Maersk Air, provide competition, while Virgin's Dublin based CityJet and its major challenger Ryanair provide significant competition. Nevertheless, Aer Lingus believes it holds a successful operating niche, helped by its distinct national identity, which appeals strongly to the Irish both at home and abroad. Indeed, the 1993 financial loss of £34 million was turned round a year later into an operating profit of £35 million. The current financial situation is just as volatile, although there is an operating profit, as indicated in Table A3 on pages 812–814.

Irish Nationalism

The essence of the successful niche central to Aer Lingus's marketing is Irish nationalism. Its transatlantic routes, where it has no other Irish based rivals, are its most profitable. To feed this route, Aer Lingus operates Dublin as a hub for all its domestic, London, other UK and European flights. These flights operate on co-ordinated timetables with the US flights to offer passengers "seamless" travel. There are believed to be over 44 million Americans of Irish ancestry. Henry Ford, John Paul Getty, Gene Kelly, Gregory Peck, the Kennedys, Ronald Reagan and Bill Clinton are just some of the more famous examples. Accordingly, there are US Immigration and Naturalisation Service clearing facilities in Dublin and Shannon airports, offering users of the Aer Lingus Dublin hub destined for Boston and New York significant time savings.

The transatlantic route is at the forefront of Aer Lingus's development programme and marketing initiatives. The highly profitable business class has 52 inch pitch sleeperettes instead of the standard 42 inch pitch business class seats found in most airlines; coupled with multi-channel personal videos, loyalty programmes for frequent fliers and luxury lounges at airports, these have given Aer Lingus an edge over rivals on its transatlantic lifeline. Because business class passengers generate up to five times as much profit as tourist class passengers, Premier class accommodation has recently been expanded

from 24 to 36 seats. In the economy cabin section, price competition with rivals has reached a peak, but by removing in-flight entertainment and reducing refreshments, Aer Lingus Ireland Vacations has been able to undercut rivals' discount deals. Regular fliers, chambers of commerce and Ireland's Air Transport Users' Committee have welcomed the attention being devoted to the Premier class; "best executive class on transatlantic routes", "best transatlantic airline", "best Ireland/UK airline", "best Ireland/Europe airline" are just some of the accolades. High take-up of the "no frills" economy service and Aer Lingus Ireland Vacations indicates that those passengers, too, are satisfied with Aer Lingus's efforts.

While pricing is often critical in the airline wars, operators such as British Airways and Singapore Airlines are perpetually seeking to create a differential advantage through improvements in customer service and customer handling: larger and more comfortable seats, better trained cabin crew, superior entertainment and food, faster check-ins, in-flight faxes and phones, limousine pick up and delivery, smart airport lounges, exercise facilities and more pleasant staff. The challenge has not gone unnoticed by Aer Lingus. Chairman Gary McGann is on record as stating that "Aer Lingus is in the service business, not a supplier of seats on aircraft—a traditional focus of many airlines—but as a supplier of a total travel experience. To compete successfully, Aer Lingus must increase its already strong focus on service and quality. The Aer Lingus brand is strong and can only be developed further through the provision of ever improved levels of customer satisfaction".

A Future of Customer Service

This reflects the view expressed in some quarters that the company will have difficulty moving away from the transatlantic economy market to compete purely on the basis of low price against operators such as Ryanair. Aer Lingus's cost base, culture and role in the Irish transport and communications system do not lend themselves to operating entirely as a price driven "no frills" airline along the lines of EasyJet. Away from premium (business) class, Aer Lingus will have difficulty developing a differential advantage as it is likely not to match discount operators' pricing. In the premium business sector, Aer Lingus believes it genuinely has a competitive

Strong Group performance

- Turnover up 12 per cent to £901 million (Eur1,144.5m)

- Profit before interest, tax and exceptional items up 14 per cent to £52.4 million (Eur66.6m)

- Profits allocated under Employee Share Participation Scheme up 24 per cent to £5.7 million (Eur7.2m)

Balance sheet growth

- Year-end net cash and liquid resources up 40 per cent at £69.8 million (Eur88.6m)

- Shareholders' funds up 37 per cent to £209 million (Eur265m)

Significant progress in core business

- Record passenger numbers—5.8 million carried, up 10 per cent

- Further expansion on transatlantic between Ireland and four US gateways; over 1 million seats offered for first time

- 9 per cent growth in transatlantic passengers to 776,000

- New route plans announced for Ireland/Los Angeles and Shannon/Paris

- 9 per cent growth in Ireland-London routes to 2.0 million passengers, with strong growth in business class in particular

- 14 per cent growth in Ireland-UK Provincial traffic to 1.1 million passengers

- 11 per cent growth on Continental Europe to 1.1 million passengers

- Additional frequencies from Dublin to Paris, Amsterdam and Frankfurt

- New route inaugurated from Cork to Amsterdam

- Positive growth across the board in cargo services

Delivery of commercial strategy

- Completion of Group restructuring with exit from Maintenance business

- Further development of Programme for a Better Airline, with significant improvements in areas such as punctuality and passenger ground services, including baggage delivery times

- Implementation of efficiency and supplier relationship programmes

- Further extension of average sector length (20 per cent growth in four years)

- Further detailed exploration of strategic alliance options

- Significant progress in major fleet renewal programme

Customer recognition of airline improvements

- Voted Airline of the Year in the Air Transport Users' Council survey of customers for the second time in three years, plus three other awards

- Voted Best Airline between Ireland-Europe/UK and Ireland Transatlantic in ITTN Awards

Table A.3 Aer Lingus Plc, Annual Report

b. Aer Lingus Group Plc, Consolidated Profit and Loss Account

	1997 IR£000	1996 IR£000
Turnover—continuing items	802,275	765,678
Cost of sales—operating	(568,812)	(557,079)
Cost of sales—exceptional items	—	4,194
	(568,812)	(552,885)
Gross Profit	233,463	212,793
Other operating expenses—operating	(189,390)	(166,939)
Other operating expenses—employee participation	(4,583)	(4,051)
	(193,973)	(170,990)
Operating Profit—continuing operations	39,490	41,803
Share of operating profit in associates	2,089	185
	41,579	41,988
Exceptional Items		
(Loss)/Profit on exit from non-core activities	(88,259)	(723)
Profit on disposal of fixed assets	5,012	978
Writedown of fixed assets	(6,000)	—
	(47,668)	42,243
(Loss)/Profit on Ordinary Activities before Interest		
Interest receivable and similar income	23,560	24,944
Interest payable and similar charges	(23,891)	(26,279)
	(47,999)	40,908
(Loss)/Profit on Ordinary Activities before Taxation		
Taxation	2,152	(8,490)
	(45,847)	32,418
(Loss)/Profit on Ordinary Activities after Taxation		
Minority interests	(82)	(424)
(Loss)/Profit for the Year	(45,929)	31,994
(Loss)/Earnings per Share (Pence)	(18.5)p	13.0p

c. Aer Lingus Group Plc, Company Balance Sheet

	1997 IR£000	1996 IR£000
Fixed Assets		
Financial Assets	168,710	168,710
Creditors: Amounts falling due within one year		
Amounts due to subsidiary undertakings	(9,001)	(12,373)
Net Current Liabilities	(9,001)	(12,373)
Net Assets	159,709	156,337
Capital and Reserves		
Called-up share capital	249,709	246,337
Profit and loss account	(90,000)	(90,000)
Shareholders' funds—equity interests	159,709	156,337

d. Aer Lingus Group Plc, Consolidated Balance Sheet

	1997 IR£000	1996 IR£000
Fixed Assets		
Intangible Assets	2,507	3,423
Tangible Assets	348,804	330,845
Financial Assets	1,624	3,486
	352,935	337,754
Current Assets		
Stocks	14,356	26,011
Debtors	126,969	99,150
Cash, short term deposits and liquid resources	355,174	378,513
	496,499	503,674
Creditors: Amounts falling due within one year	(283,581)	(296,815)
	212,918	206,859
Net Current Assets	565,853	544,613
Total Assets less Current Liabilities		
Creditors: Amounts falling due after more than one year	(254,124)	(239,936)
Investment Grants	(2,482)	(6,269)
Provisions for Liabilities and Charges	(156,207)	(106,738)
	153,040	191,670
Net Assets		
Capital and Reserves		
Called-up share capital	249,709	246,337
Revaluation reserve	—	2,685
Profit and loss account	(96,956)	(58,564)
Shareholders' funds—equity interests	152,753	190,458
Minority Interests	287	1,212
	153,040	191,670

SOURCE: Aer Lingus web site, 1999.

edge over its rivals, helped by its nationalistic profile and existing reputation for providing a good level of customer service. This may be true for the transatlantic market, where so many travellers are of Irish heritage, but perhaps less so on European and UK routes. In such a competitive and harsh marketplace, Aer Lingus cannot afford to be stuck in the middle. The future seems clear: the focus must be to enhance customer service levels, particularly in Aer Lingus's premium class. Rivals, though, will not stand still, and on most routes, Aer Lingus is still a relatively small operator. The future is not without its challenges. Understanding and serving customer requirements in a manner that takes account of rivals' strategies will be important in both the business class and the economy segments of this market.

SOURCES: Aer Lingus Annual Reports; Maurice Coleman, Aer Lingus, 1995; Jimmy Ang; The Industrial Development Agency, Dublin; Aer Lingus web site, 1999.

Avis is not the only car rental company to invest in a CRS. Key rival Hertz has its own CRS system, which it uses to compare competitors' prices worldwide. Meanwhile, Europcar has invested nearly £300 million in its Greenway reservation system, which is also linked to travel agents' CRS terminals. For Budget, the experience of trying to develop a joint CRS with Marriott and Hilton Hotels has not been a happy one. After investing over £65 million in the system, the partners are now suing the provider, a subsidiary of AMR Corp., for non-delivery. In order to fill its CRS gap, Budget has now signed up as a Wizard CRS user with WizCom (Avis's wholly owned subsidiary, which developed Wizard).

In addition to its strengths in computer technology, the company has a number of other important strengths that play an important role in establishing its position in the market, for example:

- the Avis global brand name, which gives the company a high level of buying power in its relationships with suppliers
- an extensive worldwide network of outlets, which allows customers easy access and makes it easier to build customer loyalty
- a high proportion of company owned (rather than franchised) outlets, which gives it a high level of control over standards.

Targeting the Business User

As it seeks to develop its strong position, Avis's primary focus is on the business and corporate renters. This focus is not surprising given the company's particularly strong market share of the airport and city centre business, where much of the corporate business is generated. For example, EIU figures show that in the UK Avis enjoys a 30 per cent share of the airport segment, compared with 15 per cent of the market as a whole. Targeting the corporate customer is one particular area where Wizard can help the company by providing efficient, hassle-free service. The company also uses its CRS technology to identify and target business and other frequent customers with a range of special offerings, for example:

Wizard Card This card offers corporate customers and frequent renters guaranteed preferential rates and discounts.

Avis Express This service guarantees a dedicated check-in booth for users, no queues and form-free rental. Described by the company as "the world's fastest car rental service", Avis Express is open to all Avis Wizard Card holders. Avis lists the benefits of this service as speed, efficiency, priority, availability and extra value (20 per cent discount off standard airport rates).

Avis Local Described by the company as an Avis Best Deal Promise, this service saves renters shopping around by guaranteeing the best value from the renters' local station. Additional discounts and benefits are available to Avis Club members.

Among other current initiatives is a partnership with Air UK. The Air UK and Avis deal offers Air UK customers special car rental rates and simple reservations available from all Air UK destinations. Aimed at private and business travellers, the promotion stresses the combination of convenience and quality at competitive prices.

These are just some of the marketing tools Avis is now using in its continuing efforts to maintain leadership in the car rental sector. Staying ahead will not be an easy task in a market characterised by intense competitiveness and price sensitive customers. In such an environment, Avis will continue to build upon its key strengths, so that it can live up to its positioning statement: "We try harder."

SOURCES: Jimmy Ang; "Car hire retail business", *Economic Intelligence Unit*, July 1995; "Hertz keeps its promise with £1 million", *Marketing Week*, 3 February 1995, p. 8; "The supply structure", *Car and Van Hire*, Mintel Marketing Intelligence, April 1995; "Market factors", *Car and Van Hire*, Mintel Marketing Intelligence, April 1995; "The European car rental market", *The European Car Rental Industry Research Establishment*, 1993/1994, pp. 53–56; P. Lilley, "Europcar claims it has high-tech edge", *Travel Trade Gazette Europa*, 8 September 1994, p. 14; V. Houlder, "Technology—electronic librarians", *Financial Times*, 21 April 1995, p. 21; "WizCom to provide Budget with advanced computer reservation system", *PR Newswire*, 3 May 1995; "Competitor analysis", *Vehicle Leasing and Hire*, 1995, p. 58; Avis Wizard Card and Avis Express promotional leaflets.

Questions for Discussion

1. What are Avis Rent-A-Car's competitive strengths? How does the company exploit these strengths to develop a differential advantage?

in low marks being awarded for the paper. Poor time management is generally the main reason for poor examination performance (assuming a reasonable level of revision has been undertaken!). Leave a few minutes at the end to check back through answers.

- Read the questions properly and then answer the question actually set. Remember that the questions are there to help lead students to provide the answer that tutors are seeking. It is good practice to read each question *at least twice* to check that what is required is completely clear. There are two types of problems with answers that do not tackle the question that has been set. (1) Total misunderstanding of what is required. This is extremely rare. The papers are carefully checked by the staff teaching the courses, and often by an external examiner, to minimise the chance of any ambiguities. (2) Latching onto one key word or theme in a question. Sometimes individuals spot a particular word or phrase in a question and then tell their tutors absolutely everything they know about this particular topic. In some cases they do not, however, discuss the issue in relation to the question asked! Once again, the more carefully the question is read before starting to answer it, the less likely this problem is to arise.

Format of Answers

It is important to give some thought to how ideas can best be presented in the examination. The following suggestions should help:

- Use examples to illustrate answers. Marketing is a practical subject, so it is important to demonstrate understanding of how the theoretical concepts work by referring to examples. Some questions may specifically state a named example (product, brand or company), which must be referred to in the answer. In such questions, it is essential that answers do use this named example and that the pertinent theoretical concepts are related to it. Some questions may ask students to illustrate their answers using examples of their choice. The tutors' aim in asking such questions is to require students to demonstrate their genuine understanding of the concepts taught in a course.
- It is a good idea to prepare some examples in advance of the examination. It is much easier to think about possible examples away from the pressure of the examination itself, and doing so should also save precious time. Take a break from the pain of revision and wander around the supermarket: it is surprising what can be learned there about new products and brands and how they are marketed. Spend some time watching television advertisements or browsing through magazines for example ideas. Magazines aimed at the marketing profession, such as *Marketing, Marketing Week* or *Campaign,* all have lively, interesting articles and also present up-dates on new and existing products and marketing campaigns. Copies of these magazines are available in most libraries or by order from newsagents.
- Think about the structure of answers. At the very least, make sure that each answer starts with a "scene setting" introduction and finishes with some kind of conclusion or summary. A summary helps to check that the question really has been addressed and reminds tutors of an answer's key points.
- Try to avoid the "wallpaper syndrome"—pages and pages of script completely uninterrupted by new paragraphs, headings, figures, etc. Make sure that each

answer has a clear structure, that key points stand out and are easy to follow. Have an answer plan and relate sub-headings to this plan. Make sure your writing is easy to read!

- Be sensible about diagrams. Diagrams are often a useful tool to use in answers. They can illustrate points or models in a concise and easy to follow manner. However, do not spend too long drawing them! A simple sketch is worth as many marks as a perfectly drawn and multi-coloured piece of artwork. Also, remember that the diagrams used must still be briefly explained in the text: they cannot entirely take the place of written analysis.

Commonly Asked Students' Questions

1. *How long should my answer be?*

   This is really impossible to answer. As might be expected, the quantity and quality of answers are not necessarily correlated. The variation in handwriting size also makes this impossible to judge. A typical essay answer, in say 45 minutes, for someone with average handwriting might vary from between three to six pages!

2. *What should I do if I run out of time?*

   First of all, please do not! If, despite best efforts to manage time, this problem arises and the end of the examination is approaching fast, complete as much of the rest of the paper as possible in brief note form. This is probably not going to score as many marks as a more considered and reasoned explanation, but at least it will show the areas that would have been covered.

3. *I don't have time to revise all of the topics, so which ones should I leave out?*

   Unfortunately, there is no easy answer to this one! Of course everyone has to undertake revision as efficiently as possible, but the laws of probability dictate that the more topics cut out of revision, the greater the risk that too few will be known well enough to answer the tutors' selections of questions.

4. *Should I use essay or report format?*

   Most tutors do not mind which format is adopted as long as the answer is legible, well structured and clearly addresses the question as set. Some examination papers may specify a required format in the opening instructions. Always read and understand an examination paper's covering instructions. You must adhere to these requirements and your own tutors' guidance. Remember that tutors may be marking many examination scripts, so produce clear answers that are unambiguous and easy to read.

C Careers in Marketing

lthough jobs in marketing are numerous and varied, not everyone will find a career in marketing satisfying. The work associated with a particular career should be enjoyable and stimulating. Because you will spend almost 40 per cent of your waking hours at work, you should not allow such factors as economic conditions or status to over ride your personal goals as you select a life long career. Too often, people do not weigh these factors realistically. You should give considerable thought to your choice of career, and you should adopt a well planned, systematic approach to finding a position that meets your personal and career objectives.

After determining your objectives, you should identify the organisations that are likely to offer desirable opportunities. Learn as much as possible about these organisations before setting up employment interviews; job recruiters are impressed with applicants who have done their homework. Company web sites now simplify this task.

When making initial contact with potential employers by mail, enclose a brief, clearly written letter of introduction. After an initial interview, you should send a brief letter of thanks to the interviewer. The job of getting the right job is important, and you owe it to yourself to take this process seriously.

The Résumé or Curriculum Vitae

The résumé or curriculum vitae (CV) is one of the keys to being considered for a good job. Because it states your qualifications, experiences, education and career goals, the résumé is a chance for a potential employer to assess your compatibility with the job requirements. For the employer's and individual's benefit, the résumé should be accurate and current.

To be effective, the résumé can be targeted towards a specific position, as Figure C.1 shows. This document is only one example of an acceptable résumé. The job target section is specific and leads directly to the applicant's qualifications for the job. Capabilities show what the applicant can do and that the person has an understanding of the job's requirements. Skills and strengths as

Figure C.1 A résumé targeted towards a specific position

```
                    LORRAINE WHEELER
                    35 EAST PARK ROAD
                         REEDLEY
                     LEEDS, L517 9NP
                      (0532) 482111
```

EDUCATION: B.Sc. Honours, The Best University, 1984, Marketing

DATE OF BIRTH: 2/8/59

POSITION DESIRED: PRODUCT MANAGER WITH AN INTERNATIONAL FIRM PROVIDING
FUTURE CAREER DEVELOPMENT AT THE EXECUTIVE LEVEL.

QUALIFICATIONS:

* communicates well with individuals to achieve a common goal
* handles tasks efficiently and in a timely manner
* knowledge of advertising, sales, management, marketing research, packaging, pricing, distribution and warehousing
* co-ordinates many activities at one time
* receives and carries out assigned tasks or directives
* writes complete status or research reports

EXPERIENCE:

* Assistant Editor on student newspaper
* Treasurer of the hockey club
* Student Researcher with Dr. Steven Who, Lecturer of Marketing, The Best University
* Achieved 2.1 degree

WORK RECORD:

1989 – Present	Box Clever * Account Director
1984 – 1988	Wiggins & Co. * Junior Advertising Account Executive
1981 – 1983	The Place * Retail sales and consumer relations
1979 – 1981	Do All Builders * Labourer (part time/holidays)

EDUCATION:

1981 – 1984	B. Sc. Management Science, The Best University, London. 2.1 Honours awarded. Dissertation topic: the marketing of charities.
1978 – 1980	Middlethorn Sixth Form College, Dullsville. A levels: English (A); Economics (B); General Studies (A).

they relate to the specific job should be highlighted. The achievement section indicates success at accomplishing tasks or goals within the job market and at school/college. The work experience section includes educational background, which adds credibility to the résumé but is not the major area of focus; it is the applicant's ability to function successfully in a specific job that receives the major emphasis.

Common suggestions for improving résumés include deleting useless information, improving organisation, using professional printing and typing, listing duties (not accomplishments), maintaining grammatical perfection and avoiding an excessively elaborate or fancy format.[1] One of the biggest problems in résumés, according to a survey of personnel experts, is distortions and lies; 36 per cent of the experts thought that this was a major problem.[2] People lie most often about previous salaries and tasks performed in former jobs. Present career/education details in reverse order, since your most recent exploits are of most interest to potential employers. A good CV or résumé is essential.

The Interview

Most job searches involve interviews. The Davis Company, a leading firm of careers consultants, offers the following tips for candidates being interviewed:

- Work out what are your essential and desirable criteria for the new job. Do not lose sight of these during the interview.
- Prepare well. Find out about the company's products/services and the person who is interviewing you.
- Do not be late.
- Be smart, clean and presentable. Do not look glum.
- Be comfortable in your seat.
- Answer the questions asked. Do not ramble.
- If you are not sure of the question, ask for clarification.
- Keep focused on the current question. Do not be phased by interruptions.
- Ask questions. Show interest and enthusiasm for the business.
- Listen carefully.
- Maintain eye contact, but do not stare. Do not appear furtive.
- Be positive and up-beat.
- Do not discuss politics or contentious issues.
- Do not make—or appear to make—instant judgements.
- Do not criticise strongly your current employer or college.
- Ask if there are any other questions they need to ask you.
- Clarify the rest of the interview/recruitment procedure.
- Do not be afraid to ask for the job!
- Jot down the essential points of the interview afterwards—you will only remember subsequently a tiny part of what was said.
- Go for it!

Types of Marketing Careers

A separate volume of *Marketing: Concepts and Strategies* would be needed to describe fully the multitude of marketing career options. Table C.1 presents the typical hierarchy within marketing, which commences with the junior marketing assistant, progresses to the marketing director (who may or may not have a seat on the Board) and finally reaches the senior directors of the business. The choice initially relates more to the sphere of activity. An opportunity may arise in a marketing services operation such as a management consultancy, direct mail house or marketing research agency; or with a manufacturer, wholesaler, retailer or dealer; in the public sector, service sector or not-for-profit sector; or with a consumer, services or business-to-business marketer. The following list indicates some of the wide selection of options:

- Marketing research—agency or in-house
- Selling—retail, wholesale, dealer or for a manufacturer
- Promotion—advertising, public relations, sales promotion, sponsorship, direct mail: creative, planning or strategy
- Telemarketing, telesales, direct marketing
- Business-to-business buying
- Distribution management
- Product management/brand management
- Retail management

	Predominant Sex	Age	Education	Work Experience	Perks
Marketing Assistant (£14,500)	F	25.7	degree	less than 2 years	none
Marketing Executive (£20,000)	F	28	degree	3–5 years	contributory pension
Product Brand Manager (£22,000)	F/M	28.6	degree	3–5 years	company car, medical insurance, contributory pension scheme
Group Product Manager (£32,000)	M	32.8	degree	6–10 years	company car, car running costs, medical insurance, contributory pension
Marketing Manager (£34,000)	M	35	degree	6–15 years	company car, car running costs, medical insurance, contributory pension
Marketing Director (£50,000)	M	30	degree	11+ years	company car, car running costs, medical insurance, contributory pension
Proprietor (£42,000)	M	44.7	degree	21+ years	company car, car running costs
Managing Director/ Deputy Managing Director (£80,000)	M	43	degree	21+ years	company car, car running costs, car telephone, medical insurance, contributory pension
Chairman/Chief Executive (£110,000)	M	43.5	degree	21+ years	company car, car running costs, medical insurance, contributory pension

SOURCE: Based on "The *Marketing* Salary Survey", *Marketing*, 17 January 1991, pp. 19–22, revised in 1996 and 1999.

Table C.1 A career in marketing

Each of these facets of marketing has been explored in *Marketing: Concepts and Strategies*. Careers consultants will be able to explain the opportunities currently available in more detail. The classified sections of the weekly trade magazines, such as *Marketing* or *Marketing Week*, provide a good indication of where there are openings and on what terms.

Good luck in your search for a career in marketing! We hope that *Marketing: Concepts and Strategies* has increased your understanding of and interest in the world of marketing.

Notes

Chapter 1

1. Jim Lynch in *Effective Industrial Marketing*, Norman Hart, ed. (London: Kogan Page, 1994).
2. Sally Dibb, Lyndon Simkin and John Bradley, *The Marketing Planning Workbook* (London: Routledge/ International Thomson Business Publishing, 1996).
3. Hugh J. Munro, Roderick J. Brodie and Nicole E. Coviello, "Understanding contemporary marketing: development of a classification scheme", *Journal of Marketing Management*, vol. 13, no. 6, August 1997, p. 501(22).
4. Philip Kotler, *Marketing Management: Analysis, Planning, Implementation, and Control*, 6th edn (Englewood Cliffs, N.J.: Prentice-Hall, 1988), p. 6.
5. O.C. Ferrell and George Lucas, "An evaluation of progress in the development of a definition of marketing", *Journal of the Academy of Marketing Science*, Fall 1987.
6. Christian Gronoos, "Defining marketing: a market-oriented approach", *European Journal of Marketing*, vol. 23, no. 1, January 1989, p. 52(9); and Rajendra K. Srivastava, Tasaddug Shervani and Liam Fahey, "Market-based assets and shareholder value: a framework for analysis", *Journal of Marketing*, vol. 62, no. 1, January 1998, pp. 2–18.
7. Lisa M. Wood, "Added value: marketing basics?" *Journal of Marketing Management*, vol. 12, no. 8, November 1996, p. 735(21); and Thomas Robertson, "New developments in marketing: a European perspective", *European Management Journal*, vol. 12, no. 4, p. 362(4).
8. Christian Gronoos, "From marketing mix to relationship marketing; towards a paradigm shift in marketing", *Management Decision*, 32(2), 1994, pp. 4–20; Adrian Payne, Martin Christopher, Moira Clark and Helen Peck, *Relationship Marketing for Competitive Advantage* (Oxford: Butterworth-Heinemann, 1998).
9. Gene R. Laczniak and Robert F. Lusch, "Environment and strategy in 1995: a survey of high-level executives", *Journal of Consumer Marketing*, Spring 1986, p. 28.
10. Sally Dibb and Lyndon Simkin, *The Marketing Segmentation Workbook* (London: ITBP, 1996).

Chapter 2

1. Richard C. Becherer and John G. Maurer, "The moderating effect of environmental variables on the entrepreneurial and marketing orientation of entrepreneur-led firms", *Entrepreneurship Theory and Practice*, vol. 22, no. 1, Fall 1997, pp. 47–58; Ravi S. Achrol, "Changes in the theory of interorganizational relations in marketing: toward a network paradigm", *Journal of the Academy of Marketing Science*, vol. 25, no. 1, Winter 1997, pp. 56–71.
2. Philip Kotler, "Megamarketing", *Harvard Business Review*, March–April 1986, pp. 117–124.
3. *Britain 1990: An Official Handbook* (London: Central Office of Information, 1990).
4. Joseph Plummer, "The concept of application of life style segmentation", *Journal of Marketing*, January 1974, p. 34.
5. *The IBA Code of Advertising Standards and Practice* (London: Independent Broadcasting Authority, December 1977), p. 3. (The IBA is now the ITC.)
6. Brian Bremner, "A new sales pitch: the environment", *Business Week*, 24 July 1989, p. 50.
7. Robin Knight, with Eleni Dimmler, "The greening of Europe's industries", *U.S. News & World Report*, 5 June 1989, pp. 45–46.
8. Reprinted by permission from Herbert Simon, "Technology and environment", *Management Science*, 19 (10), June 1973. Copyright 1973, The Institute of Management Sciences.

9. Wroe Alderson, *Dynamic Marketing Behavior* (Homewood, Ill.: Irwin, 1965), pp. 195–197.
10. Michael Porter, *Competitive Strategy* (New York: The Free Press, 1980).
11. P. Kotler, G. Armstrong, J. Saunders and V. Wong, *Principles of Marketing* (Hemel Hempstead: Prentice-Hall, 1999).
12. D. Abell, *Defining the Business: The Starting Point of Strategic Planning* (Englewood Cliffs, N.J.: Prentice-Hall, 1980).
13. P. Doyle, *Marketing Management and Strategy* (Hemel Hempstead: Prentice-Hall, 1998).
14. I. Ansoff and E. McDonell, *Implementing Strategic Change* (Englewood Cliffs, N.J.: Prentice-Hall, 1990).
15. D. Brownlie, "Environmental Analysis", in M. Baker (ed), *The Marketing Book* (Oxford: Butterworth-Heinemann, 1987).
16. Sally Dibb, Lyndon Simkin and John Bradley, *The Marketing Planning Workbook* (London: International Thomson Business Press, 1996).
17. J. Diffenbach, "Corporate environmental analysis in large US corporations", *Long Range Planning*, 16 (3), 1983, pp. 107–116.

Chapter 3

1. Vern Terpstra, *International Marketing*, 4th edn (Hinsdale, Ill.: Dryden Press, 1987), p. 4.
2. Dana-Nicoleta Lascu, "International marketing planning and practice", *Journal of Global Marketing*, vol. 9, no. 3, 1996; Peter S.H. Leeflang and Charles P. de Mortanges, "The international European market and strategic marketing planning: implications and expectations", *Journal of International Consumer Marketing*, 1993.
3. Theodore Levitt, "The globalisation of markets", *Harvard Business Review*, May–June 1983, p. 92.
4. Ibid.
5. Subhash C. Jain, "Standardisation of international marketing strategy: some research hypotheses", *Journal of Marketing*, January 1989, pp. 70–79.
6. "Global brands need local ad flavor", *Advertising Age*, 3 September 1984, p. 26.
7. Rajeev Batra, "Executive insights: marketing issues and challenges in transitional economies", *Journal of International Marketing*, vol. 5, no. 4, 1997, pp. 95–114; C.C.L. Wang, "Issues and advances in international consumer research: a review and assessment", *Journal of International Marketing and Marketing Research*, vol. 24, no. 1, February 1999, pp. 3–21.
8. Vern Terpstra, "Critical mass and international marketing strategy", *Journal of the Academy of Marketing Science*, Summer 1983, pp. 269–282.
9. Yumiko Ono, "Land of rising fun", *Wall Street Journal*, 2 October 1992, pp. A1, A10; Gayle Hanson, "Japan at play", *Insight*, 27 April 1992, pp. 6–13, 34–37.
10. Douglas Bowman and Shilpa Lele-Pingle, "Buyer behavior in business-to-business services: the case of

foreign exchange", *International Journal of Research in Marketing*, vol. 14, no. 5, December 1997, pp. 499–508.
11. Brian Bremner with Edith Hill Updike, "Made in America isn't the kiss of death anymore", *Business Week*, 13 November 1995, p. 62.
12. Nigel G. G. Campbell, John L. Graham, Alain Jolibert and Hans Gunther Meissner, "Marketing negotiations in France, Germany, the United Kingdom, and the United States", *Journal of Marketing*, April 1988, pp. 49–62.
13. Brian Oliver, "UK soccer advertising in trouble", *Advertising Age*, 8 July 1985, p. 36.
14. Laurel Wentz, "Local laws keep international marketers hopping", *Advertising Age*, 11 July 1985, p. 20.
15. Lee Smith, "Japan wants to make friends", *Fortune*, 2 September 1985, p. 84.
16. Jean-Pierre Jeannet and Hubert D. Hennessey, *Global Marketing Strategies* (Boston: Houghton Mifflin, 1995), p. 60.
17. Peter S. H. Leeflang and Charles P. de Mortanges, "The internal European market and strategic marketing planning: implications and expectations", *Journal of International Consumer Marketing*, 1993.
18. *Europe in Figures*, 4th edn (Brussels: Eurostat, 1995).
19. Laura Mazur, "Failing the Euro test", *Marketing*, 3 December 1998, p. 26–27.
20. "Euro Conversion Rates", *www.dri.gov.uk*.; Audrey Woods, "London banks ready for Euro land", *Associated Press*, Sunday, 3 January 2000.
21. Sandra Vandermerwe and Marc-André L'Huillier, "Euro-consumers in 1992", *Business Horizons*, January–February 1989, pp. 34–40.
22. Eric G. Friberg, "1992: moves Europeans are making", *Harvard Business Review*, May–June 1989, p. 89.
23. Warren J. Keegan, *Global Marketing Management*, (Englewood Cliffs, N.J.: Prentice-Hall, 1995), pp. 285–286.
24. Carla Rapaport, "Why Japan keeps on winning", *Fortune*, 15 July 1991, p. 76.
25. Leslie Helm, with Laxmi Nakarmi, Jang Jung Soo, William J. Holstein and Edith Terry, "The Koreans are Coming", *Business Week*, 25 December 1985, pp. 46–52.
26. Dori Jones Yang, with Dirk Bennett and Bill Javerski, "The other China is starting to soar", *Business Weekly*, 6 November 1989, pp. 60–62.
27. Louis Kraar, "Asia's rising export powers", *Fortune*, Special Pacific Rim 1989 issue, pp. 43–50.
28. Louis Kraar, "The risks are rising in China", *Fortune*, 6 March 1995, p. 179.
29. George Paine, "US-ASEAN dialogue in Bangkok will review economic issues", *Business America*, 21 May 1990, pp. 2–3.
30. Michael Vatiloptos, "Sense of purpose—new challenges lead member states to examine role", *Far Eastern Economic Review*, vol. 152, no. 25, 20 June 1991, pp. 24–25; "Trade rivalries calmed by pacific message", *Financial Times*, 2 August 1993, p. 13.

31. Jean-Pierre Jeannet and Hubert D. Hennessey, *Global Marketing Strategies* (Boston: Houghton Mifflin, 1995), p. 173.

32. Allan C. Reddy, "The role of marketing in the economic development of eastern European countries", *Journal of Applied Business Research,* vol. 7, no. 3, Summer 1991, pp. 106–107.

33. John A. Quelch, Erich Joachimsthaler and Jose Luis Nueno, "After the wall: marketing guidelines for eastern Europe", *Sloan Management Review,* Winter 1991, pp. 90–91.

34. *The World Bank Atlas,* 1994, data for 1992.

35. "Rising in Russia", *Fortune,* 24 January 1996, pp. 93, 95.

36. Jean-Pierre Jeannet and Hubert D. Hennessey, *Global Marketing Strategies* (Boston: Houghton Mifflin, 1995), p. 170.

37. Peter Gumbel, "Soviet reformers urge bold push to liberalise faltering economy", *Wall Street Journal,* 27 October 1989, p. A9.

38. Paul Meller, "Back to the USSR", *Marketing,* 9 August 1990, pp. 22–23.

39. John Templeman, Thane Peterson, Gail E. Schares and Jonathan Kapstein, "The shape of Europe to come", *Business Week,* 27 November 1989, pp. 60–64.

40. Kerry Luft, "Chile on hold for NAFTA entry: negotiations stalled by Mexico Crisis, U.S.'96 election", *Chicago Tribune,* 8 November 1995.

41. Richard S. Lapidus, "Global Marketing Strategies", *Journal of Global Marketing,* 1997.

42. John A. Quelch, "How to build a product licensing program", *Harvard Business Review,* May–June 1985, pp. 186–187.

43. Frank Bradley, *International Marketing Strategy* (London: Prentice-Hall, 1995), p. 393.

44. J. Adams and M. Mendelsohn, "Recent developments in franchising", *Journal of Business Law,* 1986, pp. 206–219.

45. P. Stern and J. Stanworth, "The development of franchising in Britain", *National Westminster Quarterly Review,* May 1988, pp. 38–48; D. Ayling, "Franchising has its dark side", *Accountancy,* 99, 1987, pp. 113–117.

46. Andrew Kupfer, "How to be a global manager", *Fortune,* 14 March 1988, pp. 52–58.

47. Kathryn R. Harrigan, "Joint ventures and competitive advantage", *Strategic Management Journal,* May 1988, pp. 141–158.

48. A. Dunlap Smith, "Europe's truckmakers face survival of the biggest", *Business Week,* 6 November 1989, p. 68.

49. J. Killing, "How to make a global joint venture work", *Harvard Business Review,* vol. 60, 1982, pp. 120–127.

50. Kathryn R. Harrigan, "Joint ventures and competitive strategy", *Strategic Management Journal,* May 1988, pp. 141–158.

51. S. C. Jain, "Some perspectives on international strategic alliances", in *Advances in International Marketing* (New York: JAI Press, 1987), pp. 103–120.

52. "More companies prefer liaisons to marriage", *Wall Street Journal,* 12 April 1988, p. 35.

53. Thomas Gross and John Neuman, "Strategic alliances vital in global marketing", *Marketing News,* June 1989, pp. 1–2.

54. Margaret H. Cunningham, "Marketing's new frontier: international strategic alliances", working paper, Queens University (Ontario), 1990.

55. Stephen Young, James Hamill, Colin Wheeler and J. Richard Davies, *International Market Entry and Development, Strategies and Management* (Englewood Cliffs, N.J.: Prentice-Hall, 1989).

Chapter 4

1. James F. Engel, Roger D. Blackwell and Paul W. Miniard, *Consumer Behavior,* 7th edn (Hinsdale, Ill.: Dryden Press, 1993), p. 4.

2. John A. Howard and Jagdish N. Sheth, *The Theory of Buyer Behavior* (New York: Wiley, 1969), pp. 27–28.

3. G. Foxall, "Consumer decision-making", in *The Marketing Book,* 3rd edn, M. Baker, ed. (London: Heinemann/Chartered Institute of Marketing, 1995).

4. Paul M. Herr, Frank R. Kardes and John Kim, "Effects of word-of-mouth and product-attribute information on persuasion: an accessibility-diagnosticity perspective", *Journal of Consumer Research,* March 1991, pp. 454–462.

5. Kevin L. Keller and Richard Staelin, "Effects of quality and quantity of information on decision effectiveness", *Journal of Consumer Research,* September 1987, pp. 200–213.

6. Gabriel Biehal and Dipankar Chakravarti, "Consumers' use of memory and external information in choice: macro and micro perspectives", *Journal of Consumer Research,* March 1986, pp. 382–405.

7. Bobby J. Calder and Brian Sternthal, "Television commercial wearout: an information processing view", *Journal of Marketing Research,* May 1980, pp. 173–186.

8. Michael J. Houston, Terry L. Childers and Susan E. Heckler, "Picture-word consistency and the elaborative processing of advertisements", *Journal of Marketing Research,* November 1987, pp. 359–369.

9. James R. Bettman and Mita Sujan, "Effects of framing on evaluation of comparable and noncomparable alternatives by expert and novice consumers", *Journal of Consumer Research,* September 1987, pp. 141–154.

10. Robert A. Westbrook, "Product/consumption-based affective responses and postpurchase processes", *Journal of Marketing Research,* August 1987, pp. 258–270.

11. Neil Denny, "Why complaining is our new hobby," *Marketing,* 26 November 1998, p. 16.

12. Patricia Sellers, "The ABC's of marketing to kids", *Fortune,* 8 May 1989, p. 115.

13. Judith Waldrop, "Inside America's households", *American Demographics,* March 1989, pp. 20–27.

14. Houston, Childers and Heckler, pp. 359–369.

15. Thomas S. Robertson and Hubert Gatignon, "Competitive effects on technology diffusion", *Journal of Marketing,* July 1986, pp. 1–12.
16. Robertson and Gatignon, pp. 1–12.
17. Al Ries and Jack Trout, *Positioning the Battle for Your Mind* (New York: McGraw-Hill Book Co., 1986).
18. James R. Bettman, *An Information Processing Theory of Consumer Choice* (Reading, Mass.: Addison-Wesley, 1979), pp. 18–24.
19. David Aaker and Douglas Stayman, "Implementing the concept of transformational advertising", *Psychology and Marketing,* May and June 1992, pp. 237–253.
20. James H. Myers, "Determinant buying attitudes: meaning and measurement", *Marketing Management,* Summer 1997.
21. Joseph W. Alba and J. Wesley Hutchinson, "Dimensions of consumer expertise", *Journal of Consumer Research,* March 1987, pp. 411–454.
22. Akshay R. Rao and Kent B. Monroe, "The moderating effect of prior knowledge on cue utilization in product evaluations", *Journal of Consumer Research,* September 1988, pp. 253–264.
23. Ibid.
24. John L. Lastovika and Erich A. Joachimsthaler, "Improving the detection of personality-behavior, relationships in consumer research", *Journal of Consumer Research,* March 1988, pp. 583–587.
25. Martha T. Moore, "Spring break: brand names chase sales", *USA Today,* 17 March 1989, p. B1.
26. Henry Assael, *Consumer Behavior and Marketing Action,* 4th edn (Boston: Kent Publishing, 1992), p. 369.
27. Gill Upton, "New Britain new consumers", *Marketing,* 3 December 1998, pp. 29–30.
28. Leonard L. Berry, "The time-sharing consumer", *Journal of Retailing,* Winter 1979, p. 69.
29. Mona Doyle, "The metamorphosis of the consumer", *Marketing Communications,* April 1989, pp. 18–22.
30. Randolph E. Bucklin, "Determining segmentation in sales response across consumer purchase behaviours", *Journal of Marketing Research,* May 1998.

Chapter 5

1. Keith Thompson and Helen Mitchell, "Organisational buying behaviour in changing times", *European Management Journal,* vol. 16, no. 6, December 1998, pp. 698–705; Richard E. Plank and Simon Knox, "Theory, practice, and empirical development contributions: advances in business marketing and purchasing", *Journal of Business Research,* March 1997; Wesley J. Johnston, "Advances in industrial marketing theory and research from the *Journal of Business and Industrial Marketing*", *Journal of Business Research,* March 1997.
2. J. Carlos Jarillo and Howard H. Stevenson, "Co-operative strategies: the payoffs and the pitfalls", *Long Range Planning,* February 1991, pp. 64–70.
3. Gregory D. Utah and Monroe M. Bird, "Changes in

industrial buying: implications for industrial marketers", *Industrial Marketing Management,* 9, May 1980, pp. 117–121; Reed Moyer, "Reciprocity: retrospect and prospect", *Journal of Marketing,* October 1970, pp. 47–54.
4. P. Green, P. Robinson and Y. Wind, "The determinant of vendor selection. The evaluation function approach", *Journal of Purchasing,* August 1968.
5. John I. Coppett, "Auditing your customer service activities", *Industrial Marketing Management,* November 1988, pp. 277–284; Thomas L. Powers, "Identify and fulfill customer service expectations", *Industrial Marketing Management,* November 1988, pp. 273–276.
6. Mary Jo Bitner, Bernard H. Booms and Mary Stanfield Tetreault, "The service encounter: diagnosing favorable and unfavorable incidents", *Journal of Marketing,* 54, January 1990, pp. 71–84.
7. Weld F. Royal, "Cashing in on complaints", *Sales & Marketing Management,* May 1995, pp. 88–89.
8. Jim Shaw, Joe Giglierano and Jeff Kallis, "Marketing complex technical products: the importance of intangible attributes", *Industrial Marketing Management,* 18, 1989, pp. 45–53.
9. Frederick E. Webster, Jr. and Yoram Wind, *Organizational Buying Behavior* (Englewood Cliffs, N.J.: Prentice-Hall, 1972), pp. 78–80.
10. E. Gummesson, "The new marketing: developing long-term interactive relationships", *Long Range Planning,* vol. 20, issue 3, 1987, pp. 10–20.
11. H. Hakansson, *International Marketing and Purchasing of Industrial Goods* (Chichester: Wiley, 1982).
12. M. Christopher, A. Payne and D. Ballantyne, *Relationship Marketing* (Oxford: Butterworth-Heinemann, 1991).
13. Tony Cram, *The Power of Relationship Marketing,* (London: Pitman Publishing, 1994).
14. Regis McKenna, *Relationship Marketing* (Reading, Mass.: Addison-Wesley, 1991).
15. Nigel C. G. Campbell, John L. Graham, Alan Jolibert and Hans Gunthe Meissner, "Marketing negotiations in France, Germany, the United Kingdom and the United States", *Journal of Marketing,* 52, April 1988, pp. 49–62.
16. J. Carlos Jarillo and Howard H. Stevenson, "Cooperative strategies: the payoffs and the pitfalls", *Long Range Planning,* February 1991, pp. 64–70.
17. Robert W. Haas, *Industrial Marketing Management* (New York: Petrocelli Charter, 1976), pp. 37–48.
18. *Standard Industrial Classification Revision* (London: Central Statistical Office, 1979).
19. Peter Doyle and John Saunders, "Market segmentation and positioning in specialized industrial markets", *Journal of Marketing,* Spring 1985, p. 25.

Chapter 6

1. David Birks, chapter 10 in *The Marketing Book,* M. Baker, ed. (Oxford: Butterworth-Heinemann, 1994).
2. "Research" is accredited by The Market Research Society (Great Britain). Reprinted by permission.
3. Jerry Wind, "Marketing research forum: state of the

art in quantitative research", *Marketing Research,* Winter 1997.

4. Sally Dibb and Lyndon Simkin, *The Marketing Casebook* (London: Routledge, 1994).

5. Deborah Utter, "Information-driven marketing decisions: development of strategic information systems", *Journal of the Academy of Marketing Science,* Spring 1998.

6. Andrea Dunham, "Information systems are the key to managing future business needs", *Marketing News,* 23 May 1986, p. 11.

7. R. Birn, *The Effective Use of Market Research* (London: Kogan Page, 1990).

8. P. M. Chisnall, *Marketing Research* (London: McGraw-Hill, 1992).

9. Johny K. Johansson and Ikujiro Nonaha, "Market research the Japanese way", *Harvard Business Review,* May–June 1987, pp. 16–22.

10. Raymond E. Taylor, "Using the Delphi method to define marketing problems", *Business,* October–December 1984, p. 17.

11. Donald Tull and Del Hawkins, *Marketing Research* (New York: Macmillan, 1990).

12. Ronald L. Vaughn, "Demographic data banks: a new management resource", *Business Horizons,* November–December 1984, pp. 38–42. See also Chapter 5.

13. Gary Levin, "IRI says data can now link ads to sales", *Advertising Age,* 26 January 1987, pp. 3, 74.

14. Based on a survey conducted by Market Facts, Inc., 28 April 1983.

15. Peter Jackson, Adsearch, Richmond.

16. Martha Farnsworth Riche, "Who says yes?", *American Demographics,* February 1987, p. 8; George Gallup, Jr, "Survey research: current problems and future opportunities", *Journal of Consumer Marketing,* Winter 1988, pp. 27–29.

17. Jeffrey S. Conant, Denise T. Smart and Bruce J. Walker, "Main survey facilitation techniques: an assessment and proposal regarding reporting practices" (working paper, Texas A&M University, 1990).

18. Riche, p. 8.

19. Diane K. Bowers, "Telephone legislation", *Marketing Research,* March 1989, p. 47.

20. Stephen M. Billing, "Go slow, be wary when considering switch to computer assisted interviewing system", *Marketing News,* 26 November 1982, secl. 2, p. 2.

21. Tull and Hawkins.

22. Alan J. Bush and A. Parasuraman, "Mall intercept versus telephone interviewing environment", *Journal of Advertising Research,* April–May 1985, p. 42.

23. Alan J. Bush and Joseph F. Hair, Jr, "An assessment of the mall intercept as a data collecting method", *Journal of Marketing Research,* May 1985, p. 162.

24. Jeff Wiss, "Meet MAX: computerized survey taker", *Marketing News,* 22 May 1989, p. 16.

25. Yorkshire Television's *The Marketing Mix* series.

26. Hal Sokolow, "In-depth interviews increasing in importance", *Marketing News,* 13 September 1985, p. 26.

27. Norman Hart and John Stapleton, *Glossary of Marketing Terms* (Oxford: Butterworth-Heinemann), 1981.

28. Pauline Bickerton, Matthew Bickerton and Upkar Pardes, *Cybermarketing* (Oxford: Butterworth-Heinemann, 1996).

29. Tull and Hawkins.

30. A. Diamantopoulos and B. Schlegelmilch, *Taking the Fear out of Data Analysis* (London: Dryden Press, 1997).

31. Michael J. Olivette, "Marketing research in the electric utility industry", *Marketing News,* 2 January 1987, p. 13.

32. Hanjoon Lee, Frank Acits and Ralph L. Day, "Evaluation and use of marketing research by decision makers: a behavioral simulation", *Journal of Marketing Research,* May 1987, p. 187.

33. Michael Kavanaugh, "Masked Brawl", *Marketing Week,* 15 October 1998, p. 65.

34. Lynn Colemar, "It's selling disguised as research", *Marketing News,* 4 January 1988, p. 1.

35. O. C. Ferrell and Steven J. Skinner, "Ethical behavior and bureaucratic structure in marketing research organizations", *Journal of Marketing Research,* February 1988, pp. 103–104.

36. Brandt Allen, "Make information services pay its way", *Harvard Business Review,* January–February 1987, p. 57.

Chapter 7

1. P. Doyle, "Marketing in the New Millennium", *European Journal of Marketing,* 29, 1995, pp. 23–44; N. Piercy, *Market-Led Strategic Change* (Oxford: Butterworth-Heinemann, 1997).

2. David W. Stewart, "Segmentation and positioning for strategic marketing decisions", *Journal of Marketing Research,* vol. 35, no. 1, February 1998, pp. 128–129.

3. R. Frank and Y. Wind, *Market Segmentation* (Englewood Cliffs, N.J.: Prentice-Hall, 1972); Yoram Wind, "Issues and advances in segmentation research", *Journal of Marketing Research,* August 1978, pp. 317–327.

4. Donald K. Clifford, Jr and Richard E. Cavanagh, *The Winning Performance: How America's High-Growth Companies Succeed* (New York: Bantam Books, 1985), p. 53.

5. Joseph G. Albonetti and Luis V. Dominguez, "Major influences on consumer goods marketers' decision to target US Hispanics", *Journal of Advertising Research,* February–March 1989, pp. 9–11.

6. HMSO, *Social trends,* 1998.

7. John L. Lastovicka and Erich A. Joachimsthaler, "Improving the detection of personality-behavior relationships in consumer research", *Journal of Consumer Research,* March 1988, pp. 583–587.

8. Joseph T. Plummer, "The concept and application of life style segmentation", *Journal of Marketing,* January 1974, p. 33.

9. James F. Engel, Roger D. Blackwell and Paul W. Miniard, *Consumer Behavior* (Orlando, Fla.: Dryden Press, 1990), pp. 348–349.

10. Russell I. Haley, "Benefit segmentation: a decision-oriented research tool", *Journal of Marketing*, July 1968, pp. 30–35.

11. Yoram Wind and Richard Cardoza, "Industrial market segmentation", *Industrial Marketing Management*, vol. 3, 1974, pp. 153–166.

12. T. P. Beane and D. M. Ennis, "Market segmentation: a review", *European Journal of Marketing*, vol. 21 (5), 1987, pp. 20–42.

13. Thomas Bonoma and B. P. Shapiro, *Segmenting the Industrial Market* (Lexington, Mass.: Lexington Books, 1983).

14. Donald F. Blumberg, "Developing service as a line of business", *Management Review*, vol. 76, February 1987, p. 61.

15. Catherine M. Schaffer and Paul E. Green, "Cluster-based market segmentation: some further comparisons of alternative approaches", *Journal of the Market Research Society*, vol. 40, no. 2, April 1998, pp. 155–163.

16. J. Saunders, "Cluster analysis", *Journal of Marketing Management*, 10, 1994; pp. 13–28; J. Saunders, "Cluster analysis for market segmentation", *European Journal of Marketing*, 14, 1980, pp. 422–435.

17. J. Maier and J. Saunders, "The implementation of segmentation in sales management", *Journal of Personal Selling and Sales Management*, 10 (1), 1990, pp. 39–48.

18. J. Saunders, "Cluster analysis", *Journal of Marketing Management*, 10, 1994, pp. 13–28; J. Saunders, "Cluster analysis for market segmentation", *European Journal of Marketing*, 14, 1980, pp. 422–435.

19. A. Diamantopoulos and B. Schlegelmilch, *Taking the Fear out of Data Analysis* (London: Dryden Press, 1997); J. Saunders, "Cluster analysis", *Journal of Marketing Management*, 10, 1994, pp. 13–28; J. Saunders, "Cluster analysis for market segmentation", *European Journal of Marketing*, 14, 1980, pp. 422–435.

20. G. L. Lilien and P. Kotler, *Marketing Decision-Making: A Model Building Approach* (New York: Harper & Row, 1983); P. Naert and P. Leeflang, *Building Implementable Marketing Models* (Leiden: Martinus Nijhoff, 1978).

21. M. McDonald, *Marketing Plans* (Oxford: Butterworth-Heinemann, 1995).

22. S. Dibb and L. Simkin, "Marketing and marketing planning: still barriers to overcome", *EMAC*, Warwick, May 1997.

23. Peter Doyle, John Saunders and Veronica Wong, "A comparative study of Japanese marketing strategies in the British market", *Journal of International Business Studies*, 17 (1), 1986, pp. 27–46.

24. Y. Wind, "Going to market: new twist for some old tricks", *Wharton Magazine*, 4, 1980.

25. T. Harrison, *A Handbook of Advertising Techniques* (London: Kogan Page, 1987), p. 7.

26. A. Ries and J. Trout, *Positioning: The Battle for Your Mind* (New York: McGraw-Hill, 1981); Jack Trout with Steve Rivkin, *The New Positioning: The Latest on the World's #1 Business Strategy* (New York: McGraw-Hill, 1996).

27. Peter Doyle, John Saunders and Veronica Wong, "A comparative study of Japanese marketing strategies in the British market", *Journal of International Business Studies*, 17 (1), 1986.

28. Graham Hooley and John Saunders, *Competitive Positioning* (London: Prentice-Hall, 1993).

29. Sally Dibb, Lyndon Simkin and John Bradley, *The Marketing Planning Workbook* (London: ITBP, 1996).

30. Sally Dibb and Lyndon Simkin, *The Market Segmentation Workbook* (London: ITPB/Routledge, 1996).

31. Philip Kotler, *Marketing Management: Analysis, Planning, and Control*, 6th edn (Englewood Cliffs, N.J., Prentice-Hall, 1988), p. 257.

Chapter 8

1. Part of this definition is adapted from James D. Scott, Martin R. Warshaw and James R. Taylor, *Introduction to Marketing Management*, 5th edn (Homewood, Ill.: Irwin, 1985), p. 215.

2. Theodore Levitt, "Marketing intangible products and product intangibles", *Harvard Business Review*, May–June 1981, pp. 94–102.

3. Robert W. Haas, *Industrial Marketing Management*, 3rd edn (Boston: Kent Publishing, 1986), pp. 15–25.

4. M. J. Thomas, "Product development management", in *The Marketing Book*, M. Baker, ed. (London: Heinemann/ The Chartered Institute of Marketing, 1987).

5. Sonja Radas and Steven M. Shugan, "Seasonal marketing and timing new product introductions", *Journal of Marketing Research*, vol. 35, no. 3, August 1998, pp. 296–315; Marjorie E. Adams, "Enhancing new product development performance: an organisational learning perspective", *The Journal of Product Innovation Management*, September 1998.

6. "New product failure: a self-fulfilling prophecy?" *Marketing Communications*, April 1989, p. 27.

7. Levitt, "Marketing intangible products and product intangibles", p. 96.

8. Christopher W. L. Hart, "The power of unconditional service guarantees", *Harvard Business Review*, July–August 1988, pp. 54–62.

9. Peter Doyle, *Marketing Management and Strategy* (London: Prentice-Hall, 1994).

Chapter 9

1. Peter D. Bennett, ed., *Dictionary of Marketing Terms* (Chicago: American Marketing Association, 1988), p. 18.

2. James U. McNeal and Linda Zeren, "Brand name selection for consumer products", *MSU Business Topics*, Spring 1981, p. 35.

3. Peter Doyle, "Building successful brands: the strategic options", *The Journal of Consumer Marketing*, vol. 7, no. 2, 1993, pp. 5–20.

4. James Bell, "Brand management for the next millennium", *The Journal of Business Strategy*, vol. 19, no. 2, March/April 1998, pp. 7–10; Joseph Arthur

Rooney, "Branding: a trend for today and tomorrow", *The Journal of Product and Brand Management*, vol. 4, no. 4, 1995, pp. 48–56.

5. Henry Assael, *Consumer Behaviour and Marketing Action*, 4th edn (Boston: PWS-Kent, 1992).

6. Ronald Alsop, "Brand loyalty is rarely blind loyalty; rise in coupons, choices blamed for '80s erosion", *Wall Street Journal*, 19 October 1989, pp. B1, B6.

7. David A. Aaker, *Managing Brand Equity: Capitalizing on the Value of a Brand Name* (New York: Free Press, 1991), pp. 16–17.

8. Kurt Badenhausen, "Brands: the management factor," *Financial World*, 1 August 1995, pp. 50–69.

9. Chip Walker, "What's in a name?" *American Demographics*, February 1991, pp. 54–57.

10. Alan Miller, "Gains share in dollars and units during 1990 third quarter", *Private Label*, January–February 1991, pp. 85–89.

11. Taylor Nelson, Sofres Superpanel, 1999.

12. "No brand like an old brand", *Forbes*, 11 June 1990, p. 180.

13. Leonard L. Berry, Edwin E. Lefkowith and Terry Clark, "In services, what's in a name?" *Harvard Business Review*, September–October 1988, pp. 2–4.

14. Dorothy Cohen, "Trademark Strategy", *Journal of Marketing*, January 1986, p. 63.

15. Zeynep Gurhan-Canli and Durairaj Maheswaran, "The effects of extensions on brand name dilution and enhancement", *Journal of Marketing Research*, vol. 35, no. 4, November 1998, pp. 464–473.

16. "Trademark Stylesheet", U.S. Trademark Association, no. 1A.

17. Ronald F. Bush, Peter H. Bloch and Scott Dawson, "Remedies for product counterfeiting", *Business Horizons*, January–February 1989, pp. 59–65; Peter Engardio, with Todd Vogel and Dinah Lee, "Companies are knocking off the knockoff outfits", *Business Week*, 26 September 1988, pp. 86–88; and Michael Harvey, "A new way to combat product counterfeiting", *Business Horizons*, July–August 1988, pp. 19–28.

18. Graham Hurrell, "Solpadol—a successful case of brand positioning", *Journal of the Market Research Society*, July 1997.

19. Peter Doyle, *Marketing Management and Strategy* (London: Prentice-Hall, 1994) and chapter 20 in M. Baker, ed., *The Marketing Book* (Oxford: Butterworth-Heinemann, 1995).

20. Fred W. Morgan, "Tampered goods: legal developments and marketing guidelines" *Journal of Marketing*, April 1988, pp. 86–96.

21. Ibid.

22. Brian Wansink, "Can package size accelerate usage volume?" *Journal of Marketing*, vol. 60, no. 3, July 1996, pp. 1–14.

23. James U. McNeal, *Consumer Behaviour: An Integrative Approach* (Boston: Little, Brown, 1982), pp. 221–222.

24. "Not in my backyard", CNN Special Report, Cable News Network, 19 December 1988.

25. Alecia Swasy, "Ecology and buyer wants don't jibe", *Wall Street Journal*, 23 August 1989, p. B1.

26. Laura Bird, "Romancing the package", *Adweek's Marketing Week*, 21 January 1991, p. 11.

27. CGM, *Marketing Guide 14: 3D Packaging Design*, Haymarket Publishing Services Ltd, 1992.

Chapter 10

1. Roger C. Bennet and Robert G. Cooper, "The product life cycle trap", *Business Horizons*, September–October 1984, pp. 7–16.

2. "Product development: where planning and marketing meet," *Journal of Business Strategy*, September–October 1990, pp. 13–16.

3. Peter F. Drucker, "The discipline of innovation", *Harvard Business Review*, May–June 1985, pp. 67–68; Wu Couchen, "A proposed method for the design of consumer products", *Journal of International Marketing and Marketing Research*, February 1999.

4. Lawrence Ingrassia, "By improving scotch paper, 3M gets new product winner", *Wall Street Journal*, 31 March 1983, p. 27.

5. Jonathan B. Levine, "Keeping new ideas kicking around", *Business Week*, Innovation 1989 issue, p. 128.

6. Joseph Weber, "Going over the lab wall in search of new ideas", *Business Week*, Innovation 1989 issue, p. 132.

7. Joshua Hyatt, "Ask and you shall receive", *Inc.*, September 1989, pp. 90–101.

8. Christine Moorman and Anne S. Miner, "The convergence of planning and execution: improvisation in new product development", *Journal of Marketing*, vol. 62, no. 3, July 1998, pp. 1–20; V. Padmanabhan, Surendra Rajiv and Kannan Srinivasan, "New products, upgrades, and new releases: a rationale for sequential product introduction", *Journal of Marketing Research*, vol. 34, no. 4, November 1997, pp. 456–472.

9. "Winging it at McDonald's", *USA Today*, 5 September 1989, p. 1B.

10. Eleanor Johnson Tracy, "Testing time for test marketing", *Fortune*, 29 October 1984, pp. 75–76.

11. Cyndee Miller, "Little relief seen for new product failure rate," *Marketing News*, 21 June 1993, p. 5.

12. Adapted from Everett M. Rogers, *Diffusion of Innovations* (New York: Macmillan, 1962), pp. 81–86.

13. Graham J. Hooley and John Saunders, *Competitive Positioning: The Key to Market Success* (Englewood Cliffs, N.J.: Prentice-Hall, 1993).

14. F. Stewart DeBruicker and Gregory L. Summe, "Make sure your customers keep coming back", *Harvard Business Review*, January–February 1985, pp. 92–98.

15. Geoffrey L. Gordon, Roger J. Calantone and Anthony di Benedetto, "Mature markets and revitalization strategies: an American fable", *Business Horizons*, May–June 1991, p. 42.

16. Kim B. Clark and Takahiro Fujimoto, "The power of product integrity," *Harvard Business Review*, November–December 1990, pp. 108–118.

17. Lynn W. Phillips, Dae R. Chang and Robert D. Buzzell, "Product quality, cost position and business performance: a test of some key hypotheses", *Journal of Marketing,* Spring 1983, pp. 26–43.

18. Douglas M. Lambert and Jay U. Sterling, "Identifying and eliminating weak products", *Business,* July–September 1988, pp. 3–10.

Chapter 11

1. Leonard L. Berry, "Services marketing is different", *Business Horizons,* May–June 1980, pp. 24–29.

2. Glenn B. Voss, A. Parasuraman and Dhruv Grewal, "The roles of price, performance, and expectations in determining satisfaction in service exchanges", *Journal of Marketing,* vol. 64, no. 4, October 1998, pp. 46–61; Jochen Wirtz and John E.G. Bateson, "Consumer satisfaction with services: integrating the environment perspective in services marketing into the traditional disconfirmation paradigm", *Journal of Business Research,* vol. 44, no. 1, January 1999, pp. 55–66.

3. Donald Cowell, *The Marketing of Services* (London: Heinemann, 1984).

4. Valarie A. Zeithaml, A. Parasuraman and Leonard L. Berry, "Problems and strategies in services marketing", *Journal of Marketing,* Spring 1985, pp. 33–46.

5. John E. G. Bateson, "Why we need service marketing", in O. C. Ferrell, S. W. Brown and C. W. Lamb, Jr, eds, *Conceptual and Theoretical Development in Marketing* (Chicago: American Marketing Association, 1979), pp. 131–146.

6. Valarie A. Zeithaml, "How consumer evaluation processes differ between goods and services", in James H. Donnelly and William R. George, eds, *Marketing of Services* (Chicago: American Marketing Association, 1981), pp. 186–190.

7. Leonard L. Berry, Valarie A. Zeithaml and A. Parasuraman, "Responding to demand fluctuations: key challenge for service businesses", in Russell Belk et al., eds, *AMA Educators' Proceedings* (Chicago: American Marketing Association, 1984), pp. 231–234.

8. Brian Moores, *Are They Being Served?* (Oxford: Philip Allan, 1986).

9. James Reardon, Chip Miller, Ronald Hasty and Blaise J. Waguespack, "A comparison of alternative theories of services marketing", *Journal of Marketing Theory and Practice,* vol. 4, no. 4, Fall 1996, pp. 61–71.

10. Christopher H. Lovelock, "Classifying services to gain strategic marketing insights", *Journal of Marketing,* Summer 1983, p. 15.

11. Christopher H. Lovelock, *Services Marketing* (Englewood Cliffs, N.J.: Prentice-Hall, 1984), pp. 46–64.

12. Yoram Wind, "Financial services: increasing your marketing productivity and profitability", *Journal of Services Marketing,* Fall 1987, p. 8.

13. Cathy Goodwin, "Marketing strategies for services: globalization, client-orientation, deregulation", *International Journal of Research in Marketing,* July 1997.

14. Lovelock, *Services Marketing,* pp. 279–289.

15. Ibid.

16. Berry, Zeithaml and Parasuraman, pp. 231–234.

17. Valarie A. Zeithaml, A. Parasuraman and Leonard L. Berry, *Delivering Quality Service: Balancing Customer Perceptions and Expectations* (New York: Free Press, 1990).

18. A. Parasuraman, Leonard L. Berry and Valarie A. Zeithaml, "An empirical examination of relationships in an extended service quality model", *Marketing Science Institute Working Paper Series,* Report no. 90–122 (Cambridge, Mass.: Marketing Science Institute, 1990), p. 29.

19. Valarie A. Zeithaml, Leonard L. Berry and A. Parasuraman, "Communication and control processes in the delivery of service quality", *Journal of Marketing,* April 1988, pp. 35–48.

20. Valarie A. Zeithaml, Leonard L. Berry and A. Parasuraman, "The nature and determinants of customer expectations of service", *Journal of the Academy of Marketing Science,* Winter 1993, pp. 1–12.

21. Hartline and Ferrell, "Service quality implementation", p. 36.

22. Mary Jo Bitner, "Evaluating service encounters: the effects of physical surroundings and employee responses", *Journal of Marketing,* April 1990, p. 70.

23. Hartline and Ferrell, "Service quality implementation", pp. 17–19.

24. Myron Glassman and Bruce McAfee, "Integrating the personnel and marketing functions: the challenge of the 1990s", *Business Horizons,* May–June 1992, pp. 52–59.

25. Keith J. Blois, "Marketing for non-profit organisations", in Michael J. Baker (ed.), *The Marketing Book* (London: Heinemann, 1994), p. 405.

26. J. Whyte, "Organisation, person and idea marketing as exchange", *Quarterly Review of Marketing,* January 1985, pp. 25–30.

27. John Garrison, "Telethons—the positive story", *Fund Raising Management,* November 1987, pp. 48–52.

28. Philip Kotler, *Marketing for Non-profit Organisations,* 2nd edn (Englewood Cliffs, N.J.: Prentice-Hall, 1982), p. 37.

29. Ibid.

30. Meryl Davids, "Doing well by doing good", *Public Relations Journal,* July 1987, pp. 17–21.

31. Leyland F. Pitt and Russell Abratt, "Pricing in non-profit organisations—a framework and conceptual overview", *Quarterly Review of Marketing,* Spring–Summer 1987, pp. 13–15.

32. Kelly Walker, "Not-for-profit profits", *Forbes,* 10 September 1984, p. 165.

Chapter 12

1. Erin Anderson, George S. Day and V. Kasturi Rangan, "Strategic channel design", *Sloan Management Review,* vol. 38, no. 4, Summer 1997, p. 59(11).

2. O.C. Ferrell and William M. Pride, national sample of 2,042 households.

3. Wroe Alderson, *Marketing Behavior and Executive Action* (Homewood, Ill.: Irwin, 1957), pp. 201–211.
4. James D. Hlavacek and Tommy J. McCuistion, "Industrial distributors: when, who, and how?" *Harvard Business Review,* March–April 1983, p. 97.
5. S. Altan Erdem and L. Jean Harrison-Walker, "Managing channel relationships: toward an identification of effective promotional strategies in vertical marketing systems", *Journal of Marketing Theory and Practice,* vol. 5, no. 2, Spring 1997, pp. 80–87.
6. Jordan D. Lewis, "Using alliances to build market power", *Planning Review,* September–October 1990, pp. 4–9, 48.
7. Leo Aspinwall, "The marketing characteristics of goods", in *Four Marketing Theories* (Boulder: University of Colorado Press, 1961), pp. 27–32.
8. Allan J. Magrath, "Differentiating yourself via distribution", *Sales & Marketing Management,* March 1991, pp. 50–57.
9. David W. Cravens, Thomas N. Ingram and Raymond W. LaForge, "Evaluating multiple sales channel strategies", *Journal of Business and Industrial Marketing,* Summer–Fall 1991, pp. 3–4.
10. Bert Rosenbloom, *Marketing Channels: A Management View* (Hinsdale, Ill.: Dryden, 1987), p. 160.
11. Ibid., p. 161.
12. Donald J. Bowersox and M. Bixby Cooper, *Strategic Marketing Channel Management* (New York: McGraw-Hill, 1992), pp. 177–178.
13. Wroe Alderson, *Dynamic Marketing Behavior* (Homewood, Ill.: Irwin, 1965), p. 239.
14. Steven J. Skinner, Julie B. Gassenheimer and Scott W. Kelley, "Cooperation in supplier-dealer relations", *Journal of Retailing,* Summer 1992, pp. 174–193; H. Hakansson, *International Marketing and Purchasing of Industrial Goods* (Chicester: Wiley, 1982).
15. J. Joseph Cronin Jr., Thomas L. Baker and Jon M. Hawes, "An assessment of the role performance measurement of power-dependency in marketing channels", *Journal of Business Research,* vol. 30, no. 3, July 1994, pp. 201–210.
16. Nirmalya Kumar, Lisa K. Scheer and Jan-Benedict Steenkamp, "Interdependence, punitive capability, and the reciprocation of punitive actions in channel relationships", *Journal of Marketing Research,* vol. 35, no. 2, May 1998, pp. 225–235; Robert F. Lusch, "Interdependency, contracting, and relational behavior in marketing channels", *Journal of Marketing,* October 1996.
17. Jakki Mohr and John R. Nevin, "Communication strategies in marketing channels: a theoretical perspective", *Journal of Marketing,* October 1990, pp. 36–51.
18. Lanny J. Ryan, Gaye C. Dawson and Thomas Galek, "New distribution channels for microcomputer software", *Business,* October–December 1985, pp. 21–22.
19. Adel I. El-Ansary, "Perspectives on channel system performance", in *Contemporary Issues in Marketing Channels,* ed. Robert F. Lusch and Paul H. Zinszer (Norman: University of Oklahoma Press, 1979), p. 50.

20. Kenneth G. Hardy and Allan J. Magrath, "Ten ways for manufacturers to improve distribution management", *Business Horizons,* November–December 1988, p. 68.
21. Ronald D. Michman and Stanley D. Sibley, *Marketing Channels and Strategies* (Columbus, Ohio: Grid Publishing, 1980), pp. 412–417.
22. Janet E. Keith, Donald W. Jackson and Lawrence A. Crosby, "Effect of alternative types of influence strategies under different dependence structures," *Journal of Marketing,* July 1990, pp. 30–41.
23. John F. Gaski and John R. Nevin, "The differential effects of exercised and unexercised power sources in a marketing channel", *Journal of Marketing Research,* July 1985, p. 139.
24. Rosenbloom, *Marketing Channels,* p. 98.
25. Ibid., pp. 96–97.

Chapter 13

1. Clarence Casson, "1988 wholesaler giants; making all the right moves", Building Supply Home Centers, September 1988, p. 56.
2. Rajesh Tyagi and Chandrasekhar Das, "Manufacturer and warehouse selection for stable relationships in dynamic wholesaling and location problems", *International Journal of Physical Distribution and Logistics Management,* 25 (6), 1995, pp. 54–72.
3. Rebecca Rolfes, "Wholesaling without borders", *Medical Marketing & Media,* February 1991, pp. 74–76.
4. *US Census of Wholesale Trade,* May 1985, p. 207.
5. Bert Rosenbloom, *Marketing Channels: A Management View* (Hinsdale, Ill.: Dryden Press, 1987), p. 63.
6. *US Census of Wholesale Trade,* May 1985, p. 207.
7. Rosenbloom, p. 61.
8. Ibid.
9. Ibid., p. 62.
10. Thomas V. Bonoma, "Get more out of your trade shows", *Harvard Business Review,* January–February 1983, pp. 75–83.
11. Rosenbloom, p. 185.
12. "Trade shows—part 1; a major sales and marketing tool", *Small Business Report,* June 1988, pp. 34–39.
13. Rosenbloom, p. 185.
14. Richard K. Swandby and Jonathan M. Cox, "Trade show trends: exhibiting growth paces economic strengths", *Business Marketing,* May 1985, p. 50.
15. "Why Cargo Club was off target", *Marketing,* 23 March 1995, p. 3.
16. Joseph Weber, "Mom and Pop move out of wholesaling", *Business Week,* 9 January 1989, p. 91.
17. Ibid.
18. Carol C. Bienstock, "Measuring physical distribution service quality", *Journal of the Academy of Marketing Science,* Winter 1997.
19. Carl M. Guelzo, *Introduction to Logistics Management* (Englewood Cliffs, N.J.: Prentice-Hall, 1986), p. 32.
20. John T. Mentzer, Roger Gomes and Robert E. Krapfel, Jr., "Physical distribution service: a fundamental marketing concept?", *Journal of the Academy of Marketing Science,* Winter 1989, p. 59.

21. Lloyd M. Rinehart, M. Bixby Cooper and George D. Wagenheim, "Furthering the integration of marketing and logistics through customer service in the channel", *Journal of the Academy of Marketing Science,* Winter 1989, p. 67.
22. Charles A. Taff, *Management of Physical Distribution and Transportation* (Homewood, Ill.: Irwin, 1984), p. 250.
23. Judith Graham, "IKEA furnishing its US identity", *Advertising Age,* 14 September 1989, p. 79; and Jonathan Reynolds, "IKEA: a competitive company with style", *Retail & Distribution Management (UK),* May/June 1988, pp. 32–34.
24. Rinehart, Cooper and Wagenheim, p. 67.
25. Guelzo, pp. 35–36.
26. Taff, p. 240.
27. Carol Doherty, Jens Maier and Lyndon Simkin, "DPP modelling in retail marketing: an application", *OMEGA,* 20 (3), 1992, pp. 25–33.
28. Guelzo, p. 102.
29. Adapted from John F. Magee, *Physical Distribution Systems* (New York: McGraw-Hill, Inc., 1967). Reprinted by permission of the author.
30. The EOQ formula for the optimal order quantity is EOQ = 2DR/I, where EOQ = optimum average order size, D = total demand, R = cost of processing an order and I = cost of maintaining one unit of inventory per year. For a more complete description of EOQ methods and terminology, see Frank S. McLaughlin and Robert C. Pickardt, *Quantitative Techniques for Management Decisions* (Boston: Houghton Mifflin, 1978), pp. 104–119.
31. "Watch for these red flags", *Traffic Management,* January 1983, p. 8.
32. David N. Burt, "Managing suppliers up to speed", *Harvard Business Review,* July–August 1989, p. 128.
33. Ibid., p. 129.
34. Peter D. Bennett, ed., *Dictionary of Marketing Terms* (Chicago: American Marketing Association, 1988), p. 204.
35. John J. Coyle, Edward Bardi and C. John Langley, Jr., *The Management of Business Logistics* (St. Paul, Minn.: West, 1988), pp. 327–329.
36. Thomas A. Foster and Joseph V. Barks, "Here comes the best", *Distribution,* September 1984, p. 25.
37. Allen R. Wastler, "Intermodal leaders ponder riddle of winning more freight", *Traffic World,* 19 June 1989, pp. 14–15.
38. Julie J. Gentry, "Using logistics alliances to gain a strategic advantage in the marketplace", *Journal of Marketing Theory and Practice,* Spring 1996; Judith Schmitz Whipple, "Logistical alliance formation motives: similarities and differences within the channel", *Journal of Marketing Theory and Practice,* Spring 1996.

Chapter 14

1. H. Carter, *The Study of Urban Geography* (London: Edward Arnold, 1972), pp. 205–247.
2. J. A. Dawson, *Shopping Centre Development* (Harlow: Longman, 1983), Chapter 2.
3. Ibid.
4. Russell Schiller, "Out of town exodus", in *The Changing Face of British Retailing* (London: Newman Books, 1987), pp. 64–73.
5. Kenneth C. Schneider, "Telemarketing as a promotional tool—its effects and side effects", *Journal of Consumer Marketing,* Winter 1985, pp. 29–39.
6. "*V/T* census of the industry issue—1988", *Vending Times,* 1988, p. 49. Reprinted by permission.
7. Ronald Alsop, "Food giants take to mails to push fancy product lines", *Wall Street Journal,* 28 February 1985, p. 85.
8. *Marketing Pocket Book 1999* and Office for National Statistics.
9. Al Urbanski, "The franchise option", *Sales & Marketing Management,* February 1988, pp. 28–33.
10. Jim Forward and Christina Fulop, "Large established firms' entry into franchising", *Retail, Distribution and Consumer Research,* 6 (1), 1996, pp. 34–52.
11. Statistical Abstract of the US, 1989, p. 760.
12. Mary Joyce, "Retailing triumphs and blunders: victims of competition in the new age of marketing management", *Journal of the Academy of Marketing Science,* vol. 26, no. 3, Summer 1998, pp. 253–254.
13. C. H. Anderson, *Retailing* (St. Paul, Minn.: West, 1993).
14. R. L. Davies and D. S. Rogers, *Store Location and Store Assessment Research* (Chichester: Wiley, 1984).
15. R. L. Davies, *Marketing Geography* (London: Methuen, 1976).
16. L. Simkin, "SLAM: store location assessment model—theory and practice", *OMEGA,* 17 (1), 1989, pp. 53–58; Lyndon Simkin, "Tackling barriers to effective implementation of modelling in retail marketing applications", *Retail, Distribution and Consumer Research,* 6 (3), 1996, pp. 225–241.
17. Ruth Schmidt, Rupert Segal and Christy Cartwright, "Two-stop shopping or polarisation", *International Journal of Retail and Distribution Management,* 22 (1), 1994, pp. 12–19.
18. C. Glenn Walters and Blaise J. Bergiel, *Marketing Channels,* 2nd edn (Glenview, Ill.: Scott, Foresman, 1982), p. 205.
19. J. R. Maier and L. Simkin, "Prioritising stock phasing for multiple retailers", *OMEGA,* 18 (1), 1988, pp. 33–40.
20. D. Cook and R. D. Walters, *Retail Marketing* (London: Prentice-Hall, 1991).
21. George H. Lucas, Jr., and Larry G. Gresham, "How to position for retail success", *Business,* April–June 1988, pp. 3–13.
22. G. J. Davies and J. M. Brooks, *Positioning Strategy in Retailing* (London: Paul Chapman, 1989).
23. Leslie Wayne, "Rewriting the rules of retailing", *The New York Times,* 15 October 1989, p. F6.
24. Terence Conran, "The retail image", in *The Retail Report* (London: Healey & Baker, 1985).
25. Francine Schwadel, "Little touches spur Wal-Mart's rise; shoppers react to logo, decor, employee vests", *Wall Street Journal,* 22 September 1989, p. B1.

26. Peter McGoldrick, *Retail Marketing* (London: McGraw-Hill, 1990).

27. Stanley C. Hollander, "The wheel of retailing", *Journal of Marketing,* July 1960, p. 37.

28. W. S. Howe, "UK retailer vertical power, market competition and consumer welfare", *International Journal of Retail and Distribution Management,* 18 (2), 1990, pp. 16–25.

29. Lynne Richardson, John Swan and James Hulton, "The effects of the presence and use of channel power sources on distributor satisfaction", *Retail, Distribution and Consumer Research,* 5 (2), 1995, pp. 185–202.

30. K. K. Tse, "Marks & Spencer: a manufacturer without factories", *International Trends in Retailing,* 6 (2), 1989, pp. 23–36.

31. R. M. Grant, "Manufacturer-retailer relations: the shifting balance of power", in Gerry Johnson, *Business Strategy and Retailing* (Chichester: Wiley, 1987), pp. 43–58.

32. Gerry Johnson, *Business Strategy and Retailing* (Chichester: Wiley, 1987).

33. Lynd Morley, "Mapping the future", *Retail Technology,* 2(7), 1988, pp. 40–2.

34. Tony Rudd, "Trends in physical distribution", in *The Changing Face of British Retailing* (London: Newman Books, 1987), pp. 84–93.

35. C. Doherty, J. R. Maier and L. Simkin, "DPP decision support in retail merchandising", *OMEGA* 21 (1), 1993, pp. 25–33.

36. Nicholas Alexander, "Expansion within the single European market: a motivational structure", *Retail, Distribution and Consumer Research,* 5 (4), 1999, pp. 488–504.

37. Terry Robinson and Colin M. Clarke-Hill, "International alliances in European retailing", *Retail, Distribution and Consumer Research,* 5 (2), 1995, pp. 167–184.

Chapter 15

1. Richard W. Pollay, "On the value of reflections on the values in 'The distorted mirror'", *Journal of Marketing,* July 1987, pp. 104–109.

2. Morris B. Holbrook, "Mirror, mirror, on the wall, what's unfair in the reflections on advertising", *Journal of Marketing,* July 1987, pp. 95–103.

3. Richard N. Farmer, "Would you want your granddaughter to marry a Taiwanese marketing man?" *Journal of Marketing,* October 1987, pp. 111–116.

4. Colin Coulson-Thomas, *Marketing Communications* (London: Heinemann, 1986); Kusum L. Ailawadi and Scott A. Neslin, "The effect of promotion on consumption: buying more and consuming it faster", *Journal of Marketing Research,* vol. 35, no. 3, August 1998, pp. 390–398.

5. James Engel, Martin Warshaw and Thomas Kinnear, *Promotional Strategy: Managing the Marketing Communications Process* (Boston: Irwin, 1994).

6. John Rossiter and Larry Percy, *Advertising and Promotion Management* (New York: McGraw-Hill, 1987).

7. In case you do not read Chinese, this says, "In the factory we make cosmetics, and in the store we sell hope". Prepared by Chih Kang Wang.

8. Terence A. Shimp and M. Wayne Delozier, *Promotion Management and Marketing Communication* (Hinsdale, Ill.: Dryden Press, 1986), pp. 25–26.

9. Carlos E. Garcia, "Hispanic market is accessible if research is designed correctly", *Marketing News,* 4 January 1988, p. 46.

10. David Jones, "Setting promotional goals: a communications' relationship model", *Journal of Consumer Marketing,* 11 (1), 1994, pp. 38–49.

11. Adapted from Everett M. Rogers, *Diffusion of Innovations* (New York: Free Press, 1962), pp. 81–86, 98–102.

12. Lawrence J. Marks and Michael A. Kamins, "Product sampling and advertising sequence, belief strength, confidence and attitudes", *Journal of Marketing Research,* August 1988, pp. 266–281.

13. Rogers, pp. 247–250.

14. Rossiter and Percy.

15. J. Richard Shannon, "The new promotions mix: a proposed paradigm, process, and application", *Journal of Marketing Theory and Practice,* Winter 1996.

16. M. Flandin, E. Martin and L. Simkin, "Advertising effectiveness research: a survey of agencies, clients and conflicts", *International Journal of Advertising,* 11 March 1992, pp. 203–214.

17. Todd Hunt and James Grunig, *Public Relations Techniques* (Fort Worth: Harcourt Brace, 1994).

18. Sally Dibb, Lyndon Simkin and Adam Vancini, "Competition, strategy, technology and people: the challenges facing PR", *International Journal of Advertising,* 15 (2), 1996, pp. 116–127.

19. This definition is adapted from John F. Luick and William L. Ziegler, *Sales Promotion and Modern Merchandising* (New York: McGraw-Hill, 1968), p. 4.

20. Roger A. Kerin and William L. Cron, "Assessing trade show functions and performance: an exploratory study", *Journal of Marketing,* July 1987, pp. 87–94.

21. Michael Kavanagh, "Free ISPs spur Net market growth", *Marketing Week,* 11 March 1999, pp. 30–31.

22. M.J. Evans, L. O'Malley and M. Patterson, "Direct marketing communications in the UK: a study of growth, past, present and future", *Journal of Marketing Communications,* 2, 1996, pp. 51–65.

23. Lisa O'Malley, Maurice Patterson and Martin Evans, *Exploring Direct Marketing* (London: ITBP, 1999), p. 9.

24. Marcy Magiera, "Holy Batvideo! Christmas already?" *Advertising Age,* 11 September 1989, p. 6.

25. *Marketing Week,* 5 July 1996, p. 13.

26. Alvin A. Achenbaum and F. Kent Mitchel, "Pulling away from push marketing", *Harvard Business Review,* May–June 1987, p. 38.

Chapter 16

1. S. Dibb, L. Simkin and R. Yuen, "Pan-European advertising: think Europe—act local", *International Journal of Advertising,* 13 (2), 1994, pp. 125–136.

2. *Students' Briefs* (London: The Advertising Association, 1988).
3. *CBS This Morning*, CBS (TV), 11 April 1990.
4. Demetrios Vakratsas and Tim Ambler, "How advertising works: what do we really know?" *Journal of Marketing*, vol. 63, no. 1, January 1999, pp. 26–43.
5. Scott Hume, "Pizza Hut is frosted; new ad takes slap at McDonald's test product", *Advertising Age,* 18 September 1989, p. 4.
6. Torin Douglas, *The Complete Guide to Advertising* (London: Macmillan, 1985).
7. Peter Jackson, Adsearch, Richmond-upon-Thames.
8. *Campaign,* 19 July 1996, p. 1.
9. Laurie Freeman, "P&G to unveil refill package", *Advertising Age,* 6 November 1989, pp. 1, 69.
10. *Marketing,* 5 March 1999, p. 1.
11. Pauline Bickerton, Matthew Bickerton and Upkor Pardesi, *Cybermarketing* (Oxford: Butterworth-Heinemann, 1996).
12. James E. Littlefield and C. A. Kirkpatrick, *Advertising Mass Communication in Marketing* (Boston: Houghton Mifflin, 1970), p. 178.
13. S. Watson Dunn and Arnold M. Barban, *Advertising: Its Role in Modern Marketing,* 6th edn (Hinsdale, Ill.: Dryden Press, 1986), p. 493.
14. Patrick Quinn, *Low Budget Advertising* (London: Heinemann, 1988).
15. M. Flandin, E. Martin and L. Simkin, "Advertising effectiveness research: a survey of agencies, clients and conflicts", *International Journal of Advertising,* 11 (3), 1992, pp. 203–214.
16. Ronald Alsop, "TV ads that are likeable get plus ratings for persuasiveness", *Wall Street Journal,* 20 February 1986, p. 21.
17. Marvin E. Goldberg and Gerald J. Gorn, "Happy and sad TV programmes: how they affect reactions to commercials", *Journal of Consumer Research,* December 1987, pp. 387–403.
18. *Marketing,* 24 May 1990, p. 5.
19. *Public Relations Practice—Its Role and Parameters* (London: The Institute of Public Relations, 1984).
20. The Advertising Association, London, 1990; *The Independent,* 12 August 1990; Robin Cobb, "The art of gentle persuasion", *Marketing,* 6 September 1990, pp. 25–26; Bill Britt, "PR leads from front as buy-up battles rage", *Marketing,* 1 February 1990, p. 13; P. J. Kitchen and T. Proctor, "The increasing importance of public relations in fast moving consumer goods firms", *Journal of Marketing Management,* 7(4), 1991, pp. 357–370.
21. David Wragg, *Public Relations for Sales and Marketing Management* (London: Kogan Page, 1987).
22. J. White, *How to Understand and Manage Public Relations* (London: Business Books, 1991).
23. Frank Jefkins, *Public Relations Techniques* (London: Heinemann, 1988).
24. S. Dibb, L. Simkin and A. Vancini, "Competition, strategy, technology and people: the challenges facing PR", *International Journal of Advertising,* 15 (2), 1996, pp. 116–127.
25. BBC and ITN news broadcasts, February and March 1993.
26. Marc G. Weinberger and Jean B. Romeo, "The impact of negative product news", *Business Horizons,* January–February 1989, p. 44.
27. Dibb, Simkin and Yuen.
28. M. Flandin, E. Martin and L. Simkin, "Advertising effectiveness research: a survey of agencies, clients and conflicts", *International Journal of Advertising,* 11(3), 1992, pp. 203–214.
29. John Wringe, managing director of Cogent, talking to IB365 students at Warwick Business School, 1996.
30. Dibb, Simkin and Vancini.
31. S. Sleight, *Sponsorship: What It Is and How to Use It* (Maidenhead: McGraw-Hill, 1989).
32. M. G. Crowley, "Prioritising the sponsorship audience," *European Journal of Marketing,* 25, 1991, pp. 11–21.
33. Tony Meenaghan, "Current developments and future directions in sponsorship", *Journal of Advertising,* vol. 17, no. 1, 1998, pp. 3–28.

Chapter 17

1. *Marketing,* 28 June 1990, p. 13.
2. Julian Cummins, *Sales Promotion* (London: Kogan Page, 1989).
3. Myron Gable and B. J. Reed, "The current status of women in professional selling", *Journal of Personal Selling & Sales Management,* May 1987, pp. 33–39.
4. William A. Weeks and Darrel D. Muehing, "Students' perceptions of personal selling", *Industrial Marketing Management,* May 1987, pp. 145–151.
5. Geoff Lancaster and David Jobber, *Selling and Sales Management* (London: Pitman, 1994).
6. "Getting ahead and staying ahead as the competition heats up", *Agency Sales Magazine,* June 1987, pp. 38–42.
7. Chris de Winter, *Telephone Selling* (London: Heinemann, 1988).
8. Thomas W. Leigh and Patrick F. McGraw, "Mapping the procedural knowledge of industrial sales personnel: a script-theoretic investigation", *Journal of Marketing,* January 1989, pp. 16–34.
9. Thayer C. Taylor, "Xerox: who says you can't be big and fast?" *Sales & Marketing Management,* November 1987, pp. 62–65.
10. Leigh and McGraw, pp. 16–34.
11. John Nemec, "Do you have grand finales?" *American Salesman,* June 1987, pp. 3–6.
12. William C. Moncrief, "Five types of industrial sales jobs", *Industrial Marketing Management,* 17, 1988, p. 164.
13. A. J. Magrath, "Are you overdoing 'lean and mean'?", *Sales & Marketing Management,* January 1988, pp. 46–53.
14. Tony Adams, *Successful Sales Management* (London: Heinemann, 1988).
15. Coleman, pp. 6, 21.
16. Patrick C. Fleenor, "Selling and sales management in action: assessment centre selection of sales representatives," *Journal of Personal Selling & Sales Management,* May 1987, pp. 57–59.

17. René Y. Darmon, "The impact of incentive compensation on the salesperson's work habits: an economic model", *Journal of Personal Selling & Sales Management*, May 1987, pp. 21–32.
18. Aimee Stern, "Commissions catch on at department stores", *Adweek's Marketing Week*, 1 February 1988, p. 5.
19. Terese Hudson, "Holding meetings sharpens employees' sales skills", *Savings Institutions*, July 1987, pp. 109–111.
20. Dan Woog, "Taking sales high tech", *High Tech Marketing*, May 1987, pp. 17–22.
21. Sandra Hile Hart, William C. Moncrief and A. Parasuraman, "An empirical investigation of salespeople's performance, effort and selling method during a sales contest", *Journal of the Academy of Marketing Science*, Winter 1989, pp. 29–39.
22. Robert Martinott, "The traveling salesman goes high tech", *Chemical Week*, 10 June 1987, pp. 22–24.
23. John F. Luick and William L. Ziegler, *Sales Promotion and Modern Merchandising* (New York: McGraw-Hill, 1968), and Don E. Schultz and William A. Robinson, *Sales Promotion Management* (Chicago: Crain Books, 1982).
24. Thomas McCann, "Promotions will gain more clout in the '90s," *Marketing News*, 6 November 1989, pp. 4, 24.
25. Cummins, p. 14.
26. "Factfile," *Marketing*, 12 July 1990, p. 18.
27. P. R. Smith, *Marketing Communication: An Integrated Approach* (London: Kogan Page, 1993).
28. K. Peattie and S. Peattie, "Sales promotion: playing to win?" *Journal of Marketing Management*, 9, 1993, pp. 225–269.
29. W. E. Phillips and Bill Robinson, "Continued sales (price) promotion destroys brands: yes; no", *Marketing News*, 16 January 1989, pp. 4, 8.
30. Cummins, p. 14.
31. Emin Babakus, Peter Tat and William Cunningham, "Coupon redemption: a motivational perspective", *Journal of Consumer Marketing*, Spring 1988, p. 40.
32. Donna Campanella, "Sales promotion: couponmania", *Marketing and Media Decisions*, June 1987, pp. 118–122.
33. Alison Fahey, "Coupon war fallout", *Advertising Age*, 4 September 1989, p. 2.
34. Campanella, pp. 118–122.
35. Ibid.
36. Joe Agnew, "P-O-P [P-O-S] displays are becoming a matter of consumer convenience", *Marketing News*, 9 October 1987, p. 14.
37. Ibid., p. 16.
38. Alison Fahey, "Study shows retailers rely on P-O-P [P-O-S]", *Advertising Age*, 27 November 1989, p. 83.
39. "Sampling accelerates adoption of new products", *Marketing News*, 11 September 1987, p. 21.
40. Peter Tat, William A. Cunningham and Emin Babakus, "Consumer perceptions of rebates", *Journal of Advertising Research*, August–September 1988, p. 48.
41. Gerrie Anthea, "Sales promotion putting up the premium", *Marketing*, 16 April 1987.
42. Steven W. Colford, "Marriott sets largest promo", *Advertising Age*, 2 October 1989, p. 58.
43. Eileen Norris, "Everyone will grab at a chance to win", *Advertising Age*, 22 August 1983, p. M10.
44. Ed Crimmins, "A co-op myth: it is a tragedy that stores don't spend all their accruals", *Sales & Marketing Management*, 7 February 1983, pp. 72–73.
45. Gillian Upton, "Sales promotion: getting results Barbados style", *Marketing*, 16 April 1987, pp. 37–40.
46. D. Bird, *Commonsense Direct Marketing* (London: Kogan Page, 1989).
47. Tom Duncan, "A communication-based marketing model for managing relationships", *Journal of Marketing*, April 1998; James W. Peltier, "The use of need-based segmentation for developing segment-specific direct marketing strategies", *Journal of Direct Marketing*, Autumn 1997.
48. B. North, "Consumer companies take direct stance", *Marketing*, 20 May 1993, pp. 24–25.
49. Michael Kavanagh, "Free ISPs spur Net market growth", *Marketing Week*, 11 March 1999, pp. 30–31.
50. Rob Lawson, NOP, London, 1999.
51. Lisa O'Malley, Maurice Patterson and Martin Evans, *Exploring Direct Marketing* (London: ITBP, 1999), chapter 9.
52. J. December and N. Randall, *The World Wide Web* (Unleashed Sams Publishing, 1994).
53. A. Schofield, "The definition of direct marketing: a rejoinder to Bauer and Miglautsch", *Journal of Direct Marketing*, 9(2), 1995, pp. 37–8.
54. P. McGoldrick, *Retail Marketing* (Maidenhead: McGraw-Hill, 1997).
55. M.J. Evans, L. O'Malley and M. Patterson, "Direct marketing communications in the UK: a study of growth, past, present and future", *Journal of Marketing Communications*, 2, 1996, pp. 51–65.
56. Lisa O'Malley, Maurice Patterson and Martin Evans, *Exploring Direct Marketing* (London: ITBP, 1999), p. 9.

Chapter 18

1. Praveen K. Kopalle, Ambar G. Rao and Joao L. Assuncao, "Asymmetric reference price effects and dynamic pricing policies", *Marketing Science*, vol. 15, no. 1, 1996, pp. 60–85.
2. Ramarao Desiraju, "Strategic service pricing and yield management", *Journal of Marketing*, January 1999.
3. Philip Buxton, "Can marketing save falling retail giants?", *Marketing Week*, 28 January 1999, pp. 19–20.
4. Stephen J. Hoch, Xavier Dreze and Mary Park, "EDLP—hi-lo, and margin arithmetic", *Journal of Marketing*, 58 (4), 1994, pp. 16–22; Allan Mitchell, "Two sides of the same argument", *Marketing Week*, 16 February 1996, pp. 26–27.

5. Michael J. O'Connor, "What is the logic of a price war?", Arthur Andersen & Company, *International Trends in Retailing*, Spring 1986.
6. Saeed Samier, "Pricing in marketing strategies of U.S. and foreign based companies", *Journal of Business Research*, 1987, pp. 15–23.
7. Robert P. Ford, "Pricing operating services", *Bankers Magazine*, May–June 1987.
8. George S. Day and Liam Fahey, "Valuing market strategies", *Journal of Marketing*, July 1988, pp. 45–57.
9. David Landis, "It's cutting prices to win lost ground", *USA Today*, 4 October 1989, pp. 1B, 2B.
10. JCB company literature, 1992.
11. *What Car?*, February 1999.
12. J. Winkler, "Pricing", M. Baker, ed., in *The Marketing Book* (London: Heinemann, 1987).
13. Joseph P. Guiltinan, "The price-bundling of services: a normative framework", *Journal of Marketing*, April 1987, pp. 74–85.
14. Susan M. Petroshius and Kent B. Monroe, "Effect of product-line pricing characteristics on product evaluations", *Journal of Consumer Research*, March 1988, pp. 511–519.
15. Valerie A. Zeithaml, "Consumer perceptions of price, quality and value: a means-end model and synthesis of evidence", *Journal of Marketing*, July 1988, pp. 2–22.
16. David E. Griffith, "The price of competitiveness in competitive pricing", *Journal of the Academy of Marketing Science*, Spring 1997; K. Sivakumar, "Quality tier competition: how price change influences brand choice and category choice", *Journal of Marketing*, July 1997.
17. James B. Wilcox, Roy D. Howell, Paul Kuzdrall and Robert Britney, "Price quantity discounts: some implications for buyers and sellers", *Journal of Marketing*, July 1987, pp. 60–61.
18. Robert G. Eccles, "Control with fairness in transfer pricing", *Harvard Business Review*, November–December 1983, pp. 149–161.
19. Michael H. Morris, "Separate prices as a marketing tool", *Industrial Marketing Management*, 16, 1987, pp. 79–86.

Chapter 19

1. Jack Trout, "Prices: simple guidelines to get them right", *The Journal of Business Strategy*, vol. 19, no. 6, November/December 1998, pp. 13–16.
2. Asim Ansari, S. Siddarth and Charles B. Weinberg, "Pricing a bundle of products or services: the case of nonprofits", *Journal of Marketing Research*, vol. 33, no. 1, February 1996, pp. 86–93.
3. Reprinted from Peter D. Bennett, ed., *Dictionary of Marketing Terms* (American Marketing Association, 1988), p. 54. Used by permission.
4. Bennett, p. 150. Reprinted by permission.
5. Herman Simon, "Pricing opportunities and how to exploit them", *Sloan Management Review*, Winter 1992, pp. 55–65.

6. Kent B. Monroe, "Effect of product line pricing characteristics on product evaluation", *Journal of Consumer Research*, March 1987, p. 518.
7. Marylin Chase, "Burroughs-Wellcome cuts price of AZT under pressure from AIDS activists", *Wall Street Journal*, 19 September 1989, p. A3.
8. National Federation of Consumer Groups, *A Handbook of Consumer Law*, Which? Books (London, 1989).
9. Daewoo; *The Evening Telegraph*, 1 March 1996, p. 30.
10. "Frantic cheap phone buy-up reveals a lot about Japanese marketing", *Ann Arbor News* (Ann Arbor, Mich.), 14 February 1988, p. C9.
11. David E. Griffith, "The price of competitiveness in competitive pricing", *Journal of the Academy of Marketing Science*, Spring 1997.

Chapter 20

1. Michael G. Harvey, "A marketing mix for the 21st century", *Journal of Marketing Theory and Practice*, Fall 1996.
2. Peter Doyle and John Saunders, "Market segmentation and positioning in specialised industrial markets", *Journal of Marketing*, Spring 1995, p. 25.
3. Erik Jan Hultink, "Industrial new product launch strategies and product development performance", *The Journal of Product Innovation Management*, July 1997.
4. Erin Anderson and Anne T. Coughlan, "International market entry and expansion via independent or integrated channels of distribution", *Journal of Marketing*, January 1987, pp. 71–82.
5. Hiram C. Barksdale, Jr., Terry E. Powell and Ernestine Hargrove, "Complaint voicing by industrial buyers", *Industrial Marketing Management*, May 1984, pp. 93–99.
6. James D. Hlavacek and Tommy J. McCuiston, "Industrial distributors: when, who, and how?" *Harvard Business Review*, March–April 1983, p. 97.
7. Gary L. Frazier, Robert E. Spekman and Charles R. O'Neal, "Just-in-time exchange relationships in industrial markets", *Journal of Marketing*, October 1988, pp. 52–67.
8. Daniel H. McQuiston, "Novelty, complexity and importance as casual determinants of industrial buyer behavior", *Journal of Marketing*, April 1989, pp. 66–79.
9. Steve Sulerno, "The close of the new salesmanship", *PSA*, April 1985, p. 63.
10. "Aircraft industry emerging from engineering dominance", *Marketing News*, 2 August 1985, p. 7.
11. Roger A. Kerin and William I., Cron. "Assessing trade show functions and performance: an exploratory study", *Journal of Marketing*, July 1987, pp. 87–94.
12. John C. Narver and Stanley F. Slater, "Creating a market-oriented business", *The Channel of Communications*, Summer 1989, pp. 5–8.
13. Robert Jacobson and David A. Aaker, "The strategic

role of product quality", *Journal of Marketing*, October 1987, pp. 31–44.

14. Douglas G. Brooks, "Bidding for the sake of follow-on contracts", *Journal of Marketing*, January 1978, p. 35.

15. Don Cowell, *The Marketing of Services* (Oxford: Butterworth-Heinemann, 1994).

16. Christopher Lovelock, *Managing Services* (Englewood Cliffs, N.J.: Prentice-Hall, 1992).

17. Walter van Waterschoot and Christophe Van den Bulte, "The 4P classification of the marketing mix revisited", *Journal of Marketing*, October 1992.

18. G. Lynn Shostack, "Breaking free from product marketing", *Journal of Marketing*, April 1977, pp. 73–80.

19. Sak Onkvisit and John J. Shaw, "Service marketing: image, branding, and competition", *Business Horizons*, January–February 1989, p. 16.

20. Tom Peters, "More expensive, but worth it", *U.S. News & World Report*, 3 February 1986, p. 54.

21. Valarie A. Zeithaml, "Consumer perceptions of price, quality, and value: a means-end model and synthesis of evidence", *Journal of Marketing*, July 1988, pp. 2–22.

22. Leonard L. Berry, "8 keys to top service at financial institutions", *American Banker*, August 1987.

23. A. Parasuraman, Valarie A. Zeithaml and Leonard L. Berry, "SERVQUAL: a multiple item scale for measuring consumer perceptions of service quality", *Journal of Retailing*, Spring 1988, pp. 12–40.

24. Stephen W. Brown and Teresa A. Swartz, "A gap analysis of professional service quality", *Journal of Marketing*, April 1989, pp. 92–98.

25. Ibid.

26. G. Lynn Shostack, "Service positioning through structural change", *Journal of Marketing*, January 1987, pp. 34–43.

27. William R. George and Leonard L. Berry, "Guidelines for the advertising of services", *Business Horizons*, July–August 1981, pp. 52–56.

28. Sally Dibb and Lyndon Simkin, "The strength of branding and positioning in services", *International Journal of Service Industry Management*, 4 (1), 1993, pp. 25–33.

29. Sally Dibb and Lyndon Simkin, "Strategy and tactics: marketing leisure facilities", *The Service Industries Journal*, 13 (3), 1993, pp. 110–124; Dibb and Simkin, "The strength of branding and positioning in services", pp. 25–35.

30. James L. Heskett, "Lessons in the Service Sector", *Harvard Business Review*, March/April 1987, pp. 118–127.

31. George and Berry, pp. 55–70.

32. William R. George and J. Patrick Kelly, "The promotion and selling of services", *Business*, July–September 1983, pp. 14–20.

33. John M. Rathmell, *Marketing in the Services Sector* (Cambridge, Mass.: Winthrop, 1974), p. 100.

34. George and Kelly, pp. 14–20; George and Berry, pp. 55–70.

35. Doris C. Van Doren and Louise W. Smith, "Marketing in the restructured professional services field", *Journal of Services Marketing*, Summer 1987, pp. 69–70.

36. James B. Ayers, "Lessons from industry for health-care", *Administrative Radiology*, July 1987, p. 53.

37. Joseph R. Guiltinan, "The price bundling of services: a normative framework", *Journal of Marketing*, April 1987, p. 74.

38. James H. Donnelly, Jr., "Marketing intermediaries in channels of distribution for services", *Journal of Marketing*, January, 1976, pp. 55–70.

39. Ibid.

40. Nigel A. L. Brooks, "Strategic issues for financial services marketing", *Journal of Services Marketing*, Summer 1987, p. 65.

41. Dibb and Simkin, "Strategy and tactics", pp. 110–124.

42. Adrian Payne, *The Essence of Services Marketing* (Hemel Hempstead: Prentice-Hall, 1993).

43. Warren J. Keegan, *Global Marketing Management*, 4th edn (Englewood Cliffs, N.J.: Prentice-Hall, 1989), pp. 378–382.

44. Colin Egan, De Montfort University.

45. Kamran Kashani, "Beware the pitfalls of global marketing", *Harvard Business Review*, September–October 1989, pp. 93–94.

46. Allecia Swasy, "After early stumbles, P&G is making inroads overseas", *Wall Street Journal*, 6 February 1989, p. B1.

47. Douglass G. Norvell and Robert Morey, "Ethno-domination in the channels of distribution of Third World nations", *Journal of the Academy of Marketing Science*, Summer 1983, pp. 204–235.

48. Erin Anderson and Anne T. Coughlan, "International market entry and expansion via independent or integrated channels of distribution", *Journal of Marketing*, January 1987, pp. 71–82.

49. David Jobber, *Principles and Practice of Marketing* (London: McGraw-Hill, 1995).

50. Sally Dibb, Lyndon Simkin and John Bradley, *The Marketing Planning Workbook* (London: Routledge, 1996).

Chapter 21

1. B. A. Weitz and R. Wensley, *Readings in Strategic Marketing* (Chicago: Dryden, 1988).

2. P. Rajan Varadarajan, "Strategy content and process perspectives revisited", *Journal of the Academy of Marketing Science*, vol. 27, no. 1, Winter 1999, pp. 88–100.

3. Sally Dibb, Lyndon Simkin and John Bradley, *The Marketing Planning Workbook* (London: Routledge, 1996).

4. Derek F. Abell and John S. Hammond, *Strategic Market Planning* (Englewood Cliffs, N.J.: Prentice-Hall, 1979), p. 10.

5. P. Rajan Varadarajan, Terry Clark and William Pride, "Determining your company's destiny", working paper, Texas A&M University, 1990.

6. J. Paul Peter and James H. Donnelly, Jr., *A Preface to*

Marketing Management, 5th edn (Homewood, Ill.: Irwin, 1991), p. 9.

7. Adapted from Peter and Donnelly, *A Preface to Marketing Management,* pp. 8–12.
8. Zachary Schiller, with Russell Mitchell, Wendy Zellner, Lois Therrien, Andrea Rothman and Walecia Konrad, "The great American health pitch", *Business Week,* 9 October 1989, p. 116.
9. Derek F. Abell, "Strategic windows", *Journal of Marketing,* July 1978, p. 21.
10. Abell and Hammond, p. 213.
11. Liam Fahey, William K. King and Vodake K. Naraganan, "Environmental scanning and forecasting in strategic planning—the state of the art", *Long Range Planning,* February 1981, p. 38.
12. David M. Georgaff and Robert G. Mundick, "Managers' guide to forecasting", *Harvard Business Review,* January–February 1986, p. 120.
13. "Energy efficient house design", *House Builder Magazine,* September 1986.
14. "The 'bumpy road to clean fuels'", *U.S. News & World Report,* 26 June 1989, pp. 10–11.
15. Ibid.
16. Philip Kotler, "Strategic planning and the marketing process", *Business,* May–June 1980, pp. 6–7.
17. Nigel Piercy, *Market-Led Strategic Change* (Oxford: Butterworth-Heinemann Ltd, 1992).
18. Roger A. Kerin, Vijay Majahan and P. Rajan Varadarajan, *Contemporary Perspectives on Strategic Marketing Planning* (Boston: Allyn & Bacon, 1990).
19. Ronald Grover, "When Columbia met Sony … a love story", *Business Week,* 9 October 1989, pp. 44–45.
20. David Woodruff, "Has Dow Chemical found the right formula?" *Business Week,* 7 August 1989, pp. 62, 64.
21. Mark Maremont, with Judith H. Dobrzynski, "Meet Asil Nadir, the billion-dollar fruit king", *Business Week,* 18 September 1989, p. 32.
22. Graham Hooley and John Saunders, *Competitive Positioning: The Key to Market Success* (London: Prentice-Hall, 1993).
23. Al Ries and Jack Trout, *Marketing Warfare* (New York: McGraw-Hill, 1986); John Saunders, "Marketing and competitive success", in Michael Baker, ed., *The Marketing Book* (London: Heinemann, 1987).
24. Hirokazu Takada, "Multiple time series analysis of competitive marketing behavior", *Journal of Business Research,* October 1998.
25. Peter Doyle, *Marketing Management and Strategy* (London: Prentice-Hall, 1994).
26. David A. Aaker, *Strategic Market Management,* 2nd edn (New York: Wiley, 1988), p. 35.
27. John Saunders, "Marketing and competitive success", Michael J. Baker, ed., in *The Marketing Book* (London: Heinemann, 1987), pp. 10–28.
28. Joseph P. Guiltinan and Gordon W. Paul, *Marketing Management: Strategies and Programmes* (New York: McGraw-Hill, 1982), p. 31.
29. George S. Day, "Diagnosing the Product Portfolio", *Journal of Marketing,* April 1977, pp. 30–31.
30. Sally Dibb and Lyndon Simkin, *The Market Segmentation Workbook* (London: Routledge, 1996).
31. Robert Jacobson, "Distinguishing among competing theories of the market share effect", *Journal of Marketing,* October 1988, pp. 68–80.
32. George S. Day, *Analysis for Strategic Market Decisions* (St. Paul, Minn.: West, 1986), pp. 117–118.
33. Robert D. Buzzell and Bradley T. Gale, *The PIMS Principles: Linking Strategy to Performance* (New York: Free Press, 1987).
34. Day, *Analysis for Strategic Market Decisions,* p. 10.
35. David W. Cravens, "Strategic marketing's new challenge", *Business Horizons,* March–April 1983, p. 19.
36. Yoram Wind, Vijay Majahan and Donald J. Swire, "An empirical comparison of standardised portfolio models", *Journal of Marketing,* Spring 1983, pp. 89–99.

Chapter 22

1. Peter S.H. Leeflang, "An empirical investigation of marketing planning", *Journal of Euro-Marketing,* 1996.
2. Ronald D. Michman, "Linking futuristics with marketing planning, forecasting, and strategy", *Journal of Consumer Marketing,* Summer 1984, pp. 17, 23.
3. Sally Dibb, Lyndon Simkin and John Bradley, *The Marketing Planning Workbook* (London: Routledge, 1996).
4. Lyndon Simkin, "People and processes in marketing planning: the benefits of controlling implementation in marketing planning", *Journal of Marketing Management,* vol. 12, no. 5, 1996, pp. 375–390; Lyndon Simkin, "Delivering effective marketing planning", *Sloan Management Review,* forthcoming; Lyndon Simkin, "Barriers impeding effective implementation of marketing plans—a new research and training agenda", *European Journal of Marketing,* forthcoming.
5. Vasudevan Ramanujam and N. Venkatraman, "Planning and performance: a new look at an old question", *Business Horizons,* May–June 1987, pp. 19–25.
6. David J. Luck, O. C. Ferrell and George Lucas, *Marketing Strategy and Plans,* 3rd edn (Englewood Cliffs, N.J.: Prentice-Hall, 1989), p. 328.
7. Malcolm McDonald, *Marketing Plans: How to Prepare Them, How to Use Them* (Oxford: Butterworth Heinemann, 1989).
8. Lyndon Simkin and Anthony Chang, "Understanding competitors' strategies," *Marketing Intelligence & Planning,* 15 (3), 1997, pp. 124–134.
9. Yoram Wind and Thomas S. Robertson, "Marketing strategy: new directions for theory and research", *Journal of Marketing,* Spring 1983, p. 12.
10. M. E. Porter, *Competitive Strategy: Techniques for Analysing Industries and Competitors* (New York: Free Press, 1980).
11. Lyndon Simkin, "Addressing organisational pre-

requisites in marketing planning programmes", *Marketing Intelligence and Planning,* vol. 14, no. 5, 1996, pp. 39–46.

12. Sally Dibb and Lyndon Simkin, *The Marketing Casebook* (London: Routledge, 1994).
13. David Hurwood, Elliot S. Grossman and Earl Bailey, *Sales Forecasting* (New York: Conference Board, 1978), p. 2.
14. D. S. Tull and D. I. Hawkins, *Marketing Research* (New York: Macmillan, 1990).
15. Kenneth E. Marino, *Forecasting Sales and Planning Profits* (Chicago: Probus Publishing, 1986), p. 155.
16. Hurwood, Grossman and Bailey, p. 61.
17. G. L. Lilien and P. Kotler, *Marketing Decision-Making* (New York: Harper & Row, 1983).
18. P. Naert and P. Leeflang, *Building Implementable Marketing Models* (Leiden: Martinus Nijhoff, 1978).
19. *Accurate Business Forecasting* (Boston's *Harvard Business Review* Booklet, 1991).
20. William A. Band, "A marketing audit provides an opportunity for improvement", *Sales & Marketing Management in Canada,* March 1984, pp. 24–26.
21. Ely S. Lurin, "Audit determines the weak link in marketing chain", *Marketing News,* 12 September 1986, pp. 35–37.
22. Ibid.

Chapter 23

1. Rohit Despande and Frederick E. Webster, Jr., "Organisational culture and marketing: defining the research agenda", *Journal of Marketing,* January 1989, pp. 3–15.
2. Michael D. Hutt and Thomas W. Speh, "The marketing strategy centre: diagnosing the industrial marketer's inter-disciplinary role", *Journal of Marketing,* Fall 1984, pp. 16–53.
3. John Bussy, "Manufacturers strive to slice time needed to develop products", *Wall Street Journal,* 23 February 1988, p. 18.
4. Nigel F. Piercy, "Marketing implementation: the implications of marketing paradigm weakness for the strategy execution process", *Journal of the Academy of Marketing Science,* vol. 26, no. 3, Summer 1998, pp. 222–236.
5. John C. Narver and Stanley F. Slater, "Creating a market orientated business", *The Channel of Communications,* Summer 1989, pp. 5–8.
6. Larry Reibstein, "IBM's plan to decentralise may set a trend—but imitation has a price", *Wall Street Journal,* 19 February 1988, p. 17.
7. Kenneth W. Thomas and Betty A. Velthouse, "Cognitive elements of empowerment: an 'interpretive' model of intrinsic task motivation", *Academy of Management Review,* October 1990, pp. 666–681.
8. O. C. Ferrell, George H. Lucas and David J. Luck, *Strategic Marketing Management: Text and Cases* (Cincinnati: South-Western Publishing, 1994), pp. 193–194.
9. Michael D. Hartline and O. C. Ferrell, "Service quality implementation: the effects of organizational socialization and managerial actions on the behav-

iors of customer-contact employees", *Marketing Science Institute Working Paper Series,* Report no. 93–122 (Cambridge, Mass.: Marketing Science Institute, 1993), pp. 36–48.
10. Ibid., pp. 36–40.
11. Dave Ulrich, "Strategic human resources planning: why and how?", *Human Resources Planning,* 10, no. 1, 1987, pp. 25–57.
12. Steven Lysonski, "A boundary theory investigation of the product manager's role", *Journal of Marketing,* Winter 1985, pp. 26–40.
13. Based on Orville C. Walker, Jr. and Robert W. Ruekert, "Marketing's role in the implementation of business strategies: a critical review and conceptual framework", *Journal of Marketing,* July 1987, pp. 15–33.
14. Nigel F. Piercy, "Marketing implementation: the implications of marketing paradigm weakness for the strategy execution process", *Journal of the Academy of Marketing Science,* vol. 26, no. 3, Summer 1998, pp. 222–236; David Strutton, "Marketing strategies: new approaches, new techniques", *Journal of the Academy of Marketing Science,* Summer 1997.
15. Robert Howard, "Values make the company: an interview with Robert Haas", *Harvard Business Review,* September–October 1990, pp. 132–144.
16. Ferrell, Lucas and Luck, *Strategic Marketing Management,* pp. 190–200.
17. Myron Glassman and Bruce McAfee, "Integrating the personnel and marketing functions: the challenge of the 1990s", *Business Horizons,* May–June 1992, pp. 52–59.
18. Ferrell, Lucas and Luck, *Strategic Marketing Management,* pp. 190–200.
19. P. Kotler, G. Armstrong, J. Saunders and V. Wong, *Principles of Marketing* (Hemel Hempstead: Prentice-Hall, 1998).
20. M. Christopher, A. Payne and D. Ballantyne, *Relationship Marketing* (Oxford: Butterworth-Heinemann, 1991); C. Gronroos, "From marketing mix to relationship marketing: towards a paradigm shift in marketing", *Management Decision,* 32 (2), pp. 4–20.
21. L.L. Berry, "Relationship marketing", in L.L. Berry, G.L. Shostack and G. Upah (eds.), *Emerging Perspectives on Services* (Chicago, Ill.: American Marketing Association, 1983), pp. 25–28.
22. A. Payne, "Relationship marketing—making the customer count", *Managing Service Quality,* vol. 4, no. 6, 1994, pp. 29–31.
23. W.R. George, "Internal marketing and organisational behaviour: a partnership in developing customer-conscious employees at every level", *Journal of Business Research,* vol. 20, 1990, pp. 63–70; I. Lings and F. Brooks, "Implementing and measuring the effectiveness of internal marketing", *Journal of Marketing Management,* vol. 14, no. 4, 1998, pp. 325–351.
24. E. Gummesson, "Using internal marketing to develop a new culture", *Journal of Business and Industrial Marketing,* vol. 2, no. 3, 1987, pp. 23–28.
25. J. Reynoso and B. Moores, "Internal relationships",

in F. Buttle (ed.), *Relationship Marketing: Theory and Practice* (London: Chapman, 1996).

26. M. McDonald, "Ten barriers to marketing planning", *Journal of Business & Industrial Marketing,* vol. 7, no. 1, 1992, pp. 5–18; M. McDonald, "Strategic marketing planning: a state-of-the-art review", *Marketing Intelligence & Planning,* vol. 10, no. 4, 1992, pp. 4–22; L. Simkin, "People and processes in marketing planning: the benefits of controlling implementation", *Journal of Marketing Management,* vol. 12, 1996, pp. 375–390; L. Simkin, "Addressing organisational prerequisites in marketing planning programmes", *Marketing Intelligence & Planning,* vol. 14, no. 5, 1996, pp. 39–46.

27. Sybil F. Stershic, "Internal marketing campaign reinforces service goals", *Marketing News,* 31 July 1989, p. 11.

28. Adapted from Joseph R. Jablonski, *Implementing Total Quality Management* (Albuquerque, N. Mex.: Technical Management Consortium, 1990).

29. Hartline and Ferrell, "Service quality implementation", pp. 36–40.

30. Philip B. Crosby, *Quality is Free—The Art of Making Quality Certain* (New York: McGraw-Hill, 1979), pp. 9–10.

31. N. Piercy, *Market-Led Strategic Change* (Oxford: Butterworth-Heinemann, 1992).

32. Fred Steingraber, "Total quality management: a new look at a basic issue", *Vital Speeches of the Day,* May 1990, pp. 415–416.

33. Hartline and Ferrell, "Service Quality Implementation," pp. 36–48.

34. David C. Jones, "Motivation the catalyst in profit formula", *National Underwriter,* 13 July 1987, pp. 10, 13.

35. Jerry McAdams, "Rewarding sales and marketing performance", *Management Review,* April 1987, p. 36.

36. "Higher education in doughnuts", *Ann Arbor News,* 9 March 1988, p. B7.

37. Bernard J. Jaworski, "Toward a theory of marketing control: environmental context, control types, and consequences", *Journal of Marketing,* July 1988, pp. 23–39.

38. See Theo Haimann, William G. Scott and Patrick E. Connor, *Management,* 5th edn (Boston: Houghton Mifflin, 1985), pp. 478–492.

39. Jeffrey A. Tannenbaum, "Video games revive—and makers hope this time the fad will last", *Wall Street Journal,* 8 March 1988, p. 35.

40. "Carbonates and concentrates", *Marketing Intelligence,* January 1990, pp. 2.10–2.17.

41. Kevin Kelly and Neil Gross, "A weakened Komatsu tries to come back swinging", *Business Week,* 22 February 1988, p. 48.

42. Jo-Anne Flack, "Measure of success", *Marketing Week,* 4 March 1999, pp. 45–49.

Chapter 24

1. Dinah Payne, Cecily Raiborn and Jorn Askvik, "A global code of business ethics", *Journal of Business Ethics,* vol. 16, no. 16, December 1997, pp. 1727–1735.

2. Anusorn Singhapakdi, Scott J. Vitell, Kumar Rallapalli and Kenneth L. Kraft, "The perceived role of ethics and social responsibility: a scale development", *Journal of Business Ethics,* November 1996.

3. Andrew Stark, *Harvard Business Review,* May–June 1993, p. 38.

4. Jim Impoco, "Working for Mr. Clean Jeans", *U.S. News & World Report,* 2 August 1993, p. 50.

5. Donald P. Robin and R. Eric Reidenbach, "Social responsibility, ethics in marketing strategy, closing the gap between concept and application", *Journal of Marketing,* January 1987, pp. 44–58.

6. Vernon R. Loucks, Jr., "A CEO looks at ethics", *Business Horizons,* March–April 1987, p. 4.

7. Clare Sambrook, "Do free flights really build brands?" *Marketing,* 15 October 1992, p. 11.

8. N. Craig Smith, "Marketing strategies for the ethics era", *Sloan Management Review,* vol. 36, no. 4, Summer 1995, p. 85(13).

9. Tim Barnett, "Ethical ideology and the ethical judgements of marketing professionals", *Journal of Business Ethics,* May 1998.

10. O. C. Ferrell and John Fraedrich, *Business Ethics* (Boston: Houghton Mifflin, 1994), p. 52.

11. F. Neil Brady, *Ethical Managing: Rules and Results* (New York: Macmillan, 1990), pp. 4–6.

12. O. C. Ferrell and Larry G. Gresham, "A contingency framework for understanding ethical decision making in marketing," *Journal of Marketing,* Summer 1985, p. 90.

13. John Fraedrich and O. C. Ferrell, "Cognitive consistency of marketing managers in ethical situations," *Journal of the Academy of Marketing Science,* 1992, pp. 245–252.

14. Joseph W. Weiss, *Business Ethics: A Managerial, Stakeholder Approach* (Belmont, Calif.: Wadsworth, 1994), p. 13.

15. O. C. Ferrell, Larry G. Gresham and John Fraedrich, "A synthesis of ethical decision models for marketing", *Journal of Macromarketing,* Fall 1989, pp. 58–59.

16. "Good Guys Finish First," *Business Ethics,* March/April 1995, p. 13.

17. Ferrell and Gresham, p. 92.

18. Damon Darlin, "Where trademarks are up for grabs", *Wall Street Journal,* 5 December 1989, p. B1.

19. "Persil Power trouble shooter nets Rockitt global group director role", *Marketing Week,* 17 May 1996, p. 10; Julian Lee and Claire Murphy, "P&G and Sears to fight Persil", *Marketing,* 2 May 1996, p. 1; Claire Cozens, "Unilever braced for price war with P&G", *Corporate Finance,* March 1996, pp. 9–11; Harriet Green, "Persil opts for change of direction", *Campaign,* 31 May 1996, p. 7.

20. Robert McLuhan, "Iceland's new strategy proves popular with consumers", *Marketing,* 1 April 1999, p. 24.

21. Scott Hume, "Squawk over KFC ads—company challenges Y&R with new strategy", *Advertising Age,* 15

January 1990, p. 16; Archie B. Carroll, *Business and Society: Ethics and Stakeholder Management* (Cincinnati: South-Western Publishing, 1989), pp. 228–230.

22. Cyndee Miller, "Sexy sizzle backfires: Calvin Klein advertised jeans, but real message is for the marketer", *Marketing News*, 25 September 1995, pp. 1–2.

23. Rob Gray, "Perils of sending brands to school", *Marketing*, 22 April 1999, pp. 30–31.

24. Linda K. Trevino and Stuart Youngblood, "Bad apples in bad barrels: a causal analysis of ethical decision making behaviour", *Journal of Applied Psychology*, 75 (4), 1990, pp. 378–385.

25. Ibid.

26. Gene R. Laczniak and Patrick E. Murphy, *Ethical Marketing Decisions: The Higher Road* (Boston: Allyn and Bacon, 1993), p. 14.

27. Tom Rusk and D. Patrick Miller, *The Power of Ethical Persuasion: From Conflict to Partnership at Work and in Private Life* (New York: Viking, 1993).

28. Carroll, *Business and Society*, p. 45.

29. Margaret A. Stroup, Ralph L. Newbert and Jerry W. Anderson, Jr., "Doing good, doing better: two views of social responsibility", *Business Horizons*, March–April 1987, p. 23.

30. "Good guys finish first," *Business Ethics*, March/April 1995, p. 13.

31. Alexandra Jardine, "Shell stresses ethical action to salvage brand reputation", *Marketing*, 18 March 1999, p. 9.

32. "Lasting value Levi Strauss", *Business Ethics*, November–December 1993, p. 28.

33. Ron Trujillo, "Good ethics pay off", *USA Today*, 23 October 1995, p. 2B.

34. "McD ads draw protests from nutritional experts", *Nation's Restaurant News*, 22 June 1987, p. 26.

35. John Eisenhammer, "Where cars will go when they die", *Independent on Sunday*, 21 February 1993, pp. 24–25.

36. Sir Adrian Cadbury, "Ethical managers make their own rules", *Harvard Business Review*, September–October 1987, p. 33.

Name Index

Dibb, Sally, 17, 32*n*, 202, 232*n*, 365*n*, 420*n*, 591*n*, 695*n*, 696*n*, 785, 809*n*
Dibb-Simkin, James, 365*n*
DiBenederro, C. Anthony, 385*n*
Dickson, P.R., 789*n*
Diet Caffeine-Free Coke, 238
Diet Coke, 238, 306, 470
D'Ietern, 815
Dillons, 426 *(table)*, 441 *(table)*
Dimplex electric heaters, 167, 168
Diner's Club, 206
Direct Collection, 448
Direct Line, 62, 282, 661, 670
Disco, 446 *(table)*
Discos snacks, 293
Discovery cars, 242
Disney, 265–266, 270 *(table)*, 279, 643, 703, 752, 818–820
Disney, Walt, 265, 703
The Disney Afternoon tv programmes, 266
Disney Channel, 266, 818
Disneyland Paris, 265, 458, 703, 818
Disney-MGM Studios Theme Park, 818
Disney Stores, 266
Disney Sunday Movie, 266
Disney University, 818
Disney Vacation Club, 266
Disney World, 266
Dixons, 261, 415, 416, 426 *(table)*, 437, 442, 807
DMB&B, 504 *(table)*
Dobie, Kathryn, 571*n*
Do It All stores, 764
Dolby stereo Surroundsound, 344
Donald Duck, 266
Done, K., 243*n*
Donkey Kong Country II, 559
Donkey Kong Land phone cards, 559
Doole, Isobel, 80
Dorfman, Dan, 613*n*
Doritos snacks, 71
Dorothy Perkins, 426 *(table)*
Dourado, Phil, 200*n*
Dow Chemical, 664
Doyle, Peter, 32, 268, 282, 567*n*, 784, 787
Dr. Martens footwear, 476
Dr. Pepper soft drinks, 235
Dr. Scheller Cosmetics, 298 *(illus.)*
Drambuie Liqueur, 273
Dreamcast, 491
Dreft detergent, 256 *(illus.)*, 279
Dreher beer, 264
Dresser Industries, 744
Drisaldi, Jerry, 414*n*
Drucker, Peter, 6, 788

DTI Enterprise Initiative, 481
Duckhams oil, 513
Duckworth, Jonathan, 690*n*
Du Lac, 641
Dun & Bradstreet, 78, 333
Dunkin, Amy, 455*n*, 613*n*
Dunkin' Donuts, 737–738
Dunkin' Donuts University, 738
Dunn, S. Watson, 498*n*, 502*n*
Dunne, J.M., 203*n*
Dunning, Liz, 289*n*
Duofold, 571
DuPont, 165, 166, 679
Duracell batteries, 62, 236
Dutch Automobile Association, 160 *(illus.)*
Duval beer, 643
DVL Smith Ltd., 186 *(table)*
Dwek, Robert, 560*n*

E45 Skin Confidence, 504 *(table)*
Eastern Airlines, 664
Eastern Electricity, 377
East Midlands Electricity (EMEB), 202, 661
EasyJet, 429, 648, 810, 811, 815
EasyPlay football game, 173
Easy Reader watches, 754
Ebert, Roger, 266
Eco-Foam, 414
Ecover, 211 *(table)*, 282
Edeka Group, 424 *(table)*
Editions, 447
Edwards, Paul, 416*n*
Egan, Colin, 71
Egan, Sir John, 419
Egg e-commerce financial services, 309
EIASMI (European Institute for Advanced Studies in Management), 790
806 cars, 242
Eisenhammer, John, 47*n*
Eisman, Regina, 647*n*
Eisner, Michael, 819
Ektar film, 260
El Corte Ingles, 422
Eldon Square shopping mall, 419
Electrolux, 69, 136, 806, 808–809
Elephant Tape, 316
Elida Fabergé, 481, 493 *(table)*
Elite cars, 573
Ellis-Brown, Gordon, 351*n*
Ellis-Simon, Pamela, 266*n*
EMEB (East Midlands Electricity), 202, 661
EMI, 208
Empire, 448 *(table)*
ENI, 96 *(table)*
EPCOT Centre, 818
Equitable Life, 504 *(table)*

Era detergent, 256 and *illus.*
Erasmus University, 587
Ericsson, 69, 84 *(illus.)*, 95 *(table)*, 96 *(table)*, 685, 810
ERRA (European Recovery and Recycling Association), 47
Erteco, 101 *(table)*
ESA Market Research Ltd., 186 *(table)*
Escher, M.C., 119 *(illus.)*
Escort cars, 30
ESOMAR (European Society for Opinion and Marketing Research), 193, 196
Espace, 528 *(illus.)*, 529
Espace cars, 242
ESPN, 818
Esso, 164, 276, 361, 541, 670
Estée Lauder, 493, 540
EuroDisney, 265, 458, 703, 818
Eurodollar, 815, 816 *(table)*
Euromarche, 102
Euromonitor, 428
Euronova, 446 *(table)*
Europa Foods, 441 *(table)*
Europcar Interrant, 815, 816 *(table)*, 817
European Financial Times, 96*n*
European Football Championships, 716
European Institute for Advanced Studies in Management (EIASMI), 790
European Marketing Academy, 784
European Protection Systems, 46 *(illus.)*
European Recovery and Recycling Association (ERRA), 47
European Society for Opinion and Marketing Research (ESOMAR), 193, 196
Eurotraveller, 276
Eurotunnel, 308
Evans, 426 *(table)*
Everest, 236
EverReady, 62
Everything Under £1, 435
Evian, 207 and *illus.*, 520, 664
Excel cars, 90
Experian demographic analysis, 179
Exxon, 405

Fab detergent, 804
Face Values, 447, 448 *(table)*
Fairly, Peter, 166*n*, 679*n*
Fairtrade Mark, 755–756
Fairy Liquid detergent, 270, 305, 569
Fairy washing powder, 570 *(illus.)*
Family Album, 448 *(table)*

Levi Strauss, 57, 74, 757, 773
Levy, Paul, 565n
Lexus, 659
Lidl, 441 (table)
Lidl & Schwartz, 424 (table)
Lifestyle brands, 275, 413
Lifestyles uk, 220–221, 221
Lifetime channel, 818
Lilley, P., 817n
Lipton's Yellow Label tea, 297
Liquid Paper, 259
Little Chef restaurants, 3–4, 4 (illus.)
Littlewoods, 419, 423, 432, 448 (table), 552
Liverpool Football Club, 467, 716
Lloyd, C., 480n
Lloyds TSB, 6, 17, 96 (table), 309, 375
London Business School, 295
London Signature Hotels, 718
Longworth, Richard, 621n
Look Again, 447, 448 (table)
Looney Tunes snacks, 293
L'Oréal, 47, 236, 493 (table)
Lotus, 685, 702, 703
Lotus cars, 235
Louis Chevalier, 412
Louis-Dreyfus, Julia, 303
Löwenbrau, 93
Lowndes Queensway, 660
Lowry, L.S., 251
Lucas, George H., 728n
Luck, David J., 728n
Lucky Strike cigarettes, 68
Lufthansa, 95 (table), 500 (illus.), 648, 810, 816
Lunn Poly, 466
Lupo cars, 315
Lux soap, 10, 249
Lynn, Matthew, 69n, 223n
Lyons, Veronica, 241n
Lyons Maid, 478

M6 Cash and Carry, 411
Maccoby, Michael, 149n
Mace, 363, 427
MacFarlane, Elaine, 257
Maersk Air, 811
Magic Kingdom theme park, 818
Magiera, Marcy, 266n
Magnet, Myron, 266n
Mail Boxes Etc., 435 (table)
Major, John, 584
Makro, 394, 412, 427
Mana, 446 (table)
Manchester Business School, 415
Manchester United Football Club, 472
Mandese, Joe, 559n
Manweb, 377

Maremont, Mark, 455n, 613n
Market Hall, 393
Market Identifiers, 159
Marketing Direction Ltd., 186 (table)
Marketing magazine, 178, 821, 826
Marketing Outpost stores, 29, 136
The Marketing Pocket Books, 178
Marketing Science Institute, 785
Marketing Sciences Ltd., 186 (table)
Marketing Week magazine, 178, 821, 826
Market-Led Strategic Change: Transforming the Process of Going to Market, 792 (illus.)
Market Locations, 160
Market Profiles, 167
Market Research Society, 169, 196
Market Research Solutions Ltd., 186 (table)
Marks & Spencer, 138, 139, 235 (illus.), 275, 358, 360, 363, 371, 400, 419, 423, 424 (table), 425, 426, 435, 439, 541, 548, 552, 606, 607, 689, 764
Marlboro cigarettes, 67, 81, 270 (table), 653
Marquis crystal, 591
Marriott, 543, 817
Mars, 176, 258, 275, 472, 519, 688, 699
Mars candy bars, 688, 699
Mars Confectionery, 493 (table)
Marsh, Harriett, 759n
Marshall, Anthony, 565n
Marshall, Colin, 519
Marshall, Sharon, 759n
Marshall Ward, 448 (table)
Martin, David, 448n
Martin Hamblin Group, 186 (table)
Mary Kay Cosmetics, 431
Massachusetts Mutual, 685
Massey Ferguson, 156 (illus.)
MasterCard, 249
Mastercare, 415
Matsui appliances, 275
Matsushita, 95 (table), 605
Mattel toys, 310
Matutano snacks, 71
Maverick cars, 6, 242, 277
Max Factor, 586
MAX (Machine Answered eXamination), 189–190
Maxwell, Robert, 312
Maytag Corp., 560, 806
Mazda, 276
The MBL Group Plc., 186 (table)

MCA, 341
McBurnie, Tony, 223n
McCann-Erickson, 504 (table), 754
McClenahen, John, 149n
McCord, 448 (table)
McDermott, Susan, 653
McDLT sandwiches, 775
McDonald, Dick, 727
McDonald, Mac, 727
McDonald, Malcom, 231, 689
McDonald's, 44, 74, 91, 266, 270 (table), 278, 302, 304, 324, 335, 363, 433, 434, 435 (table), 454, 464, 484, 493 (table), 504 (table), 514, 638, 727, 742, 772, 775, 776, 781–782
McDowall, Roddy, 303
McEnaney, T., 649n
McGan, Anthony F., 498n
McGann, Gary, 811
McGoldrick, Peter, 32, 415
McGrath, Neal, 809n
McGraw-Hill, 685, 810
McIlvain, George E., 340n
McKelvey, Siobhan, 165n
McKesson, 393
McKinlay, Margaret, 661n
McKinsey, 785n
McLaren racing team, 67
McLuhan, Robert, 117n, 588n, 756n
M&C Saatchi, 519
Mead, G., 478n
Meadows, Maureen, 17
MEB (Midlands Electricity Board), 39, 661
Mechan, Colin, 277n
Media Initiatives Agency, 481
Media Vest, 504 (table)
Meister, Jeanne C., 819n
Mele, Jim, 621n
Meller, Paul, 585n
Mennen Speed Stick deodorant, 804
Menumaster, 560
Mercedes-Benz, 242, 253, 371, 621, 659
Mercier, 585
Merck Sharp & Dohme, 685
Meridian, 138
Merrerfield, D., 102n
Merrick, Neil, 391n
Merrill Lynch, 431
Merrydown, 759
Merry Hill shopping mall, 421
Merseyside, 427
Metro, 424 (table)
Metro Centre shopping mall, 421, 422 (illus.)
Metro France, 101 (table)

Nutile, Tom, 259n
Nynas, 153, 164

Oblivion theme park ride, 703
O'Brien, Elaine, 33
The Observer, 586
Octavia cars, 315
Office Depot France, 101 *(table)*
Office World, 425
Ogilvy & Mather, 505, 585, 772
Ohmae, K., 789n
Oil of Olay bar soap, 256 *(illus.)*
Old Spice deodorant, 256 *(illus.)*
O'Leary, Noreen, 519n
Olins, R., 69n
Olivetti, 95 *(table)*
Olympics, 468, 481, 512
Omega cars, 573
Omega courier services, 406
Omega Express, 392 and *illus.*
Oneal, Michael, 819n
106 cars, 202
166 cars, 315
One Stop, 441 *(table)*
One 2 One, 117, 504 *(table)*,
    513
1-2-3 spreadsheet software, 703
One Up, 426 *(table)*
On-Line computer banking, 309
The Open University, 521
Operation Desert Storm, 414
Operation Smile, 804, 805–806
Optimedia, 504 *(table)*
Options magazine, 312
Oral-B toothbrushes, 259
Orange, 117, 282
Orbital Sciences Corp., 148
O'Reilly, Tony, 411, 412
Orgel, D., 446n
Oster, Patrick, 809n
O'Sullivan, Tom, 401n, 716n, 771n
Otto Versand, 432, 447, 448
    (table)
Our Price, 426 *(table)*
Outfit, 426 *(table)*
Ovitz, Michael, 265n
Owen, David, 613n
Owen, Michael, 513
Owens, John, 346n
Oxfam, 13, 47, 249, 335, 548
Oxford Independent newspaper,
    779, 780
Oxydol detergent, 256 *(illus.)*

Pacific Gas and Electric, 377
Palmolive detergent, 804
Pampers, 569
Panasonic, 167, 168, 542, 605
Pantene shampoos, 255, 256
    (illus.)

Paperchase, 426 *(table)*
Paper Mate pens, 259
Paramount, 341
Parasuraman, A., 177n, 323n,
    331n, 332n
Parets, Robyn, 717n
Paris Disney World, 703
Parker pens, 259, 569, 571
PAS (Public Attitude Surveys Ltd.),
    186 *(table)*
Passat cars, 572
Pasta 'n' Sauce, 504 *(table)*
Patti, Charles H., 488n
Paustian, Chuck, 522n
Pavlides, 641
Paxton, Chris, 168
Payne, A., 73n, 790n
Payne, Martin, 361n
PC World, 294, 415, 416, 426
    (table)
PC World Business Direct, 415
Peapod, 786
Peck, Gregory, 811
Pedder, Alan, 679
Pegram Walters Group, 186
    (table)
Pell, Jonathan, 30n
Pellet, Jennifer, 30n, 136n
PepsiCo, 71, 72, 81, 207,
    292–293, 433, 454, 637, 664,
    705–706
Percy, Larry, 538n
Perrier, 466, 519–520, 639 *(illus.)*,
    762
Perrier Jouet, 585
Persil Power washing powder, 762
Persil washing powder, 250, 456,
    536
Pert Plus shampoo, 256 *(illus.)*
Peter Craig, 448 *(table)*
Peters, Michael, 316
Petrofina, 47
Peugeot, 202, 203, 242, 493 *(table)*
Peugeot/Citroën, 202
P&G (Procter & Gamble), 44,
    200, 214, 221, 241, 255–256,
    266, 270, 276, 279, 286,
    304, 360, 364, 454, 486,
    491, 493 *(table)*, 495, 504
    (table), 569, 570 *(illus.)*, 640,
    724, 763
Pham, Alex, 259n
Pharmacia & Upjohn, 257
Philadelphia Eagles NFL team, 782
Philips, 95 *(table)*, 112, 295, 685,
    806, 807
Philipson, Claes, 613n
Phillips, Stan, 481n
Phoenix music festivals, 716
Picard Sugelés, 101 *(table)*, 102

Pickford, Andrew, 69n
Pierce, David Hyde, 303
Piercy, Nigel, 32, 718, 733n, 785,
    792–794
Pierre Cardin, 93
Pillsbury, 20, 477
Pingo Doce, 446 *(table)*
Piper Heidsieck, 585
Piranha alcoholic drinks, 759
Pitcher, George, 309n, 377n, 467n,
    607n, 716n
Pivco, 167, 168
Pizza Hut, 484, 636, 704
The Planet on Sunday, 173
Planters nuts, 284
Play House, 752–753
Playhouse, 426 *(table)*
Play Station, 458 and *illus.*, 716,
    763 *(illus.)*
Plummer, Joseph, 219n
Pocahontas, 265
P&O ferry operator, 308
Polaroid, 403, 599, 638
Pollock, Bill, 155n
Polly Peck International, 665
Polo mints, 268–269, 269 *(illus.)*,
    305
Pope, Kyle, 467n
POPULUS software, 189
Porritt, Jonathan, 771
Porsche, 21, 58, 100, 208, 210,
    228, 235, 668, 700
Porsche, Ferdinand, 99, 646
Porsche, Ferry, 99, 100, 647
Porsche AG, 99–100, 646–647
Porsche sunglasses, 571
Porter, Michael, 59, 666n, 698,
    700, 700n, 702n, 786
Portman Group, 759
Posthouse, 155, 718
Post-It notes, 298, 300, 316
Pot Noodles, 130
Pot Rice, 130
Poundstretcher, 427
Power, Christopher P., 300n
Powerfest, 559
PowerGen, 39, 202, 377, 661
PPC (Polystyrene Packaging
    Council), 414
PPP medical insurer, 346
Practical Car and Van Rental, 815
Practical Parenting magazine,
    106
Prahalad, C.K., 789n
Pratt & Whitney, 685
Pregnancy Plus magazine, 106
Prell shampoo, 256 *(illus.)*
Prentice, Chris, 365n
Pressley, Milton M., 184n
Presto, 441 *(table)*

Sanchez, Jesus, 613*n*
Sandoz, 810
Sanitas, 617
Sansweet, Stephen J., 267*n*
Santa Isabel, 446 *(table)*
Sanyo, 89
Saphikon, 300
Saporito, B., 136*n*
Saro-Wiwa, Ken, 771
SAS Cargo Systems, 414
SAS (Scandinavian Airlines), 95
    (table), 419, 810, 811
Saunders, Roger, 289
Savacentre, 424, 426 *(table)*, 441
    (table)
Save the Children, 780
Savory American Creams, 71
Saxa cars, 202
Scandinavian Airlines (SAS), 95
    (table), 419, 810, 811
Scania cars, 69
Scantel Ltd., 186 *(table)*
Scarman House, 155
Schering-Plough, 810
Schweppes Beverages, 368
SCM, 165, 166, 679
Scotcade, 447, 448 *(table)*
Scottish Courage, 716
Scottish & Newcastle, 716
Scottish Power, 377
Scott Paper, 275, 355
Seagram's, 585, 708
Sears, 241, 266, 425, 426 *(table)*,
    447, 448 *(table)*, 662
Secret deodorant, 256
    (illus.)
Secrett, Charles, 771
Securicor, 62, 392 and *illus.*
Sega, 491, 559, 741
Seles, Monica, 744
Selfridges, 437
Sellotape, 308, 316, 317
Sellotape Office, 316
Sensor razors, 260, 297–298
Sesam, 446 *(table)*
7-Eleven stores, 427
7 Up soft drinks, 235
Shama, Avraham, 259*n*
Sharan cars, 242
Sharp, Anita, 72*n*
Shearer, Alan, 513
Shearer, Brent, 166*n*, 679*n*
Shell, 96 *(table)*, 126, 164, 361,
    467, 769, 771, 772, 781
Shelter, 13, 335, 476
Sheraton, 276
Shipley, David, 350
Shogun cars, 242, 262
Shostack, Lynn, 632*n*, 633*n*
Shott's Alcoholic Seltzers, 759

Showcase multiplex cinemas, 303,
    344
Shredded Wheat cereal, 486
Shreddies, 504 *(table)*
Shuttle cars, 242
SHV Holdings, 412
Sibley, S.D., 370*n*
Siemens, 69, 95 *(table)*, 96 *(table)*,
    685, 810
Siemens Nixdorf, 412
Sihler, Helmut, 100
Silo, 415–416
Silver Swirls crayons, 717
Simintiras, Antonis, 521
Simkin, Lyndon, 32*n*, 232*n*, 365*n*,
    420*n*, 591*n*, 695*n*, 696*n*,
    732*n*, 785, 809*n*
Simmons, Jacqueline, 565*n*
Simmons, James C., 82*n*
Simon, H., 789*n*, 790*n*
Simon Godfrey Associates (SGA),
    186 *(table)*
Simple toiletries, 285–286
Sinclair C5 electric cars, 168, 203,
    210, 301
Singapore Airlines, 811
Sintra cars, 242
Skips snacks, 293
Skoda cars, 235, 315
Skol beer, 715, 716
Sky, 513
Skyshop brands, 419
Slater, S.F., 789*n*, 790*n*
Slimline cameras, 739
Slingsby, Helen, 289*n*, 586*n*
Slywotzky, A., 788*n*, 790*n*
Smart Cards, 361
Smit, B., 446*n*
Smith, A. Dunlap, 136*n*
Smith, Geoffrey, 559*n*
Smith, Stewart, 155*n*, 243*n*,
    316*n*
Smith and Nephew, 285–286
SmithKline Beecham, 96 *(table)*,
    257
Smiths Quavers, 293
Smiths snack foods, 293
Snickers candy bars, 688, 699
Snowdon, Ros, 173*n*, 759*n*
Snow White (movie), 266
Sock Shop, 419, 668
Soda Heist, 759
Soil Association, 755
SOLA, 124, 125 *(illus.)*
Solo Lower Fat Crisps, 293
Solomon, B., 30*n*
Somerfield, 37, 61, 350, 423, 441
    (table)
Sony, 6, 10, 74, 89, 112, 208, 251
    (illus.), 270 *(table)*, 277, 282,

345, 355, 463, 512, 549, 559,
    560, 570, 699, 736, 737
    (illus.)
Sor Bits mints, 638
So Soft butter, 277
The Source Book, 180 *(table)*
Southern Electric, 377
South West, 377
Spacesavers, 504 *(table)*
Space Star cars, 315
Spacey, Kevin, 303
Spain, Patrick J., 259*n*, 806*n*
SPA Ltd., 535
SPAR, 363, 371, 427
Special Brew beer, 716
Special K cereal, 489
Special Olympics, 454
Speedo, 335
Spethmann, Betsy, 565*n*
Spice Girls, 452, 467
Spillman, Susan, 267*n*
Sporty Spice, 467
SSang Yoeng Musso cars, 242
S.T. Dupont, 571
Stafford, Pat, 617
Stage 1, 426 *(table)*
Stage 2, 426 *(table)*
Stagecoach, 62
Stakis, 718
Stanstead Airport, 419
Staples, 426 *(table)*
Staybridge Suites, 719
Stedman, Craig, 522*n*
Steinbrink, John P., 532*n*
Stella Artois beer, 643, 716
Stern, Louis W., 385*n*
Stevens, James, 137*n*
Stewart, Rod, 249
Stewart, T.A., 137*n*
Sticks snacks, 293
Sting, 338
Sting CT pesticide, 482
The Sting (movie), 467
Stocking Fillas, 448 *(table)*
Stop & Shop, 445
Storehouse, 426 *(table)*
Stork SB margarine, 182
Strategic Planning Institute (SPI),
    631, 675, 676 *(illus.)*, 677
    (illus.)
Strathclyde Business School, 785
Style Plus, 448 *(table)*
S type cars, 206, 654
Subway, 435 *(table)*
Suchard, 640–641
Sullivan, Allanna, 467*n*
Sumitomo, 810
Summer Selection, 448 *(table)*
Summey, John H., 340*n*
Sunday Telegraph magazine, 464

Subject Index

Note: Terms and page numbers in **boldface type** indicate key terms and the pages on which they are defined.

effectiveness of, 227
product positioning and, 210
profiling market segments and, 227–228
segmentation variables (bases) for, *see* Segmentation variables (bases)
targeting strategy and, 210
total market approach contrasted with, 205
Market share, as pricing objective, 572
Market tests, 708, 708–709
Mark-up pricing, 604, 604–605
Materials handling, 397, 397–398
Maturity stage, of product life cycle, 259, 259–260
marketing strategy in, 308–311
Mechanical observation devices, 192, 194
Media plans, 492, 492–493, 493–494 *(table)*, 495, 496–498 *(table)*
Medium of transmission, 457
Medium range plans, 692
Megacarriers, 407
Merchandise, free, 544
Merchandise allowances, 544
Merchants, 352
Merchant wholesalers, 382, 382–383, 383 *(illus.)*
Mexico, 92
Micro marketing environment, 59, 59–62, 60 *(illus.)*
Misleading pricing, 602, 602–603
Mission, 659
Modified re-buy purchases, 148
Money, premium (push), 544
Money refunds, 542
Monopolistic competition, 57, 57 *(table)*
Monopoly, 56, 56–57, 57 *(table)*
Moral philosophies, 758
Motivation
of marketing personnel, 735–736
of salespeople, 533–534
Motives, 121
in consumer buying decision process, 121–122, 122 *(illus.)*, 123 *(illus.)*
as segmentation variable for consumer markets, 218
Motor vehicle transportation, 404 *(table)*

MRO items, 253
Multinational companies, 73
Multinational enterprises, 96, 96 *(table)*, 96–97
Multinational marketing, 73
Multiple packaging, 286, 286–287
Multisegment strategy, 229, 229–231 *(illus.)*, 229–232, 232 *(table)*
Multivariable segmentation, 225, 225–226, 226 *(illus.)*

Natural accounts, 744, 744–745
Negotiated pricing, 629
Negotiation, 334
in organisational buying, 148
New business order getters, 527
New product development, 297–305, 298 *(illus.)*, 299, 299 *(illus.)*, 300 *(table)*
business analysis in, 301, 302 *(table)*
commercialisation and, 304–305
concept testing for, 301
idea generation in, 299–300
product development and, 301–302, 303
screening ideas for, 300–301
test marketing for, 302, 304
Newspapers, as advertising medium, 496 *(table)*
News releases, 507
New task purchases, 148
Noise, in communication, 457
Non-business marketing, 334, 334–341
controlling activities in, 339–341, 340 *(table)*, 341 *(illus.)*
differences from business marketing, 334–336
marketing strategies for, 336–339
objectives of, 336, 337 *(illus.)*
Non-cumulative discounts, 578
Nonprice competition, 569, 569–570, 570 *(illus.)*, 571
Non-store retailing, 429, 429–432, 430 *(table)*
Non-tariff barriers, 85
Non-traceable common costs, 745
North American Free Trade Agreement (NAFTA), 92

Objections, in personal selling, 525–526
Objective(s)
of advertising campaigns, 490
of pricing, 570–572, 573–574
promotional, 470
in segmentation analysis, 226
strategic, 663–665
See also Marketing objectives; Organisational objectives
Objective and task approach, 491, 491–492
Objective of physical distribution, 395
Observation methods, 192, 192–194
Odd-even pricing, 601
Offensive warfare, 669
Office of Fair Trading, 39
Oligopoly, 57, 57 *(table)*
On-site computer interviewing, 189, 189–190
Operating variables, as segmentation variables for organisational markets, 224–225
Operational implications, in marketing plans, 701
Opportunities, 761
marketing, 18–20, 661, 662
organisational, 662–663
of sales promotion, 537
strategic, 62–63
Opportunity cost, 339
Order getters, 526, 526–527
Order processing, 396, 396–397
Order takers, 527
Organisation(s)
centralised and decentralised, 722–723
internal factors affecting marketing strategy and, 20
marketing activities used by, 10–11, 11 *(illus.)*
marketing ethics and, 760–761
marketing performed by, 8–9
marketing's importance to, 11
in micro marketing environment, 59
missions, goals, and corporate strategy of, 659–660
multinational, 73, 96 *(table)*, 96–97
performance of, 12
promoting, 482

Retail parks, **421**, 422 *(illus.)*
Retail positioning, **436**, 436–437
Retail power, balance of, 439–443
Retail technology, **440**, 440,
    441–442 *(table)*, 442
Return on investment, as pricing
    objective, 570–571
Revision tips, for examination
    papers, 820–822
Roles, **127**
    in consumer buying decision
        process, 127–128
Routine response behaviour, **108**
Routing salespeople, 535
Run outs, **312**, 312–313

Safety stock, **399**
Sales
    advertising to reduce fluctuations
        in, 487, 489
    forecasting, 237–238
Sales analysis, **741**, 741–743
Sales branches, **389**, 391
Sales contests, **544**, 544–545
Sales era, **14**, 15
Salesforce, 528–536
    compensating, 531–533, 532
        (table)
    controlling and evaluating
        performance of, 535–536
    managing sales territories and,
        534–535
    motivating, 533–534
    objectives for, 529
    recruiting and selecting,
        529–530
    size of, 529
    training, 530–531
Salesforce forecasting surveys, **706**,
    706–707
Sales forecasts, **704**, 704–709
    developing, 704–709
    multiple methods for, 709
Sales measurements, **742**,
    742–743
Sales offices, **389**, 391
Salespeople, types of, 526–527
Sales per square metre, **747**
Sales potential, **701**–702, **703**,
    703–704
Sales promotion, **466**, **536**,
    536–545
    consumer methods for, 537–543
    nature of, 536–537, 537 *(illus.)*
    opportunities and limitations of,
        537
    trade methods for, 543–545
Sales territory management,
    534–535

Salience, **112**
Samples, **182**
    free, 542
Sampling, **182**, 182–184
    in organisational buying, 148
Scheduling salespeople, 535
Scientific decision-making, **172**
Scrambled merchandising, **438**,
    438–439
Screening ideas, **300**, 300–301
Search, in business-to-business
    buying decision process,
    155–156
Search qualities, of services, 323
Seasonal analysis, **708**
Seasonal discounts, **578**,
    578–579
Secondary data, **177**
    collection of, 177–179, 180
        (table)
Secondary use packaging, **286**
Security, of transport modes, 406
Segmentation variables (bases),
    210, 210–227
    for business-to-business markets,
        222 *(table)*, 222–225
    for consumer markets, 211
        (table), 211–220, 212
        (illus.), 214 *(illus.)*, 215
        (table), 217 *(table)*, 218
        (illus.), 219 *(table)*, 221
    segmentation analysis stages and,
        226–227
    single variable versus
        multivariable segmentation
        and, 225–226, 226 *(illus.)*
Selective demand, stimulating, 483,
    488 *(illus.)*
Selective distortion, **120**
Selective distribution, **307**, 364
Selective exposure, **119**
Selective retention, **120**
Self-concept, **121**
Selling, personal, 465
Selling agents, **387**, 387–388
Service(s), **10**, **249**, 318–342, **320**
    characteristics of, 321, 323
        (table), 323–324, 325
    classification of, 324–327, 326
        (table), 327 *(illus.)*
    growth and importance of,
        320–321, 321 *(table)*, 322
        (table)
    industrial, 253
    marketing mix for, *see* Extended
        marketing mix for services
    marketing strategies for,
        327–329, 328 *(illus.)*
    non-business marketing of, *see*
        Non-business marketing

    product-related, 261
    quality of, 330–333
    of wholesalers, 380 *(table)*,
        380–382
Service expectations, **330**,
    332–333
Service product quality, **631**
Service providers, **631**
Service quality, **330**, 330–333, **631**
    customer evaluation of, 330, 331
        (table)
    exceptional, delivering, 331–333,
        332 *(illus.)*
Service quality factors, **331**
Shareholder value, **787**
Shopping mall/pavement intercept
    interviews, **189**
Shopping products, **250**, 250–251,
    251 *(illus.)*
Short range plans, **692**
Significant others, **760**
Singapore, 89–90
Single source data, **504**
Single variable segmentation, **225**
Situational analysis, 796–799
    company's internal position in,
        796–798, 797–798 *(table)*
    competition in, 799
    external environment in, 799
    market analysis in, 798–799
Situational factors, **115**
    in consumer buying decision
        process, 115–116
    as segmentation variables for
        organisational markets, 225
Situational involvement, **118**
Slovak Republic, 90–92
Social classes, **128**
    consumer buying decision
        process and, 128–129, 130
        (table), 131 *(table)*
Social factors, **127**
    in consumer buying decision
        process, 127–132
    in international marketing
        environment, 83, 84
        (illus.)
Social responsibility, **766**,
    768–777, 769 *(illus.)*
    impact on marketing, 768–770,
        771
    issues related to, 770 *(table)*,
        770–773
    marketing ethics and, 776
        (table), 776–777
    strategies for dealing with,
        773–776
Societal/green forces, **44**, 44–45
    consumer movement and, 45, 47
        (illus.)